tenth edition

Fundamental Financial Accounting Concepts

Thomas P. Edmonds
University of Alabama–Birmingham

Christopher T. Edmonds
University of Alabama–Birmingham

Mark A. Edmonds
University of Alabama–Birmingham

Frances M. McNair
Mississippi State University

Philip R. Olds
Virginia Commonwealth University

©Westend61/Getty Images

FUNDAMENTAL FINANCIAL ACCOUNTING CONCEPTS

Published by McGraw-Hill Education, 2 Penn Plaza, New York, NY 10121. Copyright © 2019 by McGraw-Hill Education. All rights reserved. Printed in the United States of America. No part of this publication may be reproduced or distributed in any form or by any means, or stored in a database or retrieval system, without the prior written consent of McGraw-Hill Education, including, but not limited to, in any network or other electronic storage or transmission, or broadcast for distance learning.

Some ancillaries, including electronic and print components, may not be available to customers outside the United States.

This book is printed on acid-free paper.

2 3 4 5 6 7 8 9 LWI 21 20 19 18

ISBN   978-1-260-09183-0
MHID   1-260-09183-X

Cover Image: ©*Westend61/Getty Images*

All credits appearing on page or at the end of the book are considered to be an extension of the copyright page.

The Internet addresses listed in the text were accurate at the time of publication. The inclusion of a website does not indicate an endorsement by the authors or McGraw-Hill Education, and McGraw-Hill Education does not guarantee the accuracy of the information presented at these sites.

mheducation.com/highered

This book is dedicated to our students, whose questions have so frequently caused us to reevaluate our method of presentation that they have, in fact, become major contributors to the development of this text.

NOTE FROM THE AUTHORS

Technology is having a profound effect on what we teach and how we teach it. The specific impacts on this text are discussed next.

● HOW TECHNOLOGY IMPACTS <u>WHAT</u> WE TEACH

Technology has changed accounting practice. Gone are the days where accountants used pens, paper, and calculators to maintain records and prepare statements. Indeed, most companies use computer software that simplifies data entry, recordkeeping, and statement preparation. Today's accountants spend less time preparing financial information and more time consulting and advising clients. To remain relevant, accounting education must move beyond the traditional preparer approach.

The first step in learning how to advise clients is to understand how business professionals incorporate accounting in the decision-making process. Business professionals tend to think about bottom-line consequences. If I do this or that, how will it affect my company's net income, total assets, cash flow, and so on. To promote bottom-line thinking, we take the student one step beyond the recording process. Specifically, we employ a *financial statements model* to show them how the journal entries affect financial statements. The model arranges the balance sheet, income statement, and statement of cash flows horizontally across a single line of text as shown next:

Balance Sheet					Income Statement					Statement of Cash Flows
Assets	=	Liab.	+	Equity	Rev.	−	Exp.	=	Net Inc.	

Typically, we show the statements model immediately after each journal entry. For example, the settlement of the liability for interest would be shown as follows:

Account Title	Debit	Credit
Interest Payable	8,400	
Cash		8,400

Balance Sheet					Income Statement					Statement of Cash Flows
Assets	=	Liab.	+	Equity	Rev.	−	Exp.	=	Net Inc.	
(8,400)		(8,400)		NA	NA		NA		NA	(8,400) OA

This approach provides a direct visual connection between journal entries and financial statements and enables students to see how *each individual accounting event affects decision making*. It shifts the focus from memorizing procedures to developing real-world thinking patterns. In today's world, computers prepare statements, humans evaluate consequences.

Most textbooks, including this one, still provide coverage of debits and credits, journal entries, trial balances, and statement preparation. It can be insightful to know what the computer is doing behind the scenes. Even so, accounting education must go beyond procedure. An accountant who can prepare a journal entry but has no idea how that entry affects financial statements cannot provide the insight and counsel expected of today's practicing accountant.

● HOW TECHNOLOGY IMPACTS HOW WE TEACH

Technology has provided many teaching tools that improve the quality of education while reducing the tasks associated with course management. Some examples include algorithmic test banks and homework management systems. The newest tool is a comprehensive set of lecture videos.

YouTube has demonstrated that videos can be a more effective medium for learning than reading. When learning almost anything, most of us reach for a video instead of the owner's manual. Even so, be aware that **all videos are not created equal.** When you search YouTube for an instructional video, you usually have to flip through several videos to find a really good one. Similarly, you must be prepared to look through several textbook video offerings to identify a set of high-quality videos. For comparison purposes, the following is a description of the key features of the lecture videos included in this text:

- *Our videos have been developed by members of the author team.* These videos have the feel of a live lecture. Delivering an effective lecture requires not only knowledge but also the proper tone, inflection, emphasis, attitude, and confidence. Scripted videos presented by a professional orator cannot compete with the spontaneous delivery of an experienced teacher.
- *We provide comprehensive instructional coverage.* We offer a lecture video for every learning objective in our text. Indeed, we refer to our set of videos as a video textbook. You can obtain the knowledge required to accomplish all learning objectives by watching the videos or by reading the text. The content is the same. It is only the method of delivery that differs.
- *We have assessment quizzes that accompany each lecture video.* After watching a video, a student is required to answer 5 to 10 multiple-choice questions. These questions are graded electronically, and students and instructors are able to obtain immediate feedback. Using this feedback, instructors can identify student weaknesses and focus class time on subjects where students are experiencing difficulty, thus more effectively helping students learn from their mistakes. The faster the feedback, the more effective the learning experience. Further, including assessment quiz scores as part of the course grade will motivate students to take video assignments seriously.
- *Our videos enable self-paced learning.* Our videos allow students to pause for contemplation and note-taking. This permits students to replay the instructor's coverage of difficult concepts or fast-forward through content they have already mastered. You can even set the speed at which the video plays; slowing it down to .75x or speeding it up to 2x. No longer is the lecture too fast for some and too slow for others. Now, every lecture can be further tailored to the needs of each individual student.

- **Our videos are just the right length.** The length of the video is of critical importance. If it is too long, you will lose students' interest. If too short, there is insufficient time to make your point. Our experience suggests that the average length of an effective video is approximately 10 minutes. Self-assessment questions follow the video and may take up to 20 minutes to complete. Therefore, each video assignment should require approximately 30 minutes. A typical homework assignment may cover two to three video assignments.
- **Our videos facilitate learning for students with disabilities.** Consistent with the Americans with Disabilities Act, all our videos are closed-captioned. This provides a learning tool for students who are visually and hearing impaired. Students with hearing impairment can see and read the video content, and those with visual impairment can listen to the lecture. Also, international students, who are less proficient in the English language, find videos with closed captions to be useful.

• Implementing lecture video content

The following are some examples of how you can use instructional videos to improve the classroom environment.

• Supplement your traditional lecture-based course

You do not have to change the way you teach your class to reap many of the benefits available from video instruction. Students who have to miss class or who have trouble comprehending certain concepts can benefit from watching video lectures. Also, many students who attend class will be able to build confidence by watching videos that reinforce the concepts presented in class. Because the videos are tied directly to the learning objectives, you can develop a plan for students who are struggling with specific topics. Alternatively, you may offer video instruction to enable advanced students to cover additional topics.

• Flipped courses

Instructional videos enable instructors to flip the traditional teaching model. Specifically, instead of providing a lecture in class and then assigning homework, *flipped courses* deliver the lecture at home and use the classroom as a place for students to work problems and ask questions. Video content provides an excellent venue for the delivery of at-home lectures.

• Distance learning courses

More and more students are taking classes online, but many students struggle with these courses. Generally, students prefer to learn from a live lecture, but due to timing or location are unable to attend class. Prerecorded lecture videos solve this problem by allowing students to access quality lectures on demand.

• Mass-section courses

Students often find it difficult to see and hear in large mass-section courses. Also, the lecture must be set at an average pace, which by its nature is too fast for some students and too slow for others. Prerecorded lecture videos help resolve these issues.

- **Comprehensive set of technological teaching tools**

Video content is one component of a comprehensive set of technological teaching tools. Some of the other tools that accompany our text include:

- Connect
- SmartBook
- Test banks (via Connect or TestGen)
- Guided exercises
- Excel simulations

These tools can be used independently or in conjunction with one another. A detailed description of each tool is included in the following sections of the front matter.

We appreciate your interest in our text and welcome comments, questions, and suggestions.

Tom Edmonds: tedmonds@gmail.com

Chris Edmonds: cedmonds@gmail.com

Mark Edmonds: medmonds@gmail.com

Phil Olds: prolds@vcu.edu

ABOUT THE AUTHORS

Courtesy of Thomas Edmonds

Thomas P. Edmonds

Thomas P. Edmonds, Ph.D., is Professor Emeritus in the Department of Accounting and Finance at the University of Alabama at Birmingham (UAB). He has been actively involved in teaching accounting principles throughout his academic career. Dr. Edmonds has coordinated the accounting principles courses at the University of Houston and UAB. He has taught introductory accounting in mass sections and in distance learning programs. He has received five prestigious teaching awards, including the Alabama Society of CPAs Outstanding Educator Award, the UAB President's Excellence in Teaching Award, and the distinguished Ellen Gregg Ingalls Award for excellence in classroom teaching. He has written numerous articles that have appeared in many publications, including *Issues in Accounting,* the *Journal of Accounting Education, Advances in Accounting Education, Accounting Education: A Journal of Theory, Practice and Research,* the *Accounting Review, Advances in Accounting,* the *Journal of Accountancy, Management Accounting,* the *Journal of Commercial Bank Lending,* the *Banker's Magazine,* and the *Journal of Accounting, Auditing, and Finance.* Dr. Edmonds has served as a member of the editorial board for *Advances in Accounting: Teaching and Curriculum Innovations* and *Issues in Accounting Education.* He has published five textbooks, five practice problems (including two computerized problems), and a variety of supplemental materials including study guides, work papers, and solutions manuals. Dr. Edmonds's writing is influenced by a wide range of business experience. He is a successful entrepreneur. He has worked as a management accountant for Refrigerated Transport, a trucking company. Dr. Edmonds also worked in the not-for-profit sector as a commercial lending officer for the Federal Home Loan Bank. In addition, he has acted as a consultant to major corporations, including First City Bank of Houston (now Citi Bank), AmSouth Bank in Birmingham (now Regions Bank), Texaco, and Cortland Chemicals. Dr. Edmonds began his academic training at Young Harris Community College in Young Harris, Georgia. He received a B.B.A. degree with a major in finance from Georgia State University in Atlanta, Georgia. He obtained an M.B.A. degree with a concentration in finance from St. Mary's University in San Antonio, Texas. His Ph.D. degree with a major in accounting was awarded by Georgia State University. Dr. Edmonds's work experience and academic training have enabled him to bring a unique user perspective to this textbook.

Courtesy of Christopher Edmonds

Christopher T. Edmonds

Christopher T. Edmonds, Ph.D., is an associate professor in the Department of Accounting and Finance at the University of Alabama at Birmingham (UAB). He coordinates the mass-section face-to-face and online principles of accounting courses. Dr. Edmonds specializes in developing flipped and online accounting courses and frequently speaks on these topics at universities and conferences. His passion for helping students learn inspired him to create hundreds of short videos teaching the fundamental concepts of accounting. Dr. Edmonds has received six prestigious teaching awards including the UAB Faculty Student Success Award, UAB Transformative Online Course Award, UAB Loudell Ellis Robinson Classroom Teaching Award, UAB Disability Support Recognition Award, and the Virginia Tech Favorite Faculty Award. He has published three textbooks where he is the lead video author and has written numerous articles that have appeared in publications including *The Accounting Review, Journal of Accounting and Public Policy, Issues in Accounting Education, Advances in Accounting Education, Advances in Accounting,* and *Review of Quantitative Finance and Accounting.* Dr. Edmonds began his academic training at Colorado State University. He obtained an M.B.A. degree from UAB. His Ph.D. degree with a major in accounting was awarded by Virginia Polytechnic Institute and State University.

Mark A. Edmonds

Mark A. Edmonds, Ph.D., CPA, is an assistant professor in the Department of Accounting and Finance at the University of Alabama at Birmingham. He has taught principles and advanced accounting classes in face-to-face, flipped, and online formats. Dr. Edmonds began his career providing assurance services for the internationally recognized accounting firm Ernst & Young. At the conclusion of his professional service, he obtained his Ph.D. from Southern Illinois University Carbondale. He serves as the education adviser on the board of the Institute of Internal Auditors Birmingham Chapter. Dr. Edmonds's research focuses on alternative learning strategies and auditor decision making.

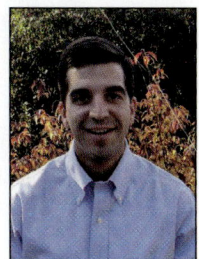

Courtesy of UAB

Frances M. McNair

Frances M. McNair holds the KPMG Peat Marwick Professorship in Accounting at Mississippi State University (MSU). She has been involved in teaching principles of accounting for the past 20 years and currently serves as the coordinator for the principles of accounting courses at MSU. Dr. McNair was selected by the Mississippi Society of CPAS as outstanding educator for 2014. She joined the MSU faculty in 1987 after receiving her Ph.D. from the University of Mississippi. The author of various articles that have appeared in the *Journal of Accountancy, Management Accounting, Business and Professional Ethics Journal, The Practical Accountant, Taxes,* and other publications, she also coauthored the book *The Tax Practitioner* with Dr. Denzil Causey. Dr. McNair is currently serving on committees of the American Taxation Association, the American Accounting Association, and the Institute of Management Accountants, as well as numerous School of Accountancy and MSU committees.

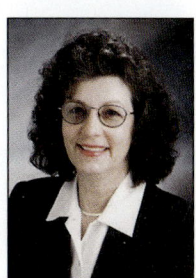

Courtesy of Francis McNair

Philip R. Olds

Professor Olds is an associate professor of accounting at Virginia Commonwealth University (VCU). He serves as the coordinator of the introduction to accounting courses at VCU. Professor Olds received his A.S. degree from Brunswick Junior College in Brunswick, Georgia (now Costal Georgia Community College). He received a B.B.A. in accounting from Georgia Southern College (now Georgia Southern University), and his M.P.A. and Ph.D. degrees are from Georgia State University. After graduating from Georgia Southern, he worked as an auditor with the U.S. Department of Labor in Atlanta, Georgia. A former CPA in Virginia, Professor Olds has published articles in various professional journals and presented papers at national and regional conferences. He also served as the faculty adviser to the VCU chapter of Beta Alpha Psi for five years. In 1989, he was recognized with an Outstanding Faculty Vice-President Award by the national Beta Alpha Psi organization. Professor Olds has received both the Distinguished Teaching Award and the Distinguished Service Award from the VCU School of Business. Most recently, he received the university's award for maintaining High Ethical and Academic Standards While Advocating for Student-Athletes and Their Quest Towards a Degree.

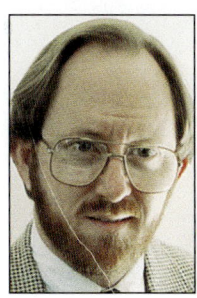

Courtesy of Philip Olds

WHAT WE DID TO MAKE IT BETTER

As discussed in the "Note from the Authors" this text has been revised to include lecture videos that provide coverage of all of the learning objectives included in the text. These videos have been developed by a member of the author team and have the feel of a live lecture as opposed to scripted PowerPoint presentations. The videos provide unparalleled opportunities for instructional innovation, including the development of flipped and distance learning courses. The videos can also be used in traditional courses to help students who need additional instruction. For example, students who are unable to keep up in class or who have to miss class now have a video lecture that can be used to catch up. Each video is accompanied by an assessment quiz containing between 5 and 10 multiple-choice questions. The videos and assessment quizzes can be assigned to individual students or to the class as a whole through *Connect*. The instructor has complete control over student access to video content and the accompanying assessment quizzes.

Specific chapter changes:

Chapter 1 An Introduction to Accounting

- Revised lecture videos and assessment quizzes
- Changed learning objectives
- Changed heading for The Financial Analyst section
- Changed heading to more clearly define sections in exercises and problems
- New "Focus on International Issues" feature
- Changed formatting to more clearly distinguish Section 1 versus Section 2 exercises and problems
- Changed formatting to highlight The Financial Analyst section
- Updated exercises, problems, and cases

Chapter 2 Accounting for Accruals and Deferrals

- Revised lecture videos and assessment quizzes
- New "Focus on International Issues" feature
- Clarified wording of learning objectives
- Revised chapter opening to provide a brief explanation of Financial Accounting Standards Board (FASB) issued Accounting Standards Codification 606 regarding revenue recognition
- Changed formatting to show learning objectives as first-level headings
- Changed formatting to more clearly distinguish Section 1 versus Section 2 exercises and problems
- Changed formatting to highlight The Financial Analyst section
- Removed all references to accrued interest revenue
- Updated exercises, problems, and cases

Chapter 3 The Double-Entry Accounting System

- Revised lecture videos and assessment quizzes
- Revised The Curious Accountant section
- Updated exercises, problems, and cases

Chapter 4 Accounting for Merchandising Businesses

- Revised lecture videos and assessment quizzes
- Revised learning objectives to better match video lectures
- Revised The Curious Accountant section
- New Exhibit 4.6 showing trend data for Dow Jones Industrial companies
- Updated Reality Bytes
- Revised real-world data in, and corresponding text related to, Exhibit 4.10
- Updated exercises, problems, and cases

Chapter 5 Accounting for Inventories

- Revised lecture videos and assessment quizzes
- Revised learning objectives to better match video lectures
- Revised The Curious Accountant section
- New Exhibit 5.1 showing trend data for Dow Jones Industrial companies
- Updated Reality Bytes section
- Revised real-world data in, and corresponding text related to, Exhibit 5.6
- Updated exercises, problems, and cases

Chapter 6 Internal Control and Accounting for Cash

- New Curious Accountant section
- Revised learning objectives to better match video lectures
- Revised real-world data in, and corresponding text related to, Exhibit 6.1
- Updated exercises, problems, and cases

Chapter 7 Accounting for Receivables

- Revised lecture videos and assessment quizzes
- New Curious Accountant section
- New Reality Bytes section
- New "Focus on International Issues"
- Revised real-world data in, and corresponding text related to, Exhibit 7.7
- Revised real-world data in, and corresponding text related to, Exhibit 7.8
- Added exercises for LO 7-12
- Resequenced exercises and problems so they match the order in which the learning objectives appear in the text
- Updated exercises, problems, and cases

Chapter 8 Accounting for Long-Term Operational Assets

- Revised lecture videos and assessment quizzes
- Revised The Curious Accountant section
- New Exhibits 8.1 and 8.2 showing trend data for Dow Jones Industrial companies
- Added exercises for the Sales to Property, Plant and Equipment ratio
- Resequenced exercises and problems so they match the order in which the learning objectives appear in the text
- Revised real-world data in, and corresponding text related to, Exhibit 8.8
- Updated exercises, problems, and cases

Chapter 9 Accounting for Current Liabilities and Payroll

- Revised The Curious Accountant section
- Revised Reality Bytes section
- New Exhibits 8.1 and 8.2 showing trend data for Dow Jones Industrial companies
- Revised real-world data in, and corresponding text related to, Exhibit 9.6
- Updated exercises, problems, and cases

Chapter 10 Accounting for Long-Term Debt

- New Curious Accountant section
- New Reality Bytes section
- New Exhibit 10.3 showing trend data for Dow Jones Industrial companies
- Revised real-world data and corresponding text in The Financial Analyst section
- Updated exercises, problems, and cases

Chapter 11 Proprietorships, Partnerships, and Corporations

- Revised lecture videos and assessment quizzes
- Revised learning objectives to better match video lectures
- Revised The Curious Accountant section
- New Exhibit 11.3 showing trend data for Dow Jones Industrial companies
- Updated Reality Bytes section
- Resequenced exercises and problems so they match the order in which the learning objectives appear in the text
- Updated exercises, problems, and cases

Chapter 12 Statement of Cash Flows

- Revised The Curious Accountant section
- New Reality Bytes section
- New Exhibit 12.4 showing trend data for Dow Jones Industrial companies
- Updated exercises, problems, and cases

Chapter 13 Financial Statement Analysis

- New The Curious Accountant section
- Updated exercises, problems, and ATC cases

> "The beauty is in the details. The authors cover all the steps in buying goods, dealing with freight and discounts, and they cover the sales issues."
>
> DON LUCY,
> INDIAN RIVER STATE COLLEGE CENTRAL

HOW DOES THE BOOK

REAL-WORLD EXAMPLES

The text provides a variety of real-world examples of financial accounting as an essential part of the management process. There are descriptions of accounting practices from real organizations such as Coca-Cola, Enron, General Motors, and Amazon.com. These companies are highlighted in blue in the text.

> "Excellent real-world example included."
>
> PAUL GOODCHILD,
> UNIVERSITY OF CENTRAL MISSOURI

THE CURIOUS ACCOUNTANT

Each chapter opens with a short vignette. These pose a question about a real-world accounting issue related to the topic of the chapter. The answer to the question appears in a separate sidebar a few pages further into the chapter.

FOCUS ON INTERNATIONAL ISSUES

These boxed inserts expose students to IFRS and other international issues in accounting.

THE FINANCIAL ANALYST

Financial statement analysis is highlighted in each chapter under this heading.

CHECK YOURSELF

These short question/answer features occur at the end of each main topic and ask students to stop and think about the material just covered. The answer follows to provide immediate feedback before students go on to a new topic.

REALITY BYTES

This feature expands on the topics by showing how companies use the concepts discussed in the chapter to make real-world business decisions.

xiv

Fundamental Financial Accounting Concepts

MOTIVATE STUDENTS?

● ANNUAL REPORTS

Excerpts from the 2016 annual report for Target Corporation is shown in Appendix B.

Business Application Problems related to the annual report are included at the end of each chapter.

A financial statement analysis project for the annual report is located in Appendix D. Also, a general purpose annual report project is included for instructors to assign for any company.

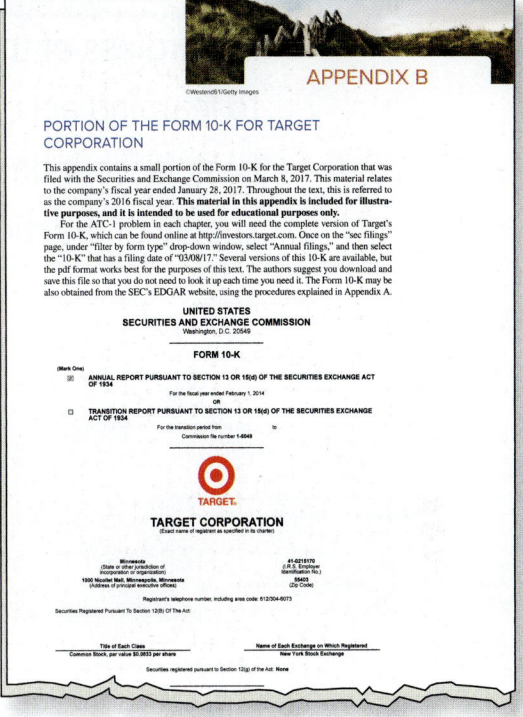

● A LOOK BACK / A LOOK FORWARD

Students need a roadmap to make sense of where the chapter topics fit into the "whole" picture. A Look Back reviews the chapter materials and a Look Forward introduces students to what is to come.

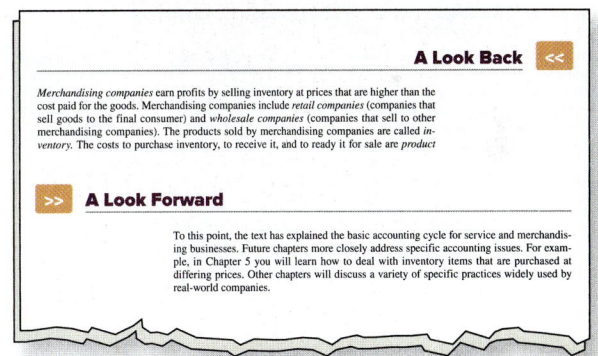

"Strong chapter introduction for students who may understand what a cash flow statement is and for those who may not."

PAUL GOODCHILD,
UNIVERSITY OF CENTRAL MISSOURI

Edmonds/Edmonds/Edmonds/McNair/Olds

HOW ARE CHAPTER CONCEPTS

Regardless of the instructional approach, there is no shortcut to learning accounting. Students must practice to master basic accounting concepts. The text includes a prodigious supply of practice materials and exercises and problems.

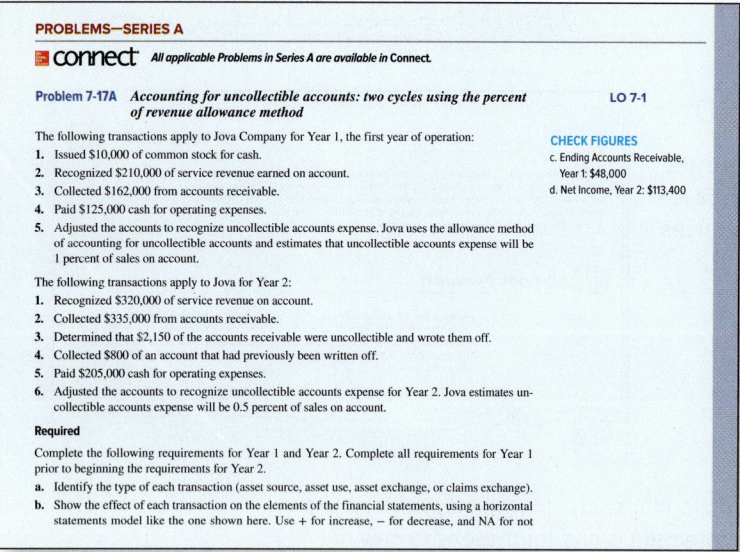

SELF-STUDY REVIEW PROBLEM

These example problems include a detailed, worked-out solution and provide support for students before they work problems on their own. These review problems are included in an animated audio presentation in the *Connect* Library.

EXERCISE SERIES A & B AND PROBLEM SERIES A & B

There are two sets of problems and exercises: Series A and B. Instructors can assign one set for homework and another set for classwork.

• Check Figures

The figures provide key answers for selected problems.

• Excel

Many problems can be solved using the Excel™ templates available in the *Connect* Library. A logo appears in the margins next to these problems.

"The self-study problems and supplements on the web are very useful for students."

BARRY BUCHOFF,
TOWSON UNIVERSITY

"Good/Excellent exercises and problems at the end of chapter with Excel."

ROBERT KACHUR,
RICHARD STOCKTON COLLEGE OF
NEW JERSEY

Fundamental Financial Accounting Concepts

REINFORCED?

● ANALYZE, THINK, COMMUNICATE (ATC)

Each chapter includes an innovative section titled Analyze, Think, Communicate (ATC). This section offers Business Applications Cases, Group Assignments, Real-World Cases, Writing Assignments, Ethical Dilemma Problems, Research Assignments, and Spreadsheet Assignments.

We use icons to help students identify the type of question being asked.

 • Target Corp.

 • Group Work   • Excel

 • Real World Company   • Ethics

 • Research   • Writing

©McGraw-Hill Education

● COMPREHENSIVE PROBLEM

Beginning in Chapter 1, a comprehensive problem builds in each successive chapter, with the ending account balances in one chapter becoming the beginning account balances in the next chapter.

● MASTERING EXCEL AND USING EXCEL

The Excel applications are used to make students comfortable with this analytical tool and to show its use in accounting.

> "I love the spreadsheet assignments and the comprehensive problems at the end of each chapter. I love the check figures that are available on some of the problems."
>
> JANE GARVIN,
> IVY TECH COMMUNITY COLLEGE

Edmonds/Edmonds/Edmonds/McNair/Olds

xvii

McGraw-Hill Connect® is a highly reliable, easy-to-use homework and learning management solution that utilizes learning science and award-winning adaptive tools to improve student results.

Homework and Adaptive Learning

- Connect's assignments help students contextualize what they've learned through application, so they can better understand the material and think critically.
- Connect will create a personalized study path customized to individual student needs through SmartBook®.
- SmartBook helps students study more efficiently by delivering an interactive reading experience through adaptive highlighting and review.

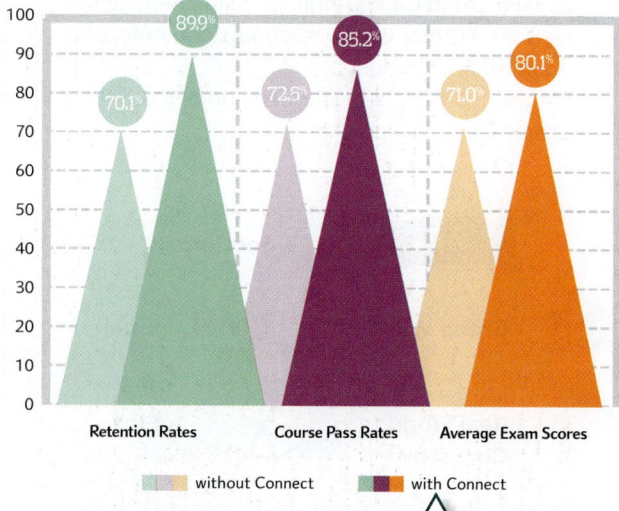

Using **Connect** improves retention rates by **19.8 percentage points,** passing rates by **12.7 percentage points, and** exam scores by **9.1 percentage points.**

Over **7 billion questions** have been answered, making McGraw-Hill Education products more intelligent, reliable, and precise.

73% of instructors who use **Connect** require it; instructor satisfaction **increases** by 28% when **Connect** is required.

Quality Content and Learning Resources

- Connect content is authored by the world's best subject matter experts, and is available to your class through a simple and intuitive interface.
- The Connect eBook makes it easy for students to access their reading material on smartphones and tablets. They can study on the go and don't need internet access to use the eBook as a reference, with full functionality.
- Multimedia content such as videos, simulations, and games drive student engagement and critical thinking skills.

©McGraw-Hill Education

Robust Analytics and Reporting

©Hero Images/Getty Images

- Connect Insight® generates easy-to-read reports on individual students, the class as a whole, and on specific assignments.
- The Connect Insight dashboard delivers data on performance, study behavior, and effort. Instructors can quickly identify students who struggle and focus on material that the class has yet to master.
- Connect automatically grades assignments and quizzes, providing easy-to-read reports on individual and class performance.

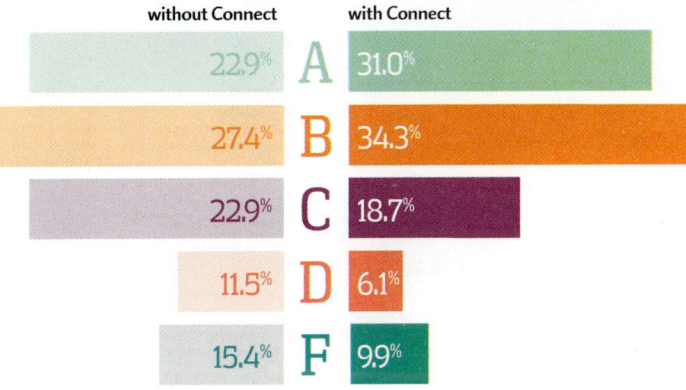

Impact on Final Course Grade Distribution

	without Connect		with Connect
A	22.9%		31.0%
B	27.4%		34.3%
C	22.9%		18.7%
D	11.5%		6.1%
F	15.4%		9.9%

More students earn **As** and **Bs** when they use **Connect**.

Trusted Service and Support

- Connect integrates with your LMS to provide single sign-on and automatic syncing of grades. Integration with Blackboard®, D2L®, and Canvas also provides automatic syncing of the course calendar and assignment-level linking.
- Connect offers comprehensive service, support, and training throughout every phase of your implementation.
- If you're looking for some guidance on how to use Connect, or want to learn tips and tricks from super users, you can find tutorials as you work. Our Digital Faculty Consultants and Student Ambassadors offer insight into how to achieve the results you want with Connect.

www.mheducation.com/connect

HOW CAN TECHNOLOGY HELP

• Online assignments

Connect helps students learn more efficiently by providing feedback and practice material when they need it, where they need it. *Connect* grades homework automatically and gives immediate feedback on any questions students may have missed. Our assignable, gradable end-of-chapter content includes a general journal application that looks and feels like what you would find in a general ledger software package. Also, select questions have been redesigned to test students' knowledge more fully. They now include tables for students to work through rather than requiring that all calculations be done offline.

End-of-chapter content in *Connect* includes:

- Quizzes (multiple-choice questions)
- Exercises
- Problems
- Analyze, Think, Communicate
- Comprehensive Problems

Exercise 3-4A Applying debit/credit terminology to accounting events LO 3-1

Required
a. In parallel columns, list the accounts that would be debited and credited for each of the following unrelated transactions:

(1) Acquired cash from the issue of common stock.
(2) Provided services for cash.
(3) Paid cash for salaries expense.
(4) Purchased supplies for cash.
(5) Paid in advance for two-year lease on office space.
(6) Provided services on account.
(7) Recognized expense for prepaid rent that had been used up by the end of the accounting period.
(8) Recorded accrued salaries at the end of the accounting period.

b. Use a horizontal statements model to show how each event affects the balance sheet, income statement, and statement of cash flows. Indicate whether the event increases (+), decreases (−), or does not affect (NA) each element of the financial statements. Also, in the Cash Flow column, use the letters OA to designate operating activity, IA for investing activity, and FA for financing activity. The first event is shown as an example.

Complete this question by entering your answers in the tabs below.

| Required A | Required B |

In parallel columns, list the accounts that would be debited and credited for each of the following unrelated transactions.

	Event	Account Debited	Account Credited
(1)	Acquired cash from the issue of common stock.	Cash	Common stock
(2)	Provided services for cash.	Cash	Service revenue
(3)	Paid cash for salaries expense.	Salaries expense	Cas
(4)	Purchased supplies for cash.		
(5)	Paid in advance for two-year lease on office space.		Cash
(6)	Provided services on account.		

• Lecture videos

One or more lecture videos are available for every learning objective introduced throughout the text. The videos have been developed by a member of the author team and have the touch and feel of a live lecture. The videos are accompanied by a set of self-assessment quizzes. Students can watch the videos and then test themselves to determine if they understand the material presented in the video. Students can repeat the process, switching back and forth between the video and self-assessment quizzes, until they are satisfied that they understand the material.

> "This is the best part of the entire Connect material. I think access to these Lecture Videos would be positive, especially for online students."
>
> CHERYL CORKE, GENESEE COMMUNITY COLLEGE

IMPROVE STUDENT SUCCESS?

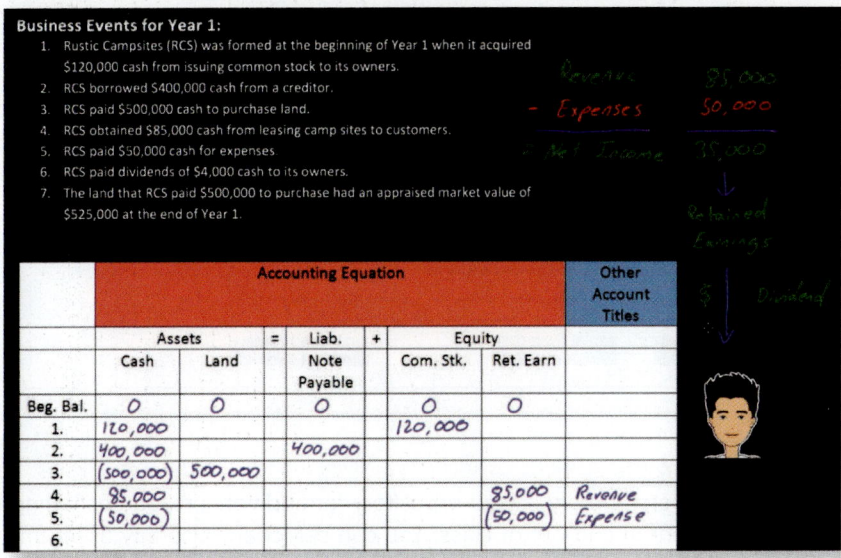

• Excel Simulations

Simulated Excel questions, assignable within *Connect*, allow students to practice their Excel skills—such as basic formulas and formatting—within the content of financial accounting. These questions feature animated, narrated Help and Show Me tutorials (when enabled), as well as automatic feedback and grading for both students and professors.

• Guided Examples

The **Guided Examples** in *Connect* provide a video-based, step-by-step walk-through of select exercises similar to those assigned. These short videos are available to students as hints by instructors and provide reinforcement when students need it most.

• General Ledger

General Ledger Problems provide a much-improved student experience when working with accounting cycle questions, offering improved navigation and less scrolling. Students can audit their mistakes by easily linking back to their original entries and can see how the numbers flow through the various financial statements. Many General Ledger Problems include an analysis tab that allows students to demonstrate their critical thinking skills and a deeper understanding of accounting concepts.

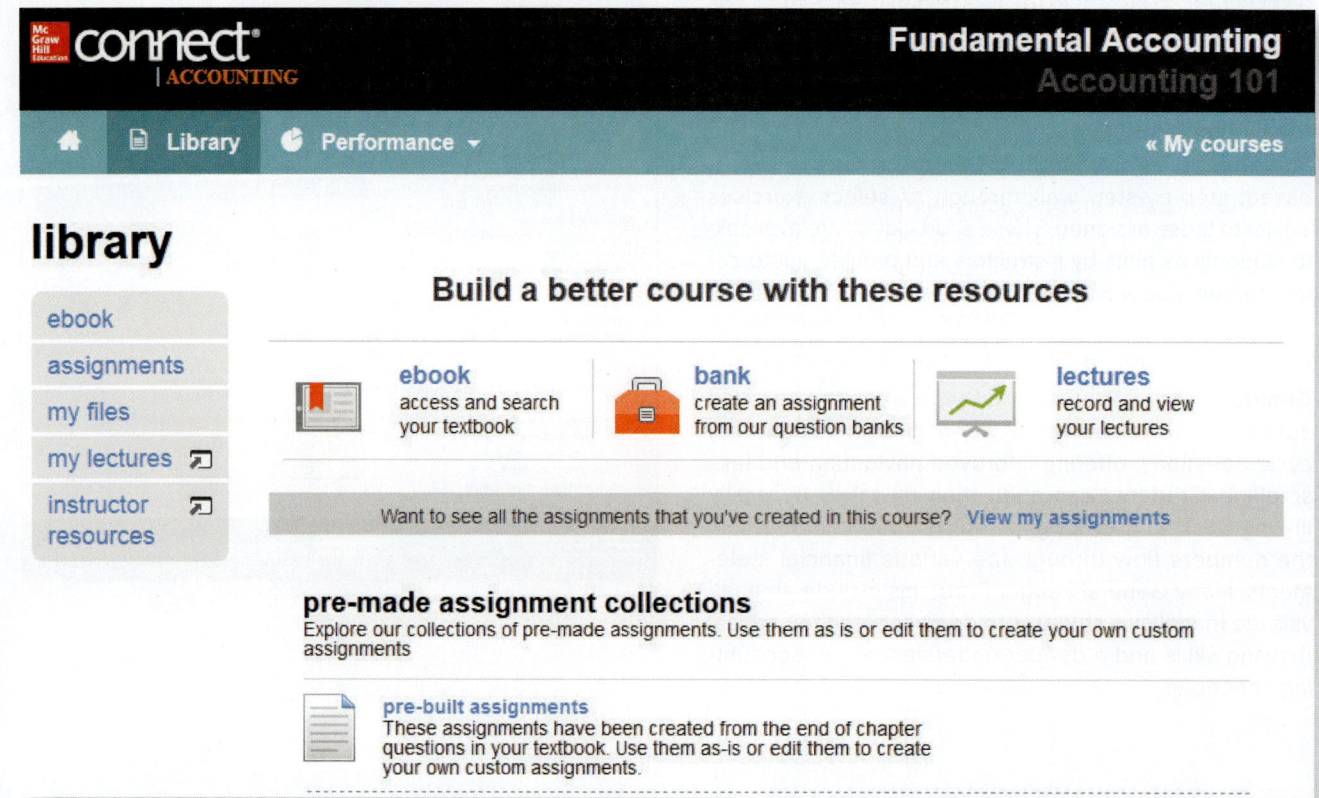

- **Instructor Library**

The *Connect* Instructor Library is your repository for additional resources to improve student engagement in and out of class. You can select and use any asset that enhances your lecture. The *Connect* Instructor Library includes access to:

- Solutions Manual
- Instructor's Manual
- Test Bank
- Instructor PowerPoint® slides
- Media-rich eBook

TEGRITY: LECTURES 24/7

Tegrity is a service that makes class time available 24/7 by automatically capturing every lecture. With a simple one-click start-and-stop process, you capture all computer screens and corresponding audio in a format that is easily searchable, frame by frame. Students can replay any part of any class with easy-to-use browser-based viewing on a PC, Mac, or other mobile device.

Help turn your students' study time into learning moments immediately supported by your lecture. With Tegrity, you also increase listening and class participation by easing students' concerns about note-taking. Lecture Capture will make it more likely you will see students' faces, not the tops of their heads. To learn more about Tegrity, visit http://www.mheducation.com/highered/platforms/tegrity.html.

• Custom Publishing through Create

McGraw-Hill Create™ is a new, self-service website that allows instructors to create custom course materials by drawing upon McGraw-Hill's comprehensive, cross-disciplinary content. Instructors can add their own content quickly and easily and tap into other rights-secured third-party sources as well, then arrange the content in a way that makes the most sense for their course. Instructors can even personalize their book with the course name and information and choose the best format for their students: color print, black-and-white print, or an eBook.

Through Create, instructors can

- Select and arrange the content in a way that makes the most sense for their course.
- Combine material from different sources and even upload their own content.
- Choose the best format for their students: print or eBook.
- Edit and update their course materials as often as they like.

Begin creating now at **www.mcgrawhillcreate.com**.

• McGraw-Hill Customer Experience Group Contact Information

At McGraw-Hill, we understand that getting the most from new technology can be challenging. That's why our services don't stop after you purchase our products. You can contact our Product Specialists 24 hours a day to get product training online. Or you can search the knowledge bank of Frequently Asked Questions on our support website. For Customer Support, call **800-331-5094,** or visit **www.mhhe.com/support**. One of our Technical Support Analysts will be able to assist you in a timely fashion.

SUPPLEMENTS FOR INSTRUCTORS

Assurance of Learning Ready

Many educational institutions today are focused on the notion of *assurance of learning*, an important element of many accreditation standards. *Fundamental Financial Accounting Concepts 10e* is designed specifically to support your assurance of learning initiatives with a simple, yet powerful, solution.

Each chapter in the book begins with a list of numbered learning objectives, which appear throughout the chapter, as well as in the end-of-chapter assignments. Every Test Bank question for *Fundamental Financial Accounting Concepts* maps to a specific chapter learning objective in the textbook. Each Test Bank question also identifies topic area, level of difficulty, Bloom's Taxonomy level, and AICPA and AACSB skill area. You can use our Test Bank software, *EZ Test Online*, or *Connect Plus Accounting* to easily search for learning objectives that directly relate to the learning objectives for your course. You can then use the reporting features of *EZ Test* to aggregate student results in a similar fashion, making the collection and presentation of Assurance of Learning data simple and easy.

AACSB Statement

McGraw-Hill Education is a proud corporate member of AACSB International. Understanding the importance and value of AACSB accreditation, *Fundamental Financial Accounting Concepts 10e* recognizes the curricula guidelines detailed in the AACSB standards for business accreditation by connecting selected questions in the text and the Test Bank to the general knowledge and skill guidelines in the revised AACSB standards.

The statements contained in *Fundamental Financial Accounting Concepts 10e* are provided only as a guide for the users of this textbook. The AACSB leaves content coverage and assessment within the purview of individual schools, the mission of the school, and the faculty. While *Fundamental Financial Accounting Concepts 10e* and the teaching package make no claim of any specific AACSB qualification or evaluation, we have, within the text and test bank, labeled selected questions according to the eight general knowledge and skill areas.

McGraw-Hill's *Connect*

Connect offers a number of powerful tools and features to make managing your classroom easier. *Connect* with Edmonds 10e offers enhanced features and technology to help both you and your students make the most of your time inside and outside the classroom.

TestGen

TestGen is a complete, state-of-the-art test generator and editing application software that allows instructors to quickly and easily select test items from McGraw-Hill's test bank content. The instructors can then organize, edit, and customize questions and answers to rapidly generate tests for paper or online administration. Questions can include stylized text, symbols, graphics, and equations that are inserted directly into questions using built-in mathematical templates. TestGen's random generator provides the option to display different text or calculated number values each time questions are used. With both quick-and-simple test creation and flexible and robust editing tools, TestGen is a complete test generator system for today's educators.

This test bank is also available in Word format and contains multiple-choice questions, essay questions, and short problems. Each test item is coded for level of difficulty, learning objective, AACSB and AICPA skill area, and Bloom's Taxonomy level.

ACKNOWLEDGMENTS

Our grateful appreciation is extended to those who reviewed previous editions:

Special thanks to the talented people who prepared the supplements. These take a great deal of time and effort to write and we appreciate our contributors' efforts. LuAnn Bean, Ph.D., of Nathan M. Bisk College of Business–Florida Institute of Technology prepared the Instructor's Manual and PowerPoints; Helen Roybark, Ph.D., of Radford University and Beth Kobylarz provided text accuracy checking; Jack Terry developed the Excel templates; Jeannie Folk revised the Test Bank; and Matt Stallings of the University of St. Thomas provided Test Bank accuracy checking.

We extend our sincere appreciation to Tim Vertovec, Rebecca Olson, Dana Pauley, Erin Quinones, Danielle Andries, Zachary Rudin, and Laura Fuller. We deeply appreciate the long hours you committed to the formation of a high-quality text.

- **Thomas P. Edmonds • Christopher T. Edmonds • Mark A. Edmonds**
- **Frances M. McNair • Philip R. Olds**

We would like to express our appreciation to the people who have provided assistance in the development of this textbook.

We express our sincere thanks to the following individuals who provided extensive reviews for the current and previous editions:

Reviewers

Stacey Adams, *Antelope Valley College*
Charles Richard Aldridge, *Western Kentucky University*
Mary Allen, *Boise State University*
Sheila Ammons, *Austin Community College*
Susan Anderson, *Appalachian State University*
Marie Archambault, *Marshall University*
Kashi Balachandran, *Stern School, New York University*
Patricia Bancroft, *Bridgewater State University*
Debra Barbeau, *Southern Illinois University–Carbondale*
Charles Baril, *James Madison University*
Beryl Barkman, *University of Massachusetts–Dartmouth*
Cheryl Bartlett, *Albuquerque TVI Community College*
Ira Bates, *Florida A&M University*
Jim Bates, *Mountain Empire Community College*
Deborah Beard, *Southeast Missouri State University*
Judy Beebe, *Western Oregon University*
Linda Bell, *William Jewell College*
Judy Benish, *Fox Valley Tech*
Debbie Benson, *Kennesaw State University*
J. Lawrence Bergin, *Winona State University*
Wilbur Berry, *Jacksonville State University*
Eddy Birrer, *Gonzaga University*
Nancy Bledsoe, *Millsaps College*
Amy Bourne, *Oregon State University*
Cendy Boyd, *Northeast Louisiana State*
Lindsey Boyer, *Central Piedmont Community College*
Arthur Boyett, *Francis Marion University*
Cassie Bradley, *Troy State University*
Rodger Brannan, *University of Minnesota, Duluth*
Helen Brubeck, *San Jose State University*
Roscoe Eugene Bryson, *University of Alabama in Huntsville*
Connie Buchanan, *Southwest Texas Junior College*
Barry Buchoff, *Towson University*
Georgia Buckles, *Manchester Community College*
Radie Bunn, *Southwest Missouri State University*
Jackie Burke, *Hofstra University*
Gregory Bushong, *Wright State University*
Sandra Byrd, *Missouri State University*
Judith Cadle, *Tarleton State University*
James Cahsell, *Miami University*
Scott Cairns, *Shippensburg College*

Edmonds/Edmonds/Edmonds/McNair/Olds

Mark Camma, *Atlantic Cape Community College*
Elizabeth Cannata, *Johnson & Wales University*
Eric Carlsen, *Kean University*
Frederic J. Carlson, *LeTourneau University*
Joan Carroll, *SUNY–College at Oswego*
Valrie Chambers, *Texas A&M University, Corpus Christi*
Bruce Chase, *Radford University*
Alan Cherry, *Loyola Marymount University*
Bea Chiang, *College of New Jersey*
Ginger Clark, *University of Cincinnati*
Paul Clikeman, *University of Richmond*
Ronald Colley, *State University of West Georgia*
Cheryl Corke, *Genesse Community College*
Samantha Cox, *Wake Technical Community College*
William Cress, *University of Wisconsin–La Crosse*
Kathy Crusto-Way, *Tarrant County College Southeast*
Sue Cullers, *Tarleton State University*
Jill D'Aquila, *Iona College*
Wagih Dafashy, *College of William & Mary*
Laura DeLaune, *Louisiana State University*
Guenther Dermanelian, *Johnson & Wales University*
Robert Derstine, *Villanova University*
Walter Doehring, *Genesee Community College*
George Dow, *Valencia Community College*
Lola Dudley, *Eastern Illinois University*
Melanie Earls, *Mississippi State University*
Catherine Eason, *Queens University of Charlotte*
Alan Eastman, *Indiana University of Pennsylvania*
M. J. Edwards, *Adirondack Community College*
Susan Eldridge, *University of Nebraska, Omaha*
Terry Elliott, *Morehead State University*
Denise English, *Boise State University*
Tom English, *Boise State University*

Ruth Epps, *Virginia Commonwealth University*
Caroline Falconetti, *Nassau Community College*
John Farlin, *Ohio Dominican University*
Philip Fink, *University of Toledo*
David Fordham, *James Madison University*
Ken Fowler, *San Jose State University*
Lou Fowler, *Missouri Western State College*
Peter Frischmann, *Idaho State University*
Ralph Fritzsch, *Midwestern State University*
Mark Fronke, *Cerritos College*
Ross Fuerman, *Suffolk University*
Mary Anne Gaffney, *Temple University*
David Ganz, *University of Missouri–St. Louis*
Michael Garner, *Salisbury State University*
Jane Garvin, *Ivy Tech Community College*
William T. Geary, *College of William and Mary*
Sheri Geddes, *Hope College*
Lucille Genduso, *Nova Southeastern University*
Frank Gersich, *Gustavus Adolphus College*
Daniel Gibbons, *Waubonsee Community College*
Claudia Gilbertson, *North Hennepin Community College*
Frank Giove, *Niagara University*
Lorraine Glasscock, *University of North Alabama*
Diane Glowacki, *Tarrant County College*
Paul Goodchild, *University of Central Missouri*
John Gould, *Western Carolina University*
Joseph Guardino, *Kingsborough Community College*
Jeffry Haber, *Iona College*
Abo-El-Yazeed Habib, *Minnesota State University, Mankato*
Larry Hagler, *East Carolina University*
Penny Hanes, *Virginia Tech University*
Deborah Hanks, *Cardinal Stritch University*

Leon Hanouille, *Syracuse University*
Heidi Hansel, *Kirkwood Community College*
Coby Harmon, *University of California, Santa Barbara*
Judith Harris, *Nova Southeastern University*
Phillip Harsha, *Southwest Missouri State University*
Charles Hart, *Copiah–Lincoln Community College*
Michael Haselkorn, *Harvard Extension, Cambridge*
Paul Haugen, *Wisconsin Indianhead Technical College*
Thomas Hayes, *University of Louisiana, Monroe*
Inez Heal, *Youngstown State University*
Kenneth Hiltebeitel, *Villanova University*
Nitham Hindi, *Shippensburg College*
Jan Holmes, *Louisiana State University*
Bambi Hora, *University of Central Oklahoma*
Kenneth Horowitz, *Mercer County Community College*
M. A. Houston, *Wright State University*
Susan Hughes, *Butler University*
Karen Hull, *Kansas Wesleyan University*
Kurt Hull, *California State University, Los Angeles*
Richard Hulme, *California State Polytechnic University, Pomona*
Gary Todd Jackson, *Northeastern State University*
Sharon Jackson, *Samford University*
Agatha Jeffers, *Montclair State University*
Scott Jerris, *San Francisco State University*
Pamela Jones, *Mississippi State University*
David Juriga, *Saint Louis Community College*
Robert Kachur, *Richard Stockton College of New Jersey*
Shelley Stall Kane, *Wake Technical Community College*
Khondkar Karim, *Monmouth University*

Cindi Khanlarian, *University of North Carolina Greensboro*

Bonita Kramer, *Montana State University*

Nathan Kranowski, *Radford University*

Leah Kratz, *Eastern Mennonite University*

Joan Lacher, *Nassau Community College*

Steven LaFave, *Augsburg College*

Helen LaFrancois, *University of Massachusetts Dartmouth*

Ellen Landgraf, *Loyola University, Chicago*

Robert Landry, *Massasoit Community College*

Joseph Larkin, *Saint Joseph's University*

Laurie Larson, *Valencia Community College*

William Lathen, *Boise State University*

Doug Laufer, *Metropolitan State College of Denver*

Daniel Law, *Gonzaga University*

David Law, *Youngstown State University*

Marilynn Leathart, *John Carroll University*

Chuo-Hsuan (Jason) Lee, *SUNY–Plattsburgh*

Patsy Lee, *University of Texas, Arlington*

June Li, *University of Minnesota, Duluth*

William Link, *University of Missouri–St. Louis*

Philip Little, *Coastal Carolina University*

Larry Logan, *University of Massachusetts Dartmouth*

Patricia Lopez, *Valencia Community College*

Angelo Luciano, *Columbia College Chicago*

Don Lucy, *Indian River State College Central*

James Lukawitz, *University of Memphis*

Catherine Lumbattis, *Southern Illinois University Carbondale*

Nancy Lynch, *West Virginia University*

Mary MacAusland, *Reading Area Community College*

Mostafa Maksy, *Northeastern Illinois University*

Mary Manktelow, *James Madison University*

Joseph Marcheggiani, *Butler University*

Diane Marker, *University of Toledo*

Herb Martin, *Hope College*

Elizabeth Matz, *University of Pittsburgh, Bradford*

Alan Mayer-Sommer, *Georgetown University*

Lynn Mazzola, *Nassau Community College*

Ruth Ann McEwen, *Suffolk University*

Dwight McIntyre, *Clemson University*

Dawn McKinley, *William Rainey Harper College*

Shaen McMurtrie, *Northern Oklahoma College*

Nancy Meade, *Radford University*

Trini Melcher, *California State University, San Marcos*

Sara Melendy, *Gonzaga University*

Pam Meyer, *University of Louisiana, Lafayette*

R. L. C. Miller, *California State University, Fullerton*

Elizabeth Minbiole, *Northwood University*

Susan Minke, *Indiana University–Purdue University Fort Wayne*

George Minmier, *University of Memphis*

Cheryl Mitchem, *Virginia State University*

Patrick Montgomery, *University of Wisconsin, Platteville*

Lu Montondon, *Southwest Texas State University*

Gerald Motl, *Xavier University*

Elizabeth Mulig, *Columbus State University*

Steve Muller, *Valencia Community College*

Carol Murphy, *Quinsigamond Community College*

Irvin Nelson, *Utah State University*

Bruce Neumann, *University of Colorado, Denver*

Christine Noel, *Colorado State University–Pueblo*

Tim Nygaard, *Madisonville Community College*

Ron O'Brien, *Fayetteville Technical Community College*

Brian O'Doherty, *East Carolina University*

Bruce Oliver, *Rochester Institute of Technology*

Joseph Onyeocha, *South Carolina State University*

Ashton Oravetz, *Tyler Junior College*

Stephen Owusu-Ansah, *University of Texas, Pan American*

Lawrence Ozzello, *University of Wisconsin–Eau Claire*

Angel Pannell, *Mississippi State University*

Eileen Peacock, *Oakland University*

Kathy Perdue, *DeVry Institute of Technology at Decatur*

Viola Persia, *SUNY Stony Brook*

Jack Peterson, *Utah State University*

Thomas Phillips, Jr., *Louisiana Tech University*

Cynthia Phipps, *Lake Land College*

Ronald Pierno, *Florida State University*

Cathy Pitts, *Highline Community College*

Wendy Potratz, *University of Wisconsin–Oshkosh*

Atul Rai, *Wichita State University*

Mary Raven, *Mount Mary College*

Thomas Rearick, *Indiana University*

Craig Reeder, *Florida A&M University*

Jane Reimers, *Florida State University*

Ann Rich, *Quinnipiac University*

Laura Rickett, *Kent State University*

Michael Riordan, *James Madison University*

Patricia Robinson, *Johnson and Wales University*

Carol Rogers, *Central New Mexico Community College*

Luther Ross, *Central Piedmont Community College*

Pamela Rouse, *Butler University*

Ann Rowell, *Central Piedmont Community College*

Ken Ruby, *Idaho State University*

Nadine Russell

P. N. Saksena, *Indiana University, South Bend*

Linda Schain, *Hofstra University*

Nancy Schneider, *Lynchburg College*

Henry Schulman, *Grossmont College*
Jeffrey Schwartz, *Montgomery College*
Joanne Segovia, *Minnesota State University, Moorhead*
Cindy Seipel, *New Mexico State University*
Suzanne Sevalstad, *University of Nevada, Las Vegas*
Kim Shaughnessy, *James Madison University*
Carol Shaver, *Louisiana Tech University*
John Shaver, *Louisiana Tech University*
Lewis Shaw, *Suffolk University*
Mary Sheil, *Kennesaw State University*
Eileen Shifflett, *James Madison University*
Nathan Slavin, *Hofstra University*
Jill Smith, *Idaho State University*
Sondra Smith, *University of West Georgia*
Talitha Smith, *Auburn University*
Nancy Snow, *University of Toledo*
Paul E. Solomon
Mary Soroko, *St. Cloud State University*
Linda Specht, *Trinity University*
John Sperry, *Virginia Commonwealth University*
Barbara Squires, *Corning Community College*
Vic Stanton, *University of California Berkeley*
Paul Steinbart, *Saint Louis University, Saint Louis*
Scott Steinkamp, *College of Lake County*
Tim Stephens, *DeVry Institute of Technology at Addison*
Mary Stevens, *University of Texas at El Paso*
Sue Stickland, *University of Texas, Arlington*
Leonard Stokes, *Siena College*
Ronald Strittmater, *North Hennepin Community College*
Gloria Stuart, *Georgia Southern University*
Janice Swanson, *Southern Oregon University*

James Swayze, *University of Nevada, Las Vegas*
Ellen Sweatt, *Georgia Perimeter College*
Jan Sweeney, *Baruch College CUNY*
Rasoul Taghizadeh, *Lexington Community College*
Bill Talbot, *Montgomery College*
Kerri Tassin, *Missouri State University*
Maurice Tassin, *Louisiana Tech University*
Steve Teeter, *Utah Valley State College*
Kim Temme, *Maryville University*
Peter Theuri, *Northern Kentucky University*
James Thompson, *Oklahoma City University*
Ada Till, *Prairie View A&M University*
Karen Turner, *University of Northern Colorado*
Suneel Udpa, *St. Mary's College of California*
Donna Ulmer, *St. Louis Community College, Meramec*
Denise Dickins Veitch, *Florida Atlantic University*
George Violette, *University of Southern Maine*
Beth Vogel, *Mount Mary College*
Sharon Walters, *Morehead State University*
Andrea Weickgenannt, *Northern Kentucky University*
J. D. Weinhold, *Concordia College*
Judith Welch, *University of Central Florida*
T. Sterling Wetzel, *Oklahoma State University, Stillwater*
Thomas Whalen, *Suffolk University*
Thomas Whitacre, *University of South Carolina*
Jennifer Wilbanks, *State Fair Community College*
Macil C. Wilkie, Jr., *Grambling State University*
Marvin Williams, *University of Houston*
Stephen Willits, *Bucknell University*
Marie Winks, *Lynchburg College*

Kenneth Winter, *University of Wisconsin–La Crosse*
Alan Winters, *Clemson University*
Gail Wright, *Bryant University*
Marjorie Yuschak, *Rutgers University*
Judith Zander, *Grossmont College*
Haiwen Zhang, *University of Minnesota*
Ping Zhon, *Baruch College*

Focus Group Participants
Mark Anderson, *University of Texas at Dallas*
Brenda Benson, *Blinn College*
Anna Marie Boulware, *St. Charles Community College*
Norris Dorsey, *California State University, Northridge*
Caroline Falconetti, *Nassau Community College*
Judith Harris, *Nova Southeastern University*
Carol Hutchinson, *AB Tech*
Douglas Larson, *Salem State College*
Joseph Lupino, *St. Mary's College of California*
Al Nagy, *John Carroll University*
Ron Pierno, *Florida State University*
Linda Poulson, *Elon University*
Atul Rai, *Wichita State University*
Gayle Richardson, *Bakersfield College*
Dwight Riley, *Richland College*
Megan Schaupp, *West Virginia University–Morgantown*
Rex Schildhouse, *Miramar College*
Virginia Smith, *Saint Mary's College of California*
Warren Smock, *Ivy Tech Community College*
Kathy Sobieralski, *University of Maryland, University College*
Rasoul Taghizadeh, *Bluegrass Community and Technical College*
LaVerne Thomas-Vertrees, *St. Louis Community College*
Al Wallace, *Owensboro Community & Technical College*

BRIEF CONTENTS

Chapter 1 An Introduction to Accounting 2

Chapter 2 Accounting for Accruals and Deferrals 70

Chapter 3 The Double-Entry Accounting System 146

Chapter 4 Accounting for Merchandising Businesses 212

Chapter 5 Accounting for Inventories 272

Chapter 6 Internal Control and Accounting for Cash 316

Chapter 7 Accounting for Receivables 362

Chapter 8 Accounting for Long-Term Operational Assets 418

Chapter 9 Accounting for Current Liabilities and Payroll 478

Chapter 10 Accounting for Long-Term Debt 536

Chapter 11 Proprietorships, Partnerships, and Corporations 594

Chapter 12 Statement of Cash Flows 646

Chapter 13 Financial Statement Analysis (Available online in *Connect*) 13-0

Appendix A Accessing the EDGAR Database through the Internet 700

Appendix B Portion of the Form 10-K for Target Corporation 701

Appendix C Summary of Financial Ratios 708

Appendix D Annual Report and Financial Statement Analysis Projects 711

Appendix E Accounting for Investment Securities 719

Appendix F Time Value of Money 728

Glossary 736

Index 745

CONTENTS

Note from the Authors iv

©McGraw-Hill Education/
Jill Braaten, photographer

Chapter 1 An Introduction to Accounting 2

SECTION 1: Collecting and Organizing Information 3

The Role of Accounting in Society 4
- *Using Free Markets to Set Resource Priorities* 4
- *Accounting Provides Information* 5
- *Types of Accounting Information* 6
- *Nonbusiness Resource Usage* 6
- *Careers in Accounting* 6
- *Measurement Rules* 8

Reporting Entities 8

Elements of Financial Statements 10
- *Using Accounts to Gather Information* 10
- *Creating an Accounting Equation* 11

Recording Business Events under the Accounting Equation 13
- *Asset Source Transactions* 13
- *Asset Exchange Transactions* 14
- *Another Asset Source Transaction* 14
- *Asset Use Transactions* 15
- *Summary of Transactions* 16

Interpreting Information Shown in the Accounting Equation 17
- *The Left versus the Right Side of the Accounting Equation* 17
- *Cash and Retained Earnings* 17
- *Business Liquidations Resulting from Net Losses* 18
- *Business Liquidations Resulting from the Mismanagement of Assets* 19
- *Two Views of the Right Side of the Accounting Equation* 19

Recap: Types of Transactions 20

SECTION 2: Reporting Information 21

Preparing an Income Statement, a Statement of Changes in Stockholders' Equity, and a Balance Sheet 21
- *Income Statement and the Matching Concept* 21
- *Statement of Changes in Stockholders' Equity* 23
- *Balance Sheet* 23

Preparing a Statement of Cash Flows 24

The Closing Process 25

The Horizontal Financial Statements Model 28

The Financial Analyst 29
- *Real-World Financial Reports* 29
- *Annual Report for Target Corporation* 30
- *Special Terms in Real-World Reports* 32

A Look Back 32
A Look Forward 32
Self-Study Review Problem 33
Key Terms 36
Questions 36
Multiple-Choice Questions 37
Section 1 Exercises–Series A 37
Section 2 Exercises–Series A 42
Sections 1 and 2 Problems–Series A 47
Section 1 Exercises–Series B 50
Section 2 Exercises–Series B 55
Sections 1 and 2 Problems–Series B 59
Analyze, Think, Communicate 63
Comprehensive Problem 69

Chapter 2 Accounting for Accruals and Deferrals 70

©B. O'Kane/Alamy

SECTION 1: Accounting for Accruals 71

Accounting for Receivables 72
- *Recognizing Accounts Receivable 73*
- *Other Events 74*

Accounting for Payables (Year-End Adjusting Entry) 74
- *Summary of Events and General Ledger 76*

Preparing Financial Statements with Accruals 76
- *Income Statement 76*
- *Statement of Changes in Stockholders' Equity 76*

Steps in an Accounting Cycle 79
- *The Closing Process 79*
- *Steps in an Accounting Cycle 79*
- *The Matching Concept 80*

SECTION 2: Accounting for Deferrals 81

Second Accounting Cycle 82

Accounting for Supplies 82

Accounting for Prepaid Items 84

Accounting for Unearned Revenue 86

Preparing Financial Statements with Deferrals 87
- *Vertical Statements Model 90*
- *Closing for the Year 2 Accounting Period 91*

Transaction Classification 93

Corporate Governance 94

The Financial Analyst 94
- *Importance of Ethics 94*
- *The Sarbanes–Oxley Act 94*
- *Common Features of Criminal and Ethical Misconduct 95*

A Look Back 97
A Look Forward 98
Appendix 98
Self-Study Review Problem 102
Key Terms 104
Questions 104
Multiple-Choice Questions 105
Section 1 Exercises–Series A 105
Section 2 Exercises–Series A 109
Sections 1 and 2 Problems–Series A 117
Section 1 Exercises–Series B 122
Section 2 Exercises–Series B 126
Sections 1 and 2 Problems–Series B 135
Analyze, Think, Communicate 140
Comprehensive Problem 144

Chapter 3 The Double-Entry Accounting System 146

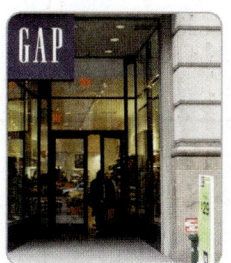
©Jstone/Shutterstock RF

Chapter Opening 146

Debit/Credit Terminology 148

Recording Transactions in T-Accounts 148
- *Asset Source Transactions 148*
- *Asset Exchange Transactions 151*
- *Asset Use Transactions 152*
- *Claims Exchange Transactions 154*
- *Adjusting the Accounts 155*
- *Overview of Debit/Credit Relationships 157*

The General Journal 158
Trial Balance and Financial Statements 160
 Closing Entries 161
 Post-Closing Trial Balance 164
The Financial Analyst 165
 Assessing the Effective Use of Assets 165
 Assessing Debt Risk 165
 Real-World Data 166
Scope of Coverage 168

A Look Back 168
A Look Forward 169
Appendix 169
Self-Study Review Problem 170
Key Terms 173
Questions 174
Multiple-Choice Questions 174
Exercises—Series A 174
Problems—Series A 182
Exercises—Series B 189
Problems—Series B 197
Analyze, Think, Communicate 204
Comprehensive Problem 210

Chapter 4 Accounting for Merchandising Businesses 212

©Jim West/Alamy

Chapter Opening 212
Accounting for Inventory Transactions 215
 Allocating Inventory Cost between Asset and Expense Accounts 216
 Perpetual Inventory System 216
 Effects of Year 1 Events on Financial Statements 216
 Ledger Accounts and Financial Statements 218
Transportation Cost, Purchase Returns and Allowances, and Cash Discounts Related to Inventory Purchases 220
 Effects of the Year 2 Events on Financial Statements 220
 Accounting for Purchase Returns and Allowances 221
 Purchase Discounts 222
 The Cost of Financing Inventory 223
 Accounting for Transportation Costs 223
 Adjustment for Lost, Damaged, or Stolen Inventory 226

Gains, Losses, and a Multistep Income Statement 227
Events Affecting Sales 231
 Accounting for Sales Returns and Allowances 232
 Accounting for Sales Discounts 233
The Financial Analyst 234
 Common Size Financial Statements 234
 Ratio Analysis 234
 Real-World Data 236
A Look Back 237
A Look Forward 238
Appendix 238
Self-Study Review Problem 241
Key Terms 242
Questions 242
Multiple-Choice Questions 243
Exercises—Series A 243
Problems—Series A 252
Exercises—Series B 255
Problems—Series B 263
Analyze, Think, Communicate 266
Comprehensive Problem 271

xxxiii

©Michael Conroy/AP Images

Chapter 5 Accounting for Inventories 272

Chapter Opening 272
Inventory Cost Flow Methods 274
   Specific Identification 274
   First-In, First-Out (FIFO) 274
   Last-In, First-Out (LIFO) 274
   Weighted Average 274
   Physical Flow 274
   Effect of Cost Flow on Financial Statements 275
   Multiple Layers with Multiple Quantities 276
   Allocating Cost of Goods Available for Sale 276
   Effect of Cost Flow on Financial Statements 278
   Inventory Cost Flow When Sales and Purchases Occur Intermittently 280
Lower-of-Cost-or-Market Rule 282
Avoiding Fraud in Merchandising Businesses 284
Estimating the Ending Inventory Balance 285

The Financial Analyst 287
   Average Number of Days to Sell Inventory 287
   Is It a Marketing or an Accounting Decision? 287
   The Wallet Company Illustration 288
   Real-World Data 288
   Effects of Cost Flow on Ratio Analysis 289
A Look Back 289
A Look Forward 290
Self-Study Review Problem 290
Key Terms 291
Questions 291
Multiple-Choice Questions 292
Exercises—Series A 292
Problems—Series A 297
Exercises—Series B 301
Problems—Series B 307
Analyze, Think, Communicate 310
Comprehensive Problem 314

©jvdwolf/123RF

Chapter 6 Internal Control and Accounting for Cash 316

Chapter Opening 316
Key Features of Internal Control Systems 318
   Segregation of Duties 319
   Quality of Employees 319
   Bonded Employees 319
   Required Absences 319
   Procedures Manual 319
   Authority and Responsibility 320
   Prenumbered Documents 320
   Physical Control 320
   Performance Evaluations 320
   Limitations 320

Accounting for Cash 321
   Controlling Cash 321
   Checking Account Documents 323
Reconciling the Bank Account 325
   Determining True Cash Balance 325
   Adjustments to the Bank Balance 325
   Adjustments to the Book Balance 325
   Correction of Errors 326
   Certified Checks 326
   Illustrating a Bank Reconciliation 327

Updating GSRI's Accounting Records   328
Cash Short and Over   329
Using Petty Cash Funds   330
The Financial Analyst   332
Notes to the Financial Statements   333
Management's Discussion and Analysis   333
Role of the Independent Auditor   333
The Securities and Exchange Commission   335

A Look Back   336
A Look Forward   336
Self-Study Review Problem   337
Key Terms   337
Questions   338
Multiple-Choice Questions   338
Exercises—Series A   338
Problems—Series A   343
Exercises—Series B   347
Problems—Series B   351
Analyze, Think, Communicate   355
Comprehensive Problem   360

Chapter 7 Accounting for Receivables   362

©Bloomberg/Getty Images

Chapter Opening   362
Estimating Uncollectible Accounts Expense Using the Percent of Revenue Method   364
Accounting Events Affecting the Year 1 Period   364
Recording and Reporting Uncollectible Accounts Events in the Double-Entry System   367
Financial Statements   367
Accounting Events Affecting the Year 2 Period   368
Recording and Reporting Uncollectible Accounts Events in the Double-Entry System   371
Analysis of Financial Statements   372
Estimating Uncollectible Accounts Expense Using the Percent of Receivables Method   372
Aging Accounts Receivable   373
Matching Revenues and Expenses versus Asset Measurement   374
Recognizing Uncollectible Accounts Expense Using the Direct Write-Off Method   375

Accounting for Notes Receivable   376
Recording and Reporting Transactions Related to Notes Receivable   377
Financial Statements   380
Accounting for Credit Card Sales   381
The Financial Analyst   382
Average Number of Days to Collect Accounts Receivable   383
Real-World Data   383

A Look Back   386
A Look Forward   386
Self-Study Review Problem   387
Key Terms   388
Questions   388
Multiple-Choice Questions   389
Exercises—Series A   389
Problems—Series A   395
Exercises—Series B   400
Problems—Series B   407
Analyze, Think, Communicate   412
Comprehensive Problem   416

xxxv

Chapter 8 Accounting for Long-Term Operational Assets 418

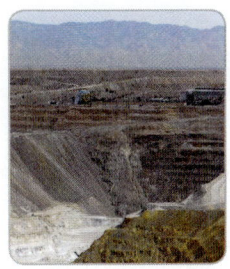
©Brad Sauter/Shutterstock

Chapter Opening 418
Tangible versus Intangible Assets 420
    Tangible Long-Term Assets 420
    Intangible Assets 420
Determining the Cost of Long-Term Assets 421
    Basket Purchase Allocation 421
Methods of Recognizing Depreciation Expense 422
    Dryden Enterprises Illustration 423
    Straight-Line Depreciation 423
    Financial Statements 425
    Double-Declining-Balance Depreciation 426
    Units-of-Production Depreciation 428
    Accounting for the Disposal of Long-Term Operational Assets 430
    Comparing the Depreciation Methods 430
Income Tax Considerations 431
Revision of Estimates 433
    Revision of Life 433
    Revision of Salvage 434
Continuing Expenditures for Plant Assets 434
    Costs That Are Expensed 434
    Costs That Are Capitalized 434

Natural Resources 436
Intangible Assets 437
    Trademarks 438
    Patents 438
    Copyrights 438
    Franchises 439
    Goodwill 439
    Expense Recognition for Intangible Assets 440
    Balance Sheet Presentation 441
The Financial Analyst 442
    Effect of Judgment and Estimation 442
A Look Back 444
A Look Forward 444
Self-Study Review Problem 444
Key Terms 446
Questions 446
Multiple-Choice Questions 447
Exercises—Series A 447
Problems—Series A 454
Exercises—Series B 459
Problems—Series B 466
Analyze, Think, Communicate 471
Comprehensive Problem 476

Chapter 9 Accounting for Current Liabilities and Payroll 478

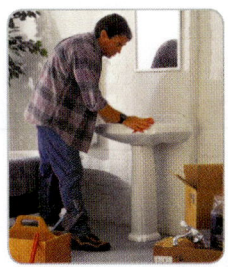
©Ingram Publishing

Chapter Opening 478
Accounting for Notes Payable 480
Accounting for Sales Tax 482
Contingent Liabilities 483

Warranty Obligations 484
    General Ledger T-Accounts and Financial Statements 486
Accounting for Payroll 487
    Identifying Employees 487

Employees' Gross Earnings 488
Deductions from Employees' Gross Earnings 488
Federal Income Taxes 488
Federal Income Tax Documents 489
Social Security and Medicare Taxes (FICA) 490
Voluntary Withholdings (Deductions) 491
Computing Employee Net Pay 492
Employer Payroll Taxes 493
Recording and Reporting Payroll Taxes 493
Employee Fringe Benefits 494

The Financial Analyst 494
Preparing a Classified Balance Sheet 495
Liquidity versus Solvency 497

A Look Back 498
A Look Forward 499
Appendix 499
Self-Study Review Problem 505
Key Terms 507
Questions 508
Multiple-Choice Questions 508
Exercises—Series A 508
Problems—Series A 515
Exercises—Series B 519
Problems—Series B 525
Analyze, Think, Communicate 529
Comprehensive Problem 534

Chapter 10 Accounting for Long-Term Debt 536

©Dorann Weber/Moment Mobile/Getty Images

Chapter Opening 536
Installment Notes Payable 538
Line of Credit 541
Bond Liabilities 542
Advantages of Issuing Bonds 542
Security of Bonds 543
Timing of Maturity 543
Special Features 544
Bond Ratings 545
Restrictive Covenants 545
Bonds Issued at Face Value 545
Journal Entries and Financial Statement Effects 545
Financial Statements 547

Amortization Using the Straight-Line Method 548
Bonds Issued at a Discount 548
Bonds Issued at a Premium 553
Bond Redemptions 554

Amortization Using the Effective Interest Rate Method 555
Amortizing Bond Discounts 556
Amortizing Bond Premiums 557

The Financial Analyst 559
Financial Leverage and Tax Advantage of Debt Financing 559
EBIT and Ratio Analysis 560
Times-Interest-Earned Ratio 561

A Look Back 562
A Look Forward 562
Self-Study Review Problem 562
Key Terms 563
Questions 563
Multiple-Choice Questions 564
Exercises—Series A 564
Problems—Series A 571
Exercises—Series B 575
Problems—Series B 581
Analyze, Think, Communicate 585
Comprehensive Problem 591

xxxvii

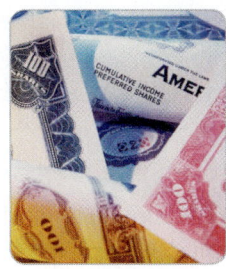
©Stockbyte/Getty Images

Chapter 11 Proprietorships, Partnerships, and Corporations 594

Chapter Opening 594
Forms of Business Organizations 596
Regulation 596
Double Taxation 597
Limited Liability 598
Continuity 598
Transferability of Ownership 598
Management Structure 598
Ability to Raise Capital 598
Appearance of Capital Structure in Financial Statements 599
Accounting for Capital Stock 600
Par Value 600
Stated Value 601
Stock: Authorized, Issued, and Outstanding 601
Other Valuation Terminology 601
Common versus Preferred Stock 601
Common Stock 601
Preferred Stock 601
Other Classes of Stock 603
Accounting for Stock Transactions on the Day of Issue 604
Issuing Par Value Stock 604
Stock Classfication 604
Stock Issued at Stated Value 605
Stock Issued with No Par Value 605
Financial Statement Presentation 605

Treasury Stock 606
Cash Dividends 609
Declaration Rate 609
Date of Record 609
Payment Date 609
Stock Dividends and Splits 610
Stock Dividends 610
Stock Splits 611
Appropriation of Retained Earnings 611
Financial Statement Presentation 612
The Financial Analyst 613
Receiving Dividends 613
Increasing the Price of Stock 613
Price-Earnings Ratio 614
Exercising Control through Stock Ownership 615

A Look Back 615
A Look Forward 616
Self-Study Review Problem 617
Key Terms 617
Questions 618
Multiple-Choice Questions 619
Exercises—Series A 619
Problems—Series A 624
Exercises—Series B 628
Problems—Series B 635
Analyze, Think, Communicate 639
Comprehensive Problem 644

©NYCStock/Shutterstock

Chapter 12 Statement of Cash Flows 646

Chapter Opening 646
An Overview of the Statement of Cash Flows 648
Operating Activities 648
Investing Activities 649

Financing Activities 649
Noncash Investing and Financing Activities 650
Reporting Format for the Statement of Cash Flows 650

Preparing a Statement of Cash Flows 651
Preparing the Operating Activities Section of a Statement of Cash Flows Using the Indirect Method 652
- *Indirect Method—Reconciliation Approach* 654
- *Indirect Method—Rule-Based Approach* 658

Preparing the Operating Activities Section of a Statement of Cash Flows Using the Direct Method 661

Preparing the Investing Activities Section of a Statement of Cash Flows 661
- *Reconciliation of Investment Securities* 662
- *Reconciliation of Store Fixtures* 662
- *Reconciliation of Land* 662

Preparing the Financing Activities Section of a Statement of Cash Flows 663
- *Reconciliation of Mortgage Payable* 664
- *Reconciliation of Bonds Payable* 664
- *Reconciliation of Common Stock* 665
- *Reconciliation of Retained Earnings* 665
- *Reconciliation of Treasury Stock* 665

Preparing the Schedule of Noncash Investing and Financing Activities 668
The Financial Analyst 668
- *Real-World Data* 668

A Look Back 670
A Look Forward 671
Self-Study Review Problem 671
Key Terms 673
Questions 673
Multiple-Choice Questions 674
Exercises—Series A 674
Problems—Series A 679
Exercises—Series B 684
Problems—Series B 689
Analyze, Think, Communicate 694

Chapter 13 Financial Statement Analysis (Available online in *Connect*) 13-0

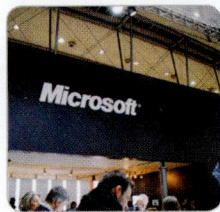
©Aleksej Penkov/123RF

Chapter Opening 13-0
Factors in Communicating Useful Information 13-2
- *The Users* 13-2
- *The Types of Decisions* 13-2
- *Information Analysis* 13-2

Methods of Analysis 13-2
- *Horizontal Analysis* 13-3
- *Vertical Analysis* 13-5

Ratio Analysis 13-6
- *Objectives of Ratio Analysis* 13-6

Measures of Debt-Paying Ability 13-7
- *Liquidity Ratios* 13-7
- *Solvency Ratios* 13-10

Measures of Profitability 13-13
- *Measures of Managerial Effectiveness* 13-13
- *Stock Market Ratios* 13-15

Limitations of Financial Statement Analysis 13-18
- *Different Industries* 13-18
- *Changing Economic Environment* 13-19
- *Accounting Principles* 13-19

A Look Back 13-20
Self-Study Review Problem 13-21
Key Terms 13-23
Questions 13-23

Multiple-Choice Questions 13-23	Exercises—Series B 13-34
Exercises—Series A 13-23	Problems—Series B 13-39
Problems—Series A 13-28	Analyze, Think, Communicate 13-45

Appendix A   Accessing the EDGAR Database through the Internet   700

Appendix B   Portion of the Form 10-K for Target Corporation   701

Appendix C   Summary of Financial Ratios   708

Appendix D   Annual Report and Financial Statement Analysis Projects   711

Appendix E   Accounting for Investment Securities   719

Appendix F   Time Value of Money   728

Glossary   736

Index   745

CHAPTER 1

An Introduction to Accounting

LEARNING OBJECTIVES

After you have mastered the material in this chapter, you will be able to:

SECTION 1: COLLECTING AND ORGANIZING INFORMATION

LO 1-1 Identify the ways accounting benefits society.
LO 1-2 Identify reporting entities.
LO 1-3 Identify the components of the accounting equation.
LO 1-4 Show how business events affect the accounting equation.
LO 1-5 Interpret information shown in an accounting equation.
LO 1-6 Classify business events as asset source, use, or exchange transactions.

SECTION 2: REPORTING INFORMATION

LO 1-7 Prepare an income statement, a statement of changes in stockholders' equity, and a balance sheet.
LO 1-8 Prepare a statement of cash flows.
LO 1-9 Close revenue, expense, and dividend accounts.
LO 1-10 Record business events using a horizontal financial statements model.

 Video lectures and accompanying self-assessment quizzes are available in Connect *for all learning objectives.*

The Curious Accountant

Who owns **Starbucks**? Who owns the **American Cancer Society** (ACS)? Many people and organizations other than owners are interested in the operations of Starbucks and the ACS. These parties are called **stakeholders**. Among others, they include lenders, employees, suppliers, customers, benefactors, research institutions, local governments, cancer patients, lawyers, bankers, financial analysts, and government agencies such as the Internal Revenue Service and the Securities and Exchange Commission. Organizations communicate information to stakeholders through **financial reports**.

How do you think the financial reports of Starbucks differ from those of the ACS? (Answers on page 11.)

©McGraw-Hill Education/Jill Braaten, photographer

SECTION 1:
COLLECTING AND ORGANIZING INFORMATION

Why should you study accounting? Because it can help you succeed in business. Businesses use accounting to keep score. Imagine trying to play football without knowing how many points a touchdown is worth. Like sports, business is competitive. If you do not know how to keep score, you likely will not succeed.

Accounting is an information system that reports on the economic activities and financial condition of a business or other organization. The importance of accounting information is paramount. It helps predict business success, and could make you a wealthy Wall Street investor. Indeed, it is so important that accounting is frequently called the *language of business*.

LO 1-1

Identify the ways accounting benefits society.

THE ROLE OF ACCOUNTING IN SOCIETY

How should society allocate its resources? Should we spend more to harvest food or cure disease? Should we build computers or cars? Should we invest money in IBM or General Motors? Accounting provides information that helps answer such questions.

Using Free Markets to Set Resource Priorities

Suppose you want to start a business. You may have heard "you need to have money to make money." In fact, you will need more than just money to start and operate a business. You will likely need such resources as equipment, land, materials, and employees. If you do not have these resources, how can you get them? In the United States, you compete for resources in open markets.

A **market** is a group of people or entities organized to exchange items of value. The market for business resources involves three distinct participants: consumers, conversion agents, and resource owners. *Consumers* use resources. Resources are frequently not in a form consumers want. For example, nature provides trees but consumers want houses. *Conversion agents* (businesses) transform resources such as trees into desirable products such as houses. *Resource owners* control the distribution of resources to conversion agents. Thus, resource owners provide resources (inputs) to conversion agents, who provide goods and services (outputs) to consumers.

For example, a home builder (conversion agent) transforms labor and materials (inputs) into houses (output) that consumers use. The transformation adds value to the inputs, creating outputs worth more than the sum of the inputs. For example, a house that required $220,000 of materials and labor to build could have a market value of $250,000.

©David Buffington/Getty Images RF

Common terms for the added value created in the transformation process include **profit, income,** or **earnings.** Accountants measure the added value as the difference between the cost of a product or service and the selling price of that product or service. The profit on the house described above is $30,000, the difference between its $220,000 cost and $250,000 market value.

Conversion agents who successfully and efficiently (at low cost) satisfy consumer preferences are rewarded with high earnings. These earnings are shared with resource owners, so conversion agents who exhibit high earnings potential are more likely to compete successfully for resources.

Return to the original question. How can you get the resources you need to start a business? You must go to open markets and convince resource owners that you can produce profits. Exhibit 1.1 illustrates the market trilogy involved in resource allocation.

The specific resources businesses commonly use to satisfy consumer demand are financial resources, physical resources, and labor resources.

Financial Resources

Businesses (conversion agents) need **financial resources** (money) to get started and to operate. *Investors* and *creditors* provide financial resources.

- **Investors** provide financial resources in exchange for ownership interests in businesses. Owners expect businesses to return to them a share of the business, including a portion of earned income.

- **Creditors** lend financial resources to businesses. Instead of a share of the business, creditors expect the businesses to repay borrowed resources plus a specified fee called **interest.**

EXHIBIT 1.1

Market Trilogy in Resource Allocation

Investors and creditors prefer to provide financial resources to businesses with high earnings potential because such companies are better able to share profits and make interest payments. Profitable businesses are also less likely to experience bankruptcy.

Physical Resources

In their most primitive form, **physical resources** are natural resources. Physical resources often move through numerous stages of transformation. For example, standing timber may be successively transformed into harvested logs, raw lumber, and finished houses. Owners of physical resources seek to sell those resources to businesses with high earnings potential because profitable businesses are able to pay higher prices and make repeat purchases.

Labor Resources

Labor resources include both intellectual and physical labor. Like other resource providers, workers prefer businesses that have high income potential because these businesses are able to pay higher wages and offer continued employment.

Accounting Provides Information

How do providers of financial, physical, and labor resources identify conversion agents (businesses) with high profit potential? Investors, creditors, and workers rely heavily on accounting information to evaluate which businesses are worthy of receiving resources. In addition, other people and organizations have an interest in accounting information about businesses. The many **users** of accounting information are commonly called **stakeholders.** Stakeholders include resource providers, financial analysts, brokers, attorneys, government regulators, and news reporters.

The link between conversion agents (businesses) and those stakeholders who provide resources is direct: Businesses pay resource providers. Resource providers use accounting information to identify companies with high earnings potential because those companies are more likely to return higher profits, make interest payments, repay debt, pay higher prices, and provide stable, high-paying employment.

The link between conversion agents and other stakeholders is indirect. Financial analysts, brokers, and attorneys may use accounting information when advising their clients. Government agencies may use accounting information to assess companies' compliance with income tax laws and other regulations. Reporters may use accounting information in news reports.

Types of Accounting Information

Stakeholders such as investors, creditors, lawyers, and financial analysts exist outside of and separate from the businesses in which they are interested. The accounting information these *external users* need is provided by **financial accounting.** In contrast, the accounting information needed by *internal users,* stakeholders such as managers and employees who work within a business, is provided by **managerial accounting.**

The information needs of external and internal users frequently overlap. For example, external and internal users are both interested in the amount of income a business earns. Managerial accounting information, however, is usually more detailed than financial accounting reports. For example, investors are concerned about the overall profitability of Wendy's versus Burger King; whereas a Wendy's regional manager is interested in the profits of individual Wendy's restaurants. In fact, a regional manager is also interested in nonfinancial measures, such as the number of employees needed to operate a restaurant, the times at which customer demand is high versus low, and measures of cleanliness and customer satisfaction.

Nonbusiness Resource Usage

The U.S. economy is not purely market-based. Factors other than profitability often influence resource allocation priorities. For example, governments allocate resources for national defense, to redistribute wealth, or to protect the environment. Foundations, religious groups, the Peace Corps, and other benevolent organizations prioritize resource usage based on humanitarian concerns.

Organizations that are not motivated by profit are called **not-for-profit entities** (also called *nonprofit* or *nonbusiness organizations*). Stakeholders interested in nonprofit organizations also need accounting information. Accounting systems measure the cost of the goods and services not-for-profit organizations provide, the efficiency and effectiveness of the organizations' operations, and the ability of the organizations to continue to provide goods and services. This information serves a host of stakeholders, including taxpayers, contributors, lenders, suppliers, employees, managers, financial analysts, attorneys, and beneficiaries.

The focus of accounting, therefore, is to provide information that is useful to a variety of business and nonbusiness user groups for decision making. The different types of accounting information and the stakeholders that commonly use the information are summarized in Exhibit 1.2.

Careers in Accounting

An accounting career can take you to the top of the business world. In a recent *Forbes* article, Jeffery Sanders reveals that a significantly higher percentage of Fortune 500 CEOs advance from financial backgrounds than any other discipline. Sanders notes that large companies prefer CEOs who understand the financial ramifications of business decisions.

What do accountants do? Accountants identify, record, analyze, and communicate information about the economic events that affect organizations. They may work in either public accounting or private accounting.

Public Accounting

You are probably familiar with the acronym CPA. CPA stands for certified *public* accountant. Public accountants provide services to various clients. They are usually paid a fee that

EXHIBIT 1.2
Accounting as Information Provider

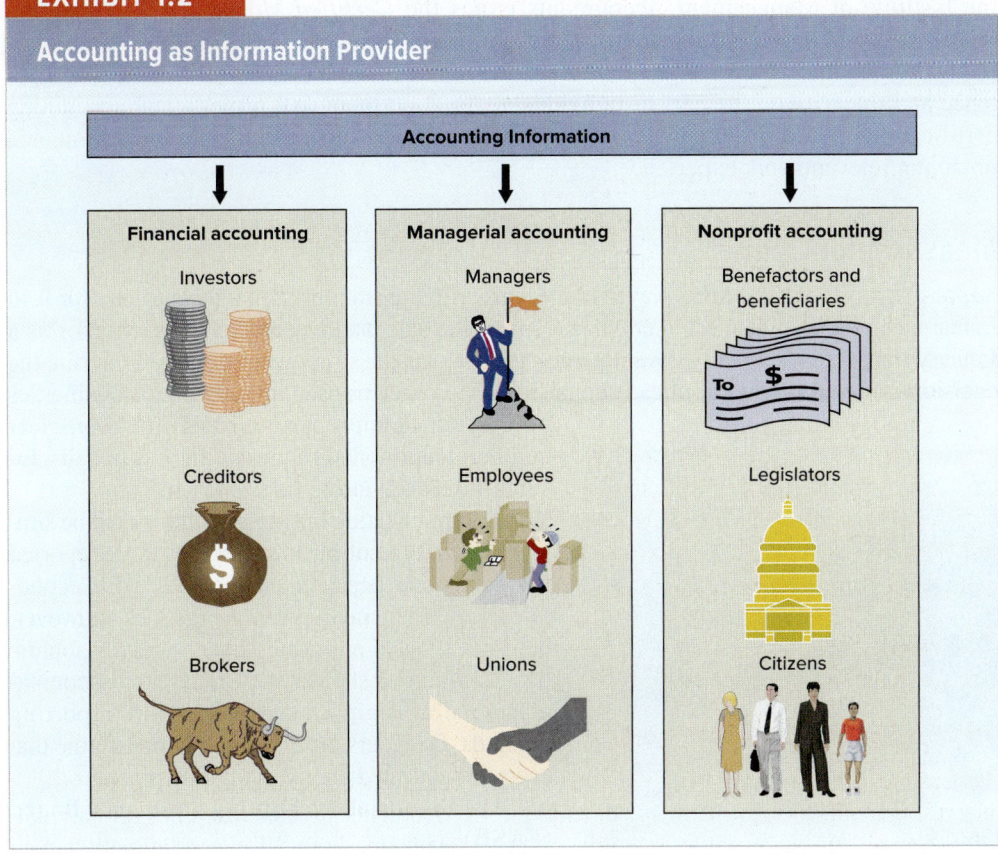

varies depending on the service provided. Services typically offered by public accountants include (1) audit services, (2) tax services, and (3) consulting services.

- *Audit services* involve examining a company's accounting records in order to issue an opinion about whether the company's financial statements conform to generally accepted accounting principles. The auditor's opinion adds credibility to the statements, which are prepared by the company's management.
- *Tax services* include both determining the amount of tax due and tax planning to help companies minimize tax expense.
- *Consulting services* cover a wide range of activities that include everything from installing sophisticated computerized accounting systems to providing personal financial advice.

All public accountants are not certified. Each state government, as well as Washington, DC, and four U.S. territories, establish certification requirements applicable in that jurisdiction. Although the requirements vary from jurisdiction to jurisdiction, CPA candidates normally must have a college education, pass a demanding technical examination, and obtain work experience relevant to practicing public accounting.

Private Accounting

Accountants employed in the private sector usually work for a specific company or nonprofit organization. Private sector accountants perform a wide variety of functions for their employers. Their duties include classifying and recording transactions, billing customers and collecting amounts due, ordering merchandise, paying suppliers, preparing and analyzing financial statements, developing budgets, measuring costs, assessing performance, and making decisions.

Private accountants may earn any of several professional certifications. For example, the Institute of Management Accountants issues the *Certified Management Accounting (CMA)* designation. The Institute of Internal Auditors issues the *Certified Internal Auditor (CIA)* designation. These designations are widely recognized indicators of technical competence and integrity on the part of individuals who hold them. All professional accounting certifications call for meeting education requirements, passing a technical examination, and obtaining relevant work experience.

Measurement Rules

Suppose a store sells an MP3 player in December to a customer who agrees to pay for it in January. Should the business *recognize* (report) the sale as a December transaction or as a January transaction? It really does not matter as long as the storeowner discloses the rule the decision is based on and applies it consistently to other transactions. Because businesses may use different reporting rules, however, clear communication also requires full and fair disclosure of the accounting rules chosen.

Communicating business results would be simpler if each type of business activity were reported using only one measurement method. World economies and financial reporting practices, however, have not evolved uniformly. Even in highly sophisticated countries such as the United States, companies exhibit significant diversity in reporting methods. Providers of financial reports assume that users are educated about accounting practices.

The **Financial Accounting Standards Board (FASB)**[1] is a privately funded organization with the primary authority for establishing accounting standards in the United States. The measurement rules established by the FASB are called **generally accepted accounting principles (GAAP).** Financial reports issued to the public must follow GAAP. This textbook introduces these principles so you will be able to understand business activity reported by companies in the United States.

©Lars Niki RF

Companies are not required to follow GAAP when preparing *management accounting* reports. Although there is considerable overlap between financial and managerial accounting, managers are free to construct internal reports in whatever fashion best suits the effective operation of their companies.

REPORTING ENTITIES

LO 1-2

Identify reporting entities.

Think of accountants in the same way you would think of news reporters. A news reporter gathers and discloses information about some person, place, or thing. Likewise, an accountant gathers and discloses financial information about specific people or businesses. The people or businesses accountants report on are called **reporting entities.** When studying accounting, you should think of yourself as the accountant. Your first step is to identify the person or business on which you are reporting. This is not always as easy as it may seem. To illustrate, consider the following scenario.

---

[1]The FASB consists of seven full-time members appointed by the supporting organization, the Financial Accounting Foundation (FAF). The FAF membership is intended to represent the broad spectrum of individuals and institutions that have an interest in accounting and financial reporting. FAF members include representatives of the accounting profession, industry, financial institutions, the government, and the investing public.

FOCUS ON INTERNATIONAL ISSUES

IS THERE GLOBAL GAAP?

As explained in this chapter, accounting is a measurement and communication discipline based on rules referred to as *generally accepted accounting principles (GAAP)*. The rules described in this text are based on GAAP used in the United States, but what rules do the rest of the world use? Is there a global GAAP, or does each country establish its own unique GAAP?

Until recently, each country developed its own unique GAAP. Global companies were required to prepare multiple sets of financial statements to satisfy each country's GAAP. The use of multiple accounting standards across the globe made comparing company performance difficult and expensive. To address the need for a common set of financial standards, the International Accounting Standards Committee was formed in 1973. The committee was reorganized as the **International Accounting Standards Board (IASB)** in 2001. The IASB issues **International Financial Reporting Standards (IFRS)**, which are rapidly gaining support worldwide. In 2005, companies in the countries who were members of the European Union were required to use the IFRS as established by the IASB, which is headquartered in London. Today, over 100 countries require or permit companies to prepare their financial statements using IFRS.

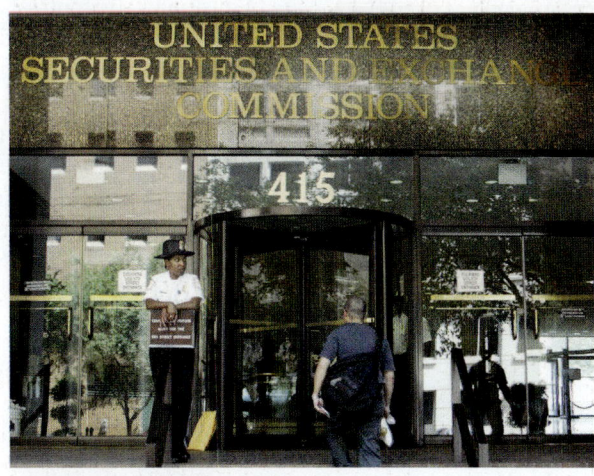
©Mark Wilson/Getty Images

As of 2018, most of the major economic countries have switched from their local GAAP to IFRS. One notable exception is the United States, but even here, there is an active process in place to reduce the differences between IFRS and U.S. GAAP.

There are many similarities between the IASB and the FASB. Both the FASB and the IASB are required to include members with a variety of backgrounds, including auditors, users of financial information, academics, and so forth. Also, both groups primarily require that their members work full-time for their respective boards; they cannot serve on the board while being compensated by another organization. (The IASB does allow up to three of its members to be part-time.) Members of each board serve five-year terms and can be reappointed once. The funds to support both boards, and the large organizations that support them, are obtained from a variety of sources, including selling publications and private contributions. To help maintain independence of the board's members, fund-raising is performed by separate sets of trustees.

Despite their similarities, there are significant differences between the IASB and the FASB. One of these relates to size and geographic diversity. The FASB has only seven members, all from the United States. The IASB has 16 members, and these must include at least 4 from Asia, 4 from Europe, 4 from North America, 1 from Africa, and 1 from South America.

Not only is the structure of the standards-setting boards different, but the standards and principles they establish may also differ significantly. In this chapter, you will learn that GAAP employs the *historical cost concept*. This means that the assets of most U.S. companies are shown on the balance sheet at the amount for which they were purchased. For example, land that has a market value of millions of dollars may be shown on **Ford**'s financial statements with a value of only a few hundred thousand dollars. This occurs because GAAP requires Ford to show the land at its cost rather than its market value. In contrast, IFRS permits companies to show market values on their financial statements. This means that the exact same assets may show radically different values if the statements are prepared under IFRS rather than GAAP.

Throughout this text, where appropriate, we will note the differences between U.S. GAAP and IFRS. However, by the time you graduate, it is likely that among the major industrialized nations, there will be a global GAAP.

Jason Winston recently started a business. During the first few days of operation, Mr. Winston transferred cash from his personal account into a business account for a company he named Winston Enterprises. Mr. Winston's brother, George, invested cash in Winston Enterprises, for which he received an ownership interest in the company. Winston Enterprises borrowed cash from First Federal Bank. Winston Enterprises paid cash to purchase a building from Commercial Properties, Inc. Winston Enterprises earned cash revenues from its customers and paid its employees cash for salaries expense.

How many reporting entities are described in this scenario? Assuming all of the customers are counted as a single entity and all of the employees are counted as a single entity, there are a total of seven entities named in the scenario. These entities include: (1) Jason Winston, (2) Winston Enterprises, (3) George Winston, (4) First Federal Bank, (5) Commercial

Properties, Inc., (6) the customers, and (7) the employees. A separate set of accounting records would be maintained for each entity.

Your ability to learn accounting will be greatly influenced by how you approach the entity concept. Based on your everyday experiences, you likely think from the perspective of a customer. In contrast, this text is written from the perspective of a business entity. These opposing perspectives dramatically affect how you view business events. For example, as a customer, you consider a sales discount a great bargain. The view is different from the perspective of the business granting the discount. A sales discount means an item did not sell at the expected price. To move the item, the business had to accept less money than it originally planned to receive. From this perspective, a sales discount is not a good thing. To understand accounting, train yourself to interpret transactions from the perspective of a business rather than a consumer. Each time you encounter an accounting event, ask yourself, "How does this affect the business?"

CHECK YOURSELF 1.1

In a recent business transaction, land was exchanged for cash. Did the amount of cash increase or decrease?

Answer The answer depends on the reporting entity to which the question pertains. One entity sold land. The other entity bought land. For the entity that sold land, cash increased. For the entity that bought land, cash decreased.

ELEMENTS OF FINANCIAL STATEMENTS

LO 1-3

Identify the components of the accounting equation.

The individuals and organizations that need information about a business are called *stakeholders*. Stakeholders include owners, lenders, government agencies, employees, news reporters, and others. Businesses communicate information to stakeholders through four financial statements:[2] (1) an income statement, (2) a statement of changes in equity, (3) a balance sheet, and (4) a statement of cash flows.

The information reported in **financial statements** is organized into 10 categories known as **elements.** Eight financial statement elements are discussed in this chapter: assets, liabilities, equity, contributed capital, revenue, expenses, distributions, and net income. The other 2 elements, gains and losses, are discussed in a later chapter. In practice, the business world uses various titles to identify several of the financial statement elements. For example, businesspeople use net income, net *earnings,* and net *profit* interchangeably to describe the same element. Contributed capital may be called *common stock,* and equity may be called *stockholders' equity, owner's capital,* and *partners' equity.* Furthermore, the transfer of assets from a business to its owners may be called *distributions, withdrawals,* or *dividends.* Think of accounting as a language. Different terms can describe the same business event. Detailed definitions of the elements and their placement on financial statements will be discussed in the following sections of the chapter.

Using Accounts to Gather Information

Detailed information about the elements is maintained in records commonly called **accounts.** For example, information regarding the element *assets* may be organized in separate accounts for cash, equipment, buildings, land, and so forth. The types and number of accounts used

---

[2]In practice these statements have alternate names. For example, the income statement may be called *results of operations* or *statement of earnings.* The balance sheet is sometimes called the *statement of financial position.* The statement of changes in equity might be called *statement of capital* or *statement of stockholders' equity.* Since the Financial Accounting Standards Board (FASB) called for the title *statement of cash flows,* companies do not use alternate names for that statement.

An Introduction to Accounting 11

Answers to The Curious Accountant

Anyone who owns stock in **Starbucks** owns a part of the company. Starbucks has many owners. In contrast, nobody actually owns the **American Cancer Society** (ACS). The ACS has a board of directors that is responsible for overseeing its operations, but the board is not its owner.

Ultimately, the purpose of a business entity is to increase the wealth of its owners. To this end, it "spends money to make money." The expense that Starbucks incurs for advertising is a cost incurred in the hope that it will generate revenues when it sells coffee. The financial statements of a business show, among other things, whether and how the company made a profit during the current year. For example, Starbucks' income statements show how much revenue was generated from "company-owned stores" operations versus from "licensed stores."

The ACS is a not-for-profit entity. It operates to provide services to society at large, not to make a profit. It cannot increase the wealth of its owners, because it has no owners. When the ACS spends money to assist cancer patients, it does not spend this money in the expectation that it will generate revenues. The revenues of the ACS come from contributors who wish to support efforts related to fighting cancer. Because the ACS does not spend money to make money, it has no reason to prepare an *income statement* like that of Starbucks. The ACS' statement of activities shows how much revenue was received from contributions versus from "investment income."

Not-for-profit entities do prepare financial statements that are similar in appearance to those of commercial enterprises. The financial statements of not-for-profit entities are called the *statement of financial position,* the *statement of activities,* and the *cash flow statement.*

by a business depends on the information needs of its stakeholders. Some businesses provide very detailed information; others report highly summarized information. The more detail desired, the greater the number of accounts needed. Think of accounts like the notebooks students keep for their classes. Some students keep detailed notes about every class they take in a separate notebook. Other students keep only the key points for all of their classes in a single notebook. Similarly, some businesses use more accounts than other businesses.

Diversity also exists regarding the names used for various accounts. For example, employee pay may be called salaries, wages, commissions, and so forth. Do not become frustrated with the diversity of terms used in accounting. Remember, accounting is a language. The same word can have different meanings. Similarly, different words can be used to describe the same phenomenon. The more you study and use accounting, the more familiar it will become to you.

Creating an Accounting Equation

Businesses use resources to conduct their operations. For example, **Carmike Cinemas, Inc.** uses buildings, seating, screens, projection equipment, vending machines, cash registers, and so on in order to make money from ticket sales. The resources a business uses to make money are called **assets**. So, where do businesses get assets? There are three distinct sources.

First, a business can borrow assets from creditors. Usually, a business acquires cash from creditors and then uses the cash to purchase the assets it needs to conduct its operations. When a business receives cash from creditors, it accepts an obligation to return the cash to the creditors at some future date. In accounting terms, the obligations a business has to its creditors are called **liabilities**.

The second source of assets is investors. When a business acquires assets from investors, it commits to keep the assets safe and to use the assets in a manner that benefits the investors. The business also grants the investor an ownership interest in the business, thereby allowing the investor (owner) to share in the profits generated by the business. The specific commitments made to the investors are described in certificates called **common stock.** In accounting terms investors are called **stockholders.** Further, the business' commitment to the stockholders is called **stockholders' equity.**

The third source of assets is operations. Businesses use assets in order to produce higher amounts of other assets. For example, **Best Buy** may sell a TV that cost the company $500 for $600. The $100 difference between the sales price and the cost of the TV results in an increase in Best Buy's total assets. This explains how operations can be a source of assets. Of course operations may also result in a decrease in assets. If Best Buy has to discount the sales price of the TV to $450 in order to sell it, the company's total assets decrease by $50.

Net increases in assets generated from operations are commonly called *earnings* or *income*. Net decreases in assets caused by operations are called *losses*. As a result of their ownership status, the stockholders reap the benefits and suffer the sacrifices that a business experiences from its operations. A business may distribute all or part of the assets generated through operations to the shareholders. The distribution of assets generated through earnings is called a *dividend*.

Notice that paying dividends is an option—not a legal requirement. Instead of paying dividends, a business may retain the assets it generates through operations. If a business retains the assets, it commits to use those assets for the benefit of the stockholders. This increase in the business' commitments to its stockholders is normally called **retained earnings.** Also, note that earnings that have been retained in the past can be used to pay dividends in the future. However, a company that does not have current or prior retained earnings cannot pay dividends.

As a result of providing assets to a business, the creditors and investors are entitled to make potential **claims**[3] on the assets owned by the business. The relationship between a business' assets and the claims on its assets is frequently expressed in an equality called the **accounting equation.** Based on the relationships described above, the accounting equation can be developed as follows:

Assets = Claims

Assets = Liabilities + Stockholders' equity

Assets = Liabilities + Common stock + Retained earnings

✓ CHECK YOURSELF 1.2

Gupta Company has $250,000 of assets, $60,000 of liabilities, and $90,000 of common stock. What percentage of the assets was provided by retained earnings?

Answer First, using algebra, determine the dollar amount of retained earnings:
Assets = Liabilities + Common stock + Retained earnings
Retained earnings = Assets − Liabilities − Common stock
Retained earnings = $250,000 − $60,000 − $90,000
Retained earnings = $100,000
Second, determine the percentage:
Percentage of assets provided by retained earnings = Retained earnings/Total assets
Percentage of assets provided by retained earnings = $100,000/$250,000 = 40%

---

[3] A claim is a legal action to obtain money, property, or the enforcement of a right against another party.

RECORDING BUSINESS EVENTS UNDER THE ACCOUNTING EQUATION

An **accounting event** is an economic occurrence that changes an enterprise's assets, liabilities, or stockholders' equity. A **transaction** is a particular kind of event that involves transferring something of value between two entities. Examples of transactions include acquiring assets from owners, borrowing money from creditors, and purchasing or selling goods and services. The following section of the text explains how several different types of accounting events affect a company's accounting equation.

Show how business events affect the accounting equation.

Asset Source Transactions

As previously mentioned, businesses obtain assets (resources) from three sources. They acquire assets from owners (stockholders); they borrow assets from creditors; and they earn assets through profitable operations. Asset source transactions increase total assets and total claims. A more detailed discussion of the effects of asset source transactions is provided below:

EVENT 1 Rustic Camp Sites (RCS) was formed on January 1, Year 1, when it acquired $120,000 cash from issuing common stock.

When RCS issued stock, it received cash and gave each investor (owner) a stock certificate as a receipt. Because this transaction provided $120,000 of assets (cash) to the business, it is an **asset source transaction.** It increases the business' assets (cash) and its stockholders' equity (common stock).

	Assets	=	Liab.	+	Stockholders' Equity
	Cash + Land	=	N. Pay.	+	Com. Stk. + Ret. Earn.
Acquired cash through stock issue	120,000 + NA	=	NA	+	120,000 + NA

Notice the elements have been divided into accounts. For example, the element *assets* is divided into a Cash account and a Land account. Do not be concerned if some of these account titles are unfamiliar. They will be explained as new transactions are presented. Recall that the number of accounts a company uses depends on the nature of its business and the level of detail management needs to operate the business. For example, Sears would have an account called Cost of Goods Sold, but GEICO Insurance would not. Why? Because Sears sells goods (merchandise) but GEICO does not.

Also, notice that a stock issue transaction affects the accounting equation in two places, both under an asset (cash) and also under the source of that asset (common stock). All transactions affect the accounting equation in at least two places. It is from this practice that the **double-entry bookkeeping** system derives its name.

EVENT 2 RCS acquired an additional $400,000 of cash by borrowing from a creditor.

This transaction is also an *asset source transaction.* It increases assets (cash) and liabilities (notes payable). The account title Notes Payable is used because the borrower (RCS) is required to issue a promissory note to the creditor (a bank). A promissory note describes, among other things, the amount of interest RCS will pay and for how long it will borrow the money.[4] The effect of the borrowing transaction on the accounting equation is indicated below.

	Assets	=	Liab.	+	Stockholders' Equity	
	Cash + Land	=	N. Pay.	+	Com. Stk. +	Ret. Earn.
Acquired cash by issuing note	400,000 + NA	+	400,000	+	NA +	NA

Asset Exchange Transactions

Businesses frequently trade one asset for another asset. In such cases, the amount of one asset decreases and the amount of the other asset increases. Total assets are unaffected by asset exchange transactions. Event 3 is an asset exchange transaction.

EVENT 3 **RCS paid $500,000 cash to purchase land.**

This asset exchange transaction reduces the asset account Cash and increases the asset account Land. The amount of total assets is not affected. An **asset exchange transaction** simply reflects changes in the composition of assets. In this case, the company traded cash for land. The amount of cash decreased by $500,000 and the amount of land increased by the same amount.

	Assets	=	Liab.	+	Stockholders' Equity	
	Cash + Land	=	N. Pay.	+	Com. Stk. +	Ret. Earn.
Paid cash to buy land	(500,000) + 500,000	=	NA	+	NA +	NA

Another Asset Source Transaction

EVENT 4 **RCS obtained $85,000 cash by leasing camp sites to customers.**

The *economic benefit* a company derives from providing goods and services to its customers is called **revenue.** In this example the economic benefit is an increase in the asset cash. Businesses may receive other benefits that will be discussed later. However, at this point we will limit our definition of revenue to being *an increase in assets* that results from providing goods and services to customers. For this event, the increase in the asset account Cash is balanced by an increase in the equity account Revenue. The effects on the accounting equation are as follows:

	Assets	=	Liab.	+	Stockholders' Equity		
	Cash + Land	=	N. Pay.	+	Com. Stk. +	Ret. Earn.	Acct. Title
Acquired cash by earning revenue	85,000 + NA	=	NA	+	NA +	85,000	Revenue

Note carefully that the $85,000 shown in the retained earnings column is *not* in the Retained Earnings account. It is in the Revenue account. It will be transferred to the Retained Earnings account at the end of the accounting period. Transferring the Revenue account balance to the Retained Earnings account is part of a process called *closing the accounts.*

---

[4]For simplicity, the computation of interest is ignored in this chapter. Interest computation is discussed in the appendix to Chapter 2 and in subsequent chapters.

Asset Use Transactions

Businesses use assets for a variety of purposes. For example, assets may be used to pay off liabilities or they may be transferred to owners. Assets may also be used in the process of generating earnings. All **asset use transactions** decrease the total amount of assets and the total amount of claims on assets (liabilities or stockholders' equity).

EVENT 5 RCS paid $50,000 cash for operating expenses such as salaries, rent, and interest. RCS could establish a separate account for each type of expense. However, the management team does not currently desire this level of detail. Remember, the number of accounts a business uses depends on the level of information managers need to make decisions.

An economic sacrifice a business incurs in the process of generating revenue is called an **expense.** In this example, the economic sacrifice is a decrease in the asset Cash. While expenses may result in other types of sacrifice, at this point we will limit our definition of expense to being a *use of assets* that is necessary to generate revenue. For this event, the decrease in the asset account is balanced by a decrease in the amount of stockholders' equity (retained earnings). The effects on the accounting equation are as follows:

	Assets			=	Liab.	+	Stockholders' Equity			
	Cash	+	Land	=	N. Pay.	+	Com. Stk.	+	Ret. Earn.	Acct. Title
Used cash to pay expenses	(50,000)	+	NA	=	NA	+	NA	+	(50,000)	Expense

Like revenues, expenses are not recorded directly into the Retained Earnings account. The $50,000 of expense is recorded in the Expense account. It will be transferred to the Retained Earnings account at the end of the accounting period as part of the closing process. The current balance in the Retained Earnings account is zero.

EVENT 6 RCS paid $4,000 in cash dividends to its owners.

To this point, operating RCS has caused the amount of total assets to increase by $35,000 ($85,000 of revenue − $50,000 of operating expenses). Because the owners bear the risk and reap the rewards of operating the business, the $35,000 increase in assets benefits them. RCS can use the additional assets to grow the business, or the company can transfer the earned assets to the owners. If a business transfers some or all of its earned assets to owners, the transfer is called a **dividend.** The $4,000 dividend paid by RCS reduces the asset account Cash and the amount of stockholders' equity (retained earnings). The effects on the accounting equation are as follows:

	Assets			=	Liab.	+	Stockholders' Equity			
	Cash	+	Land	=	N. Pay.	+	Com. Stk.	+	Ret. Earn.	Acct. Title
Used cash to pay dividends	(4,000)	+	NA	=	NA	+	NA	+	(4,000)	Dividends

Like revenues and expenses, dividends are not recorded directly into the Retained Earnings account. The $4,000 dividend is recorded in the Dividends account. It will be transferred to retained earnings at the end of the accounting period as part of the closing process. The current balance in the Retained Earnings account is zero.

EVENT 7 The land that RCS paid $500,000 to purchase had an appraised market value of $525,000 on December 31, Year 1.

Although the appraised value of the land is higher than the original cost, RCS will not increase the amount recorded in its accounting records above the land's $500,000 historical cost. In general, accountants do not recognize changes in market value. The **historical cost concept** requires that most assets be reported at the amount paid for them (their historical cost) regardless of increases in market value.

Surely, investors would rather know what an asset is worth instead of how much it originally cost. So why do accountants maintain records and report financial information based on historical cost? Accountants rely heavily on verification. Information is considered to be more useful if it can be independently verified. For example, two people looking at the legal documents associated with RCS' land purchase will both conclude that RCS paid $500,000 for the land. That historical cost is a verifiable fact. The appraised value, in contrast, is an opinion. Even two persons who are experienced appraisers are not likely to come up with the same amount for the land's market value. Accountants do not report market values in financial statements because such values are not reliable.

There are exceptions to the application of the historical cost rule. When market value can be clearly established, GAAP not only permits but requires its use. For example, securities that are traded on the New York Stock Exchange must be shown at market value rather than historical cost. We will discuss other notable exceptions to the historical cost principle later in the text. However, as a general rule, you should assume that assets shown in a company's financial statements are valued at historical cost.

Summary of Transactions

The complete collection of a company's accounts is called the **general ledger.** A summary of the accounting events and the general ledger accounts is shown in Exhibit 1.3. The Revenue, Expense, and Dividend account data appear in the retained earnings column. These account titles are shown immediately to the right of the dollar amounts listed in the retained earnings column.

EXHIBIT 1.3

Accounting Events

1	RCS issued common stock, acquiring $120,000 cash from its owners.
2	RCS borrowed $400,000 cash.
3	RCS paid $500,000 cash to purchase land.
4	RCS received $85,000 cash from earning revenue.
5	RCS paid $50,000 cash for expenses.
6	RCS paid dividends of $4,000 cash to the owners.
7	The land that RCS paid $500,000 to purchase had an appraised market value of $525,000 on December 31, Year 1.

General Ledger Accounts Organized under the Accounting Equation

Event No.	Cash	+	Land	=	Notes Payable	+	Common Stock	+	Retained Earnings	Other Account Titles
Beg. bal.	0		0		0		0		0	
1	120,000						120,000			
2	400,000				400,000					
3	(500,000)		500,000							
4	85,000								85,000	Revenue
5	(50,000)								(50,000)	Expense
6	(4,000)								(4,000)	Dividend
7	NA		NA		NA		NA		NA	
	51,000	+	500,000	=	400,000	+	120,000	+	31,000	

INTERPRETING INFORMATION SHOWN IN THE ACCOUNTING EQUATION

Before showing how financial information is reported to stakeholders, we highlight some interesting features of the accounting equation.

The Left versus the Right Side of the Accounting Equation

To illustrate the relationship between the left and right sides of the accounting equation, assume Educate Inc. begins an accounting period with balances shown in the following accounting equation:

Assets	=	Liabilities	+	Common Stock	+	Retained Earnings
2,000	=	1,200	+	500	+	300

Now assume that Educate Inc. uses all of its cash to purchase land. Immediately after this purchase, the company's accounting equation is as follows:

Assets			=	Liabilities	+	Common Stock	+	Retained Earnings
Cash		Land						
0	+	2,000	=	1,200	+	500	+	300

At this point, the company has zero cash. This highlights the fact that the amounts in liabilities, common stock, and retained earnings do not represent cash. Instead, they represent the original sources of the company's assets. Indeed, the right side of the accounting equation could be expressed as percentages instead of dollars. Specifically, the equation could be written as follows:

Assets			=	Liabilities	+	Common Stock	+	Retained Earnings
Cash		Land						
0	+	2,000	=	60%	+	25%	+	15%

This equation shows that 60 percent of Educate's assets came from creditors, 25 percent came from owners, and 15 percent from prior period earnings. However, this does not explain what has happened to the company's assets since they were acquired. Specifically, the right side of the equation does not show that the company acquired cash and then used the cash to purchase land. The right side identifies the sources of assets, not their composition.

Cash and Retained Earnings

While the amount of retained earnings does not represent the amount of cash a company has on hand, it does limit the amount of cash that can be used to pay dividends. To illustrate, assume Creative Associates begins an accounting period with balances shown in the following accounting equation:

Assets			=	Liabilities	+	Common Stock	+	Retained Earnings
Cash		Land						
400	+	1,900	=	700	+	1,000	+	600

LO 1-5

Interpret information shown in an accounting equation.

Given that the company has $600 in retained earnings, can the company pay a $500 cash dividend? The answer is no. Remember, there is no cash in retained earnings. The only cash the company has is listed on the left side of the equation. In this case, the maximum cash dividend that can be paid is $400 because that is all the cash the company has. Suppose Creative Associates decides it no longer needs the land and sells it for $1,900 cash. After this event, the accounting equation appears as follows:

Assets		=	Liabilities	+	Common Stock	+	Retained Earnings
Cash	Land						
2,300 +	0	=	700	+	1,000	+	600

Given that Creative Associates now has $2,300 in cash, can the company pay a $700 dividend? The answer is no. Based on the information in the accounting equation, Creative Associates has retained only $600 of its earnings. Because dividends are a distribution of assets that were generated through earnings, the maximum dividend Creative can distribute at this time is $600. In summary, the payment of dividends is limited by both the amount of cash and the amount of retained earnings. In other words, to pay a cash dividend a company must have both cash and retained earnings.

Business Liquidations Resulting from Net Losses

If a business ceases to operate, its remaining assets are sold and the sale proceeds are returned to the creditors and investors through a process called business **liquidation.** Creditors have priority in business liquidations. This means the business uses its assets first to settle the obligations to the creditors. Any assets remaining after the creditors have been paid are then distributed to the investors.

To illustrate, assume Cruz Company was started on January 1, Year 1, when it acquired $200 cash from creditors and $100 cash from investors. Equation 1 shows Cruz's financial position immediately after these events.

EQUATION 1

Assets	=	Liabilities	+	Common Stock	+	Retained Earnings
300	=	200	+	100	+	0

Assume Cruz had a net operating loss of $75 during Year 1. At the beginning of Year 2, Cruz's accounting equation is as follows:

Assets	=	Liabilities	+	Common Stock	+	Retained Earnings
225	=	200	+	100	+	(75)

If Cruz is forced to liquidate at this point, the creditors would receive $200 and the owners (investors) would receive only $25.

Return to the original scenario shown in Equation 1 where Cruz acquires $200 cash from creditors and $100 cash from investors. Now suppose instead of experiencing a $75 loss, Cruz experiences a $120 loss. In this scenario, Cruz's accounting equation at the beginning of Year 2 is as follows:

Assets	=	Liabilities	+	Common Stock	+	Retained Earnings
180	=	200	+	100	+	(120)

If Cruz is forced to liquidate at this point, the investors would receive zero and the creditors would receive only $180 even though the business owes them $200. Simply stated, Cruz cannot distribute assets that it does not have. This case shows that creditors, as well as investors, are at risk of losing some or all of the resources they provide to businesses. However, creditors are at lesser risk because they are first in line to receive assets in case of liquidation.

In practice, the relationships between creditors and investors are determined by complex legal documents that may conflict with the general conditions described above. We will discuss some of these exceptions in later chapters.

Business Liquidations Resulting from the Mismanagement of Assets

It is interesting to note that even profitable companies can be forced to liquidate. To illustrate, assume Bandera Company acquires $300 cash from creditors and $500 cash from investors and earns $200 of net income during its first year of operations. Also assume Bandera pays $950 to purchase land. Based on these events, Bandera would have the following accounting equation at the beginning of its second year of operation:

Assets	=	Liabilities	+	Common Stock	+	Retained Earnings
Cash	Land					
50 + 950	=	300	+	500	+	200

At this point, if the liabilities come due and the creditors demand payment, Bandera could be forced into bankruptcy. Assuming the land could not be sold immediately, Bandera has only $50 cash available to settle a $300 debt. A company must properly manage its assets, as well as its liabilities and stockholders' equity, in order to remain a going concern.

The **going concern** doctrine assumes that a business is able to continue its operations into the foreseeable future. Many procedures and practices used by accountants are based on a going concern assumption. If a company's going concern status becomes uncertain, accountants are required to notify creditors and investors.

Two Views of the Right Side of the Accounting Equation

Another important point to recognize is that there are two views of the right side of the accounting equation. One view is that the right side shows the sources of assets. Clearly, when a company borrows money from a bank the business receives an asset, cash. Therefore, we say creditors are a source of assets. However, borrowing money creates an obligation for the business to return the amount borrowed to creditors. Thus, we can view the liabilities of a company as its obligations to return assets to its creditors. In summary, liabilities can be viewed as sources of assets or, alternatively, as obligations of the business.

Similarly, a business may acquire assets from its owners by issuing stock or it may earn assets through its operations. Therefore, common stock and retained earnings can be viewed as sources of assets. However, the business has a **stewardship** function, which means that it has a duty to protect and use the assets for the benefit of the owners. As a result, common stock and retained earnings can be viewed as sources of assets or, alternatively, as commitments to the investors. In summary, the right side of the accounting equation can be viewed either as sources of assets or as the obligations and commitments of the business.

RECAP: TYPES OF TRANSACTIONS

LO 1-6

Classify business events as asset source, use, or exchange transactions.

The transactions described earlier have each been classified into one of three categories: (1) asset source transactions; (2) asset exchange transactions; and (3) asset use transactions. A fourth category, claims exchange transactions, is introduced in a later chapter. In summary:

- *Asset source transactions* increase the total amount of assets and increase the total amount of claims. In its first year of operation, RCS acquired assets from three sources: first, from owners (Event 1); next, by borrowing (Event 2); and finally, through earnings activities (Event 4).

- *Asset exchange transactions* decrease one asset and increase another asset. The total amount of assets is unchanged by asset exchange transactions. RCS experienced one asset exchange transaction; it used cash to purchase land (Event 3).

- *Asset use transactions* decrease the total amount of assets and the total amount of claims. RCS used assets to pay expenses (Event 5) and to pay dividends (Event 6).

As you proceed through this text, practice classifying transactions into one of the four categories. Businesses engage in thousands of transactions every day. It is far more effective to learn how to classify the transactions into meaningful categories than to attempt to memorize the effects of thousands of transactions.

The Curious Accountant

©xxlphoto/123RF

The RCS case includes only seven business events, one of which is not recognized in the ledger accounts. These events are assumed to have taken place over the course of a year. In contrast, real-world companies engage in thousands, even millions, of transactions in a single day. For example, think of the number of sales events **Amazon.com** processes in a day or how many tickets **United Airlines** sells. Presenting this many events in an accounting equation format would produce such a volume of data that users would be overwhelmed with details. To facilitate communication, accountants summarize and organize the transaction data into reports called *financial statements*. This section discusses the information contained in financial statements and explains how they are prepared. While the RCS illustration contains only a few transactions, the financial statements prepared for this company contain the same basic content as those of much larger companies.

SECTION 2:
REPORTING INFORMATION

As indicated earlier, accounting information is normally presented to external users in four general-purpose financial statements. The information in the ledger accounts is used to prepare these financial statements. The data in the ledger accounts in Exhibit 1.3 are color-coded to help you understand the source of information in the financial statements. The numbers in *green* are used in the *statement of cash flows*. The numbers in *red* are used to prepare the *balance sheet*. Finally, the numbers in *blue* are used to prepare the *income statement*. The numbers reported in the statement of changes in stockholders' equity have not been color-coded because they appear in more than one statement. The next section explains how the information in the accounts is presented in financial statements.

PREPARING AN INCOME STATEMENT, A STATEMENT OF CHANGES IN STOCKHOLDERS' EQUITY, AND A BALANCE SHEET

Section 1 of this chapter focused on how accountants collect information about business events. Section 2 focuses on how that information is *reported* to stakeholders. Information is normally reported annually in four financial statements including the (1) income statement, (2) statement of changes in stockholders' equity, (3) balance sheet, and (4) statement of cash flows. To illustrate the reporting process, we return to the Rustic Camp Sites example summarized in Exhibit 1.3. You should reacquaint yourself with this exhibit before reading about the statements shown in Exhibit 1.4.

LO 1-7

Prepare an income statement, a statement of changes in stockholders' equity, and a balance sheet.

Income Statement and the Matching Concept

The **income statement** matches revenue (benefits) with the expenses (sacrifices) that were incurred to generate the revenue. If revenues exceed expenses, the difference is called **net income.** If expenses are greater than revenues, the difference is called **net loss.** The practice of pairing revenues with expenses on the income statement is called the **matching concept.**

The income statement in Exhibit 1.4 shows that RCS earned $85,000 of revenue and incurred $50,000 of expenses, resulting in a net income of $35,000. Using our definition of revenue as increases in assets and expenses as decreases in assets, we can conclude that the net income figure of $35,000 represents an increase in the total amount of RCS' assets.[5]

---

[5]The definitions for revenue and expense are expanded in subsequent chapters as additional relationships among the elements of financial statements are introduced.

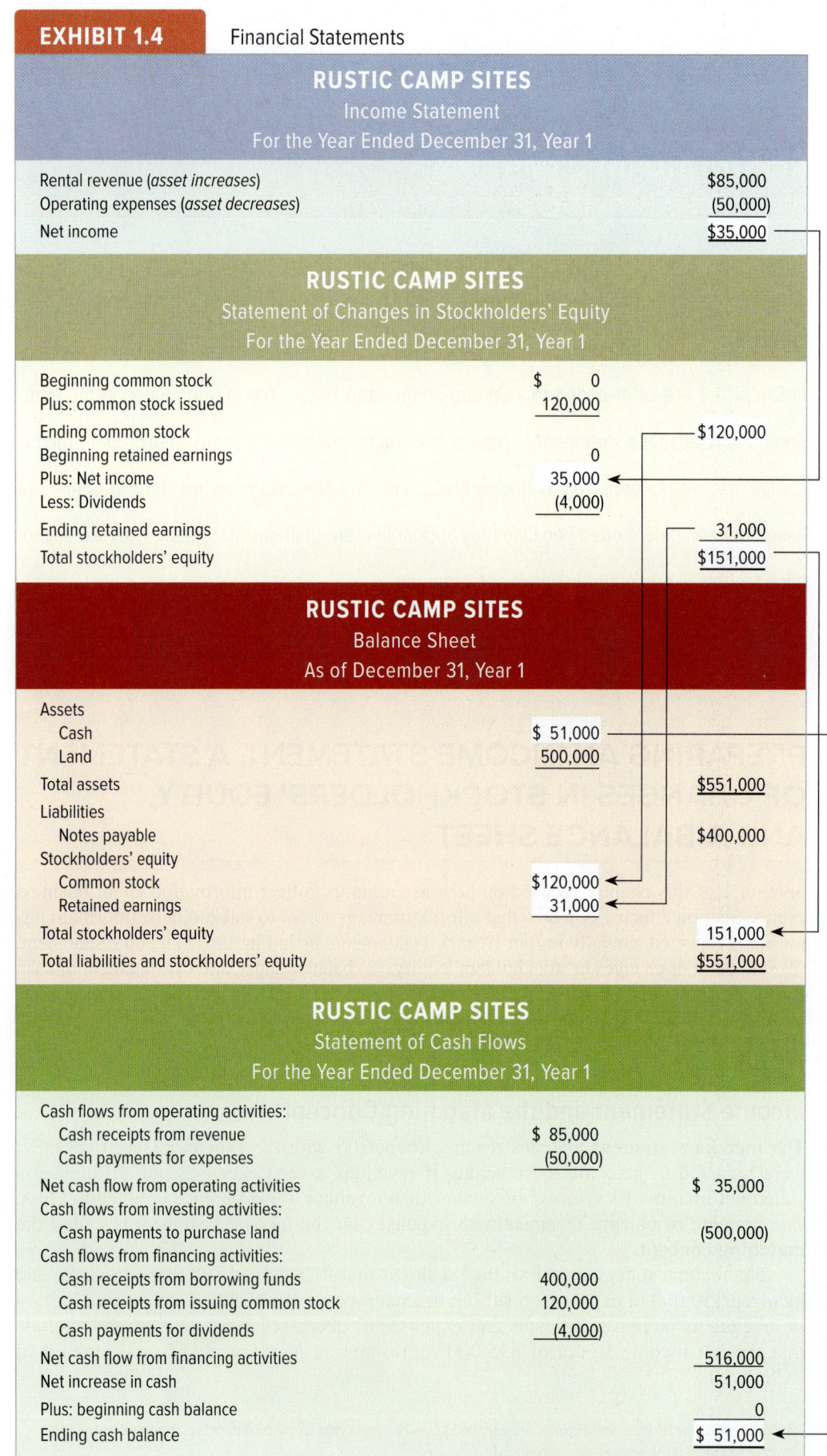

EXHIBIT 1.4 Financial Statements

Observe the phrase *For the Year Ended December 31, Year 1*, in the heading of the income statement. The income statement is a report about the company's operations that occurred over a span of time called the **accounting period.** While accounting periods of one year are normal for external financial reporting, income can be measured weekly, monthly, quarterly, semiannually, or using any other desired time period. Accordingly, the terminology used to describe the date should clearly indicate the time period covered by the statement.

Notice that the cash RCS paid to its stockholders is not reported as an expense on the income statement because the dividends were not incurred for the purpose of generating revenue. For example, a company pays employees so that they will work to produce revenue. Because the salary payment was made for the purpose of producing revenue, it is called an expense. In contrast, a business pays dividends to reward stockholders for the investment they made in the business. The stockholders are not being paid to produce revenue. A business first determines how much income it has earned and then decides how much of that income it will distribute to reward stockholders. The portion of earnings (income) distributed to owners is called a dividend. In summary, dividends are paid after the amount of income is determined. Therefore, dividends are not included on the income statement.

CHECK YOURSELF 1.3

Mahoney, Inc. was started when it issued common stock to its owners for $300,000. During its first year of operation, Mahoney received $523,000 cash for services provided to customers. Mahoney paid employees $233,000 cash. Advertising costs paid in cash amounted to $102,000. Other cash operating expenses amounted to $124,000. Finally, Mahoney paid a $25,000 cash dividend to its stockholders. What amount of net income would Mahoney report on its earnings statement?

Answer The amount of net income is $64,000 ($523,000 Revenue − $233,000 Salaries Expense − $102,000 Advertising Expense − $124,000 Other Operating Expenses). The cash received from issuing stock is not revenue because it was not acquired from earnings activities. In other words, Mahoney did not work (perform services) for this money; it was contributed by owners of the business. The dividends are not expenses because the decrease in cash was not incurred for the purpose of generating revenue. Instead, the dividends represent a transfer of wealth to the owners.

Statement of Changes in Stockholders' Equity

The **statement of changes in stockholders' equity** shown in Exhibit 1.4 explains the effects of transactions on stockholders' equity during the accounting period. It starts with the beginning balance in the common stock account. In the case of RCS, the beginning balance in the common stock account is zero because the company did not exist before the Year 1 accounting period. The $120,000 of stock issued during the accounting period is added to the beginning balance to determine the ending balance in the common stock account.

In addition to reporting the changes in common stock, the statement describes the changes in retained earnings for the accounting period. RCS had no beginning balance in retained earnings. During the period, the company earned $35,000 and paid $4,000 in dividends to the stockholders, producing an ending retained earnings balance of $31,000 ($0 + $35,000 − $4,000). Because equity consists of common stock and retained earnings, the ending total equity balance is $151,000 ($120,000 + $31,000). This statement is also dated with the phrase *For the Year Ended December 31, Year 1,* because it describes what happened to stockholders' equity during the Year 1 accounting period.

Balance Sheet

The **balance sheet** draws its name from the accounting equation. Total assets balance with (equal) liabilities plus stockholders' equity. The Year 1 balance sheet for RCS is shown in Exhibit 1.4. In this case, total assets equal total liabilities plus stockholders' equity ($551,000 = $400,000 + $151,000).

The order in which assets are shown in the balance sheet is important. Assets are displayed in the balance sheet based on their level of liquidity. Financial **liquidity** is measured by how fast an asset can be converted to cash. Because, in the normal course of business, inventory can be sold for cash quicker than land can be sold, inventory is considered to be more liquid than land. On the balance sheet, the most liquid asset, cash, is listed first, and the remaining assets are listed in the order of how rapidly they are normally converted into cash.

Observe carefully that the balance sheet is dated with the phrase *As of December 31, Year 1*, indicating that it describes the company's financial condition at a specific *point in time*. To distinguish between *span of time* versus *point in time* statements, it may be helpful to draw a parallel to how income is reported for individuals. Most people think of income in annual terms. For example, when you start work your salary will be stated in terms of how much you will earn per year. For budgeting purposes, you may also consider how much income you earn per month or per week. As these examples suggest, income is always measured in relation to some *span of time*. In contrast, the amount of your assets and liabilities is cumulative. For example, the amount of cash you own today (at this specific *point in time*) is equal to all of the cash you have collected minus all of the cash you have disbursed throughout your entire life.

For financial reporting purposes, the income statement, statement of changes in stockholders' equity, and the statement of cash flows provide information about events that occurred over some *span of time*. In contrast, the balance sheet provides information about conditions that exist at a specific *point in time*.

> ### CHECK YOURSELF 1.4
>
> To gain a clear understanding of the balance sheet, try to create one that describes your personal financial condition. First list your assets, then your liabilities. Determine the amount of your equity by subtracting your liabilities from your assets.
>
> **Answer**   Answers for this exercise will vary depending on the particular assets and liabilities each student identifies. Common student assets include automobiles, computers, TVs, smartphones, clothes, textbooks, smart speakers, and home assistants. Common student liabilities include car loans, mortgages, student loans, and credit card debt. The difference between the assets and the liabilities is the equity.

PREPARING A STATEMENT OF CASH FLOWS

LO 1-8

Prepare a statement of cash flows.

The **statement of cash flows** explains how a company obtained and used *cash* during the accounting period. Receipts of cash are called *cash inflows,* and payments are *cash outflows.* The statement classifies cash receipts (inflows) and payments (outflows) into three categories: financing activities, investing activities, and operating activities.

Businesses normally start with an idea. Implementing the idea usually requires cash. For example, suppose you decide to start an apartment rental business. First, you would need cash to finance acquiring the apartments. Acquiring cash to start a business is a financing activity. **Financing activities** include obtaining cash (inflow) from owners or paying cash (outflow) to owners (dividends). Financing activities also include borrowing cash (inflow) from creditors and repaying the principal (outflow) to creditors. In contrast, interest paid to creditors is an expense, and therefore, the associated cash flow is reported in the operating activities section of the statement of cash flows.

After obtaining cash from financing activities, you would invest the money by building or buying apartments. **Investing activities** involve paying cash (outflow) to purchase long-term assets or receiving cash (inflow) from selling long-term assets. Long-term assets are normally used for more than one year. Cash outflows to purchase land or cash inflows from selling a building are examples of investing activities.

After investing in the productive assets (apartments), you would engage in operating activities. **Operating activities** involve receiving cash (inflow) from revenue and paying cash (outflow) for expenses. Note that cash spent to purchase short-term assets such as office supplies is reported in the operating activities section because the office supplies would likely be used (expensed) within a single accounting period.

The primary cash inflows and outflows related to the types of business activity introduced in this chapter are summarized in Exhibit 1.5. The exhibit will be expanded as additional types of events are introduced in subsequent chapters.

The statement of cash flows for Rustic Camp Sites in Exhibit 1.4 shows that the amount of cash increased by $51,000 during the year. The beginning balance in the Cash account was zero; adding the $51,000 increase to the beginning balance results in a $51,000 ending balance. Notice that the $51,000 ending cash balance on the statement of cash flows is the same as the amount of cash reported in the asset section on the December 31 year-end balance sheet.

The statement of cash flows in Exhibit 1.4 is dated with the phrase *For the Year Ended December 31, Year 1*. Specifically, this statement of cash flows explains what caused the balance in the Cash account to increase by $51,000 during the Year 1 accounting period. The next statement of cash flows will explain what happens to the Cash account during the Year 2 accounting period and so on with subsequent accounting periods.

In summary, the balance sheet shows the amounts that exist in the accounts at the end of each accounting period, while the income statement, the statement of changes in stockholders' equity, and the statement of cash flows explain what caused the account balances to change from one accounting period to the next. To reflect these differences, balance sheets are dated with a phrase that begins with "As of," while the other statements are dated with a phrase that begins with "For the Period Ended."

Take note that information in one statement may relate to information in another statement. For example, the amount of net income reported on the income statement also appears on the statement of changes in stockholders' equity. Accountants use the term **articulation** to describe the interrelationships among the various elements of the financial statements. The key articulated relationships in RCS' financial statements are highlighted with the arrows shown in Exhibit 1.4.

EXHIBIT 1.5

Classification Scheme for Statement of Cash Flows

Cash flows from operating activities:
Cash receipts (inflows) from customers
Cash payments (outflows) to suppliers

Cash flows from investing activities:
Cash receipts (inflows) from the sale of long-term assets
Cash payments (outflows) for the purchase of long-term assets

Cash flows from financing activities:
Cash receipts (inflows) from borrowing funds
Cash receipts (inflows) from issuing common stock
Cash payments (outflows) to repay borrowed funds
Cash payments (outflows) for dividends

✓ CHECK YOURSELF 1.5

Classify each of the following cash flows as an operating activity, investing activity, or financing activity.

1. Acquired cash from owners.
2. Borrowed cash from creditors.
3. Paid cash to purchase land.
4. Earned cash revenue.
5. Paid cash for salaries expenses.
6. Paid cash dividend.
7. Paid cash for interest.

Answer (1) financing activity; (2) financing activity; (3) investing activity; (4) operating activity; (5) operating activity; (6) financing activity; (7) operating activity.

THE CLOSING PROCESS

In practice, the information about revenues, expenses, and dividends is *not* recorded directly into the Retained Earnings account. Instead information is recorded in separate Revenue, Expense, and Dividend accounts during the accounting period. Keeping these accounts separate permits the capture of information that pertains to a specific accounting period. This information is needed to prepare the income statement and the statement of changes in

LO 1-9

Close revenue, expense, and dividend accounts.

equity. At the end of the accounting period, after the statements are prepared, the information is transferred from the separate accounts to the Retained Earnings account.

The process of transferring information from the Revenue, Expense, and Dividend accounts to the Retained Earnings account is called **closing.** Because the Revenue, Expense, and Dividend information is held in the accounts temporarily, these accounts are called **temporary accounts.** At the beginning of each new accounting period, the temporary accounts have zero balances. In contrast, the Retained Earnings account balance carries forward from one accounting period to the next. Because this account is not closed, it is called a **permanent account.** Exhibit 1.6 shows a summary of Rustic Camp Sites' Year 1 transaction data and the before-closing general ledger account balances.

EXHIBIT 1.6

Summary of Year 1 Accounting Events and Before-Closing Account Balances

Accounting Events

1. Collected $120,000 cash from issue of common stock.
2. Borrowed $400,000 cash.
3. Paid $500,000 cash to purchase land.
4. Received $85,000 cash from earning revenue.
5. Paid $50,000 cash for expenses.
6. Paid $4,000 cash dividend to stockholders.
7. Land that cost $500,000 has a market value of $525,000.

General Ledger Accounts Before Closing

Assets	=	Liabilities	+	Stockholders' Equity		
Asset Accounts	=	Liability Accounts	+	Permanent Equity Accounts	+	Temporary Equity Accounts

Cash		Notes Payable		Common Stock		Revenue	
Bal.	0	Bal.	0	Bal.	0	Bal.	0
(1)	120,000	(2)	400,000	(1)	120,000	(4)	85,000
(2)	400,000	Bal.	400,000	Bal.	120,000	Bal.	85,000
(3)	(500,000)						
(4)	85,000			Retained Earnings		Expense	
(5)	(50,000)			Bal.	0	Bal.	0
(6)	(4,000)					(5)	(50,000)
Bal.	51,000					Bal.	(50,000)

Land						Dividend	
Bal.	0					Bal.	0
(3)	500,000					(6)	(4,000)
Bal.	500,000					Bal.	(4,000)

At the end of the accounting period, after the financial statements have been prepared, the temporary accounts will be closed as follows.

Cl. 1 Close the Revenue account to the Retained Earnings account.

Assets	=	Liabilities	+	Stockholders' Equity		
Asset Accounts	=	Liability Accounts	+	Permanent Equity Accounts	+	Temporary Equity Accounts
NA		NA		Retained Earnings		Revenue	
				85,000		(85,000)	

Cl. 2 Close the Expense account to the Retained Earnings account.

Assets	=	Liabilities	+	Stockholders' Equity		
Asset Accounts	=	Liability Accounts	+	Permanent Equity Accounts	+	Temporary Equity Accounts
NA		NA		Retained Earnings (50,000)		Expense 50,000

Cl. 3 Close the Dividends account to the Retained Earnings account.

Assets	=	Liabilities	+	Stockholders' Equity		
Asset Accounts	=	Liability Accounts	+	Permanent Equity Accounts	+	Temporary Equity Accounts
NA		NA		Retained Earnings (4,000)		Dividends 4,000

After posting the closing entries to the ledger accounts, the balance in the Retained Earnings account will be $31,000 and the balances in the Revenue, Expense, and Dividend accounts will be zero. A summary of the closing entries and the after-closing general ledger account balances are shown in Exhibit 1.7. The ending account balances for the Year 1 accounting period

EXHIBIT 1.7

Summary of the Year 1 Closing Entries and the After-Closing Account Balances

Closing Entries

- **Cl. 1** Close the Revenue account to the Retained Earnings account.
- **Cl. 2** Close the Expense account to the Retained Earnings account.
- **Cl. 3** Close the Dividends account to the Retained Earnings account.

General Ledger Accounts After Closing

Assets	=	Liabilities	+	Stockholders' Equity		
Asset Accounts	=	Liability Accounts	+	Permanent Equity Accounts	+	Temporary Equity Accounts

Cash		Notes Payable		Common Stock		Revenue	
Bal.	0	Bal.	0	Bal.	0	Bal.	0
(1)	120,000	(2)	400,000	(1)	120,000	(4)	85,000
(2)	400,000	Bal.	400,000	Bal.	120,000	Bal.	85,000
(3)	(500,000)					Cl. 1	(85,000)
(4)	85,000			Retained Earnings		Bal.	0
(5)	(50,000)			Bal.	0		
(6)	(4,000)			Cl. 1	85,000	Expense	
Bal.	51,000			Cl. 2	(50,000)	Bal.	0
				Cl. 3	(4,000)	(5)	(50,000)
Land				Bal.	31,000	Bal.	(50,000)
Bal.	0					Cl. 2	50,000
(3)	500,000					Bal.	0
Bal.	500,000						
						Dividend	
						Bal.	0
						(6)	(4,000)
						Bal.	(4,000)
						Cl. 3	4,000
						Bal.	0

will become the beginning account balances for the Year 2 accounting period. Because the Revenue, Expense, and Dividend accounts will open with a zero balance, they are ready for the collection of information that applies exclusively to the Year 2 accounting period.

> **CHECK YOURSELF 1.6**
>
> After closing on December 31, Year 1, Walston Company had $4,600 of assets, $2,000 of liabilities, and $700 of common stock. During January of Year 2, Walston earned $750 of revenue and incurred $300 of expense. Walston closes its books each year on December 31.
>
> 1. Determine the balance in the Retained Earnings account as of December 31, Year 1.
> 2. Determine the balance in the Retained Earnings account as of January 1, Year 2.
> 3. Determine the balance in the Retained Earnings account as of January 31, Year 2.
>
> **Answer**
>
> 1. Assets = Liabilities + Common Stock + Retained Earnings
>
> $4,600 = $2,000 + $700 + Retained Earnings
>
>   Retained Earnings = $1,900
>
> 2. The balance in the Retained Earnings account on January 1, Year 2, is the same as it was on December 31, Year 1. This year's ending balance becomes next year's beginning balance. Therefore, the balance in the Retained Earnings account on January 1, Year 2, is $1,900.
>
> 3. The balance in the Retained Earnings account on January 31, Year 2, is still $1,900. The revenue earned and expenses incurred during January are not recorded in the Retained Earnings account. Instead, they are recorded in the Year 2 temporary equity accounts. Balances in these temporary accounts will be closed to retained earnings at the end of the accounting period (December 31, Year 2).

THE HORIZONTAL FINANCIAL STATEMENTS MODEL

LO 1-10

 Record business events using a horizontal financial statements model.

Financial statements are the scorecard for business activity. If you want to succeed in business, you must know how your business decisions affect your company's financial statements. This text uses a **horizontal statements model** to help you understand how business events affect financial statements. This model shows a set of financial statements horizontally across a single page of paper. The balance sheet is displayed first, adjacent to the income statement, and then the statement of cash flows. Because the effects of equity transactions can be analyzed by referring to certain balance sheet columns, and because of limited space, the statement of changes in stockholders' equity is not shown in the horizontal statements model.

The model frequently uses abbreviations. For example, activity classifications in the statement of cash flows are identified using OA for operating activities, IA for investing activities, and FA for financing activities. NC designates the net change in cash. The statements model uses "NA" when an account is not affected by an event. The background of the *balance sheet* is red, the *income statement* is blue, and the *statement of cash flows* is green. To demonstrate the usefulness of the horizontal statements model, we use it to display the seven accounting events that RCS experienced during its Year 1 operations.

1. RCS acquired $120,000 cash from the issuance of common stock.
2. RCS borrowed $400,000 cash.
3. RCS paid $500,000 cash to purchase land.
4. RCS received $85,000 cash from earning revenue.
5. RCS paid $50,000 cash for expenses.
6. RCS paid $4,000 of cash dividends to the owners.
7. The market value of the land owned by RCS was appraised at $525,000 on December 31, Year 1.

	Balance Sheet							Income Statement					
	Assets	=	Liab.	+	Stockholders' Equity								
Event No.	Cash + Land	=	N. Pay.	+	Com. Stk.	+	Ret. Earn.	Rev.	−	Exp.	=	Net Inc.	Statement of Cash Flows
Beg. bal.	0 + 0	=	0	+	0	+	0	0	−	0	=	0	NA
1	120,000 + NA	=	NA	+	120,000	+	NA	NA	−	NA	=	NA	120,000 FA
2	400,000 + NA	=	400,000	+	NA	+	NA	NA	−	NA	=	NA	400,000 FA
3	(500,000) + 500,000	=	NA	+	NA	+	NA	NA	−	NA	=	NA	(500,000) IA
4	85,000 + NA	=	NA	+	NA	+	85,000	85,000	−	NA	=	85,000	85,000 OA
5	(50,000) + NA	=	NA	+	NA	+	(50,000)	NA	−	50,000	=	(50,000)	(50,000) OA
6	(4,000) + NA	=	NA	+	NA	+	(4,000)	NA	−	NA	=	NA	(4,000) FA
7	NA + NA	=	NA	+	NA	+	NA	NA	−	NA	=	NA	NA
Totals	51,000 + 500,000	=	400,000	+	120,000	+	31,000	85,000	−	50,000	=	35,000	51,000 NC

Recognize that statements models are learning tools. Because they are helpful in understanding how accounting events affect financial statements, they are used extensively in this book. However, the models omit many of the details used in published financial statements. For example, the horizontal model shows only a partial set of statements. Also, because the statements are presented in aggregate, the description of dates (i.e., "as of" versus "for the period ended") does not distinguish periodic from cumulative data.

The Financial Analyst

This section of each chapter introduces topics related to analyzing real-world financial reports. We focus first on the types of businesses that operate in the real world. We also discuss the annual report that is used to communicate information to stakeholders.

Real-World Financial Reports

As previously indicated, organizations exist in many different forms, including *business* entities and *not-for-profit* entities. Business entities are typically service, merchandising, or manufacturing companies. **Service businesses,** which include doctors, attorneys, accountants, dry cleaners, and housekeepers, provide services to their customers. **Merchandising businesses,** sometimes called *retail* or *wholesale companies,* sell goods to customers that other entities make. **Manufacturing businesses** make the goods that they sell to their customers.

Some business operations include combinations of these three categories. For example, an automotive repair shop might change oil (service function), sell parts such as oil filters (retail function), and rebuild engines (manufacturing function). The nature of the reporting entity affects the form and content of the information reported in an entity's financial statements. For example, governmental entities provide statements of activities, while business entities provide income statements. Similarly, income statements of retail companies show an expense item called *cost of goods sold,* but service companies that do not sell goods have no such item in their income statements. You should expect some diversity when reviewing real-world financial statements.

Throughout this book, we usually present income statements that end with "Net income." Due to an accounting rule that became effective at the end of 2009, income statements of large, real-world companies often appear to have three lines for net income.

The partial income statements for **Merck & Company**, a large pharmaceutical company, shown in Exhibit 1.8, illustrate this issue. Notice that the third line from the bottom of the statement is called "Net income." However, "Net income attributable to noncontrolling interests" is subtracted from this first net income to arrive at "Net income attributable to Merck & Co., Inc." The illustrations in this text always assume that there is no net income attributable to noncontrolling interests; therefore, our examples simply end with the term "Net income."

EXHIBIT 1.8 — Real-World Financial Reporting

MERCK & CO., INC. AND SUBSIDIARIES
Consolidated Statement of Income (partial)
Years Ended December 31
($ in millions except per share amounts)

	2016	2015	2014
Sales	$39,807	$39,498	$42,237
Costs, expenses, and other			
Materials and production	13,891	14,934	16,768
Marketing and administrative	9,762	10,313	11,606
Research and development	7,194	6,704	7,180
Restructuring costs	651	619	1,013
Other (income) expense, net	810	1,527	(11,613)
	32,308	34,097	24,954
Income before taxes	7,499	5,401	17,283
Taxes on income	1,787	942	5,349
Net income	5,712	4,459	11,934
Less: Net income attributable to noncontrolling interests	21	17	14
Net income attributable to Merck & Co., Inc.	$ 5,691	$ 4,442	$11,920

Some real-world companies with complex operations report information related to *comprehensive income.* Comprehensive income is determined by adding or subtracting certain items to or from net income. A description of the items used to determine comprehensive income is complex and beyond the scope of this course. Even so, the reader should be aware that, as of 2011, companies that must report comprehensive income may do so in one of two ways. First, comprehensive income items can be added to the bottom of the primary statement of earnings. Alternatively, a separate statement showing the determination of comprehensive income can be presented immediately following the primary statement of earnings. If a company chooses to report comprehensive income in a separate statement, the company's annual report will contain five financial statements. This text limits coverage to the four major financial statements that appear in real-world annual reports. The statement of comprehensive income is not covered.

Annual Report for Target Corporation

Organizations normally provide information, including financial statements, to *stakeholders* yearly in a document known as an **annual report.** The annual report for **Target Corporation** is referred to in some of the end-of-chapter assignments, and it is worth your while to review it as an example of a real-world annual report. This report can be found online at http://investors.target.com. On the web page that appears, under the "Investors" link, click on "sec filings." Next, under "filter by form type," select "Annual filings" and then select the most recent "10-K" form from the list that appears. The pdf

REALITY BYTES

The Snapchat application for smartphones was launched in 2011, and was being used widely by 2012. On February 2, 2017, the parent company of Snapchat, Snap, Inc., announced formally that it planned to become a public company through an initial public offering of its stock, commonly referred to as an "IPO."

The company's IPO in 2017 was one of the most highly anticipated new stock offerings of the past several years. However, the documents filed by the company with the Securities and Exchange Commission showed that while its revenues were growing rapidly, its net losses were also growing. In fact, the company had never made a profit, and its cumulative losses through 2016 were over $2 billion. Even so, *The Wall Street Journal* reported that the price of the company's stock at its IPO was expected to indicate that the value of the company was around $25 billion. Clearly, investors' primary focus was not on past earnings.

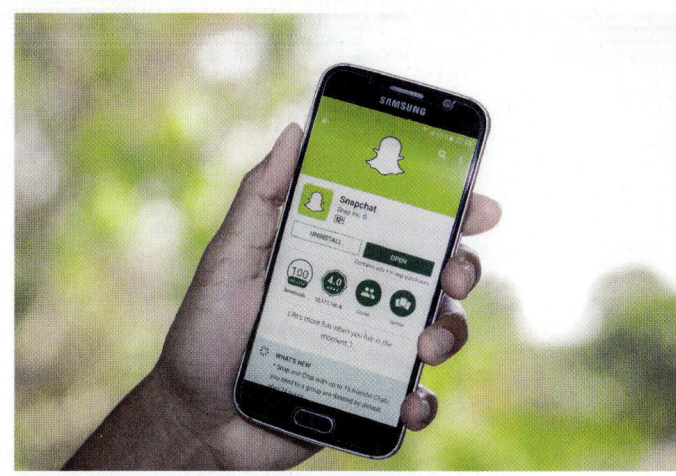
©Chonlachai/Shutterstock RF

Investors frequently use more information than just what is reported in a company's annual report. The annual report focuses on historical data, but investors are more interested in the future than the past. The historical information contained in the annual report is important because the past is frequently a strong predictor of what will occur in the future, but it does not provide a complete picture of a company's prospects.

A new company that has never earned a profit, like Snap, may have an idea that is so innovative that investors rush to buy its stock, even though they believe it will be a few years before the company has positive earnings. Although Snap has consistently reported losses in the past, it has become one of the leading providers of social media technology. Investors and creditors may also be motivated by nonfinancial considerations such as social consciousness, humanitarian concerns, or personal preferences. For example, people who buy stock in the Green Bay Packers, the only publicly traded NFL team, are motivated by team spirit, not profit.

While accounting information is very important, it is only part of the information pool that investors and creditors use to make decisions.

---

format is the easiest to work with. This report includes the company's financial statements (see pages 32–35 of the 2016 annual report). Immediately following the statements are a set of notes that provide additional details about the items described in the statements (see pages 36–58 of the 2016 annual report). The annual report contains the *auditors' report*, which is discussed in Chapter 6. Annual reports also include written commentary describing management's assessment of significant events that affected the company during the reporting period. This commentary is called *management's discussion and analysis (MD&A)*.

The U.S. Securities and Exchange Commission (SEC) requires public companies to file an annual report in a document known as a 10-K. The SEC is discussed in more detail later.

©Digital Vision/PunchStock RF

©McGraw-Hill Education/Andrew Resek, photographer

©Monty Rakusen/Getty Images RF

Even though the annual report is usually flashier (contains more color and pictures) than the 10-K, the 10-K is normally more comprehensive with respect to content. As a result, the 10-K report frequently substitutes for the annual report, but the annual report cannot substitute for the 10-K. In an effort to reduce costs, many companies now use the 10-K report as their annual report.

Special Terms in Real-World Reports

The financial statements of real-world companies include numerous items relating to advanced topics that are not covered in introductory accounting textbooks, especially the first chapter of an introductory accounting textbook. Do not, however, be discouraged from browsing through real-world annual reports. You will significantly enhance your learning if you look at many annual reports and attempt to identify as many items as you can. As your accounting knowledge grows, you will likely experience increased interest in real-world financial reports and the businesses they describe.

We encourage you to look for annual reports in the library or ask your employer for a copy of your company's report. The Internet is another excellent source for obtaining annual reports. Most companies provide links to their annual reports on their home pages. Look for links labeled "About the company" or "Investor relations" or other phrases that logically lead to the company's financial reports. The best way to learn accounting is to use it. Accounting is the language of business, and learning the language will serve you well in almost any area of business you pursue.

A Look Back

This chapter introduced the role of accounting in society and business: to provide information helpful to operating and evaluating the performance of organizations. Accounting is a measurement discipline. To communicate effectively, users of accounting must agree on the rules of measurement. *Generally accepted accounting principles (GAAP)* constitute the rules used by the accounting profession in the United States to govern financial reporting. GAAP is a work in progress that continues to evolve.

This chapter discussed eight elements of financial statements: *assets, liabilities, equity, common stock (contributed capital), revenue, expenses, dividends (distributions),* and *net income*. The elements represent broad classifications reported on financial statements. Four basic financial statements appear in the reports of public companies: the *balance sheet,* the *income statement,* the *statement of changes in stockholders' equity,* and the *statement of cash flows*. The chapter discussed the form and content of each statement, as well as the interrelationships among the statements.

This chapter introduced a *horizontal financial statements model* as a tool to help you understand how business events affect a set of financial statements. This model is used throughout the text. You should carefully study this model before proceeding to Chapter 2.

A Look Forward

To keep matters as simple as possible and to focus on the interrelationships among financial statements, this chapter considered only cash events. Obviously, many real-world events do not involve an immediate exchange of cash. For example, customers use telephone service throughout the month without paying for it until the next month. Such phone usage represents an expense in one month with a cash exchange in the following month. Events such as this are called *accruals*. Understanding the effects that accrual events have on the financial statements is included in Chapter 2.

An Introduction to Accounting   33

Video lectures and accompanying self-assessment quizzes are available in Connect for all learning objectives.

SELF-STUDY REVIEW PROBLEM

This problem extends the Rustic Camp Sites illustration shown in the main body of Chapter 1. The Year 1 after-closing account balances shown in Exhibit 1.7 become the beginning balances for the Year 2 accounting period illustrated in this problem.

During Year 2 Rustic Camp Sites experienced the following transactions:

1. RCS acquired $32,000 cash by issuing common stock.
2. RCS received $116,000 cash for providing services to customers (leasing camp sites).
3. RCS paid $13,000 cash for salaries expense.
4. RCS paid a $9,000 cash dividend to the owners.
5. RCS sold land that had cost $200,000 for $200,000 cash.
6. RCS paid $49,000 cash for other operating expenses.

Required

a. Record the transaction data in an accounting equation like the one below. The Year 2 beginning balances have been drawn from the Year 1 ending balances (see Exhibit 1.7). The Revenue, Expense, and Dividend accounts have zero beginning balances because these accounts are designed to capture revenue, expense, and dividend events only for the Year 2 accounting period. When recording revenue, expense, and dividend transactions, provide the title of the equity account affected by the transaction in the column titled "Account Titles." Otherwise, write "NA" in the "Account Titles" column to indicate that the transaction does not affect Revenue, Expense, or Dividend accounts. The first transaction is shown as an example.

	Assets			=	Liabilities		Stockholders' Equity			
	Cash	+	Land	=	Notes Pay.	+	Com. Stk.	+	Ret. Earn.	Account Titles
Beg. Bal	51,000	+	500,000	=	400,000	+	120,000	+	31,000	
Event No. 1	32,000	+	NA	=	NA	+	32,000	+	NA	NA

b. Identify each event as an asset source, use, or exchange transaction.
c. Use the information in the accounting equation to prepare an income statement, a statement of changes in stockholders' equity, and a balance sheet.
d. Create a statement of cash flows. (*Hint*: It may be helpful to review each of the six transactions and classify the impact on cash flow as being an operating, investing, or financing activity before attempting to create the statement.)
e. As of December 31, Year 2, can RCS pay a $100,000 cash dividend? What is the maximum dividend the company can pay?
f. As of December 31, Year 2, what percentage of total assets were acquired from the owners of the business?
g. Could RCS be forced into bankruptcy if the note payable is due on January 1, Year 3?
h. Show how each of the six events affects the financial statements by recording the effects of each event in a financial statements model like the one shown below. In the Statement of Cash Flows column, classify the cash flows as operating activities (OA), investing activities (IA), or financing

	Balance Sheet							Income Statement			
	Assets	=	Liab.	+	Stockholders' Equity						Statement of Cash Flows
Event No.	Cash + Land	=	N. Pay.	+	Com. Stk.	+	Ret. Earn.	Rev. − Exp.	=	Net Inc.	
Beg. bal.	51,000 + 500,000	=	400,000	+	120,000	+	31,000	NA − NA	=	NA	NA

activities (FA). The beginning balances have been recorded as an example. They are the ending balances shown on RCS' December 31, Year 1, financial statements illustrated in the chapter. Note that the revenue and expense accounts have a zero beginning balance. Amounts in these accounts apply only to a single accounting period.

Solution

a.

	Assets				Liabilities		Stockholders' Equity			Account
	Cash	+	Land	=	Notes Pay.	+	Com. Stk.	+	Ret. Earn.	
Beg. Bal	51,000	+	500,000	=	400,000	+	120,000	+	31,000	
Event No.										
1	32,000	+	NA	=	NA	+	32,000	+	NA	NA
2	116,000	+	NA	=	NA	+	NA	+	116,000	Revenue
3	(13,000)	+	NA	=	NA	+	NA	+	(13,000)	Salaries Expense
4	(9,000)	+	NA	=	NA	+	NA	+	(9,000)	Dividend
5	200,000	+	(200,000)	=	NA	+	NA	+	NA	NA
6	(49,000)	+	NA	=	NA	+	NA	+	(49,000)	Other Expenses
Totals*	328,000	+	300,000	=	400,000	+	152,000	+	76,000	

*Totals represent amounts before the accounts have been closed.

b.

1. RCS acquired $32,000 cash by issuing common stock. – ASSET SOURCE
2. RCS received $116,000 cash for providing services to customers. – ASSET SOURCE
3. RCS paid $13,000 cash for salaries expense. – ASSET USE
4. RCS paid a $9,000 cash dividend to the owners. – ASSET USE
5. RCS sold land that had cost $200,000 for $200,000 cash. – ASSET EXCHANGE
6. RCS paid $49,000 cash for other operating expenses. – ASSET USE

c.

RUSTIC CAMP SITES
Income Statement
For the Year Ended December 31, Year 2

Revenue	$116,000
Salary Expense	(13,000)
Other Expenses	(49,000)
Net Income	$ 54,000

RUSTIC CAMP SITES
Statement of Changes in Stockholders' Equity
For the Year Ended December 31, Year 2

Beginning Common Stock	$120,000	
Plus: Stock Issued	32,000	
Ending Common Stock		$152,000
Beginning Retained Earnings	31,000	
Plus: Net Income	54,000	
Minus: Dividend	(9,000)	
Ending Retained Earnings		76,000
Total Stockholders' Equity		$228,000

RUSTIC CAMP SITES
Balance Sheet
As of December 31, Year 2

Assets		
Cash	$328,000	
Land	300,000	
Total Assets		$628,000
Liabilities		
Notes Payable	400,000	
Total Liabilities		$400,000
Stockholders' Equity		
Common Stock	152,000	
Retained Earnings	76,000	
Total Stockholders' Equity		228,000
Total Liabilities and Stockholders' Equity		$628,000

d.

1. RCS acquired $32,000 cash by issuing common stock. – FINANCING ACTIVITY
2. RCS received $116,000 cash for providing services to customers. – OPERATING ACTIVITY
3. RCS paid $13,000 cash for salaries expense. – OPERATING ACTIVITY
4. RCS paid a $9,000 cash dividend to the owners. – FINANCING ACTIVITY
5. RCS sold land that had cost $200,000 for $200,000 cash. – INVESTING ACTIVITY
6. RCS paid $49,000 cash for other operating expenses. – OPERATING ACTIVITY

RUSTIC CAMP SITES
Statement of Cash Flows
For the Year Ended December 31, Year 2

Cash Flows from Operating Activities:		
Cash Receipts from Customers	$116,000	
Cash Payments for Salary Expense	(13,000)	
Cash Payments for Other Expenses	(49,000)	
Net Cash Flow from Operating Activities		$ 54,000
Net Cash Flow from Investing Activities		
Cash Receipt from Sale of Land		200,000
Net Cash Flow from Financing Activities		
Cash Receipt from Stock Issue	32,000	
Cash Payment for Dividend	(9,000)	
Net Cash Flow from Financing Activities		23,000
Net Change in Cash		277,000
Plus: Beginning Cash Balance		51,000
Ending Cash Balance		$328,000

e. RCS cannot pay a $100,000 cash dividend as of December 31, Year 2. The maximum dividend the company can pay on this date is $76,000 because dividend payments are restricted by the amount of total retained earnings.

f. RCS acquired $152,000 of assets from owners ($120,000 stock issue in Year 1 and a $32,000 stock issue in Year 2). Total assets as of December 31, Year 2, amount to $628,000 ($328,000 cash + $300,000 land). Accordingly, 24.2 percent of assets ($152,000 common stock ÷ $628,000 total assets) were acquired from owners.

g. RCS could be forced into bankruptcy on January 1, Year 3. On that date the note payable is $400,000 while the company has only $328,000 of cash available to repay the debt. In practice most companies do not carry sufficient cash to repay all of their liabilities. Most debt is simply refinanced. In other words, the existing debt is repaid by acquiring funds through new borrowing.

h.

Event No.	Balance Sheet							Income Statement				Statement of Cash Flows
	Assets			= Liab. +	Stockholders' Equity								
	Cash	+	Land	= N. Pay. +	Com. Stk.	+	Ret. Earn.	Rev. −	Exp.	=	Net Inc.	
Beg. bal.	51,000	+	500,000	= 400,000 +	120,000	+	31,000	NA −	NA	=	NA	NA
1.	32,000	+	NA	= NA +	32,000	+	NA	NA −	NA	=	NA	32,000 FA
2.	116,000	+	NA	= NA +	NA	+	116,000	116,000 −	NA	=	116,000	116,000 OA
3.	(13,000)	+	NA	= NA +	NA	+	(13,000)	NA −	13,000	=	(13,000)	(13,000) OA
4.	(9,000)	+	NA	= NA +	NA	+	(9,000)	NA −	NA	=	NA	(9,000) FA
5.	200,000	+	(200,000)	= NA +	NA	+	NA	NA −	NA	=	NA	200,000 IA
6.	(49,000)	+	NA	= NA +	NA	+	(49,000)	NA −	49,000	=	(49,000)	(49,000) OA
Totals	328,000	+	300,000	= 400,000 +	152,000	+	76,000	116,000 −	60,000	=	54,000	277,000 NC*

*The letters NC on the last line of the column designate the net change in cash.

KEY TERMS

Account 10
Accounting 3
Accounting equation 12
Accounting event 13
Accounting period 23
Annual report 30
Articulation 25
Asset 11
Asset exchange transaction 14
Asset source transaction 13
Asset use transaction 15
Balance sheet 23
Claims 12
Closing 26
Common stock 12
Creditor 4
Dividend 15
Double-entry bookkeeping 13
Earnings 4

Elements 10
Expense 15
Financial accounting 6
Financial Accounting Standards Board (FASB) 8
Financial reports 2
Financial resources 4
Financial statements 10
Financing activities 24
General ledger 16
Generally accepted accounting principles (GAAP) 8
Going concern assumption 19
Historical cost concept 15
Horizontal statements model 28
Income 4
Income statement 21

Interest 4
International Accounting Standards Board (IASB) 9
International Financial Reporting Standards (IFRS) 9
Investing activities 24
Investor 4
Labor resources 5
Liabilities 11
Liquidation 18
Liquidity 24
Managerial accounting 6
Manufacturing businesses 29
Market 4
Matching concept 21
Merchandising businesses 29
Net income 21

Net loss 21
Not-for-profit entities 6
Operating activities 24
Permanent accounts 26
Physical resources 5
Profit 4
Reporting entities 8
Retained earnings 12
Revenue 14
Service businesses 29
Stakeholders 5
Statement of cash flows 24
Statement of changes in stockholders' equity 23
Stewardship 19
Stockholders 12
Stockholders' equity 12
Temporary accounts 26
Transaction 13
Users 5

QUESTIONS

1. Explain the term *stakeholder*. Distinguish between stakeholders with a direct versus an indirect interest in the companies that issue financial reports.
2. Why is accounting called the *language of business*?
3. What is the primary mechanism used to allocate resources in the United States?
4. In a business context, what does the term *market* mean?
5. What market trilogy components are involved in the process of transforming resources into finished products?
6. Give an example of a financial resource, a physical resource, and a labor resource.
7. What type of income or profit does an investor expect to receive in exchange for providing financial resources to a business? What type of income does a creditor expect from providing financial resources to an organization or business?
8. How do financial and managerial accounting differ?

An Introduction to Accounting

9. Describe a not-for-profit or nonprofit enterprise. What is the motivation for this type of entity?
10. What are the U.S. rules of accounting information measurement called?
11. Explain how a career in public accounting differs from a career in private accounting.
12. Distinguish between elements of financial statements and accounts.
13. What role do assets play in business profitability?
14. To whom do the assets of a business belong?
15. Describe the differences between creditors and investors.
16. Name the accounting term used to describe a business' obligations to creditors.
17. What is the accounting equation? Describe each of its three components.
18. Who ultimately bears the risk and collects the rewards associated with operating a business?
19. What does a *double-entry bookkeeping system* mean?
20. Discuss the two views of the right side of the accounting equation.
21. If a company has $2,000 cash, $1,200 liabilities, and $800 retained earnings, can it pay a dividend of $1,000?
22. How does acquiring capital from owners affect the accounting equation?
23. What is the difference between assets that are acquired by issuing common stock and those that are acquired using retained earnings?
24. How does earning revenue affect the accounting equation?
25. What are the three primary sources of assets?
26. What is the source of retained earnings?
27. How does distributing assets (paying dividends) to owners affect the accounting equation?
28. What are the similarities and differences between dividends and expenses?
29. What four general-purpose financial statements do business enterprises use?
30. Which of the general-purpose financial statements provides information about the enterprise at a specific designated date?
31. What causes a net loss?
32. What is a business liquidation?
33. What is the going concern doctrine?
34. Explain the matching concept.
35. What three categories of cash receipts and cash payments do businesses report on the statement of cash flows? Explain the types of cash flows reported in each category.
36. How are asset accounts usually arranged in the balance sheet?
37. Discuss the term *articulation* as it relates to financial statements.
38. How do temporary accounts differ from permanent accounts? Name three temporary accounts. Is retained earnings a temporary or a permanent account?
39. Why are temporary accounts closed at the end of the accounting period?
40. What is the historical cost concept and how does it relate to verifiability?
41. Identify the three types of accounting transactions discussed in this chapter. Provide an example of each type of transaction, and explain how it affects the accounting equation.
42. What type of information does a business typically include in its annual report?
43. What is U.S. GAAP? What is IFRS?

MULTIPLE-CHOICE QUESTIONS

Multiple-choice questions are available in Connect.

EXERCISES—SERIES A

 All applicable Exercises in Series A are available in Connect.

Exercise 1-1A *The role of accounting in society*

LO 1-1

Free economies use open markets to allocate resources.

Required

Identify the three participants in a free business market. Write a brief memo explaining how these participants interact to ensure that goods and services are distributed in a manner that satisfies consumers. Your memo should include answers to the following questions: If you work as a public accountant, what role would you play in the allocation of resources? Which professional certification would be most appropriate to your career?

Exercise 1-2A *Careers in accounting*

LO 1-1

While public and private accounting overlap, various professional certifications are designed to attest to competency for specific areas of interest.

Required

a. Name the most common professional certification held by public accountants. Describe the general requirements for attaining this certification.

b. Name two types of professional certification, other than CPA, held by private accountants. Describe the general requirements for attaining these certifications.

LO 1-2

Exercise 1-3A *Identifying the reporting entities*

Karen White helped organize a charity fund to help cover the medical expenses of her friend, Vicky Hill, who was seriously injured in a bicycle accident. The fund was named the Vicky Hill Recovery Fund (VHRF). Karen contributed $1,000 of her own money to the fund. The $1,000 was paid to WKUX, a local radio station that designed and played an advertising campaign to educate the public about Vicky's predicament. The campaign resulted in the collection of $20,000 cash, and VHRF paid $12,000 to Mercy Hospital to cover Vicky's outstanding hospital cost. The remaining $8,000 was donated to the National Cyclist Fund.

Required

Identify the entities mentioned in the scenario and explain what happened to the cash accounts of each entity you identify.

LO 1-3

Exercise 1-4A *Define Terms and Identify Missing information in the accounting equation*

Required

a. Match the terms (identified as a through g) with the definitions and phrases (marked 1 through 7). For example, the term "a. Assets" matches with definition 7. Economic resources that will be used by a business to produce revenue.

a.	Assets	1.	Individuals or institutions that have contributed assets or services to a business in exchange for an ownership interest in the business.
b.	Common Stock	2.	Common Stock + Retained Earnings.
c.	Creditors	3.	Certificates that evidence ownership in a company.
d.	Liability	4.	Assets − Liabilities − Common Stock.
e.	Retained Earnings	5.	An obligation to pay cash in the future.
f.	Stockholders	6.	Individuals or institutions that have loaned goods or services to a business.
g.	Stockholders' Equity	7.	Economic resources that will be used by a business to produce revenue.

b. Calculate the missing amounts in the following table:

Company	Assets	=	Liabilities	+	Common Stock	+	Retained Earnings
A	$?		$25,000		$ 48,000		$50,000
B	40,000		?		7,000		30,000
C	75,000		15,000		?		42,000
D	125,000		45,000		60,000		?

LO 1-4

Exercise 1-5A *Effect of events on the accounting equation*

Olive Enterprises experienced the following events during Year 1:

1. Acquired cash from the issue of common stock.
2. Paid cash to reduce the principal on a bank note.
3. Sold land for cash at an amount equal to its cost.
4. Provided services to clients for cash.
5. Paid utilities expenses with cash.
6. Paid a cash dividend to the stockholders.

Required

Explain how each of the events would affect the accounting equation by writing the letter I for "increase," the letter D for "decrease," and NA for does "not affect" under each of the components of the accounting equation. The first event is shown as an example.

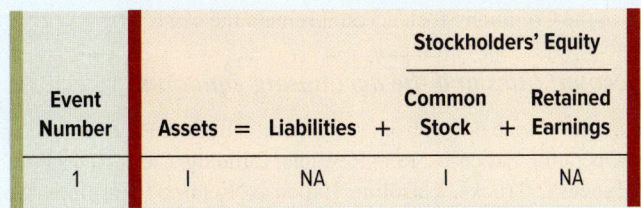

Exercise 1-6A *Effect of transactions on general ledger accounts*

LO 1-4

At the beginning of Year 2, Better Corp.'s accounting records had the following general ledger accounts and balances:

Event	Assets		=	Liabilities	+	Stockholders' Equity		Acct. Titles for RE
	Cash	Land		Notes Payable		Common Stock	Retained Earnings	
Balance 0/01/ Year 2								

BETTER CORP. Accounting Equation

Better Corp. completed the following transactions during Year 2:
1. Purchased land for $5,000 cash.
2. Acquired $25,000 cash from the issue of common stock.
3. Received $75,000 cash for providing services to customers.
4. Paid cash operating expenses of $42,000.
5. Borrowed $10,000 cash from the bank.
6. Paid a $5,000 cash dividend to the stockholders.
7. Determined that the market value of the land purchased in Event 1 is $35,000.

Required

a. Record the transactions in the appropriate general ledger accounts. Record the amounts of revenue, expense, and dividends in the Retained Earnings column. Provide the appropriate titles for these accounts in the last column of the table.
b. As of December 31, Year 2, determine the total amount of assets, liabilities, and stockholders' equity and present this information in the form of an accounting equation.
c. What is the amount of total assets, liabilities, and stockholders' equity as of January 1, Year 3?

Exercise 1-7A *Missing information and recording events*

LO 1-4

As of December 31, Year 1, Moss Company had total cash of $195,000, notes payable of $90,500, and common stock of $84,500. During Year 2, Moss earned $42,000 of cash revenue, paid $24,000 for cash expenses, and paid a $3,000 cash dividend to the stockholders.

Required

a. Determine the amount of retained earnings as of December 31, Year 1.
b. Create an accounting equation and record the beginning account balances under the appropriate elements.

c. Record the revenue, expense, and dividend events under the appropriate elements of the accounting equation created in Requirement b.

d. Prove the equality of the accounting equation as of December 31, Year 2.

e. Identify the beginning and ending balances in the Cash and Common Stock accounts. Explain why the beginning and ending balances in the Cash account are different but the beginning and ending balances in the Common Stock account remain the same.

LO 1-3

Exercise 1-8A *Account titles and the accounting equation*

The following account titles were drawn from the general ledger of Holt Food Supplies, Incorporated (HFSI): Computers, Operating Expenses, Rent Revenue, Building, Cash, Notes Payable, Land, Utilities Payable, Utilities Expense, Trucks, Gasoline Expense, Retained Earnings, Supplies, Accounts Payable, Office Furniture, Salaries Expense, Common Stock, Service Revenue, Interest Expense, Dividends, Supplies Expense.

Required

a. Create an accounting equation using the elements assets, liabilities, and stockholders' equity. List each account title under the element of the accounting equation to which it belongs.

b. Will all businesses have the same number of accounts? Explain your answer.

LO 1-4, 1-5

Exercise 1-9A *Record events and interpret information in an accounting equation*

Jones Enterprises was started when it acquired $6,000 cash from creditors and $10,000 from owners. The company immediately purchased land that cost $12,000.

Required

a. Record the events under an accounting equation.

b. After all events have been recorded, Jones' obligations to creditors represent what percentage of total assets?

c. After all events have been recorded, Jones' stockholders' equity represents what percentage of total assets?

d. Assume the debt is due. Given that Jones has $10,000 in stockholders' equity, can the company repay the creditors at this point? Why or why not?

LO 1-5

Exercise 1-10A *Interpreting information in an accounting equation*

	Assets	=	Liabilities	+	Common Stock	+	Retained Earnings
Allen	$10,000	=	$7,500	+	$2,000	+	$ 500
White	$12,000	=	$3,000	+	$7,200	+	$1,800

Required

a. Based on this information alone, can you determine whether White can pay a $2,000 cash dividend? Why or why not?

b. Reconstruct the accounting equation for each company using percentages on the right side of the equation instead of dollar values. Which company is more financially stable? Why?

c. Assume Allen incurs a $3,500 operating loss. The remaining assets are sold for the value shown on the books, and the cash proceeds are distributed to the creditors and investors. How much money will be paid to creditors and how much will be paid to investors?

d. Assume White incurs a $3,500 operating loss. The remaining assets are sold for the value shown on the books, and the cash proceeds are distributed to the creditors and investors. How much money will be paid to creditors and how much will be paid to investors?

LO 1-4, 1-5

Exercise 1-11A *Calculate missing amounts and interpret results*

The following table shows the transactions experienced by J G Gutter Works (JGGW), during Year 7. The table contains missing data which are labeled with alphabetic characters (a) through (j). Assume all transactions shown in the accounting equation are cash transactions.

	Assets				Liabilities		Stockholders' Equity			Account
	Cash	+	Land	=	Notes Pay.	+	Com. Stk.	+	Ret. Earn.	
Beg. Bal.	(a)	+	90,000	=	(b)	+	(c)	+	25,000	
Event No. 1	(d)	+	NA	=	NA	+	68,000	+	NA	NA
2	(e)	+	NA	=	NA	+	NA	+	(f)	Revenue
3	(57,000)	+	NA	=	NA	+	NA	+	(57,000)	Expenses
4	(14,000)	+	NA	=	NA	+	NA	+	(g)	Dividend
5	(50,000)	+	(h)	=	NA	+	NA	+	NA	NA
6	(10,000)	+	NA	=	(10,000)	+	NA	+	NA	NA
Totals*	77,000	+	(i)	=	40,000	+	123,000	+	(j)	

Required

a. Determine the correct amount represented by each character (a) through (j).
b. Is there sufficient cash available to repay the debt on January 1, Year 8?
c. Based on the information in the table, what is the maximum cash dividend JGGW could pay on January 1, Year 8?

Exercise 1-12A *Differences between interest and dividends*   LO 1-5

Assume that Harris Company acquires $3,600 cash from creditors and $4,200 cash from investors.

Required

a. Explain the primary differences between investors and creditors.
b. If Harris has a net income of $2,000 and then liquidates, what amount of cash will the creditors receive? What amount of cash will the investors receive?
c. If Harris has a net loss of $2,000 cash and then liquidates, what amount of cash will the creditors receive? What amount of cash will the investors receive?
d. If Harris has a net loss of $4,900 cash and then liquidates, what amount of cash will the creditors receive? What amount of cash will the investors receive?

Exercise 1-13A *Classifying events as asset source, use, or exchange*   LO 1-6

Nevada Company experienced the following events during its first year of operations:

1. Acquired an additional $1,000 cash from the issue of common stock.
2. Paid $2,400 cash for utilities expense.
3. Paid a $1,500 cash dividend to the stockholders.
4. Provided additional services for $6,000 cash.
5. Purchased additional land for $2,500 cash.
6. The market value of the land was determined to be $24,000 at the end of the accounting period.
7. Acquired $16,000 cash from the issue of common stock.
8. Paid $3,500 cash for salary expense.
9. Borrowed $10,000 cash from New South Bank.
10. Paid $6,000 cash to purchase land.
11. Provided boarding services for $10,500 cash.

Required

Classify each event as an asset source, use, or exchange transaction or as not applicable.

EXERCISES—SERIES A

LO 1-7

Exercise 1-14A *Missing information for determining net income*

The December 31, Year 1, balance sheet for Deen Company showed total stockholders' equity of $156,000. Total stockholders' equity increased by $65,000 between December 31, Year 1, and December 31, Year 2. During Year 2, Deen Company acquired $20,000 cash from the issue of common stock. Deen Company paid a $5,000 cash dividend to the stockholders during Year 2.

Required

Determine the amount of net income or loss Deen reported on its Year 2 income statement. (*Hint:* Remember that stock issues, net income, and dividends all change total stockholders' equity.)

LO 1-7

Exercise 1-15A *Preparing an income statement and a balance sheet*

Majka Company was started on January 1, Year 1. During Year 1, the company experienced the following three accounting events: (1) earned cash revenues of $33,700, (2) paid cash expenses of $14,900, and (3) paid a $3,200 cash dividend to its stockholders. These were the only events that affected the company during Year 1.

Required

a. Create an accounting equation and record the effects of each accounting event under the appropriate general ledger account headings.

b. Prepare an income statement, statement of changes in stockholders' equity, and a balance sheet dated December 31, Year 1, for Majka Company.

c. Explain why the income statement uses different terminology to date the income statement than is used to date the balance sheet.

LO 1-7

Exercise 1-16A *Historical cost versus market value*

Sung Company purchased land in April Year 1 at a cost of $500,000. The estimated market value of the land is $800,000 as of December 31, Year 7. Sung purchased marketable equity securities (bought the common stock of a company that is independent of Sung) in May Year 1 at a cost of $340,000. These securities have a market value of $360,000 as of December 31, Year 7. Generally accepted accounting principles requires that the land be shown on the December 31, Year 7, balance sheet at $500,000, while the marketable equity securities are required to be reported at $360,000.

Required

Write a brief memo that explains the contradiction regarding why GAAP requires Sung to report historical cost with respect to the land versus market value with respect to the marketable securities. This answer may require speculation on your part. Use your knowledge about the historical cost and verifiability to formulate a logical response.

LO 1-8

Exercise 1-17A *Statement of cash flows*

On January 1, Year 1, Moore, a fast-food company, had a balance in its Cash account of $45,800. During the Year 1 accounting period, the company had (1) net cash inflow from operating activities of $24,800, (2) net cash outflow for investing activities of $16,000, and (3) net cash outflow from financing activities of $6,800.

Required

a. Prepare a statement of cash flows.

b. Provide a reasonable explanation as to what may have caused the net cash inflow from operating activities.

c. Provide a reasonable explanation as to what may have caused the net cash outflow from investing activities.

d. Provide a reasonable explanation as to what may have caused the net cash outflow from financing activities.

Exercise 1-18A Prepare a statement of cash flows

LO 1-8

All-Star Automotive Company experienced the following accounting events during Year 1:

1. Performed services for $25,000 cash.
2. Purchased land for $6,000 cash.
3. Hired an accountant to keep the books.
4. Received $50,000 cash from the issue of common stock.
5. Borrowed $5,000 cash from State Bank.
6. Paid $14,000 cash for salary expense.
7. Sold land for $9,000 cash.
8. Paid $10,000 cash on the loan from State Bank.
9. Paid $2,800 cash for utilities expense.
10. Paid a cash dividend of $5,000 to the stockholders.

Required

a. Indicate how each of the events would be classified on the statement of cash flows as operating activities (OA), investing activities (IA), financing activities (FA), or not applicable (NA).
b. Prepare a statement of cash flows. Assume All-Star Automotive had a beginning cash balance of $9,000.

Exercise 1-19A Preparing financial statements

LO 1-7, 1-8

Dakota Company experienced the following events during Year 2:

1. Acquired $30,000 cash from the issue of common stock.
2. Paid $12,000 cash to purchase land.
3. Borrowed $10,000 cash.
4. Provided services for $20,000 cash.
5. Paid $1,000 cash for utilities expense.
6. Paid $15,000 cash for other operating expenses.
7. Paid a $2,000 cash dividend to the stockholders.
8. Determined that the market value of the land purchased in Event 2 is now $12,700.

Required

a. The January 1, Year 2, general ledger account balances are shown in the following accounting equation. Record the eight events in the appropriate general ledger accounts. Record the amounts of revenue, expense, and dividends in the Retained Earnings column. Provide the appropriate titles for these accounts in the last column of the table. The first event is shown as an example.

DAKOTA COMPANY
Accounting Equation

Event	Assets		=	Liabilities	+	Stockholders' Equity		Acct. Titles for RE
	Cash	Land		Notes Payable		Common Stock	Retained Earnings	
Beg. Bal. 1/1/Year 2	2,000	12,000		–0–		6,000	8,000	
1	30,000					30,000		

b. Prepare an income statement, statement of changes in equity, year-end balance sheet, and statement of cash flows for the Year 2 accounting period.
c. Determine the percentage of assets that were provided by retained earnings. How much cash is in the retained earnings account?

Chapter 1

LO 1-8

Exercise 1-20A *Relating accounting events to entities*

Riley Company paid $60,000 cash to purchase land from Smally Company. Smally originally paid $60,000 for the land.

Required

a. Was this event an asset source, use, or exchange transaction for Riley Company?
b. Was this event an asset source, use, or exchange transaction for Smally Company?
c. Was the cash flow an operating, investing, or financing activity on Riley Company's statement of cash flows?
d. Was the cash flow an operating, investing, or financing activity on Smally Company's statement of cash flows?

LO 1-4, 1-5, 1-7, 1-8, 1-9

Exercise 1-21A *Preparing financial statements—retained earnings emphasis*

On January 1, Year 2, the following information was drawn from the accounting records of Carter Company: cash of $800; land of $3,500; notes payable of $600; and common stock of $1,000.

Required

a. Determine the amount of retained earnings as of January 1, Year 2.
b. After looking at the amount of retained earnings, the chief executive officer (CEO) wants to pay a $1,000 cash dividend to the stockholders. Can the company pay this dividend? Why or why not?
c. As of January 1, Year 2, what percentage of the assets were acquired from creditors?
d. As of January 1, Year 2, what percentage of the assets were acquired from investors?
e. As of January 1, Year 2, what percentage of the assets were acquired from retained earnings?
f. Create an accounting equation using percentages instead of dollar amounts on the right side of the equation.
g. During Year 2, Carter Company earned cash revenue of $1,800, paid cash expenses of $1,200, and paid a cash dividend of $500. Prepare an income statement, statement of changes in stockholders' equity, a balance sheet, and a statement of cash flows dated December 31, Year 2. (*Hint:* It is helpful to record these events under an accounting equation before preparing the statements.)
h. Comment on the terminology used to date each statement.
i. An appraiser determines that, as of December 31, Year 2, the market value of the land is $4,200. How will this fact change the financial statements?
j. What is the balance in the Revenue account on January 1, Year 3?

LO 1-7, 1-8

Exercise 1-22A *Preparing financial statements—cash flow emphasis*

As of January 1, Year 2, Room Designs Inc. had a balance of $9,900 in Cash, $3,500 in Common Stock, and $6,400 in Retained Earnings. These were the only accounts with balances in the ledger on January 1, Year 2. Further analysis of the company's cash account indicated that during the Year 2 accounting period, the company had (1) net cash inflow from operating activities of $9,800, (2) net cash outflow for investing activities of $16,500, and (3) net cash inflow from financing activities of $11,000. All revenue and expense events were cash events. The following accounts and balances represent the financial condition of Room Designs Inc. as of December 31, Year 2.

Required

a. Assume that the net cash inflow from financing activities of $11,000 was caused by three events. Based on the information above, identify these events and determine the cash flow associated with each event.
b. What did the company purchase that resulted in the cash outflow from investing activities?
c. Prepare an income statement, statement of changes in stockholders' equity, balance sheet, and statement of cash flows.

ROOM DESIGNS INC.
General Ledger

Assets	=	Liabilities	+	Stockholders' Equity		
Cash		**Notes Payable**		**Common Stock**		**Revenue**
Bal. 14,200		Bal. 9,000		Bal. 7,500		Bal. 18,100
Land				**Retained Earnings**		**Expenses**
Bal. 16,500				Bal. 6,400		Bal. 8,300
						Dividends
						Bal. 2,000

Exercise 1-23A   *Retained earnings and the closing process*   LO 1-9

As of December 31, Year 1, Flowers Company had total assets of $130,000, total liabilities of $50,000, and common stock of $70,000. The company's Year 1 income statement contained revenue of $30,000 and expenses of $18,000. The Year 1 statement of changes in stockholders' equity stated that $3,000 of dividends were paid to investors.

Required

a. Determine the before-closing balance in the Retained Earnings account on December 31, Year 1.
b. Determine the after-closing balance in the Retained Earnings account on December 31, Year 1.
c. Determine the before-closing balances in the Revenue, Expense, and Dividend accounts on December 31, Year 1.
d. Determine the after-closing balances in the Revenue, Expense, and Dividend accounts on December 31, Year 1.
e. Explain the difference between common stock and retained earnings.
f. On January 1, Year 2, Flowers Company raised $30,000 by issuing additional common stock. Immediately after the additional capital was raised. Flowers reported total equity of $110,000. Are the stockholders of Flowers in a better financial position than they were on December 31, Year 1?

Exercise 1-24A   *The closing process*   LO 1-9

Sammy's Pizza opened on January 1, Year 1. Sammy's reported the following for cash revenues and cash expenses for the years Year 1 to Year 3:

	Cash Revenues	Cash Expenses
Year 1	$20,000	$11,000
Year 2	$30,000	$14,000
Year 3	$40,000	$22,000

Required

a. What would Sammy's Pizza report for net income and retained earnings for the years Year 1, Year 2, and Year 3?
b. Explain the difference between net income and retained earnings.
c. Assume that Sammy's Pizza paid a $5,000 dividend to stockholders in Year 2. What would Sammy's Pizza report for net income and retained earnings for Year 2 and Year 3?

Exercise 1-25A   *Retained earnings and the closing process*   LO 1-9

Critz Company was started on January 1, Year 1. During the month of January, Critz earned $7,500 of revenue and incurred $4,800 of expenses. During the remainder of Year 1, Critz earned $86,000 and incurred $51,000 of expenses. Critz closes its books on December 31 of each year.

Required

a. Determine the balance in the Retained Earnings account as of January 31, Year 1.
b. Determine the balance in the Revenue and Expense accounts as of January 31, Year 1.
c. Determine the balance in the Retained Earnings account as of December 31, Year 1, before closing.
d. Determine the balances in the Revenue and Expense accounts as of December 31, Year 1, before closing.
e. Determine the balance in the Retained Earnings account as of January 1, Year 2.
f. Determine the balance in the Revenue and Expense accounts as of January 1, Year 2.

LO 1-6, 1-10

Exercise 1-26A *Types of transactions and the horizontal statements model*

The Candle Shop experienced the following events during its first year of operations, Year 1:

1. Acquired cash by issuing common stock.
2. Paid a cash dividend to the stockholders.
3. Paid cash for operating expenses.
4. Borrowed cash from a bank.
5. Provided services and collected cash.
6. Purchased land with cash.
7. Determined that the market value of the land is higher than the historical cost.

Required

a. Indicate whether each event is an asset source, use, or exchange transaction.
b. Use a horizontal statements model to show how each event affects the balance sheet, income statement, and statement of cash flows. Indicate whether the event "increases" (I), "decreases" (D), or does "not affect" (NA) each element of the financial statements. Also, in the Statement of Cash Flows column, classify the cash flows as operating activities (OA), investing activities (IA), or financing activities (FA). The first transaction is shown as an example.

Event No.	Cash	+	Land	=	N. Pay.	+	C. Stock.	+	Ret. Ear.	Rev.	−	Exp.	=	Net Inc.	Statement of Cash Flows
1	I	+	NA	=	NA	+	I	+	NA	NA	−	NA	=	NA	I FA

LO IFRS

Exercise 1-27A *International Financial Reporting Standards*

Composite Fabricators, Inc. is a U.S.-based company that develops its financial statements under GAAP. The total amount of the company's assets shown on its balance sheet for the current year was approximately $370 million. The president of Composite Fabricators is considering the possibility of relocating the company to a country that practices accounting under IFRS. The president has hired an international accounting firm to determine what the company's statements would look like if they were prepared under IFRS. One striking difference is that, under IFRS, the assets shown on the balance sheet would be valued at approximately $430 million.

Required

a. Would Composite Fabricators' assets really be worth $60 million more if it moves its headquarters?
b. Discuss the underlying conceptual differences between U.S. GAAP and IFRS that cause the difference in the reported asset values.

PROBLEMS—SERIES A

All applicable Problems in Series A are available in Connect.

Problem 1-28A *Accounting's role in not-for-profits*

LO 1-1

Beverly Moore is struggling to pass her introductory accounting course. Beverly is intelligent but she likes to party. Studying is a low priority for Beverly. When one of her friends tells her that she is going to have trouble in business if she doesn't learn accounting, Beverly responds that she doesn't plan to go into business. She says that she is arts-oriented and plans someday to be a director of a museum. She is in the school of business to develop her social skills, not her quantitative skills. Beverly says she won't have to worry about accounting because museums are not intended to make a profit.

Required

a. Write a brief memo explaining whether you agree or disagree with Beverly's position regarding accounting and not-for-profit organizations.
b. Distinguish between financial accounting and managerial accounting.
c. Identify some of the stakeholders of not-for-profit institutions that would expect to receive financial accounting reports.
d. Identify some of the stakeholders of not-for-profit institutions that would expect to receive managerial accounting reports.

Problem 1-29A *Accounting entities*

LO 1-1

CHECK FIGURE
1. Entities mentioned: Bob Wilder and Wilder Co.

The following business scenarios are independent from one another:

1. Bob Wilder starts a business by transferring $10,000 from his personal checking account into a checking account for his business, Wilder Co.
2. A business that Sam Pace owns earns $4,600 of cash revenue from customers.
3. Jim Sneed borrows $30,000 from the National Bank and uses the money to purchase a car from Iuka Ford.
4. OZ Company pays its five employees $2,500 each to cover their salaries.
5. Gil Roberts loans his son Jim $5,000 cash.
6. Gane, Inc. paid $100,000 cash to purchase land from Atlanta Land Co.
7. Rob Moore and Gil Thomas form the MT partnership by contributing $20,000 each from their personal bank accounts to a partnership bank account.
8. Stephen Woo pays cash to purchase $5,000 of common stock that is issued by Izzard, Inc.
9. Natural Stone pays a $5,000 cash dividend to each of its seven shareholders.
10. Billows, Inc. borrowed $5,000,000 from the National Bank.

Required

a. For each scenario, create a list of all of the entities mentioned in the description.
b. Describe what happens to the cash account of each entity you identified in Requirement *a*.

Problem 1-30A *Classifying events as asset source, use, or exchange*

LO 1-6

The following unrelated events are typical of those experienced by business entities:

1. Acquire cash by issuing common stock.
2. Pay other operating supplies expense.
3. Agree to represent a client in an IRS audit and to receive payment when the audit is complete.
4. Receive cash from customers for services rendered.
5. Pay employee salaries with cash.
6. Pay back a bank loan with cash.
7. Pay interest to a bank with cash.

8. Transfer cash from a checking account to a money market account.
9. Sell land for cash at its original cost.
10. Pay a cash dividend to stockholders.
11. Learn that a financial analyst determined the company's price-earnings ratio to be 26.
12. Borrow cash from the local bank.
13. Pay office supplies expense.
14. Make plans to purchase office equipment.
15. Trade a used car for a computer with the same value.

Required

Identify each of the events as an asset source, use, or exchange transaction. If an event would not be recorded under generally accepted accounting principles, identify it as not applicable (NA). Also indicate for each event whether total assets would increase, decrease, or remain unchanged. Organize your answer according to the following table. The first event is shown in the table as an example.

Event No.	Type of Event	Effect on Total Assets
1	Asset source	Increase

LO 1-7, 1-8

Problem 1-31A *Relating titles and accounts to financial statements*

Required

Identify the financial statements on which each of the following items (titles, date descriptions, and accounts) appears by placing a check mark in the appropriate column. If an item appears on more than one statement, place a check mark in every applicable column.

Item	Income Statement	Statement of Changes in Stockholders' Equity	Balance Sheet	Statement of Cash Flows
Financing activities				
Ending common stock				
Interest expense				
As of (date)				
Land				
Beginning cash balance				
Notes payable				
Beginning common stock				
Service revenue				
Utility expense				
Stock issue				
Operating activities				
For the period ended (date)				
Net income				
Investing activities				
Net loss				
Ending cash balance				
Salary expense				
Consulting revenue				
Dividends				

Problem 1-32A Preparing financial statements for two complete accounting cycles

LO 1-4, 1-7, 1-8, 1-9

Mark's Consulting Services experienced the following transactions for Year 1, its first year of operations, and Year 2. Assume that all transactions involve the receipt or payment of cash.

CHECK FIGURES
a. Net Income Year 1: $13,000
b. Retained Earnings Year 2: $33,500

Transactions for Year 1

1. Acquired $20,000 by issuing common stock.
2. Received $35,000 for providing services to customers.
3. Borrowed $25,000 cash from creditors.
4. Paid expenses amounting to $22,000.
5. Purchased land for $30,000 cash.

Transactions for Year 2

Beginning account balances for Year 2 are:

Cash	$28,000
Land	30,000
Notes payable	25,000
Common stock	20,000
Retained earnings	13,000

1. Acquired an additional $24,000 from the issue of common stock.
2. Received $95,000 for providing services in Year 2.
3. Paid $15,000 to reduce notes payable.
4. Paid expenses amounting to $71,500.
5. Paid a $3,000 dividend to the stockholders.
6. Determined that the market value of the land is $47,000.

Required

a. Write an accounting equation, and record the effects of each accounting event under the appropriate headings for each year. Record the amounts of revenue, expense, and dividends in the Retained Earnings column. Provide appropriate titles for these accounts in the last column of the table.
b. Prepare an income statement, statement of changes in stockholders' equity, year-end balance sheet, and statement of cash flows for each year.
c. Determine the amount of cash in the Retained Earnings account at the end of Year 1 and Year 2.
d. Compare the information provided by the income statement with the information provided by the statement of cash flows. Point out similarities and differences.
e. Determine the balance in the Retained Earnings account immediately after Event 2 in Year 1 and in Year 2 are recorded.

Problem 1-33A Interrelationships among financial statements

LO 1-5, 1-7, 1-8

Pratt Corp. started the Year 2 accounting period with total assets of $30,000 cash, $12,000 of liabilities, and $5,000 of retained earnings. During the Year 2 accounting period, the Retained Earnings account increased by $7,550. The bookkeeper reported that Pratt paid cash expenses of $26,000 and paid a $2,000 cash dividend to stockholders, but she could not find a record of the amount of cash revenue that Pratt received for performing services. Pratt also paid $3,000 cash to reduce the liability owed to a bank, and the business acquired $4,000 of additional cash from the issue of common stock. Assume all transactions are cash transactions.

CHECK FIGURES
a. Net Income: $9,550
c. Total Assets: $38,550

Required

a. Prepare the Year 2 income statement.
b. Prepare the Year 2 statement of changes in stockholders' equity
c. Prepare the Year 2 balance sheet.
d. Prepare the Year 2 statement of cash flows.
e. Determine the percentage of total assets that were provided by creditors, investors, and earnings.
f. If the company were liquidated on December 31, Year 2, how much cash would be distributed to the creditors? How much cash would be distributed to the owners?

Chapter 1

LO 1-5, 1-6, 1-7, 1-8, 1-9, 1-10

CHECK FIGURES
a. Net Income: $23,000
e. Net Cash Flow from Operating Activities: $23,000

Problem 1-34A *Show how events affect the horizontal statements model*

Maben Company was started on January 1, Year 1, and experienced the following events during its first year of operation:

1. Acquired $30,000 cash from the issue of common stock.
2. Borrowed $40,000 cash from National Bank.
3. Earned cash revenues of $48,000 for performing services.
4. Paid cash expenses of $25,000.
5. Paid a $1,000 cash dividend to the stockholders.
6. Acquired an additional $20,000 cash from the issue of common stock.
7. Paid $10,000 cash to reduce the principal balance of the bank note.
8. Paid $53,000 cash to purchase land.
9. Determined that the market value of the land is $75,000.

Required

a. Use a horizontal statements model to show how each event affects the balance sheet, income statement, and statement of cash flows. Also, in the Cash Flows column, classify the cash flows as operating activities (OA), investing activities (IA), or financing activities (FA). The first event is shown as an example.

		Balance Sheet							Income Statement				
Event No.	Cash	+	Land	=	N. Pay.	+	C. Stock.	+	Ret. Ear.	Rev.	−	Exp.	=	Net Inc.	Statement of Cash Flows
1	30,000	+	NA	=	NA	+	30,000	+	NA	NA	−	NA	=	NA	30,000 FA

b. Determine the amount of total assets that Maben would report on the December 31, Year 1, balance sheet.
c. Identify the asset source transactions and related amounts for Year 1.
d. Determine the net income that Maben would report on the Year 1 income statement. Explain why dividends do not appear on the income statement.
e. Determine the net cash flows from operating activities, financing activities, and investing activities that Maben would report on the Year 1 statement of cash flows.
f. Determine the percentage of assets that were provided by investors, creditors, and earnings.
g. What is the balance in the Retained Earnings account immediately after Event 3 is recorded?

MULTIPLE-CHOICE QUESTIONS

Multiple-choice questions are available in **Connect.**

EXERCISES—SERIES B

LO 1-1

Exercise 1-1B *The role of accounting in society*

Resource owners provide three types of resources to conversion agents that transform the resources into products or services that satisfy consumer demands.

Required

Identify the three types of resources. Write a brief memo explaining how resource owners select the particular conversion agents to which they will provide resources. Your memo should include answers to the following questions: If you work as a private accountant, what role would you play in the allocation of resources? Which professional certification would be most appropriate for your career?

An Introduction to Accounting 51

Exercise 1-2B Careers in accounting

LO 1-1

Accounting is commonly divided into two sectors. One sector is called public accounting. The other sector is called private accounting.

Required
a. Identify three areas of service provided by public accountants.
b. Describe the common duties performed by private accountants.

Exercise 1-3B Identifying the reporting entities

LO 1-1

Ray Steen recently started a business. During the first few days of operation, Mr. Steen transferred $100,000 from his personal account into a business account for a company he named Steen Enterprises. Steen Enterprises borrowed $60,000 from First Bank. Mr. Steen's father-in-law, Stan Rhoades, invested $75,000 into the business for which he received a 25 percent ownership interest. Steen Enterprises purchased a building from Zoro Realty Company. The building cost $150,000 cash. Steen Enterprises earned $56,000 in revenue from the company's customers and paid its employees $31,000 for salaries expense.

Required
Identify the entities that were mentioned in the scenario and explain what happened to the cash accounts of each entity you identify.

Exercise 1-4B Defining terms and identifying missing information in the accounting equation

LO 1-2

Required
a. Match the terms (identified as a through g) with the definitions and phrases (marked 1 through 7). For example, the term "a. Stockholders' Equity" matches with definition 2. Common Stock + Retained Earnings.

a.	Stockholders' Equity	1.	Individuals or institutions that have contributed assets or services to a business in exchange for an ownership interest in the business.
b.	Liability	2.	Common Stock + Retained Earnings.
c.	Stockholders	3.	Certificates that evidence ownership in a company.
d.	Common Stock	4.	Assets – Liabilities – Common Stock.
e.	Retained Earnings	5.	An obligation to pay cash in the future.
f.	Creditors	6.	Individuals or institutions that have loaned goods or services to a business.
g.	Assets	7.	Economic resources that will be used by a business to produce revenue.

b. Calculate the missing amounts in the following table:

					Stockholders' Equity	
Company	Assets	=	Liabilities	+	Common Stock	+ Retained Earnings
A	$?		$30,000		$50,000	$62,000
B	50,000		?		10,000	25,000
C	85,000		20,000		?	40,000
D	215,000		60,000		100,000	?

Exercise 1-5B Effect of events on the accounting equation

LO 1-2

Morrison Co. experienced the following events during Year 1:

1. Acquired cash from the issue of common stock.
2. Borrowed cash.
3. Collected cash from providing services.
4. Purchased land with cash.

5. Paid operating expenses with cash.
6. Paid a cash dividend to the stockholders.

Required

Explain how each of these events affect the accounting equation by writing the letter I for increase, the letter D for decrease, and NA for does not affect under each of the components of the accounting equation. The first event is shown as an example.

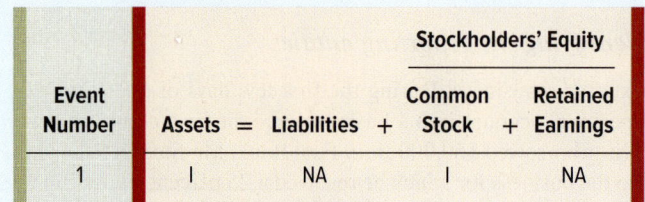

LO 1-2

Exercise 1-6B *Effect of transactions on general ledger accounts*

At the beginning of Year 2, Master Corp.'s accounting records had the following general ledger accounts and balances:

MASTER CORP.
Accounting Equation

Event	Assets		=	Liabilities	+	Stockholders' Equity		Acct. Titles for RE
	Cash	Land		Notes Payable		Common Stock	Retained Earnings	
Balance 1/1/Year 2	20,000	50,000		35,000		25,000	10,000	

Master Corp. completed the following transactions during Year 2:

1. Purchased land for $12,000 cash.
2. Acquired $20,000 cash from the issue of common stock.
3. Received $50,000 cash for providing services to customers.
4. Paid cash operating expenses of $42,000.
5. Borrowed $20,000 cash from the bank.
6. Paid a $2,000 cash dividend to the stockholders.
7. Determined that the market value of the land purchased in Event 1 is $70,000.

Required

a. Record the transactions in the appropriate general ledger accounts. Record the amounts of revenue, expense, and dividends in the Retained Earnings column. Provide the appropriate titles for these accounts in the last column of the table.
b. As of December 31, Year 2, determine the total amount of assets, liabilities, and stockholders' equity and present this information in the form of an accounting equation.
c. What is the amount of total assets, liabilities, and stockholders' equity as of January 1, Year 3?

LO 1-2

Exercise 1-7B *Missing information and recording events*

As of December 31, Year 1, Dunn Company had total cash of $156,000, notes payable of $85,600, and common stock of $52,400. During Year 2, Dunn earned $36,000 of cash revenue, paid $20,000 for cash expenses, and paid a $3,000 cash dividend to the stockholders.

Required

a. Determine the amount of retained earnings as of December 31, Year 1.
b. Create an accounting equation and record the beginning account balances under the appropriate elements.
c. Record the revenue, expense, and dividend events under the appropriate elements of the accounting equation created in Requirement b.
d. Prove the equality of the accounting equation as of December 31, Year 2.
e. Identify the beginning and ending balances in the Cash and Common Stock accounts. Explain why the beginning and ending balances in the Cash account are different, but the beginning and ending balances in the Common Stock account remain the same.

Exercise 1-8B *Account titles and the accounting equation*   LO 1-2

The following account titles were drawn from the general ledger of Pest Control, Incorporated (PCI): Cash, Notes Payable, Land, Accounts Payable, Office Furniture, Salaries Expense, Common Stock, Service Revenue, Interest Expense, Utilities Payable, Utilities Expense, Trucks, Supplies, Operating Expenses, Rent Revenue, Computers, Building, Supplies Expense, Gasoline Expense, Retained Earnings, Dividends.

Required

a. Create an accounting equation using the elements assets, liabilities, and stockholders' equity. List each account title under the element of the accounting equation to which it belongs.
b. Will all businesses have the same number of accounts? Explain your answer.

Exercise 1-9B *Components of the accounting equation*   LO 1-3

Lewis Enterprises was started when it acquired $4,000 cash from creditors and $6,000 from owners. The company immediately purchased land that cost $9,000.

Required

a. Record the events under an accounting equation.
b. After all events have been recorded, Lewis' obligations to creditors represents what percentage of total assets?
c. After all events have been recorded, Lewis' stockholders' equity represents what percentage of total assets?
d. Assume the debt is due. Given that Lewis has $6,000 in stockholders' equity, can the company repay the creditors at this point? Why or why not?

Exercise 1-10B *Components of the accounting equation*   LO 1-3

The financial condition of White Inc. is expressed in the following accounting equation:

        Assets   = Liabilities + Common stock + Retained earnings
$800 Cash + $9,200 Land = $7,000   + $2,000   + $1,000

Required

a. Are dividends paid to creditors or investors? Explain why.
b. How much cash is in the Retained Earnings account?
c. Determine the maximum dividend White can pay.
d. If the obligation to creditors is due, can White repay the loan? Why or why not?
e. Suppose the land sinks into the sea as a result of an earthquake and a resulting tsunami. The business is then liquidated. How much cash will creditors receive? How much cash will investors receive? (Assume there are no legal fees or other costs of liquidation.)

Chapter 1

LO 1-4, 1-5

Exercise 1-11B Calculate missing amounts and interpret results

The following table shows the transactions experienced by Walter Enterprises during Year 8. The table contains missing data that are labeled with alphabetic characters (a) through (i). Assume all transactions shown in the accounting equation are cash transactions.

	Assets				Liabilities		Stockholders' Equity			Account
	Cash	+	Land	=	Notes Pay.	+	Com. Stk.	+	Ret. Earn.	
Beg. Bal.	(a)	+	70,000	=	(b)	+	(c)	+	20,000	
Event No.										
1	(d)	+	NA	=	NA	+	50,000	+	NA	NA
2	(e)	+	NA	=	NA	+	NA	+	(f)	Revenue
3	(30,000)	+	NA	=	NA	+	NA	+	(30,000)	Expenses
4	(18,000)	+	NA	=	NA	+	NA	+	(g)	Dividend
5	(65,000)	+	(h)	=	NA	+	NA	+	NA	NA
6	(5,000)	+	NA	=	(5,000)	+	NA	+	NA	NA
Totals*	90,000	+	(i)	=	35,000	+	130,000	+	(j)	

Required

a. Determine the correct amount represented by each character (a) through (f).
b. Is there sufficient cash available to repay the debt on January 1, Year 8?
c. Based on the information in the table, what is the maximum cash dividend Walter could pay on January 1, Year 9?

LO 1-5

Exercise 1-12B Distribution in a business liquidation

Assume that Clayton Company acquires $1,200 cash from creditors and $1,700 cash from investors.

Required

a. Explain the primary differences between investors and creditors.
b. If Clayton has a net income of $800 and then liquidates, what amount of cash will the creditors receive? What amount of cash will the investors receive?
c. If Clayton has a net loss of $800 cash and then liquidates, what amount of cash will the creditors receive? What amount of cash will the investors receive?
d. If Clayton has a net loss of $1,900 cash and then liquidates, what amount of cash will the creditors receive? What amount of cash will the investors receive?

LO 1-6

Exercise 1-13B Classifying events as asset source, use, or exchange

Trip's Business Services experienced the following events during its first year of operations:

1. Acquired $20,000 cash from the issue of common stock.
2. Borrowed $12,000 cash from First Bank.
3. Paid $5,000 cash to purchase land.
4. Received $25,000 cash for providing boarding services.
5. Acquired an additional $5,000 cash from the issue of common stock.
6. Purchased additional land for $4,000 cash.
7. Paid $10,000 cash for salary expense.
8. Signed a contract to provide additional services in the future.
9. Paid $1,200 cash for rent expense.
10. Paid a $1,000 cash dividend to the stockholders.
11. Determined the market value of the land to be $18,000 at the end of the accounting period.

Required

Classify each event as an asset source, use, or exchange transaction, or as not applicable (NA).

EXERCISES—SERIES B

Exercise 1-14B *Missing information for determining net income* LO 1-7

The December 31, Year 1, balance sheet for James Company showed total stockholders' equity of $156,000. Total stockholders' equity increased by $65,000 between December 31, Year 1, and December 31, Year 2. During Year 2 James Company acquired $20,000 cash from the issue of common stock. James Company paid a $5,000 cash dividend to the stockholders during Year 2.

Required

Determine the amount of net income or loss James Company reported on its Year 2 income statement. (*Hint:* Remember that stock issues, net income, and dividends all change total stockholders' equity.)

Exercise 1-15B *Preparing an income statement and a balance sheet* LO 1-7

Petre Company was started on January 1, Year 1. During Year 1, the company experienced the following three accounting events: (1) earned cash revenues of $14,500, (2) paid cash expenses of $9,200, and (3) paid a $500 cash dividend to its stockholders. These were the only events that affected the company during Year 1.

Required

a. Create an accounting equation and record the effects of each accounting event under the appropriate general ledger account headings.

b. Prepare an income statement, statement of changes in stockholders' equity, and a balance sheet dated December 31, Year 1, for Petre Company.

c. Explain why the income statement uses different terminology to date the income statement than is used to date the balance sheet.

Exercise 1-16B *Historical cost versus market value* LO 1-7

Lakeside, Inc. purchased land in January Year 1 at a cost of $250,000. The estimated market value of the land is $425,000 as of December 31, Year 8.

Required

a. Name the December 31, Year 8, financial statement(s) on which the land will be shown.
b. At what dollar amount will the land be shown in the financial statement(s)?
c. Name the key concept that will be used in determining the dollar amount that will be reported for land that is shown in the financial statement(s).

Exercise 1-17B *Statement of cash flows* LO 1-8

On January 1, Year 1, Palmer, a fast-food company, had a balance in its Cash account of $32,000. During the Year 1 accounting period, the company had (1) net cash inflow from operating activities of $15,600, (2) net cash outflow for investing activities of $23,000, and (3) net cash outflow from financing activities of $4,500.

Required

a. Prepare a statement of cash flows.
b. Provide a reasonable explanation as to what may have caused the net cash inflow from operating activities.
c. Provide a reasonable explanation as to what may have caused the net cash outflow from investing activities.
d. Provide a reasonable explanation as to what may have caused the net cash outflow from financing activities.

Exercise 1-18B *Prepare a statement of cash flows* LO 1-8

National Service Company experienced the following accounting events during Year 1:

1. Paid $4,000 cash for salary expense.
2. Borrowed $8,000 cash from State Bank.

3. Received $30,000 cash from the issue of common stock.
4. Purchased land for $8,000 cash.
5. Performed services for $14,000 cash.
6. Paid $4,200 cash for utilities expense.
7. Sold land for $7,000 cash.
8. Paid a cash dividend of $1,000 to the stockholders.
9. Hired an accountant to keep the books.
10. Paid $3,000 cash on the loan from State Bank.

Required

a. Indicate how each of the events would be classified on the statement of cash flows as operating activities (OA), investing activities (IA), financing activities (FA), or not applicable (NA).

b. Prepare a statement of cash flows for Year 1. Assume National Service had a beginning cash balance of $9,000 on January 1, Year 1.

LO 1-7, 1-8

Exercise 1-19B *Preparing financial statements*

Tennessee Company experienced the following events during Year 2:

1. Acquired $50,000 cash from the issue of common stock.
2. Paid $15,000 cash to purchase land.
3. Borrowed $25,000 cash.
4. Provided services for $60,000 cash.
5. Paid $12,000 cash for rent expense.
6. Paid $22,000 cash for other operating expenses.
7. Paid a $5,000 cash dividend to the stockholders.
8. Determined that the market value of the land purchased in Event 2 is now $16,500.

Required

a. The January 1, Year 2, general ledger account balances are shown in the following accounting equation. Record the eight events in the appropriate general ledger accounts. Record the amounts of revenue, expense, and dividends in the Retained Earnings column. Provide the appropriate titles for these accounts in the last column of the table. The first event is shown as an example.

TENNESSEE COMPANY
Accounting Equation

Event	Assets		=	Liabilities	+	Stockholders' Equity		Acct. Titles for RE
	Cash	Land		Notes Payable		Common Stock	Retained Earnings	
Beg. Bal. 1/1/Year 1	15,000	10,000		0		20,000	5,000	
1	50,000					50,000		

b. Prepare an income statement, statement of changes in equity, year-end balance sheet, and statement of cash flows for the Year 2 accounting period.

c. Determine the percentage of assets that were provided by retained earnings. How much cash is in the retained earnings account?

LO 1-8

Exercise 1-20B *Relating accounting events to entities*

Arnett Company was started in Year 1 when it acquired $30,000 cash by issuing common stock to Dan Arnett.

Required

a. Was this event an asset source, use, or exchange transaction for Arnett Company?
b. Was this event an asset source, use, or exchange transaction for Dan Arnett?
c. Was the cash flow an operating, investing, or financing activity on Arnett Company's Year 1 statement of cash flows?
d. Was the cash flow an operating, investing, or financing activity on Dan Arnett's Year 1 statement of cash flows?

Exercise 1-21B   Preparing financial statements—retained earnings emphasis

LO 1-4, 1-5, 1-7, 1-8, 1-9

On January 1, Year 2, the following information was drawn from the accounting records of Zeke Company: cash of $200; land of $1,800; notes payable of $600; and common stock of $1,000.

Required

a. Determine the amount of retained earnings as of January 1, Year 2.
b. After looking at the amount of retained earnings, the chief executive officer (CEO) wants to pay a $300 cash dividend to the stockholders. Can the company pay this dividend? Why or why not?
c. As of January 1, Year 2, what percentage of the assets were acquired from creditors?
d. As of January 1, Year 2, what percentage of the assets were acquired from investors?
e. As of January 1, Year 2, what percentage of the assets were acquired from retained earnings?
f. Create an accounting equation using percentages instead of dollar amounts on the right side of the equation.
g. During Year 2, Zeke Company earned cash revenue of $500, paid cash expenses of $300, and paid a cash dividend of $50. Prepare an income statement, statement of changes in stockholders' equity, a balance sheet, and a statement of cash flows dated December 31, Year 2. (*Hint:* It is helpful to record these events under an accounting equation before preparing the statements.)
h. Comment on the terminology used to date each statement.
i. An appraiser determines that as of December 31, Year 2, the market value of the land is $2,000. How will this fact change the financial statements?
j. What is the balance in the Revenue account on January 1, Year 3?

Exercise 1-22B   Preparing financial statements—cash flow emphasis

LO 1-7, 1-8

As of January 1, Year 2, Shundra Inc. had a balance of $4,500 in Cash, $2,500 in Common Stock, and $2,000 in Retained Earnings. These were the only accounts with balances in the ledger on January 1, Year 2. Further analysis of the company's cash account indicated that during the Year 2 accounting period, the company had (1) net cash inflow from operating activities of $5,100, (2) net cash outflow for investing activities of $13,000, and (3) net cash inflow from financing activities of $7,600. All revenue and expense events were cash events. The following accounts and balances represent the general ledger of Shundra Inc. as of December 31, Year 2, before closing.

SHUNDRA INC.
General Ledger

Assets	=	Liabilities	+	Stockholders' Equity			
Cash		Notes Payable		Common Stock		Revenue	
Bal. 4,200		Bal. 3,000		Bal. 8,000		Bal. 9,900	
Land				Retained Earnings		Expenses	
Bal. 13,000				Bal. 2,000		Bal. 4,800	
						Dividends	
						Bal. 900	

Required

a. Assume that the net cash inflow from financing activities of $7,600 was caused by three events. Based on the information above, identify these events and determine the cash flow associated with each event.
b. What did the company purchase that resulted in the cash outflow from investing activities?
c. Prepare an income statement, statement of changes in stockholders' equity, balance sheet, and statement of cash flows.

Exercise 1-23B *Retained earnings and the closing process*

LO 1-9

As of December 31, Year 1, Big Horn Company had total assets of $100,000, total liabilities of $30,000, and common stock of $50,000. The company's Year 1 income statement contained revenue of $16,000 and expenses of $11,000. The Year 1 statement of changes in stockholders' equity stated that $2,000 of dividends were paid to investors.

Required

a. Determine the before-closing balance in the Retained Earnings account on December 31, Year 1.
b. Determine the after-closing balance in the Retained Earnings account on December 31, Year 1.
c. Determine the before-closing balances in the Revenue, Expense, and Dividend accounts on December 31, Year 1.
d. Determine the after-closing balances in the Revenue, Expense, and Dividend accounts on December 31, Year 1.
e. Explain the difference between common stock and retained earnings.
f. On January 1, Year 2, Big Horn Company raised $40,000 by issuing additional common stock. Immediately after the additional capital was raised. Big Horn reported total equity of $110,000. Are the stockholders of Big Horn in a better financial position than they were on December 31, Year 1?

Exercise 1-24B *The closing process*

LO 1-9

Pam's Crafts opened on January 1, Year 1. Pam's reported the following for cash revenues and cash expenses for the years Year 1 to Year 3:

	Cash Revenues	Cash Expenses
Year 1	$40,000	$21,000
Year 2	$50,000	$32,000
Year 3	$70,000	$48,000

Required

a. What would Pam's Crafts report for net income and retained earnings for the years Year 1, Year 2, and Year 3?
b. Explain the difference between net income and retained earnings.
c. Assume that Pam's Crafts paid a $6,000 dividend to stockholders in Year 2. What would Pam's Crafts report for net income and retained earnings for Year 2 and Year 3?

Exercise 1-25B *Retained earnings and the closing process*

LO 1-9

Carr Company was started on January 1, Year 1. During the month of January, Carr earned $4,600 of revenue and incurred $3,000 of expenses. During the remainder of Year 1, Carr earned $52,000 and incurred $42,000 of expenses. Carr closes its books on December 31 of each year.

Required

a. Determine the balance in the Retained Earnings account as of January 31, Year 1.
b. Determine the balance in the Revenue and Expense accounts as of January 31, Year 1.
c. Determine the balance in the Retained Earnings account as of December 31, Year 1, before closing.

d. Determine the balances in the Revenue and Expense accounts as of December 31, Year 1, before closing.
e. Determine the balance in the Retained Earnings account as of January 1, Year 2.
f. Determine the balance in the Revenue and Expense accounts as of January 1, Year 2.

Exercise 1-26B   *Types of transactions and the horizontal statements model*   LO 1-6, 1-10

Pet Partners experienced the following events during its first year of operations, Year 1:

1. Acquired cash by issuing common stock.
2. Borrowed cash from a bank.
3. Signed a contract to provide services in the future.
4. Purchased land with cash.
5. Paid cash for operating expenses.
6. Paid a cash dividend to the stockholders.
7. Determined that the market value of the land is higher than the historical cost.

Required

a. Indicate whether each event is an asset source, use, or exchange transaction.
b. Use a horizontal statements model to show how each event affects the balance sheet, income statement, and statement of cash flows. Indicate whether the event increases (I), decreases (D), or does not affect (NA) each element of the financial statements. Also, in the Statement of Cash Flows column, classify the cash flows as operating activities (OA), investing activities (IA), or financing activities (FA). The first transaction is shown as an example.

Event No.	Balance Sheet								Income Statement				Statement of Cash Flows
	Cash	+	Land	=	N. Pay.	+	C. Stock.	+	Ret. Ear.	Rev.	−	Exp.	=	Net Inc.	
1	I	+	NA	=	NA	+	I	+	NA	NA	−	NA	=	NA	I FA

Exercise 1-27B   *International Financial Reporting Standards*   LO IFRS

Corrugated Boxes Inc. is a U.S.-based company that develops its financial statements under GAAP. The total amount of the company's assets shown on its balance sheet for the current year was approximately $305 million. The president of Corrugated is considering the possibility of relocating the company to a country that practices accounting under IFRS. The president has hired an international accounting firm to determine what the company's statements would look like if they were prepared under IFRS. One striking difference is that under IFRS the assets shown on the balance sheet would be valued at approximately $345 million.

Required

a. Would Corrugated Boxes' assets really be worth $40 million more if it moves its headquarters?
b. Discuss the underlying conceptual differences between U.S. GAAP and IFRS that cause the difference in the reported asset values.

PROBLEMS—SERIES B

Problem 1-28B   *Applying GAAP to financial reporting*   LO 1-1

Jan Perkins is a business consultant. She analyzed the business processes of one of her clients, Diamond Companies, in November Year 1. She prepared a report containing her recommendation for changes in some of the company's business practices. She presented Diamond with the report in December Year 1. Jan guarantees that her clients will save money by following her advice. She does not collect for the services she provides until the client is satisfied with the results of her work. In this case, she received cash payment from Diamond in February Year 2.

Required

a. Define the acronym GAAP.

b. Assume that Jan's accountant tells her that GAAP permits Jan to recognize the revenue from Diamond in either Year 1 or Year 2. What GAAP rule would justify reporting the same event in two different ways? Write a brief memo explaining the logic behind this rule.

c. If Jan were keeping records for managerial reporting purposes, would she be bound by GAAP rules? Write a brief memo to explain how GAAP applies to financial versus managerial reporting.

LO 1-1

Problem 1-29B *Accounting entities*

The following business scenarios are independent from one another:

1. Chris Hann purchased an automobile from Classic Auto Sales for $10,000.
2. Sal Pearl loaned $15,000 to the business in which he is a stockholder.
3. First State Bank paid interest to Strong Co. on a certificate of deposit that Strong Co. has invested at First State Bank.
4. Cindy's Restaurant paid the current utility bill of $135 to Midwest Utilities.
5. Sun Corp. borrowed $50,000 from City National Bank and used the funds to purchase land from Carriage Realty.
6. Sue Wang purchased $10,000 of common stock of International Sales Corporation from the corporation.
7. Chris Gordon loaned $6,000 cash to his daughter.
8. Motor Service Co. earned $20,000 in cash revenue.
9. Poy Imports paid $4,000 for salaries to each of its four employees.
10. Borg Inc. paid a cash dividend of $4,000 to its sole shareholder, Mark Borg.

Required

a. For each scenario, create a list of all the entities mentioned in the description.

b. Describe what happens to the cash account of each entity you identified in Requirement *a*.

LO 1-6

Problem 1-30B *Classifying events as asset source, use, or exchange*

The following unrelated events are typical of those experienced by business entities:

1. Pay cash for operating expenses.
2. Pay an office manager's salary with cash.
3. Receive cash for services that have been performed.
4. Pay cash for utilities expense.
5. Acquire land by accepting a liability (financing the purchase).
6. Pay cash to purchase a new office building.
7. Discuss plans for a new office building with an architect.
8. Repay part of a bank loan.
9. Acquire cash by issuing common stock.
10. Purchase land with cash.
11. Purchase equipment with cash.
12. Pay monthly rent on an office building.
13. Hire a new office manager.
14. Borrow cash from a bank.
15. Pay a cash dividend to stockholders.

Required

Identify each of the events as an asset source, use, or exchange transaction. If an event would not be recorded under generally accepted accounting principles, identify it as not applicable (NA). Also indicate for each event whether total assets would increase, decrease, or remain unchanged.

Organize your answer according to the following table. The first event is shown in the table as an example.

Event No.	Type of Event	Effect on Total Assets
1	Asset use	Decrease

Problem 1-31B *Relating titles and accounts to financial statements*   LO 1-7, 1-8

Required

Identify the financial statements on which each of the following items (titles, date descriptions, and accounts) appears by placing a check mark in the appropriate column. If an item appears on more than one statement, place a check mark in every applicable column.

Item	Income Statement	Statement of Changes in Stockholders' Equity	Balance Sheet	Statement of Cash Flows
For the period ended (date)				
Net income				
Investing activities				
Net loss				
Ending cash balance				
Salary expense				
Consulting revenue				
Dividends				
Financing activities				
Ending common stock				
Interest expense				
As of (date)				
Land				
Beginning cash balance				
Notes payable				
Beginning common stock				
Service revenue				
Utility expense				
Stock issue				
Operating activities				

Problem 1-32B *Preparing financial statements for two complete accounting cycles*   LO 1-4, 1-7, 1-8, 1-9

Marco's Consulting experienced the following transactions for Year 1, its first year of operations, and Year 2. *Assume that all transactions involve the receipt or payment of cash.*

Transactions for Year 1

1. Acquired $50,000 by issuing common stock.
2. Received $100,000 cash for providing services to customers.
3. Borrowed $15,000 cash from creditors.
4. Paid expenses amounting to $60,000.
5. Purchased land for $40,000 cash.

Transactions for Year 2

Beginning account balances for Year 2 are:

Cash	$65,000
Land	40,000
Notes payable	15,000
Common stock	50,000
Retained earnings	40,000

1. Acquired an additional $20,000 from the issue of common stock.
2. Received $130,000 for providing services.
3. Paid $10,000 to creditors to reduce loan.
4. Paid expenses amounting to $75,000.
5. Paid a $15,000 dividend to the stockholders.
6. Determined that the market value of the land is $50,000.

Required

a. Write an accounting equation, and record the effects of each accounting event under the appropriate headings for each year. Record the amounts of revenue, expense, and dividends in the Retained Earnings column. Provide appropriate titles for these accounts in the last column of the table.
b. Prepare an income statement, statement of changes in stockholders' equity, year-end balance sheet, and statement of cash flows for each year.
c. Determine the amount of cash that is in the Retained Earnings account at the end of Year 1 and Year 2.
d. Examine the balance sheets for the two years. How did assets change from Year 1 to Year 2?
e. Determine the balance in the Retained Earnings account immediately after Event 2 in Year 1 and in Year 2 are recorded.

LO 1-5, 1-7, 1-8

Problem 1-33B *Interrelationships among financial statements*

Blix Corp. started the Year 2 accounting period with total assets of $50,000 cash, $20,000 of liabilities, and $20,000 of retained earnings. During the Year 2 accounting period, the Retained Earnings account increased by $8,500. The bookkeeper reported that Blix Corp. paid cash expenses of $15,000 and paid a $4,000 cash dividend to stockholders, but she could not find a record of the amount of cash revenue that Blix Corp. received for performing services. Blix Corp. also paid $2,000 cash to reduce the liability owed to a bank, and the business acquired $8,000 of additional cash from the issue of common stock. Assume all transactions are cash transactions.

Required

a. Prepare the Year 2 income statement.
b. Prepare the Year 2 statement of changes in stockholders' equity
c. Prepare the Year 2 balance sheet,
d. Prepare the Year 2 statement of cash flows.
e. Determine the percentage of total assets that were provided by creditors, investors, and earnings.
f. If the company were liquidated on December 31, Year 2, how much cash would be distributed to the creditors? How much cash would be distributed to the owners?

LO 1-5, 1-6, 1-7, 1-8, 1-9, 1-10

Problem 1-34B *Show how the events affect the horizontal statements model*

Daley Company was started on January 1, Year 1, and experienced the following events during its first year of operation:

1. Acquired $52,000 cash from the issue of common stock.
2. Borrowed $20,000 cash from National Bank.

3. Earned cash revenues of $42,000 for performing services.
4. Paid cash expenses of $23,000.
5. Paid a $6,000 cash dividend to the stockholders.
6. Acquired an additional $10,000 cash from the issue of common stock.
7. Paid $10,000 cash to reduce the principal balance of the bank note.
8. Paid $45,000 cash to purchase land.
9. Determined that the market value of the land is $55,000.

Required

a. Use a horizontal statements model to show how each event affects the balance sheet, income statement, and statement of cash flows. Also, in the Statement of Cash Flows column, classify the cash flows as operating activities (OA), investing activities (IA), or financing activities (FA). The first event is shown as an example.

Event No.	Balance Sheet									Income Statement					Statement of Cash Flows
	Cash	+	Land	=	N. Pay.	+	C. Stock.	+	Ret. Ear.	Rev.	−	Exp.	=	Net Inc.	
1	52,000	+	NA	=	NA	+	52,000	+	NA	NA	−	NA	=	NA	52,000 FA

b. Determine the amount of total assets that Daley would report on the December 31, Year 1, balance sheet.
c. Identify the asset source transactions and related amounts for Year 1.
d. Determine the net income that Daley would report on the Year 1 income statement. Explain why dividends do not appear on the income statement.
e. Determine the net cash flows from operating activities, financing activities, and investing activities that Daley would report on the Year 1 statement of cash flows.
f. Determine the percentage of assets provided by investors, creditors, and earnings.
g. What is the balance in the Retained Earnings account immediately after Event 3 is recorded?

ANALYZE, THINK, COMMUNICATE

ATC 1-1 Business Applications Case *Understanding real-world annual reports*

Required

Obtain the **Target Corporation's** annual report at http://investors.target.com using the instructions in Appendix B, and use it to answer the following questions:

a. What was Target's net income for 2016 (the year ended January 28, 2017)?
b. Did Target's net income increase or decrease from 2015 to 2016? By how much?
c. What was Target's accounting equation for 2016?
d. Which of the following had the largest percentage change from 2015 to 2016: sales, cost of sales, or selling, general, and administrative expenses? Show all computations.

ATC 1-2 Group Assignment *Missing information*

The following selected financial information is available for Best, Inc. Amounts are in millions of dollars.

Income Statements	Year 4	Year 3	Year 2	Year 1
Revenue	$ 860	$1,520	$ (a)	$1,200
Cost and expenses	(a)	(a)	(2,400)	(860)
Income from continuing operations	(b)	450	320	(a)
Unusual items	-0-	175	(b)	(b)
Net income	$ 20	$ (b)	$ 175	$ 300

Balance Sheets

Assets				
Cash and marketable securities	$ 350	$1,720	$ (c)	$ 940
Other assets	1,900	(c)	2,500	(c)
Total assets	2,250	$2,900	$ (d)	$3,500
Liabilities	$ (c)	$ (d)	$1,001	$ (d)
Stockholders' equity				
Common stock	880	720	(e)	800
Retained earnings	(d)	(e)	800	(e)
Total stockholders' equity	1,520	1,345	(f)	2,200
Total liabilities and stockholders' equity	$2,250	$ (f)	$3,250	$3,500

Required

a. Divide the class into groups of four or five students each. Organize the groups into four sections. Assign Task 1 to the first section of groups, Task 2 to the second section, Task 3 to the third section, and Task 4 to the fourth section.

Group Tasks

(1) Fill in the missing information for Year 1.
(2) Fill in the missing information for Year 2.
(3) Fill in the missing information for Year 3.
(4) Fill in the missing information for Year 4.

b. Each section should select two representatives. One representative is to put the financial statements assigned to that section on the board, underlining the missing amounts. The second representative is to explain to the class how the missing amounts were determined.

c. Each section should list events that could have caused the unusual items category on the income statement.

ATC 1-3 Real-World Case   *Classifying cash flow activities at five companies*

The following cash transactions occurred in five real-world companies:

1. During the third quarter of 2016 (July 1 through September 30) **Ford Motor Company** paid approximately $31.5 billion in expenses related to the production for the vehicles it sold.
2. **International Business Machines (IBM), Inc.** purchased the mobile and cloud-based web properties of **The Weather Company** in 2016. Assume this was a cash purchase.
3. **Apple, Inc.** borrowed $12 billion in 2016 by issuing bonds payable (long-term debt).
4. **Whole Foods Market, Inc.** collected $15.7 billion in cash from sales it made during its 2016 fiscal year.
5. During its 2016 fiscal year, **Microsoft Corporation** paid $11 billion of dividends.
6. In January 2017, **McDonald's, Inc.** announced plans to sell a major stake in its operations in China and Hong Kong for $1.7 billion. Assume the sale was for cash and that it was completed in 2017.

Required

Determine if each of the above transactions should be classified as an *operating, investing,* or *financing* activity. Also, identify the amount of each cash flow and whether it was an *inflow* or an *outflow*.

ATC 1-4 Business Applications Case *Forecasting from financial reports*

The following information was drawn from the annual report of Machine Imports Company (MIC):

	For the Years Year 1	Year 2
Income Statement		
Revenues	$ 600,000	$ 690,000
Operating expenses	(480,000)	(552,000)
*Infrequent item—lottery win	–	62,000
Net income	$ 120,000	$ 200,000
Balance Sheet		
Assets	$ 880,000	$ 880,000
Liabilities	$ 200,000	$ –
Stockholders' equity:		
Common stock	380,000	380,000
Retained earnings	300,000	500,000
Total liabilities and stockholders' equity	$ 880,000	$ 880,000

*By definition, infrequent items are not likely to recur in the future.

Required

a. Compute the percentage of growth in net income from Year 1 to Year 2. Can stockholders expect a similar increase between Year 2 and Year 3?

b. Assuming that MIC collected $200,000 cash from earnings (i.e., net income), explain how this money was spent in Year 2.

c. Assuming that MIC experiences the same percentage of growth from Year 2 to Year 3 as it did from Year 1 to Year 2, determine the amount of income from continuing operations that the owners can expect to see on the Year 3 income statement.

d. During Year 3, MIC experienced a $40,000 loss due to storm damage (note that this would be shown as an infrequent item on the income statement). Liabilities and common stock were unchanged from Year 2 to Year 3. Use the information you computed in Requirement *c,* plus the additional information provided in the previous two sentences, to prepare an income statement and balance sheet as of December 31, Year 3.

ATC 1-5 Writing Assignment *Elements of financial statements defined*

Sam and his sister Blair both attend the state university. As a reward for their successful completion of the past year (Sam had a 3.2 GPA in business, and Blair had a 3.7 GPA in art), their father gave each of them 100 shares of The Walt Disney Company stock. They have just received their first annual report. Blair does not understand what the information means and has asked Sam to explain it to her. Sam is currently taking an accounting course, and she knows he will understand the financial statements.

Required

Assume you are Sam. Write Blair a memo explaining the following financial statement items to her. In your explanation, describe each of the two financial statements and explain the financial information each contains. Also, define each of the elements listed for each financial statement and explain what it means.

ATC 1-6 Ethical Dilemma *Loyalty versus the bottom line*

Assume that Kevin has been working for you for five years. He has had an excellent work history and has received generous pay raises in response. The raises have been so generous that Kevin is quite overpaid for the job he is required to perform. Unfortunately, he is not qualified to take on other, more responsible jobs available within the company. A recent job applicant is willing to accept a salary $5,000 per year less than the amount currently being paid to Kevin. The applicant is well qualified to take over Kevin's duties and has a very positive attitude. The following financial statements were reported by your company at the close of its most recent accounting period:

Required

a. Reconstruct the financial statements (shown below), assuming that Kevin was replaced at the beginning of the most recent accounting period. Both Kevin and his replacement are paid in cash. No other changes are to be considered.

b. Discuss the short- and long-term ramifications of replacing Kevin. There are no right answers. However, assume you are required to make a decision. Use your judgment and common sense to support your choice.

Financial Statements

Income Statements

Revenue		$ 57,000
Expense		(45,000)
Net income		$ 12,000

Statement of Changes in Stockholders' Equity

Beginning common stock	$20,000	
Plus: stock issued	5,000	
Ending common stock		$25,000
Begnning retained earnings	50,000	
Net income	12,000	
Dividends	(2,000)	
Ending retained earnings		60,000
Total stockholders' equity		$85,000

Balance Sheet

Assets		
Cash		$ 85,000
Equity		
Common stock		$ 25,000
Retained earnings		60,000
Total stockholders' equity		$ 85,000

Statement of Cash Flows

Operating activities		
Inflow from customers	$ 57,000	
Outflow to suppliers expenses	(45,000)	
Net inflow from operations		$ 12,000
Investing activities		0
Financing activities		
Inflow from stock issue	5,000	
Outflow for dividends	(2,000)	
Net inflow from financing activities		3,000
Net change in cash		15,000
Plus: beginning cash balance		70,000
Ending cash balance		$ 85,000

ATC 1-7 Research Assignment *Finding real-world accounting information*

This chapter introduced the basic four financial statements companies use annually to keep their stakeholders informed of their accomplishments and financial situation. Complete the requirements below using the most recent (20xx) financial statements available on Sonic Drive-In's website. Obtain the statements on the Internet by following the steps below. (The formatting of the company's website may have changed since these instructions were written.)

1. Go to www.sonicdrivein.com.
2. Click on the "Investors" link at the bottom of the page.
3. Click on the "*20xx Annual Report*" link at the lower left side of the page.
4. Go to the company's financial statements that begin around page 25 of the annual report.

Required

a. What was the company's *net income* in each of the last three years?
b. What amount of total *assets* did the company have at the end of the most recent year?
c. How much *retained earnings* did the company have at the end of the most recent year?
d. For the most recent year, what was the company's *cash flow from operating activities*, *cash flow from investing activities*, and *cash flow from financing activities*?

ATC 1-8 Spreadsheet Assignment *Using Excel*

The financial statements for Simple Company are reported here using an Excel spreadsheet.

Required

Re-create the financial statements using your own Excel spreadsheet.

a. For each number with an arrow by it, enter a formula in that particular cell address to solve for the number shown. (Do not enter the arrow.)
b. When complete, print the spreadsheet with formulas rather than absolute numbers.

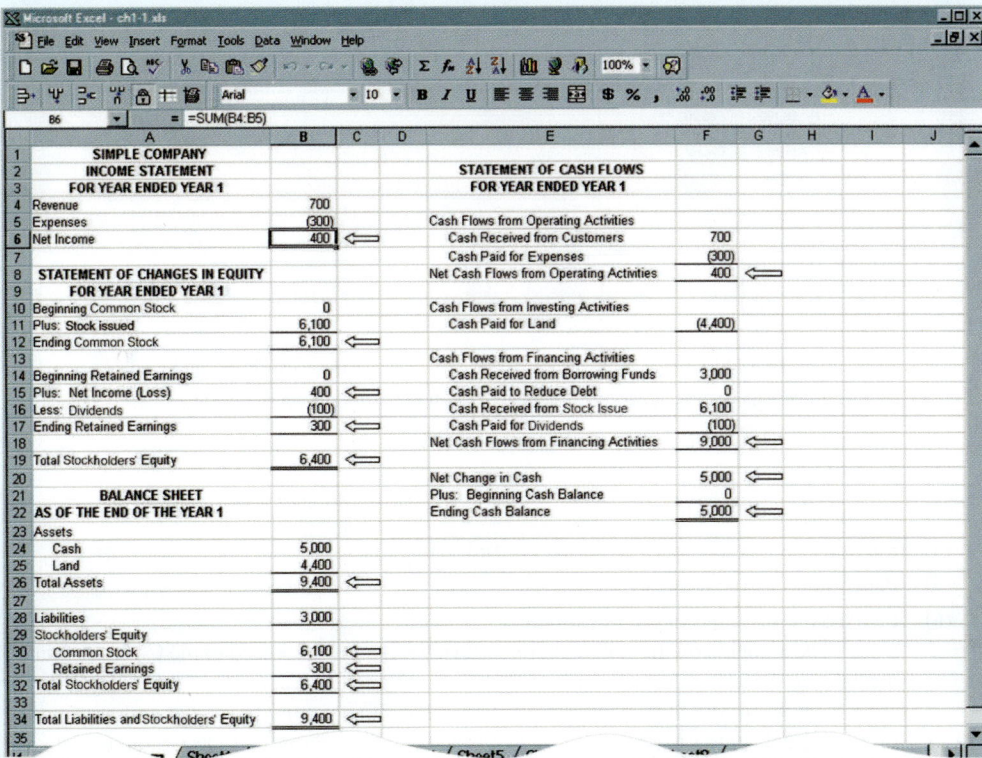

Source: Microsoft Office Excel 1997

Spreadsheet Tips

(1) Widen a column by positioning the cursor on the vertical line between two column headings until cross-hairs appear. Either double-click to automatically widen it, or click and drag the cross-hairs to the desired width.

(2) Negative numbers can be parenthesized by choosing Format and then Cells. Under Number, choose Custom and under Type, choose the first option containing parentheses.

(3) The SUM function is one way to add a series of numbers. For example, the formula for net income in cell B6 is SUM(B4:B5).

(4) Single and double lines can be drawn using the Borders icon.

(5) Print a spreadsheet on one page by choosing File, Page Setup, and Fit to 1.

(6) Print without gridlines by choosing File, Page Setup, and Sheet, and then uncheck Gridlines. Another option is to choose Tools and Options and uncheck Gridlines.

(7) Print formulas by choosing Tools, Options, and Formulas.

ATC 1-9 Spreadsheet Assignment *Mastering Excel*

Required

a. Enter the following headings for the horizontal statements model onto a blank spreadsheet.

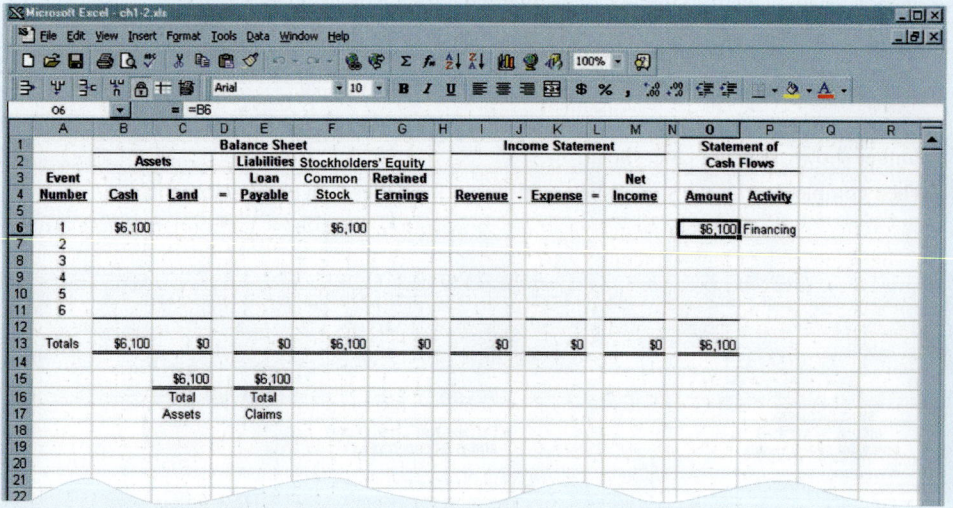

Source: Microsoft Office Excel 1997

b. Under the appropriate headings, record the effects of each of the following accounting events for the first month of operations. The first event has been recorded as an example.

(1) Acquired $6,100 from the issue of common stock.

(2) Paid $4,400 to purchase land.

(3) Borrowed $3,000 cash.

(4) Provided services to customers and received $700 in cash.

(5) Paid $300 for expenses.

(6) Paid a $100 dividend to the stockholders.

(*Note:* The amounts on the statement of cash flows can be referenced to the Cash account on the balance sheet. In other words, recording the cash amounts twice is not necessary. Instead, enter formulas in the Statement of Cash Flows column equating those cell addresses to the respective cell in the Cash column. Notice that the formula in cell O6 (statement of cash flows) is set equal to cell B6 (cash on the balance sheet). Once the formula is completed for cell O6, it can be easily copied to cells O7 through O11.)

c. Using formulas, sum each of the quantitative columns to arrive at the end-of-month amounts reported on the financial statements.

Spreadsheet Tips

(1) Center the heading *Balance Sheet* across columns by entering the entire heading in cell B1. Position the cursor on B1 until a fat cross appears. Click and drag the cursor across B1 through G1. Click on the Merge and Center icon (it is highlighted in the screen in the toolbar).

(2) Enter arithmetic signs as headings by placing an apostrophe in front of the sign. For example, to enter the equal sign in cell D4, enter '=.

(3) Copy cells by positioning the cursor in the bottom right corner of the cell to copy from (such as cell O6) until a thin cross appears. Click and drag the cursor down through the desired locations to copy to (through cell O11).

(4) To enter the dollar sign, choose Format, Cells, and Currency.

COMPREHENSIVE PROBLEM

The following information is available for Pacilio Security Services, Inc. for Year 1, its first year of operations. Pacilio provides security services for local sporting events.

The following summary transactions occurred during Year 1:

1. Acquired $6,000 from the issue of common stock.
2. Borrowed $5,000 from the Small Business Government Agency. The loan is interest-free.
3. Performed security services at local sporting events during the year for $9,000 cash.
4. Paid salaries expense of $3,000 for the year.
5. Purchased land for $4,000.
6. Paid other operating expenses of $2,000 for the year.
7. Paid a cash dividend to the shareholders of $2,500.
8. The market value of the land was determined to be $4,500 at December 31, Year 1.

Required

a. Record the above transactions in an accounting equation. Provide the appropriate account titles for the amounts shown in the Retained Earnings column.

b. Prepare an income statement, statement of changes in stockholders' equity, balance sheet, and statement of cash flows for Year 1.

CHAPTER 2

Accounting for Accruals and Deferrals

LEARNING OBJECTIVES

After you have mastered the material in this chapter, you will be able to:

SECTION 1: SHOW HOW ACCRUALS AFFECT FINANCIAL STATEMENTS

LO 2-1 Show how receivables affect financial statements.

LO 2-2 Show how payables affect financial statements.

LO 2-3 Prepare financial statements that include accruals.

LO 2-4 Identify the steps in the accounting cycle.

SECTION 2: SHOW HOW DEFERRALS AFFECT FINANCIAL STATEMENTS

LO 2-5 Show how accounting for supplies affects financial statements.

LO 2-6 Show how accounting for prepaid items affects financial statements.

LO 2-7 Show how accounting for unearned revenues affects financial statements.

LO 2-8 Prepare financial statements that include deferrals.

LO 2-9 Classify accounting events into one of four categories.

LO 2-10 Discuss the primary components of corporate governance.

APPENDIX

LO 2-11 Compute depreciation expense and show how it affects financial statements.

LO 2-12 Compute interest expense and show how it affects financial statements.

 Video lectures and accompanying self-assessment quizzes are available in Connect *for all learning objectives.*

SECTION 1:
ACCOUNTING FOR ACCRUALS

Suppose a painting company signs a contract to paint a house. Two weeks after signing the contract, a painter starts the job. The job is completed in one week. The company sends the client a bill a few days after the job is complete. The company receives payment from the client 10 days after the bill was sent. Should the paint company recognize revenue on the day the contract was signed, when the work started, when the work was finished, when the bill was sent, or when the cash was collected? To provide guidance in answering such questions, the Financial Accounting Standards Board (FASB) issued Accounting Standards Codification 606, which provides the following core principal:

> [A]n entity should recognize revenue to depict the transfer of promised goods or services to customers in an amount that reflects the consideration to which the entity expects to be entitled in exchange for those goods or services.

In lay terms, this means that revenue should be recognized in the period in which it is earned regardless of whether cash has or has not been collected. More specifically, companies may recognize revenue in the income statement in a different accounting period than the period in which they collect the related cash. Furthermore, companies frequently make cash payments for expenses in accounting periods other than the periods in which the expenses are recognized in the income statement. Recognizing revenue when it is earned and expenses when they are incurred, regardless of when cash changes hands, is commonly called **accrual accounting.**

To illustrate, assume Johnson Company provides services to customers in Year 1 but collects cash for those services in Year 2. When should Johnson recognize the services revenue?

First, note that accrual accounting is not used by all companies. Indeed, many small private companies use cash basis accounting. Users of *cash basis* accounting recognize (report) revenues and expenses in the period in which cash is collected or paid. Under cash basis accounting, Johnson would recognize the revenue in Year 2 when it collects the cash.

In contrast, users of accrual accounting recognize revenues and expenses in the period in which they occur, regardless of when cash is collected or paid. Under accrual accounting, Johnson would recognize the revenue in Year 1 (the period in which it performed the services) even though it does not collect the cash until Year 2.

Accrual accounting is required by generally accepted accounting principles (GAAP). Virtually all major companies operating in the United States use it. Its two distinguishing features are called *accruals* and *deferrals.*

- The term **accrual** describes a revenue or an expense event that is recognized *before* cash is exchanged. Johnson's recognition of revenue in Year 1 that is related to cash collected in Year 2 is an example of an accrual.
- The term **deferral** describes a revenue or an expense event that is recognized *after* cash has been exchanged. Suppose Johnson pays cash in Year 1 to purchase office supplies it uses in Year 2. In this case, the cash payment occurs in Year 1, although supplies expense is recognized in Year 2. This example is a deferral.

The Curious Accountant

©B. O'Kane/Alamy

On September 15, 2019, Karen Furman purchased a subscription to *Fitness* magazine for her sister's birthday. She paid $12 for a one-year subscription to the **Meredith Corporation**, the company that publishes *Fitness, American Baby, Better Homes and Gardens, The Ladies Home Journal,* and several other magazines. The company also owns 17 television stations. Karen's sister will receive her first issue of the magazine in October.

How should Meredith Corporation account for the receipt of this cash? How would this event be reported on its December 31, 2019, financial statements? (Answers on page 92.)

ACCOUNTING FOR RECEIVABLES

LO 2-1

 Show how receivables affect financial statements.

This section of the text describes seven events experienced by Cato Consultants, a training services company that uses accrual accounting. Recall that in a double-entry accounting system every event affects at least two ledger accounts. At the end of the accounting period, the information that has been collected in the ledger accounts is used to prepare financial statements. We analyze the events in this chapter by first identifying the two accounts affected by each event. Next, we show how the changes in the two accounts affect the accounting equation. Finally, we show how the event affects the financial statements.

EVENT 1 Cato Consultants was started on January 1, Year 1, when it acquired $5,000 cash by issuing common stock.

This event increases the company's asset account (cash) and its stockholders' equity account (common stock). The effects of this event on the accounting equation are shown here:

Assets	=	Liabilities	+	Stockholders' Equity
Cash				Common Stock
5,000	=	NA	+	5,000

The issue of stock for cash is an **asset source transaction.** On the balance sheet assets and stockholders' equity increase. The transaction does not affect the income statement. Because the company is being financed by acquiring cash from the owners, the cash inflow is classified as a financing activity (FA). These effects are shown in the following financial statements model:

Balance Sheet							Income Statement					Statement of Cash Flows
Assets	=	Liab.	+	C. Stk.	+	R. Earn.	Rev.	−	Exp.	=	Net Inc.	
5,000	=	NA	+	5,000	+	NA	NA	−	NA	=	NA	5,000 FA

Recognizing Accounts Receivable

EVENT 2 During Year 1, Cato Consultants provided $84,000 of consulting services to its clients. Cato has completed the work and sent bills to the clients, but has not yet collected any cash. This type of transaction is frequently described as providing services *on account*.

Accrual accounting requires companies to recognize revenue in the period in which the work is done regardless of when cash is collected. In this case, revenue is recognized in Year 1 even though cash has not been collected. Recall that revenue is an economic benefit (an increase in assets) that results from providing goods and services to customers. The specific asset that increases is called **Accounts Receivable.** The balance in Accounts Receivable represents the amount of cash the company expects to collect in the future. The effects on the accounting equation are as follows:

Assets	=	Liabilities	+	Stockholders' Equity
Accounts Receivable				Revenue
84,000	=	NA	+	84,000

Because the revenue recognition causes assets (accounts receivable) to increase, it is classified as an asset source transaction. On the balance sheet, assets and stockholders' equity increase. The increase in revenue increases net income and ultimately retained earnings. The collection of cash will occur in some future event. Because cash was not collected or paid, the statement of cash flows is not affected for Event 2. The effects on the financial statements are shown in the following financial statements model:

Balance Sheet							Income Statement						Statement of Cash Flows
Assets	=	Liab.	+	C. Stk.	+	R. Earn.	Rev.	−	Exp.	=	Net Inc.	
84,000	=	NA	+	NA	+	84,000	84,000	−	NA	=	84,000	NA

EVENT 3 Cato collected $60,000 cash from customers in partial settlement of its accounts receivable.

This event causes one asset account (cash) to increase and another asset account (accounts receivable) to decrease. The effect of the collection of receivables on the accounting equation is as follows:

Assets		=	Liabilities	+	Stockholders' Equity
Cash	Accounts Receivable				
60,000	(60,000)	=	NA	+	NA

The collection of an account receivable is an **asset exchange transaction.** The amount of total assets is not affected. Notice that the company does not recognize revenue when the cash is collected. Remember that the revenue was recognized when the work was done (see Event 2). Revenue would be double counted if it were recognized again when the cash is collected. Accordingly, this event does not affect the income statement. Because the cash collection was derived from normal business operations, it is classified as an operating activity (OA). The effects on the financial statements are shown in the following financial statements model:

Balance Sheet							Income Statement						Statement of Cash Flows
Assets	=	Liab.	+	C. Stk.	+	R. Earn.	Rev.	−	Exp.	=	Net Inc.	
NA	=	NA	+	NA	+	NA	NA	−	NA	=	NA	60,000 OA

Other Events

EVENT 4 Cato paid an instructor a $10,000 cash salary for teaching courses.

This event causes a decrease in the asset account Cash. Recognizing salary expense causes a corresponding decrease in stockholders' equity. The effects on the accounting equation are as follows:

Assets	=	Liabilities	+	Stockholders' Equity
Cash				Salary Expense
(10,000)	=	NA	+	(10,000)

Cash payment for salary expense is an **asset use transaction.** On the balance sheet, assets and stockholders' equity decrease. Recognizing the expense decreases net income on the income statement and ultimately retained earnings on the balance sheet. Because Cato paid cash for a normal operating expense, the statement of cash flows reflects a cash outflow from operating activities (OA). The effects on the financial statements are shown in the following financial statements model:

Balance Sheet									Income Statement					Statement of Cash Flows
Assets	=	Liab.	+	C. Stk.	+	R. Earn.	Rev.	−	Exp.	=	Net Inc.		
(10,000)	=	NA	+	NA	+	(10,000)	NA	−	10,000	=	(10,000)	(10,000)	OA

EVENT 5 Cato paid $2,000 cash for advertising costs. The advertisements appeared in Year 1.

The event causes the asset account Cash to decrease. Recognizing advertising expense causes a corresponding decrease in stockholders' equity. The effects on the accounting equation are as follows:

Assets	=	Liabilities	+	Stockholders' Equity
Cash				Advertising Expense
(2000)	=	NA	+	(2,000)

The cash payment for advertising expense is an asset use transaction. On the balance sheet, assets and stockholders' equity decrease. Recognizing the expense decreases net income on the income statement and ultimately retained earnings on the balance sheet. Because Cato paid cash for a normal operating expense, the statement of cash flows reflects a cash outflow from operating activities. The effects on the financial statements are as follows:

Balance Sheet									Income Statement					Statement of Cash Flows
Assets	=	Liab.	+	C. Stk.	+	R. Earn.	Rev.	−	Exp.	=	Net Inc.		
(2,000)	=	NA	+	NA	+	(2,000)	NA	−	2,000	=	(2,000)	(2,000)	OA

ACCOUNTING FOR PAYABLES (YEAR-END ADJUSTING ENTRY)

LO 2-2

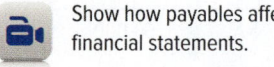

Show how payables affect financial statements.

Accrual accounting requires that companies recognize expenses in the period in which they are incurred regardless of when cash is paid. As a result, expenses may be recognized before cash is paid. For example, Cato must recognize an expense for all of the work its employees performed in Year 1 even if the employees are not paid until Year 2. Expenses that are recognized before cash is paid are called **accrued expenses.** The accounting for Event 6 illustrates the effect of recognizing accrued salary expense.

EVENT 6 At the end of Year 1, Cato recorded accrued salary expense of $6,000. The salary expense is for courses the instructor taught in Year 1. However, Cato will not pay the instructor cash until Year 2.

As of December 31, Year 1, Cato has an unrecorded salary expense. Also on this date, Cato has an unrecorded liability. In other words, on December 31, Year 1, Cato has an obligation to pay the instructor $6,000 in Year 2. Accordingly, Cato must update its ledger account balances prior to using them to prepare the financial statements. The entry required to update the account balances is called an **adjusting entry.** The effect of the adjustment for accrued salary expense on the accounting equation is as follows:

Assets	=	Liabilities	+	Stockholders' Equity
Cash		Salaries payable		Salary Expense
NA	=	6,000	+	(6,000)

Recognizing accrued expense is a **claims exchange transaction.** The claims of creditors increase and the claims of stockholders decrease. Total claims remain unchanged. Specifically, the liability account **Salaries Payable** increases. The balance in the Salaries Payable account represents the amount of cash the company is obligated to pay the instructor in the future. Also, recognizing salary expense decreases net income and ultimately retained earnings. Because cash was not paid or collected, there is no impact on the statement of cash flows. The effect of recognizing accrued salary expense on the financial statements is as follows:

Balance Sheet							Income Statement				Statement of Cash Flows
Assets	=	Liab.	+	C. Stk.	+	R. Earn.	Rev.	−	Exp.	=	Net Inc.	
NA	=	6,000	+	NA	+	(6,000)	NA	−	6,000	=	(6,000)	NA

Expenses were previously defined as assets consumed in the process of generating revenue. However, in this case, Cato's adjusting entry to recognize accrued salaries expense is not directly related to the use of assets. Instead of a decrease in assets, Cato recorded an increase in liabilities (salaries payable). *An **expense** can therefore be more broadly defined as an economic sacrifice (a decrease in assets or an increase in liabilities) resulting from operating activities undertaken to generate revenue.*

Also, be careful not to confuse liabilities with expenses. Although liabilities may increase when a company recognizes expenses, liabilities are *not* expenses. Liabilities are obligations. They can arise from acquiring assets as well as recognizing expenses. For example, when a business borrows money from a bank, it recognizes an increase in assets (cash) and liabilities (notes payable). However, in this case the increase in liabilities is not related to the recognition of expenses.

EVENT 7 During Year 1, Cato signed contracts for $42,000 of consulting services to be performed in Year 2.

The $42,000 for consulting services to be performed in Year 2 is not recognized in the Year 1 financial statements. Revenue is recognized for work actually completed, not work expected to be completed. This event does not affect any of the financial statements.

> ### CHECK YOURSELF 2.1
>
> During Year 1, Anwar Company earned $345,000 of revenue on account and collected $320,000 cash from accounts receivable. Anwar paid cash expenses of $300,000 and cash dividends of $12,000. Determine the amount of net income Anwar should report on the Year 1 income statement and the amount of cash flow from operating activities Anwar should report on the Year 1 statement of cash flows.
>
> **Answer** Net income is $45,000 ($345,000 revenue − $300,000 expenses). The cash flow from operating activities is $20,000, the amount of revenue collected in cash from customers (accounts receivable) minus the cash paid for expenses ($320,000 − $300,000). Dividend payments are classified as financing activities and do not affect the determination of either net income or cash flow from operating activities.

Summary of Events and General Ledger

The previous section of this chapter described seven events Cato Consultants experienced during the Year 1 accounting period. These events and their effects on the accounting equation and the associated general ledger accounts are shown in Exhibit 2.1. Because the balances in the accounts reflect the company's financial condition immediately after the adjusting entry has been recorded, they are called the *adjusted ledger account* balances. The information in these accounts is used to prepare the financial statements.

PREPARING FINANCIAL STATEMENTS WITH ACCRUALS

LO 2-3

Prepare financial statements that include accruals.

The financial statements for Cato Consultants' Year 1 accounting period are represented in a vertical statements model in Exhibit 2.2. A vertical statements model arranges a set of financial statement information vertically on a single page. Like horizontal statements models, vertical statements models are learning tools. They illustrate interrelationships among financial statements. The models do not, however, portray the full, formal presentation formats companies use in published financial statements. For example, statements models may use summarized formats with abbreviated titles and dates. As you read the following explanations of each financial statement, trace the color-coded financial data from Exhibit 2.1 to Exhibit 2.2.

Income Statement

The income statement reflects accrual accounting. Recall that accrual accounting recognizes revenue in the accounting period in which it is earned even when the associated cash is collected in a subsequent accounting period. In this case, the Year 1 income statement shows $84,000 of consulting revenue even though Cato has received only $60,000 cash from its customers in Year 1. Similarly, expenses include all sacrifices incurred to produce revenue regardless of whether cash has been paid. In this case, the Year 1 income statement includes $6,000 of salary expense even though Cato will not pay cash for these expenses until Year 2. These accrual reporting practices will cause differences between the amount of *net income* shown on the income statement and the amount of *cash flow from operating activities* shown on the statement of cash flows. Detailed comparisons are shown later.

Statement of Changes in Stockholders' Equity

The statement of changes in stockholders' equity explains the change in the amount of stockholders' equity that occurred during the Year 1 accounting period. In this case, total stockholders' equity increased from a beginning balance of zero to an ending balance of $71,000. The issue of stock explains $5,000 of the increase. The remaining $66,000 was caused by earnings.

Accounting for Accruals and Deferrals 77

EXHIBIT 2.1

Cato Consultants, Summary of Events and General Ledger

Panel 1 Transaction Data for Year 1

1. Cato Consultants acquired $5,000 cash by issuing common stock.
2. Cato provided $84,000 of consulting services on account.
3. Cato collected $60,000 cash from customers in partial settlement of its accounts receivable.
4. Cato paid $10,000 cash for salary expense.
5. Cato paid $2,000 cash for Year 1 advertising costs.
6. Cato recognized $6,000 of accrued salary expense.
7. Cato signed contracts for $42,000 of consulting services to be performed in Year 2.

Panel 2 Accounting Equation

Event No.	Cash	+	Accounts Receivable	=	Salaries Payable	+	Common Stock	+	Retained Earnings	Other Account Titles
Beg. bal.	0		0		0		0		0	
1	5,000						5,000			
2			84,000						84,000	Consulting revenue
3	60,000		(60,000)							
4	(10,000)								(10,000)	Salary expense
5	(2,000)								(2,000)	Advertising expense
6					6,000				(6,000)	Salary Expense
End bal.	53,000	+	24,000	=	6,000	+	5,000	+	66,000	

Panel 3 General Ledger Accounts

Assets

Cash
Bal.	0
(1)	5,000
(3)	60,000
(4)	(10,000)
(5)	(2,000)
Bal.	53,000

Accounts Receivable
(2)	84,000
(3)	(60,000)
Bal.	24,000

Liabilities

Salaries Payable
| (6) Adj. | 6,000 |
| Bal. | 6,000 |

Stockholders' Equity

Common Stock
Bal.	0
(1)	5,000
Bal.	5,000

Retained Earnings
| Bal. | 0 |

Consulting Revenue
| (2) | 84,000 |
| Bal. | 84,000 |

Salary Expense
(4)	(10,000)
(6) Adj.	(6,000)
Bal.	(16,000)

Advertising Expense
| (5) | (2,000) |
| Bal. | (2,000) |

Balance Sheet

The balance sheet discloses an entity's assets, liabilities, and stockholders' equity at a particular point in time. As of December 31, Year 1, Cato Consultants had total assets of $77,000 ($53,000 cash + $24,000 accounts receivable). These assets are equal to the obligations and commitments Cato has to its creditors and investors. Specifically, Cato has a $6,000 obligation (liability) to creditors, with the remaining $71,000 of assets available to support commitments (stockholders' equity) to stockholders.

EXHIBIT 2.2 — Vertical Statements Model

CATO CONSULTANTS
Financial Statements*

Income Statement
For the Year Ended December 31, Year 1

Consulting revenue	$84,000
Salary expense	(16,000)
Advertising expense	(2,000)
Net income	$66,000

Statement of Changes in Stockholders' Equity
For the Year Ended December 31, Year 1

Beginning common stock	$ 0	
Plus: Common stock issued	5,000	
Ending common stock		$ 5,000
Beginning retained earnings	0	
Plus: Net income	66,000	
Less: Dividends	0	
Ending retained earnings		66,000
Total stockholders' equity		$71,000

Balance Sheet
As of December 31, Year 1

Assets		
Cash	$53,000	
Accounts receivable	24,000	
Total assets		$77,000
Liabilities		
Salaries payable		$ 6,000
Stockholders' equity		
Common stock	$ 5,000	
Retained earnings	66,000	
Total stockholders' equity		71,000
Total liabilities and stockholders' equity		$77,000

Statement of Cash Flows
For the Year Ended December 31, Year 1

Cash flows from operating activities		
Cash receipts from customers	$60,000	
Cash payment for salary expense	(10,000)	
Cash payment for advertising expense	(2,000)	
Net cash flows from operating activities		$48,000
Cash flows from investing activities		0
Cash flows from financing activities		
Cash receipt from issuing common stock	5,000	
Net cash flow from financing activities		5,000
Net change in cash		53,000
Plus: Beginning cash balance		0
Ending cash balance		$53,000

*In real-world annual reports, financial statements are normally presented separately with appropriate descriptions of the date to indicate whether the statement applies to the entire accounting period or a specific point in time.

Statement of Cash Flows

The statement of cash flows explains the change in cash from the beginning to the end of the accounting period. It can be prepared by analyzing the Cash account. Because Cato Consultants was established in Year 1, its beginning cash balance was zero. By the end of the year, the cash balance was $53,000. The statement of cash flows explains this increase. The Cash account increased because Cato collected $60,000 from customers and decreased because Cato paid $12,000 for expenses. As a result, Cato's net cash inflow from operating activities was $48,000. Also, the business acquired $5,000 cash through the financing activity of issuing common stock, for a cumulative cash increase of $53,000 ($48,000 + $5,000) during Year 1.

Comparing Cash Flow from Operating Activities with Net Income

The amount of net income measured using accrual accounting differs from the amount of cash flow from operating activities. For Cato Consulting in Year 1, the differences are summarized below.

	Accrual Accounting	Cash Flow
Consulting revenue	$84,000	$60,000
Salary expense	(16,000)	(10,000)
Advertising expense	(2,000)	(2,000)
Net income	$66,000	$48,000

Many students begin their first accounting class with the misconception that revenue and expense items are cash equivalents. The Cato illustration demonstrates that a company may recognize a revenue or expense without a corresponding cash collection or payment in the same accounting period.

STEPS IN AN ACCOUNTING CYCLE

The Closing Process

Identify the steps in the accounting cycle.

Recall that the temporary accounts (revenue, expense, and dividends) are closed prior to the start of the next accounting cycle. Exhibit 2.3 shows the Year 1 closing entries and the after-closing general ledger account balances. To reinforce your understanding of the closing process, you should trace the closing entries to the ledger accounts.

After the Year 1 closing, the Consulting Revenue and Salary Expense accounts have a zero balance. These temporary accounts are now ready to capture the revenue and expense information for the Year 2 accounting period. At the end of Year 2, they will be closed again. This process will continue for every accounting cycle throughout the life of the business. In other words, the revenue and expense accounts hold information temporarily (for a single accounting period), thereby facilitating the preparation of the annual statements. While not included in this illustration, the Dividend account has these same temporary properties. Notice that after closing, the balance in the Retained Earnings account is equal to the amount shown in the year-end balance sheet. This equality affirms the fact that all temporary accounts have been closed correctly.

Steps in an Accounting Cycle

An accounting cycle, which is represented graphically in Exhibit 2.4, involves several steps. The four steps identified to this point are (1) recording transactions; (2) adjusting the accounts; (3) preparing financial statements; and (4) closing the temporary accounts. The first step occurs continually throughout the accounting period. Steps 2, 3, and 4 normally occur at the end of the accounting period.

EXHIBIT 2.3

Cato Corporation, Year 1 Closing Process

Panel 1 Closing Entries

C1 Transfers the balance from the Consulting Revenue account to the Retained Earnings account.
C2 Transfers the balance from the Salary Expense account to the Retained Earnings account.
C3 Transfers the balance from the Advertising Expense account to the Retained Earnings account.

Panel 2 General Ledger Accounts After Closing

Assets	=	Liabilities	+	Permanent Equity	+	Temporary Equity

Cash

Bal.	0
(1)	5,000
(3)	60,000
(4)	(10,000)
(5)	(2,000)
Bal.	53,000

Accounts Receivable

(2)	84,000
(3)	(60,000)
Bal.	24,000

Salaries Payable

(6) Adj.	6,000
Bal.	6,000

Common Stock

Bal.	0
(1)	5,000
Bal.	5,000

Retained Earnings

Bal.	0
Cl. 1	84,000
Cl. 2	(16,000)
Cl. 3	(2,000)
Bal.	66,000

Consulting Revenue

(2)	84,000
Bal.	84,000
Cl. 1	(84,000)
Bal.	0

Salary Expense

(4)	(10,000)
(6) Adj.	(6,000)
Bal.	(16,000)
Cl. 2	16,000
Bal.	0

Advertising Expense

(5)	(2,000)
Bal.	(2,000)
Cl. 3	2,000
Bal.	0

EXHIBIT 2.4

The Accounting Cycle

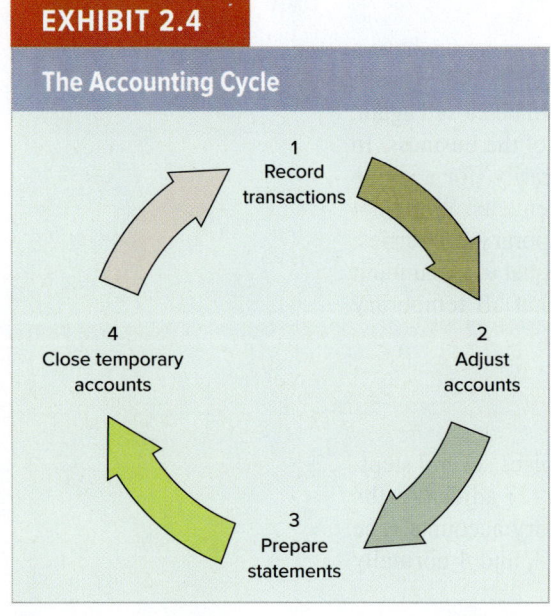

1. Record transactions
2. Adjust accounts
3. Prepare statements
4. Close temporary accounts

The Matching Concept

Cash basis accounting can distort reported net income because it sometimes fails to match expenses with the revenues they produce. To illustrate, consider the $6,000 of accrued salary expense that Cato Consultants recognized at the end of Year 1. The instructor's teaching produced revenue in Year 1. If Cato waited until Year 2 (when it paid the instructor) to recognize $6,000 of the total $16,000 salary expense, then $6,000 of the expense would not be matched with the revenue it generated. By using accrual accounting, Cato recognized all the salary expense in the same accounting period in which the consulting revenue was recognized. A primary goal of accrual accounting is to appropriately match expenses with revenues, the **matching concept.**

Appropriately matching expenses with revenues can be difficult even when using accrual accounting. For example, consider Cato's advertising expense. Money spent on advertising may generate revenue in future accounting periods, as well as in the current period. A prospective customer could save an advertising brochure for several years before calling Cato for training services. It is difficult to know when and to what extent advertising produces revenue. When the connection between an expense and the corresponding revenue is vague, accountants commonly match the expense with the period in which it is incurred. Cato matched (recognized) the entire $2,000 of advertising cost with the Year 1 accounting period even though some of that cost might generate revenue in future accounting periods. Expenses that are matched with the period in which they are incurred are frequently called **period costs**.

Matching is not perfect. Although it would be more accurate to match expenses with revenues than with periods, there is sometimes no traceable connection between expenses and revenue. Accountants must exercise judgment to select the accounting period in which to recognize revenues and expenses.

©Getty Images/Stockbyte RF

FOCUS ON INTERNATIONAL ISSUES

As explained in Chapter 1, companies in the United States must follow GAAP, as established by the Financial Accounting Standards Board (FASB), while most of the remainder of the world follows International Financial Reporting Standards (IFRS), which are established by the International Accounting Standards Board (IASB). Although there are some significant differences between GAAP and IFRS, it is the goal of the two rule-making bodies to have as much uniformity as possible. The process of trying to achieve this goal is often referred to as "convergence."

One very clear example of the attempt at convergence relates to revenue recognition. On May 28, 2014, both boards issued a converged standard related to how companies should recognize revenue earned from contract agreements. The FASB issued ASU 2014-09 (Topic 606) and the IASB issued IFRS 15. Both statements were titled "Revenue from Contracts with Customers." Although the wording of the two pronouncements was not exactly the same, the requirements were. For example, both statements list the same five-step process to be used to determine when revenue should be recognized:

1. Identify the contract(s) with a customer.
2. Identify the performance obligations in the contract.
3. Determine the transaction price.
4. Allocate the transaction price to the performance obligations in the contract.
5. Recognize revenue when (or as) the entity satisfies a performance obligation.

Although the five steps are worded exactly the same in the two pronouncements, the wording that explains each of these steps is a bit different. Keep in mind that while differences between U.S. GAAP and IFRS exist, the two rule-making bodies are working diligently to keep these differences to a minimum. Therefore, the accounting you learn in the United States is very relevant to the financial reporting of companies throughout the world.

SECTION 2:
ACCOUNTING FOR DEFERRALS

As previously discussed, cash may be exchanged before revenue or expense is recognized. In this case, the business defers recognition. This section introduces three common deferrals.

SECOND ACCOUNTING CYCLE

The effects of Cato Consultants' Year 2 events are as follows:

EVENT 1 Cato pays $6,000 to the instructor to settle the salaries payable obligation.

Cash payments to creditors are asset use transactions. When Cato pays the instructor, both the asset account Cash and the liability account Salaries Payable decrease. The effects on the accounting equation are as follows:

Assets	=	Liabilities	+	Stockholders' Equity
Cash		Salaries Payable		
(6,000)	=	(6,000)	+	NA

The event is an asset use transaction. It does not affect the income statement. The salary expense was recognized in Year 1 when the instructor taught the classes. Because the cash was paid for salaries of employees that operate the business, the cash outflow is classified as an operating activity. The effects on the financial statements are shown in the following financial statements model:

Balance Sheet							Income Statement				Statement of Cash Flows
Assets	=	Liab.	+	C. Stk.	+	R. Earn.	Rev.	−	Exp.	=	Net Inc.	
(6,000)	=	(6,000)	+	NA	+	NA	NA	−	NA	=	NA	(6,000) OA

ACCOUNTING FOR SUPPLIES

LO 2-5

Show how accounting for supplies affects financial statements.

EVENT 2 Cato purchases $800 of supplies on account.

The purchase of supplies on account is an asset source transaction. The asset account Supplies and the liability account Accounts Payable increase. The effects of this transaction on the accounting equation are shown here:

Assets	=	Liabilities	+	Stockholders' Equity
Supplies		Accounts Payable		
800	=	800	+	NA

Note that this event does not affect the income statement. Expense recognition is deferred until the supplies are used. Also, the statement of cash flows is not affected because the company did not spend cash to purchase the supplies. These effects are shown in the following financial statements model:

Balance Sheet							Income Statement				Statement of Cash Flows
Assets	=	Liab.	+	C. Stk.	+	R. Earn.	Rev.	−	Exp.	=	Net Inc.	
800	=	800	+	NA	+	NA	NA	−	NA	=	NA	NA

Year-End Adjustment

ADJ.1 After determining through a physical count that it has $150 of unused supplies on hand as of December 31, Cato recognizes supplies expense.

If a company were to attempt to record supplies expense each time a pencil, piece of paper, envelope, or other supply item were used, the cost of such tedious recordkeeping would far outweigh its benefits. Instead, accountants transfer to expense the total cost of all supplies used during the entire accounting period in a single year-end adjusting entry. The cost of supplies used is determined as follows:

Beginning balance of supplies	$ 0
Plus: Supplies purchases	800
Supplies available for use	800
Less: Ending balance of supplies	(150)
Supplies used	$650

Recognizing Cato's supplies expense is an asset use transaction. The asset account Supplies and the stockholders' equity account Retained Earnings decrease. The effects of this transaction on the accounting equation are shown here:

Assets	=	Liabilities	+	Stockholders' Equity
Supplies				Supplies Expense
(650)	=	NA	+	(650)

The recognition of supplies expense would cause the amount of net income shown on the income statement to decrease. Because the expense recognition did not involve the payment of cash, the statement of cash flows is not affected.

Balance Sheet							Income Statement						Statement of
Assets	=	Liab.	+	C. Stk.	+	R. Earn.	Rev.	−	Exp.	=	Net Inc.	Cash Flows
(650)	=	NA	+	NA	+	(650)	NA	−	650	=	(650)	NA

CHECK YOURSELF 2.2

Treadmore Company started the Year 1 accounting period with $580 of supplies on hand. During Year 1, the company paid cash to purchase $2,200 of supplies. A physical count of supplies indicated that there were $420 of supplies on hand at the end of Year 1. Treadmore pays cash for supplies at the time they are purchased. Based on this information alone, determine the amount of supplies expense to be recognized on the income statement and the amount of cash flow to be shown in the operating activities section of the statement of cash flows.

Answer The amount of supplies expense recognized on the income statement is the amount of supplies that were used during the accounting period. This amount is computed below:

$580 Beginning balance + $2,200 Supplies purchases = $2,780 Supplies available for use
$2,780 Supplies available for use − $420 Ending supplies balance = $2,360 Supplies used

The cash flow from operating activities is the amount of cash paid for supplies during the accounting period. In this case, Treadmore paid $2,200 cash to purchase supplies. This amount would be shown as a cash outflow.

Show how accounting for prepaid items affects financial statements.

ACCOUNTING FOR PREPAID ITEMS

EVENT 3 On March 1, Year 2, Cato pays $12,000 cash to lease office space for one year beginning immediately.

Accrual accounting draws a distinction between the terms cost and expense. A **cost** might be either an asset or an expense. If a company has already consumed a purchased resource in the process of earning revenue, the cost of the resource is an expense. For example, companies normally pay for electricity the month after using it. The cost of electric utilities is therefore usually recorded as an expense. In contrast, if a company purchases a resource it will use in the future to generate revenue, the cost of the resource represents an asset. Accountants record such a cost in an asset account and defer recognizing an expense until the resource has been used to produce revenue. Deferring the expense recognition provides more accurate matching of revenues and expenses.

The cost of the office space described in Event 3 is an asset. It is recorded in the asset account Prepaid Rent. Cato expects to benefit from incurring this cost by using the office to generate revenue over the next 12 months. Expense recognition is deferred until Cato actually uses the office space to help generate revenue. Other commonly deferred expenses include prepaid insurance and prepaid taxes. As these titles imply, deferred expenses are frequently called **prepaid items.** Exhibit 2.5 illustrates the relationship between costs, assets, and expenses.

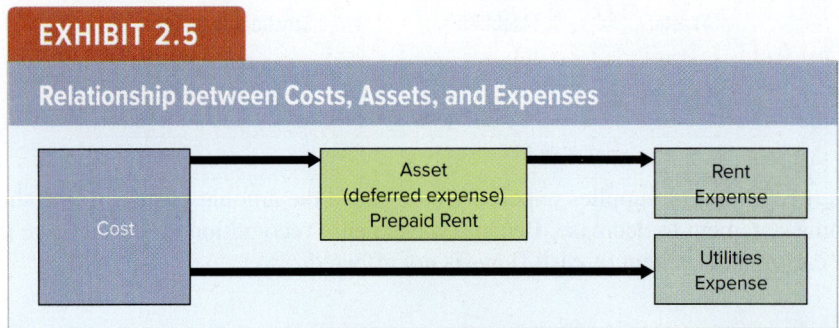

EXHIBIT 2.5

Relationship between Costs, Assets, and Expenses

Purchasing prepaid rent is an asset exchange transaction. The asset account Cash decreases and the asset account Prepaid Rent increases. The effect on the accounting equation is as follows:

Assets	=	Liabilities	+	Stockholders' Equity
Cash	Prepaid Rent			
(12,000)	12,000	=	NA	+	NA

This is an asset exchange event. The amount of total assets is not affected. Note that this event does not affect the income statement. Expense recognition is deferred until the office space is used. Because the cash outflow was incurred to purchase prepaid rent (a short-term asset) that will be used to operate the business, it is classified as an operating activity on the statement of cash flows. The effects of this transaction on the financial statements are shown here:

Balance Sheet							Income Statement					Statement of Cash Flows
Assets	=	Liab.	+	C. Stk.	+	R. Earn.	Rev.	−	Exp.	=	Net Inc.	
NA	=	NA	+	NA	+	NA	NA	−	NA	=	NA	(12,000) OA

Year-End Adjustment

ADJ.2 Cato recognizes rent expense for the office space used during the Year 2 accounting period.

At the end of Year 2, Cato is required to expense the amount of office space that has been used. Recall that Cato paid $12,000 on March 1, Year 2, to rent office space for one year (see Event 3). The portion of the lease cost that represents using office space from March 1 through December 31 is computed as follows:

$12,000 Cost of annual lease ÷ 12 Months = $1,000 Cost per month

$1,000 Cost per month × 10 Months used = $10,000 Rent expense

Recognizing the rent expense decreases the asset account Prepaid Rent and the amount of stockholders' equity. The effects on the accounting equation are as follows:

Assets	=	Liabilities	+	Stockholders' Equity
Prepaid Rent				Rent Expense
(10,000)	=	NA	+	(10,000)

The expense reduces net income shown on the income statement and ultimately the amount of stockholders' equity (retained earnings) shown on the balance sheet. The statement of cash flows is not affected. Recall that the cash flow effect was recorded in Event 3. The effects on the financial statements are as follows:

Balance Sheet							Income Statement					Statement of
Assets	=	Liab.	+	C. Stk.	+	R. Earn.	Rev.	−	Exp.	=	Net Inc.	Cash Flows
(10,000)	=	NA	+	NA	+	(10,000)	NA	−	10,000	=	(10,000)	NA

Note that while $12,000 cash was paid for rent, only $10,000 of that amount is recognized as an expense in Year 2. The deferral of the additional $2,000 causes a difference between the amounts of cash flow from operating activities versus the amount of net income reported in Year 2.

CHECK YOURSELF 2.3

Rujoub Inc. paid $18,000 cash for one year of insurance coverage that began on November 1, Year 1. Based on this information alone, determine the cash flow from operating activities that Rujoub would report on the Year 1 and Year 2 statements of cash flows. Also, determine the amount of insurance expense Rujoub would report on the Year 1 income statement and the amount of prepaid insurance (an asset) that Rujoub would report on the December 31, Year 1, balance sheet.

Answer Since Rujoub paid all of the cash in Year 1, the Year 1 statement of cash flows would report an $18,000 cash outflow from operating activities. The Year 2 statement of cash flows would report zero cash flow from operating activities. The expense would be recognized in the periods in which the insurance is used. In this case, insurance expense is recognized at the rate of $1,500 per month ($18,000 ÷ 12 months). Rujoub used two months of insurance coverage in Year 1 and therefore would report $3,000 (2 months × $1,500) of insurance expense on the Year 1 income statement. Rujoub would report a $15,000 (10 months × $1,500) asset—prepaid insurance—on the December 31, Year 1, balance sheet. The $15,000 of prepaid insurance would be recognized as insurance expense in Year 2 when the insurance coverage is used.

ACCOUNTING FOR UNEARNED REVENUE

EVENT 4 Cato receives $18,000 cash in advance from Westberry Company for consulting services that Cato agrees to perform over a one-year period beginning June 1, Year 2.

Cato must defer (delay) recognizing any revenue until it performs the consulting services (does the work) for Westberry. From Cato's point of view, the deferred revenue is a liability because Cato is obligated to perform services in the future. The liability is called **unearned revenue.** The asset account Cash and the liability account Unearned Revenue both increase. The effects on the accounting equation are shown as follows:

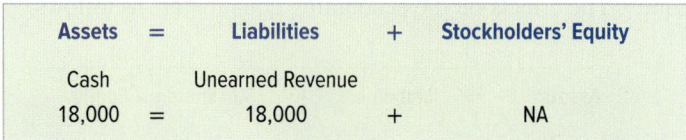

The cash receipt is an asset source transaction. Collecting the cash has no effect on the income statement. The revenue will be reported on the income statement after Cato performs the services. The statement of cash flows reflects a cash inflow from operating activities. The effects of this transaction on the financial statements are shown here:

Balance Sheet							Income Statement					Statement of Cash Flows
Assets	=	Liab.	+	C. Stk.	+	R. Earn.	Rev.	−	Exp.	=	Net Inc.	
18,000	=	18,000	+	NA	+	NA	NA	−	NA	=	NA	18,000 OA

Year-End Adjustment

ADJ. 3 Cato recognizes the portion of the unearned revenue it earned during the accounting period.

The $18,000 cash advance requires Cato to provide consulting services from June 1, Year 2, to May 31, Year 3. By December 31, Cato has earned 7 months (June 1 through December 31) of the revenue related to this contract. Rather than recording the revenue continuously as the consulting services are being performed, Cato can simply recognize the amount earned in a single adjustment to the accounting records *at the end of the accounting period*. The amount of the adjustment is computed as follows:

$18,000 \div 12$ months $= \$1,500$ revenue earned per month

$\$1,500 \times 7$ months $= \$10,500$ revenue to be recognized in Year 2

The adjusting entry moves $10,500 from the liability Unearned Revenue account to the Consulting Revenue account. The effects on the accounting equation are as follows:

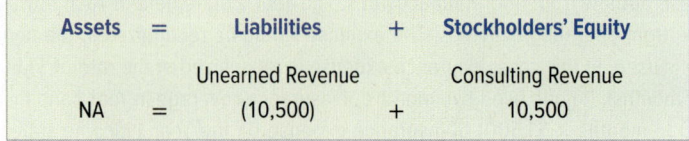

This adjusting entry is a claims exchange event. Assets are not affected. On the balance sheet, the liabilities decrease and stockholders' equity (retained earnings) increases. Cash flow is not affected by the adjustment. Recall that the impact on cash occurred previously

when Cato received the cash from Westberry in Event 4. The effects of this transaction on the financial statements are as follows:

Balance Sheet							Income Statement					Statement of Cash Flows
Assets	=	Liab.	+	C. Stk.	+	R. Earn.	Rev.	−	Exp.	=	Net Inc.	
NA	=	(10,500)	+	NA	+	10,500	10,500	−	NA	=	10,500	NA

Recall that revenue was previously defined as an economic benefit a company obtains by providing customers with goods and services. In this case, the economic benefit is a decrease in the liability account Unearned Revenue. **Revenue** can therefore be more precisely defined as *an increase in assets or a decrease in liabilities that a company obtains by providing customers with goods or services.*

CHECK YOURSELF 2.4

Sanderson & Associates received a $24,000 cash advance as a retainer to provide legal services to a client. The contract called for Sanderson to render services during a one-year period beginning October 1, Year 1. Based on this information alone, determine the cash flow from operating activities Sanderson would report on the Year 1 and Year 2 statements of cash flows. Also determine the amount of revenue Sanderson would report on the Year 1 and Year 2 income statements.

Answer Because Sanderson collected all of the cash in Year 1, the Year 1 statement of cash flows would report a $24,000 cash inflow from operating activities. The Year 2 statement of cash flows would report zero cash flow from operating activities. Revenue is recognized in the period in which it is earned. In this case, revenue is earned at the rate of $2,000 per month ($24,000 ÷ 12 months = $2,000 per month). Sanderson rendered services for three months in Year 1 and nine months in Year 2. Sanderson would report $6,000 (3 months × $2,000) of revenue on the Year 1 income statement and $18,000 (9 months × $2,000) of revenue on the Year 2 income statement.

PREPARING FINANCIAL STATEMENTS WITH DEFERRALS

The information required to prepare the financial statements is shown in Exhibit 2.6. Notice that the transaction data described at the top of the exhibit contain additional transactions 5 through 12. Transactions similar to these have been covered in previous chapters and will not be discussed further here. However, data for these transactions have been recorded in the general ledger accounts shown in the exhibit. To confirm your understanding, you should trace each transaction to the appropriate ledger accounts. The information in the ledger accounts has been labeled with the event or adjusting entry number to simplify the tracing process.

Recall that all adjustments are made at the end of the accounting period so that all account balances are updated prior to their use in preparing the financial statements. Notice that the Year 2 beginning balances shown in the general ledger accounts are derived from the Year 1 ending balances shown in Exhibit 2.3. Likewise, the Year 2 ending balances will become the Year 3 beginning balances. However, the Revenue, Expense, and Dividend accounts have zero beginning balances because they are designed to capture transaction data for a single accounting period. Therefore, the balances in these accounts are transferred to the Retained Earnings account at the end of the accounting period through the closing process. Prior to closing, the balances in the ledger accounts shown in Exhibit 2.6 are used to prepare the Year 2 financial statements shown in Exhibit 2.7.

LO 2-8

 Prepare financial statements that include deferrals.

EXHIBIT 2.6

Ledger Accounts with Year 2 Transaction Data

1. Cato paid $6,000 to the instructor to settle the salaries payable obligation.
2. Cato purchased $800 of supplies on account.
3. On March 1, Cato paid $12,000 cash to lease office space for one year.
4. Cato received $18,000 cash in advance from Westberry Company for consulting services to be performed for one year beginning June 1.
5. Cato provided $96,400 of consulting services on account.
6. Cato collected $105,000 cash from customers as partial settlement of accounts receivable.
7. Cato paid $32,000 cash for salary expense.
8. Cato incurred $21,000 of other operating expenses on account.
9. Cato paid $18,200 in partial settlement of accounts payable.
10. Cato paid $79,500 to purchase land it planned to use in the future as a building site for its home office.
11. Cato paid $21,000 in cash dividends to its stockholders.
12. Cato acquired $2,000 cash from issuing additional shares of common stock.

The year-end adjustments are:

Adj. 1 After determining through a physical count that it had $150 of unused supplies on hand as of December 31, Cato recognized supplies expense.
Adj. 2 Cato recognized rent expense for the office space used during the accounting period.
Adj. 3 Cato recognized the portion of the unearned revenue it earned during the accounting period.
Adj. 4 Cato recognized $4,000 of accrued salary expense.

Assets = Liabilities + Stockholders' Equity

Cash
Bal.	53,000
(1)	(6,000)
(3)	(12,000)
(4)	18,000
(6)	105,000
(7)	(32,000)
(9)	(18,200)
(10)	(79,500)
(11)	(21,000)
(12)	2,000
Bal.	9,300

Accounts Receivable
Bal.	24,000
(5)	96,400
(6)	(105,000)
Bal.	15,400

Supplies
Bal.	0
(2)	800
Adj. 1	(650)
Bal.	150

Prepaid Rent
Bal.	0
(3)	12,000
Adj. 2	(10,000)
Bal.	2,000

Land
Bal.	0
(10)	79,500
Bal.	79,500

Accounts Payable
Bal.	0
(2)	800
(8)	21,000
(9)	(18,200)
Bal.	3,600

Unearned Revenue
Bal.	0
(4)	18,000
Adj. 3	(10,500)
Bal.	7,500

Salaries Payable
Bal.	6,000
(1)	(6,000)
Adj. 4	(4,000)
Bal.	4,000

Common Stock
Bal.	5,000
(12)	2,000
Bal.	7,000

Retained Earnings
Bal.	66,000

Dividends
Bal.	0
(11)	(21,000)
Bal.	(21,000)

Consulting Revenue
Bal.	0
(5)	96,400
Adj. 3	10,500
Bal.	106,900

Other Operating Expenses
Bal.	0
(8)	(21,000)
Bal.	(21,000)

Salary Expense
Bal.	0
(7)	(32,000)
Adj. 4	(4,000)
Bal.	(36,000)

Rent Expense
Bal.	0
Adj. 2	(10,000)
Bal.	(10,000)

Supplies Expense
Bal.	0
Adj. 1	(650)
Bal.	(650)

EXHIBIT 2.7 — Vertical Statements Model

CATO CONSULTANTS
Financial Statements
Income Statements
For the Years Ended December 31

	Year 1	Year 2
Consulting revenue	$84,000	$106,900
Operating expenses	(18,000)	(67,650)
Net income	$66,000	$ 39,250

Statements of Changes in Stockholders' Equity
For the Years Ended December 31

	Year 1	Year 2
Beginning common stock	$ 0	$ 5,000
Plus: Common stock issued	5,000	2,000
Ending common stock	5,000	7,000
Beginning retained earnings	0	66,000
Plus: Net income	66,000	39,250
Less: Dividends	0	(21,000)
Ending retained earnings	66,000	84,250
Total stockholders' equity	$71,000	$ 91,250

Balance Sheets
As of December 31

	Year 1	Year 2
Assets		
Cash	$53,000	$ 9,300
Accounts receivable	24,000	15,400
Supplies	0	150
Prepaid rent	0	2,000
Land	0	79,500
Total assets	$77,000	$106,350
Liabilities		
Accounts payable	$ 0	$ 3,600
Unearned revenue	0	7,500
Salaries payable	6,000	4,000
Total liabilities	6,000	15,100
Stockholders' equity		
Common stock	5,000	7,000
Retained earnings	66,000	84,250
Total stockholders' equity	71,000	91,250
Total liabilities and stockholders' equity	$77,000	$106,350

continued

EXHIBIT 2.7 *Concluded*

Statements of Cash Flows
For the Years Ended December 31

	Year 1	Year 2
Cash Flows from Operating Activities		
Cash receipts from customers	$60,000	$123,000
Cash payments for operating expenses	(12,000)	(68,200)
Net cash flow from operating activities	48,000	54,800
Cash Flows from Investing Activities		
Cash payment to purchase land	0	(79,500)
Cash Flows from Financing Activities		
Cash receipts from issuing common stock	5,000	2,000
Cash payments for dividends	0	(21,000)
Net cash flow from financing activities	5,000	(19,000)
Net change in cash	53,000	(43,700)
Plus: Beginning cash balance	0	53,000
Ending cash balance	$53,000	$ 9,300

Vertical Statements Model

Financial statement users obtain helpful insights by analyzing company trends over multiple accounting cycles. Exhibit 2.7 presents for Cato Consultants a multicycle **vertical statements model** of Year 1 and Year 2 accounting data. To conserve space, we have combined all the expenses for each year into single amounts labeled "Operating Expenses," determined as follows:

	Year 1	Year 2
Other operating expenses	$ 0	$21,000
Salary expense	16,000	36,000
Rent expense	0	10,000
Advertising expense	2,000	0
Supplies expense	0	650
Total operating expenses	$18,000	$67,650

Similarly, we combined the cash payments for operating expenses on the statement of cash flows as follows:

	Year 1	Year 2
Supplies and other operating expenses	$ 0	$18,200*
Salary expense	10,000	38,000
Rent expense	0	12,000
Advertising expense	2,000	0
Total cash payments for operating expenses	$12,000	$68,200

*Amount paid in partial settlement of accounts payable.

Recall that the level of detail reported in financial statements depends on user information needs. Most real-world companies combine many account balances together to report highly summarized totals under each financial statement caption. Before reading further, trace the remaining financial statement items from the ledger accounts in Exhibit 2.6 to where they are reported in Exhibit 2.7.

The vertical statements model in Exhibit 2.7 shows significant interrelationships among the financial statements. For each year, trace the amount of net income from the income statement to the statement of changes in stockholders' equity. Next, trace the ending balances of common stock and retained earnings reported on the statement of changes in stockholders' equity to the stockholders' equity section of the balance sheet. Also, confirm that the amount of cash reported on the balance sheet equals the ending cash balance on the statement of cash flows.

Other relationships connect the two accounting periods. For example, trace the ending retained earnings balance from the Year 1 statement of stockholders' equity to the beginning retained earnings balance on the Year 2 statement of stockholders' equity. Also, trace the ending cash balance on the Year 1 statement of cash flows to the beginning cash balance on the Year 2 statement of cash flows. Finally, confirm that the change in cash between the Year 1 and Year 2 balance sheets ($53,000 − $9,300 = $43,700 decrease) agrees with the net change in cash reported on the Year 2 statement of cash flows.

Closing for the Year 2 Accounting Period

At the end of the Year 2 accounting period, the Revenue, Expense, and Dividend accounts would be closed to the Retained Earnings Account. After the closing entries are posted, the balance in the Retained Earnings account is $84,250, which is equal to the amount of retained earnings shown on the Year 2 balance sheet. The after-closing balances in the Revenue, Expense, and Dividend accounts will be zero, which makes them ready to capture information that pertains only to the Year 3 accounting period.

REALITY BYTES

WHY DID THAT BIG EXPENSE CAUSE THE STOCK PRICE TO RISE?

If you follow business news, which you should if you are a business major, you have probably heard about a company reporting a big write-off of assets that causes a decrease in its earnings, sometimes called a "special charge." Such an announcement sends a signal to readers that the company's earnings will decrease as a result of the write-off. However, in many cases, this seemingly bad news does not cause the company's stock price to fall. In fact, it sometimes causes it to increase. Why?

Consider the following January 20, 2017, announcement from Ford Motor Company:

"For the year ended December 31, 2016, we expect to record a pre-tax remeasurement loss of approximately $3.0 billion related to our pension plans and OPEB plans. . . . On an after-tax basis, the remeasurement loss will reduce our full-year net income by about $2.0 billion in 2016."

©Bloomberg/Getty Images

Despite this seemingly bad financial news, Ford's stock price was 1.1 percent higher one week after the announcement, while General Motors' stock price had not changed and Toyota Motor Corporation's stock was 1.4 percent lower.

There are at least a couple of reasons why this seemingly bad news may have very little impact on a company's stock price. First, while write-offs do decrease earnings, they often do not decrease the company's cash flows, and cash flow is at least as important to investors as earnings. Ford's special charge was mostly the result of it changing the way it accounted for pension expenses. The new method did not require any more or fewer cash payments than did the old method.

The second reason that writing off assets can sometimes have a positive effect on a company's stock price is because extra expenses that are recognized today may mean there will be fewer expenses recognized in the future. Thus, future earnings will be higher than they otherwise would have been. This subject will be explained further in later chapters, but keep in mind that investors are more interested in the future than they are in the past, so lower current earnings that lead to higher future earnings is often viewed as good news.

So, when you hear a company make a big announcement about its business, always ask yourself two questions: How does this event affect cash flows? And, how will this event affect future earnings?

Answers to The Curious Accountant

Because the **Meredith Corporation** receives cash from customers before actually sending any magazines to them, the company has not earned any revenue when it receives the cash. Meredith has a liability called *unearned revenue*. If Meredith closed its books on December 31, then $3 of Karen's subscription would be recognized as revenue in 2019. The remaining $9 would appear on the balance sheet as a liability.

Meredith actually ends its accounting year on June 30 each year. The actual June 30, 2016, balance sheet for the company is presented in Exhibit 2.8. The liability for unearned revenue was $327.9 million ($199.4 + $128.5)—which represented about 18.9 percent of total liabilities!

Will Meredith need cash to pay these subscription liabilities? Not exactly. The liabilities will not be paid directly with cash. Instead, they will be satisfied by providing magazines to the subscribers. However, Meredith will need cash to pay for producing and distributing the magazines supplied to the customers. Even so, the amount of cash required to provide magazines will probably differ significantly from the amount of unearned revenues. In most cases, subscription fees do not cover the cost of producing and distributing magazines. By collecting significant amounts of advertising revenue, publishers can provide magazines to customers at prices well below the cost of publication. The amount of unearned revenue is not likely to coincide with the amount of cash needed to cover the cost of satisfying the company's obligation to produce and distribute magazines. Even though the association between unearned revenues and the cost of providing magazines to customers is not direct, a knowledgeable financial analyst can use the information to make estimates of future cash flows and revenue recognition.

EXHIBIT 2.8 Balance Sheet for Meredith Corporation

MEREDITH CORPORATION AND SUBSIDIARIES
Consolidated Balance Sheets
As of June 30 (amounts in thousands)

	2016	2015
Assets		
Current assets		
Cash and cash equivalents	$ 24,970	$ 22,833
Accounts receivable		
(net of allowances of $8,331 in 2016 and $8,495 in 2015)	273,927	284,646
Inventories	20,678	24,681
Current portion of subscription acquisition costs	133,338	122,350
Current portion of broadcast rights	4,220	4,516
Other current assets	24,023	23,505
Total current assets	481,156	482,531
Property, plant, and equipment		
Land	24,697	24,858
Buildings and improvements	149,950	151,320
Machinery and equipment	332,314	324,185
Leasehold improvements	14,317	14,284
Construction in progress	8,774	12,975
Total property, plant, and equipment	530,052	527,622
Less accumulated depreciation	(339,099)	(313,886)
Net property, plant, and equipment	190,953	213,736

continued

EXHIBIT 2.8 Concluded

MEREDITH CORPORATION AND SUBSIDIARIES
Consolidated Balance Sheets
As of June 30 (amounts in thousands)

	2016	2015
Subscription acquisition costs	95,960	103,842
Broadcast rights	4,565	1,795
Other assets	58,645	67,750
Intangible assets, net	913,877	972,382
Goodwill	883,129	1,001,246
Total assets	**$2,628,285**	**$2,843,282**
Liabilities and shareholders' equity		
Current liabilities		
Current portion of long-term debt	$ 75,000	$ 62,500
Current portion of long-term broadcast rights payable	4,649	4,776
Accounts payable	82,107	93,944
Accrued expenses		
Compensation and benefits	71,135	71,233
Distribution expenses	10,779	13,056
Other taxes and expenses	34,863	79,366
Total accrued expenses	116,777	163,655
Current portion of unearned subscription revenues	199,359	206,126
Total current liabilities	477,892	531,001
Long-term debt	620,000	732,500
Long-term broadcast rights payable	5,524	2,998
Unearned subscription revenues	128,534	151,221
Deferred income taxes	336,346	311,645
Other noncurrent liabilities	170,946	162,067
Total liabilities	1,739,242	1,891,432
Shareholders' equity		
Series preferred stock, par value $1 per share	—	—
Common stock, par value $1 per share	39,272	37,657
Class B stock, par value $1 per share, convertible to common stock	5,284	6,963
Additional paid-in capital	54,282	49,019
Retained earnings	818,706	870,859
Accumulated other comprehensive income (loss)	(28,501)	(12,648)
Total shareholders' equity	889,043	951,850
Total liabilities and shareholders' equity	**$2,628,285**	**$2,843,282**

TRANSACTION CLASSIFICATION

Chapters 1 and 2 introduced four types of transactions. Although businesses engage in an infinite number of different transactions, all transactions fall into one of four types. By learning to identify transactions by type, you can understand how unfamiliar events affect financial statements. The four types of transactions are:

LO 2-9

Classify accounting events into one of four categories.

1. *Asset source transactions:* An asset account increases, and a corresponding claims account increases.
2. *Asset use transactions:* An asset account decreases, and a corresponding claims account decreases.
3. *Asset exchange transactions:* One asset account increases, and another asset account decreases.
4. *Claims exchange transactions:* One claims account increases, and another claims account decreases.

CORPORATE GOVERNANCE

The Financial Analyst

Corporate governance is the set of relationships between the board of directors, management, shareholders, auditors, and other stakeholders that determine how a company is operated. Clearly, financial analysts are keenly interested in these relationships. This section discusses the key components of corporate governance.

Importance of Ethics

The accountant's role in society requires trust and credibility. Accounting information is worthless if the accountant is not trustworthy. Similarly, tax and consulting advice is useless if it comes from an incompetent person. The high ethical standards required by the profession state "a certified public accountant assumes an obligation of self-discipline above and beyond requirements of laws and regulations." The **American Institute of Certified Public Accountants (AICPA)** requires its members to comply with the **Code of Professional Conduct.** The preface of the Code includes six Principles of Professional Conduct that are summarized in Exhibit 2.9. The importance of ethical conduct is universally recognized across a broad spectrum of accounting organizations. The Institute of Management Accountants requires its members to follow a set of Standards of Ethical Conduct. The Institute of Internal Auditors also requires its members to subscribe to the organization's Code of Ethics.

Discuss the primary components of corporate governance.

LO 2-10

EXHIBIT 2.9

Principles of Professional Conduct: AICPA Code of Professional Conduct

Responsibilities Principle
In carrying out their responsibilities as professionals, members should exercise sensitive professional and moral judgments in all their activities.

The Public Interest Principle
Members should accept the obligation to act in a way that will serve the public interest, honor the public trust, and demonstrate commitment to professionalism.

Integrity Principle
To maintain and broaden public confidence, members should perform all professional responsibilities with the highest sense of integrity.

Objectivity and Independence Principle
A member should maintain objectivity and be free of conflicts of interest in discharging professional responsibilities. A member in public practice should be independent in fact and appearance when providing auditing and other attestation services.

Due Care Principle
A member should observe the profession's technical and ethical standards, strive continually to improve competence and the quality of services, and discharge professional responsibility to the best of the member's ability.

Scope and Nature of Services Principle
A member in public practice should observe the Principles of the Code of Professional Conduct in determining the scope and nature of services to be provided.

Sarbanes–Oxley Act

Credible financial reporting relies on a system of checks and balances. Corporate management is responsible for preparing financial reports, while outside independent accountants (CPAs) audit the reports. The massive surprise bankruptcies of Enron in late

2001 and WorldCom several months later suggested major audit failures on the part of the independent auditors. An audit failure means a company's auditor does not detect, or fails to report, that the company's financial reports are not in compliance with GAAP. The audit failures at Enron, WorldCom, and others prompted Congress to pass the Sarbanes–Oxley Act (SOX).

Prior to SOX, independent auditors often provided nonaudit services, such as installing computer systems, for their audit clients. The fees they earned for these services sometimes greatly exceeded the fees charged for the audit itself. This practice had been questioned prior to the audit failures at Enron and WorldCom. Critics felt the independent audit firm was subject to pressure from the company to conduct a less rigorous audit or risk losing lucrative nonaudit work. To strengthen the audit function, SOX included the following provisions:

- Prior to the enactment of SOX, independent auditors were self-regulated by the membership of the American Institute of Certified Public Accountants and by state boards of accountancy. Beyond self-regulation, SOX established the Public Company Accounting Oversight Board (PCAOB) to regulate accounting professionals that audit the financial statements of public companies.
- Independent auditors must register with the PCAOB or cease all participation in public company audits and abide by the board's pronouncements.
- The PCAOB has the responsibility to conduct inspections of registered firms. To ensure enforcement, the board has a full range of sanctions at its disposal, including suspension or revocation of registration, censure, and significant fines.
- To reduce the likelihood of conflicts of interest, SOX prohibits all registered public accounting firms from providing audit clients, contemporaneously with the audit, certain nonaudit services, including internal audit outsourcing, financial-information-system design and implementation services, and expert services.
- SOX provides significant corporate governance reforms regarding audit committees and their relationship to the auditor, making the audit committee responsible for the appointment, compensation, and oversight of the issuer's auditor.

Other provisions of SOX clarify the legal responsibility that company management has for a company's financial reports. The company's chief executive officer (CEO) and chief financial officer (CFO) must certify in writing that they have reviewed the financial reports being issued and that the reports present fairly the company's financial status. An executive who falsely certifies the company's financial reports is subject to a fine up to $5 million and imprisonment up to 20 years.

Common Features of Criminal and Ethical Misconduct

Unfortunately, it takes more than a code of conduct to stop fraud. People frequently engage in activities that they know are unethical or even criminal. The auditing profession has identified three elements that are typically present when fraud occurs, including:

1. The availability of an opportunity.
2. The existence of some form of pressure leading to an incentive.
3. The capacity to rationalize.

The three elements are frequently arranged in the shape of a triangle, as shown in Exhibit 2.10.

Opportunity is shown at the top of the triangle because without opportunity fraud could not exist. The most effective way to reduce opportunities for ethical or criminal misconduct is to implement an effective set of internal controls. **Internal controls** are policies and procedures that a business implements to reduce opportunities for fraud and to assure that its objectives will be accomplished. Specific controls are tailored to meet the individual needs of particular businesses. For example, banks use elaborate vaults to protect cash and safety deposit boxes, but universities have little use for this type of equipment. Even so, many of the

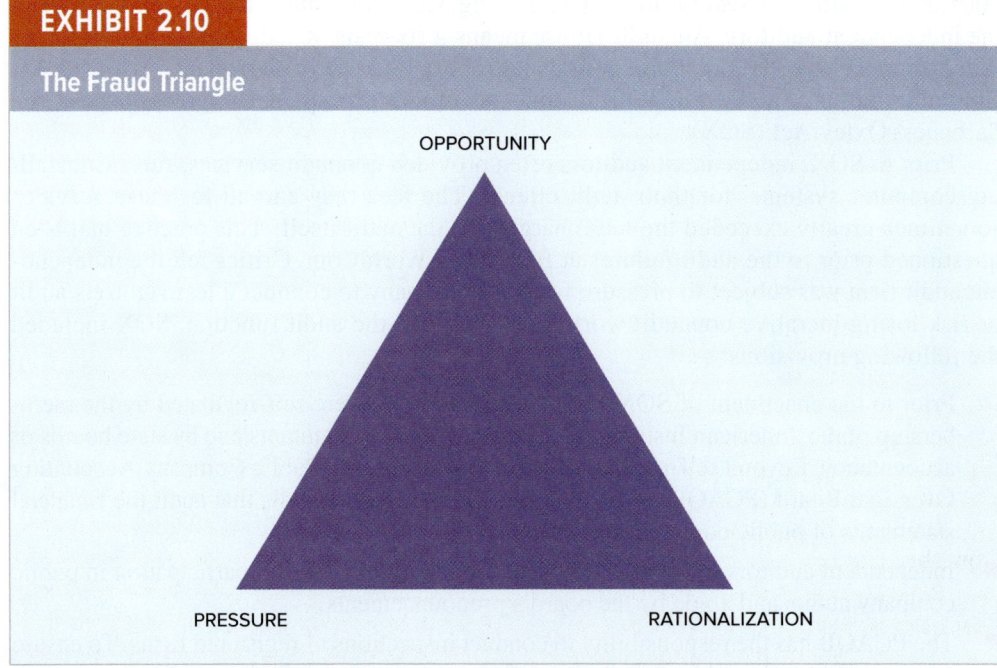

EXHIBIT 2.10

The Fraud Triangle

same procedures are used by a wide variety of businesses. The internal control policies and procedures that have gained widespread acceptance are discussed in a subsequent chapter.

Only a few employees turn to the dark side even when internal control is weak and opportunities abound. So, what causes one person to commit fraud and another to remain honest? The second element of the fraud triangle recognizes **pressure** as a key ingredient of misconduct. A manager who is told "either make the numbers or you are fired" is more likely to cheat than one who is told to "tell it like it is." Pressure can come from a variety of sources, including:

- Personal vices such as drug addiction, gambling, and promiscuity.
- Intimidation from superiors.
- Personal debt from credit cards, consumer and mortgage loans, or poor investments.
- Family expectations to provide a standard of living that is beyond one's capabilities.
- Business failure caused by poor decision making or temporary factors such as a poor economy.
- Loyalty or trying to be agreeable.

The third and final element of the fraud triangle is **rationalization.** Few individuals think of themselves as evil. They develop rationalizations to justify their misconduct. Common rationalizations include the following:

- Everybody does it.
- The company is not paying me enough. I'm only taking what I deserve.
- I'm only borrowing the money. I'll pay it back.
- The company can afford it. Look what it is paying the officers.
- I'm taking what my family needs to live like everyone else.

Most people are able to resist pressure and the tendency to rationalize ethical or legal misconduct. However, some people will yield to temptation. What can accountants do to protect themselves and their companies from unscrupulous characters? The answer lies in personal integrity. The best indicator of personal integrity is past performance. Accordingly, companies must exercise due care in performing appropriate background investigations before hiring people to fill positions of trust.

Ethical misconduct is a serious offense in the accounting profession. A single mistake can destroy an accounting career. If you commit a white-collar crime, you normally lose the opportunity to hold a white-collar job. Second chances are rarely granted; it is extremely important that you learn how to recognize and avoid the common features of ethical misconduct. To help you prepare for the real-world situations you are likely to encounter, we include ethical dilemmas in the end-of-chapter materials. When working with these dilemmas, try to identify the (1) opportunity, (2) pressure, and (3) rationalization associated with the particular ethical situation described. If you are not an ethical person, accounting is not the career for you.

A Look Back

This chapter introduced the *accrual accounting* concept. Accrual accounting causes the amount of revenues and expenses reported on the income statement to differ significantly from the amount of cash flow from operating activities reported on the statement of cash flows because of timing differences. These differences are readily apparent when relevant events are recorded in a horizontal financial statements model. To review, study the following transactions and the corresponding statements model. Set up a statements model on a piece of paper and try to record the effects of each event before reading the explanation.

Events
1. Provided $600 of services on account.
2. Collected $400 cash from accounts receivable.
3. Accrued $350 of salary expense.
4. Paid $225 cash in partial settlement of salaries payable.

Event No.	Cash	+	Accts. Rec.	=	Sal. Pay.	+	Ret. Earn.	Rev.	−	Exp.	=	Net Inc.	Statement of Cash Flows
1	NA	+	600	=	NA	+	600	600	−	NA	=	600	NA
2	400	+	(400)	=	NA	+	NA	NA	−	NA	=	NA	400 OA
3	NA	+	NA	=	350	+	(350)	NA	−	350	=	(350)	NA
4	(225)	+	NA	=	(225)	+	NA	NA	−	NA	=	NA	(225) OA
Totals	175	+	200	=	125	+	250	600	−	350	=	250	175 NC

Notice the $250 of net income differs from the $175 cash flow from operating activities. The entries in the statements model demonstrate the reasons for the difference. Although $600 of revenue is recognized, only $400 of cash was collected. The remaining $200 will be collected in the future and is currently shown on the balance sheet as Accounts Receivable. Also, although $350 of salary expense is recognized, only $225 was paid in cash. The remaining $125 will be paid in the future. This obligation is shown as Salaries Payable on the balance sheet. Study these relationships carefully to develop a clear understanding of how accrual accounting affects financial reporting.

Also, the definitions of revenue and expense have been expanded. The complete definitions of these two elements are as follows:

1. **Revenue:** Revenue is the *economic benefit* derived from operating the business. Its recognition is accompanied by an increase in assets or a decrease in liabilities resulting from providing products or services to customers.

2. **Expense:** An expense is an *economic sacrifice* incurred in the process of generating revenue. Its recognition is accompanied by a decrease in assets or an increase in liabilities resulting from consuming assets and services in an effort to produce revenue.

Finally, this chapter introduced the issues surrounding corporate governance. Codes of ethics, the relevant provisions of Sarbanes–Oxley, and the fraud triangle are discussed.

A Look Forward

To this point, we have used plus and minus signs to illustrate the effects of business events on financial statements. In real businesses, so many transactions occur that recording them with simple mathematical notations is impractical. In practice, accountants usually maintain records using a system of rules known as *double-entry bookkeeping*. Chapter 3 introduces the basic components of this bookkeeping system. You will learn how to record business events using a debit/credit format. You will be introduced to ledgers, journals, and trial balances. When you finish Chapter 3, you will have a clear understanding of how accountants maintain records of business activity.

APPENDIX

Companies frequently purchase assets that are used for several years. These assets are frequently called long-term assets. Also, companies incur liabilities that require the computation of interest. Accounting for these issues is introduced in this appendix. A more detailed discussion of these subjects will be included in subsequent chapters.

Accounting Events for Year 1

Assume that on January 1, Year 1, Libby Company had beginning balances of $43,000 in its Cash and Retained Earnings accounts. During Year 1, Libby experienced the following transactions:

EVENT 1 On January 1, Year 1, Libby paid $43,000 cash to purchase a forklift.

Libby expected to rent the forklift to its customers during the coming four years and then to sell the used forklift for $3,000. The expected period of use is commonly called the **useful life.** The amount Libby expects to receive from the sale of the asset at the end of its useful life is called the **salvage value.**

The purchase of the forklift is an asset exchange transaction. The balance in the Cash account decreases and the balance in a new asset account called Forklift increases. The purchase does not affect the income statement. Because the asset has a long-term useful life, the cash outflow necessary to buy the asset is an investing activity. The effects of the purchase on the financial statements are shown here:

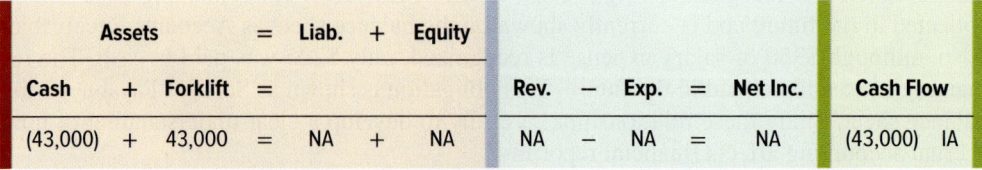

EVENT 2 On February 1, Year 1, Libby borrowed $5,000 cash from the State Bank.

As evidence of the debt, Libby issues a promissory note that describes the company's obligations to the bank. The note stipulates a one-year term and an annual interest rate of 6 percent. Issuing the note is an asset source transaction. The asset account Cash increases and a new liability account called Notes Payable increases. The income statement is not affected.

The statement of cash flows shows a $5,000 cash inflow from financing activities. The effects on the financial statements are shown here:

Assets	=	Liab.	+	Equity						
Cash + Forklift	=	Note Payable	+		Rev.	−	Exp.	=	Net Inc.	Cash Flow
5,000 + NA	=	5,000	+	NA	NA	−	NA	=	NA	5,000 FA

EVENT 3 During Year 1, Libby earned $16,000 cash by renting the forklift to its customers.

The effects of this event on the financial statements are shown here:

Assets	=	Liab.	+	Equity						
Cash + Forklift	=		+	Retained Earnings	Rev.	−	Exp.	=	Net Inc.	Cash Flow
16,000 + NA	=	NA	+	16,000	16,000	−	NA	=	16,000	16,000 OA

EVENT 4 On December 31, Year 1, Libby adjusts its accounts to recognize the expense of using the forklift during Year 1.

LO 2-11

Compute depreciation expense and show how it affects financial statements.

To measure the net economic benefit of running the business, Libby must estimate how much of the cost of the forklift it used in the process of earning revenue. Recall that the forklift has a four-year useful life and a $3,000 salvage value. Because the salvage value is expected to be recovered at the end of the forklift's useful life, only $40,000 ($43,000 cost − $3,000 salvage) worth of the forklift is ultimately expected to be used. Assuming the forklift is used evenly over its four-year life, it is logical to allocate an equal amount of the $40,000 to expense each year the forklift is used. The allocation is computed as follows:

(Asset cost − Salvage value)/Useful life = Depreciation expense
($43,000 − $3,000) / 4 years = $10,000 per year

As indicated above, the portion of the cost that represents the use of the asset is commonly called **depreciation expense.** The method of computing the depreciation expense that is described above is called **straight-line depreciation.** Recognizing depreciation expense is an asset use transaction. Assets and equity decrease. On the income statement, expenses increase and net income decreases. There are no cash flow consequences. Recall that the cash outflow occurred at the time the asset was purchased. There is no cash flow when the expense is recognized. The effects on the financial statements are shown next:

Assets	=	Liab.	+	Equity						
Cash + Book Value of Forklift	=		+	Retained Earnings	Rev.	−	Exp.	=	Net Inc.	Cash Flow
NA + (10,000)	=	NA	+	(10,000)	NA	−	10,000	=	(10,000)	NA

The asset account, Forklift, is not decreased directly. Instead, the asset reduction is recorded in a contra asset account called Accumulated Depreciation. This approach is used because it increases the usefulness of the information. The book value of the asset is the difference between the balances in the Forklift account and the related Accumulated Depreciation account as follows:

Forklift	$43,000
Accumulated Depreciation	(10,000)
Book Value	$33,000

The book value may also be called the **carrying value.** On the balance sheet, the book value of the asset is added to the other asset account balances to determine the total amount of assets.

Depreciation expense is recognized each year the forklift is used. Like other expense accounts, the Depreciation Expense account is a temporary account that is closed to retained earnings at the end of each accounting cycle. In other words, each year $10,000 is recognized in the Depreciation Expense account and then closed to the Retained Earnings account. In this case, the Depreciation Expense account will be $10,000 each year.

In contrast, the Accumulated Depreciation account is a permanent account. As its name implies, the total amount in the Accumulated Depreciation account increases (accumulates) each time depreciation expense is recognized. For example, at the end of Year 2, Libby will recognize $10,000 of depreciation expense and the balance in the Accumulated Depreciation account will increase to $20,000. At the end of Year 3, Libby will recognize $10,000 of depreciation expense and the balance in the Accumulated Depreciation account will increase to $30,000, and so on.

EVENT 5 On December 31, Year 1, Libby adjusts its books to recognize the amount of interest expense incurred during Year 1.

Recall that Libby borrowed $5,000 on February 1, Year 1. As a result, Libby owes the bank interest for the 11 months the loan was outstanding during the year. The accrued interest is $275 ($5,000 × .06 × 11/12). The adjusting entry is a claims exchange event. The liability account Interest Payable increases, and the equity account Retained Earnings decreases. The income statement would report interest expense. However, there is no effect on cash flow because the actual cash payment for interest will be made on the maturity date in Year 2. The effects on the financial statements are shown here:

LO 2-12

Compute interest expense and show how it affects financial statements.

Assets			=	Liab.	+	Equity						
Cash	+	Forklift	=	Interest Payable	+	Retained Earnings	Rev.	−	Exp.	=	Net Inc.	Cash Flow
NA	+	NA	=	275	+	(275)	NA	−	275	=	(275)	NA

The events experienced by Libby during Year 1 are summarized in Exhibit 2.11.

EXHIBIT 2.11

Transaction Data Recorded in Accounts

Event No.		Assets			=	Liabilities			+	Equity	
		Cash	+	Forklift	=	Notes Payable	+	Interest Payable	+	Retained Earnings	
Beg. bal.		43,000		0		0		0		43,000	
1	Purchase forklift	(43,000)		43,000							
2	Borrowed cash	5,000				5,000					
3	Recognize revenue	16,000								16,000	Revenue
4	Recognize depreciation			(10,000)						(10,000)	Depreciation Expense
5	Accrued interest							275		(275)	Interest Expense
End bal.		21,000	+	33,000	=	5,000	+	275	+	48,725	

Accounting Events for Year 2

Libby would record three journal entries on January 31, Year 2 (the maturity date). The first entry recognizes $25 ($5,000 × .06 × 1/12) of interest expense that accrued in Year 2 for the month of January. The effects on the financial statements are shown here:

Assets	=	Liab.	+	Equity						
Cash + Forklift	=	Interest Payable	+	Retained Earnings	Rev.	−	Exp.	=	Net Inc.	Cash Flow
NA + NA	=	25	+	(25)	NA	−	25	=	(25)	NA

The second entry records Libby's cash payment for interest payable. This entry is an asset use transaction that reduces both the Cash and Interest Payable accounts for the total amount of interest due, $300. The interest payment includes the 11 months interest accrued in Year 1 and one month accrued in Year 2 ($275 + $25 = $300). There is no effect on the income statement because Libby recognized the interest expense previously. The statement of cash flows would report a $300 cash outflow from operating activities. The effects on the financial statements are shown here:

Assets	=	Liab.	+	Equity						
Cash + Forklift	=	Interest Payable	+		Rev.	−	Exp.	=	Net Inc.	Cash Flow
(300) + NA	=	(300)	+	NA	NA	−	NA	=	NA	(300) OA

The third entry on January 31, Year 2, reflects repaying the principal. This entry is an asset use transaction. The Cash account and the Notes Payable account each decrease by $5,000. There is no effect on the income statement. The statement of cash flows would show a $5,000 cash outflow from financing activities. The effects on the financial statements are shown here:

Assets	=	Liab.	+	Equity						
Cash + Forklift	=	Note Payable	+		Rev.	−	Exp.	=	Net Inc.	Cash Flow
(5,000) + NA	=	(5,000)	+	NA	NA	−	NA	=	NA	(5,000) FA

Libby's balance sheets, income statements, and statements of cash flows for Year 1 and Year 2 are shown in Exhibit 2.12. The statements assume revenue for Year 2 is also $16,000 cash and the company made the appropriate adjusting entry to recognize depreciation expense.

EXHIBIT 2.12 Financial Statements

LIBBY COMPANY
Financial Statements
December 31, Year 1 and Year 2

	Year 1	Year 2
Income Statement		
Revenue	$ 16,000	$16,000
Depreciation expense	(10,000)	(10,000)
Interest expense	(275)	(25)
Net income	$ 5,725	$ 5,975

continued

EXHIBIT 2.12 Concluded

Balance Sheets

	Year 1	Year 2
Assets		
Cash	$21,000	$31,700
Forklift less accumulated depreciation	33,000	23,000
Total assets	$54,000	$54,700
Liabilities		
Notes Payable	$ 5,000	$ 0
Interest Payable	275	0
Total Liabilities	5,275	0
Stockholders' Equity		
Retained Earnings	48,725	54,700
Total Liab. and Stockholders' Equity	$54,000	$54,700

Statement of Cash Flows

	Year 1	Year 2
Cash flows from operating activities		
Inflow from customers	$16,000	$16,000
Cash flow from investing activities		
Outflow to purchase forklift	(43,000)	0
Cash flows from financing activities		
Inflow (outflow) from issue of note	5,000	(5,000)
Outflow for interest	0	(300)
Net change in cash	(22,000)	10,700
Plus beginning cash balance	43,000	21,000
Ending cash balance	$21,000	$31,700

 Video lectures and accompanying self-assessment quizzes are available in **Connect** for all learning objectives.

SELF-STUDY REVIEW PROBLEM

Gifford Company experienced the following accounting events during Year 1:

1. Started operations on January 1 when it acquired $20,000 cash by issuing common stock.
2. Earned $18,000 of revenue on account.
3. On March 1, collected $36,000 cash as an advance for services to be performed in the future.
4. Paid cash operating expenses of $17,000.
5. Paid a $2,700 cash dividend to stockholders.
6. On December 31, Year 1, adjusted the books to recognize the revenue earned by providing services related to the advance described in Event 3. The contract required Gifford to provide services for a one-year period starting March 1.
7. Collected $15,000 cash from accounts receivable.

Gifford Company experienced the following accounting events during Year 2:

1. Recognized $38,000 of cash revenue.
2. On April 1, paid $12,000 cash for an insurance policy that provides coverage for one year beginning immediately.
3. Collected $2,000 cash from accounts receivable.
4. Paid cash operating expenses of $21,000.

5. Paid a $5,000 cash dividend to stockholders.
6. On December 31, Year 2, adjusted the books to recognize the remaining revenue earned by providing services related to the advance described in Event 3 of Year 1.
7. On December 31, Year 2, Gifford adjusted the books to recognize the amount of the insurance policy used during Year 2.

Required

a. Record the events in a financial statements model like the following one. The first event is recorded as an example.

Event No.	Cash	+	Accts. Rec.	+	Prep. Ins.	=	Unearn. Rev.	+	Com. Stk.	+	Ret. Earn.	Rev.	−	Exp.	=	Net Inc.	Cash Flow
1	20,000	+	NA	+	NA	=	NA	+	20,000	+	NA	NA	−	NA	=	NA	20,000 FA

b. What amount of revenue would Gifford report on the Year 1 income statement?
c. What amount of cash flow from customers would Gifford report on the Year 1 statement of cash flows?
d. What amount of unearned revenue would Gifford report on the Year 1 and Year 2 year-end balance sheets?
e. What are the Year 2 opening balances for the revenue and expense accounts?
f. What amount of total assets would Gifford report on the December 31, Year 1, balance sheet?
g. What obligations and commitments would Gifford report on the December 31, Year 2, balance sheet?

Solution to Requirement *a*

The financial statements model follows:

Event No.	Cash	+	Accts. Rec.	+	Prep. Ins.	=	Unearn. Rev.	+	Com. Stk.	+	Ret. Earn.	Rev.	−	Exp.	=	Net Inc.	Cash Flow
Year 1																	
1	20,000	+	NA	+	NA	=	NA	+	20,000	+	NA	NA	−	NA	=	NA	20,000 FA
2	NA	+	18,000	+	NA	=	NA	+	NA	+	18,000	18,000	−	NA	=	18,000	NA
3	36,000	+	NA	+	NA	=	36,000	+	NA	+	NA	NA	−	NA	=	NA	36,000 OA
4	(17,000)	+	NA	+	NA	=	NA	+	NA	+	(17,000)	NA	−	17,000	=	(17,000)	(17,000) OA
5	(2,700)	+	NA	+	NA	=	NA	+	NA	+	(2,700)	NA	−	NA	=	NA	(2,700) FA
6*	NA	+	NA	+	NA	=	(30,000)	+	NA	+	30,000	30,000	−	NA	=	30,000	NA
7	15,000	+	(15,000)	+	NA	=	NA	+	NA	+	NA	NA	−	NA	=	NA	15,000 OA
Bal.	51,300	+	3,000	+	NA	=	6,000	+	20,000	+	28,300	48,000	−	17,000	=	31,000	51,300 NC

Asset, liability, and equity account balances carry forward — Rev. & exp. accts. are closed

Event No.	Cash	+	Accts. Rec.	+	Prep. Ins.	=	Unearn. Rev.	+	Com. Stk.	+	Ret. Earn.	Rev.	−	Exp.	=	Net Inc.	Cash Flow
Year 2																	
Bal.	51,300	+	3,000	+	NA	=	6,000	+	20,000	+	28,300	NA	−	NA	=	NA	NA
1	38,000	+	NA	+	NA	=	NA	+	NA	+	38,000	38,000	−	NA	=	38,000	38,000 OA
2	(12,000)	+	NA	+	12,000	=	NA	+	NA	+	NA	NA	−	NA	=	NA	(12,000) OA
3	2,000	+	(2,000)	+	NA	=	NA	+	NA	+	NA	NA	−	NA	=	NA	2,000 OA
4	(21,000)	+	NA	+	NA	=	NA	+	NA	+	(21,000)	NA	−	21,000	=	(21,000)	(21,000) OA
5	(5,000)	+	NA	+	NA	=	NA	+	NA	+	(5,000)	NA	−	NA	=	NA	(5,000) FA
6*	NA	+	NA	+	NA	=	(6,000)	+	NA	+	6,000	6,000	−	NA	=	6,000	NA
7†	NA	+	NA	+	(9,000)	=	NA	+	NA	+	(9,000)	NA	−	9,000	=	(9,000)	NA
Bal.	53,300	+	1,000	+	3,000	=	0	+	20,000	+	37,300	44,000	−	30,000	=	14,000	2,000 NC

*Revenue is earned at the rate of $3,000 ($36,000 ÷ 12 months) per month. Revenue recognized in Year 1 is $30,000 ($3,000 × 10 months). Revenue recognized in Year 2 is $6,000 ($3,000 × 2 months).

†Insurance expense is incurred at the rate of $1,000 ($12,000 ÷ 12 months) per month. Insurance expense recognized in Year 2 is $9,000 ($1,000 × 9 months).

Solutions to Requirements b–g

b. Gifford would report $48,000 of revenue in Year 1 ($18,000 revenue on account plus $30,000 of the $36,000 of unearned revenue).

c. The cash inflow from customers in Year 1 is $51,000 ($36,000 when the unearned revenue was received plus $15,000 collection of accounts receivable).

d. The December 31, Year 1, balance sheet will report $6,000 of unearned revenue, which is the amount of the cash advance less the amount of revenue recognized in Year 1 ($36,000 − $30,000). The December 31, Year 2, unearned revenue balance is zero.

e. Because revenue and expense accounts are closed at the end of each accounting period, the beginning balances in these accounts are always zero.

f. Assets on the December 31, Year 1, balance sheet are $54,300 [Gifford's cash at year-end plus the balance in accounts receivable ($51,300 + $3,000)].

g. Because all unearned revenue would be recognized before the financial statements were prepared at the end of Year 2, there would be no liabilities on the Year 2 balance sheet. In this case, all of the assets are committed to the investors.

KEY TERMS

Accounts Receivable 73
Accrual 71
Accrual accounting 71
Accrued expenses 75
Adjusting entry 75
American Institute of Certified Public Accountants (AICPA) 94
Asset exchange transaction 73
Asset source transaction 72
Asset use transaction 74
Carrying value 100
Claims exchange transaction 75
Code of Professional Conduct 94
Cost 84
Deferral 71
Depreciation expense 99
Expense 75
Internal controls 95
Matching concept 80
Opportunity 95
Period costs 81
Prepaid items 84
Pressure 96
Rationalization 96
Revenue 87
Salaries Payable 75
Salvage value 98
Straight-line depreciation 99
Unearned revenue 86
Useful life 98
Vertical statements model 90

QUESTIONS

1. What does accrual accounting attempt to accomplish?
2. Define *recognition*. How is it independent of collecting or paying cash?
3. What does the term *deferral* mean?
4. If cash is collected in advance of performing services, when is the associated revenue recognized?
5. What does the term *asset source transaction* mean?
6. What effect does the issue of common stock have on the accounting equation?
7. How does the recognition of revenue on account (accounts receivable) affect the income statement compared to its effect on the statement of cash flows?
8. Give an example of an asset source transaction. What is the effect of this transaction on the accounting equation?
9. When is revenue recognized under accrual accounting?
10. Give an example of an asset exchange transaction. What is the effect of this transaction on the accounting equation?
11. What is the effect on the right side of the accounting equation when cash is collected in advance of performing services?
12. What does the term *unearned revenue* mean?
13. What effect does expense recognition have on the accounting equation?
14. What does the term *claims exchange transaction* mean?
15. What type of transaction is a cash payment to creditors? How does this type of transaction affect the accounting equation?
16. When are expenses recognized under accrual accounting?
17. Why may net cash flow from operating activities on the cash flow statement be different from the amount of net income reported on the income statement?
18. What is the relationship between the income statement and changes in assets and liabilities?
19. How does net income affect the stockholders' claims on the business' assets?
20. What is the difference between a cost and an expense?
21. When does a cost become an expense? Do all costs become expenses?
22. How and when is the cost of the *supplies used* recognized in an accounting period?
23. What does the term *expense* mean?
24. What does the term *revenue* mean?
25. What is the purpose of the statement of changes in stockholders' equity?
26. What is the main purpose of the balance sheet?
27. Why is the balance sheet dated *as of* a specific date when the income statement, statement of changes in stockholders' equity, and statement of cash flows are dated with the phrase *for the period ended*?
28. In what order are assets listed on the balance sheet?
29. What does the statement of cash flows explain?

30. What does the term *adjusting entry* mean? Give an example.
31. What types of accounts are closed at the end of the accounting period? Why is it necessary to close these accounts?
32. Give several examples of period costs.
33. Give an example of a cost that can be directly matched with the revenue produced by an accounting firm from preparing a tax return.
34. List and describe the four stages of the accounting cycle discussed in Chapter 2.

MULTIPLE-CHOICE QUESTIONS

Multiple-choice questions are available in **Connect**.

EXERCISES—SERIES A

All applicable Exercises in Series A are available in **Connect**.

Where applicable in all exercises, round computations to the nearest dollar.

Exercise 2-1A Effect of collecting accounts receivable on the accounting equation and financial statements

LO 2-1, 2-3

Holloway Company earned $18,000 of service revenue on account during Year 1. The company collected $14,000 cash from accounts receivable during Year 1.

Required
Based on this information alone, determine the following for Holloway Company. (*Hint:* Record the events in general ledger accounts under an accounting equation before satisfying the requirements.)
a. The balance of the accounts receivable that would be reported on the December 31, Year 1, balance sheet.
b. The amount of net income that would be reported on the Year 1 income statement.
c. The amount of net cash flow from operating activities that would be reported on the Year 1 statement of cash flows.
d. The amount of retained earnings that would be reported on the Year 1 balance sheet.
e. Why are the answers to Requirements *b* and *c* different?

Exercise 2-2A Effect of accrued expenses on the accounting equation and financial statements

LO 2-2, 2-3

During Year 1, Chung Corporation earned $8,000 of cash revenue and accrued $5,000 of salaries expense.

Required
(*Hint:* Record the events in general ledger accounts under an accounting equation before satisfying the requirements.) Based on this information alone:
a. Prepare the December 31, Year 1, balance sheet.
b. Determine the amount of net income that Chung would report on the Year 1 income statement.
c. Determine the amount of net cash flow from operating activities that Chung would report on the Year 1 statement of cash flows.
d. Why are the answers to Requirements *b* and *c* different?

Exercise 2-3A Effect of accruals on the financial statements

LO 2-1, 2-2, 2-3

Milea Inc. experienced the following events in Year 1, its first year of operations:
1. Received $20,000 cash from the issue of common stock.
2. Performed services on account for $56,000.
3. Paid the utility expense of $2,500.
4. Collected $48,000 of the accounts receivable.
5. Recorded $10,000 of accrued salaries at the end of the year.
6. Paid a $2,000 cash dividend to the stockholders.

Required

a. Record the events in general ledger accounts under an accounting equation. In the last column of the table, provide appropriate account titles for the Retained Earnings amounts. The first transaction has been recorded as an example.

MILEA INC.
General Ledger Accounts

Event	Assets		=	Liabilities	+	Stockholders' Equity		Acct. Titles for Ret. Earn.
	Cash	Accounts Receivable		Salaries Payable		Common Stock	Retained Earnings	
1.	20,000					20,000		

b. Prepare the income statement, statement of changes in stockholders' equity, balance sheet, and statement of cash flows for the Year 1 accounting period.

c. Why is the amount of net income different from the amount of net cash flow from operating activities?

LO 2-1, 2-2, 2-3

Exercise 2-4A *Effect of accounts receivable and accounts payable transactions on financial statements*

The following events apply to Lewis and Harper, a public accounting firm, for the Year 1 accounting period:

1. Performed $70,000 of services for clients on account.
2. Performed $40,000 of services for cash.
3. Incurred $36,000 of other operating expenses on account.
4. Paid $10,000 cash to an employee for salary.
5. Collected $47,000 cash from accounts receivable.
6. Paid $16,000 cash on accounts payable.
7. Paid a $8,000 cash dividend to the stockholders.
8. Accrued salaries were $2,000 at the end of Year 1.

Required

a. Show the effects of the events on the financial statements using a horizontal statements model like the following one. In the Cash Flow column, use OA to designate operating activity, IA for investment activity, FA for financing activity, and NC for net change in cash. Use NA to indicate the element is not affected by the event. The first event is shown as an example.

Event No.	Assets		=	Liabilities		+	Equity						
	Cash +	Accts. Rec.	=	Accts. Pay	+	Sal. Pay	+	Ret. Earn.	Rev.	−	Exp.	=	Net Inc.	Cash Flow
1	NA +	70,000	=	NA	+	NA	+	70,000	70,000	−	NA	=	70,000	NA

b. What is the amount of total assets at the end of Year 1?
c. What is the balance of accounts receivable at the end of Year 1?
d. What is the balance of accounts payable at the end of Year 1?
e. What is the difference between accounts receivable and accounts payable?
f. What is net income for Year 1?
g. What is the amount of net cash flow from operating activities for Year 1?

LO 2-3

Exercise 2-5A *Missing information related to accruals*

Castile Inc. had a beginning balance of $4,000 in its Accounts Receivable account. The ending balance of Accounts Receivable was $4,500. During the period, Castile recognized $68,000 of revenue on account. Castile's Salaries Payable account has a beginning balance of $2,600 and an ending balance of $1,500. During the period, the company recognized $46,000 of accrued salary expense.

Required

a. Based on the information provided, determine the amount of net income.
b. Based on the information provided, determine the amount of net cash flow from operating activities.

Exercise 2-6A Effect of accruals on the financial statements

LO 2-3

Cordell Inc. experienced the following events in Year 1, its first year of operation:
1. Received $40,000 cash from the issue of common stock.
2. Performed services on account for $82,000.
3. Paid a $6,000 cash dividend to the stockholders.
4. Collected $76,000 of the accounts receivable.
5. Paid $53,000 cash for other operating expenses.
6. Performed services for $19,000 cash.
7. Recognized $3,500 of accrued utilities expense at the end of the year.

Required

a. Identify the events that result in revenue or expense recognition.
b. Based on your response to Requirement *a*, determine the amount of net income reported on the Year 1 income statement.
c. Identify the events that affect the statement of cash flows.
d. Based on your response to Requirement *c*, determine the amount of cash flow from operating activities reported on the Year 1 statement of cash flows.
e. What is the before- and after-closing balance in the Service Revenue account? What other accounts would be closed at the end of the accounting cycle?
f. What is the balance of the Retained Earnings account that appears on the Year 1 balance sheet?

Exercise 2-7A Net income versus changes in cash

LO 2-3

In Year 1, Lee Inc. billed its customers $72,000 for services performed. The company collected $55,000 of the amount billed. Lee incurred $42,000 of other operating expenses on account. Lee paid $34,000 of the accounts payable. Lee acquired $44,000 cash from the issue of common stock. The company invested $18,000 cash in the purchase of land.

Required

(*Hint:* Identify the six events described in the paragraph and record them in general ledger accounts under an accounting equation before attempting to answer the questions.) Use the preceding information to answer the following questions:

a. What amount of revenue will Lee report on the Year 1 income statement?
b. What amount of cash flow from revenue will be reported on the statement of cash flows?
c. What is the net income for the period?
d. What is the net cash flow from operating activities for the period?
e. Why is the amount of net income different from the net cash flow from operating activities for the period?
f. What is the amount of net cash flow from investing activities?
g. What is the amount of net cash flow from financing activities?
h. What amounts of total assets, liabilities, and equity will be reported on the year-end balance sheet?

Exercise 2-8A Closing entries

LO 2-4

Love Company's accounting records show an after-closing balance of $42,100 in its Retained Earnings account on December 31, Year 2. During the Year 2 accounting cycle, Love earned $19,400 of revenue, incurred $9,800 of expense, and paid $500 of dividends. Revenues and expenses were recognized evenly throughout the accounting period.

Required

a. Determine the balance in the Retained Earnings account as of January 1, Year 3.
b. Determine the balance in the temporary accounts as of January 1, Year 2.
c. Determine the after-closing balance in the Retained Earnings account as of December 31, Year 1.
d. Determine the balance in the Retained Earnings account as of June 30, Year 2.

LO 2-4

Exercise 2-9A *Closing the accounts*

The following information was drawn from the accounting records of Wyckoff Company as of December 31, Year 2, before the temporary accounts had been closed. The Cash balance was $3,600, and Notes Payable amounted to $4,000. The company had revenues of $7,500 and expenses of $3,400. The company's Land account had an $8,000 balance. Dividends amounted to $1,000. There was $2,000 of common stock issued.

Required

a. Identify which accounts would be classified as permanent and which accounts would be classified as temporary.
b. Assuming that Wyckoff's beginning balance (as of January 1, Year 2) in the Retained Earnings account was $2,500, determine its balance after the temporary accounts were closed at the end of Year 2.
c. What amount of net income would Wyckoff Company report on its Year 2 income statement?
d. Explain why the amount of net income differs from the amount of the ending Retained Earnings balance.
e. What are the balances in the revenue, expense, and dividend accounts on January 1, Year 3?

LO 2-4

Exercise 2-10A *Closing accounts and the accounting cycle*

Required

a. Identify which of the following accounts are temporary (will be closed to Retained Earnings at the end of the year) and which are permanent:
   (1) Other Operating Expenses
   (2) Utilities Expense
   (3) Retained Earnings
   (4) Salaries Expense
   (5) Land
   (6) Dividends
   (7) Service Revenue
   (8) Cash
   (9) Salaries Payable
   (10) Common Stock

b. List and explain the four stages of the accounting cycle. Which stage must be first? Which stage is last?

LO 2-4

Exercise 2-11A *Matching concept*

Companies make sacrifices known as *expenses* to obtain benefits called *revenues*. The accurate measurement of net income requires that expenses be matched with revenues. In some circumstances, matching a particular expense directly with revenue is difficult or impossible. In these circumstances, the expense is matched with the period in which it is incurred.

Required

a. Identify an expense that could be matched directly with revenue.
b. Identify a period expense that would be difficult to match with revenue. Explain why.

EXERCISES—SERIES A

Exercise 2-12A Supplies and the financial statements model

LO 2-5

Pizza Express Inc. began the Year 2 accounting period with $2,500 cash, $1,400 of common stock, and $1,100 of retained earnings. Pizza Express was affected by the following accounting events during Year 2:

1. Purchased $3,600 of supplies on account.
2. Earned and collected $12,300 of cash revenue.
3. Paid $2,700 cash on accounts payable.
4. Adjusted the records to reflect the use of supplies. A physical count indicated that $250 of supplies was still on hand on December 31, Year 2.

Required

a. Show the effects of the events on the financial statements using a horizontal statements model like the following one. In the Cash Flow column, use OA to designate operating activity, IA for investing activity, FA for financing activity, and NC for net change in cash. Use NA to indicate accounts not affected by the event. The beginning balances are entered in the following example:

Event No.	Assets			=	Liab.	+	Stockholders' Equity				Rev.	−	Exp.	=	Net Inc.	Cash Flow
	Cash	+	Supplies	=	Accts. Pay	+	Com. Stk	+	Ret. Earn.							
Beg. bal.	2,500	+	0	=	0	+	1,400	+	1,100		0	−	0	=	0	0

b. Explain the difference between the amount of net income and amount of net cash flow from operating activities.

Exercise 2-13A Supplies on financial statements

LO 2-5, 2-8

Yard Professionals Inc. experienced the following events in Year 1, its first year of operation:

1. Performed services for $35,000 cash.
2. Purchased $6,000 of supplies on account.
3. A physical count on December 31, Year 1, found that there was $1,800 of supplies on hand.

Required

Based on this information alone:

a. Record the events in general ledger accounts under an accounting equation.
b. Prepare an income statement, balance sheet, and statement of cash flows for the Year 1 accounting period.
c. What is the balance in the Supplies account as of January 1, Year 2?
d. What is the balance in the Supplies Expense account as of January 1, Year 2?

Exercise 2-14A Distinguishing between an expense and a cost

LO 2-5, 2-6

Charlene Rose tells you that accountants where she works are real hair splitters. For example, they make a big issue over the difference between a cost and an expense. She says the two terms mean the same thing to her.

Required

a. Explain to Charlene the difference between a cost and expense from an accountant's perspective.
b. Explain whether each of the following events produces an asset or an expense:
   (1) Purchased a building for cash.
   (2) Paid cash to purchase supplies.

(3) Used supplies on hand to produce revenue.
(4) Paid cash in advance for insurance.
(5) Recognized accrued salaries.

LO 2-6

Exercise 2-15A *Prepaid items on financial statements*

Life, Inc. experienced the following events in Year 1, its first year of operation:
1. Performed counseling services for $36,000 cash.
2. On February 1, Year 1, paid $18,000 cash to rent office space for the coming year.
3. Adjusted the accounts to reflect the amount of rent used during the year.

Required

Based on this information alone:

a. Record the events in general ledger accounts under an accounting equation.
b. Prepare an income statement, balance sheet, and statement of cash flows for the Year 1 accounting period.
c. Ignoring all other future events, what is the amount of rent expense that would be recognized in Year 2?

LO 2-6, 2-8

Exercise 2-16A *Effect of an error on financial statements*

On April 1, Year 1, Maine Corporation paid $18,000 cash in advance for a one-year lease on an office building. Assume that Maine records the prepaid rent as an asset and that the books are closed on December 31.

Required

a. Show the payment for the one-year lease and the related adjusting entry to recognize rent expense in the accounting equation.
b. Assume that Maine Corporation failed to record the adjusting entry to reflect using the office building. How would the error affect the company's Year 1 income statement and balance sheet?

LO 2-7

Exercise 2-17A *Unearned items on financial statements*

Yard Designs (YD) experienced the following events in Year 1, its first year of operation:
1. On October 1, Year 1, YD collected $54,000 for consulting services it agreed to provide during the coming year.
2. Adjusted the accounts to reflect the amount of consulting service revenue recognized in Year 1.

Required

Based on this information alone,

a. Record the events under an accounting equation.
b. Prepare an income statement, balance sheet, and statement of cash flows for the Year 1 accounting period.
c. Ignoring all other future events, what is the amount of service revenue that would be recognized in Year 2?

LO 2-7

Exercise 2-18A *Unearned revenue defined as a liability*

Lan, an accounting major, and Pat, a marketing major, are watching a *Matlock* rerun on late-night TV. Of course, there is a murder and the suspect wants to hire Matlock as the defense attorney. Matlock will take the case but requires an advance payment of $150,000. Pat remarks that Matlock has earned a cool $150,000 without lifting a finger. Lan tells Pat that Matlock has not earned anything but has a $150,000 liability. Pat asks, "How can that be?"

Required

Assume you are Lan. Explain to Pat why Matlock has a liability and when Matlock would actually earn the $150,000.

Exercise 2-19A Supplies, unearned revenue, and the financial statements model LO 2-5, 2-7

Hart, Attorney at Law, experienced the following transactions in Year 1, the first year of operations:
1. Accepted $36,000 on April 1, Year 1, as a retainer for services to be performed evenly over the next 12 months.
2. Performed legal services for cash of $54,000.
3. Purchased $2,800 of office supplies on account.
4. Paid $2,400 of the amount due on accounts payable.
5. Paid a cash dividend to the stockholders of $5,000.
6. Paid cash for operating expenses of $31,000.
7. Determined that at the end of the accounting period $200 of office supplies remained on hand.
8. On December 31, Year 1, recognized the revenue that had been earned for services performed in accordance with Transaction 1.

Required
Show the effects of the events on the financial statements using a horizontal statements model like the following one. In the Cash Flow column, use the initials OA to designate operating activity, IA for investing activity, FA for financing activity, and NC for net change in cash. Use NA to indicate accounts not affected by the event. The first event has been recorded as an example.

Event No.	Assets			=	Liabilities			+	Stk. Equity	Rev.	−	Exp.	=	Net Inc.	Cash Flow
	Cash	+	Supplies	=	Accts. Pay	+	Unearn. Rev.	+	Ret. Earn.						
1.	36,000	+	NA	=	NA	+	36,000	+	NA	NA	−	NA	=	NA	36,000 OA

Exercise 2-20A Unearned revenue and the financial statements model LO 2-7

Clark Bell started a personal financial planning business when he accepted $36,000 cash as advance payment for managing the financial assets of a large estate. Bell agreed to manage the estate for a one-year period beginning June 1, Year 1.

Required
a. Show the effects of the advance payment and revenue recognition on the Year 1 financial statements using a horizontal statements model like the following one. In the Cash Flow column, use OA to designate operating activity, IA for investing activity, FA for financing activity, and NC for net change in cash. Use NA if the account is not affected.

Event	Assets	=	Liab.	+	Stockholders' Equity	Rev.	−	Exp.	=	Net Inc.	Cash Flow
	Cash	=	Unearn. Rev.	+	Ret. Earn.						

b. How much revenue would Bell recognize on the Year 2 income statement?
c. What is the amount of cash flow from operating activities in Year 2?

Exercise 2-21A Prepaid vs. unearned, the entity concept LO 2-6, 2-7

On October 1, Year 1, Josh Smith, attorney, accepted a $10,800 cash advance from his client, James Company, for services to be performed over the next six months.

Required
a. Record the deferral and the related December 31, Year 1, adjustment for Josh Smith in an accounting equation.
b. Record the deferral and the related December 31, Year 1, adjustment for James Company in an accounting equation.

Exercise 2-22A Identifying deferral and accrual events

LO 2-1, 2-2, 2-5, 2-6, 2-7

Required

Identify each of the following events as an accrual, a deferral, or neither:

a. Paid cash in advance for a one-year insurance policy.
b. Paid cash to settle an account payable.
c. Collected accounts receivable.
d. Paid cash for current salaries expense.
e. Paid cash to purchase supplies.
f. Provided services on account.
g. Provided services and collected cash.
h. Paid cash to purchase land.
i. Recognized accrued salaries at the end of the accounting period.
j. Paid a cash dividend to the stockholders.
k. Recognized revenue on account at the end of the period.
l. Collected cash for services to be provided in the future.

Exercise 2-23A Revenue and expense recognition

LO 2-1, 2-2, 2-4, 2-5, 2-6

Required

a. Describe an expense recognition event that results in an increase in liabilities.
b. Describe an expense recognition event that results in a decrease in assets.
c. Describe a revenue recognition event that results in a decrease in liabilities.
d. Describe a revenue recognition event that results in an increase in assets.

Exercise 2-24A Adjusting the accounts

LO 2-5, 2-6, 2-7

Norell Inc. experienced the following accounting events during its Year 1 accounting period:

1. Recognized revenue on account.
2. Issued common stock.
3. Paid cash to purchase supplies.
4. Collected a cash advance for services that will be provided during the coming year.
5. Paid a cash dividend to the stockholders.
6. Paid cash for an insurance policy that provides coverage during the next year.
7. Collected cash from accounts receivable.
8. Paid cash for operating expenses.
9. Paid cash to settle an account payable.
10. Paid cash to purchase land.

Required

a. Identify the events that would require a year-end adjusting entry.
b. Are adjusting or closing entries recorded first? Why?

Exercise 2-25A Classifying events on the statement of cash flows

LO 2-7, 2-8

The following transactions pertain to the operations of Ewing Company for Year 1:

1. Acquired $30,000 cash from the issue of common stock.
2. Provided $65,000 of services on account.
3. Paid $22,000 cash on accounts payable.
4. Performed services for $8,000 cash.
5. Collected $51,000 cash from accounts receivable.
6. Incurred $37,000 of operating expenses on account.
7. Paid $6,500 cash for one year's rent in advance.
8. Paid a $4,000 cash dividend to the stockholders.

9. Paid $1,200 cash for supplies to be used in the future.
10. Recognized $3,100 of accrued salaries expense.

Required

a. Classify the cash flows from these transactions as operating activities (OA), investing activities (IA), or financing activities (FA). Use NA for transactions that do not affect the statement of cash flows.
b. Prepare a statement of cash flows. (There is no beginning cash balance.)

Exercise 2-26A Relationship of accounts to financial statements

LO 2-8

Required

Identify whether each of the following items would appear on the income statement (IS), statement of changes in stockholders' equity (SE), balance sheet (BS), or statement of cash flows (CF). Some items may appear on more than one statement; if so, identify all applicable statements. If an item would not appear on any financial statement, label it NA.

CHECK FIGURES
a. BS
z. CF

a. Supplies
b. Cash Flow from Financing Activities
c. "As of" Date Notation
d. Ending Retained Earnings
e. Net Income
f. Dividends
g. Net Change in Cash
h. "For the Period Ended"
i. Land
j. Ending Common Stock
k. Salaries Expense
l. Prepaid Rent
m. Accounts Payable
n. Total Assets
o. Salaries Payable
p. Insurance Expense
q. Notes Payable
r. Accounts Receivable
s. Interest Receivable
t. Interest Revenue
u. Rent Expense
v. Price/Earnings Ratio
w. Taxes Payable
x. Unearned Revenue
y. Service Revenue
z. Cash Flow from Investing Activities
aa. Consulting Revenue
bb. Utilities Expense
cc. Total Liabilities
dd. Operating Cycle
ee. Cash Flow from Operating Activities
ff. Operating Expenses
gg. Supplies Expense
hh. Beginning Retained Earnings
ii. Beginning Common Stock
jj. Prepaid Insurance
kk. Salary Expense
ll. Beginning Cash Balance
mm. Ending Cash Balance

Exercise 2-27A Effect of accounting events on the income statement and statement of cash flows

LO 2-8

Required

Explain how each of the following events or series of events and the related adjusting entry will affect the amount of *net income* and the amount of *cash flow from operating activities* reported on the year-end financial statements. Identify the direction of change (increase, decrease, or NA) and the amount of the change. Organize your answers according to the following table. The first event is recorded as an example. If an event does not have a related adjusting entry, record only the effects of the event.

	Net Income		Cash Flows from Operating Activities	
Event/ Adjustment	Direction of Change	Amount of Change	Direction of Change	Amount of Change
a	NA	NA	Decrease	$9,000
Adj	Decrease	$2,250	NA	NA

a. Paid $9,000 cash on October 1 to purchase a one-year insurance policy.
b. Purchased $2,000 of supplies on account. Paid $500 cash on accounts payable. The ending balance in the Supplies account, after adjustment, was $300.
c. Provided services for $10,000 cash.
d. Collected $2,400 in advance for services to be performed in the future. The contract called for services to start on May 1 and to continue for one year.
e. Accrued salaries amounting to $5,600.
f. Sold land that cost $3,000 for $3,000 cash.
g. Acquired $15,000 cash from the issue of common stock.
h. Earned $12,000 of revenue on account. Collected $8,000 cash from accounts receivable.
i. Paid cash operating expenses of $4,500.

LO 2-8, 2-9

Exercise 2-28A *Transactions that affect the elements of financial statements*

Required

Give an example of a transaction that will do the following:
a. Increase an asset and increase equity (asset source event).
b. Decrease an asset and decrease equity (asset use event).
c. Increase an asset and decrease another asset (asset exchange event).
d. Decrease a liability and increase equity (claims exchange event).
e. Increase a liability and decrease equity (claims exchange event).
f. Increase an asset and increase a liability (asset source event).
g. Decrease an asset and decrease a liability (asset use event).

LO 2-9

Exercise 2-29A *Identifying source, use, and exchange transactions*

Required

Indicate whether each of the following transactions is an asset source (AS), asset use (AU), asset exchange (AE), or claims exchange (CE) transaction.
a. Acquired cash from the issue of stock.
b. Paid a cash dividend to the stockholders.
c. Paid cash on accounts payable.
d. Incurred other operating expenses on account.
e. Paid cash for rent expense.
f. Performed services for cash.
g. Performed services for clients on account.
h. Collected cash from accounts receivable.
i. Received cash for services to be performed in the future.
j. Purchased land with cash.

LO 2-9

Exercise 2-30A *Identifying asset source, use, and exchange transactions*

Required

a. Name an asset use transaction that will *not* affect the income statement.
b. Name an asset exchange transaction that will affect the statement of cash flows.
c. Name an asset source transaction that will *not* affect the income statement.
d. Name an asset source transaction that will *not* affect the statement of cash flows.
e. Name an asset source transaction that will affect the income statement.

LO 2-8, 2-9

Exercise 2-31A *Identifying transaction type and effect on the financial statements*

Required

Identify whether each of the following transactions is an asset source (AS), asset use (AU), asset exchange (AE), or claims exchange (CE). Also show the effects of the events on the financial statements using the horizontal statements model. Indicate whether the event increases (I), decreases (D), or does not affect (NA) each element of the financial statements. In the Cash Flow column, designate the cash flows as operating activities (OA), investing activities (IA), or financing activities (FA). The first two transactions have been recorded as examples.

Event	Type of Event	Assets	=	Liabilities	+	Stockholders' Equity Common Stock	+	Retained Earnings	Rev.	−	Exp.	=	Net Inc.	Cash Flow
a	AS	I		NA		NA		I	I		NA		I	I OA
b	AS	I		I		NA		NA	NA		NA		NA	NA

a. Provided services and collected cash.
b. Purchased supplies on account to be used in the future.
c. Paid cash in advance for one year's rent.
d. Paid cash to purchase land.
e. Paid a cash dividend to the stockholders.
f. Received cash from the issue of common stock.
g. Paid cash on accounts payable.
h. Collected cash from accounts receivable.
i. Received cash advance for services to be provided in the future.
j. Incurred other operating expenses on account.
k. Performed services on account.
l. Adjusted books to reflect the amount of prepaid rent expired during the period.
m. Paid cash for operating expenses.
n. Adjusted the books to record the supplies used during the period.
o. Recorded accrued salaries.
p. Paid cash for salaries accrued at the end of a prior period.
q. Recognized revenue on account earned at the end of the accounting period.

Exercise 2-32A Ethical conduct

LO 2-10

Required

Name and provide a brief explanation of the six Principles of Professional Conduct of the AICPA Code of Professional Conduct.

Exercise 2-33A Effect of depreciation on the accounting equation and financial statements (Appendix)

LO 2-11

The following events apply to Tracey's Restaurant for the Year 1 fiscal year:
1. Started the company when it acquired $21,000 cash from the issue of common stock.
2. Purchased a new cooktop that cost $22,000 cash.
3. Earned $32,000 in cash revenue.
4. Paid $16,000 cash for salaries expense.
5. Paid $7,000 cash for operating expenses.
6. Adjusted the records to reflect the use of the cooktop. The cooktop, purchased on January 1, Year 1, has an expected useful life of five years and an estimated salvage value of $2,000. Use straight-line depreciation. The adjusting entry was made as of December 31, Year 1.

Required

a. Record the events in general ledger accounts under an accounting equation.
b. What amount of depreciation expense would Tracey's report on the Year 2 income statement?
c. What amount of accumulated depreciation would Tracey's report on the December 31, Year 2, balance sheet?
d. Would the cash flow from operating activities be affected by depreciation in Year 2?

LO 2-11

Exercise 2-34A Depreciation affecting multiple cycles (Appendix)

On January 1, Year 1, Your Ride Inc. paid $36,000 cash to purchase a taxi cab. The taxi had a four-year useful life and a $4,000 salvage value.

Required

a. Determine the amount of depreciation expense that would appear on the Year 1 and Year 2 income statements.

b. Determine the amount of accumulated depreciation that would appear on the Year 1 and Year 2 balance sheets.

c. Explain how the purchase of equipment would affect the Year 1 and Year 2 statements of cash flows.

LO 2-12

Exercise 2-35A Effects of recognizing accrued interest on financial statements (Appendix)

Ben Bradley started Bradley Company on January 1, Year 1. The company experienced the following events during its first year of operation:

1. Earned $2,000 of cash revenue for performing services.
2. Borrowed $8,000 cash from the bank.
3. Adjusted the accounting records to recognize accrued interest expense on the bank note. The note, issued on August 1, Year 1, had a one-year term and a 6 percent annual interest rate.

Required

a. What is the amount of interest expense in Year 1?

b. What amount of cash was paid for interest in Year 1?

c. Use a horizontal statements model to show how each event affects the balance sheet, income statement, and statement of cash flows. Indicate whether the event increases (I), decreases (D), or does not affect (NA) each element of the financial statements. Also, in the Statement of Cash Flows column, designate the cash flows as operating activities (OA), investing activities (IA), or financing activities (FA). The first transaction has been recorded as an example.

Event No.	Balance Sheet								Income Statement					Statement of Cash Flows
	Cash	=	Note Pay.	+	Int. Pay.	+	C. Stk.	+	Ret. Earn.	Rev.	−	Exp.	=	Net Inc.	
1	I	=	NA	+	NA	+	NA	+	I	I	−	NA	=	I	I OA

LO 2-12

Exercise 2-36A Recognizing accrued interest expense (Appendix)

Leach Company borrowed $80,000 cash by issuing a note payable on June 1, Year 1. The note had an 8 percent annual rate of interest and a one-year term to maturity.

Required

a. What amount of interest expense will Leach recognize for the year ending December 31, Year 1?

b. Show how the December 31, Year 1, adjusting entry to recognize the accrued interest expense affects the accounting equation.

c. What amount of cash will Leach pay for interest expense in Year 1?

d. What is the amount of interest payable as of December 31, Year 1?

e. What amount of cash will Leach pay for interest expense in Year 2?

f. What amount of interest expense will Leach recognize in Year 2?

g. What is the amount of interest payable as of December 31, Year 2?

PROBLEMS—SERIES A

All applicable Problems in Series A are available in Connect.

Problem 2-37A Effect of adjusting entries on the accounting equation

LO 2-5, 2-6, 2-7

CHECK FIGURES
d. Adjustment amount: $4,000

Required

Each of the following independent events requires a year-end adjusting entry. Show how each event and its related adjusting entry affect the accounting equation. Assume a December 31 closing date. The first event is shown as an example.

Event/ Adjustment	Cash	+	Other Assets	=	Liabilities	+	Common Stock	+	Retained Earnings
a	−4,800		+4,800		NA		NA		NA
Adj.	NA		−1,200		NA		NA		−1,200

a. Paid $4,800 cash in advance on October 1 for a one-year insurance policy.
b. Received a $3,600 cash advance for a contract to provide services in the future. The contract required a one-year commitment, starting April 1.
c. Purchased $1,200 of supplies on account. At year's end, $175 of supplies remained on hand.
d. Paid $9,600 cash in advance on August 1 for a one-year lease on office space.

Problem 2-38A Closing the accounts

LO 2-3, 2-8

The following selected accounts and account balances were taken from the records of Nowell Company. Except as otherwise indicated, all balances are as of December 31, Year 2, before the closing entries were recorded.

CHECK FIGURES
Net Income: $3,100
Ending Retained Earnings: $15,300

Consulting revenue	$18,200
Cash	35,600
Cash received from common stock issued during Year 2	6,000
Travel expense	2,100
Dividends	4,000
Cash flow from investing activities	5,200
Rent expense	3,500
Payment to reduce debt principal	10,000
Retained earnings, January 1, Year 2	16,200
Salary expense	7,200
Cash flow from operating activities	2,600
Common stock, December 31, Year 2	16,000
Other operating expenses	2,300

Required

a. Prepare the income statement Nowell would include in its Year 2 annual report.
b. Identify the accounts that should be closed to the Retained Earnings account.
c. Determine the Retained Earnings account balance at December 31, Year 2. Identify the reasons for the difference between net income and the ending balance in Retained Earnings.
d. What are the balances in the Revenue, Expense, and Dividend accounts on January 1, Year 3? Explain.

Problem 2-39A Show how the events affect the financial statements using a horizontal statements model

LO 2-8

CHECK FIGURES
Net Income: $12,300
Ending Cash Balance: $19,000

The following events pertain to Super Cleaning Company:
1. Acquired $10,000 cash from the issue of common stock.
2. Provided $15,000 of services on account.

3. Provided services for $5,000 cash.
4. Received $2,800 cash in advance for services to be performed in the future.
5. Collected $12,200 cash from the account receivable created in Event 2.
6. Paid $1,900 for cash expenses.
7. Performed $1,400 of the services agreed to in Event 4.
8. Incurred $3,600 of expenses on account.
9. Paid $4,800 cash in advance for one-year contract to rent office space.
10. Paid $2,800 cash on the account payable created in Event 8.
11. Paid a $1,500 cash dividend to the stockholders.
12. Recognized rent expense for nine months' use of office space acquired in Event 9.

Required

Show the effects of the events on the financial statements using a horizontal statements model like the following one. In the Cash Flow column, use the letters OA to designate operating activity, IA for investing activity, FA for financing activity, and NC for net change in cash. Use NA to indicate accounts not affected by the event. The first event is shown as an example.

Event No.	Cash	+	Accts. Rec.	+	Prep. Ins.	=	Accts Pay.	+	Unearn. Rev.	+	Common Stock	+	Ret. Earn.	Rev.	−	Exp.	=	Net Inc.	Cash Flow
1	10,000	+	NA	+	NA	=	NA	+	NA	+	10,000	+	NA	NA	−	NA	=	NA	10,000 FA

LO 2-3, 2-8

CHECK FIGURES
b. $44,100
h. $42,450

Problem 2-40A *Effect of events on financial statements*

Waddell Company had the following balances in its accounting records as of December 31, Year 1:

Assets		Liabilities and Equity	
Cash	$35,000	Accounts Payable	$ 7,500
Accounts Receivable	9,000	Common Stock	40,000
Land	51,000	Retained Earnings	47,500
Total	$95,000	Total	$95,000

The following accounting events apply to Waddell Company's Year 2 fiscal year:

Jan. 1 Acquired $20,000 cash from the issue of common stock.
Feb. 1 Paid $6,000 cash in advance for a one-year lease for office space.
Mar. 1 Paid a $2,000 cash dividend to the stockholders.
April 1 Purchased additional land that cost $15,000 cash.
May 1 Made a cash payment on accounts payable of $5,500.
July 1 Received $9,600 cash in advance as a retainer for services to be performed monthly over the coming year.
Sept. 1 Sold land for $30,000 cash that had originally cost $30,000.
Oct. 1 Purchased $2,500 of supplies on account.
Dec. 31 Earned $58,000 of service revenue on account during the year.
   31 Received cash collections from accounts receivable amounting to $46,000.
   31 Incurred other operating expenses on account during the year that amounted to $28,000.
   31 Recognized accrued salaries expense of $6,500.
   31 Had $50 of supplies on hand at the end of the period.
   31 The land purchased on April 1 had a market value of $20,000.

Required

Based on the preceding information, answer the following questions for Waddell Company. All questions pertain to the Year 2 financial statements. (*Hint:* Enter items in general ledger accounts under the accounting equation before answering the questions.)

a. What amount would Waddell report for land on the balance sheet?
b. What amount of net cash flow from operating activities would be reported on the statement of cash flows?
c. What amount of rent expense would be reported on the income statement?
d. What amount of total liabilities would be reported on the balance sheet?
e. What amount of supplies expense would be reported on the income statement?
f. What amount of unearned revenue would be reported on the balance sheet?
g. What amount of net cash flow from investing activities would be reported on the statement of cash flows?
h. What amount of total expenses would be reported on the income statement?
i. What amount of service revenue would be reported on the income statement?
j. What amount of cash flows from financing activities would be reported on the statement of cash flows?
k. What amount of net income would be reported on the income statement?
l. What amount of retained earnings would be reported on the balance sheet?

Problem 2-41A Identifying and arranging elements on financial statements

LO 2-3, 2-8

The following accounts and balances were drawn from the records of Barker Company at December 31, Year 2:

CHECK FIGURES
Total Assets: $93,200
Net Income: $18,500

Supplies	$ 1,000	Beginning retained earnings	$ 9,300
Cash flow from investing act.	(5,200)	Cash flow from financing act.	(5,000)
Prepaid insurance	1,200	Rent expense	2,500
Service revenue	65,200	Dividends	3,000
Other operating expenses	41,000	Cash	48,000
Supplies expense	1,100	Accounts receivable	14,200
Insurance expense	2,100	Prepaid rent	4,800
Beginning common stock	40,000	Unearned revenue	6,400
Cash flow from operating act.	15,600	Land	24,000
Common stock issued	5,000	Accounts payable	17,000

Required

Use the accounts and balances from Barker Company to construct an income statement, statement of changes in stockholders' equity, balance sheet, and statement of cash flows (show only totals for each activity on the statement of cash flows).

Problem 2-42A Missing information in financial statements

LO 2-3, 2-8

Required

Fill in the blanks (indicated by the alphabetic letters in parentheses) in the following financial statements. Assume the company started operations January 1, Year 1, and all transactions involve cash.

	For the Years		
	Year 1	Year 2	Year 3
Income Statements			
Revenue	$ 700	$ 1,300	$2,000
Expense	(a)	(700)	(1,300)
Net income	$ 200	$ (m)	$ 700

continued

Statements of Changes in Stockholders' Equity

Beginning common stock	$ 0	$ (n)	$ 6,000
Plus: Common stock issued	5,000	1,000	2,000
Ending common stock	5,000	6,000	(t)
Beginning retained earnings	0	100	200
Plus: Net income	(b)	(o)	700
Less: Dividends	(c)	(500)	(300)
Ending retained earnings	100	(p)	600
Total stockholders' equity	$ (d)	$ 6,200	$ 8,600

Balance Sheets

Assets

Cash	$ (e)	$ (q)	$ (u)
Land	0	(r)	8,000
Total assets	$ (f)	$11,200	$10,600
Liabilities	$ (g)	$ 5,000	$ 2,000
Stockholders' equity			
Common stock	(h)	(s)	8,000
Retained earnings	(i)	200	600
Total stockholders' equity	(j)	6,200	8,600
Total liabilities and stockholders' equity	$8,100	$11,200	$10,600

Statements of Cash Flows

Cash flows from operating activities			
Cash receipts from customers	$ (k)	$ 1,300	$ (v)
Cash payments for expenses	(l)	(700)	(w)
Net cash flows from operating activities	200	600	700
Cash flows from investing activities			
Cash payments for land	0	(8,000)	0
Cash flows from investing activities			
Cash receipts from loan	3,000	3,000	0
Cash payments to reduce debt	0	(1,000)	(x)
Cash receipts from stock issue	5,000	1,000	(y)
Cash payments for dividends	(100)	(500)	(z)
Net cash flows from financing activities	7,900	2,500	(1,300)
Net change in cash	8,100	(4,900)	(600)
Plus: Beginning cash balance	0	8,100	3,200
Ending cash balance	$8,100	$ 3,200	$ 2,600

LO 2-3, 2-8, 2-9

CHECK FIGURES
Net Income, Year 1: $2,400
Net Income, Year 2: $8,650

Problem 2-43A *Events for two complete accounting cycles*

Alcorn Service Company was formed on January 1, Year 1.

Events Affecting the Year 1 Accounting Period

1. Acquired $20,000 cash from the issue of common stock.
2. Purchased $800 of supplies on account.
3. Purchased land that cost $14,000 cash.
4. Paid $800 cash to settle accounts payable created in Event 2.
5. Recognized revenue on account of $10,500.
6. Paid $3,800 cash for other operating expenses.
7. Collected $7,000 cash from accounts receivable.

Information for Year 1 Adjusting Entries

8. Recognized accrued salaries of $3,600 on December 31, Year 1.
9. Had $100 of supplies on hand at the end of the accounting period.

Events Affecting the Year 2 Accounting Period

1. Acquired $15,000 cash from the issue of common stock.
2. Paid $3,600 cash to settle the salaries payable obligation.
3. Paid $9,000 cash in advance to lease office space.
4. Sold the land that cost $14,000 for $14,000 cash.
5. Received $6,000 cash in advance for services to be performed in the future.
6. Purchased $2,400 of supplies on account during the year.
7. Provided services on account of $24,500.
8. Collected $12,600 cash from accounts receivable.
9. Paid a cash dividend of $2,000 to the stockholders.
10. Paid other operating expenses of $2,850.

Information for Year 2 Adjusting Entries

11. The advance payment for rental of the office space (see Event 3) was made on March 1 for a one-year term.
12. The cash advance for services to be provided in the future was collected on October 1 (see Event 5). The one-year contract started on October 1.
13. Had $300 of supplies remaining on hand at the end of the period.
14. Recognized accrued salaries of $4,800 at the end of the accounting period.

Required

a. Identify each event affecting the Year 1 and Year 2 accounting periods as asset source (AS), asset use (AU), asset exchange (AE), or claims exchange (CE). Record the effects of each event under the appropriate general ledger account headings of the accounting equation.

b. Prepare an income statement, statement of changes in stockholders' equity, balance sheet, and statement of cash flows for Year 1 and Year 2, using the vertical statements model.

Problem 2-44A *Ethics*   LO 2-10

Pete Chalance is an accountant with a shady past. Suffice it to say that he owes some very unsavory characters a lot of money. Despite his past, Pete works hard at keeping up a strong professional image. He is a manager at Smith and Associates, a fast-growing CPA firm. Pete is highly regarded around the office because he is a strong producer of client revenue. Indeed, on several occasions he exceeded his authority in establishing prices with clients. This is typically a partner's job but who could criticize Pete, who is most certainly bringing in the business. Indeed, Pete is so good that he is able to pull off the following scheme. He bills clients at inflated rates and then reports the ordinary rate to his accounting firm. Say, for example, the normal charge for a job is $2,500. Pete will smooth talk the client, then charge him $3,000. He reports the normal charge of $2,500 to his firm and keeps the extra $500 for himself. He knows it isn't exactly right because his firm gets its regular charges and the client willingly pays for the services rendered. He thinks to himself, as he pockets his ill-gotten gains, who is getting hurt anyway?

Required

The text discusses three common features (conditions) that motivate ethical misconduct. Identify and explain each of the three features as they appear in the above scenario.

Problem 2-45A *Effect of events on financial statements (Appendix)*   LO 2-3, 2-8, 2-11, 2-12

Porser Company had the following balances in its accounting records as of December 31, Year 1:

Assets		Claims	
Cash	$26,000	Accounts payable	$ 5,000
Accounts receivable	9,000	Common stock	28,000
Land	42,000	Retained earnings	44,000
Total	$77,000	Total	$77,000

The following accounting events apply to Porser Company's Year 2 fiscal year:

Jan. 1 Acquired $15,000 cash from the issue of common stock.
1 Purchased a truck that cost $22,000 and had a $2,000 salvage value and a four-year useful life.
Feb. 1 Borrowed $12,000 by issuing a note that had a 9 percent annual interest rate and a one-year term.
1 Paid $3,000 cash in advance for a one-year lease for office space.
Mar. 1 Paid a $2,000 cash dividend to the stockholders.
April 1 Purchased land that cost $28,000 cash.
May 1 Made a cash payment on accounts payable of $4,000.
July 1 Received $5,400 cash in advance as a retainer for services to be performed monthly over the next 12 months.
Sept. 1 Sold land for $42,000 that originally cost $42,000.
Oct. 1 Purchased $5,000 of supplies on account.
Dec. 31 Earned $42,000 of service revenue on account during the year.
31 Received cash collections from accounts receivable amounting to $40,000.
31 Incurred other operating expenses on account during the year that amounted to $6,000.
31 Incurred accrued salaries expense of $5,200.
31 Had $200 of supplies on hand at the end of the period.

Required

Based on the preceding information, answer the following questions. All questions pertain to the Year 2 financial statements. (*Hint:* Enter items in general ledger accounts under the accounting equation before answering the questions.)

a. Based on the preceding transaction, identify four additional adjustments and describe them.
b. What amount of interest expense would Porser report on the income statement?
c. What amount of net cash flow from operating activities would Porser report on the statement of cash flows?
d. What amount of rent expense would Porser report on the income statement?
e. What amount of total liabilities would Porser report on the balance sheet?
f. What amount of supplies expense would Porser report on the income statement?
g. What amount of unearned revenue would Porser report on the balance sheet?
h. What amount of net cash flow from investing activities would Porser report on the statement of cash flows?
i. What amount of interest payable would Porser report on the balance sheet?
j. What amount of total expenses would Porser report on the income statement?
k. What amount of retained earnings would Porser report on the balance sheet?
l. What amount of service revenues would Porser report on the income statement?
m. What amount of cash flows from financing activities would Porser report on the statement of cash flows?
n. What amount of net income would Porser report on the income statement?

MULTIPLE-CHOICE QUESTIONS

Multiple-choice questions are available in **Connect.**

EXERCISES—SERIES B

Where applicable in all exercises, round computations to the nearest dollar.

LO 2-1, 2-3

Exercise 2-1B *Effect of collecting accounts receivable on the accounting equation and financial statements*

Smith Company earned $12,000 of service revenue on account during Year 1. The company collected $9,800 cash from accounts receivable during Year 1.

Required

Based on this information alone, determine the following for Smith Company. (*Hint:* Record the events in general ledger accounts under an accounting equation before satisfying the requirements.)

a. The balance of the accounts receivable that Smith would report on the December 31, Year 1, balance sheet.
b. The amount of net income that Smith would report on the Year 1 income statement.
c. The amount of net cash flow from operating activities that would be reported on the Year 1 statement of cash flows.
d. The amount of retained earnings that would be reported on the Year 1 balance sheet.
e. Why are the answers to Requirements *b* and *c* different?

Exercise 2-2B *Effect of accrued expenses on the accounting equation and financial statements*

LO 2-2, 2-3

During Year 1, Star Corporation earned $5,000 of cash revenue and accrued $3,000 of salaries expense.

Required

(*Hint:* Record the events in general ledger accounts under an accounting equation before satisfying the requirements.) Based on this information alone:

a. Prepare the December 31, Year 1, balance sheet.
b. Determine the amount of net income that Star would report on the Year 1 income statement.
c. Determine the amount of net cash flow from operating activities that Star would report on the Year 1 statement of cash flows.
d. Why are the answers to Requirements *b* and *c* different?

Exercise 2-3B *Effect of accruals on the financial statements*

LO 2-1, 2-2, 2-3

Talley Inc. experienced the following events in Year 1, in its first year of operation:

1. Received $20,000 cash from the issue of common stock.
2. Performed services on account for $38,000.
3. Paid the utility expense of $2,500.
4. Collected $21,000 of the accounts receivable.
5. Recorded $15,000 of accrued salaries at the end of the year.
6. Paid a $2,000 cash dividend to the shareholders.

Required

a. Record the events in general ledger accounts under an accounting equation. In the last column of the table, provide appropriate account titles for the Retained Earnings amounts. The first transaction has been recorded as an example.

TALLEY INC.
General Ledger Accounts

Event	Assets		=	Liabilities	+	Stockholders' Equity		Acct. Titles for Ret. Earn.
	Cash	Accounts Receivable		Salaries Payable		Common Stock	Retained Earnings	
1.	20,000					20,000		

b. Prepare the income statement, statement of changes in stockholders' equity, balance sheet, and statement of cash flows for the Year 1 accounting period.
c. Why is the amount of net income different from the amount of net cash flow from operating activities?

Chapter 2

LO 2-1, 2-2, 2-3

Exercise 2-4B Effect of accounts receivable and accounts payable transactions on financial statements

The following events apply to Parker and Moates, a public accounting firm, for the Year 1 accounting period:

1. Performed $96,000 of services for clients on account.
2. Performed $65,000 of services for cash.
3. Incurred $45,000 of other operating expenses on account.
4. Paid $26,000 cash to an employee for salary.
5. Collected $70,000 cash from accounts receivable.
6. Paid $38,000 cash on accounts payable.
7. Paid a $10,000 cash dividend to the stockholders.
8. Accrued salaries were $3,000 at the end of Year 1.

Required

a. Show the effects of the events on the financial statements using a horizontal statements model like the following one. In the Cash Flow column, use OA to designate operating activity, IA for investment activity, FA for financing activity, and NC for net change in cash. Use NA to indicate the element is not affected by the event. The first event is recorded as an example.

Event No.	Assets		=	Liabilities		+	Equity						
	Cash	+ Accts. Rec.	=	Accts. Pay	+ Sal. Pay	+	Ret. Earn.	Rev.	−	Exp.	=	Net Inc.	Cash Flow
1	NA	+ 96,000	=	NA	+ NA	+	96,000	96,000	−	NA	=	96,000	NA

b. What is the amount of total assets at the end of Year 1?
c. What is the balance of accounts receivable at the end of Year 1?
d. What is the balance of accounts payable at the end of Year 1?
e. What is the difference between accounts receivable and accounts payable?
f. What is net income for Year 1?
g. What is the amount of net cash flow from operating activities for Year 1?

LO 2-3

Exercise 2-5B Missing information related to accruals

Graphic Design Inc. had a beginning balance of $2,000 in its Accounts Receivable account. The ending balance of Accounts Receivable was $2,400. During the period, Graphic Design recognized $40,000 of revenue on account. The Salaries Payable account has a beginning balance of $1,300 and an ending balance of $900. During the period, the company recognized $35,000 of accrued salary expense.

Required

a. Based on the information provided, determine the amount of net income.
b. Based on the information provided, determine the amount of net cash flow from operating activities.

LO 2-3

Exercise 2-6B Effect of accruals on the financial statements

Rosewood Inc. experienced the following events in Year 1, its first year of operation:

1. Received $50,000 cash from the issue of common stock.
2. Performed services on account for $67,000.
3. Paid a $5,000 cash dividend to the stockholders.
4. Collected $45,000 of the accounts receivable.
5. Paid $49,000 cash for other operating expenses.
6. Performed services for $10,000 cash.
7. Recognized $2,000 of accrued utilities expense at the end of the year.

Required

a. Identify the events that result in revenue or expense recognition.

b. Based on your response to Requirement *a*, determine the amount of net income reported on the Year 1 income statement.

c. Identify the events that affect the statement of cash flows.

d. Based on your response to Requirement *c*, determine the amount of cash flow from operating activities reported on the Year 1 statement of cash flows.

e. What is the before- and after-closing balance in the Service Revenue account? What other accounts would be closed at the end of the accounting cycle?

f. What is the balance of the Retained Earnings account that appears on the Year 1 balance sheet?

Exercise 2-7B *Net income versus changes in cash*   LO 2-3

In Year 1, Hall Inc. billed its customers $62,000 for services performed. The company collected $51,000 of the amount billed. Hall incurred $39,000 of other operating expenses on account. Hall paid $31,000 of the accounts payable. Hall acquired $40,000 cash from the issue of common stock. The company invested $21,000 cash in the purchase of land.

Required

(*Hint:* Identify the six events described in the paragraph and record them in general ledger accounts under an accounting equation before attempting to answer the questions.) Use the preceding information to answer the following questions:

a. What amount of revenue will be reported on the Year 1 income statement?

b. What amount of cash flow from revenue will be reported on the statement of cash flows?

c. What is the net income for the period?

d. What is the net cash flow from operating activities for the period?

e. Why is the amount of net income different from the net cash flow from operating activities for the period?

f. What is the amount of net cash flow from investing activities?

g. What is the amount of net cash flow from financing activities?

h. What amounts of total assets, liabilities, and equity will be reported on the year-end balance sheet?

Exercise 2-8B *Closing entries*   LO 2-4

Beatty Company's accounting records show an after-closing balance of $19,400 in its Retained Earnings account on December 31, Year 2. During the Year 2 accounting cycle, Beatty earned $15,100 of revenue, incurred $9,200 of expense, and paid $1,500 of dividends. Revenues and expenses were recognized evenly throughout the accounting period.

Required

a. Determine the balance in the Retained Earnings account as of January 1, Year 3.

b. Determine the balance in the temporary accounts as of January 1, Year 2.

c. Determine the after-closing balance in the Retained Earnings account as of December 31, Year 1.

d. Determine the balance in the Retained Earnings account as of June 30, Year 2.

Exercise 2-9B *Closing the accounts*   LO 2-4

The following information was drawn from the accounting records of Earles Company as of December 31, Year 2, before the temporary accounts had been closed. The Cash balance was $6,000, and Notes Payable amounted to $3,000. The company had revenues of $7,000 and expenses of $4,200. The company's Land account had a $4,000 balance. Dividends amounted to $1,000. There was $2,000 of common stock issued.

Required

a. Identify which accounts would be classified as permanent and which accounts would be classified as temporary.

b. Assuming that Earles' beginning balance (as of January 1, Year 2) in the Retained Earnings account was $5,200, determine its balance after the temporary accounts were closed at the end of Year 2.
c. What amount of net income would Earles Company report on its Year 2 income statement?
d. Explain why the amount of net income differs from the amount of the ending Retained Earnings balance.
e. What are the balances in the revenue, expense, and dividend accounts on January 1, Year 3?

LO 2-4

Exercise 2-10B *Closing accounts and the accounting cycle*

Required

a. Identify which of the following accounts are temporary (will be closed to Retained Earnings at the end of the year) and which are permanent:
   (1) Service Revenue
   (2) Dividends
   (3) Common Stock
   (4) Notes Payable
   (5) Cash
   (6) Rent Expense
   (7) Accounts Receivable
   (8) Utilities Expense
   (9) Prepaid Insurance
   (10) Retained Earnings

b. Sam bragged that he had five years of accounting experience. Susan disagreed, responding, "No. You have had one year of accounting experience five times." Explain what Susan meant. (*Hint:* Refer to the accounting cycle.)

LO 2-4

Exercise 2-11B *Matching concept*

Companies make sacrifices known as *expenses* to obtain benefits called *revenues*. The accurate measurement of net income requires that expenses be matched with revenues. In some circumstances, matching a particular expense directly with revenue is difficult or impossible. In these circumstances, the expense is matched with the period in which it is incurred.

Required

Distinguish the following items that could be matched directly with revenues from the items that would be classified as period expenses:

a. Sales commissions paid to employees.
b. Advertising expense.
c. Supplies.
d. The cost of land that has been sold.

EXERCISES—SERIES B

LO 2-5

Exercise 2-12B *Supplies and the financial statements model*

Handy Andy Inc. began the Year 2 accounting period with $9,000 cash, $5,000 of common stock, and $4,000 of retained earnings. Handy Andy was affected by the following accounting events during Year 2:
1. Purchased $9,500 of operating expenses supplies on account.
2. Earned and collected $32,500 of cash revenue.
3. Paid $7,200 cash on accounts payable.
4. Adjusted the records to reflect the use of supplies. A physical count indicated that $1,700 of supplies was still on hand on December 31, Year 2.

Required

a. Show the effects of the events on the financial statements using a horizontal statements model like the following one. In the Cash Flow column, use OA to designate operating activity, IA for investing activity, FA for financing activity, and NC for net change in cash. Use NA to indicate accounts not affected by the event. The beginning balances are entered in the following example:

Event No.	Assets			=	Liab.	+	Stockholders' Equity			Rev.	−	Exp.	=	Net Inc.	Cash Flow
	Cash	+	Supplies	=	Accts. Pay	+	Com. Stk.	+	Ret. Earn.						
Beg. bal.	9,000	+	0	=	0	+	5,000	+	4,000	0	−	0	=	0	0

b. Explain the difference between the amount of net income and amount of net cash flow from operating activities.

Exercise 2-13B *Supplies on financial statements*   LO 2-5, 2-8

Janitorial Professionals Inc. experienced the following events in Year 1, its first year of operation:
1. Performed services for $20,000 cash.
2. Purchased $4,000 of supplies on account.
3. A physical count on December 31, Year 1, found that there were $1,000 of supplies on hand.

Required

Based on this information alone:
a. Record the events in general ledger accounts under an accounting equation.
b. Prepare an income statement, balance sheet, and statement of cash flows for the Year 1 accounting period.
c. What is the balance in the Supplies account as of January 1, Year 2?
d. What is the balance in the Supplies Expense account as of January 1, Year 2?

Exercise 2-14B *Asset versus expense*   LO 2-5, 2-6

A cost can be either an asset or an expense.

Required

a. Distinguish between a cost that is an asset and a cost that is an expense.
b. List three costs that are assets.
c. List three costs that are expenses.

Exercise 2-15B *Prepaid items on financial statements*   LO 2-6

Forestry Services Inc. experienced the following events in Year 1, its first year of operation:
1. Performed counseling services for $18,000 cash.
2. On February 1, Year 1, paid $12,000 cash to rent office space for the coming year.
3. Adjusted the accounts to reflect the amount of rent used during the year.

Required

Based on this information alone:
a. Record the events in general ledger accounts under an accounting equation.
b. Prepare an income statement, balance sheet, and statement of cash flows for the Year 1 accounting period.
c. Ignoring all other future events, what is the amount of rent expense that would be recognized in Year 2?

LO 2-6, 2-8

Exercise 2-16B *Effect of an error on financial statements*

On June 1, Year 1, Ark Corporation paid $8,400 to purchase a 24-month insurance policy. Assume that Ark records the purchase as an asset and that the books are closed on December 31.

Required

a. Show the purchase of the insurance policy and the related adjusting entry to recognize insurance expense in the accounting equation.

b. Assume that Ark Corporation failed to record the adjusting entry to reflect the expiration of insurance. How would the error affect the company's Year 1 income statement and balance sheet?

LO 2-7

Exercise 2-17B *Unearned items on financial statements*

Interior Design Consultants (IDC) experienced the following events in Year 1, its first year of operation:

1. On October 1, Year 1, IDC collected $24,000 for consulting services it agreed to provide during the coming year.
2. Adjusted the accounts to reflect the amount of consulting service revenue recognized in Year 1.

Required

Based on this information alone:

a. Record the events under an accounting equation.
b. Prepare an income statement, balance sheet, and statement of cash flows for the Year 1 accounting period.
c. Ignoring all other future events, what is the amount of service revenue that would be recognized in Year 2?

LO 2-7

Exercise 2-18B *Unearned revenue defined as a liability*

Jake Lewis received $800 in advance for tutoring fees when he agreed to help Laura Dalton with her introductory accounting course. Upon receiving the cash, Jake mentioned that he would have to record the transaction as a liability on his books. Laura asked, "Why a liability? You don't owe me any money, do you?"

Required

Respond to Laura's question regarding Jake's liability.

LO 2-5, 2-7

Exercise 2-19B *Supplies, unearned revenue, and the financial statements model*

Warren, Attorney at Law, experienced the following transactions in Year 1, the first year of operations:

1. Purchased $1,500 of office supplies on account.
2. Accepted $36,000 on February 1, Year 1, as a retainer for services to be performed evenly over the next 12 months.
3. Performed legal services for cash of $84,000.
4. Paid cash for salaries expense of $32,000.
5. Paid a cash dividend to the stockholders of $8,000.
6. Paid $1,200 of the amount due on accounts payable.
7. Determined that at the end of the accounting period, $150 of office supplies remained on hand.
8. On December 31, Year 1, recognized the revenue that had been earned for services performed in accordance with Transaction 2.

Required

Show the effects of the events on the financial statements using a horizontal statements model like the following one. In the Cash Flow column, use the initials OA to designate operating activity, IA for investing activity, FA for financing activity, and NC for net change in cash. Use NA to indicate accounts not affected by the event. The first event has been recorded as an example.

Event No.	Assets			=	Liabilities			+	Stk. Equity	Rev.	−	Exp.	=	Net Inc.	Cash Flow
	Cash	+	Supplies	=	Accts. Pay	+	Unearn. Rev.	+	Ret. Earn.						
1	NA	+	1,500	=	1,500	+	NA	+	NA	NA	−	NA	=	NA	NA

Exercise 2-20B Unearned revenue and the financial statements model   LO 2-7

Brandon Baily started a personal financial planning business when he accepted $120,000 cash as advance payment for managing the financial assets of a large estate. Baily agreed to manage the estate for a one-year period beginning May 1, Year 1.

Required

a. Show the effects of the advance payment and revenue recognition on the Year 1 financial statements using a horizontal statements model like the following one. In the Cash Flows column, use OA to designate operating activity, IA for investing activity, FA for financing activity, and NC for net change in cash. Use NA if the account is not affected.

Event	Assets	=	Liab.	+	Stockholder's Equity	Rev.	−	Exp.	=	Net Inc.	Cash Flows
	Cash	=	Unearn. Rev.	+	Ret. Earn.						

b. How much revenue would Baily recognize on the Year 2 income statement?
c. What is the amount of cash flow from operating activities in Year 2?

Exercise 2-21B Prepaid vs. unearned, the entity concept   LO 2-6, 2-7

On October 1, Year 1, Stokes Company paid Eastport Rentals $4,800 for a 12-month lease on warehouse space.

Required

a. Record the deferral and the related December 31, Year 1, adjustment for Stokes Company in the accounting equation.
b. Record the deferral and the related December 31, Year 1, adjustment for Eastport Rentals in the accounting equation.

Exercise 2-22B Identifying deferral and accrual events   LO 2-1, 2-2, 2-5, 2-6, 2-7

Required

Identify each of the following events as an accrual, deferral, or neither:
a. Incurred other operating expenses on account.
b. Recorded expense for salaries owed to employees at the end of the accounting period.
c. Paid a cash dividend to the stockholders.
d. Paid cash to purchase supplies to be used over the next several months.
e. Paid cash to purchase land.
f. Provided services on account.
g. Collected accounts receivable.
h. Paid one year's rent in advance.
i. Paid cash for utilities expense.
j. Collected $2,400 in advance for services to be performed over the next 12 months.
k. Recognized revenue on account at the end of the period.

LO 2-1, 2-2, 2-5, 2-6, 2-7

Exercise 2-23B *Revenue and expense recognition*

Required

a. Describe a revenue recognition event that results in an increase in assets.
b. Describe a revenue recognition event that results in a decrease in liabilities.
c. Describe an expense recognition event that results in an increase in liabilities.
d. Describe an expense recognition event that results in a decrease in assets.

LO 2-5, 2-6, 2-7

Exercise 2-24B *Adjusting the accounts*

Patal Inc. experienced the following accounting events during its Year 1 accounting period:

1. Paid cash to settle an account payable.
2. Collected a cash advance for services that will be provided during the coming year.
3. Paid a cash dividend to the stockholders.
4. Paid cash for a one-year lease to rent office space.
5. Collected cash from accounts receivable.
6. Recognized cash revenue.
7. Issued common stock.
8. Paid cash to purchase land.
9. Paid cash to purchase supplies.
10. Recognized operating expenses on account.

Required

a. Identify the events that would require a year-end adjusting entry.
b. Are adjusting or closing entries recorded first? Why?

LO 2-8

Exercise 2-25B *Classifying events on the statement of cash flows*

The following transactions pertain to the operations of Blair Company for Year 1:

1. Acquired $30,000 cash from the issue of common stock.
2. Performed services for $12,000 cash.
3. Paid a $7,200 cash advance for a one-year contract to rent equipment.
4. Recognized $15,000 of accrued salary expense.
5. Accepted a $21,000 cash advance for services to be performed in the future.
6. Provided $60,000 of services on account.
7. Incurred $28,000 of other operating expenses on account.
8. Collected $51,000 cash from accounts receivable.
9. Paid a $5,000 cash dividend to the stockholders.
10. Paid $22,000 cash on accounts payable.

Required

a. Classify the cash flows from these transactions as operating activities (OA), investing activities (IA), or financing activities (FA). Use NA for transactions that do not affect the statement of cash flows.
b. Prepare a statement of cash flows. (There is no beginning cash balance.)

LO 2-8

Exercise 2-26B *Relationship of accounts to financial statements*

Required

Identify whether each of the following items would appear on the income statement (IS), statement of changes in stockholders' equity (SE), balance sheet (BS), or statement of cash flows (CF). Some items may appear on more than one statement; if so, identify all applicable statements. If an item would not appear on any financial statement, label it NA.

a. Consulting Revenue
b. Market Value of Land
c. Supplies Expense
d. Salaries Payable
e. Notes Payable
f. Ending Common Stock
g. Beginning Cash Balance
h. Prepaid Rent
i. Net Change in Cash
j. Land
k. Operating Expenses
l. Total Liabilities
m. "As of" Date Notation
n. Salaries Expense
o. Net Income
p. Service Revenue
q. Cash Flow from Operating Activities
r. Operating Income
s. Interest Receivable
t. Interest Revenue
u. Rent Expense
v. Delivery Expense
w. Total Stockholders' Equity
x. Unearned Revenue
y. Cash Flow from Investing Activities
z. Insurance Expense
aa. Ending Retained Earnings
bb. Interest Revenue
cc. Supplies
dd. Beginning Retained Earnings
ee. Utilities Payable
ff. Cash Flow from Financing Activities
gg. Accounts Receivable
hh. Prepaid Insurance
ii. Ending Cash Balance
jj. Utilities Expense
kk. Accounts Payable
ll. Beginning Common Stock
mm. Dividends
nn. Total Assets

Exercise 2-27B *Effect of accounting events on the income statement and statement of cash flows*

LO 2-8

Required

Explain how each of the following events or series of events and the related adjusting entry will affect the amount of *net income* and the amount of *cash flow from operating activities* reported on the year-end financial statements. Identify the direction of change (increase, decrease, or NA) and the amount of the change. Organize your answers according to the following table. The first event is recorded as an example. If an event does not have a related adjusting entry, record only the effects of the event.

	Net Income		Cash Flows from Operating Activities	
Event	Direction of Change	Amount of Change	Direction of Change	Amount of Change
a	NA	NA	NA	NA

a. Acquired $60,000 cash from the issue of common stock.
b. Earned $20,000 of revenue on account. Collected $15,000 cash from accounts receivable.
c. Paid $4,800 cash on October 1 to purchase a one-year insurance policy.
d. Collected $12,000 in advance for services to be performed in the future. The contract called for services to start on August 1 and to continue for one year.
e. Accrued salaries amounting to $5,000.
f. Sold land that cost $15,000 for $15,000 cash.
g. Provided services for $9,200 cash.
h. Purchased $2,000 of supplies on account. Paid $1,500 cash on accounts payable. The ending balance in the Supplies account, after adjustment, was $800.
i. Paid cash for other operating expenses of $2,200.

LO 2-9

Exercise 2-28B *Transactions that affect the elements of financial statements*

Required

Give an example of a transaction that will
a. Increase an asset and decrease another asset (asset exchange event).
b. Increase an asset and increase a liability (asset source event).
c. Decrease an asset and decrease a liability (asset use event).
d. Decrease an asset and decrease equity (asset use event).
e. Increase a liability and decrease equity (claims exchange event).
f. Increase an asset and increase equity (asset source event).
g. Decrease a liability and increase equity (claims exchange event).

LO 2-9

Exercise 2-29B *Identifying source, use, and exchange transactions*

Required

Indicate whether each of the following transactions is an asset source (AS), asset use (AU), asset exchange (AE), or claims exchange (CE) transaction:
a. Performed services for clients on account.
b. Paid cash for salary expense.
c. Acquired cash from the issue of common stock.
d. Incurred other operating expenses on account.
e. Performed services for cash.
f. Paid cash on accounts payable.
g. Collected cash from accounts receivable.
h. Paid a cash dividend to the stockholders.
i. Received cash for services to be performed in the future.
j. Purchased land with cash.

LO 2-9

Exercise 2-30B *Identifying asset source, use, and exchange transactions*

Required

a. Name an asset use transaction that will affect the income statement.
b. Name an asset use transaction that will *not* affect the income statement.
c. Name an asset exchange transaction that will *not* affect the statement of cash flows.
d. Name an asset exchange transaction that will affect the statement of cash flows.
e. Name an asset source transaction that will *not* affect the income statement.

LO 2-8, 2-9

Exercise 2-31B *Identifying transaction type and effect on the financial statements*

Required

Identify whether each of the following transactions is an asset source (AS), asset use (AU), asset exchange (AE), or claims exchange (CE). Also show the effects of the events on the financial statements using the horizontal statements model. Indicate whether the event increases (I), decreases (D), or does not affect (NA) each element of the financial statements. In the Cash Flows column, designate the cash flows as operating activities (OA), investing activities (IA), or financing activities (FA). The first two transactions have been recorded as examples.

Event	Type of Event	Assets	=	Liabilities	+	Common Stock	+	Retained Earnings	Rev.	−	Exp.	=	Net Inc.	Cash Flows
a	AE	I/D		NA		NA		NA	NA		NA		NA	D IA
b	AS	I		NA		I		NA	NA		NA		NA	I FA

a. Purchased land for cash.
b. Acquired cash from the issue of common stock.
c. Collected cash from accounts receivable.
d. Paid cash for operating expenses.
e. Recorded accrued salaries.
f. Purchased supplies on account.
g. Performed services on account.
h. Paid cash in advance for rent on office space.
i. Adjusted the books to record supplies used during the period.
j. Performed services for cash.
k. Paid cash for salaries accrued at the end of a prior period.
l. Paid a cash dividend to the stockholders.
m. Adjusted books to reflect the amount of prepaid rent expired during the period.
n. Incurred operating expenses on account.
o. Paid cash on accounts payable.
p. Received cash advance for services to be provided in the future.
q. Recognized revenue on account at the end of the accounting period.

Exercise 2-32B *Ethical conduct* LO 2-10

An October 31, 2012, news release from Hewlett-Packard Company (HP) included the following:

> HP recorded a non-cash charge for the impairment of goodwill and intangible assets within its Software segment of approximately $8.8 billion in the fourth quarter of its 2012 fiscal year. The majority of this impairment charge is linked to serious accounting improprieties, disclosure failures and outright misrepresentations at Autonomy Corporation that occurred prior to HP's acquisition of Autonomy and the associated impact of those improprieties, failures and misrepresentations on the expected future financial performance of the Autonomy business over the long-term.

Required

Comment on the provisions of SOX that pertain to intentional misrepresentation and describe the maximum penalty the CFO could face.

Exercise 2-33B *Effect of depreciation on the accounting equation and financial statements (Appendix)* LO 2-11

The following events apply to Highland Grill for the Year 1 fiscal year:
1. Started the company when it acquired $40,000 cash by issuing common stock.
2. Purchased a new stove that cost $24,000 cash.
3. Earned $21,000 in cash revenue.
4. Paid $3,500 of cash for salaries expense.
5. Adjusted the records to reflect the use of the stove. Purchased on January 1, Year 1, the stove has an expected useful life of four years and an estimated salvage value of $4,000. Use straight-line depreciation. The adjusting entry was made as of December 31, Year 1.

Required

a. Record the events in general ledger accounts under an accounting equation.
b. Prepare a balance sheet and a statement of cash flows for the Year 1 accounting period.
c. What is the net income for Year 1?
d. What is the amount of depreciation expense Highland Grill would report on the Year 2 income statement?
e. What amount of accumulated depreciation would Highland Grill report on the December 31, Year 2, balance sheet?
f. Would the cash flow from operating activities be affected by depreciation in Year 2?

Chapter 2

LO 2-11

Exercise 2-34B *Depreciation affecting multiple cycles (Appendix)*

On January 1, Year 1, Yallow Cab Inc. paid $29,000 cash to purchase a taxi cab. The taxi had a four-year useful life and a $5,000 salvage value.

Required

a. Determine the amount of depreciation expense that would appear on the Year 1 and Year 2 income statements.

b. Determine the amount of accumulated depreciation that would appear on the Year 1 and Year 2 balance sheets.

c. Explain how the purchase of equipment would affect the Year 1 and Year 2 statements of cash flows.

LO 2-12

Exercise 2-35B *Effects of recognizing accrued interest on financial statements (Appendix)*

Carry Connelly started Connelly Company on January 1, Year 1. The company experienced the following events during its first year of operation:

1. Earned $6,200 of cash revenue.
2. Borrowed $10,000 cash from the bank.
3. Adjusted the accounting records to recognize accrued interest expense on the bank note. The note, issued on September 1, Year 1, had a one-year term and a 9 percent annual interest rate.

Required

a. What is the amount of interest payable at December 31, Year 1?
b. What is the amount of interest expense in Year 1?
c. What is the amount of interest paid in Year 1?
d. Use a horizontal statements model to show how each event affects the balance sheet, income statement, and statement of cash flows. Indicate whether the event increases (I) decreases (D), or does not affect (NA) each element of the financial statements. Also, in the Cash Flows column, designate the cash flows as operating activities (OA), investing activities (IA), or financing activities (FA). The first transaction has been recorded as an example.

Event No.			Balance Sheet							Income Statement				Statement of Cash Flows
	Cash	=	Note Pay.	+	Int. Pay	+	C. Stk.	+	Ret. Earn.	Rev.	−	Exp.	=	Net Inc.	
1	I	=	NA	+	NA	+	NA	+	I	I	−	NA	=	I	I OA

LO 2-12

Exercise 2-36B *Recognizing accrued interest expense (Appendix)*

California Company borrowed $120,000 from the issuance of a note payable on August 1, Year 1. The note had a 7 percent annual rate of interest and a one-year term to maturity.

Required

a. What amount of interest expense will California recognize for the year ending December 31, Year 1?
b. Show how the December 31, Year 1, adjusting entry to recognize the accrued interest expense affects the accounting equation.
c. What amount of cash will California pay for interest expense in Year 1?
d. What is the amount of interest payable as of December 31, Year 1?
e. What amount of cash will California pay for interest expense in Year 2?
f. What amount of interest expense will California recognize in Year 2?
g. What is the amount of interest payable as of December 31, Year 2?

PROBLEMS—SERIES B

Problem 2-37B *Effect of adjusting entries on the accounting equation*

LO 2-5, 2-6, 2-7

CHECK FIGURE
b. Adjustment amount: $2,200

Required

Each of the following independent events requires a year-end adjusting entry. Show how each event and its related adjusting entry affect the accounting equation. Assume a December 31 closing date. The first event is recorded as an example.

Event/Adjustment	Total Assets			=	Liabilities	+	Stockholders' Equity	
	Cash	+	Other Assets				Common Stock	+ Retained Earnings
a	−6,000		+6,000		NA		NA	NA
Adj.	NA		−4,500		NA		NA	−4,500

a. Paid $6,000 cash in advance on April 1 for a one-year insurance policy.
b. Purchased $2,400 of supplies on account. At year's end, $200 of supplies remained on hand.
c. Paid $7,200 cash in advance on March 1 for a one-year lease on office space.
d. Received an $18,000 cash advance for a contract to provide services in the future. The contract required a one-year commitment starting September 1.

Problem 2-38B *Closing the accounts*

LO 2-3, 2-8

The following selected accounts and account balances were taken from the records of Wages Company. Except as otherwise indicated, all balances are as of December 31, Year 2, before the closing entries were recorded.

Cash received from common stock issued during Year 2	$4,500
Cash	10,500
Revenue	18,000
Salary expense	13,000
Cash flow from operating activities	4,500
Notes payable	6,000
Utility expense	1,800
Dividends	1,000
Cash flow from financing activities	5,000
Rent expense	1,600
Land	25,000
Retained earnings, January 1, Year 2	19,700
Common stock, December 31, Year 2	20,000

Required

a. Prepare the income statement Wages would include in its Year 2 annual report.
b. Identify the accounts that should be closed to the Retained Earnings account.
c. Determine the Retained Earnings account balance at December 31, Year 2. Identify the reasons for the difference between net income and the ending balance in Retained Earnings.
d. What are the balances in the Revenue, Expense, and Dividend accounts on January 1, Year 3? Explain.

Problem 2-39B *Show how the events affect the financial statements using a horizontal statements model*

LO 2-8

The following events pertain to Weaver Cleaning Company:
1. Acquired $15,000 cash from the issue of common stock.
2. Provided services for $6,000 cash.
3. Provided $18,000 of services on account.
4. Collected $11,000 cash from the account receivable created in Event 3.
5. Paid $1,400 cash to purchase supplies.

6. Had $100 of supplies on hand at the end of the accounting period.
7. Received $3,600 cash in advance for services to be performed in the future.
8. Performed one-half of the services agreed to in Event 7.
9. Paid $6,500 for salaries expense.
10. Incurred $2,800 of other operating expenses on account.
11. Paid $2,100 cash on the account payable created in Event 10.
12. Paid a $1,000 cash dividend to the stockholders.

Required

Show the effects of the events on the financial statements using a horizontal statements model like the following one. In the Cash Flow column, use the letters OA to designate operating activity, IA for investing activity, FA for financing activity, and NC for net change in cash. Use NA to indicate accounts not affected by the event. The first event is recorded as an example.

Event No.	Cash	+	Accts. Rec.	+	Supp.	=	Accts. Pay.	+	Unearn. Rev.	+	Com. Stk.	+	Ret. Earn.		Rev.	−	Exp.	=	Net Inc.		Cash Flow
1	15,000	+	NA	+	NA	=	NA	+	NA	+	15,000	+	NA		NA	−	NA	=	NA		15,000 FA

LO 2-3, 2-8

Problem 2-40B *Effect of events on financial statements*

Gossett Company had the following beginning balances in its accounting records as of January 1, Year 2:

Assets		Liabilities and Equity	
Cash	$ 60,000	Accounts Payable	$ 32,000
Accounts Receivable	45,000	Common Stock	60,000
Land	35,000	Retained Earnings	48,000
Totals	$140,000		$140,000

The following accounting events apply to Gossett for Year 2:

Jan. 1 Acquired an additional $30,000 cash from the issue of common stock.
April 1 Paid $7,200 cash in advance for a one-year lease for office space.
June 1 Paid a $5,000 cash dividend to the stockholders.
July 1 Purchased additional land that cost $40,000 cash.
Aug. 1 Made a cash payment on accounts payable of $21,000.
Sept. 1 Received $9,600 cash in advance as a retainer for services to be performed monthly during the next eight months.
Sept. 30 Sold land for $20,000 cash that had originally cost $20,000.
Oct. 1 Purchased $1,200 of supplies on account.
Dec. 31 Earned $75,000 of service revenue on account during the year.
    31 Received $62,000 cash collections from accounts receivable.
    31 Incurred $27,000 in other operating expenses on account during the year.
    31 Recognized accrued salaries expense of $18,000.
    31 Had $100 of supplies on hand at the end of the period.
    31 The land purchased on July 1 had a market value of $56,000.

Required

Based on the preceding information for Gossett Company, answer the following questions. All questions pertain to the Year 2 financial statements. (*Hint:* Record the events in general ledger accounts under an accounting equation before answering the questions.)

a. What amount would be reported for land on the balance sheet?
b. What amount of net cash flow from operating activities would be reported on the statement of cash flows?
c. What amount of rent expense would be reported on the income statement?

d. What amount of total liabilities would be reported on the balance sheet?
e. What amount of supplies expense would be reported on the income statement?
f. What amount of unearned revenue would be reported on the balance sheet?
g. What amount of net cash flow from investing activities would be reported on the statement of cash flows?
h. What amount of total expenses would be reported on the income statement?
i. What total amount of service revenue would be reported on the income statement?
j. What amount of cash flows from financing activities would be reported on the statement of cash flows?
k. What amount of net income would be reported on the income statement?
l. What amount of retained earnings would be reported on the balance sheet?

Problem 2-41B Identifying and arranging elements on financial statements

LO 2-3, 2-8

The following accounts and balances were drawn from the records of Shearer Company at December 31, Year 2:

Cash	$22,100	Accounts receivable	$21,000
Land	43,000	Cash flow from operating act.	8,600
Insurance expense	2,500	Beginning retained earnings	47,200
Dividends	5,000	Beginning common stock	5,500
Prepaid insurance	3,500	Service revenue	86,000
Accounts payable	15,000	Cash flow from financing act.	9,000
Supplies	2,100	Ending common stock	14,500
Supplies expense	1,000	Cash flow from investing act.	(6,000)
Rent expense	3,500	Other operating expenses	59,000

Required

Use the accounts and balances from Shearer Company to construct an income statement, statement of changes in stockholders' equity, balance sheet, and statement of cash flows (show only totals for each activity on the statement of cash flows).

Problem 2-42B Missing information in financial statements

LO 2-3, 2-8

Required

Fill in the blanks (indicated by the alphabetic letters in parentheses) in the following financial statements. Assume the company started operations January 1, Year 1, and all transactions involve cash.

	For the Years		
	Year 1	Year 2	Year 3
Income Statements			
Revenue	$ 400	$ 500	$ 800
Expense	(250)	(l)	(425)
Net income	$ (a)	$ 100	$ 375
Statements of Changes in Stockholders' Equity			
Beginning common stock	$ 0	$ (m)	$9,100
Plus: Common stock issued	(b)	1,100	310
Ending common stock	$8,000	9,100	(s)
Beginning retained earnings	0	25	75
Plus: Net income	(c)	100	375
Less: Dividends	(d)	(50)	(150)
Ending retained earnings	25	(n)	300
Total stockholders' equity	$ (e)	$9,175	$ (t)

continued

Balance Sheets

Assets			
Cash	$ (f)	$ (o)	$ (u)
Land	0	(p)	2,500
Total assets	$11,000	$11,650	$10,550
Liabilities	$ (g)	$ (q)	$ 840
Stockholders' equity			
Common stock	(h)	(r)	9,410
Retained earnings	(i)	75	300
Total stockholders' equity	8,025	9,175	9,710
Total liabilities and stockholders' equity	$11,000	$11,650	$10,550

Statements of Cash Flows

Cash flows from operating activities			
Cash receipts from customers	$ (j)	$ 500	$ (v)
Cash payments for expenses	(k)	(400)	(w)
Net cash flows from operating activities	150	100	375
Cash flows from investing activities			
Cash payments for land	0	(5,000)	0
Cash receipt from sale of land	0	0	2,500
Net cash flows from investing activities	0	(5,000)	2,500
Cash flows from financing activities			
Cash receipts from borrowed funds	2,975	0	0
Cash payments to reduce debt	0	(500)	(x)
Cash receipts from stock issue	8,000	1,100	(y)
Cash payments for dividends	(125)	(50)	(z)
Net cash flows from financing activities	10,850	550	(1,475)
Net change in cash	11,000	(4,350)	1,400
Plus: Beginning cash balance	0	11,000	6,650
Ending cash balance	$11,000	$ 6,650	$ 8,050

LO 2-3, 2-8, 2-9

Problem 2-43B *Events for two complete accounting cycles*

Iowa Service Company was formed on January 1, Year 1.

Events Affecting the Year 1 Accounting Period

1. Acquired cash of $60,000 from the issue of common stock.
2. Purchased $1,200 of supplies on account.
3. Purchased land that cost $18,000 cash.
4. Paid $800 cash to settle accounts payable created in Event 2.
5. Recognized revenue on account of $42,000.
6. Paid $21,000 cash for other operating expenses.
7. Collected $38,000 cash from accounts receivable.

Information for Year 1 Adjusting Entries

8. Recognized accrued salaries of $3,200 on December 31, Year 1.
9. Had $200 of supplies on hand at the end of the accounting period.

Events Affecting the Year 2 Accounting Period

1. Acquired an additional $20,000 cash from the issue of common stock.
2. Paid $3,200 cash to settle the salaries payable obligation.
3. Paid $3,600 cash in advance for a lease on office facilities.
4. Sold land that had cost $15,000 for $15,000 cash.
5. Received $4,800 cash in advance for services to be performed in the future.
6. Purchased $1,000 of supplies on account during the year.

7. Provided services on account of $32,000.
8. Collected $33,000 cash from accounts receivable.
9. Paid a cash dividend of $5,000 to the stockholders.
10. Paid other operating expenses of $19,500.

Information for Year 2 Adjusting Entries

11. The advance payment for rental of the office facilities (see Event 3) was made on March 1 for a one-year lease term.
12. The cash advance for services to be provided in the future was collected on October 1 (see Event 5). The one-year contract started October 1.
13. Had $300 of supplies on hand at the end of the period.
14. Recognized accrued salaries of $3,900 at the end of the accounting period.

Required

a. Identify each event affecting the Year 1 and Year 2 accounting periods as asset source (AS), asset use (AU), asset exchange (AE), or claims exchange (CE). Record the effects of each event under the appropriate general ledger account headings of the accounting equation.

b. Prepare an income statement, statement of changes in stockholders' equity, balance sheet, and statement of cash flows for Year 1 and Year 2, using the vertical statements model.

Problem 2-44B *Ethics*

LO 2-10

Raula Kato discovered a material reporting error in the accounting records of Sampoon, Inc. (SI) during the annual audit. The error was so significant that it will certainly have an adverse effect on the price of the client's stock, which is actively traded on the western stock exchange. After talking to his close friend, and president of SI, Kato agreed to withhold the information until the president had time to sell his SI stock. Kato leaked the information to his parents so they could sell their shares of stock as well. The reporting matter was a relatively complex issue that involved recently issued reporting standards. Kato told himself that if he were caught he would simply plead ignorance. He would simply say he did not have time to keep up with the rapidly changing standards and so would be off the hook.

Required

a. Write a memo that identifies specific principles of the AICPA Code of Professional Conduct that were violated by Kato.
b. Would pleading ignorance relieve Kato from his audit responsibilities?

Problem 2-45B *Effect of events on financial statements (Appendix)*

LO 2-3, 2-8, 2-11, 2-12

Oaks Company had the following balances in its accounting records as of December 31, Year 1:

Assets		Claims	
Cash	$ 61,000	Accounts payable	$ 25,000
Accounts receivable	45,000	Common stock	90,000
Land	27,000	Retained earnings	18,000
Totals	$133,000		$133,000

The following accounting events apply to Oaks' Year 2 fiscal year:

Jan. 1 Acquired an additional $70,000 cash from the issue of common stock.
      1 Purchased a delivery van that cost $26,000 and that had a $7,000 salvage value and a five-year useful life.
Mar. 1 Borrowed $21,000 by issuing a note that had an 8 percent annual interest rate and a one-year term.
April 1 Paid $6,600 cash in advance for a one-year lease for office space.
June 1 Paid a $3,000 cash dividend to the stockholders.
July 1 Purchased land that cost $25,000 cash.
Aug. 1 Made a cash payment on accounts payable of $13,000.

Sept. 1	Received $8,400 cash in advance as a retainer for services to be performed monthly during the next eight months.
Oct. 1	Purchased $900 of supplies on account.
Dec. 31	Earned $80,000 of service revenue on account during the year.
31	Received $56,000 cash collections from accounts receivable.
31	Incurred $16,000 in other operating expenses on account during the year.
31	Incurred accrued salaries expense of $5,000.
31	Had $250 of supplies on hand at the end of the period.

Required

Based on the preceding information, answer the following questions. All questions pertain to the Year 2 financial statements. (*Hint:* Record the events in general ledger accounts under an accounting equation before answering the questions.)

a. What additional four adjusting entries are required at the end of the year?
b. What amount of interest expense would Oaks report on the income statement?
c. What amount of net cash flow from operating activities would Oaks report on the statement of cash flows?
d. What amount of rent expense would Oaks report on the income statement?
e. What amount of total liabilities would Oaks report on the balance sheet?
f. What amount of supplies expense would Oaks report on the income statement?
g. What amount of unearned revenue would Oaks report on the balance sheet?
h. What amount of net cash flow from investing activities would Oaks report on the statement of cash flows?
i. What amount of interest payable would Oaks report on the balance sheet?
j. What amount of total expenses would Oaks report on the income statement?
k. What amount of retained earnings would Oaks report on the balance sheet?
l. What total amount of service revenues would Oaks report on the income statement?
m. What amount of cash flows from financing activities would Oaks report on the statement of cash flows?
n. What amount of net income would Oaks report on the income statement?

ANALYZE, THINK, COMMUNICATE

ATC 2-1 Business Applications Case *Understanding real-world annual reports*

Required

Obtain the **Target Corporation's** annual report at http://investors.target.com using the instructions in Appendix B, and use it to answer the following questions:

a. Which accounts on Target's balance sheet are accrual type accounts?
b. Which accounts on Target's balance sheet are deferral type accounts?
c. Compare Target's *net income* to its *cash provided by operating activities* for the fiscal-year ended January 28, 2017 (2016). Which is larger?
d. First, compare Target's 2015 net income to its 2016 net income. Next, compare Target's 2015 cash provided by operating activities to its 2016 cash provided by operating activities. Which changed the most from 2015 to 2016, net income or cash provided by operating activities?

ATC 2-2 Group Assignment *Missing information*

Verizon Communications, Inc. is one of the world's largest providers of communication services. The following information, taken from the company's annual reports, is available for the years 2016, 2015, and 2014:

	2016	2015	2014
Revenues	$125,980	$131,620	$127,079
Operating expenses	98,921	98,560	107,480

In 2013, Verizon's operating income was $31,968. Operating income is a subcategory of net income.

Required

a. Divide the class into groups of four or five students. Organize the groups into three sections. Assign each section of groups the financial data for one of the preceding accounting periods.

Group Tasks

(1) Determine the amount of net income for the year assigned.
(2) How does the result in item 1 above affect the retained earnings of the company?
(3) Compute the percentage growth rate for each year.
(4) Have representatives from each section put the income statement for their respective year on the board.

Class Discussion

b. Have the class discuss the trend in revenue and net income.

ATC 2-3 Business Application Case *Analyzing earnings information using real-world data*

The following data are based on information in the 2016 annual report of **Cracker Barrel Old Country Store**. As of July 29, 2016, Cracker Barrel operated 640 restaurants and gift shops in 43 states. Dollar amounts are in thousands.

	2016	2015
Assets	$1,497,664	$1,576,208
Liabilities	971,221	1,037,940
Stockholders' equity	526,443	538,268
Revenues	2,912,351	2,842,284
Expenses	2,723,052	2,678,381
Dividends	186,505	171,383
Retained earnings at end of 2014		$ 493,167

Required

a. Calculate the company's net income and retained earnings for 2015 and 2016.
b. Which increased (or decreased) by the greatest percentage amount: revenues or net income? Show your computations.
c. For each year, calculate the company's net income as a percentage of its revenues. Show your computations.
d. Did the company perform better in 2015 or 2016? Explain your answer.

ATC 2-4 Business Application Case *Analyzing cash flow information using real-world data*

The following data are based on information in the 2016 annual report of **Buffalo Wild Wings, Inc.** As of December 25, 2016, there were 1,240 Buffalo Wild Wings restaurants. The parent company owned 631 restaurants and 609 were franchised. Dollar amounts are in thousands.

	2016	2015
Assets	$1,047,219	$1,072,382
Liabilities	529,319	416,645
Stockholders' equity	517,900	655,737
Revenues	1,986,793	1,812,793
Expenses	1,892,048	1,717,653
Cash flows from operating activities	282,589	237,260
Cash flows from investing activities	(144,844)	(365,191)
Cash flows from financing activities	(99,666)	45,499
Cash balance at the beginning of 2015 was $93,329		

Required

a. Calculate the company's net change in cash for 2015 and 2016.
b. Calculate the company's ending cash balance for 2015 and 2016.
c. Notice that cash flows from investing activities were negative for each year. Do you think this represents something positive or negative about the company? Explain your answer.

ATC 2-5 Business Application Case   *Analyzing earnings information at two real-world companies*

The following data are based on information in the 2016 annual reports of **Abercrombie & Fitch, Co.** and **American Eagle Outfitters, Inc.** Dollar amounts are in thousands.

Abercrombie & Fitch is a specialty retailer of apparel and accessories for men and children. As of January 30, 2016, it operated 754 stores in the United States and 178 stores outside the United States.

American Eagle Outfitters, Inc. is a specialty retailer of clothing and accessories for men and women. As of January 30, 2016, it operated 904 stores in the United States and 143 stores outside the United States.

	Abercrombie & Fitch	American Eagle Outfitters
Assets	$2,433,039	$1,612,246
Liabilities	1,137,317	568,870
Stockholders' equity	1,295,722	1,051,376
Revenues	3,518,680	3,521,848
Expenses	3,483,104	3,303,710
Dividends	55,145	99,624
Retained earnings at the beginning of the year	2,550,673	1,543,085

Required

a. Calculate each company's net income and retained earnings for 2016.
b. For each company, calculate its net earnings as a percentage of its revenues. Show your computations.
c. Which company performed better in 2016? Explain your answer.

ATC 2-6 Business Application Case   *Analyzing cash flow information at two real-world companies*

The following data are based on information in the 2016 annual reports of **H&R Block, Inc.** and **Intuit, Inc.** Dollar amounts are in thousands.

H&R Block, Inc. has subsidiaries that provide tax, investment, retail banking, accounting, and business consulting services and products in the United States, Canada, and Australia. For the fiscal year ended April 30, 2016, the company prepared approximately 23 million tax returns.

Intuit, Inc. is the company that sells the popular tax preparation software **Turbo Tax**, along with its other major product, **QuickBooks**. In the fiscal year ended July 31, 2016, its products were used by more than 45 million customers.

	H&R Block	Intuit
Assets	$2,857,775	$ 4,250,000
Liabilities	2,834,672	3,089,000
Stockholders' equity	23,103	1,161,000
Revenues	3,038,153	4,694,000
Expenses	2,663,886	3,715,000
Cash flows from operating activities	532,394	1,401,000
Cash flows from investing activities	329,515	371,000
Cash flows from financing activities	(1,961,729)	(1,940,000)
Cash balance at the beginning of 2016	2,007,190	808,000

Accounting for Accruals and Deferrals   143

Required

a. Calculate each company's net income and net change in cash for 2016.
b. Calculate each company's ending cash balance for 2016.
c. Notice that cash flows from investing activities were positive for both companies. Write a brief explanation of your answer.
d. Notice that cash flows from financing activities were negative for both companies. Write a brief explanation as to what might have caused this.

ATC 2-7 Ethical Dilemma *What is a little deceit among friends?*

Glenn's Cleaning Services Company is experiencing cash flow problems and needs a loan. Glenn has a friend who is willing to lend him the money he needs provided she can be convinced that he will be able to repay the debt. Glenn has assured his friend that his business is viable, but his friend has asked to see the company's financial statements. Glenn's accountant produced the following financial statements:

Income Statement	
Service Revenue	$ 38,000
Operating Expenses	(70,000)
Net Loss	$ (32,000)

Balance Sheet	
Assets	$85,000
Liabilities	$35,000
Stockholders' Equity	
Common Stock	82,000
Retained Earnings	(32,000)
Total Liabilities and Stockholders' Equity	$85,000

Glenn made the following adjustments to these statements before showing them to his friend. He recorded $82,000 of revenue on account from Barrymore Manufacturing Company for a contract to clean its headquarters office building that was still being negotiated for the next month. Barrymore had scheduled a meeting to sign a contract the following week, so Glenn was sure that he would get the job. Barrymore was a reputable company, and Glenn was confident that he could ultimately collect the $82,000. Also, he subtracted $30,000 of accrued salaries expense and the corresponding liability. He reasoned that because he had not paid the employees, he had not incurred any expense.

Required

a. Reconstruct the income statement and balance sheet as they would appear after Glenn's adjustments. Comment on the accuracy of the adjusted financial statements.
b. Suppose you are Glenn and the $30,000 you owe your employees is due next week. If you are unable to pay them, they will quit and the business will go bankrupt. You are sure you will be able to repay your friend when your employees perform the $82,000 of services for Barrymore and you collect the cash. However, your friend is risk averse and is not likely to make the loan based on the financial statements your accountant prepared. Would you make the changes that Glenn made to get the loan and thereby save your company? Defend your position with a rational explanation.
c. Discuss the elements of the fraud triangle as they apply to Glenn's decision to change the financial statements to reflect more favorable results.

ATC 2-8 Research Assignment *Identifying accruals and deferrals at Netflix, Inc.*

This chapter defined and discussed accrual and deferral transactions. Complete the requirements below using the most recent financial statements available on the Internet for **Netflix, Inc.** Obtain the statements by following the steps below. (Be aware that the formatting of the company's website may have changed since these instructions were written.)

1. Go to www.netflix.com.
2. Click on "Investor Relations," which is at the bottom of the page in very small print.
3. Click on the "Annual Reports and Proxies" link at the left side of the page.
4. Click on the "20xx Annual Report." Use the .pdf version of the annual report.
5. Find the company's balance sheet and complete the requirements below. In recent years, this has been shown toward the end of the Form 10-K section of the company's annual report, around page 50. The "Index" near the beginning of the report can help you locate the financial statements.

Required

a. Make a list of all the accounts on the balance sheet that you believe are accrual type accounts.
b. Make a list of all the accounts on the balance sheet that you believe are deferral type accounts.

ATC 2-9 Spreadsheet Assignment *Using Excel*

Required

a. Refer to Problem 2-41B. Use an Excel spreadsheet to construct the required financial statements. To complete Requirement *b*, use formulas where normal arithmetic calculations are made within the financial statements (in particular the statement of changes in stockholders' equity).

b. It is interesting to speculate about what would happen if certain operating results change for better or worse. After completing Requirement *a*, change certain account balances for each of the following independent operating adjustments. After each adjustment, notice how the financial statements would differ if the change in operations were to occur. After noting the effect of each adjustment, return the data to the original amounts in Problem 2-41A and then go to the next operating adjustment.

In the following table, note the new amounts on the financial statements for the various operating changes listed:

Original	1	2	3	4	5
Net income					
Total assets					
Total liabilities					
Total stockholders' equity					
Total liabilities & stockholders' equity					

Independent Operating Adjustments

1. Revenue and the related Accounts Receivable increased $10,000.
2. Revenue and the related Accounts Receivable decreased $10,000.
3. Operating Expenses and the related Accounts Payable decreased $400.
4. Operating Expenses and the related Accounts Payable increased $400.
5. Dividends paid decreased $500 and cash changed accordingly.

ATC 2-10 Spreadsheet Assignment *Mastering Excel*

Refer to Problem 2-39B. Complete the requirements using an Excel spreadsheet. Refer to Chapter 1 problem ATC 1-8 for ideas on how to structure the spreadsheet.

COMPREHENSIVE PROBLEM

The trial balance of Pacilio Security Services, Inc. as of January 1, Year 2, was as follows:

Cash	$8,500
Land	4,000
Notes Payable	5,000
Common Stock	6,000
Retained Earnings	1,500

During Year 2, Pacilio Security Services experienced the following transactions:

1. Acquired an additional $2,000 from the issue of common stock.
2. Paid $3,000 on the debt owed to the Small Business Government Agency. The loan is interest-free.
3. Performed $21,000 of security services for numerous local events during the year; $15,000 was on account and $6,000 was cash.

4. On May 1, rented a small office building. Paid $2,400 for 12 months' rent in advance.
5. Purchased supplies on account for $650.
6. Paid salaries expense for the year of $8,000.
7. Incurred other operating expenses on account, $6,200.
8. On September 1, Year 2, a customer paid $600 for services to be provided over the next six months.
9. Collected $13,500 of accounts receivable during the year.
10. Paid $5,800 on accounts payable.
11. Paid $1,500 of advertising expenses for the year.
12. Paid a cash dividend to the shareholders of $1,000.
13. The market value of the land was determined to be $5,000 at December 31, Year 2.

Information for Adjustments

14. There was $65 of supplies on hand at the end of the year.
15. Recognized the expired rent.
16. Recognized the revenue earned from Transaction 8.
17. Accrued salaries were $1,200 at December 31, Year 2.

Required

a. Record the above transactions in an accounting equation. Provide the appropriate account titles for the amounts shown in the Retained Earnings column.
b. Prepare an income statement, statement of changes in stockholders' equity, balance sheet, and statement of cash flows for Year 2.

CHAPTER 3

The Double-Entry Accounting System

LEARNING OBJECTIVES

After you have mastered the material in this chapter, you will be able to:

LO 3-1 Record business events in T-accounts using debit/credit terminology.

LO 3-2 Record transactions using the general journal format.

LO 3-3 Prepare a trial balance and explain how it is used to prepare financial statements.

LO 3-4 Prepare closing entries in general journal format.

LO 3-5 Use a return-on-assets ratio, a debt-to-assets ratio, and a return-on-equity ratio to analyze financial statements.

APPENDIX

LO 3-6 Record depreciation and interest using journal entries and T-accounts, and show how these entries affect financial statements.

 Video lectures and accompanying self-assessment quizzes are available in Connect *for all learning objectives.*

CHAPTER OPENING

To prepare financial statements, a company must have a system for accurately capturing the vast numbers of business transactions in which it engages each year. The most widely used such system, double-entry accounting, is so effective it has been in use for hundreds of years! This chapter explains the rules for recording transactions using double-entry accounting.

Double-entry accounting rules are analogous to other rules people adopt to achieve various goals, such as rules governing traffic signals. A red signal means "stop," but it could just as easily mean "go." What matters is that all drivers agree on what red means. Similarly, double-entry accounting rules could have developed differently. In fact, the rules sometimes seem backward at first. You likely use accounting terms like *debit* or *credit* from a consumer's point of view. To learn the accounting rules, however, you must view them from a business perspective. With practice, they will become second nature and you will know them as well as you know traffic signals.

The Curious Accountant

©Jstone/Shutterstock RF

Most companies prepare financial statements at least once each year. The year about which financial statements report is called a **fiscal year.** Illustrations in this textbook usually assume the fiscal year coincides with the calendar year; that is, it ends on December 31. In practice, the fiscal years of many companies do not end on December 31. For example, **Levi Strauss**, a company that produces clothing, ends its fiscal year on the last Sunday in November. **Gap, Inc.**, a company that sells clothing, ends its fiscal year on the last Saturday in January or the first Saturday in February.

Why would these companies choose these dates to end their fiscal years? (Answers on page 163.)

DEBIT/CREDIT TERMINOLOGY

LO 3-1

Record business events in T-accounts using debit/credit terminology.

An account form known as a **T-account** is a good starting point for learning double-entry recording procedures. A T-account looks like the letter "T" drawn on a piece of paper. The account title is written across the top of the horizontal bar of the T. The left side of the vertical bar is the **debit** side, and the right side is the **credit** side. An account has been *debited* when an amount is written on the left side and *credited* when an amount is written on the right side. Accountants often abbreviate the term *debit* as "dr." and *credit* as "cr." For any given account, the difference between the total debit and credit amounts is the **account balance.**

The rules for using debits and credits to record transactions in T-accounts are as follows:

Notice that a debit can represent an increase or a decrease. Likewise, a credit can represent an increase or a decrease. Whether a debit or credit is an increase or a decrease depends on the type of account (asset, liability, or stockholders' equity) in question. The rules of debits and credits are summarized as follows:

1. Debits increase asset accounts; credits decrease asset accounts.
2. Debits decrease liability and stockholders' equity accounts; credits increase liability and stockholders' equity accounts.

RECORDING TRANSACTIONS IN T-ACCOUNTS

To illustrate the rules for debits and credits, we record the Year 2 accounting events for a small business: Collins Brokerage Services, Inc. The company's December 31, Year 1 balance sheet contained the following balances in its permanent accounts: Cash, $5,000; Common Stock, $4,000; and Retained Earnings, $1,000. The beginning balances for the temporary accounts (Revenues, Expenses, and Dividends) are zero because these accounts were closed at the end of the previous period. The events are organized into four categories, including asset source, asset exchange, asset use, and claims exchange.

Asset Source Transactions

A business may obtain assets from three primary sources: (1) from stockholders, (2) from creditors, or (3) through operating activities (earning revenue). An asset source transaction increases an asset account and a corresponding liability or stockholders' equity account. The increase in the asset account is recorded with a debit entry. The increase in a liability or stockholders' equity account is recorded with a credit entry. The following section demonstrates recording procedures for common asset source transactions experienced during Year 2.

EVENT 1 On January 1, Year 2, Collins acquired $25,000 cash from the issue of common stock.

This accounting event increases both assets and stockholders' equity. The increase in assets (Cash) is recorded with a debit, and the increase in stockholders' equity (Common Stock) is recorded with a credit, shown in T-account form as follows:

The Double-Entry Accounting System

Assets	=	Liabilities	+	Stockholders' Equity
Cash				**Common Stock**
Debit | Credit				Debit | Credit
+ |				| +
(1) 25,000 |				| 25,000 (1)

Notice the entry included both debiting an account and crediting an account. This system is called **double-entry accounting.** Recording any transaction requires at least one debit and at least one credit. The total of the debit amounts must equal the total of the credit amounts. These requirements provide accountants with a built-in error detection tool. For your convenience, the event number is shown parenthetically in the T-accounts beside the transaction amounts.

This entry has the following effects on the financial statements:

Assets	=	Liab.	+	Stk. Equity	Rev.	−	Exp.	=	Net Inc.	Cash Flow
Cash	=			Com. Stk.						
25,000	=	NA	+	25,000	NA	−	NA	=	NA	25,000 FA

EVENT 2   Purchased $850 of supplies on account.

Purchasing supplies on account increases both assets and liabilities. The increase in assets (Supplies) is recorded with a debit, and the increase in liabilities (Accounts Payable) is recorded with a credit, as shown in the following T-accounts:

Assets	=	Liabilities	+	Stockholders' Equity
Supplies		**Account Payable**		
Debit | Credit		Debit | Credit		
+ |		| +		
(2) 850 |		| 850 (2)		

This entry has the following effects on the financial statements:

Assets	=	Liab.	+	Stk. Equity	Rev.	−	Exp.	=	Net Inc.	Cash Flow
Supplies	=	Accts. pay.								
850	=	850	+	NA	NA	−	NA	=	NA	NA

EVENT 3   Collected $1,800 cash as an advance to provide future services over a one-year period starting March 1, Year 2.

Accepting the $1,800 in advance creates an obligation for Collins. The obligation is to provide future services to a customer. Collins will recognize a liability called *unearned revenue*. Recording the event increases both assets and liabilities. The increase in assets

(Cash) is recorded with a debit, and the increase in liabilities (Unearned Revenue) is recorded with a credit, as shown in the following T-accounts:

Assets	=	Liabilities	+	Stockholders' Equity
Cash		**Unearned Revenue**		
Debit / Credit		Debit / Credit		
+		+		
(3) 1,800		1,800 (3)		

This entry has the following effects on the financial statements:

Assets	=	Liab.	+	Stk. Equity	Rev.	−	Exp.	=	Net Inc.	Cash Flow
Cash	=	Unearned Revenue								
1,800	=	1,800	+	NA	NA	−	NA	=	NA	1,800 OA

EVENT 4 During Year 2, Collins provided $15,760 of services on account.

Recognizing revenue earned on account increases both assets and stockholders' equity. The increase in assets (Accounts Receivable) is recorded with a debit, and the increase in stockholders' equity (Service Revenue) is recorded with a credit, as shown in the following T-accounts:

Assets	=	Liabilities	+	Stockholders' Equity
Accounts Receivable				**Service Revenue**
Debit / Credit				Debit / Credit
+				+
(4) 15,760				15,760 (4)

This entry has the following effects on the financial statements:

Assets	=	Liab.	+	Stk. Equity	Rev.	−	Exp.	=	Net Inc.	Cash Flow
Accts. Rec.	=			Ret. Earn.						
15,760	=	NA	+	15,760	15,760	−	NA	=	15,760	NA

Summary of the Previous Asset Source Transactions

Events 1 through 4 are asset source transactions. In each case, an asset account and a corresponding liability or stockholders' equity account increased. The increase in the asset account was recorded with a debit and the increase in the liability or stockholders' equity account was recorded with a credit. Any transaction that provides assets to a business is recorded similarly.

>
> ### CHECK YOURSELF 3.1
>
> What are the three sources of assets? Which accounts are debited and credited when a business acquires an asset?
>
> **Answer** The three sources of assets are creditors, investors, and earnings. When a company acquires an asset, the asset account is debited and the source account is credited. For example, if a company earns revenue on account, the Receivables account is debited and the Revenue account is credited.

Asset Exchange Transactions

Asset exchange transactions involve trading one asset for another asset. One asset account increases; the other decreases. The total amount of assets remains unchanged. Asset exchange transactions are recorded by debiting the asset account that is increasing and crediting the asset account that is decreasing. In T-account form, asset exchange transactions have the following effects on the accounting equation:

Assets	=	Claims

Assets 1		Assets 2	
Debit	Credit	Debit	Credit
+			−

EVENT 5 During Year 2 Collins paid $26,000 cash to purchase land.

The increase in assets (Land) is recorded with a debit, and the decrease in assets (Cash) is recorded with a credit, as shown in the following T-accounts:

Assets	=	Claims

Cash		Land	
Debit	Credit	Debit	Credit
	−	+	
	26,000 (5)	(5) 26,000	

This entry has the following effects on the financial statements:

Assets			=	Liab.	+	Stk. Equity	Rev.	−	Exp.	=	Net Inc.	Cash Flow	
Cash	+	Land											
(26,000)	+	26,000	=	NA	+	NA	NA	−	NA	=	NA	(26,000)	IA

EVENT 6 Paid $1,200 cash for a one-year insurance policy with coverage starting August 1, Year 2.

The increase in assets (Prepaid Insurance) is recorded with a debit, and the decrease in assets (Cash) is recorded with a credit, as shown in the following T-accounts:

Assets		=	Claims
Cash	**Prepaid Insurance**		
Debit | Credit	Debit | Credit		
−	+		
| 1,200 (6)	(6) 1,200 |		

This entry has the following effects on the financial statements:

Assets	=	Liab.	+	Stk. Equity	Rev.	−	Exp.	=	Net Inc.	Cash Flow
Cash + Prepaid Insurance										
(1,200) + 1,200	=	NA	+	NA	NA	−	NA	=	NA	(1,200) OA

EVENT 7 Collected $13,400 cash from accounts receivable.

The increase in assets (Cash) is recorded with a debit, and the decrease in assets (Accounts Receivable) is recorded with a credit, as shown in the following T-accounts:

Assets		=	Claims
Cash	**Accounts Receivable**		
Debit | Credit	Debit | Credit		
+	−		
(7) 13,400 |	| 13,400 (7)		

This entry has the following effects on the financial statements:

Assets	=	Liab.	+	Stk. Equity	Rev.	−	Exp.	=	Net Inc.	Cash Flow
Cash + Accts. Rec.										
13,400 + (13,400)	=	NA	+	NA	NA	−	NA	=	NA	13,400 OA

Summary of the Previous Asset Exchange Transactions

Events 5 through 7 are asset exchange transactions. In each case, one asset account increased and another decreased. The asset account that increased was debited, and the asset account that decreased was credited. These asset exchange transactions did not affect the total amounts of assets, liabilities, or stockholders' equity.

Asset Use Transactions

There are three primary asset use transactions: (1) expenses may use assets, (2) settling liabilities may use assets, or (3) paying dividends may use assets. An asset use transaction decreases an asset account and also decreases a liability or stockholders equity account. The decrease in the asset account is recorded with a credit and the decrease in the liability or stockholders' equity account is recorded with a debit. Collins experienced the following asset used transactions during Year 2.

EVENT 8 Paid $9,500 cash for salaries expense.

The decrease in assets (Cash) is recorded with a credit, and the decrease in stockholders' equity (Salaries Expense) is recorded with a debit, as shown in the following T-accounts:

Assets	=	Liabilities	+	Stockholders' Equity
Cash				**Salaries Expense**
Debit / Credit				Debit / Credit
—				+ Expenses
9,500 (8)				− Equity
				(8) 9,500

The debit to Salaries Expense represents an *increase* in the salaries expense account, which is actually a *decrease* in stockholders' equity (Retained Earnings). Debit entries increase expense accounts. Expenses, however, decrease stockholders' equity (Retained Earnings). Debiting an expense account, therefore, reduces stockholders' equity.

This entry has the following effects on the financial statements:

Assets	=	Liab.	+	Stk. Equity	Rev.	−	Exp.	=	Net Inc.	Cash Flow
Cash	=			Ret. Earn.						
(9,500)	=	NA	+	(9,500)	NA	−	9,500	=	(9,500)	(9,500) OA

EVENT 9 Paid an $800 cash dividend.

The decrease in assets (Cash) is recorded with a credit, and the decrease in stockholders' equity (Dividends) is recorded with a debit, as shown in the following T-accounts:

Assets	=	Liabilities	+	Stockholders' Equity
Cash				**Dividends**
Debit / Credit				Debit / Credit
—				+ Div.
800 (9)				− Equity
				(9) 800

The debit to Dividends represents both an increase in the dividends account and a decrease in stockholders' equity (Retained Earnings). Because dividends decrease stockholders' equity, an increase in the Dividends account reduces stockholders' equity. Recall that dividends are wealth transfers, not expenses.

This entry has the following effects on the financial statements:

Assets	=	Liab.	+	Stk. Equity	Rev.	−	Exp.	=	Net Inc.	Cash Flow
Cash	=			Ret. Earn.						
(800)	=	NA	+	(800)	NA	−	NA	=	NA	(800) FA

EVENT 10 Paid $850 cash to settle accounts payable.

The decrease in assets (Cash) is recorded with a credit, and the decrease in liabilities (Accounts Payable) is recorded with a debit, as shown in the following T-accounts:

Assets	=	Liabilities	+	Stockholders' Equity
Cash		Accounts Payable		
Debit Credit		Debit Credit		
850 (10)		(10) 850		

This entry has the following effects on the financial statements:

Assets	=	Liab.	+	Stk. Equity	Rev.	−	Exp.	=	Net Inc.	Cash Flow
Cash	=	Accts. pay.								
(850)	=	(850)	+	NA	NA	−	NA	=	NA	(850) OA

Summary of Asset Use Transactions

Events 8 through 10 each reduced an asset account, as well as either a liability or stockholders' equity account. Even though debit entries to expense and dividends accounts represent increases in those accounts, the balances in expense and dividends accounts reduce stockholders' equity. Any asset use transaction is recorded with a debit to a liability or a stockholders' equity account and a credit to an asset account.

Claims Exchange Transactions

Certain transactions involve exchanging one claims account for another claims account. The total amount of claims remains unchanged. Such transactions are recorded by debiting the claims account, which is decreasing, and crediting the claims account, which is increasing.

EVENT 11 During Year 2 Collins recognized $1,900 of other operating expenses on account.

This event increases liabilities and decreases stockholders' equity. The increase in liabilities (Accounts Payable) is recorded with a credit, and the decrease in stockholders' equity (Other Operating Expense) is recorded with a debit, as shown in the following T-accounts:

Assets	=	Liabilities	+	Stockholders' Equity
		Accounts Payable		Other Operating Expense
		Debit Credit +		Debit + Expense Credit
		1,900 (11)		− Equity
				(11) 1,900

This entry has the following effects on the financial statements:

Assets	=	Liab.	+	Stk. Equity	Rev.	−	Exp.	=	Net Inc.	Cash Flow
		Accts. pay.	+	Ret. Earn.						
NA	=	1,900	+	(1,900)	NA	−	1,900	=	(1,900)	NA

Summary of Claims Exchange Transaction

Event 11 reflects an exchange on the claims side of the accounting equation. In this case, one claims account (Other Operating Expense) was debited, and another claims account (Accounts Payable) was credited. Claims exchange transactions do not affect the total amounts of either assets or claims.

Adjusting the Accounts

Assume Collins' fiscal year ends on December 31, Year 2. Collins has several unrecorded accruals and deferrals that must be recognized before the financial statements can be prepared. The appropriate adjustments are discussed below.

ADJUSTMENT 1 As of December 31, Year 2, Collins had earned $1,500 of the $1,800 of the revenue it deferred in Event 3.

Recall that Collins collected $1,800 in advance for a one-year contract starting March 1. By December 31, Year 2, Collins would have provided professional services for 10 months, earning $1,500 ($1,800 ÷ 12 = $150; $150 × 10 = $1,500) of the revenue during Year 2. This amount must be transferred from the liability account (Unearned Revenue) to an equity account (Service Revenue). Recognizing the revenue decreases liabilities and increases stockholders' equity. The decrease in liabilities (Unearned Revenue) is recorded with a debit, and the increase in stockholders' equity (Service Revenue) is recorded with a credit, as shown in the following T-accounts:

Assets	=	Liabilities	+	Stockholders' Equity
		Unearned Revenue		Service Revenue
		Debit | Credit		Debit | Credit
		−		+
		(Adj. 1) 1,500		1,500 (Adj. 1)

This adjustment has the following effects on the financial statements:

Assets	=	Liab.	+	Stk. Equity	Rev.	−	Exp.	=	Net Inc.	Cash Flow
		Unearned Revenue		Ret. Earn.						
NA	=	(1,500)	+	1,500	1,500	−	NA	=	1,500	NA

ADJUSTMENT 2 As of December 31, Year 2, Collins had $800 of accrued salary expenses that will be paid in Year 3.

Assume that Collins owes $800 to employees for work done in Year 2. Collins will pay these salaries in Year 3. The required adjusting entry increases liabilities and decreases stockholders' equity. The increase in liabilities (Salaries Payable) is recorded with a credit, and the decrease in stockholders' equity (Salaries Expense) is recorded with a debit, as shown in the following T-accounts:

Assets	=	Liabilities	+	Stockholders' Equity
		Salaries Payable		Salaries Expense
		Debit | Credit		Debit | Credit
		+		+ Expense
		800 (Adj. 2)		− Equity
				(Adj. 2) 800

This adjustment has the following effects on the financial statements:

Assets	=	Liab.	+	Stk. Equity	Rev.	−	Exp.	=	Net Inc.	Cash Flow
		Sal. Pay.	+	Ret. Earn.						
NA	=	800	+	(800)	NA	−	800	=	(800)	NA

ADJUSTMENT 3 As of December 31, Year 2, Collins had used $500 of the $1,200 of insurance coverage that was prepaid in Event 6.

Recall that Collins paid $1,200 in advance for insurance coverage for one year. The monthly insurance cost is therefore $100 ($1,200 ÷ 12 months). By December 31, Collins had *used* the insurance coverage for five months in Year 2. Insurance expense for those five months is therefore $500 ($100 × 5). Recognizing the insurance expense decreases both assets and stockholders' equity. The decrease in assets (Prepaid Insurance) is recorded with a credit, and the decrease in stockholders' equity (Insurance Expense) is recorded with a debit, as shown in the following T-accounts:

Assets	=	Liabilities	+	Stockholders' Equity
Prepaid Insurance				**Insurance Expense**
Debit Credit				Debit Credit
−				+ Expense
500 (Adj. 3)				− Equity
				(Adj. 3) 500

This adjustment has the following effects on the financial statements:

Assets	=	Liab.	+	Stk. Equity	Rev.	−	Exp.	=	Net Inc.	Cash Flow
Prep. Ins.	=			Ret. Earn.						
(500)	=	NA	+	(500)	NA	−	500	=	(500)	NA

ADJUSTMENT 4 As of December 31, Year 2, a physical count of the supplies on hand revealed that $125 of unused supplies were available for future use.

Collins used $725 ($850 − $125) of supplies during the period. Recognizing the supplies expense decreases both assets and stockholders' equity. The decrease in assets (Supplies) is recorded with a credit, and the decrease in stockholders' equity (Supplies Expense) is recorded with a debit, as shown in the following T-accounts:

Assets	=	Liabilities	+	Stockholders' Equity
Supplies				**Supplies Expense**
Debit Credit				Debit Credit
−				+ Expense
725 (Adj. 4)				− Equity
				(Adj. 4) 725

This adjustment has the following effects on the financial statements:

Assets	=	Liab.	+	Stk. Equity	Rev.	−	Exp.	=	Net Inc.	Cash Flow
Supplies	=			Ret. Earn.						
(725)	=	NA	+	(725)	NA	−	725	=	(725)	NA

CHECK YOURSELF 3.2

Can an asset exchange transaction be an adjusting entry?

Answer No. Adjusting entries always involve revenue or expense accounts. Because an asset exchange transaction involves only asset accounts, it cannot be an adjusting entry.

Overview of Debit/Credit Relationships

Panel A of Exhibit 3.1 summarizes the rules for debits and credits. Panel B illustrates these rules in T-account form.

EXHIBIT 3.1
Debit/Credit Relationships

Panel A

Account	Debits	Credits
Assets	Increase	Decrease
Liabilities	Decrease	Increase
Stockholders' Equity	Decrease	Increase
Common Stock	Decrease	Increase
Retained Earnings	Decrease	Increase
Revenue	Decrease	Increase
Expenses	Increase	Decrease
Dividends	Increase	Decrease

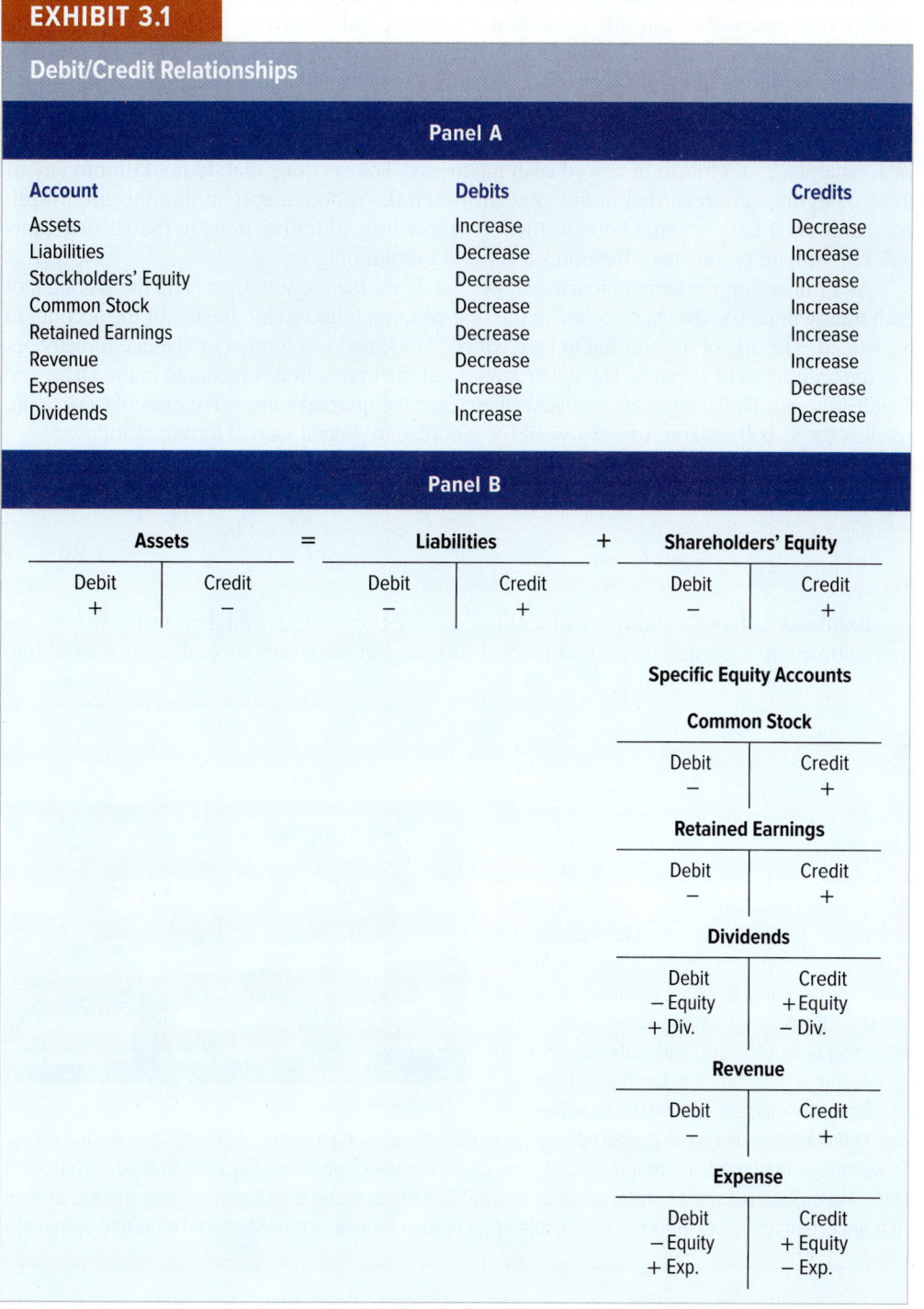

The balance in each account, which is the difference between all the debit entries and all the credit entries, is written on the plus (increase) side of that account. Asset, expense, and dividend accounts normally have *debit balances;* liability, stockholders' equity, and revenue accounts normally have *credit balances.*

THE GENERAL JOURNAL

LO 3-2

Record transactions using the general journal format.

Businesses find it impractical to record every individual transaction directly into general ledger accounts. Imagine the number of cash transactions a grocery store has each day. To simplify recordkeeping, businesses rely on **source documents,** such as cash register tapes, as the basis for entering transaction data into the accounting system. Other source documents include invoices, time cards, check registers, and deposit tickets.

Accountants further simplify recordkeeping by initially recording data from source documents into **journals.** Journals provide a chronological record of business transactions. *Transactions are recorded in journals before they are entered into ledger accounts.* Journals are therefore **books of original entry.** Companies may use different **special journals** to record specific types of recurring transactions. For example, a company may use one special journal to record sales on account, another to record purchases on account, a third to record cash receipts, and a fourth to record cash payments. Transactions that do not fall into any of these categories are recorded in the **general journal.** Although special journals are useful, companies can keep records without them by recording all transactions in the general journal. For simplicity, this text illustrates a general journal only.

At a minimum, the general journal shows the dates, the account titles, and the amounts of each transaction. The date is recorded in the first column, followed by the title of the account to be debited. The title of the account to be credited is indented and written on the line directly below the account to be debited. The dollar amount of the transaction is recorded in the Debit and Credit columns. Dollar signs are not used when recording journal entries. For example, providing services for $1,000 cash on August 1 would be recorded in general journal format as follows:

Date	Account Title	Debit	Credit
Aug. 1	Cash	1,000	
	Service Revenue		1,000

Exhibit 3.2 shows a summary of Collins' Year 2 transactions and demonstrates how the transactions are recorded in general journal format. For easy reference, the journal column

REALITY BYTES

Do all accounting systems require using debits and credits? The answer is a definite no. Many small businesses use a single-entry system. A checkbook constitutes a sufficient accounting system for many business owners. Deposits represent revenues, and payments constitute expenses. Many excellent automated accounting systems do not require data entry through a debit/credit recording scheme. **QuickBooks** is a good example of this type of system. Data are entered into the QuickBooks software program through a user-friendly computer interface that does not require knowledge of debit/credit terminology. Even so, the QuickBooks program produces traditional financial reports such as an income statement, balance sheet, and statement of cash flows. How is this possible? Before you become too ingrained in the debit/credit system, recall that throughout the first two chapters of this text, we illustrated accounting records without using debits and credits. Financial reports can be produced in many ways without using a double-entry system. Having recognized this point, we also note that the vast majority of medium- to large-sized companies use the double-entry system. Indeed, debit/credit terminology is a part of common culture. Most people have an understanding of what is happening when a business tells them that their account is being debited or credited. It is important for you to embrace the double-entry system as well as other financial reporting systems.

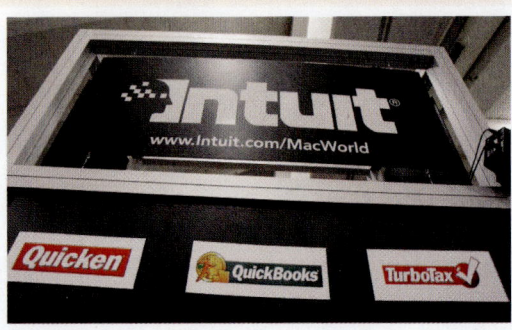

©Paul Sakuma/AP Images

EXHIBIT 3.2

Transaction Summary

Event 1   Acquired $25,000 cash from the issue of common stock.
Event 2   Purchased $850 of supplies on account.
Event 3   Collected $1,800 cash as an advance to provide future services over a one-year period starting March 1.
Event 4   Provided $15,760 of services on account.
Event 5   Purchased land for $26,000 cash.
Event 6   Paid $1,200 cash for a one-year insurance policy with coverage starting August 1.
Event 7   Collected $13,400 cash from accounts receivable.
Event 8   Paid $9,500 cash for salaries expense.
Event 9   Paid an $800 cash dividend.
Event 10 Paid $850 cash to settle accounts payable.
Event 11 Recognized $1,900 other operating expenses on account.

Adjustments

Adj. 1   Recognized $1,500 of deferred service revenue.
Adj. 2   Recognized $800 of accrued salaries expense.
Adj. 3   Recognized $500 of deferred insurance expense.
Adj. 4   Recognized $725 of deferred supplies expense.

General Journal Entries

Event No.	Account Titles	Debit	Credit
1	Cash	25,000	
	Common Stock		25,000
2	Supplies	850	
	Accounts Payable		850
3	Cash	1,800	
	Unearned Service Revenue		1,800
4	Accounts Receivable	15,760	
	Service Revenue		15,760
5	Land	26,000	
	Cash		26,000
6	Prepaid Insurance	1,200	
	Cash		1,200
7	Cash	13,400	
	Accounts Receivable		13,400
8	Salaries Expense	9,500	
	Cash		9,500
9	Dividends	800	
	Cash		800
10	Accounts Payable	850	
	Cash		850
11	Other Operating Expenses	1,900	
	Accounts Payable		1,900
Adj. 1	Unearned Service Revenue	1,500	
	Service Revenue		1,500
Adj. 2	Salaries Expense	800	
	Salaries Payable		800
Adj. 3	Insurance Expense	500	
	Prepaid Insurance		500
Adj. 4	Supplies Expense	725	
	Supplies		725

EXHIBIT 3.3
General Ledger

Assets	=	Liabilities	+	Stockholders' Equity		
Cash		**Accounts Payable**		**Common Stock**		**Service Revenue**
Bal. 5,000	26,000 (5)	(10) 850	850 (2)		4,000 Bal.		15,760 (4)
(1) 25,000	1,200 (6)		1,900 (11)		25,000 (1)		1,500 (Adj. 1)
(3) 1,800	9,500 (8)		1,900 Bal.		29,000 Bal.		17,260 Bal.
(7) 13,400	800 (9)						
	850 (10)	**Salaries Payable**		**Retained Earnings**		**Salaries Expense**
Bal. 6,850			800 (Adj. 2)		1,000 Bal.	(8) 9,500	
						(Adj. 2) 800	
Accounts Receivable		**Unearned Service Revenue**		**Dividends**		Bal. 10,300	
(4) 15,760	13,400 (7)	(Adj. 1) 1,500	1,800 (3)	(9) 800			
Bal. 2,360			300 Bal.			**Other Operating Expenses**
						(11) 1,900	
Prepaid Insurance							
(6) 1,200	500 (Adj. 3)					**Insurance Expense**
Bal. 700						(Adj. 3) 500	
Supplies						**Supplies Expense**
(2) 850	725 (Adj. 4)					(Adj. 4) 725	
Bal. 125							
Land							
(5) 26,000							

normally used for the transaction date contains the event numbers and the references for the adjusting entries. After transactions are initially recorded in a journal, the dollar amounts of each debit and credit are copied into the ledger accounts through a process called **posting.**

Most companies today use computer technology to record transactions and prepare financial statements. Computers can record and post data pertaining to vast numbers of transactions with incredible speed and unparalleled accuracy. Both manual and computerized accounting systems, however, use the same underlying design. Analyzing a manual accounting system is a useful way to gain insight into how computer-based systems work.

The collection of all the accounts used by a particular business is called the **general ledger.** The general ledger for Collins is displayed in Exhibit 3.3. In a manual system, the ledger could be a book with pages for each account where entries are recorded by hand. In more sophisticated systems, the general ledger is maintained in electronic form. Data are entered into electronic ledgers using computer keyboards or scanners. Companies typically assign each ledger account a name and a number. A list of all ledger accounts and their account numbers is called the **chart of accounts.**

TRIAL BALANCE AND FINANCIAL STATEMENTS

LO 3-3

Prepare a trial balance and explain how it is used to prepare financial statements.

To test whether debits equal credits in the general ledger, accountants regularly prepare an internal accounting schedule called a **trial balance.** A trial balance lists every ledger account and its balance. Debit balances are listed in one column, and credit balances are listed in an adjacent column. The columns are totaled and the totals are compared.

Exhibit 3.4 displays the trial balance for Collins Brokerage Services, Inc. after the adjusting entries have been posted to the ledger.

If the debit total does not equal the credit total, the accountant knows to search for an error. Even if the totals are equal, however, there may be errors in the accounting records. For example, equal trial balance totals would not disclose errors like the following: failure to record transactions; misclassifications, such as debiting the wrong account; or incorrectly recording the amount of a transaction, such as recording a $200 transaction as $2,000. Equal debits and credits in a trial balance provide evidence rather than proof of accuracy.

Supplemented with details from the Cash and Common Stock ledger accounts, the adjusted trial balance (Exhibit 3.4) provides the information to prepare the financial statements for Collins Brokerage Services, Inc. The income statement, statement of changes in stockholders' equity, balance sheet, and statement of cash flows are shown in Exhibits 3.5, 3.6, 3.7, and 3.8.

Closing Entries

Exhibit 3.9 shows **closing entries** for Collins Brokerage Services, Inc. These entries move all Year 2 data from the temporary accounts (revenues, expenses, and dividends) into the Retained Earnings account. For example, the first closing entry in Exhibit 3.9 moves the balance in the Service Revenue account to the Retained Earnings account. As shown in the adjusted trial balance (Exhibit 3.4), the Service Revenue account has a $17,260 credit balance before it is closed. Debiting the account for $17,260 brings its after-closing balance to zero. The corresponding $17,260 credit to Retained Earnings increases the balance in that account.

The second closing entry moves the balance in the Salaries Expense account to the Retained Earnings account. Before closing, the Salaries Expense account has a $10,300 debit balance; crediting the account for $10,300

LO 3-4

 Prepare closing entries in general journal format.

EXHIBIT 3.4
COLLINS BROKERAGE SERVICES, INC.
Adjusted Trial Balance
December 31, Year 2

Account Title	Debit	Credit
Cash	$ 6,850	
Accounts receivable	2,360	
Prepaid insurance	700	
Supplies	125	
Land	26,000	
Accounts payable		$ 1,900
Salaries payable		800
Unearned service revenue		300
Common stock		29,000
Retained earnings		1,000
Dividends	800	
Service revenue		17,260
Salaries expense	10,300	
Insurance expense	500	
Supplies expense	725	
Other operating expense	1,900	
Totals	$50,260	$50,260

EXHIBIT 3.5
COLLINS BROKERAGE SERVICES, INC.
Income Statement
For the Year Ended December 31, Year 2

Revenue		$ 17,260
Expenses		
Salaries expense	$(10,300)	
Other operating expenses	(1,900)	
Insurance expense	(500)	
Supplies expense	(725)	
Total expenses		(13,425)
Net income		$ 3,835

EXHIBIT 3.6
COLLINS BROKERAGE SERVICES, INC.
Statement of Changes in Stockholders' Equity
For the Year Ended December 31, Year 2

Beginning common stock	$ 4,000	
Plus: Common stock issued	25,000	
Ending common stock		$29,000
Beginning retained earnings	1,000	
Plus: Net income	3,835	
Less: Dividends	(800)	
Ending retained earnings		4,035
Total stockholders' equity		$33,035

EXHIBIT 3.7

COLLINS BROKERAGE SERVICES, INC.
Balance Sheet
As of December 31, Year 2

Assets		
Cash	$ 6,850	
Accounts receivable	2,360	
Prepaid insurance	700	
Supplies	125	
Land	26,000	
Total assets		$36,035
Liabilities		
Accounts payable	$ 1,900	
Salaries payable	800	
Unearned service revenue	300	
Total liabilities		$ 3,000
Stockholders' equity		
Common stock	29,000	
Retained earnings	4,035	
Total stockholders' equity		33,035
Total liabilities and stockholders' equity		$36,035

EXHIBIT 3.8

COLLINS BROKERAGE SERVICES, INC.
Statement of Cash Flows
For the Year Ended December 31, Year 2

Cash flows from operating activities		
Cash receipts from customers	$15,200*	
Cash payments for salaries expense	(9,500)	
Cash payments for insurance expense	(1,200)	
Cash payments for supplies	(850)	
Net cash flow from operating activities		$ 3,650
Cash flows from investing activities		
Cash payment to purchase land		(26,000)
Cash flows from financing activities		
Cash receipts from issue of common stock	25,000	
Cash payment for dividends	(800)	
Net cash flow from financing activities		24,200
Net increase in cash		1,850
Plus: Beginning cash balance		5,000
Ending cash balance		$ 6,850

*$13,400 accounts receivable collections + $1,800 unearned service revenue collection.

EXHIBIT 3.9

Closing Entries

Date	Account Titles	Debit	Credit
Dec. 31	Service Revenue	17,260	
	Retained Earnings		17,260
31	Retained Earnings	10,300	
	Salaries Expense		10,300
31	Retained Earnings	1,900	
	Other Operating Expenses		1,900
31	Retained Earnings	500	
	Insurance Expense		500
31	Retained Earnings	725	
	Supplies Expense		725
31	Retained Earnings	800	
	Dividends		800

leaves it with an after-closing balance of zero. The corresponding $10,300 debit to the Retained Earnings account reduces the balance in that account. The remaining entries close the other revenue, expense, and dividend accounts to the Retained Earnings account.

Answers to The Curious Accountant

Part 1

The process of closing the books and going through a year-end audit is time-consuming for a business. Also, it is time spent that does not produce revenue. Thus, companies whose business is highly seasonal often choose "slow" periods to end their fiscal year. **Gap, Inc.** does heavy business during the Christmas season, so it might find December 31 an inconvenient time to close its books. Toward the end of January, business activity is slow, and inventory levels are at their low points. This is a good time to count the inventory and to assess the financial condition of the company. For these reasons, Gap, Inc. has chosen to close its books to end its fiscal year around the end of January.

Now that you know why a business like Gap, Inc. might choose to end its fiscal year at the end of January, can you think of a reason why **Levi Strauss** closes its books at the end of November?

Closing entries can be recorded more efficiently than in Exhibit 3.9. For example, all revenue, expense, and dividend accounts can be closed to the retained earnings account in a single compound journal entry, like the one below.

Date	Account Title	Debit	Credit
Dec. 31	Service Revenue	17,260	
	Salary Expense		10,300
	Other Operating Expenses		1,900
	Insurance Expense		500
	Supplies Expense		725
	Dividends		800
	Retained Earnings		3,035

The form of the closing entries is not important. What matters is that all revenue, expense, and dividend amounts be moved to the Retained Earnings account. After the closing entries are posted to the ledger accounts, all revenue, expense, and dividend accounts have zero balances. The temporary accounts are then ready to capture revenue, expense, and dividend data for the next fiscal year.

Answers to The Curious Accountant

Part 2

Levi Strauss does not sell its clothes directly to consumers; rather, it sells most of its clothes through retailers. Levi Strauss must deliver its jeans to retailers before Thanksgiving if the stores are going to have goods available to sell during the Christmas season. So, Levi's "Christmas season" is probably over by early November, making the end of November a good time to end its fiscal year. Some clothing manufacturers, such as **Tommy Hilfiger** and Polo **Ralph Lauren**, close their books around the end of March. By then, goods for both the Christmas and spring seasons have been shipped to retailers. Exhibit 3.10 provides insight regarding the variety of closing dates used by a set of real-world companies.

EXHIBIT 3.10
Distribution of Fiscal Closing Dates

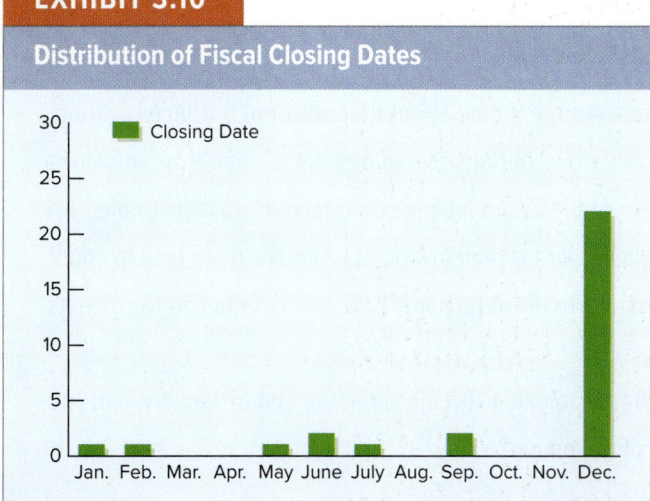

EXHIBIT 3.11

COLLINS BROKERAGE SERVICES, INC.
Post-Closing Trial Balance
December 31, Year 2

Account Title	Debit	Credit
Cash	$ 6,850	
Accounts receivable	2,360	
Prepaid insurance	700	
Supplies	125	
Land	26,000	
Accounts payable		$ 1,900
Salaries payable		800
Unearned service revenue		300
Common stock		29,000
Retained earnings		4,035
Totals	$36,035	$36,035

If all companies closed their books on December 31 each year, accountants, printers, lawyers, government agencies, and others would be overburdened by the effort to produce the accounting reports of all companies at the same time. In an effort to balance the workload, many companies close their books at the end of the natural business year. A natural business year ends when operating activities are at their lowest point. For many companies, the lowest point in the operating cycle occurs on a date other than December 31. A recent survey of the 30 companies that comprise the Dow Jones Average found that 7 (23%) of the companies closed their books in months other than December (see Exhibit 3.10).

The chart is based on data drawn from recent annual reports published by the 30 companies that comprise the Dow Jones Industrial Average.

Post-Closing Trial Balance

How often should companies prepare a trial balance? Some companies prepare a trial balance daily; others may prepare one monthly, quarterly, or annually, depending on the needs of management. The heading of a trial balance describes the status of the account balances in it. For example, the trial balance in Exhibit 3.11 is described as a *Post-Closing Trial Balance* because it reflects the account balances immediately after the closing entries were posted. In contrast, the trial balance in Exhibit 3.4 is described as an *Adjusted Trial Balance* because it shows the account balances immediately after the adjusting entries were posted. A trial balance prepared at the end of each day may be described as a *Daily Trial Balance*.

 CHECK YOURSELF 3.3

Describe an error that would not cause a trial balance to be out of balance.

Answer Many potential errors would not cause a trial balance to be out of balance, such as debiting or crediting the wrong account. For example, if revenue earned on account were recorded with a debit to Cash instead of Accounts Receivable, total assets would be correct and the totals in the trial balance would equal each other even though the balances in the Cash and Accounts Receivable accounts would be incorrect. Recording the same incorrect amount in both the debit and credit part of an entry also would not cause a trial balance to be out of balance. For example, if $20 of revenue earned on account were recorded as a $200 debit to Accounts Receivable and a $200 credit to Consulting Revenue, the totals in the trial balance would equal each other, although the Accounts Receivable and Consulting Revenue amounts would be incorrect.

The Financial Analyst

LO 3-5

Use a return-on-assets ratio, a debt-to-assets ratio, and a return-on-equity ratio to analyze financial statements.

Evaluating income performance requires considering the size of the investment base used to produce the income. In other words, you expect that someone who has $10,000,000 to invest will earn more than someone who has only $10,000 to invest. Financial analysts use financial ratios to compare the performance of companies with different-size investments. The following section of the text discusses three frequently used ratios, including the return-on-assets ratio, the debt-to-assets ratio, and the return-on-equity ratio.

Assessing the Effective Use of Assets

The relationship between the level of income and the size of the investment can be expressed as the **return-on-assets ratio,** as follows:

$$\frac{\text{Net income}[1]}{\text{Total assets}}$$

This ratio permits meaningful comparisons between different-size companies. Compare **Dollar General Corporation**, a retailer that carries mostly low-priced merchandise, to **Wal-Mart Stores, Inc.** In 2016, Dollar General reported net income of $1.2 billion, while Walmart reported net income of $13.6 billion. Walmart's earnings were more than 11 times the earnings of Dollar General. However, the return-on-asset ratios for the two companies reveal that Dollar General produced higher earnings relative to the assets invested. Walmart's ratio was 6.9 percent, while Dollar General's was 10.3 percent. Even though Dollar General earned fewer dollars of net income, the company used its assets more efficiently than Walmart.

The preceding example demonstrates the usefulness of the relationship between income and assets. Two more ratios that enhance financial statement analysis are discussed in the following paragraphs.

Assessing Debt Risk

Borrowing money can be a risky business. To illustrate, assume two companies have the following financial structures:

	Assets	=	Liabilities	+	Stockholders' Equity
Eastern Company	100	=	20	+	80
Western Company	100	=	80	+	20

Which company has the greater financial risk? If each company incurred a $30 loss, the financial structures would change as follows:

	Assets	=	Liabilities	+	Stockholders' Equity
Eastern Company	70	=	20	+	50
Western Company	70	=	80	+	(10)

Clearly, Western Company is at greater risk. Eastern Company could survive a $30 loss that reduced assets and stockholders' equity. It would still have a $50 balance in stockholders' equity and more than enough assets ($70) to satisfy the $20 obligation to creditors. In

---

[1] The use of net income in this ratio ignores the effects of debt financing and income taxation. The effect of these variables on the return-on-assets ratio is explained in a later chapter.

contrast, a $30 loss would throw Western Company into bankruptcy. The company would have a $10 deficit (negative) balance in stockholders' equity and the remaining assets ($70) would be less than the $80 obligation to creditors.

The level of debt risk can be measured in part by using a **debt-to-assets ratio,** as follows:

$$\frac{\text{Total debt}}{\text{Total assets}}$$

For example, Eastern Company's debt-to-assets ratio is 20 percent ($20 ÷ $100), while Western Company's is 80 percent ($80 ÷ $100). Why would the owners of Western Company be willing to accept greater debt risk? Assume that both companies produce $12 of revenue and each must pay 10 percent interest on money owed to creditors. Income statements for the two companies appear as follows:[2]

	Eastern Company	Western Company
Revenue	$12	$12
Interest Expense	2	8
Net Income	$10	$ 4

At first glance, the owners of Eastern Company appear better off because Eastern produced higher net income. In fact, however, the owners of *Western* Company are better off. The owners of Eastern Company get $10 of income for investing $80 of their own money into the business, a return on their invested funds of 12.5 percent ($10 ÷ $80). In contrast, the owners of Western Company obtain $4 of net income for their $20 investment, a return on invested funds of 20 percent ($4 ÷ $20).

The relationship between net income and stockholders' equity used above is the **return-on-equity ratio,** computed as

$$\frac{\text{Net income}}{\text{Stockholders' equity}}$$

Using borrowed money to increase the return on stockholders' investment is called **financial leverage.** Financial leverage explains why companies are willing to accept the risk of debt. Companies borrow money to make money. If a company can borrow money at 10 percent and invest it at 12 percent, the owners will be better off by 2 percent of the amount borrowed. A business that does not borrow may be missing an opportunity to increase its return on equity.

Real-World Data

Exhibit 3.12 shows the debt-to-assets, return-on-assets, and return-on-equity ratios for six real-world companies in two different industries. The data are drawn from the companies' 2016 annual reports. Notice that **Aflac**'s return-on-assets ratio was 2.0 percent and **Aetna**'s

EXHIBIT 3.12

Three Ratios (in Percentages) for Six Real-World Companies

Industry	Company	Debt to Assets	Return on Assets	Return on Equity
Insurance	Aetna	74	3.3	13.7
	Aflac	84	2.0	13.0
	Progressive	76	3.1	13.0
Oil	Chevron	44	(0.1)	(0.3)
	ExxonMobil	47	2.4	4.5
	Marathon Oil	56	(6.9)	(12.2)

[2]This illustration ignores the effect of income taxes on debt financing. This subject is discussed in a later chapter.

FOCUS ON INTERNATIONAL ISSUES

HOW DOES IFRS DIFFER FROM U.S. GAAP?

Chapter 1 discussed the progression toward a single global GAAP in the form of International Financial Reporting Standards (IFRS). That discussion noted that the United States does not currently allow domestic companies to use IFRS; they must follow GAAP. Let's briefly consider just how U.S. GAAP differs from IFRS.

The differences can be summarized in a few broad categories. First, some differences are relatively minor. Consider the case of bank overdrafts. Under IFRS, some bank overdrafts are included as a cash inflow and reported on the statement of cash flows. U.S. GAAP does not permit this. Conversely, some differences relate to very significant issues. Both IFRS and GAAP use historical cost as their primary method for reporting information on financial statements, but both allow exceptions in some circumstances. However, IFRS permits more exceptions to historical cost than GAAP does. Some of these differences will be discussed in later chapters.

Some of the differences affect how financial statements are presented in annual reports. IFRS requires companies to report all financial statements for the current year and the prior year—two years of comparative data. Rules of the Securities and Exchange Commission require U.S. companies to report two years of balance sheets, the current and prior year, and three years of all other statements. See the financial statements of Target Corporation in Appendix B as an example. Of course, companies can show additional years if they wish.

As you would expect in the first course of accounting, some of the differences between IFRS and GAAP are simply too complex to be covered. Examples of such items relate to business combinations (when one company buys another) and foreign currency translations (when a company has subsidiaries that operate outside the United States).

Do not be overwhelmed by the differences between IFRS and GAAP. They have many more rules alike than different. A person who has a reasonable understanding of U.S. GAAP should be able to read financial statements prepared under IFRS without too much difficulty. If you are interested in more detailed, up-to-date information about IFRS versus GAAP, the large international accounting firms have websites that can help. Two examples are: www.iasplus.com, which is presented by the firm of Deloitte Touche Tohmatsu, and www.kpmg.com/global/en/topics/global-ifrs-institute/, which is presented by the firm of KPMG.

©Corbis/PunchStock RF

was 3.3 percent. Neither ratio seems good; banks sometimes pay more than 2.0 percent interest on deposits in savings accounts. The *return-on-equity* ratios, however, show a different picture; Aflac's was 13.0 percent and Aetna's was 13.7 percent—much better than banks pay depositors.

Exhibit 3.12 shows that **ExxonMobil**'s return-on-equity ratio is about two times higher than its return-on-assets ratio (4.5 percent versus 2.4 percent). By comparison, Aflac's return-on-equity ratio is over six times higher than its return-on-assets ratio (13.0 percent versus 2.0 percent). How did this happen? Compare their debt-to-assets ratios. Aflac financed 84 percent of its assets with debt compared to Exxon's 47 percent. Financial leverage is the biggest factor causing these results, but it is not the only factor that affects this ratio.

Because financial leverage offers the opportunity to increase return on equity, why doesn't every company leverage itself to the maximum? There is a downside. When the economy turns down, companies may not be able to produce investment returns that exceed interest rates. A company that has borrowed money at a fixed rate of 8 percent that can

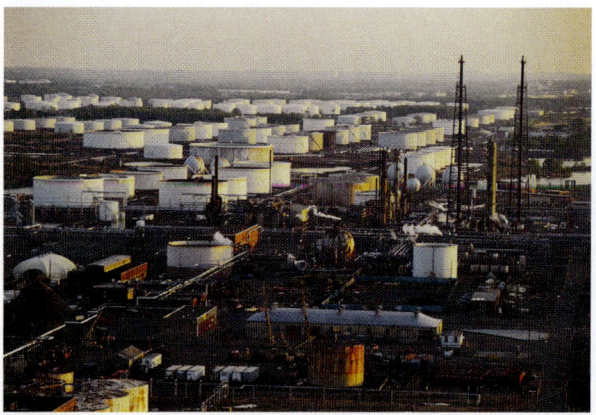
©Comstock Images/Alamy RF

earn only 6 percent on its investments will suffer from financial leverage. In other words, financial leverage is a double-edged sword. It can have a negative as well as a positive impact on a company's return-on-equity ratio.

Finally, compare the ratios in Exhibit 3.12 for companies in the oil industry to the same ratios for companies in the insurance industry. There are significant differences *between* industries, but there are considerable similarities *within* each industry. The debt-to-assets ratio is much higher for the insurance industry than for the oil industry. However, within each industry, the ratios are clustered fairly close together. Distinct differences between industries and similarities within industries are common business features. When you compare accounting information for different companies, you must consider the industries in which those companies operate.

SCOPE OF COVERAGE

Throughout this text, we introduce ratios directly related to chapter topics. Only a few of the many ratios available to users of financial statements are introduced. Introductory finance courses typically include a more extensive study of ratios and other topics related to financial statement analysis. Many business programs offer an entire course on financial statement analysis. These courses help students learn to judge whether the ratio results signal good or poor performance. Developing such judgment requires understanding how accounting policies and procedures can affect financial ratios. The ratios introduced in this text will enhance your understanding of accounting as a basis for studying more advanced topics in subsequent courses.

« A Look Back

This chapter introduced the *double-entry accounting system*. This system was first documented in the 1400s, and is used by most companies today. Key components of the double-entry system are summarized below.

1. Business events can be classified concisely using debit/credit terminology. *Debits* are used to record increases in asset accounts and decreases in liability and stockholders' equity accounts. *Credits* are used to record decreases in asset accounts and increases in liability and stockholders' equity accounts.

2. *T-accounts* are frequently used to analyze and communicate account activity. The account title is placed at the top of the horizontal bar of the T, and increases and decreases are placed on either side of the vertical bar. In a T-account, debits are recorded on the left side and credits are recorded on the right side.

3. Accountants initially record transaction data in journals. The *general journal* is used not only for data entry but also as a shorthand communication tool. Each journal entry includes at least one debit and one credit. An entry is recorded using at least two lines, with the debit recorded on the top line and the credit on the bottom line. The credit is indented to distinguish it from the debit. The general journal format is illustrated here:

4. Information is posted (copied) from the journals to *ledger* accounts. The ledger accounts provide the information used to prepare the financial statements.

5. *Trial balances* are used to check the mathematical accuracy of the recording process. Ledger accounts with their associated debit and credit balances are listed in the trial balance. The debit and credit amounts are totaled and compared. An equal amount of debits and credits provides evidence but not proof that transactions have been recorded correctly. If the debits and credits are *not* equal, it is proof that errors exist.

The double-entry system is just a way to organize accounting data. No matter how we organize the data, the objective is to summarize and report them in a way that is useful for making decisions.

A Look Forward

Chapters 1 through 3 focused on businesses that generate revenue by providing services to their customers. Examples of these types of businesses include consulting, real estate sales, medical services, and legal services. The next chapter introduces accounting practices for businesses that generate revenue by selling goods. Examples of these companies include Walmart, Best Buy, Office Depot, and Lowe's.

APPENDIX

Journal Entries for Long-Term Assets and Depreciation

To illustrate the journal entries associated with the acquisition and depreciation of long-term assets, assume Evans Company paid $34,000 cash to purchase a computer. The computer has a $4,000 salvage value and a three-year useful life. The journal entry necessary to record the purchase of the computer is shown here.

Account Title	Debit	Credit
Computer	34,000	
Cash		34,000

LO 3-6

Record depreciation and interest using journal entries and T-accounts, and show how these entries affect financial statements.

Depreciation expense is determined as follows:

($34,000 cost − $4,000 salvage) / 3-year useful life = $10,000 per year

The journal entry to record the depreciation expense at the end of each year is shown here.

Account Title	Debit	Credit
Depreciation Expense	10,000	
Accumulated Depreciation		10,000

Journal Entries for Notes Payable and Interest Expense

To illustrate the journal entries associated with issuing a promissory note and associated interest, assume Evans Company acquired $20,000 cash by issuing a note to the State Bank. The note was dated October 1, Year 1. It stipulated a one-year term and a 9 percent annual interest rate. The entry necessary to record the issue of the note on October 1 is shown here.

Account Title	Debit	Credit
Cash	20,000	
Note Payable		20,000

Accrued interest as of December 31, Year 1, is computed as follows:

$20,000 principal × .09 annual interest × 3/12 = $450

The journal entry required to record the accrued interest as of December 31, Year 1, is shown here:

Account Title	Debit	Credit
Interest Expense	450	
Interest Payable		450

The note matures on September 30, Year 2. The accrued interest expense for the nine months the note was outstanding in Year 2 is computed as follows:

$$\$20,000 \text{ principal} \times .09 \text{ annual interest} \times 9/12 = \$1,350$$

The journal entry required to record the accrued interest is shown next:

Account Title	Debit	Credit
Interest Expense	1,350	
Interest Payable		1,350

The journal entry required to pay the interest due and the principal balance of the note on September 30, Year 2, is shown next:

Account Title	Debit	Credit
Interest Payable	1,800	
Notes Payable	20,000	
Cash		21,800

SELF-STUDY REVIEW PROBLEM

A step-by-step audio-narrated series of slides is available in Connect.

The following events apply to the first year of operations for Mestro Financial Services Company:

1. Acquired $28,000 cash by issuing common stock on January 1, Year 1.
2. Purchased $1,100 of supplies on account.
3. Paid $12,000 cash in advance for a one-year lease on office space.
4. Earned $23,000 of consulting revenue on account.
5. Incurred $16,000 of general operating expenses on account.
6. Collected $20,000 cash from receivables.
7. Paid $13,000 cash on accounts payable.
8. Paid a $1,000 cash dividend to stockholders.

Information for Adjusting Entries

9. There was $200 of supplies on hand at the end of the accounting period.
10. The one-year lease on the office space was effective beginning on October 1, Year 1.
11. There was $1,200 of accrued salaries at the end of Year 1.

Required

a. Record the preceding events in general journal format.
b. Post the transaction data from the general journal into general ledger T-accounts.
c. Prepare an adjusted trial balance.
d. Prepare an income statement, statement of changes in stockholders' equity, balance sheet, and statement of cash flows.
e. Prepare the appropriate closing entries in general journal format.

Solution to Requirement a

Event No.	Account Title	Debit	Credit
1	Cash	28,000	
	Common Stock		28,000
2	Supplies	1,100	
	Accounts Payable		1,100
3	Prepaid Rent	12,000	
	Cash		12,000
4	Accounts Receivable	23,000	
	Consulting Revenue		23,000
5	General Operating Expenses	16,000	
	Accounts Payable		16,000
6	Cash	20,000	
	Accounts Receivable		20,000
7	Accounts Payable	13,000	
	Cash		13,000
8	Dividends	1,000	
	Cash		1,000
9	Supplies Expense	900	
	Supplies		900
10	Rent Expense	3,000	
	Prepaid Rent		3,000
11	Salaries Expense	1,200	
	Salaries Payable		1,200

Solution to Requirement b

MESTRO FINANCIAL SERVICES COMPANY
T-Accounts, Year 1

Assets = Liabilities + Equity

Cash
1.	28,000	3.	12,000
6.	20,000	7.	13,000
		8.	1,000
Bal.	22,000		

Accounts Receivable
4.	23,000	6.	20,000
Bal.	3,000		

Supplies
2.	1,100	9.	900
Bal.	200		

Prepaid Rent
3.	12,000	10.	3,000
Bal.	9,000		

Accounts Payable
7.	13,000	2.	1,100
		5.	16,000
		Bal.	4,100

Salaries Payable
		11.	1,200
		Bal.	1,200

Common Stock
		1.	28,000
		Bal.	28,000

Dividends
8.	1,000

Consulting Revenue
		4.	23,000

General Operating Expenses
5.	16,000

Salaries Expense
11.	1,200

Supplies Expense
9.	900

Rent Expense
10.	3,000

Solution to Requirement c

MESTRO FINANCIAL SERVICES COMPANY
Trial Balance
December 31, Year 1

Account Titles	Debit	Credit
Cash	$22,000	
Accounts receivable	3,000	
Supplies	200	
Prepaid rent	9,000	
Accounts payable		$ 4,100
Salaries payable		1,200
Common stock		28,000
Dividends	1,000	
Consulting revenue		23,000
General operating expenses	16,000	
Salaries expense	1,200	
Supplies expense	900	
Rent expense	3,000	
Totals	$56,300	$56,300

Solution to Requirement d

MESTRO FINANCIAL SERVICES COMPANY
Financial Statements

Income Statement
For the Year Ended December 31, Year 1

Consulting revenue		$23,000
Expenses		
General operating expenses	$16,000	
Salaries expense	1,200	
Supplies expense	900	
Rent expense	3,000	
Total expenses		(21,100)
Net income		$ 1,900

Statement of Changes in Stockholders' Equity
For the Year Ended December 31, Year 1

Beginning common stock	$ 0	
Plus: Common stock issued	28,000	
Ending common stock		$28,000
Beginning retained earnings	0	
Plus: Net income	1,900	
Less: Dividends	(1,000)	
Ending retained earnings		900
Total stockholders' equity		$28,900

continued

Balance Sheet
As of December 31, Year 1

Assets		
Cash	$22,000	
Accounts receivable	3,000	
Supplies	200	
Prepaid rent	9,000	
Total assets		$34,200
Liabilities		
Accounts payable	$ 4,100	
Salaries payable	1,200	
Total liabilities		$ 5,300
Stockholders' equity		
Common stock	28,000	
Retained earnings	900	
Total stockholders' equity		28,900
Total liabilities and stockholders' equity		$34,200

Statement of Cash Flows
For the Year Ended December 31, Year 1

Cash flows from operating activities		
Inflow from customers	$20,000	
Outflow for expenses	(25,000)	
Net cash flow from operating activities		$ (5,000)
Cash flows from investing activities		0
Cash flows from financing activities		
Inflow from issue of common stock	28,000	
Outflow for dividends	(1,000)	
Net cash flow from financing activities		27,000
Net change in cash		22,000
Plus: Beginning cash balance		0
Ending cash balance		$22,000

Solution to Requirement e

Date	Account Title	Debit	Credit
Dec. 31	Consulting Revenue	23,000	
	Retained Earnings		23,000
Dec. 31	Retained Earnings	21,100	
	General Operating Expenses		16,000
	Salaries Expense		1,200
	Supplies Expense		900
	Rent Expense		3,000
Dec. 31	Retained Earnings	1,000	
	Dividends		1,000

KEY TERMS

Account balance 148
Books of original entry 158
Chart of accounts 160
Closing entries 161
Credit 148

Debit 148
Debt-to-assets ratio 166
Double-entry accounting 149
Financial leverage 166
Fiscal year 147

General journal 158
General ledger 160
Journal 158
Posting 160
Return-on-assets ratio 165

Return-on-equity ratio 166
Source document 158
Special journals 158
T-account 148
Trial balance 160

QUESTIONS

1. What are the two fundamental equality requirements of the double-entry accounting system?
2. Define *debit* and *credit*. How are assets, liabilities, common stock, retained earnings, revenues, expenses, and dividends affected (increased or decreased) by debits and by credits?
3. How is the balance of an account determined?
4. What are the three primary sources of business assets?
5. What are the three primary ways a business may use assets?
6. Give an example of an asset exchange transaction.
7. How does a debit to an expense account ultimately affect retained earnings? Stockholders' equity?
8. What accounts normally have debit balances? What accounts normally have credit balances?
9. What is the primary source of information for preparing the financial statements?
10. What is the purpose of a journal?
11. What is the difference between the *general journal* and special journals?
12. What is a ledger? What is its function in the accounting system?
13. What is the purpose of closing entries?
14. Do all companies close their books on December 31? Why or why not?
15. At a minimum, what information is recorded in the general journal?
16. What is the purpose of a trial balance?
17. When should a trial balance be prepared?
18. What does the term *posting* mean?
19. What information does the return-on-assets ratio provide about a company?
20. What information does the debt-to-assets ratio provide about a company?
21. What is financial leverage?
22. Explain how financial leverage impacts the return-on-equity ratio.

MULTIPLE-CHOICE QUESTIONS

Multiple-choice questions are available in **Connect**.

EXERCISES—SERIES A

 All applicable Exercises in Series A are available in **Connect**.

LO 3-1

Exercise 3-1A *Matching debit and credit terminology with accounting elements*

Required

Complete the following table by indicating whether a debit or credit is used to increase or decrease the balance of accounts belonging to each category of financial statement elements. The appropriate debit/credit terminology has been identified for the first category (assets) as an example.

Category of Elements	Used to Increase This Element	Used to Decrease This Element
Assets	Debit	Credit
Liabilities		
Common Stock		
Retained Earnings		
Revenue		
Expense		
Dividends		

LO 3-1

Exercise 3-2A *Debit/credit terminology*

Two introductory accounting students were arguing about how to record a transaction involving an exchange of cash for land. Laura stated that the transaction should have a debit to Land and a credit to Cash; Clark argued that the reverse (debit to Cash and credit to Land) represented the appropriate treatment.

Required

Which student was correct? Defend your position.

Exercise 3-3A *Matching debit and credit terminology with account titles*   LO 3-1

Required

Indicate whether each of the following accounts normally has a debit balance or a credit balance:

a. Salaries Expense
b. Consulting Revenue
c. Unearned Revenue
d. Accounts Payable
e. Dividends
f. Land
g. Salaries Payable
h. Cash
i. Prepaid Insurance
j. Common Stock
k. Interest Revenue
l. Rent Expense

Exercise 3-4A *Applying debit/credit terminology to accounting events*   LO 3-1

Required

a. In parallel columns, list the accounts that would be debited and credited for each of the following unrelated transactions:

(1) Acquired cash from the issue of common stock.
(2) Provided services for cash.
(3) Paid cash for salaries expense.
(4) Purchased supplies for cash.
(5) Paid in advance for two-year lease on office space.
(6) Provided services on account.
(7) Recognized expense for prepaid rent that had been used up by the end of the accounting period.
(8) Recorded accrued salaries at the end of the accounting period.

b. Use a horizontal statements model to show how each event affects the balance sheet, income statement, and statement of cash flows. Indicate whether the event increases (+), decreases (−), or does not affect (NA) each element of the financial statements. Also, in the Cash Flow column, use the letters OA to designate operating activity, IA for investing activity, and FA for financing activity. The first event is shown as an example.

Assets	=	Liab.	+	Equity	Rev.	−	Exp.	=	Net Inc.	Cash Flow
+		NA		+	NA		NA		NA	+ FA

Exercise 3-5A *Debit/credit terminology*   LO 3-1

Required

For each of the following independent events, identify the account that would be debited and the account that would be credited. The accounts for the first event are identified as an example.

Event	Account Debited	Account Credited
a	Cash	Common Stock

a. Received cash by issuing common stock.
b. Received cash for services to be performed in the future.
c. Paid salaries payable.
d. Provided services on account.
e. Paid cash for operating expenses.
f. Purchased supplies on account.
g. Recognized revenue for services completed. Cash had been collected in Event *b*.
h. Recognized accrued salaries expense.
i. Recognized expense for supplies used during the period.

Chapter 3

j. Performed services for cash.
k. Paid accounts payable.
l. Received cash in payment of accounts receivable.
m. Paid a cash dividend to the stockholders.

LO 3-1

Exercise 3-6A *Identifying transaction type, its effect on the accounting equation, and whether the effect is recorded with a debit or credit*

Required

Identify whether each of the following transactions is an asset source (AS), asset use (AU), asset exchange (AE), or claims exchange (CE). Also explain how each event affects the accounting equation by placing a + for increase, − for decrease, and NA for not affected under each of the components of the accounting equation. Finally, indicate whether the effect requires a debit or credit entry. The first event is recorded as an example.

						Stockholders' Equity	
Event	Type of Event	Assets	=	Liabilities	+	Common Stock	+ Retained Earnings
a	AS	+ Debit		+ Credit		NA	NA

a. Purchased supplies on account.
b. Acquired cash from the issue of common stock.
c. Paid cash in advance for one year of rent.
d. Paid salaries payable.
e. Received cash for services to be performed in the future.
f. Paid a cash dividend to the stockholders.
g. Received cash in payment of accounts receivable.
h. Paid accounts payable.
i. Provided services for cash.
j. Recognized expense for supplies used during the period.
k. Recognized revenue for services completed for which cash had been collected previously.
l. Incurred other operating expenses on account.
m. Purchased land with cash.

LO 3-1

Exercise 3-7A *Identifying increases and decreases in T-accounts*

Required

For each of the following T-accounts, indicate the side of the account that should be used to record an increase or decrease in the account balance:

Cash		Account Payable		Common Stock	
Debit	Credit	Debit	Credit	Debit	Credit

Accounts Receivable		Salaries Payable		Dividends	
Debit	Credit	Debit	Credit	Debit	Credit

Supplies				Service Revenue	
Debit	Credit			Debit	Credit

				Other Operating Expense	
				Debit	Credit

Exercise 3-8A T-accounts and the accounting equation

LO 3-1

Required

Record each of the following Fred Co. events in T-accounts, and then explain how the event affects the accounting equation:
a. Received $20,000 cash by issuing common stock.
b. Purchased supplies for $1,000 cash.
c. Purchased land for $10,000 cash.
d. Performed services for $3,200 cash.

Exercise 3-9A Recording receivables and identifying their effect on financial statements

LO 3-1

Davos Company performed services on account for $160,000 in Year 1. Davos collected $120,000 cash from accounts receivable during Year 1, and the remaining $40,000 was collected in cash during Year 2.

Required

a. Record the Year 1 transactions in T-accounts.
b. Show the Year 1 transactions in a horizontal statements model like the following one:

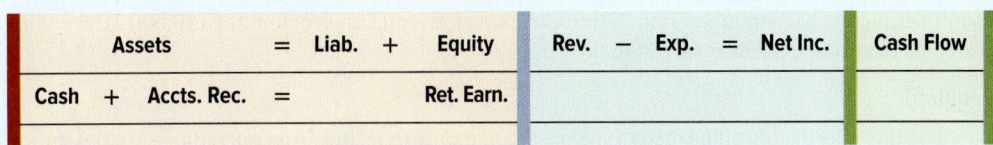

c. Determine the amount of revenue Davos would report on the Year 1 income statement.
d. Determine the amount of cash flow from operating activities Davos would report on the Year 1 statement of cash flows.
e. Open a T-account for Retained Earnings, and close the Year 1 Service Revenue account to the Retained Earnings account.
f. Record the Year 2 cash collection in the appropriate T-accounts.
g. Show the Year 2 transaction in a horizontal statements model like the one shown in Requirement *b*.
h. Assuming no other transactions occur in Year 2, determine the amount of net income and the net cash flow from operating activities for Year 2.

Exercise 3-10A Recording supplies and identifying their effect on financial statements

LO 3-1, 3-3, 3-4

Sye Chase started and operated a small family architectural firm in Year 1. The firm was affected by two events: (1) Chase provided $25,000 of services on account, and (2) he purchased $2,800 of supplies on account. There were $250 of supplies on hand as of December 31, Year 1.

Required

a. Open T-accounts and record the two transactions in the accounts.
b. Record the required year-end adjusting entry to reflect the use of supplies.
c. Show the preceding transactions in a horizontal statements model like the following one:

Assets	=	Liab.	+	Equity	Rev.	−	Exp.	=	Net Inc.	Cash Flow
Accts. Rec. + Supplies	=	Accts. Pay.	+	Ret. Earn.						

d. Explain why the amounts of net income and net cash flow from operating activities differ.
e. Record and post the required closing entries, and prepare a post-closing trial balance.

Chapter 3

LO 3-1

Exercise 3-11A *Recording unearned revenue and identifying its effect on financial statements*

Raylan received a $60,000 cash advance payment on June 1, Year 1, for consulting services to be performed in the future. Services were to be provided for a one-year term beginning June 1, Year 1.

Required

a. Record the June 1 cash receipt in T-accounts.
b. Record in T-accounts the adjustment required as of December 31, Year 1.
c. Show the preceding transaction and related adjustment in a horizontal statements model like the following one:

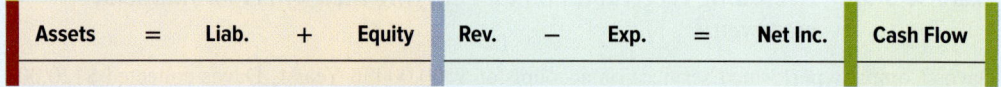

d. Determine the amount of net income on the Year 1 income statement. What is the amount of net cash flow from operating activities for Year 1?
e. What amount of liabilities would Raylan report on the Year 1 balance sheet?

LO 3-1

Exercise 3-12A *Using a T-account to determine cash flow from operating activities*

River Co. began the accounting period with a $132,000 debit balance in its Accounts Receivable account. During the accounting period, River Co. earned revenue on account of $180,000. The ending Accounts Receivable balance was $116,000.

Required

Based on this information alone, determine the amount of cash inflow from operating activities during the accounting period. (*Hint:* Use a T-account for Accounts Receivable. Enter the debits and credits for the given events, and solve for the missing amount.)

LO 3-1

Exercise 3-13A *Using a T-account to determine cash flow from operating activities*

The Garden Company began the accounting period with a $60,000 credit balance in its Accounts Payable account. During the accounting period, Garden Company incurred expenses on account of $152,000. The ending Accounts Payable balance was $64,000.

Required

Based on this information, determine the amount of cash outflow for expenses during the accounting period. (*Hint:* Use a T-account for Accounts Payable. Enter the debits and credits for the given events, and solve for the missing amount.)

LO 3-2

Exercise 3-14A *Recording events in the general journal and identifying their effect on financial statements*

Required

Record each of the following transactions in general journal form and then show the effect of the transaction in a horizontal statements model. The first transaction is shown as an example.

Account Title	Debit	Credit
Accounts Receivable	8,200	
Service Revenue		8,200

Assets	=	Liab.	+	Equity	Rev.	−	Exp.	=	Net Inc.	Cash Flow
8,200				8,200	8,200		NA		8,200	NA

a. Performed $8,200 of services on account.
b. Collected $5,600 cash on accounts receivable.
c. Paid $1,450 cash in advance for an insurance policy.

d. Paid $400 on accounts payable.
e. Recorded the adjusting entry to recognize $300 of insurance expense.
f. Received $1,600 cash for services to be performed at a later date.
g. Purchased land for $9,000 cash.
h. Purchased supplies for $350 cash.

Exercise 3-15A *Recording prepaid items and identifying their effect on financial statements*

LO 3-2

Cherokee Company began operations when it issued common stock for $80,000 cash. It paid $60,000 cash in advance for a one-year contract to lease delivery equipment for the business. It signed the lease agreement on March 1, Year 1, which was effective immediately. Cherokee received $98,000 of cash revenue in Year 1.

Required
a. Record the March 1 cash payment in general journal format.
b. Record in general journal format the adjustment required as of December 31, Year 1.
c. Show all events in a horizontal statements model like the following one:

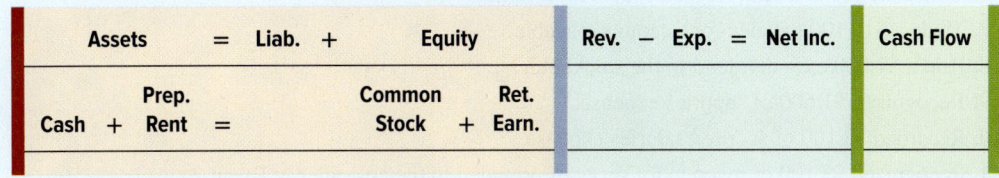

d. What amount of net income will Cherokee Company report on the Year 1 income statement? What is the amount of net cash flow from operating activities for Year 1?
e. Determine the amount of prepaid rent Cherokee Company would report on the December 31, Year 1, balance sheet.

Exercise 3-16A *Recording accrued salaries and identifying their effect on financial statements*

LO 3-2

On December 31, Year 1, BIG Company had accrued salaries of $6,400.

Required
a. Record in general journal format the adjustment required as of December 31, Year 1.
b. Show the above adjustment in a horizontal statements model like the following one:

Assets	=	Liab.	+	Equity	Rev.	−	Exp.	=	Net Inc.	Cash Flow
		Sal. Pay.	+	Ret. Earn.						

c. Determine the amount of net income BIG would report on the Year 1 income statement, assuming that BIG received $36,000 of cash revenue. What is the amount of net cash flow from operating activities for Year 1?
d. What amount of salaries payable would BIG report on the December 31, Year 1, balance sheet?

Exercise 3-17A *Recording transactions in the general journal and T-accounts*

LO 3-1, 3-2

The following events apply to Montgomery Company for Year 1, its first year of operation:
1. Received cash of $36,000 from the issue of common stock.
2. Performed $48,000 of services on account.
3. Incurred $6,500 of other operating expenses on account.
4. Paid $21,000 cash for salaries expense.
5. Collected $34,500 of accounts receivable.
6. Paid a $3,000 dividend to the stockholders.

7. Performed $9,500 of services for cash.
8. Paid $5,500 of the accounts payable.

Required

a. Record the preceding transactions in general journal form.
b. Post the entries to T-accounts and determine the ending balance in each account.
c. Determine the amount of total assets at the end of Year 1.
d. Determine the amount of net income for Year 1.

LO 3-1, 3-3

Exercise 3-18A *Recording events in T-accounts and preparing a trial balance*

The following events apply to Equipment Services Inc. in its first year of operation:

1. Acquired $60,000 cash from the issue of common stock.
2. Received an $8,200 cash advance for services to be provided in the future.
3. Purchased $2,000 of supplies on account.
4. Earned $36,000 of service revenue on account.
5. Incurred $16,100 of operating expenses on account.
6. Collected $28,500 cash from accounts receivable.
7. Made a $15,100 payment on accounts payable.
8. Paid a $2,000 cash dividend to the stockholders.
9. Recognized $1,600 of supplies expense.
10. Recorded $3,100 of accrued salaries expense.
11. Recognized $3,100 of revenue for services provided to the customer in Event 2.

Required

a. Record the events in T-accounts and determine the ending account balances.
b. Test the equality of the debit and credit balances of the T-accounts by preparing a trial balance.

LO 3-3

Exercise 3-19A *Preparing a trial balance*

Required

On December 31, Year 2, Morgan Company had the following normal account balances in its general ledger. Use this information to prepare a trial balance.

Land	$30,000
Unearned Revenue	32,000
Dividends	8,000
Prepaid Rent	5,600
Cash	90,000
Salaries Expense	18,000
Accounts Payable	7,000
Common Stock	80,000
Operating Expense	41,000
Office Supplies	2,500
Advertising Expense	3,500
Retained Earnings, Beginning	9,000
Service Revenue	86,000
Accounts Receivable	15,400

LO 3-3

Exercise 3-20A *Determining the effect of errors on the trial balance*

Required

Explain how each of the following posting errors affects a trial balance. State whether the trial balance will be out of balance because of the posting error, and indicate which side of the trial balance will have a higher amount after each independent entry is posted. If the posting error does not affect the equality of debits and credits in the trial balance, state that the error will not cause an inequality and explain why.

a. A $900 credit to Unearned Revenue was credited to Service Revenue.
b. A $3,400 credit to Accounts Payable was not posted.
c. A $900 debit to Rent Expense was posted twice.
d. A $1,250 debit to Office Supplies was debited to Office Supplies Expense.
e. A $560 debit to Cash was posted as a $650 debit.

Exercise 3-21A *Preparing closing entries*   LO 3-4

The following financial information was taken from the books of Zone Health Club, a small spa and fitness club:

Account Balances as of December 31, Year 2	
Accounts Receivable	$12,450
Accounts Payable	6,200
Salaries Payable	3,150
Cash	36,750
Dividends	2,000
Operating Expense	35,300
Prepaid Rent	1,200
Rent Expense	8,400
Retained Earnings, Beginning	41,250
Salaries Expense	14,500
Service Revenue	65,400
Supplies	650
Supplies Expense	3,150
Common Stock	7,000
Unearned Revenue	6,400
Land	15,000

Required

a. Prepare the journal entries necessary to close the temporary accounts at December 31, Year 2, for Zone Health Club.
b. What is the balance in the Retained Earnings account after the closing entries are posted?

Exercise 3-22A *Recording events in the general journal, posting to T-accounts, and preparing closing entries*   LO 3-1, 3-2, 3-3, 3-4

At the beginning of Year 2, Oak Consulting had the following normal balances in its accounts:

Account	Balance
Cash	$42,000
Accounts Receivable	25,000
Accounts Payable	8,400
Common Stock	24,000
Retained Earnings	34,600

The following events apply to Oak Consulting for Year 2:
1. Provided $185,000 of services on account.
2. Incurred $45,800 of operating expenses on account.
3. Collected $140,000 of accounts receivable.
4. Paid $120,000 cash for salaries expense.
5. Paid $31,400 cash as a partial payment on accounts payable.
6. Paid a $10,000 cash dividend to the stockholders.

Required

a. Record these transactions in a general journal.

b. Open T-accounts, and post the beginning balances and the preceding transactions to the appropriate accounts.

c. Show the beginning balances and the transactions in a horizontal statements model such as the following one:

Assets	=	Liab.	+	Equity	Rev.	−	Exp.	=	Net Inc.	Cash Flow
Cash + Acct. Rec.	=	Acct. Pay.	+	Common Stock + Ret. Earn.						

d. Record the closing entries in the general journal and post them to the T-accounts. What is the amount of net income for the year?

e. What is the amount of *change* in retained earnings for the year? Is the change in retained earnings different from the amount of net income? If so, why?

f. Prepare a post-closing trial balance.

Exercise 3-23A *Using ratio analysis to assess financial risk*

The following information was drawn from the balance sheets of two companies:

Company	Assets	=	Liabilities	+	Equity
East	200,000		84,000		116,000
West	600,000		168,000		432,000

Required

a. Compute the debt-to-assets ratio to measure the level of financial risk of both companies.

b. Compare the two ratios computed in Requirement *a* to identify which company has the higher level of financial risk.

Exercise 3-24A *IFRS and U.S. GAAP*

a. Describe some ways that U.S. GAAP and IFRS are different.

b. How are U.S. GAAP and IFRS alike for reporting purposes?

PROBLEMS—SERIES A

All applicable Problems in Series A are available in Connect.

Problem 3-25A *Identifying debit and credit balances*

Required

Indicate whether each of the following accounts normally has a debit or credit balance:

a. Interest Receivable
b. Interest Revenue
c. Prepaid Insurance
d. Land
e. Salaries Payable
f. Salaries Expense
g. Supplies Expense
h. Consulting Revenue
i. Utilities Payable
j. Supplies
k. Service Revenue
l. Accounts Payable
m. Operating Expense
n. Unearned Revenue
o. Dividends
p. Cash
q. Insurance Expense
r. Accounts Receivable
s. Utilities Expense
t. Retained Earnings
u. Common Stock

CHECK FIGURES
a. Interest Receivable: Debit
j. Supplies: Debit

Problem 3-26A Transaction type and debit/credit terminology

LO 3-1

The following events apply to Kate Enterprises:
1. Collected $16,200 cash for services to be performed in the future.
2. Acquired $50,000 cash from the issue of common stock.
3. Paid salaries to employees: $3,500 cash.
4. Paid cash to rent office space for the next 12 months: $12,000.
5. Paid cash of $17,500 for other operating expenses.
6. Paid on accounts payable: $1,752.
7. Paid cash for utilities expense: $804.
8. Recognized $45,000 of service revenue on account.
9. Paid a $2,500 cash dividend to the stockholders.
10. Purchased $3,200 of supplies on account.
11. Received $12,500 cash for services rendered.
12. Recognized $5,200 of accrued salaries expense.
13. Recognized $3,000 of rent expense. Cash had been paid in a prior transaction (see Event 4).
14. Recognized $5,000 of revenue for services performed. Cash had been previously collected (see Event 1).

Required

Identify each event as an asset source (AS), asset use (AU), asset exchange (AE), or claims exchange (CE). Also identify the account to be debited and the account to be credited when the transaction is recorded. The first event is recorded as an example.

Event No.	Type of Event	Account Debited	Account Credited
1	AS	Cash	Unearned Revenue

Problem 3-27A Showing events in a statements model, recording them in T-accounts and preparing a trial balance

LO 3-1, 3-3

The following accounting events apply to Mary's Designs for Year 1:

CHECK FIGURE
b. Total debits: $207,000

Asset Source Transactions

1. Began operations by acquiring $90,000 of cash from the issue of common stock.
2. Performed services and collected cash of $9,000.
3. Collected $36,000 of cash in advance for services to be provided over the next 12 months.
4. Provided $58,000 of services on account.
5. Purchased supplies of $5,200 on account.

Asset Exchange Transactions

6. Purchased $21,000 of land for cash.
7. Collected $49,000 of cash from accounts receivable.
8. Purchased $3,150 of supplies with cash.
9. Paid $12,000 for one year's rent in advance.

Asset Use Transactions

10. Paid $24,000 cash for salaries of employees.
11. Paid a cash dividend of $5,000 to the stockholders.
12. Paid off $3,600 of the accounts payable with cash.

Claims Exchange Transactions

13. Placed an advertisement in the local newspaper for $2,600 on account.
14. Incurred utility expense of $1,800 on account.

Adjusting Entries

15. Recognized $12,000 of revenue for performing services. The collection of cash for these services occurred in a prior transaction. (See Event 3.)
16. Recorded $8,000 of accrued salary expense at the end of Year 1.
17. Recorded supplies expense. Had $1,900 of supplies on hand at the end of the accounting period.
18. Recognized four months of expense for prepaid rent that had been used up during the accounting period.

Required

a. Record each of the preceding events in T-accounts.
b. Prepare a before-closing trial balance.
c. Use a horizontal statements model to show how each event affects the balance sheet, income statement, and statement of cash flows. Indicate whether the event increases (+), decreases (−), or does not affect (NA) each element of the financial statements. Also, in the Cash Flow column, use the letters OA to designate operating activity, IA for investing activity, and FA for financing activity. The first event is recorded as an example.

Assets	=	Liab.	+	Equity	Rev.	−	Exp.	=	Net Inc.	Cash Flow
+		NA		+	NA		NA		NA	+ FA

Problem 3-28A *Effect of journal entries on financial statements*

LO 3-2

Event No.	Account Title	Debit	Credit
1	Cash	xxx	
	Common Stock		xxx
2	Prepaid Rent	xxx	
	Cash		xxx
3	Accounts Receivable	xxx	
	Service Revenue		xxx
4	Cash	xxx	
	Unearned Revenue		xxx
5	Cash	xxx	
	Accounts Receivable		xxx
6	Supplies	xxx	
	Accounts Payable		xxx
7	Salaries Expense	xxx	
	Cash		xxx
8	Utilities Expense	xxx	
	Cash		xxx
9	Supplies Expense	xxx	
	Supplies		xxx
10	Unearned Revenue	xxx	
	Service Revenue		xxx
11	Cash	xxx	
	Service Revenue		xxx
12	Dividends	xxx	
	Cash		xxx
13	Rent Expense	xxx	
	Prepaid Rent		xxx

Required

The preceding 13 different accounting events are presented in general journal format. Use a horizontal statements model to show how each event affects the balance sheet, income statement, and statement of cash flows. Indicate whether the event increases (+), decreases (−), or does not affect (NA) each element of the financial statements. Also, in the Cash Flow column, use the letters OA to designate operating activity, IA for investing activity, and FA for financing activity. The first event is recorded as an example.

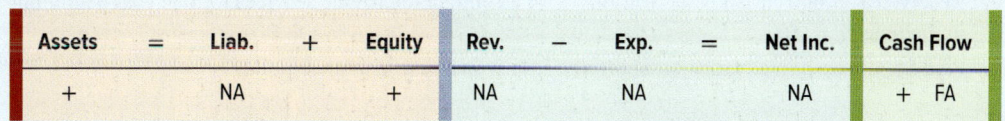

Problem 3-29A Identifying accounting events from journal entries

LO 3-2

Required
The following information is from the records of attorney Glenn Price. Write a brief explanation of the accounting event represented in each of the general journal entries.

Date	Account Titles	Debit	Credit
Jan. 1	Cash	40,000	
	Common Stock		40,000
Feb. 1	Cash	24,000	
	Service Revenue		24,000
Mar. 1	Prepaid Rent	1,600	
	Cash		1,600
Apr. 1	Accounts Receivable	48,000	
	Service Revenue		48,000
May 1	Supplies	2,000	
	Cash		2,000
June 10	Cash	8,000	
	Unearned Revenue		8,000
July 10	Cash	8,800	
	Accounts Receivable		8,800
Aug. 1	Salaries Expense	4,000	
	Cash		4,000
Oct. 1	Dividends	2,000	
	Cash		2,000
Nov. 1	Property Tax Expense	3,000	
	Cash		3,000
Dec. 31	Rent Expense	4,400	
	Prepaid Rent		4,400
31	Unearned Revenue	2,240	
	Service Revenue		2,240
31	Supplies Expense	800	
	Supplies		800

Problem 3-30A Recording adjusting entries in general journal format

LO 3-2

Required
Each of the following independent events requires a year-end adjusting entry. Record each event and the related adjusting entry in general journal format. The first event is recorded as an example. Assume a December 31 closing date.

Event No.	Date	Account Titles	Debit	Credit
a	July 1	Prepaid Rent	48,000	
		Cash		48,000
a	Dec. 31	Rent Expense (48,000 × 6/12)	24,000	
		Prepaid Rent		24,000

a. Paid $48,000 cash in advance on July 1 for a one-year lease on office space.
b. Purchased $5,000 of supplies on account on April 15. At year-end, $500 of supplies remained on hand.
c. Received a $9,600 cash advance on July 1 for a contract to provide services for one year beginning immediately.
d. Paid $5,400 cash in advance on February 1 for a one-year insurance policy.

LO 3-3

CHECK FIGURE
Corrected Cash Balance: $69,710

Problem 3-31A *Effect of errors on the trial balance*

The following trial balance was prepared from the ledger accounts of Ricardo Company:

RICARDO COMPANY
Trial Balance
April 30, Year 2

Account Title	Debit	Credit
Cash	$ 68,900	
Accounts Receivable	30,000	
Supplies	1,800	
Prepaid Insurance	3,600	
Land		$ 12,000
Accounts Payable		9,600
Common Stock		100,000
Retained Earnings		27,510
Dividends	8,000	
Service Revenue		60,000
Rent Expense	9,600	
Salaries Expense	31,500	
Operating Expense	32,400	
Totals	$185,800	$209,110

When the trial balance failed to balance, the accountant reviewed the records and discovered the following errors:

1. The company received $560 as payment for services rendered. The credit to Service Revenue was recorded correctly, but the debit to Cash was recorded as $650.
2. A $900 receipt of cash that was received from a customer on accounts receivable was not recorded.
3. A $600 purchase of supplies on account was properly recorded as a debit to the Supplies account. However, the credit to Accounts Payable was not recorded.
4. Land valued at $12,000 was contributed to the business in exchange for common stock. The entry to record the transaction was recorded as a $12,000 credit to both the Land account and the Common Stock account.
5. A $500 rent payment was properly recorded as a credit to Cash. However, the Salaries Expense account was incorrectly debited for $500.

Required
Based on this information, prepare a corrected trial balance for Ricardo Company.

LO 3-1, 3-2, 3-3, 3-4

CHECK FIGURES
d. Net Income: $50,880
Total Assets: $98,180

Problem 3-32A *Comprehensive problem: single cycle*

The following transactions pertain to Smith Training Company for Year 1:

Jan. 30 Established the business when it acquired $45,000 cash from the issue of common stock.
Feb. 1 Paid rent for office space for two years, $24,000 cash.
Apr. 10 Purchased $3,200 of supplies on account.
July 1 Received $24,000 cash in advance for services to be provided over the next year.
   20 Paid $1,500 of the accounts payable from April 10.
Aug. 15 Billed a customer $18,000 for services provided during August.
Sept. 15 Completed a job and received $8,400 cash for services rendered.

Oct. 1 Paid employee salaries of $12,000 cash.
　　 15 Received $15,000 cash from accounts receivable.
Nov. 16 Billed customers $42,000 for services rendered on account.
Dec. 1 Paid a dividend of $15,000 cash to the stockholders.
　　 31 Adjusted records to recognize the services provided on the contract of July 1.
　　 31 Recorded $3,600 of accrued salaries as of December 31.
　　 31 Recorded the rent expense for the year. (See February 1.)
　　 31 Physically counted supplies; $280 was on hand at the end of the period.

Required

a. Record the preceding transactions in the general journal.
b. Post the transactions to T-accounts and calculate the account balances.
c. Prepare a trial balance.
d. Prepare the income statement, statement of changes in stockholders' equity, balance sheet, and statement of cash flows.
e. Prepare the closing entries at December 31.
f. Prepare a trial balance after the closing entries are posted.

Problem 3-33A *Two complete accounting cycles*

LO 3-1, 3-2, 3-3, 3-4

Colton Enterprises experienced the following events for Year 1, the first year of operation:

CHECK FIGURES
Ending Cash
b. Balance, Year 1: $29,500
g. Net Income, Year 2: $20,750

1. Acquired $35,000 cash from the issue of common stock.
2. Paid $12,000 cash in advance for rent. The payment was for the period April 1, Year 1, to March 31, Year 2.
3. Performed services for customers on account for $72,000.
4. Incurred operating expenses on account of $35,000.
5. Collected $55,500 cash from accounts receivable.
6. Paid $21,000 cash for salary expense.
7. Paid $28,000 cash as a partial payment on accounts payable.

Adjusting Entries

8. Made the adjusting entry for the expired rent. (See Event 2.)
9. Recorded $2,400 of accrued salaries at the end of Year 1.

Events for Year 2

1. Paid $2,400 cash for the salaries accrued at the end of the prior accounting period.
2. Performed services for cash of $21,000.
3. Purchased $2,800 of supplies on account.
4. Paid $13,200 cash in advance for rent. The payment was for one year beginning April 1, Year 2.
5. Performed services for customers on account for $88,000.
6. Incurred operating expenses on account of $41,500.
7. Collected $89,000 cash from accounts receivable.
8. Paid $39,000 cash as a partial payment on accounts payable.
9. Paid $31,500 cash for salary expense.
10. Paid a $10,000 cash dividend to stockholders.

Adjusting Entries

11. Made the adjusting entry for the expired rent. (*Hint:* Part of the rent was paid in Year 1.)
12. Recorded supplies expense. A physical count showed that $450 of supplies were still on hand.

Required

a. Record the events and adjusting entries for Year 1 in general journal form.
b. Post the Year 1 events to T-accounts.
c. Prepare a trial balance for Year 1.
d. Prepare an income statement, statement of changes in stockholders' equity, balance sheet, and statement of cash flows for Year 1.

e. Record the entries to close the Year 1 temporary accounts to Retained Earnings in the general journal and post to the T-accounts.
f. Prepare a post-closing trial balance for December 31, Year 1.
g. Repeat requirements *a* through *f* for Year 2.

LO 3-5

Problem 3-34A *Using ratio analysis to make comparisons between companies*

The following information is available for the Maine Company and the Iowa Company:

	Maine Co.	Iowa Co.
Total assets	$695,000	$151,000
Total liabilities	417,000	106,000
Stockholders' equity	278,000	45,000
Net income	41,000	10,000

Required
a. For each company, compute the debt-to-assets ratio and the return-on-equity ratio.
b. Determine what percentage of each company's assets were financed by the owners.
c. Which company has the greatest level of financial risk?
d. Based on profitability alone, which company performed better?
e. Do the above ratios support the concept of financial leverage? Explain.

LO 3-6

Problem 3-35A *Notes payable (Appendix)*

TARVON Inc. acquired $50,000 cash by issuing a promissory note to the National Bank on May 1, Year 1. TARVON issued a promissory note with a one-year term and a 6 percent annual interest rate.

Required
Prepare the general journal entries to record:
a. The issue of the note on May 1, Year 1.
b. Accrued interest on December 31, Year 1.
c. Accrued interest on April 30, Year 2.
d. Cash paid to settle the amount of interest payable on April 30, Year 2.
e. Cash paid to settle the principal balance of the obligation to the bank on April 30, Year 2.

LO 3-6

Problem 3-36A *Comprehensive problem including depreciation (Appendix)*

Bower Consulting Company started the period with cash of $25,000, common stock of $13,000, and retained earnings of $12,000. Bower engaged in the following transactions in Year 2:

Transactions during Year 2

1. On January 1, Year 2, purchased office furniture for $12,000.
2. On March 1, paid $5,400 for an insurance policy that provides coverage for 12 months beginning immediately.
3. Purchased $1,800 of supplies for cash.
4. Provided $39,000 of services for cash.
5. Paid $9,000 for salaries expense.
6. On April 1, received $12,000 for services that will be performed over the next 12 months beginning immediately.

Information for Adjusting Entries

7. The furniture had an estimated life of four years and a $2,000 salvage value.
8. Recognized the expired insurance.
9. An inventory of supplies showed $250 of supplies on hand as of December 31.
10. Recognized the revenue associated with Event 6 as of December 31.

Required
a. Record the 10 events in general journal format.
b. Prepare an income statement, balance sheet, and statement of cash flows.

MULTIPLE-CHOICE QUESTIONS

Multiple-choice questions are available in **Connect.**

EXERCISES—SERIES B

Exercise 3-1B *Matching debit and credit terminology with accounts*   LO 3-1

Required

Complete the following table by indicating whether a debit or credit is used to increase or decrease the balance of the following accounts. The appropriate debit/credit terminology has been identified for the first account as an example.

Account Titles	Used to Increase This Account	Used to Decrease This Account
Insurance Expense	Debit	Credit
Rent Expense		
Prepaid Rent		
Interest Revenue		
Accounts Receivable		
Accounts Payable		
Common Stock		
Land		
Unearned Revenue		
Service Revenue		
Retained Earnings		

Exercise 3-2B *Debit/credit rules*   LO 3-1

Jake, Mollie, and Neil, three accounting students, are discussing the rules of debits and credits. Jake says that debits increase account balances and credits decrease account balances. Mollie says that Jake is wrong, that credits increase account balances and debits decrease account balances. Neil interrupts and declares that they are both correct.

Required

Explain what Neil means and give examples of transactions where debits increase account balances, credits decrease account balances, credits increase account balances, and debits decrease account balances.

Exercise 3-3B *Matching debit and credit terminology with account titles*   LO 3-1

Required

Indicate whether each of the following accounts normally has a debit balance or a credit balance.

a. Unearned Revenue
b. Service Revenue
c. Dividends
d. Land
e. Accounts Receivable
f. Cash
g. Common Stock
h. Prepaid Rent
i. Supplies
j. Accounts Payable
k. Interest Revenue
l. Rent Expense

Chapter 3

LO 3-1

Exercise 3-4B Applying debit/credit terminology to accounting events

Required

a. In parallel columns, list the accounts that would be debited and credited for each of the following unrelated transactions:
   (1) Provided services for cash.
   (2) Recognized accrued salaries at the end of the period.
   (3) Provided services on account.
   (4) Paid cash for operating expenses.
   (5) Acquired cash from the issue of common stock.
   (6) Purchased supplies on account.
   (7) Purchased land for cash.
   (8) Paid a cash dividend to the stockholders.

b. Use a horizontal statements model to show how each event affects the balance sheet, income statement, and statement of cash flows. Indicate whether the event increases (+), decreases (−), or does not affect (NA) each element of the financial statements. Also, in the Cash Flow column, use the letters OA to designate operating activity, IA for investing activity, and FA for financing activity. The first event is recorded as an example.

Assets	=	Liab.	+	Equity	Rev.	−	Exp.	=	Net Inc.	Cash Flow
+		NA		+	+		NA		+	+ OA

LO 3-1

Exercise 3-5B Debit/credit terminology

Required

For each of the following independent events, identify the account that would be debited and the account that would be credited. The accounts for the first event are identified as an example.

Event	Account Debited	Account Credited
a	Cash	Unearned Revenue

a. Received cash for services to be performed in the future.
b. Purchased supplies on account.
c. Paid cash in advance for one year's rent.
d. Received cash by issuing common stock.
e. Provided services on account.
f. Paid accounts payable.
g. Paid salaries payable.
h. Recognized revenue for services completed; previously collected the cash in Event *a*.
i. Paid cash for operating expenses.
j. Paid salaries expense.
k. Received cash in payment of accounts receivable.
l. Recognized expense for prepaid rent that had been used up by the end of the accounting period.
m. Paid cash dividends to the stockholders.

LO 3-1

Exercise 3-6B Identifying transaction type, its effect on the accounting equation, and whether the effect is recorded with a debit or credit

Required

Identify whether each of the following transactions is an asset source (AS), asset use (AU), asset exchange (AE), or claims exchange (CE). Also explain how each event affects the accounting equation by placing a (+) for increase, (−) for decrease, and NA for not affected under each of the components of the accounting equation. Finally, indicate whether the effect requires a debit or credit entry. The first event is recorded as an example.

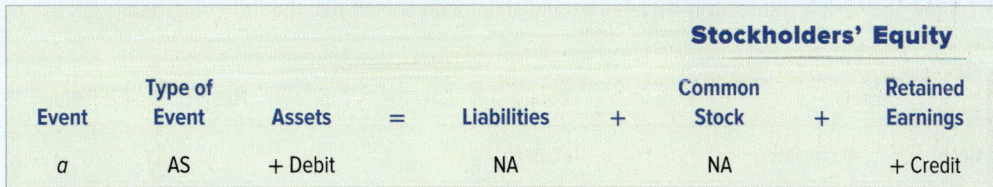

a. Provided services for cash.
b. Received cash in payment of accounts receivable.
c. Recognized revenue for services completed; cash collected previously.
d. Purchased land by paying cash.
e. Purchased supplies on account.
f. Paid salaries payable.
g. Recognized expense for prepaid rent that had been used up by the end of the accounting period.
h. Incurred other operating expenses on account.
i. Recognized expense for supplies used during the period.
j. Received cash for services to be performed in the future.
k. Paid a cash dividend to the stockholders.
l. Paid cash in advance for one year's rent.
m. Provided services on account.

Exercise 3-7B Identifying increases and decreases in T-accounts

LO 3-1

Required

For each of the following T-accounts, indicate the side of the account that should be used to record an increase or decrease in the financial statement element:

Exercise 3-8B T-accounts and the accounting equation

LO 3-1

Required

Record each of the following Wilson Co. events in T-accounts and then explain how the event affects the accounting equation:
a. Received $40,000 cash by issuing common stock.
b. Purchased supplies for $1,800 cash.
c. Performed services on account for $14,000.
d. Paid cash for $8,000 of salaries expense.

Exercise 3-9B Recording receivables and identifying their effect on financial statements

LO 3-1

Ross Company performed services on account for $30,000 in Year 1, its first year of operations. Ross collected $24,000 cash from accounts receivable during Year 1 and the remaining $6,000 in cash during Year 2.

Required

a. Record the Year 1 transactions in T-accounts.
b. Show the Year 1 transactions in a horizontal statements model like the following one:

c. Determine the amount of revenue that would be reported on the Year 1 income statement.
d. Determine the amount of cash flow from operating activities that would be reported on the Year 1 statement of cash flows.
e. Open a T-account for Retained Earnings, and close the Year 1 Service Revenue account to the Retained Earnings account.
f. Record the Year 2 cash collection in the appropriate T-accounts.
g. Show the Year 2 transaction in a horizontal statements model like the one shown in Requirement b.
h. Assuming no other transactions occur in Year 2, determine the amount of net income and the net cash flow from operating activities for Year 2.

LO 3-1, 3-3, 3-4

Exercise 3-10B *Recording supplies and identifying their effect on financial statements*

Laura Moss started and operated a small family consulting firm in Year 1. The firm was affected by two events: (1) Moss provided $36,000 of services on account, and (2) she purchased $10,000 of supplies on account. There were $1,800 of supplies on hand as of December 31, Year 1.

Required

a. Open T-accounts and record the two transactions in the accounts.
b. Record the required year-end adjusting entry to reflect the use of supplies.
c. Show the above transactions in a horizontal statements model like the following one:

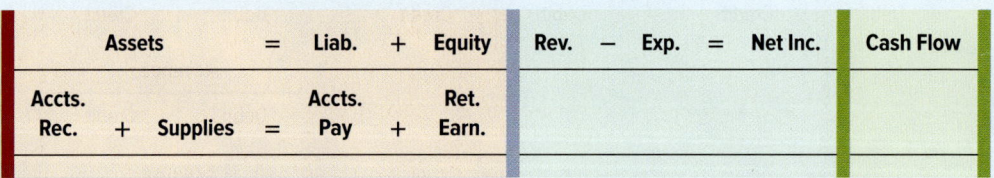

d. Explain why the amounts of net income and net cash flow from operating activities differ.
e. Record and post the required closing entries, and prepare a post-closing trial balance.

LO 3-1

Exercise 3-11B *Recording unearned revenue and identifying its effect on financial statements*

James Jones received a $90,000 cash advance on March 1, Year 1, for legal services to be performed in the future. Services were to be provided for a one-year term beginning March 1, Year 1.

Required

a. Record the March 1 cash receipt in T-accounts.
b. Record in T-accounts the adjustment required as of December 31, Year 1.
c. Show the preceding transaction and related adjustment in a horizontal statements model like the following one:

Assets	=	Liab.	+	Equity	Rev.	−	Exp.	=	Net Inc.	Cash Flow

d. Determine the amount of net income on the Year 1 income statement. What is the amount of net cash flow from operating activities for Year 1?
e. What amount of unearned revenue would Jones report on the December 31, Year 1, balance sheet?

Exercise 3-12B Using a T-account to determine cash flow from operating activities LO 3-1

Barnes Inc. began the accounting period with a $105,000 debit balance in its Accounts Receivable account. During the accounting period, Barnes earned revenue on account of $448,000. The ending Accounts Receivable balance was $86,000.

Required

Based on this information alone, determine the amount of cash inflow from operating activities during the accounting period. (*Hint:* Use a T-account for Accounts Receivable. Enter the debits and credits for the given events, and solve for the missing amount.)

Exercise 3-13B Using a T-account to determine cash flow from operating activities LO 3-1

Hun Company began the accounting period with a $36,000 credit balance in its Accounts Payable account. During the accounting period, Hun incurred expenses on account of $108,000. The ending Accounts Payable balance was $48,000.

Required

Based on this information, determine the amount of cash outflow for expenses during the accounting period. (*Hint:* Use a T-account for Accounts Payable. Enter the debits and credits for the given events, and solve for the missing amount.)

Exercise 3-14B Recording events in the general journal and identifying their effect on financial statements LO 3-2

Required

Record each of the following transactions in general journal form and then show the effect of the transaction in the horizontal statements model. The first transaction is shown as an example.

Account Title	Debit	Credit
Accounts Receivable	50,000	
Service Revenue		50,000

Assets	=	Liab.	+	Equity	Rev.	−	Exp.	=	Net Inc.	Cash Flow
50,000		NA		50,000	50,000		NA		50,000	NA

a. Performed $50,000 worth of services on account.
b. Charged $2,000 on account for operating expense.
c. Collected $27,000 cash on accounts receivable.
d. Paid $700 on accounts payable.
e. Paid $6,800 cash in advance for an insurance policy.
f. Recorded the adjusting entry to recognize $4,500 of insurance expense.
g. Received $4,000 cash for services to be performed at a later date.
h. Purchased supplies for $2,400 cash.

Exercise 3-15B Recording accrued salaries and identifying their effect on financial statements LO 3-2

On December 31, Year 1, Zeal Company had accrued salaries of $12,000.

Required

a. Record in general journal format the adjustment required as of December 31, Year 1.
b. Show the above adjustment in a horizontal statements model like the following one:

Assets	=	Liab.	+	Equity	Rev.	−	Exp.	=	Net Inc.	Cash Flow
		Sal. Pay.	+	Ret. Earn.						

c. Determine the amount of net income Zeal would report on the Year 1 income statement, assuming that Zeal received $29,000 of cash revenue. What is the amount of net cash flow from operating activities for Year 1?
d. What amount of salaries payable would Zeal report on the December 31, Year 1, balance sheet?

LO 3-2

Exercise 3-16B *Recording prepaid items and identifying their effect on financial statements*

Virginia Mining began operations by issuing common stock for $150,000. The company paid $135,000 cash in advance for a one-year contract to lease machinery for the business. The lease agreement was signed on March 1, Year 1, and was effective immediately. Virginia Mining received $172,500 of cash revenue in Year 1.

Required

a. Record the March 1 cash payment in general journal format.
b. Record in general journal format the adjustment required as of December 31, Year 1.
c. Show all Year 1 events in a horizontal statements model like the following one:

Assets	=	Liab.	+	Equity	Rev.	−	Exp.	=	Net Inc.	Cash Flow
Cash + Prep. Rent	=			Common Stock + Ret. Earn.						

d. What amount of net income would be reported on the Year 1 income statement? What is the amount of net cash flow from operating activities for Year 1?
e. Determine the amount of prepaid rent that would be reported on the December 31, Year 1, balance sheet.

LO 3-1, 3-2

Exercise 3-17B *Recording transactions in general journal and T-accounts*

The following events apply to Colton Training Co. for Year 1, its first year of operation:

1. Received cash of $60,000 from the issue of common stock.
2. Performed $100,000 worth of services on account.
3. Paid $74,000 cash for salaries expense.
4. Purchased supplies for $13,000 on account.
5. Collected $79,000 of accounts receivable.
6. Paid $9,500 of the accounts payable.
7. Paid a $6,000 dividend to the stockholders.
8. Had $2,500 of supplies on hand at the end of the period.

Required

a. Record these events in general journal form.
b. Post the entries to T-accounts and determine the ending balance in each account.
c. Determine the amount of total assets at the end of Year 1.
d. Determine the amount of net income for Year 1.

Exercise 3-18B Recording events in T-accounts and preparing a trial balance

LO 3-1, 3-3

The following events apply to Perry Carpet Cleaners in Year 1, its first year of operations:

1. Received $45,000 cash from the issue of common stock.
2. Earned $37,500 of service revenue on account.
3. Incurred $15,000 of operating expenses on account.
4. Received $30,000 cash for performing services.
5. Paid $12,000 cash to purchase land.
6. Collected $33,000 of cash from accounts receivable.
7. Received a $9,000 cash advance for services to be provided in the future.
8. Purchased $1,350 of supplies on account.
9. Made an $11,250 payment on accounts payable.
10. Paid a $7,500 cash dividend to the stockholders.
11. Recognized $750 of supplies expense.
12. Recognized $7,500 of revenue for services provided to the customer in Event 7.

Required

a. Record the events in the general journal.
b. Post the events to T-accounts and determine the ending account balances.
c. Test the equality of the debit and credit balances of the T-accounts by preparing a trial balance.

Exercise 3-19B Preparing a trial balance

LO 3-3

Required

On December 31, Year 2, Wages Company had the following normal account balances in its general ledger. Use this information to prepare a trial balance.

Common Stock	$ 50,000
Salaries Expense	32,000
Office Supplies	3,600
Advertising Expense	5,000
Retained Earnings, Beginning	28,400
Unearned Revenue	36,000
Accounts Receivable	13,000
Cash	120,000
Service Revenue	152,000
Dividends	10,000
Prepaid Insurance	12,800
Land	44,000
Rent Expense	30,000
Accounts Payable	4,000

Exercise 3-20B Determining the effect of errors on the trial balance

LO 3-3

Required

Explain how each of the following posting errors affects a trial balance. State whether the trial balance will be out of balance because of the posting error, and indicate which side of the trial balance will have a higher amount after each independent entry is posted. If the posting error does not affect the equality of debits and credits in the trial balance, state that the error will not cause an inequality and explain why.

a. A $2,000 credit to Salaries Payable was not posted.
b. A $5,400 debit to Cash was posted as a $4,500 debit.
c. A $3,000 debit to Prepaid Rent was debited to Rent Expense.
d. A $2,500 credit to Accounts Payable was posted as a credit to Cash.
e. The collection of $400 of accounts receivable was posted to Accounts Receivable twice.

LO 3-4

Exercise 3-21B *Preparing closing entries*

The following financial information was taken from the books of Serenity Spa:

Account Balances as of December 31, Year 2	
Accounts Receivable	$ 54,000
Accounts Payable	15,000
Advertising Expense	7,000
Cash	80,600
Common Stock	40,000
Dividends	10,000
Land	27,000
Prepaid Rent	6,400
Rent Expense	15,600
Retained Earnings, Beginning	38,800
Salaries Expense	64,000
Salaries Payable	23,600
Service Revenue	153,000
Supplies	800
Supplies Expense	5,000

Required

a. Prepare the journal entries necessary to close the temporary accounts December 31, Year 2, for Serenity Spa.

b. What is the balance in the Retained Earnings account after the closing entries are posted?

LO 3-1, 3-2, 3-3, 3-4

Exercise 3-22B *Recording events in the general journal, posting to T-accounts, and preparing closing entries*

At the beginning of Year 2, Event Services Co. had the following normal balances in its accounts:

Account	Balance
Cash	$60,000
Accounts Receivable	38,000
Accounts Payable	24,800
Common Stock	48,000
Retained Earnings	25,200

The following events apply to Event Services Co. for Year 2:

1. Provided $130,000 of services on account.
2. Incurred $6,200 of operating expenses on account.
3. Collected $112,000 of accounts receivable.
4. Paid $72,000 cash for salaries expense.
5. Paid $30,000 cash as a partial payment on accounts payable.
6. Paid a $16,000 cash dividend to the stockholders.

Required

a. Record these events in a general journal.

b. Open T-accounts and post the beginning balances and the preceding transactions to the appropriate accounts. Determine the balance of each account.

c. Show the beginning balances and the events in a horizontal statements model such as the following one:

Assets	=	Liab.	+	Equity		Rev.	−	Exp.	=	Net Inc.		Cash Flow
Cash + Accts. Rec.	=	Accts. Pay.	+	Common Stock + Ret. Earn.								

d. Record the closing entries in the general journal and post them to the T-accounts. What is the amount of net income for the year?
e. What is the amount of *change* in retained earnings for the year? Is the change in retained earnings different from the amount of net income? If so, why?
f. Prepare a post-closing trial balance.

Exercise 3-23B *Using ratio analysis to assess financial risk* LO 3-5

The following information was drawn from the balance sheets of two companies:

Company	Assets	=	Liabilities	+	Equity
North	$100,000		$ 24,500		$ 75,500
South	500,000		220,000		280,000

Required
a. Compute the debt-to-assets ratio to measure the level of financial risk of both companies.
b. Compare the two ratios computed in Requirement *a* to identify which company has the higher level of financial risk.

Exercise 3-24B *IFRS and U.S. GAAP* IFRS

Using one of the websites referenced in the Focus on International Issues feature earlier in this chapter, define the IASB and describe its function.

PROBLEMS—SERIES B

Problem 3-25B *Identifying debit and credit balances* LO 3-1

Required
Indicate whether each of the following accounts normally has a debit or credit balance:
a. Retained Earnings
b. Prepaid Insurance
c. Insurance Expense
d. Accounts Receivable
e. Salaries Payable
f. Cash
g. Common Stock
h. Rent Expense
i. Salaries Expense
j. Land
k. Interest Receivable
l. Interest Revenue
m. Dividends
n. Operating Expense
o. Unearned Revenue
p. Accounts Payable
q. Supplies
r. Service Revenue
s. Prepaid Rent
t. Supplies Expense

Problem 3-26B *Transaction type and debit/credit terminology* LO 3-1

The following events apply to Un Enterprises:
1. Acquired $30,000 cash from the issue of common stock.
2. Recognized $28,000 of service revenue on account.
3. Paid cash to rent office space for the next 12 months: $7,800.
4. Paid cash of $9,200 for operating expenses.
5. Collected $9,000 cash for services to be performed in the future.
6. Paid salaries to employees: $8,000 cash.
7. Paid cash for utilities expense: $1,200.
8. Paid on accounts payable: $1,200.
9. Paid a $5,000 cash dividend to the stockholders.
10. Purchased $2,000 of supplies on account.

11. Received $18,000 cash for services rendered.
12. Recognized $3,250 of rent expense related to cash paid in a prior transaction (see Event 3).
13. Recognized $6,000 of revenue for services performed for which cash had been previously collected (see Event 5).
14. Recognized $4,800 of accrued salaries expense.

Required

Identify each event as asset source (AS), asset use (AU), asset exchange (AE), or claims exchange (CE). Also identify the account to be debited and the account to be credited when the transaction is recorded. The first event is recorded as an example.

Event No.	Type of Event	Account Debited	Account Credited
1	AS	Cash	Common Stock

LO 3-1, 3-3

Problem 3-27B *Showing events in a statements model, recording them in T-accounts, and preparing a trial balance*

The following accounting events apply to Little Co. for Year 1:

Asset Source Transactions

1. Began operations when the business acquired $40,000 cash from the issue of common stock.
2. Performed services and collected cash of $2,000.
3. Collected $9,000 of cash in advance for services to be provided over the next 12 months.
4. Provided $24,000 of services on account.
5. Purchased supplies of $840 on account.

Asset Exchange Transactions

6. Purchased $8,000 of land for cash.
7. Collected $17,000 of cash from accounts receivable.
8. Purchased $1,000 of supplies with cash.
9. Paid $7,200 in advance for one year's rent.

Asset Use Transactions

10. Paid $6,000 cash for salaries of employees.
11. Paid a cash dividend of $4,000 to the stockholders.
12. Paid $840 for supplies that had been purchased on account.

Claims Exchange Transactions

13. Placed an advertisement in the local newspaper for $300 and agreed to pay for the ad later.
14. Incurred utilities expense of $250 on account.

Adjusting Entries

15. Recognized $6,000 of revenue for performing services. The collection of cash for these services occurred in a prior transaction. (See Event 3.)
16. Recorded $1,800 of accrued salary expense at the end of Year 1.
17. Recorded supplies expense. Had $240 of supplies on hand at the end of the accounting period.
18. Recognized that three months of prepaid rent had been used up during the accounting period.

Required

a. Record each of the preceding transactions in T-accounts and determine the balance of each account.
b. Prepare a before-closing trial balance.

c. Use a horizontal statements model to show how each event affects the balance sheet, income statement, and statement of cash flows. Indicate whether the event increases (+), decreases (−), or does not affect (NA) each element of the financial statements. Also, in the Cash Flow column, use the letters OA to designate operating activity, IA for investing activity, and FA for financing activity. The first event is recorded as an example.

Assets	=	Liab.	+	Equity	Rev.	−	Exp.	=	Net Inc.	Cash Flow
+		NA		+	NA		NA		NA	+ FA

Problem 3-28B Effect of journal entries on financial statements   LO 3-2

Event No.	Account Title	Debit	Credit
1	Cash	XXX	
	Common Stock		XXX
2	Accounts Receivable	XXX	
	Service Revenue		XXX
3	Cash	XXX	
	Accounts Receivable		XXX
4	Supplies	XXX	
	Accounts Payable		XXX
5	Cash	XXX	
	Unearned Revenue		XXX
6	Cash	XXX	
	Service Revenue		XXX
7	Property Tax Expense	XXX	
	Cash		XXX
8	Prepaid Rent	XXX	
	Cash		XXX
9	Salaries Expense	XXX	
	Cash		XXX
10	Unearned Revenue	XXX	
	Service Revenue		XXX
11	Rent Expense	XXX	
	Prepaid Rent		XXX
12	Supplies Expense	XXX	
	Supplies		XXX
13	Dividends	XXX	
	Cash		XXX

Required
The preceding 13 different accounting events are presented in general journal format. Use a horizontal statements model to show how each event affects the balance sheet, income statement, and statement of cash flows. Indicate whether the event increases (+), decreases (−), or does not affect (NA) each element of the financial statements. Also, in the Cash Flow column, use the letters OA to designate operating activity, IA for investing activity, and FA for financing activity. The first event is recorded as an example.

Assets	=	Liab.	+	Equity	Rev.	−	Exp.	=	Net Inc.	Cash Flow
+		NA		+	NA		NA		NA	+ FA

Chapter 3

LO 3-2

Problem 3-29B *Identifying accounting events from journal entries*

Required

The following information is from the records of Floral Design. Write a brief explanation of the accounting event represented in each of the general journal entries.

Date	Account Titles	Debit	Credit
Jan. 1	Cash	18,750	
	Common Stock		18,750
Feb. 1	Prepaid Rent	15,300	
	Cash		15,300
Mar. 1	Cash	19,500	
	Unearned Revenue		19,500
Apr. 1	Accounts Receivable	27,600	
	Service Revenue		27,600
May 1	Supplies	2,325	
	Accounts Payable		2,325
31	Salaries Expense	9,150	
	Cash		9,150
June 30	Property Tax Expense	4,500	
	Cash		4,500
Sept. 1	Cash	13,000	
	Service Revenue		13,000
Oct. 2	Cash	16,000	
	Accounts Receivable		16,000
Dec. 1	Dividends	4,000	
	Cash		4,000
Dec. 31	Supplies Expense	2,100	
	Supplies		2,100
31	Rent Expense	9,600	
	Prepaid Rent		9,600
31	Unearned Revenue	12,500	
	Service Revenue		12,500

LO 3-2

Problem 3-30B *Recording adjusting entries in general journal format*

Required

Each of the following independent events requires a year-end adjusting entry. Record each event and the related adjusting entry in general journal format. The first event is recorded as an example. Assume a December 31 closing date.

Date	Account Titles	Debit	Credit
Oct. 1	Prepaid Rent	8,400	
	Cash		8,400
Dec. 31	Rent Expense (8,400 × 3/12)	2,100	
	Prepaid Rent		2,100

a. Paid $8,400 cash in advance on October 1 for a one-year lease on office space.
b. Paid $4,800 cash in advance on May 1 for a one-year insurance policy.
c. Purchased $1,600 of supplies on account on June 15. At year end, $200 of supplies remained on hand.
d. Received a $4,800 cash advance on September 1 for a contract to provide services for one year beginning immediately.

Problem 3-31B Effect of errors on the trial balance   LO 3-3

The following trial balance was prepared from the ledger accounts of Klein Inc.:

KLEIN INC.
Trial Balance
May 31, Year 2

Account Titles	Debit	Credit
Cash	$ 7,200	
Accounts Receivable	3,000	
Supplies	420	
Prepaid Insurance	2,400	
Land	5,000	
Accounts Payable		$ 1,500
Common Stock		1,800
Retained Earnings		7,390
Dividends	400	
Service Revenue		20,830
Rent Expense	3,600	
Salaries Expense	9,000	
Operating Expenses	2,500	
Totals	$33,520	$31,520

The accountant for Klein Inc. made the following errors during May, Year 2:

1. The cash purchase of land for $3,000 was recorded as a $5,000 debit to Land and a $3,000 credit to Cash.
2. A $1,600 purchase of supplies on account was properly recorded as a debit to the Supplies account but was incorrectly recorded as a credit to the Cash account.
3. The company provided services valued at $7,800 to a customer on account. The accountant recorded the transaction in the proper accounts but in the incorrect amount of $8,700.
4. A $1,200 cash receipt from a customer on an account receivable was not recorded.
5. An $800 cash payment of an account payable was not recorded.
6. The May utility bill, which amounted to $1,050 on account, was not recorded.

Required

a. Identify the errors that would cause a difference in the total amounts of debits and credits that would appear in a trial balance. Indicate whether the Debit or Credit column would be larger as a result of the error.
b. Indicate whether each of the preceding errors would overstate, understate, or have no effect on the amount of total assets, liabilities, and equity. Your answer should take the following form:

Event No.	Assets	=	Liabilities	+	Stockholders' Equity
1	Overstate		No effect		No effect

c. Prepare a corrected trial balance.

Problem 3-32B Comprehensive problem: single cycle   LO 3-1, 3-2, 3-3, 3-4

The following transactions pertain to Price Corporation for Year 1:

Jan.   1 Began operations when the business acquired $25,000 cash from the issue of common stock.
Mar.   1 Paid rent for office space for two years: $8,400 cash.
Apr. 14 Purchased $400 of supplies on account.
June 30 Received $12,000 cash in advance for services to be provided over the next year.
July   5 Paid $300 of the accounts payable from April 14.

Aug. 1 Billed a customer $4,800 for services provided during July.
8 Completed a job and received $1,600 cash for services rendered.
Sept. 1 Paid employee salaries of $18,000 cash.
9 Received $4,250 cash from accounts receivable.
Oct. 5 Billed customers $17,000 for services rendered on account.
Nov. 2 Paid a $500 cash dividend to the stockholders.
Dec. 31 Adjusted records to recognize the services provided on the contract of June 30.
31 Recorded $1,100 of accrued salaries as of December 31.
31 Recorded the rent expense for the year. (See March 1.)
31 Physically counted supplies; $50 was on hand at the end of the period.

Required

a. Record the preceding transactions in the general journal.
b. Post the transactions to T-accounts and calculate the account balances.
c. Prepare a trial balance.
d. Prepare the income statement, statement of changes in stockholders' equity, balance sheet, and statement of cash flows.
e. Prepare the closing entries at December 31.
f. Prepare a trial balance after the closing entries are posted.

Problem 3-33B *Two complete accounting cycles*

Anchor Machining experienced the following events during Year 1:

1. Started operations by acquiring $100,000 of cash from the issue of common stock.
2. Paid $12,000 cash in advance for rent during the period from February 1, Year 1, to February 1, Year 2.
3. Received $9,600 cash in advance for services to be performed evenly over the period from September 1, Year 1, to September 1, Year 2.
4. Performed services for customers on account for $130,400.
5. Incurred operating expenses on account of $63,000.
6. Collected $113,800 cash from accounts receivable.
7. Paid $44,000 cash for salaries expense.
8. Paid $56,000 cash as a partial payment on accounts payable.

Adjusting Entries

9. Made the adjusting entry for the expired rent. (See Event 2.)
10. Recognized revenue for services performed in accordance with Event 3.
11. Recorded $4,200 of accrued salaries at the end of Year 1.

Events for Year 2

1. Paid $4,200 cash for the salaries accrued at the end of the previous year.
2. Performed services for cash of $81,000.
3. Paid $50,000 cash to purchase land.
4. Paid $10,800 cash in advance for rent during the period from February 1, Year 2, to February 1, Year 3.
5. Performed services for customers on account for $164,000.
6. Incurred operating expenses on account of $98,200.
7. Collected $152,600 cash from accounts receivable.
8. Paid $96,000 cash as a partial payment on accounts payable.
9. Paid $82,000 cash for salaries expense.
10. Paid a $10,000 cash dividend to the stockholders.

Adjusting Entries

11. Recognized revenue for services performed in accordance with Event 3 in Year 1.
12. Made the adjusting entry for the expired rent. (*Hint:* Part of the rent was paid in Year 1.)
13. Recorded $7,000 of accrued salaries at the end of Year 2.

Required

a. Record the events and adjusting entries for Year 1 in general journal form.
b. Post the events for Year 1 to T-accounts.
c. Prepare a trial balance for Year 1.
d. Prepare an income statement, statement of changes in stockholders' equity, balance sheet, and statement of cash flows for Year 1.
e. Record the entries to close the Year 1 temporary accounts to Retained Earnings in the general journal and post to the T-accounts.
f. Prepare a post-closing trial balance for December 31, Year 1.
g. Repeat requirements *a* through *f* for Year 2.

Problem 3-34B *Using ratio analysis to make comparisons between companies* LO 3-5

The following information is available for Delaware Company and Florida Company:

	Delaware Co.	Florida Co.
Total assets	$127,000	$753,000
Total liabilities	93,000	452,000
Stockholders' equity	34,000	301,000
Net income	8,000	45,000

Required

a. For each company, compute the debt-to-assets ratio and the return-on-equity ratio.
b. Determine what percentage of each company's assets were financed by the owners.
c. Which company has the greatest level of financial risk?
d. Based on profitability alone, which company performed better?
e. Do the above ratios support the concept of financial leverage? Explain.

Problem 3-35B *Notes payable (Appendix)* LO 3-6

Black Inc. acquired $10,000 cash by issuing a promissory note to the National Bank on November 1, Year 1. The note stipulated a one-year term and a 9 percent annual interest rate.

Required

Prepare the general journal entries to record:

a. The issue of the note on November 1, Year 1.
b. Accrued interest on December 31, Year 1.
c. Accrued interest on October 31, Year 2.
d. Cash paid to settle the amount of interest payable on October 31, Year 2.
e. Cash paid to settle the principal balance of the obligation to the bank on October 31, Year 2.

Problem 3-36B *Comprehensive problem including depreciation (Appendix)* LO 3-6

Vox Company started the period with cash of $22,000, common stock of $12,000, and retained earnings of $10,000. Vox engaged in the following transactions in Year 2:

Transactions during Year 2

1. On January 1, Year 2, purchased a computer for $7,500 cash.
2. On February 1, paid $6,600 cash for rent for a 12-month period beginning immediately.
3. Purchased $1,100 of supplies for cash.
4. Provided $56,000 of services for cash.
5. Paid $18,000 cash for salaries expense.
6. On May 1, received $9,000 for services that will be performed over the next 12 months.

Information for Adjusting Entries

7. The computer had an estimated life of three years and a $2,400 salvage value.
8. Recognized the expired rent.
9. An inventory of supplies showed $120 of supplies on hand as of December 31.
10. Recognized the revenue associated with Event 6 as of December 31.

Required

a. Record the 10 events in general journal format.
b. Prepare an income statement, balance sheet, and statement of cash flows.

ANALYZE, THINK, COMMUNICATE

ATC 3-1 Business Applications Case *Understanding real-world annual reports*

Required

Obtain the Target Corporation's annual report at http://investors.target.com using the instructions in Appendix B, and use it to answer the following questions:

a. What was Target's debt-to-assets ratio for its fiscal year ended January 28, 2017 (2016) and 2015?
b. What was Target's return-on-assets ratio for 2016 and 2015?
c. What was Target's return-on-equity ratio for 2016 and 2015?
d. Why was Target's return-on-equity ratio higher than its return on assets ratio for 2016 and 2015?

ATC 3-2 Group Assignment *Financial statement analysis*

The beginning account balances for Miller Company were as follows for Year 2, Year 3, and Year 4:

	January 1 Year 2	January 1 Year 3	January 1 Year 4
Cash	$12,000	$19,000	$42,600
Accounts Receivable	6,000	10,000	6,000
Land	9,000	9,000	9,000
Prepaid Rent	0	1,000	1,400
Accounts Payable	12,300	11,300	15,300
Salaries Payable	0	0	2,100
Common Stock	10,000	10,000	10,000
Retained Earnings	4,700	17,700	31,600

Miller Company experienced the following events for the accounting periods Year 2, Year 3, and Year 4:

Year 2

1. Performed services for $36,000 on account.
2. Paid rent of $6,000 for the period March 1, Year 2, to March 1, Year 3.
3. Incurred operating expenses of $18,000 on account.
4. Collected $32,000 of accounts receivable.
5. Paid $19,000 of accounts payable.
6. Recorded expired rent.

Year 3

1. Performed services on account of $48,000.
2. Paid rent of $8,400 for the period March 1, Year 3, to March 1, Year 4, and recorded the expired rent for the period January 1, Year 3, to March 1, Year 3.

3. Incurred operating expenses of $24,000 on account.
4. Collected $52,000 of accounts receivable.
5. Paid $20,000 of accounts payable.
6. Recorded expired rent.
7. Recorded accrued salaries of $2,100.

Year 4

1. Paid accrued salaries.
2. Performed services on account of $56,000.
3. Paid rent of $9,000 for the period March 1, Year 4, to March 1, Year 5, and recorded the expired rent for the period January 1, Year 4, to March 1, Year 4.
4. Incurred operating expenses of $32,000 on account.
5. Collected $55,000 of accounts receivable.
6. Paid $33,000 of accounts payable.
7. Sold land for $5,000; the land had a cost of $5,000.
8. Recorded expired rent.

Required

Divide the class into groups of four or five students. Organize the groups into three sections. Assign each section of groups the financial data for one of the preceding accounting periods.

Group Task

a. Prepare an income statement, balance sheet, and statement of cash flows. It may be helpful to open T-accounts and post transactions to these accounts before attempting to prepare the statements.

Class Discussion

b. Review the cash flows associated with the collection of receivables and the payment of payables. Comment on the company's collection and payment strategy.
c. Did net income increase or decrease between Year 2 and Year 3? What were the primary causes?
d. Did net income increase or decrease between Year 3 and Year 4? What were the primary causes?

ATC 3-3   Real-World Case   *Choice of fiscal year*

Consider the following brief descriptions of four companies from different industries. **Six Flags, Inc.** operates regional theme parks. It operates 18 parks in the United States, one in Mexico, and one in Canada. **Toll Brothers, Inc.** is a home-builder. In its 2016 fiscal year, Toll Brothers completed 6,098 home sites in 377 communities. **Toys R Us, Inc.** is the well-known, international retailer of toys. **Vail Resorts, Inc.** operates several ski resorts in Colorado, including Vail Mountain, the largest in the United States, and Breckenridge Mountain Resort.

The chapter explained that companies often choose to close their books when business is slow. Each of these companies ends its fiscal year on a different date. The closing dates, listed chronologically, are as follows:

January 30
July 31
October 31
December 31

Required

a. Try to determine which fiscal year-end matches which company. Write a brief explanation of the reason for your decisions.
b. Because many companies deliberately choose to prepare their financial statements at a slow time of year, try to identify problems this may present for someone trying to analyze the balance sheet for **Toys R Us**. Write a brief explanation of the issues you identify.

ATC 3-4 Business Applications Case *Performing ratio analysis using real-world data*

The following data were taken from **Netflix, Inc.**'s 2016 annual report. *All dollar amounts are in millions.*

	Fiscal Years Ending	
	December 31, 2016	December 31, 2015
Total assets	$13,587	$10,203
Total liabilities		
Stockholders' equity	2,680	2,223
Net income	187	123

Required

a. For each year, compute Netflix's debt-to-assets ratio, return-on-assets ratio, and return-on-equity ratio. You will need to compute total liabilities.
b. Did the company's level of financial risk increase or decrease from 2015 to 2016?
c. In which year did the company appear to manage its assets most efficiently?
d. Do the above ratios support the concept of financial leverage? Explain.

ATC 3-5 Business Applications Case *Performing ratio analysis using real-world data*

The following data were taken from the 2016 annual reports of **Biogen Idec, Inc.** and **Amgen Inc.** Both companies are leaders in biotechnology. *All dollar amounts are in millions.*

	Biogen Idec	Amgen
	December 31, 2016	December 31, 2016
Total assets	$22,876.8	$77,626
Total liabilities	10,748.2	47,751
Stockholders' equity	12,128.6	29,875
Net income	3,702.8	7,722

Required

a. For each company, compute the debt-to-assets ratio, return-on-assets ratio, and return-on-equity ratio.
b. Which company has the greatest level of financial risk? Explain.
c. Which company appears to have managed its assets most efficiently? Explain.
d. Which company performed better from the perspective of the owners? Explain.

ATC 3-6 Writing Assignment *Effect of land sale on return on assets*

Toyo Company is holding land that cost $900,000 for future use. However, plans have changed and the company may not need the land in the foreseeable future. The president is concerned about the return on assets. Current net income is $425,000 and total assets are $3,500,000.

Required

a. Write a memo to the company president explaining the effect of disposing of the land, assuming that it has a current value of $1,500,000.
b. Write a memo to the company president explaining the effect of disposing of the land, assuming it has a current value of $600,000.

ATC 3-7 Ethical Dilemma *Choice of brothers: ethics, risk, and accounting numbers in a medieval setting*

In the late 1400s, a wealthy land owner named Caster was trying to decide which of his twin sons, Rogan or Argon, to designate as the first heir to the family fortune. He decided to set up each son with a small farm consisting of 300 sheep and 20 acres of land. Each twin would be allowed to manage his property as he deemed appropriate. After a designated period, Caster would call his sons before him to account for their actions. The heir to the family fortune would be chosen on the basis of which son had produced a larger increase in wealth during the test period.

On the appointed day of reckoning, Argon boasted that he had 714 sheep under his control while Rogan had only 330. Furthermore, Argon stated that he had increased his land holdings to 27 acres. The seven-acre increase resulted from two transactions: First, on the day the contest started, Argon used 20 sheep to buy 10 additional acres; and second, he sold three of these acres for a total of 9 sheep on the day of reckoning. Also, Argon's flock had produced 75 newborn sheep during the period of accounting. He had been able to give his friends 50 sheep in return for the help they had given him in building a fence, thereby increasing not only his own wealth but the wealth of his neighbors as well. Argon boasted that the fence was strong and would keep his herd safe from predatory creatures for five years (assume the fence had been used for one year during the contest period). Rogan countered that Argon was holding 400 sheep that belonged to another herder. Argon had borrowed these sheep on the day that the contest had started. Furthermore, Argon had agreed to return 424 sheep to the herder. The 24 additional sheep represented consideration for the use of the herder's flock. Argon had agreed to return the sheep immediately after the day of reckoning.

During the test period, Rogan's flock had produced 37 newborn sheep, but 2 sheep had gotten sick and died during the accounting period. Rogan had also lost 5 sheep to predatory creatures. He had no fence, and some of his sheep strayed from the herd, thereby exposing themselves to danger. Knowing that he was falling behind, Rogan had taken a wife in order to boost his productivity. His wife owned 170 sheep on the day they were married; her sheep had produced 16 newborn sheep since the date of her marriage to Rogan. Argon had not included the wife's sheep in his count of Rogan's herd. If his wife's sheep had been counted, Rogan's herd would contain 516 instead of 330 sheep suggested by Argon's count.

Argon charged that seven of Rogan's sheep were sick with symptoms similar to those exhibited by the two sheep that were now dead. Rogan interjected that he should not be held accountable for acts of nature such as illness. Furthermore, he contended that by isolating the sick sheep from the remainder of the herd, he had demonstrated prudent management practices that supported his case to be designated first heir.

Required

a. Prepare an income statement, balance sheet, statement of sheep flow (cash flow) for each twin, using contemporary accounting standards for the current year. Note that you have to decide whether to include the sheep owned by Rogan's wife when making his financial statements (What is the accounting entity?). (*Hint:* Use the number of sheep rather than the number of dollars as the common unit of measure.)

b. Refer to the statements you prepared in Requirement *a* to answer the following questions:
   (1) Which twin has more owner's equity at the end of the accounting period?
   (2) Which twin produced the higher net income during the accounting period?
   (3) Which son should be designated heir based on conventional accounting and reporting standards?

c. What is the difference in the value of the land of the twins if the land is valued at market value (that is, three sheep per acre) rather than historical cost (that is, two sheep per acre)?

d. Did Argon's decision to borrow sheep increase his profitability? Support your answer with appropriate financial data.

e. Was Argon's decision to build a fence financially prudent? Support your answer with appropriate financial data.

f. Assuming that the loan resulted in a financial benefit to Argon, identify some reasons that the shepherd who owned the sheep may have been willing to loan them to Argon.

g. Which twin is likely to take risks to improve profitability? What would be the financial condition of each twin if one-half of the sheep in both flocks died as a result of illness? How should such risk factors be reported in financial statements?

208   Chapter 3

h. Should Rogan's decision to "marry for sheep" be considered from an ethical perspective, or should the decision be made solely on the basis of the bottom-line net income figure?

i. Prepare a report that recommends which twin should be designated heir to the family business. Include a set of financial statements that supports your recommendation. Because this is a managerial report that will not be distributed to the public, you are not bound by generally accepted accounting principles.

ATC 3-8 Research Assignment   *Investigating Nike's 10-K report*

Many companies must file financial reports with the SEC. Many of these reports are available electronically through the EDGAR database. EDGAR is an acronym for Electronic Data Gathering, Analysis, and Retrieval system, and it is accessible through the World Wide Web on the Internet. Instructions for using EDGAR are in Appendix A.

Using the most current 10-K available on EDGAR or on the company's website at www.nikebiz.com, answer the following questions about Nike Company:

a. In what year did Nike begin operations?
b. Other than the Nike brand, what business does Nike operate?
c. How many employees does Nike have?
d. Describe, in dollar amounts, Nike's accounting equation at the end of the most recent year.
e. Has Nike's performance been improving or deteriorating over the past three years? Explain your answer.

ATC 3-9 Spreadsheet Assignment   *Use of Excel*

Adams Company started operations on January 1, Year 1. Six months later on June 30, Year 1, the company decided to prepare financial statements. The company's accountant decided to problem solve for the adjusting journal entries and the final adjusted account balances by using an electronic spreadsheet. Once the spreadsheet is complete, she will record the adjusting entries in the general journal and post them to the ledger. The accountant has started the following spreadsheet but wants you to finish it for her.

Required

a. On a blank spreadsheet, enter the following trial balance in Columns A through C. Also enter the headings for Columns E through I.

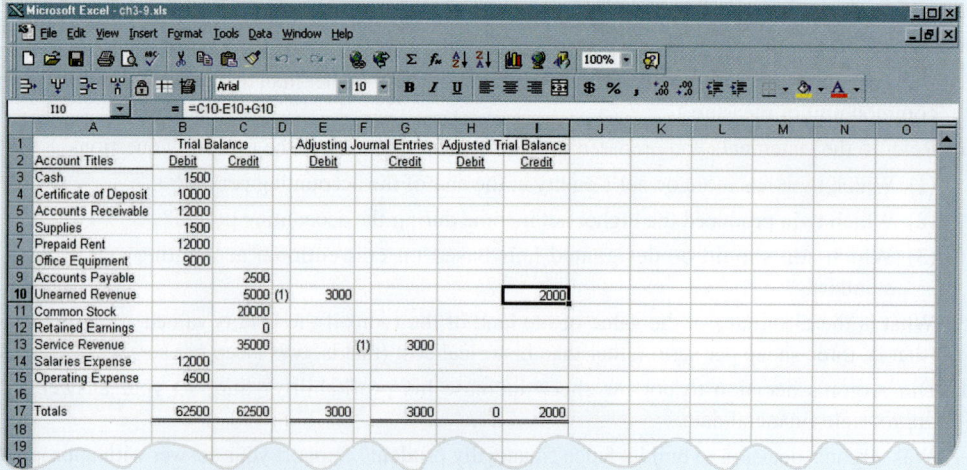

Source: Microsoft Office Excel 1997

b. Each of the following events requires an adjusting journal entry. Instead of recording entries in general journal format, record the adjusting entries in the Debit and Credit columns under the heading Adjusting Journal Entries. Entry (1) has already been recorded as an example. Be sure to number your adjusting entries on the spreadsheet. It will be necessary to insert new accounts for the adjustments. Recall that the accounting period is for six months.

(1) Received a $5,000 cash advance on April 1 for a contract to provide five months of service.
(2) Had accrued salaries on June 30 amounting to $1,500.
(3) On January 1 paid $12,000 in advance for a one-year lease on office space.
(4) Received in the mail a utility bill dated June 30 for $150.
(5) Purchased $1,500 of supplies on January 1. As of June 30, $700 of supplies remained on hand.
(6) Paid $9,000 for office equipment on January 1. The equipment was expected to have a four-year useful life and a $1,000 salvage value. Depreciation is computed on a straight-line basis.

c. Develop formulas to sum both the Debit and Credit columns under the Adjusting Journal Entries heading.

d. Develop formulas to derive the adjusted balances for the adjusted trial balance. For example, the formula for the ending balance of Unearned Revenue is =C10−E10+G10. In other words, a credit balance minus debit entries plus credit entries equals the ending balance. Once an ending balance is formulated for one credit account, that formula can be copied to all other credit accounts; the same is true for debit accounts. Once an ending balance is formulated for a debit account, that formula can be copied to all other debit accounts.

e. Develop formulas to sum both the Debit and Credit columns under the Adjusted Trial Balance heading.

Spreadsheet Tips

1. Rows and columns can be inserted by positioning the mouse on the immediate row or column after the desired position. Click on the *right* mouse button. With the *left* mouse button, choose Insert and then either Entire Column or Entire Row. Use the same method to delete columns or rows.

2. Enter the sequential numbering of the adjusting entries as labels rather than values by positioning an apostrophe in front of each entry. The first adjusting entry should be labeled '(1).

ATC 3-10   Spreadsheet Assignment   *Mastery of Excel*

At the end of the accounting period, Adams Company's general ledger contained the following adjusted balances:

Source: Microsoft Office Excel 1997

Required

1. Set up the preceding spreadsheet format. (The spreadsheet tips for ATC 3-9 also apply for this problem.)
2. Record the closing entries in the Closing Entries column of the spreadsheet.
3. Compute the Ending Trial Balance amounts.

COMPREHENSIVE PROBLEM

The trial balance of Pacilio Security Services, Inc. as of January 1, Year 3, had the following normal balances:

Cash	$8,900
Accounts Receivable	1,500
Supplies	65
Prepaid Rent	800
Land	4,000
Accounts Payable	1,050
Unearned Revenue	200
Salaries Payable	1,200
Notes Payable	2,000
Common Stock	8,000
Retained Earnings	2,815

During Year 3, Pacilio Security Services experienced the following transactions:

1. Paid the salaries payable from Year 2.
2. Paid the balance of $2,000 on the debt owed to the Small Business Government Agency. The loan is interest-free.
3. Performed $32,000 of security services for numerous local events during the year; $21,000 was on account and $11,000 was for cash.
4. On May 1, paid $3,000 for 12 months' rent in advance.
5. Purchased supplies on account for $700.
6. Paid salaries expense for the year of $9,000.
7. Incurred other operating expenses on account, $4,200.
8. On October 1, Year 3, a customer paid $1,200 for services to be provided over the next 12 months.
9. Collected $19,000 of accounts receivable during the year.
10. Paid $5,950 on accounts payable.
11. Paid $1,800 of advertising expenses for the year.
12. Paid a cash dividend to the shareholders of $4,650.
13. The market value of the land was determined to be $5,500 at December 31, Year 3.

Adjustments

14. There was $120 of supplies on hand at the end of the year.
15. Recognized the expired rent.
16. Recognized the earned revenue from Year 2 and transaction no. 8.
17. Accrued salaries were $1,000 at December 31, Year 3.

Required

a. Record the above transactions in general journal form.
b. Post the transactions to T-accounts and determine the account balances.
c. Prepare a trial balance.
d. Prepare an income statement, statement of changes in stockholders' equity, balance sheet, and statement of cash flows for Year 3.
e. Prepare the closing entries and post to the T-accounts.
f. Prepare a post-closing trial balance.

CHAPTER 4

Accounting for Merchandising Businesses

LEARNING OBJECTIVES

After you have mastered the material in this chapter, you will be able to:

LO 4-1 Record and report on inventory transactions using the perpetual system.
LO 4-2 Show how purchase returns and allowances affect financial statements.
LO 4-3 Show how cash discounts affect financial statements.
LO 4-4 Show how transportation costs affect financial statements.
LO 4-5 Show how inventory shrinkage affects financial statements.
LO 4-6 Prepare a multistep income statement.
LO 4-7 Determine the amount of net sales.
LO 4-8 Use common size financial statements and ratio analysis to evaluate managerial performance.

APPENDIX

LO 4-9 Identify the primary features of the periodic inventory system.

 Video lectures and accompanying self-assessment quizzes are available in Connect *for all learning objectives.*

CHAPTER OPENING

Previous chapters have discussed accounting for service businesses. These businesses obtain revenue by providing some kind of service such as medical or legal advice to their customers. Other examples of service companies include dry cleaning companies, housekeeping companies, and car washes. This chapter introduces accounting for merchandising businesses. **Merchandising businesses** generate revenue by selling goods. They buy the merchandise they sell from companies called suppliers. The goods purchased for resale are called **merchandise inventory.** Merchandising businesses include **retail companies** (companies that sell goods to the final consumer) and **wholesale companies** (companies that sell to other businesses). **Sears**, **JCPenney**, **Target**, and **Sam's Club** are real-world merchandising businesses.

The Curious Accountant

©Jim West/Alamy

Jason recently purchased a new Ford automobile from a dealer near his home. When he told his friend Ryan that he was able to purchase the car for $1,000 less than the sticker price, Ryan told Jason he had gotten a lousy deal. "Everybody knows there is a huge markup on cars," Ryan said. "You could have gotten a much lower price if you'd shopped around."

Jason responded, "If there is such a big profit margin on cars, why did so many of the car manufacturers get into financial trouble?" Ryan told him that he was confusing the maker of the car with the dealer. Ryan argued that although the manufacturers may not have high profit margins, the dealers do, and told him again that he had paid too much.

Exhibit 4.1 presents the income statements for **AutoNation, Inc.** and **Ford Motor Company**. Based on these statements, do you think either of these guys is correct? For example, if you pay $20,000 for a vehicle from a dealership operated by AutoNation, the largest auto retailer in the United States, how much did the car cost the company? Also, how much did the car cost the Ford Motor Company to manufacture? (Answers on page 236.)

EXHIBIT 4.1 — Comparative Income Statements

AUTONATION, INC.
Consolidated Statements of Income (Partial)
For the Years Ended December 31,
(In millions, except per share data)

	2016	2015	2014
Revenue:			
New vehicle	$12,255.8	$11,995.0	$10,972.2
Used vehicle	4,995.3	4,768.7	4,385.7
Parts and service	3,321.4	3,082.8	2,822.5
Finance and insurance, net	894.6	868.7	750.8
Other	141.9	146.8	177.6
Total revenue	21,609.0	20,862.0	19,108.8
Cost of Sales:			
New vehicle	11,620.0	11,321.9	10,322.1
Used vehicle	4,677.7	4,415.0	4,025.1
Parts and service	1,886.7	1,744.8	1,625.9
Other	111.4	118.8	147.0
Total cost of sales	18,295.8	17,600.5	16,120.1
Gross Profit:			
New vehicle	635.8	673.1	650.1
Used vehicle	317.6	353.7	360.6
Parts and service	1,434.7	1,338.0	1,196.6
Finance and insurance	894.6	868.7	750.8
Other	30.5	28.0	30.6
Total gross profit	3,313.2	3,261.5	2,988.7
Selling, general & administrative expenses	2,349.4	2,263.5	2,079.6
Depreciation and amortization	143.4	127.4	106.9
Franchise rights impairment	—	15.4	—
Other expenses (income), net	(69.1)	(17.9)	(18.6)
Operating income	889.5	873.1	820.8
Floorplan interest expense	(76.5)	(58.3)	(53.3)
Other interest expense	(115.5)	(90.9)	(86.7)
Loss on debt extinguishment	—	—	(1.6)
Interest income	1.1	0.1	0.2
Other income (losses), net	3.7	(1.3)	2.9
Income (loss) from continuing operations before income taxes	702.3	722.7	682.3
Income tax provision	270.6	279.0	262.5
Net income from continuing operations	431.7	443.7	419.8
Loss from discontinued operations, net of income taxes	(1.2)	(1.1)	(1.1)
Net income	$ 430.5	$ 442.6	$ 418.7

continued

EXHIBIT 4.1 *Concluded*

FORD MOTOR COMPANY AND SUBSIDIARIES
Consolidated Income Statements (Partial)
For the Years Ended December 31,
(In millions except per share amounts)

	2016	2015	2014
Sales and revenues			
Automotive sales	$141,546	$140,566	$135,782
Financial Services revenues	10,253	8,992	8,295
Other	1	—	—
Total sales and revenues	151,800	149,558	144,077
Costs and expenses			
Cost of sales	126,584	124,041	125,025
Selling, administrative and other expenses	12,196	10,502	11,842
Financial Services interest, operating, and other services	8,904	7,368	6,878
Total costs and expenses	147,684	141,911	143,745
Interest expense on Automotive debt	894	773	797
Non–Financial Services interest income and other income (loss), net	1,356	1,188	76
Financial Services other income/(loss), net	438	372	348
Equity in income of affiliated companies	1,780	1,818	1,275
Income before income taxes	6,796	10,252	1,234
Provision for/(Benefit from) income taxes	2,189	2,881	4
Net income	4,607	7,371	1,230
Less: Income/(Loss) attributable to noncontrolling interests	(11)	(2)	(1)
Net income attributable to Ford Motor Company	$ 4,596	$ 7,373	$ 1,231

ACCOUNTING FOR INVENTORY TRANSACTIONS

Companies report inventory costs on the balance sheet in the asset account Merchandise Inventory. All costs incurred to acquire merchandise and ready it for sale are included in the inventory account. Examples of inventory costs include the price of goods purchased, shipping and handling costs, transit insurance, and storage costs. Because inventory items are referred to as products, inventory costs are frequently called **product costs**.

Costs that are not included in inventory are usually called **selling and administrative costs**. Examples of selling and administrative costs include advertising, administrative salaries, sales commissions, and insurance. Because selling and administrative costs are usually recognized as expenses *in the period* in which they are incurred, they are sometimes called **period costs**. In contrast, product costs are expensed when inventory is sold, regardless of when it was purchased. In other words, product costs are matched directly with sales revenue, while selling and administrative costs are matched with the period in which they are incurred.

LO 4-1

 Record and report on inventory transactions using the perpetual system.

Allocating Inventory Cost between Asset and Expense Accounts

The cost of inventory that is available for sale during a specific accounting period is determined as follows:

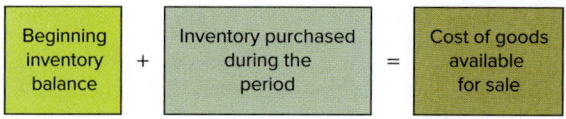

The **cost of goods available for sale** is allocated between the asset account Merchandise Inventory and an expense account called **Cost of Goods Sold.** The cost of inventory items that have not been sold (Merchandise Inventory) is reported as an asset on the balance sheet, and the cost of the items sold (Cost of Goods Sold) is expensed on the income statement. This allocation is depicted graphically as follows.

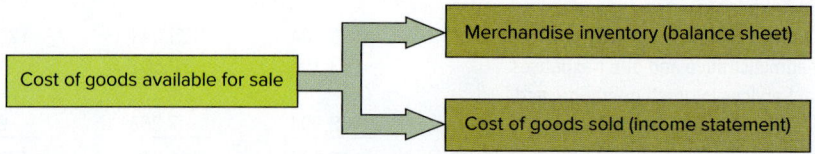

The difference between the sales revenue and the cost of goods sold is called **gross margin** or **gross profit.** The selling and administrative expenses (period costs) are subtracted from gross margin to obtain the net income.

Return to Exhibit 4.1 which displays income statements from the annual reports of AutoNation and Ford. For each company, review the most current income statement and determine the amount of gross margin on automobile sales. You should find a gross profit of $953.4 for AutoNation and a gross margin of $14,962 ($141,546 − $126,587) for Ford.

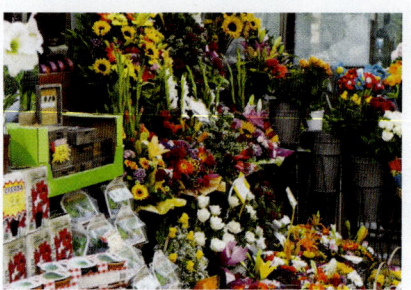
©Andreas Schindl/123RF

Perpetual Inventory System

Most modern companies maintain their inventory records using the **perpetual inventory system,** so-called because the inventory account is adjusted perpetually (continually) throughout the accounting period. Each time merchandise is purchased, the inventory account is increased; each time it is sold, the inventory account is decreased. The following illustration demonstrates the basic features of the perpetual inventory system.

June Gardener loved plants and grew them with such remarkable success that she decided to open a small retail plant store. She started June's Plant Shop (JPS) on January 1, Year 1. The following discussion explains and illustrates the effects of the five events the company experienced during its first year of operation.

Effects of Year 1 Events on Financial Statements

EVENT 1 **JPS acquired $15,000 cash by issuing common stock.**

This event is an asset source transaction. It increases both assets (cash) and stockholders' equity (common stock). The income statement is not affected. The statement of cash flows reflects an inflow from financing activities. The journal entry and its effects on the financial statements are shown next:

Account Title	Debit	Credit
Cash	15,000	
Common Stock		15,000

Accounting for Merchandising Businesses   217

Assets	=	Liab.	+	Stockholders' Equity					
Cash + Inventory + Land	=	Accts. Pay.	+	Com. Stk. + Ret. Earn.	Rev. − Exp. = Net Inc.	Cash Flow
15,000 + NA + NA	=	NA	+	15,000 + NA	NA − NA = NA	15,000 FA

EVENT 2 JPS purchased merchandise inventory (plants) for $14,000 cash.

This event is an asset exchange transaction. One asset, cash, decreases, while another asset, merchandise inventory, increases; total assets remain unchanged. Because product costs are expensed when inventory is sold, not when the goods are purchased, the event does not affect the income statement. The cash outflow, however, is reported in the operating activities section of the statement of cash flows. The journal entry and its effects on the financial statements are shown here:

Account Title	Debit	Credit
Merchandise Inventory	14,000	
Cash		14,000

Assets	=	Liab.	+	Stockholders' Equity			
Cash + Inventory + Land	=	Accts. Pay.	+	Com. Stk. + Ret. Earn.	Rev. − Exp. = Net Inc.	Cash Flow
(14,000) + 14,000 + NA	=	NA	+	NA + NA	NA − NA = NA	(14,000) OA

EVENT 3a JPS recognized sales revenue from selling inventory for $12,000 cash.

The revenue recognition is the first part of a two-part transaction. The *sales part* represents a source of assets (cash increases from earning sales revenue). Both assets (cash) and stockholders' equity (retained earnings) increase. Sales revenue on the income statement increases. The $12,000 cash inflow is reported in the operating activities section of the statement of cash flows. The journal entry and its effects on the financial statements are shown here:

Account Title	Debit	Credit
Cash	12,000	
Sales Revenue		12,000

Assets	=	Liab.	+	Stockholders' Equity			
Cash + Inventory + Land	=	Accts. Pay.	+	Com. Stk. + Ret. Earn.	Rev. − Exp. = Net Inc.	Cash Flow
12,000 + NA + NA	=	NA	+	NA + 12,000	12,000 − NA = 12,000	12,000 OA

EVENT 3b JPS recognized $8,000 of cost of goods sold.

The expense recognition is the second part of the two-part transaction. The *expense part* represents a use of assets. Both assets (merchandise inventory) and stockholders' equity (retained earnings) decrease. An expense account, Cost of Goods Sold, is reported on the income statement. This part of the transaction does not affect the statement of cash flows. A cash outflow occurred when these goods were bought, not when they were sold. The journal entry and its effects on the financial statements are shown here:

Account Title	Debit	Credit
Cost of Goods Sold	8,000	
Merchandise Inventory		8,000

Assets			=	Liab.	+	Stockholders' Equity			Rev.	−	Exp.	=	Net Inc.	Cash Flow
Cash	+ Inventory	+ Land	=	Accts. Pay.	+	Com. Stk.	+	Ret. Earn.						
NA	+ (8,000)	+ NA	=	NA	+	NA	+	(8,000)	NA	−	8,000	=	(8,000)	NA

EVENT 4 JPS paid $1,000 cash for selling and administrative expenses.

This event is an asset use transaction. The payment decreases both assets (cash) and stockholders' equity (retained earnings). The increase in selling and administrative expenses decreases net income. The $1,000 cash payment is reported in the operating activities section of the statement of cash flows. The journal entry and its effects on the financial statements are shown next:

Account Title	Debit	Credit
Selling and Administrative Expenses	1,000	
Cash		1,000

Assets			=	Liab.	+	Stockholders' Equity			Rev.	−	Exp.	=	Net Inc.	Cash Flow
Cash	+ Inventory	+ Land	=	Accts. Pay.	+	Com. Stk.	+	Ret. Earn.						
(1,000)	+ NA	+ NA	=	NA	+	NA	+	(1,000)	NA	−	1,000	=	(1,000)	(1,000) OA

EVENT 5 JPS paid $5,500 cash to purchase land for a place to locate a future store.

Buying the land increases the Land account and decreases the Cash account on the balance sheet. This is an asset exchange transaction. The income statement is not affected. The statement of cash flows shows a cash outflow to purchase land in the investing activities section of the statement of cash flows. The journal entry and its effects on the financial statements are shown next:

Account Title	Debit	Credit
Land	5,500	
Cash		5,500

Assets			=	Liab.	+	Stockholders' Equity			Rev.	−	Exp.	=	Net Inc.	Cash Flow
Cash	+ Inventory	+ Land	=	Accts. Pay.	+	Com. Stk.	+	Ret. Earn.						
(5,500)	+ NA	+ 5,500	=	NA	+	NA	+	NA	NA	−	NA	=	NA	(5,500) IA

Ledger Accounts and Financial Statements

Panel A of Exhibit 4.2 provides a summary of the Year 1 accounting events. Panel B of Exhibit 4.2 shows the general ledger T-accounts after the journal entries have been posted to them. The ledger accounts provide the data for the financial statements in Exhibit 4.3.

Although Exhibit 4.2 does not include the December 31, Year 1, closing entries, recall that the closing entries will transfer the amounts from the Revenue and Expense accounts to the Retained Earnings account. The balance in the Retained Earnings account after closing will be $3,000. Before reading further, trace the transaction data from each journal entry in Panel A to the ledger accounts in Panel B and then from the ledger accounts to the financial statements in Exhibit 4.3.

EXHIBIT 4.2

Journal Entries and General Ledger Accounts for Year 1

Panel A Accounting Events

The Year 1 transactions JPS experienced are summarized below.

- Event 1: JPS acquired $15,000 cash by issuing common stock.
- Event 2: JPS purchased merchandise inventory (plants) for $14,000 cash.
- Event 3a: JPS recognized sales revenue from selling inventory for $12,000 cash.
- Event 3b: JPS recognized $8,000 of cost of goods sold.
- Event 4: JPS paid $1,000 cash for selling and administrative expenses.
- Event 5: JPS paid $5,500 cash to purchase land.

Panel B General Ledger Accounts

Assets = Liabilities + Equity

Cash

(1)	15,000	14,000	(2)
(3a)	12,000	1,000	(4)
		5,500	(5)
Bal.	6,500		

Merchandise Inventory

(2)	14,000	8,000	(3b)
Bal.	6,000		

Land

(5)	5,500

Accounts Payable

0	Bal.

Common Stock

15,000	(1)
15,000	Bal.

Retained Earnings

Sales Revenue

12,000	(3a)

Cost of Goods Sold

(3b)	8,000

Selling and Admin. Expenses

(4)	1,000

EXHIBIT 4.3 Financial Statements

Year 1 Income Statement

Sales revenue	$12,000
Cost of goods sold	(8,000)
Gross margin	4,000
Less: Operating exp.	
Selling and admin. exp.	(1,000)
Net income	$ 3,000

12/31/Year 1 Balance Sheet

Assets		
Cash	$ 6,500	
Merchandise inventory	6,000	
Land	5,500	
Total assets		$18,000
Liabilities		$ 0
Stockholders' equity		
Common stock	$15,000	
Retained earnings	3,000*	
Total stockholders' equity		18,000
Total liab. and stk. equity		$18,000

Year 1 Statement of Cash Flows

Operating activities		
Inflow from customers	$ 12,000	
Outflow for inventory	(14,000)	
Outflow for selling & admin. exp.	(1,000)	
Net cash outflow from operating activities		$ (3,000)**
Investing activities		
Outflow to purchase land		(5,500)
Financing activities		
Inflow from stock issue		15,000
Net change in cash		6,500
Plus: Beginning cash balance		0
Ending cash balance		$ 6,500

*The balance in the Retained Earnings account is the after-closing balance (Revenue $12,000 − Cost of Goods Sold $8,000 − Selling and Admin. Expenses $1,000).

**Cash $3,000 net cash outflow from operating activities is computed as $12,000 cash inflow from Revenue minus $14,000 cash outflow for the purchase of Inventory and $1,000 cash outflow paid for Selling and Admin. Exp.

JPS had no beginning inventory in its first year, so the cost of merchandise inventory available for sale was $14,000 (the amount of inventory purchased during the period). Recall that JPS must allocate the Cost of Goods (Inventory) Available for Sale between the Cost of Goods Sold ($8,000) and the ending balance ($6,000) in the Merchandise Inventory account. The cost of goods sold is reported as an expense on the income statement and the ending balance of merchandise inventory is reported as an asset on the balance sheet. The difference between the sales revenue ($12,000) and the cost of goods sold ($8,000) is labeled gross margin ($4,000) on the income statement.

 CHECK YOURSELF 4.1

Phambroom Company began Year 4 with $35,600 in its Inventory account. During the year, it purchased inventory costing $356,800 and sold inventory that had cost $360,000 for $520,000. Based on this information alone, determine (1) the inventory balance as of December 31, Year 4, and (2) the amount of gross margin Phambroom would report on its Year 4 income statement.

Answer

1. Beginning inventory + Purchases = Goods available − Ending inventory = Cost of goods sold

   $35,600 + $356,800 = $392,400 − Ending inventory = $360,000

   Ending inventory = $32,400

2. Sales revenue − Cost of goods sold = Gross margin

   $520,000 − $360,000 = $160,000

TRANSPORTATION COST, PURCHASE RETURNS AND ALLOWANCES, AND CASH DISCOUNTS RELATED TO INVENTORY PURCHASES

Purchasing inventory often involves: (1) incurring transportation costs, (2) returning inventory or receiving purchase allowances (cost reductions), and (3) taking cash discounts (also cost reductions). During its second accounting cycle, JPS encountered these kinds of events. The final account balances on December 31, Year 1, become the January 1, Year 2, beginning balances: Cash, $6,500; Merchandise Inventory, $6,000; Land, $5,500; Common Stock, $15,000; and Retained Earnings, $3,000.

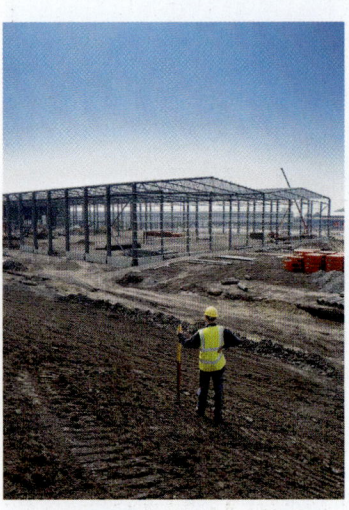
©Steve Allen/Brand X Pictures RF

Effects of the Year 2 Events on Financial Statements

JPS experienced the following events during its Year 2 accounting period. The effects of each of these events are explained and illustrated in the following discussion.

EVENT 1 **JPS borrowed $4,000 cash by issuing a note payable.**

JPS borrowed the money to enable it to purchase an additional plot of land for a future site for a store it planned to build in the near future. Borrowing the money increases the Cash account and the Notes Payable account on the balance sheet. The income statement is not affected. The statement of cash flows shows a cash flow from financing activities. The journal entry and its effects on the financial statements are shown next:

Account Title	Debit	Credit
Cash	4,000	
Notes Payable		4,000

Accounting for Merchandising Businesses 221

Assets	=	Liabilities	+	Stockholders' Equity			
Cash + Accts. Rec. + Inventory + Land	=	Accts. Pay. + Notes Pay.	+	Com. Stk. + Ret. Earn.	Rev. − Exp. = Net Inc.	Cash Flow
4,000 + NA + NA + NA	=	NA + 4,000	+	NA + NA	NA − NA = NA	4,000 FA

EVENT 2 JPS purchased on account merchandise inventory with a list price of $11,000.

The inventory purchase increases both assets (merchandise inventory) and liabilities (accounts payable) on the balance sheet. The income statement is not affected until later, when inventory is sold. Because the inventory was purchased on account, there was no cash outflow. The journal entry and its effects on the financial statements are shown next:

Account Title	Debit	Credit
Merchandise Inventory	11,000	
Accounts Payable		11,000

Assets	=	Liab.	+	Stockholders' Equity			
Cash + Accts. Rec. + Inventory + Land	=	Accts. Pay. + Notes Pay.	+	Com. Stk. + Ret. Earn.	Rev. − Exp. = Net Inc.	Cash Flow
NA + NA + 11,000 + NA	=	11,000 + NA	+	NA + NA	NA − NA = NA	NA

Accounting for Purchase Returns and Allowances

EVENT 3 JPS returned some of the inventory purchased in Event 2. The list price of the returned merchandise was $1,000.

To promote customer satisfaction, many businesses allow customers to return goods for reasons such as wrong size, wrong color, wrong design, or even simply because the purchaser changed his mind. The effect of a purchase return is the *opposite* of the original purchase. For JPS, the *purchase return* decreases both assets (merchandise inventory) and liabilities (accounts payable). There is no effect on either the income statement or the statement of cash flows. The journal entry and its effects on the financial statements are shown here:

LO 4-2

Show how purchase returns and allowances affect financial statements.

Account Title	Debit	Credit
Accounts Payable	1,000	
Merchandise Inventory		1,000

Assets	=	Liab.	+	Stockholders' Equity			
Cash + Accts. Rec. + Inventory + Land	=	Accts. Pay. + Notes Pay.	+	Com. Stk. + Ret. Earn.	Rev. − Exp. = Net Inc.	Cash Flow
NA + NA + (1,000) + NA	=	(1,000) + NA	+	NA + NA	NA − NA = NA	NA

    Sometimes dissatisfied buyers will agree to keep goods instead of returning them if the seller offers to reduce the price. Such reductions are called allowances. *Purchase allowances* affect the financial statements the same way purchase returns do. On financial statements, returns and allowances are combined in one entry, called **purchase returns and allowances**.

Purchase Discounts

EVENT 4 JPS received a cash discount on goods purchased in Event 2. The credit terms were 2/10, n/30.

LO 4-3

Show how cash discounts affect financial statements.

To encourage buyers to pay promptly, sellers sometimes offer **cash discounts.** To illustrate, assume JPS purchased the inventory in Event 2 under **credit terms** *2/10, n/30* (two-ten, net thirty). These terms mean the seller will allow a 2 percent cash discount if the purchaser pays cash within 10 days from the date of purchase. The amount not paid within the first 10 days is due at the end of 30 days from date of purchase. Recall that in Event 3, JPS returned $1,000 of the inventory purchased in Event 2, leaving a $10,000 balance ($11,000 list price − $1,000 purchase return). If JPS pays for the inventory within 10 days, the amount of the discount is $200 ($10,000 × .02).

When a cash discount is applied to a purchase, it is called a **purchase discount.** When it is applied to a sale, it is called a sales discount. Sales discounts will be discussed later in the chapter. A purchase discount reduces the cost of the inventory and the associated account payable on the balance sheet. A purchase discount does not directly affect the income statement or the statement of cash flows. The journal entry and its effects on the financial statements are shown next:

Account Title	Debit	Credit
Accounts Payable	200	
Merchandise Inventory		200

Assets	=	Liab.	+	Stockholders' Equity				
Cash + Accts. Rec. + Inventory + Land	=	Accts. Pay. + Notes Pay.	+	Com. Stk. + Ret. Earn.	Rev. − Exp. = Net Inc.	Cash Flow
NA + NA + (200) + NA	=	(200) + NA	+	NA + NA	NA − NA = NA	NA

If JPS paid the account payable after 10 days, there would be no purchase discount. In this case, the balances in the Inventory and Account Payable accounts would remain at $10,000.

EVENT 5 JPS paid the $9,800 balance due on the account payable.

The remaining balance in the accounts payable is $9,800 ($10,000 list price − $200 purchase discount). Paying cash to settle the liability reduces cash and accounts payable on the balance sheet. The income statement is not affected. The cash outflow is shown in the operating section of the statement of cash flows. The journal entry and its effects on the financial statements are shown next:

Account Title	Debit	Credit
Accounts Payable	9,800	
Cash		9,800

Assets	=	Liab.	+	Stockholders' Equity				
Cash + Accts. Rec. + Inventory + Land	=	Accts. Pay. + Notes Pay.	+	Com. Stk. + Ret. Earn.	Rev. − Exp. = Net Inc.	Cash Flow
(9,800) + NA + NA + NA	=	(9,800) + NA	+	NA + NA	NA − NA = NA	(9,800) OA

REALITY BYTES

Many real-world companies have found it more effective to impose a penalty for late payment than to use a cash discount to encourage early payment. The invoice from Arley Water Works is an example of the penalty strategy. Notice that the amount due, if paid by the due date, is $18.14. A $1.88 late charge is imposed if the bill is paid after the due date. The $1.88 late charge is in fact interest. If Arley Water Works collects the payment after the due date, the utility will receive cash of $20.02. The collection will increase cash ($20.02), reduce accounts receivable ($18.14), and increase interest revenue ($1.88).

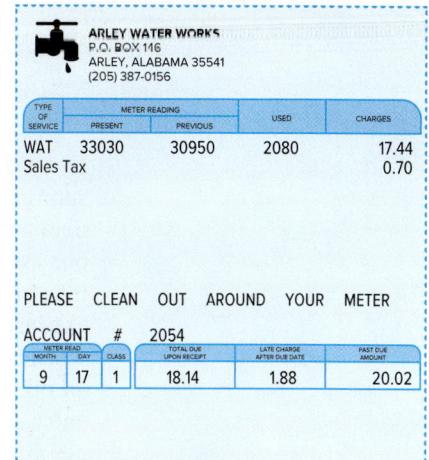

The Cost of Financing Inventory

Suppose you buy inventory this month and sell it next month. Where do you get the money to pay for the inventory at the time you buy it? One way to finance the purchase is to buy it on account and withhold payment until the last day of the term for the account payable. For example, suppose you buy inventory under terms 2/10, net/30. Under these circumstances, you could delay payment for 30 days after the day of purchase. This way, you may be able to collect enough money from the inventory you sell to pay for the inventory you purchased. Refusing the discount allows you the time needed to generate the cash necessary to pay off the liability (account payable). Unfortunately, this is usually a very expensive way to finance the purchase of inventory.

While the amount of a cash discount may appear small, the discount period is short. Consider the terms 2/10, net/30. Because you can pay on the tenth day and still receive the discount, you obtain financing for only 20 days (30-day full credit term − 10-day discount term). In other words, you must forgo a 2 percent discount to obtain a loan with a 20-day term. What is the size of the discount in annual terms? The answer is determined by the following formula:

Annual rate = Discount rate × (365 days ÷ term of the loan)

Annual rate = 2% × (365 ÷ 20)

Annual rate = 36.5%

This means that a 2 percent discount rate for 20 days is equivalent to a 36.5 percent annual rate of interest. So, if you do not have the money to pay the account payable, but can borrow money from a bank at less than 36.5 percent annual interest, you should borrow the money and pay off the account payable within the discount period.

Accounting for Transportation Costs

EVENT 6 The shipping terms for the inventory purchased in Event 2 were FOB shipping point. JPS paid the freight company $300 cash for delivering the merchandise.

The terms **FOB shipping point** and **FOB destination** identify whether the buyer or the seller is responsible for transportation costs. If goods are delivered FOB shipping point, the buyer is responsible for the freight cost. If goods are delivered FOB destination, the seller is responsible. When the buyer is responsible, the freight cost is called **transportation-in**.

LO 4-4

Show how transportation costs affect financial statements.

When the seller is responsible, the cost is called **transportation-out.** The following table summarizes freight cost terms:

Responsible Party	Buyer	Seller
Freight terms	FOB shipping point	FOB destination
Account title	Merchandise inventory	Transportation-out

Event 6 indicates the inventory was delivered FOB shipping point, so JPS (the buyer) is responsible for the $300 freight cost. Because incurring transportation-in costs is necessary to obtain inventory, these costs are added to the inventory account. The freight cost increases one asset account (Merchandise Inventory) and decreases another asset account (Cash). The income statement is not affected by this transaction because transportation-in costs are not expensed when they are incurred. Instead, they are expensed as part of *cost of goods sold* when the inventory is sold. However, the cash paid for transportation-in costs is reported as an outflow in the operating activities section of the statement of cash flows. The journal entry and its effects on the financial statements are shown next:

Account Title	Debit	Credit
Merchandise Inventory	300	
Cash		300

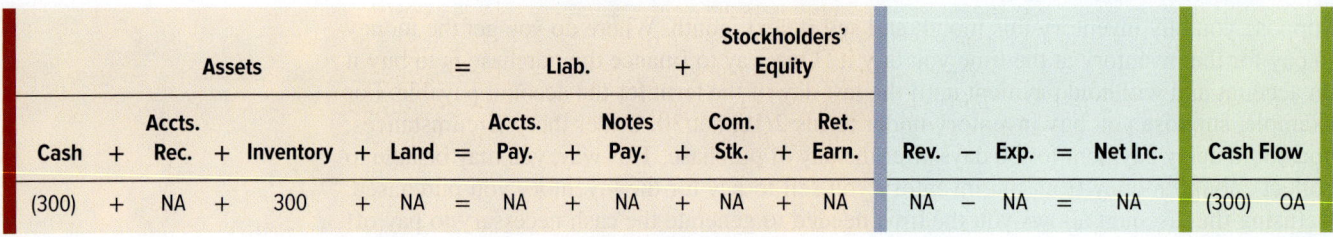

EVENT 7a JPS recognized $24,750 of revenue on the cash sale of merchandise that cost $11,500.

The sale increases assets (cash) and stockholders' equity (retained earnings). The revenue recognition increases net income. The $24,750 cash inflow from the sale is reported in the operating activities section of the statement of cash flows. The journal entry and its effects on the financial statements are shown next:

Account Title	Debit	Credit
Cash	24,750	
Sales		24,750

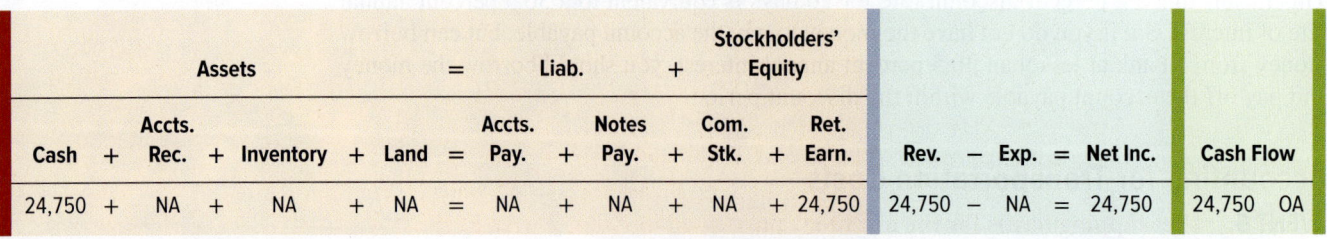

EVENT 7b JPS recognized $11,500 of cost of goods sold.

When goods are sold, the product cost—*including a proportionate share of transportation-in and adjustments for purchase returns and allowances*—is transferred from the Merchandise Inventory account to the expense account, Cost of Goods Sold. Recognizing cost of goods sold decreases both assets (merchandise inventory) and stockholders' equity (retained earnings). The expense recognition for cost of goods sold decreases net income. Cash flow is not affected. The journal entry and its effects on the financial statements are shown next:

Account Title	Debit	Credit
Cost of Goods Sold	11,500	
Merchandise Inventory		11,500

Assets	=	Liab.	+	Stockholders' Equity				
Cash + Accts. Rec. + Inventory + Land	=	Accts. Pay. + Notes Pay.	+	Com. Stk. + Ret. Earn.	Rev. − Exp. = Net Inc.	Cash Flow
NA + NA + (11,500) + NA	=	NA + NA	+	NA + (11,500)	NA − 11,500 = (11,500)	NA

EVENT 8   JPS paid $450 cash for freight costs on inventory delivered to customers.

Assume the merchandise sold in Event 7a was shipped FOB destination. Also assume JPS paid the freight cost in cash. FOB destination means the seller is responsible for the freight cost, which is called transportation-out. Transportation-out is reported on the income statement as an operating expense in the section below gross margin. The cost of freight on goods shipped to customers is incurred *after* the goods are sold. It is not part of the costs to obtain goods or ready them for sale. Recognizing the expense of transportation-out reduces assets (cash) and stockholders' equity (retained earnings). Operating expenses increase and net income decreases. The cash outflow is reported in the operating activities section of the statement of cash flows. The journal entry and its effects on the financial statements are shown next:

Account Title	Debit	Credit
Transportation-Out	450	
Cash		450

Assets	=	Liab.	+	Stockholders' Equity			
Cash + Accts. Rec. + Inventory + Land	=	Accts. Pay. + Notes Pay.	+	Com. Stk. + Ret. Earn.	Rev. − Exp. = Net Inc.	Cash Flow
(450) + NA + NA + NA	=	NA + NA	+	NA + (450)	NA − 450 = (450)	(450) OA

If the terms had been FOB shipping point, the customer would have been responsible for the transportation cost and JPS would not have recorded an expense.

EVENT 9   JPS paid $5,000 cash for selling and administrative expenses.

The effect on the balance sheet is to decrease both assets (cash) and stockholders' equity (retained earnings). Recognizing the selling and administrative expenses decreases net income. The $5,000 cash outflow is reported in the operating activities section of the statement of cash flows. The journal entry and its effects on the financial statements are shown next:

Account Title	Debit	Credit
Selling and Administrative Expenses	5,000	
Cash		5,000

226 Chapter 4

Assets	=	Liab.	+	Stockholders' Equity					
Cash + Accts. Rec. + Inventory + Land	=	Accts. Pay. + Notes Pay.	+	Com. Stk. + Ret. Earn.	Rev. − Exp. = Net Inc.	Cash Flow
(5,000) + NA + NA + NA	=	NA + NA	+	NA + (5,000)	NA − 5,000 = (5,000)	(5,000) OA

EVENT 10 JPS paid $360 cash for interest expense on the note payable described in Event 1.

The effect on the balance sheet is to decrease both assets (cash) and stockholders' equity (retained earnings). Recognizing the interest expense decreases net income. The $360 cash outflow is reported in the operating activities section of the statement of cash flows. The journal entry and its effects on the financial statements are shown next:

Account Title	Debit	Credit
Interest Expense	360	
Cash		360

Assets	=	Liab.	+	Stockholders' Equity					
Cash + Accts. Rec. + Inventory + Land	=	Accts. Pay. + Notes Pay.	+	Com. Stk. + Ret. Earn.	Rev. − Exp. = Net Inc.	Cash Flow
(360) + NA + NA + NA	=	NA + NA	+	NA + (360)	NA − 360 = (360)	(360) OA

Adjustment for Lost, Damaged, or Stolen Inventory

EVENT 11 JPS took a physical count of its inventory and found $4,100 of inventory on hand.

Show how inventory shrinkage affects financial statements.

Most merchandising companies experience some level of inventory **shrinkage,** a term that reflects decreases in inventory for reasons other than sales to customers. Inventory may be stolen by shoplifters, damaged by customers or employees, or even simply lost or misplaced. Because the *perpetual* inventory system is designed to record purchases and sales of inventory as they occur, the balance in the merchandise inventory account represents the amount of inventory that *should* be on hand at any given time. For example, based on the previous transactions, the book balance of JPS' Inventory account can be computed as follows:

Beginning balance	$ 6,000
Purchases	11,000
Purchase returns	(1,000)
Purchase discounts	(200)
Transportation-in	300
Goods available for sale	16,100
Cost of goods sold	(11,500)
Ending balance	$ 4,600

Assume that JPS takes a physical count of its inventory on hand and finds it has only $4,100 of inventory. By comparing the $4,600 book balance in the Merchandise Inventory account with the $4,100 of actual inventory counted, we determine that the company has experienced $500 of shrinkage. Under these circumstances, JPS must make an adjusting entry to write off the inventory shrinkage so that the balance of the Inventory account reported on the financial statements agrees with the amount of inventory actually on hand at the end of the period. The write-off decreases both assets (inventory) and stockholders' equity (retained earnings). The write-off increases expenses and decreases net income. Cash flow is not affected. The journal entry and its effects on the financial statements are shown next:

Account Title	Debit	Credit
Inventory Loss (Cost of Goods Sold)	500	
Inventory		500

Assets	=	Liab.	+	Stockholders' Equity				
Cash + Accts. Rec. + Inventory + Land	=	Accts. Pay. + Notes Pay.	+	Com. Stk. + Ret. Earn.	Gain − Exp. = Net Inc.	Cash Flow
NA + NA + (500) + NA	=	NA + NA	+	NA + (500)	NA − 500 = (500)	NA

Theoretically, inventory losses are operating expenses. However, because such losses are normally immaterial in amount, they are usually added to cost of goods sold for external reporting purposes.

GAINS, LOSSES, AND A MULTISTEP INCOME STATEMENT

EVENT 12   JPS sold the land that had cost $5,500 for $6,200 cash.

When JPS sells merchandise inventory for more than it cost, the difference between the sales revenue and the cost of the goods sold is called the *gross margin*. In contrast, when JPS sells land for more than it cost, the difference between the sales price and the cost of the land is called a **gain**. Why is one called *gross margin* and the other a *gain?* The terms are used to alert financial statement users to the fact that the nature of the underlying transactions is different.

LO 4-6

Prepare a multistep income statement.

JPS' primary business is selling inventory, not land. The term *gain* indicates profit resulting from transactions that are not likely to regularly recur. Similarly, had the land sold for less than cost, the difference would have been labeled **loss** rather than expense. This term also indicates the underlying transaction is not from normal, recurring operating activities. Gains and losses are shown separately on the income statement to communicate the expectation that they are nonrecurring.

The presentation of gains and losses in the income statement is discussed in more detail in a later section of the chapter. At this point, note that the sale increases cash, decreases land, and increases retained earnings on the balance sheet. The income statement shows a gain on the sale of land and net income increases. The $6,200 cash inflow is shown as an investing activity on the statement of cash flows. The journal entry and its effects on the financial statements are shown next:

Account Title	Debit	Credit
Cash	6,200	
Land		5,500
Gain on Sale of Land		700

Assets	=	Liab.	+	Stockholders' Equity				
Cash + Accts. Rec. + Inventory + Land	=	Accts. Pay. + Notes Pay.	+	Com. Stk. + Ret. Earn.	Gain − Exp. = Net Inc.	Cash Flow
6,200 + NA + NA + (5,500)	=	NA + NA	+	NA + 700	700 − NA = 700	6,200 IA

CHECK YOURSELF 4.2

Tsang Company purchased $32,000 of inventory on account with payment terms of 2/10, n/30 and freight terms FOB shipping point. Freight costs were $1,100. Tsang obtained a $2,000 purchase allowance because the inventory was damaged upon arrival. Tsang paid for the inventory within the discount period. Based on this information alone, determine the balance in the Inventory account.

Answer

List price of inventory	$32,000
Plus: Transportation-in costs	1,100
Less: Purchase returns and allowances	(2,000)
Less: Purchase discount [($32,000 − $2,000) × .02]	(600)
Balance in inventory account	$30,500

Exhibit 4.4 summarizes the accounting events and ledger T-accounts for the Year 2 accounting period. Before reading further, trace the effects of each event to the ledger accounts. Then, trace the information in the ledger accounts to the Year 2 financial statements displayed in Exhibits 4.5, 4.7, and 4.8.

EXHIBIT 4.4

Accounting Events and Ledger Accounts for Year 2

Panel A Accounting Events

Event 1	JPS borrowed $4,000 cash by issuing a note payable.
Event 2	JPS purchased on account merchandise inventory with a list price of $11,000.
Event 3	JPS returned some of the inventory purchased in Event 2. The list price of the returned merchandise was $1,000.
Event 4	JPS received a cash discount on goods purchased in Event 2. The credit terms were 2/10, n/30.
Event 5	JPS paid the $9,800 balance due on the account payable.
Event 6	The inventory purchased in Event 2 was delivered FOB shipping point. JPS paid the freight company $300 cash for delivering the merchandise.
Event 7a	JPS recognized $24,750 of revenue on the cash sale of merchandise that cost $11,500.
Event 7b	JPS recognized $11,500 of cost of goods sold.
Event 8	JPS paid $450 cash for freight costs on inventory delivered to customers.
Event 9	JPS paid $5,000 cash for selling and administrative expenses.
Event 10	JPS paid $360 cash for interest expense on the note payable described in Event 1.
Event 11	JPS took a physical count of its inventory and found $4,100 of inventory on hand.
Event 12	JPS sold the land that had cost $5,500 for $6,200 cash.

continued

EXHIBIT 4.4 Concluded

Accounting Events and Ledger Accounts for Year 2

Panel B Ledger Accounts

Assets = Liabilities + Equity

Cash

Bal.	6,500	9,800	(5)	
(1)	4,000	300	(6)	
(7a)	24,750	450	(8)	
(12)	6,200	5,000	(9)	
		360	(10)	
Bal.	25,540			

Merchandise Inventory

Bal.	6,000	1,000	(3)	
(2)	11,000	200	(4)	
(6)	300	11,500	(7b)	
		500	(11)	
Bal.	4,100			

Land

Bal.	5,500	5,500	(12)	
Bal.	–0–			

Accounts Payable

(3)	1,000	11,000	(2)	
(4)	200			
(5)	9,800			
		–0–	Bal.	

Notes Payable

	4,000	(1)	
	4,000	Bal.	

Common Stock

	15,000	Bal.

Retained Earnings

	3,000	Bal.
	7,640	(Cl)
	10,640	Bal.

Sales Revenue

(Cl)	24,750	24,750	(7a)	
		–0–	Bal.	

Gain on Sale of Land

(Cl)	700	700	(12)	
		–0–	Bal.	

Cost of Goods Sold

(7b)	11,500	12,000	(Cl)	
(11)	500			
Bal.	–0–			

Transportation-Out

(8)	450	450	(Cl)	
Bal.	–0–			

Selling and Admin. Expenses

(9)	5,000	5,000	(Cl)	
Bal.	–0–			

Interest Expense

(10)	360	360	(Cl)	
Bal.	–0–			

Total Assets = Total Liabilities + Total Equity
$29,640 $4,000 $25,640

JPS' Year 2 income statement is shown in Exhibit 4.5. Observe the form of this statement carefully. It is more informative than one which simply subtracts expenses from revenues. First, it compares sales revenue with the cost of the goods that were sold to produce that revenue. The difference between the sales revenue and the cost of goods sold is called *gross margin*. Next, the operating expenses are subtracted from the gross margin to determine the *operating income*. **Operating income** is the amount of income that is generated from the normal recurring operations of a business. Items that are not expected to recur on a regular basis are subtracted from the operating income to determine the amount of *net income*.

EXHIBIT 4.5

JUNE'S PLANT SHOP
Income Statement
For the Period Ended December 31, Year 2

Sales revenue	$24,750
Cost of goods sold*	(12,000)
Gross margin	12,750
Less: Operating expenses	
Selling and administrative expense	(5,000)
Transportation-out	(450)
Operating income	7,300
Nonoperating items	
Interest expense	(360)
Gain on the sale of land	700
Net income	$ 7,640

*$11,500 inventory sold + $500 shrinkage.

EXHIBIT 4.6

Income Statement Format Used by U.S. Companies

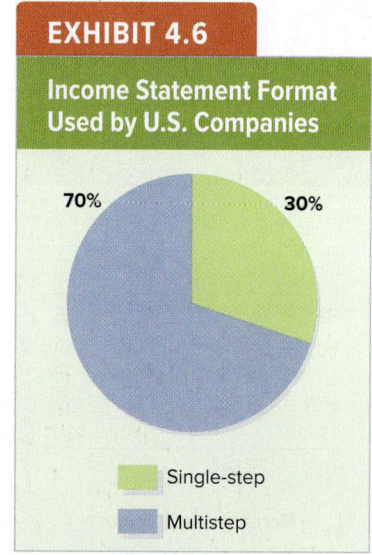

The chart is based on data drawn from recent annual reports published by the 30 companies that comprise the Dow Jones Industrial Average.

Income statements that show these additional relationships are called **multistep income statements.** Income statements that display a single comparison of all revenues minus all expenses are called **single-step income statements.** To this point in the text, we have shown only single-step income statements to promote simplicity. However, the multistep form is used more frequently in practice. Exhibit 4.6 shows the percentage of companies that use the multi-step versus the single-step format. Go to Exhibit 4.1 and identify the company that presents its income statement in the multistep format. You should have identified AutoNation as the company using the multistep format. Ford's statement is shown in the single-step format.

Note that interest is reported as a *nonoperating* item on the income statement in Exhibit 4.5. In contrast, it is shown in the *operating* activities section of the statement of cash flows in Exhibit 4.8. Generally accepted accounting principles (GAAP) requires interest to be reported in the operating activities section of the statement of cash flows. There is no corresponding requirement for the treatment of interest on the income statement. Prior to the requirement for reporting interest as an operating activity on the statement of cash flows, interest was considered to be a nonoperating item. Most companies continued to report interest as a nonoperating item on their income statements even though they were required to change how it was reported on the statement of cash flows. As a result, there is frequent inconsistency in the way interest is reported on the two financial statements.

REALITY BYTES

Good inventory management is essential for merchandising and manufacturing companies. Even if a company uses a perpetual inventory system, the amount of inventory believed to be on hand may be incorrect because of lost, damaged, or stolen goods, so a physical count is still required. Unfortunately, counting inventory is not a revenue-generating activity. If a company's employees are used to conduct the physical count, it takes time that may be better used for other activities. In fact, it may be so time-consuming that the business must close temporarily so employees will have the time to complete the inventory count.

To avoid this problem, many businesses hire outside companies to count their inventory. These outside vendors can bring in a large crew of specially trained workers and complete a count very quickly. There are many companies that provide inventory counting services, but **RGIS, LLC**, claims to be the world's largest. RGIS (an acronym for Retail Grocery Inventory Service) reports that its 34,000 employees have counted over 400 billion items in the more than four million inventory counts it has conducted since beginning operations in 1958. On second thought, counting inventory *is* a revenue-producing activity if you are a company that counts inventory for others.

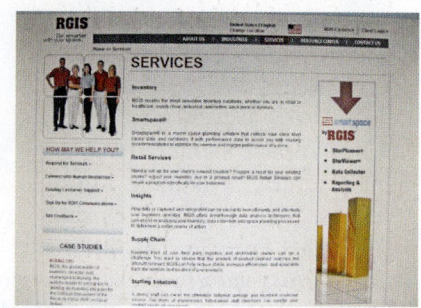

©Roberts Publishing Services

EXHIBIT 4.7

JUNE'S PLANT SHOP
Balance Sheet
As of December 31, Year 2

Assets		
Cash	$25,540	
Merchandise inventory	4,100	
Total assets		$29,640
Liabilities		
Notes payable		$ 4,000
Stockholders' equity		
Common stock	$15,000	
Retained earnings	10,640	
Total stockholders' equity		25,640
Total liabilities and stockholders' equity		$29,640

EXHIBIT 4.8

JUNE'S PLANT SHOP
Statement of Cash Flows
For the Year Ended December 31, Year 2

Operating activities		
Inflow from customers	$24,750	
Outflow for inventory*	(10,100)	
Outflow for transportation-out	(450)	
Outflow for selling and administrative expense	(5,000)	
Outflow for interest expense	(360)	
Net cash outflow for operating activities		$ 8,840
Investing activities		
Inflow from sale of land		6,200
Financing activities		
Inflow from issue of note payable		4,000
Net change in cash		19,040
Plus beginning cash balance		6,500
Ending cash balance		$25,540

*Net cost of inventory $9,800 + Transportation-in $300 = $10,100

Also note that while the gain on the sale of land is shown on the income statement, it is not included in the operating activities section of the statement of cash flows. Because the gain is a nonoperating item, it is included in the cash inflow from the sale of land shown in the investing activities section. In this case, the full cash inflow from the sale of land ($6,200) is shown in the investing activities section of the statement of cash flows in Exhibit 4.8. Finally, note that the ending inventory balance is shown on the balance sheet in Exhibit 4.7.

EVENTS AFFECTING SALES

To this point, we have assumed JPS did not offer cash discounts to its customers. However, sales, as well as purchases of inventory, can be affected by returns, allowances, and discounts. **Sales discounts** are price reductions offered by sellers to encourage buyers to pay promptly. To illustrate, assume JPS engaged in the following selected events during Year 3.

LO 4-7

Determine the amount of net sales.

232 Chapter 4

EVENT 1a JPS sold on account merchandise with a list price of $8,500. Payment terms were 1/10, n/30. The merchandise had cost JPS $4,000.

The sale increases both assets (accounts receivable) and shareholders' equity (retained earnings). Recognizing revenue increases net income. The statement of cash flows is not affected. The journal entry for this event and its effects on the financial statements follow:

Account Title	Debit	Credit
Accounts Receivable	8,500	
Sales Revenue		8,500

Assets	=	Liab.	+	Stockholders' Equity	Rev.	−	Exp.	=	Net Inc.	Cash Flow
Cash + Accts. Rec. + Inventory	=	Note Pay.	+	Com. Stk. + Retained Earnings						
NA + 8,500 + NA	=	NA	+	NA + 8,500	8,500	−	NA	=	8,500	NA

EVENT 1b JPS recognized $4,000 of cost of goods sold.

Recognizing the expense decreases assets (merchandise inventory) and stockholders' equity (retained earnings). Cost of goods sold increases and net income decreases. Cash flow is not affected. The journal entry for this event and its effects on the financial statements follow:

Account Title	Debit	Credit
Cost of Goods Sold	4,000	
Merchandise Inventory		4,000

Assets	=	Liab.	+	Stockholders' Equity	Rev.	−	Exp.	=	Net Inc.	Cash Flow
Cash + Accts. Rec. + Inventory	=	Note Pay.	+	Com. Stk. + Retained Earnings						
NA + NA + (4,000)	=	NA	+	NA + (4,000)	NA	−	4,000	=	(4,000)	NA

Accounting for Sales Returns and Allowances

EVENT 2a A customer from Event 1a returned inventory with a $1,000 list price. The merchandise had cost JPS $450.

The sales return decreases both assets (accounts receivable) and stockholders' equity (retained earnings) on the balance sheet. Sales and net income decrease. Cash flow is not affected. The journal entry for this event and its effects on the financial statements follow:

Account Title	Debit	Credit
Sales Revenue	1,000	
Accounts Receivable		1,000

Assets	=	Liab.	+	Stockholders' Equity	Rev.	−	Exp.	=	Net Inc.	Cash Flow
Cash + Accts. Rec. + Inventory	=	Note Pay.	+	Com. Stk. + Retained Earnings						
NA + (1,000) + NA	=	NA	+	NA + (1,000)	(1,000)	−	NA	=	(1,000)	NA

EVENT 2b The cost of the goods ($450) is returned to the inventory account.

Because JPS got the inventory back, the sales return increases both assets (merchandise inventory) and stockholders' equity (retained earnings). The expense (cost of goods sold) decreases and net income increases. Cash flow is not affected. The journal entry for this event and its effects on the financial statements follow:

Account Title	Debit	Credit
Merchandise Inventory	450	
Cost of Goods Sold		450

Assets	=	Liab.	+	Stockholders' Equity	Rev.	−	Exp.	=	Net Inc.	Cash Flow
Cash + Accts. Rec. + Inventory	=	Note Pay.	+	Com. Stk. + Retained Earnings						
NA + NA + 450	=	NA	+	NA + 450	NA	−	(450)	=	450	NA

Accounting for Sales Discounts

EVENT 3 JPS collected the balance of the accounts receivable generated in Event 1a. Recall the goods were sold under terms 1/10, net/30.

ALTERNATIVE 1 The collection occurs before the discount period has expired (within 10 days from the date of the sale).

JPS would give the buyer a 1 percent discount. Given the original sales amount of $8,500 and a sales return of $1,000, the amount of the discount is $75 [($8,500 − $1,000) × .01]. The sales discount reduces the amount of accounts receivable and retained earnings on the balance sheet. It also reduces the amount of revenue and the net income shown on the balance sheet. It does not affect the statement of cash flows. These effects are shown below.

Account Title	Debit	Credit
Sales Revenue	75	
Accounts Receivable		75

Assets	=	Liab.	+	Stockholders' Equity	Rev.	−	Exp.	=	Net Inc.	Cash Flow
Cash + Accts. Rec. + Inventory	=	Note Pay.	+	Com. Stk. + Retained Earnings						
NA + (75) + NA	=	NA	+	NA + (75)	(75)	−	NA	=	(75)	NA

The balance due on the account receivable is $7,425 ($8,500 original sales − $1,000 sales return − $75 discount). The collection increases the Cash account and decreases the Accounts Receivable account. The income statement is not affected. The cash inflow is shown in the operating activities section of the statement of cash flows. The journal entry for this event and its effects on the financial statements follow:

Account Title	Debit	Credit
Cash	7,425	
Accounts Receivable		7,425

Assets	=	Liab.	+	Stockholders' Equity	Rev.	−	Exp.	=	Net Inc.	Cash Flow
Cash + Accts. Rec. + Inventory	=	Note Pay.	+	Com. Stk. + Retained Earnings						
7,425 + (7,425) + NA	=	NA	+	NA + NA	NA	−	NA	=	NA	7,425 OA

Net Sales

The gross amount of sales minus **sales returns and allowances** and sales discounts is commonly called **net sales.** Companies are not required by GAAP to show sales returns and allowances and sales discounts on their income statement. Indeed, most companies show only the amount of *net sales* on the income statement. In this case, the net sales amount to $7,425 ($8,500 original sales − $1,000 sales return − $75 discount).

ALTERNATIVE 2 The collection occurs after the discount period has expired (after 10 days from the date of the sale).

Under these circumstances, there is no sales discount. The amount collected is $7,500 ($8,500 original sale − $1,000 sales return). Net sales shown on the income statement would also be $7,500.

LO 4-8

Use common size financial statements and ratio analysis to evaluate managerial performance.

The Financial Analyst

How good is a $1,000,000 increase in net income? The answer is not clear because there is no indication as to the size of the company. A million dollar increase may be excellent for a small company but would be virtually meaningless for a company the size of Exxon. Chapter 3 discussed the use of financial ratios to make comparisons of different size companies. Here, we broaden the analytical tool set to include **common size financial statements.**

Common Size Financial Statements

Common size statements display information in percentages, as well as absolute dollar amounts. To illustrate, we expand the income statements for JPS to include percentages. The results are shown in Exhibit 4.9. The percentage data are computed by defining net sales as the base figure, or 100 percent. The other amounts on the statements are then shown as a

EXHIBIT 4.9 Common Size Financial Statements

JUNE'S PLANT SHOP
Income Statement
For the Years Ended December 31,

	Year 1		Year 2	
Net sales*	$12,000	100.0%	$24,750	100.0%
Cost of goods sold	(8,000)	66.7	(12,000)	48.5
Gross margin	4,000	33.3	12,750	51.5
Less: Operating expenses				
Selling and administrative expense	(1,000)	8.3	(5,000)	20.2
Transportation-out			(450)	1.8
Operating income	3,000	25.0	7,300	29.5
Nonoperating items				
Interest expense			(360)	(1.5)
Gain on the sale of land			700	2.8
Net income	$ 3,000	25.0	$ 7,640	30.9

*Since JPS did not offer sales discounts or have sales returns and allowances during Year 1 or Year 2, the amount of sales revenue is equal to the amount of net sales. We use the term *net sales* here because it is more commonly used in business practice. Percentages do not add exactly because they have been rounded.

percentage of net sales. For example, the *cost of goods sold percentage* is the dollar amount of *cost of goods sold* divided by the dollar amount of *net sales,* which produces a percentage of 66.7 percent ($8,000 ÷ $12,000) for Year 1 and 48.5 percent ($12,000 ÷ $24,750) for Year 2. Other income statement items are computed using the same approach.

Ratio Analysis

Two of the percentages shown in Exhibit 4.9 are used frequently in business to make comparisons within a specific company or between two or more different companies. These two commonly used percentages are the **gross margin percentage** and the **net income percentage.** The gross margin percentage provides insight about a company's pricing strategy. All other things being equal, a high gross margin percentage means that a company is charging high prices in relation to its cost of goods sold. These percentages are calculated as follows:

$$\text{Gross margin percentage} = \frac{\text{Gross margin}}{\text{Net sales}}$$

$$\text{Net income percentage} = \frac{\text{Net income}}{\text{Net sales}}$$

In practice, the *net income percentage* is frequently called the **return-on-sales** ratio. The return-on-sales ratio provides insight as to how much of each sales dollar remains as net income after all expenses are paid. All other things being equal, companies with high ratios are doing a better job of controlling expenses.

Comparisons within a Particular Company

To illustrate comparisons within a particular company, assume that JPS relocated its store in an upscale mall in early Year 2. Management realized that the company would have to pay more for operating expenses but believed those expenses could be offset by charging significantly higher prices. We use the gross margin percentage and the net income percentage to assess the success of JPS' strategy. Exhibit 4.9 shows an increase in the *gross margin percentage* from 33.3 to 51.5. This confirms that JPS was able to increase prices relative to its cost of goods sold. The increase in the *return-on-sales* ratio (25 percent to 30.9 percent) confirms that the increase in gross margin was larger than the increase in total expenses. We therefore conclude that JPS' strategy to relocate was successful. This may also explain why JPS sold its land in late Year 2. Considering the success the company experienced at the new location, there was no longer a motive to build a store on the land.

Because net income is affected by nonoperating items, some financial analysts would prefer to use *operating income* instead of *net income* when computing the *return-on-sales* ratio. In this case, the nonoperating items are immaterial. Indeed, to simplify the discussion in this chapter, we always assume immateriality when computing this ratio. However, when nonoperating items are significant, it is more insightful to use *operating income* as the numerator of the *return-on-sales* ratio.

Comparisons between Companies

Does **Walmart** sell merchandise at a higher or lower price than **Target**? The *gross margin percentage* is useful in answering questions such as this. Because Walmart's 2016 fiscal year annual report shows a gross margin percentage of 24.9, while Target's report shows a gross margin percentage of 29.7, we conclude that there is validity to Walmart's claim of having low prices. The next section of the chapter provides insight as to how the *gross margin percentage* and the *return-on-sales* ratio can be used to gain insight about the operations of several real-world companies.

CHECK YOURSELF 4.3

The following sales data are from the records of two retail sales companies. All amounts are in thousands.

	Company A	Company B
Sales	$ 21,234	$ 43,465
Cost of goods sold	(14,864)	(34,772)
Gross margin	$ 6,370	$ 8,693

One company is an upscale department store, and the other is a discount store. Which company is the upscale department store?

Answer The gross margin percentage for Company A is approximately 30 percent ($6,370 ÷ $21,234). The gross margin percentage for Company B is 20 percent ($8,693 ÷ $43,465). These percentages suggest that Company A is selling goods with a higher markup than Company B, which implies that Company A is the upscale department store.

Answers to The Curious Accountant

As data from the income statement for **AutoNation** show, automobile dealers do not have big markups on the cars they sell. The new vehicles the company sold for $12,255.8 million in 2016 cost the company $11,620.0 to purchase, resulting in a gross margin of $635.8, or 5.2 percent. In other words, if you bought an "average" car from AutoNation for $20,000, the company's gross profit on it was only $1,040 ($20,000 × .052), meaning it paid **Ford** $18,960 ($20,000 − $1,040). Furthermore, the company still had other expenses to pay besides its cost of goods sold. In 2016, only 2.0 percent of each dollar of AutoNation's sales was net profit ($430.5 ÷ $21,609.0). Remember, the amount shown for sales on AutoNation's income statement is based on what customers actually paid for the cars the company sold, not the "sticker price."

Meanwhile, if Ford sold the car to AutoNation for $18,960, it earned a 10.5 percent gross margin on the sale, or $1,991 [$14,962 ÷ $141,546 = 10.5%; ($141,546 − $126,584 = $14,962)] [$18,960 × .105 = $1,991]. Like AutoNation, Ford still had other expenses to pay for besides the cost of goods sold. In 2016, Ford earned 3.0 percent of net profit on each dollar of sales ($4,596 ÷ $151,800).

Most consumers significantly overestimate the profit margins of the companies from which they buy goods. Retailers, especially, operate with small profit margins, so inventory management, discussed in Chapter 5, is very important to their success.

Real-World Data

Exhibit 4.10 shows the gross margin percentages and return-on-sales ratios for 10 companies. Three of the companies are manufacturers that produce pharmaceutical products, and the remaining seven companies sell various products at the retail level. These data are for the companies' 2016 fiscal years.

Accounting for Merchandising Businesses 237

EXHIBIT 4.10

Industry/Company	Gross Margin %	Return on Sales %
Pharmaceutical manufacturers		
GlaxoSmithKline	66.7	3.8
Johnson & Johnson	69.8	23.0
Merck & Co.	65.1	14.3
Retail pharmacies		
CVS	16.3	3.0
Rite Aid	25.5	0.5
Walgreens	25.5	3.6
Department stores		
Macy's	39.4	2.4
Walmart	24.9	2.8
Office supplies		
Office Depot	24.6	4.8
Staples	26.2	1.8

©Philip Lange/Shutterstock RF

A review of the data confirms our earlier finding that ratios for companies in the same industry are often more similar than are ratios for companies from different industries. For example, note that the manufacturers have much higher margins, both for gross profit and for net earnings, than do the retailers. Manufacturers are often able to charge higher prices than are retailers because they obtain patents that give them a legal monopoly on the products they create. When a company such as **Merck** develops a new drug, no one else can produce that drug until the patent expires, giving it lots of control over its price at the wholesale level. Conversely, when **Rite Aid** sells Merck's drug at the retail level, it faces price competition from **CVS Caremark** (CVS), a company that is trying to sell the same drug to the same consumers. One way CVS can try to get customers to shop at its store is to charge lower prices than its competitors, but this reduces its profit margins because it must pay the same price to get Merck's drug as did Rite Aid. As the data in Exhibit 4.10 show, in 2016 CVS had a lower gross margin percentage than Rite Aid, indicating it is charging lower prices for similar goods. However, CVS still managed to generate a higher return on sales percentage.

It is difficult not to notice that GlaxoSmithKline had a much lower return on sales percentage than its direct competitors. This was the result of Glaxo having an unusually high income tax expense in 2016.

In the examples presented in Exhibit 4.10, some companies with higher gross margin percentages have higher return-on-sales ratios than their competitors, but this is not always the case. In addition to the CVS and Rite Aid comparison above, notice that **Staples** had a gross margin percentage that was 6 percent lower than **Office Depot**'s [(26.2 − 24.6) ÷ 26.2], but its return-on-sales ratio was much higher.

A Look Back

Merchandising companies earn profits by selling inventory at prices that are higher than the cost paid for the goods. Merchandising companies include *retail companies* (companies that sell goods to the final consumer) and *wholesale companies* (companies that sell to other merchandising companies). The products sold by merchandising companies are called *inventory*. The costs to purchase inventory, to receive it, and to ready it for sale are *product costs,* which are first accumulated in an inventory account (balance sheet asset account) and then recognized as cost of goods sold (income statement expense account) in the period in which goods are sold. Purchases and sales of inventory can be recorded continually as goods are bought and sold (perpetual system) or at the end of the accounting period (periodic system, discussed in the chapter Appendix).

Accounting for inventory includes the treatment of cash discounts, transportation costs, returns and allowances, and shrinkage. The cost of inventory is the list price less any purchase returns and allowances and purchase discounts, plus transportation-in costs. The cost of freight paid to acquire inventory (*transportation-in*) is considered a product cost. The cost of freight paid to deliver inventory to customers (*transportation-out*) is a selling expense. *Sales returns and allowances* and *sales discounts* are subtracted from sales revenue to determine the amount of *net sales* reported on the income statement. Purchase returns and allowances reduce product cost. Theoretically, the cost of lost, damaged, or stolen inventory (shrinkage) is an operating expense. However, because these costs are usually immaterial in amount, they are typically included as part of cost of goods sold on the income statement.

Some companies use a *multistep income statement,* which reports product costs separately from selling and administrative costs. Cost of goods sold is subtracted from sales revenue to determine *gross margin.* Selling and administrative expenses are subtracted from gross margin to determine income from operations. Other companies report income using a *single-step format,* in which the cost of goods sold is listed along with selling and administrative items in a single expense category that is subtracted in total from revenue to determine income from operations.

Managers of merchandising businesses operate in a highly competitive environment. They must manage company operations carefully to remain profitable. *Common size financial statements* (statements presented on a percentage basis) and ratio analysis are useful monitoring tools. Common size financial statements permit ready comparisons among different-size companies. Although a $1 million increase in sales may be good for a small company and bad for a large company, a 10 percent increase can apply to any size company. The two most common ratios used by merchandising companies are the *gross margin percentage* (gross margin ÷ net sales) and the *net income percentage* (net income ÷ net sales). Interpreting these ratios requires an understanding of industry characteristics. For example, a discount store such as Walmart would be expected to have a much lower gross margin percentage than an upscale store such as Neiman Marcus.

Managers should be aware of the financing cost of carrying inventory. By investing funds in inventory, a firm loses the opportunity to invest them in interest-bearing assets. The cost of financing inventory is an *opportunity cost.* To minimize financing costs, a company should minimize the amount of inventory it carries, the length of time it holds the inventory, and the time it requires to collect accounts receivable after the inventory is sold.

>> A Look Forward

To this point, the text has explained the basic accounting cycle for service and merchandising businesses. Future chapters more closely address specific accounting issues. For example, in Chapter 5 you will learn how to deal with inventory items that are purchased at differing prices. Other chapters will discuss a variety of specific practices widely used by real-world companies.

APPENDIX

Periodic Inventory System

Under certain conditions, it is impractical to record inventory sales transactions as they occur. Consider the operations of a fast-food restaurant. To maintain perpetual inventory records, the restaurant would have to transfer from the Inventory account to the Cost of

LO 4-9

Identify the primary features of the periodic inventory system.

Goods Sold account the *cost* of each hamburger, order of fries, soft drink, or other food item as it was sold. Obviously, recording the cost of each item at the point of sale would be impractical without using highly sophisticated computer equipment. Recording the selling price the customer pays is captured by cash registers; the difficulty lies in capturing inventory cost.

The **periodic inventory system** offers a practical solution for recording inventory transactions in a low-technology, high-volume environment. As shown in Exhibit 4.11, inventory

EXHIBIT 4.11

General Journal Entries for Year 2 (Periodic Method)

Event No.	Account Title	Debit	Credit
1	Cash	4,000	
	Notes Payable		4,000
2	Purchases	11,000	
	Accounts Payable		11,000
3	Accounts Payable	1,000	
	Purchase Returns and Allowances		1,000
4	Accounts Payable	200	
	Purchase Discounts		200
5	Accounts Payable	9,800	
	Cash		9,800
6	Transportation-In	300	
	Cash		300
7a	Cash	24,750	
	Sales		24,750
7b	Under the periodic system, the cost of goods sold is recorded at the end of the period in the adjusting entry shown below.		
8	Transportation-Out	450	
	Cash		450
9	Selling and Administrative Expenses	5,000	
	Cash		5,000
10	Interest Expense	360	
	Cash		360
11	The effects of this event are included as part of cost of goods sold in the adjusting entry shown below.		
12	Cash	6,200	
	Land		5,500
	Gain on Sale of Land		700
Adj	Cost of Goods Sold	12,000	
	Merchandise Inventory (Ending Balance)	4,100	
	Purchase Returns and Allowances	1,000	
	Purchase Discounts	200	
	Purchases		11,000
	Transportation-In		300
	Merchandise Inventory (Beginning Balance)		6,000
CL	Revenue	24,750	
	Gain on Sale of Land	700	
	Cost of Goods Sold		12,000
	Transportation-Out		450
	Selling and Administrative Expenses		5,000
	Interest Expense		360
	Retained Earnings		7,640

EXHIBIT 4.12

Schedule of Cost of Goods Sold for Year 2

Beginning inventory	$ 6,000
Purchases	11,000
Purchase returns and allowances	(1,000)
Purchase discounts	(200)
Transportation-in	300
Cost of goods available for sale	16,100
Ending inventory	(4,100)
Cost of goods sold	$12,000

costs are recorded in a Purchases account at the time of purchase. Purchase returns and allowances and transportation-in are recorded in separate accounts. No entries for the cost of merchandise purchases or sales are recorded in the Inventory account during the period. The cost of goods sold is determined at the end of the period, as shown in Exhibit 4.12.

The perpetual and periodic inventory systems represent alternative procedures for recording the same information. The amounts of cost of goods sold and ending inventory reported in the financial statements will be the same regardless of the method used. Exhibit 4.11 presents the general journal entries JPS would make if it used the periodic inventory method for the Year 2 transactions. Cost of goods sold is recorded in an adjusting entry at the end of the accounting period.

The **schedule of cost of goods sold** presented in Exhibit 4.12 is used for internal reporting purposes. It is normally not shown in published financial statements. The amount of cost of goods sold is reported as a single line item on the income statement. The income statement in Exhibit 4.5 will be the same whether JPS maintains perpetual or periodic inventory records.

Advantages and Disadvantages of the Periodic System versus the Perpetual System

The chief advantage of the periodic method is recording efficiency. Recording inventory transactions occasionally (periodically) requires less effort than recording them continually (perpetually). Historically, practical limitations offered businesses like fast-food restaurants or grocery stores no alternative to using the periodic system. The sheer volume of transactions made recording individual decreases to the Inventory account balance as each item was sold impossible. Imagine the number of transactions a grocery store would have to record every business day to maintain perpetual records.

Although the periodic system provides a recordkeeping advantage over the perpetual system, perpetual inventory records provide significant control advantages over periodic records. With perpetual records, the book balance in the Inventory account should agree with the amount of inventory in stock at any given time. By comparing that book balance with the results of a physical inventory count, management can determine the amount of lost, damaged, destroyed, or stolen inventory. Perpetual records also permit more timely and accurate reorder decisions and profitability assessments.

When a company uses the *periodic* inventory system, lost, damaged, or stolen merchandise is automatically included in the cost of goods sold. Because such goods are not included in the year-end physical count, they are treated as sold regardless of the reason for their absence. Because the periodic system does not separate the cost of lost, damaged, or stolen merchandise from the cost of goods sold, the amount of any inventory shrinkage is unknown. This feature is a major disadvantage of the periodic system. Without knowing the amount of inventory losses, management cannot weigh the costs of various security systems against the potential benefits.

Advances in such technology as electronic bar code scanning and increased computing power have eliminated most of the practical constraints that once prevented merchandisers with high-volume, low dollar-value inventories from recording inventory transactions on a continual basis. As a result, use of the perpetual inventory system has expanded rapidly in recent years and continued growth can be expected. This text, therefore, concentrates on the perpetual inventory system.

Accounting for Merchandising Businesses

SELF-STUDY REVIEW PROBLEM

A step-by-step audio-narrated series of slides is available in Connect.

Academy Sales Company (ASC) started the Year 2 accounting period with the balances given in the financial statements model shown below. During Year 2, ASC experienced the following business events:

1. Purchased $16,000 of merchandise inventory on account, terms 2/10, n/30.
2. The goods that were purchased in Event 1 were delivered FOB shipping point. Freight costs of $600 were paid in cash by the responsible party.
3. Returned $500 of goods purchased in Event 1.
4a. Recorded the cash discount on the goods purchased in Event 1.
4b. Paid the balance due on the account payable within the discount period.
5a. Recognized $21,000 of cash revenue from the sale of merchandise.
5b. Recognized $15,000 of cost of goods sold.
6. The merchandise in Event 5a was sold to customers FOB destination. Freight costs of $950 were paid in cash by the responsible party.
7. Paid cash of $4,000 for selling and administrative expenses.
8. Sold the land for $5,600 cash.

Required

a. Record the above transactions in a financial statements model like the one shown below.

Event No.	Cash	+	Inventory	+	Land	=	Accts. Pay.	+	Com. Stk.	+	Ret. Earn.	Rev./Gain	−	Exp.	=	Net Inc.	Cash Flow
Bal.	25,000	+	3,000	+	5,000	=	−0−	+	18,000	+	15,000	NA	−	NA	=	NA	NA

b. Prepare a schedule of cost of goods sold. (See the Appendix.)
c. Prepare a multistep income statement. Include common size percentages on the income statement.
d. ASC's gross margin percentage in Year 1 was 22 percent. Based on the common size data in the income statement, did ASC raise or lower its prices in Year 2?
e. Assuming a 10 percent rate of growth, what is the amount of net income expected for Year 3?

Answer

a.

Event No.	Cash	+	Inventory	+	Land	=	Accts. Pay.	+	Com. Stk.	+	Ret. Earn.	Rev./Gain	−	Exp.	=	Net Inc.	Cash Flow
Bal.	25,000	+	3,000	+	5,000	=	−0−	+	18,000	+	15,000	NA	−	NA	=	NA	NA
1		+	16,000			=	16,000	+		+			−		=		
2	(600)	+	600			=		+		+			−		=		(600) OA
3		+	(500)			=	(500)	+		+			−		=		
4a		+	(310)			=	(310)	+		+			−		=		
4b	(15,190)	+				=	(15,190)	+		+			−		=		(15,190) OA
5a	21,000	+				=		+		+	21,000	21,000	−		=	21,000	21,000 OA
5b		+	(15,000)			=		+		+	(15,000)		−	15,000	=	(15,000)	
6	(950)	+				=		+		+	(950)		−	950	=	(950)	(950) OA
7	(4,000)	+				=		+		+	(4,000)		−	4,000	=	(4,000)	(4,000) OA
8	5,600	+		(5,000)	=		+		+	600	600	−		=	600	5,600 IA
Bal.	30,860	+	3,790	+	−0−	=	−0−	+	18,000	+	16,650	21,600	−	19,950	=	1,650	5,860 NC

b.

ACADEMY SALES COMPANY
Schedule of Cost of Goods Sold
For the Period Ended December 31, Year 2

Beginning inventory	$ 3,000
Plus purchases	16,000
Less: Purchase returns and allowances	(500)
Less: Purchases discounts	(310)
Plus: Transportation-in	600
Goods available for sale	18,790
Less: Ending inventory	(3,790)
Cost of goods sold	$15,000

c.

ACADEMY SALES COMPANY
Income Statement*
For the Period Ended December 31, Year 2

Net sales	$ 21,000	100.0%
Cost of goods sold	(15,000)	71.4
Gross margin	6,000	28.6
Less: Operating expenses		
Selling and administrative expense	(4,000)	19.0
Transportation-out	(950)	4.5
Operating income	1,050	5.0
Nonoperating items		
Gain on the sale of land	600	2.9
Net income	$ 1,650	7.9

*Percentages do not add exactly because they have been rounded.

d. All other things being equal, the higher the gross margin percentage, the higher the sales prices. Because the gross margin percentage increased from 22 percent to 28.6 percent, the data suggest that Academy raised its sales prices.

e. $1,155 [$1,050 + (.10 × $1,050)]. Note that the gain is not expected to recur.

KEY TERMS

Cash discount 222
Common size financial
  statements 234
Cost of goods available
  for sale 216
Cost of goods sold 216
Credit terms 222
FOB destination 223
FOB shipping point 223
Gains 227
Gross margin 216

Gross margin percentage 235
Gross profit 216
Losses 227
Merchandise inventory 213
Merchandising businesses 212
Multistep income
  statement 230
Net income percentage 235
Net sales 234
Operating income (or loss) 229
Period costs 215

Periodic inventory system 239
Perpetual inventory system 216
Product costs 215
Purchase discount 222
Purchase returns
  and allowances 221
Retail companies 213
Return on sales 235
Sales discount 231
Sales returns and
  allowances 234

Schedule of cost of
  goods sold 240
Selling and administrative
  costs 215
Shrinkage 226
Single-step income
  statement 230
Transportation-in 223
Transportation-out 224
Wholesale
  companies 213

QUESTIONS

1. Define *merchandise inventory*. What types of costs are included in the Merchandise Inventory account?

2. What is the difference between a product cost and a selling and administrative cost?

3. How is the cost of goods available for sale determined?

4. What portion of cost of goods available for sale is shown on the balance sheet? What portion is shown on the income statement?

5. When are period costs expensed? When are product costs expensed?

6. If PetCo had net sales of $600,000, goods available for sale of $450,000, and cost of goods sold of $375,000, what is its gross margin? What amount of inventory will be shown on its balance sheet?

7. Describe how the perpetual inventory system works. What are some advantages of using the perpetual inventory system? Is it necessary to take a physical inventory when using the perpetual inventory system?

8. What are the effects of the following types of transactions on the accounting equation? Also identify the financial statements affected. (Assume that the perpetual inventory system is used.)
   a. Acquisition of cash from the issue of common stock.
   b. Contribution of inventory by an owner of a company.
   c. Purchase of inventory with cash by a company.
   d. Sale of inventory for cash.

9. Northern Merchandising Company sold inventory that cost $12,000 for $20,000 cash. How does this event affect the accounting equation? What financial statements and accounts are affected? (Assume that the perpetual inventory system is used.)

10. If goods are shipped FOB shipping point, which party (buyer or seller) is responsible for the shipping costs?

11. Define *transportation-in*. Is it a product or a period cost?

12. Quality Cellular Co. paid $80 for freight on merchandise it had purchased for resale to customers (transportation-in) and paid $135 for freight on merchandise delivered to customers (transportation-out). What account is debited for the $80 payment? What account is debited for the $135 payment?

13. Why would a seller grant an allowance to a buyer of the seller's merchandise?

14. Dyer Department Store purchased goods with the terms 2/10, n/30. What do these terms mean?

15. Eastern Discount Stores incurred a $5,000 cash cost. How does the accounting for this cost differ if the cash were paid for inventory versus commissions to sales personnel?

16. What is the purpose of giving credit terms to customers?

17. Define *transportation-out*. Is it a product cost or a period cost for the seller?

18. Ball Co. purchased inventory with a list price of $4,000 with the terms 2/10, n/30. What amount will be debited to the Merchandise Inventory account?

19. Explain the difference between gains and revenues.

20. Explain the difference between losses and expenses.

21. Suda Company sold land that cost $40,000 for $37,000 cash. Explain how this transaction would be shown on the statement of cash flows.

22. Explain the difference between purchase returns and sales returns. How do purchase returns affect the financial statements of both buyer and seller? How do sales returns affect the financial statements of both buyer and seller?

23. How is net sales determined?

24. What is the difference between a multistep income statement and a single-step income statement?

25. What is the advantage of using common size income statements to present financial information for several accounting periods?

26. What information is provided by the net income percentage (return-on-sales ratio)?

27. What is the purpose of preparing a schedule of cost of goods sold? (Appendix)

28. Explain how the periodic inventory system works. What are some advantages of using the periodic inventory system? What are some disadvantages of using the periodic inventory system? Is it necessary to take a physical inventory when using the periodic inventory system? (See the Appendix.)

29. Why does the periodic inventory system impose a major disadvantage for management in accounting for lost, stolen, or damaged goods? (See the Appendix.)

MULTIPLE-CHOICE QUESTIONS

Multiple-choice questions are available in Connect.

EXERCISES—SERIES A

  All applicable Exercises in Series A are available in Connect.

When the instructions for *any* exercise or problem call for the preparation of an income statement, use the *multistep format* unless otherwise indicated.

Chapter 4

LO 4-1

Exercise 4-1A Comparing a merchandising company with a service company

The following information is available for two different types of businesses for the Year 1 accounting year. Hopkins CPAs is a service business that provides accounting services to small businesses. Sports Clothing is a merchandising business that sells sports clothing to college students.

Data for Hopkins CPAs
1. Borrowed $90,000 from the bank to start the business.
2. Provided $50,000 of services to clients and collected $50,000 cash.
3. Paid salary expense of $32,000.

Data for Sports Clothing
1. Borrowed $90,000 from the bank to start the business.
2. Purchased $50,000 inventory for cash.
3. Inventory costing $26,000 was sold for $50,000 cash.
4. Paid $8,000 cash for operating expenses.

Required
a. Prepare an income statement, balance sheet, and statement of cash flows for each of the companies.
b. Which of the two businesses would have product costs? Why?
c. Why does Hopkins CPAs not compute gross margin on its income statement?
d. Compare the assets of both companies. What assets do they have in common? What assets are different? Why?

LO 4-1

Exercise 4-2A Effect of inventory transactions on journals, ledgers, and financial statements: perpetual system

Dan Watson started a small merchandising business in Year 1. The business experienced the following events during its first year of operation. Assume that Watson uses the perpetual inventory system.
1. Acquired $30,000 cash from the issue of common stock.
2. Purchased inventory for $18,000 cash.
3. Sold inventory costing $15,000 for $32,000 cash.

Required
a. Record the events in general journal format.
b. Post the entries to T-accounts.
c. Determine the amount of gross margin.
d. What is the amount of net cash flow from operating activities for Year 1?

LO 4-1

Exercise 4-3A Effect of inventory transactions on the income statement and statement of cash flows: perpetual system

During Year 1, Hardy Merchandising Company purchased $40,000 of inventory on account. Hardy sold inventory on account that cost $24,500 for $38,000. Cash payments on accounts payable were $22,000. There was $26,000 cash collected from accounts receivable. Hardy also paid $5,100 cash for operating expenses. Assume that Hardy started the accounting period with $20,000 in both cash and common stock.

Required
a. Identify the events described in the preceding paragraph and show them in a horizontal statements model like the following one:

Assets	=	Liab.	+	Equity	Rev.	−	Exp.	=	Net Inc.	Cash Flow
Cash + Accts. Rec. + Inv.	=	Accts. Pay.	+	Com. Stk. + Ret. Earn.						
20,000 + NA + NA	=	NA	+	20,000 + NA	NA	−	NA	=	NA	NA

b. What is the balance of accounts receivable at the end of Year 1?
c. What is the balance of accounts payable at the end of Year 1?
d. What are the amounts of gross margin and net income for Year 1?
e. Determine the amount of net cash flow from operating activities.
f. Explain why net income and retained earnings are the same for Hardy. Normally, would these amounts be the same? Why or why not?

Exercise 4-4A Recording inventory transactions in the general journal and posting entries to T-accounts: perpetual system

LO 4-1

Milo Clothing experienced the following events during Year 1, its first year of operation:
1. Acquired $30,000 cash from the issue of common stock.
2. Purchased inventory for $15,000 cash.
3. Sold inventory costing $9,000 for $20,000 cash.
4. Paid $1,500 for advertising expense.

Required
a. Record the general journal entries for the preceding transactions.
b. Post each of the entries to T-accounts.
c. Prepare a trial balance to prove the equality of debits and credits.

Exercise 4-5A Cash discounts and purchase returns

LO 4-2, 4-3

On April 6, Year 1, Home Furnishings purchased $25,200 of merchandise from Una Imports, terms 2/10 n/45. On April 8, Home returned $2,400 of the merchandise to Una Imports for credit. Home paid cash for the merchandise on April 15, Year 1.

Required
a. What is the amount that Home must pay Una Imports on April 15?
b. Show the events in a horizontal statements model like the following one:

Assets	=	Liab.	+	Equity	Rev.	−	Exp.	=	Net Inc.	Cash Flow
Cash + Inv.	=	Accts. Pay.	+	C. Stk. + Ret. Earn.						

c. How much must Home pay for the merchandise purchased if the payment is not made until April 20, Year 1?
d. Show the payment in Requirement c in a horizontal statements model like the one above.
e. Why would Home want to pay for the merchandise by April 15?

Exercise 4-6A Understanding the freight terms FOB shipping point and FOB destination

LO 4-4

Required
For each of the following events, indicate whether the freight terms are FOB destination or FOB shipping point.
a. Sold merchandise and the buyer paid the freight costs.
b. Purchased merchandise and the seller paid the freight costs.
c. Sold merchandise and paid the freight costs.
d. Purchased merchandise and paid the freight costs.

LO 4-2, 4-3, 4-4

Exercise 4-7A *Determining the cost of inventory*

Required

For each of the following cases determine the ending balance in the inventory account. (*Hint:* First, determine the total cost of inventory available for sale. Next, subtract the cost of the inventory sold to arrive at the ending balance.)

a. Jill's Dress Shop had a beginning balance in its inventory account of $40,000. During the accounting period, Jill's purchased $75,000 of inventory, returned $5,000 of inventory, and obtained $750 of purchases discounts. Jill's incurred $1,000 of transportation-in cost and $600 of transportation-out cost. Salaries of sales personnel amounted to $31,000. Administrative expenses amounted to $35,600. Cost of goods sold amounted to $82,300.

b. Ken's Bait Shop had a beginning balance in its inventory account of $8,000. During the accounting period, Ken's purchased $36,900 of inventory, obtained $1,200 of purchases allowances, and received $360 of purchases discounts. Sales discounts amounted to $640. Ken's incurred $900 of transportation-in cost and $260 of transportation-out cost. Selling and administrative cost amounted to $12,300. Cost of goods sold amounted to $33,900.

LO 4-1, 4-2, 4-3, 4-4

Exercise 4-8A *Accounting for product costs: perpetual inventory system*

Which of the following would be *debited* to the Inventory account for a merchandising business using the perpetual inventory system?

Required

a. Transportation-out.
b. Purchase discount.
c. Transportation-in.
d. Purchase of a new computer to be used by the business.
e. Purchase of inventory.
f. Allowance received for damaged inventory.

LO 4-1, 4-2, 4-3, 4-4

Exercise 4-9A *Determining the effect of inventory transactions on the horizontal statements model: perpetual system*

Bali Sales Company experienced the following events:

1. Purchased merchandise inventory for cash.
2. Purchased merchandise inventory on account.
3. Returned merchandise purchased on account.
4. Sold merchandise inventory for cash. Label the revenue recognition 4a and the expense recognition 4b.
5. Paid cash on accounts payable not within the discount period.
6. Sold merchandise inventory on account. Label the revenue recognition 6a and the expense recognition 6b.
7. Paid cash for selling and administrative expenses.
8. Paid cash for transportation-in.
9. Collected cash from accounts receivable.
10. Paid cash for transportation-out.

Required

Identify each event as asset source (AS), asset use (AU), asset exchange (AE), or claims exchange (CE). Also explain how each event affects the financial statements by placing a + for increase, − for decrease, or NA for not affected under each of the components in the following statements model. Assume the use of the perpetual inventory system. The first event is recorded as an example.

Event No.	Event Type	Assets	=	Liab.	+	Equity	Rev.	−	Exp.	=	Net Inc.	Cash Flow
1	AE	+−	=	NA	+	NA	NA	−	NA	=	NA	− OA

Exercise 4-10A Effect of product cost and period cost: horizontal statements model LO 4-2, 4-4

The Pet Store experienced the following events for the Year 1 accounting period:

1. Acquired $60,000 cash from the issue of common stock.
2. Purchased $65,000 of inventory on account.
3. Received goods purchased in Event 2 FOB shipping point; freight cost of $900 paid in cash.
4. Sold inventory on account that cost $38,000 for $71,000.
5. Freight cost on the goods sold in Event 4 was $620. The goods were shipped FOB destination. Cash was paid for the freight cost.
6. Customer in Event 4 returned $4,200 worth of goods that had a cost of $2,150.
7. Collected $58,300 cash from accounts receivable.
8. Paid $59,200 cash on accounts payable.
9. Paid $2,600 for advertising expense.
10. Paid $3,100 cash for insurance expense.

Required

a. Which of these events affect period (selling and administrative) costs? Which result in product costs? If neither, label the transaction NA.
b. Show each event in a horizontal statements model like the following one. The first event is recorded as an example.

Assets	=	Liab.	+	Equity	Rev. − Exp. = Net Inc.	Cash Flow
Cash + Accts. Rec. + Inv.	=	Accts. Pay.	+	C. Stk. + Ret. Earn.		
60,000 + NA + NA	=	NA	+	60,000 + NA	NA − NA = NA	60,000 FA

Exercise 4-11A Effect of inventory losses: perpetual system LO 4-5

Ho Designs experienced the following events during Year 1, its first year of operation:

1. Started the business when it acquired $70,000 cash from the issue of common stock.
2. Paid $41,000 cash to purchase inventory.
3. Sold inventory costing $37,500 for $56,200 cash.
4. Physically counted inventory; had inventory of $3,200 on hand at the end of the accounting period.

Required

a. Open appropriate ledger T-accounts, and record the events in the accounts.
b. Prepare an income statement and balance sheet.
c. If all purchases and sales of merchandise are reflected as increases or decreases to the Merchandise Inventory account, why is it necessary for management to even bother to take a physical count of goods on hand (ending inventory) at the end of the year?

Exercise 4-12A Effect of purchase returns and allowances and freight costs on the journal, ledger, and financial statements: perpetual system LO 4-2, 4-4, 4-6

The trial balance for Terry's Auto Shop as of January 1, Year 2, follows:

Account Title	Debit	Credit
Cash	$16,000	
Inventory	8,000	
Common Stock		$20,000
Retained Earnings		4,000
Total	$24,000	$24,000

The following events affected the company during the Year 2 accounting period:

1. Purchased merchandise on account that cost $15,000.
2. The goods in Event 1 were purchased FOB shipping point with freight cost of $800 cash.
3. Returned $2,600 of damaged merchandise for credit on account.
4. Agreed to keep other damaged merchandise for which the company received an $1,100 allowance.
5. Sold merchandise that cost $15,000 for $31,000 cash.
6. Delivered merchandise to customers in Event 5 under terms FOB destination with freight costs amounting to $500 cash.
7. Paid $8,000 on the merchandise purchased in Event 1.
8. Paid $9,000 cash for operating expenses.

Required

a. Record the events in general journal format.
b. Open general ledger T-accounts with the appropriate beginning balances, and post the journal entries to the T-accounts.
c. Prepare a multistep income statement, balance sheet, and statement of cash flows. (Assume that closing entries have been made.)
d. Explain why a difference does or does not exist between net income and net cash flow from operating activities.

LO 4-6

Exercise 4-13A *Multistep income statement*

In Year 1, Kim Company sold land for $80,000 cash. The land had originally cost $60,000. Also, Kim sold inventory that had cost $110,000 for $198,000 cash. Operating expenses amounted to $36,000.

Required

a. Prepare a Year 1 multistep income statement for Kim Company.
b. Assume that normal operating activities grow evenly by 10 percent during Year 2. Prepare a Year 2 multistep income statement for Kim Company.
c. Determine the percentage change in net income between Year 1 and Year 2.
d. Should the stockholders have expected the results determined in Requirement *c*? Explain your answer.

LO 4-6

Exercise 4-14A *Single-step and multistep income statements*

The following information was taken from the accounts of Green Market, a small grocery store, at December 31, Year 1. The accounts are listed in alphabetical order, and all have normal balances. Dollar amounts are given in thousands.

Account	Amount
Accounts payable	$ 800
Accounts receivable	2,250
Advertising expense	600
Cash	1,850
Common stock	2,000
Cost of goods sold	2,950
Interest expense	120
Merchandise inventory	1,250
Prepaid rent	720
Retained earnings, 1/1/Year 1	2,610
Sales revenue	5,600
Salaries expense	960
Rent expense	510
Gain on sale of land	200

Required

First, prepare an income statement for the year using the single-step approach. Then, prepare another income statement using the multistep approach.

Exercise 4-15A Sales returns, discounts, gain, and a multistep income statement

LO 4-2, 4-3, 4-6

The following information was drawn from the Year 1 accounting records of Ozark Merchandisers:

1. Inventory that had cost $21,200 was sold for $39,900 under terms 2/20, net/30.
2. Customers returned merchandise to Ozark five days after the purchase. The merchandise had been sold for a price of $1,520. The merchandise had cost Ozark $920.
3. All customers paid their accounts within the discount period.
4. Selling and administrative expenses amounted to $4,200.
5. Interest expense paid amounted to $360.
6. Land that had cost $8,000 was sold for $9,250 cash.

Required

a. Determine the amount of net sales.
b. Prepare a multistep income statement.
c. Where would the interest expense be shown on the statement of cash flows?
d. How would the sale of the land be shown on the statement of cash flows?
e. Explain the difference between a gain and revenue.

Exercise 4-16A Effect of sales returns and allowances and freight costs on the journal, ledger, and financial statements: perpetual system

LO 4-2, 4-4, 4-6, 4-7

Powell Company began the Year 2 accounting period with $40,000 cash, $86,000 inventory, $60,000 common stock, and $66,000 retained earnings. During Year 2, Powell experienced the following events:

1. Sold merchandise that cost $58,000 for $99,500 on account to Prentise Furniture Store.
2. Delivered the goods to Prentise under terms FOB destination. Freight costs were $900 cash.
3. Received returned goods from Prentise. The goods cost Powell $4,000 and were sold to Prentise for $5,900.
4. Granted Prentise a $3,000 allowance for damaged goods that Prentise agreed to keep.
5. Collected partial payment of $81,000 cash from accounts receivable.

Required

a. Record the events in general journal format.
b. Open general ledger T-accounts with the appropriate beginning balances and post the journal entries to the T-accounts.
c. Prepare a multistep income statement, a balance sheet, and a statement of cash flows.
d. Why would Prentise agree to keep the damaged goods? Who benefits more?

Exercise 4-17A Comprehensive exercise with sales discounts

LO 4-2, 4-3, 4-4, 4-6, 4-7, 4-8

Junker's Stash started the Year 2 accounting period with the balances given in the financial statements model shown below. During Year 2, Junker's Stash experienced the following business events:

1. Paid cash to purchase $70,000 of merchandise inventory.
2. The goods that were purchased in Event 1 were delivered FOB destination. Freight costs of $1,400 were paid in cash by the responsible party.
3a. Sold merchandise for $72,000 under terms 1/10, n/30.
3b. Recognized $41,900 of cost of goods sold.
4a. Junker's Stash customers returned merchandise that was sold for $2,100.
4b. The merchandise returned in Event 4a had cost Junker's Stash $1,250.
5. The merchandise in Event 3a was sold to customers FOB destination. Freight costs of $1,650 were paid in cash by the responsible party.
6a. The customers paid for the merchandise sold in Event 3a within the discount period. Recognized the sales discount.
6b. Collected the balance in the accounts receivable account.
7. Paid cash of $6,850 for selling and administrative expenses.
8. Sold the land for $9,100 cash.

Required

a. Show the above transactions in a financial statements model like the one shown below:

Event No.	Cash	+	Accts. Rec.	+	Inventory	+	Land	=	Com. Stk.	+	Ret. Earn.	Rev./ Gain	−	Exp.	=	Net Inc.	Cash Flow
Bal.	80,000	+	0	+	15,000	+	11,000	=	70,000	+	36,000	NA	−	NA	=	NA	NA

b. Determine the amount of net sales.

c. Prepare a multistep income statement. Include common size percentages on the income statement.

d. The return-on-sales ratio for Junker's Stash during the prior year was 12 percent. Based on the common size data in the income statement, did the expenses for Junker's Stash increase or decrease in Year 2?

e. Explain why the term *loss* is used to describe the results due to the sale of land.

LO 4-8

Exercise 4-18A *Using ratios to make comparisons*

The following income statements were drawn from the annual reports of the Atlanta Company and the Boston Company:

	Atlanta*	Boston*
Net sales	$ 210,000	$ 230,000
Cost of goods sold	(126,000)	(179,400)
Gross margin	84,000	50,600
Less: Operating exp.		
Selling and admin. exp.	(67,200)	(32,200)
Net income	$ 16,800	$ 18,400

*All figures are reported in thousands of dollars.

Required

a. One of the companies is a high-end retailer that operates in exclusive shopping malls. The other operates discount stores located in low-cost, standalone buildings. Identify the high-end retailer and the discounter. Support your answer with appropriate ratios.

b. If Atlanta and Boston have equity of $168,000 and $122,700, respectively, which company is in the more profitable business?

LO 4-8

Exercise 4-19A *Using common size statements and ratios to make comparisons*

The following information is available for the Memphis and Billings companies:

	Memphis	Billings
Sales	$1,500,000	$1,500,000
Cost of goods sold	1,050,000	1,125,000
Operating expenses	350,000	250,000
Total assets	1,800,000	1,800,000
Stockholders' equity	720,000	720,000

Required

a. Prepare a common size income statement for each company.

b. Compute the return on assets and return on equity for each company.

c. Which company is more profitable from the stockholders' perspective?

d. One company is a high-end retailer, and the other operates a discount store. Which is the discounter? Support your selection by referring to the appropriate ratios.

Exercise 4-20A Effect of inventory transactions on the income statement and balance sheet: periodic system (Appendix)

LO 4-9

Bill Rose owns Rose Sporting Goods. At the beginning of the year, Rose Sporting Goods had $18,000 in inventory. During the year, Rose Sporting Goods purchased inventory that cost $66,000. At the end of the year, inventory on hand amounted to $28,500.

Required

Calculate the following:

a. Cost of goods available for sale during the year.
b. Cost of goods sold for the year.
c. Amount of inventory Rose Sporting Goods would report on the year-end balance sheet.

Exercise 4-21A Determining cost of goods sold: periodic system (Appendix)

LO 4-9

Tippah Antiques uses the periodic inventory system to account for its inventory transactions. The following account titles and balances were drawn from Tippah's records for Year 2: beginning balance in inventory, $42,000; purchases, $128,000; purchase returns and allowances, $12,000; sales, $520,000; sales returns and allowances, $3,900; freight-in, $1,000; and operating expenses, $130,000. A physical count indicated that $26,000 of merchandise was on hand at the end of the accounting period.

Required

a. Prepare a schedule of cost of goods sold.
b. Prepare a multistep income statement.

Exercise 4-22A Basic transactions: periodic system, single cycle (Appendix)

LO 4-9

The following transactions apply to Bob's Bike Shop for Year 1, its first year of operations:

1. Acquired $35,000 cash from the issue of common stock.
2. Acquired $9,600 of merchandise from Bob Hall, the owner, who had acquired the merchandise prior to opening the shop. Issued common stock to Bob in exchange for the merchandise inventory.
3. Purchased $85,000 of inventory on account.
4. Paid $2,800 for radio ads.
5. Sold inventory for $165,000 cash.
6. Paid $28,000 in salary to a part-time salesperson.
7. Paid $65,000 on accounts payable (see Event 3).
8. Physically counted inventory, which indicated that $28,500 of inventory was on hand at the end of the accounting period.

Required

a. Record each of these transactions in general journal form using the periodic method.
b. Post each of the transactions to ledger T-accounts.
c. Prepare an income statement, statement of changes in stockholders' equity, balance sheet, and statement of cash flows for Year 1.
d. Prepare the necessary closing entries at the end of Year 1, and post them to the appropriate T-accounts.
e. Prepare a post-closing trial balance.
f. Give an example of a business that may want to use the periodic system. Give an example of a business that may use the perpetual system.
g. Give some examples of assets other than cash that are commonly contributed to a business in exchange for stock.

PROBLEMS—SERIES A

All applicable Problems in Series A are available in Connect.

LO 4-4

Problem 4-23A *Identifying freight costs*

Required

For each of the following events, determine the amount of freight paid by The Box Company. Also indicate whether the freight cost would be classified as a product or period (selling and administrative) cost.

a. Purchased merchandise with freight costs of $650. The merchandise was shipped FOB shipping point.
b. Shipped merchandise to customers, freight terms FOB shipping point. The freight costs were $310.
c. Purchased inventory with freight costs of $1,500. The goods were shipped FOB destination.
d. Sold merchandise to a customer. Freight costs were $520. The goods were shipped FOB destination.

LO 4-1

Problem 4-24A *Identifying product and period costs*

Required

Indicate whether each of the following costs is a product cost or a period (selling and administrative) cost:

a. Goods purchased for resale.
b. Salaries of salespersons.
c. Advertising costs.
d. Transportation-out.
e. Interest on a note payable.
f. Salary of the company president.
g. Transportation-in.
h. Insurance on the office building.
i. Office supplies.
j. Costs incurred to improve the quality of goods available for sale.

LO 4-1, 4-6

Problem 4-25A *Basic transactions for three accounting cycles: perpetual system*

Blooming Flower Company was started in Year 1 when it acquired $60,000 cash from the issue of common stock. The following data summarize the company's first three years' operating activities. Assume that all transactions were cash transactions.

	Year 1	Year 2	Year 3
Purchases of inventory	$50,000	$60,000	$ 85,000
Sales	68,000	85,000	130,000
Cost of goods sold	34,000	43,000	71,000
Selling and administrative expenses	29,000	35,000	42,000

Required

Prepare an income statement (use multistep format) and balance sheet for each fiscal year. (*Hint:* Record the transaction data for each accounting period in T-accounts before preparing the statements for that year.)

Accounting for Merchandising Businesses 253

Problem 4-26A *Comprehensive cycle problem: perpetual system*   LO 4-1, 4-2, 4-3, 4-4, 4-5, 4-6, 4-7

At the beginning of Year 2, the Redd Company had the following balances in its accounts:

Cash	$ 6,900
Inventory	15,000
Land	7,000
Common stock	15,000
Retained earnings	13,900

During Year 2, the company experienced the following events:

1. Purchased inventory that cost $5,200 on account from Ross Company under terms 1/10, n/30. The merchandise was delivered FOB shipping point. Freight costs of $190 were paid in cash.
2. Returned $400 of the inventory it had purchased because the inventory was damaged in transit. The seller agreed to pay the return freight cost.
3. Paid the amount due on its account payable to Ross Company within the cash discount period.
4. Sold inventory that had cost $6,800 for $12,100 on account, under terms 2/10, n/45.
5. Received merchandise returned from a customer. The merchandise originally cost $900 and was sold to the customer for $1,680 cash. The customer was paid $1,680 cash for the returned merchandise.
6. Delivered goods FOB destination in Event 4. Freight costs of $140 were paid in cash.
7. Collected the amount due on the account receivable within the discount period.
8. Sold the land for $8,500.
9. Recognized accrued interest income of $600.
10. Took a physical count indicating that $13,400 of inventory was on hand at the end of the accounting period. *Hint:* Determine the current balance in the inventory account before calculating the amount of the inventory write down.

Required

a. Identify each of these events as asset source (AS), asset use (AU), asset exchange (AE), or claims exchange (CE). Also explain how each event would affect the financial statements by placing a + for increase, − for decrease, or NA for not affected under each of the components in the following statements model. Assume that the perpetual inventory method is used. When an event has more than one part, use letters to distinguish the effects of each part. The first event is recorded as an example.

Event No.	Event Type	Assets	=	Liab.	+	Stk. Equity	Rev.	−	Exp.	=	Net Inc.	Cash Flow
1a	AS	+	=	+	+	NA	NA	−	NA	=	NA	NA
1b	AE	+ −	=	NA	+	NA	NA	−	NA	=	NA	− OA

b. Record the events in general journal format.
c. Open ledger T-accounts, and post the beginning balances and the events to the accounts.
d. Prepare a multistep income statement, a statement of changes in stockholders' equity, a balance sheet, and a statement of cash flows.
e. Use a single general journal to close all revenue, gain, and expense accounts to the retained earnings account. Post the journal entry to the ledger accounts and prepare a post-closing trial balance.

Problem 4-27A *Multistep and common size income statements*   LO 4-6, 4-8

The following information was drawn from the records of Toner Sales Company:

	Year 1	Year 2
Net sales	$200,000	$200,000
Cost of goods sold	(90,000)	(80,000)
Operating expenses	(60,000)	(50,000)
Loss on the sale of land	−0−	(24,000)

Required

a. Prepare a multistep income statement for each year.
b. Prepare a common size income statement for each year.
c. At a recent meeting of the stockholders, Toner's president stated Year 3 would be a very good year with net income rising significantly. Write a brief memo explaining whether you agree or disagree with the president. Assume that the operating trends between Year 1 and Year 2 continue through Year 3.

LO 4-9

Problem 4-28A *Preparing schedule of cost of goods sold and multistep and single-step income statements: periodic system (Appendix)*

The following account titles and balances were taken from the adjusted trial balance of King Co. for Year 2. The company uses the periodic inventory system.

Account Title	Balance
Sales returns and allowances	$ 3,500
Miscellaneous expense	900
Transportation-out	2,200
Sales	$156,300
Advertising expense	6,200
Salaries expense	21,000
Transportation-in	3,800
Purchases	88,000
Interest expense	250
Merchandise inventory, January 1	11,200
Rent expense	12,000
Merchandise inventory, December 31	10,700
Purchase returns and allowances	2,100
Loss on sale of land	3,100
Utilities expense	1,850

Required

a. Prepare a schedule to determine the amount of cost of goods sold.
b. Prepare a multistep income statement.
c. Prepare a single-step income statement.

LO 4-9

Problem 4-29A *Comprehensive cycle problem: periodic system (Appendix)*

The following trial balance pertains to Benji's Grocery as of January 1, Year 2:

Account Title	Debit	Credit
Cash	$ 64,000	
Accounts receivable	12,000	
Merchandise inventory	90,000	
Accounts payable		$ 7,500
Common stock		89,000
Retained earnings		69,500
Totals	$166,000	$166,000

The following events occurred in Year 2. Assume that Benji's uses the periodic inventory method.

1. Purchased land for $30,000 cash.
2. Purchased merchandise on account for $230,000, terms 1/10 n/45.
3. Paid freight of $2,100 cash on merchandise purchased FOB shipping point.

4. Returned $8,600 of defective merchandise purchased in Event 2.
5. Sold merchandise for $186,000 cash.
6. Sold merchandise on account for $236,000, terms 2/10 n/30.
7. Paid cash within the discount period on accounts payable due on merchandise purchased in Event 2.
8. Paid $28,500 cash for selling expenses.
9. Collected $156,000 of the accounts receivable from Event 6 within the discount period.
10. Collected $56,000 of the accounts receivable but not within the discount period.
11. Paid $17,100 of other operating expenses.
12. A physical count indicated that $48,300 of inventory was on hand at the end of the accounting period.

Required

a. Record these transactions in a general journal.
b. Post the transactions to ledger T-accounts.
c. Prepare a schedule of costs of goods sold, income statement, statement of changes in stockholders' equity, balance sheet, and statement of cash flows for Year 2.

MULTIPLE-CHOICE QUESTIONS

Multiple-choice questions are available in Connect.

EXERCISES—SERIES B

When the instructions for *any* exercise or problem call for the preparation of an income statement, use the *multistep format* unless otherwise indicated.

Exercise 4-1B *Comparing a merchandising company with a service company*   LO 4-1

The following information is available for two different types of businesses for the Year 1 accounting year. Diamond Consulting is a service business that provides consulting services to small businesses. University Bookstore is a merchandising business that sells books to college students.

Data for Diamond Consulting

1. Borrowed $80,000 by issuing a note to the bank to start the business.
2. Performed services for clients and collected $60,000 cash.
3. Paid salary expense of $38,400.

Data for University Bookstore

1. Borrowed $80,000 by issuing a note to the bank to start the business.
2. Purchased $38,000 of inventory for cash.
3. Inventory costing $33,600 was sold for $60,000 cash.
4. Paid $4,800 cash for operating expenses.

Required

a. Prepare an income statement, balance sheet, and statement of cash flows for each of the companies.
b. What is different about the income statements of the two businesses?
c. What is different about the balance sheets of the two businesses?
d. How are the statements of cash flow different for the two businesses?

Chapter 4

LO 4-1

Exercise 4-2B Effect of inventory transactions on journals, ledgers, and financial statements: perpetual system

Jason Kidd started a small merchandising business in Year 1. The business experienced the following events during its first year of operation. Assume that Kidd uses the perpetual inventory system.

1. Acquired $90,000 cash from the issue of common stock.
2. Purchased inventory for $60,000 cash.
3. Sold inventory costing $48,000 for $82,000 cash.

Required

a. Record the events in general journal format.
b. Post the entries to T-accounts.
c. Prepare an income statement for Year 1 (use the multistep format).
d. What is the amount of total assets at the end of the period?

LO 4-1

Exercise 4-3B Effect of inventory transactions on the income statement and statement of cash flows: perpetual system

During Year 1, Rondor Merchandising Company purchased $40,000 of inventory on account. The company sold inventory on account that cost $30,000 for $50,000. Cash payments on accounts payable were $24,500. There was $38,000 cash collected from accounts receivable. Rondor also paid $9,000 cash for operating expenses. Assume that Rondor started the accounting period with $20,000 in both cash and common stock.

Required

a. Identify the events described in the preceding paragraph and record them in a horizontal statements model like the following one:

Assets				=	Liab.	+	Equity			Rev.	−	Exp.	=	Net Inc.	Cash Flow
Cash	+ Accts. Rec.	+	Inv.	=	Accts. Pay.	+	C. Stk.	+	Ret. Earn.						
20,000	+ NA	+	NA	=	NA	+	20,000	+	NA	NA	−	NA	=	NA	NA

b. What is the balance of accounts receivable at the end of Year 1?
c. What is the balance of accounts payable at the end of Year 1?
d. What are the amounts of gross margin and net income for Year 1?
e. Determine the amount of net cash flow from operating activities.
f. Explain any differences between net income and net cash flow from operating activities.

LO 4-1

Exercise 4-4B Recording inventory transactions in the general journal and posting entries to T-accounts: perpetual system

Jones Shoe shop experienced the following events during Year 1, its first year of operation:

1. Acquired $25,000 cash from the issue of common stock.
2. Purchased inventory for $32,000 cash.
3. Sold inventory costing $19,000 for $36,000 cash.
4. Paid $3,100 for advertising expense.

Required

a. Record the general journal entries for the preceding transactions.
b. Post each of the entries to T-accounts.
c. Prepare a trial balance to prove the equality of debits and credits.

Exercise 4-5B Cash discounts and purchase returns

LO 4-2, 4-3

On March 6, Year 1, Salon Express purchased merchandise from Hair Fashions with a list price of $19,000, terms 2/10, n/45. On March 10, Salon returned merchandise to Hair Fashions for credit. The list price of the returned merchandise was $8,500. Salon paid cash to settle the accounts payable on March 15, Year 1.

Required

a. What is the amount of the check that Salon must write to Hair Fashions on March 15?
b. Show the events in a horizontal statements model like the following one:

Assets	=	Liab.	+	Equity		Rev.	−	Exp.	=	Net Inc.	Cash Flow
Cash + Inv.	=	Accts. Pay.	+	C. Stk + Ret. Earn.							

c. How much would Salon pay for the merchandise purchased if the payment is not made until March 20, Year 1?
d. Show the payment of the merchandise in Requirement *c* in a horizontal statements model like the one shown above.
e. Why would Hair Fashions sell merchandise with the terms 2/10, n/45?

Exercise 4-6B Determining which party is responsible for freight cost

LO 4-4

Required

Determine which party (buyer or seller) is responsible for freight charges in each of the following situations:

a. Purchased merchandise, freight terms, FOB destination.
b. Purchased merchandise, freight terms, FOB shipping point.
c. Sold merchandise, freight terms, FOB destination.
d. Sold merchandise, freight terms, FOB shipping point.

Exercise 4-7B Purchase discounts and transportation costs

LO 4-3, 4-4

Musgrove Basket Company had an $8,500 beginning balance in its Merchandise Inventory account. The following information regarding Musgrove's purchases and sales of inventory during its Year 1 accounting period was drawn from the company's accounting records:

1. Purchased $45,000 of inventory under terms 1/10, net/60. Transportation costs amounted to $700. The goods were delivered FOB shipping point. Musgrove paid for the inventory within the discount period.
2. Purchased $40,000 of inventory under terms 2/10, net/30. Transportation costs amounted to $900. The goods were delivered to Musgrove FOB destination. Musgrove paid for the inventory after the discount period had expired.
3. Sold inventory that cost $56,000 for $94,000. Transportation costs for goods delivered to customers amounted to $3,200. The goods were delivered FOB destination.

Required

a. Determine the balance in the Inventory account at the end of the accounting period.
b. Is Musgrove or its customers responsible for the transportation costs described in Event 3?
c. Determine the gross margin.

Exercise 4-8B Accounting for product costs: perpetual inventory system

LO 4-1, 4-2, 4-3, 4-4

Which of the following would be *debited* to the Inventory account for a merchandising business using the perpetual inventory system?

Required

a. Transportation-in.
b. Allowance received for damaged inventory.
c. Purchase of inventory.
d. Purchase of office supplies.
e. Transportation-out.
f. Cash discount given on goods sold.

LO 4-1, 4-2, 4-3, 4-4

Exercise 4-9B *Determining the effect of inventory transactions on the financial statements model: perpetual system*

TRS Company experienced the following events:

1. Purchased merchandise inventory for cash.
2. Sold merchandise inventory on account. Label the revenue recognition 2a and the expense recognition 2b.
3. Returned merchandise purchased on account.
4. Purchased merchandise inventory on account.
5. Paid cash on accounts payable within the discount period.
6. Paid cash for selling and administrative expenses.
7. Sold merchandise inventory for cash. Label the revenue recognition 7a and the expense recognition 7b.
8. Paid cash for transportation-out.
9. Paid cash for transportation-in.
10. Collected cash from accounts receivable not within the discount period.

Required

Identify each event as asset source (AS), asset use (AU), asset exchange (AE), or claims exchange (CE). Also explain how each event affects the financial statements by placing a + for increase, − for decrease, or NA for not affected under each of the components in the following horizontal statements model. Assume the company uses the perpetual inventory system. The first event is recorded as an example.

Event No.	Event Type	Assets	=	Liab.	+	Equity	Rev.	−	Exp.	=	Net Inc.	Cash Flow
1	AE	+ −	=	NA	+	NA	NA	−	NA	=	NA	− OA

LO 4-2, 4-4

Exercise 4-10B *Effect of product cost and period cost: horizontal statements model*

Wild Rose Co. experienced the following events for the Year 1 accounting period:

1. Acquired $20,000 cash from the issue of common stock.
2. Purchased $36,000 of inventory on account.
3. Received goods purchased in Event 2 FOB shipping point. Freight cost of $900 paid in cash.
4. Returned $4,000 of goods purchased in Event 2 because of poor quality.
5. Sold inventory on account that cost $28,000 for $82,000.
6. Freight cost on the goods sold in Event 5 was $200. The goods were shipped FOB destination. Cash was paid for the freight cost.
7. Collected $33,000 cash from accounts receivable.
8. Paid $27,000 cash on accounts payable.
9. Paid $4,500 for advertising expense.
10. Paid $7,200 cash for insurance expense.

Accounting for Merchandising Businesses 259

Required

a. Which of these transactions affect period (selling and administrative) costs? Which result in product costs? If neither, label the transaction NA.

b. Show each event in a horizontal statements model like the following one. The first event is recorded as an example.

Assets	=	Liab.	+	Equity		Rev.	−	Exp.	=	Net Inc.		Cash Flow
Cash + Accts. Rec. + Inv.	=	Accts. Pay.	+	C. Stk. + Ret. Earn.								
20,000 + NA + NA	=	NA	+	20,000 + NA		NA	−	NA	=	NA		20,000 FA

Exercise 4-11B Effect of inventory losses: perpetual system   LO 4-5

Raabe Sales experienced the following events during Year 1, its first year of operation:

1. Started the business when it acquired $80,000 cash from the issue of common stock.
2. Paid $35,000 cash to purchase inventory.
3. Sold inventory that cost $21,000 for $40,500 cash.
4. Physically counted inventory showing $13,500 inventory was on hand at the end of the accounting period.

Required

a. Open appropriate ledger T-accounts, and record the events in the accounts.
b. Prepare an income statement and balance sheet for Year 1.
c. Explain how differences between the book balance and the physical count of inventory could arise. Why is being able to determine whether differences exist useful to management?

Exercise 4-12B Effect of purchase returns and allowances and freight costs on the journal, ledger, and financial statements: perpetual system   LO 4-2, 4-4, 4-6

The trial balance for The Bolt Co. as of January 1, Year 2, was as follows:

Account Title	Debit	Credit
Cash	$12,000	
Inventory	6,000	
Common stock		$15,000
Retained earnings		3,000
Total	$18,000	$18,000

The following events affected the company during the Year 2 accounting period:

1. Purchased merchandise on account that cost $8,200.
2. The goods in Event 1 were purchased FOB shipping point with freight cost of $600 cash.
3. Returned $800 of damaged merchandise for credit on account.
4. Agreed to keep other damaged merchandise for which the company received a $400 allowance.
5. Sold merchandise that cost $5,500 for $9,500 cash.
6. Delivered merchandise to customers under terms FOB destination with freight costs amounting to $300 cash.
7. Paid $5,000 on the merchandise purchased in Event 1.

Required

a. Record the transactions in general journal format.
b. Open general ledger T-accounts with the appropriate beginning balances, and post the journal entries to the T-accounts.
c. Prepare an income statement and statement of cash flows for Year 2.
d. Explain why a difference does or does not exist between net income and net cash flow from operating activities.

Chapter 4

LO 4-6

Exercise 4-13B Multistep income statement

In Year 1, Image Incorporated sold land for $82,000 cash. The land had originally cost $50,000. Also, Image sold inventory that had cost $176,000 for $265,000 cash. Operating expenses amounted to $41,000.

Required

a. Prepare a Year 1 multistep income statement for Image Incorporated.
b. Assume that normal operating activities grow evenly by 10% during Year 2. Prepare a Year 2 multistep income statement for Image Incorporated.
c. Determine the percentage change in net income between Year 1 and Year 2.
d. Should the stockholders have expected the results determined in Requirement c? Explain your answer.

LO 4-6

Exercise 4-14B Single-step and multistep income statements

The following information was taken from the accounts of Adams's Eatery, a delicatessen, at December 31, Year 1. The accounts are listed in alphabetical order, and each has a normal balance.

Account	Amount
Accounts payable	$1,200
Accounts receivable	800
Advertising expense	400
Cash	820
Common stock	400
Cost of goods sold	1,200
Interest expense	140
Loss on sale of land	50
Merchandise inventory	900
Prepaid rent	80
Rent expense	220
Retained earnings	1,000
Salaries expense	260
Sales revenue	2,000

Required

First, prepare an income statement for the year using the single-step approach. Then, prepare another income statement using the multistep approach.

LO 4-2, 4-3, 4-6

Exercise 4-15B Purchase returns, discounts, loss, and a multistep income statement

The following information was drawn from the Year 1 accounting records of Cozart Merchandisers.

1. Inventory with a list price of $40,000 was purchased under terms 2/10, net/30.
2. Cozart returned $4,200 of the inventory to the supplier five days after purchase.
3. The accounts payable was settled within the discount period.
4. The inventory was sold for $69,000.
5. Selling and administrative expenses amounted to $12,000.
6. Interest expense paid amounted to $800.
7. Land that cost $15,000 was sold for $20,000 cash.

Required

a. Determine the cost of the inventory sold.
b. Prepare a multistep income statement.
c. Where would the interest expense be shown on the statement of cash flows?
d. How would the sale of the land be shown on the statement of cash flows?
e. Explain the difference between a loss and an expense.

Exercise 4-16B Effect of sales returns and allowances and freight costs on the journal, ledger, and financial statements: perpetual system

LO 4-2, 4-4, 4-7

Hollis Company began the Year 2 accounting period with $36,000 cash, $80,000 inventory, $70,000 common stock, and $46,000 retained earnings. During the Year 2 accounting period, Hollis experienced the following events:

1. Sold merchandise costing $51,500 for $92,900 on account to RJ's General Store.
2. Delivered the goods to RJ's under terms FOB destination. Freight costs were $500 cash.
3. Received returned goods from RJ's. The goods cost Hollis Company $3,200 and were sold to RJ's for $4,700.
4. Granted RJ's a $1,500 allowance for damaged goods that RJ's agreed to keep.
5. Collected partial payment of $71,000 cash from accounts receivable.

Required
a. Record the transactions in general journal format.
b. Open general ledger T-accounts with the appropriate beginning balances and post the journal entries to the T-accounts.
c. Prepare an income statement, balance sheet, and statement of cash flows.
d. Why would Hollis grant the $1,500 allowance to RJ's? Who benefits more?

Exercise 4-17B Comprehensive exercise with purchases discounts

LO 4-2, 4-3, 4-4, 4-6, 4-7, 4-8

Custom Auto Parts (CAP) started the Year 2 accounting period with the balances given in the financial statements model shown below. During Year 2, CAP experienced the following business events:

1. Purchased $60,000 of merchandise inventory on account, terms 2/10, n/30.
2. The goods that were purchased in Event 1 were delivered FOB shipping point. Freight costs of $1,500 were paid in cash by the responsible party.
3. Returned $3,000 of goods purchased in Event 1.
4a. Recorded the cash discount on the goods purchased in Event 1.
4b. Paid the balance due on the account payable within the discount period.
5a. Recognized $59,000 of cash revenue from the sale of merchandise.
5b. Recognized $45,000 of cost of goods sold.
6. The merchandise in Event 5a was sold to customers FOB destination. Freight costs of $1,400 were paid in cash by the responsible party.
7. Paid cash of $9,000 for selling and administrative expenses.
8. Sold the land for $14,500 cash.

Required
a. Show the above transactions in a financial statements model like the one shown below.

Event No.	Cash	+	Inventory	+	Land	=	Accts. Pay.	+	Com. Stk.	+	Ret. Earn.	Rev./ Gain	−	Exp.	=	Net Inc.	Cash Flow
Bal.	60,000	+	8,000	+	12,000	=	−0−	+	50,000	+	30,000	NA	−	NA	=	NA	NA

b. Prepare a multistep income statement. Include common size percentages on the income statement.
c. CAP's gross margin percentage in the prior year was 34%. Based on the common size data in the income statement, did CAP raise or lower its prices in Year 2?
d. Assuming a 5% rate of growth, what is the amount of net income expected for Year 3?

LO 4-8

Exercise 4-18B *Using ratios to make comparisons*

The following income statements were drawn from the annual reports of Athens Company and Boulder Company:

	Athens*	Boulder*
Net sales	$ 32,600	$ 86,200
Cost of goods sold	(24,450)	(47,410)
Gross margin	8,150	38,790
Less: Operating exp.		
Selling and admin. exp.	(6,200)	(34,480)
Net income	$ 1,950	$ 4,310

*All figures are reported in thousands of dollars.

Required

a. One of the companies is a high-end retailer that operates in exclusive shopping malls. The other operates discount stores located in low-cost, standalone buildings. Identify the high-end retailer and the discounter. Support your answer with appropriate ratios.

b. If Athens and Boulder have equity of $22,000 and $39,000, respectively, which company is in the more profitable business?

LO 4-8

Exercise 4-19B *Using common size statements and ratios to make comparisons*

The following information is available for Billings and Phoenix companies:

	Billings	Phoenix
Sales	$3,000,000	$3,000
Cost of goods sold	1,800,000	2,100
Operating expenses	960,000	780
Total assets	3,750,000	3,750
Stockholders' equity	1,000,000	1,200

Required

a. Prepare a common size income statement for each company.

b. Compute the return on assets and return on equity for each company.

c. Which company is more profitable from the stockholders' perspective?

d. One company is a high-end retailer, and the other operates a discount store. Which is the discounter? Support your selection by referring to the appropriate ratios.

LO 4-9

Exercise 4-20B *Effect of inventory transactions on the income statement and balance sheet: periodic system (Appendix)*

Rick Dove is the owner of RD Cleaning. At the beginning of the year, RD Cleaning had $4,800 in inventory. During the year, RD Cleaning purchased inventory that cost $26,000. At the end of the year, inventory on hand amounted to $3,600.

Required

Calculate the following:

a. Cost of goods available for sale during the year.

b. Cost of goods sold for the year.

c. Inventory amount RD Cleaning would report on its year-end balance sheet.

Exercise 4-21B *Determining cost of goods sold: periodic system (Appendix)*   LO 4-9

Far East Retailers uses the periodic inventory system to account for its inventory transactions. The following account titles and balances were drawn from Far East's records for Year 2: beginning balance in inventory, $46,200; purchases, $352,400; purchase returns and allowances, $14,600; sales, $840,000; sales returns and allowances, $7,520; transportation-in, $2,150; and operating expenses, $65,100. A physical count indicated that $35,100 of merchandise was on hand at the end of the accounting period.

Required
a. Prepare a schedule of cost of goods sold.
b. Prepare a multistep income statement.

Exercise 4-22B *Basic transactions: periodic system, single cycle (Appendix)*   LO 4-9

The following events apply to Sally's Gift Shop for Year 1, its first year of operation:
1. Acquired $60,000 cash from the issue of common stock.
2. Issued common stock to Sally Quin, one of the owners, in exchange for merchandise inventory worth $3,200 Sally had acquired prior to opening the shop.
3. Purchased $56,200 of inventory on account.
4. Paid $4,500 for advertising expense.
5. Sold inventory for $98,300 cash.
6. Paid $12,000 in salary to a part-time salesperson.
7. Paid $47,000 on accounts payable (see Event 3).
8. Physically counted inventory, which indicated that $16,000 of inventory was on hand at the end of the accounting period.

Required
a. Record each of these events in general journal form. Sally's Gift Shop uses the periodic system.
b. Post each of the events to ledger T-accounts.
c. Prepare an income statement, statement of changes in stockholders' equity, balance sheet, and statement of cash flows for Year 1.
d. Prepare the necessary closing entries at the end of Year 1, and post them to the appropriate T-accounts.
e. Prepare a post-closing trial balance.
f. Discuss an advantage of using the periodic system instead of the perpetual system.
g. Why is the common stock issued on the statement of changes in stockholders' equity different from the common stock issued in the cash flow from financing activities section of the cash flow statement?

PROBLEMS—SERIES B

Problem 4-23B *Identifying freight cost*   LO 4-4

Required
For each of the following events, determine the amount of freight paid by Cycle Parts House. Also indicate whether the freight is classified as a product or period cost.
a. Purchased merchandise with costs of $500, FOB shipping point.
b. Sold merchandise to a customer. Freight costs were $800, FOB shipping point.
c. Purchased inventory with freight costs of $1,400, FOB destination.
d. Shipped merchandise to customers with freight costs of $300, FOB destination.

Problem 4-24B *Identifying product and period costs*   LO 4-4

Required
Indicate whether each of the following costs is a product cost or a period cost:
a. Cleaning supplies for the office.
b. Freight on goods purchased for resale.

c. Salary of the marketing director.
d. Freight on goods sold to customer with terms FOB destination.
e. Utilities expense incurred for office building.
f. Advertising expense.
g. Insurance on vans used to deliver goods to customers.
h. Salaries of sales supervisors.
i. Monthly maintenance expense for a copier.
j. Goods purchased for resale.

LO 4-1, 4-6

Problem 4-25B *Basic transactions for three accounting cycles: perpetual system*

Mano Company was started in Year 1 when it acquired $40,000 from the issue of common stock. The following data summarize the company's first three years' operating activities. Assume that all transactions were cash transactions.

	Year 1	Year 2	Year 3
Purchases of inventory	$30,000	$36,000	$57,000
Sales	42,000	56,000	72,000
Cost of goods sold	22,000	39,000	51,000
Selling and administrative expenses	6,500	9,100	11,200

Required

Prepare an income statement (use the multistep format) and balance sheet for each fiscal year. (*Hint:* Record the transaction data for each accounting period in T-accounts before preparing the statements for that year.)

LO 4-1, 4-2, 4-3, 4-4, 4-5, 4-6, 4-7

Problem 4-26B *Comprehensive cycle problem: perpetual system*

At the beginning of Year 2, EuRo Enterprises had the following balances in its accounts:

Cash	$16,800
Inventory	4,000
Land	2,000
Common stock	12,000
Retained earnings	10,800

During Year 2, EuRo Enterprises experienced the following events:

1. Purchased inventory that cost $11,200 on account from Ivey Company under terms 2/10, n/30. The merchandise was delivered FOB shipping point. Freight costs of $800 were paid in cash.
2. Returned $600 of the inventory that it had purchased because the inventory was damaged in transit. The seller agreed to pay the return freight cost.
3. Paid the amount due on its account payable to Ivey Company within the cash discount period.
4. Sold inventory that had cost $8,000 for $13,500. The sale was on account under terms 2/10, n/45.
5. Received merchandise returned from a customer. The merchandise had originally cost $1,200 and had been sold to the customer for $2,100 cash. The customer was paid $2,100 cash for the returned merchandise.
6. Delivered goods in Event 4 FOB destination. Freight costs of $800 were paid in cash.
7. Collected the amount due on accounts receivable within the discount period.
8. Sold the land for $3,500.
9. Recognized $500 of accrued interest revenue.
10. Took a physical count indicating that $6,500 of inventory was on hand at the end of the accounting period. *Hint:* Determine the current balance in the inventory account before calculating the amount of the inventory write down.

Required

a. Identify each of these events as asset source (AS), asset use (AU), asset exchange (AE), or claims exchange (CE). Also explain how each event affects the financial statements by placing a + for increase, − for decrease, or NA for not affected under each of the components in the following horizontal statements model. Assume that the perpetual inventory method is used. When an event has more than one part, use letters to distinguish the effects of each part. The first event is recorded as an example.

Event No.	Event Type	Assets	=	Liab.	+	Stk. Equity	Rev.	−	Exp.	=	Net Inc.	Cash Flow
1a	AS	+	=	+	+	NA	NA	−	NA	=	NA	NA
1b	AE	+ −	=	NA	+	NA	NA	−	NA	=	NA	− OA

b. Record the events in general journal format.
c. Open ledger T-accounts and post the beginning balances and the events to the accounts.
d. Prepare a multistep income statement, statement of changes in stockholders' equity, balance sheet, and statement of cash flows.
e. Use a single general journal to close all revenue, gain, and expense accounts to the retained earnings account. Post the journal entry to the ledger accounts and prepare a post-closing trial balance.

Problem 4-27B Multistep and common size income statements   LO 4-6, 4-8

The following information was drawn from the records of Moore Sales Company:

	Year 1	Year 2
Net sales	$60,000	$70,000
Cost of goods sold	(25,000)	(26,500)
Operating expenses	(13,200)	(16,100)
Gain on the sale of land	0	5,000

Required

a. Prepare a multistep income statement for each year.
b. Prepare a common size income statement for each year.
c. Assume that the operating trends between Year 1 and Year 2 continue through Year 3. Write a brief memo indicating whether you expect net income to increase or decrease in Year 3.

Problem 4-28B Preparing a schedule of cost of goods sold and multistep and single-step income statements: periodic system (Appendix)   LO 4-9

The following account titles and balances were taken from the adjusted trial balance of Hogan Sales Co. at December 31, Year 2. The company uses the periodic inventory method.

Account Title	Balance
Advertising expense	$ 20,800
Interest expense	10,000
Merchandise inventory, January 1	36,000
Merchandise inventory, December 31	40,200
Miscellaneous expense	1,600
Purchases	300,000
Purchase returns and allowances	5,400
Rent expense	36,000
Salaries expense	106,000
Sales	640,000
Sales returns and allowances	16,000
Transportation-in	12,400
Transportation-out	21,600
Gain on sale of land	8,000
Utilities expense	22,400

Required

a. Prepare a schedule to determine the amount of cost of goods sold.
b. Prepare a multistep income statement.
c. Prepare a single-step income statement.

LO 4-9

Problem 4-29B *Comprehensive cycle problem: periodic system (Appendix)*

The following trial balance pertains to Simmons Hardware as of January 1, Year 2:

Account Title	Debit	Credit
Cash	$ 28,000	
Accounts receivable	18,000	
Merchandise inventory	120,000	
Accounts payable		$ 10,000
Common stock		140,000
Retained earnings		16,000
Totals	$166,000	$166,000

The following events occurred in Year 2. Assume that Simmons Hardware uses the periodic inventory system.

1. Purchased land for $16,000 cash.
2. Purchased merchandise on account for $46,000, terms 2/10 n/30.
3. The merchandise purchased by Simmons was shipped FOB shipping point for $460 cash.
4. Returned $4,000 of defective merchandise purchased in Event 2.
5. Sold merchandise for $54,000 cash.
6. Sold merchandise on account for $100,000, terms 1/20 n/30.
7. Paid cash within the discount period on accounts payable due on merchandise purchased in Event 2.
8. Paid $2,400 cash for selling expenses.
9. Collected $70,000 of accounts receivable within the discount period.
10. Collected $24,000 of accounts receivable but not within the discount period.
11. Paid $6,400 of other operating expenses.
12. Performed a physical count indicating that $60,000 of inventory was on hand at the end of the accounting period.

Required

a. Record these transactions in a general journal.
b. Post the transactions to ledger T-accounts.
c. Prepare a schedule of cost of goods sold, income statement, statement of changes in stockholders' equity, balance sheet, and statement of cash flows for Year 2.

ANALYZE, THINK, COMMUNICATE

ATC 4-1 **Business Applications Case** *Understanding real-world annual reports*

Required

Obtain the Target Corporation's annual report at http://investors.target.com using the instructions in Appendix B, and use it to answer the following questions:

a. What was Target's gross margin percentage for the fiscal year ended January 28, 2017 (2016) and 2015?
b. What was Target's return on sales percentage for 2016 and 2015?
c. Target's return on sales percentage for 2016 was lower than it was in 2015. Ignoring taxes, how much higher would Target's 2016 net income have been if its return on sales percentage in 2016 had been the same as for 2015?

ATC 4-2 **Group Exercise** *Multistep income statement*

The following quarterly information is given for Rossie for Year 1 (amounts shown are in millions):

	First Quarter	Second Quarter	Third Quarter	Fourth Quarter
Net Sales	$736.0	$717.4	$815.2	$620.1
Gross Margin	461.9	440.3	525.3	252.3
Net Income	37.1	24.6	38.6	31.4

Required

a. Divide the class into groups and organize the groups into four sections. Assign each section financial information for one of the quarters.

  (1) Each group should compute the cost of goods sold and operating expenses for the specific quarter assigned to its section and prepare a multistep income statement for the quarter.

  (2) Each group should compute the gross margin percentage and cost of goods sold percentage for its specific quarter.

  (3) Have a representative of each group put that quarter's sales, cost of goods sold percentage, and gross margin percentage on the board.

Class Discussion

b. Have the class discuss the change in each of these items from quarter to quarter and explain why the change might have occurred. Which was the best quarter and why?

ATC 4-3 Real-World Case *Identifying companies based on financial statement information*

Presented here is selected information from the 2013 fiscal-year 10-K reports of four companies. The four companies, in alphabetical order, are: **AT&T, Inc.**, a company that provides communications and digital entertainment; **Deere & Company**, a manufacturer of heavy machinery; **Starbucks**, a company that sells coffee products; and **Tiffany & Company**, a company that operates high-end jewelry and department stores. The data for the companies, presented in the order of the amount of their sales in millions of dollars, are:

	A	B	C	D
Sales	$163,786	$26,644.0	$21,315.9	$4,104.9
Cost of goods sold	76,884	18,248.9	8,511.1	1,613.6
Net earnings	12,976	1,523.9	2,817.7	463.9
Inventory	—	3,340.5	1,378.5	2,225.0
Accounts receivable	16,794	29,741.1	768.8	206.4
Total assets	403,821	57,981.4	14,329.5	5,129.7

Required

Based on these financial data and your knowledge and assumptions about the nature of the businesses that the companies operate, determine which data relate to which companies. Write a memorandum explaining your decisions. Include a discussion of which ratios you used in your analysis, and show the computations of these ratios in your memorandum.

ATC 4-4 Real-World Case *Performing ratio analysis using real-world data*

Bloomin' Brands, Inc. is the corporation behind five restaurant chains: **Outback Steakhouse**, **Carrabba's Italian Grill**, **Bonefish Grill**, **Fleming's Prime Steakhouse and Wine Bar**, and **Roy's**. The following data were taken from its 2016 annual report. All dollar amounts are in thousands.

	Fiscal Years Ending	
	December 25, 2016	December 27, 2015
Total restaurant sales	$4,226,057	$4,349,921
Cost of goods sold	1,354,853	1,419,689
Net income	41,748	127,327

Required

a. Compute Bloomin' Brands' gross margin percentage for 2016 and 2015.
b. Compute Bloomin' Brands' return-on-sales percentage for 2016 and 2015.
c. Based on the percentages computed in Requirements *a* and *b*, did Bloomin' Brands' performance get better or worse from 2015 to 2016? Speculate as to what might have caused such a dramatic change from 2015 to 2016.
d. Compare Bloomin' Brands' gross margin percentages and return-on-sales percentages to those of the other real-world companies covered in this chapter and discuss whether or not it appears to have a better-than-average financial performance.

ATC 4-5 Business Applications Case *Performing ratio analysis using real-world data*

The Kroger Co. was founded in 1883 and is one of the largest retailers in the world, based on annual sales. Whole Foods Market claims to be the world's largest retailer of natural and organic foods. Whole Foods offers specialty products to customers with sufficient disposable income to spend on such goods.

The following data were taken from these companies' 2016 annual reports. All dollar amounts are in millions.

	Kroger Co. January 30, 2016	Whole Foods September 25, 2016
Sales	$109,830	$15,724
Cost of goods sold	85,496	10,313
Net income	2,039	507

Required

a. Before performing any calculations, speculate as to which company will have the highest gross margin and return-on-sales percentage. Explain the rationale for your decision.
b. Calculate the gross margin percentages for Kroger and Whole Foods Market.
c. Calculate the return-on-sales percentages for Kroger and Whole Foods Market.
d. Do the calculations from Requirements *b* and *c* confirm your speculations in Requirement *a*?

ATC 4-6 Written Assignment, Critical Thinking *Effect of sales returns on financial statements*

Bell Farm and Garden Equipment Co. reported the following information for Year 1:

Net sales of equipment	$ 2,450,567
Other income	6,786
Cost of goods sold	(1,425,990)
Selling, general, and administrative expense	(325,965)
Depreciation and amortization	(3,987)
Net operating income	$ 701,411

Selected information from the balance sheet as of December 31, Year 1, follows:

Cash and marketable securities	$113,545
Inventory	248,600
Accounts receivable	82,462
Property, plant, and equipment—net	335,890
Other assets	5,410
Total assets	$785,907

Assume that a major customer returned a large order to Bell on December 31, Year 1. The amount of the sale had been $146,800, with a cost of sales of $94,623. The return was recorded in the books on January 1, Year 2. The company president does not want to correct the books. He argues that it makes no difference as to whether the return is recorded in Year 1 or Year 2. Either way, the return has been duly recognized.

Required

a. Assume you are the CFO for Bell Farm and Garden Equipment Co. Write a memo to the president explaining how omitting the entry on December 31, Year 1, could cause the financial statements to be misleading to investors and creditors. Explain how omitting the return from the customer would affect net income and the balance sheet.
b. Why might the president want to record the return on January 1, Year 2, instead of December 31, Year 1?
c. Would the failure to record the customer return violate the AICPA Code of Professional Conduct? (See Exhibit 2.9 in Chapter 2.)
d. If the president of the company refuses to correct the financial statements, what action should you take?

ATC 4-7 Ethical Dilemma *Wait until I get mine*

Ada Fontanez is the president of a large company that owns a chain of athletic shoe stores. The company was in dire financial condition when she was hired three years ago. In an effort to motivate Fontanez, the board of directors included a bonus plan as part of her compensation package. According to her employment contract, on January 15 of each year, Fontanez is paid a cash bonus equal to 5 percent of the amount of net income reported on the preceding December 31 income statement. Fontanez was sufficiently motivated. Through her leadership, the company prospered. Her efforts were recognized throughout the industry, and she received numerous lucrative offers to leave the company. One offer was so enticing that she decided to change jobs. Her decision was made in late December Year 1. However, she decided to resign effective February 1, Year 2, to ensure the receipt of her January bonus. On December 31, Year 1, the chief accountant, Walter Smith, advised Fontanez that the company had a sizable quantity of damaged inventory. A warehouse fire had resulted in smoke and water damage to approximately $600,000 of inventory. The warehouse was not insured, and the accountant recommended that the loss be recognized immediately. After examining the inventory, Fontanez argued that it could be sold as *damaged goods* to customers at reduced prices. Accordingly, she refused to allow the write-off the accountant recommended. She stated that so long as she is president, the inventory stays on the books at cost. She told the accountant that he could take up the matter with the new president in February.

Required

a. How would an immediate write-off of the damaged inventory affect the December 31, Year 1, income statement, balance sheet, and statement of cash flows?
b. How would the write-off affect Fontanez's bonus?
c. If the new president is given the same bonus plan, how will Fontanez's refusal to recognize the loss affect his or her bonus?
d. Assuming that the damaged inventory is truly worthless, comment on the ethical implications of Fontanez's refusal to recognize the loss in the Year 1 accounting period.
e. Assume that the damaged inventory is truly worthless and that you are Smith. How would you react to Fontanez's refusal to recognize the loss?

ATC 4-8 Research Assignment *Analyzing Coca-Cola's profit margins*

Using Coca-Cola Company's most current Form 10-K, answer the questions below. To obtain the Form 10-K, you can use the EDGAR system, following the instructions in Appendix A, or it can be found on the company's website.

Required

a. What was Coke's gross margin percentage for the most current year?
b. What was Coke's gross margin percentage for the previous year? Has it changed significantly?
c. What was Coke's return-on-sales percentage for the most current year?
d. What percentage of Coke's total net operating revenues for the most current year were from operations in the United States?
e. Comment on the appropriateness of comparing Coke's gross margin with that of Microsoft. If Microsoft has a higher/lower margin, does that mean Microsoft is a better managed company?

ATC 4-9 Spreadsheet Analysis *Using Excel*

The following accounts, balances, and other financial information are drawn from the records of Vong Company for Year 2:

Net sales revenue	$18,800	Beginning common stock	$9,000
Unearned revenue	2,600	Land	8,000
Accounts receivable	6,000	Certificate of deposit	10,000
Cost of goods sold	6,000	Interest revenue	100
Inventory	5,000	Interest receivable	100
Accounts payable	5,800	Dividends	1,500
Notes payable	6,000	Beginning retained earnings	8,500
Interest expense	550	Cash from stock issued	3,000
Interest payable	550	Cash	7,200
Supplies	50	Gain on sale of land	1,050
Supplies expense	750	Loss on sale of property	50
Office equipment	3,500	Salaries expense	1,400
Depreciation expense	500	Salaries payable	400
Accumulated depreciation	1,000	Rent expense	1,100
Transportation-out expense	500	Prepaid rent	100
Miscellaneous operating expense	4,500		

The Cash account revealed the following cash flows:

Received cash from advances from customers	$ 2,600
Purchased office equipment	(3,500)
Received cash from issuing stock	3,000
Collected cash from accounts receivable	3,800
Purchased land	(8,000)
Received cash from borrowing funds	6,000
Paid cash for rent	(1,200)
Sold land	10,000
Paid cash for dividends	(1,500)
Paid cash for operating expenses	(1,000)
Purchased certificate of deposit	(10,000)

Required

Build an Excel spreadsheet to construct a multistep income statement, statement of changes in stockholders' equity, balance sheet, and statement of cash flows for Year 2.

ATC 4-10 **Spreadsheet Analysis** *Mastering Excel*

At the end of Year 1, the following information is available for Short and Wise Companies:

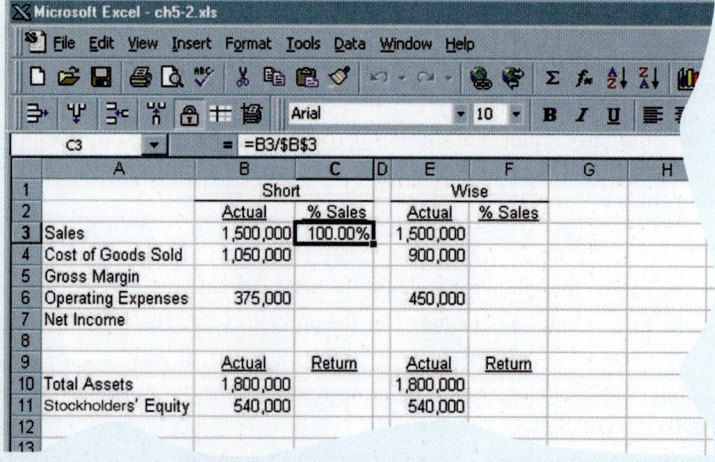

Source: Microsoft Office Excel 1997

Required

a. Set up the spreadsheet shown here. Complete the income statements by using Excel formulas.
b. Prepare a common size income statement for each company by completing the % Sales columns.

COMPREHENSIVE PROBLEM

The trial balance of Pacilio Security Services, Inc. as of January 1, Year 4, had the following normal balances:

Cash	$12,500
Accounts Receivable	3,500
Supplies	120
Prepaid Rent	1,000
Land	4,000
Unearned Revenue	900
Salaries Payable	1,000
Common Stock	8,000
Retained Earnings	11,220

In Year 4, Pacilio Security Services decided to expand its business to sell security systems and offer 24-hour alarm monitoring services. It plans to phase out its current service of providing security personnel at various events. The following summary transactions occurred during Year 4:

1. Paid the salaries payable from Year 3.
2. Acquired an additional $42,000 cash from the issue of common stock.
3. Rented a larger building on May 1; paid $6,000 for 12 months' rent in advance.
4. Paid $800 cash for supplies to be used over the next several months by the business.
5. Purchased 50 alarm systems for resale at a cost of $12,000. The alarm systems were purchased on account with the terms 2/10, n/30.
6. Returned one of the alarm systems that had a cost of $240.
7. Installed 40 alarm systems during the year for a total sales amount of $20,000. The cost of these systems amounted to $9,440. Sales of $15,000 were on account, while $5,000 were cash sales.
8. Paid the installers and other employees a total of $9,500 in salaries.
9. Sold $36,000 of monitoring services for the year. The services are billed to the customers each month.
10. Paid cash on accounts payable. The payment was made before the discount period expired. At the time of purchase, the inventory had a cost of $8,000.
11. Paid cash to settle additional accounts payable. The payment was made after the discount period expired. At the time of purchase, the inventory had a cost of $2,780.
12. Collected $43,000 of accounts receivable during the year.
13. Performed $12,000 of security services for area events; $9,000 was on account and $3,000 was for cash.
14. Paid advertising cost of $1,620 for the year.
15. Paid $1,100 for utilities expense for the year.
16. Paid a dividend of $12,000 to the shareholders.

Adjustment Information

17. Supplies of $150 were on hand at the end of the year.
18. Recognized the expired rent for the year.
19. Recognized the balance of the unearned revenue; cash was received in Year 3.
20. Accrued salaries at December 31, Year 4, were $1,500.

Required

a. Record the above transactions in general journal form. (Round amounts to the nearest dollar.)
b. Post the transactions to T-accounts.
c. Prepare a trial balance.
d. Prepare an income statement, statement of changes in stockholders' equity, balance sheet, and statement of cash flows.
e. Close the temporary accounts to retained earnings.
f. Post the closing entries to the T-accounts and prepare a post-closing trial balance.

CHAPTER 5

Accounting for Inventories

LEARNING OBJECTIVES

After you have mastered the material in this chapter, you will be able to:

LO 5-1 Determine the amount of cost of goods sold and ending inventory using the specific identification, FIFO, LIFO, and weighted-average cost flow methods.

LO 5-2 Apply the lower-of-cost-or-market rule to inventory valuation.

LO 5-3 Show how fraud can be avoided through inventory control.

LO 5-4 Use the gross margin method to estimate ending inventory.

LO 5-5 Calculate and interpret the inventory turnover ratio.

 Video lectures and accompanying self-assessment quizzes are available in Connect *for all learning objectives.*

CHAPTER OPENING

In the previous chapter, we used the simplifying assumption that identical inventory items cost the same amount. In practice, businesses often pay different amounts for identical items. Suppose The Mountain Bike Company (TMBC) sells high-end Model 201 helmets. Because all Model 201 helmets are identical, does the helmet supplier charge TMBC the same amount for each helmet? Probably not. You have likely observed that prices change frequently.

Assume TMBC purchases one Model 201 helmet at a cost of $100. Two weeks later, TMBC purchases a second Model 201 helmet. Because the supplier has raised prices, the second helmet costs $110. If TMBC sells one of its two helmets, should it record $100 or $110 as cost of goods sold? The following section of this chapter discusses several acceptable alternative methods for determining the amount of cost of goods sold from which companies may choose under generally accepted accounting principles.

The Curious Accountant

©Michael Conroy/AP Images

The Kroger Company is one of the world's largest retail chains, operating about 2,778 stores. As of January 30, 2016, the company reported approximately $6.2 billion of inventory on its balance sheet. In the notes to its financial statements, Kroger reported that it uses an inventory method that assumes its newest goods are sold first and its oldest goods are kept in inventory.

Can you think of any reason why a company selling perishable goods, such as milk and vegetables, would use an inventory method that assumes older goods are kept, while newer goods are sold? (Answers on page 287.)

INVENTORY COST FLOW METHODS

LO 5-1

Determine the amount of cost of goods sold and ending inventory using the specific identification, FIFO, LIFO, and weighted-average cost flow methods.

Recall that when goods are sold, product costs flow (are transferred) from the Inventory account to the Cost of Goods Sold account. Four acceptable methods for determining the amount of cost to transfer are (1) specific identification; (2) first-in, first-out (FIFO); (3) last-in, first-out (LIFO); and (4) weighted average.

Specific Identification

Suppose The Mountain Bike Company (TMBC) tags inventory items so it can identify which one is sold at the time of sale. TMBC could then charge the actual cost of the specific item sold to cost of goods sold. Recall that the first inventory item TMBC purchased cost $100 and the second item cost $110. Using **specific identification,** cost of goods sold would be $100 if the first item purchased was sold, or $110 if the second item purchased was sold.

When a company's inventory consists of many low-priced, high-turnover goods, the recordkeeping necessary to use specific identification isn't practical. Imagine the difficulty of recording the cost of each specific food item in a grocery store. Another disadvantage of the specific identification method is the opportunity for managers to manipulate the income statement. For example, TMBC can report a lower cost of goods sold by selling the first instead of the second item. Specific identification is, however, frequently used for high-priced, low-turnover inventory items such as automobiles. For big ticket items like cars, customer demands for specific products limit management's ability to select which merchandise is sold, and volume is low enough to manage the recordkeeping.

©Andersen Ross/Brand X/Corbis RF

First-In, First-Out (FIFO)

The **first-in, first-out (FIFO) cost flow method** requires that the cost of the items purchased *first* be assigned to cost of goods sold. Using FIFO, TMBC's cost of goods sold is $100.

Last-In, First-Out (LIFO)

The **last-in, first-out (LIFO) cost flow method** requires that the cost of the items purchased *last* be charged to cost of goods sold. Using LIFO, TMBC's cost of goods sold is $110.

Weighted Average

To use the **weighted-average cost flow method,** first calculate the average cost per unit by dividing the *total cost* of the inventory available by the *total number* of units available. In the case of TMBC, the average cost per unit of the inventory is $105 [($100 + $110) ÷ 2]. Cost of goods sold is then calculated by multiplying the average cost per unit by the number of units sold. Using weighted average, TMBC's cost of goods sold is $105 ($105 × 1).

Physical Flow

The preceding discussion pertains to the flow of *costs* through the accounting records, *not* the actual **physical flow of goods.** Goods usually move physically on a FIFO basis, which means that the first items of merchandise acquired by a company (first-in) are the first items sold to its customers (first-out). The inventory items on hand at the end of the accounting period are typically the last items in (the most recently acquired goods). If companies did not sell their oldest inventory items first, inventories would include dated, less marketable merchandise. *Cost flow,* however, can differ from *physical flow.* For example, a company may use LIFO or weighted average for financial reporting even if its goods flow physically on a FIFO basis.

Effect of Cost Flow on Financial Statements

Effect on Income Statement

The cost flow method a company uses can significantly affect the gross margin reported in the income statement. To demonstrate, assume that TMBC sold the inventory item discussed previously for $120. The amounts of gross margin using the FIFO, LIFO, and weighted-average cost flow assumptions are shown in the following table:

	FIFO	LIFO	Weighted Average
Sales	$120	$120	$120
Cost of goods sold	100	110	105
Gross margin	$ 20	$ 10	$ 15

Even though the physical flow is assumed to be identical for each method, the gross margin reported under FIFO is double the amount reported under LIFO. Companies experiencing identical economic events (same units of inventory purchased and sold) can report significantly different results in their financial statements. Meaningful financial analysis requires an understanding of financial reporting practices.

Effect on Balance Sheet

Because total product costs are allocated between costs of goods sold and ending inventory, the cost flow method a company uses affects its balance sheet as well as its income statement. FIFO transfers the first cost to the income statement, so this leaves the last cost on the balance sheet. Similarly, by transferring the last cost to the income statement, LIFO leaves the first cost in ending inventory. The weighted-average method bases both cost of goods sold and ending inventory on the average cost per unit. To illustrate, the ending inventory TMBC would report on the balance sheet using each of the three cost flow methods is shown in the following table:

EXHIBIT 5.1

Use of Inventory Cost Flow Methods

The chart is based on data drawn from recent annual reports published by the 30 companies that comprise the Dow Jones Industrial Average. The category titled "Not disclosed" consisted of companies with relatively small quantities of inventory.

	FIFO	LIFO	Weighted Average
Ending inventory	$110	$100	$105

The FIFO, LIFO, and weighted-average methods are all used extensively in business practice. The same company may even use one cost flow method for some of its products and different cost flow methods for other products. Exhibit 5.1 illustrates the relative use of the different cost flow methods among U.S. companies.

CHECK YOURSELF 5.1

Nash Office Supply (NOS) purchased two Model 303 copiers at different times. The first copier purchased cost $400 and the second copier purchased cost $450. NOS sold one of the copiers for $600. Determine the gross margin on the sale and the ending inventory balance assuming NOS accounts for inventory using (1) FIFO, (2) LIFO, and (3) weighted average.

Answer

	FIFO	LIFO	Weighted Average
Sales	$ 600	$ 600	$ 600
Cost of goods sold	(400)	(450)	(425)
Gross margin	$ 200	$ 150	$ 175
Ending inventory	$ 450	$ 400	$ 425

Multiple Layers with Multiple Quantities

The previous example illustrates different **inventory cost flow methods** using only two cost layers ($100 and $110) with only one unit of inventory in each layer. Actual business inventories are considerably more complex. Most real-world inventories are composed of multiple cost layers with different quantities of inventory in each layer. The underlying allocation concepts, however, remain unchanged.

For example, a different inventory item The Mountain Bike Company (TMBC) carries in its stores is a bike called the Eraser. TMBC's beginning inventory and two purchases of Eraser bikes are described below.

Jan. 1	Beginning inventory	10 units @ $200	=	$ 2,000
Mar. 18	First purchase	20 units @ $220	=	4,400
Aug. 21	Second purchase	25 units @ $250	=	6,250
Total cost of the 55 bikes available for sale				$12,650

The accounting records for the period show that TMBC paid cash for all Eraser bike purchases and sold 43 bikes at a cash price of $350 each.

Allocating Cost of Goods Available for Sale

The following discussion shows how to determine the cost of goods sold and ending inventory amounts using FIFO, LIFO, and weighted-average cost flow methods. We show all three methods to demonstrate how they affect the financial statements differently; TMBC would actually use only one of the methods.

Regardless of the cost flow method chosen, TMBC must allocate the cost of goods available for sale ($12,650) between cost of goods sold and ending inventory. The amounts assigned to each category will differ depending on TMBC's cost flow method. Computations for each method are shown below.

FIFO Inventory Cost Flow

Recall that TMBC sold 43 Eraser bikes during the accounting period. The FIFO method transfers to the Cost of Goods Sold account the *cost of the first 43 bikes* TMBC had available to sell. The first 43 bikes acquired by TMBC were the 10 bikes in the beginning inventory (these were purchased in the prior period) plus the 20 bikes purchased in March and 13 of the bikes purchased in August. The expense recognized for the cost of these bikes ($9,650) is computed as follows:

Jan. 1	Beginning inventory	10 units @ $200	=	$2,000
Mar. 18	First purchase	20 units @ $220	=	4,400
Aug. 21	Second purchase	13 units @ $250	=	3,250
Total cost of the 43 bikes sold				$9,650

Because TMBC had 55 bikes available for sale, it would have 12 bikes (55 available − 43 sold) in ending inventory. The cost assigned to these 12 bikes (the ending balance in the Inventory account) equals the cost of goods available for sale minus the cost of goods sold as shown below:

Cost of goods available for sale	$12,650
Cost of goods sold	9,650
Ending inventory balance	$ 3,000

We show the allocation of the cost of goods available for sale between cost of goods sold and ending inventory graphically below.

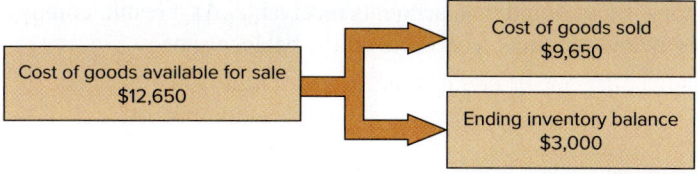

LIFO Inventory Cost Flow

Under LIFO, the cost of goods sold is the cost of the last 43 bikes acquired by TMBC, computed as follows:

Aug. 21	Second purchase	25 units @ $250	=	$ 6,250
Mar. 18	First purchase	18 units @ $220	=	3,960
Total cost of the 43 bikes sold				$10,210

The LIFO cost of the 12 bikes in ending inventory is computed as shown below:

Cost of goods available for sale	$12,650
Cost of goods sold	10,210
Ending inventory balance	$ 2,440

We show the allocation of the cost of goods available for sale between cost of goods sold and ending inventory graphically below.

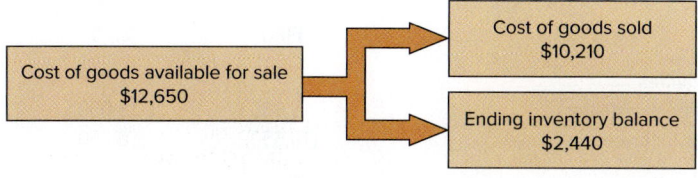

Weighted-Average Cost Flow

The weighted-average cost per unit is determined by dividing the *total cost of goods available for sale* by the *total number of units* available for sale. For TMBC, the weighted-average cost per unit is $230 ($12,650 ÷ 55). The weighted-average cost of goods sold is determined by multiplying the average cost per unit by the number of units sold ($230 × 43 = $9,890). The cost assigned to the 12 bikes in ending inventory is $2,760 (12 × $230).

We show the allocation of the cost of goods available for sale between cost of goods sold and ending inventory graphically below.

Effect of Cost Flow on Financial Statements

Exhibit 5.2 displays partial financial statements for The Mountain Bike Company (TMBC). This exhibit includes only information pertaining to the Eraser bikes inventory item described above. Other financial statement data are omitted.

Recall that assets are reported on the balance sheet in order of liquidity (how quickly they are expected to be converted to cash). Because companies frequently sell inventory on account, inventory is less liquid than accounts receivable. As a result, companies commonly report inventory below accounts receivable on the balance sheet.

EXHIBIT 5.2

TMBC COMPANY
Comparative Financial Statements

Partial Income Statements

	FIFO	LIFO	Weighted Average
Sales	$15,050	$15,050	$15,050
Cost of goods sold	(9,650)	(10,210)	(9,890)
Gross margin	5,400	4,840	5,160

Partial Balance Sheets

	FIFO	LIFO	Weighted Average
Assets			
Cash	$ xx	$ xx	$ xx
Accounts receivable	xx	xx	xx
Inventory	3,000	2,440	2,760

Partial Statements of Cash Flows

	FIFO	LIFO	Weighted Average
Operating Activities			
Cash inflow from customers	$ 15,050	$ 15,050	$ 15,050
Cash outflow for inventory	(10,650)	(10,650)	(10,650)

Exhibit 5.2 demonstrates that the amounts reported for gross margin on the income statement and inventory on the balance sheet differ significantly. The cash flow from operating activities on the statement of cash flows, however, is identical under all three methods. Regardless of the cost flow reporting method, TMBC paid $10,650 cash ($4,400 first purchase + $6,250 second purchase) to purchase inventory and received $15,050 cash for inventory sold.

The Impact of Income Tax

Based on the financial statement information in Exhibit 5.2, which cost flow method should TMBC use? Most people initially suggest FIFO because FIFO reports the highest gross margin and the largest balance in ending inventory. However, other factors are relevant. FIFO produces the highest gross margin; it also produces the highest net income and the highest income tax expense. In contrast, LIFO results in recognizing the lowest gross margin, lowest net income, and the lowest income tax expense.

©Michel Kemp/Alamy

Will investors favor a company with more assets and higher net income or one with lower tax expense? Recognize that specific identification, FIFO, LIFO, and weighted average are *different methods of reporting the same information*. TMBC experienced only one set of events pertaining to Eraser bikes. Exhibit 5.2 reports those same events three different ways. However, if the FIFO reporting method causes TMBC to pay more taxes than the LIFO method, using FIFO will cause a real reduction in the value of the company. Paying more money in taxes leaves less money in the company. Knowledgeable investors would be more attracted to TMBC if it uses LIFO because the lower tax payments allow the company to keep more value in the business.

Research suggests that, as a group, investors are knowledgeable. They make investment decisions based on economic substance regardless of how information is reported in financial statements.

The Income Statement vs. the Tax Return

In some instances, companies may use one accounting method for financial reporting and a different method to compute income taxes (the tax return must explain any differences). With respect to LIFO, however, the Internal Revenue Service requires that companies using LIFO for income tax purposes must also use LIFO for financial reporting. A company could not, therefore, get both the lower tax benefit provided by LIFO and the financial reporting advantage offered under FIFO.

Inflation vs. Deflation

Our illustration assumes an inflationary environment (rising inventory prices). In a deflationary environment, the impact of using LIFO versus FIFO is reversed. LIFO produces tax advantages in an inflationary environment, while FIFO produces tax advantages in a deflationary environment. Companies operating in the computer industry—where prices are falling—would obtain a tax advantage by using FIFO. In contrast, companies that sell medical supplies in an inflationary environment would obtain a tax advantage by using LIFO.

Full Disclosure and Consistency

Generally accepted accounting principles allow each company to choose the inventory cost flow method best suited to its reporting needs. Because results can vary considerably among methods, however, the GAAP principle of **full disclosure** requires that financial statements disclose the method chosen. In addition, so that a company's financial statements are comparable from year to year, the GAAP principle of **consistency** generally requires that companies use the same cost flow method each period. The limited exceptions to the consistency principle are described in more advanced accounting courses.

CHECK YOURSELF 5.2

The following information was drawn from the inventory records of Fields, Inc.

Beginning inventory	200 units @ $20
First purchase	400 units @ $22
Second purchase	600 units @ $24

Assume that Fields sold 900 units of inventory.
1. Determine the amount of cost of goods sold using FIFO.
2. Would using LIFO produce a higher or lower amount of cost of goods sold? Why?

Answer
1. Cost of goods sold using FIFO

Beginning inventory	200 units @ $20	=	$ 4,000
First purchase	400 units @ $22	=	8,800
Second purchase	300 units @ $24	=	7,200
Total cost of goods sold			$20,000

2. The inventory records reflect an inflationary environment of steadily rising prices. Because LIFO charges the latest costs (in this case, the highest costs) to the income statement, using LIFO (as opposed to FIFO) would produce a higher amount of cost of goods sold.

Inventory Cost Flow When Sales and Purchases Occur Intermittently

In the previous illustrations, all purchases were made before any goods were sold. This section addresses more realistic conditions, when sales transactions occur intermittently with purchases. Consider a third product that The Mountain Bike Company (TMBC) carries in its inventory: an energy bar called NeverStop. NeverStop is sold at concession booths sponsored by TMBC at bike races. TMBC purchases and sells NeverStop in bulk boxes. It refers to each box as a unit of product. TMBC's beginning inventory, purchases, and sales of NeverStop for the period are described below.

Date	Transaction	Description
Jan. 1	Beginning inventory	100 units @ $20.00
Feb. 14	Purchased	200 units @ $21.50
Apr. 5	Sold	220 units @ $30.00
June 21	Purchased	160 units @ $22.50
Aug. 18	Sold	100 units @ $30.00
Sep. 2	Purchased	280 units @ $23.50
Nov. 10	Sold	330 units @ $30.00

FIFO Cost Flow

Exhibit 5.3 displays the computations for cost of goods sold and inventory if TMBC uses the FIFO cost flow method. The inventory records are maintained in layers. Each time a sales

EXHIBIT 5.3

Inventory Balance and Cost of Goods Sold Using FIFO Cost Flow Method

Date	Description	Units		Cost		Total	Cost of Goods Sold
Jan. 1	Beginning balance	100	@	$20.00	=	$2,000	
Feb. 14	Purchase	200	@	21.50	=	4,300	
Apr. 5	Sale of 220 units	(100)	@	20.00	=	(2,000)	
		(120)	@	21.50	=	(2,580)	$ 4,580
	Inventory balance after sale	80	@	21.50	=	1,720	
June 21	Purchase	160	@	22.50	=	3,600	
Aug. 18	Sale of 100 units	(80)	@	21.50	=	(1,720)	
		(20)	@	22.50	=	(450)	2,170
	Inventory balance after sale	140	@	22.50	=	3,150	
Sept. 2	Purchase	280	@	23.50	=	6,580	
Nov. 10	Sale of 330 units	(140)	@	22.50	=	(3,150)	
		(190)	@	23.50	=	(4,465)	7,615
	Ending inventory balance	90	@	23.50	=	$ 2,115	
	Total cost of goods sold						$14,365

transaction occurs, the unit cost in the first layer of inventory is assigned to the items sold. If the number of items sold exceeds the number of items in the first layer, the unit cost of the next layer is assigned to the remaining number of units sold, and so on. For example, the cost assigned to the 220 units of inventory sold on April 5 is determined as follows:

100 units of inventory in the first layer × $20.00 per unit	=	$2,000
+ 120 units of inventory in the second layer × $21.50 per unit	=	2,580
220 units for total cost of goods sold for the April 5 sale	=	$4,580

The cost of goods sold for subsequent sales transactions is similarly computed.

Using FIFO, and assuming a selling price of $30 per unit, gross margin for the period is computed as follows:

Sales (650 units @ $30 each)	$19,500
Cost of goods sold	14,365
Gross margin	$ 5,135

Weighted-Average and LIFO Cost Flows

When maintaining perpetual inventory records, using the weighted-average or LIFO cost flow methods leads to timing difficulties. For example, under LIFO, the cost of the *last* items purchased *during an accounting period* is the first amount transferred to cost of goods sold. When sales and purchases occur intermittently, the cost of the last items purchased isn't known at the time earlier sales occur. For example, when TMBC sold merchandise in April, it did not know what the replacement inventory purchased in September would cost.

Accountants can solve cost flow timing problems by keeping perpetual records of the quantities (number of units) of items purchased and sold separately from the related costs.

FOCUS ON INTERNATIONAL ISSUES

LIFO IN OTHER COUNTRIES

This chapter introduced a rather strange inventory cost flow assumption called LIFO. As explained, the primary advantage of LIFO is to reduce a company's income taxes. Given the choice, companies that use LIFO to reduce their taxes would probably prefer to use another method when preparing their GAAP-based financial statements, but the IRS does not permit this. Thus, they are left with no choice but to use the seemingly counterintuitive LIFO assumption for financial reporting purposes in order to reap the benefits of LIFO in their income tax reporting.

©Imaginechina/AP Images

What happens in countries other than the United States? International Financial Reporting Standards (IFRS) do not allow the use of LIFO. Most industrialized nations are now using IFRS. You can see the impact of this disparity if you review the annual report of a U.S. company that uses LIFO *and* has significant operations in other countries. Very often it will explain that LIFO is used to calculate inventory (and cost of goods sold) for domestic operations, but another method is used for activities outside the United States.

For example, here is an excerpt from General Electric's 2016 Form 10-K, Note 1.

All inventories are stated at the lower of cost or realizable values. Cost for a portion of GE U.S. inventories is determined on a last-in, first-out (LIFO) basis. Cost of other GE inventories is determined on a first-in, first-out (FIFO) basis. LIFO was used for 34% of GE inventories in both 2015 and 2016.

If the company has its headquarters in the United States, why not simply use LIFO in its foreign operations? In addition to having to prepare financial statements for the United States, the company probably has to prepare statements for its local operations using the reporting standards of the local country.

Prior to the establishment of IFRS, each country was responsible for issuing its own, local GAAP. Even then, most countries did not allow for the use of LIFO.

Keeping records of quantities moving in and out of inventory, even though cost information is unavailable, provides many of the benefits of a perpetual inventory system. For example, management can determine the quantity of lost, damaged, or stolen goods and the point at which to reorder merchandise. At the end of the accounting period, when the cost of all inventory purchases is available, costs are assigned to the quantity data that have been maintained perpetually. Although further discussion of the weighted-average and LIFO cost flow methods is beyond the scope of this text, recognize that timing problems associated with intermittent sales are manageable.

LOWER-OF-COST-OR-MARKET RULE

LO 5-2

Apply the lower-of-cost-or-market rule to inventory valuation.

Regardless of whether a company uses FIFO, LIFO, weighted average, or specific identification, once the cost of ending inventory has been determined, generally accepted accounting principles require that the cost be compared with the end of period market value and that the inventory be reported at *lower of cost or market. Market* is defined as the amount the company would have to pay to *replace* the merchandise. If the replacement cost is less than the actual cost, regardless of whether the decline in market value is due to physical damage, deterioration, obsolescence, or a general price-level decline, the loss must be recognized in the current period.

The **lower-of-cost-or-market rule** can be applied to (1) each individual inventory item, (2) major classes or categories of inventory, or (3) the entire stock of inventory in the aggregate. The most common practice is the individualized application. To illustrate applying the rule to individual inventory items, assume that The Mountain Bike Company (TMBC) has in ending inventory 100 T-shirts it purchased at a cost of $14 each. If the year-end replacement cost of the shirts is above $14, TMBC will report the ending inventory at cost

REALITY BYTES

To avoid spoilage or obsolescence, most companies use a first-in, first-out (FIFO) approach for the flow of physical goods. The older goods (first units purchased) are sold before the newer goods are sold. For example, Safeway and other food stores stack older merchandise at the front of the shelf where customers are more likely to pick it up first. As a result, merchandise is sold before it becomes dated. However, when timing is not an issue, convenience may dictate the use of the last-in, first-out (LIFO) method. Examples of products that frequently move on a LIFO basis include rock, gravel, dirt, or other nonwasting assets. Indeed, rock, gravel, and dirt are normally stored in piles that are unprotected from weather. New inventory is simply piled on top of the old. Inventory that is sold is taken from the top of the pile because it is convenient to do so. Accordingly, the last inventory purchased is the first inventory sold. For example, Vulcan Materials Co., which claims to be the nation's largest producer of construction aggregates (stone and gravel), uses LIFO. Regardless of whether the flow of physical goods occurs on a LIFO or FIFO basis, costs can flow differently. The flow of inventory through the physical facility is a separate issue from the flow of costs through the accounting system.

©Martial Colomb/Getty Images RF

(100 × $14 = $1,400). However, if outsourcing permits the manufacturer to reduce the unit price of the shirts to $11, then TMBC's replacement cost falls below the historical cost, and the inventory must be written down to $1,100 (100 × $11).

Exhibit 5.4 illustrates computing the ending inventory value on an item-by-item basis for a company that has four different inventory items. The company must write down the $30,020 historical cost of its ending inventory to $28,410. This $1,610 write-down reduces the company's gross margin for the period. If the company keeps perpetual inventory records, the effect of the write-down and the journal entry to record it are as follows:

Assets	=	Liab.	+	Equity	Rev.	−	Exp.	=	Net Inc.	Cash Flow
(1,610)	=	NA	+	(1,610)	NA	−	1,610	=	(1,610)	NA

Account Title	Debit	Credit
Cost of Goods Sold (Inventory Loss)	1,610	
Inventory		1,610

EXHIBIT 5.4

Determination of Ending Inventory at Lower of Cost or Market

Item	Quantity (a)	Unit Cost (b)	Unit Market (c)	Total Cost (a × b)	Total Market (a × b)	Lower of Cost or Market
A	320	$21.50	$22.00	$ 6,880	$ 7,040	$ 6,880
B	460	18.00	16.00	8,280	7,360	7,360
C	690	15.00	14.00	10,350	9,660	9,660
D	220	20.50	23.00	4,510	5,060	4,510
				$30,020	$29,120	$28,410

FOCUS ON INTERNATIONAL ISSUES

THE LOWER-OF-COST-OR-MARKET RULE AND IFRS

Suppose a company has inventory with a historical cost of $1,000,000, the market value of which falls to $700,000. The company would have to write down the inventory and take a loss of $300,000. Now suppose that before the inventory was sold the market value recovered to $900,000. What would the company do? Nothing under U.S. GAAP; the inventory would remain on the books at $700,000 until it is sold or its market value declines further. However, under IFRS the inventory would be written up from $700,000 to $900,000, and a gain of $200,000 would be recognized.

Conceptually, the loss should be reported as an operating expense on the income statement. However, if the amount is immaterial, it can be included in cost of goods sold.

AVOIDING FRAUD IN MERCHANDISING BUSINESSES

LO 5-3

Show how fraud can be avoided through inventory control.

For merchandising businesses, inventory is often the largest single asset reported on the balance sheet, and cost of goods sold is normally the largest single expense reported on the income statement. For example, a recent income statement for **Publix** (a large grocery store chain) reported $32.4 billion of sales and approximately $23.5 billion of cost of goods sold, which means cost of goods sold for Publix was about 72 percent of revenue. In contrast, the next largest expense (operating and administrative expense) was approximately $6.4 billion, or 20 percent of revenue. While cost of goods sold represents only one expense account, the operating and administrative expense category actually combines many, perhaps hundreds, of individual expense accounts, such as depreciation, salaries, utilities, and so on. Because the inventory and cost of goods sold accounts are so significant, they are attractive targets for concealing fraud. For example, suppose a manager attempts to perpetrate a fraud by deliberately understating expenses. The understatement is less likely to be detected if it is hidden in the $23.5 billion Cost of Goods Sold account than if it is recorded in one of the smaller operating expense accounts.

Because the inventory and cost of goods sold accounts are susceptible to abuse, auditors and financial analysts carefully examine them for signs of fraud. Using tools to detect possible inventory misstatements requires understanding how overstatement or understatement of inventory affects the financial statements. To illustrate, assume that a company overstates its year-end inventory balance by $1,000. This inventory overstatement results in a $1,000 understatement of cost of goods sold, as shown in the following schedule:

	Ending Inventory Is Accurate	Ending Inventory Is Overstated	Effect
Beginning inventory	$ 4,000	$ 4,000	
Purchases	6,000	6,000	
Cost of goods available for sale	10,000	10,000	
Ending inventory	(3,000)	(4,000)	$1,000 Overstated
Cost of goods sold	$ 7,000	$ 6,000	$1,000 Understated

The understatement of cost of goods sold results in the overstatement of gross margin, which leads to an overstatement of net earnings, as indicated in the following income statement:

	Ending Inventory Is Accurate	Ending Inventory Is Overstated	Effect
Sales	$11,000	$11,000	
Cost of goods sold	(7,000)	(6,000)	$1,000 Understated
Gross Margin	$ 4,000	$ 5,000	$1,000 Overstated

On the balance sheet, assets (inventory) and stockholders' equity (retained earnings) are overstated as follows:

	Ending Inventory Is Accurate	Ending Inventory Is Overstated	Effect
Assets			
Cash	$1,000	$ 1,000	
Inventory	3,000	4,000	$1,000 Overstated
Other assets	5,000	5,000	
Total assets	$9,000	$10,000	
Stockholders' equity			
Common stock	$5,000	$ 5,000	
Retained earnings	4,000	5,000	$1,000 Overstated
Total stockholders' equity	$9,000	$10,000	

Managers may be tempted to overstate the physical count of the ending inventory in order to report higher amounts of gross margin on the income statement and larger amounts of assets on the balance sheet. How can companies discourage managers from deliberately overstating the physical count of the ending inventory? The first line of defense is to assign the task of recording inventory transactions to different employees from those responsible for counting inventory.

Recall that under the perpetual system, increases and decreases in inventory are recorded at the time inventory is purchased and sold. If the records are maintained accurately, the balance in the inventory account should agree with the amount of physical inventory on hand. If a manager were to attempt to manipulate the financial statements by overstating the physical count of inventory, there would be a discrepancy between the accounting records and the physical count. In other words, a successful fraud requires controlling both the physical count and the recording process. If the counting and recording duties are performed by different individuals, fraud requires collusion, which reduces the likelihood of its occurrence. The separation of duties is an internal control procedure discussed further in the next chapter.

Because motives for fraud persist, even the most carefully managed companies cannot guarantee that no fraud will ever occur. As a result, auditors and financial analysts have developed tools to test for financial statement manipulation. The gross margin method of estimating the ending inventory balance is such a tool.

©Getty Images RF

ESTIMATING THE ENDING INVENTORY BALANCE

The **gross margin method** assumes that the percentage of gross margin to sales remains relatively stable over time. To the extent that this assumption is accurate, the gross margin ratio from prior periods can be used to accurately estimate the current period's ending inventory. To illustrate, first review the information in Exhibit 5.5, which pertains to The T-Shirt Company.

The estimated cost of ending inventory can be computed as follows:

LO 5-4

 Use the gross margin method to estimate ending inventory.

1. Calculate the expected gross margin ratio using financial statement data from prior periods. Accuracy may be improved by averaging gross margin and sales data over several accounting periods. For The T-Shirt Company, assume the average gross margin for the prior five years ÷ the average sales for the same five-year period = 25% expected gross margin ratio.

2. Multiply the expected gross margin ratio by the current period's sales ($22,000 × 0.25 = $5,500) to estimate the amount of gross margin.

3. Subtract the estimated gross margin from sales ($22,000 − $5,500 = $16,500) to estimate the amount of cost of goods sold.

4. Subtract the estimated cost of goods sold from the amount of goods available for sale ($23,600 − $16,500 = $7,100) to estimate the amount of ending inventory.

EXHIBIT 5.5

THE T-SHIRT COMPANY
Schedule for Estimating the Ending Inventory Balance
For the Six Months Ending June 30, Year 2

Beginning inventory	$ 5,100	
Purchases	18,500	
Cost of goods available for sale		$23,600
Sales through June 30, Year 2	22,000	
Less: Estimated gross margin*	?	
Estimated cost of goods sold		?
Estimated ending inventory		$?

*Historically, gross margin has amounted to approximately 25 percent of sales.

The estimated amount of ending inventory ($7,100) can be compared to the book balance and the physical count of inventory. If the book balance or the physical count is significantly higher than the estimated inventory balance, the analysis suggests the possibility of financial statement manipulation.

Other analytical comparisons are also useful. For example, the current year's gross margin ratio can be compared to last year's ratio. If cost of goods sold has been understated (ending inventory overstated), the gross margin ratio will be inflated. If this year's ratio is significantly higher than last year's, further analysis is required.

Although it may seem common because of the intense publicity generated when it occurs, fraud is the exception rather than the norm. In fact, growth in the inventory account balance usually results from natural business conditions. For example, a company that is adding new stores is expected to report growth in its inventory balance. Nevertheless, significant growth in inventory that is not explained by accompanying sales growth signals the need to analyze further for evidence of manipulation.

Because one year's ending inventory balance becomes the next year's beginning inventory balance, inaccuracies carry forward from one accounting period to the next. Persistent inventory overstatements result in an inventory account balance that spirals higher and higher. A fraudulently increasing inventory balance is likely to be discovered eventually.

To avoid detection, a manager who has previously overstated inventory will need to write the inventory back down in a subsequent accounting period. Therefore, significant decreases, as well as increases, in the inventory balance or the gross margin ratio should be investigated. A manager may try to justify inventory write-downs by claiming that the inventory was lost, damaged, stolen, or had declined in value below historical cost. While there are valid reasons for writing down inventory, the possibility of fraud should be investigated.

✓ CHECK YOURSELF 5.3

A physical count of Cantrell Inc.'s inventory revealed an ending balance of $6,020. The company's auditor decided to use the gross margin method to test the accuracy of the physical count. The accounting records indicate that the beginning inventory balance had been $20,000. During the period, Cantrell had purchased $70,000 of inventory and had recognized $140,000 of sales revenue. Cantrell's gross margin percentage is normally 40 percent of sales. Develop an estimate of the amount of ending inventory and comment on the accuracy of the physical count.

Answer Goods available for sale is $90,000 ($20,000 beginning inventory + $70,000 purchases). Estimated cost of goods sold is $84,000 [$140,000 sales − ($140,000 × 0.40) gross margin]. Estimated ending inventory is $6,000 ($90,000 goods available for sale − $84,000 cost of goods sold). The difference between the physical count and the estimated balance ($6,020 − $6,000 = $20) is immaterial. Therefore, the gross margin estimate is consistent with the physical count.

Answers to The Curious Accountant

Even though **Kroger** uses the last-in, first-out *cost flow assumption* for financial reporting purposes, it, like most other companies, actually sells its oldest inventory first. As explained in the text material, GAAP allows a company to report its costs of goods sold in an order that is different from the actual physical flow of its goods. The primary reason some companies use the LIFO assumption is to reduce income taxes. Over the years, Kroger has saved approximately $429 million in taxes by using the LIFO versus the FIFO cost flow assumption when computing its taxable income.

The Financial Analyst

Assume a grocery store sells two brands of kitchen cleansers, Zjax and Cosmos. Zjax costs $1 and sells for $1.25, resulting in a gross margin of $0.25 ($1.25 − $1.00). Cosmos costs $1.20 and sells for $1.60, resulting in a gross margin of $0.40 ($1.60 − $1.20). Is it more profitable to stock Cosmos than Zjax? Not if the store can sell significantly more cans of Zjax.

Suppose the lower price results in higher customer demand for Zjax. If the store can sell 7,000 units of Zjax but only 3,000 units of Cosmos, Zjax will provide a total gross margin of $1,750 (7,000 units × $0.25 per unit), while Cosmos will provide only $1,200 (3,000 units × $0.40 per unit). How fast inventory sells is as important as the spread between cost and selling price. To determine how fast inventory is selling, financial analysts calculate a ratio that measures the *average number of days it takes to sell inventory*.

LO 5-5

Calculate and interpret the inventory turnover ratio.

Average Number of Days to Sell Inventory

The first step in calculating the average number of days it takes to sell inventory is to compute the **inventory turnover,** as follows:

$$\frac{\text{Cost of goods sold}}{\text{Inventory}}$$

The result of this computation is the number of times the balance in the Inventory account is turned over (sold) each year. To more easily interpret the inventory turnover ratio, analysts often take a further step and determine the **average number of days to sell inventory** (also called the **average days in inventory**), computed as

$$\frac{365}{\text{Inventory turnover}}$$

Is It a Marketing or an Accounting Decision?

As suggested, overall profitability depends upon two elements: gross margin and inventory turnover. The most profitable combination would be to carry high margin inventory that turns over rapidly. To be competitive, however, companies must often concentrate on one or the other of the elements. For example, *discount merchandisers* such as **Costco** offer lower prices to stimulate greater sales. In contrast, fashionable stores such as **Neiman Marcus** charge higher prices to compensate for their slower inventory turnover. These upscale stores justify their higher prices by offering superior style, quality, convenience, service, etc. While decisions about pricing, advertising, service, and so on are often viewed as marketing decisions, effective choices require understanding the interaction between the gross margin percentage and inventory turnover.

The Wallet Company Illustration

To examine the interaction between the gross margin percentage and inventory turnover from an accounting perspective, consider the case of The Wallet Company (TWC). TWC sells men's wallets. The following information was drawn from the company's accounting records:

	Year 7	Year 6
Sales revenue	$390,000	$320,000
Cost of goods sold	273,000	208,000
Gross margin	117,000	112,000
Average inventory balance	40,000	40,000

Comparing Year 7 with Year 6 data, how was TWC able to increase its total gross margin by $5,000 ($117,000 − $112,000)? First, note that TWC lowered the sales price of its products. This conclusion is supported by the fact that the company's gross margin percentage decreased from 35% ($112,000 gross margin / $320,000 sales revenue) to 30% ($117,000 gross margin / $390,000 sales revenue).

Next, note that inventory turnover increased from 5.2 ($208,000 cost of goods sold / $40,000 inventory balance) in Year 6 to 6.8 ($273,000 cost of goods sold / $40,000 inventory balance) in Year 7. Higher inventory turnover means that it requires less time to sell the inventory, restock it, and sell it again. In TWC's case, the number of days required to sell inventory in Year 6 was 70.19 (365 days in a year / 5.2 inventory turnover). In contrast, the number of days required to sell the inventory in Year 7 was only 53.7 (365 days in a year / 6.8 inventory turnover).

Decreasing the number of days required to sell inventory means that TWC sold inventory more rapidly in Year 7 than it did in Year 6. Increasing the speed at which inventory is sold means that more units are sold during an accounting period. In other words, higher inventory turnover lowers the number of days required to sell inventory and increases the number of units sold. The number of units sold is commonly called the sales volume. In summary, TWC was able to increase its profitability by lowering the sales price of its products, thereby increasing the sales volume.

Real-World Data

Exhibit 5.6 shows the *average number of days to sell inventory* for seven real-world companies in three different industries. The numbers pertain to the 2016 fiscal year. The data raise several questions.

First, why do **D.R. Horton** and **Toll Brothers** take so long to sell their inventories compared with the other companies? Both of these companies build and sell houses. It takes a lot longer to build a house than it does to make a hamburger. Furthermore, once a house is built, it may take months to find a buyer. Finally, inventory of home builders includes the land on which the houses are constructed. A large subdivision may take several years to complete, but all of the land may have been purchased months, or even years, before the first house was started.

EXHIBIT 5.6

Industry	Company	Average Number of Days to Sell Inventory
Fast Food	McDonald's	4
	Starbucks	59
	Restaurant Brands International	15
Department Stores	Macy's	126
	Walmart	43
Home Construction	D.R. Horton	320
	Toll Brothers	648

Why does Starbucks hold its inventory so much longer than the other two fast-food businesses? Starbucks' inventory is mostly coffee. It is more difficult for Starbucks to obtain coffee than it is for McDonald's or Restaurant Brands to obtain beef. Restaurant Brands International is the parent company of Burger King and Tim Horton. Very little coffee is grown in the United States (Hawaii is the only state that produces coffee). Because purchasing coffee requires substantial delivery time, Starbucks cannot order its inventory at the last minute. This problem is further complicated by the fact that coffee harvests are seasonal. Cattle, on the other hand, can be processed into hamburgers year-round. As a result, Starbucks must hold inventory longer than McDonald's or Restaurant Brands.

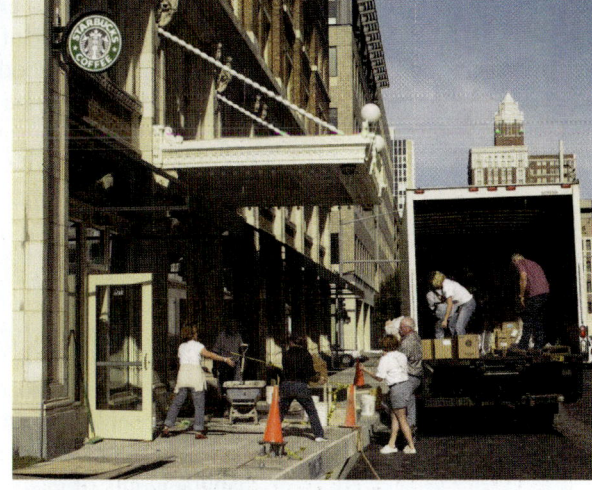
©Steve Pope/AP Images

Why do department stores such as Macy's and Walmart take longer to sell inventory than McDonald's? Part of the answer is that food is perishable and clothing is not. But there is also the fact that department stores carry many more inventory items than do fast-food restaurants. It is much easier to anticipate customer demand if a company sells only 20 different items than if the company sells 20,000 different items. The problem of anticipating customer demand is solved by holding larger quantities of inventory.

Finally, notice that Walmart sells it merchandise in 43 days, while Macy's takes 126. This would seem to be an advantage for Walmart, but recall from Chapter 4 that in its 2016 fiscal year, Walmart's gross margin percentage was 24.9 while Macy's was 39.4. Macy's higher gross margin percentage helps to make up for the additional time it takes to sell merchandise. Different companies use different business strategies to achieve their objectives. In the end, Macy's return on sales percentage, at 2.4 percent, was lower than Walmart's, which was 6.9 percent, so Macy's higher gross margin did not lead to higher bottom-line profit.

Effects of Cost Flow on Ratio Analysis

Because the amounts of ending inventory and cost of goods sold are affected by the cost flow method (FIFO, LIFO, etc.) a company uses, the gross margin and inventory turnover ratios are also affected by the cost flow method used. Further, because cost of goods sold affects the amount of net income and retained earnings, many other ratios are also affected by the inventory cost flow method that a company uses. Financial analysts must consider that the ratios they use can be significantly influenced by which accounting methods a company chooses.

A Look Back «

This chapter discussed the specific identification, first-in, first-out (FIFO), last-in, first-out (LIFO), and weighted-average inventory cost flow methods. Under *specific identification,* the actual cost of the goods is reported on the income statement and the balance sheet. Under *FIFO,* the cost of the items purchased first is reported on the income statement, and the cost of the items purchased last is reported on the balance sheet. Under *LIFO,* the cost of the items purchased last is reported on the income statement, and the cost of the items purchased first is reported on the balance sheet. Finally, under the *weighted-average method,* the average cost of inventory is reported on both the income statement and the balance sheet.

Generally accepted accounting principles often allow companies to account for the same types of events in different ways. The different cost flow methods presented in this chapter—FIFO, LIFO, weighted average, and specific identification—are examples of alternative accounting procedures allowed by GAAP. Financial analysts must be aware that financial statement amounts are affected by the accounting methods that a company uses, as well as the economic activity it experiences.

This chapter also explained how to calculate the time it takes a company to sell its inventory. The measure of how fast inventory sells is called *inventory turnover;* it is computed by dividing cost of goods sold by inventory. The result of this computation is the number of times the balance in the inventory account is turned over each year. The *average number of days to sell inventory* can be determined by dividing the number of days in a year (365) by the inventory turnover ratio.

A Look Forward

Chapter 6 examines accounting for cash and the system of internal controls. Internal controls are the accounting practices and procedures that companies use to protect assets and ensure that transactions are recorded accurately. You will learn that companies account for small disbursements of cash, called *petty cash disbursements,* differently than they do for large disbursements. You will also learn how to prepare a formal bank reconciliation.

SELF-STUDY REVIEW PROBLEM

A step-by-step audio-narrated series of slides is available in **Connect.**

Erie Jewelers sells gold earrings. Its beginning inventory of Model 407 gold earrings consisted of 100 pairs of earrings at $50 per pair. Erie purchased two batches of Model 407 earrings during the year. The first batch purchased consisted of 150 pairs at $53 per pair; the second batch consisted of 200 pairs at $56 per pair. During the year, Erie sold 375 pairs of Model 407 earrings.

Required

Determine the amount of product cost Erie would allocate to cost of goods sold and ending inventory assuming that Erie uses (a) FIFO, (b) LIFO, and (c) weighted average.

Solution to Requirements a–c

Goods Available for Sale						
Beginning inventory	100	@	$50	=	$ 5,000
First purchase	150	@	53	=	7,950
Second purchase	200	@	56	=	11,200
Goods available for sale	450				$24,150

a. **FIFO**

Cost of Goods Sold	Pairs		Cost per Pair		Cost of Goods Sold
From beginning inventory	100	@	$50	=	$ 5,000
From first purchase	150	@	53	=	7,950
From second purchase	125	@	56	=	7,000
Total pairs sold	375				$19,950

Ending inventory = Goods available for sale − Cost of goods sold
Ending inventory = $24,150 − $19,950 = $4,200

b. LIFO

Cost of Goods Sold	Pairs	Cost per Pair		Cost of Goods Sold
From second purchase	200	@ $56	=	$11,200
From first purchase	150	@ 53	=	7,950
From beginning inventory	25	@ 50	=	1,250
Total pairs sold	375			$20,400

Ending inventory = Goods available for sale − Cost of goods sold
Ending inventory = $24,150 − $20,400 = $3,750

c. Weighted average

Goods available for sale ÷ Total pairs = Cost per pair
$24,150 ÷ 450 = $53.6667
Cost of goods sold 375 units @ $53.6667 = $20,125
Ending inventory 75 units @ $53.6667 = $4,025

KEY TERMS

Average number of days to sell inventory (or average days in inventory) 287
Consistency 279
First-in, first-out (FIFO) cost flow method 274
Full disclosure 279
Gross margin method 285
Inventory cost flow methods 276
Inventory turnover 287
Last-in, first-out (LIFO) cost flow method 274
Lower-of-cost-or-market rule 282
Physical flow of goods 274
Specific identification 274
Weighted-average cost flow method 274

QUESTIONS

1. Name and describe the four cost flow methods discussed in this chapter.
2. What are some advantages and disadvantages of the specific identification method of accounting for inventory?
3. What are some advantages and disadvantages of using the FIFO method of inventory valuation?
4. What are some advantages and disadvantages of using the LIFO method of inventory valuation?
5. In an inflationary period, which inventory cost flow method will produce the highest net income? Explain.
6. In an inflationary period, which inventory cost flow method will produce the largest amount of total assets on the balance sheet? Explain.
7. What is the difference between the flow of costs and the physical flow of goods?
8. Does the choice of cost flow method (FIFO, LIFO, or weighted average) affect the statement of cash flows? Explain.
9. Assume that Key Co. purchased 1,000 units of merchandise in its first year of operations for $25 per unit. The company sold 850 units for $40. What is the amount of cost of goods sold using FIFO? LIFO? Weighted average?
10. Assume that Key Co. purchased 1,500 units of merchandise in its second year of operation for $27 per unit. Its beginning inventory was determined in Question 9. Assuming that 1,500 units are sold, what is the amount of cost of goods sold using FIFO? LIFO? Weighted average?
11. Refer to Questions 9 and 10. Which method might be preferable for financial statements? For income tax reporting? Explain.
12. In an inflationary period, which cost flow method—FIFO or LIFO—produces the larger cash flow? Explain.
13. Which inventory cost flow method produces the highest net income in a deflationary period?
14. How does the phrase *lower-of-cost-or-market* apply to inventory valuation?
15. If some merchandise declines in value because of damage or obsolescence, what effect will the lower-of-cost-or-market rule have on the income statement? Explain.
16. What is a situation in which estimates of the amount of inventory may be useful or even necessary?

17. How can management manipulate net income using inventory fraud?
18. If the amount of goods available for sale is $123,000, the amount of sales is $130,000, and the gross margin is 25 percent of sales, what is the amount of ending inventory?
19. Assume that inventory is overstated by $1,500 at the end of Year 1 but is corrected in Year 2. What effect will this have on the Year 1 income statement? The Year 1 balance sheet? The Year 2 income statement? The Year 2 balance sheet?
20. What information does inventory turnover provide?
21. What is an example of a business that would have a high inventory turnover? A low inventory turnover?

MULTIPLE-CHOICE QUESTIONS

Multiple-choice questions are available in **Connect.**

EXERCISES—SERIES A

All applicable Exercises in Series A are available in **Connect.**

LO 5-1

Exercise 5-1A *Effect of inventory cost flow assumption on financial statements*

Required

For each of the following situations, indicate whether FIFO, LIFO, or weighted average applies:

a. In a period of falling prices, net income would be highest.
b. In a period of falling prices, the unit cost of goods would be the same for ending inventory and cost of goods sold.
c. In a period of rising prices, net income would be highest.
d. In a period of rising prices, cost of goods sold would be highest.
e. In a period of rising prices, ending inventory would be highest.

LO 5-1

Exercise 5-2A *Allocating product cost between cost of goods sold and ending inventory*

Jones Co. started the year with no inventory. During the year, it purchased two identical inventory items at different times. The first purchase cost $1,060 and the other, $1,380. Jones sold one of the items during the year.

Required

Based on this information, how much product cost would be allocated to cost of goods sold and ending inventory on the year-end financial statements, assuming use of

a. FIFO?
b. LIFO?
c. Weighted average?

LO 5-1

Exercise 5-3A *Allocating product cost between cost of goods sold and ending inventory: multiple purchases*

Cortez Company sells chairs that are used at computer stations. Its beginning inventory of chairs was 100 units at $60 per unit. During the year, Cortez made two batch purchases of this chair. The first was a 150-unit purchase at $68 per unit; the second was a 200-unit purchase at $72 per unit. During the period, it sold 270 chairs.

Required

Determine the amount of product costs that would be allocated to cost of goods sold and ending inventory, assuming that Cortez uses

a. FIFO.
b. LIFO.
c. Weighted average.

Exercise 5-4A Effect of inventory cost flow (FIFO, LIFO, and weighted average) on gross margin

LO 5-1

The following information pertains to Mason Company for Year 2:

Beginning inventory	90 units @ $40
Units purchased	310 units @ $45

Ending inventory consisted of 30 units. Mason sold 370 units at $90 each. All purchases and sales were made with cash. Operating expenses amounted to $4,100.

Required

a. Compute the gross margin for Mason Company using the following cost flow assumptions: (1) FIFO, (2) LIFO, and (3) weighted average.
b. What is the amount of net income using FIFO, LIFO, and weighted average? (Ignore income tax considerations.)
c. Compute the amount of ending inventory using (1) FIFO, (2) LIFO, and (3) weighted average.

Exercise 5-5A Effect of inventory cost flow on ending inventory balance and gross margin

LO 5-1

The Shirt Shop had the following transactions for T-shirts for Year 1, its first year of operations:

Jan. 20	Purchased 400 units @ $ 8	=	$3,200
Apr. 21	Purchased 200 units @ $10	=	2,000
July 25	Purchased 280 units @ $13	=	3,640
Sept. 19	Purchased 90 units @ $15	=	1,350

During the year, The Shirt Shop sold 810 T-shirts for $20 each.

Required

a. Compute the amount of ending inventory The Shirt Shop would report on the balance sheet, assuming the following cost flow assumptions: (1) FIFO, (2) LIFO, and (3) weighted average.
b. Record the above transactions in general journal form and post to T-accounts assuming (1) FIFO, (2) LIFO, and (3) weighted-average methods. Use a separate set of journal entries and T-accounts for each method. Assume all transactions are cash transactions.
c. Compute the difference in gross margin between the FIFO and LIFO cost flow assumptions.

Exercise 5-6A Income tax effect of shifting from FIFO to LIFO

LO 5-1

The following information pertains to the inventory of Parvin Company during Year 2:

Jan. 1	Beginning inventory	400 units @ $30
Apr. 1	Purchased	2,000 units @ $35
Oct. 1	Purchased	600 units @ $38

During Year 2, Parvin sold 2,700 units of inventory at $90 per unit and incurred $41,500 of operating expenses. Parvin currently uses the FIFO method but is considering a change to LIFO. All transactions are cash transactions. Assume a 30 percent income tax rate. Parvin started the period with cash of $75,000, inventory of $12,000, common stock of $50,000, and retained earnings of $37,000.

Required

a. Record the above transactions in general journal form and post to T-accounts using (1) FIFO and (2) LIFO. Use a separate set of journal entries and T-accounts for each method.
b. Prepare income statements using FIFO and LIFO.

c. Determine the amount of income tax that Parvin would pay using each cost flow method.
d. Determine the cash flow from operating activities under FIFO and LIFO.
e. Why is the cash flow from operating activities different under FIFO and LIFO?

LO 5-1

Exercise 5-7A *Effect of FIFO versus LIFO on income tax expense*

The Brick Company had cash sales of $280,000 for Year 1, its first year of operation. On April 2, the company purchased 210 units of inventory at $390 per unit. On September 1, an additional 160 units were purchased for $425 per unit. The company had 110 units on hand at the end of the year. The company's income tax rate is 40 percent. All transactions are cash transactions.

Required

a. The preceding paragraph describes five accounting events: (1) a sales transaction, (2) the first purchase of inventory, (3) a second purchase of inventory, (4) the recognition of cost of goods sold expense, and (5) the payment of income tax expense. Show the amounts of each event in horizontal statements models like the following ones, assuming first a FIFO and then a LIFO cost flow.

Effect of Events on Financial Statements

Panel 1: FIFO Cost Flow

Event No.	Balance Sheet	Income Statement	Statement of Cash Flows
	Cash + Inventory = Ret. Earn.	Rev. − Exp. = Net Inc.	

Panel 2: LIFO Cost Flow

Event No.	Balance Sheet	Income Statement	Statement of Cash Flows
	Cash + Inventory = Ret. Earn.	Rev. − Exp. = Net Inc.	

b. Compute net income using FIFO.
c. Compute net income using LIFO.
d. Explain the difference, if any, in the amount of income tax expense incurred using the two cost flow assumptions.
e. Which method, FIFO or LIFO, produced the larger amount of assets on the balance sheet?

LO 5-1

Exercise 5-8A *Recording inventory transactions using the perpetual method: intermittent sales and purchases*

The following inventory transactions apply to Green Company for Year 2:

Jan. 1	Purchased	260 units @ $50
Apr. 1	Sold	130 units @ $85
Aug. 1	Purchased	390 units @ $56
Dec. 1	Sold	490 units @ $96

The beginning inventory consisted of 180 units at $48 per unit. All transactions are cash transactions.

Required

a. Record these transactions in general journal format assuming Green uses the FIFO cost flow assumption and keeps perpetual records.
b. Compute cost of goods sold for Year 2.

Exercise 5-9A *Effect of cost flow on ending inventory: intermittent sales and purchases*   LO 5-1

The Hat Store had the following series of transactions for Year 2:

Date	Transaction	Description
Jan. 1	Beginning inventory	50 units @ $40
Mar. 15	Purchased	200 units @ $42
May 30	Sold	170 units @ $95
Aug. 10	Purchased	275 units @ $46
Nov. 20	Sold	340 units @ $96

Required

a. Determine the quantity and dollar amount of inventory at the end of the year, assuming The Hat Store uses the FIFO cost flow assumption and keeps perpetual records.

b. Write a memo explaining why The Hat Store would have difficulty applying the weighted-average method on a perpetual basis.

Exercise 5-10A *Lower-of-cost-or-market rule: perpetual system*   LO 5-2

The following information pertains to Hagen Metal Works' ending inventory for the current year:

Item	Quantity	Unit Cost	Unit Market Value
C	90	$24	$16
D	75	22	20
K	40	25	28
M	22	15	17

Required

a. Determine the value of the ending inventory using the lower-of-cost-or-market rule applied to (1) each individual inventory item and (2) the inventory in aggregate.

b. Prepare any necessary journal entries, assuming the decline in value is immaterial. Hagen Metal Works uses the perpetual inventory system. (Make entries for both methods.)

Exercise 5-11A *Lower-of-cost-or-market rule*   LO 5-2

Brooks Company carries three inventory items. The following information pertains to the ending inventory:

Item	Quantity	Unit Cost	Unit Market Value
A	120	$60	$55
F	170	80	75
K	110	30	40

Required

a. Determine the ending inventory that Brooks will report on the balance sheet, assuming that it applies the lower-of-cost-or-market rule to individual inventory items.

b. Prepare the necessary journal entry, assuming the decline in value was immaterial.

Exercise 5-12A *Effect of inventory error on financial statements: perpetual system*   LO 5-3

Stubbs Company failed to count $55,000 of inventory in its Year 1 year-end physical count.

Required

Write a memo explaining how Stubbs Company's balance sheet will be affected in Year 1. Assume Stubbs uses the perpetual inventory system.

LO 5-3

Exercise 5-13A Effect of inventory error on elements of financial statements

The ending inventory for Carver Co. was incorrectly adjusted, which caused it to be understated by $15,300 for Year 2.

Required

Was each of the following amounts overstated, understated, or not affected by the error?

Item No.	Year	Amount
1	Year 2	Beginning inventory
2	Year 2	Purchases
3	Year 2	Goods available for sale
4	Year 2	Cost of goods sold
5	Year 2	Gross margin
6	Year 2	Net income
7	Year 3	Beginning inventory
8	Year 3	Purchases
9	Year 3	Goods available for sale
10	Year 3	Cost of goods sold
11	Year 3	Gross margin
12	Year 3	Net income

LO 5-4

Exercise 5-14A Estimating ending inventory

A substantial portion of inventory owned by Prentiss Sporting Goods was recently destroyed when the roof collapsed during a rainstorm. Prentiss also lost some of its accounting records. Prentiss must estimate the loss from the storm for insurance reporting and financial statement purposes. Prentiss uses the periodic inventory system. The following accounting information was recovered from the damaged records:

Beginning inventory	$ 60,000
Purchases to date of storm	190,000
Sales to date of storm	250,000

The value of undamaged inventory counted was $3,600. Historically, Prentiss' gross margin percentage has been approximately 25 percent of sales.

Required

Estimate the following:
a. Gross margin in dollars.
b. Cost of goods sold.
c. Ending inventory.
d. Amount of lost inventory.

LO 5-4

Exercise 5-15A Estimating ending inventory: perpetual system

Brad Essary owned a small company that sold garden equipment. The equipment was expensive, and a perpetual system was maintained for control purposes. Even so, lost, damaged, and stolen merchandise normally amounted to 5 percent of the inventory balance. On June 14, Essary's warehouse was destroyed by fire. Just prior to the fire, the accounting records contained a $280,000 balance in the Inventory account. However, inventory costing $42,000 had been sold and delivered to customers but had not been recorded in the books at the time of the fire. The fire did not affect the showroom, which contained inventory that cost $58,000.

Required

Estimate the amount of inventory destroyed by fire.

LO 5-5

Exercise 5-16A Inventory turnover and average days to sell

The following accounting information pertains to two grocery store chains. One grocery store chain has a market strategy of selling only high-end organic food products while the other grocery store sells less expensive foods that are traditionally grown with the use of pesticides, synthetic fertilizers, and/or genetically modified organisms.

Accounting for Inventories 297

	Traditional	Organic
Sales	$600,000	?
Cost of Goods Sold	?	$300,000
Gross Margin	?	$200,000
Gross Margin Percentage	35%	?

The company selling traditional produced foods has an average inventory balance of $45,000, while the company selling organic foods has an average inventory balance of $40,000.

a. Complete the table by filling in the missing amounts.
b. Which grocery store chain is taking a lower cost/higher volume strategy as it relates to sales?
c. Calculate the inventory turnover and average days to sell inventory for each grocery store chain. Based on your calculations, which grocery chain will be required to reorder inventory more frequently?

Exercise 5-17A *Explaining multiple inventory methods at one real-world company* — IFRS

The following information related to accounting for inventory was taken from the 2016 annual report of **Costco Wholesale Corporation**:

Merchandise inventories consist of the following at the end of 2016 and 2015:

	2016	2015
United States	$6,422	$6,427
Foreign	2,547	2,481
Merchandise inventories	$8,969	$8,908

Merchandise inventories are valued at the lower of cost or market, as determined primarily by the retail inventory method, and are stated using the last-in, first-out (LIFO) method for substantially all U.S. merchandise inventories. Merchandise inventories for all foreign operations are primarily valued by the retail inventory method and are stated using the first-in, first-out (FIFO) method.

Required

Write a brief report explaining the reason (reasons) that best explains (explain) why Costco uses the LIFO cost flow method for its inventories in the United States, but the FIFO cost method for its other inventories.

Exercise 5-18A *GAAP versus IFRS* — IFRS

Generally accepted accounting principles (GAAP) and International Financial Reporting Standards (IFRS) treat the LIFO inventory cost flow method differently.

Required

a. Briefly describe the position GAAP takes with respect to LIFO.
b. Briefly describe the position IFRS takes with respect to LIFO.
c. Explain the primary force that motivates the different positions.

PROBLEMS—SERIES A

 All applicable Problems in Series A are available in **Connect**.

Problem 5-19A *Effect of different inventory cost flow methods on financial statements* — LO 5-1

The accounting records of Wall's China Shop reflected the following balances as of January 1, Year 2:

Cash	$80,100
Beginning inventory	33,000 (220 units @ $150)
Common stock	50,000
Retained earnings	63,100

CHECK FIGURES
a. Cost of Goods Sold FIFO: $62,650
b. Net Income LIFO: $22,012

The following five transactions occurred in Year 2:

1. First purchase (cash): 150 units @ $155
2. Second purchase (cash): 160 units @ $160
3. Sales (all cash): 410 units @ $320
4. Paid $38,000 cash for salaries expense
5. Paid cash for income tax at the rate of 25 percent of income before taxes

Required

a. Compute the cost of goods sold and ending inventory, assuming (1) FIFO cost flow, (2) LIFO cost flow, and (3) weighted-average cost flow. Compute the income tax expense for each method.
b. Record the five transactions in general journal form and post to T-accounts assuming (1) FIFO cost flow, (2) LIFO cost flow, and (3) weighted-average cost flow.
c. Use a vertical model to show the Year 2 income statement, balance sheet, and statement of cash flows under FIFO, LIFO, and weighted average. (*Hint:* Record the events under an accounting equation before preparing the statements.)

Problem 5-20A *Allocating product costs between cost of goods sold and ending inventory: intermittent purchases and sales of merchandise*

Pam's Creations had the following sales and purchase transactions during Year 2. Beginning inventory consisted of 60 items at $350 each. The company uses the FIFO cost flow assumption and keeps perpetual inventory records.

Date	Transaction	Description
Mar. 5	Purchased	50 items @ $370
Apr. 10	Sold	30 items @ $450
June 19	Sold	60 items @ $450
Sep. 16	Purchased	70 items @ $390
Nov. 28	Sold	45 items @ $480

Required

a. Record the inventory transactions in general journal format.
b. Calculate the gross margin Pam's Creations would report on the Year 2 income statement.
c. Determine the ending inventory balance Pam's Creations would report on the December 31, Year 2, balance sheet.

Problem 5-21A *Inventory valuation based on the lower-of-cost-or-market rule*

At the end of the year, Randy's Parts Co. had the following items in inventory:

Item	Quantity	Unit Cost	Unit Market Value
P1	60	$ 85	$ 90
P2	40	70	72
P3	80	130	120
P4	70	125	130

Required

a. Determine the amount of ending inventory using the lower-of-cost-or-market rule applied to each individual inventory item.
b. Provide the general journal entry necessary to write down the inventory based on Requirement *a*. Assume that Randy's Parts Co. uses the perpetual inventory system.
c. Determine the amount of ending inventory, assuming that the lower-of-cost-or-market rule is applied to the total inventory in aggregate.
d. Provide the general journal entry necessary to write down the inventory based on Requirement *c*. Assume that Randy's Parts Co. uses the perpetual inventory system.
e. Explain how the inventory loss would be reported when the periodic inventory system is used.

Problem 5-22A *Estimating ending inventory: gross margin method*   LO 5-4

The inventory of Don's Grocery was destroyed by a tornado on October 6 of the current year. Fortunately, some of the accounting records were at the home of one of the owners and were not damaged. The following information was available for the period of January 1 through October 6:

Beginning inventory, January 1	$ 140,000
Purchases through October 6	670,000
Sales through October 6	1,100,000

CHECK FIGURES
a. Gross Margin: $330,000
b. Total Inventory Loss: $25,000

Gross margin for Don's has traditionally been 30 percent of sales.

Required

a. For the period ending October 6, compute the following:
   (1) Estimated gross margin.
   (2) Estimated cost of goods sold.
   (3) Estimated inventory at October 6.
b. Assume that $15,000 of the inventory was not damaged. What is the amount of the loss from the tornado?
c. If Don's had used the perpetual inventory system, how would it have determined the amount of the inventory loss?

Problem 5-23A *Estimating ending inventory: gross margin method*   LO 5-4

Toyland wishes to produce quarterly financial statements, but it takes a physical count of inventory only at year-end. The following historical data were taken from the Year 1 and Year 2 accounting records:

	Year 1	Year 2
Net sales	$150,000	$190,000
Cost of goods sold	76,000	89,200

CHECK FIGURE
b. Estimated ending inventory: $20,040

At the end of the first quarter of Year 3, Toyland's ledger had the following account balances:

Sales	$210,000
Purchases	90,000
Beginning inventory 1/1/Year 3	32,100
Ending inventory 3/31/Year 3	16,000

Based on purchases and sales, the Toyland accountant thinks inventory is low.

Required

Using the information provided, estimate the following for the first quarter of Year 3:
a. Cost of goods sold. (Use the average cost of goods sold percentage.)
b. Ending inventory at March 31.
c. What could explain the difference between actual and estimated inventory?

Problem 5-24A *Effect of inventory errors on financial statements*   LO 5-3

The following income statement was prepared for Frame Supplies for Year 1:

FRAME SUPPLIES
Income Statement
For the Year Ended December 31, Year 1

Sales	$ 250,000
Cost of goods sold	(140,000)
Gross margin	110,000
Operating expenses	(69,500)
Net income	$ 40,500

During the year-end audit, the following errors were discovered:

1. A $2,500 payment for repairs was erroneously charged to the Cost of Goods Sold account. (Assume that the perpetual inventory system is used.)
2. Sales to customers for $1,800 at December 31, Year 1, were not recorded in the books for Year 1. Also, the $980 cost of goods sold was not recorded.
3. A mathematical error was made in determining ending inventory. Ending inventory was understated by $2,150. (The Inventory account was mistakenly written down to the Cost of Goods Sold account.)

Required

Determine the effect, if any, of each of the errors on the following items. Give the dollar amount of the effect and whether it would overstate (O), understate (U), or not affect (NA) the account. The first item for each error is recorded as an example.

Error No. 1	Amount of Error	Effect
Sales, Year 1	NA	NA
Ending inventory, December 31, Year 1		
Gross margin, Year 1		
Beginning inventory, January 1, Year 2		
Cost of goods sold, Year 1		
Net income, Year 1		
Retained earnings, December 31, Year 1		
Total assets, December 31, Year 1		

Error No. 2	Amount of Error	Effect
Sales, Year 1	$1,800	U
Ending inventory, December 31, Year 1		
Gross margin, Year 1		
Beginning inventory, January 1, Year 2		
Cost of goods sold, Year 1		
Net income, Year 1		
Retained earnings, December 31, Year 1		
Total assets, December 31, Year 1		

Error No. 3	Amount of Error	Effect
Sales, Year 1	NA	NA
Ending inventory, December 31, Year 1		
Gross margin, Year 1		
Beginning inventory, January 1, Year 2		
Cost of goods sold, Year 1		
Net income, Year 1		
Retained earnings, December 31, Year 1		
Total assets, December 31, Year 1		

LO 5-5

Problem 5-25A *Using ratios to make comparisons*

The following accounting information pertains to Boardwalk Taffy and Beach Sweets. The only difference between the two companies is that Boardwalk Taffy uses FIFO, while Beach Sweets uses LIFO.

	Boardwalk Taffy	Beach Sweets
Cash	$ 120,000	$ 120,000
Accounts receivable	480,000	480,000
Merchandise inventory	350,000	300,000
Accounts payable	360,000	360,000
Cost of goods sold	2,000,000	2,050,000
Building	500,000	500,000
Sales	3,000,000	3,000,000

Required

a. Compute the gross margin percentage for each company and identify the company that *appears* to be charging the higher prices in relation to its cost.

b. For each company, compute the inventory turnover ratio and the average days to sell inventory. Identify the company that *appears* to be incurring the higher financing cost.

c. Explain why a company with the lower gross margin percentage needs to have a higher inventory turnover ratio assuming a period of inflation.

EXERCISES—SERIES B

Exercise 5-1B   *Effect of inventory cost flow assumption on financial statements*   LO 5-1

Required

For each of the following situations, fill in the blank with *FIFO, LIFO,* or *weighted average:*

a. _____ would produce the highest amount of net income in an inflationary environment.
b. _____ would produce the highest amount of assets in an inflationary environment.
c. _____ would produce the lowest amount of net income in a deflationary environment.
d. _____ would produce the same unit cost for assets and cost of goods sold in an inflationary environment.
e. _____ would produce the lowest amount of net income in an inflationary environment.
f. _____ would produce an asset value that was the same regardless of whether the environment was inflationary or deflationary.
g. _____ would produce the lowest amount of assets in an inflationary environment.
h. _____ would produce the highest amount of assets in a deflationary environment.

Exercise 5-2B   *Allocating product cost between cost of goods sold and ending inventory*   LO 5-1

Harris Co. started the year with no inventory. During the year, it purchased two identical inventory items. The inventory was purchased at different times. The first purchase cost $3,600 and the other, $4,200. One of the items was sold during the year.

Required

Based on this information, how much product cost would be allocated to cost of goods sold and ending inventory on the year-end financial statements, assuming use of

a. FIFO?
b. LIFO?
c. Weighted average?

Exercise 5-3B   *Allocating product cost between cost of goods sold and ending inventory: multiple purchases*   LO 5-1

Marley Company sells coffee makers used in business offices. Its beginning inventory of coffee makers was 400 units at $50 per unit. During the year, Marley made two batch purchases of coffee makers. The first was a 500-unit purchase at $55 per unit; the second was a 600-unit purchase at $58 per unit. During the period, Marley sold 1,200 coffee makers.

Required

Determine the amount of product costs that would be allocated to cost of goods sold and ending inventory, assuming that Marley uses

a. FIFO.
b. LIFO.
c. Weighted average.

Exercise 5-4B   *Effect of inventory cost flow (FIFO, LIFO, and weighted average) on gross margin*   LO 5-1

The following information pertains to Stanley Company for Year 2:

Beginning inventory	90 units @ $15
Units purchased	320 units @ $19

Ending inventory consisted of 40 units. Stanley sold 370 units at $30 each. All purchases and sales were made with cash.

Required

a. Compute the gross margin for Stanley Company using the following cost flow assumptions: (1) FIFO, (2) LIFO, and (3) weighted average.

b. What is the dollar amount of difference in net income between using FIFO versus LIFO? (Ignore income tax considerations.)

c. Determine the cash flow from operating activities, using each of the three cost flow assumptions listed in Requirement a. Ignore the effect of income taxes. Explain why these cash flows have no differences.

LO 5-1

Exercise 5-5B *Effect of inventory cost flow on ending inventory balance and gross margin*

Scott Sales had the following transactions for jackets in Year 1, its first year of operations:

Jan. 20	Purchased 80 units @ $15	=	$1,200
Apr. 21	Purchased 420 units @ $16	=	6,720
July 25	Purchased 250 units @ $20	=	5,000
Sept. 19	Purchased 150 units @ $22	=	3,300

During the year, Scott Sales sold 830 jackets for $40 each.

Required

a. Compute the amount of ending inventory Scott would report on the balance sheet, assuming the following cost flow assumptions: (1) FIFO, (2) LIFO, and (3) weighted average.

b. Record the above transactions in general journal form and post to T-accounts using (1) FIFO, (2) LIFO, and (3) weighted average. Use a separate set of journal entries and T-accounts for each method. Assume all transactions are cash transactions.

c. Compute the difference in gross margin between the FIFO and LIFO cost flow assumptions.

LO 5-1

Exercise 5-6B *Income tax effect of shifting from FIFO to LIFO*

The following information pertains to the inventory of the Bryant Company:

Jan. 1	Beginning Inventory	300 units @ $25
Apr. 1	Purchased	2,800 units @ $30
Oct. 1	Purchased	1,000 units @ $32

During the year, Bryant sold 3,500 units of inventory at $50 per unit and incurred $21,000 of operating expenses. Bryant currently uses the FIFO method but is considering a change to LIFO. All transactions are cash transactions. Assume a 30 percent income tax rate. Bryant started the period with cash of $36,000, inventory of $7,500, common stock of $20,000, and retained earnings of $23,500.

Required

a. Record the above transactions in general journal form and post to T-accounts using (1) FIFO and (2) LIFO. Use a separate set of journal entries and T-accounts for each method.

b. Prepare income statements using FIFO and LIFO.

c. Determine the amount of income tax Bryant would save if it changed cost flow methods.

d. Determine the cash flow from operating activities under FIFO and LIFO.

e. Explain why cash flow from operating activities is lower under FIFO when that cost flow method produced the higher gross margin.

Exercise 5-7B *Effect of FIFO versus LIFO on income tax expense*   LO 5-1

Home Gifts Inc. had cash sales of $112,500 for Year 1, its first year of operation. On April 2, the company purchased 150 units of inventory at $180 per unit. On September 1, an additional 200 units were purchased for $200 per unit. The company had 50 units on hand at the end of the year. The company's income tax rate is 40 percent. All transactions are cash transactions.

Required

a. The preceding paragraph describes five accounting events: (1) a sales transaction, (2) the first purchase of inventory, (3) a second purchase of inventory, (4) the recognition of cost of goods sold expense, and (5) the payment of income tax expense. Show the amounts of each event in horizontal statements models like the following ones, assuming first a FIFO and then a LIFO cost flow.

Effect of Events on Financial Statements
Panel 1: FIFO Cost Flow

Event No.	Balance Sheet	Income Statement	Statement of Cash Flows
	Cash + Inventory = Com. Stk. + Ret. Earn.	Rev. − Exp. = Net Inc.	

Panel 2: LIFO Cost Flow

Event No.	Balance Sheet	Income Statement	Statement of Cash Flows
	Cash + Inventory = Com. Stk. + Ret. Earn.	Rev. − Exp. = Net Inc.	

b. Compute net income using FIFO.
c. Compute net income using LIFO.
d. Explain the difference, if any, in the amount of income tax expense incurred using the two cost flow assumptions.
e. How does the use of the FIFO versus the LIFO cost flow assumptions affect the statement of cash flows?

Exercise 5-8B *Recording inventory transactions using the perpetual system: intermittent sales and purchases*   LO 5-1

The following inventory transactions apply to Duncan Steel Company for Year 2:

Jan. 1	Purchased	200 units @ $12
Apr. 1	Sold	150 units @ $20
Aug. 1	Purchased	300 units @ $15
Dec. 1	Sold	450 units @ $25

The beginning inventory consisted of 180 units at $10 per unit. All transactions are cash transactions.

Required

a. Record these transactions in general journal format assuming Duncan Steel Company uses the FIFO cost flow assumption and keeps perpetual records.
b. Compute the ending balance in the Inventory account.

Chapter 5

LO 5-1

Exercise 5-9B *Effect of cost flow on ending inventory: intermittent sales and purchases*

Nash Auto Parts, Inc. had the following transactions for Year 2:

Date	Transaction	Description
Jan. 1	Beginning inventory	40 units @ $22
Mar. 15	Purchased	150 units @ $24
May 30	Sold	175 units @ $48
Aug. 10	Purchased	320 units @ $26
Nov. 20	Sold	300 units @ $50

Required

a. Determine the quantity and dollar amount of inventory at the end of the year, assuming Nash Auto Parts, Inc. uses the FIFO cost flow assumption and keeps perpetual records.

b. Write a memo explaining why Nash Auto Parts, Inc. would have difficulty applying the LIFO method on a perpetual basis. Include a discussion of how to overcome these difficulties.

LO 5-2

Exercise 5-10B *Lower-of-cost-or-market rule: perpetual system*

The following information pertains to James Hardware's ending inventory for the current year:

Item	Quantity	Unit Cost	Unit Market Value
M	200	$10	$ 8
N	100	12	10
O	40	8	9
P	30	5	10

Required

a. Determine the value of the ending inventory using the lower-of-cost-or-market rule applied to (1) each individual inventory item and (2) the inventory in aggregate.

b. Prepare any necessary journal entries, assuming the decline in value is immaterial, using the (1) individual method and (2) aggregate method. James Hardware uses the perpetual inventory system.

LO 5-2

Exercise 5-11B *Lower-of-cost-or-market rule*

Harvey Company carries three inventory items. The following information pertains to the ending inventory:

Item	Quantity	Unit Cost	Unit Market Value
A	400	$20	$18
B	500	25	24
C	300	10	12

Required

a. Determine the ending inventory that will be reported on the balance sheet, assuming that Harvey applies the lower-of-cost-or-market rule to individual inventory items.

b. Prepare the necessary journal entry, assuming the decline in value is immaterial.

Exercise 5-12B *Effect of inventory error on financial statements: perpetual system*   LO 5-3

Bosh Company failed to count $22,000 of inventory in its Year 1 year-end physical count.

Required

Explain how this error will affect Bosh's Year 1 financial statements, assuming that Bosh uses the perpetual inventory system.

Exercise 5-13B *Effect of inventory misstatement on elements of financial statements*   LO 5-3

The ending inventory for Oak Co. was erroneously written down, causing an understatement of $6,500 at the end of Year 2.

Required

Was each of the following amounts overstated, understated, or not affected by the error?

Item No.	Year	Amount
1	Year 2	Beginning inventory
2	Year 2	Purchases
3	Year 2	Goods available for sale
4	Year 2	Cost of goods sold
5	Year 2	Gross margin
6	Year 2	Net income
7	Year 3	Beginning inventory
8	Year 3	Purchases
9	Year 3	Goods available for sale
10	Year 3	Cost of goods sold
11	Year 3	Gross margin
12	Year 3	Net income

Exercise 5-14B *Estimating ending inventory using the gross margin method*   LO 5-4

Frank Jones, the owner of Frank's Hunting Supplies, is surprised at the amount of actual inventory at the end of the year. He thought there should be more inventory on hand based on the amount of sales for the year. The following information is taken from the books of Frank's Hunting Supplies:

Beginning inventory	$250,000
Purchases for the year	500,000
Sales for the year	850,000
Inventory at the end of the year (based on actual count)	40,000

Historically, Frank has made a 20 percent gross margin on his sales. Frank thinks there may be some problem with the inventory. Evaluate the situation based on the historical gross profit percentage.

Required

Estimate the following:
a. Gross margin in dollars.
b. Cost of goods sold in dollars.
c. Estimated ending inventory.
d. Inventory shortage.
e. Provide an explanation for the shortage.

LO 5-4

Exercise 5-15B Estimating ending inventory: perpetual system

Beth Malone owned a small company that sold boating equipment. The equipment was expensive, and a perpetual system was maintained for control purposes. Even so, lost, damaged, and stolen merchandise normally amounted to 5 percent of the inventory balance. On June 14, Beth's warehouse was destroyed by fire. Just prior to the fire, the accounting records contained a $130,000 balance in the Inventory account. However, inventory that cost $20,000 had been sold and delivered to customers the day of the fire but had not been recorded in the books at the time of the fire. The fire did not affect the showroom, which contained inventory that cost $50,000.

Required

Estimate the amount of inventory destroyed by fire.

LO 5-5

Exercise 5-16B Inventory turnover and average days to sell

The following accounting information pertains to two retail stores that specialize in selling winter ski gear. Aspen Sports operates only a few locations and has a market strategy of selling only high-end ski gear. Discount Ski has many locations but sells lower-quality products than Aspen Sports.

	Discount Ski	Aspen Sports
Sales	$800,000	?
Cost of Goods Sold	?	$200,000
Gross Margin	?	$300,000
Gross Margin Percentage	20%	?

Discount Ski has an average inventory balance of $60,000, while Aspen Sports' average inventory balance is $55,000.

a. Complete the table above by filling in the missing amounts.
b. Which retail store is using a higher cost/lower volume strategy regarding sales?
c. Calculate the inventory turnover and the average days to sale inventory for each retail store. Based on your calculations, which retail store will need to reorder inventory more frequently?

IFRS

Exercise 5-17B Explaining multiple inventory methods at one real-world company

The following note related to accounting for inventory was taken from the 2016 annual report of **Wal-Mart Stores, Inc.**:

> *Inventories* The Company values inventories at the lower of cost or market as determined primarily by the retail inventory method of accounting, using the last-in, first-out ("LIFO") method for substantially all of the Walmart U.S. segment's inventories. The inventory at the Walmart International segment is valued primarily by the retail inventory method of accounting, using the first-in, first-out ("FIFO") method. The retail inventory method of accounting results in inventory being valued at the lower of cost or market since permanent markdowns are immediately recorded as a reduction of the retail value of inventory. The inventory at the Sam's Club segment is valued based on the weighted-average cost using the LIFO method. At January 31, 2016 and January 31, 2015, the Company's inventories valued at LIFO approximated those inventories as if they were valued at FIFO.

Required

Write a brief report explaining the reason (reasons) that best explains (explain) why Walmart uses the LIFO cost flow method for its operations in the United States, but the FIFO method for its non-U.S. operations.

IFRS

Exercise 5-18B GAAP versus IFRS

Po River Winery Inc. has inventory that cost $500,000. The aging process for the inventory requires several years. At the company's closing date (December 31, Year 1), the inventory had a market value of $400,000. During Year 2, the market value recovered to an estimated $480,000.

Required

a. Assuming Po River uses GAAP, determine the book value and the amount of any gain or loss recognized on the Year 1 and Year 2 financial statements.
b. Assuming Po River uses IFRS, determine the book value and the amount of any gain or loss recognized on the Year 1 and Year 2 financial statements.

PROBLEMS—SERIES B

Problem 5-19B Effect of different inventory cost flow methods on financial statements
LO 5-1

The accounting records of Allen Insulation, Inc. reflected the following balances as of January 1, Year 2:

Cash	$36,000
Beginning inventory	24,000 (200 units @ $120)
Common stock	25,000
Retained earnings	35,000

The following five transactions occurred in Year 2:
1. First purchase (cash)   130 units @ $124
2. Second purchase (cash)   220 units @ $128
3. Sales (all cash)   350 units @ $320
4. Paid $24,000 cash for operating expenses
5. Paid cash for income tax at the rate of 40 percent of income before taxes

Required

a. Compute the cost of goods sold and ending inventory, assuming (1) FIFO cost flow, (2) LIFO cost flow, and (3) weighted-average cost flow. Compute income tax expense for each method.

b. Record the above transactions in general journal form and post to T-accounts assuming (1) FIFO cost flow, (2) LIFO cost flow, and (3) weighted-average cost flow.

c. Use a vertical model to show the Year 2 income statement, balance sheet, and statement of cash flows under FIFO, LIFO, and weighted average.

Problem 5-20B Allocating product costs between cost of goods sold and ending inventory: intermittent purchases and sales of merchandise
LO 5-1

Donovan, Inc. had the following sales and purchase transactions during Year 2. Beginning inventory consisted of 120 items at $80 each. Donovan uses the FIFO cost flow assumption and keeps perpetual inventory records.

Date	Transaction	Description
Mar. 5	Purchased	100 items @ $90
Apr. 10	Sold	70 items @ $175
June 19	Sold	80 items @ $175
Sep. 16	Purchased	50 items @ $95
Nov. 28	Sold	60 items @ $180

Required

a. Record the inventory transactions in general journal format.
b. Calculate the gross margin Donovan would report on the Year 2 income statement.
c. Determine the ending inventory balance Donovan would report on the December 31, Year 2, balance sheet.

Problem 5-21B Inventory valuation based on the lower-of-cost-or-market rule
LO 5-2

At the end of the year, Ronaldo Jewelers had the following items in inventory:

Item	Quantity	Unit Cost	Unit Market Value
D1	30	$80	$90
D2	10	60	55
D3	41	30	32
D4	20	90	75

Required

a. Determine the amount of ending inventory using the lower-of-cost-or-market rule applied to each individual inventory item.

b. Provide the general journal entry necessary to write down the inventory based on Requirement *a*. Assume that Ronaldo Jewelers uses the perpetual inventory system.

c. Determine the amount of ending inventory, assuming that the lower-of-cost-or-market rule is applied to the inventory in aggregate.

d. Provide the general journal entry necessary to write down the inventory based on Requirement *c*. Assume that Ronaldo Jewelers uses the perpetual inventory system.

LO 5-4

Problem 5-22B *Estimating ending inventory: gross margin method*

A hurricane destroyed the inventory of Coleman Feed Store on September 21 of the current year. Although some of the accounting information was destroyed, the following information was discovered for the period of January 1 through September 21:

Beginning inventory, January 1	$120,000
Purchases through September 21	450,000
Sales through September 21	800,000

The gross margin for Coleman Feed Store has traditionally been 35 percent of sales.

Required

a. For the period ending September 21, compute the following:
   (1) Estimated gross margin.
   (2) Estimated cost of goods sold.
   (3) Estimated inventory at September 21.

b. Assume that $8,000 of the inventory was not damaged. What is the amount of the loss from the hurricane?

c. Coleman Feed Store uses the perpetual inventory system. If some of the accounting records had not been destroyed, how would Coleman determine the amount of the inventory loss?

LO 5-4

Problem 5-23B *Estimating ending inventory: gross margin method*

Sam Todd, owner of Todd Company, is reviewing the quarterly financial statements and thinks the cost of goods sold is out of line with past years. The following historical data are available for Year 1 and Year 2:

	Year 1	Year 2
Net sales	$220,000	$250,000
Cost of goods sold	99,000	117,200

At the end of the first quarter of Year 3, Todd Company's ledger had the following account balances:

Sales	$280,000
Purchases	210,000
Beginning inventory, January 1, Year 3	70,000

Required

Using the information provided, estimate the following for the first quarter of Year 3:

a. Cost of goods sold. (Use average cost of goods sold percentage.)

b. Ending inventory at March 31 based on the historical cost of goods sold percentage.

c. Inventory shortage if the inventory balance as of March 31 is $125,000.

Problem 5-24B *Effect of inventory errors on financial statements* **LO 5-3**

The following income statement was prepared for Rice Company for Year 1:

RICE COMPANY
Income Statement
For the Year Ended December 31, Year 1

Sales	$ 75,000
Cost of goods sold	(41,250)
Gross margin	33,750
Operating expenses	(10,120)
Net income	$ 23,630

During the year-end audit, the following errors were discovered:

1. An $1,800 payment for repairs was erroneously charged to the Cost of Goods Sold account. (Assume that the perpetual inventory system is used.)
2. Sales to customers for $3,400 at December 31, Year 1, were not recorded in the books for Year 1. Also, the $1,870 cost of goods sold was not recorded
3. A mathematical error was made in determining ending inventory. Ending inventory was understated by $1,700. (The Inventory account was written down in error to the Cost of Goods Sold account.)

Required

Determine the effect, if any, of each of the errors on the following items. Give the dollar amount of the effect and whether it would overstate (O), understate (U), or not affect (NA) the account. The effect on sales is recorded as an example.

Error No. 1	Amount of Error	Effect
Sales, Year 1	NA	NA
Ending inventory, December 31, Year 1		
Gross margin, Year 1		
Beginning inventory, January 1, Year 2		
Cost of goods sold, Year 1		
Net income, Year 1		
Retained earnings, December 31, Year 1		
Total assets, December 31, Year 1		

Error No. 2	Amount of Error	Effect
Sales, Year 1	$3,400	U
Ending inventory, December 31, Year 1		
Gross margin, Year 1		
Beginning inventory, January 1, Year 2		
Cost of goods sold, Year 1		
Net income, Year 1		
Retained earnings, December 31, Year 1		
Total assets, December 31, Year 1		

Error No. 3	Amount of Error	Effect
Sales, Year 1	NA	NA
Ending inventory, December 31, Year 1		
Gross margin, Year 1		
Beginning inventory, January 1, Year 2		
Cost of goods sold, Year 1		
Net income, Year 1		
Retained earnings, December 31, Year 1		
Total assets, December 31, Year 1		

LO 5-5

Problem 5-25B *Using ratios to make comparisons*

The following accounting information pertains to Mobile and Casper companies. The only difference between the two companies is that Mobile uses FIFO, while Casper uses LIFO.

	Mobile Co.	Casper Co.
Cash	$ 70,000	$ 70,000
Accounts receivable	230,000	230,000
Merchandise inventory	220,000	190,000
Accounts payable	210,000	210,000
Cost of goods sold	1,350,000	1,380,000
Building	300,000	300,000
Sales	1,800,000	1,800,000

Required

a. Compute the gross margin percentage for each company and identify the company that *appears* to be charging the higher prices in relation to its cost.
b. For each company, compute the inventory turnover ratio and the average days to sell inventory. Identify the company that *appears* to be incurring the higher financing cost.
c. Explain why a company with the lower gross margin percentage needs to have a higher inventory turnover ratio assuming a period of inflation.

ANALYZE, THINK, COMMUNICATE

ATC 5-1 Business Applications Case *Understanding real-world annual reports*

Required

Obtain the Target Corporation's annual report at http://investors.target.com using the instructions in Appendix B, and use it to answer the following questions:

a. What was Target's inventory turnover ratio and average days to sell inventory for the fiscal year ended January 28, 2017 (2016) and 2015?
b. Is the company's management of inventory getting better or worse?
c. What cost flow method(s) did Target use to account for inventory?

ATC 5-2 Group Assignment *Inventory cost flow*

The accounting records of Blue Bird Co. showed the following balances at January 1, Year 2:

Cash	$30,000
Beginning inventory (100 units @ $50, 70 units @ $55)	8,850
Common stock	20,000
Retained earnings	18,850

Transactions for Year 2 were as follows:

> Purchased 100 units @ $54 per unit.
> Sold 220 units @ $80 per unit.
> Purchased 250 units @ $58 per unit.
> Sold 200 units @ $90 per unit.
> Paid operating expenses of $3,200.
> Paid income tax expense. The income tax rate is 30%.

Required

a. Organize the class into three sections, and divide each section into groups of three to five students. Assign each section one of the cost flow methods, FIFO, LIFO, or weighted average. The company uses the perpetual inventory system.

Group Tasks

Determine the amount of ending inventory, cost of goods sold, gross margin, and net income after income tax for the cost flow method assigned to your section. Also prepare an income statement using that cost flow assumption.

Class Discussion

b. Have a representative of each section put its income statement on the board. Discuss the effect that each cost flow method has on assets (ending inventory), net income, and cash flows. Which method is preferred for tax reporting? For financial reporting? What restrictions are placed on the use of LIFO for tax reporting?

ATC 5-3 Real-World Case Inventory management issues at the Penske Automotive Group

The following data were extracted from the 2016 financial statements of **Penske Automotive Group, Inc.** This company operates automobile dealerships, mostly in the United States, Canada, and Western Europe, and commercial truck dealerships in Australia, New Zealand, and the United Kingdom. The company had 355 dealerships as of the end of 2016. Dollar amounts are in millions.

	December 31, 2016	December 31, 2015
Revenue	$20,118.5	$19,284.9
Cost of sale	17,151.9	16,417.4
Gross profit	2,966.6	2,867.5
Operating income before taxes	574.9	566.5
Net income	342.9	326.1
Ending inventory	3,408.2	3,463.5

Required

a. Compute Penske's gross margin percentage for 2016 and 2015.
b. Compute Penske's average days to sell inventory for 2016 and 2015.
c. How much higher or lower would *Penske's earnings before taxes* have been in 2016 if its gross margin percentage had been the same as it was in 2015? Show all supporting computations.

ATC 5-4 Business Applications Case Performing ratio analysis using real-world data

Costco Wholesale Corporation operated 715 stores as of August 28, 2016. The following data were taken from the company's annual report. All dollar amounts are in millions.

	Fiscal Years Ending	
	August 28, 2016	August 30, 2015
Net sales	$116,073	$113,666
Cost of goods sold	102,901	101,065
Net income	2,350	2,377
Merchandise inventory	8,969	8,908

Required

a. Compute Costco's inventory turnover ratio for 2016 and 2015.
b. Compute Costco's average days to sell inventory for 2016 and 2015.
c. Based on your computations in Requirements *a* and *b*, did Costco's inventory management get better or worse from 2015 to 2016?

ATC 5-5 Business Applications Case   *Performing ratio analysis using real-world data*

Ruby Tuesday's, Inc. operated 646 casual dining restaurants across the United States as of May 31, 2016. **Signet Jewelers Limited** claims to be the world's largest retailer of diamond jewelry. Its stores include Zales, Jared, Kay Jewelers, and Piercing Pagoda. As of January 30, 2016, it had over 3,500 retail outlets.

The following data were taken from these companies' 2016 annual reports. All dollar amounts are in thousands.

	Ruby Tuesday's May 31, 2016	Signet Jewelers January 30, 2016
Revenue	$1,091,228	$6,550,200
Cost of goods sold	298,529	4,109,800
Net income	(50,682)	467,900
Merchandise inventory	13,799	2,453,900

Required

a. Before performing any calculations, speculate as to which company will take the longest to sell its inventory. Explain the rationale for your decision.
b. Calculate the inventory turnover ratios for Ruby Tuesday's and Signet.
c. Calculate the average days to sell inventory for Ruby Tuesday's and Signet.
d. Do the calculations from Requirements *b* and *c* confirm your speculations in Requirement *a*?

ATC 5-6 Writing Assignment   *Use of LIFO*

The following information is available for Leno Company:

Sales	$695,000
Goods available for sale	535,000
Ending inventory (using FIFO)	246,000

Leno Company currently uses the FIFO cost flow method for financial statement reporting and tax reporting. It is considering changing to the LIFO cost flow method for tax reporting purposes. If Leno uses LIFO, its ending inventory would be $175,000.

Required

a. Why would Leno want to change to LIFO for tax reporting?
b. Discuss any changes that Leno would have to make for GAAP reporting if it does change to LIFO for tax reporting.

ATC 5-7 Ethical Dilemma   *Show them only what you want them to see*

Clair Coolage is the chief accountant for a sales company called Far Eastern Imports. The company has been highly successful and is trying to increase its capital base by attracting new investors. The company operates in an inflationary environment and has been using the LIFO inventory cost flow method to minimize its net earnings and thereby reduce its income taxes. Katie Bailey, the vice president of finance, asked Coolage to estimate the change in net earnings that would occur if the company switched to FIFO. After reviewing the company's books, Coolage estimated that pretax income would increase by $1,200,000 if the company adopted the FIFO cost flow method. However, the switch would result in approximately $400,000 of additional taxes. The overall effect would result in an increase of $800,000 in net earnings. Bailey told Coolage to avoid the additional taxes by preparing the tax return on a LIFO basis but to prepare a set of statements on a FIFO basis to be distributed to potential investors.

Required

a. Comment on the legal and ethical implications of Bailey's decision.
b. How will the switch to FIFO affect Far Eastern's balance sheet?
c. If Bailey reconsiders and makes a decision to switch to FIFO for tax purposes as well as financial reporting purposes, net income will increase by $800,000. Comment on the wisdom of paying $400,000 in income taxes to obtain an additional $800,000 of net income.

ATC 5-8 Research Assignment *Analyzing inventory at Gap Company*

Using either **Gap**'s most current Form 10-K or the company's annual report, answer the questions below. To obtain the Form 10-K, use either the EDGAR system, following the instructions in Appendix A, or the company's website. The company's annual report is available on its website.

Required

a. How many stores did Gap operate at year-end? (Do not include "Franchise store locations.")
b. What was the average amount of inventory per store? Use *all* stores operated by The Gap, Inc., not just those called *The Gap*. (*Hint:* The answer to this question must be computed. The number of stores in operation at the end of the most recent year can be found in the MD&A of the 10-K.)
c. Using the quarterly financial information in the 10-K, complete the following chart:

Quarter	Sales during Each Quarter
1	$
2	
3	
4	

d. Referring to the chart in Requirement *c*, explain why Gap's sales vary so widely throughout its fiscal year. Do you believe that Gap's inventory level varies throughout the year in relation to sales?

ATC 5-9 Spreadsheet Analysis *Using Excel*

At January 1, Year 2, the accounting records of Ginger's Boutique had the following balances:

Cash	$1,000
Inventory	2,250 (150 units @ $15)
Common stock	2,000
Retained earnings	1,250

During January, Ginger's Boutique entered into five cash transactions:
1. Purchased 120 units of inventory @ $16 each.
2. Purchased 160 units of inventory @ $17 each.
3. Sold 330 units of inventory @ $30 each.
4. Incurred $1,700 of operating expenses.
5. Paid income tax at the rate of 30 percent of income before taxes.

Required

a. Set up rows 1 through 10 of the following spreadsheet to compute cost of goods sold and ending inventory, assuming (1) FIFO, (2) LIFO, and (3) weighted-average cost flows. Notice that the FIFO cost flow has already been completed for you. Use columns O through W to complete the LIFO and weighted-average cost flow computations. Be sure to use formulas for all calculations.

314   Chapter 5

Source: Microsoft Office Excel 1997

b. In rows 13 through 31, compute the amount of net income and net cash flow from operations under FIFO, LIFO, and weighted average. The FIFO column has been provided as an example.

ATC 5-10 Spreadsheet Assignment   *Mastering Excel*

Required

Complete ATC 5-5 using an Excel spreadsheet.

COMPREHENSIVE PROBLEM

The trial balance of Pacilio Security Services, Inc. as of January 1, Year 5, had the following normal balances:

Cash	$62,860
Accounts receivable	20,500
Supplies	150
Prepaid rent	2,000
Merchandise inventory (9 @ $240)	2,160
Land	4,000
Accounts payable	980
Salaries payable	1,500
Common stock	50,000
Retained earnings	39,190

During Year 5, Pacilio Security Services experienced the following transactions:

1. Paid the salaries payable from Year 4.
2. On January 15, purchased 20 standard alarm systems for cash at a cost of $250 each.
3. On February 1, paid the accounts payable of $980, but not within the discount period. (The company uses the gross method.)
4. On March 1, leased a business van. Paid $4,800 for one year's lease in advance.
5. Paid $7,200 on May 1 for one year's rent on the office in advance.
6. Purchased with cash $500 of supplies to be used over the next several months by the business.
7. Purchased with cash another 25 alarm systems on August 1 for resale at a cost of $260 each.
8. On September 5, purchased on account 30 standard alarm systems at a cost of $265.
9. Installed 60 standard alarm systems for $33,000. Sales of $22,000 were on account, while $11,000 were cash sales. (*Note:* Be sure to record cost of goods sold using the perpetual FIFO method.)
10. Made a full refund to a dissatisfied customer who returned her alarm system. The sale had been a cash sale for $550 with a cost of $260.
11. Paid installers and other employees a total of $21,000 cash for salaries.
12. Sold $45,000 of monitoring services during the year. The services are billed to the customers each month.
13. Sold an additional monitoring service for $1,200 for one year's service. The customer paid the full amount of $1,200 on October 1.
14. Collected $74,000 of accounts receivable during the year.
15. Paid an additional $6,000 to settle some of the accounts payable.
16. Paid $3,500 of advertising expense during the year.
17. Paid $2,320 of utilities expense for the year.
18. Paid a dividend of $15,000 to the shareholders.

Adjustments

19. There was $200 of supplies on hand at the end of the year.
20. Recognized the expired rent for both the van and the office building for the year.
21. Recognized the revenue earned from transaction 13.
22. Accrued salaries at December 31, Year 5, were $1,000.

Required

a. Record the above transactions in general journal form.
b. Post the transactions to T-accounts.
c. Prepare a trial balance.
d. Prepare an income statement, statement of changes in stockholders' equity, balance sheet, and statement of cash flows.
e. Close the temporary accounts to retained earnings.
f. Post the closing entries to the T-accounts and prepare an after-closing trial balance.

CHAPTER 6

Internal Control and Accounting for Cash

LEARNING OBJECTIVES

After you have mastered the material in this chapter, you will be able to:

LO 6-1 Identify the key elements of a strong system of internal control.

LO 6-2 Identify special internal controls for cash.

LO 6-3 Prepare a bank reconciliation.

LO 6-4 Show how a petty cash fund affects financial statements.

LO 6-5 Describe the auditor's role in financial reporting.

 Video lectures and accompanying self-assessment quizzes are available in Connect for all learning objectives.

CHAPTER OPENING

To operate successfully, businesses must establish systems of control. How can **Walmart**'s upper-level managers ensure that every store will open on time? How can the president of **General Motors** be confident that the company's financial reports fairly reflect the company's operations? How can the owner of a restaurant prevent a server from serving food to his friends and relatives without charging them for it? The answer: by exercising effective control over company activities. The policies and procedures used to provide reasonable assurance that the objectives of an enterprise will be accomplished are called **internal controls.**

Internal controls can be divided into two categories: (1) **accounting controls** are designed to safeguard company assets and ensure reliable accounting records; and (2) **administrative controls** are concerned with evaluating performance and assessing the degree of compliance with company policies and public laws.

The Curious Accountant

©jvdwolf/123RF

When many people think about the threats to a company's financial resources they imagine someone trying to steal its cash or other assets, or a hacker trying to drain its bank account. Although these are legitimate threats, the biggest threats facing business often come from within.

Consider the case of the **Volkswagen AG** (VW) emissions scandal that became widely known to the public in September 2015, when the Environmental Protection Agency (EPA) filed charges claiming VW had intentionally installed software to provide inaccurate results related to mileage and emissions performance in some of its vehicles with diesel engines. Within months of the charges by the EPA, VW admitted that its emissions defeating software had been installed on about 11 million vehicles worldwide.

Companies' responsibilities under the Sarbanes–Oxley Act (SOX) were introduced in Chapter 2, and SOX is discussed further in this chapter. Do you think SOX was intended to require companies to protect their customers from the type of emissions reporting frauds reported here? If not, are there other aspects of financial accounting systems that should protect a company's customers and investors? (Answers on page 322.)

KEY FEATURES OF INTERNAL CONTROL SYSTEMS

LO 6-1

Identify the key elements of a strong system of internal control.

During the early 2000s, a number of accounting-related scandals cost investors billions. In 2001, Enron's share price went from $85 to $0.30 after it was revealed that the company had billions of dollars in losses that were not reported on the financial statements. Several months later, WorldCom reported an $11 billion accounting fraud, which included hundreds of millions in personal loans to then-CEO, Bernie Ebbers.

The Enron and WorldCom accounting scandals had such devastating effects that they led Congress to pass the Sarbanes–Oxley Act of 2002 (SOX). SOX requires public companies to evaluate their internal control and to publish those findings with their SEC filings.

Internal control is the process designed to ensure reliable financial reporting, effective and efficient operations, and compliance with applicable laws and regulations. Safeguarding assets against theft and unauthorized use, acquisition, or disposal is also part of internal control.

Section 404 of Sarbanes–Oxley requires a statement of management's responsibility for establishing and maintaining adequate internal control over financial reporting by public companies. This section includes an assessment of the controls and the identification of the framework used for the assessment. The framework established by the Committee of Sponsoring Organizations (COSO) of the Treadway Commission in 1992 is the de facto standard by which SOX compliance is judged. COSO's framework, titled *Internal Control—An Integrated Framework,* recognizes five interrelated components, including:

©Charles Bennett/AP Images

1. *Control Environment.* The integrity and ethical values of the company, including its code of conduct, involvement of the board of directors, and other actions that set the tone of the organization.

2. *Risk Assessment.* Management's process of identifying potential risks that could result in misstated financial statements and developing actions to address those risks.

3. *Control Activities.* These are the activities usually thought of as "the internal controls." They include such things as segregation of duties, account reconciliations, and information processing controls designed to safeguard assets and enable an organization to prepare reliable financial statements in a timely manner.

4. *Information and Communication.* The internal and external reporting process, including an assessment of the technology environment.

5. *Monitoring.* Assessing the quality of a company's internal control over time and taking actions as necessary to ensure it continues to address the risks of the organization.

In 2004, COSO updated the framework to help entities design and implement effective enterprisewide approaches to risk management. The updated document is titled *Enterprise Risk Management (ERM)—An Integrated Framework.* The ERM framework introduces an enterprisewide approach to risk management, as well as concepts such as risk appetite, risk tolerance, and portfolio view. While SOX applies only to U.S. public companies, the ERM framework has been adopted by both public and private organizations around the world.

The ERM framework does not replace the internal control framework. Instead, it incorporates the internal control framework within it. Accordingly, companies may decide to look to the ERM framework both to satisfy their internal control needs and to move toward a fuller risk management process.

While a detailed discussion of the COSO documents is beyond the scope of this text, the following overview of the more common *control activities* of the internal control framework is insightful.

Segregation of Duties

The likelihood of fraud or theft is reduced if employees must work together to accomplish it. Clear **segregation of duties** is frequently used as a deterrent to corruption. When duties are segregated, the work of one employee can act as a check on the work of another employee. For example, a person selling seats to a movie may be tempted to steal money received from customers who enter the theater. This temptation is reduced if the person staffing the box office is required to issue tickets that a second employee collects as people enter the theater. If ticket stubs collected by the second employee are compared with the cash receipts from ticket sales, any cash shortages will become apparent. Furthermore, friends and relatives of the ticket agent cannot easily enter the theater without paying. Theft or unauthorized entry would require collusion between the ticket agent and the usher who collects the tickets. Both individuals would have to be dishonest enough to steal, yet trustworthy enough to convince each other they would keep the embezzlement secret. Whenever possible, the functions of *authorization, recording,* and *custody of assets* should be performed by separate individuals.

Quality of Employees

A business is only as good as the people it employs. Cheap labor is not a bargain if the employees are incompetent. Employees should be properly trained. In fact, they should be trained to perform a variety of tasks. The ability of employees to substitute for one another prevents disruptions when co-workers are absent because of illnesses, vacations, or other commitments. The capacity to rotate jobs also relieves boredom and increases respect for the contributions of other employees. Every business should strive to maximize the productivity of every employee. Ongoing training programs are essential to a strong system of internal control.

Bonded Employees

The best way to ensure employee honesty is to hire individuals with *high levels of personal integrity.* Employers should screen job applicants using interviews, background checks, and recommendations from prior employers or educators. Even so, screening programs may fail to identify character weaknesses. Further, unusual circumstances may cause honest employees to go astray. Therefore, employees in positions of trust should be bonded. A **fidelity bond** provides insurance that protects a company from losses caused by employee dishonesty.

Required Absences

Employees should be required to take regular vacations and their duties should be rotated periodically. Employees may be able to cover up fraudulent activities if they are always present at work. Consider the case of a parking meter collection agent who covered the same route for several years with no vacation. When the agent became sick, a substitute collected more money each day than the regular reader usually reported. Management checked past records and found that the ill meter reader had been understating the cash receipts and pocketing the difference. If management had required vacations or rotated the routes, the embezzlement would have been discovered much earlier.

Procedures Manual

Appropriate accounting procedures should be documented in a **procedures manual.** The manual should be routinely updated. Periodic reviews should be conducted to ensure that employees are following the procedures outlined in the manual.

Authority and Responsibility

Employees are motivated by clear lines of authority and responsibility. They work harder when they have the authority to use their own judgment, and they exercise reasonable caution when they are held responsible for their actions. Businesses should prepare an **authority manual** that establishes a definitive *chain of command.* The authority manual should guide both specific and general authorizations. **Specific authorizations** apply to specific positions within the organization. For example, investment decisions are authorized at the division level, while hiring decisions are authorized at the departmental level. In contrast, **general authority** applies across different levels of management. For example, employees at all levels may be required to fly economy class or to make purchases from specific vendors.

Prenumbered Documents

How would you know if a check were stolen from your checkbook? If you keep a record of your check numbers, the missing number would tip you off immediately. Businesses also use prenumbered checks to avoid the unauthorized use of their bank accounts. In fact, prenumbered forms are used for all important documents such as purchase orders, receiving reports, invoices, and checks. To reduce errors, prenumbered forms should be as simple and easy to use as possible. Also, the documents should allow for authorized signatures. For example, credit sales slips should be signed by the customer to clearly establish who made the purchase, reducing the likelihood of unauthorized transactions.

Physical Control

Employees walk away with billions of dollars of business assets each year. To limit losses, companies should establish adequate physical control over valuable assets. For example, inventory should be kept in a storeroom and not released without proper authorization. Serial numbers on equipment should be recorded along with the name of the individual who is responsible for the equipment. Unannounced physical counts should be conducted randomly to verify the presence of company-owned equipment. Certificates of deposit and marketable securities should be kept in fireproof vaults. Access to these vaults should be limited to authorized personnel. These procedures protect the documents from fire and limit access to only those individuals who have the appropriate security clearance to handle the documents.

In addition to safeguarding assets, there should be physical control over the accounting records. The accounting journals, ledgers, and supporting documents should be kept in a fireproof safe. Only personnel responsible for recording transactions in the journals should have access to them. With limited access, there is less chance that someone will change the records to conceal fraud or embezzlement.

Performance Evaluations

Because few people can evaluate their own performance objectively, internal controls should include independent verification of employee performance. For example, someone other than the person who has control over inventory should take a physical count of inventory. Internal and external audits serve as independent verification of performance. Auditors should evaluate the effectiveness of the internal control system, as well as verify the accuracy of the accounting records. In addition, the external auditors attest to the company's use of generally accepted accounting principles in the financial statements.

Limitations

A system of internal controls is designed to prevent or detect errors and fraud. However, no control system is foolproof. Internal controls can be circumvented by collusion among employees. Two or more employees working together can hide embezzlement by covering for each other. For example, if an embezzler goes on vacation, fraud will not be reported by a replacement who is in collusion with the embezzler. No system can prevent all fraud. However, a good system of internal controls minimizes illegal or unethical activities by reducing temptation and increasing the likelihood of early detection.

CHECK YOURSELF 6.1

What are nine features of an internal control system?

Answer The nine features follow:

1. Separating duties so that fraud or theft requires collusion.
2. Hiring and training competent employees.
3. Bonding employees to recover losses through insurance.
4. Requiring employees to be absent from their jobs so that their replacements can discover errors or fraudulent activity that might have occurred.
5. Establishing proper procedures for processing transactions.
6. Establishing clear lines of authority and responsibility.
7. Using prenumbered documents.
8. Implementing physical controls such as locking cash in a safe.
9. Conducting performance evaluations through independent internal and external audits.

ACCOUNTING FOR CASH

For financial reporting purposes, **cash** generally includes currency and other items that are payable *on demand*, such as checks, money orders, bank drafts, and certain savings accounts. Savings accounts that impose substantial penalties for early withdrawal should be classified as *investments* rather than cash. Postdated checks or IOUs represent *receivables* and should not be included in cash. As illustrated in Exhibit 6.1, most companies combine currency and other receivable-on-demand items in a single balance sheet account with varying titles.

Companies must maintain a sufficient amount of cash to pay employees, suppliers, and other creditors. When a company fails to pay its legal obligations, its creditors can force the company into bankruptcy. Even so, management should avoid accumulating more cash than is needed. The failure to invest excess cash in earning assets reduces profitability. Cash inflows and outflows must be managed to prevent a shortage or surplus of cash.

LO 6-2

Identify special internal controls for cash.

Controlling Cash

Controlling cash, more than any other asset, requires strict adherence to internal control procedures. Cash has universal appeal. A relatively small suitcase filled with high-denomination currency can represent significant value. Furthermore, the rightful owner of currency is difficult to prove. In most cases, possession constitutes ownership. As a result, cash is highly susceptible to theft and must be carefully protected. Cash is most susceptible to embezzlement when it is received or disbursed. The following controls should be employed to reduce the likelihood of theft.

Cash Receipts

A record of all cash collections should be prepared immediately upon receipt. The amount of cash on hand should be counted regularly. Missing amounts of money can be detected by comparing the actual cash on hand with the book balance. Employees who receive cash should give customers a copy of a written receipt. Customers usually review their receipts to ensure they have gotten credit for the amount paid and call any errors to the receipts clerk's attention. This not only reduces errors but also provides a control on the clerk's honesty. Cash receipts should be deposited in a bank on a timely basis. Cash collected late in the day should be deposited in a night depository. Every effort should be made to minimize the amount of cash on hand. Keeping large amounts of cash on hand not only increases the risk of loss from theft but also places employees in danger of being harmed by criminals who may be tempted to rob the company.

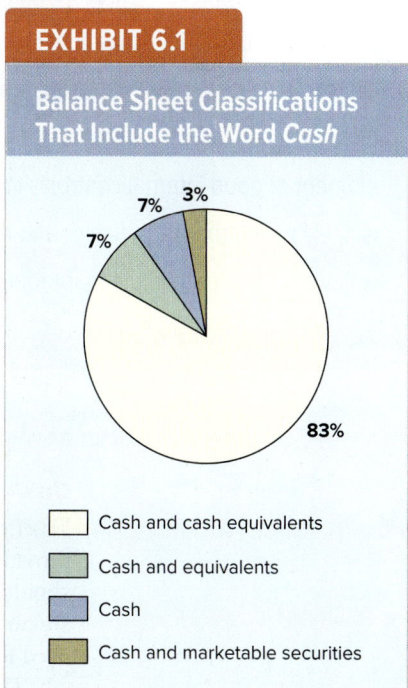

EXHIBIT 6.1

Balance Sheet Classifications That Include the Word *Cash*

- Cash and cash equivalents
- Cash and equivalents
- Cash
- Cash and marketable securities

Note: The chart is based on data drawn from the recent annual reports published by the 30 companies that comprise the Dow Jones Industrial Average.

Answers to The Curious Accountant

©Hirotaka Ihara/123RF

The Sarbanes–Oxley Act (SOX) placed a lot of emphasis on companies having a good system of internal controls, primarily to ensure proper financial reporting. But SOX was intended mostly to protect a company's investors, not its customers. Fraud that involves providing misleading information on emissions tests is not a financial reporting issue, but it can lead to financial problems. As this chapter has explained, good internal controls are about more than accurate financial reporting; they should also protect the company's resources, and customers are a major company resource.

The fraud that occurred at **Volkswagen** was bad for customers and the environment, but it was very costly to the company and its investors. By early 2017, *The Wall Street Journal* estimated that the emissions scandal would ultimately cost VW over $25 billion in direct compensation to car owners and fines to governments. This figure does not include the potential cost of lost sales. As a point of reference, in 2014, the year before the scandal became public news, VW's net earnings were approximately $12 billion. As for stock investors, in the two years from February 2, 2015, until February 2, 2017, VW's stock price fell by 29.4 percent. During this same period, the Standard and Poor's 500 index rose by 10.8 percent.

The problem at VW did not occur overnight, nor was it the work of one employee. VW initiated its "clean diesel" program in 2008, and as early as 2009, emissions-defeating devices had already been installed in cars. By early 2017, 37 officials at VW were under investigation, including its former CEO, Martin Winterkorn. Another executive had been arrested in the United States. The CEO at Bosch, a parts supplier for VW, was also alleged to have known about the scheme, and **Bosch** agreed to pay $327.5 million to settle claims that it assisted in developing the software used to defeat emissions tests. One element of good internal control is to have a separation of duties so that if one person is behaving inappropriately, another is likely to see the misbehavior and take corrective action. This system does not work if many high-level employees are all willing to participate in the inappropriate behavior. Even the best systems of internal controls still rely on people.

Source: The emissions testing problems for VW vehicles was reported widely in the press. The specifics for this Curious Accountant were from online postings of *The Wall Street Journal* dated January 9, 11, and 27, 2017.

Cash Payments

To effectively control cash, a company should make all disbursements using checks, thereby providing a record of cash payments. All checks should be prenumbered, and unused checks should be locked up. Using prenumbered checks allows companies to easily identify lost or stolen checks by comparing the numbers on unused and canceled checks with the numbers used for legitimate disbursements.

The duties of approving disbursements, signing checks, and recording transactions should be segregated. If one person is authorized to approve, sign, and record checks, he or she could falsify supporting documents, write an unauthorized check, and record a cover-up transaction in the accounting records. By separating these duties, the check signer reviews the documentation provided

REALITY BYTES

THE COST OF PROTECTING CASH

Could you afford to buy a safe like the one shown here? The vault is only one of many expensive security devices used by banks to safeguard cash. By using checking accounts, companies are able to avoid many of the costs associated with keeping cash safe. In addition to providing physical control, checking accounts enable companies to maintain a written audit trail of cash receipts and payments. Checking accounts represent the most widely used internal control device in modern society. It is difficult to imagine a business operating without the use of checking accounts.

©Digital Vision/Getty Images RF

by the approving individual before signing the check. Likewise, the recording clerk reviews the work of both the approving person and the check signer when the disbursement is recorded in the accounting records. Thus, writing unauthorized checks requires trilevel collusion.

Supporting documents with authorized approval signatures should be required when checks are presented to the check signer. For example, a warehouse receiving order should be matched with a purchase order before a check is approved to pay a bill from a supplier. Before payments are approved, invoice amounts should be checked and payees verified as valid vendors. Matching supporting documents with proper authorization discourages employees from creating phony documents for a disbursement to a friend or fictitious business. Also, the approval process serves as a check on the accuracy of the work of all employees involved.

Supporting documents should be marked *Paid* when the check is signed. If the documents are not indelibly marked, they could be retrieved from the files and resubmitted for a duplicate unauthorized payment. A payables clerk could collude with the payee to split extra cash paid out by submitting the same supporting documents for a second payment.

All spoiled and voided checks should be defaced and retained. If defaced checks are not retained, an employee could steal a check and then claim it was written incorrectly and thrown away. The clerk could then use the stolen check to make an unauthorized payment.

Checking Account Documents

The previous section explained the need for businesses to use checking accounts. Next, we will describe the four main types of forms associated with a bank checking account.

Signature Card

A bank **signature card** shows the bank account number and the signatures of the people authorized to sign checks. The card is retained in the bank's files. If a bank employee is unfamiliar with the signature on a check, he or she can refer to the signature card to verify the signature before cashing the check.

Deposit Ticket

Each deposit of cash or checks is accompanied by a **deposit ticket,** which normally identifies the account number and the name of the account. The depositor lists the individual amounts of currency, coins, and checks, as well as the total deposited, on the deposit ticket.

Bank Check

A written check affects three parties: (1) the person or business writing the check (the *payer*); (2) the bank on which the check is drawn; and (3) the person or business to whom the check is payable (the *payee*). Companies often write **checks** using multicopy, prenumbered forms, with the name of the issuing business preprinted on the face of each check. A remittance notice is usually attached to the check forms. This portion of the form provides the issuer space to record what the check is for (e.g., what invoices are being paid), the amount being disbursed, and the date of payment. When signed by the person whose signature is on the signature card, the check authorizes the bank to transfer the face amount of the check from the payer's account to the payee.

Bank Statement

Periodically, the bank sends the depositor a **bank statement.** The bank statement is presented from the bank's point of view. Checking accounts are liabilities to a bank because the bank is obligated to pay back the money that customers have deposited in their accounts. Therefore, in the bank's accounting records a customer's checking account has a *credit* balance. As a result, **bank statement debit memos** describe transactions that reduce the customer's account balance (the bank's liability). **Bank statement credit memos** describe activities that increase the customer's account balance (the bank's liability). Because a checking account is an asset (cash) to the depositor, a *bank statement debit memo* requires a *credit entry* to the Cash account on the depositor's books. Likewise, when a bank tells you it has credited your account, you will debit your Cash account in response.

Bank statements normally report (a) the balance of the account at the beginning of the period; (b) additions for customer deposits made during the period; (c) other additions described in credit memos (e.g., for interest earned); (d) subtractions for the payment of checks drawn on the account during the period; (e) other subtractions described in debit memos (e.g., for service charges); (f) a running balance of the account; and (g) the balance of the account at the end of the period. The sample bank statement in Exhibit 6.2 illustrates these items with references to the preceding letters in parentheses.

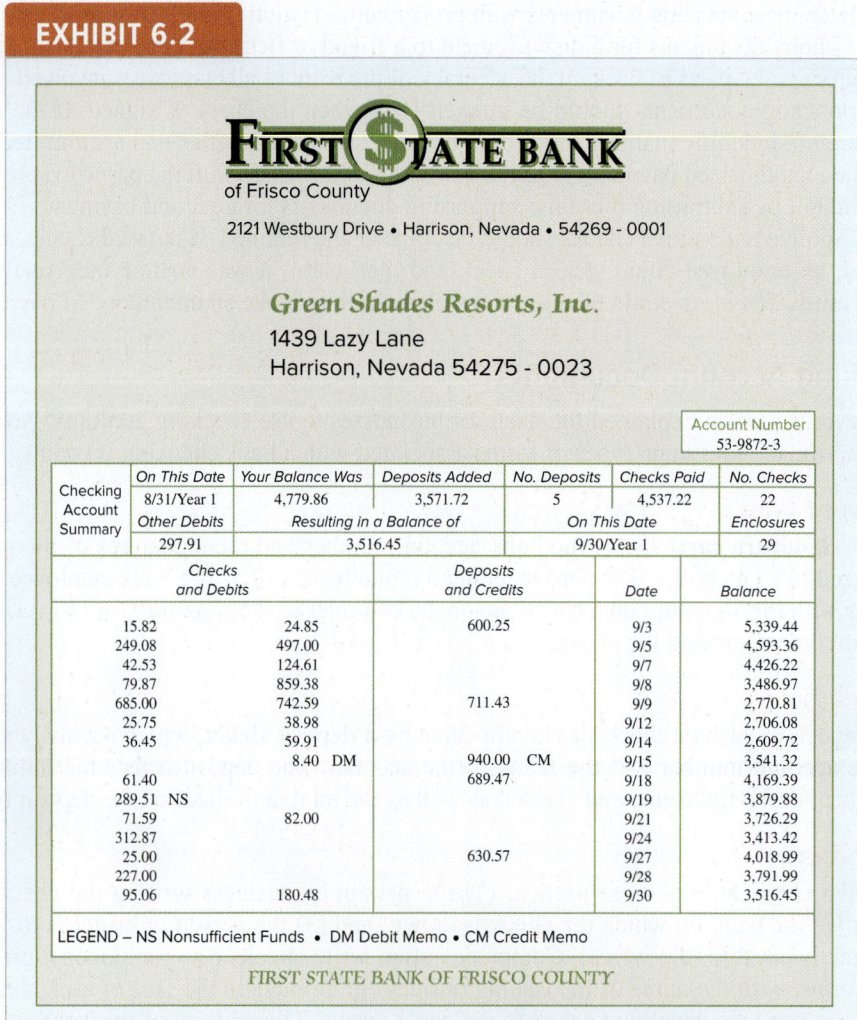

EXHIBIT 6.2

RECONCILING THE BANK ACCOUNT

Usually the ending balance reported on the bank statement differs from the balance in the depositor's Cash account as of the same date. The discrepancy is normally attributable to timing differences. For example, a depositor deducts the amount of a check from its Cash account when it writes the check. However, the bank does not deduct the amount of the check from the depositor's account until the payee presents it for payment, which may be days, weeks, or even months after the check is written. As a result, the balance on the depositor's books is lower than the balance on the bank's books. Companies prepare a **bank reconciliation** to explain the differences between the cash balance reported on the bank statement and the cash balance recorded in the depositor's accounting records.

LO 6-3

Prepare a bank reconciliation.

Determining True Cash Balance

A bank reconciliation normally begins with the cash balance reported by the bank, which is called the **unadjusted bank balance.** The adjustments necessary to determine the amount of cash that the depositor actually owns as of the date of the bank statement are then added to and subtracted from the unadjusted bank balance. The final total is the **true cash balance.** The true cash balance is independently reached a second time by making adjustments to the **unadjusted book balance.** The bank account is reconciled when the true cash balance determined from the perspective of the unadjusted *bank* balance agrees with the true cash balance determined from the perspective of the unadjusted *book* balance. The procedures a company uses to determine the *true cash balance* from the two different perspectives are outlined here.

Adjustments to the Bank Balance

A typical format for determining the true cash balance beginning with the unadjusted bank balance is

> Unadjusted bank balance
> \+ Deposits in transit
> − Outstanding checks
> = True cash balance

Deposits in Transit

Companies frequently leave deposits in the bank's night depository or make them on the day following the receipt of cash. Such deposits are called **deposits in transit.** Because these deposits have been recorded in the depositor's accounting records but have not yet been added to the depositor's account by the bank, they must be added to the unadjusted bank balance.

Outstanding Checks

These are disbursements that have been properly recorded as cash deductions on the depositor's books. However, the bank has not deducted the amounts from the depositor's bank account because the checks have not yet been presented by the payee to the bank for payment; that is, the checks have not cleared the bank. **Outstanding checks** must be subtracted from the unadjusted bank balance to determine the true cash balance.

Adjustments to the Book Balance

A typical format for determining the true cash balance beginning with the unadjusted book balance is as follows:

> Unadjusted book balance
> \+ Accounts receivable collections
> \+ Interest earned
> − Bank service charges
> − Non-sufficient-funds (NSF) checks
> = True cash balance

Accounts Receivable Collections

To collect cash as quickly as possible, many companies have their customers send payments directly to the bank. The bank adds the collection directly to the depositor's account and notifies the depositor about the collection through a credit memo that is included on the bank statement. The depositor adds the amount of the cash collections to the unadjusted book balance in the process of determining the true cash balance.

Interest Earned

Banks pay interest on certain checking accounts. The amount of the interest is added directly to the depositor's bank account. The bank notifies the depositor about the interest through a credit memo that is included on the bank statement. The depositor adds the amount of the interest revenue to the unadjusted book balance in the process of determining the true cash balance.

Service Charges

Banks frequently charge depositors fees for services performed. They may also charge a penalty if the depositor fails to maintain a specified minimum cash balance throughout the period. Banks deduct such fees and penalties directly from the depositor's account and advise the depositor of the deduction through a debit memo that is included on the bank statement. The depositor deducts such **service charges** from the unadjusted book balance to determine the true cash balance.

Non-Sufficient-Funds (NSF) Checks

Non-sufficient-funds (NSF) checks are checks that a company obtains from its customers and deposits in its checking account. However, when the checks are submitted to the customers' banks for payment, the banks refuse payment because there is insufficient money in the customers' accounts. When such checks are returned, the amounts of the checks are deducted from the company's bank account balance. The company is advised of NSF checks through debit memos that appear on the bank statement. The depositor deducts the amounts of the NSF checks from the unadjusted book balance in the process of determining the true cash balance.

Correction of Errors

In the course of reconciling the bank statement with the Cash account, the depositor may discover errors in the bank's records, the depositor's records, or both. If an error is found on the bank statement, an adjustment for it is made to the unadjusted bank balance to determine the true cash balance, and the bank should be notified immediately to correct its records. Errors made by the depositor require adjustments to the book balance to arrive at the true cash balance.

©Ryan McVay/Getty Images RF

Certified Checks

A **certified check** is guaranteed for payment by a bank. Whereas a regular check is deducted from the customer's account when it is presented for payment, a certified check is deducted from the customer's account when the bank certifies that the check is good. Certified checks, therefore, *have* been deducted by the bank in determining the unadjusted bank balance, whether they have cleared the bank or remain outstanding as of the date of the bank statement. Because certified checks are deducted both from bank and depositor records immediately, they do not cause differences between the depositor and bank balances. As a result, certified checks are not included in a bank reconciliation.

Illustrating a Bank Reconciliation

The following example illustrates a bank reconciliation for Green Shades Resorts, Inc. (GSRI). The bank statement for GSRI is displayed in Exhibit 6.2. Exhibit 6.3 illustrates the completed bank reconciliation. The items on the reconciliation are described in the discussion that follows.

Adjustments to the Bank Balance

As of September 30, Year 1, the bank statement showed an unadjusted balance of $3,516.45. A review of the bank statement disclosed three adjustments that had to be made to the unadjusted bank balance to determine GSRI's true cash balance.

1. Comparing the deposits on the bank statement with deposits recorded in GSRI's accounting records indicated there was $724.11 of deposits in transit.
2. An examination of the returned checks disclosed that the bank had erroneously deducted a $25 check written by Green Valley Resorts from GSRI's bank account. This amount must be added back to the unadjusted bank balance to determine the true cash balance.
3. The checks returned with the bank statement were sorted and compared to the cash records. Three checks with amounts totaling $235.25 were outstanding.

After these adjustment are made, GSRI's true cash balance is determined to be $4,030.31.

Adjustments to the Book Balance

As indicated in Exhibit 6.3, GSRI's unadjusted book balance as of September 30, Year 1, was $3,361.22. This balance differs from GSRI's true cash balance because of four unrecorded accounting events:

1. The bank collected a $940 account receivable for GSRI.
2. GSRI's accountant made a $27 recording error.

EXHIBIT 6.3

GREEN SHADES RESORTS, INC.
Bank Reconciliation
September 30, Year 1

Unadjusted bank balance, September 30, Year 1	$3,516.45
Add: Deposits in transit	724.11
Bank error: Check drawn on Green Valley Resorts charged to GSRI	25.00
Less: Outstanding checks	

Check No.	Date	Amount
639	Sept. 18	$ 13.75
646	Sept. 20	29.00
672	Sept. 27	192.50

Total	(235.25)
True cash balance, September 30, Year 1	$4,030.31
Unadjusted book balance, September 30, Year 1	$3,361.22
Add: Receivable collected by bank	940.00
Error made by accountant (Check no. 633 recorded as $63.45 instead of $36.45)	27.00
Less: Bank service charges	(8.40)
NSF check	(289.51)
True cash balance, September 30, Year 1	$4,030.31

3. The bank charged GSRI an $8.40 service fee.
4. GSRI had deposited a $289.51 check from a customer who did not have sufficient funds to cover the check.

Two of these four adjustments increase the unadjusted cash balance. The other two decrease the unadjusted cash balance. After the adjustments have been recorded, the Cash account reflects the true cash balance of $4,030.31 ($3,361.22 unadjusted cash balance + $940.00 receivable collection + $27.00 recording error − $8.40 service charge − $289.51 NSF check). Because the true balance determined from the perspective of the bank statement agrees with the true balance determined from the perspective of GSRI's books, the bank statement has been successfully reconciled with the accounting records.

Updating GSRI's Accounting Records

Each of the adjustments to the book balance must be recorded in GSRI's financial records. The effects of each adjustment on the financial statements are as follows:

ADJUSTMENT 1 Recording the $940 receivable collection increases Cash and reduces Accounts Receivable.

The event is an asset exchange transaction. The journal entry and its effects on the financial statements are shown next:

Account Title	Debit	Credit
Cash	940.00	
Accounts Receivable		940.00

Assets			=	Liab.	+	Equity	Rev.	−	Exp.	=	Net Inc.	Cash Flow
Cash	+	Accts. Rec.										
940.00	+	(940.00)	=	NA	+	NA	NA	−	NA	=	NA	940.00 OA

ADJUSTMENT 2 Assume the $27 recording error occurred because GSRI's accountant accidentally transposed two numbers when recording check no. 633 for utilities expense.

The check was written to pay utilities expense of $36.45 but was recorded as a $63.45 disbursement. Because cash payments are overstated by $27.00 ($63.45 − $36.45), this amount must be added back to GSRI's Cash balance and deducted from the Utilities Expense account, which increases net income. The journal entry and its effects on the financial statements are shown next:

Account Title	Debit	Credit
Cash	27.00	
Utilities Expense		27.00

Assets	=	Liab.	+	Equity	Rev.	−	Exp.	=	Net Inc.	Cash Flow
Cash	=			Ret. Earn.						
27.00	=	NA	+	27.00	NA	−	(27.00)	=	27.00	27.00 OA

ADJUSTMENT 3 The $8.40 service charge is an expense that reduces assets, stockholders' equity, net income, and cash.

The journal entry and its effects on the financial statements are shown next:

Account Title	Debit	Credit
Bank Service Charge Expense	8.40	
Cash		8.40

Assets	=	Liab.	+	Equity	Rev.	−	Exp.	=	Net Inc.	Cash Flow
Cash	=			Ret. Earn.						
(8.40)	=	NA	+	(8.40)	NA	−	8.40	=	(8.40)	(8.40) OA

ADJUSTMENT 4 The $289.51 NSF check reduces GSRI's cash balance.

When it originally accepted the customer's check, GSRI increased its Cash account. Because there is not enough money in the customer's bank account to pay the check, GSRI didn't actually receive cash, so GSRI must reduce its Cash account. GSRI will still try to collect the money from the customer. In the meantime, it will show the amount of the NSF check as an account receivable. The adjusting entry to record the NSF check is an asset exchange transaction. Cash decreases and Accounts Receivable increases. The journal entry and its effects on the financial statements are shown next:

Account Title	Debit	Credit
Accounts Receivable	289.51	
Cash		289.51

Assets			=	Liab.	+	Equity	Rev.	−	Exp.	=	Net Inc.	Cash Flow
Cash	+	Accts. Rec.										
(289.51)	+	289.51	=	NA	+	NA	NA	−	NA	=	NA	(289.51) OA

Cash Short and Over

Sometimes employees make mistakes when collecting cash from or making change for customers. When such errors occur, the amount of money in the cash register will not agree with the amount of cash receipts recorded on the cash register tape. For example, suppose that when a customer paid for $17.95 of merchandise with a $20 bill, the sales clerk returned $3.05 in change instead of $2.05. If, at the end of the day, the cash register tape shows total receipts of $487.50, the cash drawer would contain only $486.50. The actual cash balance is less than the expected cash balance by $1. Any shortage of cash or excess of cash is recorded in a special account called **Cash Short and Over.** In this example, the shortage is recorded with the following journal entry:

Account Title	Debit	Credit
Cash	486.50	
Cash Short and Over	1.00	
Sales		487.50

A cash shortage is an expense. It is recorded by debiting the Cash Short and Over account. An overage of cash represents revenue and is recorded by crediting the Cash Short and Over account. As with other expense and revenue items, the balance of the Cash Short and Over account is closed to the Retained Earnings account at the end of the accounting period.

CHECK YOURSELF 6.2

The following information was drawn from Reliance Company's October bank statement. The unadjusted bank balance on October 31 was $2,300. The statement showed that the bank had collected a $200 account receivable for Reliance. The statement also included $20 of bank service charges for October and a $100 check payable to Reliance that was returned NSF. A comparison of the bank statement with company accounting records indicates that there was a $500 deposit in transit and $1,800 of checks outstanding at the end of the month. Based on this information, determine the true cash balance on October 31.

Answer Because the unadjusted book balance is not given, start with the unadjusted bank balance to determine the true cash balance. The collection of the receivable, the bank service charges, and the NSF check are already recognized in the unadjusted bank balance, so these items are not used to determine the true cash balance. To determine the true cash balance, add the deposit in transit to the unadjusted bank balance and then subtract the outstanding checks. The true cash balance is $1,000 ($2,300 unadjusted bank balance + $500 deposit in transit − $1,800 outstanding checks).

USING PETTY CASH FUNDS

LO 6-4

Show how a petty cash fund affects financial statements.

Although businesses use checks for most disbursements, they often pay for small items such as postage, delivery charges, taxi fares, employees' supper money, and so on with currency. They frequently establish a **petty cash fund** to maintain effective control over these small cash disbursements. The fund is established for a specified dollar amount, such as $300, and is controlled by one employee, called the *petty cash custodian*.

Petty cash funds are usually maintained on an **imprest basis,** which means that the money disbursed is periodically replenished. The fund is created by drawing a check on the regular checking account, cashing it, and giving the currency to the petty cash custodian. The custodian normally keeps the currency under lock and key. The amount of the petty cash fund depends on what it is used for, how often it is used, and how often it is replenished. It should be large enough to handle disbursements for a reasonable time period, such as several weeks or a month.

Establishing a petty cash fund merely transfers money from a bank to a safety box inside the company offices. The establishment is an asset exchange event. The Cash account decreases, and an account called Petty Cash increases. The journal entry and its effects on the financial statements are shown next:

Account Title	Debit	Credit
Petty Cash	300.00	
Cash		300.00

Assets	=	Liab.	+	Equity	Rev.	−	Exp.	=	Net Inc.	Cash Flow
Cash + Petty Cash										
(300.00) + 300.00	=	NA	+	NA	NA	−	NA	=	NA	NA

EXHIBIT 6.4

Petty cash voucher no. _____

To: _____ Date _____, 20___

Explanation: Account No. _____   Amount _____

Approved by _____   Received by _____

When money is disbursed from the petty cash fund, the custodian should complete a **petty cash voucher,** such as the one in Exhibit 6.4. Any supporting documents, such as an invoice, restaurant bill, or parking fee receipt, should be attached to the petty cash voucher. The person who receives the currency should sign the voucher as evidence of receiving the money. The total of the amounts recorded on the petty cash vouchers plus the remaining coins and currency should equal the balance of the petty cash ledger account. *No journal entry is made in the accounting records when petty cash funds are disbursed.* The effects on the financial statements are recorded only when the petty cash fund is replenished or increased (when additional currency is put into the petty cash safety box).

When the amount of currency in the petty cash fund is relatively low, the fund is replenished. The petty cash vouchers are totaled, the amount of any cash short or over is determined, and a check is issued to the bank to obtain the currency needed to return the fund to its imprest balance. For example, suppose the $300 petty cash fund is replenished when the total of the petty cash vouchers is $216. The vouchers can be classified according to different types of expenses or listed in total as miscellaneous expense. Assuming the company classifies petty cash expenditures as miscellaneous expense, the journal entries to record replenishing the fund are as follows:

Account Title	Debit	Credit
Miscellaneous Expense	216.00	
Petty Cash		216.00
To record expenses paid from the petty cash fund		
Petty Cash	216.00	
Cash		216.00
To replenish the petty cash fund		

If desired, the effect of the entries could be recorded more efficiently. Because the credit to the Petty Cash account is offset by a debit to the same account, a single entry debiting miscellaneous expense and crediting cash would have the same effect on the accounts. The entry more frequently used in practice to record replenishing petty cash is

Account Title	Debit	Credit
Miscellaneous Expense	216.00	
Cash		216.00

The replenishment affects the financial statements in the same manner as any other cash expense. It reduces assets, stockholders' equity, net income, and cash flow, as follows:

Assets	=	Liab.	+	Equity	Rev.	−	Exp.	=	Net Inc.	Cash Flow
Cash	=			Ret. Earn.						
(216.00)	=	NA	+	(216.00)	NA	−	216.00	=	(216.00)	(216.00) OA

If management desires more detailed information about petty cash expenditures, the vouchers can be sorted into postage, $66; delivery charges, $78.40; taxi fares, $28; and supper money, $43.60, in which case the journal entry to replenish the fund would be recorded as follows:

Account Title	Debit	Credit
Postage Expense	66.00	
Delivery Expense	78.40	
Taxi Fares Expense	28.00	
Employee Meal Expense	43.60	
Cash		216.00

Once the vouchers are checked, the fund replenished, and the journal entry recorded, the vouchers should be indelibly marked *Paid* so they cannot be reused.

Sometimes, cash shortages and overages are discovered when the money in the petty cash fund is physically counted. Suppose that a physical count discloses $212.30 in petty cash vouchers and only $87 in currency and coins. Assuming an imprest petty cash balance of $300, the journal entry necessary to replenish the fund is as follows:

Account Title	Debit	Credit
Miscellaneous Expense	212.30	
Cash Short and Over	.70	
Cash		213.00
To replenish the petty cash fund		

If cash shortages or overages do not occur frequently and are of insignificant amounts, companies are likely to include them in miscellaneous expense or miscellaneous revenue.

CHECK YOURSELF 6.3

Cornerstone Corporation established a $400 petty cash fund that was replenished when it contained $30 of currency and coins and $378 of receipts for miscellaneous expenses. Based on this information, determine the amount of cash short or over to be recognized. Explain how the shortage or overage would be reported in the financial statements. Also determine the amount of petty cash expenses that were recognized when the fund was replenished.

Answer The fund contained $408 of currency and receipts ($30 currency + $378 of receipts), resulting in a cash overage of $8 ($408 − $400). The overage would be reported as miscellaneous revenue on the income statement. The amount of petty cash expenses recognized would equal the amount of the expense receipts, which is $378.

The Financial Analyst

Companies communicate information to analysts and other users through a document called the *annual report*. These reports are usually printed in color on high-quality paper and contain lots of photographs. However, in an effort to reduce cost, some companies issue their annual reports in black and white on low-grade paper or in electronic form. A company's annual report contains much more than the financial statements. Annual reports often have 40 or more pages. The financial statements require only four to six pages. What is printed on all those other pages? In general, the annual report of a large company has four major sections: (1) financial statements, (2) notes to the financial statements, (3) management's discussion and analysis, and (4) auditors' report. The notes and management's discussion and analysis make up the bulk of the report.

LO 6-5

 Describe the auditor's role in financial reporting.

Notes to the Financial Statements

Accountants frequently have to make estimates when preparing financial statements. Also, GAAP may offer alternative ways of reporting certain transactions. **Notes to the financial statements** explain some of the estimates that were made, as well as which reporting options were used. Reading the notes is critical to understanding the financial statements. The financial statements include a caveat such as "the accompanying notes are an integral part of these financial statements."

Management's Discussion and Analysis

Management's discussion and analysis (MD&A) is located at the beginning of the annual report. MD&A is the section of the annual report in which management explains the company's past performance and future plans. For example, MD&A typically compares current-year earnings with those of past periods and explains the reasons for significant changes. If the company is planning significant acquisitions of assets or other businesses, this information is usually included in MD&A. Likewise, any plans to discontinue part of the existing business are outlined in MD&A.

Role of the Independent Auditor

As previously explained, financial statements are prepared in accordance with certain rules called *generally accepted accounting principles (GAAP)*. Thus, when General Electric publishes its financial statements, it is saying, "here are our financial statements prepared according to GAAP." How can a financial analyst know that a company really did follow GAAP? Analysts and other statement users rely on **audits** conducted by **certified public accountants (CPAs).**

The primary roles of an independent auditor (CPA) are summarized below:

1. Conducts a financial audit (a detailed examination of a company's financial statements and underlying accounting records).
2. Assumes both legal and professional responsibilities to the public, as well as to the company paying the auditor.
3. Determines if financial statements are *materially* correct rather than *absolutely* correct.
4. Presents conclusions in an audit report that includes an opinion as to whether the statements are prepared in conformity with GAAP. In rare cases, the auditor issues a disclaimer.
5. Maintains professional confidentiality of client records. The auditor is not, however, exempt from legal obligations such as testifying in court.

The Financial Statements Audit

What is an audit? There are several different types of audits. The type most relevant to this course is a **financial statements audit.** The financial audit is a detailed examination of a company's financial statements and the documents that support those statements. It also tests the reliability of the accounting system used to produce the financial reports. A financial audit is conducted by an **independent auditor** who must be a CPA.

The term *independent auditor* typically refers to a *firm* of certified public accountants. CPAs are licensed by state governments to provide services to the public. They are to be independent of the companies they audit. To help ensure independence, CPAs may not be employees of the companies they audit. Further, they cannot have investments in the companies they audit. Although CPAs are paid by the companies they audit, the audit fee may not be based on the outcome of the audit.

Although the independent auditors are chosen by, paid by, and can be fired by their client companies, the auditors are primarily responsible to *the public*. In fact, auditors have a legal responsibility to those members of the public who have a financial interest in the company being audited. If investors in a company lose money, they sometimes sue the independent auditors in an attempt to recover their losses, especially if the losses were related to financial failure. A lawsuit against auditors will succeed only if the auditors failed in their professional responsibilities when conducting the audit. Auditors are not responsible for the success or failure of a company. Instead, they are responsible for the appropriate auditing of the reporting of that success or failure. While recent debacles such as Bernard Madoff Investments produce spectacular headlines, auditors are actually not sued very often, considering the number of audits they perform.

Materiality and Financial Statements Audits

Auditors do not guarantee that financial statements are absolutely correct—only that they are *materially* correct. This is where things get a little fuzzy. What is a *material error?* The concept of materiality is very subjective. If **Walmart** inadvertently overstated its sales by $1 million, would this be material? In its 2016 fiscal year, Walmart had approximately $486 billion of sales! A $1 million error in computing sales at Walmart is like a $1 error in computing the pay of a person who makes $486,000 per year—not material at all! An error, or other reporting problem, is **material** if knowing about it would influence the decisions of an *average prudent investor*.

Financial audits are not directed toward the discovery of fraud. Auditors are, however, responsible for providing *reasonable assurance* that statements are free from material misstatements, whether caused by errors or fraud. Also, auditors are responsible for evaluating whether internal control procedures are in place to help prevent fraud. If fraud is widespread in a company, normal audit procedures should detect it.

Accounting majors take at least one and often two or more courses in auditing to understand how to conduct an audit. An explanation of auditing techniques is beyond the scope of this course, but at least be aware that auditors do not review how the company accounted for every transaction. Along with other methods, auditors use statistics to choose representative samples of transactions to examine.

Types of Audit Opinions

Once an audit is complete, the auditors present their conclusions in a report that includes an *audit opinion*. There are three basic types of audit opinions.

An **unqualified opinion,** despite its negative-sounding name, is the most favorable opinion auditors can express. It means the auditor believes the financial statements are in compliance with GAAP without material qualification, reservation, or exception. Most audits result in unqualified opinions because companies correct any material reporting deficiencies the auditors find before the financial statements are released.

The most negative report an auditor can issue is an **adverse opinion.** An adverse opinion means that one or more departures from GAAP are so material the financial statements do not present a fair picture of the company's status. The auditor's report explains the unacceptable accounting practice(s) that resulted in the adverse opinion being issued. Adverse opinions are very rare because public companies are required by law to follow GAAP.

A **qualified opinion** falls between an unqualified and an adverse opinion. A qualified opinion means that for the most part, the company's financial statements are in compliance with GAAP, but the auditors have reservations about something in the statements. The auditors' report explains why the opinion is qualified. A qualified opinion usually does not imply a serious accounting problem, but users should read the auditors' report and draw their own conclusions.

If an auditor is unable to perform the audit procedures necessary to determine whether the statements are prepared in accordance with GAAP, the auditor cannot issue an opinion on the financial statements. Instead, the auditor issues a **disclaimer of opinion.** A disclaimer is neither negative nor positive. It simply means that the auditor is unable to obtain enough information to confirm compliance with GAAP.

Regardless of the type of report they issue, auditors are only expressing their judgment about whether the financial statements present a fair picture of a company. They do not provide opinions regarding the investment quality of a company.

The ultimate responsibility for financial statements rests with the executives of the reporting company. Just like auditors, management can be sued by investors who believe they lost money due to improper financial reporting. This is one reason all businesspersons should understand accounting fundamentals.

Confidentiality

The **confidentiality** rules in the code of ethics for CPAs prohibit auditors from *voluntarily disclosing* information they have acquired as a result of their accountant–client relationships. However, accountants may be required to testify in a court of law. In general, federal law does not recognize an accountant–client privilege, as it does with attorneys and clergy. Some federal courts have taken exception to this position, especially as it applies to tax cases. State law varies with respect to accountant–client privilege. Furthermore, if auditors terminate a client relationship because of ethical or legal disagreements and they are subsequently contacted by a successor auditor, they may be required to inform the successor of the reasons for the termination. In addition, auditors must consider the particular circumstances of a case when assessing the appropriateness of disclosing confidential information. Given the diverse legal positions governing accountant–client confidentiality, auditors should seek legal counsel prior to disclosing any information obtained in an accountant–client relationship.

To illustrate, assume that Joe Smith, CPA, discovers that his client Jane Doe is misrepresenting information reported in her financial statements. Smith tries to convince Doe to correct the misrepresentations, but she refuses to do so. Smith is required by the code of ethics to terminate his relationship with Doe. However, Smith is not permitted to disclose Doe's dishonest reporting practices unless he is called on to testify in a legal hearing or to respond to an inquiry by Doe's successor accountant.

With respect to the discovery of significant fraud, the auditor is required to inform management at least one level above the position of the employee who is engaged in the fraud and to notify the board of directors of the company. Suppose that Joe Smith, CPA, discovers that Mary Adams, employee of Western Company, is embezzling money from Western. Smith is required to inform Adams' supervisor and to notify Western's board of directors. However, Smith is prohibited from publicly disclosing the fraud.

The Securities and Exchange Commission

The annual reports of public companies often differ from those of private companies because public companies are registered with the **Securities and Exchange Commission (SEC).** Public companies, sometimes called SEC companies, have to follow the reporting rules of the SEC as well as GAAP. SEC rules require some additional disclosures not required by GAAP. For example, an MD&A section is required by the SEC, but not by GAAP. As a result, annual reports of non-SEC companies usually do not include MD&A.

The SEC is a government agency authorized to establish and enforce the accounting rules for public companies. Although the SEC can overrule GAAP, it has very seldom done so. Recall that GAAP is established by the Financial Accounting Standards Board, a private professional accounting organization. While SEC rules seldom conflict with GAAP, they frequently require additional disclosures. All companies whose stock trades on public stock exchanges, and some whose stock does not, are required to register with the SEC. The SEC has no jurisdiction over non-SEC companies.

SEC companies must file specific information directly with the SEC annually, quarterly, and in-between if required. The most common reports are filed on Form 10-K (annually) and Form 10-Q (quarterly). The 10-Qs are less detailed than the 10-Ks. While there is significant overlap between the 10-Ks (SEC report) and the annual reports that companies issue directly to the public, the 10-Ks usually contain more information but fewer photographs. Most of the reports filed with the SEC are available electronically through the SEC's EDGAR database. EDGAR is an acronym for Electronic Data Gathering, Analysis, and Retrieval, and it is accessible through the World Wide Web on the Internet. Appendix A provides instructions for using EDGAR.

The SEC regulates audit standards as well as financial reporting. Prior to passage of the Sarbanes–Oxley Act in July 2002, the SEC left much of the regulation and oversight of independent auditors to the American Institute of Certified Public Accountants, a private professional organization. However, a key provision of Sarbanes–Oxley establishes the Public Company Accounting Oversight Board (PCAOB). This board assumes the primary responsibility for establishing and enforcing auditing standards for CPA firms that audit SEC companies. The board has five financially astute members, three of whom cannot be CPAs.

A Look Back

The policies and procedures used to provide reasonable assurance that the objectives of an enterprise will be accomplished are called *internal controls,* and they can be subdivided into two categories: accounting controls and administrative controls. *Accounting controls* are composed of procedures designed to safeguard the assets and ensure that the accounting records contain reliable information. *Administrative controls* are designed to evaluate performance and the degree of compliance with company policies and public laws. While the mechanics of internal control systems vary from company to company, the more prevalent features include the following: segregation of duties, quality of employees, bonded employees, required absence, a procedures manual, authority and responsibility, prenumbered documents, physical control, and performance evaluations.

Because cash is such an important business asset and because it is tempting to steal, much of the discussion of internal controls in this chapter focused on cash controls. Special procedures should be employed to control the receipts and payments of cash. One of the most common control policies is to use *checking accounts* for all except petty cash disbursements.

A *bank reconciliation* should be prepared each month to explain differences between the bank statement and a company's internal accounting records. A common reconciliation format determines the true cash balance based on both bank and book records. Items that typically appear on a bank reconciliation include the following:

Unadjusted bank balance	xxx	Unadjusted book balance	xxx
Add		Add	
Deposits in transit	xxx	Interest revenue	xxx
		Collection of receivables	xxx
Subtract		Subtract	
Outstanding checks	xxx	Bank service charges	xxx
		NSF checks	xxx
True cash balance	xxx	True cash balance	xxx

Agreement of the two true cash balances provides evidence that accounting for cash transactions has been accurate.

Another common internal control policy for protecting cash is using a *petty cash fund.* Normally, an employee who is designated as the petty cash custodian is entrusted with a small amount of cash. The custodian reimburses employees for small expenditures made on behalf of the company in exchange for authorized receipts from the employees at the time they are reimbursed. The total of these receipts plus the remaining currency in the fund should always equal the amount of funds entrusted to the custodian. Journal entries to recognize the expenses incurred are made at the time the fund is replenished.

Finally, the chapter discussed the auditor's role in financial reporting, including the materiality concept and the types of audit opinions that may be issued.

A Look Forward

Accounting for receivables and payables was introduced in Chapter 2 using relatively simple illustrations. For example, we assumed that customers who purchased services on account always paid their bills. In real business practice, some customers do not pay their bills. Among other topics, Chapter 7 examines how companies account for uncollectible accounts receivable.

SELF-STUDY REVIEW PROBLEM

A step-by-step audio-narrated series of slides is available in **Connect.**

The following information pertains to Terry's Pest Control Company (TPCC) for July:

1. The unadjusted bank balance at July 31 was $870.
2. The bank statement included the following items:
   (a) A $60 credit memo for interest earned by TPCC.
   (b) A $200 NSF check made payable to TPCC.
   (c) A $110 debit memo for bank service charges.
3. The unadjusted book balance at July 31 was $1,400.
4. A comparison of the bank statement with company accounting records disclosed the following:
   (a) A $400 deposit in transit at July 31.
   (b) Outstanding checks totaling $120 at the end of the month.

Required

a. Prepare a bank reconciliation.
b. Prepare in general journal format the entries necessary to adjust TPCC's cash account to its true balance.

Solution to Requirement a

TERRY'S PEST CONTROL COMPANY
Bank Reconciliation
July 31

Unadjusted bank balance	$ 870
Add: Deposits in transit	400
Less: Outstanding checks	(120)
True cash balance	$ 1,150
Unadjusted book balance	$1,400
Add: Interest revenue	60
Less: NSF check	(200)
Less: Bank service charges	(110)
True cash balance	$ 1,150

Solution to Requirement b

Ref.	Account Title	Debit	Credit
1.	Cash	60	
	Interest Revenue		60
2.	Accounts Receivable	200	
	Cash		200
3.	Service Charge Expense	110	
	Cash		110

KEY TERMS

Accounting controls 316
Administrative controls 316
Adverse opinion 334
Audit 333
Authority manual 320
Bank reconciliation 325
Bank statement 324
Bank statement credit memo 324
Bank statement debit memo 324
Cash 321
Cash Short and Over 329
Certified check 326
Certified public accountant (CPA) 333
Checks 323
Confidentiality 335
Deposit ticket 323
Deposits in transit 325
Disclaimer of opinion 334
Fidelity bond 319
Financial statements audit 333

338 Chapter 6

General authority 320
Imprest basis 330
Independent auditor 333
Internal controls 316
Management's discussion and analysis (MD&A) 333
Material 334

Non-sufficient-funds (NSF) checks 326
Notes to the financial statements 333
Outstanding checks 325
Petty cash fund 330
Petty cash voucher 331

Procedures manual 319
Qualified opinion 334
Securities and Exchange Commission (SEC) 335
Segregation of duties 319
Service charges 326
Signature card 323

Specific authorizations 320
True cash balance 325
Unadjusted bank balance 325
Unadjusted book balance 325
Unqualified opinion 334

QUESTIONS

1. What motivated Congress to pass the Sarbanes–Oxley Act (SOX) of 2002?
2. Define the term *internal control*.
3. Explain the relationship between SOX and COSO.
4. Name and briefly define the five components of COSO's internal control framework.
5. Explain how COSO's *Enterprise Risk Management—An Integrated Framework* project relates to COSO's *Internal Control—An Integrated Framework* project.
6. What is the difference between accounting controls and administrative controls?
7. What are several features of an effective internal control system?
8. What is meant by *segregation of duties*? Give an illustration.
9. What are the attributes of a high-quality employee?
10. What is a fidelity bond? Explain its purpose.
11. Why is it important that every employee periodically take a leave of absence or vacation?
12. What are the purpose and importance of a procedures manual?
13. What is the difference between specific and general authorizations?
14. Why should documents (checks, invoices, receipts) be prenumbered?
15. What procedures are important in the physical control of assets and accounting records?
16. What is the purpose of independent verification of performance?
17. What items are considered cash?
18. Why is cash more susceptible to theft or embezzlement than other assets?
19. Giving written copies of receipts to customers can help prevent what type of illegal acts?
20. What procedures can help protect cash receipts?
21. What procedures can help protect cash disbursements?
22. What effect does a debit memo in a bank statement have on the Cash account? What effect does a credit memo in a bank statement have on the Cash account?
23. What information is normally included in a bank statement?
24. Why might a bank statement reflect a balance that is larger than the balance recorded in the depositor's books? What could cause the bank balance to be smaller than the book balance?
25. What is the purpose of a bank reconciliation?
26. What is an outstanding check?
27. What is a deposit in transit?
28. What is a certified check?
29. How is an NSF check accounted for in the accounting records?
30. What is the purpose of the Cash Short and Over account?
31. What is the purpose of a petty cash fund?
32. What types of expenditures are usually made from a petty cash fund?
33. What is a financial statement audit? Who is qualified to perform it?
34. What is an independent auditor? Why must auditors be independent?
35. What makes an error in the financial statements material?
36. What three basic types of auditors' opinions can be issued on audited financial statements? Describe each.
37. What are the implications of an unqualified audit opinion?
38. When might an auditor issue a disclaimer on financial statements?
39. In what circumstances can an auditor disclose confidential information about a client without the client's permission?
40. What is the purpose of internal controls in an organization?

MULTIPLE-CHOICE QUESTIONS

Multiple-choice questions are available in Connect.

EXERCISES—SERIES A

 All applicable Exercises in Series A are available in Connect.

LO 6-1

Exercise 6-1A *SOX and COSO's internal control frameworks*

Required
a. Discuss the requirements of Section 404 of the Sarbanes–Oxley Act and how it relates to COSO.
b. What type of companies do these rules apply to?

Exercise 6-2A *Features of a strong internal control system*   LO 6-1

Required

List and describe nine features of a strong internal control system discussed in this chapter.

Exercise 6-3A *Internal control procedures to prevent embezzlement*   LO 6-1

Anna Chun was in charge of the returns department at The Luggage Company. She was responsible for evaluating returned merchandise. She sent merchandise that was reusable back to the warehouse, where it was restocked in inventory. Chun was also responsible for taking the merchandise that she determined to be defective to the city dump for disposal. She had agreed to buy a friend a tax planning program at a discount through her contacts at work. That is when the idea came to her. She could simply classify one of the reusable returns as defective and bring it home instead of taking it to the dump. She did so and made a quick $150. She was happy, and her friend was ecstatic; he was able to buy a $400 software package for only $150. He told his friends about the deal, and soon Chun had a regular set of customers. She was caught when a retail store owner complained to the marketing manager that his pricing strategy was being undercut by The Luggage Company's direct sales to the public. The marketing manager was suspicious because The Luggage Company had no direct marketing program. When the outside sales were ultimately traced back to Chun, the company discovered that it had lost over $10,000 in sales revenue because of her criminal activity.

Required

Identify an internal control procedure that could have prevented the company's losses. Explain how the procedure would have stopped the embezzlement.

Exercise 6-4A *Internal control procedures to prevent deception*   LO 6-1

Regional Medical Centers (RMC) hired a new physician, Fred Clark, who was an immediate success. Everyone loved his bedside manner; he could charm the most cantankerous patient. Indeed, he was a master salesman, as well as an expert physician. Unfortunately, Clark misdiagnosed a case that resulted in serious consequences to the patient. The patient filed suit against RMC. In preparation for the defense, RMC's attorneys discovered that Clark was indeed an exceptional salesman. He had worked for several years as district marketing manager for a pharmaceutical company. In fact, he was not a physician at all! He had changed professions without going to medical school. He had lied on his application form. His knowledge of medical terminology had enabled him to fool everyone. RMC was found negligent and lost a $3 million lawsuit.

Required

Identify the relevant internal control procedures that could have prevented the company's losses. Explain how these procedures would have prevented Clark's deception.

Exercise 6-5A *Internal controls for small businesses*   LO 6-1

Required

Assume you are the owner of a small business that has only two employees.

a. Which of the internal control procedures are most important to you?
b. How can you overcome the limited opportunity to use the segregation-of-duties control procedure?

Exercise 6-6A *Internal control for cash*   LO 6-2

Required

a. Why are special controls needed for cash?
b. What is included in the definition of *cash*?

Exercise 6-7A *Treatment of NSF check*   LO 6-3

Han's Supplies' bank statement contained a $270 NSF check that one of its customers had written to pay for supplies purchased.

Required

a. Show the effects of recognizing the NSF check on the financial statements by recording the appropriate amounts in a horizontal statements model like the following one:

Assets	= Liab. + Equity	Rev. − Exp. = Net Inc.	Cash Flow
Cash + Accts. Rec.			

b. Is the recognition of the NSF check on Han's books an asset source, use, or exchange transaction?
c. Suppose the customer redeems the check by giving Han's $290 cash in exchange for the bad check. The additional $20 paid a service fee charged by Han's. Show the effects on the financial statements in the horizontal statements model in Requirement *a*.
d. Is the receipt of cash referenced in Requirement *c* an asset source, use, or exchange transaction?
e. Record in general journal form the adjusting entry for the NSF check and the entry for redemption of the check by the customer.

LO 6-3

Exercise 6-8A *Adjustments to the balance per books*

Required

Identify which of the following items are added to or subtracted from the unadjusted *book balance* to arrive at the true cash balance. Distinguish the additions from the subtractions by placing a + beside the items that are added to the unadjusted book balance and a − beside those subtracted from it. The first item is recorded as an example.

Reconciling Items	Book Balance Adjusted?	Added or Subtracted?
Credit memo	Yes	+
Interest revenue		
Deposits in transit		
Debit memo		
Service charge		
Charge for printing checks		
NSF check from customer		
Note receivable collected by the bank		
Outstanding checks		

LO 6-3

Exercise 6-9A *Adjustments to the balance per bank*

Required

Identify which of the following items are added to or subtracted from the unadjusted *bank balance* to arrive at the true cash balance. Distinguish the additions from the subtractions by placing a + beside the items that are added to the unadjusted bank balance and a − beside those subtracted from it. The first item is recorded as an example.

Reconciling Items	Book Balance Adjusted?	Added or Subtracted?
Bank service charge	No	NA
Outstanding checks		
Deposits in transit		
Debit memo		
Credit memo		
Certified checks		
Petty cash voucher		
NSF check from customer		
Interest revenue		

Exercise 6-10A *Adjusting the cash account*

LO 6-3

As of June 30, Year 1, the bank statement showed an ending balance of $19,500. The unadjusted Cash account balance was $15,200. The following information is available:

1. Deposit in transit: $2,400.
2. Credit memo in bank statement for interest earned in June: $30.
3. Outstanding check: $6,690.
4. Debit memo for service charge: $20.

Required

a. Determine the true cash balance by preparing a bank reconciliation as of June 30, Year 1, using the preceding information.
b. Record in general journal format the adjusting entries necessary to correct the unadjusted book balance.

Exercise 6-11A *Determining the true cash balance, starting with the unadjusted bank balance*

LO 6-3

The following information is available for Trinkle Company for the month of June:

1. The unadjusted balance per the bank statement on June 30 was $81,500.
2. Deposits in transit on June 30 were $3,150.
3. A debit memo was included with the bank statement for a service charge of $40.
4. A $5,611 check written in June had not been paid by the bank.
5. The bank statement included a $950 credit memo for the collection of a note. The principal of the note was $900, and the interest collected amounted to $50.

Required

Determine the true cash balance as of June 30. (*Hint:* It is not necessary to use all of the preceding items to determine the true balance.)

Exercise 6-12A *Determining the true cash balance, starting with the unadjusted book balance*

LO 6-3

Nickleson Company had an unadjusted cash balance of $7,750 as of May 31. The company's bank statement, also dated May 31, included a $72 NSF check written by one of Nickleson's customers. There were $800 in outstanding checks and $950 in deposits in transit as of May 31. According to the bank statement, service charges were $50, and the bank collected an $800 note receivable for Nickleson. The bank statement also showed $13 of interest revenue earned by Nickleson.

Required

Determine the true cash balance as of May 31. (*Hint:* It is not necessary to use all of the preceding items to determine the true balance.)

Exercise 6-13A *Effect of establishing a petty cash fund*

LO 6-4

Chen Company established a $200 petty cash fund on January 1, Year 1.

Required

a. Is the establishment of the petty cash fund an asset source, use, or exchange transaction?
b. Show the establishment of the petty cash fund in a horizontal statements model like the following one:

Assets	=	Liab.	+	Equity	Rev.	−	Exp.	=	Net Inc.	Cash Flow
Cash + Petty Cash										

c. Record the establishment of the fund in general journal format.

LO 6-4

Exercise 6-14A *Effect of petty cash events on the financial statements*

Fresh Foods established a petty cash fund of $100 on January 2. On January 31, the fund contained cash of $9.20 and vouchers for the following cash payments:

Maintenance expense	$61.50
Office supplies	12.50
Transportation expense	15.00

The three distinct accounting events affecting the petty cash fund for the period were (1) establishment of the fund, (2) reimbursements made to employees, and (3) recognition of expenses and replenishment of the fund.

Required

a. Show each of the three events in a horizontal statements model like the following one. In the Cash Flow column, indicate whether the item is an operating activity (OA), investing activity (IA), or a financing activity (FA). Use NA to indicate that an account was not affected by the event.

Assets	=	Liab.	+	Equity	Rev.	−	Exp.	=	Net Inc.	Cash Flow
Cash + Petty Cash										

b. Record the events in general journal format.

LO 6-4

Exercise 6-15A *Determining the amount of petty cash expense*

Consider the following events:

1. A petty cash fund of $200 was established on April 1, Year 1.
2. Employees were reimbursed when they presented petty cash vouchers to the petty cash custodian.
3. On April 30, Year 1, the petty cash fund contained vouchers totaling $196.50 plus $2.20 of currency.

Required

Answer the following questions:

a. How did the establishment of the petty cash fund affect (increase, decrease, or have no effect on) total assets?
b. What is the amount of total petty cash expenses to be recognized during April?
c. When are petty cash expenses recognized (at the time of establishment, reimbursement, or replenishment)?

LO 6-5

Exercise 6-16A *Confidentiality and the auditor*

Suzanne Hurley discovered significant fraud in the accounting records of a high-profile client. Due to her client's prestige, the story aired in the mainstream media. Unable to resolve her client's remaining concerns with the company's management team, Hurley ultimately resigned from the audit engagement. She knows she will be asked by several interested parties, including her friends and relatives, the successor auditor, and the prosecuting attorneys in a court of law, to tell what she knows. She has asked you for advice.

Required

Write a memo that explains Hurley's disclosure responsibilities to each of the interested parties.

PROBLEMS—SERIES A

connect *All applicable Problems in Series A are available in Connect.*

Problem 6-17A *Using internal control to restrict illegal or unethical behavior*

LO 6-1, 6-2

Required

For each of the following fraudulent acts, describe one or more internal control procedures that could have prevented (or helped prevent) the problems.

a. Everyone in the office has noticed what a dedicated employee Carley Trap is. She never misses work, not even for a vacation. Trap is in charge of the petty cash fund. She transfers funds from the company's bank account to the petty cash account on an as-needed basis. During a surprise audit, the petty cash fund was found to contain fictitious receipts. Over a three-year period, Trap had used more than $4,000 of petty cash to pay for personal expenses.

b. Doug Clampet was hired as the vice president of the manufacturing division of a corporation. His impressive resume listed a master's degree in business administration from a large state university and numerous collegiate awards and activities, but in truth Clampet only had a high school diploma. Soon, the company was in poor financial condition because of his inadequate knowledge and bad decisions.

c. Stone Manufacturing has good internal control over its manufacturing materials inventory. However, office supplies are kept on open shelves in the employee break room. The office supervisor has noticed that he is having to order paper, tape, staplers, and pens with increasing frequency.

Problem 6-18A *Preparing a bank reconciliation*

LO 6-3

Rick Hall owns a card shop: Hall's Cards. The following cash information is available for the month of August Year 1.

As of August 31, the bank statement shows a balance of $16,140. The August 31 unadjusted balance in the Cash account of Hall's Cards is $14,100. A review of the bank statement revealed the following information:

1. A deposit of $4,150 on August 31, Year 1, does not appear on the August bank statement.
2. It was discovered that a check to pay for baseball cards was correctly written and paid by the bank for $4,500 but was recorded on the books as $5,400.
3. When checks written during the month were compared with those paid by the bank, three checks amounting to $5,370 were found to be outstanding.
4. A debit memo for $80 was included in the bank statement for the purchase of a new supply of checks.

Required

a. Prepare a bank reconciliation at the end of August showing the true cash balance.
b. Prepare any necessary journal entries to adjust the books to the true cash balance.

Problem 6-19A *Missing information in a bank reconciliation*

LO 6-3

The following data apply to Pro Beauty Supply Inc. for May Year 1:

1. Balance per the bank on May 31: $9,150.
2. Deposits in transit not recorded by the bank: $1,510.
3. Bank error; check written by Best Beauty Supply was charged to Pro Beauty Supply's account: $560.
4. The following checks written and recorded by Pro Beauty Supply were not included in the bank statement:

3013	$ 510
3054	640
3056	1,520

5. Note collected by the bank: $500.
6. Service charge for collection of note: $20.
7. The bookkeeper recorded a check written for $320 to pay for the May utilities expense as $230 in the cash disbursements journal.
8. Bank service charge in addition to the note collection fee: $40.
9. Customer checks returned by the bank as NSF: $310.

Required
Determine the amount of the unadjusted cash balance per Pro Beauty Supply's books.

LO 6-3

Problem 6-20A *Adjustments to the cash account based on the bank reconciliation*

Required
Determine whether the following items included in Wong Company's January Year 1 bank reconciliation will require adjusting or correcting entries on Wong's books. When an entry is required, record it in general journal format.

a. Service charges of $50 for the month of January were listed on the bank statement.
b. The bank charged a $250 check drawn on Wing Restaurant to Wong's account. The check was included in Wong's bank statement.
c. A check of $62 was returned to the bank because of insufficient funds and was noted on the bank statement. Wong received the check from a customer and thought it was good when it was deposited into the account.
d. A $990 deposit was recorded by the bank as $980.
e. Four checks totaling $810 written during the month of January were not included with the January bank statement.
f. A $75 check written to OfficeMax for office supplies was recorded in the general journal as $57.
g. The bank statement indicated that the bank had collected a $450 note for Wong.
h. Wong recorded $900 of receipts on January 31, Year 1, which were deposited in the night depository of the bank. These deposits were not included in the bank statement.

LO 6-3

CHECK FIGURE
a. True Cash Balance, July 31, Year 1: $16,234

Problem 6-21A *Bank reconciliation and adjustments to the cash account*

The following information is available for Park Valley Spa for July Year 1:

Bank Statement
STATE BANK
Bolta Vista, NV 10001

Park Valley Spa
10 Main Street
Bolta Vista, NV 10001

Account number
12-4567
July 31, Year 1

Beginning balance 6/30/Year 1	$ 9,031
Total deposits and other credits	29,800
Total checks and other debits	23,902
Ending balance 7/31/Year 1	14,929

Checks and Debits		Deposits and Credits	
Check No.	Amount	Date	Amount
2350	$3,761	July 1	$1,102
2351	1,643	July 10	6,498
2352	8,000	July 15	4,929
2354	2,894	July 21	6,174
2355	1,401	July 26	5,963
2357	6,187	July 30	2,084
DM	16	CM	3,050

The following is a list of checks and deposits recorded on the books of the Park Valley Spa for July Year 1:

Date	Check No.	Amount of Check	Date	Amount of Deposit
July 2	2351	$1,643	July 8	$6,498
July 4	2352	8,000	July 14	4,929
July 10	2353	1,500	July 21	6,174
July 10	2354	2,894	July 26	5,963
July 15	2355	1,401	July 29	2,084
July 20	2356	745	July 30	3,550
July 22	2357	6,187		

Other Information

1. Check no. 2350 was outstanding from June.
2. The credit memo was for collection of notes receivable.
3. All checks were paid at the correct amount.
4. The debit memo was for printed checks.
5. The June 30 bank reconciliation showed a deposit in transit of $1,102.
6. The unadjusted Cash account balance at July 31 was $13,200.

Required

a. Prepare the bank reconciliation for Park Valley Spa at the end of July.
b. Record in general journal form any necessary entries to the Cash account to adjust it to the true cash balance.

Problem 6-22A *Effect of adjustments to cash on the accounting equation* LO 6-3

After reconciling its bank account, Watson Company made the following adjusting entries:

Entry No.	Account Titles	Debit	Credit
1	Cash	20	
	Supplies Expense		20
	To correct overstatement of expense		
2	Cash	845	
	Accounts Receivable		845
	To record bank collection		
3	Cash	44	
	Interest Revenue		44
	To record interest revenue		
4	Service Charge Expense	35	
	Cash		35
	To record bank service charge		
5	Accounts Receivable	174	
	Cash		174
	To record NSF check from Beat		

Required

Identify the event depicted in each journal entry as asset source (AS), asset use (AU), asset exchange (AE), or claims exchange (CE). Also explain how each entry affects the accounting equation by placing a + for increase, − for decrease, or NA for not affected under the following components of the accounting equation. The first event is recorded as an example.

Event No.	Type of Event	Assets	=	Liabilities	+	Common Stock	+	Retained Earnings
						Stockholders' Equity		
1	AS	+		NA		NA		+

LO 6-1, 6-2, 6-3

Problem 6-23A Bank reconciliation and internal control

Following is a bank reconciliation for Zocar Enterprises for June 30, Year 1:

	Cash Account	Bank Statement
Balance as of 6/30/Year 1	$ 1,918	$ 3,000
Deposit in transit		600
Outstanding checks		(1,507)
Note collected by bank	2,000	
Bank service charge	(25)	
NSF check	(1,800)	
Adjusted cash balance as of 6/30/Year 1	$ 2,093	$ 2,093

When reviewing the bank reconciliation, Zocar's auditor was unable to locate any reference to the NSF check on the bank statement. Furthermore, the clerk who reconciles the bank account and records the adjusting entries could not find the actual NSF check that should have been included in the bank statement. Finally, there was no specific reference in the accounts receivable supporting records identifying a party who had written a bad check.

Required

a. Prepare the adjusting entry that the clerk would have made to record the NSF check.
b. Assume that the clerk who prepares the bank reconciliation and records the adjusting entries also makes bank deposits. Explain how the clerk could use a fictitious NSF check to hide the theft of cash.
c. How could Zocar avoid the theft of cash that is concealed by the use of fictitious NSF checks?

LO 6-4

Problem 6-24A Petty cash fund

Austin Co. established a petty cash fund by issuing a check for $300 and appointing Steve Mack as petty cash custodian. Mack had vouchers for the following petty cash payments during the month:

Stamps	$62
Miscellaneous items	20
Employee supper money	70
Taxi fare	50
Window-washing service	75

There was $21 of currency in the petty cash box at the time it was replenished.

Required

a. Prepare all general journal entries necessary to (1) establish the fund, (2) reimburse employees, (3) recognize expenses, and (4) replenish the fund. (*Hint:* Journal entries may not be required for all the events.)
b. Explain how the Cash Short and Over account required in this case will affect the income statement.
c. Identify the event depicted in each journal entry recorded in Requirement *a* as asset source (AS), asset use (AU), asset exchange (AE), or claims exchange (CE).

d. Show the effects of the events in Requirement *a* on the financial statements using a horizontal statements model like the following one. In the Cash Flow column, indicate whether the item is an operating activity (OA), investing activity (IA), or financing activity (FA). Use NA to indicate that an account was not affected by the event.

Assets	=	Liab.	+	Equity	Rev.	−	Exp.	=	Net Inc.	Cash Flow
Cash + Petty Cash										

Problem 6-25A *Auditor responsibilities*

LO 6-5

You have probably heard it is unwise to bite the hand that feeds you. Independent auditors are chosen by, paid by, and can be fired by the companies they audit. What keeps the auditor independent? In other words, what stops an auditor from blindly following the orders of a client?

Required

Write a memo that explains the reporting responsibilities of an independent auditor.

EXERCISES—SERIES B

Exercise 6-1B *SOX and COSO's internal control frameworks*

LO 6-1

Required

a. Explain what the acronym SOX refers to.
b. Define the acronym COSO and explain how it relates to SOX.
c. Name and briefly define the five components of COSO's internal control framework.
d. Define the acronym ERM and explain how it relates to COSO's internal control framework.

Exercise 6-2B *Internal control procedures*

LO 6-1

Required

a. Name and describe the two categories of internal controls.
b. What is the purpose of internal controls?

Exercise 6-3B *Internal control procedures*

LO 6-1

Stan Oden is opening a new business that will sell sporting goods. It will initially be a small operation, and he is concerned about the security of his assets. He will not be able to be at the business all of the time and will have to rely on his employees and internal control procedures to ensure that transactions are properly accounted for and assets are safeguarded. He will have a store manager and two other employees who will be sales personnel and stock personnel and who will also perform any other duties necessary. Stan will be in the business on a regular basis. He has come to you for advice.

Required

Write a memo to Stan outlining the procedures he should implement to ensure his store assets are protected and that the financial transactions are properly recorded.

Exercise 6-4B *Internal controls to prevent theft*

LO 6-1

Sally Knox worked as the parts manager for East River Automobiles, a local automobile dealership. Sally was very dedicated and never missed a day of work. Because East River was a small operation, she was the only employee in the parts department. Her duties consisted of ordering parts for stock and those needed for repairs, receiving the parts and checking them in, distributing them as needed to the shop or to customers for purchase, and keeping track of and taking the year-end inventory of parts.

East River decided to expand and needed to secure additional financing. The local bank agreed to a loan contingent on an audit of the dealership. One requirement of the audit was to oversee the inventory count of both automobiles and parts on hand. Sally was clearly nervous, explaining she had just inventoried all parts in the parts department. She supplied the auditors with a detailed list. The inventory showed parts on hand worth $225,000. The auditors decided they needed to verify a substantial part of the inventory.

When the auditors began their counts, a pattern began to develop. Each type of part seemed to be one or two items short when the actual count was taken. This raised more concern. Although Sally assured the auditors the parts were just misplaced, the auditors continued the count. After completing the count of parts on hand, the auditors could document only $155,000 of actual parts. Suddenly, Sally quit her job and moved to another state.

Required

a. What do you suppose caused the discrepancy between the actual count and the count that Sally had supplied?
b. What procedures could be put into place to prevent this type of problem?

Exercise 6-5B Internal controls for equipment

Required
List the internal control procedures that pertain to the protection of business equipment.

Exercise 6-6B Features of internal control procedures for cash

Required
List and discuss effective internal control procedures that apply to cash.

Exercise 6-7B Treatment of NSF check

The bank statement of Hibbert Supplies included a $300 NSF check that one of Hibbert's customers had written to pay for services that were provided by Hibbert.

Required

a. Show the effects of recognizing the NSF check on the financial statements by recording the appropriate amounts in a horizontal statements model like the following one:

Assets	=	Liab.	+	Equity	Rev.	−	Exp.	=	Net Inc.	Cash Flow
Cash + Accts. Rec.										

b. Is the recognition of the NSF check on Hibbert's books an asset source, use, or exchange transaction?
c. Suppose the customer redeems the check by giving Hibbert $325 cash in exchange for the bad check. The additional $25 paid a service fee charged by Hibbert. Show the effects on the financial statements in the horizontal statements model in Requirement *a*.
d. Is the receipt of cash referred to in Requirement *c* an asset source, use, or exchange transaction?
e. Record in general journal form the adjusting entry for the NSF check and the subsequent entry for redemption of the check by the customer.

Exercise 6-8B Adjustments to the balance per books

Required
Identify which of the following items are added to or subtracted from the unadjusted *book balance* to arrive at the true cash balance. Distinguish the additions from the subtractions by placing a + beside the items that are added to the unadjusted book balance and a − beside those subtracted from it. The first item is recorded as an example.

Reconciling Items	Book Balance Adjusted?	Added or Subtracted?
Automatic debit for utility bill	Yes	−
Charge for printing new checks		
NSF check from customer		
ATM fee		
Outstanding checks		
Interest revenue earned on the account		
Deposits in transit		
Service charge		

Exercise 6-9B Adjustments to the balance per bank

LO 6-3

Required

Identify which of the following items are added to or subtracted from the unadjusted *bank balance* to arrive at the true cash balance. Distinguish the additions from the subtractions by placing a + beside the items that are added to the unadjusted bank balance and a − beside those subtracted from it. The first item is recorded as an example.

Reconciling Items	Book Balance Adjusted?	Added or Subtracted?
Credit memo	No	N/A
ATM fee		
Petty cash voucher		
NSF check from customer		
Interest revenue		
Bank service charge		
Outstanding checks		
Deposits in transit		
Debit memo		

Exercise 6-10B Adjusting the cash account

LO 6-3

As of May 31, Year 1, the bank statement showed an ending balance of $26,100. The unadjusted Cash account balance was $27,350. The following information is available:

1. Deposit in transit: $6,981.
2. Credit memo in bank statement for interest earned in May: $36.
3. Outstanding check: $5,720.
4. Debit memo for service charge: $25.

Required

a. Determine the true cash balance by preparing a bank reconciliation as of May 31, Year 1, using the preceding information.
b. Record in general journal format the adjusting entries necessary to correct the unadjusted book balance.

Exercise 6-11B Determining the true cash balance, starting with the unadjusted bank balance

LO 6-3

The following information is available for Jenkins Company for the month of August:

1. The unadjusted balance per the bank statement on August 31 was $35,200.
2. Deposits in transit on August 31 were $3,750.
3. A debit memo was included with the bank statement for a service charge of $35.
4. A $2,120 check written in August had not been paid by the bank.
5. The bank statement included a $1,550 credit memo for the collection of a note. The principal of the note was $1,500, and the interest collected was $50.

Required

Determine the true cash balance as of August 31. (*Hint:* It is not necessary to use all of the preceding items to determine the true balance.)

LO 6-3

Exercise 6-12B *Determining the true cash balance, starting with the unadjusted book balance*

Burson Company had an unadjusted cash balance of $8,120 as of April 30. The company's bank statement, also dated April 30, included a $200 NSF check written by one of Burson's customers. There were $1,525 in outstanding checks and $900 in deposits in transit as of April 30. According to the bank statement, service charges were $50, and the bank collected a $500 note receivable for Burson. The bank statement also showed $31 of interest revenue earned by Burson.

Required

Determine the true cash balance as of April 30. (*Hint:* It is not necessary to use all of the preceding items to determine the true balance.)

LO 6-4

Exercise 6-13B *Effect of establishing a petty cash fund*

Mountain Timber Company established a $180 petty cash fund on January 1, Year 1.

Required

a. Is the establishment of the petty cash fund an asset source, use, or exchange transaction?
b. Show the establishment of the petty cash fund in a horizontal statements model like the following one:

Assets	= Liab. + Equity	Rev. − Exp. = Net Inc.	Cash Flow
Cash + Petty Cash			

c. Record the establishment of the fund in general journal format.

LO 6-4

Exercise 6-14B *Effect of petty cash events on the financial statements*

Payton Inc. established a petty cash fund of $150 on January 2. On January 31, the fund contained cash of $8.20 and vouchers for the following cash payments:

Postage and office supplies	$76.30
Entertainment expense	36.50
Maintenance expense	25.00

The three distinct accounting events affecting the petty cash fund for the period were (1) establishment of the fund, (2) reimbursements made to employees, and (3) recognition of expenses and replenishment of the fund.

Required

a. Show each of the three events in a horizontal statements model like the following one. In the Cash Flow column, indicate whether the item is an operating activity (OA), investing activity (IA), or a financing activity (FA). Use NA to indicate that an account was not affected by the event.

Assets	= Liab. + Equity	Rev. − Exp. = Net Inc.	Cash Flow
Cash + Petty Cash			

b. Record the events in general journal format.

Exercise 6-15B *Determining the amount of petty cash expense*

LO 6-4

Consider the following events:

1. A petty cash fund of $200 was established on April 1, Year 1.
2. Employees were reimbursed when they presented petty cash vouchers to the petty cash custodian.
3. On April 30, Year 1, the petty cash fund contained vouchers totaling $171.40 plus $26.10 of currency.

Required

Answer the following questions:

a. How did the establishment of the petty cash fund affect (increase, decrease, or have no effect on) total assets?
b. What is the amount of total petty cash expenses to be recognized during April?
c. When are petty cash expenses recognized (at the time of establishment, reimbursement, or replenishment)?

Exercise 6-16B *Materiality and the auditor*

LO 6-5

Sarah Bale is an auditor. Her work at two companies disclosed inappropriate recognition of revenue. Both cases involved dollar amounts in the $100,000 range. In one case, Bale considered the item material and required her client to restate earnings. In the other case, Bale dismissed the misstatement as being immaterial.

Required

Write a memo that explains how a $100,000 misstatement of revenue is acceptable for one company but unacceptable for a different company.

PROBLEMS—SERIES B

Problem 6-17B *Using internal control to restrict illegal or unethical behavior*

LO 6-1, 6-2

Required

For each of the following fraudulent acts, describe one or more internal control procedures that could have prevented (or helped prevent) the problems.

a. Linda Hinson, the administrative assistant in charge of payroll, created a fictitious employee, wrote weekly checks to the fictitious employee, and then personally cashed the checks for her own benefit.
b. Jim Stewart, the receiving manager of Western Lumber, created a fictitious supplier named B&A Building Supply. B&A regularly billed Western Lumber for supplies purchased. Stewart had printed shipping slips and billing invoices with the name of the fictitious company and opened a post office box as the mailing address. Stewart simply prepared a receiving report and submitted it for payment to the accounts payable department. The accounts payable clerk then paid the invoice when it was received because Stewart acknowledged receipt of the supplies.
c. Jalie Thomas works at a local hobby shop and usually operates the cash register. She has developed a way to give discounts to her friends. When they come by, she rings a lower price or does not charge the friend for some of the material purchased. At first, Thomas thought she would get caught, but no one seemed to notice. Indeed, she has become so sure that there is no way for the owner to find out that she has started taking home some supplies for her own personal use.

Problem 6-18B *Preparing a bank reconciliation*

LO 6-3

Bill Lewis owns a construction business, Lewis Supply Co. The following cash information is available for the month of October Year 1.

As of October 31, the bank statement shows a balance of $21,400. The October 31 unadjusted balance in the Cash account of Lewis Supply Co. is $18,400. A review of the bank statement revealed the following information:

1. A deposit of $2,600 on October 31, Year 1, does not appear on the October 31 bank statement.
2. A debit memo for $75 was included in the bank statement for the purchase of a new supply of checks.

3. When checks written during the month were compared with those paid by the bank, three checks amounting to $2,075 were found to be outstanding.
4. It was discovered that a check to pay for repairs was correctly written and paid by the bank for $1,500 but was recorded on the books as $5,100.

Required

a. Prepare a bank reconciliation at the end of October showing the true cash balance.
b. Prepare any necessary journal entries to adjust the books to the true cash balance.

LO 6-3

Problem 6-19B *Missing information in a bank reconciliation*

The following data apply to Woods Sports Inc. for April Year 1:

1. Balance per the bank on April 30: $13,750.
2. Deposits in transit not recorded by the bank: $3,600.
3. Bank error; check written by Glen Woods on his personal checking account was drawn on Woods Sports Inc.'s account: $800.
4. The following checks written and recorded by Woods Sports Inc. were not included in the bank statement:

1901	$ 265
1920	650
1921	1,200

5. Credit memo for note collected by the bank: $1,100.
6. Service charge for collection of note: $50.
7. The bookkeeper recorded a check written for $760 to pay for April's office supplies as $670 in the cash disbursements journal.
8. Bank service charge in addition to the note collection fee: $45.
9. NSF checks returned by the bank: $175.

Required

Determine the amount of the unadjusted cash balance per Woods Sports Inc.'s books.

LO 6-3

Problem 6-20B *Adjustments to the cash account based on the bank reconciliation*

Determine whether the following items in China Imports' bank reconciliation require adjusting or correcting entries on China Imports' books. When an entry is required, record it in general journal format.

a. The bank statement indicated that China Imports earned $60 of interest revenue.
b. China Imports' accountant mistakenly recorded a $430 check that was written to purchase supplies as $350.
c. Bank service charges for the month were $45.
d. The bank reconciliation disclosed that $800 had been stolen from China Imports' business.
e. Outstanding checks amounted to $2,600.
f. The bank collected $4,000 of China Imports' accounts receivable. China Imports had instructed its customers to send their payments directly to the bank.
g. The bank mistakenly gave Imports Inc. credit for a $800 deposit made by China Imports.
h. Deposits in transit were $6,200.
i. China Imports' bank statement contained a $525 NSF check. China Imports had received the check from a customer and had included it in one of its bank deposits.

Problem 6-21B *Bank reconciliation and adjustments to the cash account* **LO 6-3**

The following information is available for Pyle Garage for March Year 1:

```
                    BANK STATEMENT
                  HAZARD STATE BANK
                    215 MAIN STREET
                   HAZARD, GA 30321
```

Pyle Garage
629 Main Street
Hazard, GA 30321

Account number
62-00062
March 31, Year 1

Beginning balance 3/1/Year 1	$15,000.00
Total deposits and other credits	7,000.00
Total checks and other debits	6,000.00
Ending balance 3/31/Year 1	16,000.00

Checks and Debits		Deposits and Credits	
Check No.	Amount	Date	Amount
1462	$1,163.00	March 1	$1,000.00
1463	62.00	March 2	1,340.00
1464	1,235.00	March 6	210.00
1465	750.00	March 12	1,940.00
1466	1,111.00	March 17	855.00
1467	964.00	March 22	1,480.00
DM	15.00	CM	175.00
1468	700.00		

The following is a list of checks and deposits recorded on the books of Pyle Garage for March Year 1:

Date	Check No.	Amount of Check	Date	Amount of Deposit
March 1	1463	$ 62.00	March 1	$1,340.00
March 5	1464	1,235.00	March 5	210.00
March 6	1465	750.00		
March 9	1466	1,111.00	March 10	1,940.00
March 10	1467	964.00		
March 14	1468	70.00	March 16	855.00
March 19	1469	1,500.00	March 19	1,480.00
March 28	1470	102.00	March 29	2,000.00

Other Information

1. Check no. 1462 was outstanding from February.
2. A credit memo for collection of accounts receivable was included in the bank statement.
3. All checks were paid at the correct amount.
4. The bank statement included a debit memo for service charges.
5. The February 28 bank reconciliation showed a deposit in transit of $1,000.
6. Check no. 1468 was for the purchase of equipment.
7. The unadjusted Cash account balance at March 31 was $16,868.

Required

a. Prepare the bank reconciliation for Pyle Garage at the end of March.
b. Record in general journal form any necessary entries to the Cash account to adjust it to the true cash balance.

LO 6-3

Problem 6-22B *Effect of adjustments to cash on the accounting equation*

After reconciling its bank account, Addy Equipment Company made the following adjusting entries:

Entry No.	Account Titles	Debit	Credit
1	Accounts Receivable	250	
	Cash		250
	To record NSF check from Wilson		
2	Rent Expense	35	
	Cash		35
	To correct understatement of expense		
3	Service Charge Expense	15	
	Cash		15
	To record bank service charge		
4	Cash	175	
	Accounts Receivable		175
	To record bank collection		
5	Cash	40	
	Interest Revenue		40
	To record interest revenue		

Required

Identify the event depicted in each journal entry as an asset source (AS), asset use (AU), asset exchange (AE), or claims exchange (CE). Also explain how each entry affects the accounting equation by placing a + for increase, − for decrease, or NA for not affected under the following components of the accounting equation. The first event is recorded as an example.

Event No.	Type of Event	Assets	=	Liabilities	+	Stockholders' Equity Common Stock	+	Retained Earnings
1	AE	+/−		NA		NA		NA

LO 6-1, 6-2, 6-3

Problem 6-23B *Bank reconciliation and internal control*

The following is a bank reconciliation for BBQ Express for May 31, Year 1:

	Cash Account	Bank Statement
Balance as of 5/31/Year 1	$25,000	$22,000
Deposit in transit		4,250
Outstanding checks		(465)
Note collected by bank	1,815	
Bank service charge	(30)	
Automatic payment on loan	(1,000)	
Adjusted cash balance as of 5/31/Year 1	$25,785	$25,785

Because of limited funds, BBQ Express employed only one accountant who was responsible for receiving cash, recording receipts and disbursements, preparing deposits, and preparing the bank reconciliation. The accountant left the company on June 8, Year 1, after preparing the May 31 bank reconciliation. His replacement compared the checks returned with the bank statement to the cash disbursements journal and found the total of the outstanding checks to be $4,600.

Required

a. Prepare a corrected bank reconciliation.
b. What is the total amount of cash missing, and how was the difference between the "true cash" per the bank and the "true cash" per the books hidden on the reconciliation prepared by the former employee?
c. What could BBQ Express do to avoid cash theft in the future?

Problem 6-24B *Petty cash fund*

LO 6-4

The following data pertain to the petty cash fund of Marsh Company:

CHECK FIGURE
a. Cash Short: $3

1. The petty cash fund was established on an imprest basis at $250 on March 1.
2. On March 31, a physical count of the fund disclosed $13 in currency and coins, vouchers authorizing meal allowances totaling $120, vouchers authorizing purchase of postage stamps of $21, and vouchers for payment of delivery charges of $93.

Required

a. Prepare all general journal entries necessary to (1) establish the fund, (2) reimburse employees, and (3) recognize the expenses and replenish the fund as of March 31. (*Hint:* Journal entries may not be required for all three events.)
b. Explain how the Cash Short and Over account required in this case affects the income statement.
c. Identify the event depicted in each journal entry recorded in Requirement *a* as asset source (AS), asset use (AU), asset exchange (AE), or claims exchange (CE).
d. Show the effects on the financial statements of the events in Requirement *a* using a horizontal statements model like the following one. In the Cash Flow column, indicate whether the item is an operating activity (OA), investing activity (IA), or financing activity (FA). Use NA to indicate that an account was not affected by the event.

Assets	=	Liab.	+	Equity	Rev.	−	Exp.	=	Net Inc.	Cash Flow
Cash + Petty Cash										

Problem 6-25B *Types of audit reports*

LO 6-5

Connie Stevens is a partner in a regional accounting firm. Stevens was hired by a client to audit the company's books. After extensive work, Stevens determined that she was unable to perform the appropriate audit procedures.

Required

a. Name the type of audit report that Stevens should issue with respect to the work that she did accomplish.
b. If Stevens had been able to perform the necessary audit procedures, there are three types of audit reports she could have issued depending on the outcome of the audit. Name and describe these three types of audit reports.

ANALYZE, THINK, COMMUNICATE

ATC 6-1 Business Applications Case *Understanding real-world annual reports*

Required

Obtain the Target Corporation's annual report at http://investors.target.com using the instructions in Appendix B, and use it to answer the following questions:

a. Who are the independent auditors for Target?
b. What type of opinion did the independent auditors issue on Target's financial statements?

c. On what date does it appear the independent auditors completed their work related to Target's financial statements for the fiscal year ended January 28, 2017 (2016)?
d. Does the auditors' report give any information about how the audit was conducted? If so, what does it suggest was done?
e. Does the auditors' report tell the reader that the audit was concerned with materiality rather than absolute accuracy in the financial statements?

ATC 6-2 Group Assignment *Bank reconciliations*

The following cash and bank information is available for three companies at June 30, Year 1:

Cash and Adjustment Information	Peach Co.	Apple Co.	Pear Co.
Unadjusted cash balance per books, 6/30	$45,620	$32,450	$23,467
Outstanding checks	1,345	2,478	2,540
Service charge	50	75	35
Balance per bank statement, 6/30	48,632	37,176	24,894
Credit memo for collection of notes receivable	4,500	5,600	3,800
NSF check	325	145	90
Deposits in transit	2,500	3,200	4,800
Credit memo for interest earned	42	68	12

Required

a. Organize the class into three sections and divide each section into groups of three to five students. Assign Peach Co. to section 1, Apple Co. to section 2, and Pear Co. to section 3.

Group Tasks

(1) Prepare a bank reconciliation for the company assigned to your group.
(2) Prepare any necessary journal entries for the company assigned to your group.
(3) Select a representative from a group in each section to put the bank reconciliation and required journal entries on the board.

Class Discussion

b. Discuss the cause of the difference between the unadjusted cash balance and the ending balance for the bank statement. Also, discuss types of adjustments that are commonly made to the bank balance and types of adjustments commonly made to the unadjusted book balance.

ATC 6-3 Real-World Case *Evaluating management's responsibilities*

The following excerpt was taken from **Alphabet, Inc.**'s 10-K report for its 2016 fiscal year. Alphabet, Inc. is the parent company of **Google, Inc.**

CONTROLS AND PROCEDURES

Evaluation of Disclosure Controls and Procedures

Our management, with the participation of our chief executive officer and chief financial officer, evaluated the effectiveness of our disclosure controls and procedures. . . .

Based on this evaluation, our chief executive officer and chief financial officer concluded that, as of December 31, 2016, our disclosure controls and procedures are designed at a reasonable assurance level and are effective to provide reasonable assurance that information we are required to disclose in reports that we file or submit under the Exchange Act is recorded, processed, summarized, and reported within the time periods specified in the SEC's rules and forms, and that such information is accumulated and communicated to our management, including our chief executive officer and chief financial officer, as appropriate, to allow timely decisions regarding required disclosure. . . .

Management's Report on Internal Control over Financial Reporting

Our management is responsible for establishing and maintaining adequate internal control over financial reporting, as defined in Rule 13a-15(f) of the Exchange Act. Our management conducted an evaluation of the effectiveness of our internal control over financial reporting based on the framework in Internal Control — Integrated Framework issued by the Committee of Sponsoring Organizations of the Treadway Commission (2013 framework). Based on this evaluation, management concluded that our internal control over financial reporting was effective as of December 31, 2016. Management reviewed the results of its assessment with our Audit Committee. The effectiveness of our internal control over financial reporting as of December 31, 2016, has been audited by Ernst & Young LLP, an independent registered public accounting firm, as stated in its report which is included in Item 8 of this Annual Report on Form 10-K.

Limitations on Effectiveness of Controls and Procedures

In designing and evaluating the disclosure controls and procedures, management recognizes that any controls and procedures, no matter how well designed and operated, can provide only reasonable assurance of achieving the desired control objectives. In addition, the design of disclosure controls and procedures must reflect the fact that there are resource constraints and that management is required to apply its judgment in evaluating the benefits of possible controls and procedures relative to their costs.

Required

Based on information in the text, list some of the elements of internal control you would expect the company's management to have established. You do not need to read the report of the Treadway Commission.

ATC 6-4   Business Applications Case   *Decisions about materiality*

The accounting firm of Eckert & Bell, CPAs, recently completed the audits of three separate companies. During these audits, the following events were discovered, and Eckert & Bell is trying to decide if each event is material. If an item is material, the CPA firm will insist that the company modify the financial statements.

1. In 2019, Carter Company reported service revenues of $4,000,000 and earnings before tax of $240,000. Because of an accounting error, the company recorded $24,000 as revenue in 2019 for services that will not be performed until early 2020.
2. Avery Company plans to report a cash balance of $210,000. Because of an accounting error, this amount is $15,000 too high. Avery also plans to report total assets of $12,000,000 and net earnings of $1,245,000.
3. Lewis Company's 2019 balance sheet shows a cash balance of $250,000 and total assets of $9,500,000. For 2019, the company had a net income of $850,000. These balances are all correct, but they would have been $7,000 higher if the president of the company had not claimed business travel expenses that were, in fact, the cost of personal vacations for him and his family. He charged the costs of these trips on the company's credit card. The president of Lewis Company owns 25 percent of the business.

Required

Write a memorandum to the partners of Eckert & Bell, explaining whether each of these events is material.

ATC 6-5   Business Applications Case   *Limitations of audit opinion*

The statement of financial position (balance sheet) of Omni-Pave Company reports assets of $7,800,000. Ellen Martin advises you that a major accounting firm has audited the statements and attested that they were prepared in accordance with generally accepted accounting principles. She tells you that she can buy the total owner's interest in the business for only $5,400,000 and is seriously considering the opportunity. She says that the auditor's unqualified opinion validates the $7,800,000 value of the assets. Ellen believes she would be foolish to pass up the opportunity to purchase the assets at a price of only $5,400,000.

Required

a. What part of the accounting equation is Ellen failing to consider?
b. Comment on Ellen's misconceptions regarding the auditor's role in providing information that is useful in making investment decisions.

ATC 6-6 Writing Assignment *Internal control procedures*

Sarah Johnson was a trusted employee of Evergreen Trust Bank. She was involved in everything. She worked as a teller, accounted for the cash at the other teller windows, and recorded many of the transactions in the accounting records. She was so loyal that she never took a day off, even when very sick. She routinely worked late to see that all the day's work was posted into the accounting records, and never took a day's vacation because they might need her at the bank.

Adam and Jammie, CPAs, were hired to perform an audit, the first complete audit that had been done in several years. Johnson seemed somewhat upset by the upcoming audit, saying that everything had been properly accounted for and that the audit was a needless expense. When Adam and Jammie examined some of the bank's internal control procedures, the firm discovered problems. In fact, as the audit progressed, it became apparent that a large amount of cash was missing. Numerous adjustments had been made to customer accounts with credit memorandums, and many of the transactions had been posted several days late. In addition, there were numerous cash payments for "office expenses."

When the audit was complete, it was determined that more than $100,000 of funds was missing or improperly accounted for. All fingers pointed to Johnson. The bank's president, who was a close friend of Johnson, was bewildered. How could this type of thing happen at this bank?

Required

Prepare a written memo to the bank president, outlining the procedures that should be followed to prevent this type of problem in the future.

ATC 6-7 Ethical Dilemma *I need just a little extra money*

John Riley, a certified public accountant, has worked for the past eight years as a payroll clerk for Southeast Industries, a small furniture manufacturing firm in the northeast. John recently experienced unfortunate circumstances. His teenage son required minor surgery and the medical bills not covered by John's insurance have financially strained John's family.

John works hard and is a model employee. Although he received regular performance raises during his first few years with Southeast, John's wages have not increased in three years. John asked his supervisor, Bill Jameson, for a raise. Bill agreed that John deserved a raise, but told him he could not currently approve one because of sluggish sales.

A disappointed John returned to his duties while the financial pressures in his life continued. Two weeks later, Larry Tyler, an assembly worker at Southeast, quit over a dispute with management. John conceived an idea. John's duties included not only processing employee terminations but also approving time cards before paychecks were issued and then distributing the paychecks to firm personnel. John decided to delay processing Larry's termination, to forge timecards for Larry for the next few weeks, and to cash the checks himself. Because he distributed paychecks, no one would find out, and John reasoned that he was really entitled to the extra money anyway. In fact, no one did discover his maneuver and John stopped the practice after three weeks.

Required

a. Does John's scheme affect Southeast's balance sheet? Explain your answer.
b. Review the AICPA's Articles of Professional Conduct (see Chapter 2) and comment on any of the standards that have been violated.
c. Identify the three elements of unethical and criminal conduct recognized in the fraud triangle.

ATC 6-8 Research Assignment *Investigating cash and management issues at Smucker's*

Using the most current annual report available on the company's website, answer the following questions about the J. M. Smucker Company.

Required

a. Instead of "Cash," the company's balance sheet uses the account name "Cash and cash equivalents." How does the company define cash equivalents?

b. The annual report has two reports in which management clearly acknowledges its responsibility for the company's financial reporting and internal controls. What are the names of these reports and on what pages are they located?

ATC 6-9 Spreadsheet Assignment *Using Excel*

At the end of Year 1, the following accounting information is available for Bainbridge and Crist companies:

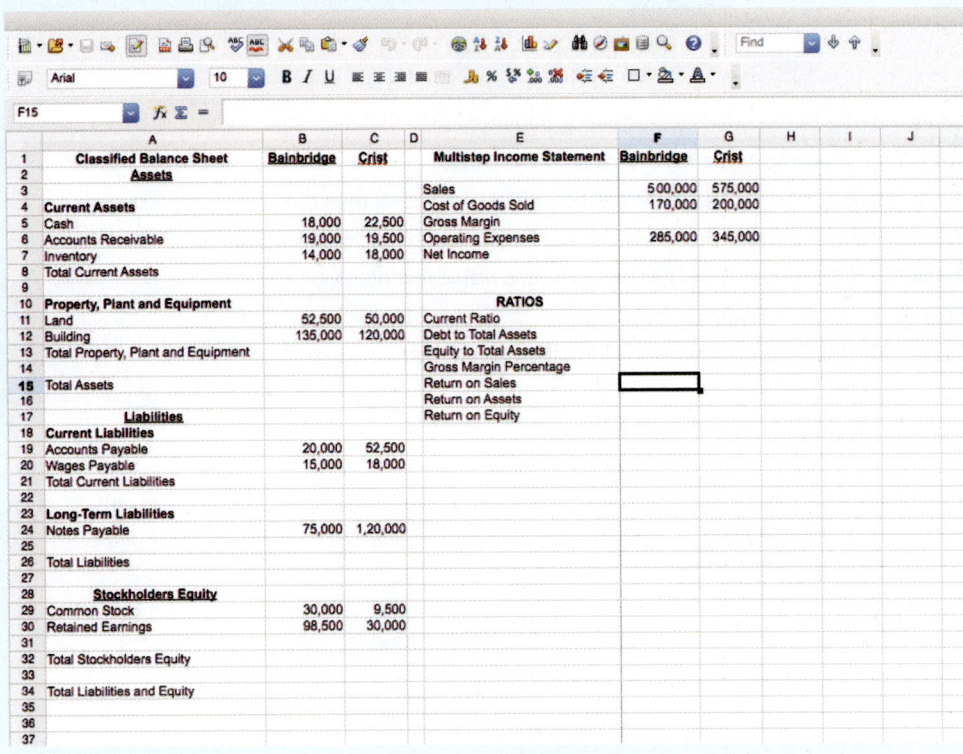

Source: Microsoft Office Excel 2010

Required

a. Set up the preceding spreadsheet. Complete the balance sheet and income statement. Use Excel formulas for rows that "total" on the balance sheet and for gross margin and net income on the income statement.

b. Calculate the designated ratios using Excel formulas.

c. Assume that sales increased 10 percent and that the additional sales were made on account. Adjust the balance sheet and income statement for the effects. Notice that Retained Earnings will also need to be adjusted to keep the balance sheet in balance. What is the resultant effect on the ratios?

COMPREHENSIVE PROBLEM

The trial balance of Pacilio Security Services, Inc. as of January 1, Year 6, had the following normal balances:

Cash	$74,210
Accounts Receivable	13,500
Supplies	200
Prepaid Rent	3,200
Merchandise Inventory (24 @ $265; 1 @ $260)	6,620
Land	4,000
Accounts Payable	1,950
Unearned Revenue	900
Salaries Payable	1,000
Common Stock	50,000
Retained Earnings	47,880

During Year 6, Pacilio Security Services experienced the following transactions:

1. Paid the salaries payable from Year 5.
2. On March 1, Year 6, Pacilio established a $100 petty cash fund to handle small expenditures.
3. Paid $4,800 on March 1, Year 6, for a one-year lease on the company van in advance.
4. Paid $7,200 on May 2, Year 6, for one year's office rent in advance.
5. Purchased $400 of supplies on account.
6. Purchased 100 alarm systems for $28,000 cash during the year.
7. Sold 102 alarm systems for $57,120. All sales were on account. (Compute cost of goods sold using the FIFO cost flow method.)
8. Paid $2,100 on accounts payable during the year.
9. Replenished the petty cash fund on August 1. At this time, the petty cash fund had only $7 of currency left. It contained the following receipts: office supplies expense, $23; cutting grass, $55; and miscellaneous expense, $14.
10. Billed $52,000 of monitoring services for the year.
11. Paid installers and other employees a total of $25,000 cash for salaries.
12. Collected $89,300 of accounts receivable during the year.
13. Paid $3,600 of advertising expense during the year.
14. Paid $2,500 of utilities expense for the year.
15. Paid a dividend of $10,000 to the shareholders.

Adjustments

16. There was $160 of supplies on hand at the end of the year.
17. Recognized the expired rent for both the van and the office building for the year. (The rent for both the van and the office remained the same for Year 5 and Year 6.)
18. Recognized the balance of the revenue earned in Year 6 where cash had been collected in Year 5.
19. Accrued salaries at December 31, Year 6, were $1,400.

Required

a. Record the above transactions in general journal form.
b. Post the transactions to the T-accounts.
c. Prepare a bank reconciliation at the end of the year. The following information is available for the bank reconciliation:

   (1) Checks written but not paid by the bank, $8,350.
   (2) A deposit of $6,500 made on December 31, Year 6, had been recorded but was not shown on the bank statement.

(3) A debit memo for $55 for a new supply of checks. (*Hint:* Use Office Supplies Expense account.)

(4) A credit memo for $30 for interest earned on the checking account.

(5) An NSF check for $120.

(6) The balance shown on the bank statement was $80,822.

d. Record and post any adjustments necessary from the bank reconciliation.

e. Prepare a trial balance.

f. Prepare an income statement, statement of changes in stockholders' equity, balance sheet, and statement of cash flows.

g. Close the temporary accounts to retained earnings.

h. Post the closing entries to the T-accounts and prepare a post-closing trial balance.

CHAPTER 7

Accounting for Receivables

LEARNING OBJECTIVES

After you have mastered the material in this chapter, you will be able to:

LO 7-1 Use the percent of revenue method to account for uncollectible accounts expense.
LO 7-2 Use the percent of receivables method to estimate uncollectible accounts expense.
LO 7-3 Use aging of accounts receivable to estimate uncollectible accounts expense.
LO 7-4 Show how the direct write-off method of accounting for uncollectible accounts affects financial statements.
LO 7-5 Show how accounting for notes receivable and accrued interest affects financial statements.
LO 7-6 Show how accounting for credit card sales affects financial statements.
LO 7-7 Calculate and interpret the accounts receivable turnover ratio.

 Video lectures and accompanying self-assessment quizzes are available in Connect *for all learning objectives.*

CHAPTER OPENING

Many people buy on impulse. If they must wait, the desire to buy wanes. To take advantage of impulse buyers, most merchandising companies offer customers credit because it increases their sales. A disadvantage of this strategy occurs when some customers are unable or unwilling to pay their bills. Nevertheless, the widespread availability of credit suggests that the advantages of increased sales outweigh the disadvantages of some uncollectible accounts.

When a company allows a customer to "buy now and pay later," the company's right to collect cash in the future is called an **account receivable.** Typically, amounts due from individual accounts receivable are relatively small and the collection period is short. Most accounts receivable are collected within 30 days. When a longer credit term is needed or when a receivable is large, the seller usually requires the buyer to issue a note reflecting a credit agreement between the parties. The note specifies the maturity date, interest rate, and other credit terms. Receivables evidenced by such notes are called **notes receivable.** Accounts and notes receivable are reported as assets on the balance sheet.

The Curious Accountant

©Bloomberg/Getty Images

Lockheed Martin Corporation develops and maintains various types of technology related to security. Its biggest customer, by far, is the U.S. government for whom it provides aeronautics and space-system products and services. In 2016, 71 percent of its revenue came from sales to the U.S. government, and another 27 percent came from sales to governments of other countries.

Suppose the U.S. government contracted with Lockheed Martin to provide management services related to a governmental hardware and software system, and that the cost of these services will be $10 million per month. Assume the government offers to pay for the services on the day they are provided (a cash purchase) or 60 days later (a purchase on account). Assume that Lockheed Martin is absolutely sure the government will pay its account when due.

Do you think the company should care whether the government pays for the services upon delivery or 60 days later? Why? (Answers on page 365.)

ESTIMATING UNCOLLECTIBLE ACCOUNTS EXPENSE USING THE PERCENT OF REVENUE METHOD

LO 7-1

Use the percent of revenue method to account for uncollectible accounts expense.

Most companies do not expect to collect the full amount (face value) of their accounts receivable. Even carefully screened credit customers sometimes don't pay their bills. The **net realizable value** of accounts receivable represents the amount of receivables a company estimates it will actually collect. The net realizable value is the *face value* less an *allowance for doubtful accounts*.

The **allowance for doubtful accounts** represents a company's estimate of the amount of uncollectible receivables. To illustrate, assume a company with total accounts receivable of $50,000 estimates that $2,000 of its receivables will not be collected. The net realizable value of receivables is computed as follows:

Accounts receivable	$50,000
Less: Allowance for doubtful accounts	(2,000)
Net realizable value of receivables	$48,000

A company cannot know today, of course, the exact amount of the receivables it will not be able to collect in the future. The *allowance for doubtful accounts* and the *net realizable value* are necessarily *estimated amounts*. The net realizable value, however, more closely measures the cash that will ultimately be collected than does the face value. To avoid overstating assets, companies report receivables on their balance sheets at the net realizable value.

Reporting accounts receivable in the financial statements at net realizable value is commonly called the **allowance method of accounting for uncollectible accounts.** As indicated above, the allowance method requires accountants to estimate the amount of uncollectible accounts. How do accountants make these estimates? One approach is to base the estimates on a percentage of revenue. The following section of this chapter illustrates accounting for uncollectible accounts when the percentage of revenue approach is employed.

Accounting Events Affecting the Year 1 Period

Allen's Tutoring Services (ATS) is a small company that provides tutoring services to college students. ATS started operations on January 1, Year 1. During Year 1, ATS experienced three types of accounting events. These events are discussed below.

EVENT 1   Revenue Recognition
Allen's Tutoring Services (ATS) recognized $3,750 of service revenue earned on account during Year 1.

This is an asset source transaction. ATS obtained assets (accounts receivable) by providing services to customers. Both assets and stockholders' equity (retained earnings) increase. The event increases revenue and net income. Cash flow is not affected. The journal entry and its effects on the financial statements are shown here:

Account Title	Debit	Credit
Accounts Receivable	3,750	
Service Revenue		3,750

Assets	=	Liab.	+	Equity		Rev.	−	Exp.	=	Net Inc.		Cash Flow
Accts. Rec.	=			Ret. Earn.								
3,750	=	NA	+	3,750		3,750	−	NA	=	3,750		NA

Answers to The Curious Accountant

Lockheed Martin would definitely prefer to make the sale to the government in cash rather than on account. Even though it may be certain to collect its accounts receivable, the sooner the company gets its cash, the sooner the cash can be reinvested.

The interest cost related to a small accounts receivable of $50 that takes 60 days to collect may seem immaterial. At 2 percent, the lost interest amounts to $.17. However, when one considers that Lockheed Martin had approximately $8.2 billion of accounts receivable on December 31, 2016, and took an average of 63 days to collect them, the cost of financing receivables for a real-world company becomes apparent. At 2 percent, the cost of waiting 63 days to collect $8.2 billion of cash is $28.3 million ($8.2 billion × .02 × 63/365). For a full year, the cost to Lockheed Martin would be $164 million ($8.2 billion × .02). In 2016, the weighted-average interest rate on Lockheed Martin's debt was approximately 2 percent.

EVENT 2 Collection of Receivables
ATS collected $2,750 cash from accounts receivable in Year 1.

This event is an asset exchange transaction. The asset cash increases; the asset accounts receivable decreases. Total assets remains unchanged. Net income is not affected because the revenue was recognized in the previous transaction. The cash inflow is reported in the operating activities section of the statement of cash flows. The journal entry and its effects on the financial statements are shown here:

Account Title	Debit	Credit
Cash	2,750	
Accounts Receivable		2,750

Assets			=	Liab.	+	Equity	Rev.	−	Exp.	=	Net Inc.	Cash Flow
Cash	+	Accts. Rec.										
2,750	+	(2,750)	=	NA	+	NA	NA	−	NA	=	NA	2,750 OA

EVENT 3 Recognizing Uncollectible Accounts Expense
ATS recognized uncollectible accounts expense for accounts expected to be uncollectible in the future.

While ATS has collected cash for some of the revenue earned in Year 1, some of the remaining receivables may never be collected. ATS will not know the *actual amount* of uncollectible accounts until Year 1 when the customers fail to pay. However, the company can estimate the amount of revenue that it expects will be uncollectible. The *estimated amount* of uncollectible accounts can then be recognized as an expense on the Year 1 income statement. Recognizing the estimated expense improves the matching of revenues and expenses and therefore increases the accuracy of the financial statements.

Many accountants determine the estimated uncollectible accounts expense by taking a percentage of revenue. This approach is commonly called the **percent of revenue method.** The percentage used to make the estimate is usually based on the company's past collection experiences. However, the percentage may be adjusted for anticipated future circumstances. For example, the percentage may be reduced if the company plans to adopt more rigorous credit approval standards. Alternatively, the percentage may be increased if economic forecasts signal an economic downturn that would make customer defaults more likely.

Because this is ATS' first year of operation, there is no prior experience for determining the estimated percentage of uncollectible accounts. Instead, ATS will have to base its estimate on industry averages. To illustrate the accounting procedures for recognizing uncollectible accounts expense, assume that ATS estimates that 2 percent of revenue will be uncollectible. Under these circumstances, ATS would recognize $75 ($3,750 of revenue × 2%) of uncollectible accounts expense on the Year 1 income statement.

The estimated amount of **uncollectible accounts expense** is recognized in a year-end adjusting entry. The adjusting entry reduces the net realizable value of receivables, stockholders' equity, and the amount of reported net income. The statement of cash flows is not affected. The journal entry and its effects on the financial statements are shown next:

Account Title	Debit	Credit
Uncollectible Accounts Expense	75	
Allowance for Doubtful Accounts		75

Assets	=	Liab.	+	Equity	Rev.	−	Exp.	=	Net Inc.	Cash Flow
Net Realizable Value of Receivables	=			Ret. Earn.						
(75)	=	NA	+	(75)	NA	−	75	=	(75)	NA

The Accounts Receivable account is not reduced directly because none of the receivables have *actually* been determined to be uncollectible. The decrease in the net realizable value of receivables represents an *estimate* of what will be uncollectible some time in the future. To distinguish the actual balance in accounts receivable from the net realizable value, accountants use a **contra asset account** called Allowance for Doubtful Accounts. The allowance account is called a *contra account* because it has a credit balance instead of the debit balance normally seen in asset accounts. Indeed, the credit balance in the Allowance for Doubtful Accounts is subtracted from the debit balance in the Accounts Receivable account to determine the net realizable value of receivables that is shown on the balance sheet. The net realizable value of receivables for ATS is determined as follows:

Accounts receivable	$1,000*
Less: Allowance for doubtful accounts	(75)
Net realizable value of receivables	$ 925

*($3,750 revenue on account − $2,750 of collections)

Generally accepted accounting principles require disclosure of both the net realizable value and the amount of the allowance account. Many companies disclose these amounts directly in the balance sheet in a manner similar to that shown in the text box above. Other companies disclose allowance information in the notes to the financial statements.

Recording and Reporting Uncollectible Accounts Events in the Double-Entry System, Year 1

Exhibit 7.1, Panel A, shows a summary of the Year 1 transactions for ATC. Panel B shows the general ledger T-accounts after the journal entries have been posted to them. Panel C contains the financial statements. Although Exhibit 7.1 does not illustrate the Year 1 year-end closing entries, recall that the closing entries will transfer the amounts from the revenue and expense accounts to the Retained Earnings account. The balance in the Retained Earnings account after closing will be $3,675, as reported on the year-end balance sheet.

Financial Statements

As previously indicated, estimating uncollectible accounts improves the usefulness of the Year 1 financial statements in two ways. First, the balance sheet reports the amount of cash ($1,000 − $75 = $925) the company actually expects to collect (net realizable value of accounts receivable). Second, the income statement provides a clearer picture of managerial

EXHIBIT 7.1
The Big Picture

Panel A Transactions Summary

- **Event 1** ATS earned $3,750 of revenue on account.
- **Event 2** ATS collected $2,750 cash from accounts receivable.
- **Event 3** ATS adjusted its accounts to reflect management's estimate that uncollectible accounts expense would be $75.

Panel B General Ledger Accounts

Assets = Liabilities + Equity

Cash
(2)	2,750	
Bal.	2,750	

Accounts Receivable
(1)	3,750	2,750	(2)	
Bal.	1,000			

Allowance for Doubtful Accounts
		75	(3)
		75	Bal.

Retained Earnings

Service Revenue
	3,750	(1)

Uncollectible Accts. Expense
(3)	75	

Panel C Financial Statements for Year 1

Income Statement
Service revenue	$3,750
Uncollectible accts. exp.	(75)
Net income	$3,675

Balance Sheet
Assets		
Cash		$2,750
Accounts receivable	$1,000	
Less: Allowance	(75)	
Net realizable value		925
Total assets		$3,675
Stockholders' equity		
Retained earnings		$3,675

Statement of Cash Flows
Operating Activities	
Inflow from customers	$ 2,750
Investing Activities	0
Financing Activities	0
Net change in cash	2,750
Plus: Beginning cash balance	0
Ending cash balance	$2,750

performance because it better *matches* the uncollectible accounts expense with the revenue it helped produce. The statements in Exhibit 7.1 show that the cash flow from operating activities ($2,750) differs from net income ($3,675). The statement of cash flows reports only cash collections, whereas the income statement reports revenues earned on account less the estimated amount of uncollectible accounts expense.

CHECK YOURSELF 7.1

Pamlico Inc. began operations on January 1, Year 1. During Year 1, it earned $400,000 of revenue on account. The company collected $370,000 of accounts receivable. At the end of the year, Pamlico estimates uncollectible accounts expense will be 1 percent of revenue. Based on this information alone, what is the net realizable value of accounts receivable as of December 31, Year 1?

Answer Accounts receivable at year-end are $30,000 ($400,000 sales on account − $370,000 collection of receivables). The recognition of uncollectible accounts expense would result in a $4,000 ($400,000 × 0.01) balance in the allowance account. The net realizable value of accounts receivable is therefore $26,000 ($30,000 − $4,000).

Accounting Events Affecting the Year 2 Period

To further illustrate accounting for uncollectible accounts, we discuss six accounting events affecting Allen's Tutoring Services (ATS) during Year 2.

EVENT 1 Write-Off of Uncollectible Accounts Receivable
ATS wrote off $70 of uncollectible accounts receivable.

This is an asset exchange transaction. The amount of the uncollectible accounts is removed from the Accounts Receivable account and from the Allowance for Doubtful Accounts account. Because the balances in both the Accounts Receivable and the Allowance accounts decrease, the net realizable value of receivables—and therefore total assets—remains unchanged. The write-off does not affect the income statement. Because the uncollectible accounts expense was recognized in the previous year, the expense would be double counted if it were recognized again at the time an uncollectible account is written off. Finally, the statement of cash flows is not affected by the write-off. The journal entry and its effects on the financial statements are shown here:

Account Title	Debit	Credit
Allowance for Doubtful Accounts	70	
Accounts Receivable		70

Assets	=	Liab.	+	Equity	Rev.	−	Exp.	=	Net Inc.	Cash Flow
Net Realizable Value of Receivables										
NA	=	NA	+	NA	NA	−	NA	=	NA	NA

The computation of the *net realizable value,* before and after the write-off, is shown below:

	Before Write-Off	After Write-Off
Accounts receivable	$1,000	$930
Less: Allowance for doubtful accounts	(75)	(5)
Net realizable value	$ 925	$925

EVENT 2 Revenue Recognition
ATS provided $10,000 of tutoring services on account during Year 2.

Assets (accounts receivable) and stockholders' equity (retained earnings) increase. Recognizing revenue increases net income. Cash flow is not affected. The journal entry and its effects on the financial statements are shown here:

Account Title	Debit	Credit
Accounts Receivable	10,000	
Service Revenue		10,000

Assets	=	Liab.	+	Equity	Rev.	−	Exp.	=	Net Inc.	Cash Flow
Accts. Rec.	=			Ret. Earn.						
10,000	=	NA	+	10,000	10,000	−	NA	=	10,000	NA

EVENT 3 Collection of Accounts Receivable
ATS collected $8,430 cash from accounts receivable.

The balance in the Cash account increases, and the balance in the Accounts Receivable account decreases. Total assets are unaffected. Net income is not affected because revenue was recognized previously. The cash inflow is reported in the operating activities section of the statement of cash flows. The journal entry and its effects on the financial statements are shown here:

Account Title	Debit	Credit
Cash	8,430	
Accounts Receivable		8,430

Assets			=	Liab.	+	Equity	Rev.	−	Exp.	=	Net Inc.	Cash Flow
Cash	+	Accts. Rec.										
8,430	+	(8,430)	=	NA	+	NA	NA	−	NA	=	NA	8,430 OA

EVENT 4 Recovery of an Uncollectible Account: Reinstate Receivable
ATS recovered a receivable that it had previously written off.

Occasionally, a company receives payment from a customer whose account was previously written off. In such cases, the customer's account should be reinstated and the cash received should be recorded the same way as any other collection on account. The account receivable is reinstated because a complete record of the customer's payment history may be useful if the customer requests credit again at some future date. To illustrate, assume that ATS received a $10 cash payment from a customer whose account had previously been written off. The first step is to **reinstate** the account receivable by reversing the previous write-off. The balances in the Accounts Receivable and the Allowance accounts increase. Because the Allowance is a contra asset account, the increase in it offsets the increase in the Accounts Receivable account, and total assets are unchanged. Net income and cash flow are unaffected. The journal entry and its effects on the financial statements are shown next:

Account Title	Debit	Credit
Accounts Receivable	10	
Allowance for Doubtful Accounts		10

Assets	=	Liab.	+	Equity	Rev.	−	Exp.	=	Net Inc.	Cash Flow
Net Realizable Value of Receivables										
NA	=	NA	+	NA	NA	−	NA	=	NA	NA

EVENT 5   **Recovery of an Uncollectible Account: Collection of Receivable**
ATS recorded collection of the reinstated receivable.

The collection of $10 is recorded like any other collection of a receivable account: Cash increases and Accounts Receivable decreases. The journal entry and its effects on the financial statements are shown next:

Account Title	Debit	Credit
Cash	10	
Accounts Receivable		10

Assets			=	Liab.	+	Equity	Rev.	−	Exp.	=	Net Inc.	Cash Flow
Cash	+	Accts. Rec.										
10	+	(10)	=	NA	+	NA	NA	−	NA	=	NA	10 OA

©photastic/Shutterstock

EVENT 6   **Adjustment for Recognition of Uncollectible Accounts Expense**
Using the percent of revenue method, ATS recognized uncollectible accounts expense for Year 2.

Assuming management continues to estimate uncollectible accounts expense at 2 percent of revenue, ATS will recognize $200 ($10,000 revenue × .02) of uncollectible accounts expense in a year-end adjusting entry. The adjusting entry and its effects on the financial statements are shown next:

Account Title	Debit	Credit
Uncollectible Accounts Expense	200	
Allowance for Doubtful Accounts		200

Assets	=	Liab.	+	Equity	Rev.	−	Exp.	=	Net Inc.	Cash Flow
Net Realizable Value of Receivables	=			Ret. Earn.						
(200)	=	NA	+	(200)	NA	−	200	=	(200)	NA

Recording and Reporting Uncollectible Accounts Events in the Double-Entry System, Year 2

Panel A of Exhibit 7.2 shows a summary of the Year 2 accounting events for ATS. Panel B of the exhibit shows the general ledger T-accounts after the journal entries have been posted to them. Panel C contains the financial statements. Exhibit 7.2 does not include the closing entries. Closing the accounts will transfer the amounts from the revenue and expense accounts to the Retained Earnings account, resulting in a $13,475 ending balance in this account, as shown on the Year 2 balance sheet.

EXHIBIT 7.2
The Big Picture

Panel A Transactions Summary

Event 1	ATS wrote off $70 of uncollectible accounts receivable.
Event 2	ATS earned $10,000 of revenue on account.
Event 3	ATS collected $8,430 cash from accounts receivable.
Event 4	ATS reinstated a $10 account receivable it had previously written off.
Event 5	ATS recorded the collection of $10 from the reinstated receivable referenced in Event 4.
Event 6	ATS adjusted its accounts to recognize $200 of uncollectible accounts expense.

Panel B General Ledger Accounts

Assets = Liabilities + Equity

Cash

Bal.	2,750		
(3)	8,430		
(5)	10		
Bal.	11,190		

Accounts Receivable

Bal.	1,000	70	(1)
(2)	10,000	8,430	(3)
(4)	10	10	(5)
Bal.	2,500		

Allowance for Doubtful Accounts

(1)	70	75	Bal.
		10	(4)
		200	(6)
		215	Bal.

Retained Earnings

		3,675	Bal.

Service Revenue

		10,000	(2)

Uncollectible Accts. Expense

(6)	200		

Panel C Financial Statements for Year 2

Income Statement

Service revenue	$10,000
Uncollectible accts. exp.	(200)
Net income	$ 9,800

Balance Sheet

Assets		
Cash		$11,190
Accounts receivable	$2,500	
Less: Allowance	(215)	
Net realizable value		2,285
Total assets		$13,475
Stockholders' equity		
Retained earnings		$13,475

Statement of Cash Flows

Operating Activities	
Inflow from customers	$ 8,440
Investing Activities	0
Financing Activities	0
Net change in cash	8,440
Plus: Beginning cash balance	2,750
Ending cash balance	$11,190

Analysis of Financial Statements

Exhibit 7.2 Panel C displays the Year 2 financial statements. The amount of uncollectible accounts expense ($200) differs from the ending balance of the Allowance account ($215). The balance in the Allowance account was $15 before the Year 2 adjusting entry for uncollectible accounts expense was recorded. At the end of Year 1, Allen's Tutoring Services estimated there would be $75 of uncollectible accounts as a result of Year 1 credit sales. Actual write-offs, however, amounted to $70 and $10 of that amount was recovered, indicating the actual uncollectible accounts expense for Year 1 was only $60. Hindsight shows the expense for Year 1 was overstated by $15. However, if no estimate had been made, the amount of uncollectible accounts expense would have been understated by $60. In some accounting periods, estimated uncollectible accounts expense will likely be overstated; in others, it may be understated. The allowance method cannot produce perfect results, but it does improve the accuracy of the financial statements.

Because no dividends were paid, retained earnings at the end of Year 2 equals the December 31, Year 1, retained earnings plus Year 2 net income (that is, $3,675 + $9,800 = $13,475). Again, the cash flow from operating activities ($8,440) differs from net income ($9,800) because the statement of cash flows does not include the effects of revenues earned on account or the recognition of uncollectible accounts expense.

 CHECK YOURSELF 7.2

Maher Company had beginning balances in Accounts Receivable and Allowance for Doubtful Accounts of $24,200 and $2,000, respectively. During the accounting period, Maher earned $230,000 of revenue on account and collected $232,500 of cash from receivables. The company also wrote off $1,950 of uncollectible accounts during the period. Maher estimates uncollectible accounts expense will be 1 percent of credit sales. Based on this information, what is the net realizable value of receivables at the end of the period?

Answer The balance in the Accounts Receivable account is $19,750 ($24,200 + $230,000 − $232,500 − $1,950). The amount of uncollectible accounts expense for the period is $2,300 ($230,000 × 0.01). The balance in the Allowance for Doubtful Accounts is $2,350 ($2,000 − $1,950 + $2,300). The net realizable value of receivables is therefore $17,400 ($19,750 − $2,350).

ESTIMATING UNCOLLECTIBLE ACCOUNTS EXPENSE USING THE PERCENT OF RECEIVABLES METHOD

LO 7-2

 Use the percent of receivables method to estimate uncollectible accounts expense.

Some accountants believe they can better estimate the amount of uncollectible expense by basing their estimates on a percentage of accounts receivable rather than a percentage of revenue. This approach is commonly called the **percent of receivables method** of estimating uncollectible accounts expense. The approach focuses on estimating the most accurate balance for the Allowance for Doubtful Accounts account that appears on the year-end balance sheet.

To illustrate, assume that before adjusting its accounts on December 31, Year 1, Pyramid Corporation had a $56,000 balance in its Accounts Receivable account and a $500 credit balance in its Allowance for Doubtful Accounts account. Further assume that Pyramid estimates it will be unable to collect 6 percent of its accounts receivable. In other words, Pyramid estimates that $3,360 ($56,000 × .06) of the accounts receivable will be uncollectible. Accordingly, the *ending credit balance* in the Allowance for Doubtful Accounts account that appears on the December 31, Year 1, balance sheet must be $3,360.

Because the Allowance account currently has a $500 credit balance, Pyramid must record an adjusting entry that adds a $2,860 ($3,360 − $500) credit to the Allowance account before preparing the financial statements. The offsetting debit in the adjusting entry is to Uncollectible Accounts Expense. In other words, *the amount of the uncollectible accounts expense is determined by calculating the amount necessary to achieve the required ending balance in the Allowance account.*

Account Title	Debit	Credit
Uncollectible Accounts Expense	2,860	
Allowance for Doubtful Accounts		2,860

Assets	=	Liab.	+	Equity	Rev.	−	Exp.	=	Net Inc.	Cash Flow
Net Realizable Value of Receivables	=			Ret. Earn.						
(2,860)	=	NA	+	(2,860)	NA	−	2,860	=	(2,860)	NA

✓ CHECK YOURSELF 7.3

During Year 1, Oron Company earned $100,000 of revenue. Before adjusting its accounts on December 31, Year 1, Oron had a $20,000 balance in its Accounts Receivable Account and a $50 credit balance in its Allowance for Doubtful Accounts account. Determine the amount of uncollectible accounts expense Oron will recognize on its Year 1 income statement assuming the company estimates uncollectible accounts expense to be 4 percent of receivables.

Answer The ending balance in the Allowance for Doubtful Accounts account after the adjusting entries are posted to the ledger accounts is an $800 ($20,000 accounts receivable × .04) credit balance. Because there is an unadjusted credit balance of $50 in the Allowance account, the adjusting entry must include a $750 credit to the Allowance account. A corresponding $750 debit to the Uncollectible Accounts Expense account would be required. Accordingly, the amount of uncollectible expense recognized on the Year 1 income statement is $750.

Aging Accounts Receivable

History suggests that an account receivable that is past its due date is less likely to be collected than one that is not yet currently due. The longer an account receivable remains past due, the less likely it is to be collected. Accordingly, the accuracy of the amount of estimated uncollectible expense can be improved by **aging of accounts receivable,** which involves applying higher uncollectible percentage estimates to older receivables. To illustrate, assume that Pyramid Corporation prepared the aging of accounts receivable schedule shown in Exhibit 7.3.

The amount of accounts receivable that is estimated to be uncollectible (the ending balance in the Allowance for Doubtful Accounts account) is determined by applying different percentages to each category in the aging schedule. The percentage for each category is based on a company's previous collection experience for each of the categories. The percentages become progressively higher as the accounts become older. Exhibit 7.4 illustrates computing the ending balance required for Pyramid Corporation's December 31, Year 1, balance sheet.

LO 7-3

Use aging of accounts receivable to estimate uncollectible accounts expense.

EXHIBIT 7.3

PYRAMID CORPORATION
Accounts Receivable Aging Schedule
December 31, Year 1

Customer Name	Total Balance	Current	0–30	31–60	61–90	Over 90
J. Davis	$ 6,700	$ 6,700				
B. Diamond	4,800	2,100	$ 2,700			
K. Eppy	9,400	9,400				
B. Gilman	2,200				$1,000	$1,200
A. Kelly	7,300	7,300				
L. Niel	8,600	1,000	6,000	$ 1,600		
L. Platt	4,600			4,600		
J. Turner	5,500			3,000	2,000	500
H. Zachry	6,900		3,000	3,900		
Total	$56,000	$26,500	$11,700	$13,100	$3,000	$1,700

EXHIBIT 7.4

Balance Required in the Allowance for Doubtful Accounts at December 31, Year 1

Number of Days Past Due	Receivables Amount	Percentage Likely to Be Uncollectible	Required Allowance Account Balance
Current	$26,500	.01	$ 265
0–30	11,700	.05	585
31–60	13,100	.10	1,310
61–90	3,000	.25	750
Over 90	1,700	.50	850
Total	$56,000		$3,760

The computations in Exhibit 7.4 show that the *ending balance* in the Allowance for Doubtful Accounts account shown must be $3,760. Because Pyramid has an unadjusted $500 credit balance in its Allowance account, the amount of uncollectible expense to be recognized in the adjusting entry is $3,260 ($3,760 required ending balance − $500 current unadjusted balance). Except for the amount of the estimated expense, the journal entry and the effects on the financial statement would be the same as previously shown. Remember that aging is designed to improve the estimated amount of uncollectible accounts expense. It does not affect how the recognition of the expense affects the financial statements.

Matching Revenues and Expenses versus Asset Measurement

The *percent of revenue* method, with its focus on determining the uncollectible accounts expense, is often called the income statement approach. The *percent of receivables* method, focused on determining the best estimate of the allowance balance, is frequently called the balance sheet approach. Which estimating method is better? In any given year, the results will vary slightly between approaches. In the long run, however, the percentages used in either approach are based on a company's actual history of uncollectible accounts. Accountants routinely revise their estimates as more data become available, using hindsight to determine if the percentages should be increased or decreased. Either approach provides acceptable results.

RECOGNIZING UNCOLLECTIBLE ACCOUNTS EXPENSE USING THE DIRECT WRITE-OFF METHOD

If uncollectible accounts are not material, generally accepted accounting principles allow companies to account for them using the **direct write-off method.** Under the direct write-off method, a company simply recognizes uncollectible accounts expense *in the period in which it identifies and writes off uncollectible accounts.* No estimates, allowance account, or adjusting entries are needed.

The direct write-off method fails to match revenues with expenses. Revenues are recognized in one period and any related uncollectible accounts expense is recognized in a later period. Also, the direct write-off method overstates assets because receivables are reported at *face value* rather than *net realizable value.* If the amount of uncollectible accounts is immaterial, however, companies accept the minor reporting inaccuracies as a reasonable trade-off for recording convenience.

To illustrate the direct write-off method, return to Allen's Tutoring Services (ATS) Year 1 accounting period. Assume ATS decided the direct write-off method was appropriate to account for its receivables. Recall that, during Year 1, ATS recognized $3,750 of revenue on account. The journal entry and its effects on the financial statements are shown next:

LO 7-4

Show how the direct write-off method of accounting for uncollectible accounts affects financial statements.

Account Title	Debit	Credit
Accounts Receivable	3,750	
Service Revenue		3,750

Assets	=	Liab.	+	Equity	Rev.	−	Exp.	=	Net Inc.	Cash Flow
Accts. Rec.	=			Ret. Earn.						
3,750	=	NA	+	3,750	3,750	−	NA	=	3,750	NA

ATS believed only an immaterial amount of the $3,750 of accounts receivable would prove uncollectible. It therefore made no year-end adjusting entry for estimated uncollectible accounts. Instead, ATS recognizes uncollectible accounts expense when it determines an account is uncollectible.

In the Year 2 accounting period, ATS determined that $70 of accounts receivable were uncollectible. ATS recognized the uncollectible accounts expense in the entry to write off the uncollectible receivables. With the direct write-off method, the write-off reduces the asset account Accounts Receivable and decreases the stockholders' equity account Retained Earnings. On the income statement, expenses increase and net income decreases. The statement of cash flows is not affected by the write-off. The journal entry and its effects on the financial statements are shown below:

Account Title	Debit	Credit
Uncollectible Accounts Expense	70	
Accounts Receivable		70

Assets	=	Liab.	+	Equity	Rev.	−	Exp.	=	Net Inc.	Cash Flow
Accts. Rec.	=			Ret. Earn.						
(70)	=	NA	+	(70)	NA	−	70	=	(70)	NA

Also, in Year 2 ATS recovered a $10 account receivable it had previously written off. Recording the recovery of a previously written-off account requires two entries. First, ATS must *reinstate* the receivable (merely reverse the write-off entry above) because it has proven to be collectible after all. Second, ATS must record collecting the reinstated account. With the direct write-off method, reinstating the receivable increases the asset account Accounts Receivable and increases the stockholders' equity account Retained Earnings. On the income statement, expenses decrease and net income increases. The statement of cash flows is not affected. The journal entry and its effects on the financial statements are shown next:

Account Title	Debit	Credit
Accounts Receivable	10	
Uncollectible Accounts Expense		10

Assets	=	Liab.	+	Equity	Rev.	−	Exp.	=	Net Inc.	Cash Flow
Accts. Rec.	=			Ret. Earn.						
10	=	NA	+	10	NA	−	(10)	=	10	NA

Like the collection of any other receivable, collection of the reinstated account receivable increases the asset account Cash and decreases the asset account Accounts Receivable. The income statement is not affected. The cash inflow is reported in the operating activities section of the statement of cash flows. The journal entry and its effects on the financial statements are shown next:

Account Title	Debit	Credit
Cash	10	
Accounts Receivable		10

Assets			=	Liab.	+	Equity	Rev.	−	Exp.	=	Net Inc.	Cash Flow
Cash	−	Accts. Rec.										
10		(10)	=	NA	+	NA	NA	−	NA	=	NA	10 OA

ACCOUNTING FOR NOTES RECEIVABLE

Show how accounting for notes receivable and accrued interest affects financial statements.

Companies typically do not charge their customers interest on accounts receivable that are not past due. When a company extends credit for a long time or when the amount of credit it extends is large, however, the cost of granting free credit and the potential for disputes about payment terms both increase. To address these concerns, the parties frequently enter into a credit agreement, the terms of which are legally documented in a **promissory note.**

To illustrate, assume in Year 3 Allen's Tutoring Services (ATS) generates excess cash that it loans to an individual, Stanford Cummings, so Cummings can buy a car. ATS and Cummings agree that Cummings will repay the money borrowed plus interest at the end of one year. They also agree that ATS will hold the title to the car to secure the debt. Exhibit 7.5 illustrates a promissory note that outlines this credit agreement. For ATS, the credit arrangement represents a *note receivable*.

EXHIBIT 7.5

Promissory Note

Promissory Note

$15,000 (3)   *November 1, Year 3*
Amount   **Date**

For consideration received, <u>Stanford Cummings (1)</u> hereby promises to pay to the order of:

<u>   Allen's Tutoring Services (2)   </u>

<u> Fifteen thousand and no/100 (3)   </u>   **Dollars**

payable on   <u>October 31, Year 4 (5)   </u>

plus interest thereon at the rate of <u>6</u> percent per year. (4)

Collateral Description   <u>Automobile title (6)   </u>

Signature   <u>*Stanford Cummings* (1)   </u>

Features of this note are discussed next. Each feature is cross-referenced with a number that corresponds to an item on the promissory note in Exhibit 7.5. Locate each feature in Exhibit 7.5 and read the corresponding description of the feature that follows:

1. Maker—The person responsible for making payment on the due date is the **maker** of the note. The maker may also be called the *borrower* or *debtor*.
2. Payee—The person to whom the note is made payable is the **payee**. The payee may also be called the *creditor* or *lender*. The payee loans money to the maker and expects the return of the principal and the interest due.
3. Principal—The amount of money loaned by the payee to the maker of the note is the **principal**.
4. Interest—The economic benefit earned by the payee for loaning the principal to the maker is **interest,** which is normally expressed as an annual percentage of the principal amount. For example, a note with a 6 percent interest rate requires interest payments equal to 6 percent of the principal amount every year the loan is outstanding.
5. Maturity Date—The date on which the maker must repay the principal and make the final interest payment to the payee is the **maturity date**.
6. Collateral—Assets belonging to the maker that are assigned as security to ensure that the principal and interest will be paid when due are called **collateral.** In this example, if Cummings fails to pay ATS the amount due, ownership of the car Cummings purchased will be transferred to ATS.

Recording and Reporting Transactions Related to Notes Receivable

We illustrate accounting for notes receivable using the credit agreement evidenced by the promissory note in Exhibit 7.5. Allen's Tutoring Services engaged in many transactions during Year 3; we discuss here only transactions directly related to the note receivable.

EVENT 1   Loan of Money

The note shows that ATS loaned $15,000 to Stanford Cummings on November 1, Year 3. This event is an asset exchange. The asset account Cash decreases and the asset account Notes Receivable increases. The income statement is not affected. The statement of cash flows shows a cash outflow for investing activities. The journal entry and its effects on the financial statements are shown next:

Account Title	Debit	Credit
Notes Receivable	15,000	
Cash		15,000

		Assets					=	Liab.	+	Equity		Rev.	−	Exp.	=	Net Inc.		Cash Flow	
Date	Cash	+	Notes Rec.	+	Int. Rec.	=				Ret. Earn.									
11/01/Year 3	(15,000)	+	15,000	+	NA	=	NA	+	NA		NA	−	NA	=	NA		(15,000)	IA

EVENT 2 Accrual of Interest

For ATS, loaning money represents an investment in the note receivable. ATS will collect the principal ($15,000) plus interest of 6 percent of the principal amount (0.06 × $15,000 = $900), or a total of $15,900, on October 31, Year 4, one year from the date the loan was made.

Conceptually, lenders *earn* interest continually even though they do not *collect* cash continually. Each day, the amount of interest due, called **accrued interest,** is greater than the day before. Companies would find it highly impractical to attempt to record (recognize) accrued interest continually as the amount due increased.

Businesses typically solve the recordkeeping problem by recording accrued interest only when it is time to prepare financial statements or when the interest is due. At such times, the accounts are *adjusted* to reflect the amount of interest currently due. For example, ATS recorded the asset exchange immediately upon investing in the Note Receivable on November 1, Year 3. ATS did not, however, recognize any interest earned on the note until the balance sheet date, December 31, Year 3. At year-end, ATS made an entry to recognize the interest it had earned during the previous two months (November 1 through December 31). This entry is an **adjusting entry** because it adjusts (updates) the account balances prior to preparing financial statements.

ATS computed the amount of accrued interest by multiplying the principal amount of the note by the annual interest rate and by the length of time for which the note has been outstanding.

Principal × Annual interest rate × Time outstanding = Interest revenue
$15,000 × 0.06 × (2/12) = $150

ATS recognized the $150 of interest revenue in Year 3 although ATS will not collect the cash until Year 4. This practice illustrates the **matching concept.** Interest revenue is recognized in (matched with) the period in which it is earned regardless of when the related cash is collected. The adjusting entry is an asset source transaction. The asset account Interest Receivable increases, and the stockholders' equity account Retained Earnings increases. The income statement reflects an increase in revenue and net income. The statement of cash flows is not affected because ATS will not collect cash until the maturity date (October 31, Year 4). The adjusting entry and its effects on the financial statements are shown next:

Account Title	Debit	Credit
Interest Receivable	150	
Interest Revenue		150

		Assets					=	Liab.	+	Equity		Rev.	−	Exp.	=	Net Inc.		Cash Flow
Date	Cash	+	Notes Rec.	+	Int. Rec.	=				Ret. Earn.								
12/31/Year 3	NA	+	NA	+	150	=	NA	+	150		150	−	NA	=	150		NA	

EVENT 3   Collection of Principal and Interest on the Maturity Date

ATS collected $15,900 cash on the maturity date. The collection included $15,000 for the principal plus $900 for the interest. Recall that ATS previously accrued interest in the December 31, Year 3, adjusting entry for the two months in Year 3 that the note was outstanding. Since year-end, ATS has earned an additional 10 months of interest revenue. ATS must recognize this interest revenue before recording the cash collection. The amount of interest earned in Year 4 is computed as follows:

$$\text{Principal} \times \text{Annual interest rate} \times \text{Time outstanding} = \text{Interest revenue}$$
$$\$15{,}000 \times 0.06 \times (10/12) = \$750$$

The journal entry and effects on the financial statements are shown next:

Account Title	Debit	Credit
Interest Receivable	750	
Interest Revenue		750

	Assets	=	Liab.	+	Equity	Rev. − Exp. = Net Inc.	Cash Flow
Date	Cash + Notes Rec. + Int. Rec.	=			Ret. Earn.		
10/31/Year 4	NA + NA + 750	=	NA	+	750	750 − NA = 750	NA

The total amount of accrued interest is now $900 ($150 accrued in Year 3 plus $750 accrued in Year 4). The $15,900 cash collection is an asset exchange transaction. The asset account Cash increases, and two asset accounts, Notes Receivable and Interest Receivable, decrease. The income statement is not affected. The statement of cash flows shows a $15,000 inflow from investing activities (recovery of principal) and a $900 inflow from operating activities (interest collection). The journal entry and effects on the financial statements are shown next:

Account Title	Debit	Credit
Cash	15,900	
Notes Receivable		15,000
Interest Receivable		900

	Assets	=	Liab.	+	Equity	Rev. − Exp. = Net Inc.	Cash Flow
Date	Cash + Notes Rec. + Int. Rec.	=			Ret. Earn.		
10/31/Year 4	15,900 + (15,900) + (900)	=	NA	+	NA	NA − NA = NA	15,000 IA 900 OA

To clarify the illustration, we showed the interest accrual and the cash collection as two separate entries. Experienced accountants often record the two events in a single journal entry as follows:

Account Title	Debit	Credit
Cash	15,900	
Notes Receivable		15,000
Interest Receivable		150
Interest Revenue		750

Financial Statements

The financial statements reveal key differences between the timing of revenue recognition and the exchange of cash. These differences are highlighted next:

	Year 3	Year 4	Total
Interest revenue recognized	$150	$750	$900
Cash inflow from operating activities	0	900	900

Accrual accounting calls for recognizing revenue in the period in which it is earned regardless of when cash is collected.

Income Statement

Although generally accepted accounting principles require reporting receipts of, or payments for, interest on the statement of cash flows as operating activities, they do not specify how to classify interest on the income statement. In fact, companies traditionally report interest on the income statement as a nonoperating item. Interest is therefore frequently reported in two different categories within the same set of financial statements.

Balance Sheet

As with other assets, companies report interest receivable and notes receivable on the balance sheet in order of their liquidity. **Liquidity** refers to how quickly assets are expected to be converted to cash during normal operations. In the preceding example, Allen's Tutoring Services expects to convert its accounts receivable to cash before it collects the interest receivable and note receivable. Companies commonly report interest and notes receivable after accounts receivable. Exhibit 7.6 shows a partial balance sheet for ATS to illustrate the presentation of receivables.

CHECK YOURSELF 7.4

On October 1, Year 1, Mei Company accepted a promissory note for a loan it made to the Asia Pacific Company. The note had a $24,000 principal amount, a four-month term, and an annual interest rate of 4 percent. Determine the amount of interest revenue and the cash inflow from operating activities Mei will report in its Year 1 and Year 2 financial statements. Also provide in general journal form the year-end adjusting entry needed to recognize Year 1 interest revenue.

Answer The computation of accrued interest revenue is shown next. The interest rate is stated in annual terms even though the term of the note is only four months. Interest rates are commonly expressed as an annual percentage regardless of the term of the note. The *time outstanding* in the following formulas is therefore expressed as a fraction of a year. Mei charged annual interest of 4 percent, but the note was outstanding for only 3/12 of a year in Year 1 and 1/12 of a year in Year 2.

Year 1

Principal × Annual interest rate × Time outstanding = Interest revenue
$24,000 × 0.04 × (3/12) = $240

Year 2

Principal × Annual interest rate × Time outstanding = Interest revenue
$24,000 × 0.04 × (1/12) = $80

In Year 1, Mei's cash inflow from interest will be zero.

In Year 2, Mei will report a $320 ($240 + $80) cash inflow from operating activities for interest. The adjusting entry to recognize Year 1 accrued interest is as follows:

Interest Receivable	240	
Interest Revenue		240

EXHIBIT 7.6

Typical Balance Sheet Presentation of Receivables

ALLEN'S TUTORING SERVICES
Partial Balance Sheet
As of December 31, Year 3

Cash	xxxx
Accounts receivable	xxxx
Less: Allowance for doubtful accounts	(xxxx)
Net realizable value of accounts receivable	xxxx
Interest receivable	xxxx
Notes receivable	xxxx

ACCOUNTING FOR CREDIT CARD SALES

Maintaining accounts and notes receivable is expensive. In addition to uncollectible accounts expense, companies extending credit to their customers incur considerable costs for such clerical tasks as running background checks and maintaining customer records. Many businesses find it more efficient to accept third-party credit cards instead of offering credit directly to their customers. Credit card companies service the merchant's credit sales for a fee that typically ranges between 1 and 5 percent of gross sales.

LO 7-6

Show how accounting for credit card sales affects financial statements.

The credit card company usually provides customers with plastic cards that permit cardholders to charge purchases at various retail outlets. When a sale takes place, the seller records the transaction on a receipt the customer usually signs. The receipt is forwarded to the credit card company, which immediately pays the merchant.

The credit card company deducts its service fee from the gross amount of the sale and pays the merchant the net balance (gross amount of sale less credit card fee) in cash. The credit card company collects the gross sale amount directly from the customer. The merchant avoids the risk of uncollectible accounts, as well as the cost of maintaining customer credit records. To illustrate, assume that Allen's Tutoring Services experiences the following events.

©Piotr Adamowicz/123RF

EVENT 1   **Recognition of Revenue and Expense on Credit Card Sales**
ATS accepts a credit card payment for $1,000 of services rendered.

Assume the credit card company charges a 5 percent fee for handling the transaction ($1,000 × 0.05 = $50). ATS' income increases by the amount of revenue ($1,000) and decreases by the amount of the credit card expense ($50). Net income increases by $950. The event increases an asset, accounts receivable, due from the credit card company, and stockholders' equity (retained earnings) by $950 ($1,000 revenue − $50 credit card expense). Cash flow is not affected. The journal entry and its effects on the financial statements are shown next:

Account Title	Debit	Credit
Accounts Receivable—Credit Card Company	950	
Credit Card Expense	50	
Service Revenue		1,000

Assets	=	Liab.	+	Equity	Rev.	−	Exp.	=	Net Inc.	Cash Flow
Accts. Rec.	=			Ret. Earn.						
950	=	NA	+	950	1,000	−	50	=	950	NA

382 Chapter 7

EVENT 2 Collection of Credit Card Receivable
The collection of the receivable due from the credit card company is recorded like any other receivable collection.

When ATS collects the net amount of $950 ($1,000 − $50) from the credit card company, one asset account (Cash) increases and another asset account (Accounts Receivable) decreases. Total assets are not affected. The income statement is not affected. A $950 cash inflow is reported in the operating activities section of the statement of cash flows. The journal entry and its effects on the financial statements are shown next:

Account Title	Debit	Credit
Cash	950	
Accounts Receivable—Credit Card Company		950

Assets	=	Liab.	+	Equity	Rev.	−	Exp.	=	Net Inc.	Cash Flow
Cash + Accts. Rec.										
950 + (950)	=	NA	+	NA	NA	−	NA	=	NA	950 OA

The Financial Analyst

LO 7-7

Calculate and interpret the accounts receivable turnover ratio.

As mentioned earlier, two costs of extending credit to customers are uncollectible accounts expense and recordkeeping costs. These costs can be significant. Large companies spend literally millions of dollars to buy the equipment and pay the staff necessary to operate entire departments devoted to managing accounts receivable. Further, there is an implicit interest cost associated with extending credit. When a customer is permitted to delay payment, the creditor forgoes the opportunity to invest the amount the customer owes.

Exhibit 7.7 presents part of a note from the 2016 annual report of **Rent-A-Center**. This excerpt provides insight into the credit costs real companies incur. First, observe that Rent-A-Center was owed $73.4 million of receivables. These receivables represent money that could

EXHIBIT 7.7

RENT-A-CENTER, INC. December 31, 2016
Partial Note C Regarding Accountants Receivable and Allowance for Doubtful Accounts (amounts shown in thousands)

Receivables consist of the following:

	2016	2015
Installment sales receivable	$ 55,834	$ 57,010
Trade and notes receivables	14,067	15,924
Other receivables	3,477	—
Total	73,378	72,934
Less allowance for doubtful accounts	(3,593)	(3,614)
Net receivables	$ 69,785	$ 69,320

Changes in the Company's allowance for doubtful accounts are as follows:

	2016	2015
Beginning balance	$ 3,614	$ 4,023
Bad debt expense	15,449	15,260
Accounts written off	(16,095)	(16,317)
Recoveries	625	648
Ending balance	$ 3,593	$ 3,614

be in the bank earning interest if all sales had been made in cash. If Rent-A-Center could have earned interest at 5 percent on that money, the opportunity cost of this lost interest is approximately $3.7 million ($73.4 million × .05) a year. Next, observe that Rent-A-Center expects to have uncollectible accounts amounting to $3.6 million (balance in the allowance account). These are significant costs to a company that incurred a net loss of $105.2 million in 2016.

Average Number of Days to Collect Accounts Receivable

The longer it takes to collect accounts receivable, the greater the opportunity cost of lost income. Also, business experience indicates that the older an account receivable becomes, the less likely it is to be collected. Finally, taking longer to collect an account typically costs more for salaries, equipment, and supplies used in the process of trying to collect it. Businesses are therefore concerned about how long it takes to collect their receivables.

Two ratios help management, or other users, measure a company's collection period. One is the **accounts receivable turnover ratio,** computed as:[1]

$$\frac{\text{Sales}}{\text{Net accounts receivable}}$$

Net accounts receivable is also known as net realizable value of receivable, which is the amount of accounts receivable minus the allowance for doubtful accounts. Dividing a company's sales by its net accounts receivable tells how many times the net accounts receivable balance is "turned over" (converted into cash) each year. The higher the turnover, the shorter the collection period. To simplify its interpretation, the accounts receivable turnover ratio is often taken one step further to determine the **average number of days to collect accounts receivable,** sometimes called the *average collection period.* This is computed as:

$$\frac{365}{\text{Accounts receivable turnover ratio}}$$

This ratio measures how many days, on average, it takes a company to collect its accounts receivable. Because longer collection periods increase costs, shorter periods are obviously more desirable. To illustrate computing the *average number of days to collect accounts receivable* for Allen's Tutoring Services, refer to the Year 2 financial statements in Exhibit 7.2. On average, the company takes 83 days to collect its receivables, computed in two steps:

1. The accounts receivable turnover is 4.376 ($10,000 ÷ $2,285) times.
2. The average number of days to collect receivables is 83 (365 ÷ 4.376) days.

In the preceding computations, the net realizable value of accounts receivable was used because that is the amount typically reported in published financial statements. The results would not have been materially different had total accounts receivable been used.

Real-World Data

What is the collection period for real companies? The time required to collect receivables varies among industries and among companies within industries. The fourth column in Exhibit 7.8 displays the average number of days to collect receivables for seven companies in three different industries. These numbers are for 2016.

Because customers in fast-food restaurants typically pay cash when they purchase hamburgers or coffee, why do these companies have accounts receivable? The accounts receivable for **McDonald's** and **Restaurant Brands** arise because these companies sell goods to restaurants that are independent franchisees. (Restaurant Brands is the parent company of

---

[1]To be more precise, the ratio could be computed using only credit sales and average accounts receivable. Usually, however, companies do not report credit sales separately from cash sales in published financial statements. Average accounts receivable, if desired, is computed as [(Beginning receivables + Ending receivables) ÷ 2]. For this course, use the simpler computation shown here (Sales ÷ Accounts receivable).

EXHIBIT 7.8

Industry	Company	Average Days to Sell Inventory	Average Days to Collect Receivables	Length of Operating Cycle
Fast Food	McDonald's	4	22	26
	Starbucks	59	13	72
	Restaurant Brands International	15	36	51
Department Stores	Macy's	126	7	133
	Walmart	43	4	47
Home Construction	D.R. Horton	320	0	320
	Toll Brothers	648	0	648

Burger King and **Tim Horton**.) So, for example, McDonald's accounts receivable represents future collections from restaurant owners, not only from customers who purchase hamburgers.

Although there are many franchised **Starbucks** coffee shops, most of the company's revenues come from shops that are owned and operated by the company itself. Starbucks does not have accounts receivable from its own shops; its receivables come from sales to outside customers and from credit card sales in its own shops. In addition to accounts receivable related to franchised coffee shops, Starbucks sells coffee products such as coffee beans to retailers such as grocery stores. Most of these companies do not pay Starbucks "cash on delivery," but purchase their goods on account. One way companies manage their cash flow is to take time to pay their bills, and large companies such as **Kroger** can essentially force their suppliers to sell them goods on credit.

Some companies allow their customers extended time to pay their bills because the customers would otherwise have difficulty coming up with the money. Many small companies do not have cash available to pay up front. Buying on credit is the only way they can obtain the inventory they need. If a manufacturer or wholesaler wants to sell to such companies, credit sales represent the only option available.

The length of the **operating cycle** is the average time it takes a business to convert inventory to accounts receivable plus the time it takes to convert accounts receivable into cash. The average number of days to collect receivables is one component of the operating cycle for a particular company. The other component is the average number of days to sell inventory, which was explained in Chapter 5. The length of the operating cycles for the real-world companies in Exhibit 7.8 is shown in the last column.

What is the significance of the different operating cycle lengths in Exhibit 7.8? As previously explained, the longer the operating cycle takes, the more it costs the company. Exhibit 7.8 shows it takes **Macy's** an average of 86 days longer than **Walmart** to complete an operating cycle. All other things being equal, approximately how much did this longer time reduce Macy's earnings? Assume Macy's could invest excess cash at 8 percent (or alternatively, assume it pays 8 percent to finance its inventory and accounts receivable). Using the accounting information reported in Macy's 2016 financial statements, we can answer the question as follows:

Macy's investment in inventory × **Interest rate** × **Time** = **Cost**

$5,506,000,000 × 8% × 86/365 = $103,784,329

With 2.7 operating cycles per year (365 ÷ 133), the extended operating cycle costs Macy's $280 million annually. Based on the assumptions used here, Macy's would have increased its after-tax earnings by approximately 17 percent, if it could have reduced its operating cycle by 86 days. Although this illustration is a rough estimate, it demonstrates that it is important for businesses to minimize the length of their operating cycles.

REALITY BYTES

This chapter explains that, in general, companies want to collect their receivables as quickly as possible. There is a notable exception to this generalization. If a company charges its customers interest on unpaid receivables, the company makes money on the unpaid balance. Many sellers of "big-ticket" goods like furniture, large appliances, and automobiles offer to finance their customers' purchases, allowing customers extended time to pay off their receivables in exchange for the customers' paying additional charges for interest.

For example, most people probably think of Harley-Davidson as a company that makes its profits selling motorcycles, and that is largely true. However, Harley-Davidson also made a substantial amount of profit from financing the motorcycles that it sells. During 2014, 2015, and 2016, the company earned 76 percent of its operating income from motorcycle sales and 24 percent from financing those sales. This amounted to $834 million of income before taxes. Therefore, the fact that it took Harley-Davidson 165 days to collect its receivables in 2016 was probably not a reason for concern.

©Karen Bleier/AFP/Getty Images

CHECK YOURSELF 7.5

Randolph Corporation had sales for the year of $535,333 and an accounts receivable balance at year-end of $22,000. Determine Randolph's average number of days to collect accounts receivable.

Answer The accounts receivable turnover is 24.33 ($535,333 ÷ $22,000) times per year. The average number of days to collect accounts receivable is 15 (365 ÷ 24.33).

FOCUS ON INTERNATIONAL ISSUES

A ROSE BY ANY OTHER NAME . . .

If a person who studied U.S. GAAP wanted to look at the financial statements of a non-U.S. company, choosing statements of a company from another English-speaking country might seem logical. Presumably, this would eliminate language differences, and only the differences in GAAP would remain. However, this is not true.

When an accountant in the United States uses the term *turnover,* she or he is usually thinking of a financial ratio, such as the accounts receivable turnover ratio. However, in the United Kingdom, the term *turnover* refers to what U.S. accountants call *sales.* UK balance sheets do

(All): ©Press Association/AP Images

not usually show an account named *Inventory;* rather, they use the term *Stocks.* In the United States, accountants typically use the term *stocks* to refer to certificates representing ownership in a corporation. Finally, if an accountant or banker from the United Kingdom should ever ask you about your *gearing ratio,* he or she probably is not interested in your bicycle but in your debt-to-assets ratio.

Although IFRS has significantly increased the uniformity of financial reporting throughout the world, it does not seek to impose absolute uniformity. IFRS often allows alternate ways of accounting for the same business event, as will be discussed in Chapter 8. Even when different companies choose the same IFRS option for accounting for a given event, they are allowed some flexibility in the application of the IFRS rule, as are companies in the United States who follow GAAP. And, obviously, companies in different countries are allowed to prepare financial reports in their own language. As we will see in Chapter 9, companies in different countries may even use significantly different formats for their balance sheets.

A Look Back

We first introduced accounting for receivables in Chapter 2. This chapter presented additional complexities related to accounts receivable, such as the *allowance method of accounting for uncollectible accounts.* The allowance method improves matching of expenses with revenues. It also provides a more accurate measure of the value of accounts receivable on the balance sheet.

Under the allowance method, estimated uncollectible accounts expense is recorded in an adjusting entry at the end of the period in which a company has made credit sales. There are two methods commonly used to estimate the amount of uncollectible accounts expense: the percent of revenue method and the percent of receivables method. With the percent of revenue method, uncollectible accounts expense is measured as a percentage of the period's sales. With the percent of receivables method, a company analyzes its accounts receivable at the end of the period, usually classifying them by age, to estimate the amount of the accounts receivable balance that is likely to be uncollectible. The balance in the Allowance for Doubtful Accounts account is then adjusted to equal the estimated amount of uncollectible accounts. Uncollectible accounts expense decreases the net realizable value of receivables (accounts receivable − allowance for doubtful accounts), stockholders' equity, and net income.

The allowance method of accounting for uncollectible accounts is conceptually superior to the *direct write-off method,* in which uncollectible accounts expense is recognized when an account is determined to be uncollectible. The direct write-off method fails to match revenues with expenses and overstates accounts receivable on the balance sheet. It is easier to use, however, and is permitted by generally accepted accounting principles if the amount of uncollectible accounts expense is immaterial.

The chapter also introduced notes receivable and accounting for *accrued interest.* When the term of a promissory note extends over more than one accounting period, companies must record adjusting entries to recognize interest in the appropriate accounting period, even if the cash exchange of interest occurs in a different accounting period.

We also discussed accounting for credit card sales, a vehicle that shifts uncollectible accounts expense to the credit card issuer. Many companies find the benefits of accepting major credit cards to be worth the credit card expense consequently incurred.

Finally, we addressed the costs of making credit sales. In addition to uncollectible accounts expense, interest is a major cost of financing receivables. The length of the collection period provides a measure of the quality of receivables. Short collection periods usually indicate lower amounts of uncollectible accounts and interest cost. Long collection periods imply higher costs. The collection period can be measured in two steps. First, divide sales by the accounts receivable balance to determine the accounts receivable turnover ratio. Then divide the number of days in the year (365) by the accounts receivable turnover ratio.

A Look Forward

Chapter 8 discusses accounting for long-term assets such as buildings and equipment. As with inventory cost flow, discussed in Chapter 5, GAAP allows companies to use different accounting methods to report on similar types of business events. Life would be easier for accounting students if all companies used the same accounting methods. However, the business world is complex. For the foreseeable future, people are likely to continue to have diverse views as to the best way to account for a variety of business transactions. To function effectively in today's business environment, it is important for you to be able to recognize differences in reporting practices.

SELF-STUDY REVIEW PROBLEM

A step-by-step audio-narrated series of slides is available in **Connect.**

During Year 4 Calico Company experienced the following accounting events:

1. Provided $120,000 of services on account.
2. Collected $85,000 cash from accounts receivable.
3. Wrote off $1,800 of accounts receivable that were uncollectible.
4. Loaned $3,000 to an individual, Emma Gardner, in exchange for a note receivable.
5. Paid $90,500 cash for operating expenses.
6. Estimated that uncollectible accounts expense would be 2 percent of credit sales. Recorded the year-end adjusting entry.
7. Recorded the year-end adjusting entry for accrued interest on the note receivable (see Event 4). Calico made the loan on August 1. It had a six-month term and a 6 percent rate of interest.

Calico's ledger balances on January 1, Year 4, were as follows:

Event No.	Cash	+	Net Realizable Value of Receivables	+	Notes Rec.	+	Int. Rec.	=	Liab.	+	Com. Stk.	+	Ret. Earn.
Bal.	12,000	+	15,800	+	NA	+	NA	=	NA	+	20,000	+	7,800

Required

a. Record the Year 4 events in ledger accounts using the horizontal format shown in the preceding example.
b. Determine net income for Year 4.
c. Determine net cash flow from operating activities for Year 4.
d. Determine the net realizable value of accounts receivable at December 31, Year 4.
e. What amount of interest revenue will Calico recognize on its note receivable in Year 5?

Solution to Requirement a

Event No.	Cash	+	Net Realizable Value of Receivables	+	Notes Rec.	+	Int. Rec.	=	Liab.	+	Com. Stk.	+	Ret. Earn.
Bal.	12,000	+	15,800	+	NA	+	NA	=	NA	+	20,000	+	7,800
1	NA	+	120,000	+	NA	+	NA	=	NA	+	NA	+	120,000
2	85,000	+	(85,000)	+	NA	+	NA	=	NA	+	NA	+	NA
3	NA	+	NA	+	NA	+	NA	=	NA	+	NA	+	NA
4	(3,000)	+	NA	+	3,000	+	NA	=	NA	+	NA	+	NA
5	(90,500)	+	NA	+	NA	+	NA	=	NA	+	NA	+	(90,500)
6	NA	+	(2,400)	+	NA	+	NA	=	NA	+	NA	+	(2,400)
7	NA	+	NA	+	NA	+	75*	=	NA	+	NA	+	75
Totals	3,500	+	48,400	+	3,000	+	75	=	NA	+	20,000	+	34,975

*$3,000 × .06 × 5/12 = $75.

Solution to Requirements b–e

a. Net income is $27,175 ($120,000 − $90,500 − $2,400 + $75).
b. Net cash flow from operating activities is an outflow of $5,500 ($85,000 − $90,500).
c. The net realizable value of accounts receivable is $48,400 ($50,800 − $2,400).
d. In Year 5, Calico will recognize interest revenue for one month: $3,000 × .06 × 1/12 = $15.

KEY TERMS

Account receivable 362
Accounts receivable turnover ratio 383
Accrued interest 378
Adjusting entry 378
Aging of accounts receivable 373
Allowance for doubtful accounts 364
Allowance method of accounting for uncollectible accounts 364
Average number of days to collect accounts receivable 383
Collateral 377
Contra asset account 366
Direct write-off method 375
Interest 377
Liquidity 380
Maker 377
Matching concept 378
Maturity date 377
Net realizable value 364
Notes receivable 363
Operating cycle 384
Payee 377
Percent of receivables method 372
Percent of revenue method 366
Principal 377
Promissory note 376
Reinstate 369
Uncollectible accounts expense 366

QUESTIONS

1. What is the difference between accounts receivable and notes receivable?
2. What is the *net realizable value* of receivables?
3. What type of account is the Allowance for Doubtful Accounts?
4. What are two ways in which estimating uncollectible accounts improves the accuracy of the financial statements?
5. When using the allowance method, why is uncollectible accounts expense an estimated amount?
6. What is the most common format for reporting accounts receivable on the balance sheet? What information does this method provide beyond showing only the net amount?
7. Why is it necessary to make an entry to reinstate a previously written-off account receivable before the collection is recorded?
8. What are some factors considered in estimating the amount of uncollectible accounts receivable?
9. What is the effect on the accounting equation of recognizing uncollectible accounts expense?
10. What is the effect on the accounting equation of writing off an uncollectible account receivable when the allowance method is used? When the direct write-off method is used?
11. How does the recovery of a previously written-off account affect the income statement when the allowance method is used? How does the recovery of a previously written-off account affect the statement of cash flows when the allowance method is used?
12. What is the advantage of using the allowance method of accounting for uncollectible accounts? What is the advantage of using the direct write-off method?
13. How do companies determine the percentage estimate of uncollectible accounts when using the percent of revenue method?
14. What is an advantage of using the percent of receivables method of estimating uncollectible accounts expense?
15. What is "aging of accounts receivable"?
16. What is the difference between the allowance method and the direct write-off method of accounting for uncollectible accounts?
17. When is it acceptable to use the direct write-off method of accounting for uncollectible accounts?
18. What is a promissory note?
19. Define the following terms:
    a. Maker
    b. Payee
    c. Principal
    d. Interest
    e. Maturity date
    f. Collateral
20. What is the formula for computing interest revenue?
21. What is accrued interest?
22. When is an adjusting entry for accrued interest generally recorded?
23. Assume that on July 1, Year 1, Big Corp. loaned Little Corp. $12,000 for a period of one year at 6 percent interest. What amount of interest revenue will Big report for Year 1? What amount of cash will Big receive upon maturity of the note?
24. In which section of the statement of cash flows will Big report the cash collected in Question 23?
25. Why is it generally beneficial for a business to accept major credit cards as payment for goods and services even when the fee charged by the credit card company is substantial?
26. What types of costs do businesses avoid when they accept major credit cards as compared with handling credit sales themselves?
27. How is the accounts receivable turnover ratio computed? What information does the ratio provide?
28. How is the average number of days to collect accounts receivable computed? What information does the ratio provide?
29. Is accounting terminology standard in all countries? What term is used in the United Kingdom to refer to *sales*? What term is used to refer to *inventory*? What is a *gearing ratio*? Is it important to know about these differences?
30. What is the operating cycle of a business?

MULTIPLE-CHOICE QUESTIONS

Multiple-choice questions are available in **Connect**.

EXERCISES—SERIES A

 All applicable Exercises in Series A are available in **Connect**.

Exercise 7-1A *Analysis of financial statement effects of accounting for uncollectible accounts under the allowance method*

LO 7-1

Businesses using the allowance method for the recognition of uncollectible accounts expense commonly experience four accounting events:

1. Recognition of uncollectible accounts expense through a year-end adjusting entry.
2. Write-off of uncollectible accounts.
3. Recognition of revenue on account.
4. Collection of cash from accounts receivable.

Required

Show the effect of each event on the elements of the financial statements, using a horizontal statements model like the one shown next. Use the following coding scheme to record your answers: increase is +, decrease is −, not affected is NA. In the Cash Flow column, indicate whether the item is an operating activity (OA), investing activity (IA), or financing activity (FA). The first transaction is entered as an example.

Event No.	Assets	=	Liab.	+	Equity	Rev.	−	Exp.	=	Net Inc.	Cash Flow
1	−		NA		−	NA		+		−	NA

Exercise 7-2A *Accounting for uncollectible accounts: allowance method*

LO 7-1

Holmes Cleaning Service began operation on January 1, Year 1. The company experienced the following events for its first year of operations:

Events Affecting Year 1:

1. Provided $84,000 of cleaning services on account.
2. Collected $76,000 cash from accounts receivable.
3. Paid salaries of $28,500 for the year.
4. Adjusted the accounts to reflect management's expectations that uncollectible accounts expense would be $1,650. The expense was determined using the percent of revenue method.

Required

a. Prepare general journal entries for Events 1 through 4.
b. Post the general journal entries to T-accounts.
c. Prepare an income statement, balance sheet, and statement of cash flows for Year 1.

Exercise 7-3A *Analyzing account balances for a company using the allowance method of accounting for uncollectible accounts*

LO 7-1

The following account balances come from the records of Ourso Company:

	Beginning Balance	Ending Balance
Accounts Receivable	$2,800	$3,600
Allowance for Doubtful Accounts	280	350

During the accounting period, Ourso recorded $14,000 of sales revenue on account. The company also wrote off a $150 account receivable.

Required

a. Determine the amount of cash collected from receivables.

b. Determine the amount of uncollectible accounts expense recognized during the period.

LO 7-1

Exercise 7-4A Effect of recognizing uncollectible accounts expense on financial statements: percent of revenue allowance method

Rosie Dry Cleaning was started on January 1, Year 1. It experienced the following events during its first two years of operation:

Events Affecting Year 1

1. Provided $45,000 of cleaning services on account.
2. Collected $39,000 cash from accounts receivable.
3. Adjusted the accounting records to reflect the estimate that uncollectible accounts expense would be 1 percent of the cleaning revenue on account.

Events Affecting Year 2

1. Wrote off a $300 account receivable that was determined to be uncollectible.
2. Provided $62,000 of cleaning services on account.
3. Collected $61,000 cash from accounts receivable.
4. Adjusted the accounting records to reflect the estimate that uncollectible accounts expense would be 1 percent of the cleaning revenue on account.

Required

a. Record the events for Year 1 in T-accounts.

b. Determine the following amounts:
   (1) Net income for Year 1.
   (2) Net cash flow from operating activities for Year 1.
   (3) Balance of accounts receivable at the end of Year 1.
   (4) Net realizable value of accounts receivable at the end of Year 1.

c. Repeat Requirements *a* and *b* for the Year 2 accounting period.

LO 7-1

Exercise 7-5A Analyzing financial statement effects of accounting for uncollectible accounts using the percent of revenue allowance method

Grover Inc. uses the allowance method to account for uncollectible accounts expense. Grover Inc. experienced the following four accounting events in Year 1:

1. Recognized $92,000 of revenue on account.
2. Collected $78,000 cash from accounts receivable.
3. Wrote off uncollectible accounts of $720.
4. Recognized uncollectible accounts expense. Grover estimated that uncollectible accounts expense will be 1 percent of sales on account.

Required

a. Show the effect of each event on the elements of the financial statements, using a horizontal statements model like the one shown next. Use + for increase, − for decrease, and NA for not affected. In the Cash Flow column, indicate whether the item is an operating activity (OA), investing activity (IA), or financing activity (FA). The first transaction is entered as an example.

Event No.	Assets	=	Liab.	+	Equity	Rev.	−	Exp.	=	Net Inc.	Cash Flow
1	+		NA		+	+		NA		+	NA

b. Record the above transactions in general journal form.

Exercise 7-6A Effect of recovering a receivable previously written off

LO 7-1

The accounts receivable balance for Renue Spa at December 31, Year 1, was $61,000. Also on that date, the balance in the Allowance for Doubtful Accounts was $3,750. During Year 2, $2,100 of accounts receivable were written off as uncollectible. In addition, Renue unexpectedly collected $500 of receivables that had been written off in a previous accounting period. Services provided on account during Year 2 were $215,000, and cash collections from receivables were $218,000. Uncollectible accounts expense was estimated to be 2 percent of the sales on account for the period.

Required

a. Record the transactions in general journal form and post to T-accounts.
b. Based on the preceding information, compute (after year-end adjustment):
   (1) Balance of Allowance for Doubtful Accounts at December 31, Year 2.
   (2) Balance of Accounts Receivable at December 31, Year 2.
   (3) Net realizable value of Accounts Receivable at December 31, Year 2.
c. What amount of uncollectible accounts expense will Renue report for Year 2?
d. Explain how the $500 recovery of receivables affects the income statement.

Exercise 7-7A Effect of recognizing uncollectible accounts on the financial statements: percent of receivables allowance method

LO 7-2

Leach Inc. experienced the following events for the first two years of its operations:

Year 1:

1. Issued $10,000 of common stock for cash.
2. Provided $78,000 of services on account.
3. Provided $36,000 of services and received cash.
4. Collected $69,000 cash from accounts receivable.
5. Paid $38,000 of salaries expense for the year.
6. Adjusted the accounting records to reflect uncollectible accounts expense for the year. Leach estimates that 5 percent of the ending accounts receivable balance will be uncollectible.

Year 2:

1. Wrote off an uncollectible account for $650.
2. Provided $88,000 of services on account.
3. Provided $32,000 of services and collected cash.
4. Collected $81,000 cash from accounts receivable.
5. Paid $65,000 of salaries expense for the year.
6. Adjusted the accounts to reflect uncollectible accounts expense for the year. Leach estimates that 5 percent of the ending accounts receivable balance will be uncollectible.

Required

a. Record the Year 1 events in general journal form and post them to T-accounts.
b. Prepare the income statement, statement of changes in stockholders' equity, balance sheet, and statement of cash flows for Year 1.
c. What is the net realizable value of the accounts receivable at December 31, Year 1?
d. Repeat Requirements a, b, and c for Year 2.

Exercise 7-8A Accounting for uncollectible accounts: percent of receivables allowance method

LO 7-2, 7-3

Vulcan Service Co. experienced the following transactions for Year 1, its first year of operations:

1. Provided $91,000 of services on account.
2. Collected $72,000 cash from accounts receivable.
3. Paid $36,000 of salaries expense for the year.

4. Adjusted the accounts using the following information from an accounts receivable aging schedule:

Number of Days Past Due	Amount	Percent Likely to Be Uncollectible	Allowance Balance
Current	$7,800	.01	
0–30	4,500	.05	
31–60	2,000	.10	
61–90	2,200	.20	
Over 90 days	2,500	.50	

Required

a. Record the above transactions in general journal form and post to T-accounts.
b. Prepare the income statement for Vulcan Service Co. for Year 1.
c. What is the net realizable value of the accounts receivable at December 31, Year 1?

LO 7-4

Exercise 7-9A *Accounting for uncollectible accounts: direct write-off method*

Patel Service Co. does make a few sales on account but is mostly a cash business. Consequently, it uses the direct write-off method to account for uncollectible accounts. During Year 1, Patel Service Co. earned $35,000 of cash revenue and $4,500 of revenue on account. Cash operating expenses were $19,000. After numerous attempts to collect a $120 account receivable from Sam Stephens, the account was determined to be uncollectible in Year 1.

Required

a. Show the effects of (1) cash revenue, (2) revenue on account, (3) cash expenses, and (4) write-off of the uncollectible account on the financial statements using a horizontal statements model like the one shown here. In the Cash Flow column, indicate whether the item is an operating activity (OA), investing activity (IA), or financing activity (FA). Use NA to indicate that an element is not affected by the event.

Assets	=	Liab.	+	Equity	Rev.	−	Exp.	=	Net Inc.	Cash Flow
Cash + Accts. Rec.										

b. What amount of net income did Patel Service Co. report on the Year 1 income statement?
c. Prepare the general journal entries for the four accounting events listed in Requirement a.

LO 7-1, 7-4

Exercise 7-10A *Accounting for uncollectible accounts: percent of revenue allowance versus direct write-off method*

Joey's Bike Shop sells new and used bicycle parts. Although a majority of its sales are cash sales, it makes a significant amount of credit sales. During Year 1, its first year of operations, Joey's Bike Shop experienced the following:

Sales on account	$260,000
Cash sales	580,000
Collections of accounts receivable	235,000
Uncollectible accounts charged off during the year	1,250

Required

a. Assume that Joey's Bike Shop uses the allowance method of accounting for uncollectible accounts and estimates that 1 percent of its sales on account will not be collected. Answer the following questions:

(1) What is the Accounts Receivable balance at December 31, Year 1?
(2) What is the ending balance of the Allowance for Doubtful Accounts at December 31, Year 1, after all entries and adjusting entries are posted?
(3) What is the amount of uncollectible accounts expense for Year 1?
(4) What is the net realizable value of accounts receivable at December 31, Year 1?

b. Assume that Joey's Bike Shop uses the direct write-off method of accounting for uncollectible accounts. Answer the following questions:
(1) What is the Accounts Receivable balance at December 31, Year 1?
(2) What is the amount of uncollectible accounts expense for Year 1?
(3) What is the net realizable value of accounts receivable at December 31, Year 1?

Exercise 7-11A *Accounting for notes receivable* LO 7-5

Rainey Enterprises loaned $20,000 to Small Co. on June 1, Year 1, for one year at 6 percent interest.

Required

a. Record these general journal entries for Rainey Enterprises:
(1) The loan to Small Co.
(2) The adjusting entry at December 31, Year 1.
(3) The adjusting entry and collection of the note on June 1, Year 2.

b. Show the effects of the three above transactions in a horizontal statements model like the one shown next:

Date	Assets	=	Liab.	+	Equity	Rev.	−	Exp.	=	Net Inc.	Cash Flow
	Cash + Notes Rec. + Int. Rec. =				Ret. Earn.						

Exercise 7-12A *Notes receivable—accrued interest* LO 7-5

On May 1, Year 1, Benz's Sandwich Shop loaned $10,000 to Mark Henry for one year at 6 percent interest.

Required

Answer the following questions:
a. What is Benz's interest income for Year 1?
b. What is Benz's total amount of receivables at December 31, Year 1?
c. How will the loan and interest be reported on Benz's Year 1 statement of cash flows?
d. What is Benz's interest income for Year 2?
e. What is the total amount of cash that Benz's will collect in Year 2 from Mark Henry?
f. How will the loan and interest be reported on Benz's Year 2 statement of cash flows?
g. What is the total amount of interest that Benz's earned on the loan to Mark Henry?

Exercise 7-13A *Effect of credit card sales on financial statements* LO 7-6

Ultra Day Spa provided $120,000 of services during Year 1. All customers paid for the services with credit cards. Ultra submitted the credit card receipts to the credit card company immediately. The credit card company paid Ultra cash in the amount of face value less a 5 percent service charge.

Required

a. Show the credit card sales and the subsequent collection of accounts receivable in a horizontal statements model like the one shown next. In the Cash Flow column, indicate whether the item is an operating activity (OA), investing activity (IA), or financing activity (FA). Use NA to indicate that an element is not affected by the event.

Assets	= Liab. + Equity	Rev. − Exp. = Net Inc.	Cash Flow
Cash + Accts. Rec.			

b. Based on this information alone, answer the following questions:
   (1) What is the amount of total assets at the end of the accounting period?
   (2) What is the amount of revenue reported on the income statement?
   (3) What is the amount of cash flow from operating activities reported on the statement of cash flows?
   (4) What costs would a business incur if it maintained its own accounts receivable? What cost does a business incur by accepting credit cards?

LO 7-6

Exercise 7-14A *Recording credit card sales*

Luna Company accepted credit cards in payment for $6,000 of services performed during July Year 1. The credit card company charged Luna a 4 percent service fee; it paid Luna as soon as it received the invoices.

Required

a. Prepare the general journal entry to record the service revenue.
b. Prepare the general journal entry for the collection of the receivable from the credit card company.
c. Based on this information alone, what is the amount of net income earned during the month of July?

LO 7-1, 7-5, 7-6

Exercise 7-15A *Comprehensive single-cycle problem*

The following post-closing trial balance was drawn from the accounts of Little Grocery Supplier (LGS) as of December 31, Year 1:

	Debit	Credit
Cash	$ 9,000	
Accounts Receivable	41,000	
Allowance for Doubtful Accounts		$ 2,500
Inventory	78,000	
Accounts Payable		21,000
Common Stock		50,000
Retained Earnings		54,500
Totals	$128,000	$128,000

Transactions for Year 2

1. LGS acquired an additional $20,000 cash from the issue of common stock.
2. LGS purchased $85,000 of inventory on account.
3. LGS sold inventory that cost $91,000 for $160,000. Sales were made on account.
4. The company wrote off $900 of uncollectible accounts.
5. On September 1, LGS loaned $18,000 to Eden Co. The note had an 8 percent interest rate and a one-year term.
6. LGS paid $19,000 cash for operating expenses.
7. The company collected $161,000 cash from accounts receivable.
8. A cash payment of $92,000 was paid on accounts payable.
9. The company paid a $5,000 cash dividend to the stockholders.
10. Accepted credit cards for sales amounting to $7,000. The cost of goods sold was $4,000. The credit card company charges a 4% service charge. The cash has not been received.
11. Uncollectible accounts are estimated to be 1 percent of sales on account.
12. Recorded the accrued interest at December 31, Year 2 (see item 5).

Required

a. Record the above transactions in general journal form.
b. Open T-accounts and record the beginning balances and the Year 2 transactions.
c. Prepare an income statement, statement of changes in stockholders' equity, balance sheet, and statement of cash flows for Year 2.

Exercise 7-16A *Accounts receivable turnover and average days to collect accounts receivable*   LO 7-7

The following information is available for Market, Inc. and Supply, Inc. at December 31:

Accounts	Market, Inc.	Supply, Inc.
Accounts Receivable	$ 56,200	$ 75,400
Allowance for Doubtful Accounts	2,248	2,256
Sales Revenue	606,960	867,100

Required

a. What is the accounts receivable turnover for each of the companies?
b. What is the average days to collect the receivables?
c. Assuming both companies use the percent of receivables allowance method, what is the estimated percentage of uncollectible accounts for each company?

PROBLEMS—SERIES A

 All applicable Problems in Series A are available in Connect.

Problem 7-17A *Accounting for uncollectible accounts: two cycles using the percent of revenue allowance method*   LO 7-1

The following transactions apply to Jova Company for Year 1, the first year of operation:
1. Issued $10,000 of common stock for cash.
2. Recognized $210,000 of service revenue earned on account.
3. Collected $162,000 from accounts receivable.
4. Paid $125,000 cash for operating expenses.
5. Adjusted the accounts to recognize uncollectible accounts expense. Jova uses the allowance method of accounting for uncollectible accounts and estimates that uncollectible accounts expense will be 1 percent of sales on account.

The following transactions apply to Jova for Year 2:
1. Recognized $320,000 of service revenue on account.
2. Collected $335,000 from accounts receivable.
3. Determined that $2,150 of the accounts receivable were uncollectible and wrote them off.
4. Collected $800 of an account that had previously been written off.
5. Paid $205,000 cash for operating expenses.
6. Adjusted the accounts to recognize uncollectible accounts expense for Year 2. Jova estimates uncollectible accounts expense will be 0.5 percent of sales on account.

CHECK FIGURES
c. Ending Accounts Receivable, Year 1: $48,000
d. Net Income, Year 2: $113,400

Required

Complete the following requirements for Year 1 and Year 2. Complete all requirements for Year 1 prior to beginning the requirements for Year 2.

a. Identify the type of each transaction (asset source, asset use, asset exchange, or claims exchange).
b. Show the effect of each transaction on the elements of the financial statements, using a horizontal statements model like the one shown here. Use + for increase, − for decrease, and NA for not

affected. Also, in the Cash Flow column, indicate whether the item is an operating activity (OA), investing activity (IA), or financing activity (FA). The first transaction is entered as an example. (*Hint:* Closing entries do not affect the statements model.)

Event No.	Assets	=	Liab.	+	Equity	Rev.	−	Exp.	=	Net Inc.	Cash Flow
1	+		NA		+	+		NA		+	NA

c. Record the transactions in general journal form and post them to T-accounts (begin Year 2 with the ending T-account balances from Year 1).

d. Prepare the income statement, statement of changes in stockholders' equity, balance sheet, and statement of cash flows.

e. Prepare closing entries and post these closing entries to the T-accounts. Prepare the post-closing trial balance.

LO 7-1

Problem 7-18A *Determining account balances and preparing journal entries: percent of revenue allowance method of accounting for uncollectible accounts*

CHECK FIGURE
d. Net Realizable Value: $43,100

During the first year of operation, Year 1, Direct Service Co. recognized $290,000 of service revenue on account. At the end of Year 1, the accounts receivable balance was $46,000. For this first year in business, the owner believes uncollectible accounts expense will be about 1 percent of sales on account.

Required

a. What amount of cash did Direct Service collect from accounts receivable during Year 1?

b. Assuming Direct Service uses the allowance method to account for uncollectible accounts, what amount should Direct Service record as uncollectible accounts expense for Year 1?

c. Prepare the general journal entries to:
   (1) Record service revenue on account.
   (2) Record collections from accounts receivable.
   (3) Record the entry to recognize uncollectible accounts expense.

d. What is the net realizable value of receivables at the end of Year 1?

e. Show the effects of the transactions in Requirement *c* on the financial statements by recording the appropriate amounts in a horizontal statements model like the one shown next. In the Cash Flow column, indicate whether the item is an operating activity (OA), investing activity (IA), or financing activity (FA). Use NA for not affected.

Assets	=	Liab.	+	Equity	Rev.	−	Exp.	=	Net Inc.	Cash Flow
Cash + Net Realizable Value of Receivables										

LO 7-2

Problem 7-19A *Determination of account balances and preparation of journal entries—percent of receivables allowance method of accounting for uncollectible accounts*

CHECK FIGURE
a. Net Realizable Value: $66,864

The following information is available for Quality Book Sales' sales on account and accounts receivable:

Accounts receivable balance, January 1, Year 2	$ 78,500
Allowance for doubtful accounts, January 1, Year 2	$ 4,710
Sales on account, Year 2	$550,000
Collection on accounts receivable, Year 2	$556,000

After several collection attempts, Quality Book Sales wrote off $2,850 of accounts that could not be collected. Quality Book Sales estimates that 4 percent of the ending accounts receivable balance will be uncollectible.

Required

a. Compute the following amounts:
   (1) Using the allowance method, the amount of uncollectible accounts expense for Year 2.
   (2) Net realizable value of receivables at the end of Year 2.
b. Record the general journal entries to:
   (1) Record sales on account for Year 2.
   (2) Record cash collections from accounts receivable for Year 2.
   (3) Write off the accounts that are not collectible.
   (4) Record the estimated uncollectible accounts expense for Year 2.
c. Explain why the uncollectible accounts expense amount is different from the amount that was written off as uncollectible.

Problem 7-20A *Accounting for uncollectible accounts: percent of receivables allowance method*

LO 7-2, 7-3

Roth Inc. experienced the following transactions for Year 1, its first year of operations:
1. Issued common stock for $50,000 cash.
2. Purchased $140,000 of merchandise on account.
3. Sold merchandise that cost $110,000 for $250,000 on account.
4. Collected $236,000 cash from accounts receivable.
5. Paid $118,000 on accounts payable.
6. Paid $50,000 of salaries expense for the year.
7. Paid other operating expenses of $28,000.
8. Roth adjusted the accounts using the following information from an accounts receivable aging schedule:

CHECK FIGURES
b. Net Income: $61,430
Total Assets: $133,430

Number of Days Past Due	Amount	Percent Likely to Be Uncollectible	Allowance Balance
Current	$10,000	.01	
0–30	2,000	.05	
31–60	1,200	.10	
61–90	500	.20	
Over 90 days	300	.50	

Required

a. Record the above transactions in general journal form and post to T-accounts.
b. Prepare the income statement, statement of changes in stockholders' equity, balance sheet, and statement of cash flows for Roth Inc. for Year 1.
c. What is the net realizable value of the accounts receivable at December 31, Year 1?

Problem 7-21A *Multistep income statement and balance sheet*

LO 7-1, 7-5

Required

Use the following information to prepare a multistep income statement and a balance sheet for Sherman Equipment Co. for Year 2. (*Hint:* Some of the items will *not* appear on either statement, and ending retained earnings must be calculated.)

CHECK FIGURES
Total Assets: $273,800
Total Liabilities: $58,000

Salaries Expense	$ 69,000	Operating Expenses	62,000
Common Stock	100,000	Cash Flow from Investing Activities	78,400
Notes Receivable (short term)	24,000	Prepaid Rent	12,500
Allowance for Doubtful Accounts	7,800	Land	40,000
Uncollectible Accounts Expense	8,100	Cash	48,100
Supplies	1,200	Inventory	98,300
Interest Revenue	5,400	Accounts Payable	46,000
Sales Revenue	320,000	Salaries Payable	12,000
Dividends	3,500	Cost of Goods Sold	148,000
Interest Receivable (short term)	1,500	Accounts Receivable	56,000
Beginning Retained Earnings	81,000		

Chapter 7

LO 7-4, 7-5

Problem 7-22A Accounting for notes receivable and uncollectible accounts using the direct write-off method

The following transactions apply to Hooper Co. for Year 1, its first year of operations:

1. Issued $60,000 of common stock for cash.
2. Provided $90,000 of services on account.
3. Collected $78,000 cash from accounts receivable.
4. Loaned $20,000 to Mosby Co. on November 30, Year 1. The note had a one-year term to maturity and a 6 percent interest rate.
5. Paid $26,000 of salaries expense for the year.
6. Paid a $2,000 dividend to the stockholders.
7. Recorded the accrued interest on December 31, Year 1 (see item 4).
8. Determined that $920 of accounts receivable were uncollectible.

Required

a. Record the above transactions in general journal form.
b. Post the entries to T-accounts.
c. Prepare the income statement, balance sheet, and statement of cash flows for Year 1.
d. Show the effects of the above transactions in a horizontal statements model like the one shown next:

Event	Assets	= Liab. +	Equity	Rev. − Exp. = Net Inc.	Cash Flows
	Cash + Accts. Rec. + Notes Rec. + Int. Rec. =		Com. Stk. + Ret. Earn.		

LO 7-1, 7-5

Problem 7-23A Missing information

The following information comes from the accounts of James Company:

Account Title	Beginning Balance	Ending Balance
Accounts Receivable	$36,000	$34,000
Allowance for Doubtful Accounts	1,800	1,600
Note Receivable	40,000	40,000
Interest Receivable	1,400	2,800

Required

a. There were $190,000 of sales on account during the accounting period. Write-offs of uncollectible accounts were $1,450. What was the amount of cash collected from accounts receivable? What amount of uncollectible accounts expense was reported on the income statement? What was the net realizable value of receivables at the end of the accounting period?
b. The note receivable has a two-year term with a 7 percent interest rate. What amount of interest revenue was recognized during the period? How much cash was collected from interest?

LO 7-2, 7-6

Problem 7-24A Accounting for credit card sales and uncollectible accounts: percent of receivables allowance method

CHECK FIGURES
c. Net Income: $280,300
Total Assets: $480,300

Northwest Sales had the following transactions in Year 1:

1. The business was started when it acquired $200,000 cash from the issue of common stock.
2. Northwest purchased $900,000 of merchandise for cash in Year 1.
3. During the year, the company sold merchandise for $1,200,000. The merchandise cost $710,000. Sales were made under the following terms:

a.	$520,000	Cash sales
b.	380,000	Credit card sales (The credit card company charges a 4 percent service fee.)
c.	300,000	Sales on account

4. The company collected all the amount receivable from the credit card company.
5. The company collected $210,000 of accounts receivable.
6. The company paid $190,000 cash for selling and administrative expenses.
7. Determined that 5 percent of the ending accounts receivable balance would be uncollectible.

Required

a. Show the effects of each of the transactions on the elements of the financial statements, using a horizontal statements model like the one shown next. Use + for increase, − for decrease, and NA for not affected. The first transaction is entered as an example. (*Hint:* Closing entries do not affect the statements model.)

Event No.	Assets	=	Liab.	+	Equity	Rev.	−	Exp.	=	Net Inc.	Cash Flow
1	+		NA		+	NA		NA		NA	+ FA

b. Prepare general journal entries for each of the transactions and post them to T-accounts.
c. Prepare an income statement, statement of changes in stockholders' equity, balance sheet, and statement of cash flows for Year 1.

Problem 7-25A Effect of transactions on the elements of financial statements

LO 7-4, 7-5, 7-6

Required

Identify each of the following independent transactions as asset source (AS), asset use (AU), asset exchange (AE), or claims exchange (CE). Also explain how each event affects assets, liabilities, stockholders' equity, net income, and cash flow by placing a + for increase, − for decrease, or NA for not affected under each of the categories. The first event is recorded as an example.

Event	Type of Event	Assets	Liabilities	Common Stock	Retained Earnings	Net Income	Cash Flow
a	AS	+	NA	NA	+	+	NA

a. Provided services on account.
b. Wrote off an uncollectible account (use the direct write-off method).
c. Loaned cash to H. Phillips for one year at 6 percent interest.
d. Collected cash from customers paying their accounts.
e. Paid cash for land.
f. Sold merchandise at a price above cost. Accepted payment by credit card. The credit card company charges a service fee. The receipts have not yet been forwarded to the credit card company.
g. Provided services for cash.
h. Paid cash for operating expenses.
i. Paid cash for salaries expense.
j. Recovered an uncollectible account that had been previously written off (assume the direct write-off method is used to account for uncollectible accounts).
k. Paid cash to creditors on accounts payable.
l. Recorded three months of accrued interest on the note receivable (see item *c*).
m. Submitted receipts to the credit card company (see item *f*) and collected cash.
n. Sold land at its cost.

LO 7-1, 7-4, 7-5, 7-6

Problem 7-26A *Comprehensive accounting cycle problem (uses percent of revenue allowance method)*

The following trial balance was prepared for Tile, Etc., Inc. on December 31, Year 1, after the closing entries were posted:

Account Title	Debit	Credit
Cash	$110,000	
Accounts Receivable	125,000	
Allowance for Doubtful Accounts		$ 18,000
Inventory	425,000	
Accounts Payable		95,000
Common Stock		450,000
Retained Earnings		97,000
Totals	$660,000	$660,000

Tile, Etc. had the following transactions in Year 2:

1. Purchased merchandise on account for $580,000.
2. Sold merchandise that cost $420,000 for $890,000 on account.
3. Sold for $245,000 cash merchandise that had cost $160,000.
4. Sold merchandise for $190,000 to credit card customers. The merchandise had cost $96,000. The credit card company charges a 4 percent fee.
5. Collected $620,000 cash from accounts receivable.
6. Paid $610,000 cash on accounts payable.
7. Paid $145,000 cash for selling and administrative expenses.
8. Collected cash for the full amount due from the credit card company (see item 4).
9. Loaned $60,000 to J. Parks. The note had an 8 percent interest rate and a one-year term to maturity.
10. Wrote off $7,500 of accounts as uncollectible.
11. Made the following adjusting entries:
    (a) Recorded uncollectible accounts expense estimated at 1 percent of sales on account.
    (b) Recorded seven months of accrued interest on the note at December 31, Year 2 (see item 9).

Required

a. Prepare general journal entries for these transactions, and post the entries to T-accounts. Also, prepare an income statement, a statement of changes in stockholders' equity, a balance sheet, and a statement of cash flows for Year 2.
b. Compute the net realizable value of accounts receivable at December 31, Year 2.
c. If Tile, Etc. used the direct write-off method, what amount of uncollectible accounts expense would it report on the income statement?

EXERCISES—SERIES B

LO 7-1

Exercise 7-1B *Analysis of financial statement effects of accounting for uncollectible accounts under the allowance method*

Hardin Services Co. experienced the following events in Year 1:

1. Provided services on account.
2. Collected cash for accounts receivable.
3. Attempted to collect an account and, when unsuccessful, wrote off the amount to uncollectible accounts expense.

Required

Show the effect of each event on the elements of the financial statements, using a horizontal statements model like the one shown next. Use + for increase, − for decrease, and NA for not affected. In the Cash Flow column, indicate whether the item is an operating activity (OA), investing activity (IA), or financing activity (FA).

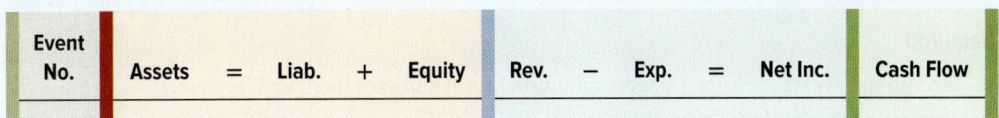

Exercise 7-2B *Accounting for bad debts: allowance method*   LO 7-1

Sandy's Accounting Service began operation on January 1, Year 1. The company experienced the following events for its first year of operations:

Events Affecting Year 1:

1. Provided $96,000 of accounting services on account.
2. Collected $80,000 cash from accounts receivable.
3. Paid salaries of $32,000 for the year.
4. Adjusted the accounts to reflect management's expectations that uncollectible accounts expense would be $1,600.

Required

a. Prepare general journal entries for Events 1 through 4.
b. Post the general journal entries to T-accounts.
c. Prepare an income statement, balance sheet, and statement of cash flows for Year 1.

Exercise 7-3B *Analyzing account balances for a company using the allowance*   LO 7-1
method of accounting for uncollectible accounts

The following account balances come from the records of Stone Company:

	Beginning Balance	Ending Balance
Accounts Receivable	$4,000	$4,500
Allowance for Doubtful Accounts	150	250

During the accounting period, Stone recorded $21,000 of service revenue on account. The company also wrote off a $180 account receivable.

Required

a. Determine the amount of cash collected from receivables.
b. Determine the amount of uncollectible accounts expense recognized during the period.

Exercise 7-4B *Effect of recognizing uncollectible accounts expense on financial*   LO 7-1
statements: percent of revenue allowance method

Reliable Auto Service was started on January 1, Year 1. The company experienced the following events during its first two years of operation:

Events Affecting Year 1

1. Provided $45,000 of repair services on account.
2. Collected $32,000 cash from accounts receivable.
3. Adjusted the accounting records to reflect the estimate that uncollectible accounts expense would be 1 percent of the service revenue on account.

Events Affecting Year 2

1. Wrote off a $320 account receivable that was determined to be uncollectible.
2. Provided $65,000 of repair services on account.
3. Collected $66,000 cash from accounts receivable.
4. Adjusted the accounting records to reflect the estimate that uncollectible accounts expense would be 1 percent of the service revenue on account.

Required

a. Record the events for Year 1 in general journal form and post them to T-accounts.
b. Determine the following amounts:
   (1) Net income for Year 1.
   (2) Net cash flow from operating activities for Year 1.
   (3) Balance of accounts receivable at the end of Year 1.
   (4) Net realizable value of accounts receivable at the end of Year 1.
c. Repeat Requirements *a* and *b* for the Year 2 accounting period.

LO 7-1

Exercise 7-5B *Analyzing financial statement effects of accounting for uncollectible accounts using the percent of revenue allowance method*

Tull Bros. uses the allowance method to account for uncollectible accounts expense. Tull experienced the following four events in Year 1:

1. Recognized $68,000 of revenue on account.
2. Collected $62,000 cash from accounts receivable.
3. Determined that $500 of accounts receivable were not collectible and wrote them off.
4. Recognized uncollectible accounts expense for the year. Tull estimates that uncollectible accounts expense will be 2 percent of its sales.

Required

a. Show the effect of each of these events on the elements of the financial statements, using a horizontal statements model like the following one. Use + for increase, − for decrease, and NA for not affected. In the Cash Flow column, indicate whether the item is an operating activity (OA), investing activity (IA), or financing activity (FA).

Event No.	Assets	=	Liab.	+	Equity	Rev.	−	Exp.	=	Net Inc.	Cash Flow
	Cash + Net Realizable Value of Rec.	=			Ret. Earn.						

b. Record the above transactions in general journal form.

LO 7-1

Exercise 7-6B *Effect of recovering a receivable previously written off*

The accounts receivable balance for Edd's Shoe Repair at December 31, Year 1, was $76,000. Also on that date, the balance in the Allowance for Doubtful Accounts was $3,200. During Year 2, $2,900 of accounts receivable were written off as uncollectible. In addition, Edd's Shoe Repair unexpectedly collected $200 of receivables that had been written off in a previous accounting period. Sales on account during Year 2 were $210,000, and cash collections from receivables were $215,000. Uncollectible accounts expense was estimated to be 1 percent of the sales on account for the period.

Required

a. Record the transactions in general journal form and post them to T-accounts.
b. Based on the preceding information, compute (after year-end adjustment):
   (1) Balance of Allowance for Doubtful Accounts at December 31, Year 2.
   (2) Balance of Accounts Receivable at December 31, Year 2.
   (3) Net realizable value of Accounts Receivable at December 31, Year 2.
c. What amount of uncollectible accounts expense will Edd's Shoe Repair report for Year 2?
d. Explain how the $200 recovery of receivables affected the accounting equation.

Exercise 7-7B Effect of recognizing uncollectible accounts on the financial statements: percent of receivables allowance method

LO 7-2

Juno Inc. experienced the following events for the first two years of its operations:

Year 1:

1. Issued $5,000 of common stock for cash.
2. Provided $80,000 of services on account.
3. Provided $22,000 of services and received cash.
4. Collected $65,000 cash from accounts receivable.
5. Paid $24,000 of salaries expense for the year.
6. Adjusted the accounting records to reflect uncollectible accounts expense for the year. Juno estimates that 5 percent of the ending accounts receivable balance will be uncollectible.

Year 2:

1. Wrote off an uncollectible account of $620.
2. Provided $95,000 of services on account.
3. Provided $15,000 of services and collected cash.
4. Collected $90,000 cash from accounts receivable.
5. Paid $35,000 of salaries expense for the year.
6. Adjusted the accounts to reflect uncollectible accounts expense for the year. Juno estimates that 5 percent of the ending accounts receivable balance will be uncollectible.

Required

a. Record the Year 1 events in general journal form and post them to T-accounts.
b. Prepare the income statement, statement of changes in stockholders' equity, balance sheet, and statement of cash flows for Year 1.
c. What is the net realizable value of the accounts receivable at December 31, Year 1?
d. Repeat Requirements *a*, *b*, and *c* for Year 2.

Exercise 7-8B Accounting for uncollectible accounts: percent of receivables allowance method

LO 7-2, 7-3

Pollard Service Co. experienced the following transactions for Year 1, its first year of operations:

1. Provided $86,000 of services on account.
2. Collected $72,000 cash from accounts receivable.
3. Paid $39,000 of salaries expense for the year.
4. Pollard adjusted the accounts using the following information from an accounts receivable aging schedule:

Number of Days Past Due	Amount	Percent Likely to Be Uncollectible	Allowance Balance
Current	$7,500	.01	
0–30	2,000	.05	
31–60	1,500	.10	
61–90	1,000	.30	
Over 90 days	2,000	.50	

Required

a. Record the above transactions in general journal form and post them to T-accounts.
b. Prepare the income statement for Pollard Service Co. for Year 1.
c. What is the net realizable value of the accounts receivable at December 31, Year 1?

Exercise 7-9B Accounting for uncollectible accounts: direct write-off method

LO 7-4

Applied Business Systems has a small number of sales on account but is mostly a cash business. Consequently, it uses the direct write-off method to account for uncollectible accounts. During Year 1, Applied Business Systems earned $46,000 of cash revenue and $9,000 of revenue on account. Cash operating expenses were $32,100. After numerous attempts to collect a $325 account receivable from J.C. Mims, the account was determined to be uncollectible in Year 2.

Required

a. Show the effects of (1) cash revenue, (2) revenue on account, (3) cash expenses, and (4) write-off of the uncollectible account on the financial statements using a horizontal statements model like the one shown next. In the Cash Flow column, indicate whether the item is an operating activity (OA), investing activity (IA), or financing activity (FA). Use NA to indicate that an element is not affected by the event.

Assets	=	Liab.	+	Equity	Rev.	−	Exp.	=	Net Inc.	Cash Flow
Cash + Accts. Rec.										

b. What amount of net income did Applied Business Systems report on the Year 1 income statement?

c. Prepare the general journal entries for the four accounting events listed in Requirement *a*.

LO 7-1, 7-4

Exercise 7-10B *Accounting for uncollectible accounts: percent of revenue allowance versus direct write-off method*

Classic Auto Parts sells new and used auto parts. Although a majority of its sales are cash sales, it makes a significant amount of credit sales. During Year 1, its first year of operations, Classic Auto Parts experienced the following:

Sales on account	$320,000
Cash sales	680,000
Collections of accounts receivable	295,000
Uncollectible accounts charged off during the year	1,400

Required

a. Assume that Classic Auto Parts uses the allowance method of accounting for uncollectible accounts and estimates that 1 percent of its sales on account will not be collected. Answer the following questions:

(1) What is the Accounts Receivable balance at December 31, Year 1?

(2) What is the ending balance of the Allowance for Doubtful Accounts at December 31, Year 1, after all entries and adjusting entries are posted?

(3) What is the amount of uncollectible accounts expense for Year 1?

(4) What is the net realizable value of accounts receivable at December 31, Year 1?

b. Assume that Classic Auto Parts uses the direct write-off method of accounting for uncollectible accounts. Answer the following questions:

(1) What is the Accounts Receivable balance at December 31, Year 1?

(2) What is the amount of uncollectible accounts expense for Year 1?

(3) What is the net realizable value of accounts receivable at December 31, Year 1?

LO 7-5

Exercise 7-11B *Accounting for notes receivable*

Cachet Enterprises loaned $30,000 to Craft Co. on September 1, Year 1, for one year at 6 percent interest.

Required

a. Record these general journal entries for Cachet Enterprises:

(1) The loan to Craft Co.

(2) The adjusting entry at December 31, Year 1.

(3) The adjusting entry and collection of the note on September 1, Year 2.

b. Show the effects of the three preceding transactions in a horizontal statements model like the one shown next.

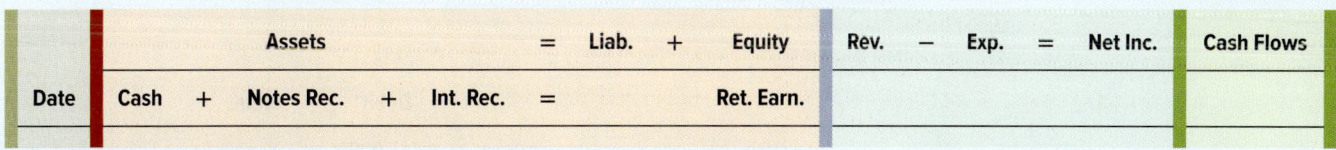

Exercise 7-12B *Notes receivable—accrued interest* LO 7-5

On March 1, Year 1, Taylor's Deli loaned $18,000 to Style Studio for one year at 5 percent interest.

Required

Answer the following questions:

a. What is Taylor's interest income for Year 1?
b. What is Taylor's total amount of receivables at December 31, Year 1?
c. How will the loan and interest be reported on Taylor's Year 1 statement of cash flows?
d. What is Taylor's interest income for Year 2?
e. What is the total amount of cash that Taylor's will collect in Year 2 from Style Studio?
f. How will the loan and interest be reported on Taylor's Year 2 statement of cash flows?
g. What is the total amount of interest Taylor's Deli earned from the loan to Style Studio?

Exercise 7-13B *Effect of credit card sales on financial statements* LO 7-6

Advanced Carpet Cleaning provided $76,000 of services during Year 1, its first year of operations. All customers paid for the services with major credit cards. Advanced Carpet submitted the credit card receipts to the credit card company immediately. The credit card company paid Advanced Carpet cash in the amount of face value less a 3 percent service charge.

Required

a. Show the credit card sales and the subsequent collection of accounts receivable in a horizontal statements model like the one shown next. In the Cash Flow column, indicate whether the item is an operating activity (OA), investing activity (IA), or financing activity (FA). Use NA to indicate that an element is not affected by the event.

Assets	=	Liab.	+	Equity	Rev.	−	Exp.	=	Net Inc.	Cash Flow
Cash + Accts. Rec.										

b. Answer the following questions:
   (1) What is the amount of total assets at the end of the accounting period?
   (2) What is the amount of revenue reported on the income statement?
   (3) What is the amount of cash flow from operating activities reported on the statement of cash flows?
   (4) Why would Advanced Carpet Cleaning accept credit cards instead of providing credit directly to its customers? In other words, why would Advanced Carpet be willing to pay 3 percent of sales to have the credit card company handle its sales on account?

Exercise 7-14B *Recording credit card sales* LO 7-6

Jung Company accepted credit cards in payment for $8,650 of services performed during March Year 1. The credit card company charged Jung a 4 percent service fee. The credit card company paid Jung as soon as it received the invoices.

Required

a. Prepare the general journal entry to record the service revenue.
b. Prepare the general journal entry for the collection of the receivable from the credit card company.
c. Based on this information alone, what is the amount of net income earned during the month of March?

LO 7-1, 7-5, 7-6

Exercise 7-15B *Comprehensive single-cycle problem*

The following post-closing trial balance was drawn from the accounts of Southern Timber Co. as of December 31, Year 1:

	Debit	Credit
Cash	$16,000	
Accounts receivable	18,000	
Allowance for doubtful accounts		$ 2,000
Inventory	25,000	
Accounts payable		9,200
Common stock		30,000
Retained earnings		17,800
Totals	$59,000	$59,000

Transactions for Year 2

1. Acquired an additional $20,000 cash from the issue of common stock.
2. Purchased $80,000 of inventory on account.
3. Sold inventory that cost $61,000 for $98,000. Sales were made on account.
4. Wrote off $1,500 of uncollectible accounts.
5. On September 1, Southern loaned $10,000 to Pine Co. The note had a 6 percent interest rate and a one-year term.
6. Paid $24,500 cash for salaries expense.
7. Collected $99,000 cash from accounts receivable.
8. Paid $78,000 cash on accounts payable.
9. Paid a $5,000 cash dividend to the stockholders.
10. Accepted credit cards for sales amounting to $5,000. The cost of goods sold was $3,500. The credit card company charges a 4% service charge. The cash has not been received.
11. Estimated uncollectible accounts expense to be 1 percent of sales on account.
12. Recorded the accrued interest at December 31, Year 1.

Required

a. Record the preceding transactions in general journal form.
b. Open T-accounts and record the beginning balances and the Year 2 transactions.
c. Prepare an income statement, statement of changes in stockholders' equity, balance sheet, and statement of cash flows for Year 2.

LO 7-7

Exercise 7-16B *Accounts receivable turnover and average days to collect accounts receivable*

The following information is available for Bradford Inc. and Windsor Inc. at December 31:

Accounts	Bradford	Windsor
Accounts Receivable	$ 92,500	$ 220,200
Allowance for Doubtful Accounts	3,250	8,100
Sales Revenue	716,500	1,978,200

Required

a. What is the accounts receivable turnover for each of the companies?
b. What is the average days to collect the receivables?
c. Assuming both companies use the percent of receivables allowance method, what is the estimated percentage of uncollectible accounts for each company?

PROBLEMS—SERIES B

Problem 7-17B Accounting for uncollectible accounts—two cycles using the percent of revenue allowance method

LO 7-1

The following transactions apply to Sports Consulting for Year 1, the first year of operation:

1. Issued $5,000 of common stock for cash.
2. Recognized $70,000 of service revenue earned on account.
3. Collected $62,000 from accounts receivable.
4. Adjusted accounts to recognize uncollectible accounts expense. Sports uses the allowance method of accounting for uncollectible accounts and estimates that uncollectible accounts expense will be 2 percent of sales on account.

The following transactions apply to Sports Consulting for Year 2:

1. Recognized $84,000 of service revenue on account.
2. Collected $70,000 from accounts receivable.
3. Determined that $1,100 of the accounts receivable were uncollectible and wrote them off.
4. Collected $200 of an account that had been previously written off.
5. Paid $51,200 cash for operating expenses.
6. Adjusted accounts to recognize uncollectible accounts expense for Year 2. Sports estimates that uncollectible accounts expense will be 1 percent of sales on account.

CHECK FIGURES
c. Ending Accounts Receivable, Year 1: $8,000
d. Net Income, Year 2: $31,960

Required

Complete all the following requirements for Year 1 and Year 2. Complete all requirements for Year 1 prior to beginning the requirements for Year 2.

a. Identify the type of each transaction (asset source, asset use, asset exchange, or claims exchange).
b. Show the effect of each transaction on the elements of the financial statements, using a horizontal statements model like the one shown next. Use + for increase, − for decrease, and NA for not affected. Also, in the Cash Flow column, indicate whether the item is an operating activity (OA), investing activity (IA), or financing activity (FA). The first transaction is entered as an example. (*Hint:* Closing entries do not affect the statements model.)

Event No.	Assets	=	Liab.	+	Equity	Rev.	−	Exp.	=	Net Inc.	Cash Flow
1	+		NA		+	+		NA		+	NA

c. Record the transactions in general journal form and post them to T-accounts (begin Year 2 with the ending T-account balances from Year 1).
d. Prepare the income statement, statement of changes in stockholders' equity, balance sheet, and statement of cash flows.
e. Prepare closing entries and post these closing entries to the T-accounts. Prepare a post-closing trial balance.

Problem 7-18B Determination of account balances and preparation of journal entries—percent of receivables allowance method of accounting for uncollectible accounts

LO 7-2

During the first year of operation, Year 1, Home Renovation recognized $261,000 of service revenue on account. At the end of Year 1, the accounts receivable balance was $46,300. Even though this is his first year in business, the owner believes he will collect all but about 4 percent of the ending balance.

Required

a. What amount of cash was collected by Home Renovation during Year 1?
b. Assuming the use of an allowance system to account for uncollectible accounts, what amount should Home Renovation record as uncollectible accounts expense in Year 1?

c. Prepare the journal entries to
   (1) Record service revenue on account.
   (2) Record collection of accounts receivable.
   (3) Record the entry to recognize uncollectible accounts expense.
d. What is the net realizable value of receivables at the end of Year 1?
e. Show the effect of the transactions listed in Requirement c on the financial statements by recording the appropriate amounts in a horizontal statements model like the one shown next. When you record amounts in the Cash Flow column, indicate whether the item is an operating activity (OA), investing activity (IA), or financing activity (FA). The letters NA indicate that an element is not affected by the event.

Assets	=	Liab.	+	Equity	Rev.	−	Exp.	=	Net Inc.	Cash Flow
Cash + Net Realizable Value of Receivables										

LO 7-1

Problem 7-19B *Determining account balances and preparing journal entries: percent of revenue allowance method of accounting for uncollectible accounts*

The following information pertains to Kee Cabinet Company's sales on account and accounts receivable:

Accounts Receivable Balance, January 1, Year 2	$ 96,200
Allowance for Doubtful Accounts, January 1, Year 2	6,250
Sales on Account, Year 2	726,000
Cost of Goods Sold, Year 2	473,000
Collections of Accounts Receivable, Year 2	715,000

After several collection attempts, Kee Cabinet Company wrote off $3,100 of accounts that could not be collected. Kee estimates that uncollectible accounts expense will be 0.5 percent of sales on account.

Required

a. Prepare the general journal entries to:
   (1) Record sales on account for Year 2.
   (2) Record cash collections from accounts receivable for Year 2.
   (3) Write off the accounts that are not collectible.
   (4) Record the estimated uncollectible accounts expense for Year 2.
b. Compute the following amounts:
   (1) Using the allowance method, the amount of uncollectible accounts expense for Year 2.
   (2) Net realizable value of receivables at the end of Year 2.
c. Explain why the uncollectible accounts expense amount is different from the amount that was written off as uncollectible.

LO 7-2, 7-3

Problem 7-20B *Accounting for uncollectible accounts: percent of receivables allowance method*

Thorne Inc. experienced the following transactions for Year 1, its first year of operations:

1. Issued common stock for $60,000 cash.
2. Purchased $210,000 of merchandise on account.
3. Sold merchandise that cost $165,000 for $310,000 on account.
4. Collected $288,000 cash from accounts receivable.
5. Paid $190,000 on accounts payable.
6. Paid $46,000 of salaries expense for the year.

Accounting for Receivables

7. Paid other operating expenses of $62,000.
8. Thorne adjusted the accounts using the following information from an accounts receivable aging schedule:

Number of Days Past Due	Amount	Percent Likely to Be Uncollectible	Allowance Balance
Current	$5,700	.01	
0–30	8,500	.05	
31–60	4,000	.10	
61–90	2,600	.20	
Over 90 days	1,200	.50	

Required

a. Record the above transactions in general journal form and post them to T-accounts.
b. Prepare the income statement, statement of changes in stockholders' equity, balance sheet, and statement of cash flows for Thorne Inc. for Year 1.
c. What is the net realizable value of the accounts receivable at December 31, Year 1?

Problem 7-21B   Multistep income statement and balance sheet

LO 7-1, 7-5

Required

Use the following information to prepare a multistep income statement and a balance sheet for Trias Company for Year 2. (*Hint:* Some of the items will *not* appear on either statement, and ending retained earnings must be calculated.)

Operating Expenses	$ 45,000	Allowance for Doubtful Accounts	$ 6,500
Accounts Payable	48,000	Sales Revenue	350,000
Land	45,000	Uncollectible Accounts Expense	9,600
Dividends	10,000	Accounts Receivable	92,000
Beginning Retained Earnings	120,100	Salaries Payable	10,500
Interest Revenue	12,000	Supplies	4,500
Inventory	105,000	Prepaid Rent	16,000
Notes Receivable (short term)	15,000	Common Stock	60,000
Cash	16,700	Cost of Goods Sold	225,000
Interest Receivable (short term)	2,100	Salaries Expense	61,200
Cash Flow from Investing Activities	(91,600)	Unearned Revenue	40,000

Problem 7-22B   Accounting for notes receivable and uncollectible accounts using the direct write-off method

LO 7-4, 7-5

The following transactions apply to Cheng Co. for Year 1, its first year of operations:

1. Issued $60,000 of common stock for cash.
2. Provided $94,000 of services on account.
3. Collected $84,500 cash from accounts receivable.
4. Loaned $10,000 to Swan Co. on October 1, Year 1. The note had a one-year term to maturity and a 6 percent interest rate.
5. Paid $41,000 of salaries expense for the year.
6. Paid a $3,000 dividend to the stockholders.
7. Recorded the accrued interest on December 31, Year 1 (see item 4).
8. Determined that $990 of accounts receivable were uncollectible. The company uses the direct write-off method.

CHECK FIGURES
c. Net Income $52,160
d. Ending Cash $90,500

Required

a. Record the above transactions in general journal form.
b. Post the entries to T-accounts.
c. Prepare the income statement, balance sheet, and statement of cash flows for Year 1.
d. Show the effects of the above transactions in a horizontal statements model like the one shown next.

	Assets				= Liab. +	Equity		Rev. − Exp. = Net Inc.	Cash Flows
Event	Cash +	Accts. Rec. +	Notes Rec. +	Int. Rec. =		Com. Stk. + Ret. Earn.			

LO 7-1, 7-5

Problem 7-23B Missing information

The following information comes from the accounts of Legoria Company:

Account Title	Beginning Balance	Ending Balance
Accounts Receivable	$36,000	$32,000
Allowance for Doubtful Accounts	2,000	2,200
Notes Receivable	50,000	50,000
Interest Receivable	2,000	5,000

Required

a. There were $160,000 in sales on account during the accounting period. Write-offs of uncollectible accounts were $1,200. What was the amount of cash collected from accounts receivable? What amount of uncollectible accounts expense was reported on the income statement? What was the net realizable value of receivables at the end of the accounting period?

b. The note has a 6 percent interest rate and 24 months to maturity. What amount of interest revenue was recognized for the year? How much cash was collected for interest?

LO 7-2, 7-6

Problem 7-24B Accounting for credit card sales and uncollectible accounts: percent of receivables allowance method

Diamond Supply Company had the following transactions in Year 1:

1. Acquired $50,000 cash from the issue of common stock.
2. Purchased $120,000 of merchandise for cash in Year 1.
3. Sold merchandise that cost $95,000 for $180,000 during the year under the following terms:

$ 50,000	Cash sales
115,000	Credit card sales (Credit card company charges a 3 percent service fee.)
15,000	Sales on account

4. Collected all the amount receivable from the credit card company.
5. Collected $11,300 of accounts receivable.
6. Paid selling and administrative expenses of $51,500.
7. Determined that 5 percent of the ending accounts receivable balance would be uncollectible.

Required

a. Show the effects of each of the transactions on the elements of the financial statements, using a horizontal statements model like the one shown next. Use + for increase, − for decrease, and NA for not affected. The first transaction is entered as an example. (*Hint:* Closing entries do not affect the statements model.)

Event No.	Assets	=	Liab.	+	Equity	Rev.	−	Exp.	=	Net Inc.	Cash Flow
1	+		NA		+	NA		NA		NA	+ FA

b. Prepare general journal entries for each of the transactions and post them to T-accounts.
c. Prepare an income statement, statement of changes in stockholders' equity, balance sheet, and statement of cash flows for Year 1.

Problem 7-25B Effect of transactions on the elements of financial statements

LO 7-4, 7-5, 7-6

Required

Identify each of the following independent transactions as an asset source (AS), asset use (AU), asset exchange (AE), or claims exchange (CE). Also explain how each event affects assets, liabilities, stockholders' equity, net income, and cash flow by placing a + for increase, − for decrease, or NA for not affected under each of the categories. The first event is recorded as an example.

Event	Type of Event	Assets	Liabilities	Common Stock	Retained Earnings	Net Income	Cash Flow
a	AS/AU	+/−	NA	NA	+	+	NA

a. Sold merchandise at a price above cost. Accepted payment by credit card. The credit card company charges a service fee. The receipts have not yet been forwarded to the credit card company.
b. Sold land for cash at its cost.
c. Paid cash to satisfy salaries payable.
d. Submitted receipts to the credit card company (see item *a*) and collected cash.
e. Loaned Carl Maddox cash. The loan had a 5 percent interest rate and a one-year term to maturity.
f. Paid cash to creditors on accounts payable.
g. Accrued three months' interest on the note receivable (see item *e*).
h. Provided services for cash.
i. Paid cash for salaries expense.
j. Provided services on account.
k. Wrote off an uncollectible account (use direct write-off method).
l. Collected cash from customers paying their accounts.
m. Recovered an uncollectible account that was previously written off (assume direct write-off method was used).
n. Paid cash for land.
o. Paid cash for other operating expenses.

Problem 7-26B Comprehensive accounting cycle problem (uses percent of revenue allowance method)

LO 7-1, 7-5, 7-6

The following trial balance was prepared for Village Cycle Sales and Service on December 31, Year 1, after the closing entries were posted:

Account Title	Debit	Credit
Cash	$ 46,200	
Accounts Receivable	21,300	
Allowance for Doubtful Accounts		$ 1,350
Inventory	85,600	
Accounts Payable		28,000
Common Stock		80,000
Retained Earnings		43,750
Totals	$153,100	$153,100

Village Cycle had the following transactions in Year 2:

1. Purchased merchandise on account for $260,000.
2. Sold merchandise that cost $243,000 on account for $340,000.
3. Performed $80,000 of services for cash.

4. Sold merchandise for $60,000 to credit card customers. The merchandise cost $41,250. The credit card company charges a 5 percent fee.
5. Collected $348,000 cash from accounts receivable.
6. Paid $265,000 cash on accounts payable.
7. Paid $115,000 cash for selling and administrative expenses.
8. Collected cash for the full amount due from the credit card company (see item 4).
9. Loaned $50,000 to Lee Supply. The note had a 9 percent interest rate and a one-year term to maturity.
10. Wrote off $830 of accounts as uncollectible.
11. Made the following adjusting entries:
    (a) Recorded three months' interest on the note at December 31, Year 2 (see item 9).
    (b) Estimated uncollectible accounts expense to be .5 percent of sales on account.

Required

Prepare general journal entries for these transactions, and post the entries to T-accounts. Also, prepare an income statement, a statement of changes in stockholders' equity, a balance sheet, and a statement of cash flows for Year 2.

ANALYZE, THINK, COMMUNICATE

ATC 7-1 Business Applications Case *Understanding real-world annual reports*

Required

Obtain the **Target Corporation's** annual report at http://investors.target.com using the instructions in Appendix B, and use it to answer the following questions:

Anyone who has shopped at Target knows that many of its customers use a credit card to pay for their purchases; there is even a Target brand credit card. However, Target did not report any accounts receivables or credit card receivables on its January 28, 2017 (2016), balance sheet.

a. Review Target's Form 10-K and determine where Target is reporting its credit card receivables.
b. How long does it usually take Target to collect its credit card receivables?
c. How much credit cards receivables did Target have as of January 28, 2017, and January 30, 2016, respectively?
d. In "Item 1. Business" section of its Form 10-K, Target discloses that it has a financial interest in the credit card that bears its name. Discuss this relationship.

Hint: It will be easier to answer these questions if you do a word search on Target's Form 10-K rather than trying to find the answers by reading through the report.

ATC 7-2 Group Assignment *Missing information*

The following selected financial information is available for three companies:

	Expo	White	Zina
Total sales	$125,000	$210,000	?
Cash sales	?	26,000	$120,000
Sales on account	40,000	?	75,000
Accounts receivable, January 1, Year 2	6,200	42,000	?
Accounts receivable, December 31, Year 2	5,600	48,000	7,500
Allowance for doubtful accounts, January 1, Year 2	?	?	405
Allowance for doubtful accounts, December 31, Year 2	224	1,680	?
Uncollectible accounts expense, Year 2	242	1,200	395
Uncollectible accounts written off	204	1,360	365
Collections of accounts receivable, Year 2	?	?	75,235

Required

a. Divide the class into three sections and divide each section into groups of three to five students. Assign one of the companies to each of the sections.

Group Tasks

(1) Determine the missing amounts for your company.
(2) Determine the percentage of accounts receivable estimated to be uncollectible at the end of the Year 1 and Year 2 for your company.
(3) Determine the percentage of total sales that are sales on account for your company.
(4) Determine the accounts receivable turnover for your company.

Class Discussion

b. Have a representative of each section put the missing information on the board and explain how it was determined.
c. Which company has the highest percentage of sales that are on account?
d. Which company is doing the best job of collecting its accounts receivable? What procedures and policies can a company use to better collect its accounts receivable?

ATC 7-3 Real-World Case Time needed to collect accounts receivable

Presented here are the average days to collect accounts receivable for four companies in different industries. The data are for 2016.

Company	Average Days to Collect Accounts Receivable
Boeing (aircraft manufacturer)	34
Colgate-Palmolive Company (consumer products manufacturer)	34
Ethan Allen (furniture retailer)	4
General Motors (auto sales only)	22

Required

Write a brief memorandum that provides possible answers to each of the following questions:

a. Why would a company that manufactures and sells airplanes (Boeing) and a company that manufactures and sells automobiles (General Motors) collect their accounts receivables in such relatively short times?
b. Why would a company that sells furniture (Ethan Allen) collect its receivables so much quicker than a company that sells toothpaste and soap (Colgate-Palmolive)?

ATC 7-4 Business Applications Case Performing ratio analysis using real-world data

The following data were taken from Hershey Foods Corporation's 2016 annual report. All dollar amounts are in thousands.

	Fiscal Years Ending	
	December 31, 2016	December 31, 2015
Sales	$7,440,181	$7,386,626
Accounts receivable	581,381	599,073

Required

a. Compute Hershey's accounts receivable turnover ratios for 2016 and 2015.
b. Compute Hershey's average days to collect accounts receivables for 2016 and 2015.
c. Based on the ratios computed in Requirements *a* and *b*, did Hershey's performance get better or worse from 2015 to 2016?
d. Assume it took Hershey 30 days to collect its receivables. Using an interest rate of 3.0 percent, calculate how much it cost Hershey's to finance its receivables for 30 days in 2016.

ATC 7-5 Business Applications Case *Performing ratio analysis using real-world data*

AutoZone, Inc. claims to be the nation's leading auto parts retailer. It sells replacement auto parts directly to the consumer. **BorgWarner, Inc.** has over 30,000 employees and produces automobile parts, such as transmissions and cooling systems, for the world's vehicle manufacturers. The following data were taken from these companies' 2016 annual reports. All dollar amounts are in thousands.

	Fiscal Years Ending	
	AutoZone August 27, 2016	BorgWarner December 31, 2016
Sales	$10,635,676	$9,071,000
Accounts receivable	287,680	1,689,300

Required

a. Before performing any calculations, speculate as to which company will take the longest to collect its accounts receivable. Explain the rationale for your decision.
b. Calculate the accounts receivable turnover ratios for AutoZone and BorgWarner.
c. Calculate the average days to collect accounts receivable for AutoZone and BorgWarner.
d. Do the calculations from Requirements *b* and *c* confirm your speculations in Requirement *a*?

ATC 7-6 Writing Assignment *Cost of charge sales*

Paul Smith is opening a plumbing supply store in University City. He plans to sell plumbing parts and materials to both wholesale and retail customers. Because contractors (wholesale customers) prefer to charge parts and materials and pay at the end of the month, Paul expects he will have to offer charge accounts. He plans to offer charge sales to the wholesale customers only and to require retail customers to pay with either cash or credit cards. Paul wondered what expenses his business would incur relative to the charge sales and the credit cards.

Required

a. What issues will Paul need to consider if he allows wholesale customers to buy plumbing supplies on account?
b. Write a memo to Paul Smith outlining the potential cost of accepting charge customers. Discuss the difference between the allowance method for uncollectible accounts and the direct write-off method. Also discuss the cost of accepting credit cards.

ATC 7-7 Ethical Dilemma *How bad can it be?*

Alonzo Saunders owns a small training services company that is experiencing growing pains. The company has grown rapidly by offering liberal credit terms to its customers. Although his competitors require payment for services within 30 days, Saunders permits his customers to delay payment for up to 90 days. Saunders' customers thereby have time to fully evaluate the training that employees receive before they must pay for that training. Saunders guarantees satisfaction. If a customer is unhappy, the customer does not have to pay. Saunders works with reputable companies, provides top-quality training, and rarely encounters dissatisfied customers.

The long collection period, however, has created a cash flow problem. Saunders has a $100,000 accounts receivable balance but needs cash to pay current bills. He has recently negotiated a loan agreement with National Bank of Brighton County that should solve his cash flow problems. The loan agreement requires that Saunders pledge the accounts receivable as collateral for the loan. The bank agreed to loan Saunders 70 percent of the receivables balance, thereby giving him access to $70,000 cash. Saunders is satisfied with this arrangement because he estimates he needs approximately $60,000.

On the day Saunders was to execute the loan agreement, he heard a rumor that his biggest customer was experiencing financial problems and might declare bankruptcy. The customer owed Saunders $45,000. Saunders promptly called the customer's chief accountant and learned "off the record" that the rumor was true. The accountant told Saunders that the company's net worth was negative and most of its assets were pledged as collateral for bank loans. In his opinion, Saunders was unlikely to collect the balance due. Saunders' immediate concern was the impact the circumstances would have on his loan agreement with the bank.

Saunders uses the direct write-off method to recognize uncollectible accounts expense. Removing the $45,000 receivable from the collateral pool would leave only $55,000 of receivables, reducing the available credit to $38,500 ($55,000 × 0.70). Even worse, recognizing the uncollectible accounts expense would so adversely affect his income statement that the bank might further reduce the available credit by reducing the percentage of receivables allowed under the loan agreement. Saunders will have to attest to the quality of the receivables at the date of the loan but reasons that, because the information he obtained about the possible bankruptcy was "off the record," he is under no obligation to recognize the uncollectible accounts expense until the receivable is officially uncollectible.

Required

a. How are income and assets affected by the decision not to act on the bankruptcy information?
b. Review the AICPA's Articles of Professional Conduct (see Chapter 2) and comment on any of the standards that would be violated by the actions Saunders is contemplating.
c. Identify the elements of unethical and criminal conduct recognized in the fraud triangle (see Chapter 2), and explain how they apply to this case.

ATC 7-8 Research Assignment *Comparing Whirlpool Corporation's and Papa John's time to collect accounts receivable*

Using the most current annual reports or Forms 10-K for **Whirlpool Corporation** and **Papa John's International, Inc.**, complete the requirements that follow. To obtain the Forms 10-K, use either the EDGAR system, following the instructions in Appendix A, or the companies' websites. The annual reports can be found on the companies' websites.

Required

a. What was Whirlpool's average days to collect accounts receivable? Show your computations.
b. What percentage of accounts receivable did Whirlpool estimate would not be collected?
c. What was Papa John's average days to collect accounts receivable? Show your computations.
d. What percentage of accounts receivable did Papa John's estimate would not be collected?
e. Briefly explain why Whirlpool would take longer than Papa John's to collect its accounts receivable.

ATC 7-9 Spreadsheet Assignment *Using Excel*

Set up the following spreadsheet comparing the Vong and Crist companies:

Source: Microsoft Office Excel 1997

Required

For each company, compute gross profit, gross profit percentage, net realizable value, accounts receivable turnover, and average days to collect.

COMPREHENSIVE PROBLEM

The trial balance of Pacilio Security Services, Inc. as of January 1, Year 7, had the following normal balances:

Cash	$78,972
Petty Cash	100
Accounts Receivable	33,440
Supplies	160
Prepaid Rent	3,200
Merchandise Inventory (23 @ $280)	6,440
Land	4,000
Accounts Payable	250
Salaries Payable	1,400
Common Stock	50,000
Retained Earnings	74,662

During Year 7, Pacilio Security Services experienced the following transactions:

1. Paid the salaries payable from Year 6.
2. Paid $4,800 on March 1, Year 7, for one year's lease in advance on the company van.
3. Paid $8,400 on May 2, Year 7, for one year's office rent in advance.
4. Purchased $550 of supplies on account.
5. Paid cash to purchase 105 alarm systems at a cost of $285 each.
6. Pacilio has noticed its accounts receivable balance is growing more than desired and some collection problems exist. It appears that uncollectible accounts expense is approximately 3 percent of total credit sales. Pacilio has decided it will, starting this year, adopt the allowance method of accounting for uncollectible accounts. It will record an adjusting entry to recognize the estimate at the end of the year.
7. In trying to collect several of its delinquent accounts, Pacilio has learned that these customers have either declared bankruptcy or moved and left no forwarding address. These uncollectible accounts amount to $1,900.
8. Sold 110 alarm systems for $63,800. All sales were on account. (Compute cost of goods sold using the FIFO cost flow method.)
9. Paid the balance of the accounts payable.
10. Pacilio began accepting credit cards for some of its monitoring service sales. The credit card company charges a fee of 4 percent. Total monitoring services for the year were $68,000. Pacilio accepted credit cards for $24,000 of this amount. The other $44,000 was sales on account.
11. On July 1, Year 7, Pacilio replenished the petty cash fund. The fund contained $21 of currency and receipts of $50 for yard mowing, $22 for office supplies expense, and $9 for miscellaneous expenses.
12. Collected the amount due from the credit card company.
13. Paid installers and other employees a total of $45,000 cash for salaries.
14. Collected $116,800 of accounts receivable during the year.
15. Paid $9,500 of advertising expense during the year.
16. Paid $5,200 of utilities expense for the year.
17. Paid a dividend of $20,000 to the shareholders.

Adjustments

18. There was $250 of supplies on hand at the end of the year.
19. Recognized the expired rent for both the van and the office for the year.
20. Recognized the uncollectible accounts expense for the year using the allowance method.
21. Accrued salaries at December 31, Year 7, were $2,100.

Required

a. Record the preceding transactions in general journal form.
b. Post the transactions to the T-accounts.
c. Prepare a trial balance.
d. Prepare an income statement, statement of changes in stockholders' equity, balance sheet, and statement of cash flows.
e. Close the temporary accounts to retained earnings.
f. Post the closing entries to the T-accounts and prepare a post-closing trial balance.

CHAPTER 8

Accounting for Long-Term Operational Assets

LEARNING OBJECTIVES

After you have mastered the material in this chapter, you will be able to:

LO 8-1 Identify and determine the cost of long-term operational assets.

LO 8-2 Calculate straight-line depreciation and show how it affects financial statements.

LO 8-3 Calculate double-declining-balance depreciation and show how it affects financial statements.

LO 8-4 Calculate units-of-production depreciation and show how it affects financial statements.

LO 8-5 Show how gains and losses on disposals of long-term operational assets affect financial statements.

LO 8-6 Identify some of the tax issues that affect long-term operational assets.

LO 8-7 Show how revising estimates affects financial statements.

LO 8-8 Show how continuing expenditures for operational assets affect financial statements.

LO 8-9 Calculate depletion and show how it affects financial statements.

LO 8-10 Identify and determine the cost of intangible assets.

LO 8-11 Show how the amortization of intangible assets affects financial statements.

LO 8-12 Show how expense recognition choices and industry characteristics affect financial performance measures.

 Video lectures and accompanying self-assessment quizzes are available in Connect *for all learning objectives.*

CHAPTER OPENING

Companies use assets to produce revenue. Some assets, like inventory or office supplies, are called **current assets** because they are used relatively quickly (within a single accounting period). Other assets, like equipment or buildings, are used for extended periods of time (two or more accounting periods). These assets are called **long-term operational assets.**[1] Accounting

[1]Classifying assets as current versus long term is explained in more detail in Chapter 9.

for long-term assets raises several questions. For example, what is the cost of the asset? Is it the list price only or should the cost of transportation, transit insurance, setup, and so on be added to the list price? Should the cost of a long-term asset be recognized as expense in the period the asset is purchased or should the cost be expensed over the useful life of the asset? What happens in the accounting records when a long-term asset is retired from use? This chapter answers these questions. It explains accounting for long-term operational assets from the date of purchase through the date of disposal.

The Curious Accountant

Most companies have various types of long-term assets that they use to operate their business. Common types of long-term assets include buildings, machinery, and equipment. But there are other types as well. A major category of long-term assets for a mining company is the mineral reserves from which they extract ore.

©Brad Sauter/Shutterstock

Freeport-McMoRan Copper & Gold, Inc. (referred to as FCX) is one of the largest mining operations in the world. It produces copper, gold, and molybdenum from 12 major mines located on four continents. As of December 31, 2016, it owned proven mineral reserves that cost $3.9 billion, as well as buildings, machinery, and equipment that cost $13.0 billion.

As you learned in Chapters 2 and 4, except for land, over time most assets are consumed in a company's efforts to produce revenues, and as they are consumed, the asset account is decreased and an expense account is increased. How do you think the way a mining company uses its buildings and equipment differs from the way it uses its mineral reserves, and how do you think these differences affect the way these assets are accounted for? (Answers on page 437.)

LO 8-1

Identify and determine the cost of long-term operational assets.

TANGIBLE VERSUS INTANGIBLE ASSETS

Long-term assets may be tangible or intangible. **Tangible assets** have a physical presence; they can be seen and touched. Tangible assets include equipment, machinery, natural resources, and land. In contrast, intangible assets have no physical form. Although they may be represented by physical documents, **intangible assets** are, in fact, rights or privileges. They cannot be seen or touched. For example, a patent represents an exclusive legal *privilege* to produce and sell a particular product. It protects inventors by making it illegal for others to profit by copying their inventions. Although a patent may be represented by legal documents, the privilege is the actual asset. Because the privilege cannot be seen or touched, the patent is an intangible asset.

Tangible Long-Term Assets

Tangible long-term assets are classified as (1) property, plant, and equipment; (2) natural resources; or (3) land.

Property, Plant, and Equipment

Property, plant, and equipment is sometimes called *plant assets* or *fixed assets*. Examples of property, plant, and equipment include furniture, cash registers, machinery, delivery trucks, computers, mechanical robots, and buildings. The level of detail used to account for these assets varies. One company may include all office equipment in one account, whereas another company might divide office equipment into computers, desks, chairs, and so on. The term used to recognize expense for property, plant, and equipment is **depreciation.**

Natural Resources

Mineral deposits, oil and gas reserves, timber stands, coal mines, and stone quarries are examples of **natural resources.** Conceptually, natural resources are inventories. When sold, the cost of these assets is frequently expensed as *cost of goods sold*. Although inventories are usually classified as short-term assets, natural resources are normally classified as long term because the resource deposits generally have long lives. For example, it may take decades to extract all of the diamonds from a diamond mine. The term used to recognize expense for natural resources is **depletion.**

Land

Land is classified separately from other property because land is not subject to depreciation or depletion. Land has an infinite life. It is not worn out or consumed as it is used. When buildings or natural resources are purchased simultaneously with land, the amount paid must be divided between the land and the other assets because of the nondepreciable nature of the land.

Intangible Assets

Intangible assets fall into two categories, those with *identifiable useful lives* and those with *indefinite useful lives*.

Intangible Assets with Identifiable Useful Lives

Intangible assets with identifiable useful lives include patents and copyrights. These assets may become obsolete (a patent may become worthless if new technology provides a superior product) or may reach the end of their legal lives. The term used when recognizing expense for intangible assets with identifiable useful lives is called **amortization.**

Intangible Assets with Indefinite Useful Lives

The benefits of some intangible assets may extend so far into the future that their useful lives cannot be estimated. For how many years will the Coca-Cola trademark attract customers? When will the value of a McDonald's franchise end? There are no answers to

Accounting for Long-Term Operational Assets 421

these questions. Intangible assets such as renewable franchises, trademarks, and goodwill have indefinite useful lives. The costs of such assets are not expensed unless the value of the assets becomes impaired.

DETERMINING THE COST OF LONG-TERM ASSETS

The **historical cost concept** requires that an asset be recorded at the amount paid for it. This amount includes the purchase price plus any costs necessary to get the asset in the location and condition for its intended use. Common cost components are:

- **Buildings:** (1) purchase price, (2) sales taxes, (3) title search and transfer document costs, (4) realtor's and attorney's fees, and (5) remodeling costs.
- **Land:** (1) purchase price, (2) sales taxes, (3) title search and transfer document costs, (4) realtor's and attorney's fees, (5) costs for removal of old buildings, and (6) grading costs.
- **Equipment:** (1) purchase price (less discounts), (2) sales taxes, (3) delivery costs, (4) installation costs, and (5) costs to adapt for intended use.

The cost of an asset does not include payments for fines, damages, and so on that could have been avoided.

CHECK YOURSELF 8.1

Sheridan Construction Company purchased a new bulldozer that had a $260,000 list price. The seller agreed to allow a 4 percent cash discount in exchange for immediate payment. The bulldozer was delivered FOB shipping point at a cost of $1,200. Sheridan hired a new employee to operate the dozer for an annual salary of $36,000. The employee was trained to operate the dozer for a one-time training fee of $800. The cost of the company's theft insurance policy increased by $300 per year as a result of adding the dozer to the policy. The dozer had a five-year useful life and an expected salvage value of $26,000. Determine the asset's cost.

Answer

List price	$260,000
Less: Cash discount ($260,000 × 0.04)	(10,400)
Shipping cost	1,200
Training cost	800
Total asset cost (amount capitalized)	$251,600

Basket Purchase Allocation

Acquiring a group of assets in a single transaction is known as a **basket purchase.** The total price of a basket purchase must be allocated among the assets acquired. Accountants commonly allocate the purchase price using the **relative market value method.** To illustrate, assume that Beatty Company purchased land and a building for $240,000 cash. A real estate appraiser determined the market value of each asset to be

Building	$270,000
Land	90,000
Total	$360,000

The appraisal indicates that the land is worth 25 percent ($90,000 ÷ $360,000) of the total value and the building is worth 75 percent ($270,000 ÷ $360,000). Using these percentages, the actual purchase price is allocated as follows:

Building	0.75 × $240,000 =	$180,000
Land	0.25 × $240,000 =	60,000
Total		$240,000

METHODS OF RECOGNIZING DEPRECIATION EXPENSE

The life cycle of an operational asset involves (1) acquiring the funds to buy the asset, (2) purchasing the asset, (3) using the asset, and (4) retiring (disposing of) the asset. These stages are illustrated in Exhibit 8.1. The stages involving (1) acquiring funds and (2) purchasing assets have been discussed previously. This section of the chapter describes how accountants recognize the *use* of assets (Stage 3). As they are used, assets suffer from wear and tear called *depreciation*. Ultimately, assets depreciate to the point that they are no longer useful in the process of earning revenue. This process usually takes several years. The amount of an asset's cost that is allocated to expense during an accounting period is called **depreciation expense.**

An asset that is fully depreciated by one company may still be useful to another company. For example, a rental car that is no longer useful to Hertz may still be useful to a local delivery company. As a result, companies are frequently able to sell their fully depreciated assets to other companies or individuals. The expected market value of a fully depreciated asset is called its **salvage value.** The total amount of depreciation a company recognizes for an asset, its **depreciable cost,** is the difference between its original cost and its salvage value.

For example, assume a company purchases an asset for $5,000. The company expects to use the asset for 5 years (the **estimated useful life**) and then to sell it for $1,000 (salvage value). The depreciable cost of the asset is $4,000 ($5,000 − $1,000). The portion of the depreciable cost ($4,000) that represents its annual usage is recognized as depreciation expense.

Accountants must exercise judgment to estimate the amount of depreciation expense to recognize each period. For example, suppose you own a personal computer. You know how much the computer cost, and you know you will eventually need to replace it. How would you determine the amount the computer depreciates each year you use it? Businesses may use any of several acceptable methods to estimate the amount of depreciation expense to recognize each year.

The method used to recognize depreciation expense should match the asset's usage pattern. More expense should be recognized in periods when the asset is used more, and less in periods when the asset is used less. Because assets are used to produce revenue, matching expense recognition with asset usage also matches expense recognition with revenue recognition. Three alternative methods for recognizing depreciation expense are (1) straight-line, (2) double-declining-balance, and (3) units-of-production.

The *straight-line* method produces the same amount of depreciation expense each accounting period. *Double-declining-balance,* an accelerated method, produces more depreciation expense in the early years of an asset's life, with a declining amount of expense in later years. *Units-of-production* produces varying amounts of depreciation expense in different accounting periods (more in some accounting periods and less in others). Exhibit 8.2 contrasts the different depreciation methods that U.S. companies use.

EXHIBIT 8.1
Life Cycle of an Operational Asset

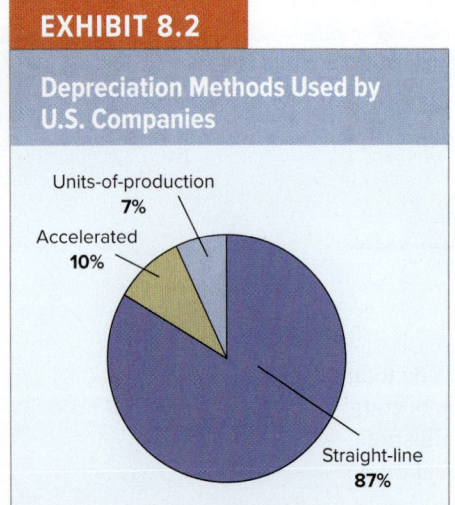

EXHIBIT 8.2
Depreciation Methods Used by U.S. Companies

The chart is based on data drawn from recent annual reports published by the 30 companies that comprise the Dow Jones Industrial Average. The percentages add to more than 100% because one company used two depreciation methods and therefore was included in two categories.

Dryden Enterprises Illustration

To illustrate the different depreciation methods, consider a van purchased by Dryden Enterprises. Dryden plans to use the van as rental property. The van had a list price of $23,500. Dryden obtained a 10 percent cash discount from the dealer. The van was delivered FOB shipping point, and Dryden paid an additional $250 for transportation costs. Dryden also paid $2,600 for a custom accessory package to increase the van's appeal as a rental vehicle. The cost of the van is computed as follows:

List price	$23,500	
Less: Cash discount	(2,350)	$23,500 × 0.10
Plus: Transportation costs	250	
Plus: Cost of customization	2,600	
Total	$24,000	

The van has an estimated *salvage value* of $4,000 and an *estimated useful life* of four years. The following section examines three different patterns of expense recognition for this van.

Straight-Line Depreciation

The first scenario assumes the van is used evenly over its four-year life. The revenue from renting the van is assumed to be $8,000 per year. The matching concept calls for the expense recognition pattern to match the revenue stream. Because the same amount of revenue is recognized in each accounting period, Dryden should use **straight-line depreciation** because it produces equal amounts of depreciation expense each year.

The first phase of the asset life cycle is to acquire funds to purchase the asset. Assume Dryden acquired $25,000 cash on January 1, Year 1, by issuing common stock. The journal entry and its effects on the financial statements are shown next:

LO 8-2

Calculate straight-line depreciation and show how it affects financial statements.

Account Title	Debit	Credit
Cash	25,000	
Common Stock		25,000

Assets			=	Equity			Rev.	−	Exp.	=	Net Inc.	Cash Flow
Cash	+	Book Value of Van	=	Com. Stk.	+	Ret. Earn.						
25,000	+	NA	=	25,000	+	NA	NA	−	NA	=	NA	25,000 FA

The second phase of the life cycle is to purchase the van. Assume Dryden bought the van on January 1, Year 1, using funds from the stock issue. The cost of the van, previously computed, was $24,000 cash. The journal entry and its effects on the financial statements are shown next:

Account Title	Debit	Credit
Van	24,000	
Cash		24,000

Assets			=	Equity			Rev.	−	Exp.	=	Net Inc.	Cash Flow
Cash	+	Book Value of Van	=	Com. Stk.	+	Ret. Earn.						
(24,000)	+	24,000	=	NA	+	NA	NA	−	NA	=	NA	(24,000) IA

Dryden used the van by renting it to customers. The rent revenue each year is $8,000 cash. The annual journal entry and its effects on the financial statements are shown next:

Account Title	Debit	Credit
Cash	8,000	
Rent Revenue		8,000

Assets	=	Equity	Rev.	−	Exp.	=	Net Inc.	Cash Flow
Cash + Book Value of Van	=	Com. Stk. + Ret. Earn.						
8,000 + NA	=	NA + 8,000	8,000	−	NA	=	8,000	8,000 OA

Although illustrated only once, these effects occur four times—once for each year Dryden earns revenue by renting the van.

At the end of each year, Dryden adjusts its accounts to recognize depreciation expense. The amount of depreciation recognized using the straight-line method is calculated as follows:

$$(\text{Asset cost} - \text{Salvage value}) \div \text{Useful life} = \text{Depreciation expense}$$
$$(\$24,000 - \$4,000) \div 4 \text{ years} = \$5,000 \text{ per year}$$

Recognizing depreciation expense is an asset use transaction that reduces assets and equity. The asset reduction is reported using a **contra asset account** called **Accumulated Depreciation.** Like other contra asset accounts, the Accumulated Depreciation account has a credit balance. The **book value** of a long-term tangible asset is determined by subtracting the credit balance in the Accumulated Depreciation account from the debit balance in the associated asset account. The book value may also be called the **carrying value.**

While recognizing depreciation expense decreases net income, it *does not affect cash flow*. The $24,000 cash outflow occurred in January Year 1 when Dryden purchased the van. In contrast, the $5,000 depreciation expense is recognized each year as the van is used. The December 31, Year 1, journal entry recognizing depreciation expense and its effects on the financial statements are shown next:

Account Title	Debit	Credit
Depreciation Expense	5,000	
Accumulated Depreciation		5,000

Assets	=	Equity	Rev.	−	Exp.	=	Net Inc.	Cash Flow
Cash + Book Value of Van	=	Com. Stk. + Ret. Earn.						
NA + (5,000)	=	NA + (5,000)	NA	−	5,000	=	(5,000)	NA

The book value of the van as of December 31, Year 1, is $19,000, computed as shown next:

Van	$24,000
Accumulated depreciation	(5,000)
Book value	$19,000

Depreciation expense is recognized each year the van is used. Like other expense accounts, the Depreciation Expense account is a temporary account that is closed to retained earnings at the end of each accounting cycle. In other words, each year $5,000 is recognized in the Depreciation Expense account and then closed to the Retained Earnings account. As a result, the Depreciation Expense account will never have a balance that is larger than $5,000.

In contrast, the Accumulated Depreciation account is a permanent account. As its name implies, the total amount in the Accumulated Depreciation account increases (accumulates) each time depreciation expense is recognized. For example, at the end of Year 2 Dryden will recognize $5,000 of depreciation expense and the balance in the Accumulated Depreciation account will increase to $10,000. At the end of Year 3, Dryden will recognize $5,000 of depreciation expense and increase the balance in the Accumulated Depreciation account to $15,000, and so on.

Financial Statements

Exhibit 8.3 displays a vertical statements model that shows the financial results for the Dryden illustration from Year 1 through Year 4. Study the exhibit until you understand how all the figures were derived. The amount of depreciation expense ($5,000) reported on the income statement is constant each year from Year 1 through Year 4. The amount of accumulated depreciation reported on the balance sheet grows from $5,000 to $10,000, to $15,000, and finally to $20,000. The Accumulated Depreciation account is a *contra asset account* that is subtracted from the Van account in determining total assets.

EXHIBIT 8.3 — Financial Statements Under Straight-Line Depreciation

DRYDEN ENTERPRISES
Financial Statements

	Year 1	Year 2	Year 3	Year 4
Income Statements				
Rent revenue	$ 8,000	$ 8,000	$ 8,000	$ 8,000
Depreciation expense	(5,000)	(5,000)	(5,000)	(5,000)
Net income	$ 3,000	$ 3,000	$ 3,000	$ 3,000
Balance Sheets				
Assets				
Cash	$ 9,000	$17,000	$25,000	$33,000
Van	24,000	24,000	24,000	24,000
Accumulated depreciation	(5,000)	(10,000)	(15,000)	(20,000)
Total assets	$28,000	$31,000	$34,000	$37,000
Stockholders' equity				
Common stock	$25,000	$25,000	$25,000	$25,000
Retained earnings	3,000	6,000	9,000	12,000
Total stockholders' equity	$28,000	$31,000	$34,000	$37,000
Statements of Cash Flows				
Operating Activities				
Inflow from customers	$ 8,000	$ 8,000	$ 8,000	$ 8,000
Investing Activities				
Outflow to purchase van	(24,000)			
Financing Activities				
Inflow from stock issue	25,000			
Net Change in Cash	9,000	8,000	8,000	8,000
Beginning cash balance	0	9,000	17,000	25,000
Ending cash balance	$ 9,000	$17,000	$25,000	$33,000

Notice the differences between cash flow from operating activities and the income statement. For example, in Year 1 Dryden paid $24,000 cash to purchase the van. However, only $5,000 of this cost is shown as an operating expense on the income statement. Further, there is no effect on cash flow from operating activities. Instead, the entire $24,000 cash outflow is shown as an investing activity. These differences highlight the fact that cash flow from operating activities and the income statement are purposefully designed to inform users about different aspects of the business' operations.

Double-Declining-Balance Depreciation

Calculate double-declining-balance depreciation and show how it affects financial statements.

For the second scenario, assume demand for the van is strong when it is new, but fewer people rent the van as it ages. As a result, the van produces smaller amounts of revenue as time goes by. To match expenses with revenues, it is reasonable to recognize more depreciation expense in the van's early years and less as it ages.

Double-declining-balance depreciation produces a large amount of depreciation in the first year of an asset's life and progressively smaller levels of expense in each succeeding year. Because the double-declining-balance method recognizes depreciation expense more rapidly than the straight-line method does, it is called an **accelerated depreciation method.**

©Guy Sagi/123RF

Depreciation expense recognized using double-declining-balance is computed in three steps.

1. *Determine the straight-line rate.* Divide one by the asset's useful life. Because the estimated useful life of Dryden's van is four years, the straight-line rate is 25 percent (1 ÷ 4) per year.

2. *Determine the double-declining-balance rate.* Multiply the straight-line rate by 2 (*double* the rate). The double-declining-balance rate for the van is 50 percent (25 percent × 2).

3. *Determine the depreciation expense.* Multiply the double-declining-balance rate by the book value of the asset *at the beginning of the period* (recall that book value is historical cost minus *accumulated depreciation*). The following table shows the amount of depreciation expense Dryden will recognize over the van's useful life (Year 1 – Year 4).

Year	Book Value at Beginning of Period	×	Double the Straight-Line Rate	=	Annual Depreciation Expense	
Year 1	($24,000 – $ 0)	×	0.50	=	$12,000	
Year 2	(24,000 – 12,000)	×	0.50	=	6,000	
Year 3	(24,000 – 18,000)	×	0.50	=	3,000	2,000
Year 4	(24,000 – 20,000)	×	0.50	=	2,000	0

Regardless of the depreciation method used, *an asset cannot be depreciated below its salvage value.* This restriction affects depreciation computations for the third and fourth years. Because the van had a cost of $24,000 and a salvage value of $4,000, the total amount of depreciable cost (historical cost − salvage value) is $20,000 ($24,000 − $4,000). Because $18,000 ($12,000 + $6,000) of the depreciable cost is recognized in the first two years, only $2,000 ($20,000 − $18,000) remains to be recognized after the second year. Depreciation expense recognized in the third year is therefore $2,000 even though double-declining-balance computations suggest that $3,000 should be recognized. Similarly, zero depreciation expense is recognized in the fourth year even though the computations indicate a $2,000 charge.

Effects on the Financial Statements

Exhibit 8.4 displays financial statements for the life of the asset assuming Dryden uses double-declining-balance depreciation. The illustration assumes a cash revenue stream of $15,000, $9,000, $5,000, and $3,000 for Year 1, Year 2, Year 3, and Year 4, respectively. Trace the depreciation expense from the preceding table to the income statements. Reported depreciation expense is greater in the earlier years, and smaller in the later years of the asset's life.

The double-declining-balance method smoothes the amount of net income reported over the asset's useful life. In the early years, when heavy asset use produces higher revenue, depreciation expense is also higher. Similarly, in the later years, lower levels of revenue are matched with lower levels of depreciation expense. Net income is constant at $3,000 per year.

The depreciation method a company uses *does not* affect how it acquires the financing, invests the funds, and retires the asset. For Dryden's van, the accounting effects of these life cycle phases are the same as under the straight-line approach. Similarly, the *recording procedures* are not affected by the depreciation method. Different depreciation methods affect only the amounts of depreciation expense recorded each year, not which accounts are used. The general journal entries are therefore not illustrated for the double-declining-balance or the units-of-production depreciation methods.

EXHIBIT 8.4 Financial Statements under Double-Declining-Balance Depreciation

DRYDEN ENTERPRISES
Financial Statements

	Year 1	Year 2	Year 3	Year 4
Income Statements				
Rent revenue	$15,000	$ 9,000	$ 5,000	$ 3,000
Depreciation expense	(12,000)	(6,000)	(2,000)	0
Net income	$ 3,000	$ 3,000	$ 3,000	$ 3,000
Balance Sheets				
Assets				
Cash	$16,000	$25,000	$30,000	$33,000
Van	24,000	24,000	24,000	24,000
Accumulated depreciation	(12,000)	(18,000)	(20,000)	(20,000)
Total assets	$28,000	$31,000	$34,000	$37,000
Stockholders' equity				
Common stock	$25,000	$25,000	$25,000	$25,000
Retained earnings	3,000	6,000	9,000	12,000
Total stockholders' equity	$28,000	$31,000	$34,000	$37,000
Statements of Cash Flows				
Operating Activities				
Inflow from customers	$15,000	$ 9,000	$ 5,000	$ 3,000
Investing Activities				
Outflow to purchase van	(24,000)			
Financing Activities				
Inflow from stock issue	25,000			
Net Change in Cash	16,000	9,000	5,000	3,000
Beginning cash balance	0	16,000	25,000	30,000
Ending cash balance	$16,000	$25,000	$30,000	$33,000

CHECK YOURSELF 8.2

Olds Company purchased an asset that cost $36,000 on January 1, Year 1. The asset had an expected useful life of five years and an estimated salvage value of $5,000. Assuming Olds uses the double-declining-balance method, determine the amount of depreciation expense and the amount of accumulated depreciation Olds would report on the Year 3 financial statements.

Answer

Year	Book Value at Beginning of Period	×	Double the Straight-Line Rate*	=	Annual Depreciation Expense
Year 1	($36,000 − $ 0)	×	0.40	=	$14,400
Year 2	(36,000 − 14,400)	×	0.40	=	8,640
Year 3	(36,000 − 23,040)	×	0.40	=	5,184
Total accumulated depreciation at December 31, Year 3					$28,224

*Double-declining-balance rate = 2 × Straight-line rate = 2 × (1 ÷ 5 years) = 0.40

Units-of-Production Depreciation

LO 8-4

Calculate units-of-production depreciation and show how it affects financial statements.

Suppose rental demand for Dryden's van depends on general economic conditions. In a robust economy, travel increases, and demand for renting vans is high. In a stagnant economy, demand for van rentals declines. In such circumstances, revenues fluctuate from year to year. To accomplish the matching objective, depreciation should also fluctuate from year to year. A method of depreciation known as **units-of-production depreciation** accomplishes this goal by basing depreciation expense on actual asset usage.

Computing depreciation expense using units-of-production begins with identifying a measure of the asset's productive capacity. For example, the number of miles Dryden expects its van to be driven may be a reasonable measure of its productive capacity. If the depreciable asset were a saw, an appropriate measure of productive capacity could be the number of board feet the saw was expected to cut during its useful life. In other words, the basis for measuring production depends on the nature of the depreciable asset.

To illustrate computing depreciation using the units-of-production depreciation method, assume that Dryden measures productive capacity based on the total number of miles the van will be driven over its useful life. Assume Dryden estimates this productive capacity to be 100,000 miles. The first step in determining depreciation expense is to compute the cost per unit of production. For Dryden's van, this amount is total depreciable cost (historical cost − salvage value) divided by total units of expected productive capacity (100,000 miles). The depreciation cost per mile is therefore $0.20 [($24,000 cost − $4,000 salvage) ÷ 100,000 miles]. Annual depreciation expense is computed by multiplying the cost per mile by the number of miles driven. Odometer readings indicate the van was driven 40,000 miles, 20,000 miles, 30,000 miles, and 15,000 miles in Year 1, Year 2, Year 3, and Year 4, respectively. Based on these data, Dryden developed the following schedule of depreciation charges:

Year	Cost per Mile (a)	Miles Driven (b)	Depreciation Expense (a × b)
Year 1	$.20	40,000	$8,000
Year 2	.20	20,000	4,000
Year 3	.20	30,000	6,000
Year 4	.20	15,000	3,000 2,000

As pointed out in the discussion of the double-declining-balance method, an asset cannot be depreciated below its salvage value. Because $18,000 of the $20,000 ($24,000 cost − $4,000 salvage) depreciable cost is recognized in the first three years of using the van, only $2,000 ($20,000 − $18,000) remains to be charged to depreciation in the fourth year, even though the depreciation computations suggest the charge should be $3,000. As the preceding table indicates, the general formula for computing units-of-production depreciation is

$$\frac{\text{Cost} - \text{Salvage value}}{\text{Total estimated units of production}} \times \text{Units of production in current year} = \text{Annual depreciation expense}$$

Exhibit 8.5 displays financial statements that assume Dryden uses units-of-production depreciation. The exhibit assumes a cash revenue stream of $11,000, $7,000, $9,000, and $5,000 for Year 1, Year 2, Year 3, and Year 4, respectively. Trace the depreciation expense from the preceding schedule to the income statements. Depreciation expense is greater in years the van is driven more, and smaller in years the van is driven less, providing a reasonable matching of depreciation expense with revenue produced. Net income is again constant at $3,000 per year.

EXHIBIT 8.5 Financial Statements under Units-of-Production Depreciation

DRYDEN ENTERPRISES
Financial Statements

	Year 1	Year 2	Year 3	Year 4
Income Statements				
Rent revenue	$11,000	$ 7,000	$ 9,000	$ 5,000
Depreciation expense	(8,000)	(4,000)	(6,000)	(2,000)
Net income	$ 3,000	$ 3,000	$ 3,000	$ 3,000
Balance Sheets				
Assets				
Cash	$12,000	$19,000	$28,000	$33,000
Van	24,000	24,000	24,000	24,000
Accumulated depreciation	(8,000)	(12,000)	(18,000)	(20,000)
Total assets	$28,000	$31,000	$34,000	$37,000
Stockholders' equity				
Common stock	$25,000	$25,000	$25,000	$25,000
Retained earnings	3,000	6,000	9,000	12,000
Total stockholders' equity	$28,000	$31,000	$34,000	$37,000
Statements of Cash Flows				
Operating Activities				
Inflow from customers	$11,000	$ 7,000	$ 9,000	$ 5,000
Investing Activities				
Outflow to purchase van	(24,000)			
Financing Activities				
Inflow from stock issue	25,000			
Net Change in Cash	12,000	7,000	9,000	5,000
Beginning cash balance	0	12,000	19,000	28,000
Ending cash balance	$12,000	$19,000	$28,000	$33,000

LO 8-5

Show how gains and losses on disposals of long-term operational assets affect financial statements.

Accounting for the Disposal of Long-Term Operational Assets

Regardless of which method of depreciation a company chooses to use, the van will ultimately cease to be useful for the purpose of generating revenue. At this point, the company will have to dispose of the asset. To illustrate accounting for the disposal of the asset, assume Dryden retires the van from service and sells it on January 1, Year 5, for $4,500 cash. On this date, the van's book value is $4,000 ($24,000 cost − $20,000 accumulated depreciation). Under these circumstances, Dryden would recognize a $500 gain ($4,500 sales price − $4,000 book value) on the sale. Recording the disposal of the asset requires the following journal entry:

Account Title	Debit	Credit
Cash	4,500	
Accumulated Depreciation	20,000	
Van		24,000
Gain on Sale of Van		500

The debit to the Cash account records the amount of the cash received from the sale of the asset. The debit to the Accumulated Depreciation account removes the amount of accumulated depreciation associated with the van from the accounting records. The credit to the Van account removes the original cost of the van from the accounting records. The credit to the Gain account recognizes the gain that was generated from the sale of the van. The effects of the compound journal entry on the financial statements is shown next:

Assets			=	Equity			Rev. or Gain.	−	Exp. Or Loss.	=	Net Inc.	Cash Flow
Cash	+	Book Value of Van	=	Com. Stk.	+	Ret. Earn.						
4,500	+	(4,000)	=	NA	+	500	500	−	NA	=	500	4,500 IA

Total assets increase by $500 because the amount of cash collected is more than the book value of the van. The gain causes the amount of net income, and ultimately stockholders' equity, to increase. The amount of the gain is not reported on the statement of cash flows. Instead, the entire $4,500 is shown in the statement of cash flows as an inflow from investing activities. Because selling vans is not part of Dryden's normal operations, the gain will be reported separately, after operating income, on the income statement.

Comparing the Depreciation Methods

The total amount of depreciation expense Dryden recognized using each of the three methods was $20,000 ($24,000 cost − $4,000 salvage value). The different methods affect the *timing,* but not the *total amount,* of expense recognized. The different methods simply assign the $20,000 to different accounting periods. Exhibit 8.6 presents graphically the differences among the three depreciation methods discussed earlier. A company should use the method that most closely matches expenses with revenues.

EXHIBIT 8.6

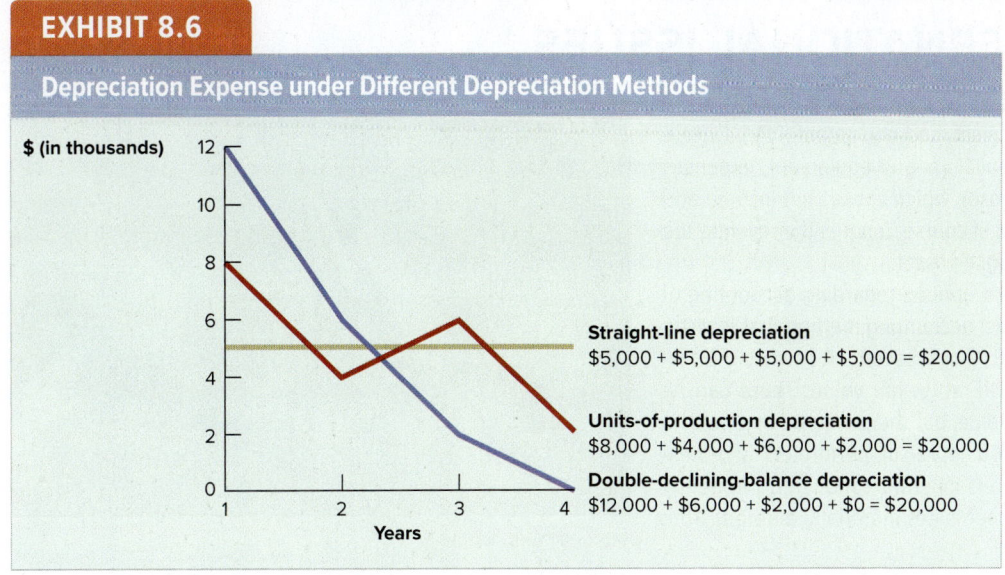

Depreciation Expense under Different Depreciation Methods

Straight-line depreciation
$5,000 + $5,000 + $5,000 + $5,000 = $20,000

Units-of-production depreciation
$8,000 + $4,000 + $6,000 + $2,000 = $20,000

Double-declining-balance depreciation
$12,000 + $6,000 + $2,000 + $0 = $20,000

INCOME TAX CONSIDERATIONS

The matching principle is not relevant to income tax reporting. The objective of tax reporting is to minimize tax expense. For tax purposes, the most desirable depreciation method is the one that produces the highest amount of depreciation expense. Higher expenses mean lower taxes.

The maximum depreciation currently allowed by tax law is computed using an accelerated depreciation method known as the **modified accelerated cost recovery system (MACRS).** MACRS specifies the useful life for designated categories of assets. For example, under the law, companies must base depreciation computations for automobiles, light trucks, technological equipment, and other similar asset types on a 5-year useful life. In contrast, a 7-year life must be used for office furniture, fixtures, and many types of conventional machinery. The law classifies depreciable property, excluding real estate, into one of six categories: 3-year property, 5-year property, 7-year property, 10-year property, 15-year property, and 20-year property. Tables have been established for each category that specify the percentage of cost that can be expensed (deducted) in determining the amount of taxable income. A tax table for 5- and 7-year property is shown next as an example.

LO 8-6

Identify some of the tax issues that affect long-term operational assets.

Year	5-Year Property, %	7-Year Property, %
1	20.00	14.29
2	32.00	24.49
3	19.20	17.49
4	11.52	12.49
5	11.52	8.93
6	5.76	8.92
7		8.93
8		4.46

The amount of depreciation a company can deduct each year for tax purposes is determined by multiplying the cost of a depreciable asset by the percentage shown in the table. For example, the depreciation expense for Year 1 of a 7-year property asset is the cost of the asset multiplied by 14.29 percent. Depreciation for Year 2 is the cost multiplied by 24.49 percent.

FOCUS ON INTERNATIONAL ISSUES

As you have learned, U.S. GAAP requires companies to use historical cost when accounting for property, plant, and equipment (PPE). Once a company begins depreciating its buildings and equipment, expenses increase (due to depreciation expense), which causes net income and retained earnings to decrease. This, of course, ignores the revenue the company hopes to generate by using the asset.

Under IFRS, a company has two options regarding accounting of PPE. First, it can use a historical cost accounting method that is virtually identical to that required by U.S. GAAP. Second, it can use the "revaluation model," which reports PPE at its fair value. There can be different ways of determining fair value, but the preferred approach is to base fair value on a market-based appraisal, performed by professional appraisers. These revaluations must be conducted frequently enough that the fair value of an asset is not materially different from its recorded book value.

©Skip Nall/Getty Images RF

Basically, the revaluation model works as follows. The company periodically compares the current book value of its PPE to the fair value at that same date. This fair value relates to the value of the used asset, not the amount required to replace it with a new asset. If the fair value of an asset is higher than its currently recorded book value, the recorded amount for the asset is increased, which increases total assets. However, the increase in the asset's fair value is *not* reported on the company's income statement, as would a gain from selling the asset. Rather, the increase is reported in a special section of stockholders' equity, which balances the increase that was recorded for assets. However, if the new fair value is *lower* than the asset's current book value, the decrease is charged to net income, as well as to assets. This is another example of the conservatism principle at work. Not surprisingly, there are exceptions to these rules. Once a new fair value is established, future depreciation expense is based on these values.

One concern might be that companies, hoping to manipulate earnings, would pick and choose some assets to account for under historical costs and others to account for under the revaluation model. This is not permitted. Although a company does not have to use a single method for all its assets, it must use a single method for all the assets in a given class of assets. For example, historical costs could be used for all factory equipment, and the revaluation model used for all its buildings.

As significant as the difference between the historical cost method and the fair value approach might be, the majority of companies continue to use historical costs. Professors H. B. Christensen and V. Nikolaev conducted a study of the use of revaluation accounting for nonfinancial assets by companies in Germany and the United Kingdom. Their research found that only 3.2 percent of the 1,539 companies surveyed used the revaluation model for property, plant, and equipment.

Source: Christensen, H. B. and Nikolaev, V., "Who Uses Fair Value Accounting for Nonfinancial Assets after IFRS Adoption?" The University of Chicago Booth School of Business Working Paper No. 09-12, February 2009.

The tables present some apparent inconsistencies. For example, if MACRS is an accelerated depreciation method, why is less depreciation permitted in Year 1 than in Years 2 and 3? Also, why is depreciation computed in Year 6 for property with a 5-year life and in Year 8 for property with a 7-year life? These conditions are the consequence of using the **half-year convention.**

The half-year convention is designed to simplify computing taxable income. Instead of requiring taxpayers to calculate depreciation from the exact date of purchase to the exact date of disposal, the tax code requires one-half year's depreciation to be charged in the year in which an asset is acquired and one-half year's depreciation in the final year of depreciation. As a result, the percentages shown in the table for the first and last years represent depreciation for one-half year instead of the actual time of usage.

To illustrate computing depreciation using MACRS, assume that Wilson Company purchased furniture (7-year property) for $10,000 cash on July 21. Tax depreciation charges over the useful life of the asset are computed as shown:

Year	Table Factor, %	×	Cost	=	Depreciation Amount
1	14.29		$10,000		$1,429
2	24.49		10,000		2,449
3	17.49		10,000		1,749
4	12.49		10,000		1,249
5	8.93		10,000		893
6	8.92		10,000		892
7	8.93		10,000		893
8	4.46		10,000		446
Total over useful life					$10,000

As an alternative to MACRS, the tax code permits using straight-line depreciation. For certain types of assets such as real property (buildings), the tax code requires using straight-line depreciation.

There is no requirement that depreciation methods used for financial reporting be consistent with those used in preparing the income tax return. For example, a company may use straight-line depreciation in its financial statements and MACRS for the tax return. A company making this choice would reduce taxes in the early years of an asset's life because it would report higher depreciation charges on the tax return than in the financial statements. In later years, however, taxes will be higher because, under MACRS, the amount of depreciation declines as the asset becomes older. Taxes are delayed but not avoided. The amount of taxes delayed for future payment represent a **deferred tax liability.** Delaying tax payments is advantageous. During the delay period, the money that would have been used to pay taxes can be used instead to make revenue-generating investments.

REVISION OF ESTIMATES

In order to report useful financial information on a timely basis, accountants must make many estimates of future results, such as the salvage value and useful life of depreciable assets. Estimates are frequently revised when new information surfaces. Because revisions of estimates are common, generally accepted accounting principles call for incorporating the revised information into present and future calculations. Prior reports are not corrected.

LO 8-7

Show how revising estimates affects financial statements.

To illustrate, assume that McGraw Company purchased a machine on January 1, Year 1, for $50,000. McGraw estimated the machine would have a useful life of eight years and a salvage value of $3,000. Using the straight-line method, McGraw determined the annual depreciation charge as follows:

($50,000 − $3,000) ÷ 8 years = $5,875 per year

At the beginning of the fifth year, accumulated depreciation on the machine is $23,500 ($5,875 × 4). The machine's book value is $26,500 ($50,000 − $23,500). At this point, what happens if McGraw changes its estimates of useful life or the salvage value? Consider the following revision examples independently of each other.

Revision of Life

Assume McGraw revises the expected life to 14 years, rather than 8. The machine's *remaining* life would then be 10 more years instead of 4 more years. Assume salvage value remains $3,000. Depreciation for each remaining year is

($26,500 book value − $3,000 salvage) ÷ 10-year remaining life = $2,350

Revision of Salvage

Alternatively, assume the original expected life remained 8 years, but McGraw revised its estimate of salvage value to $6,000. Depreciation for each of the remaining 4 years would be

($26,500 book value − $6,000 salvage) ÷ 4-year remaining life = $5,125

The revised amounts are determined for the full year, regardless of when McGraw revised its estimates. For example, if McGraw decides to change the estimated useful life on October 1, Year 3, the change would be effective as of January 1, Year 3. The year-end adjusting entry for depreciation would include a full year's depreciation calculated on the basis of the revised estimated useful life.

CONTINUING EXPENDITURES FOR PLANT ASSETS

LO 8-8

Show how continuing expenditures for operational assets affect financial statements.

Most plant assets require additional expenditures for maintenance or improvement during their useful lives. Accountants must determine if these expenditures should be expensed or capitalized (recorded as assets).

Costs That Are Expensed

The costs of routine maintenance and minor repairs that are incurred to *keep* an asset in good working order are expensed in the period in which they are incurred. Because they reduce net income when incurred, accountants often call repair and maintenance costs **revenue expenditures** (companies subtract them from revenue).

With respect to the previous example, assume McGraw spent $500 for routine lubrication and to replace minor parts. The journal entry and its effects on the financial statements are shown next:

Account Title	Debit	Credit
Repairs Expense	500	
Cash		500

Assets	=	Equity			Rev.	−	Exp.	=	Net Inc.	Cash Flow
Cash	=	Com. Stk.	+	Ret. Earn.						
(500)	=	NA	+	(500)	NA	−	500	=	(500)	(500) OA

Costs That Are Capitalized

Substantial amounts spent to improve the quality or extend the life of an asset are described as **capital expenditures.** Capital expenditures are accounted for in one of two ways, depending on whether the cost incurred *improves the quality* or *extends the life* of the asset.

Improving Quality

Expenditures such as adding air conditioning to an existing building or installing a trailer hitch on a vehicle improve the quality of service these assets provide. If a capital expenditure improves an asset's quality, the amount is added to the historical cost of the asset. The additional cost is expensed through higher depreciation charges over the asset's remaining useful life.

To demonstrate, return to the McGraw Company example. Recall that the machine originally cost $50,000, had an estimated salvage value of $3,000, and had a predicted life of 8 years. Recall further that accumulated depreciation at the beginning of the fifth year is $23,500 ($5,875 × 4) so the book value is $26,500 ($50,000 − $23,500). Assume McGraw makes a major expenditure of $4,000 in the machine's fifth year to improve its productive capacity. The journal entry and its effects on the financial statements are shown next:

Account Title	Debit	Credit
Machine	4,000	
Cash		4,000

Assets	=	Equity	Rev.	−	Exp.	=	Net Inc.	Cash Flow
Cash + Book Value of Mach.	=	Com. Stk. + Ret. Earn.						
(4,000) + 4,000	=	NA + NA	NA	−	NA	=	NA	(4,000) IA

After recording the expenditure, the machine account balance is $54,000 and the asset's book value is $30,500 ($54,000 − $23,500). The depreciation charges for each of the remaining 4 years are

($30,500 book value − $3,000 salvage) ÷ 4-year remaining life = $6,875

Extending Life

Expenditures such as replacing the roof of an existing building or putting a new engine in an older vehicle extend the useful life of these assets. If a capital expenditure extends the life of an asset rather than improving the asset's quality of service, accountants view the expenditure as canceling some of the depreciation previously charged to expense. The event is still an asset exchange; cash decreases, and the book value of the machine increases. However, the increase in the book value of the machine results from reducing the balance in the contra asset account, Accumulated Depreciation.

To illustrate, assume that instead of increasing productive capacity, McGraw's $4,000 expenditure had extended the useful life of the machine by 2 years. The journal entry and its effects on the financial statements are shown next:

Account Title	Debit	Credit
Accumulated Depreciation–Machine	4,000	
Cash		4,000

Assets	=	Equity	Rev.	−	Exp.	=	Net Inc.	Cash Flow
Cash + Book Value of Mach.	=	Com. Stk. + Ret. Earn.						
(4,000) + 4,000	=	NA + NA	NA	−	NA	=	NA	(4,000) IA

After the expenditure is recorded, the book value is the same as if the $4,000 had been added to the Machine account ($50,000 cost − $19,500 adjusted balance in Accumulated Depreciation = $30,500). Depreciation expense for each of the remaining 6 years follows:

($30,500 book value − $3,000 salvage) ÷ 6-year remaining life = $4,583

> **CHECK YOURSELF 8.3**
>
> On January 1, Year 1, Dager Inc. purchased an asset that cost $18,000. It had a 5-year useful life and a $3,000 salvage value. Dager uses straight-line depreciation. On January 1, Year 3, it incurred a $1,200 cost related to the asset. With respect to this asset, determine the amount of expense and accumulated depreciation Dager would report in the Year 3 financial statements under each of the following assumptions:
>
> 1. The $1,200 cost was incurred to repair damage resulting from an accident.
> 2. The $1,200 cost improved the operating capacity of the asset. The total useful life and salvage value remained unchanged.
> 3. The $1,200 cost extended the useful life of the asset by one year. The salvage value remained unchanged.
>
> **Answer**
>
> 1. Dager would report the $1,200 repair cost as an expense. Dager would also report depreciation expense of $3,000 [($18,000 − $3,000) ÷ 5]. Total expenses related to this asset in Year 3 would be $4,200 ($1,200 repair expense + $3,000 depreciation expense). Accumulated depreciation at the end of Year 3 would be $9,000 ($3,000 depreciation expense × 3 years).
>
> 2. The $1,200 cost would be capitalized in the asset account, increasing both the book value of the asset and the annual depreciation expense.
>
> | | After-Effects of Capital Improvement |
> |---|---|
> | Amount in asset account ($18,000 + $1,200) | $19,200 |
> | Less: Salvage value | (3,000) |
> | Accumulated depreciation on January 1, Year 3 | (6,000) |
> | Remaining depreciable cost before recording Year 3 depreciation | $10,200 |
> | Depreciation for Year 3 ($10,200 ÷ 3 years) | $ 3,400 |
> | Accumulated depreciation at December 31, Year 3 ($6,000 + $3,400) | $ 9,400 |
>
> 3. The $1,200 cost would be subtracted from the Accumulated Depreciation account, increasing the book value of the asset. The remaining useful life would increase to 4 years, which would decrease the depreciation expense.
>
> | | After-Effects of Capital Improvement |
> |---|---|
> | Amount in asset account | $18,000 |
> | Less: Salvage value | (3,000) |
> | Accumulated depreciation on January 1, Year 3 ($6,000 − $1,200) | (4,800) |
> | Remaining depreciable cost before recording Year 3 depreciation | $10,200 |
> | Depreciation for Year 3 ($10,200 ÷ 4 years) | $ 2,550 |
> | Accumulated depreciation at December 31, Year 3 ($4,800 + $2,550) | $ 7,350 |

NATURAL RESOURCES

LO 8-9

Calculate depletion and show how it affects financial statements.

The cost of natural resources includes not only the purchase price but also related items such as the cost of exploration, geographic surveys, and estimates. The process of expensing natural resources is commonly called depletion.[2] The most common method used to calculate depletion is units-of-production.

[2] In practice, the depletion charge is considered a product cost and allocated between inventory and cost of goods sold. This text uses the simplifying assumption that all resources are sold in the same accounting period in which they are extracted. The full depletion charge is therefore expensed in the period in which the resources are extracted.

Answers to The Curious Accountant

As assets lose their productive capacity, either from being used or due to obsolescence, the asset account is reduced and an expense account is increased. Assets such as buildings and equipment may decline faster if they are used, but, due to obsolescence, they usually continue to decline even if they are not used. For this reason, a time-based depreciation method, such as straight-line or double-declining-balance, is almost always used for buildings and more often than not for equipment. In contrast, a mineral reserve does not lose its capacity unless ore is extracted. After all, the gold the FCX is mining today has been in the earth for millions of years. For this reason, companies typically use the units-of-production method to calculate depletion on mineral reserves. In both cases, the objective should be to achieve the best matching of expenses incurred with the revenues they generate.

To illustrate, assume Apex Coal Mining paid $4,000,000 cash to purchase a mine with an estimated 16,000,000 tons of coal. The unit depletion charge is

$$\$4,000,000 \div 16,000,000 \text{ tons} = \$0.25 \text{ per ton}$$

If Apex mines 360,000 tons of coal in the first year, the depletion charge is

$$360,000 \text{ tons} \div \$0.25 \text{ per ton} = \$90,000$$

The depletion of a natural resource has the same effect on the accounting equation as other expense recognition events. Assets (in this case, a *coal mine*) and stockholders' equity decrease. The depletion expense reduces net income. The journal entries necessary to record the acquisition and depletion of the coal mine and their effects on the financial statements are shown next:

Account Title	Debit	Credit
Coal Mine	4,000,000	
Cash		4,000,000
Depletion Expense	90,000	
Coal Mine		90,000

Assets			=	Equity			Rev.	−	Exp.	=	Net Inc.	Cash Flow
Cash	+	Coal Mine	=	Com. Stk.	+	Ret. Earn.						
(4,000,000)	+	4,000,000	=	NA	+	NA	NA	−	NA	=	NA	(4,000,000) IA
NA	+	(90,000)	=	NA	+	(90,000)	NA	−	90,000	=	(90,000)	NA

INTANGIBLE ASSETS

LO 8-10

Intangible assets provide rights, privileges, and special opportunities to businesses. Common intangible assets include trademarks, patents, copyrights, franchises, and goodwill. Some of the unique characteristics of these intangible assets are described in the following sections.

 Identify and determine the cost of intangible assets.

FOCUS ON INTERNATIONAL ISSUES

RESEARCH *AND* DEVELOPMENT VS. RESEARCH *OR* DEVELOPMENT

For many years, some thought the companies that followed U.S. GAAP were at a disadvantage when it came to research and development (R&D) costs, because these companies had to immediately expense such cost, while the accounting rules of some other countries allowed R&D cost to be capitalized. Remember, recording costs as an asset—capitalizing it—means that net income is not immediately reduced. The global movement toward using IFRS is reducing, but not eliminating, the different accounting treatments for R&D.

Like U.S. GAAP, IFRS requires *research* costs to be expensed, but it allows *development* costs to be capitalized. This IFRS rule itself can present challenges, because sometimes it is not clear where research ends and development begins. Basically, once research has produced a product, patent, and so forth that the company believes will result in a revenue-generating outcome, any additional costs to get it ready for market are development costs.

©Adam Gault/Getty Images

Trademarks

A **trademark** is a name or symbol that identifies a company or a product. Familiar trademarks include the *Polo* emblem, the name *Coca-Cola*, and the *Nike* slogan, "Just do it." Trademarks are registered with the federal government and have an indefinite legal lifetime.

The costs incurred to design, purchase, or defend a trademark are capitalized in an asset account called Trademarks. Companies want their trademarks to become familiar, but they also face the risk of a trademark being used as the generic name for a product. To protect a trademark, companies in this predicament spend large sums on legal fees and extensive advertising programs to educate consumers. Well-known trademarks that have been subject to this problem include *Coke*, *Xerox*, *Kleenex*, and *Vaseline*.

Patents

A **patent** grants its owner an exclusive legal right to produce and sell a product that has one or more unique features. Patents issued by the U.S. Patent Office have a legal life of 20 years. Companies may obtain patents through purchase, lease, or internal development. The costs capitalized in the Patent account are usually limited to the purchase price and legal fees to obtain and successfully defend the patent. The research and development costs incurred to develop patentable products are usually expensed in the period in which they are incurred.

Copyrights

A **copyright** protects writers' works, musical compositions, works of art, and other intellectual property for the exclusive benefit of the creator or persons assigned the right by the creator. The cost of a copyright includes the purchase price and any legal costs associated with obtaining and defending the copyright. Copyrights granted by the federal government extend for the life of the creator plus 70 years. A radio commercial could legally use a Bach composition as background music; it could not, however, use the theme song from the most recent Academy Award–winning movie without obtaining permission from the copyright owner. The cost of a copyright is often expensed early because future royalties may be uncertain.

REALITY BYTES

In 2017, Reckitt Benckiser Group, PLC reported that it had paid $17.9 billion to acquire Mead Johnson Nutrition Co. (M-J), even though the company's assets were reported on its December 31, 2016, balance sheet to be only $4.1 billion. Reckitt is a British-based company that owns numerous consumer brands, including Air Wick, French's, Lysol, and Dr. Scholl's. M-J's brands include Enfamil infant formulas. Why would Reckitt pay the owners of M-J over four times the value of the assets shown on the company's balance sheet?

©The McGraw-Hill Companies, Inc./Jill Braaten, photographer

Reckitt was willing to pay well above the book value of the assets for several reasons. First, the value of the assets on M-J's balance sheet represented the historical cost of the assets. The current market value of these assets was probably higher than their historical cost, especially for intangible assets such as its trademarks and research in progress. Second, Reckitt believed that the two companies combined could operate at a lower cost than the two could as separate companies, thus increasing the total earnings they could generate. It estimated these savings would be over $200 million per year by the third year after the acquisition. Third, M-J had a bigger presence than Reckitt in developing markets, especially China, so this would make it easier to get Reckitt's existing products into those markets. Finally, Reckitt probably believed that M-J had *goodwill* that enables a company to use its assets in a manner that will generate above-average earnings. In other words, Reckitt was paying for a hidden asset not shown on M-J's balance sheet.

Source: Companies' reports.

Franchises

Franchises grant exclusive rights to sell products or perform services in certain geographic areas. Franchises may be granted by governments or private businesses. Franchises granted by governments include federal broadcasting licenses. Private business franchises include fast-food restaurant chains and brand labels such as Healthy Choice. The legal and useful lives of a franchise are frequently difficult to determine. Judgment is often crucial to establishing the estimated useful life for franchises.

Goodwill

Goodwill is the value attributable to favorable factors such as reputation, location, and superior products. Consider the most popular restaurant in your town. If the owner sold the restaurant, do you think the acquisition price would be simply the total value of the chairs, tables, kitchen equipment, and building? Certainly not, because much of the restaurant's value lies in its popularity; in other words, its ability to generate a high return is based on the goodwill (reputation) of the business.

Calculating goodwill can be complex; here we present a simple example to illustrate how it is determined. Suppose the accounting records of a restaurant named Bendigo's show

Assets = Liabilities + Stockholders' equity
$200,000 = $50,000 + $150,000

Assume a buyer agrees to acquire the restaurant by paying the owner $300,000 cash and assuming the existing liabilities. In other words, the restaurant is acquired at a price of $350,000 ($300,000 cash + $50,000 assumed liabilities). Now assume that the assets of the business (tables, chairs, kitchen equipment, etc.) have a fair value of only $280,000. Why would the buyer pay $350,000 to purchase assets with a fair value of $280,000? Obviously, the buyer is purchasing more than just the assets. The buyer is acquiring the business' goodwill. The amount of the goodwill is the difference between the purchase price and the fair value of the assets. In this case, the goodwill is $70,000 ($350,000 − $280,000). The journal entry to record the acquisition and its effects on the financial statements are shown here:

Account Title	Debit	Credit
Restaurant Assets	280,000	
Goodwill	70,000	
Cash		300,000
Liabilities		50,000

Assets	=	Liab.	+	Equity	Rev.	−	Exp.	=	Net Inc.	Cash Flow
Cash + Rest. Assets + Goodwill										
(300,000) + 280,000 + 70,000	=	50,000	+	NA	NA	−	NA	=	NA	(300,000) IA

The fair value of the restaurant assets represents the historical cost to the new owner. It becomes the basis for future depreciation charges.

Expense Recognition for Intangible Assets

As mentioned earlier, intangible assets fall into two categories, those with *identifiable useful lives* and those with *indefinite useful lives*. Expense recognition for intangible assets depends on which classification applies.

Show how the amortization of intangible assets affects financial statements.

Expensing Intangible Assets with Identifiable Useful Lives

The costs of intangible assets with identifiable useful lives are normally expensed on a straight-line basis using a process called *amortization*. An intangible asset should be amortized over the shorter of two possible time periods: (1) its legal life or (2) its useful life.

To illustrate, assume that Flowers Industries purchased a newly granted patent for $44,000 cash. Although the patent has a legal life of 20 years, Flowers estimates that it will be useful for only 11 years. The annual amortization charge is therefore $4,000 ($44,000 ÷ 11 years). The journal entries to record the patent purchase and first year amortization and their effects on the financial statements are shown next:

Account Title	Debit	Credit
Patent	44,000	
Cash		44,000
Amortization Expense, Patent	4,000	
Patent		4,000

Assets	=	Equity	Rev.	−	Exp.	=	Net Inc.	Cash Flow
Cash + Patent	=	Com. Stk. + Ret. Earn.						
(44,000) + 44,000	=	NA + NA	NA	−	NA	=	NA	(44,000) IA
NA + (4,000)	=	NA + (4,000)	NA	−	4,000	=	(4,000)	NA

Impairment Losses for Intangible Assets with Indefinite Useful Lives

Intangible assets with indefinite useful lives must be tested for impairment annually. The impairment test consists of comparing the fair value of the intangible asset to its carrying value (book value). If the fair value is less than the book value, an impairment loss must be recognized.

To illustrate, return to the example of the Bendigo's restaurant acquisition. Recall that the buyer of Bendigo's paid $70,000 for goodwill. Assume the restaurant experiences a significant decline in revenue because many of its former regular customers are dissatisfied with the food prepared by the new chef. Suppose the decline in revenue is so substantial that the new owner believes the Bendigo's name is permanently impaired. The owner decides to hire a different chef and change the name of the restaurant. In this case, the business has suffered a permanent decline in value of goodwill. The company must recognize an impairment loss.

The restaurant's name has lost its value, but the owner believes the location continues to provide the opportunity to produce above-average earnings. Some, but not all, of the goodwill has been lost. Assume the fair value of the remaining goodwill is determined to be $40,000. The impairment loss to recognize is $30,000 ($70,000 − $40,000). The loss reduces the intangible asset (goodwill), stockholder's equity (retained earnings), and net income. The statement of cash flows is not affected. The journal entry and its effects on the financial statements follow:

Account Title	Debit	Credit
Impairment Loss	30,000	
Goodwill		30,000

Assets	=	Liab.	+	Equity	Rev.	−	Exp./Loss	=	Net Inc.	Cash Flow
Goodwill	=			Ret. Earn.						
(30,000)	=	NA	+	(30,000)	NA	−	(30,000)	=	(30,000)	NA

Balance Sheet Presentation

This chapter explained accounting for the acquisition, expense recognition, and disposal of a wide range of long-term assets. Exhibit 8.7 illustrates the typical balance sheet presentation of many of the assets discussed.

EXHIBIT 8.7

Balance Sheet Presentation of Operational Assets

Partial Balance Sheet

Long-Term Assets		
Plant and equipment		
Buildings	$4,000,000	
Less: Accumulated depreciation	(2,500,000)	$1,500,000
Equipment	1,750,000	
Less: Accumulated depreciation	(1,200,000)	550,000
Total plant and equipment		$2,050,000
Land		850,000
Natural resources		
Mineral deposits (Less: Depletion)	2,100,000	
Oil reserves (Less: Depletion)	890,000	
Total natural resources		2,990,000
Intangibles		
Patents (Net of amortization)	38,000	
Goodwill	175,000	
Total intangible assets		213,000
Total long-term assets		$6,103,000

LO 8-12

Show how expense recognition choices and industry characteristics affect financial performance measures.

The Financial Analyst

Managers may have differing opinions about which allocation method (straight-line, accelerated, or units-of-production) best matches expenses with revenues. As a result, one company may use straight-line depreciation, while another company in similar circumstances uses double-declining-balance. Because the allocation method a company uses affects the amount of expense it recognizes, analysts reviewing financial statements must consider the accounting procedures companies use in preparing the statements.

Assume that two companies, Alpha and Zeta, experience identical economic events in Year 1 and Year 2. Both generate revenue of $50,000 and incur cost of goods sold of $30,000 during each year. In Year 1, each company pays $20,000 for an asset with an expected useful life of five years and no salvage value. How will the companies' financial statements differ if one uses straight-line depreciation and the other uses the double-declining-balance method? To answer this question, first compute the depreciation expense for both companies for Year 1 and Year 2.

Effect of Judgment and Estimation

If Alpha Company uses the straight-line method, depreciation for Year 1 and Year 2 is

(Cost − Salvage) ÷ Useful life = Depreciation expense per year
($20,000 − $0) ÷ 5 years = $4,000

In contrast, if Zeta Company uses the double-declining-balance method, Zeta recognizes the following amounts of depreciation expense for Year 1 and Year 2.

	(Cost − Accumulated Depreciation)	×	2 × (Straight-Line Rate)	=	Depreciation Expense
Year 1	($20,000 − $ 0)	×	[2 × (1 ÷ 5)]	=	$8,000
Year 2	($20,000 − $8,000)	×	[2 × (1 ÷ 5)]	=	$4,800

Based on these computations, the income statements for the two companies are

Income Statements

	Year 1 Alpha Co.	Year 1 Zeta Co.	Year 2 Alpha Co.	Year 2 Zeta Co.
Sales	$ 50,000	$ 50,000	$ 50,000	$ 50,000
Cost of goods sold	(30,000)	(30,000)	(30,000)	(30,000)
Gross margin	20,000	20,000	20,000	20,000
Depreciation expense	(4,000)	(8,000)	(4,000)	(4,800)
Net income	$ 16,000	$ 12,000	$ 16,000	$ 15,200

The relevant sections of the balance sheets are

Plant Assets

	Year 1 Alpha Co.	Year 1 Zeta Co.	Year 2 Alpha Co.	Year 2 Zeta Co.
Asset	$20,000	$20,000	$20,000	$ 20,000
Accumulated depreciation	(4,000)	(8,000)	(8,000)	(12,800)
Book value	$16,000	$12,000	$12,000	$ 7,200

The depreciation method is not the only aspect of expense recognition that can vary between companies. Companies may also make different assumptions about the useful lives and salvage values of long-term operational assets. Thus, even if the same depreciation method is used, depreciation expense may still differ.

Because the depreciation method and the underlying assumptions regarding useful life and salvage value affect the determination of depreciation expense, they also affect the amounts of net income, retained earnings, and total assets. Financial statement analysis is affected if it is based on ratios that include these items. Previously defined ratios that are affected include the (1) debt-to-assets ratio, (2) return-on-assets ratio, (3) return-on-equity ratio, and (4) return-on-sales ratio.

To promote meaningful analysis, GAAP requires companies to disclose all significant accounting policies used to prepare their financial statements. This disclosure is provided in the notes that accompany the financial statements.

Effect of Industry Characteristics

As indicated in previous chapters, industry characteristics affect financial performance measures. For example, companies in manufacturing industries invest heavily in machinery, while insurance companies rely more on human capital. Manufacturing companies therefore have relatively higher depreciation charges than insurance companies. To illustrate how the type of industry affects financial reporting, examine Exhibit 8.8. This exhibit compares the ratio of sales to property, plant, and equipment for two companies in each of three different industries. These data are for 2016.

©Northfoto/Shutterstock

The table indicates that for every $1.00 invested in property, plant, and equipment, Manpower produced $132.43 of sales. In contrast, Verizon and Southwest Airlines produced only $1.49 and $1.20, respectively, for each $1.00 they invested in operational assets. Does this mean the management of Manpower is doing a better job than the management of Verizon or Southwest Airlines? Not necessarily. It means that these companies operate in different economic environments. In other words, it takes significantly more equipment to operate a cable company or an airline than it takes to operate an employment agency.

Effective financial analysis requires careful consideration of industry characteristics, accounting policies, and the reasonableness of assumptions such as useful life and salvage value.

EXHIBIT 8.8

Industry Data Reflecting the Use of Long-Term Tangible Assets

Industry	Company	Sales ÷ Property, Plant, and Equipment
Broadband Communications	Comcast Corp.	2.39
	Verizon Communications	1.49
Airlines	Alaska Air Group	1.04
	Southwest Airlines	1.20
Employment Agencies	Kelly Services	65.31
	Manpower, Inc.	132.43

A Look Back

This chapter explains that the primary objective of recognizing depreciation is to match the cost of a long-term tangible asset with the revenues the asset is expected to generate. The matching concept also applies to natural resources (depletion) and intangible assets (amortization). The chapter explains how alternative methods can be used to account for the same event (e.g., straight-line versus double-declining-balance depreciation). Companies experiencing exactly the same business events could produce different financial statements. The alternative accounting methods for depreciating, depleting, or amortizing assets include the (1) straight-line, (2) double-declining-balance, and (3) units-of-production methods.

The *straight-line method* produces equal amounts of expense in each accounting period. The amount of the expense recognized is determined using the formula [(cost − salvage) ÷ number of years of useful life]. The *double-declining-balance method* produces proportionately larger amounts of expense in the early years of an asset's useful life and increasingly smaller amounts of expense in the later years of the asset's useful life. The formula for calculating double-declining-balance depreciation is [book value at beginning of period × (2 × the straight-line rate)]. The *units-of-production method* produces expense in direct proportion to the number of units produced during an accounting period. The formula for the amount of expense recognized each period is [(cost − salvage) ÷ total estimated units of production = allocation rate × units of production in current accounting period].

The chapter also discussed *MACRS depreciation*, an accelerated tax reporting method. MACRS is not acceptable under GAAP for public reporting. A company may use MACRS depreciation for tax purposes and straight-line or one of the other methods for public reporting. As a result, differences may exist between the amount of tax expense and the amount of tax liability. Such differences are reported as *deferred income taxes*.

This chapter showed how to account for *changes in estimates* such as the useful life or the salvage value of a depreciable asset. Changes in estimates do not affect the amount of depreciation recognized previously. Instead, the remaining book value of the asset is expensed over its remaining useful life.

After an asset has been placed into service, companies typically incur further costs for maintenance, quality improvement, and extensions of useful life. *Maintenance costs* are expensed in the period in which they are incurred. *Costs that improve the quality* of an asset are added to the cost of the asset, increasing the book value and the amount of future depreciation charges. *Costs that extend the useful life* of an asset are subtracted from the asset's Accumulated Depreciation account, increasing the book value and the amount of future depreciation charges.

A Look Forward

In Chapter 9, we move from the assets section of the balance sheet to issues in accounting for short-term liabilities. You will also study the basic components of a payroll accounting system.

SELF-STUDY REVIEW PROBLEM

A step-by-step audio-narrated series of slides is available in **Connect.**

The following information pertains to a machine purchased by Bakersfield Company on January 1, Year 1:

Purchase price	$ 63,000
Delivery cost	$ 2,000
Installation charge	$ 3,000
Estimated useful life	8 years
Estimated units the machine will produce	130,000
Estimated salvage value	$ 3,000

The machine produced 14,400 units during Year 1 and 17,000 units during Year 2.

Required

Determine the depreciation expense Bakersfield would report for Year 1 and Year 2 using each of the following methods:

a. Straight-line
b. Double-declining-balance
c. Units-of-production
d. MACRS, assuming that the machine is classified as a seven-year property

Solution to Requirements a–d

a. Straight-line

Purchase price	$63,000
Delivery cost	2,000
Installation charge	3,000
Total cost of machine	68,000
Less: Salvage value	(3,000)
	$65,000 ÷ 8 = $8,125 Depreciation per year
Year 1	$ 8,125
Year 2	$ 8,125

b. Double-declining-balance

Year	Cost	−	Accumulated Depreciation at Beginning of Year	×	2 × S-L Rate	=	Annual Depreciation
Year 1	$68,000	−	$ 0	×	(2 × 0.125)	=	$17,000
Year 2	68,000	−	17,000	×	(2 × 0.125)	=	12,750

c. Units-of-production

(1) (Cost − Salvage value) ÷ Estimated units of production = Depreciation cost per unit produced

$$\frac{\$68,000 - \$3,000}{130,000} = \$0.50 \text{ per unit}$$

(2) Cost per unit × Annual units produced = Annual depreciation expense

Year 1 $0.50 × 14,400 = $7,200
Year 2   0.50 × 17,000 = 8,500

d. MACRS

Cost × MACRS percentage = Annual depreciation
Year 1 $68,000 × 0.1429 = $ 9,717
Year 2   68,000 × 0.2449 =   16,653

KEY TERMS

Accelerated depreciation method 426
Accumulated depreciation 424
Amortization 420
Basket purchase 421
Book value 424
Capital expenditures 434
Carrying value 424
Contra asset account 424
Copyright 438
Current assets 418
Deferred tax liability 433
Depletion 420
Depreciable cost 422
Depreciation 420
Depreciation expense 422
Double-declining-balance depreciation 426
Estimated useful life 422
Franchise 439
Goodwill 439
Half-year convention 432
Historical cost concept 421
Intangible assets 420
Long-term operational assets 418
Modified accelerated cost recovery system (MACRS) 431
Natural resources 420
Patent 438
Property, plant, and equipment 420
Relative market value method 421
Revenue expenditures 434
Salvage value 422
Straight-line depreciation 423
Tangible assets 420
Trademark 438
Units-of-production depreciation 428

QUESTIONS

1. What is the difference between the functions of long-term operational assets and investments?
2. What is the difference between tangible and intangible assets? Give an example of each.
3. What is the difference between goodwill and specifically identifiable intangible assets?
4. Define *depreciation*. What kind of asset depreciates?
5. Why do you think natural resources are called *wasting assets*?
6. Is land a depreciable asset? Why or why not?
7. Define *amortization*. Which kinds of assets are amortized?
8. Explain the historical cost concept as it applies to long-term operational assets. Why is the book value of an asset likely to be different from the current fair market value of the asset?
9. What different kinds of expenditures might be included in the recorded cost of a building?
10. What is a basket purchase of assets? When a basket purchase is made, how is cost assigned to individual assets?
11. What are the stages in the life cycle of a long-term operational asset?
12. Explain straight-line, units-of-production, and double-declining-balance depreciation. When is it appropriate to use each of these depreciation methods?
13. What effect does the recognition of depreciation expense have on total assets? On total equity?
14. Does the recognition of depreciation expense affect cash flows? Why or why not?
15. MalMax purchased a depreciable asset. What would be the difference in total assets at the end of the first year if MalMax chooses straight-line depreciation versus double-declining-balance depreciation?
16. John Smith mistakenly expensed the cost of a long-term tangible fixed asset. Specifically, he charged the cost of a truck to a delivery expense account. How will this error affect the income statement and the balance sheet in the year in which the mistake is made?
17. What is *salvage value*?
18. What type of account (classification) is Accumulated Depreciation?
19. How is the book value of an asset determined?
20. Why is depreciation that has been recognized over the life of an asset shown in a contra account? Why not just reduce the asset account?
21. Assume that a piece of equipment cost $5,000 and had accumulated depreciation recorded of $3,000. What is the book value of the equipment? Is the book value equal to the fair market value of the equipment? Explain.
22. Why would a company choose to depreciate one piece of equipment using the double-declining-balance method and another piece of equipment using straight-line depreciation?
23. Explain MACRS depreciation. When is its use appropriate?
24. Does the method of depreciation required to be used for tax purposes reflect the use of a piece of equipment? Can you use double-declining-balance depreciation for tax purposes?
25. Define *deferred taxes*. Where does the account *Deferred Taxes* appear in the financial statements?
26. Why may it be necessary to revise the estimated life of a plant asset? When the estimated life is revised, does it affect the amount of depreciation per year? Why or why not?
27. How are capital expenditures made to improve the quality of a capital asset accounted for? Would the answer change if the expenditure extended the life of the asset but did not improve quality? Explain.
28. When a long-term operational asset is sold at a gain, how is the balance sheet affected? Is the statement of cash flows affected? If so, how?
29. Define *depletion*. What is the most commonly used method of computing depletion?
30. List several common intangible assets. How is the life determined that is to be used to compute amortization?
31. List some differences between U.S. GAAP and IFRS for long-term operational assets.
32. How do differences in expense recognition and industry characteristics affect financial performance measures?

MULTIPLE-CHOICE QUESTIONS

Multiple-choice questions are available in **Connect.**

EXERCISES—SERIES A

All applicable Exercises in Series A are available in Connect.

Unless specifically included, ignore income tax considerations in all exercises and problems.

Exercise 8-1A *Long-term operational assets used in a business*   LO 8-1

Required

Give some examples of long-term operational assets that each of the following companies is likely to own: *(a)* **Caterpillar**, *(b)* **Amtrak**, *(c)* **Facebook**, and *(d)* **Bank of America Corp**.

Exercise 8-2A *Identifying long-term operational assets*   LO 8-1

Required

Which of the following items should be classified as long-term operational assets?

a. Prepaid insurance
b. Coal mine
c. Office equipment
d. Accounts receivable
e. Supplies
f. Copyright
g. Delivery van
h. Land used in the business
i. Goodwill
j. Cash
k. Filing cabinet
l. Tax library of accounting firm

Exercise 8-3A *Classifying tangible and intangible assets*   LO 8-1

Required

Identify each of the following long-term operational assets as either tangible (T) or intangible (I):

a. Pizza oven
b. Land
c. Franchise
d. Filing cabinet
e. Copyright
f. Silver mine
g. Office building
h. Drill press
i. Patent
j. Oil well
k. Desk
l. Goodwill

Exercise 8-4A *Determining the cost of an asset*   LO 8-1

Southwest Milling Co. purchased a front-end loader to move stacks of lumber. The loader had a list price of $140,000. The seller agreed to allow a 4 percent discount because Southwest Milling paid cash. Delivery terms were FOB shipping point. Freight cost amounted to $1,200. Southwest Milling had to hire a specialist to calibrate the loader. The specialist's fee was $1,800. The loader operator is paid an annual salary of $60,000. The cost of the company's theft insurance policy increased by $800 per year as a result of acquiring the loader. The loader had a four-year useful life and an expected salvage value of $6,000.

Required

a. Determine the amount to be capitalized in an asset account for the purchase of the loader.
b. Record the purchase in general journal format.

Exercise 8-5A *Allocating costs on the basis of relative market values*   LO 8-1

Carver Inc. purchased a building and the land on which the building is situated for a total cost of $700,000 cash. The land was appraised at $320,000 and the building at $480,000.

Required

a. Determine the amount of the purchase cost to allocate to the land and the amount to allocate to the building.
b. Would the company recognize a gain on the purchase? Why or why not?
c. Record the purchase in a statements model like the following one:

Assets	=	Liab.	+	Equity	Rev.	−	Exp.	=	Net Inc.	Cash Flow
Cash + Land + Building										

d. Record the purchase in general journal format.

LO 8-1

Exercise 8-6A *Allocating costs for a basket purchase*

Pitney Co. purchased an office building, land, and furniture for $500,000 cash. The appraised value of the assets was as follows:

Land	$180,000
Building	300,000
Furniture	120,000
Total	$600,000

Required

a. Compute the amount to be recorded on the books for each asset.
b. Show the purchase in a horizontal statements model like the following one:

c. Prepare the general journal entry to record the purchase.

LO 8-2

Exercise 8-7A *Effect of depreciation on the accounting equation and financial statements*

The following events apply to Gulf Seafood for the Year 1 fiscal year:

1. The company started when it acquired $60,000 cash by issuing common stock.
2. Purchased a new cooktop that cost $40,000 cash.
3. Earned $72,000 in cash revenue.
4. Paid $25,000 cash for salaries expense.
5. Adjusted the records to reflect the use of the cooktop. Purchased on January 1, Year 1, the cooktop has an expected useful life of four years and an estimated salvage value of $4,000. Use straight-line depreciation. The adjusting entry was made as of December 31, Year 1.

Required

a. Record the events in general journal format and post to T-accounts.
b. Prepare a balance sheet and a statement of cash flows for the Year 1 accounting period.
c. What is the net income for Year 1?
d. What amount of depreciation expense would Gulf Seafood report on the Year 2 income statement?
e. What amount of accumulated depreciation would Gulf Seafood report on the December 31, Year 2, balance sheet?
f. Would the cash flow from operating activities be affected by depreciation in Year 2?

Exercise 8-8A *Effect of double-declining-balance depreciation on financial statements*

LO 8-3

Golden Manufacturing Company started operations by acquiring $150,000 cash from the issue of common stock. On January 1, Year 1, the company purchased equipment that cost $120,000 cash, had an expected useful life of six years, and had an estimated salvage value of $4,000. Golden Manufacturing earned $72,000 and $83,000 of cash revenue during Year 1 and Year 2, respectively. Golden Manufacturing uses double-declining-balance depreciation.

Required
Prepare income statements, balance sheets, and statements of cash flows for Year 1 and Year 2. Use a vertical statements format. (*Hint:* Record the events in T-accounts prior to preparing the statements.)

Exercise 8-9A *Computing and recording straight-line versus double-declining-balance depreciation*

LO 8-2, 8-3

At the beginning of Year 1, Copeland Drugstore purchased a new computer system for $52,000. It is expected to have a five-year life and a $7,000 salvage value.

Required
a. Compute the depreciation for each of the five years, assuming that the company uses
   (1) Straight-line depreciation.
   (2) Double-declining-balance depreciation.
b. Record the purchase of the computer system and the depreciation expense for the first year under straight-line and double-declining-balance methods in a financial statements model like the following one:

Assets	=	Equity	Rev.	−	Exp.	=	Net Inc.	Cash Flow
Cash + Book Value of Comp. Sys.	=	Ret. Earn.						

c. Prepare the journal entries to recognize depreciation for each of the five years, assuming that the company uses
   (1) Straight-line depreciation.
   (2) Double-declining-balance depreciation.

Exercise 8-10A *Double-declining-balance and units-of-production depreciation: gain or loss on disposal*

LO 8-3, 8-4, 8-5

Exact Photo Service purchased a new color printer at the beginning of Year 1 for $38,000. The printer is expected to have a four-year useful life and a $3,500 salvage value. The expected print production is estimated at 1,500,000 pages. Actual print production for the four years was as follows:

Year 1	390,000
Year 2	410,000
Year 3	420,000
Year 4	300,000
Total	1,520,000

The printer was sold at the end of Year 4 for $1,650.

Required
a. Compute the depreciation expense for each of the four years, using double-declining-balance depreciation.
b. Compute the depreciation expense for each of the four years, using units-of-production depreciation.
c. Calculate the amount of gain or loss from the sale of the asset under each of the depreciation methods.

Chapter 8

LO 8-2, 8-5

Exercise 8-11A Events related to the acquisition, use, and disposal of a tangible plant asset: straight-line depreciation

City Taxi Service purchased a new auto to use as a taxi on January 1, Year 1, for $36,000. In addition, City paid sales tax and title fees of $1,200 for the vehicle. The taxi is expected to have a five-year life and a salvage value of $4,000.

Required

a. Using the straight-line method, compute the depreciation expense for Year 1 and Year 2.
b. Prepare the general journal entry to record the Year 1 depreciation.
c. Assume that the taxi was sold on January 1, Year 3, for $22,000. Prepare the journal entry for the sale of the taxi in Year 3.

LO 8-5

Exercise 8-12A Effect of the disposal of plant assets on the financial statements

Un Company sold office equipment with a cost of $23,000 and accumulated depreciation of $12,000 for $14,000.

Required

a. What is the book value of the asset at the time of sale?
b. What is the amount of gain or loss on the disposal?
c. How would the sale affect net income (increase, decrease, no effect) and by how much?
d. How would the sale affect the amount of total assets shown on the balance sheet (increase, decrease, no effect) and by how much?
e. How would the event affect the statement of cash flows (inflow, outflow, no effect) and in what section?

LO 8-5

Exercise 8-13A Effect of gains and losses on the accounting equation and financial statements

On January 1, Year 1, Prairie Enterprises purchased a parcel of land for $28,000 cash. At the time of purchase, the company planned to use the land for a warehouse site. In Year 3, Prairie Enterprises changed its plans and sold the land.

Required

a. Assume that the land was sold for $29,500 in Year 3.
   (1) Show the effect of the sale on the accounting equation.
   (2) What amount would Prairie report on the Year 3 income statement related to the sale of the land?
   (3) What amount would Prairie report on the Year 3 statement of cash flows related to the sale of the land?
b. Assume that the land was sold for $24,000 in Year 3.
   (1) Show the effect of the sale on the accounting equation.
   (2) What amount would Prairie report on the Year 3 income statement related to the sale of the land?
   (3) What amount would Prairie report on the Year 3 statement of cash flows related to the sale of the land?

LO 8-6

Exercise 8-14A Computing depreciation for tax purposes

Crossroads Eye Care Company purchased $60,000 of equipment on March 1, Year 1.

Required

a. Compute the amount of depreciation expense that is deductible under MACRS for Year 1 and Year 2, assuming that the equipment is classified as a seven-year property.
b. Compute the amount of depreciation expense that is deductible under MACRS for Year 1 and Year 2, assuming that the equipment is classified as a five-year property.

Exercise 8-15A Revision of estimated useful life   LO 8-7

On January 1, Year 1, Poultry Processing Company purchased a freezer and related installation equipment for $42,000. The equipment had a three-year estimated life with a $3,000 salvage value. Straight-line depreciation was used. At the beginning of Year 3, Poultry Processing revised the expected life of the asset to four years rather than three years. The salvage value was revised to $2,000.

Required

Compute the depreciation expense for each of the four years, Year 1 through Year 4.

Exercise 8-16A Distinguishing between revenue expenditures and capital expenditures   LO 8-8

Bill's Wrecker Service has just completed a minor repair on a tow truck. The repair cost was $1,550, and the book value prior to the repair was $6,500. In addition, the company spent $12,000 to replace the roof on a building. The new roof extended the life of the building by five years. Prior to the roof replacement, the general ledger reflected the Building account at $85,000 and related Accumulated Depreciation account at $32,000.

Required

After the work was completed, what book value should appear on the balance sheet for the tow truck and the building?

Exercise 8-17A Effect of revenue expenditures versus capital expenditures on financial statements   LO 8-8

Sellers Construction Company purchased a compressor for $28,000 cash. It had an estimated useful life of four years and a $4,000 salvage value. At the beginning of the third year of use, the company spent an additional $6,000 related to the equipment. The company's financial condition just prior to this expenditure is shown in the following statements model:

Assets			=	Equity			Rev.	−	Exp.	=	Net Inc.	Cash Flow
Cash	+	Book Value of Compressor	=	Com. Stk.	+	Ret. Earn.						
45,000	+	16,000	=	40,000	+	21,000	NA	−	NA	=	NA	NA

Required

Record the $6,000 expenditure in the statements model under each of the following *independent* assumptions:

a. The expenditure was for routine maintenance.
b. The expenditure extended the compressor's life.
c. The expenditure improved the compressor's operating capacity.

Exercise 8-18A Effect of revenue expenditures versus capital expenditures on financial statements   LO 8-8

On January 1, Year 1, Webb Construction Company overhauled four cranes, resulting in a slight increase in the life of the cranes. Such overhauls occur regularly at two-year intervals and have been treated as a maintenance expense in the past. Management is considering whether to capitalize this year's $22,000 cash cost in the Cranes asset account or to expense it as a maintenance expense. Assume that the cranes have a remaining useful life of two years and no expected salvage value. Assume straight-line depreciation.

Required

a. Determine the amount of additional depreciation expense Webb would recognize in Year 1 and Year 2 if the cost were capitalized in the Cranes account.
b. Determine the amount of expense Webb would recognize in Year 1 and Year 2 if the cost were recognized as maintenance expense.

c. Determine the effect of the overhaul on cash flow from operating activities for Year 1 and Year 2 if the cost were capitalized and expensed through depreciation charges.

d. Determine the effect of the overhaul on cash flow from operating activities for Year 1 and Year 2 if the cost were recognized as maintenance expense.

LO 8-9

Exercise 8-19A *Computing and recording depletion expense*

Colorado Mining paid $600,000 to acquire a mine with 40,000 tons of coal reserves. The following statements model reflects Colorado Mining's financial condition just prior to purchasing the coal reserves. The company extracted 15,000 tons of coal in Year 1 and 18,000 tons in Year 2.

Assets			=	Equity			Rev.	−	Exp.	=	Net Inc.	Cash Flow
Cash	+	Coal Res.	=	Com. Stk.	+	Ret. Earn.						
800,000	+	NA	=	800,000	+	NA	NA	−	NA	=	NA	NA

Required

a. Compute the depletion charge per unit.
b. Record the acquisition of the coal reserves and the depletion expense for Years 1 and 2 in a financial statements model like the preceding one.
c. Prepare the general journal entries to record the depletion expense for Years 1 and 2.

LO 8-10

Exercise 8-20A *Computing and recording goodwill*

Arizona Corp. acquired the business Data Systems for $320,000 cash and assumed all liabilities at the date of purchase. Data's books showed tangible assets of $260,000, liabilities of $40,000, and stockholders' equity of $220,000. An appraiser assessed the fair market value of the tangible assets at $250,000 at the date of acquisition. Arizona Corp.'s financial condition just prior to the acquisition is shown in the following statements model:

Assets					=	Liab.	+	Equity	Rev.	−	Exp.	=	Net Inc.	Cash Flow
Cash	+	Tang. Assets	+	Goodwill										
450,000	+	NA	+	NA	=	NA	+	450,000	NA	−	NA	=	NA	NA

Required

a. Compute the amount of goodwill acquired.
b. Record the acquisition in a financial statements model like the preceding one.
c. When will the goodwill be written off under the impairment rules?
d. Record the acquisition in general journal format.

LO 8-10, 8-11

Exercise 8-21A *Computing and recording the amortization of intangibles*

Dynamo Manufacturing paid cash to acquire the assets of an existing company. Among the assets acquired were the following items:

Patent with 4 remaining years of legal life	$40,000
Goodwill	35,000

Dynamo's financial condition just prior to the acquisition of these assets is shown in the following statements model:

Assets					=	Liab.	+	Equity	Rev.	−	Exp.	=	Net Inc.	Cash Flow
Cash	+	Patent	+	Goodwill										
90,000	+	NA	+	NA	=	NA	+	90,000	NA	−	NA	=	NA	NA

Required

a. Compute the annual amortization expense for these items.
b. Show the acquisition of the intangible assets and the related amortization expense for Year 1 in a horizontal statements model like the one shown earlier.
c. Prepare the journal entries to record the acquisition of the intangible assets and the related amortization for Year 1.

Exercise 8-22A Identifying companies using property, plant, and equipment   LO 8-12

Executive Jets, LLC operates a charter flight-service company in the northwestern United States. Classic Steps, LLC is a company that provides dance lessons to students of all ages. Classic Steps has dance studios in several cities throughout the western United States. The following data are from the companies' most recent financial statements but are not identified as to which company they relate.

	Company 1	Company 2
Sales	$10,000,000	$10,000,000
Depreciation expense	70,000	500,000
Net earnings	850,000	800,000
Current assets	950,000	900,000
Property, plant, and equipment	700,000	6,000,000
Total assets	2,500,000	7,900,000

Required

a. Calculate the ratio of sales to property, plant, and equipment for each company.
b. Based on the ratios calculated in requirement a, decide which is the airline company and which is the dance studio. Explain your answer.
c. Based on the ratios calculated in requirement a, which company appears to be using its property, plant, and equipment more efficiently? Explain you answer.
d. Explain why two companies with such different amounts of property, plant, and equipment might have the same amount of current assets.

Exercise 8-23A R&D costs: GAAP vs. IFRS   IFRS

The Paris Corp. incurred $3,600,000 of research cost and $800,000 of development cost during the current year.

Required

a. Determine the amount of expense recognized on its income statement assuming Paris uses U.S. GAAP.
b. Determine the amount of expense recognized on its income statement assuming Paris uses IFRS.

Exercise 8-24A Accounting for land and buildings under IFRS   IFRS

Assume the following. Queensland Company purchased a parcel of land on January 1, Year 1, for $400,000. It constructed a building on the land at a cost of $2,000,000. The building was occupied on January 1, Year 4, and is expected to have a useful life of 40 years and an estimated salvage value of $600,000.

As of December 31, Year 5 and Year 6, the fair value of the land had not been formally revalued because the real estate market had not changed significantly. Due to a jump in real estate prices, during Year 7 the value of the land had increased to $450,000, and the fair value of the building was $2,000,000. The salvage value of the building is still estimated at $600,000. The land and the building were reevaluated by the company in Year 7.

Required

a. Under U.S. accounting rules, what amount would be reported on the company's Year 6 and Year 7 balance sheets for the land and for the building? Show any necessary computations.
b. Under U.S. accounting rules, what amount of depreciation expense would be reported in Year 7 for the building? Show any necessary computations.
c. Under the IFRS revaluation model, what amount would be reported on the company's Year 6 and Year 7 balance sheets for the land and for the building? Show any necessary computations.
d. Under the IFRS revaluation model, what amount of depreciation expense would be reported in Year 7 for the building? Show any necessary computations.

PROBLEMS—SERIES A

All applicable Problems in Series A are available in Connect.

LO 8-1

CHECK FIGURES
Total cost of equipment: $62,800
Cost allocated to copier: $16,500

Problem 8-25A *Accounting for acquisition of assets including a basket purchase*

Trinkle Co., Inc. made several purchases of long-term assets in Year 1. The details of each purchase are presented here.

New Office Equipment

1. List price: $60,000; terms: 2/10 n/30; paid within discount period.
2. Transportation-in: $1,500.
3. Installation: $2,500.
4. Cost to repair damage during unloading: $650.
5. Routine maintenance cost after six months: $350.

Basket Purchase of Copier, Computer, and Scanner for $30,000 with Fair Market Values

1. Copier, $22,000.
2. Computer, $10,000.
3. Scanner, $8,000.

Land for New Warehouse with an Old Building Torn Down

1. Purchase price, $250,000.
2. Demolition of building, $18,000.
3. Lumber sold from old building, $6,000.
4. Grading in preparation for new building, $22,000.
5. Construction of new building, $510,000.

Required

In each of these cases, determine the amount of cost to be capitalized in the asset accounts.

LO 8-2, 8-3, 8-4

CHECK FIGURES
a. Company A, Net Income: $28,750
c. Company C, Book Value: $16,700

Problem 8-26A *Determining the effect of depreciation expense on financial statements*

Three different companies each purchased trucks on January 1, Year 1, for $50,000. Each truck was expected to last four years or 200,000 miles. Salvage value was estimated to be $5,000. All three trucks were driven 66,000 miles in Year 1, 42,000 miles in Year 2, 40,000 miles in Year 3, and 60,000 miles in Year 4. Each of the three companies earned $40,000 of cash revenue during each of the four years. Company A uses straight-line depreciation, company B uses double-declining-balance depreciation, and company C uses units-of-production depreciation.

Required

Answer each of the following questions. Ignore the effects of income taxes.
a. Which company will report the highest amount of net income for Year 1?
b. Which company will report the lowest amount of net income for Year 4?
c. Which company will report the highest book value on the December 31, Year 3, balance sheet?
d. Which company will report the highest amount of retained earnings on the December 31, Year 4, balance sheet?
e. Which company will report the lowest amount of cash flow from operating activities on the Year 3 statement of cash flows?

LO 8-2, 8-3, 8-5

Problem 8-27A *Effect of straight-line versus double-declining-balance depreciation on the recognition of expense and gains or losses*

Becker Office Service purchased a new computer system in Year 1 for $40,000. It is expected to have a five-year useful life and a $5,000 salvage value. The company expects to use the system more extensively in the early years of its life.

Required

a. Calculate the depreciation expense for each of the five years, assuming the use of straight-line depreciation.
b. Calculate the depreciation expense for each of the five years, assuming the use of double-declining-balance depreciation.
c. Would the choice of one depreciation method over another produce a different amount of cash flow for any year? Why or why not?
d. Assume that Becker Office Service sold the computer system at the end of the fourth year for $15,000. Compute the amount of gain or loss using each depreciation method.
e. Explain any differences in gain or loss due to using the different methods.

CHECK FIGURES
a. Depreciation Expense, Year 2: $7,000
b. Depreciation Expense, Year 2: $9,600

Problem 8-28A Accounting for depreciation over multiple accounting cycles: straight-line depreciation

LO 8-2, 8-5

Bensen Company started business by acquiring $60,000 cash from the issue of common stock on January 1, Year 1. The cash acquired was immediately used to purchase equipment for $50,000 that had a $10,000 salvage value and an expected useful life of four years. The equipment was used to produce the following revenue stream (assume that all revenue transactions are for cash). At the beginning of the fifth year, the equipment was sold for $8,800 cash. Bensen uses straight-line depreciation.

CHECK FIGURES
Net Income, Year 1: $16,100
Total Assets, Year 4: $137,900

	Year 1	Year 2	Year 3	Year 4	Year 5
Revenue	$26,100	$28,500	$32,000	$31,300	$0

Required

Prepare income statements, statements of changes in stockholders' equity, balance sheets, and statements of cash flows for each of the five years. Present the statements in the form of a vertical statements model.

Problem 8-29A Computing and recording units-of-production depreciation

LO 8-4, 8-5

Sabel Co. purchased assembly equipment for $500,000 on January 1, Year 1. Sabel's financial condition immediately prior to the purchase is shown in the following horizontal statements model:

Assets			=	Equity			Rev.	−	Exp.	=	Net Inc.	Cash Flow
Cash	+	Book Value of Equip.	=	Com. Stk.	+	Ret. Earn.						
800,000	+	NA	=	800,000	+	NA	NA	−	NA	=	NA	NA

The equipment is expected to have a useful life of 200,000 machine hours and a salvage value of $20,000. Actual machine-hour use was as follows:

Year 1	56,000
Year 2	61,000
Year 3	42,000
Year 4	36,000
Year 5	10,000

Required

a. Compute the depreciation for each of the five years, assuming the use of units-of-production depreciation.
b. Assume that Sabel earns $230,000 of cash revenue during Year 1. Record the purchase of the equipment and the recognition of the revenue and the depreciation expense for the first year in a financial statements model like the preceding one.
c. Assume that Sabel sold the equipment at the end of the fifth year for $20,600. Record the general journal entry for the sale.

CHECK FIGURES
a. Depreciation Expense, Year 1: $134,400
c. Gain on Sale: $600

456 Chapter 8

LO 8-2, 8-3, 8-4, 8-6

Problem 8-30A *Calculating depreciation expense using four different methods*

Banko Inc. manufactures sporting goods. The following information applies to a machine purchased on January 1, Year 1:

Purchase price	$ 70,000
Delivery cost	$ 3,000
Installation charge	$ 1,000
Estimated life	5 years
Estimated units	140,000
Salvage estimate	$ 4,000

During Year 1, the machine produced 36,000 units, and during Year 2 it produced 38,000 units.

Required

Determine the amount of depreciation expense for Year 1 and Year 2 using each of the following methods:

CHECK FIGURES
a. Depreciation Expense, Year 1: $14,000
d. Depreciation Expense, Year 2: $18,123

a. Straight-line
b. Double-declining-balance
c. Units-of-production
d. MACRS, assuming that the machine is classified as seven-year property

LO 8-2, 8-7, 8-8

Problem 8-31A *Purchase and use of tangible asset: three accounting cycles, straight-line depreciation*

CHECK FIGURES
Net Income, Year 1: $34,100
Total Assets, Year 3: $174,450

The following transactions relate to Academy Towing Service. Assume the transactions for the purchase of the wrecker and any capital improvements occur on January 1 of each year.

Year 1

1. Acquired $70,000 cash from the issue of common stock.
2. Purchased a used wrecker for $32,000. It has an estimated useful life of three years and a $5,000 salvage value.
3. Paid sales tax on the wrecker of $3,000.
4. Collected $56,100 in towing fees.
5. Paid $12,000 for gasoline and oil.
6. Recorded straight-line depreciation on the wrecker for Year 1.
7. Closed the revenue and expense accounts to Retained Earnings at the end of Year 1.

Year 2

1. Paid for a tune-up for the wrecker's engine, $900.
2. Bought four new tires, $1,250.
3. Collected $62,000 in towing fees.
4. Paid $18,000 for gasoline and oil.
5. Recorded straight-line depreciation for Year 2.
6. Closed the revenue and expense accounts to Retained Earnings at the end of Year 2.

Year 3

1. Paid to overhaul the wrecker's engine, $4,800, which extended the life of the wrecker to a total of four years. The salvage value did not change.
2. Paid for gasoline and oil, $19,100.
3. Collected $65,000 in towing fees.
4. Recorded straight-line depreciation for Year 3.
5. Closed the revenue and expense accounts at the end of Year 3.

Required

a. Use a horizontal statements model like the following one to show the effect of these transactions on the elements of financial statements. Use + for increase, − for decrease, and NA for not affected. The first event is recorded as an example.

Accounting for Long-Term Operational Assets 457

Year 1 Event No.	Assets	=	Liabilities	+	Equity	Net Inc.	Cash Flow
1	+		NA		+	NA	+ FA

b. For each year, record the transactions in general journal form and post them to T-accounts.
c. Use a vertical model to present financial statements for Year 1, Year 2, and Year 3.

Problem 8-32A   Recording continuing expenditures for plant assets

LO 8-2, 8-8

Morris Inc. recorded the following transactions over the life of a piece of equipment purchased in Year 1:

Jan. 1, Year 1   Purchased equipment for $90,000 cash. The equipment was estimated to have a five-year life and $5,000 salvage value and was to be depreciated using the straight-line method.
Dec. 31, Year 1 Recorded depreciation expense for Year 1.
Sept. 30, Year 2 Undertook routine repairs costing $900.
Dec. 31, Year 2 Recorded depreciation expense for Year 2.
Jan. 1, Year 3   Made an adjustment costing $2,500 to the equipment. It improved the quality of the output but did not affect the life and salvage value estimates.
Dec. 31, Year 3 Recorded depreciation expense for Year 3.
June 1, Year 4   Incurred $850 cost to oil and clean the equipment.
Dec. 31, Year 4 Recorded depreciation expense for Year 4.
Jan. 1, Year 5   Had the equipment completely overhauled at a cost of $9,000. The overhaul was estimated to extend the total life to seven years. The salvage value did not change.
Dec. 31, Year 5 Recorded depreciation expense for Year 5.
Oct. 1, Year 6   Received and accepted an offer of $19,000 for the equipment.

CHECK FIGURES
b. Year 3: Depreciation Expense: $17,833
d. Gain on Sale: $2,820

Required

a. Use a horizontal statements model like the following one to show the effects of these transactions on the elements of the financial statements. Use + for increase, − for decrease, and NA for not affected. The first event is recorded as an example.

Date	Assets	=	Liabilities	+	Equity	Net Inc.	Cash Flow
Jan. 1, Year 1	+ −		NA		NA	NA	− IA

b. Determine the amount of depreciation expense to be reported on the income statements for Year 1 through Year 5.
c. Determine the book value (cost − accumulated depreciation) Morris will report on the balance sheets at the end of each year for Year 1 through Year 6.
d. Determine the amount of the gain or loss Morris will report on the disposal of the equipment on October 1, Year 6.
e. Prepare the journal entry for the disposal of the equipment on October 1, Year 6.

Problem 8-33A   Continuing expenditures with statements model

LO 8-2, 8-8

Tower Company owned a service truck that was purchased at the beginning of Year 1 for $31,000. It had an estimated life of three years and an estimated salvage value of $4,000. Tower Company uses straight-line depreciation. Its financial condition as of January 1, Year 3, is shown in the following financial statements model:

CHECK FIGURE
b. Depreciation Expense: $8,000

Assets			=	Equity			Rev.	−	Exp.	=	Net Inc.	Cash Flow
Cash	+	Book Value of Truck	=	Com. Stk.	+	Ret. Earn.						
20,000	+	13,000	=	9,000	+	24,000	NA	−	NA	=	NA	NA

458 Chapter 8

In Year 3, Tower Company spent the following amounts on the truck:

Jan. 4 Overhauled the engine for $6,000. The estimated life was extended one additional year, and the salvage value was revised to $3,000.
July 6 Obtained oil change and transmission service, $250.
Aug. 7 Replaced the fan belt and battery, $350.
Dec. 31 Purchased gasoline for the year, $7,500.
Dec. 31 Recognized Year 3 depreciation expense.

Required

a. Record the Year 3 transactions in a statements model like the preceding one.
b. Prepare journal entries for the Year 3 transactions.

LO 8-7, 8-9

CHECK FIGURES
a. Silver Mine Depletion, Year 1: $210,000
b. Total Natural Resources: $4,844,000

Problem 8-34A Accounting for depletion

Flannery Company engages in the exploration and development of many types of natural resources. In the last two years, the company has engaged in the following activities:

Jan. 1, Year 1 Purchased for $1,500,000 a silver mine estimated to contain 100,000 tons of silver ore.
July 1, Year 1 Purchased for $1,700,000 cash a tract of land containing timber estimated to yield 1,000,000 board feet of lumber. At the time of purchase, the land had an appraised of $100,000.
Feb. 1, Year 2 Purchased for $2,700,000 a gold mine estimated to yield 50,000 tons of gold-veined ore.
Sept. 1, Year 2 Purchased oil reserves for $1,300,000. The reserves were estimated to contain 270,000 barrels of oil, of which 10,000 would be unprofitable to pump.

Required

a. Prepare the journal entries to account for the following:
   (1) The Year 1 purchases.
   (2) Depletion on the Year 1 purchases, assuming that 14,000 tons of silver were mined and 500,000 board feet of lumber were cut.
   (3) The Year 2 purchases.
   (4) Depletion on the four natural resource assets, assuming that 20,000 tons of silver ore, 300,000 board feet of lumber, 4,000 tons of gold ore, and 50,000 barrels of oil were extracted.
b. Prepare the portion of the December 31, Year 2, balance sheet that reports natural resources.
c. Assume that in Year 3 the estimates changed to reflect only 20,000 tons of gold ore remaining. Prepare the depletion journal entry in Year 3 to account for the extraction of 10,000 tons of gold ore.

LO 8-10, 8-11

CHECK FIGURE
b. Amortization Expense: $4,000

Problem 8-35A Accounting for intangible assets

Mitre Company acquired Midwest Transportation Co. for $1,400,000. The fair market values of the assets acquired were as follows. No liabilities were assumed.

Equipment	$510,000
Land	150,000
Building	520,000
Franchise (10-year life)	40,000

Required

a. Calculate the amount of goodwill acquired.
b. Prepare the journal entry to record the amortization of the franchise fee at the end of Year 1.

LO 8-11

Problem 8-36A Accounting for goodwill

Rossie Equipment Manufacturing Co. acquired the assets of Alba Inc., a competitor, in Year 1. It recorded goodwill of $70,000 at acquisition. Because of defective machinery Alba had produced prior to the acquisition, it has been determined that all of the acquired goodwill has been permanently impaired.

Required

Prepare the journal entry to record the permanent impairment of the goodwill.

EXERCISES—SERIES B

Unless specifically included, ignore income tax considerations in all exercises and problems.

Exercise 8-1B Long-term operational assets used in a business
LO 8-1

Required

Give some examples of long-term operational assets that each of the following companies is likely to own: *(a)* Sears, *(b)* Princess Cruise Lines, *(c)* Southwest Airlines, and *(d)* Harley-Davidson Co.

Exercise 8-2B Identifying long-term operational assets
LO 8-1

Required

Which of the following items should be classified as long-term operational assets?

a. Cash
b. Buildings
c. Production machinery
d. Accounts receivable
e. Prepaid rent
f. Franchise
g. Inventory
h. Patent
i. Tract of timber
j. Land
k. Computer
l. Goodwill

Exercise 8-3B Classifying tangible and intangible assets
LO 8-1

Required

Identify each of the following long-term operational assets as either tangible (T) or intangible (I).

a. Retail store building
b. Shelving for inventory
c. Trademark
d. Gas well
e. Drilling rig
f. FCC license for TV station
g. 18-wheel truck
h. Timber
i. Log loader
j. Dental chair
k. Goodwill
l. Computer software

Exercise 8-4B Determining the cost of an asset
LO 8-1

Oregon Logging Co. purchased an electronic saw to cut various types and sizes of logs. The saw had a list price of $160,000. The seller agreed to allow a 5 percent discount because Oregon paid cash. Delivery terms were FOB shipping point. Freight cost amounted to $3,200. Oregon had to hire an individual to operate the saw. Oregon had to build a special platform to mount the saw. The cost of the platform was $2,500. The saw operator was paid an annual salary of $50,000. The cost of the company's theft insurance policy increased by $1,800 per year as a result of acquiring the saw. The saw had a five-year useful life and an expected salvage value of $25,000.

Required

a. Determine the amount to be capitalized in an asset account for the purchase of the saw.
b. Record the purchase in general journal format.

Exercise 8-5B Allocating costs on the basis of relative market values
LO 8-1

Florida Company purchased a building and the land on which the building is situated for a total cost of $800,000 cash. The land was appraised at $300,000 and the building at $700,000.

Required

a. What is the accounting term for this type of acquisition?
b. Determine the amount of the purchase cost to allocate to the land and the amount to allocate to the building.
c. Would the company recognize a gain on the purchase? Why or why not?
d. Record the purchase in a statements model like the following one:

	Assets			=	Liab.	+	Equity	Rev.	−	Exp.	=	Net Inc.	Cash Flow
Cash	+	Land	+	Building									

e. Record the purchases in general journal format.

LO 8-1

Exercise 8-6B *Allocating costs for a basket purchase*

Usrey Company purchased a restaurant building, land, and equipment for $600,000 cash. The appraised value of the assets was as follows:

Land	$200,000
Building	480,000
Equipment	120,000
Total	$800,000

Required

a. Compute the amount to be recorded on the books for each of the assets.
b. Show the purchase in a horizontal statements model like the following one:

	Assets					=	Liab.	+	Equity	Rev.	−	Exp.	=	Net Inc.	Cash Flow
Cash	+	Land	+	Building	+	Equip.									

c. Prepare the general journal entry to record the purchase.

LO 8-2

Exercise 8-7B *Effect of depreciation on the accounting equation and financial statements*

The following events apply to The Soda Shop for the Year 1 fiscal year:
1. The company started when it acquired $20,000 cash from the issue of common stock.
2. Purchased a new ice cream machine that cost $20,000 cash.
3. Earned $36,000 in cash revenue.
4. Paid $21,000 cash for salaries expense.
5. Paid $6,000 cash for operating expenses.
6. Adjusted the records to reflect the use of the machine to make ice cream sodas. The machine, purchased on January 1, Year 1, has an expected useful life of five years and an estimated salvage value of $5,000. Use straight-line depreciation. The adjusting entry was made as of December 31, Year 1.

Required

a. Record the events in general journal format and post to T-accounts.
b. What amount of depreciation expense would The Soda Shop report on the Year 2 income statement?
c. What amount of accumulated depreciation would The Soda Shop report on the December 31, Year 2, balance sheet?
d. Would the cash flow from operating activities be affected by depreciation in Year 2?

LO 8-3

Exercise 8-8B *Effect of double-declining-balance depreciation on financial statements*

Hinds Company started operations by acquiring $120,000 cash from the issue of common stock. On January 1, Year 1, the company purchased equipment that cost $110,000 cash. The equipment had an expected useful life of five years and an estimated salvage value of $10,000. Hinds Company earned $85,000 and $72,000 of cash revenue during Year 1 and Year 2, respectively. Hinds Company uses double-declining-balance depreciation.

Accounting for Long-Term Operational Assets   461

Required

Prepare income statements, balance sheets, and statements of cash flows for Year 1 and Year 2. Use a vertical statements format. (*Hint:* Record the events in T-accounts prior to preparing the statements.)

Exercise 8-9B Computing and recording straight-line versus double-declining-balance depreciation

LO 8-2, 8-3

At the beginning of Year 1, Hill Manufacturing purchased a new computerized drill press for $75,000. It is expected to have a five-year life and a $15,000 salvage value.

Required

a. Compute the depreciation for each of the five years, assuming that the company uses
   (1) Straight-line depreciation.
   (2) Double-declining-balance depreciation.
b. Record the purchase of the drill press and the depreciation expense for the first year under the straight-line and double-declining-balance methods in a financial statements model like the following one:

Assets	=	Equity	Rev.	−	Exp.	=	Net Inc.	Cash Flow
Cash + Book Value of Drill Press	=	Ret. Earn.						

c. Prepare the journal entries to recognize depreciation for each of the five years, assuming that the company uses
   (1) Straight-line depreciation.
   (2) Double-declining-balance depreciation.

Exercise 8-10B Double-declining-balance and units-of-production depreciation: gain or loss on disposal

LO 8-3, 8-4, 8-5

Design Service Co. purchased a new color copier at the beginning of Year 1 for $47,000. The copier is expected to have a five-year useful life and a $7,000 salvage value. The expected copy production was estimated at 2,000,000 copies. Actual copy production for the five years was as follows:

Year 1	560,000
Year 2	490,000
Year 3	430,000
Year 4	350,000
Year 5	210,000
Total	2,040,000

The copier was sold at the end of Year 5 for $7,600.

Required

a. Compute the depreciation expense for each of the five years, using double-declining-balance depreciation.
b. Compute the depreciation expense for each of the five years, using units-of-production depreciation. (Round cost per unit to three decimal places.)
c. Calculate the amount of gain or loss from the sale of the asset under each of the depreciation methods.

Exercise 8-11B Events related to the acquisition, use, and disposal of a tangible plant asset: straight-line depreciation

LO 8-2, 8-5

Pete's Pizza purchased a delivery van on January 1, Year 1, for $35,000. In addition, Pete's paid sales tax and title fees of $1,500 for the van. The van is expected to have a four-year life and a salvage value of $6,500.

Required

a. Using the straight-line method, compute the depreciation expense for Year 1 and Year 2.
b. Prepare the general journal entry to record the Year 1 depreciation.
c. Assume the van was sold on January 1, Year 4, for $21,000. Prepare the journal entry for the sale of the van in Year 4.

LO 8-5

Exercise 8-12B *Effect of the disposal of plant assets on the financial statements*

A plant asset with a cost of $50,000 and accumulated depreciation of $41,000 is sold for $10,000.

Required

a. What is the book value of the asset at the time of sale?
b. What is the amount of gain or loss on the disposal?
c. How would the sale affect net income (increase, decrease, no effect) and by how much?
d. How would the sale affect the amount of total assets shown on the balance sheet (increase, decrease, no effect) and by how much?
e. How would the event affect the statement of cash flows (inflow, outflow, no effect) and in what section?

LO 8-5

Exercise 8-13B *Effect of gains and losses on the accounting equation and financial statements*

On January 1, Year 1, Heflin Enterprises purchased a parcel of land for $20,000 cash. At the time of purchase, the company planned to use the land for future expansion. In Year 2, Heflin Enterprises changed its plans and sold the land.

Required

a. Assume that the land was sold for $22,500 in Year 2.
  (1) Show the effect of the sale on the accounting equation.
  (2) What amount would Heflin report on the income statement related to the sale of the land?
  (3) What amount would Heflin report on the statement of cash flows related to the sale of the land?
b. Assume that the land was sold for $18,500 in Year 2.
  (1) Show the effect of the sale on the accounting equation.
  (2) What amount would Heflin report on the income statement related to the sale of the land?
  (2) What amount would Heflin report on the statement of cash flows related to the sale of the land?

LO 8-6

Exercise 8-14B *Computing depreciation for tax purposes*

Ripley Lumber Company purchased $240,000 of equipment on September 1, Year 1.

Required

a. Compute the amount of depreciation expense that is deductible under MACRS for Year 1 and Year 2, assuming that the equipment is classified as a seven-year property.
b. Compute the amount of depreciation expense that is deductible under MACRS for Year 1 and Year 2, assuming that the equipment is classified as a five-year property.

LO 8-7

Exercise 8-15B *Revision of estimated useful life*

On January 1, Year 1, Mead Machining Co. purchased a compressor and related installation equipment for $72,500. The equipment had a three-year estimated life with a $12,500 salvage value. Straight-line depreciation was used. At the beginning of Year 3, Mead revised the expected life of the asset to four years rather than three years. The salvage value was revised to $2,500.

Required

Compute the depreciation expense for each of the four years.

Exercise 8-16B Distinguishing between revenue expenditures and capital expenditures

LO 8-8

Efficient Shredding Service has just completed a minor repair on a shredding machine. The repair cost was $1,900, and the book value prior to the repair was $6,000. In addition, the company spent $12,000 to replace the roof on a building. The new roof extended the life of the building by five years. Prior to the roof replacement, the general ledger reflected the Building account at $110,000 and related Accumulated Depreciation account at $30,000.

Required

After the work was completed, what book value should Efficient have reported on the balance sheet for the shredding machine and the building?

Exercise 8-17B Effect of revenue expenditures versus capital expenditures on financial statements

LO 8-8

Ford Construction Company purchased a forklift for $150,000 cash. It had an estimated useful life of four years and a $10,000 salvage value. At the beginning of the third year of use, the company spent an additional $9,000 that was related to the forklift. The company's financial condition just prior to this expenditure is shown in the following statements model:

Assets			=	Equity			Rev.	−	Exp.	=	Net Inc.	Cash Flow
Cash	+	Book Value of Forklift	=	Com. Stk.	+	Ret. Earn.						
15,000	+	80,000	=	45,000	+	50,000	NA	−	NA	=	NA	NA

Required

Record the $9,000 expenditure in the statements model under each of the following *independent* assumptions:

a. The expenditure was for routine maintenance.
b. The expenditure extended the forklift's life.
c. The expenditure improved the forklift's operating capacity.

Exercise 8-18B Effect of revenue expenditures versus capital expenditures on financial statements

LO 8-8

On January 1, Year 1, Midstate Power Company overhauled four turbine engines that generate power for customers. The overhaul resulted in a slight increase in the capacity of the engines to produce power. Such overhauls occur regularly at two-year intervals and have been treated as a maintenance expense in the past. Management is considering whether to capitalize this year's $22,000 cash cost in the engine asset account or to expense it as a maintenance expense. Assume that the engines have a remaining useful life of two years and no expected salvage value. Assume straight-line depreciation.

Required

a. Determine the amount of additional depreciation expense Midstate would recognize in Year 1 and Year 2 if the cost were capitalized in the Engine account.
b. Determine the amount of expense Midstate would recognize in Year 1 and Year 2 if the cost were recognized as maintenance expense.
c. Determine the effect of the overhaul on cash flow from operating activities for Year 1 and Year 2 if the cost were capitalized and expensed through depreciation charges.
d. Determine the effect of the overhaul on cash flow from operating activities for Year 1 and Year 2 if the cost were recognized as maintenance expense.

LO 8-9

Exercise 8-19B *Computing and recording depletion expense*

Fulton Sand and Gravel paid $800,000 to acquire 1,200,000 cubic yards of sand reserves. The following statements model reflects Fulton's financial condition just prior to purchasing the sand reserves. The company extracted 650,000 cubic yards of sand in Year 1 and 450,000 cubic yards in Year 2.

Assets			=	Equity			Rev.	−	Exp.	=	Net Inc.	Cash Flow
Cash	+	Sand Res.	=	Com. Stk.	+	Ret. Earn.						
900,000	+	NA	=	900,000	+	NA	NA	−	NA	=	NA	NA

Required

a. Compute the depletion charge per cubic yard.
b. Record the acquisition of the sand reserves and the depletion expense for Years 1 and 2 in a financial statements model like the preceding one.
c. Prepare the general journal entries to record the depletion expense for Years 1 and 2.

LO 8-10

Exercise 8-20B *Computing and recording goodwill*

Horn Co. acquired the business Medical Supply Co. for $275,000 cash and assumed all liabilities at the date of acquisition. Medical's books showed tangible assets of $250,000, liabilities of $10,000, and equity of $240,000. An appraiser assessed the fair market value of the tangible assets at $265,000 at the date of acquisition. Horn's financial condition just prior to the acquisition is shown in the following statements model:

Assets					=	Liab.	+	Equity	Rev.	−	Exp.	=	Net Inc.	Cash Flow
Cash	+	Tang. Assets	+	Goodwill										
450,000	+	NA	+	NA	=	NA	+	450,000	NA	−	NA	=	NA	NA

Required

a. Compute the amount of goodwill acquired.
b. Record the acquisition in a financial statements model like the preceding one.
c. Record the acquisition in general journal format.

LO 8-10, 8-11

Exercise 8-21B *Computing and recording the amortization of intangibles*

Garth Manufacturing paid cash to acquire the assets of an existing company. Among the assets acquired were the following items:

Patent with 5 remaining years of legal life	$48,000
Goodwill	35,000

Garth's financial condition just prior to the purchase of these assets is shown in the following statements model:

Assets					=	Liab.	+	Equity	Rev.	−	Exp.	=	Net Inc.	Cash Flow
Cash	+	Patent	+	Goodwill										
94,000	+	NA	+	NA	=	NA	+	94,000	NA	−	NA	=	NA	NA

Required

a. Compute the annual amortization expense for these items if applicable.
b. Show the acquisition of the intangible assets and the related amortization expense for Year 1 in a horizontal statements model like the preceding one.
c. Prepare the journal entries to record the acquisition of the intangible assets and the related amortization for Year 1.

Exercise 8-22B *Identifying companies using property, plant, and equipment*   LO 8-12

Tri-Cities Equipment Rentals, LLC rents equipment such as cranes and bulldozers to construction companies, while Sam's Tax Services, LLC provides income tax and accounting services to individuals and small businesses. Sam's has offices in several cities throughout the mid-Atlantic states. The data that follow are from the companies' most recent financial statements, but are not identified as to which company they relate.

	Company 1	Company 2
Sales	$13,500,000	$13,500,000
Depreciation expense	700,000	90,000
Net earnings	1,050,000	1,100,000
Current assets	1,000,000	850,000
Property, plant, and equipment	8,100,000	900,000
Total assets	10,700,000	2,700,000

Required

a. Calculate the ratio of sales to property, plant, and equipment for each company.
b. Based on the ratios calculated in requirement *a*, decide which is the equipment rental company and which is the tax and accounting business. Explain your answer.
c. Based on the ratios calculated in requirement *a*, which company appears to be using its property, plant, and equipment more efficiently? Explain your answer.
d. Explain why two companies with such different amounts of property, plant, and equipment might have the same amount of current assets.

Exercise 8-23B *Depreciable assets under IFRS*   IFRS

The Transnational Business Inc. (TBI) purchased an asset that cost $60,000 on January 1, Year 1. The asset had a four-year useful life and a $10,000 salvage value.

Required

a. Determine the amount of expense recognized on the Year 1 income statement, assuming TBI uses U.S. GAAP.
b. Determine the amount of expense or gain recognized on the income statement, assuming TBI uses the IFRS revaluation model and the asset is determined to have a fair value of $55,000 as of December 31, Year 1.
c. Determine the amount of expense or gain recognized on the income statement, assuming TBI uses the IFRS revaluation model and the asset is determined to have a fair value of $65,000 as of December 31, Year 1.

Exercise 8-24B *Accounting for land and buildings under IFRS*   IFRS

Assume the following. Madrid Company purchased a parcel of land on January 1, Year 1, for $600,000. It constructed a building on the land at a cost of $3,000,000. The building was occupied on January 1, Year 4, and is expected to have a useful life of 40 years and an estimated salvage value of $1,000,000.

As of December 31, Year 5 and Year 6, the fair value of the land had not been formally revalued because the real estate market had not changed significantly. Due to a jump in real estate prices, during Year 7 the value of the land had increased to $650,000, and the fair value of the building was $3,000,000. The salvage value of the building is still estimated at $1,000,000. The land and the building were reevaluated by the company in Year 7.

Required

a. Under U.S. accounting rules, what amount would be reported on the company's Year 6 and Year 7 balance sheets for the land and for the building? Show any necessary computations.
b. Under U.S. accounting rules, what amount of depreciation expense would be reported in Year 7 for the building? Show any necessary computations.
c. Under the IFRS revaluation model, what amount would be reported on the company's Year 6 and Year 7 balance sheets for the land and for the building? Show any necessary computations.
d. Under the IFRS revaluation model, what amount of depreciation expense would be reported in Year 7 for the building? Show any necessary computations.

PROBLEMS—SERIES B

LO 8-1

Problem 8-25B *Accounting for acquisition of assets including a basket purchase*

Floyd Company made several purchases of long-term assets in Year 1. The details of each purchase are presented here.

New Office Equipment

1. List price: $50,000; terms: 1/10 n/30; paid within the discount period.
2. Transportation-in: $1,200.
3. Installation: $1,000.
4. Cost to repair damage during unloading: $700.
5. Routine maintenance cost after eight months: $240.

Basket Purchase of Office Furniture, Copier, Computers, and Laser Printers for $70,000 with Fair Market Values

1. Office furniture, $48,000.
2. Copier, $12,000.
3. Computers and printers, $20,000.

Land for New Headquarters with Old Barn Torn Down

1. Purchase price, $100,000.
2. Demolition of barn, $7,000.
3. Lumber sold from old barn, $2,000.
4. Grading in preparation for new building, $11,000.
5. Construction of new building, $310,000.

Required

In each of these cases, determine the amount of cost to be capitalized in the asset accounts.

LO 8-2, 8-3, 8-4

Problem 8-26B *Determining the effect of depreciation expense on financial statements*

Three different companies each purchased a machine on January 1, Year 1, for $64,000. Each machine was expected to last five years or 200,000 hours. Salvage value was estimated to be $6,000. All three machines were operated for 50,000 hours in Year 1, 55,000 hours in Year 2, 40,000 hours in Year 3, 44,000 hours in Year 4, and 31,000 hours in Year 5. Each of the three companies earned $30,000 of cash revenue during each of the five years. Company A uses straight-line depreciation, company B uses double-declining-balance depreciation, and company C uses units-of-production depreciation.

Required

Answer each of the following questions. Ignore the effects of income taxes.
a. Which company will report the highest amount of net income for Year 1?
b. Which company will report the lowest amount of net income for Year 3?
c. Which company will report the highest book value on the December 31, Year 3, balance sheet?
d. Which company will report the highest amount of retained earnings on the December 31, Year 4, balance sheet?
e. Which company will report the lowest amount of cash flow from operating activities on the Year 3 statement of cash flows?

Problem 8-27B Effect of straight-line versus double-declining-balance depreciation on the recognition of expense and gains or losses

LO 8-2, 8-3, 8-5

National Laundry Services purchased a new steam press on January 1 for $42,000. It is expected to have a five-year useful life and a $4,000 salvage value. National expects to use the steam press more extensively in the early years of its life.

Required

a. Calculate the depreciation expense for each of the five years, assuming the use of straight-line depreciation.
b. Calculate the depreciation expense for each of the five years, assuming the use of double-declining-balance depreciation.
c. Would the choice of one depreciation method over another produce a different amount of cash flow for any year? Why or why not?
d. Assume that National Laundry Services sold the steam press at the end of the third year for $22,000. Compute the amount of gain or loss using each depreciation method.

Problem 8-28B Accounting for depreciation over multiple accounting cycles: straight-line depreciation

LO 8-2, 8-5

Scott Company began operations when it acquired $40,000 cash from the issue of common stock on January 1, Year 1. The cash acquired was immediately used to purchase equipment for $40,000 that had a $4,000 salvage value and an expected useful life of four years. The equipment was used to produce the following revenue stream (assume all revenue transactions are for cash). At the beginning of the fifth year, the equipment was sold for $4,500 cash. Scott uses straight-line depreciation.

	Year 1	Year 2	Year 3	Year 4	Year 5
Revenue	$9,500	$10,000	$10,500	$8,500	$0

Required

Prepare income statements, statements of changes in stockholders' equity, balance sheets, and statements of cash flows for each of the five years.

Problem 8-29B Computing and recording units-of-production depreciation

LO 8-4, 8-5

Friendly Corporation purchased a delivery van for $28,500 in Year 1. The firm's financial condition immediately prior to the purchase is shown in the following horizontal statements model:

Assets			=	Equity			Rev.	−	Exp.	=	Net Inc.	Cash Flow
Cash	+	Book Value of Van	=	Com. Stk.	+	Ret. Earn.						
50,000	+	NA	=	50,000	+	NA	NA	−	NA	=	NA	NA

The van was expected to have a useful life of 200,000 miles and a salvage value of $2,500. Actual mileage was as follows:

Year 1	60,000
Year 2	50,000
Year 3	55,000

Required

a. Compute the depreciation for each of the three years, assuming the use of units-of-production depreciation.

b. Assume that Friendly earns $26,000 of cash revenue during Year 1. Record the purchase of the van and the recognition of the revenue and the depreciation expense for the first year in a financial statements model like the one shown earlier.

c. Assume that Friendly sold the van at the end of the third year for $8,000. Record the general journal entry for the sale.

LO 8-2, 8-3, 8-4, 8-6

Problem 8-30B *Calculating depreciation expense using four different methods*

Todd Service Company purchased a copier on January 1, Year 1, for $25,000 and paid an additional $500 for delivery charges. The copier was estimated to have a life of four years or 1,000,000 copies. Salvage value was estimated at $1,500. The copier produced 250,000 copies in Year 1 and 270,000 copies in Year 2.

Required

Compute the amount of depreciation expense for the copier for calendar years Year 1 and Year 2, using the following methods:
a. Straight-line
b. Units-of-production
c. Double-declining-balance
d. MACRS, assuming that the copier is classified as five-year property

LO 8-3, 8-7, 8-8

Problem 8-31B *Purchase and use of tangible asset: three accounting cycles, double-declining-balance depreciation*

The following transactions pertain to Accounting Solutions Inc. Assume the transactions for the purchase of the computer and any capital improvements occur on January 1 each year.

Year 1

1. Acquired $80,000 cash from the issue of common stock.
2. Purchased a computer system for $35,000. It has an estimated useful life of five years and a $5,000 salvage value.
3. Paid $2,450 sales tax on the computer system.
4. Collected $65,000 in fees from clients.
5. Paid $1,500 in fees to service the computers.
6. Recorded double-declining-balance depreciation on the computer system for Year 1.
7. Closed the revenue and expense accounts to Retained Earnings at the end of Year 1.

Year 2

1. Paid $1,000 for repairs to the computer system.
2. Bought off-site backup services to maintain the computer system, $1,500.
3. Collected $68,000 in fees from clients.
4. Paid $1,500 in fees to service the computers.
5. Recorded double-declining-balance depreciation for Year 2.
6. Closed the revenue and expense accounts to Retained Earnings at the end of Year 2.

Year 3

1. Paid $6,000 to upgrade the computer system, which extended the total life of the system to six years. The salvage value did not change.
2. Paid $1,200 in fees to service the computers.
3. Collected $70,000 in fees from clients.
4. Recorded double-declining-balance depreciation for Year 3.
5. Closed the revenue and expense accounts at the end of Year 3.

Required

a. Use a horizontal statements model like the following one to show the effect of these transactions on the elements of the financial statements. Use + for increase, − for decrease, and NA for not affected. The first event is recorded as an example.

Year 1 Event No.	Assets	=	Liabilities	+	Equity	Net Inc.	Cash Flow
1	+		NA		+	NA	+ FA

b. For each year, record the transactions in general journal form and post them to T-accounts.
c. Use a vertical model to present financial statements for Year 1, Year 2, and Year 3.

Problem 8-32B Recording continuing expenditures for plant assets

LO 8-2, 8-8

Tringle Inc. recorded the following transactions over the life of a piece of equipment purchased in Year 1:

Jan. 1, Year 1	Purchased the equipment for $38,000 cash. The equipment is estimated to have a five-year life and $3,000 salvage value and was to be depreciated using the straight-line method.
Dec. 31, Year 1	Recorded depreciation expense for Year 1.
May 5, Year 2	Undertook routine repairs costing $900.
Dec. 31, Year 2	Recorded depreciation expense for Year 2.
Jan. 1, Year 3	Made an adjustment costing $4,000 to the equipment. It improved the quality of the output but did not affect the life and salvage value estimates.
Dec. 31, Year 3	Recorded depreciation expense for Year 3.
Mar. 1, Year 4	Incurred $410 cost to oil and clean the equipment.
Dec. 31, Year 4	Recorded depreciation expense for Year 4.
Jan. 1, Year 5	Had the equipment completely overhauled at a cost of $9,000. The overhaul was estimated to extend the total life to seven years and revised the salvage value to $2,500.
Dec. 31, Year 5	Recorded depreciation expense for Year 5.
July 1, Year 6	Sold the equipment for $8,500 cash.

Required

a. Use a horizontal statements model like the following one to show the effects of these transactions on the elements of the financial statements. Use + for increase, − for decrease, and NA for not affected. The first event is recorded as an example.

Date	Assets	=	Liabilities	+	Equity	Net Inc.	Cash Flow
Jan. 1, Year 1	+ −		NA		NA	NA	− IA

b. Determine the amount of depreciation expense Tringle will report on the income statements for Year 1 through Year 5.
c. Determine the book value (cost − accumulated depreciation) Tringle will report on the balance sheets at the end of each year for Year 1 through Year 5.
d. Determine the amount of the gain or loss Tringle will report on the disposal of the equipment on July 1, Year 6.
e. Prepare the journal entry for the disposal of the equipment on July 1, Year 6.

Problem 8-33B Accounting for continuing expenditures

LO 8-2, 8-8

Delta Manufacturing paid $62,000 to purchase a computerized assembly machine on January 1, Year 1. The machine had an estimated life of eight years and a $2,000 salvage value. Delta's financial condition as of January 1, Year 4, is shown in the following financial statements model. Delta uses the straight-line method for depreciation.

Assets			=	Equity			Rev.	−	Exp.	=	Net Inc.	Cash Flow
Cash	+	Book Value of Mach.	=	Com. Stk.	+	Ret. Earn.						
15,000	+	39,500	=	10,500	+	44,000	NA	−	NA	=	NA	NA

Delta Manufacturing made the following expenditures on the computerized assembly machine in Year 4:

Jan. 2   Added an overdrive mechanism for $8,000 that would improve the overall quality of the performance of the machine but would not extend its life. The salvage value was revised to $2,500.
Aug. 1   Performed routine maintenance, $1,250.
Oct. 2   Replaced some computer chips (considered routine), $800.
Dec. 31   Recognized Year 4 depreciation expense.

Required

a. Record the Year 4 transactions in a statements model like the preceding one.
b. Prepare journal entries for the Year 4 transactions.

LO 8-7, 8-9

Problem 8-34B   *Accounting for depletion*

Metals Exploration Corporation engages in the exploration and development of many types of natural resources. In the last two years, the company has engaged in the following activities:

Jan. 1, Year 1   Purchased a coal mine estimated to contain 300,000 tons of coal for $900,000.
July 1, Year 1   Purchased for $2,000,000 cash a tract of land containing timber estimated to yield 3,000,000 board feet of lumber. At the time of purchase, the land had an appraised value of $200,000.
Feb. 1, Year 2   Purchased a silver mine estimated to contain 30,000 tons of silver for $850,000.
Aug. 1, Year 2   Purchased for $875,000 oil reserves estimated to contain 270,000 barrels of oil, of which 20,000 would be unprofitable to pump.

Required

a. Prepare the journal entries to account for the following:
  (1) The Year 1 purchases.
  (2) Depletion on the Year 1 purchases, assuming that 80,000 tons of coal were mined and 1,000,000 board feet of lumber were cut.
  (3) The Year 2 purchases.
  (4) Depletion on the four reserves, assuming that 68,000 tons of coal, 1,200,000 board feet of lumber, 9,000 tons of silver, and 80,000 barrels of oil were extracted.
b. Prepare the portion of the December 31, Year 2, balance sheet that reports natural resources.
c. Assume that in Year 3 the estimates changed to reflect only 50,000 tons of coal remaining. Prepare the depletion journal entry for Year 3 to account for the extraction of 40,000 tons of coal.

LO 8-10, 8-11

Problem 8-35B   *Accounting for intangible assets*

Doug's Diner acquired a fast-food restaurant for $1,500,000. The fair market values of the assets acquired were as follows. No liabilities were assumed.

Equipment	$380,000
Land	200,000
Building	680,000
Franchise (5-year life)	120,000

Required

a. Calculate the amount of goodwill acquired.
b. Prepare the journal entry to record the amortization of the franchise fee at the end of Year 1.

LO 8-11

Problem 8-36B   *Accounting for goodwill*

Bostick Co. acquired the assets of Belk Co. for $1,200,000 in Year 1. The estimated fair market value of the assets at the acquisition date was $1,000,000. Goodwill of $200,000 was recorded at acquisition. In Year 2, because of negative publicity, one-half of the goodwill acquired from Belk Co. was judged to be permanently impaired.

Required

a. How will Bostick account for the impairment of the goodwill?
b. Prepare the journal entry to record the permanent impairment of goodwill.

ANALYZE, THINK, COMMUNICATE

ATC 8-1 Business Applications Case   *Understanding real-world annual reports*

Required

Obtain the Target Corporation's annual report at http://investors.target.com using the instructions in Appendix B, and use it to answer the following questions:

a. What method of depreciation does Target use?
b. What types of intangible assets does Target have?
c. What are the estimated lives that Target uses for the various types of long-term assets?
d. As of January 28, 2017 (2016 fiscal year), what is the original cost of Target's land, buildings and improvements, and fixtures and equipment?
e. What was Target's depreciation expense and amortization expense for 2016?

ATC 8-2 Group Assignment   *Different depreciation methods*

Sweet's Bakery makes cakes, pies, and other pastries that it sells to local grocery stores. The company experienced the following transactions during Year 1.

1. Started business by acquiring $60,000 cash from the issue of common stock.
2. Purchased bakery equipment for $46,000.
3. Had sales in Year 1 amounting to $42,000.
4. Paid $8,200 of cash for supplies, which were all used during the year to make baked goods.
5. Incurred other operating expenses of $12,000 for Year 1.
6. Recorded depreciation assuming the equipment had a four-year life and a $6,000 salvage value. The MACRS recovery period is five years.
7. Paid income tax. The rate is 30 percent.

Required

a. Organize the class into three sections and divide each section into groups of three to five students. Assign each section a depreciation method: straight-line, double-declining-balance, or MACRS.

Group Task

Prepare an income statement and balance sheet using the preceding information and the depreciation method assigned to your group.

Class Discussion

b. Have a representative of each section put its income statement on the board. Are there differences in net income? In the amount of income tax paid? How will these differences in the amount of depreciation expense change over the life of the equipment?

ATC 8-3 Real-World Case   *Identifying companies based on financial statement information*

The following ratios are for four companies in different industries. Some of these ratios have been discussed in the textbook, others have not, but their names explain how the ratio was computed. These data are for the companies' 2016 fiscal years. The four sets of ratios, presented randomly are:

Ratio	Company 1	Company 2	Company 3	Company 4
Current assets ÷ Total assets	7%	18%	31%	19%
Average days to sell inventory	72 days	12 days	163 days	108 days
Average days to collect receivables	60 days	3 days	47 days	9 days
Return-on-assets	7%	8%	3%	5%
Gross margin	39%	22%	22%	50%
Sales ÷ Property, plant, and equipment	1.1 times	3.4 times	4.5 times	23.5 times
Sales ÷ Number of full-time employees	$ 279,980	$ 46,350	$ 397,743	$ 64,717

The four companies to which these ratios relate, listed in alphabetical order, are:

Molson Coors Brewing Company is a company that produces beer and related products.

Darden Restaurants, Inc. operates approximately 2,150 restaurants under 10 different names, including Olive Garden, Bahama Breeze, and LongHorn Steakhouse.

Deere & Company is a company that manufactures heavy construction equipment.

Weight Watchers International, Inc. is a company that provides weight loss services and products. Its fiscal year-end was December 31, 2016, during which 81 percent of its revenues came from services and 19 percent from product sales.

Required

Determine which company should be matched with each set of ratios. Write a memorandum explaining the rationale for your decisions.

ATC 8-4   Business Applications Case   *Performing ratio analysis using real-world data*

American Greetings Corporation manufactures and sells greeting cards and related items such as gift wrapping paper. CSX Corporation is one of the largest railway networks in the nation. The following data were taken from one of the companies' February 29, 2016, annual report and from the other's December 30, 2016, annual report. Revealing which data relate to which company was intentionally omitted. For one company, the dollar amounts are in thousands, while for the other they are in millions.

	Company 1	Company 2
Sales	$1,900,790	$11,069
Depreciation costs	50,303	1,301
Net earnings	129,842	1,714
Current assets	559,868	2,487
Property, plant, and equipment	467,710	31,150
Total assets	1,603,449	35,414

Required

a. Calculate depreciation costs as a percentage of sales for each company.
b. Calculate property, plant, and equipment as a percentage of total assets for each company.
c. Based on the information now available to you, decide which data relate to which company. Explain the rationale for your decision.
d. Which company appears to be using its assets most efficiently? Explain your answer.

ATC 8-5   Business Applications Case   *Performing ratio analysis using real-world data*

Companies in the gas and oil business use a lot of property, plant, and equipment. Not only is there the significant investment they must make in equipment used to find, extract, and process the oil and natural gas, but they must also purchase the rights to the energy reserves themselves.

Chesapeake Energy Corporation "We own interests in approximately 22,700 oil and natural gas wells. . . . Our daily production for 2016 averaged 635 mboe, . . ." One "mboe" is the energy equivalent to that in 1,000 barrels of oil.

Anadarko Petroleum Corporation "Anadarko Petroleum Corporation is among the world's largest independent exploration and production companies, with approximately 1.7 billion BOE of proved reserves at December 31, 2016." One "BOE" is equivalent to the energy contained in one barrel of oil.

The following information was taken from the companies' December 31, 2016, annual reports. All dollar amounts are in millions.

	Chesapeake Energy Corporation	Anadarko Petroleum Corporation
Sales	$7,872	$7,869
Depreciation and depletion costs	1,107	4,301
Property, plant, and equipment (net of accumulated depreciation)	10,609	32,168
Total assets	13,028	45,564
Depreciation method	Straight-line	Straight-line
Depletion method	Units of production	Units of production
Estimated life of assets		
Buildings	10 to 39 years	up to 40 years
Machinery and equipment	3 to 20 years	3 to 15 years
Net income	$(4,401)	$(3,071)

Required

a. Calculate depreciation costs as a percentage of sales for each company.
b. Calculate property, plant, and equipment as a percentage of total assets for each company.
c. Based only on the percentages calculated in Requirements *a* and *b*, which company appears to be using its assets most efficiently? Explain your answer.
d. Calculate the return-on-assets ratio for each company. Based on this ratio, which company appears to be using its assets most efficiently? Explain your answer.
e. Identify some of the problems a financial analyst would encounter in comparing the use of long-term assets at Chesapeake versus Anadarko.

ATC 8-6   Writing Assignment   *Impact of historical cost on asset presentation on the balance sheet*

Assume you are examining the balance sheets of two companies and note the following information:

	Company A	Company B
Equipment	$1,130,000	$900,000
Accumulated Depreciation	(730,000)	(500,000)
Book Value	$ 400,000	$400,000

Maxie Smith, a student who has had no accounting courses, remarks that Company A and Company B have the same amount of equipment.

Required

In a short paragraph, explain to Maxie that the two companies do not have equal amounts of equipment. In your discussion comments regarding the possible age of each company's equipment, you may want to include the impact of the historical cost concept on balance sheet information, as well as the impact of different depreciation methods on book value.

ATC 8-7   Ethical Dilemma   *What's an expense?*

Several years ago, Wilson Blowhard founded a communications company. The company became successful and grew by expanding its customer base and acquiring some of its competitors. In fact, most of its growth resulted from acquiring other companies. Mr. Blowhard is adamant about continuing the company's growth and increasing its net worth. To achieve these goals, the business' net income must continue to increase at a rapid pace.

If the company's net worth continues to rise, Mr. Blowhard plans to sell the company and retire. He is, therefore, focused on improving the company's profit any way he can.

In the communications business, companies often use the lines of other communications companies. This line usage is a significant operating expense for Mr. Blowhard's company. Generally accepted accounting principles require operating costs like line use be expensed as they are incurred each year. Each dollar of line cost reduces net income by a dollar.

After reviewing the company's operations, Mr. Blowhard concluded that the company did not currently need all of the line use it was paying for. It was really paying the owner of the lines now so that the line use would be available in the future for all of Mr. Blowhard's expected new customers. Mr. Blowhard instructed his accountant to capitalize all of the line cost charges and depreciate them over 10 years. The accountant reluctantly followed Mr. Blowhard's instructions, and the company's net income for the current year showed a significant increase over the prior year's net income. Mr. Blowhard had found a way to report continued growth in the company's net income and increase the value of the company.

Required

a. How does Mr. Blowhard's scheme affect the amount of income that the company would otherwise report in its financial statements, and how does the scheme affect the company's balance sheet? Explain your answer.
b. Review the AICPA's Articles of Professional Conduct (see Chapter 2) and comment on any of the principles that were violated.
c. Review the elements of the fraud triangle (see Chapter 2) and comment on which of these features are evident in this case.

ATC 8-8 Research Assignment *Comparing Microsoft's and Intel's operational assets*

This chapter discussed how companies in different industries often use different proportions of current versus long-term assets to accomplish their business objective. The technology revolution resulting from the silicon microchip has often been led by two well-known companies: **Microsoft** and **Intel.** Although often thought of together, these companies are really very different. Using either the most current Forms 10-K or annual reports for Microsoft Corporation and Intel Corporation, complete the requirements asked for below. Obtain the Forms 10-K using either the EDGAR system, following the instructions in Appendix A, or the company's website. Microsoft's annual report is available on its website; Intel's annual report is its Form 10-K.

Required

a. Fill in the missing data in the following table. The percentages must be computed; they are not included in the companies' 10-Ks. (*Note:* The percentages for current assets and property, plant, and equipment will not sum to 100.)

	Current Assets	Property, Plant, and Equipment	Total Assets
Microsoft			
Dollar Amount	$ _____	$ _____	$ _____
% of Total Assets	_____ %	_____ %	100%
Intel			
Dollar Amount	$ _____	$ _____	$ _____
% of Total Assets	_____ %	_____ %	100%

b. Briefly explain why these two companies have different percentages of their assets in current assets versus property, plant, and equipment.

ATC 8-9 Spreadsheet Assignment *Reporting to the IRS versus financial statement reporting*

Crist Company operates a lawn-mowing service. Crist has chosen to depreciate its equipment for financial statement purposes using the straight-line method. However, to save cash in the short run, Crist has elected to use the MACRS method for income tax reporting purposes.

Required

a. Set up the following spreadsheet to reflect the two different methods of reporting. Notice that the first two years of revenues and operating expenses are provided.

b. Enter the effects of the following items for Year 1.

   (1) At the beginning of Year 1, Crist purchased for $10,000 cash a lawn mower it expects to use for five years. Salvage value is estimated to be $2,000. As stated, Crist uses the straight-line method of depreciation for financial statement purposes, and the MACRS method for income tax purposes. Use formulas to calculate the depreciation expense for each method.

   (2) No equipment was sold during Year 1; therefore, no gain or loss would be reported this year.

   (3) The income tax rate is 30 percent. For simplicity, assume that the income tax payable was paid in Year 1.

   (4) Complete the schedules for income reporting, reporting of equipment, and reporting of cash flows for Year 1. Use formulas for all calculations.

c. Enter the effects of the following items for Year 2.

   (1) Crist used the mower for the entire Year 2. Enter Year 2 depreciation expense amounts for the income reporting section of your spreadsheet.

   (2) At December 31, Crist sold the lawn mower for $7,000. Calculate the gain or loss on the sale for the income reporting section. Use formulas to make the calculations.

   (3) The income tax rate is 30 percent. For simplicity, assume that the income tax payable was paid in Year 2.

   (4) Complete the schedules for income reporting and reporting of cash flows for Year 2.

d. Calculate the Total columns for the income reporting and reporting of cash flows sections.

e. Respond to the following:

   (1) In Year 1, by adopting the MACRS method of depreciation for tax purposes instead of the straight-line method, what is the difference in the amount of cash paid for income taxes?

   (2) In the long term, after equipment has been disposed of, is there any difference in total income under the two methods?

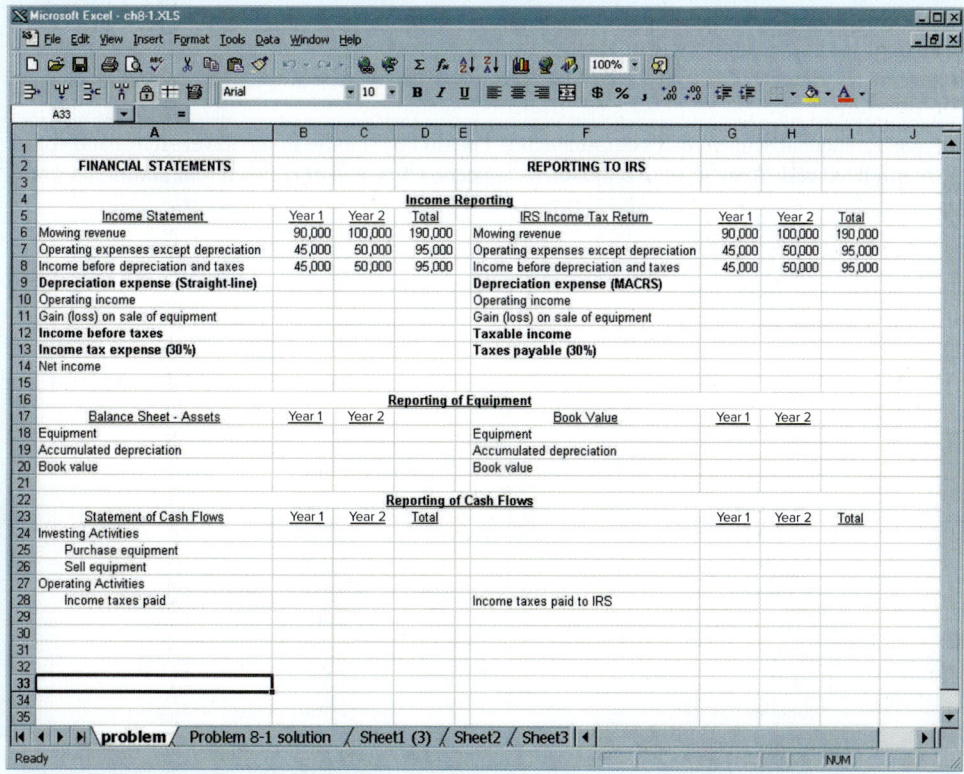

Source: Microsoft Office Excel 1997

(3) In the long term, after equipment has been disposed of, is there any difference between total income tax expense and total income tax paid?

(4) Explain why Crist Company would use two different depreciation methods, particularly the straight-line method for the financial statements and an accelerated method (MACRS) for reporting to the IRS.

ATC 8-10 Spreadsheet Assignment *Alternative methods of depreciation*

Short Company purchased a computer on January 1, Year 1, for $5,000. An additional $100 was paid for delivery charges. The computer was estimated to have a life of five years or 10,000 hours. Salvage value was estimated at $300. During the five years, the computer was used as follows:

Year 1	2,500 hours
Year 2	2,400 hours
Year 3	2,000 hours
Year 4	1,700 hours
Year 5	1,400 hours

Required

a. Prepare a five-year depreciation schedule for the computer using the straight-line depreciation method. Be sure to use formulas for all computations including depreciation expense. Set up the following headings for your schedule:

		Beginning				Ending	
Year	Cost	Accumulated Depreciation	Book Value	Depreciation Expense	Cost	Accumulated Depreciation	Book Value

b. Prepare another five-year depreciation schedule for the computer using the units-of-production method. Use (copy) the headings used in Requirement *a*.

c. Prepare another five-year depreciation schedule for the computer using the double-declining-balance method. Use (copy) the headings used in Requirement *a*.

d. Prepare another five-year depreciation schedule for the computer using the MACRS method. Use (copy) the headings used in Requirement *a*.

Spreadsheet Tip

After Year 1, enter subsequent dates automatically. Position the mouse in the lower right-hand corner of the highlighted cell "Year 1" until a thin cross appears. Click and drag down four additional rows.

COMPREHENSIVE PROBLEM

The trial balance of Pacilio Security Services, Inc. as of January 1, Year 8, had the following normal balances:

Cash	$93,708
Petty cash	100
Accounts receivable	22,540
Allowance for doubtful accounts	1,334
Supplies	250
Prepaid rent	3,600
Merchandise inventory (18 @ $285)	5,130
Land	4,000
Salaries payable	2,100
Common stock	50,000
Retained earnings	75,894

During Year 8, Pacillo Security Services experienced the following transactions:

1. Paid the salaries payable from Year 7.
2. Purchased equipment and a van for a lump sum of $36,000 cash on January 2, Year 8. The equipment was appraised for $10,000 and the van was appraised for $30,000.
3. Paid $9,000 on May 1, Year 8, for one year's office rent in advance.
4. Purchased $300 of supplies on account.
5. Purchased 120 alarm systems at a cost of $280 each. Paid cash for the purchase.
6. After numerous attempts to collect from customers, wrote off $2,350 of uncollectible accounts receivable.
7. Sold 115 alarm systems for $580 each. All sales were on account. (Be sure to compute cost of goods sold using the FIFO cost flow method.)
8. Billed $86,000 of monitoring services for the year. Credit card sales amounted to $36,000, and the credit card company charged a 4 percent fee. The remaining $50,000 were sales on account.
9. Replenished the petty cash fund on June 30. The fund had $12 cash and receipts of $45 for yard mowing, $28 for office supplies expense, and $11 for miscellaneous expenses.
10. Collected the amount due from the credit card company.
11. Paid installers and other employees a total of $52,000 cash for salaries.
12. Collected $115,500 of accounts receivable during the year.
13. Paid $12,500 of advertising expense during the year.
14. Paid $6,800 of utilities expense for the year.
15. Sold the land, which was purchased in 2011, for $12,000.
16. Paid the accounts payable.
17. Paid a dividend of $10,000 to the shareholders.

Adjustments

18. Determined that $180 of supplies were on hand at the end of the year.
19. Recognized the expired rent for both the old van and the office building for the year. The lease on the van was not renewed. Rent paid on March 1, Year 7, for the van was $4,800.
20. Recognized uncollectible accounts expense for the year using the allowance method. Pacilio estimates that 3 percent of sales on account will not be collected.
21. Recognized depreciation expense on the equipment and the van. The equipment has a five-year life and a $2,000 salvage value. The van has a four-year life and a $6,000 salvage value. The company uses double-declining-balance for the van and straight-line for the equipment.
22. Accrued salaries at December 31, Year 8, were $1,500.

Required

a. Record the preceding transactions in general journal form.
b. Post the transactions to T-accounts.
c. Prepare a trial balance.
d. Prepare an income statement, statement of changes in stockholders' equity, balance sheet, and statement of cash flows.
e. Close the temporary accounts to retained earnings.
f. Post the closing entries to the T-accounts and prepare a post-closing trial balance.

CHAPTER 9

Accounting for Current Liabilities and Payroll

LEARNING OBJECTIVES

After you have mastered the material in this chapter, you will be able to:

LO 9-1 Show how notes payable and related interest expense affect financial statements.

LO 9-2 Show how sales tax liabilities affect financial statements.

LO 9-3 Define contingent liabilities and explain how they are reported in financial statements.

LO 9-4 Explain how warranty obligations affect financial statements.

LO 9-5 Determine payroll taxes and explain how they affect financial statements.

LO 9-6 Prepare a classified balance sheet.

LO 9-7 Use the current ratio to assess the level of liquidity.

APPENDIX

LO 9-8 Show how discount notes and related interest charges affect financial statements.

 Video lectures and accompanying self-assessment quizzes are available in Connect *for all learning objectives.*

CHAPTER OPENING

Chapter 7 explained the need to estimate the net realizable value of receivables (the amount of receivables a company expects to actually collect). Do companies also estimate the net realizable value of payables (the amount they expect to actually pay)? The answer is no. Unless there is evidence to the contrary, companies are assumed to be going concerns that will continue to operate. Under this **going concern assumption,** companies expect to pay their obligations in full. Accounts and notes payable are therefore reported at face value. In addition to reporting liabilities for which the amounts due are known, companies report liabilities for which the amounts due are uncertain. Liabilities that are uncertain as to amount are contingent liabilities.

Chapter 2 discussed several types of liabilities with known amounts due, including accounts payable, salaries payable, and unearned revenue. This chapter introduces other liabilities with known amounts due: notes payable, sales tax payable, and payroll liabilities; and contingent liabilities including warranties payable and vacation pay. We limit the discussion in this chapter to *current liabilities,* those that are payable within one year or the operating cycle, whichever is longer.

The Curious Accountant

Rusty Rohr had worked as a plumber or plumber's assistant since high school. When he turned 30, he started his own plumbing business. In addition to working himself, he hired two friends, each of whom he planned to pay $25 per hour plus reasonable benefits. One reason Rusty wanted his own business was because he felt small companies often did not provide employees reasonable benefits. Rusty planned to charge customers $50 per hour for plumbing services. He believed charging double the rate he paid his employees would cover his operating expenses and still provide a profit on the employees' work.

Rusty hired a local accounting firm for his accounting needs, including handling his company's payroll records. After getting the business established, he and his employees kept busy, but the business was not as profitable as Rusty had expected. His accountant explained that the total compensation cost of his employees was averaging around $35 per hour. Rusty knew the employees would cost more than their $25 per hour wage rate because of their fringe benefits, but he had not expected the benefits cost to be 40 percent of their base pay.

What could cause Rusty's compensation expenses to be so unexpectedly high? (Answers on page 495.)

©Ingram Publishing

ACCOUNTING FOR NOTES PAYABLE

LO 9-1

Show how notes payable and related interest expense affect financial statements.

Our discussion of promissory notes in Chapter 7 focused on the payee, the company with a note receivable on its books. In this chapter, we focus on the maker of the note, the company with a note payable on its books. Because the maker of the note issues (gives) the note to the payee, the maker is sometimes called the **issuer**.

To illustrate, assume that on September 1, Year 1, Herrera Supply Company (HSC) borrowed $90,000 (the principal amount) from National Bank. As evidence of the debt, Herrera issued a **note payable** that had a one-year term and an annual interest rate of 9 percent.

Issuing the note is an asset source transaction. The asset account Cash increases and the liability account Notes Payable increases. The income statement is not affected. The statement of cash flows shows a $90,000 cash inflow from financing activities. The journal entry and its effects on the financial statements are shown next:

Account Title	Debit	Credit
Cash	90,000	
Notes Payable		90,000

	Assets	=	Liabilities	+	Stockholders' Equity		Rev.	−	Exp.	=	Net Inc.	Cash Flow
Date	Cash	=	Notes Pay. + Int. Pay.	+	Com. Stk. + Ret. Earn.							
09/01/Year 1	90,000	=	90,000 + NA	+	NA + NA		NA	−	NA	=	NA	90,000 FA

On December 31, Year 1, HSC would record an adjusting entry to recognize four months (September 1 through December 31) of accrued interest expense. The accrued interest is $2,700 [$90,000 × 0.09 × (4 ÷ 12)]. The adjusting entry is a claims exchange. The liability account Interest Payable increases, and the equity account Retained Earnings decreases. The income statement would report interest expense, even though HSC had not paid any cash for interest in Year 1. The journal entry and its effects on the financial statements are shown next:

Account Title	Debit	Credit
Interest Expense	2,700	
Interest Payable		2,700

	Assets	=	Liabilities	+	Stockholders' Equity		Rev.	−	Exp.	=	Net Inc.	Cash Flow
Date	Cash	=	Notes Pay. + Int. Pay.	+	Com. Stk. + Ret. Earn.							
12/31/Year 1	NA	=	NA + 2,700	+	NA + (2,700)		NA	−	2,700	=	(2,700)	NA

HSC would record three journal entries on August 31, Year 2 (the maturity date). The first entry recognizes $5,400 of interest expense that accrued in Year 2 from January 1 through August 31 [$90,000 × 0.09 × (8 ÷ 12)]. The entry and its effects on the financial statements are shown next:

Account Title	Debit	Credit
Interest Expense	5,400	
Interest Payable		5,400

	Assets	=	Liabilities	+	Stockholders' Equity		Rev.	−	Exp.	=	Net Inc.		Cash Flow
Date	Cash	=	Notes Pay. + Int. Pay.	+	Com. Stk. + Ret. Earn.								
08/31/Year 2	NA	=	NA + 5,400	+	NA + (5,400)		NA	−	5,400	=	(5,400)		NA

The second entry records HSC's cash payment for interest on August 31, Year 2. This entry is an asset use transaction that reduces both the Cash and Interest Payable accounts for the total amount of interest due: $8,100 [$90,000 × 0.09 × (12 ÷ 12)]. The interest payment includes the four months' interest accrued in Year 1 and the eight months accrued in Year 2 ($2,700 + $5,400 = $8,100). There is no effect on the income statement because HSC recognized the interest expense in two previous journal entries. The statement of cash flows would report an $8,100 cash outflow from operating activities. The journal entry and its effects on the financial statements are shown next:

Account Title	Debit	Credit
Interest Payable	8,100	
Cash		8,100

	Assets	=	Liabilities	+	Stockholders' Equity		Rev.	−	Exp.	=	Net Inc.		Cash Flow
Date	Cash	=	Notes Pay. + Int. Pay.	+	Com. Stk. + Ret. Earn.								
08/31/Year 2	(8,100)	=	NA + (8,100)	+	NA + NA		NA	−	NA	=	NA		(8,100) OA

The third entry on August 31, Year 2, reflects repaying the principal. This entry is an asset use transaction. The Cash account and the Notes Payable account each decrease by $90,000. There is no effect on the income statement. The statement of cash flows would show a $90,000 cash outflow from financing activities. Recall that paying interest is classified as an operating activity even though repaying the principal is a financing activity. The journal entry and its effects on the financial statements are shown next:

Account Title	Debit	Credit
Notes Payable	90,000	
Cash		90,000

	Assets	=	Liabilities	+	Stockholders' Equity		Rev.	−	Exp.	=	Net Inc.		Cash Flow
Date	Cash	=	Notes Pay. + Int. Pay.	+	Com. Stk. + Ret. Earn.								
08/31/Year 2	(90,000)	=	(90,000) + NA	+	NA + NA		NA	−	NA	=	NA		(90,000) FA

Alternatively, HSC could combine the three separate journal entries recorded on the maturity date (August 31, Year 2) into a single compound journal entry as shown next:

Account Title	Debit	Credit
Interest Expense	5,400	
Interest Payable	2,700	
Notes Payable	90,000	
Cash		98,100

CHECK YOURSELF 9.1

On October 1, Year 1, Mellon Company issued an interest-bearing note payable to Better Banks Inc. The note had a $24,000 principal amount, a four-month term, and an annual interest rate of 4 percent. Determine the amount of interest expense and the cash outflow from operating activities Mellon will report in its Year 1 and Year 2 financial statements. Also provide, in general journal form, the adjusting entry necessary to recognize interest expense in Year 1.

Answer The computation of accrued interest expense is shown below. Unless otherwise specified, the interest rate is stated in annual terms, even though the term of the note is only four months. Interest rates are commonly expressed as an annual percentage regardless of the term of the note. The *time outstanding* in the following formulas is therefore expressed as a fraction of a year. Mellon paid interest at an annual rate of 4 percent, but the note was outstanding for only 3/12 of a year in Year 1 and 1/12 of a year in Year 2.

Year 1

Principal	×	Annual interest rate	×	Time outstanding	=	Interest expense
$24,000	×	0.04	×	(3/12)	=	$240

Year 2

Principal	×	Annual interest rate	×	Time outstanding	=	Interest expense
$24,000	×	0.04	×	(1/12)	=	$80

Mellon will report a $320 ($240 + $80) cash outflow from operating activities for interest in Year 2. The adjusting entry required to recognize accrued interest at the end of Year 1 is as follows:

Interest Expense	240	
Interest Payable		240

ACCOUNTING FOR SALES TAX

LO 9-2

Show how sales tax liabilities affect financial statements.

Most states require retail companies to collect a sales tax on items sold to their customers. The retailer collects the tax from its customers and remits the tax to the state at regular intervals. The retailer has a current liability for the amount of sales tax collected but not yet paid to the state.

To illustrate, assume Herrera Supply Company (HSC) sells merchandise to a customer for $2,000 cash in a state where the sales tax rate is 6 percent. The journal entry to record the sale and its effects on the financial statements are shown next:

Account Title	Debit	Credit
Cash	2,120	
Sales Tax Payable		120
Sales Revenue[1]		2,000

Assets	=	Liab.	+	Equity		Rev.	−	Exp.	=	Net Inc.		Cash Flow
Cash	=	Sales Tax Pay.	+	Com. Stk. + Ret. Earn.								
2,120	=	120	+	NA + 2,000		2,000	−	NA	=	2,000		2,120 OA

[1]The entry to record cost of goods sold for this sale is intentionally omitted.

Remitting the tax (paying cash to the tax authority) is an asset use transaction. Both the Cash account and the Sales Tax Payable account decrease. The journal entry and its effects on the financial statements are shown next:

Account Title	Debit	Credit
Sales Tax Payable	120	
Cash		120

Assets	=	Liab.	+	Equity		Rev.	−	Exp.	=	Net Inc.	Cash Flow
Cash	=	Sales Tax Pay.	+ Com. Stk. + Ret. Earn.								
(120)	=	(120)	+ NA + NA			NA	−	NA	=	NA	(120) OA

CONTINGENT LIABILITIES

A **contingent liability** is a potential obligation arising from a past event. The amount or existence of the obligation depends on some future event. A pending lawsuit, for example, is a contingent liability. Depending on the outcome, a defendant company could be required to pay a monetary settlement or could be relieved of any obligation. Generally accepted accounting principles require that companies classify contingent liabilities into three different categories depending on the likelihood of their becoming actual liabilities. The categories and the accounting for each are described in the following:

 Define contingent liabilities and explain how they are reported in financial statements.

1. If the likelihood of a future obligation arising is *probable* (likely) and its amount can be *reasonably estimated,* a liability is recognized in the financial statements. Contingent liabilities in this category include warranties, vacation pay, and sick leave.

2. If the likelihood of a future obligation arising is *reasonably possible* but not likely, or if it is probable but *cannot be reasonably estimated,* no liability is reported on the balance sheet. The potential liability is, however, disclosed in the notes to the financial statements. Contingent liabilities in this category include legal challenges, environmental damages, and government investigations.

3. If the likelihood of a future obligation arising is *remote,* no liability need be recognized in the financial statements or disclosed in the notes to the statements.[2]

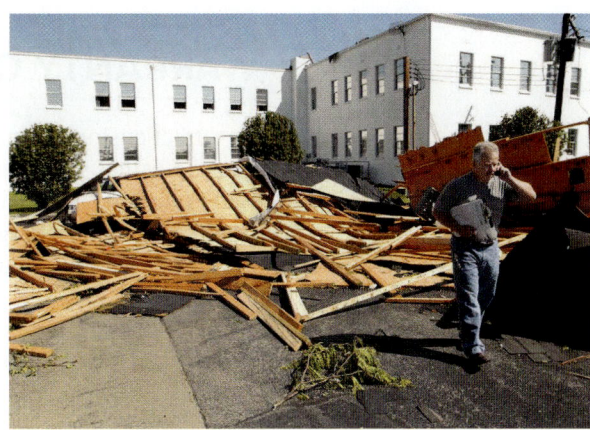
©Ed Reinke/AP Images

Determining whether a contingent liability is probable, reasonably possible, or remote requires professional judgment. Even seasoned accountants seek the advice of attorneys, engineers, insurance agents, and government regulators before classifying significant contingent liabilities. Professional judgment is also required to distinguish between contingent liabilities and **general uncertainties.** All businesses face uncertainties such as competition and damage from floods or storms. Such uncertainties are not contingent liabilities, however, because they do not arise from past events.

Exhibit 9.1 summarizes the three categories of contingent liabilities and the accounting for each category.

---

[2]Companies may, if desired, voluntarily disclose contingent liabilities classified as remote.

EXHIBIT 9.1

Reporting Contingent Liabilities

WARRANTY OBLIGATIONS

 Explain how warranty obligations affect financial statements.

To attract customers, many companies guarantee their products or services. Such guarantees are called **warranties,** and they take many forms. Usually, they extend for a specified period of time. Within this period, the seller promises to replace or repair defective products without charge. Although the amount and timing of warranty obligations are uncertain, warranties usually represent liabilities that must be reported in the financial statements.

To illustrate accounting for warranty obligations, assume Herrera Supply Company (HSC) had cash of $2,000, inventory of $6,000, common stock of $5,000, and retained earnings of $3,000 on December 31, Year 1. The Year 2 accounting period is affected by three accounting events: (1) sale of merchandise under warranty; (2) recognition of warranty obligations to customers who purchased the merchandise; and (3) settlement of a customer's warranty claim.

EVENT 1 During Year 2, HSC sold for $7,000 cash merchandise that had cost $4,000.

In the following statements model, revenue from the sale is labeled 1a, while the cost of the sale is labeled 1b. The journal entries for the sales transaction and their effects on the financial statements are shown next:

Account Title	Debit	Credit
Cash	7,000	
Sales Revenue		7,000
Cost of Goods Sold	4,000	
Inventory		4,000

Event No.	Assets			=	Liab.	+	Equity	Rev.	−	Exp.	=	Net Inc.	Cash Flow
	Cash	+	Inventory	=			Ret. Earn.						
1a	7,000	+	NA	=	NA	+	7,000	7,000	−	NA	=	7,000	7,000 OA
1b	NA	+	(4,000)	=	NA	+	(4,000)	NA	−	4,000	=	(4,000)	NA

EVENT 2 HSC guaranteed the merchandise sold in Event 1 to be free from defects for one year following the date of sale.

Although the exact amount of future warranty claims is unknown, HSC must inform financial statement users of the company's obligation. HSC must estimate the amount of the warranty liability and report the estimate in the Year 2 financial statements. Assume the warranty obligation is estimated to be $100. Recognizing this obligation increases liabilities (warranties payable) and reduces stockholders' equity (retained earnings). Recognizing the warranty expense reduces net income. The statement of cash flows is not affected when the obligation and the corresponding expense are recognized. The journal entry and its effects on the financial statements are shown next:

Account Title	Debit	Credit
Warranty Expense	100	
Warranties Payable		100

Event No.	Assets	=	Liab.	+	Equity	Rev.	−	Exp.	=	Net Inc.	Cash Flow
			Warr. Pay.	+	Ret. Earn.						
2	NA	=	100	+	(100)	NA	−	100	=	(100)	NA

EVENT 3 HSC paid $40 cash to repair defective merchandise returned by a customer.

The cash payment for the repair is not an expense. Warranty expense was recognized in the period in which the sale was made (when the Warranties Payable account was credited). The payment reduces an asset (cash) and a liability (warranties payable). The income statement is not affected by the repairs payment. However, there is a $40 cash outflow reported in the operating activities section of the statement of cash flows. The journal entry and its effects on the financial statements are shown next:

Account Title	Debit	Credit
Warranties Payable	40	
Cash		40

Event No.	Assets	=	Liab.	+	Equity	Rev.	−	Exp.	=	Net Inc.	Cash Flow
	Cash	=	Warr. Pay.	+	Ret. Earn.						
3	(40)	=	(40)	+	NA	NA	−	NA	=	NA	(40) OA

General Ledger T-Accounts and Financial Statements

Panel A of Exhibit 9.2 summarizes the Year 2 accounting events. Panel B presents the ledger accounts in T-account form. The event numbers are shown parenthetically in the T-accounts to facilitate your review. The closing entries (Event 4 in Panel A) are included and referenced with the abbreviation "cl." The financial statements are shown in Panel C of the exhibit. You should study Exhibit 9.2 to strengthen your understanding of how the warranty events affect the financial statements.

EXHIBIT 9.2
The Big Picture

Panel A: Transaction Summary

1. Sold merchandise that cost $4,000 for $7,000 cash.
2. Recognized a $100 warranty obligation and the corresponding expense.
3. Paid $40 to satisfy a warranty claim.
4. Closed the revenue and expense accounts (referenced *cl.*).

Panel B: General Ledger

Assets = Liabilities + Equity

Cash					Warranties Payable				Common Stock	
Bal.	2,000	40	(3)	(3)	40	100	(2)		5,000	Bal.
(1a)	7,000					60	Bal.			
Bal.	8,960									

Retained Earnings		
	3,000	Bal.
	2,900	(cl.)
	5,900	Bal.

Inventory			
Bal.	6,000	4,000	(1b.)
Bal.	2,000		

Sales Revenue			
(cl.)	7,000	7,000	(1a.)
		0	Bal.

Cost of Goods Sold			
(1b)	4,000	4,000	(cl.)
Bal.	0		

Warranty Expense			
(2)	100	100	(cl.)
Bal.	0		

Panel C: Financial Statements for Year 2

Income Statement

Sales revenue	$ 7,000
Cost of goods sold	(4,000)
Gross margin	3,000
Warranty expense	(100)
Net income	$ 2,900

Balance Sheet

Assets	
Cash	$ 8,960
Inventory	2,000
Total assets	$10,960
Liabilities	
Warranties payable	$ 60
Stockholders' equity	
Common stock	5,000
Retained earnings	5,900
Total liab. and stockholders' equity	$10,960

Statement of Cash Flows

Operating Activities	
Inflow from customers	$7,000
Outflow for warranty	(40)
Net Inflow from	
Operating activities	6,960
Investing Activities	0
Financing Activities	0
Net change in cash	6,960
Plus: Beginning cash balance	2,000
Ending cash balance	$8,960

CHECK YOURSELF 9.2

Flotation Systems Inc. (FSI) began operations in Year 1. Its sales were $360,000 in Year 1 and $410,000 in Year 2. FSI estimates the cost of its one-year product warranty will be 2 percent of sales. Actual cash payments for warranty claims amounted to $5,400 during Year 1 and $8,500 during Year 2. Prepare the journal entries required to record warranty expense and cash paid to settle warranty claims for Year 1 and Year 2. Determine the amount of warranties payable FSI would report on its Year 1 and Year 2 year-end balance sheets.

Answer Journal Entries for Year 1

Account Title	Debit	Credit
Warranty Expense ($360,000 × .02)	7,200	
Warranties Payable		7,200
Warranties Payable	5,400	
Cash		5,400

Journal Entries for Year 2

Account Title	Debit	Credit
Warranty Expense ($410,000 × .02)	8,200	
Warranties Payable		8,200
Warranties Payable	8,500	
Cash*		8,500

*The Year 2 cash payment exceeds the Year 2 accrued expense because some of the warranty expense accrued in Year 1 was actually paid in Year 2.

FSI would report Warranties Payable on the December 31, Year 1, balance sheet of $1,800 ($7,200 − $5,400). Warranties Payable on the December 31, Year 2, balance sheet is $1,500 ($1,800 + $8,200 − $8,500).

ACCOUNTING FOR PAYROLL

If you've had a job, you know the amount of your paycheck is less than the amount of your salary. Employers are required to withhold part of each employee's earnings. The money withheld is used to pay such items as income taxes, union dues, and medical insurance premiums for which the *employee* is responsible. The *employer* is also required to make matching payments for certain items such as Social Security and to pay additional amounts for unemployment taxes. This section of the chapter explains how employers account for *employee withholdings,* as well as *employer payroll expenses.*

LO 9-5

Determine payroll taxes and explain how they affect financial statements.

Identifying Employees

Businesses use the services of independent contractors as well as employees. They must distinguish between the two because payroll taxes apply only to employees. When a business supervises, directs, and controls an individual's work, the individual is an **employee** of the business. When a business pays an individual for specific services, but the individual supervises and controls the work, then that individual is an **independent contractor.**

REALITY BYTES

Many of the items we purchase come with a manufacturer's warranty, but companies that sell electronics and electrical appliances often offer to sell you an extended warranty that provides protection after the manufacturer's warranty has expired. Why do they offer this option to customers, and how do these warranties differ from the standard manufacturers' warranties?

Companies such as **Best Buy** offer to sell customers extended warranties because they make a significant profit on them. If you buy an extended warranty from Best Buy, the retailer is not actually the one who is promising to repair your product; that will be done by a third party. Best Buy simply receives a commission for selling the warranty. In recent fiscal years, such commissions accounted for 2 to 3 percent of the company's total revenues, and because it had to incur very little expense to earn these revenues, they are mostly profit.

©The McGraw-Hill Companies, Inc./Andrew Resek, photographer

The typical manufacturer's warranty, as you have learned in this chapter, is an expense recognized at the time of the sale. However, companies that provide extended warranties must recognize the warranty revenue over the life of the warranty, not immediately upon sale. Remember, this is referring to the third-party warranty provider, not Best Buy. Because Best Buy is simply earning a commission from selling the warranty, it gets to recognize all of the revenue at the time of the sale.

The distinction between independent contractor and employee depends upon control and supervision rather than the type of work performed. A company's chief financial officer (CFO) is a company *employee;* the company's outside auditor is an *independent contractor.* Although both individuals provide accounting services, the company controls the CFO's work while the auditor is independent. If a business hired Rusty Rohr's company (see The Curious Accountant at the start of the chapter) for plumbing services, Rusty would be an independent contractor with respect to his customer. Rusty's workers, however, are employees of Rusty's plumbing company.

Employees' Gross Earnings

The compensation earned by employees who are paid based on the number of hours they work is normally called **wages.** The compensation earned by employees who are paid a set amount per week, month, or other earnings period regardless of the number of hours worked is normally called **salaries.** The total amount of wages or salaries earned, before any deductions for withholding, represents employees' **gross earnings.** Gross earnings is the sum of regular pay plus any bonuses, overtime, or other additions.

Deductions from Employees' Gross Earnings

Employers withhold money from employees' gross earnings and are obligated (have liabilities) to pay the funds withheld on behalf of the employees. Employers determine each employee's net pay (cash paid to the employee) by *deducting* the withholdings from the gross earnings. This section of the chapter introduces common withholdings.

Federal Income Taxes

To help the federal government collect income taxes due on a timely basis, the tax laws adopted by Congress require employers to withhold income taxes from employee earnings. The employers then pay the withheld taxes directly to the government.

For example, assume an employee earns $2,000. Assume further that the employee owes $300 of income tax on these earnings. On payday, the employer withholds $300 of the earnings and pays the employee $1,700 cash. The employer then has a $300 liability (obligation) to the federal government for the income tax withheld. The employer will use the money withheld to pay the employee's federal income tax liability. The journal entry to record paying the employee and its effects on the financial statements are shown next:

Account Title	Debit	Credit
Salary Expense	2,000	
Employee Income Tax Payable		300
Cash		1,700

Assets	=	Liab.	+	Equity		Rev.	−	Exp.	=	Net Inc.	Cash Flow
Cash	=	EIT Pay.	+	Com. Stk. + Ret. Earn.							
(1,700)	=	300	+	NA + (2,000)		NA	−	2,000	=	(2,000)	(1,700) OA

When the employer pays the liability, both cash and liabilities will decrease. The income statement will not be affected. The statement of cash flows will show a cash outflow from operating activities. The journal entry and its effects on the financial statements are shown next:

Account Title	Debit	Credit
Employee Income Tax Payable	300	
Cash		300

Assets	=	Liab.	+	Equity		Rev.	−	Exp.	=	Net Inc.	Cash Flow
Cash	=	EIT Pay.	+	Com. Stk. + Ret. Earn.							
(300)	=	(300)	+	NA + NA		NA	−	NA	=	NA	(300) OA

The federal tax laws require employers to withhold funds for employee Social Security and Medicare (FICA) taxes, as well as income taxes. Employers may also be required to withhold amounts to pay state, county, and municipal government taxes from employees' paychecks. These withholdings have the same effects on the financial statements as those described earlier for federal income taxes.

Federal Income Tax Documents

The amount withheld from an employee's salary depends on the employee's *gross pay* and the number of *withholding allowances* the employee claims. Each allowance reduces the amount the employer must withhold. Employees are generally allowed to claim one allowance for themselves and one for each legal dependent. For example, a married person with two dependent children could claim four allowances (the employee, the dependent spouse, and the two dependent children). Exhibit 9.3 shows an **Employee's Withholding Allowance Certificate, Form W-4,** the form used to document the number of allowances claimed by an employee.

The federal government provides tax withholding tables that indicate the amount to withhold for any amount of earnings and any number of allowances. At the end of the calendar year, the employer must notify each employee of the amount of his or her gross earnings for the yea, as well as the amounts the employer withheld. Employers provide this information to employees on a **Wage and Tax Statement, Form W-2,** illustrated in

EXHIBIT 9.3

Employee's Withholding Allowance Certificate Form W-4

---------- Separate here and give Form W-4 to your employer. Keep the top part for your records. ----------

Form W-4
Department of the Treasury
Internal Revenue Service

Employee's Withholding Allowance Certificate
▶ Whether you are entitled to claim a certain number of allowances or exemption from withholding is subject to review by the IRS. Your employer may be required to send a copy of this form to the IRS.

OMB No. 1545-0074
2017

1	Your first name and middle initial	Last name		2	Your social security number
	Home address (number and street or rural route)		3 ☐ Single ☐ Married ☐ Married, but withhold at higher Single rate. Note: If married, but legally separated, or spouse is a nonresident alien, check the "Single" box.		
	City or town, state, and ZIP code		4 If your last name differs from that shown on your social security card, check here. You must call 1-800-772-1213 for a replacement card. ▶ ☐		

5	Total number of allowances you are claiming (from line **H** above **or** from the applicable worksheet on page 2)	5	
6	Additional amount, if any, you want withheld from each paycheck	6	$
7	I claim exemption from withholding for 2017, and I certify that I meet **both** of the following conditions for exemption.		
	• Last year I had a right to a refund of **all** federal income tax withheld because I had **no** tax liability, **and**		
	• This year I expect a refund of **all** federal income tax withheld because I expect to have **no** tax liability.		
	If you meet both conditions, write "Exempt" here . . . . ▶	7	

Under penalties of perjury, I declare that I have examined this certificate and, to the best of my knowledge and belief, it is true, correct, and complete.

Employee's signature
(This form is not valid unless you sign it.) ▶   **Date** ▶

8	Employer's name and address (Employer: Complete lines 8 and 10 only if sending to the IRS.)	9 Office code (optional)	10 Employer identification number (EIN)

For Privacy Act and Paperwork Reduction Act Notice, see page 2.   Cat. No. 10220Q   Form **W-4** (2017)

Exhibit 9.4. The employer sends one copy of Form W-2 to the Social Security Administration and other copies to the employee.

Employers are required to file the **Employer's Quarterly Federal Tax Return, Form 941** no later than one month after each quarter ends. This form reports the amounts due and paid to the government for federal withholdings. Failure to pay withheld taxes in a timely manner is serious. The government has the right to impose significant penalties and can even close a business, seize its assets, and take legal action against those who fail to pay taxes due.

Social Security and Medicare Taxes (FICA)

Congress adopted the Federal Insurance Contributions Act (FICA) to provide funding for the Social Security and Medicare programs. **Social Security** provides qualified individuals with old age, survivor's, and disability insurance (OASDI); **Medicare** provides health insurance. During their working years, employees pay a percentage of their earnings (up to a specified limit) to the federal government for Social Security. At retirement, a qualified person is entitled to receive monthly Social Security payments. Workers who become disabled before retirement are eligible to receive disability benefits. If a worker or retired person dies, any legal dependents are eligible to receive survivor benefits.

In order to meet the required benefit payments, Congress has frequently increased the amount of earnings to which the rates apply. Future changes in FICA tax rates and earnings maximums are likely. These changes will affect only the amount of FICA taxes, however, not how to account for them. *To simplify computations, this text assumes a Social Security rate of 6 percent on the first $110,000 of income and a Medicare*

©zimmytws/123RF

EXHIBIT 9.4

Wage and Tax Statement Form W-2

[Form W-2 Wage and Tax Statement 2017, Copy A For Social Security Administration, Department of the Treasury—Internal Revenue Service, Cat. No. 10134D]

rate of 1.5 percent on all earnings.[3] For example, an employee earning $100,000 per year will have the following FICA taxes withheld from his or her salary:

Social Security	$100,000	×	6.0%	=	$6,000
Medicare	100,000	×	1.5%	=	1,500
Total withheld					$7,500

Not only employees are required to pay FICA taxes; the FICA legislation requires employers to pay a matching amount. The total FICA tax paid to the federal government for an employee earning $100,000 per year is $15,000 ($7,500 × 2), half paid by the employee and half paid by the employer. We discuss accounting for employer taxes later in the chapter.

Voluntary Withholdings (Deductions)

One reason governments require employers to withhold taxes from employee earnings is that many people have difficulty managing their spending. If employees received their gross earnings amount, they might not be able to pay their taxes because they would spend the money on other things first. Many people have this tendency with regard to other spending

---

[3]The actual 2017 rate for Social Security is 6.2% on the first $127,200 of income. The actual 2017 rate for Medicare is 1.45% on the first $200,000 of income and 2.35% above $200,000.

responsibilities as well. To ensure they make important payments, they voluntarily allow their employer to withhold money from their salaries. The employer then uses the money withheld to make payment in the employees' names for such items as medical insurance premiums, union dues, charitable contributions, and contributions to private retirement funds or savings accounts. Even employees who manage their personal finances without difficulty find it convenient to allow their employers to withhold funds and make payments on their behalf.

Withholding voluntary deductions from an employee's gross earnings represents a service on the employer's part. The employer must deduct the amounts authorized by each employee and remit the withheld money to the proper recipients. The employer must maintain additional records and undertake additional transactions to ensure the proper amounts are withheld and paid as specified on a timely basis. Employers normally itemize all deductions from gross pay on the pay stub to explain how an employee's net pay was determined.

Computing Employee Net Pay

Net pay is the employee's gross earnings less all deductions (withholdings). Net pay, often called take-home pay, is the amount of cash the employee receives from the employer.

To illustrate, assume that Herrera Supply Company (HSC) has an employee named Sarah Jennings. Ms. Jennings earns a monthly salary of $6,000. Based on Ms. Jennings' Form W-4, the tax tables require withholding $450 per month for income taxes. Because Ms. Jennings earns less than $110,000 per year, her full monthly salary is subject to FICA withholdings. Ms. Jennings has authorized HSC to deduct $320 per month for medical insurance and $25 per month for a charitable contribution to the American Cancer Society. Ms. Jennings' net pay is computed as follows:

Gross monthly salary		$6,000
Deductions		
Federal income taxes	$450	
FICA Tax—Social Security ($6,000 × 6%)	360	
FICA Tax—Medicare ($6,000 × 1.5%)	90	
Medical insurance premiums	320	
American Cancer Society	25	
Total deductions		1,245
Net pay		$4,755

The journal entry to recognize salary expense for Ms. Jennings and its effects on HSC's financial statements are shown next:

Account Title	Debit	Credit
Salary Expense	6,000	
Employee Income Tax Payable		450
FICA Tax—Social Security Payable		360
FICA Tax—Medicare Payable		90
Medical Insurance Premiums Payable		320
American Cancer Society Payable		25
Cash		4,755

Assets	=	Liab.	+	Equity		Rev.	−	Exp.	=	Net Inc.		Cash Flow
Cash	=	Various Payables	+	Com. Stk. + Ret. Earn.								
(4,755)	=	1,245	+	NA + (6,000)		NA	−	6,000	=	(6,000)		(4,755) OA

Employer Payroll Taxes

As mentioned earlier, employers are required to match employees' FICA taxes, and FICA tax rates are subject to change. This text uses the same assumed tax rates for employers as it uses for employees. *Assume a Social Security rate of 6 percent on the first $110,000 of each employee's earnings and a Medicare rate of 1.5 percent on all earnings.* The employer's portion of FICA taxes is a payroll tax expense to the employer.

Employers also incur a payroll tax expense for *unemployment* taxes. Congress adopted the **Federal Unemployment Tax Act (FUTA)** to finance temporary relief to qualified *unemployed* persons. The tax is determined by multiplying the wages of employees (up to a specified maximum limit) by a specified rate. The FUTA tax provides money to both state and federal government workforce agencies. States may enact supplemental unemployment tax laws based on higher maximum earnings or tax rates and could assess employees, rather than employers, for all or part of the supplemental coverage.

As of January 2017, the unemployment tax rate was 6.0 percent of the first $7,000 of wages earned by each employee during a calendar year. FUTA allows employers a credit of up to 5.4 percent for amounts paid to a state unemployment program, leaving a rate of 0.6 percent to be paid to the federal government. For example, on a tax of $420 (6.0% × $7,000), an employer would pay $42 (0.6% × $7,000) to the federal government and $378 (5.4% × $7,000) to the state government. State governments receive a larger percentage because they are responsible for administering the unemployment programs. The rates may be reduced to reward employers with few or no unemployment claims.

Recording and Reporting Payroll Taxes

To illustrate computing employer payroll tax expense, return to HSC's employee, Ms. Jennings, who earns $6,000 per month. HSC's February payroll tax expense for Ms. Jennings is computed as follows:

FICA tax expense—Social Security ($6,000 × 6%)	$360
FICA tax expense—Medicare ($6,000 × 1.5%)	90
Federal unemployment tax expense ($1,000 × 0.6%)	6
State unemployment tax expense ($1,000 × 5.4%)	54
Total payroll tax expense	$510

The unemployment taxes apply only to the first $7,000 of income earned each year by each employee. Because Ms. Jennings earned $6,000 in January, unemployment tax only applies to $1,000 of her February salary. The journal entry to record the payroll tax expense and its effects on the financial statements are shown next:

Account Title	Debit	Credit
Payroll Tax Expense	510	
FICA Tax—Social Security Payable		360
FICA Tax—Medicare Payable		90
Federal Unemployment Tax Payable		6
State Unemployment Tax Payable		54

Assets	=	Liab.	+	Equity		Rev.	−	Exp.	=	Net Inc.	Cash Flow
Cash	=	Various Payables	+	Com. Stk. + Ret. Earn.							
NA	=	510	+	NA + (510)		NA	−	510	=	(510)	NA

>
> **CHECK YOURSELF 9.3**
>
> Bill Chavez, an employee of Bombay Company, earns a salary of $110,000 per year. Based on the tax rates assumed in this chapter, determine the annual payroll tax expense Bombay Company would incur with respect to Mr. Chavez. How much payroll tax would Mr. Chavez be required to pay?
>
> **Answer**
>
> | Payroll Tax Expense for Bombay Company | |
> |---|---:|
> | FICA tax expense—Social Security ($110,000 × 6%) | $6,600 |
> | FICA tax expense—Medicare ($110,000 × 1.5%) | 1,650 |
> | Federal unemployment tax expense ($7,000 × 0.6%) | 42 |
> | State unemployment tax expense ($7,000 × 5.4%) | 378 |
> | Total payroll tax expense | $8,670 |
>
> Mr. Chavez would not pay any payroll taxes. Payroll taxes apply to employers, not employees.

Employee Fringe Benefits

In addition to salaries and wages, many employers provide their employees with a variety of fringe benefits such as paid vacations, sick leave, maternity leave, and medical, dental, life, and disability insurance. These benefits plus payroll taxes frequently amount to as much as 25 percent of the employees' gross salaries and wages. Fringe benefits are reported as expenses on the income statement.

To illustrate, assume HSC provides the following fringe benefits to an employee, Alice Worthington. Ms. Worthington accrues $200 per month in vacation pay. HSC pays $250 per month for Ms. Worthington's medical insurance and contributes $150 per month to a pension (retirement) program for Ms. Worthington. The monthly entry to record the accrued fringe benefits expenses and its effects on the financial statements are shown next:

Account Title	Debit	Credit
Vacation Pay Expense	200	
Employee Medical Insurance Expense	250	
Employee Pension Expense	150	
Vacation Pay Payable		200
Employee Medical Insurance Payable		250
Employee Pension Liability		150

Assets	=	Liab.	+	Equity		Rev.	−	Exp.	=	Net Inc.		Cash Flow
Cash	=	Various Payables	+	Com. Stk. + Ret. Earn.								
NA	=	600	+	NA + (600)		NA	−	600	=	(600)		NA

The Financial Analyst

Because meeting obligations on time is critical to business survival, financial analysts and creditors are interested in whether companies will have enough money available to pay bills when they are due. Most businesses provide information about their bill-paying ability by classifying their assets and liabilities according to liquidity. The more quickly an asset is converted to cash or consumed, the more *liquid* it is. Assets are usually divided into two

LO 9-6

Prepare a classified balance sheet.

Answers to The Curious Accountant

As the chapter explains, not only do employees have 7.65 percent of their wages withheld for Social Security taxes, but their employers also must pay 7.65 percent, which is $1.91 per hour for someone being paid $25 per hour. Additionally, federal and state unemployment insurance taxes must be paid. Workers' compensation insurance must be provided to assist workers who are injured on the job. In addition, there are the benefits that Rusty voluntarily provides his workers, such as health care, vacation pay, and contributions to their retirement plans. According to the U.S. Bureau of Labor Statistics (BLS), in 2016 the average pay for plumbers was around $25 per hour. The BLS further reported that benefits for workers in private industry averaged 43.3 percent of their base pay.

Based on the information provided by the BLS survey, fringe benefits and payroll taxes would increase Rusty's payroll costs per hour by around $10.83 ($25 × 0.433), bringing the total cost to $35.83. An additional problem is that Rusty can charge his customers only for "billable hours," but he must pay his employees for 40 hours per week. Obviously plumbers cannot work 40 billable hours per week because they must travel from job to job. The $25 markup Rusty is charging his customers ($50 − $25) has to pay for these nonbillable hours, as well as his employees' fringe benefits and, he hopes, a profit.

major classifications: *current* and *noncurrent*. Current items are also referred to as *short term* and noncurrent items as *long term*.

Preparing a Classified Balance Sheet

A **current (short-term) asset** is expected to be converted to cash or consumed within one year or an operating cycle, whichever is longer. An **operating cycle** is defined as the average time it takes a business to convert cash to inventory, inventory to accounts receivable, and accounts receivable back to cash. The financial tools used to measure the length of an operating cycle for particular businesses are discussed in Chapter 7. For most businesses, the operating cycle is less than one year. As a result, the one-year rule normally prevails with respect to classifying assets as current. The current assets section of a balance sheet typically includes the following items:

> Current Assets
>   Cash
>   Marketable securities
>   Accounts receivable
>   Short-term notes receivable
>   Interest receivable
>   Inventory
>   Supplies
>   Prepaid items

Given the definition of current assets, it seems reasonable to assume that **current (short-term) liabilities** would be those due within one year or an operating cycle, whichever is longer. This assumption is usually correct. However, an exception is made for long-term renewable debt. For example, consider a liability that was issued with a 20-year term to maturity. After 19 years, the liability becomes due within one year and is, therefore, a current liability. Even so, the liability will be classified as long term if the company plans to issue new long-term debt and to use the proceeds from that debt to repay the maturing liability. This situation is described as *refinancing short-term debt on a long-term basis*. In general, if a business does not plan to use any of its current assets to repay a debt, that debt is listed as long term even if it is due within one year. The current liabilities section of a balance sheet typically includes the following items:

> **Current Liabilities**
> Accounts payable
> Short-term notes payable
> Wages payable
> Taxes payable
> Interest Payable

Balance sheets that distinguish between current and noncurrent items are called **classified balance sheets.** To enhance the usefulness of accounting information, most real-world balance sheets are classified. Exhibit 9.5 displays an example of a classified balance sheet.

EXHIBIT 9.5

LIMBAUGH COMPANY
Classified Balance Sheet
As of December 31, Year 1

Assets

Current Assets
Cash		$ 20,000	
Accounts receivable		35,000	
Inventory		230,000	
Prepaid rent		3,600	
Total current assets			$288,600

Property, Plant, and Equipment
Office equipment	$ 80,000		
Less: Accumulated depreciation	(25,000)	55,000	
Building	340,000		
Less: Accumulated depreciation	(40,000)	300,000	
Land		120,000	
Total property, plant, and equipment			475,000
Total assets			$763,600

Liabilities and Stockholders' Equity

Current Liabilities
Accounts payable	$ 32,000	
Notes payable	120,000	
Salaries payable	32,000	
Unearned revenue	9,800	
Total current liabilities		$193,800

Long-Term Liabilities
Notes payable		100,000
Total liabilities		293,800

Stockholders' Equity
Common stock	200,000	
Retained earnings	269,800	469,800
Total liabilities and stockholders' equity		$763,600

Liquidity versus Solvency

Liquidity describes the ability to generate sufficient short-term cash flows to pay obligations as they come due. **Solvency** is the ability to repay liabilities in the long run. Liquidity and solvency are both important to the survival of a business. Financial analysts rely on several ratios to help them evaluate a company's liquidity and solvency. The *debt-to-assets* ratio introduced in Chapter 3 is one tool used to measure solvency. The primary ratio used to evaluate liquidity is the current ratio.

LO 9-7

Use the current ratio to assess the level of liquidity.

The **current ratio** is defined as:

$$\frac{\text{Current assets}}{\text{Current liabilities}}$$

Because current assets normally exceed current liabilities, this ratio is usually greater than 100 percent. For example, if a company has $250 in current assets and $100 in current liabilities, current assets are 250 percent of current liabilities. The current ratio is traditionally expressed as a decimal rather than as a percentage, however; most analysts would describe this example as a current ratio of 2.5 to 1 ($250 ÷ $100 = $2.50 in current assets for every $1 in current liabilities). This book uses the traditional format when referring to the current ratio.

The current ratio is among the most widely used ratios in analyzing financial statements. Current ratios can be too high, as well as too low. A low ratio suggests that the company may have difficulty paying its short-term obligations. A high ratio suggests that a

FOCUS ON INTERNATIONAL ISSUES

WHY ARE THESE BALANCE SHEETS BACKWARD?

As discussed in earlier chapters, most industrialized countries require companies to use international financial accounting standards (IFRS), which are similar to the GAAP used in the United States. The globalization of accounting standards should, therefore, make it easier to read a company's annual report regardless of its country of origin. However, there are still language differences between companies; German companies prepare their financial reports using IFRS, but in German, while UK companies use English.

Suppose language is not an issue. For example, companies in the United States, the United Kingdom (UK), and even India, prepare their annual reports in English. Thus, one would expect to find few differences between financial reports prepared by companies in these countries.

©david pearson/Alamy

However, if a person who learned accounting in the United States looks at the balance sheet of a UK company, he or she might think the statement is a bit "backward," and likewise, the balance sheet of an Indian company might seem upside down.

Like U.S. companies, UK companies report assets at the top, or left, of the balance sheet, and liabilities and stockholders' equity on the bottom or right. However, unlike the United States, UK companies typically show long-term assets before current assets. Even more different are balance sheets of Indian companies, which begin with stockholders' equity and then liabilities at the top or left, and then show assets on the bottom or right. Like the UK statements, those in India show long-term assets before current assets. Realize that most of the accounting rules established by IFRS or U.S. GAAP deal with measurement issues. Assets can be measured using the same rules but they may be disclosed in different manners. IFRS requires companies to classify assets and liabilities as current versus noncurrent, but the order in which these categories are listed on the balance sheet is not specified.

For an example of a financial statement for a UK company, go to www.itvplc.com. Click on "Investors" and then "Reports and Results." For an example of an Indian company's annual report, go to www.colgatepalmolive.co.in. Click on "For Investors," then "Financials Reports," and then on "Annual Report."

company is not maximizing its earnings potential because investments in liquid assets usually do not earn as much money as investments in other assets. Companies must try to maintain an effective balance between liquid assets (so they can pay bills on time) and nonliquid assets (so they can earn a good return).

Real-World Data

Exhibit 9.6 presents the current ratios and debt-to-assets ratios for six companies in three different industries. These data are for the 2016 fiscal year.

EXHIBIT 9.6

Industry	Company	Current Ratio	Debt-to-Assets Ratio
Electric utilities	American Electric Power	0.64	0.73
	Dominion Resources	0.52	0.76
Clothing stores	American Eagle Outfitters	1.56	0.35
	The Gap	1.57	0.66
Building supplies	Home Depot	1.36	0.85
	Lowe's	1.01	0.75

Upon reviewing the data in Exhibit 9.6, one might conclude that the two electric utilities have more credit risks than the two clothing stores. After all, Dominion Resources and American Electric Power have much lower current ratios and higher debt-to-assets ratios, but they do not necessarily have higher credit risk. The ratios of clothing stores and electric utilities may not be comparable because their industries are very different. If the economy turns downward, people are more likely to continue to use electricity than they are to spend money on new clothes. Because utility companies have a stable source of revenue, creditors are likely to feel comfortable with higher levels of debt for them than they would for clothing companies. Utilities have traditionally had relatively high debt-to-assets ratios.

What about the high debt-to-assets ratios of the companies in the building supplies business. When the economy is bad, housing construction is often one of the first industries to feel the effects, so why are Home Depot's and Lowes' debt-to-assets ratios so high? In this situation, the cause is due to macroeconomic policy. In 2016, and the few preceding years, interest rates were very low due to the policies of the Federal Reserve. The low interest rates caused many companies to increase their financing through debt, and decrease their financing through equity. This was accomplished by buying back some of their outstanding common stock, an issue discussed in Chapter 11. Just three years earlier, in 2013, Home Depot's and Lowes' debt-to-assets ratios were only 0.57 and 0.58, respectively. Finally, notice that while the building supplies companies have debt-to-assets ratios in line with the electric utilities, their current ratios are much higher, and similar to each other's. As the data in Exhibit 9.6 demonstrate, financial ratios are often grouped by industry.

A Look Back

Chapter 9 discussed accounting for current liabilities and payroll. Current liabilities are obligations due within one year or the company's operating cycle, whichever is longer. The chapter expanded the discussion of promissory notes begun in Chapter 7. Chapter 7 introduced accounting for the note payee, the lender; Chapter 9 discussed accounting for the note maker (issuer), the borrower. Notes payable and related interest payable are reported as liabilities on the balance sheet. Chapter 9 also discussed accounting for sales tax liabilities, warranty obligations, and contingent liabilities.

Payroll costs and payroll taxes constitute a major expense for most businesses. An employer is responsible for withholding money from an employee's salary. The most common withholdings are for federal income taxes, FICA taxes, insurance premiums, savings or retirement contributions, union dues, and charitable donations. The employer uses the withholdings to pay the employees' obligations. The difference between the *gross pay* and the money withheld is called net pay. The *net pay* is the amount of cash the employer pays to the employee.

In addition to making payments for its employees, the employer is responsible for certain taxes on its employees' salaries and wages. These taxes are called payroll taxes. They include matching FICA Social Security and Medicare taxes, and federal and state unemployment taxes. Governments periodically change the rates of these taxes. The accounting for them, however, is not affected by rate changes. The rates used in this text are as follows: FICA Social Security—6 percent of the first $110,000 of each employee's wages with a matching payment for the employer; FICA Medicare—1.5 percent of the total wages of each employee with a matching payment for the employer; federal unemployment taxes—0.6 percent (6.0 percent less a 5.4 percent credit for state unemployment taxes) of the first $7,000 of each employee's wages; and state unemployment—5.4 percent of the first $7,000 of each employee's wages.

Finally, Chapter 9 discussed assessing companies' liquidity. The current ratio is current assets divided by current liabilities. The higher the current ratio, the more liquid the business.

A Look Forward

Chapter 10 investigates issues related to accounting for long-term liabilities. As you will learn, income tax consequences enter into decisions to borrow money.

APPENDIX

Accounting for Discount Notes

All notes payable discussed previously have been "add-on" **interest-bearing notes.** The amount due at maturity for add-on notes is the *face value* of the note *plus accrued interest*. In contrast, the interest on a **discount note** is included in the face value of the note. A $5,000 face value discount note is repaid with $5,000 cash at maturity. This payment includes both principal and accrued interest.

Show how discount notes and related interest charges affect financial statements.

Accounting Events Affecting Year 1

To illustrate, assume Beacon Management Services experienced the following four events in Year 1: (1) borrowed money by issuing a discount note; (2) recognized operating expenses; (3) recognized revenue; and (4) recognized accrued interest.

EVENT 1 **Beacon Management Services was started when it issued a $10,000 face value discount note to State Bank on March 1, Year 1.**

The note had a 9 percent *discount rate* and a one-year term to maturity. As with interest-bearing notes, the *issuer* of a discount note exchanges the promissory note for cash. Accounting for the discount note requires dividing the face amount between the **discount** and the **principal,** or **proceeds** (amount of cash borrowed). The discount is computed by multiplying the face value of the note by the interest rate by the time period. Subtracting the discount from the face value of the note determines the principal (proceeds). The computations follow:

Face value of note	$10,000
Less discount ($10,000 × 0.09 × 1) =	900
Proceeds (amount borrowed)	$ 9,100

On the issue date, both assets and liabilities increase by the amount borrowed (the $9,100 principal). The borrowing transaction on the issue date has no effect on the income statement. The $9,100 cash inflow is reported in the financing activities section of the statement of cash flows. The journal entry to record issuing the discount note and its effects on the financial statements are shown next:

Account Title	Debit	Credit
Cash	9,100	
Discount on Notes Payable	900	
Notes Payable		10,000

Event No.	Assets	=	Liabilities			+	Equity			Rev.	−	Exp.	=	Net Inc.	Cash Flow
	Cash	=	Notes Pay.	−	Disc. on N/P	+	Com. Stk.	+	Ret. Earn.						
1	9,100	=	10,000	−	900	+	NA	+	NA	NA	−	NA	=	NA	9,100 FA

The discount is recorded in a **contra liability account** called **Discount on Notes Payable**. The *carrying value* of the liability is the difference between the Notes Payable and Discount accounts. Carrying value, also called *book value*, is the amount at which the liability is carried on the books. In this case, the Notes Payable account in Beacon's ledger has a $10,000 credit balance, while the Discount on Notes Payable account has a $900 debit balance. The carrying value on the issue date is as follows:

Notes Payable	$10,000
Discount on Notes Payable	(900)
Carrying value of liability	$ 9,100

EVENT 2 Beacon incurred $8,000 of cash operating expenses.

Paying these expenses reduces both assets and stockholders' equity. The effect on the income statement is to increase expenses and decrease net income. The cash outflow is reported in the operating activities section of the statement of cash flows. The journal entry and its effects on the financial statements are shown next:

Account Title	Debit	Credit
Operating Expenses	8,000	
Cash		8,000

Event No.	Assets	=	Liabilities			+	Equity			Rev.	−	Exp.	=	Net Inc.	Cash Flow
	Cash	=	Notes Pay.	−	Disc. on N/P	+	Com. Stk.	+	Ret. Earn.						
2	(8,000)	=	NA	−	NA	+	NA	+	(8,000)	NA	−	(8,000)	=	(8,000)	(8,000) OA

EVENT 3 Beacon recognized $12,000 of cash service revenue.

Recognizing revenue increases both assets and stockholders' equity. Net income increases. The cash inflow is reported in the operating activities section of the statement of cash flows. The journal entry and its effects on the financial statements are shown next:

Account Title	Debit	Credit
Cash	12,000	
Service Revenue		12,000

Event No.	Assets	=	Liabilities			+	Equity			Rev.	−	Exp.	=	Net Inc.	Cash Flow
	Cash	=	Notes Pay.	−	Disc. on N/P	+	Com. Stk.	+	Ret. Earn.						
3	12,000	=	NA	−	NA	+	NA	+	12,000	12,000	−	NA	=	12,000	12,000 OA

EVENT 4 Beacon recorded an adjusting entry to recognize interest accrued since March 1.

On December 31, Year 1, Beacon must adjust its accounting records to recognize the 10 months of interest expense it incurred in Year 1. For this note, interest expense accrues at $75 per month ($900 discount ÷ 12). As of December 31, $750 ($75 × 10) of interest expense has accrued. Because no cash payment is due until the note matures in Year 2, the reduction in equity from recognizing the interest expense is accompanied by an increase in liabilities.

The increase in liabilities is recorded by *reducing the contra liability account,* Discount on Notes Payable. Recall that the carrying value of the liability was $9,100 on the day the note was issued. The adjusting entry to record the accrued interest expense removes $750 from the Discount account, leaving a discount balance of $150 ($900 − $750) after the adjusting entry is posted.

The bookkeeping technique of converting the discount to interest expense over the term of the loan is described as **amortizing** the discount. After amortizing 10 months' interest expense, the carrying value of the liability reported on the December 31, Year 1, balance sheet (see Exhibit 9.7) is $9,850 ($10,000 face value − $150 discount). The effect of the interest recognition on the income statement is to increase expenses and decrease net income by $750. The statement of cash flows is not affected by the accrual. Beacon recognizes the cash effects of the interest on the maturity date when it pays the maturity (face) value of the note to State Bank.

The journal entry to amortize the discount and its effects on the financial statements are shown next:

Account Title	Debit	Credit
Interest Expense	750	
Discount on Notes Payable		750

Event No.	Assets	=	Liabilities			+	Equity			Rev.	−	Exp.	=	Net Inc.	Cash Flow
	Cash	=	Notes Pay.	−	Disc. on N/P	+	Com. Stk.	+	Ret. Earn.						
4	NA	=	NA	−	(750)	+	NA	+	(750)	NA	−	750	=	(750)	NA

General Ledger T-Accounts and Financial Statements

Panel A of Exhibit 9.7 summarizes the Year 1 accounting events. Panel B presents the ledger accounts in T-account form. The event numbers are shown in the T-accounts to facilitate your review. The closing entries are included and referenced with the abbreviation "cl." The financial statements are shown parenthetically in Panel C of the exhibit. You should study Exhibit 9.7 to strengthen your understanding of how the accounting for discount notes affects the financial statements.

EXHIBIT 9.7

The Big Picture

Panel A: Transaction Summary

1. Beacon issued a $10,000 face value, one-year, discount note with a 9 percent discount rate.
2. Beacon paid $8,000 cash for operating expenses.
3. Beacon earned cash service revenue of $12,000.
4. Beacon recognized $750 of accrued interest expense.
5. Beacon closed the revenue and expense accounts. The letters *cl* are the posting reference for the closing entry.

Panel B: General Ledger

Assets = Liabilities + Equity

Cash			
(1)	9,100	8,000	(2)
(3)	12,000		
Bal.	13,100		

Notes Payable			
		10,000	(1)
		10,000	Bal.

Discount on Notes Payable			
(1)	900	750	(4)
Bal.	150		

Retained Earnings			
		3,250	(cl.)
		3,250	Bal.

Service Revenue			
(cl.)	12,000	12,000	(3)
		0	Bal.

Operating Expenses			
(2)	8,000	8,000	(cl.)
Bal.	0		

Interest Expense			
(4)	750	750	(cl.)
Bal.	0		

Panel C: Financial Statements for Year 1

Income Statement

Service revenue	$12,000
Operating expenses	(8,000)
Operating income	4,000
Interest expense	(750)
Net income	$ 3,250

Balance Sheet

Assets		
Cash		$13,100
Liabilities		
Notes payable	$10,000	
Less: Disc. on notes pay.	(150)	
Total liabilities		$ 9,850
Stockholders' equity		
Retained earnings		3,250
Total liab. and stockholders' equity		$13,100

Statement of Cash Flows

Operating Activities		
Inflow from customers		$12,000
Outflow for expenses		(8,000)
Net inflow from operating activities		4,000
Investing Activities		0
Financing Activities		
Inflow from creditors		9,100
Net change in cash		13,100
Plus: Beginning cash balance		0
Ending cash balance		$13,100

Accounting Events Affecting Year 2

In Year 2, Beacon Management Services experienced the following four accounting events: (1) recognized accrued interest for Year 2; (2) paid the face value of the note; (3) recognized revenue; and (4) recognized operating expenses.

EVENT 1 Beacon recorded an adjusting entry to recognize the interest that had accrued since December 31, Year 1.

Because the note had a one-year term, interest for two months remains to be accrued at the maturity date on February 28, Year 2. Interest on this note accrues at $75 per month

($900 discount ÷ 12), so there is $150 ($75 × 2) of interest expense to recognize in Year 2. Recognizing the interest increases liabilities (the Discount account is reduced to zero) and decreases stockholders' equity. The effect on the income statement of recognizing interest is to increase expenses and decrease net income by $150. The statement of cash flows is not affected by the interest recognition. The journal entry and its effects on the financial statements are shown next:

Account Title	Debit	Credit
Interest Expense	150	
Discount on Notes Payable		150

Event No.	Assets	=	Liabilities	+	Equity	Rev.	−	Exp.	=	Net Inc.	Cash Flow
	Cash	=	Notes Pay. − Disc. on N/P	+	Com. Stk. + Ret. Earn.						
1	NA	=	NA − (150)	+	NA + (150)	NA	−	150	=	(150)	NA

EVENT 2 Beacon paid the face value of the note.

The face value ($10,000) of the note is due on the maturity date. Paying the maturity value is an asset use transaction that decreases both assets and liabilities. The income statement is not affected by the payment. The $10,000 cash payment includes $900 for interest and $9,100 for principal. On the statement of cash flows, a $900 outflow for interest is reported in the operating activities section and a $9,100 outflow for repaying the loan is reported in the financing activities section. The journal entry and its effects on the financial statements are shown next:

Account Title	Debit	Credit
Notes Payable	10,000	
Cash		10,000

Event No.	Assets	=	Liabilities	+	Equity	Rev.	−	Exp.	=	Net Inc.	Cash Flow
	Cash	=	Notes Pay. − Disc. on N/P	+	Com. Stk. + Ret. Earn.						
2	(10,000)	=	(10,000) − NA	+	NA + NA	NA	−	NA	=	NA	(900) OA (9,100) FA

EVENT 3 Beacon recognized $13,000 of cash service revenue.

Recognizing the revenue increases both assets and stockholders' equity. Net income also increases. The cash inflow is reported in the operating activities section of the statement of cash flows. The journal entry and its effects on the financial statements are shown next:

Account Title	Debit	Credit
Cash	13,000	
Service Revenue		13,000

Event No.	Assets	=	Liabilities	+	Equity	Rev.	−	Exp.	=	Net Inc.	Cash Flow
	Cash	=	Notes Pay. − Disc. on N/P	+	Com. Stk. + Ret. Earn.						
3	13,000	=	NA − NA	+	NA + 13,000	13,000	−	NA	=	13,000	13,000 OA

EVENT 4 Beacon incurred $8,500 of cash operating expenses.

This event decreases both assets and stockholders' equity. Net income also decreases. The cash outflow is reported in the operating activities section of the statement of cash flows. The journal entry and its effects on the financial statements are shown next:

Account Title	Debit	Credit
Operating Expenses	8,500	
Cash		8,500

Event No.	Assets	=	Liabilities	+	Equity	Rev.	−	Exp.	=	Net Inc.	Cash Flow
	Cash	=	Notes Pay. − Disc. on N/P	+	Com. Stk. + Ret. Earn.						
4	(8,500)	=	NA − NA	+	NA + (8,500)	NA	−	8,500	=	(8,500)	(8,500) OA

General Ledger T-Accounts and Financial Statements

Panel A of Exhibit 9.8 summarizes the Year 2 accounting events. Panel B presents the ledger accounts in T-account form. The event numbers are shown in the T-accounts to facilitate

EXHIBIT 9.8
The Big Picture

Panel A: Transaction Summary

Event 1 Recognized $150 of accrued interest for Year 2.
Event 2 Paid the $10,000 face value of note.
Event 3 Recognized $13,000 of revenue.
Event 4 Recognized $8,500 of operating expenses.

Panel B: General Ledger

Assets = **Liabilities** + **Equity**

Cash
Bal.	13,100	10,000	(2)	
(3)	13,000	8,500	(4)	
Bal.	7,600			

Notes Payable
(2)	10,000	10,000	Bal.	
		0	Bal.	

Discount on Notes Payable
Bal.	150	150	(1)	
Bal.	0			

Retained Earnings
		3,250	Bal.	
		4,350	(cl.)	
		7,600	Bal.	

Service Revenue
(cl.)	13,000	13,000	(3)	
		0	Bal.	

Operating Expenses
(4)	8,500	8,500	(cl.)	
Bal.	0			

Interest Expense
(1)	150	150	(cl.)	
Bal.	0			

continued

EXHIBIT 9.8 Concluded

Panel C: Financial Statements for Year 2

Income Statement

Service revenue	$13,000
Operating expenses	(8,500)
Operating income	4,500
Interest expense	(150)
Net income	$ 4,350

Balance Sheet

Assets	
Cash	$7,600
Liabilities	$ 0
Stockholders' equity	
Retained earnings	7,600
Total liab. and stockholders' equity	$7,600

Statement of Cash Flows

Operating Activities	
Inflow from customers	$13,000
Outflow for expenses	(8,500)
Outflow for interest	(900)
Net inflow from operating activities	3,600
Investing Activities	0
Financing Activities	
Outflow to creditors	(9,100)
Net change in cash	(5,500)
Plus: Beginning cash balance	13,100
Ending cash balance	$ 7,600

your review. The closing entries are included and referenced with the abbreviation "cl." The financial statements are shown parenthetically in Panel C of the exhibit.

You should study Exhibit 9.8 to strengthen your understanding of how accounting for discount notes affects the financial statements. Observe that no liabilities are reported in the balance sheet because Beacon has paid off the note and interest before the closing date. Because Beacon has not paid dividends since its inception, retained earning represents the sum of net income recognized for Year 1 and Year 2.

SELF-STUDY REVIEW PROBLEM

A step-by-step audio-narrated series of slides is available in **Connect.**

Perfect Picture Inc. (PPI) experienced the following transactions during Year 1. The transactions are summarized (transaction data pertain to the full year) and limited to those that affect the company's current liabilities.

1. PPI had cash sales of $820,000. The state requires that PPI charge customers an 8 percent sales tax (ignore cost of goods sold).
2. PPI paid the state sales tax authority $63,000.
3. On March 1, PPI issued a note payable to County Bank. PPI received $50,000 cash (principal balance). The note had a one-year term and a 6 percent annual interest rate.
4. On December 31, PPI recognized accrued interest on the note issued in Event 3.
5. On December 31, PPI recognized warranty expense at the rate of 3 percent of sales.
6. PPI paid $22,000 cash to settle warranty claims.
7. PPI has five employees. Four of the employees each earn $40,000 per year. The fifth employee, the store manager, earns $120,000 per year. The annual amount withheld for income tax for all employees is $54,000. Each of the five employees has volunteered to have $50 per month withheld as a charitable contribution to the United Way. Record the net pay as a liability.
8. Based on the salary data described in Event 7, PPI recognized payroll tax expense for FICA and unemployment taxes.
9. During the year, PPI remitted the following amounts of cash in partial settlement of the indicated liabilities:

Employee income tax payable	$ 52,000
FICA tax—Social Security payable	27,000
FICA tax—Medicare payable	7,000
United Way payable	2,500
Salaries payable	190,250
Federal unemployment tax payable	200
State unemployment tax payable	1,500

10. PPI pays $320 per month for medical insurance premiums for each employee. The company also contributes an amount equal to 4 percent of salaries to a pension fund for each employee. Each employee accrues vacation pay at a rate of $300 per month.

11. During the year, PPI remitted the following amount of cash in partial settlement of the indicated liabilities:

Medical insurance payable	$18,000
Employee pension fund payable	8,200
Vacation pay payable	16,400

Required

a. Prepare in general journal form the entries to record the transactions described above.
b. Prepare the current liabilities section of the December 31, Year 1, balance sheet.

Solution to Requirement *a*

Event No.	Account Title	Debit	Credit
1	Cash	885,600	
	Sales Revenue		820,000
	Sales Tax Payable		65,600
2	Sales Tax Payable	63,000	
	Cash		63,000
3	Cash	50,000	
	Notes Payable		50,000
4	Interest Expense ($50,000 × 0.06 × 10/12)	2,500	
	Interest Payable		2,500
5	Warranty Expense ($820,000 × 0.03)	24,600	
	Warranties Payable		24,600
6	Warranties Payable	22,000	
	Cash		22,000
7	Salary Expense [(4 × $40,000) + $120,000]	280,000	
	Employee Income Tax Payable		54,000
	FICA Tax—Social Security Payable*		16,200
	FICA Tax—Medicare Payable ($280,000 × 0.015)		4,200
	United Way Payable ($50 × 5 × 12)		3,000
	Salaries Payable		202,600
8	Payroll Tax Expense	22,500	
	FICA Tax—Social Security Payable*		16,200
	FICA Tax—Medicare Payable ($280,000 × 0.015)		4,200
	Federal Unemployment Tax Payable ($7,000 × 5 × 0.006)		210
	State Unemployment Tax Payable ($7,000 × 5 × 0.054)		1,890
			continued

*Recall that the chapter assumes Social Security tax is applied to a maximum limit of $110,000.
[($40,000 × 0.06 = $2,400 × 4 = $9,600) + ($110,000 × 0.06 = $6,600)] = $16,200

Event No.	Account Title	Debit	Credit
9	Employee Income Tax Payable	52,000	
	FICA Tax—Social Security Payable	27,000	
	FICA Tax—Medicare Payable	7,000	
	United Way Payable	2,500	
	Salaries Payable	190,250	
	Federal Unemployment Tax Payable	200	
	State Unemployment Tax Payable	1,500	
	Cash		280,450
10	Fringe Benefits Expense	48,400	
	Medical Insurance Payable ($320 × 12 × 5)		19,200
	Employee Pension Fund Payable ($280,000 × 0.04)		11,200
	Vacation Pay Payable ($300 × 12 × 5)		18,000
11	Medical Insurance Payable	18,000	
	Employee Pension Fund Payable	8,200	
	Vacation Pay Payable	16,400	
	Cash		42,600

Solution to Requirement b

PERFECT PICTURE INC.
Partial Balance Sheet
December 31, Year 1

Current Liabilities

Sales tax payable ($65,600 − $63,000)	$ 2,600
Notes payable	50,000
Interest payable	2,500
Warranties payable ($24,600 − $22,000)	2,600
Employee income tax payable ($54,000 − $52,000)	2,000
FICA—Social Security payable ($16,200 + $16,200 − $27,000)	5,400
FICA—Medicare payable ($4,200 + $4,200 − $7,000)	1,400
United Way payable ($3,000 − $2,500)	500
Salaries payable ($202,600 − $190,250)	12,350
Federal unemployment tax payable ($210 − $200)	10
State unemployment tax payable ($1,890 − $1,500)	390
Medical insurance payable ($19,200 − $18,000)	1,200
Employee pension fund payable ($11,200 − $8,200)	3,000
Vacation pay payable ($18,000 − $16,400)	1,600
Total current liabilities	$85,550

KEY TERMS

Amortizing 501
Classified balance sheets 496
Contingent liability 483
Contra liability account 500
Current (short-term) asset 495
Current (short-term) liability 495
Current ratio 497
Discount 499
Discount note 499

Discount on Notes Payable 500
Employee 487
Employee's Withholding Allowance Certificate, Form W-4 489
Employer's Quarterly Federal Tax Return, Form 941 490
Federal Unemployment Tax Act (FUTA) 493
General uncertainties 483

Going concern assumption 478
Gross earnings 488
Independent contractor 487
Interest-bearing notes 499
Issuer 480
Liquidity 497
Medicare 490
Net pay 492
Note payable 480
Operating cycle 495
Principal 499

Proceeds 499
Salaries 488
Social Security 490
Solvency 497
Wage and Tax Statement, Form W-2 489
Wages 488
Warranties 484

QUESTIONS

1. What type of transaction is a cash payment to creditors? How does this type of transaction affect the accounting equation?
2. What is a current liability? Distinguish between a current liability and a long-term debt.
3. What is included in the entry to record accrued interest expense? How does it affect the accounting equation?
4. Who is the maker of a note payable?
5. What is the going concern assumption? Does it affect the way liabilities are reported in the financial statements?
6. Why is it necessary to make an adjusting entry at the end of the accounting period for unpaid interest on a note payable?
7. Assume that on October 1, Year 1, Big Company borrowed $10,000 from the local bank at 6 percent interest. The note is due on October 1, Year 2. How much interest does Big pay in Year 1? How much interest does Big pay in Year 2? What amount of cash does Big pay back in Year 2?
8. When a business collects sales tax from customers, is it revenue? Why or why not?
9. What is a contingent liability?
10. List the three categories of contingent liabilities.
11. Are contingent liabilities recorded on a company's books? Explain.
12. What is the difference in accounting procedures for a liability that is probable and estimable and one that is reasonably possible but not estimable?
13. What type of liabilities are not recorded on a company's books?
14. What does the term *warranty* mean?
15. What effect does recognizing future warranty obligations have on the balance sheet? On the income statement?
16. When is warranty cost reported on the statement of cash flows?
17. What is the difference between an employee and an independent contractor?
18. What is the difference between wages and salaries?
19. What is the purpose of the W-2 form? What is the purpose of the W-4 form?
20. What two taxes are components of the FICA tax? What programs do they fund?
21. Who pays the FICA tax? Is there a ceiling on the amount of tax that is paid?
22. What is the difference between gross pay and net pay for an employee?
23. Why are amounts withheld from employees' pay considered liabilities of the employer?
24. What is the purpose of the Federal Unemployment Tax? What is the maximum amount of wages subject to the tax?
25. What items are included in compensation cost for a company in addition to the gross salaries of the employees?
26. Give two examples of fringe benefits.
27. What is a classified balance sheet?
28. What is the difference between the liquidity and the solvency of a business?
29. The higher the company's current ratio, the better the company's financial condition. Do you agree with this statement? Explain.
30. What is the difference between an interest-bearing note and a discount note?
31. How is the carrying value of a discount note computed?
32. Will the effective rate of interest be the same on a $10,000 face value, 6 percent interest-bearing note and a $10,000 face value, 6 percent discount note? Is the amount of cash received upon making these two loans the same? Why or why not?
33. How does the *amortization* of a discount affect the income statement, balance sheet, and statement of cash flows?
34. How does issuing an $8,000 discount note with an 8 percent discount rate and a one-year term to maturity affect the accounting equation?
35. What type of account is Discount on Notes Payable?

MULTIPLE-CHOICE QUESTIONS

Multiple-choice questions are available in Connect.

EXERCISES—SERIES A

All applicable Exercises in Series A are available in Connect.

LO 9-1

Exercise 9-1A *Recognizing accrued interest expense*

Abardeen Corporation borrowed $90,000 from the bank on October 1, Year 1. The note had an 8 percent annual rate of interest and matured on March 31, Year 2. Interest and principal were paid in cash on the maturity date.

Required

a. What amount of cash did Abardeen pay for interest in Year 1?
b. What amount of interest expense was recognized on the Year 1 income statement?
c. What amount of total liabilities was reported on the December 31, Year 1, balance sheet?
d. What total amount of cash was paid to the bank on March 31, Year 2, for principal and interest?
e. What amount of interest expense was reported on the Year 2 income statement?

Exercise 9-2A *Effects of recognizing accrued interest on financial statements*   LO 9-1

Bill Darby started Darby Company on January 1, Year 1. The company experienced the following events during its first year of operation:

1. Earned $16,200 of cash revenue.
2. Borrowed $12,000 cash from the bank.
3. Adjusted the accounting records to recognize accrued interest expense on the bank note. The note, issued on September 1, Year 1, had a one-year term and an 8 percent annual interest rate.

Required

a. What is the amount of interest payable at December 31, Year 1?
b. What is the amount of interest expense in Year 1?
c. What is the amount of interest paid in Year 1?
d. Use a horizontal statements model to show how each event affects the balance sheet, income statement, and statement of cash flows. Indicate whether the event increases (I), decreases (D), or does not affect (NA) each element of the financial statements. In the Statement of Cash Flows column, designate the cash flows as operating activities (OA), investing activities (IA), or financing activities (FA). The first transaction has been recorded as an example.

Event No.	Balance Sheet									Income Statement					Statement of Cash Flows
	Cash	=	Notes Pay.	+	Int. Pay.	+	Com. Stk.	+	Ret. Earn.	Rev.	−	Exp.	=	Net Inc.	
1	I	=	NA	+	NA	+	NA	+	I	I	−	NA	=	I	I OA

Exercise 9-3A *Recording sales tax*   LO 9-2

Vail Book Mart sells books and other supplies to students in a state where the sales tax rate is 8 percent. Vail Book Mart engaged in the following transactions for Year 1. Sales tax of 8 percent is collected on all sales.

1. Book sales, not including sales tax, for Year 1 amounted to $250,000 cash.
2. Cash sales of miscellaneous items in Year 1 were $85,000, not including tax.
3. Cost of goods sold was $190,000 for the year.
4. Paid $117,000 in operating expenses for the year.
5. Paid the sales tax collected to the state agency.

Required

a. What is the total amount of sales tax Vail Book Mart collected and paid for the year?
b. Prepare the journal entries for the preceding transactions.
c. What is Vail Book Mart's net income for the year?

Exercise 9-4A *Recognizing sales tax payable*   LO 9-2

The following selected transactions apply to Topeca Supply for November and December Year 1. November was the first month of operations. Sales tax is collected at the time of sale but is not paid to the state sales tax agency until the following month.

1. Cash sales for November Year 1 were $165,000, plus sales tax of 7 percent.
2. Topeca Supply paid the November sales tax to the state agency on December 10, Year 1.
3. Cash sales for December Year 1 were $180,000, plus sales tax of 7 percent.

Required

a. Record the preceding transactions in general journal form.

b. Show the effect of the preceding transactions on a horizontal statements model like the one shown next.

Assets	=	Liabilities	+	Equity		Income Statement		Cash Flow
Cash	=	Sales Tax Pay.	+	Com. Stk. + Ret. Earn.		Rev. − Exp. = Net Inc.		

c. What was the total amount of sales tax paid in Year 1?

d. What was the total amount of sales tax collected in Year 1?

e. What amount of sales tax expense will be reported on the Year 1 income statement?

LO 9-3

Exercise 9-5A Contingent liabilities

The following three independent sets of facts relate to contingent liabilities:

1. In November of the current year, an automobile manufacturing company recalled all pickup trucks manufactured during the past two years. A flaw in the battery cable was discovered and the recall provides for replacement of the defective cables. The estimated cost of this recall is $2 million.

2. The EPA has notified a company of violations of environmental laws relating to hazardous waste. These actions seek cleanup costs, penalties, and damages to property. The company is reasonably certain there will be cost associated with the cleanup, but cannot estimate the amount. The cleanup cost could be as high as $4,000,000 or as little as $500,000, and insurance could reimburse all or part of the cost. There is no way to more accurately estimate the cost to the company at this time.

3. Holland Company does not carry property damage insurance because of the cost. The company has suffered substantial losses each of the past three years. However, it has had no losses for the current year. Management thinks this is too good to be true and is sure there will be significant losses in the coming year. However, the exact amount cannot be determined.

Required

a. Discuss the various categories of contingent liabilities.

b. For each item in the preceding list, determine the correct accounting treatment. Prepare any required journal entries.

LO 9-4

Exercise 9-6A Effect of warranties on income and cash flow

To support herself while attending school, Daun Deloch sold stereo systems to other students. During the first year of operations, Daun purchased the stereo systems for $140,000 and sold them for $250,000 cash. She provided her customers with a one-year warranty against defects in parts and labor. Based on industry standards, she estimated that warranty claims would amount to 2 percent of sales. During the year, she paid $2,820 cash to replace a defective tuner.

Required

Prepare an income statement and statement of cash flows for Daun's first year of operation. Based on the information given, what is Daun's total warranties liability at the end of the accounting period?

LO 9-4

Exercise 9-7A Effect of warranty obligations and payments on financial statements

The Chair Company provides a 120-day parts-and-labor warranty on all merchandise it sells. The Chair Company estimates the warranty expense for the current period to be $2,650. During this period, a customer returned a product that cost $1,830 to repair.

Required

a. Show the effects of these transactions on the financial statements using a horizontal statements model like the example shown next. Use + for increase, − for decrease, and NA for not affected.

In the Cash Flow column, indicate whether the item is an operating activity (OA), investing activity (IA), or financing activity (FA).

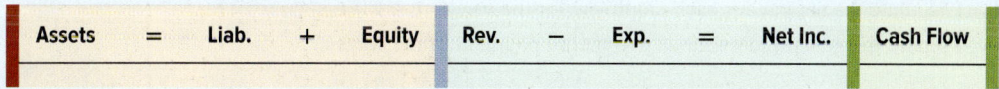

b. Prepare the journal entry to record the warranty expense for the period.
c. Prepare the journal entry to record payment for the actual repair costs.
d. Why do companies estimate warranty expense and record the expense before the repairs are actually made?

Exercise 9-8A Current liabilities

LO 9-1, 9-2, 9-4

The following transactions apply to Ozark Sales for Year 1:

1. The business was started when the company received $50,000 from the issue of common stock.
2. Purchased equipment inventory of $380,000 on account.
3. Sold equipment for $510,000 cash (not including sales tax). Sales tax of 8 percent is collected when the merchandise is sold. The merchandise had a cost of $330,000.
4. Provided a six-month warranty on the equipment sold. Based on industry estimates, the warranty claims would amount to 2 percent of sales.
5. Paid the sales tax to the state agency on $400,000 of the sales.
6. On September 1, Year 1, borrowed $50,000 from the local bank. The note had a 4 percent interest rate and matured on March 1, Year 2.
7. Paid $6,200 for warranty repairs during the year.
8. Paid operating expenses of $78,000 for the year.
9. Paid $250,000 of accounts payable.
10. Recorded accrued interest on the note issued in transaction no. 6.

Required

a. Show the effect of these transactions on the financial statements using a horizontal statements model like the one shown next. Use + for increase, − for decrease, and NA for not affected. In the Cash Flow column, indicate whether the item is an operating activity (OA), investing activity (IA), or financing activity (FA). The first transaction is recorded as an example.

Assets	=	Liabilities	+	Equity	Rev.	−	Exp.	=	Net Inc.	Cash Flow
+		NA		+	NA		NA		NA	+ FA

b. Prepare the journal entries for the preceding transactions and post them to the appropriate T-accounts.
c. Prepare the income statement, balance sheet, and statement of cash flows for Year 1.
d. What is the total amount of current liabilities at December 31, Year 1?

Exercise 9-9A Calculating payroll

LO 9-5

Zolnick Enterprises has two hourly employees: Kelly and Jon. Both employees earn overtime at the rate of 1½ times the hourly rate for hours worked in excess of 40 per week. Assume the Social Security tax rate is 6 percent on the first $110,000 of wages, and the Medicare tax rate is 1.5 percent on all earnings. Federal income tax withheld for Kelly and Jon was $260 and $220, respectively, for the first week of January. The following information is for the first week in January Year 1:

Employee	Hours Worked	Wage Rate per Hour
Kelly	54	$32
Jon	44	$26

Required

a. Calculate the gross pay for each employee for the week.
b. Calculate the net pay for each employee for the week.
c. Prepare the general journal entry to record payment of the wages.

LO 9-5

Exercise 9-10A *Calculating payroll*

Old Town Entertainment has two employees in Year 1. Clay earns $3,600 per month, and Philip, the manager, earns $10,800 per month. Neither is paid extra for working overtime. Assume the Social Security tax rate is 6 percent on the first $110,000 of earnings and the Medicare tax rate is 1.5 percent on all earnings. The federal income tax withholding is 15 percent of gross earnings for Clay and 20 percent for Philip. Both Clay and Philip have been employed all year.

Required

a. Calculate the net pay for both Clay and Philip for March.
b. Calculate the net pay for both Clay and Philip for December.
c. Is the net pay the same in March and December for both employees? Why or why not?
d. What amounts will Old Town report on the Year 1 W-2s for each employee?

LO 9-5

Exercise 9-11A *Calculating employee and employer payroll taxes*

Sky Co. employed Tom Mills in Year 1. Tom earned $5,100 per month and worked the entire year. Assume the Social Security tax rate is 6 percent for the first $110,000 of earnings, and the Medicare tax rate is 1.5 percent. Tom's federal income tax withholding amount is $900 per month. Use 5.4 percent for the state unemployment tax rate and .06 percent for the federal unemployment tax rate on the first $7,000 of earnings per employee.

Required

a. Answer the following questions:
   (1) What is Tom's net pay per month?
   (2) What amount does Tom pay monthly in FICA payroll taxes?
   (3) What is the total payroll tax expense for Sky Co. for January Year 1? February Year 1? March Year 1? December Year 1?
b. Assume that instead of $5,100 per month Tom earned $9,600 per month. Answer the questions in Requirement *a*.

LO 9-5

Exercise 9-12A *Fringe benefits and payroll expense*

The two employees of Silver Co. receive various fringe benefits. Silver Co. provides vacation at the rate of $315 per day. Each employee earns one day of vacation per month worked. In addition, Silver Co. pays a total amount of $650 per month in medical insurance premiums. Silver also contributes a total amount of $400 per month into an employee retirement plan. The federal unemployment tax rate is 6%, while the state tax rate is 4%. Unemployment taxes apply to the first $7,000 of earnings per employee. Assume a Social Security tax rate of 6% and a Medicare tax rate of 1.5%.

Required

a. Prepare the monthly journal entry for the accrued fringe benefits per month.
b. Show the effect of accrued fringe benefits per month on a horizontal statements model like the one shown next.

Assets =	Liabilities	+	Equity	Income Statement	Cash Flow
Cash =	Various Payables	+	Com. Stk. + Ret. Earn.	Rev. − Exp. = Net Inc.	

c. If the two employees each worked 250 days, what is Silver Co.'s total payroll cost (salary, payroll taxes, and fringe benefits) for the year? (Assume that each employee earns $315 per day.)

Exercise 9-13A Comprehensive single-cycle problem

LO 9-1, 9-2, 9-4, 9-5

The following transactions apply to Park Co. for Year 1:

1. Received $50,000 cash from the issue of common stock.
2. Purchased inventory on account for $180,000.
3. Sold inventory for $250,000 cash that had cost $140,000. Sales tax was collected at the rate of 5 percent on the inventory sold.
4. Borrowed $50,000 from First State Bank on March 1, Year 1. The note had a 7 percent interest rate and a one-year term to maturity.
5. Paid the accounts payable (see transaction 2).
6. Paid the sales tax due on $190,000 of sales. Sales tax on the other $60,000 is not due until after the end of the year.
7. Salaries for the year for one employee amounted to $46,000. Assume the Social Security tax rate is 6 percent and the Medicare tax rate is 1.5 percent. Federal income tax withheld was $5,300.
8. Paid $5,800 for warranty repairs during the year.
9. Paid $36,000 of other operating expenses during the year.
10. Paid a dividend of $2,000 to the shareholders.

Adjustments

11. The products sold in transaction 3 were warranted. Park estimated that the warranty cost would be 3 percent of sales.
12. Record the accrued interest at December 31, Year 1.
13. Record the accrued payroll tax at December 31, Year 1. Assume no payroll taxes have been paid for the year and that the unemployment tax rate is 6 percent (federal unemployment tax rate is .06 percent and the state unemployment tax rate is 5.4 percent on the first $7,000 of earnings per employee).

Required

a. Record the preceding transactions in general journal form.
b. Post the transactions to T-accounts.
c. Prepare an income statement, statement of changes in stockholders' equity, balance sheet, and statement of cash flows for Year 1.

Exercise 9-14A Preparing a classified balance sheet

LO 9-6

Required

Use the following information to prepare a classified balance sheet for Alpha Co. at the end of Year 1:

Accounts receivable	$26,500
Accounts payable	12,200
Cash	20,500
Common stock	30,000
Land	10,000
Long-term notes payable	17,500
Merchandise inventory	26,300
Retained earnings	23,600

Exercise 9-15A Using the current ratio to make comparisons

LO 9-7

The following information was drawn from the balance sheets of the Kansas and Montana companies:

	Kansas	Montana
Current assets	$59,000	$78,000
Current liabilities	40,000	43,000

Required

a. Compute the current ratio for each company.
b. Which company has the greater likelihood of being able to pay its bills?
c. Assume that both companies have the same amount of total assets. Speculate as to which company would produce the higher return-on-assets ratio.

LO 9-8

Exercise 9-16A *Effect of a discount note on financial statements (Appendix)*

Helen Parish started a design company on January 1, Year 1. On April 1, Year 1, Parish borrowed cash from a local bank by issuing a one-year $120,000 face value note with annual interest based on an 8 percent discount. During Year 1, Parish provided services for $72,000 cash.

Required

Answer the following questions. (*Hint:* Record the events in T-accounts prior to answering the questions.)

a. What is the amount of total liabilities on the December 31, Year 1, balance sheet?
b. What is the amount of net income on the Year 1 income statement?
c. What is the amount of cash flow from operating activities on the Year 1 statement of cash flows?
d. Provide the general journal entries necessary to record issuing the note on April 1, Year 1; recognizing accrued interest on December 31, Year 1; and repaying the loan on March 31, Year 2.

LO 9-1, 9-8

Exercise 9-17A *Comparing effective interest rates on discount versus interest-bearing notes (Appendix)*

Sheldon Jones borrowed money by issuing two notes on March 1, Year 1. The financing transactions are described next.

1. Borrowed funds by issuing a $52,000 face value discount note to Farmers Bank. The note had an 8 percent discount rate, a one-year term to maturity, and was paid off on March 1, Year 2.
2. Borrowed funds by issuing a $52,000 face value, interest-bearing note to Valley Bank. The note had an 8 percent stated rate of interest, a one-year term to maturity, and was paid off on March 1, Year 2.

Required

a. Show the effects of issuing the two notes on the financial statements using separate horizontal financial statement models like those shown next. Record the transaction amounts under the appropriate categories. In the Cash Flow column, indicate whether the item is an operating activity (OA), investing activity (IA), or financing activity (FA). Record only the events occurring on the date of issue. Do not record accrued interest or the repayment at maturity.

Discount Note

Assets =	Liabilities	+ Equity	Rev. − Exp. = Net Inc.	Cash Flow
Cash = Notes Pay. − Disc. on Notes Pay. + Ret. Earn.				

Interest-Bearing Note

Assets =	Liabilities	+ Equity	Rev. − Exp. = Net Inc.	Cash Flow
Cash = Notes Pay. + Ret. Earn.				

b. What is the total amount of interest to be paid on each note?
c. What amount of cash was received from each note when it was issued?
d. Which note has the higher effective interest rate? Support your answer with appropriate computations.

Exercise 9-18A *Recording accounting events for a discount note (Appendix)* LO 9-8

Harden Co. issued a $60,000 face value discount note to National Bank on July 1, Year 1. The note had a 6 percent discount rate and a one-year term to maturity.

Required

Prepare general journal entries for the following:

a. The issuance of the note on July 1, Year 1.
b. The adjustment for accrued interest at the end of the year, December 31, Year 1.
c. Recording interest expense for Year 2 and repaying the principal on June 30, Year 2.

PROBLEMS—SERIES A

connect All applicable Problems in Series A are available in Connect.

Problem 9-19A *Effect of accrued interest on financial statements* LO 9-1

Malco Enterprises issued $10,000 of common stock when the company was started. In addition, Malco borrowed $36,000 from a local bank on July 1, Year 1. The note had a 6 percent annual interest rate and a one-year term to maturity. Malco Enterprises recognized $72,500 of revenue on account in Year 1 and $85,200 of revenue on account in Year 2. Cash collections of accounts receivable were $61,300 in Year 1 and $71,500 in Year 2. Malco paid $39,000 of other operating expenses in Year 1 and $45,000 of other operating expenses in Year 2. Malco repaid the loan and interest at the maturity date.

CHECK FIGURES
a. $1,080
b. $22,300

Required

Based on this information, answer the following questions. (*Hint:* Record the events in the accounting equation before answering the questions.)

a. What amount of interest expense would Malco report on the Year 1 income statement?
b. What amount of net cash flow from operating activities would Malco report on the Year 1 statement of cash flows?
c. What amount of total liabilities would Malco report on the December 31, Year 1, balance sheet?
d. What amount of retained earnings would Malco report on the December 31, Year 1, balance sheet?
e. What amount of net cash flow from financing activities would Malco report on the Year 1 statement of cash flows?
f. What amount of interest expense would Malco report on the Year 2 income statement?
g. What amount of net cash flow from operating activities would Malco report on the Year 2 statement of cash flows?
h. What amount of total assets would Malco report on the December 31, Year 2, balance sheet?
i. What amount of net cash flow from investing activities would Malco report on the Year 2 statement of cash flows?
j. If Malco Enterprises paid a $2,000 dividend during Year 2, what retained earnings balance would it report on the December 31, Year 2, balance sheet?

Problem 9-20A *Account for short-term debt and sales tax—two accounting cycles* LO 9-1, 9-2

The following transactions apply to Walnut Enterprises for Year 1, its first year of operations:

CHECK FIGURES
c. Net Income, Year 1: $65,750
f. Total Assets, Year 2: $164,460

1. Received $50,000 cash from the issue of a short-term note with a 6 percent interest rate and a one-year maturity. The note was made on April 1, Year 1.
2. Received $130,000 cash plus applicable sales tax from performing services. The services are subject to a sales tax rate of 6 percent.
3. Paid $62,000 cash for other operating expenses during the year.
4. Paid the sales tax due on $110,000 of the service revenue for the year. Sales tax on the balance of the revenue is not due until Year 2.
5. Recognized the accrued interest at December 31, Year 1.

The following transactions apply to Walnut Enterprises for Year 2:

1. Paid the balance of the sales tax due for Year 1.
2. Received $201,000 cash plus applicable sales tax from performing services. The services are subject to a sales tax rate of 6 percent.
3. Repaid the principal of the note and applicable interest on April 1, Year 2.
4. Paid $102,500 of other operating expenses during the year.
5. Paid the sales tax due on $185,000 of the service revenue. The sales tax on the balance of the revenue is not due until Year 3.

Required

a. Record the Year 1 transactions in general journal form.
b. Post the transactions to T-accounts.
c. Prepare a balance sheet, statement of changes in stockholders' equity, income statement, and statement of cash flows for Year 1.
d. Prepare the closing entries and post them to the T-accounts.
e. Prepare a post-closing trial balance.
f. Repeat Requirements *a* through *e* for Year 2.

Problem 9-21A Contingent liabilities

Required

a. Give an example of a contingent liability that is probable and reasonably estimable. How would this type of liability be shown in the accounting records?
b. Give an example of a contingent liability that is reasonably possible or probable but not reasonably estimable. How would this type of liability be shown in the accounting records?
c. Give an example of a contingent liability that is remote. How is this type of liability shown in the accounting records?

Problem 9-22A Current liabilities

The following selected transactions were taken from the books of Ripley Company for Year 1:

1. On February 1, Year 1, borrowed $70,000 cash from the local bank. The note had a 6 percent interest rate and was due on June 1, Year 1.
2. Cash sales for the year amounted to $240,000 plus sales tax at the rate of 7 percent.
3. Ripley provides a 90-day warranty on the merchandise sold. The warranty expense is estimated to be 1 percent of sales.
4. Paid the sales tax to the state sales tax agency on $210,000 of the sales.
5. Paid the note due on June 1 and the related interest.
6. On November 1, Year 1, borrowed $20,000 cash from the local bank. The note had a 6 percent interest rate and a one-year term to maturity.
7. Paid $2,100 in warranty repairs.
8. A customer has filed a lawsuit against Ripley for $1 million for breach of contract. The company attorney does not believe the suit has merit.

Required

a. Answer the following questions:
   (1) What amount of cash did Ripley pay for interest during Year 1?
   (2) What amount of interest expense is reported on Ripley's income statement for Year 1?
   (3) What is the amount of warranty expense for Year 1?
b. Prepare the current liabilities section of the balance sheet at December 31, Year 1. (*Hint:* First post the liabilities transactions to T-accounts.)
c. Show the effect of these transactions on the financial statements using a horizontal statements model like the one shown next. Use + for increase, − for decrease, and NA for not affected. In the Cash Flow column, indicate whether the item is an operating activity (OA),

investing activity (IA), or financing activity (FA). The first transaction has been recorded as an example.

Assets	=	Liabilities	+	Equity	Rev.	−	Exp.	=	Net Inc.	Cash Flow
+		+		NA	NA		NA		NA	+ FA

Problem 9-23A Accounting for payroll and payroll taxes

LO 9-5

Electronics Service Co. pays salaries monthly on the last day of the month. The following information is available from Electronics for the month ended December 31, Year 1:

Administrative salaries	$96,000
Sales salaries	57,000
Office salaries	38,000

Assume the Social Security tax rate is 6 percent on the first $110,000 of salaries. Duke reached the $110,000 amount in September. His salary in December amounted to $11,500 and is included in the $96,000. No one else will reach the $110,000 amount for the year. None of the employee salaries are subject to unemployment tax in December.

Other amounts withheld from salaries in December were as follows:

Federal income tax	$21,500
State income tax	11,200
Employee savings plan	4,000

Required

a. Prepare the journal entry to record the payment of payroll on December 31, Year 1.
b. Prepare the journal entry to record the payroll tax expense for Electronics Service Co. for December Year 1.

Problem 9-24A Computation of net pay and payroll expense

LO 9-5

CHECK FIGURE
e. $4,055.24

The following information is available for the employees of Webber Packing Company for the first week of January Year 1:

1. Kayla earns $28 per hour and 1½ times her regular rate for hours over 40 per week. Kayla worked 52 hours the first week in January. Kayla's federal income tax withholding is equal to 15 percent of her gross pay. Webber pays medical insurance of $50 per week for Kayla and contributes $50 per week to a retirement plan for her.
2. Paula earns a weekly salary of $1,600. Paula's federal income tax withholding is 18 percent of her gross pay. Webber pays medical insurance of $80 per week for Paula and contributes $100 per week to a retirement plan for her.
3. Vacation pay is accrued at the rate of 2 hours per week (based on the regular pay rate) for Kayla and $60 per week for Paula.

Assume the Social Security tax rate is 6 percent on the first $110,000 of salaries and the Medicare tax rate is 1.5 percent of total salaries. The state unemployment tax rate is 5.4 percent and the federal unemployment tax rate is 0.6 percent of the first $7,000 of salary for each employee.

Required

a. Compute the gross pay for Kayla for the first week in January.
b. Compute the net pay for both Kayla and Paula for the first week in January.
c. Prepare the journal entry to record the payment of the payroll for the week.
d. Prepare the journal entry to record the payroll tax expense and fringe benefit expense for Webber Packing Company for the week.
e. What is the total cost of compensation expense for the first week of January Year 1 for Webber Packing Company?

Chapter 9

LO 9-6

Problem 9-25A *Multistep income statement and classified balance sheet*

Required

Use the following information to prepare a multistep income statement and a classified balance sheet for Eller Equipment Co. for Year 1. (*Hint:* Some of the items will *not* appear on either statement, and ending retained earnings must be calculated.)

CHECK FIGURES
Total Current Assets: $212,700
Total Current Liabilities: $67,500

Salaries expense	$ 72,000	Beginning retained earnings	$134,150
Common stock	50,000	Warranties payable (short term)	2,500
Notes receivable (short term)	10,000	Gain on sale of equipment	8,500
Allowance for doubtful accounts	6,500	Operating expenses	96,000
Accumulated depreciation	42,300	Cash flow from investing activities	125,000
Notes payable (long term)	80,000	Prepaid rent	14,000
Salvage value of building	6,000	Land	70,000
Interest payable (short term)	1,500	Cash	26,300
Uncollectible accounts expense	7,150	Inventory	110,500
Supplies	1,800	Accounts payable	32,000
Equipment	97,500	Interest expense	8,600
Interest revenue	3,600	Salaries payable	5,200
Sales revenue	510,000	Unearned revenue	26,300
Dividends	11,500	Cost of goods sold	310,000
Warranty expense	9,600	Accounts receivable	56,000
Interest receivable (short term)	600	Depreciation expense	1,000

LO 9-7

Problem 9-26A *Using ratios to make comparisons*

The following accounting information exists for Aspen and Willow companies:

CHECK FIGURE
a. Aspen Current Ratio: 1.53 to 1.0

	Aspen	Willow
Cash	$ 30,000	$ 20,000
Wages payable	30,000	25,000
Merchandise inventory	65,000	35,000
Building	95,000	95,000
Accounts receivable	35,000	40,000
Long-term notes payable	145,000	110,000
Land	60,000	55,000
Accounts payable	55,000	50,000
Sales revenue	325,000	265,000
Expenses	295,000	230,000

Required

a. Identify the current assets and current liabilities and compute the current ratio for each company.
b. Assuming that all assets and liabilities are listed here, compute the debt-to-assets ratios for each company.
c. Determine which company has the greater financial risk in both the short term and the long term.

LO 9-8

Problem 9-27A *Accounting for a discount note across two accounting cycles (Appendix)*

CHECK FIGURES
c. Net Income, Year 1: $160,200
Total Assets, Year 2: $323,400

Don Terry opened Terry Company, an accounting practice, in Year 1. The following summarizes transactions that occurred during Year 1:

1. Issued a $120,000 face value discount note to First National Bank on July 1, Year 1. The note had an 8 percent discount rate and a one-year term to maturity.
2. Recognized cash revenue of $310,000.
3. Incurred and paid $145,000 of operating expenses.
4. Adjusted the books to recognize interest expense at December 31, Year 1.
5. Prepared the necessary closing entries at December 31, Year 1.

The following summarizes transactions that occurred in Year 2:

1. Recognized $346,000 of cash revenue.
2. Incurred and paid $178,000 of operating expenses.
3. Recognized the interest expense for Year 2 and paid the face value of the note.
4. Prepared the necessary closing entries at December 31, Year 2.

Required

a. Show the effects of each of the transactions on the elements of the financial statements, using a horizontal statements model like the one shown next. Use + for increase, − for decrease, and NA for not affected. The first transaction is entered as an example. (*Hint:* Closing entries do not affect the statements model.)

Event No.	Assets	=	Liab.	+	Equity	Rev.	−	Exp.	=	Net Inc.	Cash Flow
1	+		+		NA	NA		NA		NA	+ FA

b. Prepare entries in general journal form for the transactions for Year 1 and Year 2, and post them to T-accounts.
c. Prepare an income statement, statement of changes in stockholders' equity, balance sheet, and statement of cash flows for Year 1 and Year 2.

EXERCISES—SERIES B

Exercise 9-1B *Recognizing accrued interest expense*   LO 9-1

Union Corporation borrowed $60,000 from the bank on November 1, Year 1. The note had a 6 percent annual rate of interest and matured on April 30, Year 2. Interest and principal were paid in cash on the maturity date.

Required

a. What amount of cash did Union pay for interest in Year 1?
b. What amount of interest expense was reported on the Year 1 income statement?
c. What amount of total liabilities was reported on the December 31, Year 1, balance sheet?
d. What total amount of cash was paid to the bank on April 30, Year 2, for principal and interest?
e. What amount of interest expense was reported on the Year 2 income statement?

Exercise 9-2B *Effects of recognizing accrued interest on financial statements*   LO 9-1

Danny Bell started Bell Company on January 1, Year 1. The company experienced the following events during its first year of operation:

1. Earned $3,000 of cash revenue for performing services.
2. Borrowed $4,800 cash from the bank.
3. Adjusted the accounting records to recognize accrued interest expense on the bank note. The note, issued on August 1, Year 1, had a one-year term and a 6 percent annual interest rate.

Required

a. What is the amount of interest expense in Year 1?
b. What amount of cash was paid for interest in Year 1?
c. Use a horizontal statements model to show how each event affects the balance sheet, income statement, and statement of cash flows. Indicate whether the event increases (I), decreases (D), or does not affect (NA) each element of the financial statements. In the Statement of Cash Flows column, designate the cash flows as operating activities (OA), investing activities (IA), or financing activities (FA). The first transaction has been recorded as an example.

Event No.	Balance Sheet								Income Statement					Statement of Cash Flows
	Cash	=	Notes Pay.	+	Int. Pay.	+	Com. Stk.	+ Ret. Earn.	Rev.	−	Exp.	=	Net Inc.	
1	I	=	NA	+	NA	+	NA	+ I	I	−	NA	=	I	I OA

LO 9-2

Exercise 9-3B *Recording sales tax*

The Tiger Book Store sells books and other supplies to students in a state where the sales tax rate is 7 percent. The Tiger Book Store engaged in the following transactions for Year 1. Sales tax of 7 percent is collected on all sales.

1. Book sales, not including sales tax, for Year 1 amounted to $215,000 cash.
2. Cash sales of miscellaneous items in Year 1 were $160,000, not including tax.
3. Cost of goods sold amounted to $195,000 for the year.
4. Paid $95,000 in operating expenses for the year.
5. Paid the sales tax collected to the state agency.

Required

a. What is the total amount of sales tax the Tiger Book Store collected and paid for the year?
b. Prepare the journal entries for the preceding transactions.
c. What is the Tiger Book Store's net income for the year?

LO 9-2

Exercise 9-4B *Recognizing sales tax payable*

The following selected transactions apply to Fast Stop for November and December Year 1. November was the first month of operations. Sales tax is collected at the time of sale but is not paid to the state sales tax agency until the following month.

1. Cash sales for November Year 1 were $85,000 plus sales tax of 8 percent.
2. Fast Stop paid the November sales tax to the state agency on December 10, Year 1.
3. Cash sales for December Year 1 were $98,000 plus sales tax of 8 percent.

Required

a. Record the preceding transactions in general journal form.
b. Show the effect of the preceding transactions on a horizontal statements model like the one shown next.

Assets	=	Liabilities	+	Equity		Income Statement		Cash Flow
Cash	=	Sales Tax Pay.	+	Com. Stk. + Ret. Earn.		Rev. − Exp. = Net Inc.		

c. What was the total amount of sales tax paid in Year 1?
d. What was the total amount of sales tax collected in Year 1?
e. What is the amount of the sales tax liability as of December 31, Year 1?
f. On what financial statement will the sales tax liability appear?

LO 9-3

Exercise 9-5B *Contingent liabilities*

The following legal situations apply to Zier Corp. for Year 1:

1. A customer slipped and fell on a slick floor while shopping in the retail store. The customer has filed a $5 million lawsuit against the company. Zier's attorney knows that the company will have to pay some damages but is reasonably certain that the suit can be settled for $750,000.
2. The EPA has assessed a fine against Zier of $320,000 for hazardous emissions from one of its manufacturing plants. The EPA had previously issued a warning to Zier and required Zier to make

repairs within six months. Zier began to make the repairs, but was not able to complete them within the six-month period. Because Zier has started the repairs, Zier's attorney thinks the fine will be reduced to $120,000. He is approximately 80 percent certain that he can negotiate the fine reduction because of the repair work that has been completed.

3. One of Zier's largest manufacturing facilities is located in "tornado alley." Property is routinely damaged by storms. Zier estimates it may have property damage of as much as $450,000 this coming year.

Required

For each of the preceding items, determine the correct accounting treatment. Prepare any required journal entries.

Exercise 9-6B *Effect of warranties on income and cash flow* LO 9-4

To support himself while attending school, Steve Owens sold computers to other students. During the year, Steve purchased computers for $150,000 and sold them for $280,000 cash. He provided his customers with a one-year warranty against defects in parts and labor. Based on industry standards, he estimated that warranty claims would amount to 5 percent of sales. During the year, he paid $1,545 cash to replace a defective hard drive.

Required

a. Prepare the journal entries to record the
   (1) Purchase of inventory.
   (2) Sale of computers.
   (3) Warranty expense.
   (4) Payment for repairs.
b. Post the preceding transactions to T-accounts.
c. Prepare an income statement and statement of cash flows for Steve's first year of operation.
d. Explain the difference between net income and the amount of cash flow from operating activities.

Exercise 9-7B *Effect of warranty obligations and payments on financial statements* LO 9-4

The Malon Appliance Co. provides a 120-day parts-and-labor warranty on all merchandise it sells. Malon estimates the warranty expense for the current period to be $2,450. During this period, a customer returned a product that cost $1,950 to repair.

Required

a. Show the effects of these transactions on the financial statements using a horizontal statements model like the example shown next. Use + for increase, − for decrease, and NA for not affected. In the Cash Flow column, indicate whether the item is an operating activity (OA), investing activity (IA), or financing activity (FA).

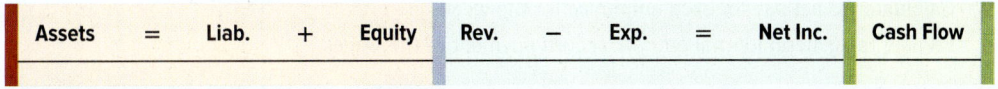

b. Prepare the journal entry to record the warranty expense for the period.
c. Prepare the journal entry to record payment for the actual repair costs.
d. Discuss the advantage of estimating the amount of warranty expense.

Exercise 9-8B *Current liabilities* LO 9-1, 9-2, 9-4

The following transactions apply to Farmer's Equipment Sales Corp. for Year 1:

1. The business was started when Farmer's received $60,000 from the issue of common stock.
2. Purchased $160,000 of merchandise on account.
3. Sold merchandise for $220,000 cash (not including sales tax). Sales tax of 8 percent is collected when the merchandise is sold. The merchandise had a cost of $140,000.

4. Provided a six-month warranty on the merchandise sold. Based on industry estimates, the warranty claims would amount to 4 percent of merchandise sales.
5. Paid the sales tax to the state agency on $180,000 of the sales.
6. On September 1, Year 1, borrowed $40,000 from the local bank. The note had a 6 percent interest rate and matures on March 1, Year 2.
7. Paid $6,600 for warranty repairs during the year.
8. Paid operating expenses of $61,000 for the year.
9. Paid $145,000 of accounts payable.
10. Recorded accrued interest at the end of the year.

Required

a. Show the effect of these transactions on the financial statements using a horizontal statements model like the one shown next. Use + for increase, − for decrease, and NA for not affected. In the Cash Flow column, indicate whether the item is an operating activity (OA), investing activity (IA), or financing activity (FA). The first transaction is recorded as an example.

Assets	=	Liabilities	+	Equity	Rev.	−	Exp.	=	Net Inc.	Cash Flow
+		NA		+	NA		NA		NA	+ FA

b. Prepare the journal entries for the preceding transactions and post them to the appropriate T-accounts.
c. Prepare the income statement, balance sheet, and statement of cash flows for Year 1.
d. What is the total amount of current liabilities at December 31, Year 1?

LO 9-5

Exercise 9-9B *Calculating payroll*

Wilkins Enterprises has two hourly employees: Marcia and Clark. Both employees earn overtime at the rate of 1½ times the hourly rate for hours worked in excess of 40 per week. Assume the Social Security tax rate is 6 percent on the first $110,000 of wages, and the Medicare tax rate is 1.5 percent on all earnings. Federal income tax withheld for Marcia and Clark was $280 and $250, respectively. The following information is for the first week in January Year 1:

Employee	Hours Worked	Wage Rate per Hour
Marcia	54	$25
Clark	48	$35

Required

a. Calculate the gross pay for each employee for the week.
b. Calculate the net pay for each employee for the week.
c. Prepare the general journal entry to record payment of the wages.

LO 9-5

Exercise 9-10B *Calculating payroll*

Easy Stop has two employees in Year 1. Catherine earns $4,500 per month and Jordan, the manager, earns $11,000 per month. Neither is paid extra if they work overtime. Assume the Social Security tax rate is 6 percent on the first $110,000 of earnings, and the Medicare tax rate is 1.5 percent on all earnings. The federal income tax withholding is 15 percent of gross earnings for Catherine and 20 percent for Jordan. Both Catherine and Jordan have been employed all year.

Required

a. Calculate the net pay for both Catherine and Jordan for March.
b. Calculate the net pay for both Catherine and Jordan for December.
c. Is the net pay the same in March and December for both employees? Why or why not?
d. What amounts will Easy Stop report on the Year 1 W-2s for each employee?

Exercise 9-11B Calculating employee and employer payroll taxes

LO 9-5

Culver Co. employed Jen Sing in Year 1. Jen earned $5,200 per month and worked the entire year. Assume the Social Security tax rate is 6 percent on the first $110,000 of earnings, and the Medicare tax rate is 1.5 percent. Jen's federal income tax withholding amount is $800 per month. Use 6.0 percent for the unemployment tax rate for the first $7,000 of earnings per employee.

Required

a. Answer the following questions:
   (1) What is Jen's net pay per month?
   (2) What amount does Jen pay monthly in FICA payroll taxes?
   (3) What is the total payroll tax expense for Culver Co. for January Year 1? February Year 1? March Year 1? December Year 1?

b. Assume that instead of $5,200 per month, Jen earned $10,000 per month. Answer the questions in Requirement a.

Exercise 9-12B Fringe benefits and payroll expense

LO 9-5

The two employees at Oswald Co. receive various fringe benefits. Oswald Co. provides vacation at the rate of $500 per day, and each employee earns one day of vacation per month worked. In addition, Oswald Co. pays a total amount of $780 per month in medical insurance premiums. Oswald also contributes a total amount of $400 per month into an employee retirement plan. The federal unemployment tax rate is 6%, while the state unemployment rate is 4.5%. Unemployment taxes apply to the first $7,000 of earnings per employee. Assume a Social Security tax rate of 6.0% and a Medicare tax rate of 1.5%.

Required

a. Prepare the computation for the accrued fringe benefits per month.
b. Show the effect of accrued fringe benefits per month on a statements model like the one shown next:

Assets =	Liabilities	+	Equity	Income Statement	Cash Flow
Cash =	Various Payables	+ Com. Stk. +	Ret. Earn.	Rev. − Exp. = Net Inc.	

c. If the two employees each worked 250 days for the year, what is Oswald Co.'s total payroll cost (salary, payroll taxes, and fringe benefits) for the year? (Assume that each employee earns $500 per day.)

Exercise 9-13B Comprehensive single-cycle problem

LO 9-1, 9-2, 9-4, 9-5

The following transactions apply to Ritter Co. for Year 1:

1. Received $40,000 cash from the issue of common stock.
2. Purchased inventory on account for $128,000.
3. Sold inventory for $200,000 cash that had cost $110,000. Sales tax was collected at the rate of 5 percent on the inventory sold.
4. Borrowed $40,000 from First State Bank on October 1, Year 1. The note had a 6 percent interest rate and a one-year term to maturity.
5. Paid the accounts payable (see transaction 2).
6. Paid the sales tax due on $160,000 of sales. Sales tax on the other $40,000 is not due until after the end of the year.
7. Salaries for the year for one employee amounted to $45,000. Assume the Social Security tax rate is 6 percent and the Medicare tax rate is 1.5 percent. Federal income tax withheld was $5,600.
8. Paid $3,200 for warranty repairs during the year.
9. Paid $24,000 of other operating expenses during the year.
10. Paid a dividend of $5,000 to the shareholders.

Adjustments

11. The products sold in transaction 3 were warranted. Ritter estimated that the warranty cost would be 3 percent of sales.
12. Record the accrued interest at December 31, Year 1.
13. Record the accrued payroll tax at December 31, Year 1. Assume no payroll taxes have been paid for the year and that the unemployment tax rate is 6.0 percent (the federal unemployment tax rate is 0.6 percent and the state unemployment tax rate is 5.4 percent on the first $7,000 of earnings per employee).

Required

a. Record the preceding transactions in general journal form.
b. Post the transactions to T-accounts.
c. Prepare an income statement, statement of changes in stockholders' equity, balance sheet, and statement of cash flows for Year 1.

LO 9-6

Exercise 9-14B   *Preparing a classified balance sheet*

Required

Use the following information to prepare a classified balance sheet for Latimer Co. at the end of Year 1:

Accounts receivable	$36,200
Accounts payable	12,400
Cash	29,650
Common stock	50,000
Long-term notes payable	45,500
Merchandise inventory	38,300
Office equipment	36,400
Retained earnings	36,250
Prepaid insurance	3,600

LO 9-7

Exercise 9-15B   *Using the current ratio to make comparisons*

The following information was drawn from the balance sheets of the Augusta and Reno companies:

	Augusta Company	Reno Company
Current assets	$45,000	$72,000
Current liabilities	28,000	54,000

Required

a. Compute the current ratio for each company.
b. Which company has the greater likelihood of being able to pay its bills?
c. Assume that both companies have the same amount of total assets. Speculate as to which company would produce the higher return-on-assets ratio.

LO 9-8

Exercise 9-16B   *Effect of a discount note on financial statements (Appendix)*

Mark Miller started a moving company on January 1, Year 1. On March 1, Year 1, Miller borrowed cash from a local bank by issuing a one-year $80,000 face value note with annual interest based on a 12 percent discount. During Year 1, Miller provided services for $65,400 cash.

Required

Answer the following questions. Record the events in T-accounts prior to answering the questions.

a. What is the amount of total liabilities on the December 31, Year 1, balance sheet?
b. What is the amount of net income on the Year 1 income statement?
c. What is the amount of cash flow from operating activities on the Year 1 statement of cash flows?
d. Provide the general journal entries necessary to record issuing the note on March 1, Year 1; recognizing accrued interest on December 31, Year 1; and repaying the loan on February 28, Year 2.

Accounting for Current Liabilities and Payroll

Exercise 9-17B *Comparing effective interest rates on discount versus interest-bearing notes (Appendix)*

LO 9-1, 9-8

Jim Hanks borrowed money by issuing two notes on January 1, Year 1. The financing transactions are described next.

1. Borrowed funds by issuing a $60,000 face value discount note to State Bank. The note had an 8 percent discount rate, a one-year term to maturity, and was paid off on December 31, Year 1.
2. Borrowed funds by issuing a $60,000 face value, interest-bearing note to Community Bank. The note had an 8 percent stated rate of interest, a one-year term to maturity, and was paid off on December 31, Year 1.

Required

a. Show the effects of issuing the two notes on the financial statements using separate horizontal financial statement models like those shown next. Record the transaction amounts under the appropriate categories. In the Cash Flow column, indicate whether the item is an operating activity (OA), investing activity (IA), or financing activity (FA). Record only the events occurring on the date of issue. Do not record accrued interest or the repayment at maturity.

Discount Note

Assets	=	Liabilities	+	Equity	Rev.	−	Exp.	=	Net Inc.	Cash Flow
Cash	=	Notes Pay. − Disc. on Notes Pay.	+	Ret. Earn.						

Interest-Bearing Note

Assets	=	Liabilities	+	Equity	Rev.	−	Exp.	=	Net Inc.	Cash Flow
Cash	=	Notes Pay.	+	Ret. Earn.						

b. What is the total amount of interest to be paid on each note?
c. What amount of cash was received from each note when it was issued?
d. Which note has the higher effective interest rate? Support your answer with appropriate computations.

Exercise 9-18B *Recording accounting events for a discount note (Appendix)*

LO 9-8

Bricca Co. issued a $60,000 face value discount note to First Bank on June 1, Year 1. The note had a 6 percent discount rate and a one-year term to maturity.

Required

Prepare general journal entries for the following transactions:

a. The issuance of the note on June 1, Year 1.
b. The adjustment for accrued interest at the end of the year, December 31, Year 1.
c. Recording interest expense for Year 2 and repaying the principal on May 31, Year 2.

PROBLEMS—SERIES B

Problem 9-19B *Effect of accrued interest on financial statements*

LO 9-1

Ingals Co. issued $10,000 of common stock when the company was started. In addition, Ingals borrowed $20,000 from the local bank on April 1, Year 1. The note had an 8 percent annual interest rate and a one-year term to maturity. Ingals Co. recognized $54,000 of revenue on account in Year 1 and $65,000 of revenue on account in Year 2. Cash collections from accounts receivable were $46,000 in Year 1 and $63,000 in Year 2. Ingals Co. paid $27,000 of salaries expense in Year 1 and $36,000 of salaries expense in Year 2. Ingals Co. paid the loan and interest at the maturity date.

Required

Based on the preceding information, answer the following questions. (*Hint:* Record the events in the accounting equation before answering the questions.)

a. What amount of net cash flow from operating activities would Ingals report on the Year 1 cash flow statement?
b. What amount of interest expense would Ingals report on the Year 1 income statement?
c. What amount of total liabilities would Ingals report on the December 31, Year 1, balance sheet?
d. What amount of retained earnings would Ingals report on the December 31, Year 1, balance sheet?
e. What amount of cash flow from financing activities would Ingals report on the Year 1 statement of cash flows?
f. What amount of interest expense would Ingals report on the Year 2 income statement?
g. What amount of cash flows from operating activities would Ingals report on the Year 2 cash flows statement?
h. What amount of total assets would Ingals report on the December 31, Year 2, balance sheet?

LO 9-1, 9-2

Problem 9-20B *Accounting for short-term debt and sales tax—two accounting cycles*

The following transactions apply to Barclay Co. for Year 1, its first year of operations:

1. Received $50,000 cash from the issue of a short-term note with a 5 percent interest rate and a one-year maturity. The note was made on April 1, Year 1.
2. Received $140,000 cash plus applicable sales tax from performing services. The services are subject to a sales tax rate of 6 percent.
3. Paid $84,000 cash for other operating expenses during the year.
4. Paid the sales tax due on $110,000 of the service revenue for the year. Sales tax on the balance of the revenue is not due until Year 2.
5. Recognized the accrued interest at December 31, Year 1.

The following transactions apply to Barclay Co. for Year 2:

1. Paid the balance of the sales tax due for Year 1.
2. Received $155,000 cash plus applicable sales tax from performing services. The services are subject to a sales tax rate of 6 percent.
3. Repaid the principal of the note and applicable interest on April 1, Year 2.
4. Paid $96,000 of other operating expenses during the year.
5. Paid the sales tax due on $135,000 of the service revenue. The sales tax on the balance of the revenue is not due until Year 3.

Required

a. Record the Year 1 transactions in general journal form.
b. Post the transactions to T-accounts.
c. Prepare a balance sheet, statement of changes in stockholders' equity, income statement, and statement of cash flows for Year 1.
d. Prepare the closing entries and post them to the T-accounts.
e. Prepare a post-closing trial balance.
f. Repeat Requirements *a* through *e* for Year 2.

LO 9-3

Problem 9-21B *Contingent liabilities*

Required

How should each of the following situations be reported in the financial statements?

a. It has been determined that one of the company's products has caused a safety hazard. It is considered probable that liabilities have been incurred and a reasonable estimate of the amount can be made.
b. A company warehouse is located in a section of the city that has routinely flooded in the past. Consequently, the company can no longer find a source of insurance for the warehouse. No flood has yet occurred this year.
c. Because of newly passed legislation, a company will have to upgrade its facilities over the next two years. Significant expenditures will occur, but at this time the amount has not been determined.

Problem 9-22B Current liabilities

LO 9-1, 9-2, 9-3, 9-4

The following selected transactions were taken from the books of Dodson Company for Year 1:

1. On March 1, Year 1, borrowed $60,000 cash from the local bank. The note had a 6 percent interest rate and was due on September 1, Year 1.
2. Cash sales for the year amounted to $240,000 plus sales tax at the rate of 7 percent.
3. Dodson provides a 90-day warranty on the merchandise sold. The warranty expense is estimated to be 2 percent of sales.
4. Paid the sales tax to the state sales tax agency on $200,000 of the sales.
5. Paid the note due on September 1 and the related interest.
6. On October 1, Year 1, borrowed $50,000 cash from the local bank. The note had a 7 percent interest rate and a one-year term to maturity.
7. Paid $3,800 in warranty repairs.
8. A customer has filed a lawsuit against Dodson for $150,000 for breach of contract. The company attorney does not believe the suit has merit.

Required

a. Answer the following questions:
   (1) What amount of cash did Dodson pay for interest during the year?
   (2) What amount of interest expense is reported on Dodson's income statement for the year?
   (3) What is the amount of warranty expense for the year?
b. Prepare the current liabilities section of the balance sheet at December 31, Year 1. (*Hint:* First post the liabilities transactions to T-accounts.)
c. Show the effect of these transactions on the financial statements using a horizontal statements model like the one shown next. Use + for increase, − for decrease, and NA for not affected. In the Cash Flow column, indicate whether the item is an operating activity (OA), investing activity (IA), or financing activity (FA). The first transaction is recorded as an example.

Assets	=	Liabilities	+	Equity	Rev.	−	Exp.	=	Net Inc.	Cash Flow
+	=	+	+	NA	NA	−	NA	=	NA	+ FA

Problem 9-23B Accounting for payroll and payroll taxes

LO 9-5

Maddox Co. pays salaries monthly on the last day of the month. The following information is available from Maddox Co. for the month ended December 31, Year 1.

Administrative salaries	$85,000
Sales salaries	66,000
Office salaries	48,000

Assume the Social Security tax rate is 6 percent on the first $110,000 of salaries, while the Medicare tax rate is 1.5 percent on all salaries. James reached the $110,000 amount in October. His salary in December amounted to $11,000 and is included in the $85,000. No one else will reach the $110,000 amount for the year. None of the employee salaries are subject to unemployment tax in December.

Other amounts withheld from salaries in December were as follows:

Federal income tax	$24,500
State income tax	7,200
Employee savings plan	3,000

Required

a. Prepare the journal entry to record the payment of payroll on December 31, Year 1.
b. Prepare the journal entry to record the payroll tax expense for Maddox Co. for December Year 1.

LO 9-5

Problem 9-24B Computation of net pay and payroll expense

The following information is available for the employees of Yui Company for the first week of January Year 1:

1. Sam earns $32 per hour and 1½ times his regular rate for hours over 40 per week. He worked 46 hours the first week in January. Sam's federal income tax withholding is equal to 10 percent of his gross pay. Yui pays medical insurance of $75 per week for Sam and contributes $50 per week to a retirement plan for him.
2. Adam earns a weekly salary of $1,200. Adam's federal income tax withholding is 15 percent of his gross pay. Yui pays medical insurance of $110 per week for Adam and contributes $100 per week to a retirement plan for him.
3. Vacation pay is accrued at the rate of 1/4 of the regular pay rate per hour for Sam and $60 per week for Adam.

Assume the Social Security tax rate is 6 percent on the first $110,000 of salaries, and the Medicare tax rate is 1.5 percent of total salaries. The state unemployment tax rate is 5.4 percent and the federal unemployment tax rate is 0.6 percent of the first $7,000 of salary for each employee.

Required

a. Compute the gross pay for Sam for the first week in January.
b. Compute the net pay for both Sam and Adam for the first week in January.
c. Prepare the journal entry to record the payment of the payroll for the week.
d. Prepare the journal entry to record the payroll tax expense and fringe benefit expense for Yui for the week.
e. What is the total cost of compensation expense for the first week of January Year 1 for Yui Company?

LO 9-6

Problem 9-25B Multistep income statement and classified balance sheet

Required

Use the following information to prepare a multistep income statement and a classified balance sheet for Brown Company for Year 1. (*Hint:* Some of the items will *not* appear on either statement, and ending retained earnings must be calculated.)

Operating expenses	$ 45,000	Cash	$ 46,000
Land	75,000	Interest receivable (short term)	1,600
Accumulated depreciation	46,000	Cash flow from investing activities	(96,000)
Accounts payable	35,000	Allowance for doubtful accounts	14,000
Unearned revenue	27,000	Interest payable (short term)	6,000
Warranties payable (short term)	4,500	Sales revenue	900,000
Equipment	96,000	Uncollectible accounts expense	25,000
Notes payable (long term)	140,000	Interest expense	16,000
Salvage value of equipment	10,000	Accounts receivable	88,000
Dividends	15,000	Salaries payable	48,000
Warranty expense	7,200	Supplies	4,500
Beginning retained earnings	41,100	Prepaid rent	18,000
Interest revenue	4,200	Common stock	90,000
Gain on sale of equipment	7,000	Cost of goods sold	575,000
Inventory	126,000	Salaries expense	102,000
Notes receivable (short term)	12,500	Building	110,000

LO 9-7

Problem 9-26B Using ratios to make comparisons

The following accounting information exists for Collie and Spaniel companies:

	Collie	Spaniel
Cash	$ 12,000	$ 15,000
Wages payable	10,000	12,000
Merchandise inventory	20,000	55,000
Building	90,000	80,000
Accounts receivable	22,000	25,000
Long-term notes payable	80,000	100,000
Land	35,000	40,000
Accounts payable	25,000	35,000
Sales revenue	220,000	250,000
Expenses	190,000	230,000

Required

a. Identify the current assets and current liabilities and compute the current ratio for each company.
b. Assuming that all assets and liabilities are listed here, compute the debt-to-assets ratios for each company.
c. Determine which company has the greater financial risk in both the short term and the long term.

Problem 9-27B Accounting for a discount note—two accounting cycles (Appendix)

LO 9-8

Ball Company was started in Year 1. The following summarizes transactions that occurred during Year 1:

1. Issued a $40,000 face value discount note to Golden Savings Bank on April 1, Year 1. The note had a 6 percent discount rate and a one-year term to maturity.
2. Recognized revenue from services performed for cash, $130,000.
3. Incurred and paid $98,000 cash for selling and administrative expenses.
4. Amortized the discount on the note at the end of the year, December 31, Year 1.
5. Prepared the necessary closing entries at December 31, Year 1.

The following summarizes transactions that occurred in Year 2:

1. Recognized $215,000 of service revenue in cash.
2. Incurred and paid $151,000 for selling and administrative expenses.
3. Amortized the remainder of the discount for Year 2 and paid the face value of the note.
4. Prepared the necessary closing entries at December 31, Year 2.

Required

a. Show the effects of each of the transactions on the elements of the financial statements, using a horizontal statements model like the one shown next. Use + for increase, − for decrease, and NA for not affected. The first transaction is entered as an example. (*Hint:* Closing entries do not affect the statements model.)

Event No.	Assets	=	Liab.	+	Equity	Rev.	−	Exp.	=	Net Inc.	Cash Flow
1	+	=	+	+	NA	NA	−	NA	=	NA	+ FA

b. Prepare entries in general journal form for the transactions for Year 1 and Year 2, and post them to T-accounts.
c. Prepare an income statement, statement of changes in stockholders' equity, balance sheet, and statement of cash flows for Year 1 and Year 2.

ANALYZE, THINK, COMMUNICATE

ATC 9-1 Business Applications Case *Understanding real-world annual reports*

Required

Obtain the **Target Corporation's** annual report at http://investors.target.com using the instructions in Appendix B, and use it to answer the following questions:

a. What was Target's current ratio for its fiscal year ended January 28, 2017 (2016) and 2015?
b. Did the current ratio get stronger or weaker from 2015 to 2016? Explain briefly why this happened.
c. Target's balance sheet reports "Accrued and other current liabilities." What is included in this category? (See the notes to the financial statements.)

ATC 9-2 Group Assignment *Accounting for payroll*

The following payroll information is available for three companies for Year 1. Each company has two employees. Assume that the Social Security tax rate is 6 percent on the first $110,000 of earnings and that the Medicare tax rate is 1.5 percent on all earnings.

Brooks Company

Brooks Company	Hourly Rate	Regular Hours	Overtime Rate	Overtime Hours
Employee No. 1	$40	2,000	$60	300
Employee No. 2	20	2,000	30	100

Other benefits provided for the employees:
Medical insurance $250 per month for each employee
Pension benefits $100 per month for one employee

Federal income tax withheld is 15 percent of gross earnings for each employee. The state unemployment tax rate is 5.4 percent and the federal unemployment tax rate is 0.6 percent on the first $7,000 of earnings per employee.

Hill Company

Hill Company	Weekly Rate/Hourly Rate	Weeks/Hours Worked	Overtime Rate	Overtime Hours
Employee No. 1	$2,000	52	NA	NA
Employee No. 2	18/hr.	2,000	$27/hr.	60

Other benefits provided for the employees:
Medical and dental insurance $325 per month for each employee
Pension benefits $150 per month for one employee and
                               $100 per month for the other employee

Federal income tax withheld is 15 percent of gross earnings for each employee. The state unemployment tax rate is 5.4 percent and the federal unemployment tax rate is 0.6 percent on the first $7,000 of earnings per employee.

Valley Company

Valley Company	Monthly Rate/Hourly Rate	Monthly/Hours Worked	Overtime Rate	Overtime Hours
Employee No. 1	$10,500	12	NA	NA
Employee No. 2 (part time)	20/hr.	860	NA	NA

Other benefits provided for the employees:
Medical and dental insurance $375 per month for only one employee
Pension benefits   10% of gross salary for the full-time employee

Federal income tax withheld is 15 percent of gross earnings for each employee. The state unemployment tax rate is 5.4 percent and the federal unemployment tax rate is 0.6 percent on the first $7,000 of earnings per employee.

Required

a. Divide the class into groups of four or five students. Organize the groups into three sections. Assign each section of groups the payroll data for one of the above companies.

Group Tasks

(1) Determine the gross and net payroll for your company for the year.

(2) Determine the total compensation cost for your company for the year.

(3) Have a representative from each section put the compensation on the board broken down by salaries cost, payroll tax, and fringe benefit cost.

Class Discussion

b. Have the class discuss how the categories of compensation cost are similar and why some are more or less than those of the other companies.

ATC 9-3   Real-World Case   *Unusual types of liabilities*

In the liabilities section of its 2016 balance sheet, **Bank of America** reported "noninterest-bearing deposits" in U.S. offices of over $438 billion. Bank of America is a very large banking company. In the liabilities section of its 2016 balance sheet, **Newmont Mining Corporation** reported "reclamation and remediation liabilities" of more than $2.0 billion. Newmont Mining is involved in gold mining and refining activities. In its 2016 balance sheet, **Delta Air Lines**' largest current liability reported was $4.6 billion for "air traffic liability."

Required

a. For each of the preceding liabilities, write a brief explanation of what you believe the nature of the liability to be and how the company will pay it off. To develop your answers, think about the nature of the industry in which each of the companies operates.

b. Of the three liabilities described, which do you think poses the most risk for the company? In other words, for which liability are actual costs most likely to exceed the liability reported on the balance sheet? Uncertainty creates risk.

ATC 9-4   Business Applications Case   *Performing ratio analysis using real-world data*

Newell Brands, Inc. is the marketer of the well-known Rubbermaid plastic containers, but it also markets many other consumer brands, including Sharpie, Calphalon, Parker and Waterman writing instruments, and Lenox hand and power tools. The 2016 numbers are larger than those for 2015 because Newell acquired Jarden Corporation in 2016. Jarden's brands include Breville and Mr. Coffee. The following data were taken from the company's 2016 annual report. Dollar amounts are in millions.

	Fiscal Years Ending	
	December 31, 2016	**December 31, 2015**
Current assets	$ 7,484.5	$2,493.5
Current liabilities	4,292.0	1,988.6
Total assets	33,898.4	7,221.0
Total liabilities	22,453.1	5,394.6

Required

a. Compute Newell's current ratios for 2016 and 2015.

b. Compute Newell's debt-to-assets ratios for 2016 and 2015.

c. Based on the ratios computed in Requirements *a* and *b*, did Newell's liquidity get better or worse from 2015 to 2016?

d. Based on the ratios computed in Requirements *a* and *b*, did Newell's solvency get better or worse from 2015 to 2016?

ATC 9-5 Business Applications Case *Performing ratio analysis using real-world data*

Advanced Micro Devices, Inc. (AMD) is "a global semiconductor company with facilities around the world." AMD began operations in 1969. Texas Instruments, Inc. is the company that invented the integrated circuit over 45 years ago. It has more than 100,000 customers in over 30 countries. The following data were taken from the companies' 2016 annual reports. Dollar amounts are in millions.

	Advanced Micro Devices	Texas Instruments
Current assets	$2,530	$ 7,457
Current liabilities	1,346	2,264
Total assets	3,321	16,431
Total liabilities	2,905	5,958

Required

a. Compute the current ratio for each company.
b. Compute the debt-to-assets ratio for each company.
c. Based on the ratios computed in Requirements *a* and *b*, which company had the better liquidity in 2016?
d. Based on the ratios computed in Requirements *a* and *b*, which company had the better solvency in 2016?

ATC 9-6 Writing Assignment *Payroll tax costs*

Nancy, who graduated from State University in June Year 1, has just landed her first real job. She is excited because her salary is $4,000 per month. Nancy is single and has been planning all month about how she will spend her $4,000. When she received her first paycheck on June 30, Year 1, she was very disappointed. The amount of her check was only $3,100. Explain to Nancy why (generally) her check will not be for $4,000.

ATC 9-7 Ethical Dilemma *Who pays FICA taxes?*

Scott Putman owns and operates a lawn care company. Like most companies in the lawn care business, his company experiences a high level of employee turnover. However, he finds it relatively easy to replace employees because he pays above-market wages. He attributes his ability to pay high wages to a little accounting trick he discovered several years ago. Instead of paying his half of each employee's FICA taxes to the government, he decided to pay that money to the employees in the form of higher wages. He then doubles their FICA tax payroll deduction and uses half of the deduction to pay his share of the Social Security tax. For example, suppose he plans to pay an employee $2,000 per month. Technically, the employee would have to pay 7.5 percent FICA and Medicare tax ($2,000 × .075 = $150) and Mr. Putman's company would have to make a $150 matching payment. Instead of doing it this way, he devised the following plan. He pays the employee $2,150 and then deducts $300 for FICA and Medicare tax from the employee's salary. The end result is the same. Either way, the employee ends up with net pay of $1,850 ($2,000 − $150 = $1,850 or $2,150 − $300 = $1,850). Also, the government gets $300 FICA tax, regardless of how it gets divided between the employee and the employer. Mr. Putman is convinced that he is right in what he is doing. Certainly, it benefits his company by allowing him to offer higher starting salaries. Further, he believes it is a more honest way of showing the real cost of Social Security and Medicare.

Required

a. Is Mr. Putnam right in his assumption that the total tax paid is the same under his approach as it would be if proper accounting procedures were applied? Explain.
b. Assuming that Mr. Putman is a CPA, do his actions violate any of the articles of the AICPA Code of Professional Conduct shown in Chapter 2 (Exhibit 2.9)? If so, discuss some of the articles that are violated.
c. Discuss Mr. Putman's actions within the context of the fraud triangle's elements of ethical misconduct that were outlined in Chapter 2.

ATC 9-8 Research Assignment *Analyzing AutoZone's liquidity*

Using either the most current Form 10-K for AutoZone, Inc. or the company's annual report, answer the following questions. To obtain the Form 10-K, either use the EDGAR system (following the instructions in Appendix A), or the company's website. The company's annual report is available on its website.

Required

a. What is AutoZone's current ratio?
b. Which of AutoZone's current assets had the largest balance?
c. What percentage of AutoZone's total assets consisted of current assets?
d. If AutoZone were a company that manufactured auto parts rather than a retailer of auto parts, how do you think its balance sheet would be different?

ATC 9-9 Spreadsheet Assignment

The following information is available for Lumberton Co. for the week ending June 28, Year 1. All employees are paid time and one-half for all hours over 40. Each employee has a cumulative salary of over $7,000, but less than $110,000. Assume the Social Security tax rate is 6 percent on the first $110,000 of wages and that the Medicare tax rate is 1.5 percent of total wages. The company contributes the retirement cost to a retirement plan for the employee.

Employee	Rate of Pay	Hours	Fed WH %	Contributions to Retirement Plans
Jillian	$15 per hour	32	12%	$20 per week
Carl	18	46	10	10% of gross pay
Yolanda	16	45	10	10% of gross pay

Required

a. Set up a spreadsheet to compute the net pay for each of the preceding employees. You will need to insert the appropriate Excel formulas.

Source: Microsoft Office Excel 2010

b. What is the total amount of compensation cost (salary cost plus payroll tax cost) for Lumberton Co. for the week ending June 28, Year 1?

c. Lumberton is considering adding group health insurance coverage for its employees to its benefits package. If the average cost of health insurance per employee is $3,900 per year, how much additional cost would be added to the weekly compensation cost for Lumberton? Assume the addition of health insurance and recompute the total compensation cost for Lumberton for the week ending June 28, Year 1.

ATC 9-10 Spreadsheet Assignment *Mastering Excel*

Refer to Problem 9-17A. Complete Requirements *a*, *b*, *c*, and *d* using an Excel spreadsheet. Refer to Chapter 1, Problem ATC 1-8, for ideas on how to structure the spreadsheet.

COMPREHENSIVE PROBLEM

The trial balance of Pacilio Security Services, Inc. as of January 1, Year 9, had the following normal balances:

Cash	$93,380
Petty Cash	100
Accounts receivable	21,390
Allowance for doubtful accounts	2,485
Supplies	180
Prepaid rent	3,000
Merchandise inventory (23 @ $280)	6,440
Equipment	9,000
Van	27,000
Accumulated depreciation	14,900
Salaries payable	1,500
Common stock	50,000
Retained earnings	91,605

During Year 9, Pacilio Security Services experienced the following transactions:

1. Paid the salaries payable from Year 8.
2. Paid $9,000 on May 2, Year 9, for one year's office rent in advance.
3. Purchased $425 of supplies on account.
4. Purchased 145 alarm systems at a cost of $290 each. Paid cash for the purchase.
5. After numerous attempts to collect from customers, wrote off $2,060 of uncollectible accounts receivable.
6. Sold 130 alarm systems for $580 each plus sales tax of 5 percent. All sales were on account. (Be sure to compute cost of goods sold using the FIFO cost flow method.)
7. Billed $107,000 of monitoring services for the year. Credit card sales amounted to $42,000, and the credit card company charged a 4 percent fee. The remaining $65,000 were sales on account. Sales tax is not charged on this service.
8. Replenished the petty cash fund on June 30. The fund had $5 cash and has receipts of $60 for yard mowing, $15 for office supplies expense, and $17 for miscellaneous expenses.
9. Collected the amount due from the credit card company.
10. Paid the sales tax collected on $69,600 of the alarm sales.
11. Paid installers and other employees a total of $65,000 for salaries for the year. Assume the Social Security tax rate is 6 percent and the Medicare tax rate is 1.5 percent. Federal income taxes withheld amounted to $7,500. Cash was paid for the net amount of salaries due.
12. Pacilio now offers a one-year warranty on its alarm systems. Paid $1,950 in warranty repairs during the year.
13. On September 1, borrowed $12,000 from State Bank. The note had an 8 percent interest rate and a one-year term to maturity.
14. Collected $136,100 of accounts receivable during the year.

15. Paid $15,000 of advertising expense during the year.
16. Paid $7,200 of utilities expense for the year.
17. Paid the payroll taxes, both the amounts withheld from the salaries plus the employer share of Social Security tax and Medicare tax, on $60,000 of the salaries plus $7,000 of the federal income tax that was withheld. (Unemployment taxes were not paid at this time.)
18. Paid the accounts payable.
19. Paid a dividend of $10,000 to the shareholders.

Adjustments

20. There was $165 of supplies on hand at the end of the year.
21. Recognized the expired rent for the office building for the year.
22. Recognized uncollectible accounts expense for the year using the allowance method. The company revised its estimate of uncollectible accounts based on prior years' experience. This year, Pacilio estimates that 2.75 percent of sales on account will not be collected.
23. Recognized depreciation expense on the equipment and the van. The equipment has a five-year life and a $2,000 salvage value. The van has a four-year life and a $6,000 salvage value. The company uses double-declining-balance for the van and straight-line for the equipment. (A full year's depreciation was taken in Year 8, the year of acquisition.)
24. The alarm systems sold in transaction 6 were covered with a one-year warranty. Pacilio estimated that the warranty cost would be 3 percent of alarm sales.
25. Recognized the accrued interest on the note payable at December 31, Year 9.
26. The unemployment tax on salaries has not been paid. Recorded the accrued unemployment tax on the salaries for the year. The unemployment tax rate is 4.5 percent. ($14,000 of salaries is subject to this tax.)
27. Recognized the employer Social Security and Medicare payroll tax that has not been paid on $5,000 of salaries expense.

Required

a. Record the preceding transactions in general journal form. Round all amounts to the nearest whole dollar.
b. Post the transactions to the T-accounts.
c. Prepare a trial balance.
d. Prepare an income statement, statement of changes in stockholders' equity, a classified balance sheet, and statement of cash flows.
e. Close the temporary accounts to retained earnings.
f. Post the closing entries to the T-accounts and prepare a post-closing trial balance.

CHAPTER 10

Accounting for Long-Term Debt

LEARNING OBJECTIVES

After you have mastered the material in this chapter, you will be able to:

LO 10-1 Show how an installment note affects financial statements.

LO 10-2 Show how a line of credit affects financial statements.

LO 10-3 Describe bond features and show how bonds issued at face value affect financial statements.

LO 10-4 Use the straight-line method to amortize bond discounts.

LO 10-5 Use the straight-line method to amortize bond premiums.

LO 10-6 Use the effective interest rate method to amortize bond discounts.

LO 10-7 Use the effective interest rate method to amortize bond premiums.

LO 10-8 Explain the advantages and disadvantages of debt financing.

 Video lectures and accompanying self-assessment quizzes are available in Connect *for all learning objectives.*

CHAPTER OPENING

Most businesses finance their investing activities with long-term debt. Recall that current liabilities mature within one year or a company's operating cycle, whichever is longer. Other liabilities are **long-term liabilities.** Long-term debt agreements vary with respect to requirements for paying interest charges and repaying principal (the amount borrowed). Interest payments may be due monthly, annually, at some other interval, or at the maturity date. Interest charges may be based on a **fixed interest rate** that remains constant during the term of the loan or on a **variable interest rate** that fluctuates up or down during the loan period.

Principal repayment is generally required either in one lump sum at the maturity date or in installments that are spread over the life of the loan. For example, each monthly payment on your car loan probably includes both paying interest and repaying some of the principal. Repaying a portion of the principal with regular payments that also include interest is often called loan **amortization.**[1] This chapter explains accounting for interest and principal with respect to the major forms of long-term debt financing.

---

[1]In Chapter 8, the term *amortization* described the expense recognized when the cost of an intangible asset is systematically allocated to expense over the useful life of the asset. This chapter shows that the term *amortization* refers more broadly to a variety of allocation processes. Here it means the systematic process of allocating interest to the periods in which the loan is outstanding.

The Curious Accountant

In 2016, **Rent-A-Center, Inc.** reported a net loss of $105 million. The previous year it had reported a loss of $954 million. The company had $47 million of interest expense in 2016. As a point of reference, revenue for Rent-A-Center for 2016 was only $2.9 billion, so these losses were substantial.

With such a huge loss on its income statement, do you think Rent-A-Center was able to make the interest payments on its debt? If so, how? (Answers on page 539.)

©Dorann Weber/Moment Mobile/Getty Images

INSTALLMENT NOTES PAYABLE

LO 10-1

Show how an installment note affects financial statements.

Loans that require payments of principal and interest at regular intervals (amortizing loans) are typically represented by **installment notes.** The terms of installment notes usually range from two to five years. To illustrate accounting for installment notes, assume Blair Company was started on January 1, Year 1, when it borrowed $100,000 cash from National Bank. In exchange for the money, Blair issued the bank a five-year installment note with a 9 percent fixed interest rate. The journal entry to record issuing the note and its effects on the financial statements are as follows:

Date	Account Title	Debit	Credit
Year 1 Jan. 1	Cash	100,000	
	Installment Note Payable		100,000

	Assets	=	Liab.	+	Equity			Rev.	−	Exp.	=	Net Inc.	Cash Flow
Date	Cash	=	Note Pay.	+	Com. Stk.	+	Ret. Earn.						
Year 1 Jan. 1	100,000	=	100,000	+	NA	+	NA	NA	−	NA	=	NA	100,000 FA

The loan agreement required Blair to pay five equal installments of $25,709[2] on December 31 of Year 1 through Year 5. Exhibit 10.1 shows the allocation of each payment between principal and interest. When Blair pays the final installment, both the principal and interest will be paid in full. The amounts shown in Exhibit 10.1 are computed as follows:

1. The Interest Expense (Column D) is computed by multiplying the Principal Balance on Jan. 1 (Column B) by the interest rate. For example, interest expense for Year 1 is $100,000 × 0.09 = $9,000; for Year 2 it is $83,291 × 0.09 = $7,496; and so on.

2. The Principal Repayment (Column E) is computed by subtracting the Interest Expense (Column D) from the Cash Payment on Dec. 31 (Column C). For example, the Principal Repayment for Year 1 is $25,709 − $9,000 = $16,709; for Year 2 it is $25,709 − $7,496 = $18,213; and so on.

EXHIBIT 10.1

Amortization Schedule for Installment Note Payable

Accounting Period Column A	Principal Balance on Jan. 1 Column B	Cash Payment on Dec. 31 Column C	Interest Expense Column D	Principal Repayment Column E	Principal Balance on Dec. 31 Column F
Year 1	$100,000	$25,709	$9,000	$16,709	$83,291
Year 2	83,291	25,709	7,496	18,213	65,078
Year 3	65,078	25,709	5,857	19,852	45,226
Year 4	45,226	25,709	4,070	21,639	23,587
Year 5	23,587	25,710*	2,123	23,587	0

*All computations are rounded to the nearest dollar. To fully liquidate the liability, the final payment is one dollar more than the others because of rounding differences.

[2]The amount of the annual payment is determined using the present value concepts presented in Appendix F at the end of this textbook. Usually the lender (bank or other financial institution) calculates the amount of the payment for the customer.

Answers to The Curious Accountant

Even though **Rent-A-Center** reported a $105 million loss in 2016, it was able to make the interest payments on its debt with no difficulty for two reasons. First, interest is paid with cash, not accrual earnings. Many of the expenses on the company's income statement did not require the use of cash in 2016. For example, Rent-A-Center reported a depreciation and amortization expense of $80 million, which did not require cash. Also, it reported $151 million of charges for impairments of goodwill, but this charge also did not require any cash payments.

Second, the net loss the company incurred was *after* the interest expense of $47 million had been deducted. The company's statement of cash flows shows that net cash flow from operating activities in 2016, *after making interest payments,* was a positive $354 million. The capacity of operations to support interest payments is measured by the amount of earnings before interest deductions. For example, look at the Year 1 income statement for Blair Company in Exhibit 10.2. This statement shows only $3,000 of net income, but $12,000 of cash revenue was available for the payment of interest. Similarly, Rent-A-Center's 2016 net loss is not an indication of the company's ability to pay interest in the short run.

EXHIBIT 10.2

BLAIR COMPANY
Financial Statements

	Year 1	Year 2	Year 3	Year 4	Year 5
Income Statements					
Rent revenue	$ 12,000	$12,000	$12,000	$12,000	$12,000
Interest expense	(9,000)	(7,496)	(5,857)	(4,070)	(2,123)
Net income	$ 3,000	$ 4,504	$ 6,143	$ 7,930	$ 9,877
Balance Sheets					
Assets					
Cash	$ 86,291	$72,582	$58,873	$45,164	$31,454
Liabilities					
Note payable	$ 83,291	$65,078	$45,226	$23,587	$ 0
Stockholders' equity					
Retained earnings	3,000	7,504	13,647	21,577	31,454
Total liabilities and stk. equity	$ 86,291	$72,582	$58,873	$45,164	$31,454
Statements of Cash Flows					
Operating Activities					
Inflow from customers	$ 12,000	$12,000	$12,000	$12,000	$12,000
Outflow for interest	(9,000)	(7,496)	(5,857)	(4,070)	(2,123)
Investing Activities	0	0	0	0	0
Financing Activities					
Inflow from note issue	100,000	0	0	0	0
Outflow to repay note	(16,709)	(18,213)	(19,852)	(21,639)	(23,587)
Net change in cash	86,291	(13,709)	(13,709)	(13,709)	(13,710)
Plus: Beginning cash balance	0	86,291	72,582	58,873	45,164
Ending cash balance	$ 86,291	$72,582	$58,873	$45,164	$31,454

3. The Principal Balance on Dec. 31 (Column F) is computed by subtracting the Principal Repayment (Column E) from the Principal Balance on Jan. 1 (Column B). For example, the Principal Balance on Dec. 31 for Year 1 is $100,000 − $16,709 = $83,291; on December 31, Year 2, the principal balance is $83,291 − $18,213 = $65,078; and so on. The Principal Balance on Dec. 31 (ending balance) for Year 1 ($83,291) is also the Principal Balance on Jan. 1 (beginning balance) for Year 2; the principal balance on December 31, Year 2, is the principal balance on January 1, Year 3, and so on.

Although the amounts for interest expense and principal repayment differ each year, the effects of the annual payment on the financial statements are the same. On the balance sheet, assets (cash) decrease by the total amount of the payment; liabilities (notes payable) decrease by the amount of the principal repayment; and stockholders' equity (retained earnings) decreases by the amount of interest expense. Net income decreases from recognizing interest expense. On the statement of cash flows, the portion of the cash payment applied to interest is reported in the operating activities section, and the portion applied to principal is reported in the financing activities section. The journal entry to record the December 31, Year 1, cash payment and its effects on the financial statements are as follows:

Date	Account Title	Debit	Credit
Year 1 Dec. 31	Interest Expense	9,000	
	Installment Note Payable	16,709	
	Cash		25,709

	Assets	=	Liab.	+	Equity		Rev.	−	Exp.	=	Net Inc.	Cash Flow
Date	Cash	=	Note Pay.	+	Com. Stk. + Ret. Earn.							
Year 1 Dec. 31	(25,709)	=	(16,709)	+	NA + (9,000)		NA	−	9,000	=	(9,000)	(9,000) OA (16,709) FA

Exhibit 10.2 displays income statements, balance sheets, and statements of cash flows for Blair Company for the accounting periods Year 1 through Year 5. The illustration assumes that Blair earned $12,000 of rent revenue each year. Because some of the principal is repaid each year, the note payable amount reported on the balance sheet and the amount of the interest expense on the income statement both decline each year.

CHECK YOURSELF 10.1

On January 1, Year 1, Krueger Company issued a $50,000 installment note to State Bank. The note had a 10-year term and an 8 percent interest rate. Krueger agreed to repay the principal and interest in 10 annual payments of $7,451.47 at the end of each year. Determine the amount of principal and interest Krueger paid during the first and second year that the note was outstanding.

Answer

Accounting Period	Principal Balance January 1 A	Cash Payment December 31 B	Applied to Interest C = A × 0.08	Applied to Principal B − C
Year 1	$50,000.00	$7,451.47	$4,000.00	$3,451.47
Year 2	46,548.53	7,451.47	3,723.88	3,727.59

LINE OF CREDIT

A **line of credit** enables a company to borrow or repay funds as needed. For example, a business may borrow $50,000 one month and make a partial repayment of $10,000 the next month. Credit agreements usually specify a limit on the amount that can be borrowed. Exhibit 10.3 shows that credit agreements are widely used.

Interest rates on lines of credit normally vary with fluctuations in some designated interest rate benchmark such as the rate paid on U.S. Treasury bills. For example, a company may pay 4 percent interest one month and 4.5 percent the next month, even if the principal balance remains constant.

Lines of credit typically have one-year terms. Although they are classified on the balance sheet as short-term liabilities, lines of credit are frequently extended indefinitely by simply renewing the credit agreement.

To illustrate accounting for a line of credit, assume Lagoon Company owns a wholesale jet-ski distributorship. In the spring, Lagoon borrows money using a line of credit to finance building up its inventory. Lagoon repays the loan over the summer months using cash generated from jet-ski sales. Borrowing or repaying events occur on the first of the month. Interest payments occur at the end of each month. Exhibit 10.4 presents all Year 1 line of credit events.

Each borrowing event (March 1, April 1, and May 1) is an asset source transaction. Both cash and the line of credit liability increase. Each repayment (June 1, July 1, and August 1) is an asset use transaction. Both cash and the line of credit liability decrease. Each month's interest expense recognition and payment is an asset use transaction. Assets (cash) and stockholders' equity (retained earnings) decrease, as does net income. The journal entries to record the events are shown in Panel A of Exhibit 10.5. The effects of the events on the financial statements are shown in Panel B.

LO 10-2

Show how a line of credit affects financial statements.

EXHIBIT 10.3

Percentage of Dow Companies Disclosing Credit Agreements

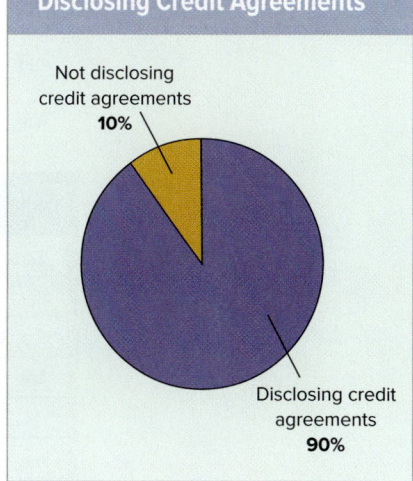

Source: The chart is based on data drawn from recent annual reports published by the 30 companies that comprise the Dow Jones Industrial Average.

EXHIBIT 10.4

Summary of Line of Credit Events

Date	Amount Borrowed (Repaid)	Loan Balance at End of Month	Effective Interest Rate per Month (%)	Interest Expense (rounded to nearest $1)
Mar. 1	$ 20,000	$ 20,000	0.09 ÷ 12	$150
Apr. 1	30,000	50,000	0.09 ÷ 12	375
May 1	50,000	100,000	0.105 ÷ 12	875
June 1	(10,000)	90,000	0.10 ÷ 12	750
July 1	(40,000)	50,000	0.09 ÷ 12	375
Aug. 1	(50,000)	0	0.09 ÷ 12	0

EXHIBIT 10.5

Panel A: Journal Entries

Date	Account Title	Debit	Credit
Mar. 1	Cash	20,000	
	Note Payable		20,000
Mar. 31	Interest Expense	150	
	Cash		150
Apr. 1	Cash	30,000	
	Note Payable		30,000

continued

EXHIBIT 10.5 Concluded

Date	Account	Debit	Credit
Apr. 30	Interest Expense	375	
	Cash		375
May 1	Cash	50,000	
	Note Payable		50,000
May 31	Interest Expense	875	
	Cash		875
June 1	Note Payable	10,000	
	Cash		10,000
June 30	Interest Expense	750	
	Cash		750
July 1	Note Payable	40,000	
	Cash		40,000
July 31	Interest Expense	375	
	Cash		375
Aug. 1	Note Payable	50,000	
	Cash		50,000

Panel B: Effects on Financial Statements

Date	Assets	=	Liabilities	+	Equity	Rev.	−	Exp.	=	Net Inc.	Cash Flow	
Mar. 1	20,000	=	20,000	+	NA	NA	−	NA	=	NA	20,000	FA
31	(150)	=	NA	+	(150)	NA	−	150	=	(150)	(150)	OA
Apr. 1	30,000	=	30,000	+	NA	NA	−	NA	=	NA	30,000	FA
30	(375)	=	NA	+	(375)	NA	−	375	=	(375)	(375)	OA
May 1	50,000	=	50,000	+	NA	NA	−	NA	=	NA	50,000	FA
31	(875)	=	NA	+	(875)	NA	−	875	=	(875)	(875)	OA
June 1	(10,000)	=	(10,000)	+	NA	NA	−	NA	=	NA	(10,000)	FA
30	(750)	=	NA	+	(750)	NA	−	750	=	(750)	(750)	OA
July 1	(40,000)	=	(40,000)	+	NA	NA	−	NA	=	NA	(40,000)	FA
31	(375)	=	NA	+	(375)	NA	−	375	=	(375)	(375)	OA
Aug. 1	(50,000)	=	(50,000)	+	NA	NA	−	NA	=	NA	(50,000)	FA
31	NA	=	NA	+	NA	NA	−	NA	=	NA	NA	

BOND LIABILITIES

LO 10-3

Describe bond features and show how bonds issued at face value affect financial statements.

Many companies borrow money directly from the public by selling **bond certificates,** otherwise called *issuing* bonds. Bond certificates describe a company's obligation to pay interest and to repay the principal. The seller, or **issuer,** of a bond is the borrower; the buyer of a bond, or **bondholder,** is the lender.

From the issuer's point of view, a bond represents an obligation to pay a sum of money to the bondholder on the bond's maturity date. The amount due at maturity is the **face value** of the bond. Most bonds also require the issuer to make cash interest payments based on a **stated interest rate** at regular intervals over the life of the bond. Exhibit 10.6 shows a typical bond certificate.

Advantages of Issuing Bonds

Bond financing offers companies the following advantages:

1. Bonds usually have longer terms than notes issued to banks. While typical bank loan terms range from 2 to 5 years, bonds normally have 20-year terms to maturity. Longer

EXHIBIT 10.6
Bond Certificate

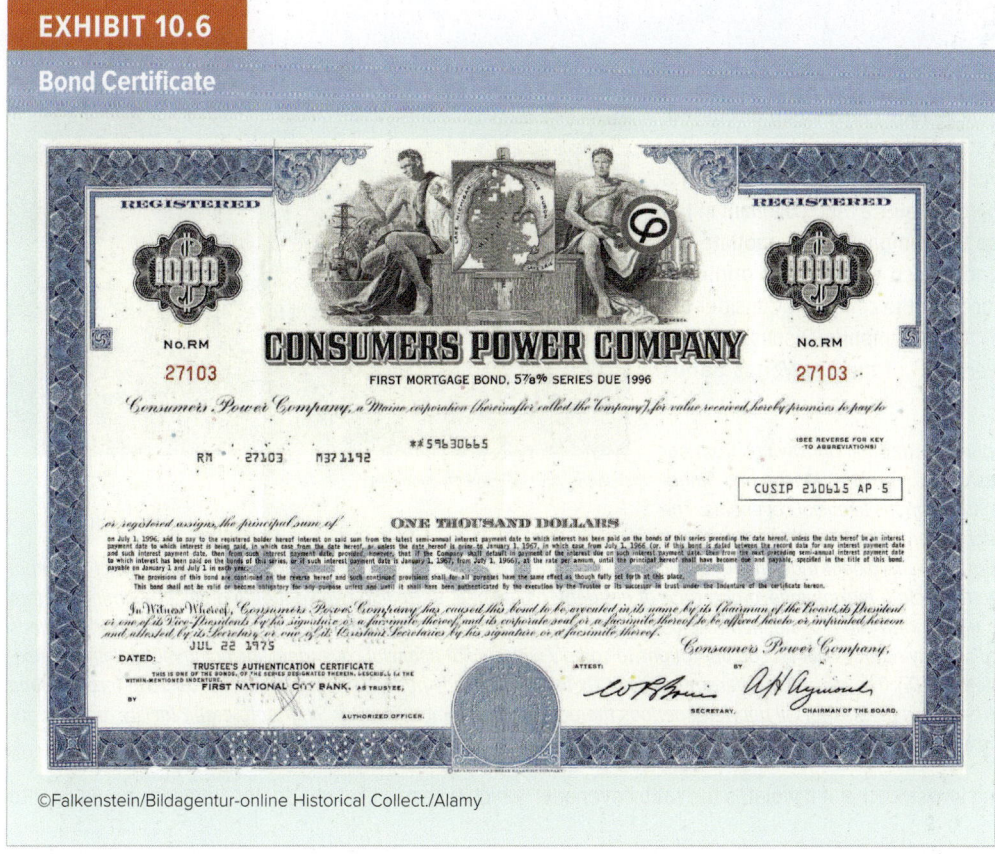

©Falkenstein/Bildagentur-online Historical Collect./Alamy

terms to maturity allow companies to implement long-term strategic plans without having to worry about frequent refinancing arrangements.

2. Bond interest rates may be lower than bank interest rates. Banks earn profits by borrowing money from the public (depositors) at low interest rates, then loaning that money to companies at higher rates. By issuing bonds directly to the public, companies can pay lower interest costs by eliminating the intermediary (banks).

Security of Bonds

Bonds may be either secured or unsecured.

1. **Secured bonds** grant their holders a priority legal claim on specified identifiable assets should the issuer default. A common type of secured bond is a **mortgage bond,** which conditionally transfers the title of designated property to the bondholder until the bond is paid.
2. **Unsecured bonds,** also called **debentures,** are issued based on the general strength of the borrower's credit. Bond certificates often specify the priority of debenture holders' claims relative to other creditors. Holders of **subordinated debentures** have lower priority claims than other creditors, whereas holders of **unsubordinated debentures** have equal claims.

Timing of Maturity

The maturity dates of bonds can be specified in various ways. Even bonds sold as separate components of a single issue may have different maturity dates.

1. **Term bonds** mature on a specified date in the future.
2. **Serial bonds** mature at specified intervals throughout the life of the total issue. For example, bonds with a total face value of $1,000,000 may mature in increments of $100,000 every year for 10 years.

REALITY BYTES

Throughout this textbook, various financial ratios have been discussed, along with explanations of how they are used by financial analysts. Ratios are also often included as covenants in loan agreements when a company borrows money. If the company violates a ratio covenant in the loan agreement, the lender can force the company to renegotiate the loan or pay back the borrowed funds much earlier than originally agreed. This can have dire consequences for the company. Consider the following excerpts taken from the "Management's Discussion and Analysis . . . - *Capital Financing Overview*" of the **Las Vegas Sands Corporation**'s 2016 Form 10-K.

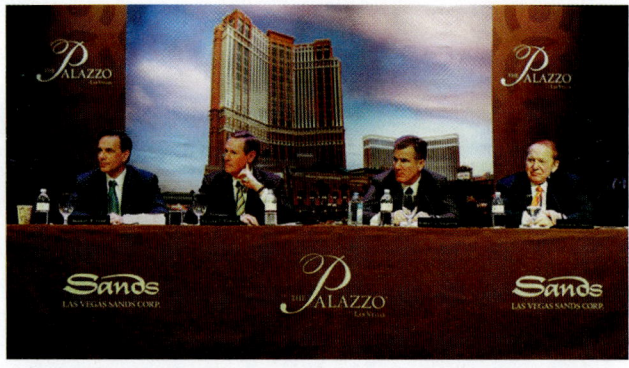

©Jacob Andrzejczak/Getty Images

> *We fund our development projects primarily through borrowings from our credit facilities . . . and operating cash flows. Our U.S., Macao and Singapore credit facilities, as amended, contain various financial covenants. The U.S. credit facility requires our Las Vegas operations to comply with a financial covenant at the end of each quarter to the extent that any revolving loans or certain letters of credit are outstanding. This financial covenant requires our Las Vegas operations to maintain a maximum leverage ratio of net debt, as defined, to trailing twelve-month adjusted earnings before interest, income taxes, depreciation and amortization, as defined ("Adjusted EBITDA"). The maximum leverage ratio is 5.5x for all quarterly periods through maturity. . . . Our Macao credit facility requires our Macao operations to comply with similar financial covenants, including maintaining a maximum leverage ratio of debt to Adjusted EBITDA. The maximum leverage ratio is 4.0x for the quarterly periods ending December 31, 2016 through June 30, 2017, and then decreases to, and remains at, 3.5x for all quarterly periods thereafter through maturity. Our Singapore credit facility requires our Marina Bay Sands operations to comply with similar financial covenants, ...*

Simply put, the company is warning investors that if it violates the ratio covenants, which it seems likely to do, the company could go into bankruptcy. Ratios matter!

To ensure there is enough cash available at maturity to pay off the debt, a bond agreement may require the issuer to make regular payments into a **sinking fund.** Money deposited in the sinking fund is usually managed by an independent trustee who invests the funds until the bonds mature. At maturity, the funds and the proceeds from the investments are used to repay the bond debt.

Special Features

Some bonds feature one or both of the following characteristics:

1. **Convertible bonds** are liabilities that can be exchanged at the option of the bondholder for common stock or some other specified ownership interest. The issuing company benefits because bondholders (investors) are willing to accept a lower interest rate in exchange for the conversion feature. Bondholders benefit because they obtain the option to share in potential rewards of ownership. If the market value of the company's stock increases, bondholders can convert their bonds to stock. If the stock price does not increase, bondholders are still guaranteed interest payments and priority claims in bankruptcy settlements.

2. **Callable bonds** allow the issuing company to redeem (pay off) the bond debt before the maturity date. If interest rates decline, this feature benefits the issuing company because it could borrow additional money at a lower rate and use the proceeds to pay off its higher rate bonds. Because an early redemption would eliminate their higher-interest bond investments, bondholders consider call features undesirable. To encourage investors to buy callable bonds, the **call price** normally exceeds the *face value* of the bonds. For example, the issuing company may agree to pay the holder of a $1,000 face-value bond a call price of $1,050 if the bond is redeemed before its maturity date. The difference between the call price and the face value ($50 [$1,050 − $1,000] in this case) is commonly called a **call premium.**

Bond Ratings

Three financial services analyze the risk of default for corporate bond issues and publish ratings of the risk as guides to bond investors. These agencies are Fitch, Moody's, and Standard & Poor's. The highest rating (lowest risk) a company can achieve is AAA, the next highest is AA, and so forth. Bond issuers try to maintain high credit ratings because lower ratings require them to pay higher interest rates.

Restrictive Covenants

In general, large loans with long terms to maturity pose more risk to lenders (creditors) than small loans with short terms. To reduce the risk that they won't get paid, lenders frequently require borrowers (debtors) to pledge designated assets as **collateral** for loans. For example, when a bank makes a car loan, it usually retains legal title to the car until the loan is fully repaid. If the borrower fails to make the monthly payments, the bank repossesses the car, sells it to someone else, and uses the proceeds to pay the original owner's debt. Similarly, assets like accounts receivable, inventory, equipment, buildings, and land may be pledged as collateral for business loans.

Besides requiring collateral, creditors often obtain additional protection by including **restrictive covenants** in loan agreements. Such covenants may restrict additional borrowing, limit dividend payments, or restrict salary increases. If the loan restrictions are violated, the borrower is in default and the loan balance is due immediately.

Finally, creditors often ask owners and executives of nonpublic companies to provide copies of their personal tax returns and financial statements. The financial condition of the owners and executives is important because they may be asked to pledge personal property as collateral for business loans.

Bonds Issued at Face Value

Assume Marsha Mason needs cash in order to seize a business opportunity. Mason knows of a company seeking a plot of land on which to store its inventory of crushed stone. Mason also knows of a suitable tract of land she could purchase for $100,000. The company has agreed to lease the land it needs from Mason for $12,000 per year. Mason lacks the funds to buy the land.

Some of Mason's friends recently complained about the low interest rates banks were paying on certificates of deposit. Mason suggested that her friends invest in bonds instead of CDs. She offered to sell them bonds with a 9 percent stated interest rate. The terms specified in the bond agreement Mason drafted included making interest payments in cash on December 31 of each year, a five-year term to maturity, and pledging the land as collateral for the bonds.[3] Her friends were favorably impressed, and Mason issued the bonds to them in exchange for cash on January 1, Year 1.

Mason used the bond proceeds to purchase the land, and then immediately contracted to lease it for five years. On December 31, Year 5, the maturity date of the bonds, Mason sold the land for its $100,000 book value and used the proceeds from the sale to repay the bond liability.

Journal Entries and Financial Statement Effects

Mason's business venture involved six distinct accounting events, described next.

EVENT 1 Issued bonds for $100,000 cash.

Assets (cash) and liabilities (bonds payable) increase. Net income is not affected. The $100,000 cash inflow is reported in the financing activities section of the statement of

---

[3] In practice, bonds are usually issued for much larger sums of money, often hundreds of millions of dollars. Also, terms to maturity are normally long, with 20 years being common. Using such large amounts for such long terms is unnecessarily cumbersome for instructional purposes. The effects of bond issues can be illustrated efficiently by using smaller amounts of debt with shorter maturities, as assumed in the case of Marsha Mason.

cash flows. The journal entry and its effects on the financial statements are shown next:

Account Title	Debit	Credit
Cash	100,000	
Bonds Payable		100,000

Assets	=	Liab.	+	Equity	Rev.	−	Exp.	=	Net Inc.	Cash Flow	
Cash	=	Bonds Pay.									
100,000	=	100,000	+	NA	NA	−	NA	=	NA	100,000	NA

EVENT 2   Paid $100,000 cash to purchase land.

The asset cash decreases and the asset land increases. The income statement is not affected. The cash outflow is reported in the investing activities section of the statement of cash flows. The journal entry and its effects on the financial statements are shown next:

Account Title	Debit	Credit
Land	100,000	
Cash		100,000

Assets			=	Liab.	+	Equity	Rev.	−	Exp.	=	Net Inc.	Cash Flow	
Cash	+	Land											
(100,000)	+	100,000	=	NA	+	NA	NA	−	NA	=	NA	(100,000)	IA

EVENT 3   Recognized $12,000 cash revenue from renting the land.

This event is repeated each year from Year 1 through Year 5. The event increases assets and stockholders' equity. Recognizing revenue increases net income. The cash inflow is reported in the operating activities section of the statement of cash flows. The journal entry and its effects on the financial statements are shown next:

Account Title	Debit	Credit
Cash	12,000	
Rent Revenue		12,000

Assets	=	Liab.	+	Equity	Rev.	−	Exp.	=	Net Inc.	Cash Flow	
Cash	=			Ret. Earn.							
12,000	=	NA	+	12,000	12,000	−	NA	=	12,000	12,000	OA

EVENT 4   Paid $9,000 cash for interest.

This event is also repeated each year from Year 1 through Year 5. The interest payment is an asset use transaction. Cash and stockholders' equity (retained earnings) decrease. The expense recognition decreases net income. The cash outflow is reported in the operating activities section of the statement of cash flows. The journal entry and its effects on the financial statements are shown next:

Account Title	Debit	Credit
Interest Expense	9,000	
Cash		9,000

Assets	=	Liab.	+	Equity	Rev.	−	Exp.	=	Net Inc.	Cash Flow
Cash	=			Ret. Earn.						
(9,000)	=	NA	+	(9,000)	NA	−	9,000	=	(9,000)	(9,000) OA

EVENT 5 Sold the land for cash equal to its $100,000 book value.

Cash increases and land decreases. Because there was no gain or loss on the sale, the income statement is not affected. The cash inflow is reported in the investing activities section of the statement of cash flows. The journal entry and its effects on the financial statements are shown next:

Account Title	Debit	Credit
Cash	100,000	
Land		100,000

Assets	=	Liab.	+	Equity	Rev.	−	Exp.	=	Net Inc.	Cash Flow
Cash + Land										
100,000 + (100,000)	=	NA	+	NA	NA	−	NA	=	NA	100,000 IA

EVENT 6 Repaid the face value of the bond liability.

Cash and bonds payable decrease. The income statement is not affected. The cash outflow is reported in the financing activities section of the statement of cash flows. The journal entry and its effects on the financial statements are shown next:

Account Title	Debit	Credit
Bonds Payable	100,000	
Cash		100,000

Assets	=	Liab.	+	Equity	Rev.	−	Exp.	=	Net Inc.	Cash Flow
Cash	=	Bonds Pay.								
(100,000)	=	(100,000)	+	NA	NA	−	NA	=	NA	(10,000) FA

Financial Statements

Exhibit 10.7 displays Mason Company's financial statements. For simplicity, the income statement does not distinguish between operating and other items. Rent revenue and interest expense are constant across all accounting periods, so Mason recognizes $3,000 of net income in each accounting period. On the balance sheet, cash increases by $3,000 each year because cash revenue exceeds cash paid for interest. Land remains constant each year at its $100,000 historical cost until it is sold in Year 5. Similarly, the bonds payable liability is reported at $100,000 from the date the bonds were issued in Year 1 until they are paid off on December 31, Year 5.

EXHIBIT 10.7

Mason Company Financial Statements

Bonds Issued at Face Value

	Year 1	Year 2	Year 3	Year 4	Year 5
Income Statements					
Rent revenue	$ 12,000	$ 12,000	$ 12,000	$ 12,000	$ 12,000
Interest expense	(9,000)	(9,000)	(9,000)	(9,000)	(9,000)
Net income	$ 3,000	$ 3,000	$ 3,000	$ 3,000	$ 3,000
Balance Sheets					
Assets					
Cash	$ 3,000	$ 6,000	$ 9,000	$ 12,000	$ 15,000
Land	100,000	100,000	100,000	100,000	0
Total assets	$103,000	$106,000	$109,000	$112,000	$ 15,000
Liabilities					
Bonds payable	$100,000	$100,000	$100,000	$100,000	$ 0
Stockholders' equity					
Retained earnings	3,000	6,000	9,000	12,000	15,000
Total liabilities and stockholders' equity	$103,000	$106,000	$109,000	$112,000	$ 15,000
Statements of Cash Flows					
Operating Activities					
Inflow from customers	$ 12,000	$ 12,000	$ 12,000	$ 12,000	$ 12,000
Outflow for interest	(9,000)	(9,000)	(9,000)	(9,000)	(9,000)
Investing Activities					
Outflow to purchase land	(100,000)				
Inflow from sale of land					100,000
Financing Activities					
Inflow from bond issue	100,000				
Outflow to repay bond liab.					(100,000)
Net Change in Cash	3,000	3,000	3,000	3,000	3,000
Plus: Beginning cash balance	0	3,000	6,000	9,000	12,000
Ending cash balance	$ 3,000	$ 6,000	$ 9,000	$ 12,000	$ 15,000

Compare Blair Company's income statements in Exhibit 10.2 with Mason Company's income statements in Exhibit 10.7. Both Blair and Mason borrowed $100,000 cash at a 9 percent stated interest rate for five-year terms. Blair, however, repaid its liability under the terms of an installment note, while Mason did not repay any principal until the end of the five-year bond term. Because Blair repaid part of the principal balance on the installment loan each year, Blair's interest expense declined each year. The interest expense on Mason's bond liability, however, remained constant because the full principal amount was outstanding for the entire five-year bond term.

AMORTIZATION USING THE STRAIGHT-LINE METHOD

LO 10-4

Use the straight-line method to amortize bond discounts.

Bonds Issued at a Discount

Return to the Mason Company illustration with one change. Assume Mason's bond certificates have a 9 percent stated rate of interest printed on them. Suppose Mason's friends find they can buy bonds from another entrepreneur willing to pay a higher rate of interest. They explain to Mason that business decisions cannot be made on the basis of friendship. Mason provides a counteroffer. There is no time to change the bond certificates, so Mason offers to accept $95,000 for the bonds today and still repay the full face value of $100,000 at the maturity date. The $5,000 difference is called a **bond discount.** Mason's friends agree to buy the bonds for $95,000.

Effective Interest Rate

The bond discount increases the interest Mason must pay. First, Mason must still make the annual cash payments described in the bond agreement. In other words, Mason must pay cash of $9,000 (0.09 × $100,000) annually even though she actually borrowed only $95,000. Second, Mason will have to pay back $5,000 more than she received ($100,000 − $95,000). The extra $5,000 (bond discount) is additional interest. Although the $5,000 of additional interest is not paid until maturity, when spread over the life of the bond, it amounts to $1,000 of additional interest expense per year.

The actual rate of interest that Mason must pay is called the **effective interest rate.** A rough estimate of the effective interest rate for the discounted Mason bonds is 10.5 percent ([$9,000 annual stated interest + $1,000 annual amortization of the discount] ÷ $95,000 amount borrowed). Selling the bonds at a $5,000 discount permits Mason to raise the 9 percent stated rate of interest to an effective rate of roughly 10.5 percent. Deeper discounts would raise the effective rate even higher. More shallow discounts would reduce the effective rate of interest. Mason can set the effective rate of interest to any level desired by adjusting the amount of the discount.

Bond Prices

It is common business practice to use discounts to raise the effective rate of interest above the stated rate. Bonds frequently sell for less than face value. Bond prices are normally expressed *as a percentage of the face value.* For example, Mason's discounted bonds sold for 95, meaning the bonds sold at 95 percent of face value ($100,000 × 0.95 = $95,000). Amounts of less than 1 percentage point are usually expressed as a fraction. Therefore, a bond priced at 98 3/4 sells for 98.75 percent of face value.

Journal Entries and Financial Statement Effects

To illustrate accounting for bonds issued at a discount, return to the Mason Company example using the assumption the bonds are issued for 95 instead of face value. We examine the same six events using this revised assumption. This revision changes some amounts reported on the financial statements. For example, Event 1 in Year 1 reflects receiving only $95,000 cash from the bond issue. Because Mason had only $95,000 available to invest in land, the illustration assumes that Mason acquired a less desirable piece of property which generated only $11,400 of rent revenue per year.

EVENT 1 Bonds with a face value of $100,000 are issued at 95.

Because Mason must pay the face value at maturity, the $100,000 face value of the bonds is recorded in the Bonds Payable account. The $5,000 discount is recorded in a separate contra liability account called **Discount on Bonds Payable.** As shown next, the contra account is subtracted from the face value to determine the **carrying value** (book value) of the bond liability on January 1, Year 1.

Bonds payable	$100,000
Less: Discount on bonds payable	(5,000)
Carrying value	$ 95,000

The bond issue is an asset source transaction. Both assets and total liabilities increase by $95,000. Net income is not affected. The cash inflow is reported in the financing activities section of the statement of cash flows. The journal entry and its effects on the financial statements are shown next:

Account Title	Debit	Credit
Cash	95,000	
Discount on Bonds Payable	5,000	
Bonds Payable		100,000

Assets	=	Liabilities	+	Equity	Rev.	−	Exp.	=	Net Inc.	Cash Flow
Cash	=	Carrying Value of Bond Liability	+	Equity						
(95,000)	=	95,000	+	NA	NA	−	NA	=	NA	95,000 FA

EVENT 2   Paid $95,000 cash to purchase land.

The asset cash decreases and the asset land increases. The income statement is not affected. The cash outflow is reported in the investing activities section of the statement of cash flows. The journal entry and its effects on the financial statements are shown next:

Account Title	Debit	Credit
Land	95,000	
Cash		95,000

Assets			=	Liab.	+	Equity	Rev.	−	Exp.	=	Net Inc.	Cash Flow
Cash	+	Land										
(95,000)	+	95,000	=	NA	+	NA	NA	−	NA	=	NA	(95,000) IA

EVENT 3   Recognized $11,400 cash revenue from renting the land.

This event is repeated each year from Year 1 through Year 5. The event is an asset source transaction that increases assets and stockholders' equity. Recognizing revenue increases net income. The cash inflow is reported in the operating activities section of the statement of cash flows. The journal entry and its effects on the financial statements are shown next:

Account Title	Debit	Credit
Cash	11,400	
Rent Revenue		11,400

Assets	=	Liab.	+	Equity	Rev.	−	Exp.	=	Net Inc.	Cash Flow
Cash	=			Ret. Earn.						
11,400	=	NA	+	11,400	11,400	−	NA	=	11,400	11,400 OA

EVENT 4   Recognized interest expense. The interest cost of borrowing has two components: the $9,000 paid in cash each year and the $5,000 discount paid at maturity.

Using **straight-line amortization,** the amount of the discount recognized as expense in each accounting period is $1,000 ($5,000 discount ÷ 5 years). Mason will therefore recognize $10,000 of interest expense each year ($9,000 at the stated interest rate plus $1,000 amortization of the bond discount). On the balance sheet, the asset cash decreases by $9,000, the carrying value of the bond liability increases by $1,000 (through a decrease in the bond discount), and retained earnings (interest expense) decreases by $10,000. The journal entry and its effects on the financial statements are shown next:

Account Title	Debit	Credit
Interest Expense	10,000	
Cash		9,000
Discount on Bonds Payable		1,000

Assets	=	Liab.	+	Equity	Rev.	−	Exp.	=	Net Inc.	Cash Flow
Cash	=	Carrying Value of Bond Liability	+	Ret. Earn.						
(9,000)	=	1,000	+	(10,000)	NA	−	10,000	=	(10,000)	(9,000) OA

EVENT 5 *Sold the land for cash equal to its $95,000 book value.*

Cash increases and land decreases. Because there was no gain or loss on the sale, the income statement is not affected. The cash inflow is reported in the investing activities section of the statement of cash flows. The journal entry and its effects on the financial statements are shown next:

Account Title	Debit	Credit
Cash	95,000	
Land		95,000

Assets			=	Liab.	+	Equity	Rev.	−	Exp.	=	Net Inc.	Cash Flow
Cash	+	Land										
95,000	+	(95,000)	=	NA	+	NA	NA	−	NA	=	NA	95,000 IA

EVENT 6 *Paid the bond liability.*

Cash and bonds payable decrease. The income statement is not affected. For reporting purposes, the cash outflow is separated into two parts on the statement of cash flows: $95,000 of the cash outflow is reported in the financing activities section because it represents repaying the principal amount borrowed; the remaining $5,000 cash outflow is reported in the operating activities section because it represents the interest arising from issuing the bonds at a discount. In practice, the amount of the discount is frequently immaterial and is combined in the financing activities section with the principal repayment. The journal entry and its effects on the financial statements are shown next:

Account Title	Debit	Credit
Bonds Payable	100,000	
Cash		100,000

Assets	=	Liab.	+	Equity	Rev.	−	Exp.	=	Net Inc.	Cash Flow
Cash	=	Bonds Pay.								
(100,000)	=	(100,000)	+	NA	NA	−	NA	=	NA	(95,000) FA / (5,000) OA

Financial Statements

Exhibit 10.8 displays Mason Company's financial statements, assuming the bonds were issued at a discount. Contrast the net income reported in Exhibit 10.8 (bonds issued at a discount) with the net income reported in Exhibit 10.7 (bonds sold at face value). Two factors cause the net income in Exhibit 10.8 to be lower. First, because the bonds were sold at a discount, Mason Company had less money to spend on its land investment. It bought less desirable land, which generated less revenue. Second, the effective interest rate was higher than the stated rate, resulting in higher interest expense. Lower revenues coupled with higher expenses result in less profitability.

On the balance sheet, the carrying value of the bond liability increases each year until the maturity date, December 31, Year 5, when it is equal to the $100,000 face value of the bonds (the amount Mason is obligated to pay). Because Mason did not pay any dividends, retained earnings ($7,000) on December 31, Year 5, is equal to the total amount of net income reported over the five-year period ($1,400 × 5). All earnings were retained in the business.

EXHIBIT 10.8

Mason Company Financial Statements

Bonds Issued at a Discount

	Year 1	Year 2	Year 3	Year 4	Year 5
Income Statements					
Rent revenue	$ 11,400	$ 11,400	$ 11,400	$ 11,400	$ 11,400
Interest expense	(10,000)	(10,000)	(10,000)	(10,000)	(10,000)
Net income	$ 1,400	$ 1,400	$ 1,400	$ 1,400	$ 1,400
Balance Sheets					
Assets					
Cash	$ 2,400	$ 4,800	$ 7,200	$ 9,600	$ 7,000
Land	95,000	95,000	95,000	95,000	0
Total assets	$ 97,400	$ 99,800	$102,200	$104,600	$ 7,000
Liabilities					
Bonds payable	$100,000	$100,000	$100,000	$100,000	$ 0
Discount on bonds payable	(4,000)	(3,000)	(2,000)	(1,000)	0
Carrying value of bond liab.	96,000	97,000	98,000	99,000	0
Stockholders' equity					
Retained earnings	1,400	2,800	4,200	5,600	7,000
Total liabilities and stockholders' equity	$ 97,400	$ 99,800	$102,200	$104,600	$ 7,000
Statements of Cash Flows					
Operating Activities					
Inflow from customers	$ 11,400	$ 11,400	$ 11,400	$ 11,400	$ 11,400
Outflow for interest	(9,000)	(9,000)	(9,000)	(9,000)	(14,000)
Investing Activities					
Outflow to purchase land	(95,000)				
Inflow from sale of land					95,000
Financing Activities					
Inflow from bond issue	95,000				
Outflow to repay bond liab.					(95,000)
Net Change in Cash	2,400	2,400	2,400	2,400	(2,600)
Plus: Beginning cash balance	0	2,400	4,800	7,200	9,600
Ending cash balance	$ 2,400	$ 4,800	$ 7,200	$ 9,600	$ 7,000

Several factors account for the differences between net income and cash flow. First, although $10,000 of interest expense is reported on each income statement, only $9,000 of cash was paid for interest each year until Year 5, when $14,000 was paid for interest ($9,000 based on the stated rate + $5,000 for discount). The $1,000 difference between interest expense and cash paid for interest in Year 1, Year 2, Year 3, and Year 4 results from amortizing the bond discount. The cash outflow for the interest related to the discount is included in the $100,000 payment made at maturity on December 31, Year 5. Even though $14,000 of cash is paid for interest in Year 5, only $10,000 is recognized as interest expense on the income statement that year. Although the total increase in cash over the five-year life of the business ($7,000) is equal to the total net income reported for the same period, there are significant timing differences between when the interest expense is recognized and when the cash outflows occur to pay for it.

CHECK YOURSELF 10.2

On January 1, Year 1, Moffett Company issued bonds with a $600,000 face value at 98. The bonds had a 9 percent annual interest rate and a 10-year term. Interest is payable in cash on December 31 of each year. What amount of interest expense will Moffett report on the Year 3 income statement? What carrying value for bonds payable will Moffett report on the December 31, Year 3, balance sheet?

Answer The bonds were issued at a $12,000 ($600,000 × 0.02) discount. The discount will be amortized over the 10-year life at the rate of $1,200 ($12,000 ÷ 10 years) per year. The amount of interest expense for Year 3 is $55,200 ($600,000 × 0.09 = $54,000 annual cash interest + $1,200 discount amortization).

The carrying value of the bond liability is equal to the face value less the unamortized discount. By the end of Year 3, $3,600 of the discount will have been amortized ($1,200 × 3 years = $3,600). The unamortized discount as of December 31, Year 3, will be $8,400 ($12,000 − $3,600). The carrying value of the bond liability as of December 31, Year 3, will be $591,600 ($600,000 − $8,400).

Effect of Semiannual Interest Payments

The previous examples assumed that interest payments were made annually. In practice, most bond agreements call for interest to be paid semiannually, which means that interest is paid in cash twice each year. If Marsha Mason's bond certificate had stipulated semiannual interest payments, her company would have paid $4,500 ($100,000 × 0.09 = $9,000 ÷ 2 = $4,500) cash to bondholders for interest on June 30 and December 31 of each year. The journal entries to record semiannual interest payments each year (for the bonds issued at a discount) are as follows:

Date	Account Title	Debit	Credit
June 30	Interest Expense	5,000	
	Discount on Bonds Payable		500
	Cash		4,500
Dec. 31	Interest Expense	5,000	
	Discount on Bonds Payable		500
	Cash		4,500

Bonds Issued at a Premium

When bonds are sold for more than their face value, the difference between the amount received and the face value is called a **bond premium.** Bond premiums reduce the effective interest rate. For example, assume Mason Company issued its 9 percent bonds at 105, receiving $105,000 cash on the issue date. The company is still required to repay only the

LO 10-5

Use the straight-line method to amortize bond premiums.

$100,000 face value of the bonds at the maturity date. The $5,000 difference between the amount received and the amount repaid at maturity reduces the total amount of interest expense. The premium is recorded in a separate liability account called **Premium on Bonds Payable.** This account is reported on the balance sheet as an addition to Bonds Payable, increasing the carrying value of the bond liability. On the issue date, the bond liability would be reported on the balance sheet as follows:

Bonds payable	$100,000
Plus: Premium on bonds payable	5,000
Carrying value	$105,000

The entire $105,000 cash inflow is reported in the financing activities section of the statement of cash flows even though the $5,000 premium is conceptually an operating activities cash flow because it pertains to interest. In practice, premiums are usually so small they are immaterial and the entire cash inflow is normally classified as a financing activity.

The journal entries to record issuing the bonds at a premium and the first interest payment are as follows (assume annual interest payments):

Date	Account Title	Debit	Credit
Jan. 1	Cash	105,000	
	Bonds Payable		100,000
	Premium on Bonds Payable		5,000
Dec. 31	Interest Expense	8,000	
	Premium on Bonds Payable	1,000	
	Cash		9,000

The effects on the financial statements are shown next:

Date	Assets	=	Liabilities	+	Equity	Rev.	−	Exp.	=	Net Inc.	Cash Flow
	Cash	=	Carrying Value of Bond Liability								
Jan. 1	105,000	=	105,000	+	NA	NA	−	NA	=	NA	(105,000) FA
Dec. 31	(9,000)	=	(1,000)		(8,000)			8,000		(8,000)	(9,000) OA

The Market Rate of Interest

When a bond is issued, the effective interest rate is determined by current market conditions. Market conditions are influenced by many factors, such as the state of the economy, government policy, and the law of supply and demand. These conditions are collectively reflected in the **market interest rate.** The *effective rate of interest* investors are willing to accept *for a particular bond* equals the *market rate of interest* for other investments with similar levels of risk at the time the bond is issued. When the market rate of interest is higher than the stated rate of interest, bonds will sell at a discount so as to increase the effective rate of interest to the market rate. When the market rate is lower than the stated rate, bonds will sell at a premium so as to reduce the effective rate to the market rate.

Bond Redemptions

In the previous illustration, Mason Company's five-year, 9 percent bonds were redeemed (paid off) on the maturity date. After Mason Company paid the bondholders the face value of the bonds, the balance in the bonds payable account was zero. The balance in the fully amortized discount account was also zero.

Companies may redeem bonds with a *call provision* prior to the maturity date. If a company calls bonds prior to maturity, it must pay the bondholders the call price. As explained previously, the call price is normally above face value. For example, suppose Mason Company's bond certificate allows it to call the bonds at 103. Assume Marsha Mason's client breaks the land rental contract two years early, at the end of Year 3. Mason is forced to sell the land and pay off the bonds. Assuming the bonds were originally issued at a $5,000 discount, Exhibit 10.8 shows there is a $2,000 balance in the Discount on Bonds Payable account at the end of Year 3.

To redeem the bonds on January 1, Year 4, Mason must pay the bondholders $103,000 ($100,000 face value × 1.03 call price). Because the book value of the bond liability is $98,000 ($100,000 face value − $2,000 remaining discount), Mason recognizes a $5,000 loss ($103,000 redemption price − $98,000 book value) when the bonds are called. The early redemption decreases cash, the carrying value of the bond liability, and stockholders' equity.

The entire $103,000 cash outflow is reported in the financing activities section of the statement of cash flows. Conceptually, some of this outflow is attributable to activities other than financing. In practice, the amounts paid in an early redemption which are not attributable to financing activities are usually immaterial and the entire cash outflow is therefore classified as a financing activity.

The general journal entry to record the bond redemption and its effects on the financial statements are shown next:

Account Title	Debit	Credit
Loss on Bond Redemption	5,000	
Bonds Payable	100,000	
Discount on Bonds Payable		2,000
Cash		103,000

Assets	=	Liabilities	+	Equity	Rev.	−	Exp.	=	Net Inc.	Cash Flow
Cash	=	Carrying Value of Bond Liability	+	Ret. Earn.						
(103,000)	=	(98,000)	+	(5,000)	NA	−	5,000	=	(5,000)	(103,000) FA

AMORTIZATION USING THE EFFECTIVE INTEREST RATE METHOD

Up to this point, we have demonstrated the straight-line method for amortizing bond discounts and premiums. While this method is easy to understand, it is inaccurate because it does not show the correct amount of interest expense incurred during each accounting period. To illustrate, return to the case of Mason Company, demonstrated in Exhibit 10.8. Recall that the exhibit shows the effects of accounting for a $100,000 face-value bond with a 9 percent stated rate of interest that was issued at a price of 95. The carrying value of the bond liability on the January 1, Year 1, issue date was $95,000. The bond discount was amortized using the straight-line method.

Recall that the straight-line method amortizes the discount equally over the life of the bond. Specifically, there is a $5,000 discount which is amortized over a five-year life, resulting in a $1,000 amortization per year. As the discount is amortized, the bond liability (carrying value of the bond) increases. Specifically, the carrying value of the bond liability shown in Exhibit 10.8 increases as follows:

Accounting Period	Year 1	Year 2	Year 3	Year 4
Carrying value as of December 31	$96,000	$97,000	$98,000	$99,000

While the carrying value of the bond liability increases steadily, the straight-line method recognizes the same amount of interest expense ($9,000 stated rate of interest + $1,000 discount amortization = $10,000 interest expense) per year. This straight-line recognition pattern is irrational because the amount of interest expense recognized should increase as the carrying value of the bond liability increases. A more accurate recognition pattern can be accomplished by using an approach called the **effective interest rate method.**

Amortizing Bond Discounts

LO 10-6

Use the effective interest rate method to amortize bond discounts.

The effective interest rate is determined by the price that the buyer of a bond is willing to pay on the issue date. In the case of Mason Company, the issue price of $95,000 for bonds with a $100,000 face value, a 9 percent stated rate of interest, and a five-year term produces an effective interest rate of approximately 10.33 percent.[4] Because the effective interest rate is based on the market price of the bonds on the day of issue, it is sometimes called *the market rate of interest.*

Interest recognition under the effective interest rate method is accomplished as follows:

1. Determine the cash payment for interest by multiplying the stated rate of interest times the face value of the bonds.

2. Determine the amount of interest expense by multiplying the effective rate of interest times the carrying value of the bond liability.

3. Determine the amount of the amortization of the bond discount by subtracting the cash payment from the interest expense.

4. Update the carrying value of the liability by adding the amount of the discount amortization to the amount of the carrying value at the beginning of the accounting period.

Applying these procedures to the Mason Company illustration produces the amortization schedule shown in Exhibit 10.9.

The recognition of interest expense at the end of each accounting period has the following effects on the financial statements. On the balance sheet, assets decrease, liabilities increase, and retained earnings decrease. On the income statement, expenses increase

EXHIBIT 10.9

Amortization Schedule for Bond Discount

	(A) Cash Payment	(B) Interest Expense	(C) Discount Amortization	(D) Carrying Value
January 1, Year 1				$ 95,000
December 31, Year 1	$ 9,000	$ 9,814	$ 814	95,814
December 31, Year 2	9,000	9,898	898	96,712
December 31, Year 3	9,000	9,990	990	97,702
December 31, Year 4	9,000	10,093	1,093	98,795
December 31, Year 5	9,000	10,205	1,205	100,000
Totals	$45,000	$50,000	$5,000	

(A) Stated rate of interest times the face value of the bonds ($100,000 × 0.09).
(B) Effective interest rate times the carrying value at the beginning of the period. For the Year 1 accounting period, the amount is $9,814 ($95,000 × 0.1033).
(C) Interest Expense − Cash Payment. For Year 1, the discount amortization is $814 ($9,814 − $9,000 = $814).
(D) Carrying value at the beginning of the period plus the portion of the discount amortized. For the accounting period ending December 31, Year 1, the amount is $95,814 ($95,000 + $814).

---

[4]In practice, the effective rate of interest is calculated using software programs, interest formulas, or interest tables. For further discussion, see Appendix F, which is located at the end of this textbook.

and net income decreases. There is a cash outflow in the operating activities section of the statement of cash flows. The journal entry and its effects on the financial statements are shown next:

Account Title	Debit	Credit
Interest Expense	9,814	
Cash		9,000
Discount on Bonds Payable		814

Assets	=	Liabilities	+	Equity	Rev.	−	Exp.	=	Net Inc.	Cash Flow
Cash	=	Carrying Value of Bond Liability	+	Ret. Earn.						
(9,000)	=	814	+	(9,814)	NA	−	9,814	=	(9,814)	(9,000) OA

Exhibit 10.10 shows the financial statements for Mason Company for Year 1 through Year 5. The statements assume the same events as those used to construct Exhibit 10.8. These events are summarized next:

1. Mason issues a $100,000 face-value bond with a 9 percent stated rate of interest. The bond has a five-year term and is issued at a price of 95. Annual interest is paid with cash on December 31 of each year.
2. Mason uses the proceeds from the bond issue to purchase land.
3. Leasing the land produces rent revenue of $11,400 cash per year.
4. On the maturity date of the bond, the land is sold and the proceeds from the sale are used to repay the bond liability.

The only difference between the two exhibits is that Exhibit 10.8 was constructed assuming that the bond discount was amortized using the straight-line method, while Exhibit 10.10 assumes that the discount was amortized using the effective interest rate method.

Notice that interest expense under the effective interest rate method (Exhibit 10.10) increases each year, while interest expense under the straight-line method (Exhibit 10.8) remains constant for all years. This result occurs because the effective interest rate method amortizes increasingly larger amounts of the discount (see Column C of Exhibit 10.9) as the carrying value of the bond liability increases. In contrast, the straight-line method amortized the bond discount at a constant rate of $1,000 per year over the life of the bond. Even so, the total amount of interest expense recognized over the life of the bond is the same ($50,000) under both methods. Because the effective interest rate method matches the interest expense with the carrying value of the bond liability, it is the theoretically preferred approach. Indeed, accounting standards require the use of the effective interest rate method when the differences between it and the straight-line method are material.

The amortization of the discount affects the carrying value of the bond, as well as the amount of interest expense. Under the effective interest rate method, the rate of growth of the carrying value of the bond increases as the maturity date approaches. In contrast, under the straight-line method the rate of growth of the carrying value of the bond remains constant at $1,000 per year throughout the life of the bond.

Finally, notice that cash flow is not affected by the method of amortization. The exact same cash flow consequences occur under both the straight-line (Exhibit 10.8) and the effective interest rate method (Exhibit 10.10).

Amortizing Bond Premiums

LO 10-7

Use the effective interest rate method to amortize bond premiums.

Bond premiums can also be amortized using the effective interest rate method. To illustrate, assume United Company issued a $100,000 face-value bond with a 10 percent stated rate of interest. The bond had a five-year term, was issued at a price of $107,985, and the effective rate

EXHIBIT 10.10
Financial Statements

Under the Assumption That Bonds Are Issued at a Discount

	Year 1	Year 2	Year 3	Year 4	Year 5
Income Statements					
Rent revenue	$ 11,400	$ 11,400	$ 11,400	$ 11,400	$ 11,400
Interest expense	(9,814)	(9,898)	(9,990)	(10,093)	(10,205)
Net income	$ 1,586	$ 1,502	$ 1,410	$ 1,307	$ 1,195
Balance Sheets					
Assets					
Cash	$ 2,400	$ 4,800	$ 7,200	$ 9,600	$ 7,000
Land	95,000	95,000	95,000	95,000	0
Total assets	$ 97,400	$ 99,800	$102,200	$104,600	$ 7,000
Liabilities					
Bonds payable	$100,000	$100,000	$100,000	$100,000	$ 0
Discount on bonds payable	(4,186)	(3,288)	(2,298)	(1,205)	0
Carrying value of bond liab.	95,814	96,712	97,702	98,795	0
Equity					
Retained earnings	1,586	3,088	4,498	5,805	7,000
Total liabilities and equity	$ 97,400	$ 99,800	$102,200	$104,600	$ 7,000
Statements of Cash Flows					
Operating Activities					
Inflow from customers	$ 11,400	$ 11,400	$ 11,400	$ 11,400	$ 11,400
Outflow for interest	(9,000)	(9,000)	(9,000)	(9,000)	(14,000)
Investing Activities					
Outflow to purchase land	(95,000)				
Inflow from sale of land					95,000
Financing Activities					
Inflow from bond issue	95,000				
Outflow to repay bond liab.					(95,000)
Net Change in Cash	2,400	2,400	2,400	2,400	(2,600)
Plus: Beginning cash balance	0	2,400	4,800	7,200	9,600
Ending cash balance	$ 2,400	$ 4,800	$ 7,200	$ 9,600	$ 7,000

of interest is 8 percent. United's accountant prepared the amortization schedule shown in Exhibit 10.11.

The recognition of interest expense at the end of each accounting period has the following effects on the financial statements. On the balance sheet, assets decrease, liabilities decrease, and retained earnings decrease. On the income statement, expenses increase and net income decreases. There is a cash outflow in the operating activities section of the statement of cash flows. The journal entry and its effects on the financial statements are shown next:

Account Title	Debit	Credit
Interest Expense	8,639	
Premium on Bonds Payable	1,361	
Cash		10,000

EXHIBIT 10.11

Amortization Schedule for Bond Premium

	(A) Cash Payment	(B) Interest Expense	(C) Discount Amortization	(D) Carrying Value
January 1, Year 1				$107,985
December 31, Year 1	$10,000	$ 8,639	$1,361	106,624
December 31, Year 2	10,000	8,530	1,470	105,154
December 31, Year 3	10,000	8,413	1,587	103,567
December 31, Year 4	10,000	8,285	1,715	101,852
December 31, Year 5	10,000	8,148	1,852	100,000
Totals	$50,000	$42,015	$7,985	

(A) Stated rate of interest times the face value of the bonds ($100,000 × 0.10).
(B) Effective interest times the carrying value at the beginning of the period. For the Year 1 accounting period, the amount is $8,639 ($107,985 × 0.08).
(C) Cash Payment − Interest Expense. For Year 1, the premium amortization is $1,361 ($10,000 − $8,639 = $1,361).
(D) Carrying value at the beginning of the period minus the portion of the premium amortized. For the accounting period ending December 31, Year 1, the amount is $106,624 ($107,985 − $1,361).

Assets	=	Liabilities	+	Equity	Rev.	−	Exp.	=	Net Inc.	Cash Flow
Cash	=	Carrying Value of Bond Liability	+	Ret. Earn.						
(10,000)	=	(1,361)	+	(8,639)	NA	−	8,639	=	(8,639)	(10,000) OA

The Financial Analyst

LO 10-8

Explain the advantages and disadvantages of debt financing.

Bond financing has advantages and disadvantages for the stockholders of a business. Assessing a company's investment potential requires understanding both the potential rewards and the potential risks of debt financing.

Financial Leverage and Tax Advantage of Debt Financing

As with other forms of credit, bonds may provide companies increased earnings through **financial leverage.** If a company can borrow money at 7 percent through a bond issue and invest the proceeds at 12 percent, the company's earnings benefit from the 5 percent (12 percent − 7 percent) **spread.**

Also, bond interest expense, like other forms of interest expense, is tax deductible, making the effective cost of borrowing less than the interest expense because the interest expense reduces the tax expense. Because dividend payments are not tax deductible, equity financing (e.g., issuing common stock) does not offer this advantage.

To illustrate, assume its organizers obtain $100,000 to start Maduro Company. During its first year of operation, Maduro earns $60,000 of revenue and incurs $40,000 of expenses other than interest expense. Consider two different forms of financing. First, assume the initial $100,000 is obtained by issuing common stock (equity financing) and Maduro pays an 8 percent dividend ($100,000 × 0.08 = $8,000 dividend). Second, assume Maduro issues $100,000 of bonds that pay 8 percent annual interest ($100,000 × 0.08 = $8,000). Assuming a 30 percent tax rate, which form of financing produces the larger increase in retained earnings? Refer to the following computations:

Computation of Addition to Retained Earnings

	Equity Financing	Debt Financing
Revenue	$ 60,000	$ 60,000
Expense (excluding interest)	(40,000)	(40,000)
Earnings before interest and taxes	20,000	20,000
Interest ($100,000 × 8%)	0	(8,000)
Pretax income	20,000	12,000
Income tax (30%)	(6,000)	(3,600)
Net income	14,000	8,400
Dividend	(8,000)	0
Addition to retained earnings	$ 6,000	$ 8,400

Debt financing produces $2,400 more retained earnings than equity financing. If equity financing is obtained, the company pays $6,000 in income taxes; debt financing requires only $3,600 of income taxes. Maduro's cost of financing, whether paid in dividends to investors or interest to creditors, is $8,000. With debt financing, however, the Internal Revenue Service receives $2,400 less.

The after-tax interest cost of debt can be computed as

$$\text{Total interest expense} \times (1.0 - \text{Tax rate})$$
$$\$8,000 \times (1.0 - 0.30) = \$5,600$$

The after-tax interest rate that Maduro is paying can be computed using the same logic:

$$\text{Debt interest rate} \times (1.0 - \text{Tax rate})$$
$$8\% \times (1.0 - 0.30) = 5.6\%$$

Unlike interest expense, there is no difference in the before-tax and after-tax effects of a dividend. For Maduro, $1 of dividends costs the company a full $1 of retained earnings, while $1 of interest has an after-tax cost of only $0.70 (assuming a 30 percent tax rate). This tax benefit only applies to profitable businesses. There are no tax savings if a company has no income because businesses that produce losses pay no taxes.

EBIT and Ratio Analysis

The tax consequences of debt financing can influence ratio analysis. For example, consider the *return-on-assets* (*ROA*) ratio discussed in Chapter 3. In that chapter, ROA was defined as:

$$\text{Net income} \div \text{Total assets}$$

Recall that the ROA ratio is used to measure the effectiveness of asset management. In general, higher ROAs suggest better performance. However, the Maduro example demonstrates that a higher ROA can be obtained by using equity financing rather than debt financing without regard to how assets are managed. Recall that Maduro obtained $100,000 of assets whether through equity or debt financing. The assets were used exactly the same way regardless of the financing method used. With equity financing, Maduro's ROA is 14 percent ($14,000 ÷ $100,000) and with debt financing it is 8.4 percent ($8,400 ÷ $100,000). The difference in the ROA results from the financing approach rather than asset management.

The effects of the financing strategy can be avoided in ROA calculations by using *earnings before interest and taxes* (*EBIT*) rather than net income when computing the ratio. For example, if Maduro uses EBIT to compute ROA, the result is 20 percent ($20,000 ÷ $100,000) regardless of whether debt or equity financing is used. Using EBIT to compute ROA provides a less biased measure of asset utilization. For simplicity, however, this text uses net income to determine ROA unless otherwise indicated.

Times-Interest-Earned Ratio

Financing with bonds also has disadvantages. The issuer is legally obligated to make interest payments on time and to repay the principal at maturity. If a company fails to make scheduled payments, the creditors (bondholders) can force the company into bankruptcy. The claims on a company's assets held by bondholders and other creditors have priority over the claims of the owners. If a company in bankruptcy is forced to liquidate its assets, creditor claims must be fully paid before any owner claims can be paid. Bond issues therefore increase the owners' risk.

Financial analysts use several ratios to help assess the risk of bankruptcy. One is the *debt-to-assets ratio,* explained in Chapter 3. Another is the **times-interest-earned** ratio, defined as

$$\text{EBIT} \div \text{Interest expense}$$

This ratio measures *how many times* a company would be able to pay its interest using its earnings. The *times-interest-earned ratio* is based on EBIT rather than net income because it is the amount of earnings before interest and taxes that is available to pay interest. The higher the ratio, the less likely a company will be unable to make its interest payments. Higher times-interest-earned ratios suggest lower levels of risk. Examples of times-interest-earned ratios and debt-to-assets ratios for six real-world companies follow. These numbers are based on financial data for Year 1.

Industry	Company	Times Interest Earned	Debt to Assets
Breakfast cereal	Kellogg's	3.3	0.87
	General Mills	8.3	0.72
Cosmetics	Avon	1.2	1.11
	Esteé Lauder	23.0	0.61
Hotels	Marriott International	6.1	0.78
	Wyndham Worldwide	7.9	0.83

Because bills are paid with cash, not income, a company may be able to make interest payments even if it has a negative times-interest-earned ratio. A company with no EBIT may yet have cash. Meaningful financial statement analysis cannot rely on any single ratio or any set of ratios. Making sound business decisions requires considering other information in addition to the insights provided from analyzing ratios. A company with inferior ratios and a patent on a newly discovered drug that cures cancer may be a far better investment than a company with great ratios and a patent on a chemotherapy product that will soon be out of date. Ratio computations are based on historical data. They are useful only to the extent that history is likely to repeat itself.

CHECK YOURSELF 10.3

Selected financial data pertaining to Shaver Company and Goode Company follow (amounts are in thousands):

	Shaver Company	Goode Company
Earnings before interest and taxes	$750,720	$2,970,680
Interest expense	234,600	645,800

Based on this information, which company is more likely to be able to make its interest payments?

Answer The times-interest-earned ratio for Shaver Company is 3.2 ($750,720 ÷ $234,600) times. The times-interest-earned ratio for Goode Company is 4.6 ($2,970,680 ÷ $645,800) times. Based on these data, Goode Company is more likely to be able to make its interest payments.

A Look Back

This chapter explained basic accounting for long-term debt. *Long-term notes payable* usually mature in two to five years and require payments that include a return of principal plus interest. *Lines of credit* enable companies to borrow limited amounts on an as-needed basis. Although lines of credit normally have one-year terms, companies frequently renew them, extending the effective maturity date to the intermediate range of five or more years. Interest on a line of credit is normally paid monthly.

Long-term debt financing for more than 10 years usually requires issuing *bonds*. Bond agreements normally commit a company to pay *semiannual interest* at a fixed percentage of the bond face value. The amount of interest required by the bond agreement is based on the *stated interest rate*. If bonds are issued when the *market interest rate* is different from the stated interest rate, companies will receive more or less than the face value in order for the effective rate of interest to be consistent with market conditions. Selling bonds at a *discount* (below face value) increases the effective interest rate above the stated rate. Selling bonds at a *premium* decreases the effective rate of interest.

This chapter explained the tax advantages of using debt versus equity financing. Interest is a *tax-deductible expense* subtracted prior to determining taxable income. In contrast, dividends paid to owners are not deductible in determining taxable income.

A Look Forward

A company seeking long-term financing might choose to use debt, such as the types of bonds or term loans that were discussed in this chapter. Owners' equity is another source of long-term financing. Several equity alternatives are available, depending on the type of business organization the owners choose to establish. For example, a company could be organized as a sole proprietorship, partnership, or corporation. Chapter 11 presents accounting issues related to equity transactions for each of these types of business structures.

SELF-STUDY REVIEW PROBLEM

***A step-by-step audio-narrated series of slides is available in* Connect.**

During Year 1 and Year 2, Herring Corp. completed the following selected transactions relating to its bond issue. The corporation's fiscal year ends on December 31.

Year 1

Jan. 1 Sold $400,000 of 10-year, 9 percent bonds at 97. Interest is payable in cash on December 31 each year.

Dec. 31 Paid the bond interest and recorded the amortization of the discount using the straight-line method.

Year 2

Dec. 31 Paid the bond interest and recorded the amortization of the discount using the straight-line method.

Required

a. Show how these events would affect Herring's financial statements by recording them in a financial statements model like the following one.

Accounting for Long-Term Debt 563

Date	Assets = Cash =	Liab. Carrying Value of Bond Liability	+ Equity + Ret. Earn.	Rev. − Exp. = Net Inc.	Cash Flow
1/1/Year 1					
12/31/Year 1					
12/31/Year 2					

b. Determine the carrying value of the bond liability as of December 31, Year 2.
c. Assuming Herring had earnings before interest and taxes of $198,360 in Year 2, calculate the times-interest-earned ratio.

Solution

a.

Date	Assets = Cash =	Liab. Carrying Value of Bond Liability	+ Equity + Ret. Earn.	Rev. − Exp. = Net Inc.	Cash Flow
1/1/Year 1	388,000 =	388,000	+ NA	NA − NA = NA	388,000 FA
12/31/Year 1	(36,000) =	1,200	+ (37,200)	NA − 37,200 = (37,200)	(36,000) OA
12/31/Year 2	(36,000) =	1,200	+ (37,200)	NA − 37,200 = (37,200)	(36,000) OA

b. The unamortized discount as of December 31, Year 2, is $9,600 ($12,000 − $1,200 − $1,200). The carrying value of the bond liability is $390,400 ($400,000 − $9,600).
c. The times-interest-earned ratio is 5.3 times ($198,360 ÷ $37,200).

KEY TERMS

Amortization 537
Bond certificates 542
Bond discount 549
Bond premium 553
Bondholder 542
Call premium 544
Call price 544
Callable bonds 544
Carrying value 549
Collateral 545
Convertible bonds 544

Debenture 543
Discount on Bonds
 Payable 549
Effective interest rate 549
Effective interest rate
 method 556
Face value 542
Financial leverage 559
Fixed interest rate 536
Installment notes 538
Issuer 542

Line of credit 541
Long-term liabilities 536
Market interest rate 554
Mortgage bond 543
Premium on Bonds
 Payable 554
Restrictive covenants 545
Secured bonds 543
Serial bonds 543
Sinking fund 544
Spread 559

Stated interest rate 542
Straight-line amortization 550
Subordinated debentures 543
Term bonds 543
Times interest earned 561
Unsecured bonds 543
Unsubordinated
 debentures 543
Variable interest rate 536

QUESTIONS

1. What is the difference between classification of a note as short term or long term?
2. At the beginning of Year 1, B Co. has a note payable of $72,000 that calls for an annual payment of $16,246, which includes both principal and interest. If the interest rate is 8 percent, what is the amount of interest expense in Year 1 and in Year 2? What is the balance of the note at the end of Year 2?
3. What is the purpose of a line of credit for a business? Why would a company choose to obtain a line of credit instead of issuing bonds?
4. What are the primary sources of debt financing for most large companies?
5. What are some advantages of issuing bonds versus borrowing from a bank?
6. What are some disadvantages of issuing bonds?

564 Chapter 10

7. Why can a company usually issue bonds at a lower interest rate than the company would pay if the funds were borrowed from a bank?
8. What effect does income tax have on the cost of borrowing funds for a business?
9. What is the concept of financial leverage?
10. Which type of bond, secured or unsecured, is likely to have a lower interest rate? Explain.
11. What is the function of restrictive covenants attached to bond issues?
12. What is the difference between term bonds and serial bonds?
13. What is the purpose of establishing a sinking fund?
14. What is the call price of a bond? Is it usually higher or lower than the face amount of the bond? Explain.
15. If Roc Co. issued $100,000 of 5 percent, 10-year bonds at the face amount, what is the effect of the issuance of the bonds on the financial statements? What amount of interest expense will Roc Co. recognize each year?
16. What mechanism is used to adjust the stated interest rate to the market rate of interest?
17. When the effective interest rate is higher than the stated interest rate on a bond issue, will the bond sell at a discount or premium? Why?
18. What type of transaction is the issuance of bonds by a company?
19. What factors may cause the effective interest rate and the stated interest rate to be different?
20. If a bond is selling at 97½, how much cash will the company receive from the sale of a $1,000 bond?
21. How is the carrying value of a bond computed?
22. Gay Co. has a balance in the Bonds Payable account of $25,000 and a balance in the Discount on Bonds Payable account of $5,200. What is the carrying value of the bonds? What is the total amount of the liability?
23. When the effective interest rate is higher than the stated interest rate, will interest expense be higher or lower than the amount of interest paid?
24. Assuming that the selling price of the bond and the face value are the same, would the issuer of a bond prefer to make annual or semiannual interest payments? Why?
25. Rato Co. called some bonds and had a loss on the redemption of the bonds of $2,850. How is this amount reported on the income statement?
26. Which method of financing, debt or equity, is generally more advantageous from a tax standpoint? Why?
27. If a company has a tax rate of 30 percent, and interest expense was $10,000, what is the after-tax cost of the debt?
28. Which type of financing, debt or equity, increases the risk factor of a business? Why?
29. What information does the times-interest-earned ratio provide?

MULTIPLE-CHOICE QUESTIONS

Multiple-choice questions are available in Connect.

EXERCISES—SERIES A

 All applicable Exercises in Series A are available in Connect.

LO 10-1

Exercise 10-1A *Interest only versus an installment note*

Sanders Co. is planning to finance an expansion of its operations by borrowing $150,000. City Bank has agreed to loan Sanders the funds. Sanders has two repayment options: (1) to issue a note with the principal due in 10 years and with interest payable annually or (2) to issue a note to repay $15,000 of the principal each year along with the annual interest based on the unpaid principal balance. Assume the interest rate is 8 percent for each option.

Required

a. What amount of interest will Sanders pay in Year 1
 (1) Under option 1?
 (2) Under option 2?
b. What amount of interest will Sanders pay in Year 2
 (1) Under option 1?
 (2) Under option 2?
c. Explain the advantage of each option.

Exercise 10-2A Amortization schedule for an installment note

LO 10-1

On January 1, Year 1, Beatie Co. borrowed $200,000 cash from Central Bank by issuing a five-year, 6 percent note. The principal and interest are to be paid by making annual payments in the amount of $47,479. Payments are to be made December 31 of each year, beginning December 31, Year 1.

Required

Prepare an amortization schedule for the interest and principal payments for the five-year period.

Exercise 10-3A Financial statement effects of an installment note

LO 10-1

Dan Dayle started a business by issuing an $80,000 face-value note to First State Bank on January 1, Year 1. The note had an 8 percent annual rate of interest and a five-year term. Payments of $20,037 are to be made each December 31 for five years.

Required

a. What portion of the December 31, Year 1, payment is applied to
   (1) Interest expense?
   (2) Principal?
b. What is the principal balance on January 1, Year 2?
c. What portion of the December 31, Year 2, payment is applied to
   (1) Interest expense?
   (2) Principal?

Exercise 10-4A Financial statement effects of an installment note

LO 10-1

A partial amortization schedule for a 10-year note payable issued on January 1, Year 1, is shown next:

Accounting Period	Principal Balance January 1	Cash Payment	Applied to Interest	Applied to Principal
Year 1	$200,000	$27,174	$12,000	$15,174
Year 2	184,826	27,174	11,090	16,084
Year 3	168,742	27,174	10,125	17,049

Required

a. Using a financial statements model like the one shown next, record the appropriate amounts for the following two events:
   (1) January 1, Year 1, issue of the note payable.
   (2) December 31, Year 1, payment on the note payable.

Event No.	Assets	=	Liab.	+	Equity	Rev.	−	Exp.	=	Net Inc.	Cash Flow
1											

b. If the company earned $62,000 cash revenue and paid $45,000 in cash expenses in addition to the interest in Year 1, what is the amount of each of the following?
   (1) Net income for Year 1.
   (2) Cash flow from operating activities for Year 1.
   (3) Cash flow from financing activities for Year 1.
c. What is the amount of interest expense on this loan for Year 4?

Exercise 10-5A Journal entries for a line of credit

LO 10-2

Singer Company has a line of credit with United Bank. Singer can borrow up to $400,000 at any time over the course of the Year 1 calendar year. The following table shows the prime rate expressed as an annual percentage along with the amounts borrowed and repaid during the first three months of Year 1. Singer agreed to pay interest at an annual rate equal to 2 percent above the bank's prime rate. Funds are borrowed or repaid on the first day of each month. Interest is payable in cash on the last day of the month. The interest rate is applied to the outstanding monthly balance. For example, Singer pays 6.5 percent (4.5 percent + 2 percent) annual interest on $140,000 for the month of February.

Month	Amount Borrowed or (Repaid)	Prime Rate for the Month
January	$80,000	4.0%
February	60,000	4.5
March	(20,000)	4.0

Required

Provide all journal entries pertaining to Singer's line of credit for the first three months of Year 1.

LO 10-3

Exercise 10-6A *Two accounting cycles for bonds issued at face value*

Doyle Company issued $500,000 of 10-year, 7 percent bonds on January 1, Year 1. The bonds were issued at face value. Interest is payable in cash on December 31 of each year. Doyle immediately invested the proceeds from the bond issue in land. The land was leased for an annual $125,000 of cash revenue, which was collected on December 31 of each year, beginning December 31, Year 1.

Required

a. Prepare the journal entries for these events, and post them to T-accounts for Year 1 and Year 2.
b. Prepare the income statement, balance sheet, and statement of cash flows for Year 1 and Year 2.

LO 10-3

Exercise 10-7A *Two accounting cycles for bonds issued at face value*

On January 1, Year 1, Bell Corp. issued $180,000 of 10-year, 6 percent bonds at their face amount. Interest is payable on December 31 of each year with the first payment due December 31, Year 1.

Required

Prepare all the general journal entries related to these bonds for Year 1 and Year 2.

LO 10-3

Exercise 10-8A *Journal entries for callable bonds*

Nivan Co. issued $500,000 of 5 percent, 10-year, callable bonds on January 1, Year 1, at their face value. The call premium was 3 percent (bonds are callable at 103). Interest was payable annually on December 31. The bonds were called on December 31, Year 5.

Required

Prepare the journal entries to record the bond issue on January 1, Year 1, and the bond redemption on December 31, Year 5. Entries for accrual and payment of interest are not required.

LO 10-3

Exercise 10-9A *Annual versus semiannual interest for bonds issued at face value*

Milan Company issued bonds with a face value of $200,000 on January 1, Year 1. The bonds had a 7 percent stated rate of interest and a six-year term. The bonds were issued at face value. Interest is payable on an annual basis.

Required

Write a memo explaining whether the total cash outflow for interest would be more, less, or the same if the bonds pay semiannual versus annual interest.

Exercise 10-10A Determining cash receipts from bond issues

LO 10-4, 10-5

Required

Compute the cash proceeds from bond issues under the following terms. For each case, indicate whether the bonds sold at a premium or discount:

a. Pear, Inc. issued $400,000 of 10-year, 8 percent bonds at 103.
b. Apple, Inc. issued $200,000 of five-year, 12 percent bonds at 97½.
c. Cherry Co. issued $100,000 of five-year, 6 percent bonds at 102½.
d. Grape, Inc. issued $120,000 of four-year, 8 percent bonds at 96.

Exercise 10-11A Stated rate of interest versus the market rate of interest

LO 10-3, 10-4, 10-5

Required

Indicate whether a bond will sell at a premium (P), discount (D), or face value (F) for each of the following conditions:

a. ____ The stated rate of interest is higher than the market rate.
b. ____ The market rate of interest is equal to the stated rate.
c. ____ The market rate of interest is less than the stated rate.
d. ____ The stated rate of interest is less than the market rate.
e. ____ The market rate of interest is higher than the stated rate.

Exercise 10-12A Identifying bond premiums and discounts

LO 10-4, 10-5

Required

In each of the following situations, state whether the bonds will sell at a premium or discount:

a. Valley issued $300,000 of bonds with a stated interest rate of 7 percent. At the time of issue, the market rate of interest for similar investments was 6 percent.
b. Spring issued $220,000 of bonds with a stated interest rate of 5 percent. At the time of issue, the market rate of interest for similar investments was 6 percent.
c. River Inc. issued $150,000 of callable bonds with a stated interest rate of 5 percent. The bonds were callable at 102. At the date of issue, the market rate of interest was 6 percent for similar investments.

Exercise 10-13A Determining the amount of bond premiums and discounts

LO 10-4, 10-5

Required

For each of the following situations, calculate the amount of bond discount or premium, if any:

a. Gray Co. issued $80,000 of 6 percent bonds at 101¼.
b. Bush, Inc. issued $200,000 of 10-year, 6 percent bonds at 97½.
c. Oak, Inc. issued $100,000 of 20-year, 6 percent bonds at 103.
d. Willow Co. issued $180,000 of 15-year, 7 percent bonds at 99.

Exercise 10-14A Straight-line amortization of a bond discount

LO 10-4

Diaz Company issued bonds with a $180,000 face value on January 1, Year 1. The bonds had a 7 percent stated rate of interest and a five-year term. Interest is paid in cash annually, beginning December 31, Year 1. The bonds were issued at 98. The straight-line method is used for amortization.

Required

a. Use a financial statements model like the one shown next to demonstrate how (1) the January 1, Year 1, bond issue and (2) the December 31, Year 1, recognition of interest expense, including the amortization of the discount and the cash payment, affect the company's financial statements. Use + for increase, − for decrease, and NA for not affected.

Event No.	Assets	=	Liab.	+	Equity	Rev.	−	Exp.	=	Net Inc.	Cash Flow
1											

b. Determine the carrying value (face value less discount or plus premium) of the bond liability as of December 31, Year 1.
c. Determine the amount of interest expense reported on the Year 1 income statement.
d. Determine the carrying value (face value less discount or plus premium) of the bond liability as of December 31, Year 2.
e. Determine the amount of interest expense reported on the Year 2 income statement.

LO 10-5

Exercise 10-15A *Straight-line amortization of a bond premium*

The Square Foot Grill, Inc. issued $200,000 of 10-year, 6 percent bonds on July 1, Year 1, at 102. Interest is payable in cash semiannually on June 30 and December 31. The straight-line method is used for amortization.

Required

a. Prepare the journal entries to record issuing the bonds and any necessary journal entries for Year 1 and Year 2. Post the journal entries to T-accounts. Prepare any necessary closing entries for Year 1.
b. Prepare the liabilities section of the balance sheet at the end of Year 1 and Year 2.
c. What amount of interest expense will Square Foot report on the financial statements for Year 1 and Year 2?
d. What amount of cash will Square Foot pay for interest in Year 1 and Year 2?

LO 10-4

Exercise 10-16A *Straight-line amortization for bonds issued at a discount*

On January 1, Year 1, Price Co. issued $190,000 of five-year, 6 percent bonds at 96½. Interest is payable annually on December 31. The discount is amortized using the straight-line method.

Required

Prepare the journal entries to record the bond transactions for Year 1 and Year 2.

LO 10-5

Exercise 10-17A *Straight-line amortization of a bond premium*

Stuart Company issued bonds with a $150,000 face value on January 1, Year 1. The bonds had a 6 percent stated rate of interest and a five-year term. Interest is paid in cash annually, beginning December 31, Year 1. The bonds were issued at 103. The straight-line method is used for amortization.

Required

a. Use a financial statements model like the one shown next to demonstrate how (1) the January 1, Year 1, bond issue and (2) the December 31, Year 1, recognition of interest expense, including the amortization of the premium and the cash payment, affect the company's financial statements. Use + for increase, − for decrease, and NA for not affected.

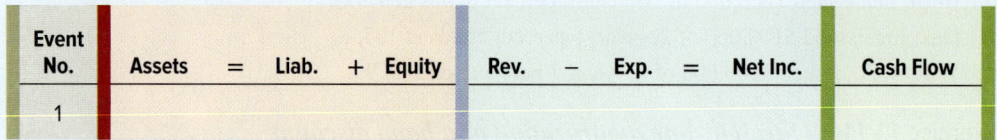

b. Determine the carrying value (face value less discount or plus premium) of the bond liability as of December 31, Year 1.
c. Determine the amount of interest expense reported on the Year 1 income statement.
d. Determine the carrying value of the bond liability as of December 31, Year 2.
e. Determine the amount of interest expense reported on the Year 2 income statement.

LO 10-5

Exercise 10-18A *Straight-line amortization for bonds issued at a premium*

On January 1, Year 1, Sayers Company issued $280,000 of five-year, 6 percent bonds at 102. Interest is payable semiannually on June 30 and December 31. The premium is amortized using the straight-line method.

Required

Prepare the journal entries to record the bond transactions for Year 1 and Year 2.

Accounting for Long-Term Debt 569

Exercise 10-19A *Effective interest amortization of a bond discount* LO 10-6

On January 1, Year 1, the Diamond Association issued bonds with a face value of $300,000, a stated rate of interest of 6 percent, and a 10-year term to maturity. Interest is payable in cash on December 31 of each year. The effective rate of interest was 7 percent at the time the bonds were issued. The bonds sold for $278,932. Diamond used the effective interest rate method to amortize the bond discount.

Required

a. Determine the amount of the discount on the day of issue.
b. Determine the amount of interest expense recognized on December 31, Year 1.
c. Determine the carrying value of the bond liability on December 31, Year 1.
d. Provide the general journal entry necessary to record the December 31, Year 1, interest expense.

Exercise 10-20A *Effective interest amortization of a bond discount* LO 10-6

On January 1, Year 1, Parker Company issued bonds with a face value of $80,000, a stated rate of interest of 8 percent, and a five-year term to maturity. Interest is payable in cash on December 31 of each year. The effective rate of interest was 9 percent at the time the bonds were issued. The bonds sold for $76,888. Parker used the effective interest rate method to amortize the bond discount.

Required

a. Prepare an amortization table as shown next:

	Cash Payment	Interest Expense	Discount Amortization	Carrying Value
January 1, Year 1				76,888
December 31, Year 1	6,400	6,920	520	77,408
December 31, Year 2	?	?	?	?
December 31, Year 3	?	?	?	?
December 31, Year 4	?	?	?	?
December 31, Year 5	?	?	?	?
Totals	32,000	35,112	3,112	

b. What item(s) in the table would appear on the Year 4 balance sheet?
c. What item(s) in the table would appear on the Year 4 income statement?
d. What item(s) in the table would appear on the Year 4 statement of cash flows?

Exercise 10-21A *Effective interest amortization of a bond premium* LO 10-7

On January 1, Year 1, Young Company issued bonds with a face value of $300,000, a stated rate of interest of 7 percent, and a 10-year term to maturity. Interest is payable in cash on December 31 of each year. The effective rate of interest was 6 percent at the time the bonds were issued. The bonds sold for $323,165. Young used the effective interest rate method to amortize the bond premium.

Required

a. Determine the amount of the premium on the day of issue.
b. Determine the amount of interest expense recognized on December 31, Year 1.
c. Determine the carrying value of the bond liability on December 31, Year 1.
d. Provide the general journal entry necessary to record the December 31, Year 1, interest expense.

Exercise 10-22A *Effective interest amortization for a bond premium* LO 10-7

On January 1, Year 1, Hart Company issued bonds with a face value of $150,000, a stated rate of interest of 8 percent, and a five-year term to maturity. Interest is payable in cash on December 31 of each year. The effective rate of interest was 7 percent at the time the bonds were issued. The bonds sold for $156,150. Hart used the effective interest rate method to amortize the bond premium.

Required

a. Prepare an amortization table as shown next:

	Cash Payment	Interest Expense	Premium Amortization	Carrying Value
January 1, Year 1				156,150
December 31, Year 1	12,000	10,931	1,069	155,081
December 31, Year 2	?	?	?	?
December 31, Year 3	?	?	?	?
December 31, Year 4	?	?	?	?
December 31, Year 5	?	?	?	?
Totals	60,000	53,850	6,150	

b. What item(s) in the table would appear on the Year 4 balance sheet?
c. What item(s) in the table would appear on the Year 4 income statement?
d. What item(s) in the table would appear on the Year 4 statement of cash flows?

LO 10-5, 10-7

Exercise 10-23A *Effective interest versus straight-line amortization*

On January 1, Year 1, the Christie Companies issued bonds with a face value of $500,000, a stated rate of interest of 10 percent, and a 20-year term to maturity. Interest is payable in cash on December 31 of each year. The effective rate of interest was 8 percent at the time the bonds were issued.

Required

Write a brief memo explaining whether the effective interest rate method or the straight-line method will produce the highest amount of interest expense recognized on the Year 1 income statement.

LO 10-8

Exercise 10-24A *Determining the after-tax cost of debt*

The following information is available for three companies:

	Rope Co.	Chain Co.	Line Co.
Face value of bonds payable	$400,000	$700,000	$600,000
Interest rate	8%	7%	6%
Income tax rate	35%	20%	25%

Required

a. Determine the annual before-tax interest cost for each company *in dollars*.
b. Determine the annual after-tax interest cost for each company *in dollars*.
c. Determine the annual after-tax interest cost for each company as *a percentage* of the face value of the bonds.

LO 10-8

Exercise 10-25A *Determining the effects of financing alternatives on ratios*

Clayton Industries has the following account balances:

Current assets	$20,000	Current liabilities	$10,000
Noncurrent assets	80,000	Noncurrent liabilities	50,000
		Stockholders' equity	40,000

The company wishes to raise $40,000 in cash and is considering two financing options: Clayton can sell $40,000 of bonds payable, or it can issue additional common stock for $40,000. To help in the decision process, Clayton's management wants to determine the effects of each alternative on its current ratio and debt-to-assets ratio.

Accounting for Long-Term Debt   571

Required

a. Help Clayton's management by completing the following chart:

Ratio	Currently	If Bonds Are Issued	If Stock Is Issued
Current ratio			
Debt-to-assets ratio			

b. Assume that after the funds are invested, EBIT amounts to $12,000. Also assume the company pays $4,000 in dividends or $4,000 in interest depending on which source of financing is used. Based on a 30 percent tax rate, determine the amount of the increase in retained earnings that would result under each financing option.

PROBLEMS—SERIES A

All applicable Problems in Series A are available in Connect.

Problem 10-26A *Effect of an installment note on financial statements*

LO 10-1

On January 1, Year 1, Brown Co. borrowed cash from First Bank by issuing a $100,000 face-value, four-year term note that had an 8 percent annual interest rate. The note is to be repaid by making annual cash payments of $30,192 that include both interest and principal on December 31 of each year. Brown used the proceeds from the loan to purchase land that generated rental revenues of $52,000 cash per year.

CHECK FIGURES
a. Year 1 Ending Principal Balance: $77,808
b. Year 1 Net Income: $44,000

Required

a. Prepare an amortization schedule for the four-year period.
b. Prepare an income statement, balance sheet, and statement of cash flows for each of the four years. (*Hint:* Record the transactions for each year in T-accounts before preparing the financial statements.)
c. Given that revenue is the same for each period, explain why net income increases each year.

Problem 10-27A *Effect of a line of credit on financial statements*

LO 10-2

Boyd Company has a line of credit with State Bank. Boyd can borrow up to $400,000 at any time over the course of the Year 1 calendar year. The following table shows the prime rate expressed as an annual percentage along with the amounts borrowed and repaid during Year 1. Boyd agreed to pay interest at an annual rate equal to 2 percent above the bank's prime rate. Funds are borrowed or repaid on the first day of each month. Interest is payable in cash on the last day of the month. The interest rate is applied to the outstanding monthly balance. For example, Boyd pays 7 percent (5 percent + 2 percent) annual interest on $100,000 for the month of January.

CHECK FIGURES
a. Interest Expense: $11,008
Total Assets: $83,992

Month	Amount Borrowed or (Repaid)	Prime Rate for the Month
January	$100,000	5%
February	70,000	6
March	(30,000)	7
April through October	No change	No change
November	(50,000)	6
December	(40,000)	5

Boyd earned $45,000 of cash revenue during Year 1.

Required

a. Prepare an income statement, balance sheet, and statement of cash flows for Year 1. (*Note:* Round computations to the nearest dollar.)
b. Write a memo to explain how the business was able to generate retained earnings when the owner contributed no assets to the business.

572 Chapter 10

LO 10-3

CHECK FIGURES
b. Interest Expense: $48,000
Loss on Bond Redemptions: $24,000

Problem 10-28A *Recording transactions for callable bonds*

Arnold Corp. issued $600,000 of 20-year, 8 percent, callable bonds on January 1, Year 1, with interest payable annually on December 31. The bonds were issued at their face amount. The bonds are callable at 104. The fiscal year of the corporation ends December 31.

Required

a. Show the effect of the following events on the financial statements by recording the appropriate amounts in a horizontal statements model like the following one. In the Cash Flow column, indicate whether the item is an operating activity (OA), investing activity (IA), or financing activity (FA). Use NA if an element was not affected by the event.

(1) Issued the bonds on January 1, Year 1.
(2) Paid interest due to bondholders on December 31, Year 1.
(3) On January 1, Year 6, Arnold Corp. called the bonds. Assume that all interim entries were correctly recorded.

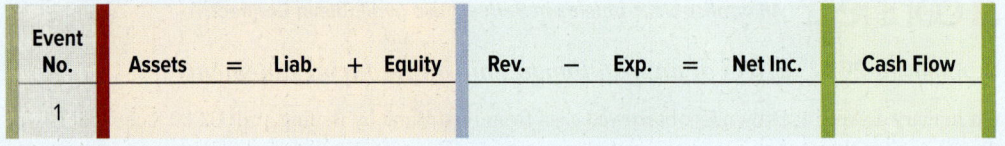

b. Prepare journal entries for the three events listed in Requirement *a*.

LO 10-5

Problem 10-29A *Straight-line amortization of a bond premium*

Pine Land Co. was formed when it acquired cash from the issue of common stock. The company then issued bonds at a premium on January 1, Year 1. Interest is payable annually on December 31 of each year, beginning December 31, Year 1. On January 2, Year 1, Pine Land Co. purchased a piece of land and leased it for an annual rental fee. The rent is received annually on December 31, beginning December 31, Year 1. At the end of the eight-year period (December 31, Year 8), the land was sold at a gain, and the bonds were paid off. A summary of the transactions for each year follows:

Year 1

1. Acquired cash from the issue of common stock.
2. Issued eight-year bonds.
3. Purchased land.
4. Received land rental income.
5. Recognized interest expense including the straight-line amortization of the premium and made the cash payment for interest on December 31.
6. Prepared the December 31 entry to close Rent Revenue.
7. Prepared the December 31 entry to close Interest Expense.

Year 2–Year 7

8. Received land rental income.
9. Recognized interest expense, including the straight-line amortization of the premium, and made the cash payment for interest on December 31.
10. Prepared the December 31 entry to close Rent Revenue.
11. Prepared the December 31 entry to close Interest Expense.

Year 8

12. Sold land at a gain.
13. Retired bonds at face value.

Required

Identify each of these 13 events and transactions as an asset source (AS), asset use (AU), asset exchange (AE), or claims exchange (CE). Explain how each event affects assets, liabilities, equity, net income, and cash flow by placing a + for increase, − for decrease, or NA for not affected under each category. In the Cash Flow column, indicate whether the item is an operating activity (OA), investing activity (IA), or financing activity (FA). The first event is recorded as an example.

Event No.	Types of Event	Assets	=	Liabilities	+	Common Stock	+	Retained Earnings	Net Income	Cash Flow
1	AS	+		NA		+		NA	NA	+ FA

Problem 10-30A Straight-line amortization of a bond discount

LO 10-4

During Year 1 and Year 2, Agatha Corp. completed the following transactions relating to its bond issue. The corporation's fiscal year is the calendar year.

CHECK FIGURES
d. Year 1 Interest Expense: $18,600
e. Year 1 Interest Paid: $18,000

Year 1

Jan. 1 Issued $300,000 of 10-year, 6 percent bonds for $294,000. The annual cash payment for interest is due on December 31.
Dec. 31 Recognized interest expense, including the straight-line amortization of the discount, and made the cash payment for interest.
Dec. 31 Closed the interest expense account.

Year 2

Dec. 31 Recognized interest expense, including the straight-line amortization of the discount, and made the cash payment for interest.
Dec. 31 Closed the interest expense account.

Required

a. When the bonds were issued, was the market rate of interest more or less than the stated rate of interest? If Agatha had sold the bonds at their face amount, what amount of cash would Agatha have received?
b. Prepare the general journal entries for these transactions.
c. Prepare the liabilities section of the balance sheet at December 31, Year 1 and Year 2.
d. Determine the amount of interest expense that will be reported on the income statements for Year 1 and Year 2.
e. Determine the amount of interest that will be paid in cash to the bondholders in Year 1 and Year 2.

Problem 10-31A Straight-line amortization of a bond discount

LO 10-4

OZ Company was started when it issued bonds with a $500,000 face value on January 1, Year 1. The bonds were issued for cash at 96. OZ uses the straight-line method of amortization. They had a 20-year term to maturity and an 8 percent annual interest rate. Interest was payable on December 31 of each year. OZ Company immediately purchased land with the proceeds (cash received) from the bond issue. OZ leased the land for $60,000 cash per year. On January 1, Year 4, the company sold the land for $500,000 cash. Immediately after the sale of the land, Oz redeemed the bonds at 98. Assume that no other accounting events occurred during Year 4.

Required

Prepare an income statement, statement of changes in equity, balance sheet, and statement of cash flows for the Year 1, Year 2, Year 3, and Year 4 accounting periods. Assume that the company closes its books on December 31 of each year. Prepare the statements using a vertical statements format. (*Hint:* Record each year's transactions in T-accounts prior to preparing the financial statements.)

574 Chapter 10

LO 10-4, 10-5

Problem 10-32A *Effect of bond transactions on financial statements*

The three typical accounting events associated with borrowing money through a bond issue are:
1. Exchanging the bonds for cash on the day of issue.
2. Making cash payments for interest expense and recording amortization when applicable.
3. Repaying the principal at maturity.

Required

a. Assuming the bonds are issued at face value, show the effect of each of the three events on the financial statements using a horizontal statements model like the following one. Use + for increase, − for decrease, and NA for not affected.

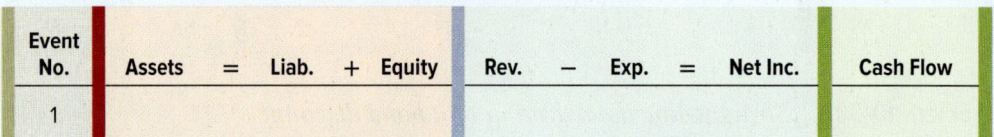

b. Repeat the requirements in Requirement *a*, but assume instead that the bonds are issued at a discount.

c. Repeat the requirements in Requirement *a*, but assume instead that the bonds are issued at a premium.

LO 10-4, 10-6

Problem 10-33A *Effective interest versus straight-line amortization*

On January 1, Year 1, Twain Corp. sold $500,000 of its own 7 percent, 10-year bonds. Interest is payable annually on December 31. The bonds were sold to yield an effective interest rate of 8 percent. Twain uses the effective interest rate method. The bonds sold for $477,422.

Required

a. Prepare the journal entry for the issuance of the bonds.
b. Prepare the journal entry for the amortization of the bond discount and the payment of the interest at December 31, Year 1. (Assume effective interest amortization.)
c. Prepare the journal entry for the amortization of the bond discount and the payment of interest on December 31, Year 1. (Assume straight-line amortization.)
d. Calculate the amount of interest expense for Year 2. (Assume effective interest amortization.)
e. Calculate the amount of interest expense for Year 2. (Assume straight-line amortization.)

LO 10-8

Problem 10-34A *Using ratios to make comparisons*

The following information pertains to Austin, Inc. and Huston Company:

Account Title	Austin	Huston
Current assets	$ 40,000	$ 40,000
Total assets	300,000	300,000
Current liabilities	15,000	20,000
Total liabilities	200,000	240,000
Stockholders' equity	100,000	60,000
Interest expense	14,000	17,000
Income tax expense	28,000	27,000
Net income	52,000	50,000

Required

a. Compute each company's debt-to-assets ratio, current ratio, and times interest earned (EBIT must be computed). Identify the company with the greater financial risk.

b. Compute each company's return-on-equity ratio and return-on-assets ratio. Use EBIT instead of net income when computing the return-on-assets ratio. Identify the company that is managing its

Accounting for Long-Term Debt 575

assets more effectively. Identify the company that is producing the higher return from the stockholders' perspective. Explain how one company was able to produce a higher return on equity than the other.

EXERCISES—SERIES B

Exercise 10-1B *Interest only versus an installment note*

LO 10-1

Pare Co. borrowed $80,000 from National Bank by issuing a note with a five-year term. Pare has two options with respect to the payment of interest and principal. Option 1 requires the payment of interest only on an annual basis with the full amount of the principal due at maturity. Option 2 calls for an annual payment that includes interest due plus a partial repayment of the principal balance. The effective annual interest rate on both notes is identical.

Required

Write a memo explaining how the two alternatives will affect *(a)* the carrying value of liabilities, *(b)* the amount of annual interest expense, *(c)* the total amount of interest that will be paid over the life of the note, and *(d)* the cash flow consequences.

Exercise 10-2B *Amortization schedule for an installment note*

LO 10-1

On January 1, Year 1, Monroe Co. borrowed $80,000 cash from First Bank by issuing a four-year, 6 percent note. The principal and interest are to be paid by making annual payments in the amount of $23,087. Payments are to be made December 31 of each year, beginning December 31, Year 1.

Required

Prepare an amortization schedule for the interest and principal payments for the four-year period.

Exercise 10-3B *Financial statement effects of an installment note*

LO 10-1

Lek Hood started a business by issuing a $70,000 face-value note to State National Bank on January 1, Year 1. The note had a 6 percent annual rate of interest and a 10-year term. Payments of $9,581 are to be made each December 31 for 10 years.

Required

a. What portion of the December 31, Year 1, payment is applied to
   (1) Interest expense?
   (2) Principal?
b. What is the principal balance on January 1, Year 2?
c. What portion of the December 31, Year 2, payment is applied to
   (1) Interest expense?
   (2) Principal?

Exercise 10-4B *Financial statement effects of an installment note*

LO 10-1

A partial amortization schedule for a five-year note payable that Mercury Co. issued on January 1, Year 1, is shown next:

Accounting Period	Principal Balance January 1	Cash Payment	Applied to Interest	Applied to Principal
Year 1	$60,000	$13,858	$3,000	$10,858
Year 2	49,142	13,858	2,457	11,401

Required

a. What rate of interest is Mercury Co. paying on the note?

b. Using a financial statements model like the one shown next, record the appropriate amounts for the following two events:
   (1) January 1, Year 1, issue of the note payable
   (2) December 31, Year 2, payment on the note payable

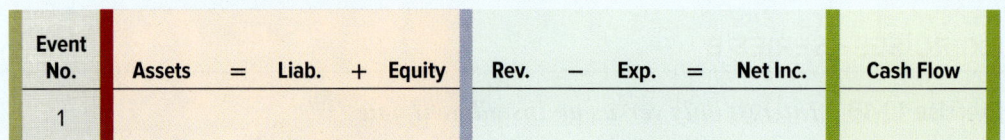

c. If the company earned $75,000 cash revenue and paid $32,000 in cash expenses in addition to the interest in Year 1, what is the amount of each of the following?
   (1) Net income for Year 1
   (2) Cash flow from operating activities for Year 1
   (3) Cash flow from financing activities for Year 1
d. What is the amount of interest expense on this loan for Year 3?

LO 10-2

Exercise 10-5B Journal entries for a line of credit

Colson Company has a line of credit with Federal Bank. Colson can borrow up to $800,000 at any time over the course of the Year 1 calendar year. The following table shows the prime rate expressed as an annual percentage along with the amounts borrowed and repaid during the first four months of Year 1. Colson agreed to pay interest at an annual rate equal to 2 percent above the bank's prime rate. Funds are borrowed or repaid on the first day of each month. Interest is payable in cash on the last day of the month. The interest rate is applied to the outstanding monthly balance. For example, Colson pays 6 percent (4 percent + 2 percent) annual interest on $80,000 for the month of January.

Month	Amount Borrowed or (Repaid)	Prime Rate for the Month
January	$80,000	4.0%
February	50,000	4.25%
March	(30,000)	4.5%
April	20,000	4.25%

Required
Provide all journal entries pertaining to Colson's line of credit for the first four months of Year 1.

LO 10-3

Exercise 10-6B Two accounting cycles for bonds issued at face value

Pluto Company issued $300,000 of 20-year, 6 percent bonds on January 1, Year 1. The bonds were issued at face value. Interest is payable in cash on December 31 of each year. Pluto immediately invested the proceeds from the bond issue in land. The land was leased for an annual $50,000 of cash revenue, which was collected on December 31 of each year, beginning December 31, Year 1.

Required
a. Prepare the journal entries and appropriate closing entries for these events and post them to T-accounts for Year 1 and Year 2.
b. Prepare the income statement, balance sheet, and statement of cash flows for Year 1 and Year 2.

LO 10-3

Exercise 10-7B Two accounting cycles for bonds issued at face value

On January 1, Year 1, Hazman Corp. issued $200,000 of 10-year, 6 percent bonds at their face value. Interest is payable on December 31 of each year with the first payment due December 31, Year 1.

Required
Prepare all the general journal entries related to these bonds for Year 1 and Year 2.

Exercise 10-8B Journal entries for callable bonds
LO 10-3

Tyler Co. issued $250,000 of 6 percent, 10-year, callable bonds on January 1, Year 1, at their face value. The call premium was 2 percent (bonds are callable at 102). Interest was payable annually on December 31. The bonds were called on December 31, Year 4.

Required

Prepare the journal entries to record the bond issue on January 1, Year 1, and the bond redemption on December 31, Year 4. Entries to accrue and pay interest are not required.

Exercise 10-9B Annual versus semiannual interest for bonds issued at face value
LO 10-3

Jupiter Co. issued bonds with a face value of $150,000 on January 1, Year 1. The bonds had a 6 percent stated rate of interest and a five-year term. The bonds were issued at face value.

Required

a. What total amount of interest will Jupiter pay in Year 1 if bond interest is paid annually each December 31?

b. What total amount of interest will Jupiter pay in Year 1 if bond interest is paid semiannually each June 30 and December 31?

c. Write a memo explaining which option Jupiter would prefer.

Exercise 10-10B Determining cash receipts from bond issues
LO 10-4, 10-5

Required

Compute the cash proceeds from bond issues under the following terms. For each case, indicate whether the bonds sold at a premium or discount:

a. Hett, Inc. issued $400,000 of 8-year, 8 percent bonds at 101.
b. Holt Co. issued $250,000 of 4-year, 6 percent bonds at 98.
c. Holmes Co. issued $300,000 of 10-year, 7 percent bonds at 102¼.
d. Hart, Inc. issued $200,000 of 5-year, 6 percent bonds at 97½.

Exercise 10-11B Stated rate of interest versus the market rate of interest
LO 10-3, 10-4, 10-5

Required

Indicate whether a bond will sell at a premium (P), discount (D), or face value (F) for each of the following conditions:

a. _____ The stated rate of interest is less than the market rate.
b. _____ The market rate of interest is equal to the stated rate.
c. _____ The market rate of interest is less than the stated rate.
d. _____ The market rate of interest is higher than the stated rate.
e. _____ The stated rate of interest is higher than the market rate.

Exercise 10-12B Identifying bond premiums and discounts
LO 10-4, 10-5

Required

In each of the following situations, state whether the bonds will sell at a premium or discount:

a. Carver issued $400,000 of bonds with a stated interest rate of 7 percent. At the time of issue, the market rate of interest for similar investments was 6 percent.

b. Herring issued $200,000 of bonds with a stated interest rate of 6 percent. At the time of issue, the market rate of interest for similar investments was 8 percent.

c. Watson, Inc. issued callable bonds with a stated interest rate of 6 percent. The bonds were callable at 102. At the date of issue, the market rate of interest was 7 percent for similar investments.

578 Chapter 10

LO 10-4, 10-5

Exercise 10-13B *Determining the amount of bond premiums and discounts*

Required

For each of the following situations, calculate the amount of bond discount or premium, if any:

a. Jones Co. issued $120,000 of 6 percent bonds at 101.
b. Jude, Inc. issued $80,000 of 10-year, 8 percent bonds at 98.
c. James, Inc. issued $200,000 of 15-year, 9 percent bonds at 102¼.
d. Jolly Co. issued $400,000 of 20-year, 8 percent bonds at 99¾.

LO 10-4

Exercise 10-14B *Straight-line amortization of a bond discount*

Frey Company issued bonds of $300,000 face value on January 1, Year 1. The bonds had a 6 percent stated rate of interest and a 10-year term. Interest is paid in cash annually, beginning December 31, Year 1. The bonds were issued at 98. Frey uses the straight-line method of amortization.

Required

a. Use a financial statements model like the one shown next to demonstrate how (1) the January 1, Year 1, bond issue and (2) the December 31, Year 1, recognition of interest expense, including the amortization of the discount and the cash payment, affect the company's financial statements. Use + for increase, − for decrease, and NA for not affected.

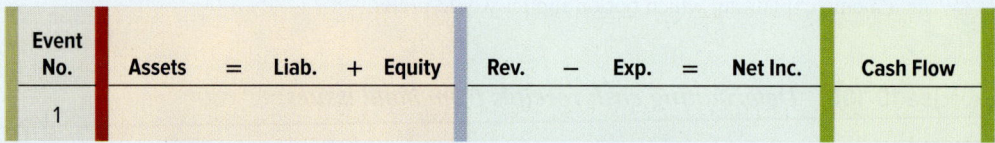

b. Determine the amount of interest expense reported on the Year 1 income statement.
c. Determine the carrying value (face value less discount or plus premium) of the bond liability as of December 31, Year 1.
d. Determine the amount of interest expense reported on the Year 2 income statement.
e. Determine the carrying value (face value less discount or plus premium) of the bond liability as of December 31, Year 2.

LO 10-4

Exercise 10-15B *Straight-line amortization of a bond discount*

Dixon Construction, Inc. issued $300,000 of 10-year, 6 percent bonds on July 1, Year 1, at 96. Interest is payable in cash semiannually on June 30 and December 31. Dixon uses the straight-line method of amortization.

Required

a. Prepare the journal entries to record issuing the bonds and any necessary journal entries for Year 1 and Year 2. Prepare any necessary closing entries for Year 1. Post the entries to T-accounts.
b. Prepare the liabilities section of the balance sheet at the end of Year 1 and Year 2.
c. What amount of interest expense will Dixon Construction report on the financial statements for Year 1 and Year 2?
d. What amount of cash will Dixon Construction pay for interest in Year 1 and Year 2?

LO 10-4

Exercise 10-16B *Straight-line amortization for bonds issued at a discount*

On January 1, Year 1, Files Co. issued $400,000 of five-year, 6 percent bonds at 97. Interest is payable annually on December 31. The discount is amortized using the straight-line method.

Required

Prepare the journal entries to record the bond transactions for Year 1 and Year 2.

LO 10-5

Exercise 10-17B *Straight-line amortization of a bond premium*

Ramsey Company issued bonds of $300,000 face value on January 1, Year 1. The bonds had a 6 percent stated rate of interest and a 10-year term. Interest is paid in cash annually, beginning December 31, Year 1. The bonds were issued at 101½. The straight-line method is used for amortization.

Required

a. Use a financial statements model like the one shown next to demonstrate how (1) the January 1, Year 1 bond issue and (2) the December 31, Year 1, recognition of interest expense, including the amortization of the premium and the cash payment, affect the company's financial statements. Use + for increase, − for decrease, and NA for not affected.

Event No.	Assets	=	Liab.	+	Equity	Rev.	−	Exp.	=	Net Inc.	Cash Flow
1											

b. Determine the carrying value (face value plus premium) of the bond liability as of December 31, Year 1.
c. Determine the amount of interest expense reported on the Year 1 income statement.
d. Determine the carrying value of the bond liability as of December 31, Year 2.
e. Determine the amount of interest expense reported on the Year 2 income statement.

Exercise 10-18B Straight-line amortization for bonds issued at a premium   LO 10-5

On January 1, Year 1, Chen Company issued $300,000 of five-year, 6 percent bonds at 101. Interest is payable annually on December 31. The premium is amortized using the straight-line method.

Required
Prepare the journal entries to record the bond transactions for Year 1 and Year 2.

Exercise 10-19B Effective interest amortization of a bond discount   LO 10-6

On January 1, Year 1, Seaside Condo Association issued bonds with a face value of $250,000, a stated rate of interest of 8 percent, and a 10-year term to maturity. Interest is payable in cash on December 31 of each year. The effective rate of interest was 10 percent at the time the bonds were issued. The bonds sold for $219,277. Seaside used the effective interest rate method to amortize the bond discount.

Required
a. Determine the amount of the discount on the day of issue.
b. Determine the amount of interest expense recognized on December 31, Year 1.
c. Determine the carrying value of the bond liability on December 31, Year 1.
d. Provide the general journal entry necessary to record the December 31, Year 1, interest expense.

Exercise 10-20B Effective interest amortization of a bond discount   LO 10-6

On January 1, Year 1, Valley Enterprises issued bonds with a face value of $60,000, a stated rate of interest of 8 percent, and a five-year term to maturity. Interest is payable in cash on December 31 of each year. The effective rate of interest was 9 percent at the time the bonds were issued. The bonds sold for $57,666. Valley used the effective interest rate method to amortize the bond discount.

Required
a. Prepare an amortization table as shown next:

	Cash Payment	Interest Expense	Discount Amortization	Carrying Value
January 1, Year 1				57,666
December 31, Year 1	4,800	5,190	390	58,056
December 31, Year 2	?	?	?	?
December 31, Year 3	?	?	?	?
December 31, Year 4	?	?	?	?
December 31, Year 5	?	?	?	?
Totals	24,000	26,334	2,334	

b. What item(s) in the table would appear on the Year 2 balance sheet?
c. What item(s) in the table would appear on the Year 2 income statement?
d. What item(s) in the table would appear on the Year 2 statement of cash flows?

LO 10-7

Exercise 10-21B *Effective interest amortization of a bond premium*

On January 1, Year 1, Omega Company issued bonds with a face value of $200,000, a stated rate of interest of 6 percent, and a 10-year term to maturity. Interest is payable in cash on December 31 of each year. The effective rate of interest was 5 percent at the time the bonds were issued. The bonds sold for $215,443. Omega used the effective interest rate method to amortize the bond discount.

Required

a. Determine the amount of the premium on the day of issue.
b. Determine the amount of interest expense recognized on December 31, Year 1.
c. Determine the carrying value of the bond liability on December 31, Year 1.
d. Provide the general journal entry necessary to record the December 31, Year 1, interest expense.

LO 10-7

Exercise 10-22B *Effective interest amortization for a bond premium*

On January 1, Year 1, Reese Incorporated issued bonds with a face value of $120,000, a stated rate of interest of 8 percent, and a five-year term to maturity. Interest is payable in cash on December 31 of each year. The effective rate of interest was 7 percent at the time the bonds were issued. The bonds sold for $124,920. Reese used the effective interest rate method to amortize the bond discount.

Required

a. Prepare an amortization table as shown next:

	Cash Payment	Interest Expense	Discount Amortization	Carrying Value
January 1, Year 1				124,920
December 31, Year 1	9,600	8,744	856	124,064
December 31, Year 2	?	?	?	?
December 31, Year 3	?	?	?	?
December 31, Year 4	?	?	?	?
December 31, Year 5	?	?	?	?
Totals	48,000	43,080	4,920	

b. What item(s) in the table would appear on the Year 3 balance sheet?
c. What item(s) in the table would appear on the Year 3 income statement?
d. What item(s) in the table would appear on the Year 3 statement of cash flows?

LO 10-4, 10-6

Exercise 10-23B *Effective interest versus straight-line amortization*

On January 1, Year 1, Wright and Associates issued bonds with a face value of $800,000, a stated rate of interest of 8 percent, and a 20-year term to maturity. Interest is payable in cash on December 31 of each year. The effective rate of interest was 9 percent at the time the bonds were issued.

Required

Write a brief memo explaining whether the effective interest rate method or the straight-line method will produce the highest amount of interest expense recognized on the Year 1 income statement.

LO 10-8

Exercise 10-24B *Determining the after-tax cost of debt*

The following information is available for three companies:

	Bass Co.	Carp Co.	Perch Co.
Face value of bonds payable	$300,000	$600,000	$500,000
Interest rate	10%	9%	8%
Income tax rate	40%	30%	35%

Required

a. Determine the annual before-tax interest cost for each company *in dollars*.
b. Determine the annual after-tax interest cost for each company *in dollars*.
c. Determine the annual after-tax interest cost for each company as *a percentage* of the face value of the bonds.

Exercise 10-25B *Determining the effects of financing alternatives on ratios*   LO 10-8

Cascade Industries has the following account balances:

Current assets	$ 30,000	Current liabilities	$15,000
Noncurrent assets	120,000	Noncurrent liabilities	75,000
		Stockholders' equity	60,000

The company wishes to raise $50,000 in cash and is considering two financing options: Cascade can sell $50,000 of bonds payable, or it can issue additional common stock for $50,000. To help in the decision process, Cascade's management wants to determine the effects of each alternative on its current ratio and debt-to-assets ratio.

Required

a. Help Cascade's management by completing the following chart:

Ratio	Currently	If Bonds Are Issued	If Stock Is Issued
Current ratio			
Debt-to-assets ratio			

b. Assume that after the funds are invested, EBIT amounts to $18,000. Also assume the company pays $5,000 in dividends or $5,000 in interest, depending on which source of financing is used. Based on a 30 percent tax rate, determine the amount of the increase in retained earnings that would result under each financing option.

PROBLEMS—SERIES B

Problem 10-26B *Effect of an installment note on financial statements*   LO 10-1

On January 1, Year 1, Kramer Co. borrowed cash from First City Bank by issuing a $90,000 face-value, three-year term note that had a 7 percent annual interest rate. The note is to be repaid by making annual payments of $34,295 that include both interest and principal on December 31. Kramer invested the proceeds from the loan in land that generated lease revenues of $45,000 cash per year.

Required

a. Prepare an amortization schedule for the three-year period.
b. Prepare an income statement, balance sheet, and statement of cash flows for each of the three years. (*Hint:* Record the transactions for each year in T-accounts before preparing the financial statements.)
c. Does cash outflow from operating activities remain constant or change each year? Explain.

Problem 10-27B *Effect of a line of credit on financial statements*   LO 10-2

Mott Company has a line of credit with Bay Bank. Mott can borrow up to $400,000 at any time over the course of the Year 1 calendar year. The following table shows the prime rate expressed as an annual percentage along with the amounts borrowed and repaid during Year 1. Mott agreed to pay interest at an annual rate equal to 1 percent above the bank's prime rate. Funds are borrowed or repaid on the first day of each month. Interest is payable in cash on the last day of the month. The interest rate is applied to the outstanding monthly balance. For example, Mott pays 6 percent (5 percent + 1 percent) annual interest on $60,000 for the month of January.

Month	Amount Borrowed or (Repaid)	Prime Rate for the Month
January	$60,000	5%
February	40,000	5
March	(30,000)	6
April through October	No change	No change
November	(20,000)	6
December	(10,000)	5

Mott earned $25,000 of cash revenue during Year 1.

Required

a. Prepare an income statement, balance sheet, and statement of cash flows for Year 1.
b. Write a memo discussing the advantages to a business of arranging a line of credit.

Problem 10-28B *Recording transactions for callable bonds*

LO 10-3

Dame Co. issued $250,000 of 10-year, 6 percent, callable bonds on January 1, Year 1, with interest payable annually on December 31. The bonds were issued at their face amount. The bonds are callable at 101½. The fiscal year of the corporation is the calendar year.

Required

a. Show the effect of the following events on the financial statements by recording the appropriate amounts in a horizontal statements model like the following one. In the Cash Flow column, indicate whether the item is an operating activity (OA), investing activity (IA), or financing activity (FA). Use NA if an element was not affected by the event.

(1) Issued the bonds on January 1, Year 1.
(2) Paid interest due to bondholders on December 31, Year 1.
(3) On January 1, Year 5, Dame Co. called the bonds. Assume that all interim entries were correctly recorded.

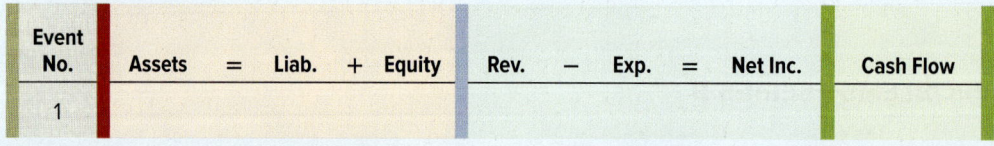

b. Prepare journal entries for the three events listed in Requirement *a*.

Problem 10-29B *Straight-line amortization of a bond discount*

LO 10-4

White Co. was formed when it acquired cash from the issue of common stock. The company then issued bonds at a discount on January 1, Year 1. Interest is payable on December 31 with the first payment made December 31, Year 1. On January 2, Year 1, White Co. purchased a piece of land that produced rent revenue annually. The rent is collected on December 31 of each year, beginning December 31, Year 1. At the end of the six-year period (January 1, Year 7), the land was sold at a gain and the bonds were paid off at face value. A summary of the transactions for each year follows:

Year 1

1. Acquired cash from the issue of common stock.
2. Issued six-year bonds.
3. Purchased land.
4. Received land rental income.
5. Recognized interest expense, including the straight-line amortization of the discount, and made the cash payment for interest on December 31.
6. Prepared December 31 entry to close Rent Revenue.
7. Prepared December 31 entry to close Interest Expense.

Year 2–Year 6

8. Received land rental income.
9. Recognized interest expense, including the straight-line amortization of the discount, and made the cash payment for interest December 31.
10. Prepared December 31 entry to close Rent Revenue.
11. Prepared December 31 entry to close Interest Expense.

Year 7

12. Sold the land at a gain.
13. Retired the bonds at face value.

Required

Identify each of these 13 events and transactions as an asset source (AS), asset use (AU), asset exchange (AE), or claims exchange (CE). Explain how each event affects assets, liabilities, equity, net income, and cash flow by placing a + for increase, − for decrease, or NA for not affected under each of the categories. In the Cash Flow column, indicate whether the item is an operating activity (OA), investing activity (IA), or financing activity (FA). The first event is recorded as an example.

Event No.	Type of Event	Assets	=	Liabilities	+	Common Stock	+	Retained Earnings	Net Income	Cash Flow
1	AS	+		NA		+		NA	NA	+ FA

Problem 10-30B *Straight-line amortization of a bond discount*   LO 10-4

During Year 1 and Year 2, Kale Co. completed the following transactions relating to its bond issue. The company's fiscal year ends on December 31.

Year 1

Mar. 1 Issued $200,000 of eight-year, 6 percent bonds for $194,000. The semiannual cash payment for interest is due on March 1 and September 1, beginning September Year 1.
Sept. 1 Recognized interest expense, including the straight-line amortization of the discount, and made the semiannual cash payment for interest.
Dec. 31 Recognized accrued interest expense, including the straight-line amortization of the discount.
Dec. 31 Closed the interest expense account.

Year 2

Mar. 1 Recognized interest expense, including the straight-line amortization of the discount, and made the semiannual cash payment for interest.
Sept. 1 Recognized interest expense, including the straight-line amortization of the discount, and made the semiannual cash payment for interest.
Dec. 31 Recognized accrued interest expense, including the amortization of the discount.
Dec. 31 Closed the interest expense account.

Required

a. When the bonds were issued, was the market rate of interest more or less than the stated rate of interest? If the bonds had sold at face value, what amount of cash would Kale Co. have received?
b. Prepare the general journal entries for these transactions.
c. Prepare the liabilities section of the balance sheet at December 31, Year 1 and Year 2.
d. Determine the amount of interest expense Kale would report on the income statements for Year 1 and Year 2.
e. Determine the amount of interest Kale would pay to the bondholders in Year 1 and Year 2.

LO 10-5

Problem 10-31B *Straight-line amortization of a bond premium*

Whitten Company was started when it issued bonds with $300,000 face value on January 1, Year 1. The bonds were issued for cash at 103. Whitten uses the straight-line method of amortization. They had a 15-year term to maturity and a 6 percent annual interest rate. Interest was payable annually. Whitten immediately purchased land with the proceeds (cash received) from the bond issue. Whitten leased the land for $36,000 cash per year. On January 1, Year 4, the company sold the land for $310,000 cash. Immediately after the sale, Whitten repurchased its bonds (repaid the bond liability) at 104. Assume that no other accounting events occurred in Year 4.

Required

Prepare an income statement, statement of changes in equity, balance sheet, and statement of cash flows for each of the Year 1, Year 2, Year 3, and Year 4 accounting periods. Assume that the company closes its books on December 31 of each year. Prepare the statements using a vertical statements format. (*Hint:* Record each year's transactions in T-accounts prior to preparing the financial statements.)

LO 10-1, 10-2, 10-4, 10-5

Problem 10-32B *Effect of financing transactions on financial statements*

Required

Show the effect of each of the following independent accounting events on the financial statements using a horizontal statements model like the following one. Use + for increase, − for decrease, and NA for not affected. The first event is recorded as an example.

Event No.	Assets	=	Liab.	+	Equity	Rev.	−	Exp.	=	Net Inc.	Cash Flow
1	+		+		NA	NA		NA		NA	FA +

a. Issued a bond at a premium.
b. Made an interest payment on a bond that had been issued at a premium and amortized the premium.
c. Borrowed funds using a line of credit.
d. Made an interest payment for funds that had been borrowed against a line of credit.
e. Made a cash payment on a note payable for both interest and principal.
f. Issued a bond at face value.
g. Made an interest payment on a bond that had been issued at face value.
h. Issued a bond at a discount.
i. Made an interest payment on a bond that had been issued at a discount and amortized the discount.

LO 10-5, 10-7

Problem 10-33B *Effective interest versus straight-line amortization*

On January 1, Year 1, Mason Corp. sold $100,000 of its own 6 percent, 10-year bonds. Interest is payable annually on December 31. The bonds were sold to yield an effective interest rate of 5 percent. Mason Corp. uses the effective interest rate method. The bonds sold for $104,330.

Required

a. Prepare the journal entry for the issuance of the bonds.
b. Prepare the journal entry for the amortization of the bond premium and the payment of the interest on December 31, Year 3. (Assume effective interest amortization.)
c. Prepare the journal entry for the amortization of the bond premium and the payment of interest on December 31, Year 3. (Assume straight-line amortization.)
d. Calculate the amount of interest expense for Year 4. (Assume effective interest amortization.)
e. Calculate the amount of interest expense for Year 4. (Assume straight-line amortization.)

Problem 10-34B *Using ratios to make comparisons*

LO 10-8

The following information pertains to Tacoma and Olympia companies:

Account Title	Tacoma Co.	Olympia Co.
Current assets	$ 60,000	$ 60,000
Total assets	1,000,000	1,000,000
Current liabilities	55,000	50,000
Total liabilities	800,000	600,000
Stockholders' equity	200,000	400,000
Interest expense	60,000	45,000
Income tax expense	95,000	100,000
Net income	145,000	155,000

Required

a. Compute each company's debt-to-assets ratio, current ratio, and times interest earned (EBIT must be computed). Identify the company with the greater financial risk.

b. Compute each company's return-on-equity ratio and return-on-assets ratio. Use EBIT instead of net income when computing the return-on-assets ratio. Identify the company that is managing its assets more effectively. Identify the company that is producing the higher return from the stockholders' perspective. Explain how one company was able to produce a higher return on equity than the other.

ANALYZE, THINK, COMMUNICATE

ATC 10-1 Business Applications Case *Understanding real-world annual reports*

Obtain the Target Corporation's annual report at http://investors.target.com using the instructions in Appendix B, and use it to answer the following questions:

Required

a. What was the average interest rate on Target's long-term debt in the fiscal-year ended January 28, 2017 (2016)?

b. Target has an "unsecured revolving credit facility" (i.e., a line of credit). What is the total amount of credit available under this facility? How much of this total amount available had Target used as of January 28, 2017?

c. Target's balance sheet shows a line titled "Other noncurrent liabilities." What are the types of debt included in this category?

ATC 10-2 Group Assignment *Missing information*

The following three companies issued the following bonds:

1. Carr, Inc. issued $100,000 of 8 percent, five-year bonds at 102¼ on January 1, 2016. Interest is payable annually on December 31.
2. Kim, Inc. issued $100,000 of 8 percent, five-year bonds at 98 on January 1, 2016. Interest is payable annually on December 31.
3. Jay, Inc. issued $100,000 of 8 percent, five-year bonds at 104 on January 1, 2016. Interest is payable annually on December 31.

Required

a. Organize the class into three sections and divide each section into groups of three to five students. Assign each of the sections one of the companies.

Group Tasks

(1) Compute the following amounts for your company (use straight-line amortization):
 (a) Cash proceeds from the bond issue
 (b) Interest paid in 2016
 (c) Interest expense for 2016

(2) Prepare the liabilities section of the balance sheet as of December 31, 2016.

Class Discussion

b. Have a representative of each section put the liabilities section for its company on the board.
c. Is the amount of interest expense different for the three companies? Why or why not?
d. Is the amount of interest paid different for each of the companies? Why or why not?
e. Is the amount of total liabilities different for each of the companies? Why or why not?

ATC 10-3 Real-World Case *Using accounting numbers to assess creditworthiness*

Advance Auto Parts, Inc. is "a leading automotive aftermarket parts provider in North America.... We were founded in 1929 as Advance Stores Company.... As of January 2, 2016, ... we operated 5,171 total stores and 122 branches primarily under the trade names 'Advance Auto Parts,' 'Autopart International,' 'Carquest' and 'Worldpac.'"

Foot Locker, Inc. "incorporated under the laws of the State of New York in 1989, is a leading global retailer of athletically inspired shoes and apparel, operating 3,383 primarily mall-based stores in the United States, Canada, Europe, Australia, and New Zealand as of January 30, 2016."

Johnson & Johnson, Inc. "and its subsidiaries have approximately 127,100 employees worldwide engaged in the research and development, manufacture and sale of a broad range of products in the health care field.... The Company's primary focus is products related to human health and well-being. Johnson & Johnson was incorporated in the State of New Jersey in 1887."

Tesla, Inc.: "We design, develop, manufacture and sell high-performance fully electric vehicles, and energy storage systems, as well as install, operate and maintain solar and energy storage products. We are the world's only vertically integrated energy company, offering end-to-end clean energy products, including generation, storage and consumption."

Each company received a different rating from **Standards & Poor's** (S&P). In descending order, the ratings for these companies were AAA, BBB-, BB+, and B-. These rating are as of March 16, 2017. All dollar amounts are in millions.

	Net Income	Cash Flow from Operations	Current Ratio	Debt-to-Assets Ratio	Times Interest Earned	Return-on-Assets Ratio
Advance Auto Parts						
2015	$473	$690	1.30	0.70	12.57	0.058
2016	460	501	1.41	0.65	13.32	0.055
Foot Locker						
2015	520	712	3.53	0.30	162.80	0.145
2016	541	745	3.72	0.32	210.25	0.143
Jonnson & Johnson						
2015	15,409	19,279	2.17	0.47	35.78	0.116
2016	16,540	18,767	2.47	0.50	28.28	0.117
Tesla						
2015	(889)	(524)	0.99	0.87	−6.37	−0.110
2016	(773)	(124)	1.07	0.79	−2.75	−0.034

Required

Determine which credit rating was assigned to which company. Write a memorandum explaining the rationale for your decisions. The logic you present to support your conclusions is more important than correctly matching the companies with their ratings.

ATC 10-4 Business Applications Case *Performing ratio analysis using real-world data*

Bojangels', Inc. operates Cajun-themed fast-food restaurants. As of December 25, 2016, Bojangels' had 309 company operated restaurants and 404 domestic franchised restaurants located in 11 states, and 3 franchised restaurants outside the United States. The following data were taken from the company's 2016 annual report. All dollar amounts are in thousands.

	Fiscal Years Ending	
Account Title	December 25, 2016	December 27, 2015
Current assets	$ 26,024	$ 28,121
Total assets	559,772	558,306
Current liabilities	48,579	45,102
Total liabilities	348,982	391,182
Interest expense	7,489	8,314
Income tax expense	19,537	16,034
Net income	37,716	26,526

Required

a. Calculate the EBIT for each year.
b. Calculate the times-interest-earned ratio for each year.
c. Calculate the current ratio and debt-to-assets ratio for each year.
d. Did the company's level of financial risk increase or decrease from 2015 to 2016? Explain.

ATC 10-5 Business Applications Case *Performing ratio analysis using real-world data*

The following data are for the 2016 fiscal year of **Alphabet, Inc.**, which is the parent company of **Google, Inc.**, and **Facebook, Inc.** All dollar amounts are in thousands.

Account Title	Alphabet, Inc.	Facebook, Inc.
Current assets	$105,408	$34,401
Total assets	167,497	64,961
Current liabilities	16,756	2,875
Total liabilities	28,461	5,767
Stockholders' equity	139,036	59,194
Interest expense	124	10
Income tax expense	4,672	2,301
Net income	19,478	10,217

Required

a. Calculate the EBIT for each company.
b. Calculate each company's debt-to-assets ratio, current ratio, and the times-interest-earned ratio.
c. Calculate each company's return-on-assets ratio using EBIT instead of net earnings. Calculate each company's return-on-equity ratio using net earnings.
d. Alphabet reported interest expense of $124 million, before taxes. What was its after-tax interest expense in dollars? (*Hint:* You will need to compute its tax rate by dividing income tax expense by *earnings before taxes,* which must be computed.)

ATC 10-6 Writing Assignment Debt versus equity financing

Mack Company plans to invest $50,000 in land that will produce annual rent revenue equal to 15 percent of the investment, starting on January 1, 2016. The revenue will be collected in cash at the end of each year, starting December 31, 2016. Mack can obtain the cash necessary to purchase the land from two sources. Funds can be obtained by issuing $50,000 of 10 percent, five-year bonds at their face amount. Interest due on the bonds is payable on December 31 of each year with the first payment due on December 31, 2016. Alternatively, the $50,000 needed to invest in land can be obtained from equity financing. In this case, the stockholders (holders of the equity) will be paid a $5,000 annual cash dividend. Mack Company is in a 30 percent income tax bracket.

Required

a. Prepare an income statement and statement of cash flows for 2016 under the two alternative financing proposals.

b. Write a short memorandum explaining why one financing alternative provides more net income but less cash flow than the other.

ATC 10-7 Ethical Dilemma I don't want to pay taxes

Dana Harbert recently started a very successful small business. Indeed, the business had grown so rapidly that she was no longer able to finance its operations by investing her own resources in the business. She needed additional capital but had no more of her own money to put into the business. A friend, Gene Watson, was willing to invest $100,000 in the business. Harbert estimated that with Watson's investment, the company would be able to increase revenue by $40,000. Furthermore, she believed that operating expenses would increase by only 10 percent. Harbert and Watson agree that Watson's investment should entitle him to receive a cash dividend equal to 20 percent of net income. A set of forecasted statements with and without Watson's investment is presented next. (Assume that all transactions involving revenue, expense, and dividends are cash transactions.)

Financial Statements

	Forecast 1 without Watson's Investment	Forecast 2 with Watson's Investment
Income Statements		
Revenue	$120,000	$160,000
Operating expenses	(70,000)	(77,000)
Income before interest and taxes	50,000	83,000
Income tax expense (effective tax rate is 30%)	(15,000)	(24,900)
Net income	$ 35,000	$ 58,100
Statements of Changes in Stockholders' Equity		
Beginning retained earnings	$ 15,000	$ 15,000
Plus: Net income	35,000	58,100
Less: Dividend to Watson (20% of $58,100)	0	(11,620)
Ending retained earnings	$ 50,000	$ 61,480
Balance Sheets		
Assets (computations explained in following paragraph)	$400,000	$511,480
Liabilities	$ 0	$ 0
Equity		
Common stock	350,000	450,000
Retained earnings	50,000	61,480
Total liabilities and equity	$400,000	$511,480

The balance for assets in Forecast 1 is computed as the beginning balance of $365,000 plus net income of $35,000. The balance for assets in Forecast 2 is computed as the beginning balance of $365,000, plus the $100,000 cash investment, plus net income of $58,100, less the $11,620 dividend. Alternatively, total assets can be computed by determining the amount of total claims (total assets = total claims).

Harbert tells Watson that there would be a $3,486 tax advantage associated with debt financing. She says that if Watson is willing to become a creditor instead of an owner, she could pay him an additional $697.20 (that is, 20 percent of the tax advantage). Watson tells Harbert that he has no interest in participating in the management of the business, but Watson wants an ownership interest to guarantee that he will always receive 20 percent of the profits of the business. Harbert suggests that they execute a formal agreement in which Watson is paid 11.62 percent interest on his $100,000 loan to the business. This agreement will be used for income tax reporting. In addition, Harbert says that she is willing to establish a private agreement to write Watson a personal check for any additional amount necessary to make Watson's total return equal to 20 percent of all profits plus a $697.20 bonus for his part of the tax advantage. She tells Watson, "It's just like ownership. The only difference is that we call it debt for the Internal Revenue Service. If they want to have some silly rule that says if you call it debt, you get a tax break, then we are foolish if we don't call it debt. I will call it anything they want, just as long as I don't have to pay taxes on it."

Required

a. Construct a third set of forecasted financial statements (Forecast 3) at 11.62 percent annual interest, assuming that Watson is treated as creditor (he loans the business $100,000).

b. Verify the tax advantage of debt financing by comparing the balances of the Retained Earnings account in Forecast 2 and Forecast 3.

c. If you were Watson, would you permit Harbert to classify the equity transaction as debt to provide a higher return to the business and to you?

d. Comment on the ethical implications of misnaming a financing activity for the sole purpose of reducing income taxes.

ATC 10-8 Research Assignment *Analyzing debt financing at Home Depot*

Interest rates in the United States were at historic lows for much of the period from 2013 through 2016. The economy was slowly recovering from the recession of 2008 and 2009, and the Federal Reserve kept interest rates low to encourage this recovery. Because of these low interest rates, many companies increased their long-term financing from debt, while lowering their financing with owners' equity. **Home Depot, Inc.**, the large building supplies company, was one of these companies.

Use Home Depot's 2016 Form 10-K to obtain the data for 2015 and 2016, and its 2014 Form 10-K to obtain the data for 2013 and 2014. NOTE: Home Depot ends its fiscal year in late January or early February, so, for the purposes of this assignment, the fiscal year ending on January 29, 2017, is considered the company's 2016 fiscal year. All other fiscal years are treated the same, so 2013 will be the year ended February 2, 2014. To obtain the 10-Ks, you can either use the EDGAR system, following the instructions in Appendix A, or they can be found on the company's website.

Required

a. For each year, 2013 through 2016, calculate the following ratios:
   Debt to assets
   Return on assets
   Return on equity

b. List the company's interest expense for each year from 2013 through 2016.

c. Write a brief memorandum discussing all of the effects that Home Depot's strategy of increasing its financing with debt had on the company from 2013 through 2016.

ATC 10-9 Spreadsheet Assignment *Using Excel*

On January 1, Year 1, Bainbridge Company borrowed $100,000 cash from a bank by issuing a 10-year, 9 percent note. The principal and interest are to be paid by making annual payments in the amount of $15,582. Payments are to be made December 31 of each year beginning December 31, Year 1.

Required

a. Set up the spreadsheet as shown below. Notice that Excel can be set up to calculate the loan payment. If you're unfamiliar with this, see the following Spreadsheet Tips section. The Beginning Principal Balance (B12) and Cash Payment (C12) can be referenced from the Loan Information section. The interest rate used to calculate Interest Expense (D12) can also be referenced from the Loan Information section.

b. Complete the spreadsheet for the 10 periods.

c. In Row 23, calculate totals for cash payments, interest expense, and applied to principal.

d. Consider how the amounts would differ if Bainbridge were to borrow the $100,000 at different interest rates and time periods. The results of the original data (option 1) have been entered in the following schedule. In the spreadsheet, delete 9 percent and 10 from cells B4 and B5, respectively. Enter the data for the second option (8 percent and 10 years) in cells B4 and B5. Enter the recomputed payment and total interest in the schedule for the second option. Continue the same process for options 3 through 9 by deleting the prior rate and number of periods in the spreadsheet and entering in the next option's data. The number of years scheduled (rows 12 through 21) will have to be shortened for the 7-year options and lengthened for the 13-year options.

	\multicolumn{9}{c}{Option}
	1	2	3	4	5	6	7	8	9
Rate	9%	8%	10%	9%	8%	10%	9%	8%	10%
Years	10	10	10	7	7	7	13	13	13
Payment	15,582								
Total interest	55,820								

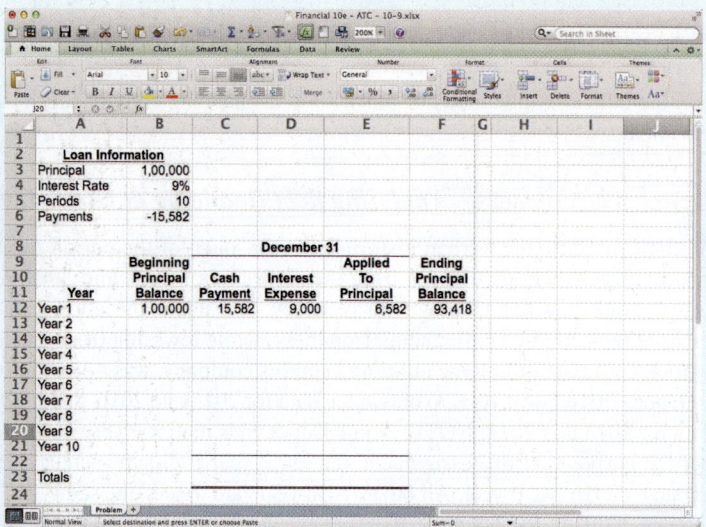

Source: Microsoft Office Excel 2010

Spreadsheet Tips

1. Excel will calculate an installment loan payment. The interest rate (%), number of periods (nper), and amount borrowed or otherwise known as present value (PV) must be entered in the payment formula. The formula for the payment is =PMT(rate,nper,pv). The rate, number of periods, and amount borrowed (present value) may be entered as actual amounts or referenced to other cells. In the preceding spreadsheet, the payment formula can be either =PMT(9%,10,100000) or =PMT(B4,B5,B3). In our case, the latter is preferred so that variables can be altered in the spreadsheet without also having to rewrite the payment formula. Notice that the payment is a negative number.

2. Using positive numbers is preferred in the amortization schedule. The loan payment (cell B6) in the loan information section shows up as a negative number. Any reference to it in the amortization schedule should be preceded by a minus sign to convert it to a positive number. For example, the formula in cell C12 for the cash payment is = −B6.

3. Recall that to copy a fixed number, a $ sign must be positioned before the column letter and row number. The complete formula then for cell C12 is = −B6.

ATC 10-10 Spreadsheet Assignment *Mastering Excel*

Wise Company was started on January 1, Year 1, when it issued 20-year, 10 percent, $200,000 face-value bonds at a price of 90. Interest is payable annually at December 31 of each year. Wise immediately purchased land with the proceeds (cash received) from the bond issue. Wise leased the land for $27,000 cash per year. The lease revenue payments are due every December 31.

Accounting for Long-Term Debt 591

Required

Set up the following horizontal statements model on a blank spreadsheet. The SCF Activity column is for the classifications operating, financing, or investing.

a. Enter the effects of the Year 1 transactions. Assume that both the interest and lease payments occurred on December 31. Notice that the entry for the lease has already been entered as an example. Calculate the ending balances.

b. Enter the effects of the Year 2 transactions. Assume that both the interest and lease payments occurred on December 31. Calculate the ending balances.

c. Enter the effects of the Year 3 transactions. Assume that both the interest and lease payments occurred on December 31. Calculate the ending balances.

Source: Microsoft Office Excel 2010

d. On January 1, 2019, Wise Company sold the land for $190,000 cash. Immediately after the sale of the land, Wise repurchased its bond at a price of 93. Assume that no other accounting events occurred during 2019. Enter the effects of the 2019 transactions. Calculate the ending balances.

COMPREHENSIVE PROBLEM

The trial balance of Pacilio Security Services, Inc. as of January 1, Year 10, had the following normal balances:

Cash	$122,475
Petty cash	100
Accounts receivable	27,400
Allowance for doubtful accounts	4,390
Supplies	165
Prepaid rent	3,000
Merchandise inventory (38 @ $290)	11,020
Equipment	9,000
Van	27,000
Accumulated depreciation	23,050
Sales tax payable	290
Employee income tax payable	500
FICA—Social Security tax payable	600
FICA—Medicare tax payable	150
Warranty payable	312
Unemployment tax payable	630
Interest payable	320
Notes payable	12,000
Common stock	50,000
Retained earnings	107,918

During Year 10, Pacilio Security Services experienced the following transactions:

1. Paid the sales tax payable from Year 9.
2. Paid the balance of the payroll liabilities due for Year 9 (federal income tax, FICA taxes, and unemployment taxes).
3. On January 1, Year 10, purchased land and a building for $150,000. The building was appraised at $125,000 and the land at $25,000. Pacilio paid $50,000 cash and financed the balance. The balance was financed with a 10-year installment note. The note had an interest rate of 7 percent and annual payments of $14,238 due on the last day of the year.
4. On January 1, Year 10, issued $50,000 of 6 percent, five year bonds. The bonds were issued at 98.
5. Purchase $660 of supplies on account.
6. Purchased 170 alarm systems at a cost of $300. Cash was paid for the purchase.
7. After numerous attempts to collect from customers, wrote off $2,450 of uncollectible accounts receivable.
8. Sold 160 alarm systems for $580 each plus sales tax of 5 percent. All sales were on account. (Be sure to compute cost of goods sold using the FIFO cost flow method.)
9. Billed $120,000 of monitoring services for the year. Credit card sales amounted to $36,000, and the credit card company charged a 4 percent fee. The remaining $84,000 were sales on account. Sales tax is not charged on this service.
10. Replenished the petty cash fund on June 30. The fund had $11 cash and receipts of $65 for yard mowing and $24 for office supplies expense.
11. Collected the amount due from the credit card company.
12. Paid the sales tax collected on $85,000 of the alarm sales.
13. Collected $167,000 of accounts receivable during the year.
14. Paid installers and other employees a total of $82,000 for salaries for the year. Assume the Social Security tax rate is 6 percent and the Medicare tax rate is 1.5 percent. Federal income taxes withheld amounted to $9,600. The net amount of salaries was paid in cash.
15. Paid $1,250 in warranty repairs during the year.
16. On September 1, paid the note and interest owed to State Bank.
17. Paid $18,000 of advertising expense during the year.
18. Paid $5,600 of utilities expense for the year.
19. Paid the payroll liabilities, both the amounts withheld from the salaries plus the employer share of Social Security tax and Medicare tax, on $75,000 of the salaries plus $8,600 of the federal income tax that was withheld. (Disregard unemployment taxes in this entry.)
20. Paid the accounts payable.
21. Paid bond interest and amortized the discount.
22. Paid the annual installment on the amortized note.
23. Paid a dividend of $10,000 to the shareholders.

Adjustments

24. There was $210 of supplies on hand at the end of the year.
25. Recognized the expired rent for the office building for the year.
26. Recognized the uncollectible accounts expense for the year using the allowance method. Pacilio now estimates that 1.5 percent of sales on account will not be collected.
27. Recognized depreciation expense on the equipment, van, and building. The equipment has a 5-year life and a $2,000 salvage value. The van has a 4-year life and a $6,000 salvage value. The building has a 40-year life and a $10,000 salvage value. The company uses double-declining-balance for the van and straight-line for the equipment and the building. The equipment and van were purchased in Year 8 and a full year of depreciation was taken for both in Year 8.
28. The alarms systems sold in transaction 8 were covered with a one-year warranty. Pacilio estimated that the warranty cost would be 2 percent of alarm sales.

29. The unemployment tax on the three employees has not been paid. Record the accrued unemployment tax on the salaries for the year. The unemployment tax rate is 4.5 percent and gross wages for all employees exceeded $7,000.
30. Recognized the employer Social Security and Medicare payroll tax that has not been paid on $7,000 of salaries expense.

Required

a. Record the preceding transactions in general journal form. Round all amounts to the nearest whole dollar.
b. Post the transactions to the T-accounts.
c. Prepare a trial balance.
d. Prepare an income statement, statement of changes in stockholders' equity, classified balance sheet, and statement of cash flows.
e. Close the temporary accounts to retained earnings.
f. Post the closing entries to the T-accounts and prepare an after-closing trial balance.

CHAPTER 11

Proprietorships, Partnerships, and Corporations

LEARNING OBJECTIVES

After you have mastered the material in this chapter, you will be able to:

LO 11-1 Identify the primary characteristics of sole proprietorships, partnerships, and corporations.

LO 11-2 Identify the characteristics of capital stock.

LO 11-3 Differentiate between common and preferred stock.

LO 11-4 Show how issuing different classes of stock affects financial statements.

LO 11-5 Show how treasury stock affects financial statements.

LO 11-6 Show how declaring and paying cash dividends affect financial statements.

LO 11-7 Show how stock dividends and stock splits affect financial statements.

LO 11-8 Show how the appropriation of retained earnings affects financial statements.

LO 11-9 Show how accounting information is used to make stock investment decisions.

 Video lectures and accompanying self-assessment quizzes are available in Connect *for all learning objectives.*

CHAPTER OPENING

You want to start a business. How should you structure it? Should it be a sole proprietorship, partnership, or corporation? Each form of business structure presents advantages and disadvantages. For example, a sole proprietorship allows maximum independence and control while partnerships and corporations allow individuals to pool resources and talents with other people. This chapter discusses these and other features of the three primary forms of business structure.

The Curious Accountant

©Stockbyte/Getty Images

Imagine your rich uncle rewarded you for doing well in your first accounting course by giving you $10,000 to invest in the common stock of one company. After reviewing many recent annual reports, you narrowed your choice to two companies with the following characteristics:

Mystery Company A: This company began operations in 2010, was incorporated in 2012, and began selling its stock to the public on March 2, 2017. It has lost money every year it has been in existence. In 2016 alone, its losses were $515 million, and by December 31, 2016, it had total lifetime losses of approximately $2.3 billion. Even so, the company provides services that are used by millions of individuals every day. At its current price of $22, you could buy 455 shares. A friend tells you that a person whose attention span is as short as yours would be crazy not to buy this company's stock.

Mystery Company B: This company has been in existence since 1892 and has made a profit most years. In 2016 alone, its net earnings were $8.2 billion, and it paid dividends of $8.8 billion. Almost every home in America uses one or more of its products or services. Its stock is selling for about $29 per share, so you can buy 345 shares. Your friend says that owning this company's stock would be about as exciting as staring at a light bulb.

The names of the real-world companies described here are disclosed later. Based on the information provided, which company's stock would you buy? (Answers on page 597.)

FORMS OF BUSINESS ORGANIZATIONS

LO 11-1

Identify the primary characteristics of sole proprietorships, partnerships, and corporations.

Sole proprietorships are owned by a single individual who is responsible for making business and profit distribution decisions. If you want to be the absolute master of your destiny, you should organize your business as a proprietorship. Establishing a sole proprietorship is usually as simple as obtaining a business license from local government authorities. Usually no legal ownership agreement is required.

Partnerships allow persons to share their talents, capital, and the risks and rewards of business ownership. Because two or more individuals share ownership, partnerships require clear agreements about how authority, risks, and profits will be shared. Prudent partners minimize misunderstandings by hiring attorneys to prepare a **partnership agreement** that defines the responsibilities of each partner and describes how income or losses will be divided. Because the measurement of income affects the distribution of profits, partnerships frequently hire accountants to ensure that records are maintained in accordance with generally accepted accounting principles (GAAP). Partnerships (and sole proprietorships) also may need professional advice to deal with tax issues.

A **corporation** is a separate legal entity created by the authority of a state government. The paperwork to start a corporation is complex. For most laypersons, engaging professional attorneys and accountants to assist with the paperwork is well worth the fees charged.

Each state has separate laws governing establishing corporations. Many states follow the standard provisions of the Model Business Corporation Act. All states require the initial application to provide **articles of incorporation,** which normally include the following information: (1) the corporation's name and proposed date of incorporation; (2) the purpose of the corporation; (3) the location of the business and its expected life (which can be *perpetuity,* meaning *endless*); (4) provisions for capital stock; and (5) the names and addresses of the members of the first board of directors, the individuals with the ultimate authority for operating the business. If the articles are in order, the state establishes the legal existence of the corporation by issuing a charter of incorporation. The charter and the articles are public documents.

Each form of business organization presents a different combination of advantages and disadvantages. Persons wanting to start a business or invest in one should consider the characteristics of each type of business structure.

Regulation

Few laws specifically affect the operations of proprietorships and partnerships. Corporations, however, are usually heavily regulated. The extent of government regulation depends on the size and distribution of a company's ownership interests. Ownership interests in corporations are normally evidenced by **stock certificates.**

Ownership of corporations can be transferred from one individual to another through exchanging stock certificates. As long as the exchanges (buying and selling of shares of stock, often called *trading*) are limited to transactions between individuals, a company is defined as a **closely held corporation.** However, once a corporation reaches a certain size, it may list its stock on a stock exchange such as the New York Stock Exchange. Trading on a stock exchange is limited to the stockbrokers who are members of the exchange. These brokers represent buyers and sellers who are willing to pay the brokers commissions for exchanging stock certificates on their behalf. Although closely held corporations are relatively free from government regulation, companies whose stock is publicly traded on the exchanges by brokers are subject to extensive regulation.

The extensive regulation of trading on stock exchanges began in the 1930s. The stock market crash of 1929 and the subsequent Great Depression led Congress to pass the **Securities Act of 1933** and the **Securities Exchange Act of 1934** to regulate issuing stock and to govern the exchanges. The 1934 act also created the Securities and Exchange Commission (SEC) to enforce the securities laws. Congress gave the SEC legal authority

Answers to The Curious Accountant

Mystery Company A is **Snap, Inc.**, as of May 2, 2017. For its initial public offering on March 2, 2017, its stock was priced at $17 per share; by the end of the day it was selling for $24.48. Two months later, the stock was trading at $21.85, a decline of 10.7 percent.

Mystery Company B is **General Electric Company**, as of May 2, 2017. Its operations include electricity generation, oil and gas, aviation, health care, and transportation. During the two months of trading when Snap's stock price declined by 10.7 percent, General Electric's stock price declined by only 4.0 percent, from $30.19 to $28.99. Of course, only the future will reveal which company is the better investment in the long run.

to establish accounting principles for corporations that are registered on the exchanges. However, the SEC has generally deferred its rule-making authority to the independent, private sector Financial Accounting Standards Board (FASB).

A number of high-profile business failures around the turn of this century raised questions about the effectiveness of financial statement audits to protect the public. The **Sarbanes–Oxley Act of 2002** was adopted to address these concerns. The act created a five-member Public Company Accounting Oversight Board (PCAOB) with the authority to set and enforce auditing, attestation, quality control, and ethics standards for auditors of public companies. The PCAOB is empowered to impose disciplinary and remedial sanctions for violations of its rules, securities laws, and professional auditing and accounting standards. Public corporations operate in a complex regulatory environment that requires the services of attorneys and professional accountants.

Double Taxation

Corporations pay income taxes on their earnings and then owners pay income taxes on distributions (dividends) received from corporations. As a result, distributed corporate profits are taxed twice—first when income is reported on the corporation's income tax return and a second time when distributions are reported on individual owners' tax returns. This phenomenon is commonly called **double taxation** and is a significant disadvantage of the corporate form of business organization.

To illustrate, assume Glide Corporation earns pretax income of $100,000. Glide is in a 30 percent tax bracket. The corporation itself will pay income tax of $30,000 ($100,000 × 0.30). If the corporation distributes the after-tax income of $70,000 ($100,000 − $30,000) to individual stockholders who are taxed at 15 percent, the $70,000 dividend will be reported on the individual tax returns, requiring tax payments of $10,500 ($70,000 × 0.15). Total income tax of $40,500 ($30,000 + $10,500) is due on $100,000 of earned income. In contrast, consider a proprietorship that is owned by an individual in a 30 percent tax bracket. If the proprietorship earns and distributes $100,000 profit, the total tax would be only $30,000 ($100,000 × 0.30).

Double taxation can be a burden for small companies. To reduce that burden, tax laws permit small closely held corporations to elect "S Corporation" status. S Corporation income is not taxed at the corporate level but instead flows through to the owners who pay individual income taxes. Also, many states have enacted laws permitting the formation of **limited liability companies (LLCs),** which offer many of the benefits of corporate ownership yet are, in general, taxed as sole proprietorships or partnerships. Because proprietorships and partnerships are not separate taxable entities, company earnings are taxable to the owners rather than the company itself.

Limited Liability

Given the disadvantages of increased regulation and double taxation, why would anyone choose the corporate form of business structure over a partnership or proprietorship? A major reason is that the corporate form limits an investor's potential liability as an owner of a business venture. Because a corporation is legally separate from its owners, creditors cannot claim owners' personal assets as payment for the company's debts. Also, plaintiffs must sue the corporation, not its owners. The most that owners of a corporation can lose is the amount they have invested in the company (the value of the company's stock).

Unlike corporate stockholders, the owners of proprietorships and partnerships are *personally liable* for actions they take in the name of their companies. In fact, partners are responsible not only for their own actions but also for those taken by any other partner on behalf of the partnership. The benefit of **limited liability** is one of the most significant reasons limited liability companies and corporations are so popular.

Continuity

Unlike partnerships or proprietorships, which terminate with the departure of their owners, a corporation's life continues when a shareholder dies or sells his or her stock. Because of **continuity** of existence, many corporations formed in the 1800s still thrive today.

Transferability of Ownership

The **transferability** of corporate ownership is easy. An investor simply buys or sells stock to acquire or give up an ownership interest in a corporation. Hundreds of millions of shares of stock are bought and sold on the major stock exchanges each day.

Transferring the ownership of proprietorships is much more difficult. To sell an ownership interest in a proprietorship, the proprietor must find someone willing to purchase the entire business. Because most proprietors also run their businesses, transferring ownership also requires transferring management responsibilities. Consider the difference in selling $1 million of ExxonMobil stock versus selling a locally owned gas station. The stock could be sold on the New York Stock Exchange within minutes. In contrast, it could take years to find a buyer who is financially capable of and interested in owning and operating a gas station.

Transferring ownership in partnerships can also be difficult. As with proprietorships, ownership transfers may require a new partner to make a significant investment and accept management responsibilities in the business. Further, a new partner must accept and be accepted by the other partners. Personality conflicts and differences in management style can cause problems in transferring ownership interests in partnerships.

Management Structure

Partnerships and proprietorships are usually managed by their owners. Corporations, in contrast, have three tiers of management authority. The *owners* (**stockholders**) represent the highest level of organizational authority. The stockholders *elect* a **board of directors** to oversee company operations. The directors then *hire* professional executives to manage the company on a daily basis. Because large corporations can offer high salaries and challenging career opportunities, they can often attract superior managerial talent.

Ability to Raise Capital

Because corporations can have millions of owners (shareholders), they have the opportunity to raise huge amounts of capital. Few individuals have the financial means to build and operate a telecommunications network such as AT&T or a marketing distribution system such as Walmart. However, by pooling the resources of millions of owners through public stock and bond offerings, corporations generate the billions of dollars of capital needed for such massive investments. In contrast, the capital resources of proprietorships and partnerships are limited to a relatively small number of private owners. Although proprietorships and partnerships can also obtain resources by borrowing, the amount creditors are willing to lend them is usually limited by the size of the owners' net worth.

Appearance of Capital Structure in Financial Statements

The ownership interest (equity) in a business is composed of two elements: (1) owner/investor contributions and (2) retained earnings. The way these two elements are reported in the financial statements differs for each type of business structure (proprietorship, partnership, or corporation).

©The McGraw-Hill Companies, Inc./John Flournoy, photographer

Presentation of Equity in Proprietorships

Owner contributions and retained earnings are combined in a single Capital account on the balance sheets of proprietorships. To illustrate, assume that Worthington Sole Proprietorship was started on January 1, Year 1, when it acquired a $5,000 capital contribution from its owner, Phil Worthington. During the first year of operation, the company generated $4,000 of cash revenues, incurred $2,500 of cash expenses, and distributed $1,000 cash to the owner. Exhibit 11.1 displays Year 1 financial statements for Worthington's company. Note on the *capital statement* that distributions are called **withdrawals.** Verify that the $5,500 balance in the Capital account on the balance sheet includes the $5,000 owner contribution and the retained earnings of $500 ($1,500 net income − $1,000 withdrawal).

EXHIBIT 11.1

WORTHINGTON SOLE PROPRIETORSHIP
Financial Statements
As of December 31, Year 1

Income Statement		Capital Statement		Balance Sheet	
Revenue	$4,000	Beginning capital balance	$ 0	Assets	
Expenses	2,500	Plus: Investment by owner	5,000	Cash	$5,500
Net income	$1,500	Plus: Net income	1,500	Equity	
		Less: Withdrawal by owner	(1,000)	Worthington, capital	$5,500
		Ending capital balance	$5,500		

CHECK YOURSELF 11.1

Weiss Company was started on January 1, Year 1, when it acquired $50,000 cash from its owner(s). During Year 1, the company earned $72,000 of net income. Explain how the equity section of Weiss' December 31, Year 1, balance sheet would differ if the company were a proprietorship versus a corporation.

Answer *Proprietorship* records combine capital acquisitions from the owner and earnings from operating the business in a single capital account. In contrast, *corporation* records separate capital acquisitions from the owners and earnings from operating the business. If Weiss were a proprietorship, the equity section of the year-end balance sheet would report a single capital component of $122,000. If Weiss were a corporation, the equity section would report two separate equity components, most likely common stock of $50,000 and retained earnings of $72,000.

EXHIBIT 11.2

SLATER AND JOHNSON PARTNERSHIP
Financial Statements
As of December 31, Year 2

Income Statement		Capital Statement		Balance Sheet	
Revenue	$5,000	Beginning capital balance	$ 0	Assets	
Expenses	3,000	Plus: Investment by owner	6,000	Cash	$7,400
Net income	$2,000	Plus: Net income	2,000	Equity	
		Less: Withdrawal by owner	(600)	Slater, capital	$2,700
		Ending capital balance	$7,400	Johnson, capital	4,700
				Total capital	$7,400

Presentation of Equity in Partnerships

The financial statement format for reporting partnership equity is similar to that used for proprietorships. Contributed capital and retained earnings are combined. However, a separate capital account is maintained for each partner in the business to reflect each partner's ownership interest.

To illustrate, assume that Sara Slater and Jill Johnson formed a partnership on January 1, Year 2. The partnership acquired $2,000 of capital from Slater and $4,000 from Johnson. The partnership agreement called for each partner to receive an annual distribution equal to 10 percent of her capital contribution. Any further earnings were to be retained in the business and divided equally between the partners. During Year 2, the company earned $5,000 of cash revenue and incurred $3,000 of cash expenses, for net income of $2,000 ($5,000 − $3,000). As specified by the partnership agreement, Slater received a $200 ($2,000 × 0.10) cash withdrawal and Johnson received $400 ($4,000 × 0.10). The remaining $1,400 ($2,000 − $200 − $400) of income was retained in the business and divided equally, adding $700 to each partner's capital account.

Exhibit 11.2 displays financial statements for the Slater and Johnson partnership. Again, note that distributions are called *withdrawals*. Also find on the balance sheet a *separate capital account* for each partner. Each capital account includes the amount of the partner's contributed capital plus her proportionate share of the earnings.

Presentation of Stockholders' Equity in Corporations

Corporations have more complex capital structures than proprietorships and partnerships. Explanations of some of the more common features of corporate capital structures and transactions follow.

ACCOUNTING FOR CAPITAL STOCK

LO 11-2

Identify the characteristics of capital stock.

Stock issued by corporations may have a variety of different characteristics. For example, a company may issue different classes of stock that grant owners different rights and privileges. Also, the number of shares a corporation can legally issue may differ from the number it actually has issued. Further, a corporation can even buy back its own stock. Finally, a corporation may assign different values to the stock it issues. Accounting for corporate equity transactions is discussed in the next section of the text.

Par Value

Many states require assigning a **par value** to stock. Historically, par value represented the maximum liability of the investors. Par value multiplied by the number of shares of stock issued represents the minimum amount of assets that must be retained in the company as protection for creditors. This amount is known as **legal capital.** To ensure that the amount of legal capital is maintained in a corporation, many states require that purchasers pay at least the par value for a share of stock initially purchased from a corporation. To minimize the amount of assets that owners must maintain in the business, many corporations issue stock with very low par values, often $1 or less. Therefore, *legal capital* as defined by par value has come to have very little relevance to investors or creditors. As a result, many states allow corporations to issue no-par stock.

Stated Value

No-par stock may have a stated value. Like par value, **stated value** is an arbitrary amount assigned by the board of directors to the stock. It also has little relevance to investors and creditors. Stock with a par value and stock with a stated value are accounted for exactly the same way. When stock has no par or stated value, accounting for it is slightly different. These accounting differences are illustrated later in this chapter.

Stock: Authorized, Issued, and Outstanding

As part of the regulatory function, states approve the maximum number of shares of stock that corporations are legally permitted to issue. This maximum number is called **authorized stock.** Authorized stock that has been sold to the public is called **issued stock.** When a corporation buys back some of its issued stock from the public, the repurchased stock is called **treasury stock.** Treasury stock is still considered to be issued stock, but it is no longer outstanding. **Outstanding stock** (total issued stock minus treasury stock) is stock owned by investors outside the corporation. For example, assume that Alpha, Incorporated is authorized to issue 150,000 shares of stock, issues 100,000 shares to investors, and then buys back 20,000 shares of treasury stock. In this scenario, there are 150,000 shares authorized, 100,000 shares issued, and 80,000 shares outstanding.

Other Valuation Terminology

The price an investor must pay to purchase a share of stock is the **market value.** The sales price of a share of stock may be more or less than the par value. Another term analysts frequently associate with stock is *book value.* **Book value per share** is calculated by dividing total stockholders' equity (assets − liabilities) by the number of shares of stock owned by investors. Book value per share differs from market value per share because equity is measured in historical dollars and market value reflects investors' estimates of a company's current value.

To illustrate, return to the scenario where Alpha, Incorporated has 150,000 shares authorized, 100,000 shares issued, and 80,000 shares outstanding. At this point, assume that Alpha has $520,000 of assets, $120,000 in liabilities, $240,000 of common stock, and $160,000 of retained earnings. Further, assume that the market value of Alpha's common stock is $6 per share. Based on this scenario, Alpha's book value per share is $5 [($520,000 assets − $120,000 liabilities) / 80,000 shares outstanding]. The most likely explanation for the market value ($6 per share) being higher than the book value ($5 per share) is that book value is a measure of historical cost, while market value is a measure of current values.

COMMON VERSUS PREFERRED STOCK

The corporate charter defines the number of shares of stock authorized, the par value or stated value (if any), and the classes of stock that a corporation can issue. Most stock issued is classified as either *common* or *preferred.*

LO 11-3

Differentiate between common and preferred stock.

Common Stock

All corporations issue **common stock.** Common stockholders bear the highest risk of losing their investment if a company is forced to liquidate. On the other hand, they reap the greatest rewards when a corporation prospers. Common stockholders generally enjoy several rights, including (1) the right to buy and sell stock, (2) the right to share in the distribution of profits, (3) the right to share in the distribution of corporate assets in the case of liquidation, (4) the right to vote on significant matters that affect the corporate charter, and (5) the right to participate in the election of directors.

Preferred Stock

Many corporations issue **preferred stock** in addition to common stock. Holders of preferred stock receive certain privileges relative to holders of common stock. In exchange for special privileges in some areas, preferred stockholders give up rights in other areas. Preferred stockholders usually have no voting rights and the amount of their dividends is usually limited. Preferences granted to preferred stockholders include the following:

1. *Preference as to assets.* Preferred stock often has a liquidation value. In case of bankruptcy, preferred stockholders must be paid the liquidation value before any assets are distributed to common stockholders. However, preferred stockholder claims still fall behind creditor claims.

2. *Preference as to dividends.* Preferred shareholders are frequently guaranteed the right to receive dividends before common stockholders. The amount of the preferred dividend is normally stated on the stock certificate. It may be stated as a dollar value (say, $5) per share or as a percentage of the par value. Most preferred stock has **cumulative dividends,** meaning that if a corporation is unable to pay the preferred dividend in any year, the dividend is not lost but begins to accumulate. Cumulative dividends that have not been paid are called **dividends in arrears.** When a company pays dividends, any preferred stock arrearages must be paid before any other dividends are paid. Noncumulative preferred stock is not often issued because preferred stock is much less attractive if missed dividends do not accumulate.

To illustrate the effects of preferred dividends, consider Dillion, Incorporated, which has the following shares of stock outstanding:

> Preferred stock, 4%, $10 par, 10,000 shares
> Common stock, $10 par, 20,000 shares

Assume the preferred stock dividend has not been paid for two years. If Dillion pays $22,000 in dividends, how much will each class of stock receive? It depends on whether the preferred stock is cumulative.

Allocation of Distribution for Cumulative Preferred Stock

	To Preferred	To Common
Dividends in arrears	$ 8,000	$ 0
Current year's dividends	4,000	10,000
Total distribution	$12,000	$10,000

Allocation of Distribution for Noncumulative Preferred Stock

	To Preferred	To Common
Dividends in arrears	$ 0	$ 0
Current year's dividends	4,000	18,000
Total distribution	$4,000	$18,000

EXHIBIT 11.3

Source: The chart is based on data drawn from recent annual reports published by the 30 companies that comprise the Dow Jones Industrial Average.

The total annual dividend on the preferred stock is $4,000 (0.04 × $10 par × 10,000 shares). If the preferred stock is cumulative, the $8,000 in arrears must be paid first. Then, $4,000 for the current year's dividend is paid next. The remaining $10,000 goes to common stockholders. If the preferred stock is noncumulative, the $8,000 of dividends from past periods is ignored. This year's $4,000 preferred dividend is paid first, with the remaining $18,000 going to common.

Other features of preferred stock may include the right to participate in distributions beyond the established amount of the preferred dividend, the right to convert preferred stock to common stock or to bonds, and the potential for having the preferred stock called (repurchased) by the corporation. Detailed discussion of these topics is left to more advanced courses. Exhibit 11.3 indicates that roughly 20 percent of U.S. companies have preferred shares outstanding.

Other Classes of Stock

There can be different classes of common or preferred stock. For example, a company could issue class A common stock that provides its stockholders with rights to vote in the elections of the members of the board of directors. The same company could also issue class B common stock that does not provide voting rights. In conclusion, a company can have many classes of stock, with each type offering the shareholders a different set of rights and privileges.

ACCOUNTING FOR STOCK TRANSACTIONS ON THE DAY OF ISSUE

LO 11-4

Show how issuing different classes of stock affects financial statements.

Issuing stock with a par or stated value is accounted for differently from issuing no-par stock. For stock with either a par or stated value, the total amount acquired from the owners is divided between two separate equity accounts. The amount of the par or stated value is recorded in the stock account. Any amount received above the par or stated value is recorded in an account called **Paid-in Capital in Excess of Par** (or **Stated**) **Value.**

Issuing Par Value Stock

To illustrate the issue of common stock with a par value, assume that Nelson Incorporated is authorized to issue 250 shares of common stock. During Year 1, Nelson issued 100 shares of $10 par common stock for $22 per share. The event increases assets and stockholders' equity by $2,200 ($22 × 100 shares). The increase in stockholders' equity is divided into two parts, $1,000 of par value ($10 per share × 100 shares) and $1,200 ($2,200 − $1,000) received in excess of par value. The income statement is not affected. The $2,200 cash inflow is reported in the financing activities section of the statement of cash flows. The journal entry and its effects on the financial statements are shown next.

Account Title	Debit	Credit
Cash	2,200	
Common Stock, $10 Par Value		1,000
Paid-in Capital in Excess of Par Value—Common		1,200

Assets	=	Liab.	+	Equity		Rev.	−	Exp.	=	Net Inc.	Cash Flow
Cash	=			Com. Stk. + PIC in Excess							
2,200	=	NA	+	1,000 + 1,200		NA	−	NA	=	NA	2,200 FA

The *legal capital* of the corporation is $1,000, the total par value of the issued common stock. The number of shares issued can be easily verified by dividing the total amount in the common stock account by the par value ($1,000 ÷ $10 = 100 shares).

Stock Classification

Assume Nelson Incorporated obtains authorization to issue 400 shares of class B, $20 par value common stock. The company issues 150 shares of this stock at $25 per share. The event increases assets and stockholders' equity by $3,750 ($25 × 150 shares). The increase in stockholders' equity is divided into two parts, $3,000 of par value ($20 per share × 150 shares) and $750 ($3,750 − $3,000) received in excess of par value. The income statement is not affected. The $3,750 cash inflow is reported in the financing activities section of the statement of cash flows. The journal entry and its effects on the financial statements are shown next:

Account Title	Debit	Credit
Cash	3,750	
Common Stock, Class B, $20 Par Value		3,000
Paid-in Capital in Excess of Par Value—Class B Common		750

Assets	=	Liab.	+	Equity		Rev.	−	Exp.	=	Net Inc.	Cash Flow
Cash	=			Com. Stk. + PIC in Excess							
3,750	=	NA	+	3,000 + 750		NA	−	NA	=	NA	3,750 FA

As the preceding event suggests, companies can issue numerous classes of common stock. The specific rights and privileges for each class are described in the individual stock certificates.

Stock Issued at Stated Value

Assume Nelson Incorporated is authorized to issue 300 shares of a third class of stock, 7 percent cumulative preferred stock with a stated value of $10 per share. Nelson issued 100 shares of the preferred stock at a price of $22 per share. The effect on the financial statements is identical to that described for the issue of the $10 par value common stock. The journal entry differs only to reflect the name of the different class of stock.

Account Title	Debit	Credit
Cash	2,200	
Preferred Stock, $10 Stated Value, 7% Cumulative		1,000
Paid-in Capital in Excess of Stated Value—Preferred		1,200

Assets	=	Liab.	+	Equity		Rev.	−	Exp.	=	Net Inc.	Cash Flow
Cash	=			Pfd. Stk. + PIC in Excess							
2,200	=	NA	+	1,000 + 1,200		NA	−	NA	=	NA	2,200 FA

Stock Issued with No Par Value

Assume that Nelson Incorporated is authorized to issue 150 shares of a fourth class of stock. This stock is no-par common stock. Nelson issues 100 shares of this no-par stock at $22 per share. The entire amount received ($22 × 100 = $2,200) is recorded in the stock account. The journal entry and its effects on the financial statements are shown next:

Account Title	Debit	Credit
Cash	2,200	
Common Stock, No Par		2,200

Assets	=	Liab.	+	Equity		Rev.	−	Exp.	=	Net Inc.	Cash Flow
Cash	=			Com. Stk. + PIC in Excess							
2,200	=	NA	+	2,200 + NA		NA	−	NA	=	NA	2,200 FA

Financial Statement Presentation

Exhibit 11.4 displays Nelson Incorporated's balance sheet after the four stock issuances described earlier. The exhibit assumes that Nelson earned and retained $5,000 of income during Year 1. The stock accounts are presented first, followed by the paid-in capital in excess of par (or stated) value accounts. A wide variety of reporting formats is used in practice. For example, another popular format is to group accounts by stock class, with the paid-in capital in excess accounts listed with their associated stock accounts. Alternatively, many companies combine the different classes of stock into a single amount and provide the detailed information in notes to the financial statements.

EXHIBIT 11.4

NELSON INCORPORATED
Balance Sheet
As of December 31, Year 1

Assets	
Cash	$15,350
Stockholders' equity	
Preferred stock, $10 stated value, 7% cumulative,	
300 shares authorized, 100 issued and outstanding	$ 1,000
Common stock, $10 par value, 250 shares authorized,	
100 issued and outstanding	1,000
Common stock, class B, $20 par value, 400 shares	
authorized, 150 issued and outstanding	3,000
Common stock, no par, 150 shares authorized,	
100 issued and outstanding	2,200
Paid-in capital in excess of stated value—Preferred	1,200
Paid-in capital in excess of par value—Common	1,200
Paid-in capital in excess of par value—Class B common	750
Total paid-in capital	10,350
Retained earnings	5,000
Total stockholders' equity	$15,350

TREASURY STOCK

LO 11-5

 Show how treasury stock affects financial statements.

When a company buys its own stock, the stock purchased is called *treasury stock*. Why would a company buy its own stock? Common reasons include (1) to have stock available to give employees pursuant to stock option plans, (2) to accumulate stock in preparation for a merger or business combination, (3) to reduce the number of shares outstanding in order to increase earnings per share, (4) to keep the price of the stock high when it appears to be falling, and (5) to avoid a hostile takeover (removing shares from the open market reduces the opportunity for outsiders to obtain enough voting shares to gain control of the company).

Conceptually, purchasing treasury stock is the reverse of issuing stock. When a business issues stock, the assets and equity of the business increase. When a business buys treasury stock, the assets and equity of the business decrease. To illustrate, return to the Nelson Incorporated example. Assume that in Year 2 Nelson paid $20 per share to buy back 50 shares of the $10 par value common stock that it originally issued at $22 per share. The purchase of treasury stock is an asset use transaction. Assets and stockholders' equity decrease by the cost of the purchase ($20 × 50 shares = $1,000). The income statement is not affected. The cash outflow is reported in the financing activities section of the statement of cash flows. The journal entry and its effects on the financial statements are shown next:

Account Title	Debit	Credit
Treasury Stock	1,000	
Cash		1,000

Assets	=	Liab.	+	Equity			Rev.	−	Exp.	=	Net Inc.	Cash Flow
Cash	=			Other Equity Accts.	−	Treasury Stk.						
(1,000)	=	NA	+	NA	−	1,000	NA	−	NA	=	NA	(1,000) FA

REALITY BYTES

HOW MUCH TREASURY STOCK CAN A COMPANY PURCHASE?

A common practice in recent years has been for companies to purchase treasury stock frequently. Whereas in past years companies wishing to distribute more of their equity back to shareholders might have increased dividends, today they are more likely to use stock buybacks. Some companies seem to take the practice to extremes. Consider the excerpt that follows, taken from the shareholders' equity section of McDonald's Corporation's recent balance sheets.

First, notice that the company has a balance in its Treasury Stock account that is much larger than the balance in its Common Stock account. How can this be? Remember, when stock is issued to shareholders it is recorded in Common Stock at its issuance price, but it is recorded in Treasury Stock at the price the company paid to buy it back. The stock prices of successful companies rise over time.

Second, notice that McDonald's has purchased so much treasury stock that its total shareholders' equity is negative. This is unusual. When a company has negative shareholders' equity, it is usually because of a negative balance in Retained Earnings, but McDonald's had $46.2 billion of retained earnings as of December 31, 2016. The fact that the company had negative shareholders' equity means that, at least on paper, its liabilities were more than its assets. While this can present a problem for a company that is struggling, McDonald's reported approximately $7.8 billion of earnings before interest and taxes (EBIT) and $6.1 billion of cash flow from operating activities in 2016, so it was able to meet its debt obligations with no difficulty.

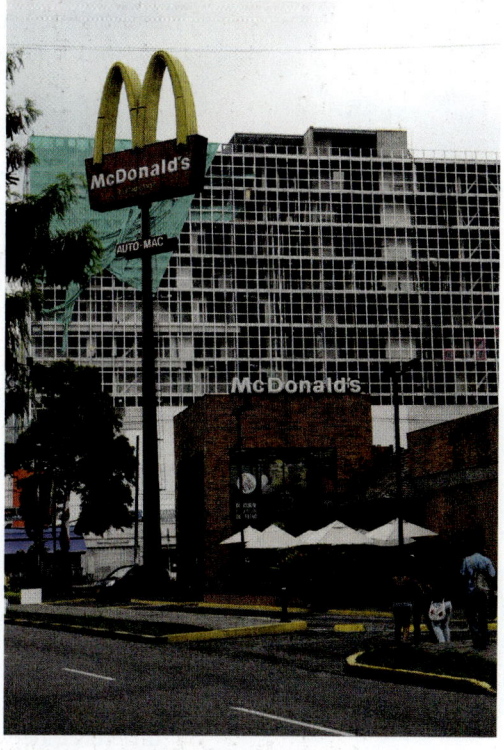
©Aaron Roeth Photography

MCDONALD'S CORPORATION
Partial Balance Sheets
For the Years Ended
(in millions)

	December 31, 2016	December 28, 2015
Shareholders' deficit		
Class A common stock	$ 16.6	$ 16.6
Additional paid-in capital	6,757.9	6,533.4
Retained earnings	46,222.7	44,594.5
Accumulated other comprehensive loss	(3,092.9)	(2,879.8)
Common stock held in treasury	(52,108.6)	(41,176.8)
Total shareholders' equity	(2,204.3)	7,087.9
Total liabilities and stockholders' equity	$31,023.9	$37,938.7

The Treasury Stock account is a contra equity account. It is deducted from the other equity accounts in determining total stockholders' equity. In this example, the Treasury Stock account is debited for the full amount paid ($1,000). The original issue price and the par value of the stock have no effect on the entry. Recording the full amount paid in the Treasury Stock account is called the **cost method of accounting for treasury stock** transactions. Although other methods could be used, the cost method is the most common.

Assume Nelson reissues 30 shares of treasury stock at a price of $25 per share. As with any other stock issue, the sale of treasury stock is an asset source transaction. In this case, assets and stockholders' equity increase by $750 ($25 × 30 shares). The income statement is not affected. The cash inflow is reported in the financing activities section of the statement of cash flows. The journal entry and its effects on the financial statements are shown next:

Account Title	Debit	Credit
Cash	750	
Treasury Stock		600
Paid-in Capital in Excess of Cost of Treasury Stock		150

Assets	=	Liab.	+	Equity			Rev.	−	Exp.	=	Net Inc.	Cash Flow
				Other Equity Accounts	Treasury Stock	PIC from Treasury Stk.						
Cash	=				−	+						
750	=	NA	+	NA	− (600)	+ 150	NA	−	NA	=	NA	750 FA

The decrease in the Treasury Stock account increases stockholders' equity. The $150 difference between the cost of the treasury stock ($20 per share × 30 shares = $600) and the sales price ($750) is *not* reported as a gain. The sale of treasury stock is a capital acquisition, not a revenue transaction. The $150 is additional paid-in capital. *Corporations do not recognize gains or losses on the sale of treasury stock.*

After selling 30 shares of treasury stock, 20 shares remain in Nelson's possession. These shares cost $20 each, so the balance in the Treasury Stock account is now $400 ($20 × 20 shares). Treasury stock is reported on the balance sheet directly below retained earnings. Although this placement suggests that treasury stock reduces retained earnings, the reduction actually applies to the entire stockholders' equity section. In the following section, we continue our discussion of Nelson Incorporated and show the presentation of treasury stock in the balance sheet. (See Exhibit 11.5.)

CHECK YOURSELF 11.2

On January 1, Year 1, Janell Company's Common Stock account balance was $20,000. On April 1, Year 1, Janell paid $12,000 cash to purchase some of its own stock. Janell resold this stock on October 1, Year 1, for $14,500. What is the effect on the company's cash and stockholders' equity from both the April 1 purchase and the October 1 resale of the stock?

Answer The April 1 purchase would reduce both cash and stockholders' equity by $12,000. The treasury stock transaction represents a return of invested capital to those owners who sold stock back to the company.

The sale of the treasury stock on October 1 would increase both cash and stockholders' equity by $14,500. The difference between the sales price of the treasury stock and its cost ($14,500 − $12,000) represents additional paid-in capital from treasury stock transactions. The stockholders' equity section of the balance sheet would include Common Stock, $20,000, and Additional Paid-in Capital from Treasury Stock Transactions, $2,500.

CASH DIVIDENDS

Cash dividends are affected by three significant dates: the *declaration date,* the *date of record,* and the *payment date.* Assume that on October 15, Year 2, the board of Nelson Incorporated declared the cash dividend on the 100 outstanding shares of its $10 stated value preferred stock. The dividend will be paid to stockholders of record as of November 15, Year 2. The cash payment will be made on December 15, Year 2.

Show how declaring and paying cash dividends affect financial statements.

Declaration Date

Although corporations are not required to declare dividends, they are legally obligated to pay dividends once they have been declared. They must recognize a liability on the **declaration date** (in this case, October 15, Year 2). The increase in liabilities is accompanied by a decrease in retained earnings. The income statement and statement of cash flows are not affected. The journal entry and the effects on the financial statements of *declaring* the $70 (0.07 × $10 × 100 shares) dividend are shown next:

Account Title	Debit	Credit
Dividends	70	
Dividends Payable		70

Assets	=	Liab.	+	Equity			Rev.	−	Exp.	=	Net Inc.	Cash Flow
Cash	=	Div. Pay.	+	Com. Stk.	+	Ret. Earn.						
NA	=	70	+	NA	+	(70)	NA	−	NA	=	NA	NA

Date of Record

Cash dividends are paid to investors who owned the preferred stock on the **date of record** (in this case, November 15, Year 2). Any stock sold after the date of record but before the payment date (in this case, December 15, Year 2) is traded **ex-dividend,** meaning the buyer will not receive the upcoming dividend. The date of record is merely a cutoff date. It does not affect the financial statements.

Payment Date

Nelson Incorporated actually paid the cash dividend on the **payment date.** This event has the same effect as paying any other liability. Assets (cash) and liabilities (dividends payable) both decrease. The income statement is not affected. The cash outflow is reported in the financing activities section of the statement of cash flows. The journal entry and its effects on the financial statements are shown next:

Account Title	Debit	Credit
Dividends Payable	70	
Cash		70

Assets	=	Liab.	+	Equity			Rev.	−	Exp.	=	Net Inc.	Cash Flow
Cash	=	Div. Pay.	+	Com. Stk.	+	Ret. Earn.						
(70)	=	(70)	+	NA	+	NA	NA	−	NA	=	NA	(70) FA

REALITY BYTES

As you have learned, dividends, unlike interest on bonds, do not have to be paid. In fact, a company's board of directors must vote to pay dividends before they can be paid. Even so, once a company establishes a practice of paying a dividend of a given amount each period, usually quarterly, the company is reluctant to not pay the dividend. The amount of dividends that companies pay, relative to their earnings, varies widely.

Large, well-established companies usually do pay dividends, while young, growing companies often do not. Consider the 30 companies that make up the Dow Jones Industrials Average. In 2016, all of these companies paid dividends. Goldman Sachs paid out the lowest percentage of its earnings in dividends (15.9 percent). At the other extreme was Chevron, which paid dividends of $4.38 per share even though it reported a net loss of $0.27 per share. The average percentage of earnings paid out as dividends for all 30 companies in the Dow was 51.6 percent in 2016.

©Trong Nguyen/Shutterstock

For comparison, consider two large, relatively young, technology companies: Alphabet, Inc., the parent company of Google, and Facebook. Although both of these companies have had large, positive earnings in recent years (Google alone had $19.5 billion in earnings in 2016), neither has ever paid a dividend to its common shareholders. They are using their cash to grow their businesses, often by purchasing other companies.

STOCK DIVIDENDS AND SPLITS

Stock Dividends

LO 11-7

Show how stock dividends and stock splits affect financial statements.

Dividends are not always paid in cash. Companies sometimes choose to issue **stock dividends,** wherein they distribute additional shares of stock to the stockholders. To illustrate, assume that Nelson Incorporated decided to issue a 10 percent stock dividend on its class B, $20 par value common stock. Because dividends apply to outstanding shares only, Nelson will issue 15 (150 outstanding shares × 0.10) additional shares of class B stock.

Assume the new shares are distributed when the market value of the stock is $30 per share. As a result of the stock dividend, Nelson will transfer $450 ($30 × 15 new shares) from retained earnings to paid-in capital.[1] The stock dividend is an equity exchange transaction. The income statement and statement of cash flows are not affected. The journal entry and its effects on the financial statements are shown next:

Account Title	Debit	Credit
Retained Earnings	450	
Common Stock, Class B, $20 Par Value		300
Paid-in Capital in Excess of Par Value—Class B Common		150

Assets	=	Liab.	+	Equity				Rev.	−	Exp.	=	Net Inc.	Cash Flow
				Com. Stk. + PIC in Excess + Ret. Earn.									
NA	=	NA	+	300 + 150 + (450)				NA	−	NA	=	NA	NA

[1] The accounting here applies to small stock dividends. Accounting for large stock dividends is explained in a more advanced course.

FOCUS ON INTERNATIONAL ISSUES

PICKY, PICKY, PICKY . . .

Considering the almost countless number of differences that could exist between U.S. GAAP and IFRS, it is not surprising that some of those that do exist relate to very specific issues. Consider the case of the timing of stock splits.

Assume a company that ends its fiscal year on December 31, 2018, declares a 2-for-1 stock split on January 15, 2019, before it has issued its 2018 annual report. Should the company apply the effects of the stock split retroactively to its 2018 financial statements, or begin showing the effects of the split on its 2019 statements? Under U.S. GAAP, the split must be applied retroactively to the 2018 statements because they had not been issued at the time of the split. Under IFRS, the 2018 statements would not show the effects of the split, but the 2019 statements would. By the way, an event that occurs between a company's fiscal year-end and the date its annual report is released is called a *subsequent event* by accountants.

Obviously no one can know every rule under GAAP, much less all of the differences between GAAP and IFRS. This is why it is important to learn how to find answers to specific accounting questions, as well as to develop an understanding of the basic accounting rules. Most important, if you are not sure you know the answer, do not assume you do.

Stock dividends have no effect on assets. They merely increase the number of shares of stock outstanding. Because a greater number of shares represents the same ownership interest in the same amount of assets, the market value per share of a company's stock normally declines when a stock dividend is distributed. A lower market price makes the stock more affordable and may increase demand for the stock, which benefits both the company and its stockholders.

Stock Splits

A corporation may also reduce the market price of its stock through a **stock split.** A stock split replaces existing shares with a greater number of new shares. Any par or stated value of the stock is proportionately reduced to reflect the new number of shares outstanding. For example, assume Nelson Incorporated declared a 2-for-1 stock split on the 165 outstanding shares (150 originally issued + 15 shares distributed in a stock dividend) of its $20 par value, class B common stock. Nelson notes in the accounting records that the 165 old $20 par shares are replaced with 330 new $10 par shares. Investors who owned the 165 shares of old common stock would now own 330 shares of the new common stock.

Stock splits have no effect on the dollar amounts of assets, liabilities, and stockholders' equity. They affect only the number of shares of stock outstanding and the par value per share. In Nelson's case, the ownership interest that was previously represented by 165 shares of stock is now represented by 330 shares. Because twice as many shares now represent the same ownership interest, the market value per share should be one-half as much as it was prior to the split. However, as with a stock dividend, the lower market price will probably stimulate demand for the stock. As a result, doubling the number of shares will likely reduce the market price to slightly more than one-half of the pre-split value. For example, if the stock were selling for $30 per share before the 2-for-1 split, it might sell for $15.50 after the split.

APPROPRIATION OF RETAINED EARNINGS

The board of directors may restrict the amount of retained earnings available to distribute as dividends. The restriction may be required by credit agreements, or it may be discretionary. A retained earnings restriction, often called an *appropriation,* is an equity exchange event. It transfers a portion of existing retained earnings to **appropriated retained earnings.** Total retained earnings remains unchanged. To illustrate, assume that Nelson Incorporated appropriates $1,000 of retained earnings for future expansion. The income statement and the

LO 11-8

Show how the appropriation of retained earnings affects financial statements.

statement of cash flows are not affected. The journal entry and its effects on the financial statements are shown next:

Account Title	Debit	Credit
Retained Earnings	1,000	
Appropriated Retained Earnings		1,000

Assets	=	Liab.	+	Equity					Rev.	−	Exp.	=	Net Inc.	Cash Flow
				Com. Stk.	+	Ret. Earn.	+	App. Ret. Earn.						
NA	=	NA	+	NA	+	(1,000)	+	1,000	NA	−	NA	=	NA	FA

Financial Statement Presentation

The Year 1 and Year 2 events for Nelson Incorporated are summarized in the following. Events 1 through 8 are cash transactions. The results of the Year 1 transactions (nos. 1–5) are reflected in Exhibit 11.4. The results of the Year 2 transactions (nos. 6–11) are shown in Exhibit 11.5.

1. Issued 100 shares of $10 par value common stock at a market price of $22 per share.
2. Issued 150 shares of class B, $20 par value common stock at a market price of $25 per share.
3. Issued 100 shares of $10 stated value, 7 percent cumulative preferred stock at a market price of $22 per share.
4. Issued 100 shares of no-par common stock at a market price of $22 per share.

EXHIBIT 11.5

NELSON INCORPORATED
Balance Sheet
As of December 31, Year 2

Assets		
Cash		$21,030
Stockholders' equity		
Preferred stock, $10 stated value, 7% cumulative, 300 shares authorized, 100 issued and outstanding	$1,000	
Common stock, $10 par value, 250 shares authorized, 100 issued, and 80 outstanding	1,000	
Common stock, class B, $10 par, 800 shares authorized, 330 issued and outstanding	3,300	
Common stock, no par, 150 shares authorized, 100 issued and outstanding	2,200	
Paid-in capital in excess of stated value—Preferred	1,200	
Paid-in capital in excess of par value—Common	1,200	
Paid-in capital in excess of par value—Class B common	900	
Paid-in capital in excess of cost of treasury stock	150	
Total paid-in capital		$10,950
Retained Earnings		
Appropriated	1,000	
Unappropriated	9,480	
Total retained earnings		10,480
Less: Treasury stock, 20 shares @ $20 per share		(400)
Total stockholders' equity		$21,030

5. Earned and retained $5,000 cash from operations.
6. Purchased 50 shares of $10 par value common stock as treasury stock at a market price of $20 per share.
7. Sold 30 shares of treasury stock at a market price of $25 per share.
8. Declared and paid a $70 cash dividend on the preferred stock.
9. Issued a 10 percent stock dividend on the 150 shares of outstanding class B, $20 par value common stock (15 additional shares). The additional shares were issued when the market price of the stock was $30 per share. There are 165 (150 + 15) class B common shares outstanding after the stock dividend.
10. Issued a 2-for-1 stock split on the 165 shares of class B, $20 par value common stock. After this transaction, there are 330 shares outstanding of the class B common stock with a $10 par value.
11. Appropriated $1,000 of retained earnings.

The illustration assumes that Nelson earned net income of $6,000 in Year 2. The ending retained earnings balance is determined as follows: Beginning balance $5,000 − $70 Cash dividend − $450 Stock dividend + $6,000 Net income = $10,480.

The Financial Analyst

Stockholders may benefit in two ways when a company generates earnings. The company may distribute the earnings directly to the stockholders in the form of dividends. Alternatively, the company may retain some or all of the earnings to finance growth and increase its potential for future earnings. If the company retains earnings, the market value of its stock should increase to reflect its greater earnings prospects. How can analysts use financial reporting to help assess the potential for dividend payments or growth in market value?

LO 11-9

Show how accounting information is used to make stock investment decisions.

Receiving Dividends

Is a company likely to pay dividends in the future? The financial statements can help answer this question. They show if dividends were paid in the past. Companies with a history of paying dividends usually continue to pay dividends. Also, to pay dividends in the future, a company must have sufficient cash and retained earnings. These amounts are reported on the balance sheet and the statement of cash flows.

Increasing the Price of Stock

Is the market value (price) of a company's stock likely to increase? Increases in a company's stock price occur when investors believe the company's earnings will grow. Financial statements provide information that is useful in predicting the prospects for earnings growth. Here also, a company's earnings history is an indicator of its growth potential. However, because published financial statements report historical information, investors must recognize their limitations. Investors want to know about the future. Stock prices are therefore influenced more by forecasts than by history.

For example:

- On January 30, 2017, **Under Armour, Inc.** announced that revenues for the fiscal year ended December 31, 2016, were 22.7 percent higher than for the previous year, and its earnings were up 11.2 percent. In reaction to this seemingly good news, the price of its stock *fell* by 23.4 percent on a day when the market as a whole barely changed. Why did the market respond in this way? Even though the company's sales were up 23 percent for 2016,

©Sorbis/Shutterstock

for the fourth quarter of 2016 its revenues were up *only* 12 percent. For the previous six years, quarterly revenue had increased over 20 percent. This caused many investors to sell their stock fearing that revenue and earnings growth in the future would not be as great as they had been in the past.

- On February 21, 2017, Wal-Mart Stores, Inc. announced that earnings for 2016 were 7.2 percent lower for 2015, and earnings for the fourth quarter of the fiscal year ended January 31, 2017, were 22.7 percent lower than for the same quarter of the prior year. The market's reaction to this seemingly negative news was to *increase* the price of the company's stock by 3 percent on a day when the market as a whole barely changed. The market reacted this way because even though earnings were down significantly, total revenues increased by around 1 percent. A 1 percent increase in revenue is not much, but many traditional retail companies were experiencing declining revenues at this time, so a 1 percent increase was good news.

In each case, investors reacted to the potential for earnings growth rather than the historical earnings reports. Because investors find forecasted statements more relevant to decision making than historical financial statements, most companies provide forecasts in addition to historical financial statements.

The value of a company's stock is also influenced by nonfinancial information that financial statements cannot provide. For example, suppose ExxonMobil announced in the middle of its fiscal year that it had just discovered substantial oil reserves on property to which it held drilling rights. Consider the following questions:

- What would happen to the price of ExxonMobil's stock on the day of the announcement?
- What would happen to ExxonMobil's financial statements on that day?

The price of ExxonMobil's stock would almost certainly increase as soon as the discovery was made public. However, nothing would happen to its financial statements on that day. There would probably be very little effect on its financial statements for that year. Only after the company began to develop the oil field and sell the oil would its financial statements reflect the discovery. Changes in financial statements tend to lag behind the announcements companies make regarding their earnings potential.

To illustrate the hypothetical Exxon story with a real-world example, consider the events at Apache Corporation in September 2016. Apache, like Exxon, is in the gas and oil business, but it is less well known. On September 7, 2016, Apache announced that it had confirmed the discovery of an oil and gas field on property it controlled in Texas. The estimated reserves of this field were three billion barrels of oil and 75 billion cubic feet of natural gas, which are worth billions of dollars. However, a comparison of Apache's quarterly balance sheet of June 30, 2016, issued just before the announcement, with its quarterly balance sheet dated September 30, 2016, issued just after the announcement, shows that reported gas and oil properties *fell* by $102 million. The stock market's reaction? From September 6, 2016 until September 8, 2016, the price of Apache's stock increased by 14.3 percent, while the stock market as a whole fell by 0.2 percent.

Price-Earnings Ratio

The **price-earnings ratio,** frequently called the *P/E ratio,* is the most commonly reported measure of a company's value. The P/E ratio is a company's market price per share of stock divided by the company's annual earnings per share (EPS).[2]

Assume Western Company recently reported annual earnings per share of $3. Western's stock is currently selling for $54 per share. Western's stock is therefore selling at a P/E ratio of 18 ($54 market price ÷ $3 EPS). What does a P/E ratio of 18 mean? If Western continued earning $3 per share of stock each year and paid out all its earnings to stockholders in the form of cash dividends, it would take 18 years for an investor to recover the price paid for the stock.

---

[2]The amount of earnings per share is provided on the face of the income statement. In its simplest form, it is computed by dividing the company's net income (net earnings) by the number of shares of common stock outstanding.

In contrast, assume the stock of Eastern Company, which reported EPS of $4, is currently selling for $48 per share. Eastern's P/E ratio is 12 ($48 market price ÷ $4 EPS). Investors who buy Eastern Company stock would get their money back six years faster (18 − 12) than investors who buy Western Company stock.

Why would investors buy a stock with a P/E ratio of 18 when they could buy one with a P/E ratio of 12? If investors expect Western Company's earnings to grow faster than Eastern Company's earnings, the higher P/E ratio makes sense. For example, suppose Western Company's earnings were to double to $6 per share, while Eastern's remained at $4 per share. Western's P/E ratio would drop to 9 ($54 market price ÷ $6 EPS), while Eastern's remains at 12. This explains why high-growth companies sell for higher P/E multiples than do low-growth companies.

Caution must be used when interpreting P/E ratios. A company can have a high P/E ratio due to very low earnings, rather than high optimism by investors. For example, if a company's EPS is $0.02, and its stock is selling for $0.50, it will have a P/E ratio of 25, which is high. In this case, the high P/E ratio is the result of very low earnings, not optimism. If a company has a net loss, the P/E ratio is not computed.

Also, be aware that P/E ratios reported in the financial press are often based on *projected* EPS, rather than historical earnings. Sometimes P/E ratios based on historical earnings are referred to as being based on trailing earnings. In this course, compute the P/E ratio using the company's most recent, actual earnings amount rather than its forecasted earnings.

Exercising Control through Stock Ownership

The more influence an investor has over the operations of a company, the more the investor can benefit from owning stock in the company. For example, consider a power company that needs coal to produce electricity. The power company may purchase some common stock in a coal mining company to ensure a stable supply of coal. What percentage of the mining company's stock must the power company acquire to exercise significant influence over the mining company? The answer depends on how many investors own stock in the mining company and how the number of shares is distributed among the stockholders.

The greater its number of stockholders, the more *widely held* a company is. If stock ownership is concentrated in the hands of a few persons, a company is *closely held*. Widely held companies can generally be controlled with smaller percentages of ownership than closely held companies. Consider a company in which no existing investor owns more than 1 percent of the voting stock. A new investor who acquires a 5 percent interest would immediately become, by far, the largest shareholder and would likely be able to significantly influence board decisions. In contrast, consider a closely held company in which one current shareholder owns 51 percent of the company's stock. Even if another investor acquired the remaining 49 percent of the company, that investor could not control the company.

Financial statements contain some, but not all, of the information needed to help an investor determine ownership levels necessary to permit control. For example, the financial statements disclose the total number of shares of stock outstanding, but they normally contain little information about the number of shareholders and even less information about any relationships between shareholders. Relationships between shareholders are critically important because related shareholders, whether bound by family or business interests, might exercise control by voting as a bloc. For publicly traded companies, information about the number of shareholders and the identity of some large shareholders is disclosed in reports filed with the Securities and Exchange Commission.

A Look Back <<

Starting a business requires obtaining financing; it takes money to make money. Although some money may be borrowed, lenders are unlikely to make loans to businesses that lack some degree of owner financing. Equity financing is therefore critical to virtually all profit-oriented businesses. This chapter has examined some of the issues related to accounting for equity transactions.

The idea that a business must obtain financing from its owners was one of the first events presented in this textbook. This chapter discussed the advantages and disadvantages of organizing a business as a sole proprietorship versus a partnership versus a corporation. These advantages and disadvantages include the following:

- *Double taxation*—Income of corporations is subject to double taxation, but that of proprietorships and partnerships is not.
- *Regulation*—Corporations are subject to more regulation than are proprietorships and partnerships.
- *Limited liability*—An investor's personal assets are not at risk as a result of owning corporate securities. The investor's liability is limited to the amount of the investment. In general, proprietorships and partnerships do not offer limited liability. However, laws in some states permit the formation of limited liability companies which operate like proprietorships and partnerships yet place some limits on the personal liability of their owners.
- *Continuity*—Proprietorships and partnerships dissolve when one of the owners leaves the business. Corporations are separate legal entities that continue to exist regardless of changes in ownership.
- *Transferability*—Ownership interests in corporations are easier to transfer than those of proprietorships or partnerships.
- *Management structure*—Corporations are more likely to have independent professional managers than are proprietorships or partnerships.
- *Ability to raise capital*—Because they can be owned by millions of investors, corporations have the opportunity to raise more capital than proprietorships or partnerships.

Corporations issue different classes of common stock and preferred stock as evidence of ownership interests. In general, *common stock* provides the widest range of privileges, including the right to vote and participate in earnings. *Preferred stockholders* usually give up the right to vote in exchange for preferences such as the right to receive dividends or assets upon liquidation before common stockholders. Stock may have a *par value* or *stated value*, which relates to legal requirements governing the amount of capital that must be maintained in the corporation. Corporations may also issue *no-par stock*, avoiding some of the legal requirements that pertain to par or stated value stock.

Stock that a company issues and then repurchases is called *treasury stock*. Purchasing treasury stock reduces total assets and stockholders' equity. Reselling treasury stock represents a capital acquisition. The difference between the reissue price and the cost of the treasury stock is recorded directly in the equity accounts. Treasury stock transactions do not result in gains or losses on the income statement.

Companies may issue *stock splits* or *stock dividends*. These transactions increase the number of shares of stock without changing the net assets of a company. The per share market value usually drops when a company issues stock splits or dividends.

>> A Look Forward

Chapter 12 examines the statement of cash flows in more detail than past chapters have. It introduces a more practical way to prepare the statement than analyzing every single entry in the Cash account, and it presents the more formal format for the statement of cash flows used by most real-world companies.

Proprietorships, Partnerships, and Corporations   617

SELF-STUDY REVIEW PROBLEM

A step-by-step audio-narrated series of slides is available in Connect.

Edwards Inc. experienced the following events:

1. Issued common stock for cash.
2. Declared a cash dividend.
3. Issued noncumulative preferred stock for cash.
4. Appropriated retained earnings.
5. Distributed a stock dividend.
6. Paid cash to purchase treasury stock.
7. Distributed a 2-for-1 stock split.
8. Issued cumulative preferred stock for cash.
9. Paid a cash dividend that had previously been declared.
10. Sold treasury stock for cash at a higher amount than the cost of the treasury stock.

Required

Show the effect of each event on the elements of the financial statements using a horizontal statements model like the one shown next. Use + for increase, − for decrease, and NA for not affected. In the Cash Flow column, indicate whether the item is an operating activity (OA), investing activity (IA), or financing activity (FA). The first transaction is entered as an example.

Event	Assets	=	Liab.	+	Equity	Rev.	−	Exp.	=	Net Inc.	Cash Flow
1	+		NA		+	NA		NA		NA	+ FA

Solution to Self-Study Review Problem

Event	Assets	=	Liab.	+	Equity	Rev.	−	Exp.	=	Net Inc.	Cash Flow
1	+		NA		+	NA		NA		NA	+ FA
2	NA		+		−	NA		NA		NA	NA
3	+		NA		+	NA		NA		NA	+ FA
4	NA		NA		−+	NA		NA		NA	NA
5	NA		NA		−+	NA		NA		NA	NA
6	−		NA		−	NA		NA		NA	− FA
7	NA		NA		NA	NA		NA		NA	NA
8	+		NA		+	NA		NA		NA	+ FA
9	−		−		NA	NA		NA		NA	− FA
10	+		NA		+	NA		NA		NA	+ FA

KEY TERMS

Appropriated retained earnings 611
Articles of incorporation 596
Authorized stock 601
Board of directors 598
Book value per share 601
Closely held corporation 596
Common stock 601
Continuity 598
Corporation 596
Cost method of accounting for treasury stock 607

Cumulative dividends 602
Date of record 609
Declaration date 609
Dividends in arrears 602
Double taxation 597
Ex-dividend 609
Issued stock 601
Legal capital 601
Limited liability 598
Limited liability companies (LLCs) 597
Market value 601
Outstanding stock 601
Paid-in Capital in Excess of Par Value 604
Par value 600
Partnership 596
Partnership agreement 596
Payment date 609
Preferred stock 602
Price-earnings (P/E) ratio 614
Sarbanes–Oxley Act of 2002 597
Securities Act of 1933 596
Securities Exchange Act of 1934 596
Sole proprietorship 596
Stated value 601
Stock certificate 596
Stock dividend 610
Stock split 611
Stockholders 598
Transferability 598
Treasury stock 601
Withdrawals 599

QUESTIONS

1. What are the three major forms of business organizations? Describe each.
2. How are sole proprietorships formed?
3. Discuss the purpose of a partnership agreement. Is such an agreement necessary for partnership formation?
4. What is meant by the phrase *separate legal entity?* To which type of business organization does it apply?
5. What is the purpose of the articles of incorporation? What information do they provide?
6. What is the function of the stock certificate?
7. What prompted Congress to pass the Securities Act of 1933 and the Securities Exchange Act of 1934? What is the purpose of these laws?
8. What are the advantages and disadvantages of the corporate form of business organization?
9. What is a limited liability company? Discuss its advantages and disadvantages.
10. How does the term *double taxation* apply to corporations? Give an example of double taxation.
11. What is the difference between contributed capital and retained earnings for a corporation?
12. What are the similarities and differences in the equity structure of a sole proprietorship, a partnership, and a corporation?
13. Why is it easier for a corporation to raise large amounts of capital than it is for a partnership?
14. What is the meaning of each of the following terms with respect to the corporate form of organization?
    (a) Legal capital
    (b) Par value of stock
    (c) Stated value of stock
    (d) Market value of stock
    (e) Book value of stock
    (f) Authorized shares of stock
    (g) Issued stock
    (h) Outstanding stock
    (i) Treasury stock
    (j) Common stock
    (k) Preferred stock
    (l) Dividends
15. What is the difference between cumulative preferred stock and non-cumulative preferred stock?
16. What is no-par stock? How is it recorded in the accounting records?
17. Assume that Best Co. has issued and outstanding 1,000 shares of $100 par value, 10 percent, cumulative preferred stock. What is the dividend per share? If the preferred dividend is two years in arrears, what total amount of dividends must be paid before the common shareholders can receive any dividends?
18. If Best Co. issued 10,000 shares of $20 par value common stock for $30 per share, what amount is credited to the Common Stock account? What amount of cash is received?
19. What is the difference between par value stock and stated value stock?
20. Why might a company repurchase its own stock?
21. What effect does the purchase of treasury stock have on the equity of a company?
22. Assume that Day Company repurchased 1,000 of its own shares for $30 per share and sold the shares two weeks later for $35 per share. What is the amount of gain on the sale? How is it reported on the balance sheet? What type of account is treasury stock?
23. What is the importance of the declaration date, record date, and payment date in conjunction with corporate dividends?
24. What is the difference between a stock dividend and a stock split?
25. Why would a company choose to distribute a stock dividend instead of a cash dividend?
26. What is the primary reason that a company would declare a stock split?
27. If Best Co. had 10,000 shares of $20 par value common stock outstanding and declared a 5-for-1 stock split, how many shares would then be outstanding and what would be their par value after the split?
28. When a company appropriates retained earnings, does the company set aside cash for a specific use? Explain.
29. What is the largest source of financing for most U.S. businesses?
30. What is meant by *equity financing?* What is meant by *debt financing?*
31. What is a widely held corporation? What is a closely held corporation?
32. What are some reasons that a corporation might not pay dividends?

MULTIPLE-CHOICE QUESTIONS

Multiple-choice questions are available in **Connect**.

EXERCISES—SERIES A

 All applicable Exercises in Series A are available in **Connect**.

Exercise 11-1A *Characteristics of sole proprietorships, partnerships, and corporations* LO 11-1

Required

The three primary types of business organization are proprietorship, partnership, and corporation. Each type has characteristics that distinguish it from the other types. In the left column of the following table write the name of the type of business organization that is most likely to possess the characteristic that is described in the right column of the table. The first item is shown as an example.

Business Type	Characteristic
Proprietorship	Owned and operated by a single individual
	Subject to double taxation
	Has a retained earnings account on its balance sheet
	One owner may be held personally liable for actions taken on behalf of the business by different owner
	Profits benefit a single individual
	Frequently uses legal agreements to define profit distribution for two or more owners
	Most highly regulated form of business
	The business dissolves with the death of its only owner
	Offers the least capacity to raise capital
	Provides the best opportunity to benefit a few people
	Has only one capital account on its balance sheet
	Provides for easy transfer of ownership
	Offers the highest level of control over operating decisions
	Has multiple capital accounts but no retained earnings account on its balance sheet
	Provides the greatest capacity to raise capital
	Least regulated form of business
	Usually operated by a professional management team that is separated from the owners
	Has two or more owners who are not stockholders

Exercise 11-2A *Effect of accounting events on the financial statements of a sole proprietorship* LO 11-1

A sole proprietorship was started on January 1, Year 1, when it received $60,000 cash from Marlin Jones, the owner. During Year 1, the company earned $35,300 in cash revenues and paid $16,200 in cash expenses. Jones withdrew $1,000 cash from the business during Year 1.

Required

Prepare an income statement, capital statement (statement of changes in equity), balance sheet, and statement of cash flows for Jones' Year 1 fiscal year.

Exercise 11-3A *Effect of accounting events on the financial statements of a partnership* LO 11-1

Faith Busby and Jeremy Beatty started the B&B partnership on January 1, Year 1. The business acquired $44,000 cash from Busby and $66,000 from Beatty. During Year 1, the partnership earned $42,000 in cash revenues and paid $18,400 for cash expenses. Busby withdrew $2,000 cash from the business, and Beatty withdrew $2,500 cash. The net income was allocated to the capital accounts of the two partners in proportion to the amounts of their original investments in the business.

Required

Prepare an income statement, capital statement, balance sheet, and statement of cash flows for B&B's Year 1 fiscal year.

LO 11-2

Exercise 11-4A *Capital stock authorized, issued, and outstanding*

Enscoe Enterprises, Inc. (EEI) has 225,000 shares authorized, 150,000 shares issued, and 30,000 shares of treasury stock. At this point, EEI has $780,000 of assets. $180,000 liabilities, $360,000 of common stock, and $240,000 of retained earnings. Further, assume that the market value of EEI's common stock is $7 per share.

Required

a. Determine the number of shares of stock that is outstanding.
b. Determine the book value per share.
c. Provide a rational explanation for the difference between the book value per share and the market value per share of EEI's common stock.

LO 11-2

Exercise 11-5A *Characteristics of capital stock*

The stockholders' equity section of Creighton Company's balance sheet is shown as follows:

CREIGHTON COMPANY
As of December 31, Year 3

Stockholders' equity	
Preferred stock, $10 stated value, 7% cumulative,	
300 shares authorized, 50 issued and outstanding	$ 500
Common stock, $10 par value, 250 shares authorized,	
100 issued and outstanding	1,000
Common stock, class B, $20 par value, 400 shares	
authorized, 150 issued and outstanding	3,000
Common stock, no par, 150 shares authorized,	
100 issued and outstanding	2,200
Paid-in capital in excess of stated value—preferred	600
Paid-in capital in excess of par value—common	1,200
Paid-in capital in excess of par value—class B common	750
Retained earnings	7,000
Total stockholders' equity	$16,250

Required

a. Assuming the preferred stock was originally issued for cash, determine the amount of cash that was collected when the stock was issued.
b. Based on the class B common stock alone, determine the amount of the company's legal capital.
c. Based on the class B common stock alone, determine the minimum amount of assets that must be retained in the company as protection for creditors.
d. Determine the number of shares of class B common stock that are available to sell as of December 31, Year 3.
e. Assuming Creighton purchases treasury stock consisting of 25 shares of its no par common stock on January 1, Year 4, determine the amount of the no-par common stock that would be outstanding immediately after the purchase.
f. Based on the stockholders' equity section shown earlier, can you determine the market value of the preferred stock? If yes, what is the market value of one share of this stock?

LO 11-3

Exercise 11-6A *Accounting for cumulative preferred dividends*

When Crossett Corporation was organized in January Year 1, it immediately issued 4,000 shares of $50 par, 6 percent, cumulative preferred stock and 50,000 shares of $20 par common stock. Its earnings history is as follows: Year 1, net loss of $35,000; Year 2, net income of $125,000; Year 3, net income of $215,000. The corporation did not pay a dividend in Year 1.

Required

a. How much is the dividend arrearage as of January 1, Year 2?
b. Assume that the board of directors declares a $25,000 cash dividend at the end of Year 2 (remember that the Year 1 and Year 2 preferred dividends are due). How will the dividend be divided between the preferred and common stockholders?

Exercise 11-7A *Cash dividends for preferred and common shareholders* LO 11-3

Weaver Corporation had the following stock issued and outstanding at January 1, Year 1:

1. 150,000 shares of $1 par common stock.
2. 15,000 shares of $100 par, 6 percent, noncumulative preferred stock.

On June 10, Weaver Corporation declared the annual cash dividend on its 15,000 shares of preferred stock and a $0.50 per share dividend for the common shareholders. The dividends will be paid on July 1 to the shareholders of record on June 20.

Required

a. Determine the total amount of dividends to be paid to the preferred shareholders and common shareholders.
b. Prepare general journal entries to record the declaration and payment of the cash dividends (be sure to date your entries).

Exercise 11-8A *Effect of issuing common stock on the balance sheet* LO 11-4

Newly formed S&J Iron Corporation has 50,000 shares of $10 par common stock authorized. On March 1, Year 1, S&J Iron issued 6,000 shares of the stock for $16 per share. On May 2, the company issued an additional 10,000 shares for $18 per share. S&J Iron was not affected by other events during Year 1.

Required

a. Record the transactions in a horizontal statements model like the following one. In the Cash Flow column, indicate whether the item is an operating activity (OA), investing activity (IA), or financing activity (FA). Use NA to indicate that an element was not affected by the event.

Assets	=	Liab.	+	Equity		Rev.	−	Exp.	=	Net Inc.	Cash Flow
Cash	=			Com. Stk. + PIC in Excess							

b. Determine the amount S&J Iron would report for common stock on the December 31, Year 1, balance sheet.
c. Determine the amount S&J Iron would report for paid-in capital in excess of par.
d. What is the total amount of capital contributed by the owners?
e. What amount of total assets would S&J Iron report on the December 31, Year 1, balance sheet?
f. Prepare journal entries to record the March 1 and May 2 transactions.

Exercise 11-9A *Recording and reporting common and preferred stock transactions* LO 11-4

Eastport Inc. was organized on June 5, Year 1. It was authorized to issue 300,000 shares of $10 par common stock and 50,000 shares of 5 percent cumulative class A preferred stock. The class A stock had a stated value of $50 per share. The following stock transactions pertain to Eastport Inc.:

1. Issued 15,000 shares of common stock for $12 per share.
2. Issued 5,000 shares of the class A preferred stock for $51 per share.
3. Issued 60,000 shares of common stock for $15 per share.

Required

a. Prepare general journal entries for these transactions.
b. Prepare the stockholders' equity section of the balance sheet immediately after these transactions.

LO 11-4

Exercise 11-10A Effect of no-par common and par preferred stock on the horizontal statements model

Mercury Corporation issued 6,000 shares of no-par common stock for $45 per share. Mercury also issued 3,000 shares of $50 par, 5 percent noncumulative preferred stock at $52 per share.

Required

a. Record these events in a horizontal statements model like the following one. In the Cash Flow column, indicate whether the item is an operating activity (OA), investing activity (IA), or financing activity (FA). Use NA to indicate that an element was not affected by the event.

Assets	=	Equity			Rev. − Exp. = Net Inc.	Cash Flow
Cash	=	Pfd. Stk. + Com. Stk. + PIC in Excess				

b. Prepare journal entries to record these transactions.

LO 11-4

Exercise 11-11A Issuing stock for assets other than cash

Tom Yuppy, a wealthy investor, exchanged a plot of land that originally cost him $25,000 for 1,000 shares of $10 par common stock issued to him by Leuig Corp. On the same date, Leuig Corp. issued an additional 2,000 shares of stock to Yuppy for $25 per share.

Required

a. What was the value of the land at the date of the stock issue?
b. Show the effect of the two stock issues on Leuig's books in a horizontal statements model like the following one. In the Cash Flow column, indicate whether the item is an operating activity (OA), investing activity (IA), or financing activity (FA). Use NA to indicate that an element was not affected by the event.

Assets	=	Equity	Rev. − Exp. = Net Inc.	Cash Flow
Cash + Land	=	Com. Stk. + PIC in Excess		

c. Prepare the journal entries to record these transactions.

LO 11-5

Exercise 11-12A Treasury stock transactions

Elroy Corporation repurchased 4,000 shares of its own stock for $30 per share. The stock has a par of $10 per share. A month later, Elroy resold 900 shares of the treasury stock for $32 per share.

Required

a. Record the two events in general journal format.
b. What is the balance of the treasury stock account after these transactions?

LO 11-5

Exercise 11-13A Recording and reporting treasury stock transactions

The following information pertains to JAE Corp. at January 1, Year 1:

Common stock, $10 par, 20,000 shares authorized, 2,000 shares issued and outstanding	$20,000
Paid-in capital in excess of par, common stock	15,000
Retained earnings	82,000

JAE Corp. completed the following transactions during Year 1:

1. Issued 3,000 shares of $10 par common stock for $25 per share.
2. Repurchased 500 shares of its own common stock for $26 per share.
3. Resold 200 shares of treasury stock for $30 per share.

Required

a. How many shares of common stock were outstanding at the end of the period?
b. How many shares of common stock had been issued at the end of the period?
c. Prepare journal entries for these transactions and post them to T-accounts.
d. Prepare the stockholders' equity section of the balance sheet reflecting these transactions. Include the number of shares authorized, issued, and outstanding in the description of the common stock.

Exercise 11-14A Effect of cash dividends on financial statements

LO 11-6

On May 1, Year 1, Love Corporation declared a $50,000 cash dividend to be paid on May 31 to shareholders of record on May 15.

Required

a. Record the events occurring on May 1, May 15, and May 31 in a horizontal statements model like the following one. In the Cash Flow column, indicate whether the item is an operating activity (OA), investing activity (IA), or financing activity (FA).

b. Prepare journal entries for all events associated with the dividend.

Exercise 11-15A Accounting for stock dividends

LO 11-7

Beacon Corporation issued a 5 percent stock dividend on 30,000 shares of its $10 par common stock. At the time of the dividend, the market value of the stock was $15 per share.

Required

a. Compute the amount of the stock dividend.
b. Show the effects of the stock dividend on the financial statements using a horizontal statements model like the following one:

c. Prepare the journal entry to record the stock dividend.

Exercise 11-16A Determining the effects of stock splits on the accounting records

LO 11-7

The market value of Yeates Corporation's common stock had become excessively high. The stock was currently selling for $240 per share. To reduce the market price of the common stock, Yeates declared a 3-for-1 stock split for the 100,000 outstanding shares of its $10 par value common stock.

Required

a. What entry will be made on the books of Yeates Corporation for the stock split?
b. Determine the number of common shares outstanding and the par value after the split.
c. Explain how the market value of the stock will be affected by the stock split.

Exercise 11-17A Determining how the appropriation of retained earnings affects financial statements

LO 11-8

On December 30, Billy's Boat Yard (BBY) had $90,000 of cash, $20,000 of liabilities, $30,000 of common stock, and $40,000 of unrestricted retained earnings. On December 31, BBY appropriated retained earnings in the amount of $18,000 for a future remodeling project.

Required

a. Record the December 31 appropriation in the following statements model:

Assets	=	Liab.	+	Stockholders' Equity						Income Statement						Cash Flow
				C. Stk	+	Ret. Earn.	+	App. Ret. Earn.		Rev.	−	Exp.	=	Net Inc.		

b. Determine the amount of dividends that BBY can pay immediately after the December 31 appropriation.
c. Determine the total amount of retained earnings immediately after the December 31 appropriation.
d. Determine the total amount of cash immediately after the December 31 appropriation.

LO 11-9

Exercise 11-18A *Corporate announcements*

Discount Drugs (one of the three largest drug makers) just reported that its Year 2 third-quarter profits are essentially the same as the Year 1 third-quarter profits. In addition to this announcement, the same day, Discount Drugs also announced that the Food and Drug Administration has just approved a new drug used to treat high blood pressure that Discount Drugs developed. This new drug has been shown to be extremely effective and has few or no side effects. It will also be less expensive than the other drugs currently on the market.

Required

Using the preceding information, answer the following questions:

a. What do you think will happen to the stock price of Discount Drugs on the day these two announcements are made? Explain your answer.
b. How will the balance sheet be affected on that day by the preceding announcements?
c. How will the income statement be affected on that day by the preceding announcements?
d. How will the statement of cash flows be affected on that day by the preceding announcements?

LO 11-9

Exercise 11-19A *Using the P/E ratio*

Lake Inc. and River, Inc. reported net incomes of $800,000 and $1,000,000, respectively, for the most recent fiscal year. Both companies had 200,000 shares of common stock issued and outstanding. The market price per share of Lake's stock was $50, while River's sold for $85 per share.

Required

a. Determine the P/E ratio for each company.
b. Based on the P/E ratios computed in requirement *a*, which company do investors believe has the greater potential for growth in income?

LO 11-9

Exercise 11-20A *The P/E ratio*

Required

Write a memo explaining why one company's P/E ratio may be higher than another company's P/E ratio.

PROBLEMS—SERIES A

connect All applicable Problems in Series A are available in **Connect**.

LO 11-1

Problem 11-21A *Different forms of business organization*

Cal Cagle was working to establish a business enterprise with four of his wealthy friends. Each of the five individuals would receive a 20 percent ownership interest in the company. A primary goal of establishing the enterprise was to minimize the amount of income taxes paid. Assume that the five investors are in a 35 percent personal tax bracket and that the corporate tax rate is 25 percent. Also assume that the new company is expected to earn $220,000 of cash income before taxes during its first year of operation. All earnings are expected to be immediately distributed to the owners.

Required

Calculate the amount of after-tax cash flow available to each investor if the business is established as a partnership versus a corporation. Write a memo explaining the advantages and disadvantages of these two forms of business organization. Explain why a limited liability company may be a better choice than either a partnership or a corporation.

Problem 11-22A *Effect of business structure on financial statements*

LO 11-1

Cascade Company was started on January 1, Year 1, when it acquired $60,000 cash from the owners. During Year 2, the company earned cash revenues of $35,000 and incurred cash expenses of $18,100. The company also paid cash distributions of $4,000.

CHECK FIGURES
a. Net Income: $16,900
b. C. Cascade: $29,160

Required

Prepare a Year 1 income statement, capital statement (statement of changes in equity), balance sheet, and statement of cash flows under each of the following assumptions. (Consider each assumption separately.)

a. Cascade is a sole proprietorship owned by Carl Cascade.
b. Cascade is a partnership with two partners, Carl Cascade and Beth Cascade. Carl Cascade invested $24,000 and Beth Cascade invested $36,000 of the $60,000 cash that was used to start the business. Beth was expected to assume the vast majority of the responsibility for operating the business. The partnership agreement called for Beth to receive 60 percent of the profits and Carl to get the remaining 40 percent. With regard to the $4,000 distribution, Beth withdrew $2,400 from the business and Carl withdrew $1,600.
c. Cascade is a corporation. It issued 5,000 shares of $5 par common stock for $60,000 cash to start the business.

Problem 11-23A *Cash dividends: Common and preferred stock*

LO 11-3, 11-6

Nowell Inc. had the following stock issued and outstanding at January 1, Year 2:

1. 150,000 shares of no-par common stock.
2. 30,000 shares of $50 par, 4 percent, cumulative preferred stock. (Dividends are in arrears for one year, Year 1.)

On March 8, Year 1, Nowell declared a $175,000 cash dividend to be paid March 31 to shareholders of record on March 20.

Required

a. What amount of dividends will be paid to the preferred shareholders versus the common shareholders?
b. Prepare the journal entries required for these transactions. (Be sure to include the dates of the entries.)

Problem 11-24A *Analyzing journal entries for treasury stock transactions*

LO 11-4, 11-5

The following correctly prepared entries without explanations pertain to Corners Corporation:

CHECK FIGURE
b. 4,800

	Account Title	Debit	Credit
1.	Cash	1,000,000	
	Common Stock		600,000
	Paid-in Capital in Excess of Par Value		400,000
2.	Treasury Stock	24,000	
	Cash		24,000
3.	Cash	21,000	
	Treasury Stock		18,000
	Paid-in Capital in Excess of Cost of Treasury Stock		3,000

The original sale (Entry 1) was for 400,000 shares, and the treasury stock was acquired for $5 per share (Entry 2).

Required

a. What was the sales price per share of the original stock issue?
b. How many shares of stock did the corporation acquire in Entry 2?
c. How many shares were reissued in Entry 3?
d. How many shares are outstanding immediately following Entries 2 and 3, respectively?

LO 11-3, 11-6

CHECK FIGURES
b. Preferred Stock, Year 1: $50,000
c. Common Shares Outstanding, Year 2: 35,100

Problem 11-25A Recording and reporting stock transactions and cash dividends across two accounting cycles

Sun Corporation received a charter that authorized the issuance of 100,000 shares of $10 par common stock and 50,000 shares of $50 par, 5 percent cumulative preferred stock. Sun Corporation completed the following transactions during its first two years of operation:

Year 1

Jan. 5 Sold 6,000 shares of the $10 par common stock for $15 per share.
    12 Sold 1,000 shares of the 5 percent preferred stock for $55 per share.
Apr. 5 Sold 30,000 shares of the $10 par common stock for $21 per share.
Dec. 31 During the year, earned $150,000 in cash revenue and paid $88,000 for cash operating expenses.
    31 Declared the cash dividend on the outstanding shares of preferred stock for Year 1. The dividend will be paid on February 15 to stockholders of record on January 10, Year 2.
    31 Closed the revenue, expense, and dividend accounts to the retained earnings account.

Year 2

Feb. 15 Paid the cash dividend declared on December 31, Year 1.
Mar. 3 Sold 15,000 shares of the $50 par preferred stock for $53 per share.
May 5   Purchased 900 shares of the common stock as treasury stock at $24 per share.
Dec. 31 During the year, earned $210,000 in cash revenues and paid $98,000 for cash operating expenses.
    31 Declared the annual dividend on the preferred stock and a $0.50 per share dividend on the common stock.
    31 Closed revenue, expense, and dividend accounts to the retained earnings account.

Required

a. Prepare journal entries for these transactions for Year 1 and Year 2 and post them to T-accounts.
b. Prepare the balance sheets at December 31, Year 1 and Year 2.
c. What is the number of common shares *outstanding* at the end of Year 1? At the end of Year 2? How many common shares had been *issued* at the end of Year 1? At the end of Year 2? Explain any differences between issued and outstanding common shares for Year 1 and for Year 2.

LO 11-2, 11-3, 11-7

CHECK FIGURES
a. Par Value per Share: $20
b. Dividend per Share: $1.20

Problem 11-26A Analyzing the stockholders' equity section of the balance sheet

The stockholders' equity section of the balance sheet for Mann Equipment Co. at December 31, Year 1, is as follows:

Stockholders' Equity

Paid-in capital	
Preferred stock, ? par value, 6% cumulative, 100,000 shares authorized, 10,000 shares issued and outstanding	$ 200,000
Common stock, $10 stated value, 200,000 shares authorized, 100,000 shares issued and outstanding	1,000,000
Paid-in capital in excess of par—Preferred	25,000
Paid-in capital in excess of stated value—Common	500,000
Total paid-in capital	$1,725,000
Retained earnings	420,000
Total stockholders' equity	$2,145,000

Note: The market value per share of the common stock is $42, and the market value per share of the preferred stock is $26.

Required

a. What is the par value per share of the preferred stock?
b. What is the dividend per share on the preferred stock?
c. What was the average issue price per share (price for which the stock was issued) of the common stock?
d. Explain the difference between the par value and the market price of the preferred stock.
e. If Mann declares a 2-for-1 stock split on the common stock, how many shares will be outstanding after the split? What amount will be transferred from the retained earnings account because of the stock split? Theoretically, what will be the market price of the common stock immediately after the stock split?

Problem 11-27A *Recording and reporting stock dividends*

LO 11-4, 11-6, 11-7

Brice Co. completed the following transactions in Year 1, the first year of operation:

CHECK FIGURE
c. Total Paid-In Capital: $608,000

1. Issued 40,000 shares of no-par common stock for $10 per share.
2. Issued 8,000 shares of $20 par, 6 percent, preferred stock for $20 per share.
3. Paid a cash dividend of $9,600 to preferred shareholders.
4. Issued a 10 percent stock dividend on no-par common stock. The market value at the dividend declaration date was $12 per share.
5. Later that year, issued a 2-for-1 split on the shares of outstanding common stock. The market price of the stock at that time was $50 per share.
6. Produced $140,000 of cash revenues and incurred $72,000 of cash operating expenses.
7. Closed the revenue, expense, and dividend accounts to retained earnings.

Required

a. Record each of these events in a horizontal statements model like the following one. In the Cash Flow column, indicate whether the item is an operating activity (OA), investing activity (IA), or financing activity (FA). Use NA to indicate that an element is not affected by the event.

Assets	=	Equity			Rev.	−	Exp.	=	Net Inc.	Cash Flow
		P. Stk. + C. Stk. + Ret. Earn.								

b. Record the Year 1 transactions in general journal form and post them to T-accounts.
c. Prepare the stockholders' equity section of the balance sheet at the end of Year 1. (Include all necessary information.)
d. Theoretically, what is the market value of the common stock after the stock split?

Problem 11-28A *Recording and reporting treasury stock transactions*

LO 11-3, 11-4, 11-5, 11-6, 11-8

Choctaw Co. completed the following transactions in Year 1, the first year of operation:

1. Issued 20,000 shares of $10 par common stock for $10 per share.
2. Issued 3,000 shares of $20 stated value preferred stock for $20 per share.
3. Purchased 1,000 shares of common stock as treasury stock for $12 per share.
4. Declared a $2,000 cash dividend on preferred stock.
5. Sold 500 shares of treasury stock for $14 per share.
6. Paid $2,000 cash for the preferred dividend declared in Event 4.
7. Earned cash revenues of $78,000 and incurred cash expenses of $41,000.
8. Closed revenue, expense, and dividend accounts to the retained earnings account.
9. Appropriated $8,000 of retained earnings.

CHECK FIGURE
b. Total Paid-In Capital: $261,000

Required

a. Prepare journal entries to record these transactions and post them to T-accounts.
b. Prepare a balance sheet as of December 31, Year 1.

LO 11-3, 11-4, 11-5, 11-6, 11-7, 11-8

Problem 11-29A *Effects of equity transactions on financial statements*

The following events were experienced by Sequoia, Inc.:

1. Issued cumulative preferred stock for cash.
2. Issued common stock for cash.
3. Issued noncumulative preferred stock for cash.
4. Paid cash to purchase treasury stock.
5. Sold treasury stock for an amount of cash that was more than the cost of the treasury stock.
6. Declared a cash dividend.
7. Declared a 2-for-1 stock split on the common stock.
8. Distributed a stock dividend.
9. Appropriated retained earnings.
10. Paid a cash dividend that was previously declared.

Required

Show the effect of each event on the elements of the financial statements using a horizontal statements model like the following one. Use + for increase, − for decrease, and NA for not affected. In the Cash Flow column, indicate whether the item is an operating activity (OA), investing activity (IA), or financing activity (FA). The first transaction is entered as an example.

Event No.	Assets	=	Liab.	+	Equity	Rev.	−	Exp.	=	Net Inc.	Cash Flow
1	+		NA		+	NA		NA		NA	+ FA

LO 11-9

Problem 11-30A *Using accounting information to make investment decisions*

Sea Coast Plumbing Company (SCPC) is a national company that provides residential plumbing services. SCPC is considering making a substantial investment in Rakeland Distributors, Inc. (RDI). RDI sells plumbing supplies throughout the United States.

Required

a. Identify two financial benefits that SCPC could receive from an investment in RDI.
b. What types of information would be helpful in evaluating SCPC's investment opportunity?
c. Speculate as to how owning RDI stock could benefit SCPC's capacity to conduct its operations.

EXERCISES—SERIES B

LO 11-1

Exercise 11-1B *Characteristics of sole proprietorships, partnerships, and corporations*

Required

The three primary types of business organization are proprietorship, partnership, and corporation. Each type has characteristics that distinguish it from the other types. In the left column of the following table, write the name of the type of business organization that is most likely to possess the characteristic that is described in the right column of the table. The first item is shown as an example.

Business Type	Characteristic
Proprietorship	Offers the highest level of control over operating decisions
	The business dissolves with the death of its only owner
	Has a retained earnings account on its balance sheet
	Has two or more owners who are not stockholders
	Profits benefit a single individual
	Frequently uses legal agreements to define profit distribution for two or more owners
	Most highly regulated form of business
	Subject to double taxation
	Has multiple capital accounts but no retained earnings account on its balance sheet
	Provides the best opportunity to benefit a few people
	Has only one capital account on its balance sheet
	Provides for easy transfer of ownership
	Owned and operated by a single individual
	Offers the least capacity to raise capital
	Provides the greatest capacity to raise capital
	Least regulated form of business
	One owner may be held personally liable for actions taken on behalf of the business by a different owner
	Usually operated by a professional management team that is separated from the owners

Exercise 11-2B *Effect of accounting events on the financial statements of a sole proprietorship*   LO 11-1

A sole proprietorship was started on January 1, Year 1, when it received $30,000 cash from Maria Lopez, the owner. During Year 1, the company earned $50,000 in cash revenues and paid $22,300 in cash expenses. Lopez withdrew $10,000 cash from the business during Year 1.

Required

Prepare an income statement, capital statement (statement of changes in equity), balance sheet, and statement of cash flows for Lopez's Year 1 fiscal year.

Exercise 11-3B *Effect of accounting events on the financial statements of a partnership*   LO 11-1

D. Reed and J. Files started the RF partnership on January 1, Year 1. The business acquired $70,000 cash from Reed and $140,000 from Files. During Year 1, the partnership earned $75,000 in cash revenues and paid $39,000 for cash expenses. Reed withdrew $2,000 cash from the business, and Files withdrew $4,000 cash. The net income was allocated to the capital accounts of the two partners in proportion to the amounts of their original investments in the business.

Required

Prepare an income statement, capital statement, balance sheet, and statement of cash flows for the RF partnership for the Year 1 fiscal year.

Exercise 11-4B *Capital stock authorized, issued, and outstanding*   LO 11-2

Bronson Inc. has 300,000 shares authorized, 175,000 shares issued, and 25,000 shares of treasury stock. At this point, Bronson has $820,000 of assets, $250,000 liabilities, $400,000 of common stock, and $170,000 of retained earnings. Further, assume that the market value of Bronson's common stock is $6 per share.

Required

a. Determine the number of shares of stock that is outstanding.
b. Determine the book value per share.
c. Provide a rational explanation for the difference between the book value per share and the market value per share of Bronson Inc. common stock.

LO 11-2

Exercise 11-5B *Characteristics of capital stock*

The stockholders' equity section of Creighton Company's balance sheet is shown as follows:

CREIGHTON COMPANY
As of December 31, Year 3

Stockholders' equity	
Preferred stock, $6 stated value, 6% cumulative,	
250 shares authorized, 100 issued and outstanding	$ 600
Common stock, $6 par value, 200 shares authorized,	
150 issued and outstanding	900
Common stock, class B, $8 par value, 450 shares authorized,	
100 issued and outstanding	800
Common stock, no par, 200 shares authorized,	
150 issued and outstanding	1,800
Paid-in capital in excess of stated value—preferred	400
Paid-in capital in excess of par value—common	900
Paid-in capital in excess of par value—class B common	800
Retained earnings	9,000
Total stockholders' equity	$15,200

Required

a. Assuming the preferred stock was originally issued for cash, determine the amount of cash that was collected when the stock was issued.
b. Based on the class B common stock alone, determine the amount of the company's legal capital.
c. Based on the class B common stock alone, determine the minimum amount of assets that must be retained in the company as protection for creditors.
d. Determine the number of shares of class B common stock that are available to sell as of December 31, Year 3.
e. Assuming Creighton purchases treasury stock consisting of 50 shares of its no par common stock on January 1, Year 4, determine the amount of the no-par common stock that would be outstanding immediately after the purchase.
f. Based on the stockholders' equity section shown earlier, can you determine the market value of the preferred stock? If yes, what is the market value of one share of this stock?

LO 11-3

Exercise 11-6B *Accounting for cumulative preferred dividends*

When Ching Corporation was organized in January Year 1, it immediately issued 10,000 shares of $50 par, 5 percent, cumulative preferred stock and 15,000 shares of $10 par common stock. The company's earnings history is as follows: Year 1, net loss of $18,000; Year 2, net income of $95,000; Year 3, net income of $90,000. The corporation did not pay a dividend in Year 1.

Required

a. How much is the dividend arrearage as of January 1, Year 2?
b. Assume that the board of directors declares a $65,000 cash dividend at the end of Year 2 (remember that the Year 1 and Year 2 preferred dividends are due). How will the dividend be divided between the preferred and common stockholders?

Exercise 11-7B Cash dividends for preferred and common shareholders   LO 11-3

ALR Corporation had the following stock issued and outstanding at January 1, Year 1:

1. 200,000 shares of $10 par common stock.
2. 8,000 shares of $100 par, 4 percent, noncumulative preferred stock.

On May 10, ALR Corporation declared the annual cash dividend on its 8,000 shares of preferred stock and a $0.50 per share dividend for the common shareholders. The dividends will be paid on June 15 to the shareholders of record on May 30.

Required

a. Determine the total amount of dividends to be paid to the preferred shareholders and common shareholders.
b. Prepare general journal entries to record the declaration and payment of the cash dividends (be sure to date your entries).

Exercise 11-8B Effect of issuing common stock on the balance sheet   LO 11-4

Newly formed Irwin Services Corporation has 100,000 shares of $10 par common stock authorized. On March 1, Year 1, Irwin Services issued 20,000 shares of the stock for $12 per share. On May 2, the company issued an additional 30,000 shares for $15 per share. Irwin Services was not affected by other events during Year 1.

Required

a. Record the transactions in a horizontal statements model like the following one. In the Cash Flow column, indicate whether the item is an operating activity (OA), investing activity (IA), or financing activity (FA). Use NA to indicate that an element was not affected by the event.

Assets	=	Liab.	+	Equity		Rev.	−	Exp.	=	Net Inc.		Cash Flow
Cash	=			Com. Stk. + PIC in Excess								

b. Determine the amount Irwin Services would report for common stock on the December 31, Year 1, balance sheet.
c. Determine the amount Irwin Services would report for paid-in capital in excess of par.
d. What is the total amount of capital contributed by the owners?
e. What amount of total assets would Irwin Services report on the December 31, Year 1, balance sheet?
f. Prepare journal entries to record the March 1 and May 2 transactions.

Exercise 11-9B Recording and reporting common and preferred stock transactions   LO 11-4

Reiss Inc. was organized on June 1, Year 1. It was authorized to issue 500,000 shares of $10 par common stock and 100,000 shares of 4 percent cumulative class A preferred stock. The class A stock had a stated value of $50 per share. The following stock transactions pertain to Reiss Inc.:

1. Issued 40,000 shares of common stock for $16 per share.
2. Issued 20,000 shares of the class A preferred stock for $52 per share.
3. Issued 60,000 shares of common stock for $20 per share.

Required

a. Prepare general journal entries for these transactions.
b. Prepare the stockholders' equity section of the balance sheet immediately after these transactions.

LO 11-4

Exercise 11-10B *Effect of no-par common and par preferred stock on the horizontal statements model*

Rice Corporation issued 10,000 shares of no-par common stock for $25 per share. Rice also issued 3,000 shares of $40 par, 6 percent noncumulative preferred stock at $42 per share.

Required

a. Record these events in a horizontal statements model like the following one. In the Cash Flow column, indicate whether the item is an operating activity (OA), investing activity (IA), or financing activity (FA). Use NA to indicate that an element was not affected by the event.

Assets	=	Equity			Rev.	−	Exp.	=	Net Inc.	Cash Flow
Cash	=	Pfd. Stk.	+ Com. Stk.	+ PIC in Excess						

b. Prepare journal entries to record these transactions.

LO 11-4

Exercise 11-11B *Issuing stock for assets other than cash*

Carroll Corporation was formed when it issued shares of common stock to two of its shareholders. Carroll issued 10,000 shares of $5 par common stock to R. Flowler in exchange for $80,000 cash (the issue price was $8 per share). Carroll also issued 3,500 shares of stock to P. Jones in exchange for a one-year-old delivery van on the same day. Jones had originally paid $39,000 for the van.

Required

a. What was the market value of the delivery van on the date of the stock issue?
b. Show the effect of the two stock issues on Carroll's books in a horizontal statements model like the following one. In the Cash Flow column, indicate whether the item is an operating activity (OA), investing activity (IA), or financing activity (FA). Use NA to indicate that an element was not affected by the event.

Assets			=	Equity			Rev.	−	Exp.	=	Net Inc.	Cash Flow
Cash	+	Van	=	Com. Stk.	+	PIC in Excess						

c. Prepare the journal entries to record these transactions.

LO 11-5

Exercise 11-12B *Treasury stock transactions*

Earles Corporation repurchased 4,000 shares of its own stock for $30 per share. The stock has a par value of $10 per share. A month later, Earles resold 2,500 shares of the treasury stock for $35 per share.

Required

a. Record the two events in general journal format.
b. What is the balance of the treasury stock account after these transactions?

LO 11-5

Exercise 11-13B *Recording and reporting treasury stock transactions*

The following information pertains to Ming Corp. at January 1, Year 1:

Common stock, $10 par, 50,000 shares authorized, 3,000 shares issued and outstanding	$30,000
Paid-in capital in excess of par, common stock	12,000
Retained earnings	46,000

Ming Corp. completed the following transactions during Year 1:

1. Issued 2,000 shares of $10 par common stock for $16 per share.
2. Repurchased 500 shares of its own common stock for $18 per share.
3. Resold 120 shares of treasury stock for $20 per share.

Required

a. How many shares of common stock were outstanding at the end of the period?
b. How many shares of common stock had been issued at the end of the period?
c. Prepare journal entries for these transactions and post them to T-accounts.
d. Prepare the stockholders' equity section of the balance sheet reflecting these transactions. Include the number of shares authorized, issued, and outstanding in the description of the common stock.

Exercise 11-14B Effect of cash dividends on financial statements

LO 11-6

On October 1, Year 1, Nicholes Corporation declared a $50,000 cash dividend to be paid on December 15 to shareholders of record on November 1.

Required

a. Record the events occurring on October 1, November 1, and December 15 in a horizontal statements model like the following one. In the Cash Flow column, indicate whether the item is an operating activity (OA), investing activity (IA), or financing activity (FA).

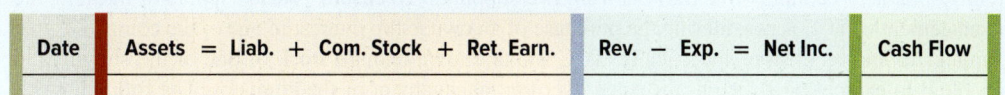

b. Prepare journal entries for all events associated with the dividend.

Exercise 11-15B Accounting for stock dividends

LO 11-7

Egrett Corporation issued a 4 percent stock dividend on 20,000 shares of its $10 par common stock. At the time of the dividend, the market value of the stock was $30 per share.

Required

a. Compute the amount of the stock dividend.
b. Show the effects of the stock dividend on the financial statements using a horizontal statements model like the following one.

c. Prepare the journal entry to record the stock dividend.

Exercise 11-16B Determining the effects of stock splits on the accounting records

LO 11-7

The market value of Granger Corporation's common stock had become excessively high. The stock was currently selling for $240 per share. To reduce the market price of the common stock, Granger declared a 3-for-1 stock split for the 200,000 outstanding shares of its $15 par common stock.

Required

a. How will Granger Corporation's books be affected by the stock split?
b. Determine the number of common shares outstanding and the par value after the split.
c. Explain how the market value of the stock will be affected by the stock split.

LO 11-8

Exercise 11-17B *Determining how the appropriation of retained earnings affects financial statements*

On December 30, Odom Enterprises (OE) had $120,000 of cash, $35,000 of liabilities, $50,000 of common stock, and $35,000 of unrestricted retained earnings. On December 31, OE appropriated retained earnings in the amount of $15,000 for a future remodeling project.

Required

a. Record the December 31 appropriation in the following statements model:

Assets	=	Liab.	+	Stockholders' Equity						Income Statement					Cash Flow
				C. Stk	+	Ret. Earn.	+	App. Ret. Earn.		Rev.	−	Exp.	=	Net Inc.	

b. Determine the amount of dividends that OE can pay immediately after the December 31 appropriation.

c. Determine the total amount of retained earnings immediately after the December 31 appropriation.

d. Determine the total amount of cash immediately after the December 31 appropriation.

LO 11-9

Exercise 11-18B *Accounting information*

The Cutting Edge (TCE) is one of the world's largest lawn mower distributors. TCE is concerned about maintaining an adequate supply of the economy-line mowers that it sells in its stores. TCE currently obtains its economy-line mowers from two suppliers. To ensure a steady supply of mowers, the management of TCE is considering the purchase of an ownership interest in one of the companies that supplies its mowers. More specifically, TCE wants to own enough stock of one of the suppliers to enable it to exercise significant influence over the management of the company. The following is a description of the two suppliers.

The first supplier, Dobbs Incorporated, is a closely held company. Large blocks of the Dobbs stock are held by individual members of the Dobbs family. TCE's investment advisor has discovered that one of the members of the Dobbs family is interested in selling her 5 percent share of the company's stock.

The second supplier, National Mowers Inc., has widely disbursed ownership with no one single stockholder owning more than 1 percent of the stock. TCE's investment advisor believes that 5 percent of this company's stock could be acquired gradually over an extended period of time without having a significant effect on the company's stock price.

Required

Provide a recommendation to TCE's management as to whether, it should pursue the purchase of 5 percent of Dobbs Incorporated, or 5 percent of National Mowers Inc. Your answer should be supported by an explanation of your recommendation.

LO 11-9

Exercise 11-19B *Using the P/E ratio*

Davis, Inc. and Royal, Inc. reported net incomes of $81,000 and $93,000, respectively, for their most recent fiscal years. Both companies had 10,000 shares of common stock issued and outstanding. The market price per share of Davis' stock was $130, while Royal's sold for $120 per share.

Required

a. Determine the P/E ratio for each company. (Round to the nearest whole number.)

b. Based on the P/E ratios computed in requirement *a*, which company do investors believe has the greater potential for growth in income?

LO 11-9

Exercise 11-20B *The P/E ratio*

Pepper Company's earnings were approximately the same in Year 1 and Year 2. Even so, the company's P/E ratio dropped significantly.

Required

Speculate about why Pepper's P/E ratio dropped significantly while its earnings remained constant.

PROBLEMS—SERIES B

Problem 11-21B *Different forms of business organization* LO 11-1

Bill Wheeler established a partnership with June Cramer. The new company, W&C Fuels, purchased coal directly from mining companies and contracted to ship the coal via waterways to a seaport where it was delivered to ships that were owned and operated by international utilities companies. Wheeler was primarily responsible for running the day-to-day operations of the business. Cramer negotiated the buy-and-sell agreements. She recently signed a deal to purchase and deliver $2,000,000 of coal to Solar Utilities. W&C Fuels purchased the coal on account from Miller Mining Company. After accepting title to the coal, W&C Fuels agreed to deliver the coal under terms FOB destination, Port of Long Beach. Unfortunately, Cramer failed to inform Wheeler of the deal in time for Wheeler to insure the shipment. While in transit, the vessel carrying the coal suffered storm damage that rendered the coal virtually worthless by the time it reached its destination. W&C Fuels immediately declared bankruptcy. The company not only was responsible for the $2,000,000 due to Miller Mining Company but also was sued by Solar for breach of contract. Cramer had a personal net worth of virtually zero, but Wheeler was a wealthy individual with a net worth approaching $2,500,000. Accordingly, Miller Mining and Solar filed suit against Wheeler's personal assets. Wheeler claimed that he was not responsible for the problem because Cramer had failed to inform him of the contracts in time to obtain insurance coverage. Cramer admitted that she was personally responsible for the disaster.

Required

Write a memo describing Wheeler's risk associated with his participation in the partnership. Comment on how other forms of ownership would have affected his level of risk.

Problem 11-22B *Effect of business structure on financial statements* LO 11-1

Best Auto Parts Company was started on January 1, Year 1, when the owners invested $120,000 cash in the business. During Year 1, the company earned cash revenues of $80,000 and incurred cash expenses of $56,000. The company also paid cash distributions of $5,000.

Required

Prepare a Year 1 income statement, capital statement (statement of changes in equity), balance sheet, and statement of cash flows using each of the following assumptions. (Consider each assumption separately.)

a. Best Auto Parts is a sole proprietorship owned by J. Smart.

b. Best Auto Parts is a partnership with two partners, Beth Song and J. Smart. Song invested $72,000 and Smart invested $48,000 of the $120,000 cash that was used to start the business. Smart was expected to assume the vast majority of the responsibility for operating the business. The partnership agreement called for Smart to receive 60 percent of the profits and Song the remaining 40 percent. With regard to the $5,000 distribution, Smart withdrew $1,500 from the business and Song withdrew $3,500.

c. Best Auto Parts is a corporation. The owners were issued 10,000 shares of $10 par common stock when they invested the $120,000 cash in the business.

Problem 11-23B *Cash dividends: Common and preferred stock* LO 11-3

Tyler Corp. had the following stock issued and outstanding at January 1, Year 2:

1. 60,000 shares of no-par common stock.
2. 15,000 shares of $100 par, 4 percent, cumulative preferred stock. (Dividends are in arrears for one year, Year 1.)

On February 1, Year 1, Tyler declared a $150,000 cash dividend to be paid March 31 to shareholders of record on March 10.

Required

a. What amount of dividends will be paid to the preferred shareholders versus the common shareholders?

b. Prepare the journal entries required for these transactions. (Be sure to include the dates of the entries.)

LO 11-4, 11-5

Problem 11-24B *Recording and reporting treasury stock transactions*

Edwards Corporation reports the following information in its January 1, Year 1, balance sheet:

> Stockholders' equity
> Common stock, $10 par value, 100,000 shares authorized, 50,000
>   shares issued and outstanding $500,000
> Paid-in capital in excess of par value   150,000
> Retained earnings   120,000
> Total stockholders' equity $770,000

During Year 1, Edwards was affected by the following accounting events:

1. Purchased 2,000 shares of treasury stock at $15 per share.
2. Reissued 1,200 shares of treasury stock at $18 per share.
3. Earned $72,000 of cash revenues.
4. Paid $41,000 of cash operating expenses.

Required

a. Provide journal entries to record these transactions.
b. Prepare the stockholders' equity section of the year-end balance sheet.

LO 11-3, 11-6

Problem 11-25B *Recording and reporting stock transactions and cash dividends across two accounting cycles*

Edgar Corporation was authorized to issue 100,000 shares of $8 par common stock and 50,000 shares of $80 par, 4 percent, cumulative preferred stock. Edgar Corporation completed the following transactions during its first two years of operation:

Year 1

Jan. 2 Issued 25,000 shares of $8 par common stock for $10 per share.
     15 Issued 2,000 shares of $80 par preferred stock for $90 per share.
Feb. 14 Issued 20,000 shares of $8 par common stock for $12 per share.
Dec. 31 During the year, earned $280,000 of cash revenues and paid $165,000 of cash operating expenses.
     31 Declared the cash dividend on outstanding shares of preferred stock for Year 1. The dividend will be paid on January 31 to stockholders of record on January 15, Year 2.
     31 Closed revenue, expense, and dividend accounts to the retained earnings account.

Year 2

Jan. 31 Paid the cash dividend declared on December 31, Year 1.
Mar. 1 Issued 4,000 shares of $80 par preferred stock for $92 per share.
June 1 Purchased 1,000 shares of common stock as treasury stock at $14 per share.
Dec. 31 During the year, earned $185,000 of cash revenues and paid $110,000 of cash operating expenses.
     31 Declared the dividend on the preferred stock and a $1.00 per share dividend on the common stock.
     31 Closed revenue, expense, and dividend accounts to the retained earnings account.

Required

a. Prepare journal entries for these transactions for Year 1 and Year 2 and post them to T-accounts.
b. Prepare the stockholders' equity section of the balance sheet at December 31, Year 1.
c. Prepare the balance sheet at December 31, Year 2.

Problem 11-26B Analyzing the stockholders' equity section of the balance sheet   LO 11-2, 11-3, 11-7

The stockholders' equity section of the balance sheet for Stinson Company at December 31, Year 1, is as follows:

Stockholders' Equity

Paid-in capital	
Preferred stock, ? par value, 5% cumulative, 100,000 shares authorized, 40,000 shares issued and outstanding	$400,000
Common stock, $20 stated value, 150,000 shares authorized, 40,000 shares issued and ? outstanding	800,000
Paid-in capital in excess of par—Preferred	30,000
Paid-in capital in excess of stated value—Common	100,000
Total paid-in capital	$1,330,000
Retained earnings	250,000
Treasury stock, 2,000 shares	(25,000)
Total stockholders' equity	$1,555,000

Note: The market value per share of the common stock is $40, and the market value per share of the preferred stock is $12.

Required

a. What is the par value per share of the preferred stock?
b. What is the dividend per share on the preferred stock?
c. What is the number of common stock shares outstanding?
d. What was the average issue price per share (price for which the stock was issued) of the common stock?
e. Explain the difference between the average issue price and the market price of the common stock.
f. If Stinson declared a 2-for-1 stock split on the common stock, how many shares would be outstanding after the split? What amount would be transferred from the retained earnings account because of the stock split? Theoretically, what would be the market price of the common stock immediately after the stock split?

Problem 11-27B Recording and reporting stock dividends   LO 11-4, 11-6, 11-7

Burk Corp. completed the following transactions in Year 1, the first year of operation:

1. Issued 30,000 shares of $10 par common stock for $15 per share.
2. Issued 6,000 shares of $100 par, 5 percent, preferred stock at $101 per share.
3. Paid the annual cash dividend to preferred shareholders.
4. Issued a 5 percent stock dividend on the common stock. The market value at the dividend declaration date was $19 per share.
5. Later that year, issued a 2-for-1 split on the 31,500 shares of outstanding common stock.
6. Earned $165,000 of cash revenues and paid $98,000 of cash operating expenses.
7. Closed the revenue, expense, and dividend accounts to retained earnings.

Required

a. Record each of these events in a horizontal statements model like the following one. In the Cash Flow column, indicate whether the item is an operating activity (OA), investing activity (IA), or financing activity (FA). Use NA to indicate that an element is not affected by the event.

Assets = Liab. +	Equity	Rev. − Exp. = Net Inc.	Cash Flow
	PIC in PIC in		
Pfd. Stk. + Com. Stk. + Excess PS + Excess CS + Ret. Earn.			

b. Record the Year 1 transactions in general journal form and post them to T-accounts.
c. Prepare the stockholders' equity section of the balance sheet at the end of Year 1.

LO 11-3, 11-4, 11-5, 11-6, 11-8

Problem 11-28B *Recording and reporting treasury stock transactions*

Rabern Corp. completed the following transactions in Year 1, the first year of operation:

1. Issued 15,000 shares of $10 par common stock at par.
2. Issued 5,000 shares of $50 stated value preferred stock at $52 per share.
3. Purchased 800 shares of common stock as treasury stock for $12 per share.
4. Declared a 5 percent cash dividend on preferred stock.
5. Sold 300 shares of treasury stock for $16 per share.
6. Paid the cash dividend on preferred stock that was declared in Event 4.
7. Earned revenue of $80,000 and incurred operating expenses of $48,000.
8. Closed revenue, expense, and dividend accounts to the retained earnings account.
9. Appropriated $6,000 of retained earnings.

Required

a. Prepare journal entries to record these transactions and post them to T-accounts.
b. Prepare the stockholders' equity section of the balance sheet as of December 31, Year 1.

LO 11-3, 11-4, 11-5, 11-6, 11-7, 11-8

Problem 11-29B *Effects of equity transactions on financial statements*

The following events were experienced by Halbart Inc.:

1. Issued common stock for cash.
2. Distributed a 2-for-1 stock split on the common stock.
3. Appropriated retained earnings.
4. Issued cumulative preferred stock for cash.
5. Sold treasury stock for an amount of cash that was more than the cost of the treasury stock.
6. Issued noncumulative preferred stock for cash.
7. Paid cash to purchase treasury stock.
8. Declared a cash dividend.
9. Distributed a stock dividend.
10. Paid the cash dividend declared in Event 8.

Required

Show the effect of each event on the elements of the financial statements using a horizontal statements model like the following one. Use + for increase, − for decrease, and NA for not affected. In the Cash Flow column, indicate whether the item is an operating activity (OA), investing activity (IA), or financing activity (FA). The first transaction is entered as an example.

Event No.	Assets	=	Liab.	+	Equity	Rev.	−	Exp.	=	Net Inc.	Cash Flow
1	+		NA		+	NA		NA		NA	+ FA

LO 11-9

Problem 11-30B *Using accounting information to make investment decisions*

An investor is trying to decide whether to purchase stock in Henderson Inc. or Glover Corporation. Glover Corporation reported annual earnings per share of $8, and the current market price of Glover stock is $64 per share. Henderson Inc. has annual earnings per share of $4, and the current market price for Henderson stock is $84 per share. Based on this information, complete the requirements to assist the investor in making his decision.

Required

a. Determine the P/E ratio for Glover Corporation.
b. Determine the P/E ratio for Henderson Inc.
c. Assume the growth prospects for the two companies are identical. Further, assume both companies plan to distribute all future earnings as cash dividends. Under these circumstances, which company represents the best investment opportunity.

ANALYZE, THINK, COMMUNICATE

ATC 11-1 Business Applications Case *Understanding real-world annual reports*

Obtain the Target Corporation's annual report at http://investors.target.com using the instruction in Appendix B, and use it to answer the following questions:

Required

a. What is the par value per share of Target's stock?
b. How many shares of Target's common stock were *outstanding* as of January 28, 2017?
c. Target's annual report provides some details about the company's executive officers. How many are identified? What is their minimum, maximum, and average age? How many are females?
d. Target's balance sheet does not show a balance for treasury stock. Does this mean the company has not repurchased any of its own stock? Explain.

ATC 11-2 Group Assignment *Missing information*

Listed here are the stockholders' equity sections of three public companies for years ending in 2015 and 2016:

	2016	2015
The Wendy's Company (in thousands)		
Stockholders' equity		
Common stock, ?? par value per share, authorized:		
1,500,000; 470,424 shares issued	$ 47,042	$ 47,042
Additional paid-in capital	2,878,589	2,874,752
Retained earnings	(290,857)	(356,632)
Accumulated other comp. income (loss)	(63,241)	(70,823)
Treasury stock, at cost: 223,850 in 2016 and 198,109 in 2015	(2,043,797)	(1,741,425)
Coca-Cola (in millions)		
Stockholders' equity		
Common stock, ?? par value per share, authorized:		
11,200; issued: 7,040 shares in 2016 and 2015	1,760	1,760
Capital surplus	14,993	14,016
Reinvested earnings	65,502	65,018
Accumulated other comp. inc. (loss)	(11,205)	(10,174)
Treasury stock, at cost: (2,752 shares in 2016 and 2,716 shares in 2015)	(47,988)	(45,066)
General Mills (in millions)		
Stockholders' equity		
Common stock, ?? par value per share, 754.6 issued in 2016 and 2015	75.5	75.5
Additional paid-in capital	1,177.0	1,296.7
Retained earnings	12,616.5	11,990.8
Accumulated other comp. inc. (loss)	(2,612.2)	(2,310.7)
Treasury stock, at cost: 158.7 and 155.9 shares in 2016 and 2015, respectively, at cost	(6,326.6)	(6,055.6)

Required

a. Divide the class in three sections and divide each section into groups of three to five students. Assign each section one of the companies.

Group Tasks

Based on the company assigned to your group, answer the following questions:

b. What is the per share par or stated value of the common stock in 2016?
c. What was the average issue price of the common stock for each year?
d. How many shares of stock are outstanding at the end of each year?
e. What is the average cost per share of the treasury stock for 2016?
f. Do the data suggest that your company was profitable in 2016?
g. Can you determine the amount of net income from the information given? What is missing?
h. What is the total stockholders' equity of your company for each year?

Class Discussion

i. Have each group select a representative to present the information about its company. Compare the share issue price and the par or stated value of the companies.
j. Compare the average issue price to the current market price for each of the companies. Speculate about what might cause the difference.

ATC 11-3 Real-World Case *Which stock is most valuable?*

Listed here are data for five companies. These data are for the companies' 2016 fiscal years. The market price per share is the closing price of the companies' stock as of March 24, 2017. Except for market price per share, all amounts are in thousands. The shares outstanding number is the weighted-average number of shares the company used to compute basic earnings per share.

Company	Net Earnings	Stockholders' Equity	Shares Outstanding	Market Price per Share
Amazon.com	$ 2,371,000	$ 19,285,000	474,000	$ 845.61
Berkshire Hathaway	24,074,000	286,359,000	1,644	252,301.00
ExxonMobil	7,840,000	173,830,000	4,177,000	81.23
PepsiCo	6,323,000	11,199,000	1,439,000	112.12
Verizon Communications	13,127,000	24,032,000	4,080,000	49.68

Required

a. Compute the earnings per share (EPS) for each company.
b. Compute the P/E ratio for each company.
c. Using the P/E ratios, rank the companies' stock in the order that the stock market appears to value the companies, from most valuable to least valuable. Identify reasons the ranking based on P/E ratios may not represent the market's optimism for some companies.
d. Compute the book value per share for each company.
e. Compare each company's book value per share to its market price per share. Based on the data, rank the companies from most valuable to least valuable. (The higher the ratio of market value to book value, the greater the value the stock market appears to be assigning to a company's stock.)

ATC 11-4 Business Applications Case *Performing ratio analysis using real-world data*

Ford Motor Company is one of the world's largest automobile manufacturing companies. The following data were taken from the company's 2016 annual report:

	Fiscal Years Ending	
	December 31, 2016	December 31, 2015
Net earnings (in millions)	$4,596	$7,373
Earnings per share	$ 1.16	$ 1.86
The following data were taken from public stock-price quotes:		
Stock price per share on February 27, 2017 (Two months after the end of Ford's 2016 fiscal year.)		$12.65
Stock price per share on February 29, 2016 (Two months after the end of Ford's 2015 fiscal year.)		$13.59

Required

a. Compute Ford's price-earnings ratio for February 27, 2017, and February 29, 2016.

b. Did the financial markets appear to be more optimistic about Ford's future performance on February 27, 2017, or February 29, 2016?

c. Based on the information provided, estimate approximately how many shares of stock Ford had outstanding as of December 31, 2016.

ATC 11-5 Business Applications Case *Performing ratio analysis using real-world data*

There were 36,899 McDonald's Company restaurants in 120 countries as of December 31, 2016. Shake Shack, Inc., a much newer fast-food restaurant company, began operations as a hot dog cart in 2001. It incorporated on September 23, 2014, and had it initial public offering of stock on February 4, 2015. As of December 31, 2016, it had 114 restaurants operating in 16 states and 13 countries. The following data were taken from the companies' December 31, 2016, annual reports:

	McDonald's	Shake Shack
Net earnings (in thousands)	$4,686,500	$12,446
Earnings per share	$ 5.49	$ 0.54
The following data were taken from public stock-price quotes:		
Stock price per share on February 27, 2017 (Two months after the end of their 2016 fiscal years.)	$ 126.99	$ 36.75

Required

a. Compute the price-earnings ratios for each company as of February 27, 2017.

b. Which company's future performance did the financial markets appear to be more optimistic about as of February 27, 2017?

c. Provide some reasons why the market may view one company's future more optimistically than the other.

ATC 11-6 Writing Assignment *Comparison of organizational forms*

Jim Baku and Scott Hanson are thinking about opening a new restaurant. Baku has extensive marketing experience but does not know that much about food preparation. However, Hanson is an excellent chef. Both will work in the business, but Baku will provide most of the funds necessary to start the business. At this time, they cannot decide whether to operate the business as a partnership or a corporation.

Required

Prepare a written memo to Baku and Hanson describing the advantages and disadvantages of each organizational form. Also, from the limited information provided, recommend the organizational form you think they should use.

ATC 11-7 Ethical Dilemma *Bad news versus very bad news*

Louise Stinson, the chief financial officer of Bostonian Corporation, was on her way to the president's office. She was carrying the latest round of bad news. There would be no executive bonuses this year. Corporate profits were down. Indeed, if the latest projections held true, the company would report a small loss on the year-end income statement. Executive bonuses were tied to corporate profits. The executive compensation plan provided for 10 percent of net earnings to be set aside for bonuses. No profits meant no bonuses. While things looked bleak, Stinson had a plan that might help soften the blow.

After informing the company president of the earnings forecast, Stinson made the following suggestion: Because the company was going to report a loss anyway, why not report a big loss? She reasoned that the directors and stockholders would not be much angrier if the company reported a large loss than if it reported a small one. There were several questionable assets that could be written down in the current year. This would increase the current year's loss but would reduce expenses in subsequent accounting periods. For example, the company was carrying damaged inventory that was estimated to have a value of $2,500,000. If this estimate were revised to $500,000, the company would have to recognize a $2,000,000 loss in the current year. However, next year when the goods were sold, the expense for cost of goods sold would be $2,000,000 less and profits would be higher by that amount. Although the directors would be angry this year, they would certainly be happy next year. The strategy would also have the benefit of adding $200,000 to next year's executive bonus pool ($2,000,000 × 0.10). Furthermore, it could not hurt this year's bonus pool because there would be no pool this year due to the company reporting a loss.

Some of the other items that Stinson is considering include (1) converting from straight-line to accelerated depreciation, (2) increasing the percentage of receivables estimated to be uncollectible in the current year and lowering the percentage in the following year, and (3) raising the percentage of estimated warranty claims in the current period and lowering it in the following period. Finally, Stinson notes that two of the company's department stores have been experiencing losses. The company could sell these stores this year and thereby improve earnings next year. Stinson admits that the sale would result in significant losses this year, but she smiles as she thinks of next year's bonus check.

Required

a. Explain how each of the three numbered strategies for increasing the amount of the current year's loss would affect the stockholders' equity section of the balance sheet in the current year. How would the other elements of the balance sheet be affected?

b. If Stinson's strategy were effectively implemented, how would it affect the stockholders' equity in subsequent accounting periods?

c. Comment on the ethical implications of running the company for the sake of management (maximization of bonuses) versus the maximization of return to stockholders.

d. Formulate a bonus plan that will motivate managers to maximize the value of the firm instead of motivating them to manipulate the reporting process.

e. How would Stinson's strategy of overstating the amount of the reported loss in the current year affect the company's current P/E ratio?

ATC 11-8 Research Assignment *Analyzing Starbucks' equity structure*

Using either Starbucks Corporation's most current Form 10-K or the company's annual report, answer the following questions. To obtain the Form 10-K, use either the EDGAR system, following the instructions in Appendix A, or the company's website. The company's annual report is available on its website.

Required

a. What is the *book value* of Starbucks' stockholders' equity that is shown on the company's balance sheet? What is its book value per share?

b. What is the par value of Starbucks' common stock?

c. Does Starbucks have any treasury stock? If so, how many shares of treasury stock does the company hold?

d. Why does the stock of a company such as Starbucks have a market value that is higher than its book value?

ATC 11-9 Spreadsheet Assignment *Using Excel*

Annette's Accessories had the following stock issued and outstanding at January 1, 2016:

> 150,000 shares of $1 par common stock
> 10,000 shares of $50 par, 8%, cumulative preferred stock

On March 5, 2016, Annette's declared a $100,000 cash dividend to be paid March 31 to shareholders of record on March 21.

Required

Set up a spreadsheet to calculate the total amount of dividends to be paid to preferred and common shareholders under the following alternative situations:

a. No dividends are in arrears for preferred shareholders.
b. One year's worth of dividends is in arrears for preferred shareholders.
c. Two years' worth of dividends is in arrears for preferred shareholders.
d. Instead of a $100,000 dividend, Annette's paid a $70,000 dividend and one year of dividends was in arrears.

Spreadsheet Tips

The following spreadsheet provides one method of setting up formulas for all possible alternatives. The spreadsheet also reflects the results of requirement *a*.

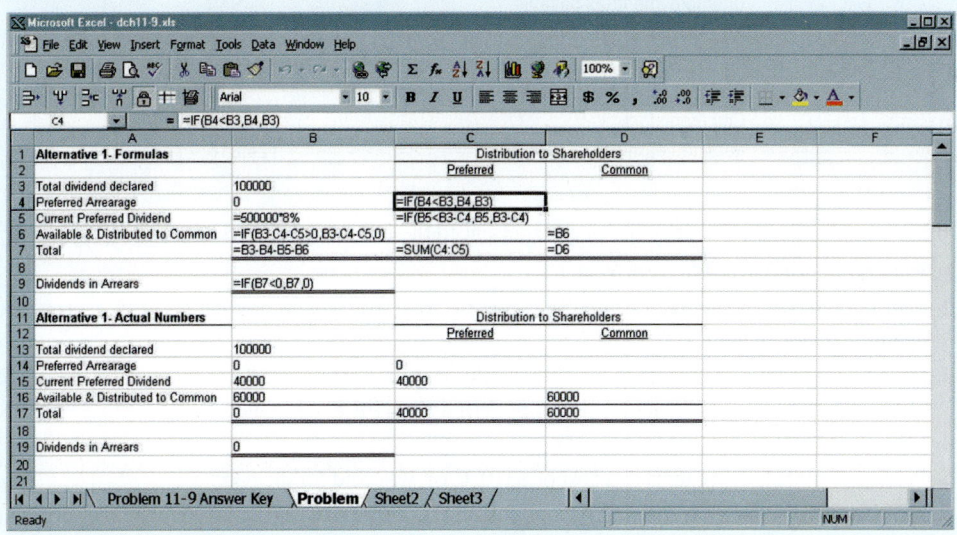

Source: Microsoft Office Excel 1997

Notice the use of the IF function. The IF function looks like =IF(condition, true, false). To use the IF function, first describe a certain condition to Excel. Next, indicate the desired result if that condition is found to be true. Finally, indicate the desired result if that condition is found to be false. Notice in cell C4 of the spreadsheet (dividends in arrears distributed to preferred shareholders) that the condition provided is B4<B3, which is asking whether the dividends in arrears are less than the total dividend. If this condition is true, the formula indicates to display B4, which is the amount of the dividends in arrears. If the condition is false, the formula indicates that B3 should be displayed, which is the total amount of the dividend.

The IF function can also be used to determine the amount of the current dividend distributed to preferred shareholders, the amount available for common shareholders, and the dividends in arrears after the dividend.

ATC 11-10 Spreadsheet Assignment *Mastering Excel*

Required

Complete requirement *a* of Problem 11-22A using an Excel spreadsheet.

COMPREHENSIVE PROBLEM

The trial balance of Pacilio Security Services, Inc. as of January 1, Year 11, had the following normal balances:

Cash	$113,718
Petty cash	100
Accounts receivable	39,390
Allowance for doubtful accounts	4,662
Supplies	210
Merchandise inventory (48 @ $300)	14,400
Equipment	9,000
Van	27,000
Building	125,000
Accumulated depreciation	28,075
Land	25,000
Sales tax payable	390
Employee income tax payable	1,000
FICA—Social Security tax payable	840
FICA—Medicare tax payable	210
Warranty payable	918
Unemployment tax payable	945
Notes payable—Building	92,762
Bonds payable	50,000
Discount on bonds payable	800
Common stock	50,000
Retained earnings	124,816

During Year 11, Pacilio Security Services experienced the following transactions:

1. Paid the sales tax payable from Year 10.
2. Paid the balance of the payroll liabilities due for Year 10 (federal income tax, FICA taxes, and unemployment taxes).
3. Issued 5,000 additional shares of the $5 par value common stock for $8 per share and 1,000 shares of $50 stated value, 5 percent cumulative preferred stock for $52 per share.
4. Purchased $500 of supplies on account.
5. Purchased 190 alarm systems at a cost of $310. Cash was paid for the purchase.
6. After numerous attempts to collect from customers, wrote off $3,670 of uncollectible accounts receivable.
7. Sold 210 alarm systems for $600 each plus sales tax of 5 percent. All sales were on account. (Be sure to compute cost of goods sold using the FIFO cost flow method.)
8. Billed $125,000 of monitoring services for the year. Credit card sales amounted to $58,000, and the credit card company charged a 4 percent fee. The remaining $67,000 were sales on account. Sales tax is not charged on this service.
9. Replenished the petty cash fund on June 30. The fund had $10 cash and receipts of $75 for yard mowing and $15 for office supplies expense.
10. Collected the amount due from the credit card company.
11. Paid the sales tax collected on $105,000 of the alarm sales.

12. Collected $198,000 of accounts receivable during the year.
13. Paid installers and other employees a total of $96,000 for salaries for the year. Assume the Social Security tax rate is 6 percent and the Medicare tax rate is 1.5 percent. Federal income taxes withheld amounted to $10,600. No employee exceeded $127,200 in total wages. The net salaries were paid in cash.
14. On October 1, declared a dividend on the preferred stock and a $1 per share dividend on the common stock to be paid to shareholders of record on October 15, payable on November 1, Year 11.
15. Paid $1,625 in warranty repairs during the year.
16. On November 1, Year 11, paid the dividends that had been previously declared.
17. Paid $18,500 of advertising expense during the year.
18. Paid $6,100 of utilities expense for the year.
19. Paid the payroll liabilities, both the amounts withheld from the salaries plus the employer share of Social Security tax and Medicare tax, on $88,000 of the salaries plus $9,200 of the federal income tax that was withheld.
20. Paid the accounts payable.
21. Paid bond interest and amortized the discount. The bond was issued in Year 10 and pays interest at 6 percent.
22. Paid the annual installment of $14,238 on the amortized note. The interest rate for the note is 7 percent.

Adjustments

23. There was $190 of supplies on hand at the end of the year.
24. Recognized the uncollectible accounts expense for the year using the allowance method. Pacilio now estimates that 1 percent of sales on account will not be collected.
25. Recognized depreciation expense on the equipment, van, and building. The equipment, purchased in Year 8, has a 5-year life and a $2,000 salvage value. The van has a 4-year life and a $6,000 salvage value. The building has a 40-year life and a $10,000 salvage value. The company uses straight-line for the equipment and the building. The van is fully depreciated.
26. The alarm systems sold in transaction 7 were covered with a one-year warranty. Pacilio estimated that the warranty cost would be 2 percent of alarm sales.
27. The unemployment tax on the three employees has not been paid. Record the accrued unemployment tax on the salaries for the year. The unemployment tax rate is 4.5 percent and gross wages for all three employees exceeded $7,000.
28. Recognized the employer Social Security and Medicare payroll tax that has not been paid on $8,000 of salaries expense.

Required

a. Record the preceding transactions in general journal form. Round all amounts to the nearest whole dollar.
b. Post the transactions to the T-accounts.
c. Prepare a trial balance.
d. Prepare an income statement, a balance sheet, and a statement of cash flows.
e. Close the temporary accounts to retained earnings.
f. Post the closing entries to the T-accounts and prepare a post-closing trial balance.

CHAPTER 12

Statement of Cash Flows

LEARNING OBJECTIVES

After you have mastered the material in this chapter, you will be able to:

LO 12-1 Prepare the operating activities section of a statement of cash flows using the indirect method.

LO 12-2 Prepare the operating activities section of a statement of cash flows using the direct method.

LO 12-3 Prepare the investing activities section of a statement of cash flows.

LO 12-4 Prepare the financing activities section of a statement of cash flows.

 Video lectures and accompanying self-assessment quizzes are available in Connect *for all learning objectives.*

CHAPTER OPENING

To make informed investment and credit decisions, financial statement users need information to help them assess the amounts, timing, and uncertainty of a company's prospective cash flows. This chapter explains more about the items reported on the statement of cash flows and describes a more practical way to prepare the statement than analyzing every entry in the cash account. As previously shown, the statement of cash flows reports how a company obtained and spent cash during an accounting period. Sources of cash are **cash inflows,** and uses are **cash outflows.** Cash receipts (inflows) and payments (outflows) are reported as either operating activities, investing activities, or financing activities.

The Curious Accountant

As described in The Curious Accountant for Chapter 11, **Snap, Inc.** began operations in 2010 and began selling its stock to the public on March 2, 2017. It has lost money every year it has been in existence. In 2016 alone, its losses were $515 million, and by December 31, 2016, it had total lifetime losses of approximately $2.3 billion.

How could Snap lose so much money and still be able to pay its bills? (Answers on page 653.)

©NYCStock/Shutterstock

AN OVERVIEW OF THE STATEMENT OF CASH FLOWS

The statement of cash flows provides information about cash coming into and going out of a business during an accounting period. Cash flows are classified into one of three categories: operating activities, investing activities, or financing activities. A separate section also displays any significant noncash investing and financing activities. Descriptions of these categories and how they are presented in the statement of cash flows follow.

Operating Activities

Routine cash inflows and outflows resulting from running (operating) a business are reported in the **operating activities** section of the statement of cash flows. Cash flows reported as operating activities include:

1. Cash receipts from revenues, including interest and dividend revenue.
2. Cash payments for expenses, including interest expense. Recall that dividend payments are not expenses. Dividend payments are reported in the financing activities section.

Under generally accepted accounting principles, the operating activities section of the statement of cash flows can be presented using either the *direct* or the *indirect* method. The **direct method** explicitly (*directly*) identifies the major *sources* and *uses* of cash. To illustrate, assume that, during Year 1, New South Company earns revenue on account of $500 and collects $400 cash from customers. Further assume the company incurs $390 of expenses on account and pays $350 cash to settle accounts payable. Exhibit 12.1 shows the operating activities section of the statement of cash flows using the *direct method*.

EXHIBIT 12.1

Operating Activities—Direct Method

Cash Flows from Operating Activities	
Cash receipts from customers	$400
Cash payments for expenses	(350)
Net cash flow from operating activities	$ 50

In contrast, the **indirect method** starts with net income as reported on the income statement, followed by the adjustments necessary to convert the accrual-based net income figure to a cash-basis equivalent. To illustrate, begin with New South Company's income statement based on the earlier assumptions:

Revenues	$500
Expenses	(390)
Net income	$110

Converting the net income of $110 to the net cash flow from operating activities of $50 requires the following adjustments:

1. New South earned $500 of revenue but collected only $400 in cash. The remaining $100 will be collected in the next accounting period. This $100 *increase in accounts receivable* must be *subtracted* from net income to determine cash flow because it increased net income but did not increase cash.
2. New South incurred $390 of expense but paid only $350 in cash. The remaining $40 will be paid in the next accounting period. This $40 *increase in accounts payable* must be *added* back to net income to determine cash flow because it decreased net income but did not use cash.

Exhibit 12.2 shows the operating activities section of the statement of cash flows using the *indirect method*.

Compare the direct method presented in Exhibit 12.1 with the indirect method presented in Exhibit 12.2. Both methods report $50 of net cash flow from operating activities. They represent two different approaches to computing the same amount.

EXHIBIT 12.2

Operating Activities—Indirect Method

Cash Flows from Operating Activities	
Net income	$110
Subtract: Increase in accounts receivable	(100)
Add: Increase in accounts payable	40
Net cash flow from operating activities	$ 50

Because people typically find the direct method easier to understand, the Financial Accounting Standards Board (FASB) recommends it. Most companies, however, use the indirect method. Why? Back when the FASB adopted a requirement for companies to include a statement of cash flows in their published financial statements, most companies used accounting systems that were compatible with the indirect method. It was therefore easier to prepare the new statement under the indirect method using existing systems than to create new recordkeeping systems compatible with the direct method.

The FASB continues to advocate the direct method and a growing number of companies use it. Because the majority of companies continue to use the indirect method, however, financial statement users should understand both methods.

✓ CHECK YOURSELF 12.1

Hammer, Inc. had a beginning balance of $22,400 in its Accounts Receivable account. During the accounting period, Hammer earned $234,700 of net income. The ending balance in the Accounts Receivable account was $18,200. Based on this information alone, determine the amount of cash flow from operating activities.

Answer

Account Title	Ending	Beginning	Change
Accounts receivable	$18,200	$22,400	$(4,200)

Applicable Rule	Cash Flow from Operating Activities	Amount
Rule 1	Net Income	$234,700
	Add: Decrease in accounts receivable	4,200
	Cash flow from operating activities	$238,900

Investing Activities

For a business, long-term assets are investments. Cash flows related to acquiring or disposing of long-term assets are therefore reported in the **investing activities** section of the statement of cash flows. Cash flows reported as investing activities include:

1. Cash receipts (inflows) from selling property, plant, equipment, or marketable securities, as well as collections from credit instruments such as notes or mortgages receivable.
2. Cash payments (outflows) for purchasing property, plant, equipment, or marketable securities, as well as for making loans to borrowers.

Financing Activities

Cash flows related to borrowing (short- or long-term) and stockholders' equity are reported in the **financing activities** section of the statement of cash flows. Cash flows reported as financing activities include:

1. Cash receipts (inflows) from borrowing money and issuing stock.
2. Cash payments (outflows) to repay debt, purchase treasury stock, and pay dividends.

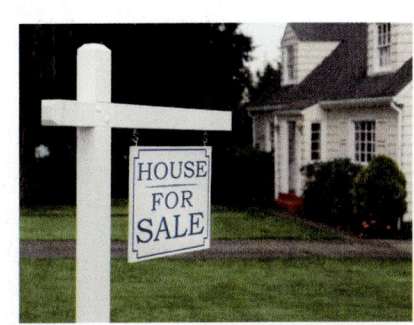
©Ryan McVay/Getty Images

The classification of cash flows is based on the type of activity, not the type of account. For example, buying another company's common stock is an investing activity, but issuing a company's own common stock is a financing activity. Receiving dividends from a common stock investment is an operating activity, and paying dividends to a company's own stockholders is a financing activity. Similarly, loaning money is an investing activity, although borrowing it is a financing activity. Focus on the type of activity rather than the type of account when classifying cash flows as operating, investing, or financing activities.

Noncash Investing and Financing Activities

Companies sometimes undertake significant **noncash investing and financing activities** such as acquiring a long-term asset in exchange for common stock. Because these types of transactions do not involve exchanging cash, they are not reported in the main body of the statement of cash flows. However, because the FASB requires that all material investing and financing activities be disclosed, whether or not they involve exchanging cash, companies must include with the statement of cash flows a separate schedule of any noncash investing and financing activities.

Reporting Format for the Statement of Cash Flows

Cash flow categories are reported in the following order: (1) operating activities, (2) investing activities, and (3) financing activities. In each category, the difference between the inflows and outflows is presented as a net cash inflow or outflow for the category. These net amounts are combined to determine the net change (increase or decrease) in the company's cash for the period. The net change in cash is combined with the beginning cash balance to determine the ending cash balance. The ending cash balance on the statement of cash flows is the same as the cash balance reported on the balance sheet. The schedule of noncash investing and financing activities is typically presented at the bottom of the statement of cash flows. Exhibit 12.3 outlines this format.

EXHIBIT 12.3 Format for Statement of Cash Flows

WESTERN COMPANY
Statement of Cash Flows
For the Year Ended December 31, Year 5

Cash flows from operating activities	
Net cash flow from operating activities	XXX
Cash flows from investing activities	
Net cash flow from investing activities	XXX
Cash flows from financing activities	
Net cash flow from financing activities	XXX
Net increase (decrease) in cash	XXX
Plus: Beginning cash balance	XXX
Ending cash balance	XXX
Schedule of Noncash Investing and Financing Activities	
List of significant noncash transactions	XXX

As indicated in Exhibit 12.4, 50% of the companies that make up the Dow Jones Industrial Average show the statement of cash flows as the third statement presented, with the remaining 50% presenting it as the fourth statement. However, a sizable number of companies present it after the income statement and balance sheet but before the statement of changes in stockholders' equity. Some companies place the statement of cash flows first, before the other three statements.

EXHIBIT 12.4

Placement of Statement of Cash Flows Relative to Other Financial Statements

Presented as the fourth statement — 50%

Presented as the third statement — 50%

Source: This chart is based on data drawn from recent annual reports published by the 30 companies that comprise the Dow Jones Industrial Average.

PREPARING A STATEMENT OF CASH FLOWS

Most of the data needed to construct a statement of cash flows can be obtained from two successive balance sheets and the intervening income statement. Certain information from the long-term asset records is also usually required. To illustrate, refer to the financial statements for New South Company presented in Exhibit 12.5. Notice that cash decreased from $400 at the end of Year 1 to $300 at the end of Year 2. The statement of cash flows explains what caused this $100 decrease.

EXHIBIT 12.5 — Financial Statements for New South Company

NEW SOUTH COMPANY
Balance Sheets
As of December 31

	Year 2	Year 1
Current assets:		
Cash	$ 300	$ 400
Accounts receivable	1,000	1,200
Interest receivable	400	300
Inventory	8,900	8,200
Prepaid insurance	1,100	1,400
Total current assets	11,700	11,500
Long-term assets		
Investment securities	5,100	3,500
Store fixtures	5,400	4,800
Accumulated depreciation	(900)	(1,200)
Land	8,200	6,000
Total long-term assets	17,800	13,100
Total assets	$29,500	$24,600
Current liabilities:		
Accounts payable—inventory purchases	$ 800	$ 1,100
Salaries payable	1,000	900
Other operating expenses payable	1,500	1,300
Interest payable	300	500
Unearned rent revenue	600	1,600
Total current liabilities	4,200	5,400

continued

EXHIBIT 12.5 Concluded

NEW SOUTH COMPANY
Balance Sheets
As of December 31

	Year 2	Year 1
Long-term liabilities		
Mortgage payable	2,200	0
Bonds payable	1,000	4,000
Total long-term liabilities	3,200	4,000
Stockholders' equity		
Common stock	10,000	8,000
Retained earnings	12,700	7,200
Treasury stock	(600)	0
Total stockholders' equity	22,100	15,200
Total liabilities and stockholders' equity	$29,500	$24,600

NEW SOUTH COMPANY
Income Statement
For the Year Ended December 31, Year 2

Sales revenue		$ 20,600
Cost of goods sold		(10,500)
Gross margin		10,100
Operating expenses		
Depreciation expense	$(1,000)	
Salaries expense	(2,700)	
Insurance expense	(1,300)	
Other operating expenses	(1,400)	
Total operating expenses		(6,400)
Income from sales business		3,700
Other income—rent revenue		2,400
Operating income		6,100
Nonoperating revenue and expense		
Interest revenue	700	
Interest expense	(400)	
Gain on sale of store fixtures	600	
Total nonoperating items		900
Net income		$ 7,000

Note 1: No investment securities were sold during Year 2.

Note 2: During Year 2, New South sold store fixtures that had originally cost $1,700. At the time of sale, accumulated depreciation on the fixtures was $1,300.

Note 3: Land was acquired during Year 2 by issuing a mortgage note payable. No land sales occurred during Year 2.

PREPARING THE OPERATING ACTIVITIES SECTION OF A STATEMENT OF CASH FLOWS USING THE INDIRECT METHOD

LO 12-1

Prepare the operating activities section of a statement of cash flows using the indirect method.

Recall that the indirect approach begins with the amount of net income. Many aspects of accrual accounting, such as recognizing revenues and expenses on account, can cause differences between the amount of net income reported on a company's income statement and the amount of net cash flow it reports from operating activities. Most of the differences between

Answers to The Curious Accountant

First, it should be remembered that GAAP requires earnings and losses be computed on an accrual basis. A company can have negative earnings and still have positive cash flows from operating activities. This was not the case at **Snap**. For 2015 and 2016, the company's cash flows from operating activities totaled a negative $918 million. Negative cash flows do not pay the bills.

In its early years of operations, Snap, like many new companies, was able to stay in business because of the cash it raised through financing activities. Obviously, a company cannot operate indefinitely without generating cash from operating activities. Individuals and institutions who are willing to buy a company's stock or loan it cash in its early years will disappear if they do not believe the company will eventually begin earning profits and generating positive cash flows from operations. Exhibit 12.6 presents Snap's statements of cash flows for 2015 and 2016.

EXHIBIT 12.6

SNAP, INC.
Consolidated Statements of Cash Flows (partial)
(in thousands)

	Year Ended December 31	
	2016	**2015**
Cash flows from operating activities		
Net loss	$ (514,643)	$(372,893)
Adjustments to reconcile net loss to net cash used in operating activities:		
Depreciation and amortization	29,115	15,307
Stock-based compensation expense	31,842	73,524
Deferred income taxes	(7,952)	(7,700)
Other	889	626
Changes in operating assets and liabilities, net of effect of acquisitions:		
Accounts receivable, net of allowance	(118,434)	(41,905)
Prepaid expenses and other current assets	(20,521)	(6,590)
Other assets	(5,064)	(4,451)
Accounts payable	6,486	(6,724)
Accrued expenses and other current liabilities	(19,728)	40,026
Other liabilities	6,765	4,158
Net cash used in operating activities	(611,245)	(306,622)
Cash flows from investing activities		
Purchases of property and equipment	(66,441)	(19,205)
Purchases of intangible assets	(572)	(9,100)
Non-marketable investments	(6,513)	(9,551)
Cash paid for acquisitions, net of cash acquired	(104,001)	(48,730)
Issuance of notes receivables from officers/stockholders	(15,000)	(7,500)
Repayment of notes receivables from officers/stockholders	15,000	—
Purchases of marketable securities	(1,565,347)	—
Sales of marketable securities	195,898	—
Maturities of marketable securities	532,690	—
Change in restricted cash	(7,048)	(1,856)
Other investing activities	—	(5,000)
Net cash used in investing activities	(1,021,334)	(100,942)

continued

EXHIBIT 12.6 Concluded

SNAP, INC.
Consolidated Statements of Cash Flows (partial)
(in thousands)

	Year Ended December 31	
	2016	2015
Cash flows from financing activities		
Proceeds from the exercise of stock options	731	60
Repurchase of Class B voting common stock and Series FP preferred stock	(10,593)	(1,000)
Proceeds from issuances of preferred stock, net of issuance costs	1,157,147	651,306
Borrowings from revolving credit facility	5,000	—
Principle payments on revolving credit facility	(5,000)	—
Payments of deferred offering costs	(5,395)	—
Net cash provided by financing activities	1,141,890	650,366
Changes in cash and cash equivalents	(490,689)	242,802
Cash and cash equivalents, beginning of period	640,810	398,008
Cash and cash equivalents, end of period	$ 150,121	$ 640,810

revenue and expense recognition and cash flows are related to changes in the balances of the noncash current assets and current liabilities.

Indirect Method—Reconciliation Approach

The following section of this chapter examines the relationships between items reported on the income statement and the related assets and liabilities. Begin by reconciling the *noncash current asset and current liability amounts* shown on the balance sheets in Exhibit 12.5. *Do not include Cash in this analysis.* The amount of the change in the cash balance is the result of not only operating activities but also investing and financing activities.

Reconciliation of Accounts Receivable

Use the information in Exhibit 12.5 to prepare the following reconciliation of Accounts Receivable. The beginning and ending balances appear on the balance sheets. The *increase due to revenue recognized on account* is the sales revenue reported on the income statement.

Table 1 Reconciliation of Accounts Receivable

Beginning balance	$ 1,200
Increase due to revenue recognized on account	20,600
Decrease due to cash collections from customers	? = (20,800)
Ending balance	$ 1,000

$200 Decrease

To balance Accounts Receivable, the *decrease due to cash collections from customers* must be $20,800.[1]

The reconciliation shows that the $200 decrease in the accounts receivable balance occurred because *cash collections from customers* were $200 more than the amount of *revenue recognized on account* ($20,800 versus $20,600). Because the amount of cash collected is

---

[1]This text uses the simplifying assumption that all sales occur on account.

more than the amount of revenue recognized, we add $200 to the amount of net income to determine net cash flow from operating activities (Reference No. 1 in Exhibit 12.7).

Reconciliation of Interest Receivable

The beginning and ending balances appear on the balance sheets in Exhibit 12.5. The *increase due to interest revenue recognized on account* is the interest revenue reported on the income statement.

Table 2 Reconciliation of Interest Receivable

Beginning balance	$300
Increase due to interest revenue recognized on account	700
Decrease due to cash collections of interest receivable	? = (600)
Ending balance	$400

To balance Interest Receivable, the *decrease due to cash collections of interest receivable* must be $600.

The reconciliation shows that the $100 increase in the interest receivable balance occurred because *cash collections of interest* were $100 less than the *interest revenue recognized on account* ($600 versus $700). Because the amount of cash collected is less than the amount of revenue recognized, we subtract the $100 from the amount of net income to determine net cash flow from operating activities (Reference No. 2 in Exhibit 12.7).

Reconciliation of Inventory and Accounts Payable

To simplify computing the amount of cash paid for inventory purchases, assume that all inventory purchases are made on account. The computation requires two steps. First, Inventory must be analyzed to determine the amount of inventory purchased. Second, Accounts Payable must be analyzed to determine the amount of cash paid to purchase inventory.

Use the financial statement information in Exhibit 12.5 to prepare the following Inventory reconciliation. The beginning and ending balances appear on the balance sheets. The *decrease due to recognizing cost of goods sold* is the cost of goods sold reported on the income statement.

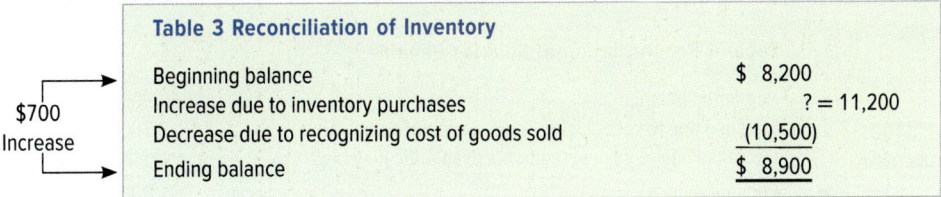

Table 3 Reconciliation of Inventory

Beginning balance	$ 8,200
Increase due to inventory purchases	? = 11,200
Decrease due to recognizing cost of goods sold	(10,500)
Ending balance	$ 8,900

To balance Inventory, the *increase due to inventory purchases* must be $11,200.

Assuming the inventory was purchased on account, the $11,200 of inventory purchases determined earlier equals the *increase due to inventory purchases* used in the reconciliation of Accounts Payable below. The beginning and ending balances appear on the balance sheets in Exhibit 12.5.

Table 4 Reconciliation of Accounts Payable*

Beginning balance	$ 1,100
Increase due to inventory purchases	11,200
Decrease due to cash settlements of accounts payable—inv.	? = (11,500)
Ending balance	$ 800

*Assume that Accounts Payable is used for purchases of inventory only.

To balance Accounts Payable, the *decrease due to cash settlements of accounts payable—inventory* (cash paid to purchase inventory) must be $11,500.

Because the amount of *cash paid to purchase inventory* is $1,000 more than the amount of *cost of goods sold* recognized on the income statement ($11,500 versus $10,500), we subtract the $1,000 difference from the amount of net income to determine net cash flow from operating activities. In Exhibit 12.7, the $1,000 subtraction is divided between a $700 increase in inventory (Reference No. 3 in Exhibit 12.7) and a $300 decrease in accounts payable (Reference No. 4 in Exhibit 12.7).

Reconciliation of Prepaid Insurance

Use the financial statement information in Exhibit 12.5 to reconcile Prepaid Insurance. The beginning and ending balances appear on the balance sheets. The *decrease due to recognizing insurance expense* is the insurance expense reported on the income statement.

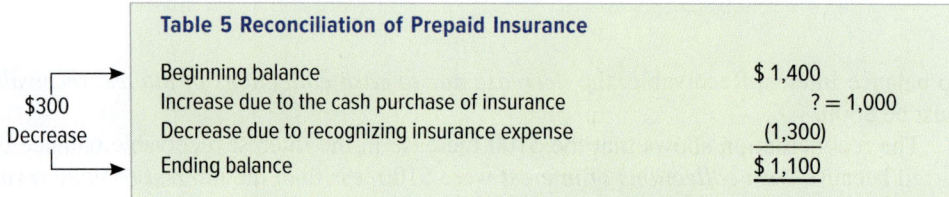

Table 5 Reconciliation of Prepaid Insurance

Beginning balance	$ 1,400
Increase due to the cash purchase of insurance	? = 1,000
Decrease due to recognizing insurance expense	(1,300)
Ending balance	$ 1,100

To balance Prepaid Insurance, the amount of the *increase due to the cash purchase of insurance* must be $1,000.

The reconciliation shows that the $300 decrease in the prepaid insurance balance occurred because *cash paid to purchase insurance* was $300 less than the amount of *insurance expense recognized* ($1,000 versus $1,300). Because the amount of cash paid is less than the amount of expense recognized, we add $300 to the amount of net income to determine the net cash flow from operating activities (Reference No. 5 in Exhibit 12.7).

Reconciliation of Salaries Payable

Use the financial statement information in Exhibit 12.5 to reconcile Salaries Payable. The beginning and ending balances appear on the balance sheets. The *increase due to recognizing salary expense on account* is the salaries expense reported on the income statement.

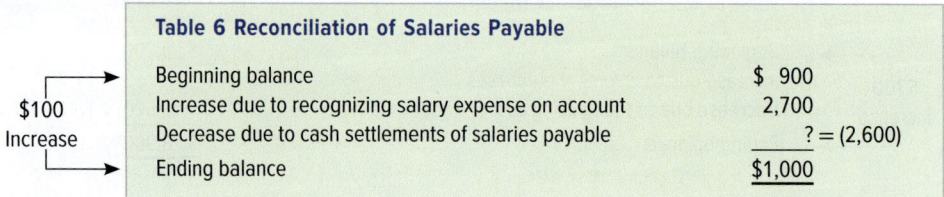

Table 6 Reconciliation of Salaries Payable

Beginning balance	$ 900
Increase due to recognizing salary expense on account	2,700
Decrease due to cash settlements of salaries payable	? = (2,600)
Ending balance	$1,000

To balance Salaries Payable, the amount of the *decrease due to cash settlements of salaries payable* (cash paid for salaries expense) must be $2,600. The reconciliation shows that the $100 increase in the salaries payable balance occurred because the *cash paid for salary expense* is $100 less than the amount of *salary expense recognized on account* ($2,600 versus $2,700). Because the amount of cash paid is less than the amount of expense recognized, we add $100 to the amount of net income to determine the cash flow from operating activities (Reference No. 6 in Exhibit 12.7).

Reconciliation of Other Operating Expenses Payable

Use the financial statement information in Exhibit 12.5 to reconcile Other Operating Expenses Payable. The beginning and ending balances appear on the balance sheets. The *increase due to recognizing other operating expenses on account* is the other operating expenses amount reported on the income statement.

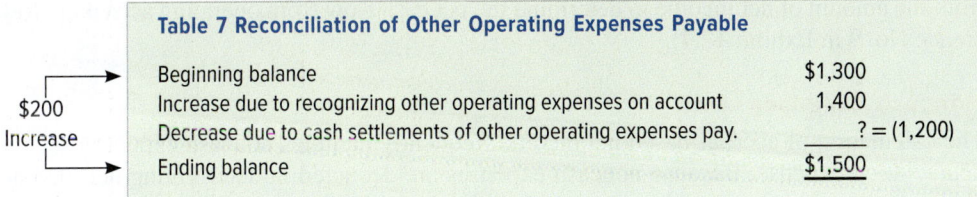

To balance Other Operating Expenses Payable, the amount of the *decrease due to cash settlements of other operating expenses payable* must be $1,200.

The reconciliation shows that the $200 increase in the other operating expenses payable balance occurred because the *cash paid for other operating expenses* was $200 less than the amount of *other operating expenses recognized on account* ($1,200 versus $1,400). Because the amount of cash paid is less than the amount of expense recognized, we add $200 to the amount of net income to determine the net cash flow from operating activities (Reference No. 7 in Exhibit 12.7).

Reconciliation of Interest Payable

Use the financial statement information in Exhibit 12.5 to reconcile Interest Payable. The beginning and ending balances appear on the balance sheets. The *increase due to recognizing interest expense on account* is the interest expense reported on the income statement.

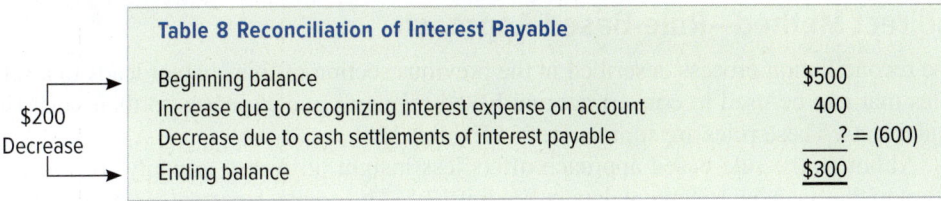

To balance Interest Payable, the amount of the *decrease due to cash settlements of interest payable* (cash paid for interest expense) must be $600.

The reconciliation shows that the $200 decrease in the interest payable balance occurred because the amount of *cash paid for interest expense* is $200 more than the amount of *interest expense recognized on account* ($600 versus $400). Because the amount of cash paid is more than the amount of interest expense recognized, we subtract $200 from the amount of net income to determine the net cash flow from operating activities (Reference No. 8 in Exhibit 12.7).

Reconciliation of Unearned Rent Revenue

Use the financial statement information in Exhibit 12.5 to reconcile Unearned Rent Revenue. The beginning and ending balances appear on the balance sheets. The *decrease due to recognizing other income—rent revenue* is the other income—rent revenue reported on the income statement.

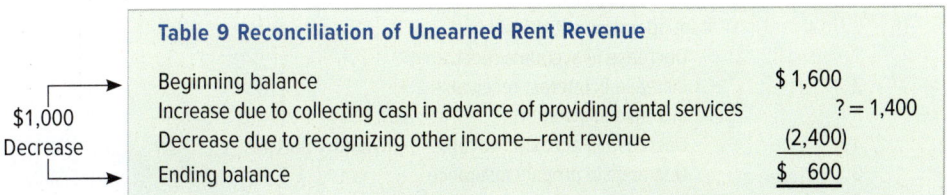

To balance Unearned Rent Revenue, the amount of the *increase due to collecting cash in advance of providing rental services* must be $1,400.

The reconciliation shows that the $1,000 decrease in the unearned rent revenue balance occurred because the amount of *cash collected in advance of providing rental services* is $1,000 less than the amount of *rent revenue recognized* ($1,400 versus $2,400). Because the amount of cash collected is less than the amount of revenue recognized, we subtract $1,000 from the amount of net income to determine the net cash flow from operating activities (Reference No. 9 in Exhibit 12.7).

Noncash Expenses

The calculation of accrual-based net income frequently includes noncash expenses such as depreciation expense. Because noncash expenses are deducted in determining net income, they must be added back to the amount of net income when computing net cash flow from operating activities (Reference No. 10 in Exhibit 12.7).

Gains and Losses

When a company retires a long-term asset, the company may receive cash from the sale of the asset being retired. If the asset is sold for more than book value (cost − accumulated depreciation), the gain increases net income; if the asset is sold for less than book value, the loss decreases net income. In either case, the cash inflow is the total amount of cash collected from selling the asset, not the amount of the gain or loss, and this cash inflow is reported in the investing activities section of the statement of cash flows. Because gains increase net income and losses decrease net income, but neither represents the amount of cash received from an asset sale, gains must be subtracted from and losses added back to net income to determine net cash flow from operating activities (Reference No. 11 in Exhibit 12.7).

Indirect Method—Rule-Based Approach

The reconciliation process described in the previous section of this chapter leads to a set of rules that can be used to convert accrual-based revenues and expenses to their cash flow equivalents. These rules are summarized in Exhibit 12.8.

Although the rule-based approach offers less insight, it is easy to apply. To illustrate, return to the financial statement data in Exhibit 12.5. The *noncash* current assets and current liabilities reported on the balance sheets are summarized in Exhibit 12.9 for your convenience. The amount of the change in each balance is shown in the *Change* column.

Refer to the income statement to identify the amounts of net income, noncash expenses, gains, and losses. The income statement for New South Company in Exhibit 12.5 includes three relevant figures: net income of $7,000; depreciation expense of $1,000; and a $600 gain on the sale of store fixtures. Applying the rules in Exhibit 12.8 produces the operating

EXHIBIT 12.7

Cash Flows from Operating Activities—Indirect Method

Reference No.	Cash Flows from Operating Activities	
	Net income	$7,000
	Adjustments to reconcile net income to net cash flow from operating activities:	
1	Decrease in accounts receivable	200
2	Increase in interest receivable	(100)
3	Increase in inventory	(700)
4	Decrease in accounts payable for inventory purchases	(300)
5	Decrease in prepaid insurance	300
6	Increase in salaries payable	100
7	Increase in other operating expenses payable	200
8	Decrease in interest payable	(200)
9	Decrease in unearned rent revenue	(1,000)
10	Depreciation expense	1,000
11	Gain on sale of store fixtures	(600)
	Net cash flow from operating activities	$5,900

activities section of the statement of cash flows shown in Exhibit 12.10. The applicable rule for each item is referenced in the first column of the exhibit.

The operating activities section of the statements of cash flows shown in Exhibits 12.10 and 12.7 are identical. The rule-based approach is an alternative way to prepare this section when using the indirect method.

EXHIBIT 12.8

Cash Flows from Operating Activities—Indirect Method

	Net income	XXX
Rule 1	Add decreases and subtract increases in noncash current assets.	XXX
Rule 2	Add increases and subtract decreases in noncash current liabilities.	XXX
Rule 3	Add noncash expenses (e.g., depreciation).	XXX
Rule 4	Add losses and subtract gains.	XXX
	Net cash flow from operating activities	XXX

EXHIBIT 12.9

Noncash Current Assets and Current Liabilities

Account Title	Year 2	Year 1	Change
Accounts receivable	$1,000	$1,200	$ (200)
Interest receivable	400	300	100
Inventory	8,900	8,200	700
Prepaid insurance	1,100	1,400	(300)
Accounts payable—inventory purchases	800	1,100	(300)
Salaries payable	1,000	900	100
Other operating expenses payable	1,500	1,300	200
Interest payable	300	500	(200)
Unearned rent revenue	600	1,600	(1,000)

EXHIBIT 12.10

Cash Flows from Operating Activities—Indirect Method, Operating Activities

NEW SOUTH COMPANY
Statement of Cash Flows
For the Year Ended December 31, Year 2

Applicable Rule	Cash Flows from Operating Activities	
	Net income	$ 7,000
	Adjustments to reconcile net income to net cash flow from operating activities:	
Rule 1	Decrease in accounts receivable	200
Rule 1	Increase in interest receivable	(100)
Rule 1	Increase in inventory	(700)
Rule 2	Decrease in accounts payable for inventory purchases	(300)
Rule 1	Decrease in prepaid insurance	300
Rule 2	Increase in salaries payable	100
Rule 2	Increase in other operating expenses payable	200
Rule 2	Decrease in interest payable	(200)
Rule 2	Decrease in unearned rent revenue	(1,000)
Rule 3	Depreciation expense	1,000
Rule 4	Gain on sale of store fixtures	(600)
	Net cash flow from operating activities	$ 5,900

CHECK YOURSELF 12.2

Q Magazine, Inc. reported $369,000 of net income for the month. At the beginning of the month, its Unearned Revenue account had a balance of $78,000. At the end of the month, the account had a balance of $67,000. Based on this information alone, determine the amount of net cash flow from operating activities.

Answer

Account Title	Ending	Beginning	Change
Unearned revenue	$67,000	$78,000	$(11,000)

Applicable Rule	Cash Flows from Operating Activities	Amount
	Net income	$369,000
Rule 2	Deduct: Decrease in unearned revenue	(11,000)
	Net cash flow from operating activities	$358,000

CHECK YOURSELF 12.3

The following account balances were drawn from the accounting records of Loeb, Inc.:

Account Title	Ending Balance	Beginning Balance
Prepaid rent	$3,000	$4,200
Interest payable	2,650	2,900

Loeb reported $7,400 of net income during the accounting period. Based on this information alone, determine the amount of net cash flow from operating activities.

Answer Based on Rule 1, the $1,200 decrease ($4,200 − $3,000) in Prepaid Rent (current asset) must be added to net income to determine the amount of net cash flow from operating activities. Rule 2 requires that the $250 decrease ($2,900 − $2,650) in interest Payable (current liability) must be deducted from net income. Accordingly, the cash flow from operating activities is $8,350 ($7,400 + $1,200 − $250). Note that paying interest is defined as an operating activity and should not be confused with dividend payments, which are classified as financing activities.

CHECK YOURSELF 12.4

Arley Company's income statement reported net income (all amounts are in millions) of $326 for the year. The income statement included depreciation expense of $45 and a net loss on the sale of long-term assets of $22. Based on this information alone, determine the net cash flow from operating activities.

Answer Based on Rule 3 and Rule 4, both the depreciation expense and the loss would have to be added to net income to determine net cash flow from operating activities. Net cash flow from operating activities would be $393 million ($326 + $45 + $22).

PREPARING THE OPERATING ACTIVITIES SECTION OF A STATEMENT OF CASH FLOWS USING THE DIRECT METHOD

The reconciliation tables developed earlier to determine net cash flow from operating activities under the *indirect method* also disclose the information needed to present the amount of net cash flow from operating activities under the *direct method*. Remember that the amount of net cash flow from operating activities is the same whether it is presented using the indirect or the direct method.

The direct method shows the specific sources and uses of cash that are associated with operating activities. It does not show adjustments to net income. To illustrate, examine Exhibit 12.11. The information in the reference column identifies the reconciliation table from which the cash flow amounts were drawn.

Table 3 is not included in Exhibit 12.11 because it does not directly involve a cash flow. Also, noncash expenses, gains, and losses are not used in the determination of net cash flow from operating activities when using the direct method.

LO 12-2

Prepare the operating activities section of a statement of cash flows using the direct method.

EXHIBIT 12.11

Cash Flows from Operating Activities—Direct Method

Reference	Cash Flows from Operating Activities	
Table 1, page 654	Inflow from customers	$ 20,800
Table 2, page 655	Inflow from interest revenue	600
Table 4, page 655	Outflow for inventory purchases	(11,500)
Table 5, page 656	Outflow to purchase insurance	(1,000)
Table 6, page 656	Outflow to pay salary expense	(2,600)
Table 7, page 657	Outflow for other operating expenses	(1,200)
Table 8, page 657	Outflow to pay interest expense	(600)
Table 9, page 657	Inflow from rent revenue	1,400
	Net cash flow from operating activities	$ 5,900

PREPARING THE INVESTING ACTIVITIES SECTION OF A STATEMENT OF CASH FLOWS

The direct and indirect methods discussed earlier pertain only to the presentation of operating activities. The *investing activities* section of the statement of cash flows is the same regardless of whether the direct or indirect method is used for operating activities. The information necessary to identify cash inflows and outflows from investing activities is obtained by reconciling changes in a company's long-term assets. In general:

- Increases in long-term asset balances suggest cash outflows to purchase assets.
- Decreases in long-term asset balances suggest cash inflows from selling assets.

It is usually necessary to analyze data from the long-term asset records to determine details about long-term asset purchases and sales. In the New South Company example, these details are presented as notes at the bottom of the balance sheets.

To illustrate, return to the financial statements in Exhibit 12.5. New South Company reports the following three long-term assets on its balance sheets. *It is not necessary to reconcile accumulated depreciation because it does not affect cash flow.*

LO 12-3

Prepare the investing activities section of a statement of cash flows.

Long-Term Asset	Year 2	Year 1
Investment securities	$5,100	$3,500
Store fixtures	5,400	4,800
Land	8,200	6,000

For each long-term asset, reconcile the beginning and ending balances by identifying purchases and sales affecting it. Review the notes for additional relevant information. Begin with investment securities.

Reconciliation of Investment Securities

Reconciliation of Investment Securities	
Beginning balance in investment securities	$3,500
Increase due to purchase of investment securities	? = 1,600
Decrease due to sale of investment securities	0
Ending balance in investment securities	$5,100

Because Note 1 below the balance sheets indicates no investment securities were sold during Year 2, the *decrease due to sale of investment securities* is zero. To balance Investment Securities, the *increase due to purchase of investment securities* must be $1,600. In the absence of contrary information, assume New South used cash to purchase the investment securities. This cash outflow is reported in the investing activities section of the statement of cash flows in Exhibit 12.12.

Reconciliation of Store Fixtures

Reconciliation of Store Fixtures	
Beginning balance in store fixtures	$ 4,800
Increase due to purchase of store fixtures	? = 2,300
Decrease due to sale of store fixtures	(1,700)
Ending balance in store fixtures	$ 5,400

Note 2 below the balance sheets indicates that the *decrease due to sale of store fixtures* is $1,700. What is the cash flow from this sale? The book value of these fixtures was $400 ($1,700 cost − $1,300 accumulated depreciation). Because the income statement reports a $600 gain on the sale of store fixtures, the cash collected from the sale was more than the book value of the store fixtures. Compute the amount of cash collected from the sale of store fixtures as follows:

$$\text{Cash inflow} = \text{Book value} + \text{Gain} = \$400 + \$600 = \$1,000$$

The $1,000 cash inflow from the sale of store fixtures is reported in the investing activities section of the statement of cash flows in Exhibit 12.12.

To balance Store Fixtures, the *increase due to purchase of store fixtures* must be $2,300. In the absence of contrary information, assume New South used cash to purchase store fixtures. The cash outflow is reported in the investing activities section of the statement of cash flows in Exhibit 12.12.

Reconciliation of Land

Reconciliation of Land	
Beginning balance in land	$6,000
Increase due to purchase of land	? = 2,200
Decrease due to sale of land	0
Ending balance in land	$8,200

Because Note 3 below the balance sheets indicates no land was sold during Year 2, the *decrease due to sale of land* is zero. To balance Land, the *increase due to purchase of land* must be $2,200. Because the land was acquired by issuing a mortgage note payable, New South did not use cash for the purchase. This type of transaction is reported in the *noncash investing and financing activities* section of the statement of cash flows, discussed in more detail later in the chapter. The cash inflows and outflows from investing activities are summarized in Exhibit 12.12.

EXHIBIT 12.12

Cash Flows from Investing Activities

Cash Flows from Investing Activities	
Cash outflow to purchase investment securities	$(1,600)
Cash inflow from the sale of store fixtures	1,000
Cash outflow to purchase store fixtures	(2,300)
Net cash outflow from investing activities	$(2,900)

CHECK YOURSELF 12.5

On January 1, Year 7, Wyatt Company had an Equipment balance of $124,000. During Year 7, Wyatt purchased equipment that cost $50,000. The balance in Equipment on December 31, Year 7, was $90,000. The Year 7 income statement included a $7,000 loss from the sale of equipment. On the date of sale, accumulated depreciation on the equipment sold was $49,000.

Required

a. Determine the cost of the equipment sold during Year 7.

b. Determine the amount of cash flow from the sale of equipment that should be reported in the investing activities section of the Year 7 statement of cash flows.

Solution

a.

Reconciliation of Equipment	
Beginning balance	$124,000
Increase due to the purchase of equipment	50,000
Decrease due to sale of equipment	? = (84,000)
Ending balance	$ 90,000

To balance Equipment, the *decrease due to sale of equipment* must be $84,000.

b. The book value of the equipment sold was $35,000 ($84,000 − $49,000 accumulated depreciation). Because Wyatt recognized a loss on the equipment sale, the amount of cash collected from the sale was less than the book value of the equipment. The cash collected from the sale of the equipment was $28,000 ($35,000 book value − $7,000 loss on sale).

PREPARING THE FINANCING ACTIVITIES SECTION OF A STATEMENT OF CASH FLOWS

LO 12-4

Because the differences between the direct and the indirect methods of presenting the statement of cash flows pertain only to operating activities, the *financing activities* section is the same under either approach. The information necessary to identify cash inflows and outflows

Prepare the financing activities section of a statement of cash flows.

from financing activities is obtained by reconciling changes in short-term notes payable, long-term liabilities, and stockholders' equity. In general:

- Increases in short-term notes payable or long-term debt balances suggest cash inflows occurred from issuing debt instruments (notes or bonds).
- Decreases in short-term notes payable or long-term debt balances suggest cash outflows occurred for payment of debt (notes or bonds).
- Increases in contributed capital (common stock, preferred stock, or paid-in capital) suggest cash inflows occurred from issuing equity instruments.
- Increases or decreases in treasury stock suggest cash outflows or inflows occurred to purchase or sell a company's own stock.
- Decreases in retained earnings from cash dividends suggest cash outflows occurred to pay dividends.

To illustrate, return to the financial statements of the New South Company in Exhibit 12.5. The following long-term liability and stockholders' equity balances are reported on the New South balance sheets:

©larryhw/123RF

Account Title	Year 2	Year 1
Mortgage payable	$ 2,200	$ 0
Bonds payable	1,000	4,000
Common stock	10,000	8,000
Retained earnings	12,700	7,200
Treasury stock	600	0

For each account, reconcile the beginning and ending balances by identifying the increases and decreases affecting it. Review the notes for additional relevant information. Begin with the mortgage payable liability.

Reconciliation of Mortgage Payable

Reconciliation of Mortgage Payable	
Beginning balance in mortgage payable	$ 0
Increase due to issuing mortgage payable	? = 2,200
Decrease due to payment of mortgage payable	0
Ending balance in mortgage payable	$2,200

As previously discussed, Note 3 indicates a mortgage note payable was issued to acquire land. The *increase due to issuing mortgage payable* is $2,200. Because New South received land, not cash, by issuing the mortgage, the transaction is reported in the noncash investing and financing activities section of the statement of cash flows.

Reconciliation of Bonds Payable

Bonds Payable	
Beginning balance in bonds payable	$4,000
Increase due to issuing bonds payable	0
Decrease due to payment of bonds payable	? = (3,000)
Ending balance in bonds payable	$1,000

Because there is no indication that New South issued bonds during Year 2, assume the *increase due to issuing bonds payable* is zero. To balance Bonds Payable, the *decrease due to payment of bonds payable* must be $3,000. The cash outflow is reported in the financing activities section in Exhibit 12.13.

Reconciliation of Common Stock

Reconciliation of Common Stock

Beginning balance in common stock	$ 8,000
Increase due to issuing common stock	? = 2,000
Ending balance in common stock	$10,000

To balance Common Stock, the *increase due to issuing common stock* has to be $2,000. The cash inflow is reported in the financing activities section in Exhibit 12.13.

Reconciliation of Retained Earnings

Reconciliation of Retained Earnings

Beginning balance in retained earnings	$ 7,200
Increase due to net income	7,000
Decrease due to payment of dividends	? = (1,500)
Ending balance in retained earnings	$12,700

The *increase due to net income* comes from the income statement. To balance Retained Earnings, the decrease due to payment of dividends must be $1,500. In the absence of information to the contrary, assume the decrease is due to the cash payment of dividends. The cash outflow for payment of dividends is reported in the financing activities section of the statement of cash flows in Exhibit 12.13.

Reconciliation of Treasury Stock

Reconciliation of Treasury Stock

Beginning balance in treasury stock	$ 0
Increase due to purchasing treasury stock	? = 600
Decrease due to reissuing treasury stock	0
Ending balance in treasury stock	$600

Because there is no indication that New South reissued treasury stock during Year 2, the *decrease due to reissuing treasury stock* is zero. To balance Treasury Stock, the increase due to purchasing treasury stock must be $600. The cash outflow is reported in the financing activities section in Exhibit 12.13.

Exhibits 12.14 and 12.15 illustrate the complete statement of cash flows for New South Company under the two alternative methods. Exhibit 12.14 presents operating activities using the indirect method. Exhibit 12.15 presents operating activities using the direct method. The investing and financing activities do not differ between methods. Under either method, the combined effects of operating, investing, and financing activities result in a net decrease in cash of $100 for Year 2. This $100 decrease is necessarily consistent with the difference between the December 31, Year 2, and the December 31, Year 1, cash balances shown in the balance sheets in Exhibit 12.5.

EXHIBIT 12.13

Cash Flows from Financing Activities

Cash Flows from Financing Activities	
Cash outflow to reduce bonds payable	$(3,000)
Cash inflow from issuing common stock	2,000
Cash outflow to pay dividends	(1,500)
Cash outflow to purchase treasury stock	(600)
Net cash outflow from financing activities	$(3,100)

EXHIBIT 12.14 — Statement of Cash Flows—Indirect Method

NEW SOUTH COMPANY
Statement of Cash Flows
For the Year Ended December 31, Year 2

Cash Flows from Operating Activities

Net income		$7,000
Adjustments to reconcile net income to net cash flow from operating activities:		
Decrease in accounts receivable	200	
Increase in interest receivable	(100)	
Increase in inventory	(700)	
Decrease in accounts payable for inventory purchases	(300)	
Decrease in prepaid insurance	300	
Increase in salaries payable	100	
Increase in other operating expenses payable	200	
Decrease in interest payable	(200)	
Decrease in unearned rent revenue	(1,000)	
Depreciation expense	1,000	
Gain on sale of store fixtures	(600)	
Net cash flow from operating activities		$5,900

Cash Flows from Investing Activities

Cash outflow to purchase investment securities	(1,600)	
Cash inflow from the sale of store fixtures	1,000	
Cash outflow to purchase store fixtures	(2,300)	
Net cash outflow from investing activities		(2,900)

Cash Flows from Financing Activities

Cash outflow to reduce bonds payable	(3,000)	
Cash inflow from issuing common stock	2,000	
Cash outflow to pay dividends	(1,500)	
Cash outflow to purchase treasury stock	(600)	
Net cash outflow from financing activities		(3,100)
Net decrease in cash		(100)
Plus: Beginning cash balance		400
Ending cash balance		$ 300

Schedule of Noncash Investing and Financing Activities

Issue mortgage for land	$2,200

EXHIBIT 12.15 — Statement of Cash Flows—Direct Method

NEW SOUTH COMPANY
Statement of Cash Flows
For the Year Ended December 31, Year 2

Cash Flows from Operating Activities

Inflow from customers	$20,800	
Inflow from interest revenue	600	
Outflow for inventory purchases	(11,500)	
Outflow to purchase insurance	(1,000)	
Outflow to pay salary expense	(2,600)	
Outflow for other operating expenses	(1,200)	
Outflow to pay interest expense	(600)	
Inflow from rent revenue	1,400	
Net cash flow from operating activities		$5,900

continued

EXHIBIT 12.15 Concluded

NEW SOUTH COMPANY
Statement of Cash Flows
For the Year Ended December 31, Year 2

Cash Flows from Investing Activities		
Cash outflow to purchase investment securities	(1,600)	
Cash inflow from the sale of store fixtures	1,000	
Cash outflow to purchase store fixtures	(2,300)	
Net cash outflow from investing activities		(2,900)
Cash Flows from Financing Activities		
Cash outflow to reduce bonds payable	(3,000)	
Cash inflow from issuing common stock	2,000	
Cash outflow to pay dividends	(1,500)	
Cash outflow to purchase treasury stock	(600)	
Net cash outflow from financing activities		(3,100)
Net decrease in cash		(100)
Plus: Beginning cash balance		400
Ending cash balance		$ 300
Schedule of Noncash Investing and Financing Activities		
Issue mortgage for land		$2,200

CHECK YOURSELF 12.6

On January 1, Year 4, Sterling Company had a balance of $250,000 in Bonds Payable. During Year 4, Sterling issued bonds with a $75,000 face value. The bonds were issued at face value. The balance in Bonds Payable on December 31, Year 4, was $150,000.

Required

a. Determine the cash outflow for repayment of bond liabilities assuming the bonds were retired at face value.

b. Prepare the financing activities section of the Year 4 statement of cash flows.

Solution

a.

Reconciliation of Bonds Payable

Beginning balance	$250,000
Increase due to issuing bonds payable	75,000
Decrease due to payment of bonds payable	? = (175,000)
Ending balance	$150,000

In order to balance Bonds Payable, the *decrease due to payment of bonds payable* must be $175,000. In the absence of information to the contrary, assume cash was used to pay the bond liabilities.

b.

Cash Flows from Financing Activities

Inflow from issuing bond liabilities	$ 75,000
Outflow for reduction of bond liabilities	(175,000)
Net cash outflow from financing activities	$(100,000)

PREPARING THE SCHEDULE OF NONCASH INVESTING AND FINANCING ACTIVITIES

As mentioned earlier, companies may engage in significant noncash investing and financing activities. For example, New South Company acquired land by issuing a $2,200 mortgage note. Because these types of transactions do not involve exchanging cash, they are not reported in the main body of the statement of cash flows. However, the Financial Accounting Standards Board (FASB) requires disclosure of all material investing and financing activities, whether or not they involve exchanging cash. Companies must therefore include with the statement of cash flows a separate schedule that reports noncash investing and financing activities. See the *Schedule of Noncash Investing and Financing Activities* at the bottom of Exhibits 12.14 and 12.15 for an example.

REALITY BYTES

How did **Amazon.com** acquire $6.9 billion of assets in 2016 *without* spending cash? Oddly enough, the answer can be found on its statement of cash flows.

The supplemental "noncash transactions" information included at the bottom of Amazon's statement of cash flows reveals that it acquired the assets by using long-term leases, a form of debt.

Had Amazon issued $6.9 billion of long-term debt for cash, and then used this cash to purchase $6.9 billion of assets, it would have reported two separate cash events in the body of its statement of cash flows. A cash inflow would have been reported in the financing activities section for the issuance of the debt, and a cash outflow would have been reported in the investing activities section for the purchase of the assets. Acquiring large amounts of assets is considered important, even if there is no immediate exchange of cash, so generally accepted accounting principles require such events to be reported with the statement of cash flows or disclosed in the notes.

©Evan Lorne/Shutterstock

The Financial Analyst

Why are financial analysts interested in the statement of cash flows? Understanding the cash flows of a business is essential because cash is used to pay the bills. A company, especially one experiencing rapid growth, can be short of cash in spite of earning substantial net income. To illustrate, assume you start a computer sales business. You borrow $2,000 and spend the money to purchase two computers for $1,000 each. You sell one of the computers on account for $1,500. If your loan required a payment at this time, you could not make it. Even though you have net income of $500 ($1,500 sales − $1,000 cost of goods sold), you have no cash until you collect the $1,500 account receivable. A business cannot survive without managing cash flow carefully. It is little wonder that financial analysts are keenly interested in cash flow.

Real-World Data

The statement of cash flows frequently provides a picture of business activity that otherwise would be lost in the complexities of accrual accounting. For example, as *The Curious Accountant* in Chapter 10 explained, even though **Rent-A-Center** reported a loss of approximately $105 million in 2016 on its income statement, its net cash flow from operating activities was a positive $354 million.

Investors consider cash flow information so important they are willing to pay for it. Even though the FASB *prohibits* companies from disclosing *cash flow per share* in audited financial statements, one prominent stock analysis service, *Value Line Investment Survey*, sells this information to a significant customer base. Clearly, Value Line's customers value information about cash flows.

Exhibit 12.16 compares income from operations to cash flows from operating activities for six real-world companies for 2013 through 2016. Several things are apparent from this exhibit. Notice that the cash flow from operating activities exceeds income from operations for all but 4 of the 24 comparisons, and all of these relate to one company, Netflix. Cash flows often exceed earnings because depreciation, a noncash expense, is usually significant. There are two dramatic examples of the differences between cash flow and earnings. First, for the four years shown in Exhibit 12.16, Twitter had had cumulative net losses of $2.2 billion, but its cash flows from operations were a positive $1.2 billion. Second, Caterpillar had cumulative net earnings of $9.6 billion for the four years reported, but its net cash flows from operations were $30.5 billion, over three times larger. The difference between cash flows from operating activities and net earnings helps explain how some companies can have significant losses over a few years and continue to stay in business and pay their bills.

©Juan Carlos Baena/Alamy

EXHIBIT 12.16

Net Income versus Cash Flow from Operations (amounts in millions)

	2016	2015	2014	2013
Caterpillar				
Net income	$ (59)	$ 2,113	$ 3,711	$ 3,803
Cash flow—operations	5,608	6,675	8,057	10,191
Chevron				
Net income	(431)	4,710	19,310	21,597
Cash flow—operations	12,846	19,456	31,475	35,002
Facebook				
Operating income	10,217	3,688	2,940	1,500
Cash flow—operations	16,108	8,599	5,457	4,222
Netflix				
Net income	187	123	267	112
Cash flow—operations	(1,474)	(749)	16	98
Twitter				
Net income	(457)	(521)	(578)	(645)
Cash flow—operations	763	383	82	1
Wendy's				
Net income	130	161	121	45
Cash flow—operations	181	212	255	330

©Anthony Correia/Shutterstock

The exhibit also shows that cash flow from operating activities can be more stable than operating income. Results for **Chevron** demonstrate this clearly. Chevron earnings ranged from a negative $431 million to a positive $21.6 billion, a range of $22.0 billion, which is 195 percent of its average earnings of $11.3 billion for these four years. However, operating cash flows were not only positive in every year, but their total variation over the four years of $22.2 billion was only 90 percent of the average cash flows from operations ($24.7 billion).

What could explain why **Netflix** had *less* cash flow from operating activities than net earnings in all four years, and even had negative cash flows in 2015 and 2016? The company was experiencing the kind of growth described earlier for your computer business. Its cash outflows were supporting growth in Netflix's "streaming content library"—essentially, its inventory. Netflix's revenues doubled from 2013 to 2016, going from $3.4 billion to 8.8 billion. To support this growth, the company had to increase its inventory. In 2016 alone, Netflix spent $8.6 billion to increase its streaming content library.

The Netflix situation highlights a potential weakness in the format of the statement of cash flows. Some accountants consider it misleading to classify all increases in long-term assets as *investing activities* and all changes in inventory as affecting cash flow from operating activities. In the case of Netflix, they would argue that the increase in inventory that relates to expanding its business should be classified as an investing activity, just as the cost of a new warehouse is. Although inventory is classified as a current asset and buildings are classified as long-term assets, in reality there is a certain level of inventory a company must permanently maintain to stay in business. The GAAP format of the statement of cash flows penalizes cash flow from operating activities for increases in inventory that are really a permanent investment in assets.

Conversely, the same critics might argue that some purchases of long-term assets are not actually *investments* but merely replacements of old, existing property, plant, and equipment. In other words, the *investing activities* section of the statement of cash flows makes no distinction between expenditures that expand the business and those that simply replace old equipment (sometimes called *capital maintenance* expenditures).

Users of the statement of cash flows must exercise the same care interpreting it as when they use the balance sheet or the income statement. Numbers alone are insufficient. Users must evaluate numbers based on knowledge of the particular business and industry they are analyzing.

Accounting information alone cannot guide a businessperson to a sound decision. Making good business decisions requires an understanding of the business in question, the environmental and economic factors affecting the operation of that business, and the accounting concepts on which the financial statements of that business are based.

<< A Look Back

This chapter examined in detail only one financial statement, the statement of cash flows. The chapter provided a more comprehensive discussion of how accrual accounting relates to cash-based accounting. Effective use of financial statements requires understanding not only accrual and cash-based accounting systems but also how they relate to each other. That relationship is why a statement of cash flows can begin with a reconciliation of net income, an accrual measurement, to net cash flow from operating activities, a cash measurement. Finally, this chapter explained how the conventions for classifying cash flows as operating, investing, or financing activities require analysis and understanding to make informed decisions with the financial information.

A Look Forward

Chapter 13, which is available only online, provides expanded coverage of financial statement analysis. Your instructor will provide guidance as to how to access this chapter if he or she decides to cover it. If your journey ends here, we sincerely hope this text provided a meaningful learning experience that will serve you well as you progress through your academic training and, ultimately, your career. Good luck and best wishes.

 SELF-STUDY REVIEW PROBLEM

A step-by-step audio-narrated series of slides is available in **Connect.**

The following financial statements pertain to Schlemmer Company:

Balance Sheets
As of December 31

	Year 2	Year 1
Cash	$ 48,400	$ 2,800
Accounts receivable	2,200	1,200
Inventory	5,600	6,000
Equipment	18,000	22,000
Accumulated depreciation—equip.	(13,650)	(17,400)
Land	17,200	10,400
Total assets	$ 77,750	$25,000
Accounts payable (inventory)	$ 5,200	$ 4,200
Long-term debt	5,600	6,400
Common stock	19,400	10,000
Retained earnings	47,550	4,400
Total liabilities and equity	$ 77,750	$25,000

Income Statement
For the Year Ended December 31, Year 2

Sales revenue	$67,300
Cost of goods sold	(24,100)
Gross margin	43,200
Depreciation expense	(1,250)
Operating income	41,950
Gain on sale of equipment	2,900
Loss on disposal of land	(100)
Net income	$44,750

Additional Data

1. During Year 2, equipment that had originally cost $11,000 was sold. Accumulated depreciation on this equipment was $5,000 at the time of sale.
2. Common stock was issued in exchange for land valued at $9,400 at the time of the exchange.

Required

Using the indirect method, prepare in good form a statement of cash flows for the year ended December 31, Year 2.

Solution

SCHLEMMER COMPANY
Statement of Cash Flows
For the Year Ended December 31, Year 2

Cash Flows from Operating Activities		
Net income		$44,750
Add:		
Decrease in inventory (1)	400	
Increase in accounts payable (2)	1,000	
Depreciation expense (3)	1,250	
Loss on disposal of land (4)	100	
Subtract:		
Increase in accounts receivable (1)	(1,000)	
Gain on sale of equipment (4)	(2,900)	
Net cash inflow from operating activities		$43,600
Cash Flows from Investing Activities		
Cash inflow from the sale of equipment (5)	8,900	
Cash outflow for the purchase of equipment (5)	(7,000)	
Cash inflow from sale of land (6)	2,500	
Net cash outflow from investing activities		4,400
Cash Flows from Financing Activities		
Cash outflow to repay long-term debt (7)	(800)	
Cash outflow to pay dividends (8)	(1,600)	
Net cash outflow from financing activities		(2,400)
Net Increase in Cash		45,600
Plus: Beginning cash balance		2,800
Ending cash balance		$48,400
Schedule of Noncash Investing and Financing Activities		
Issue of common stock for land (9)		$ 9,400

(1) Add decreases and subtract increases in current asset account balances to net income.

(2) Add increases and subtract decreases in current liability account balances to net income.

(3) Add noncash expenses (depreciation) to net income.

(4) Add losses on the sale of noncurrent assets to net income and subtract gains on the sale of long-term assets from net income.

(5) Information regarding the Equipment account is summarized in the following table:

Equipment Account Information

Beginning balance in equipment	$ 22,000
Purchases of equipment (cash outflows)	? = 7,000
Sales of equipment (cash inflows)	(11,000)
Ending balance in equipment	$ 18,000

To balance the account, equipment costing $7,000 must have been purchased. In the absence of information to the contrary, we assume cash was used to make the purchase.

Note 1 to the financial statement shows that equipment sold had a book value of $6,000 ($11,000 cost − $5,000 accumulated depreciation). The amount of the cash inflow from this sale is computed as follows:

$$\text{Cash inflow} = \text{Book value} + \text{Gain} = \$6,000 + \$2,900 = \$8,900$$

(6) The information regarding the Land account is as follows:

Land Account Information

Beginning balance in land	$10,400
Purchases of land (Issue of common stock)	9,400
Sales of land (cash inflows)	? = (2,600)
Ending balance in land	$17,200

Note 2 indicates that land valued at $9,400 was acquired by issuing common stock. Because there was no cash flow associated with this purchase, the event is shown in the *noncash investing and financing activities* section of the statement of cash flows.

To balance the account, the cost (book value) of land sold had to be $2,600. Because the income statement shows a $100 loss on the sale of land, the cash collected from the sale is computed as follows:

$$\text{Cash inflow} = \text{Book value} - \text{Loss} = \$2,600 - \$100 = \$2,500$$

(7) The information regarding the Long-Term Debt account is as follows:

Long-Term Debt Information

Beginning balance in long-term debt	$6,400
Issue of long-term debt instruments (cash inflow)	0
Payment of long-term debt (cash outflow)	? = (800)
Ending balance in long-term debt	$5,600

There is no information in the financial statements that suggests long-term debt was issued. Therefore, to balance the account, $800 of long-term debt had to be paid off, thereby resulting in a cash outflow.

(8) The information regarding the Retained Earnings account is as follows:

Retained Earnings Information

Beginning balance in retained earnings	$ 4,400
Net income	44,750
Dividends (cash outflow)	? = (1,600)
Ending balance in retained earnings	$47,550

To balance the account, $1,600 of dividends had to be paid, thereby resulting in a cash outflow.

(9) Note 2 states that common stock was issued to acquire land valued at $9,400. This is a noncash investing and financing activity.

KEY TERMS

Cash inflows 646
Cash outflows 646
Direct method 648
Financing activities 649
Indirect method 648
Investing activities 649
Noncash investing and financing activities 650
Operating activities 648

QUESTIONS

1. What is the purpose of the statement of cash flows?
2. What are the three categories of cash flows reported on the cash flow statement? Discuss each and give an example of an inflow and an outflow for each category.
3. What are noncash investing and financing activities? Provide an example. How are such transactions shown on the statement of cash flows?
4. Albring Company had a beginning balance in accounts receivable of

$12,000 and an ending balance of $14,000. Net income amounted to $110,000. Based on this information alone, determine the amount of net cash flow from operating activities.

5. Forsyth Company had a beginning balance in utilities payable of $3,300 and an ending balance of $5,200. Net income amounted to $87,000. Based on this information alone, determine the amount of net cash flow from operating activities.

6. Clover Company had a beginning balance in unearned revenue of $4,300 and an ending balance of $3,200. Net income amounted to $54,000. Based on this information alone, determine the amount of net cash flow from operating activities.

7. Which of the following activities are financing activities?

(a) Payment of accounts payable.
(b) Payment of interest on bonds payable.
(c) Sale of common stock.
(d) Sale of preferred stock at a premium.
(e) Payment of a cash dividend.

8. Does depreciation expense affect net cash flow? Explain.

9. If Best Company sold land that cost $4,200 at a $500 gain, how much cash did it collect from the sale of land?

10. If Best Company sold office equipment that originally cost $7,500 and had $7,200 of accumulated depreciation at a $100 loss, what was the selling price for the office equipment?

11. In which section of the statement of cash flows would the following transactions be reported?

(a) The amount of the change in the balance of accounts receivable.
(b) Cash purchase of investment securities.
(c) Cash purchase of equipment.
(d) Cash sale of merchandise.
(e) Cash sale of common stock.
(f) The amount of net income.
(g) Cash proceeds from loan.
(h) Cash payment on bonds payable.
(i) Cash receipt from sale of old equipment.
(j) The amount of the change in the balance of accounts payable.

12. What is the difference between preparing the statement of cash flows using the direct method and using the indirect method?

13. Which method (direct or indirect) of presenting the statement of cash flows is more intuitively logical? Why?

14. What is the major advantage of using the indirect method to present the statement of cash flows?

15. What is the advantage of using the direct method to present the statement of cash flows?

16. How would Best Company report the following transactions on the statement of cash flows?

(a) Purchased new equipment for $46,000 cash.
(b) Sold old equipment for $8,700 cash. The equipment had a book value of $4,900.

17. Can a company report negative net cash flows from operating activities for the year on the statement of cash flows but still have positive net income on the income statement? Explain.

MULTIPLE-CHOICE QUESTIONS

Multiple-choice questions are available in **Connect**.

EXERCISES—SERIES A

 All applicable Exercises in Series A are available in **Connect**.

LO 12-1

Exercise 12-1A *Use the indirect method to determine cash flows from operating activities*

An accountant for Southern Manufacturing Companies (SMC) computed the following information by making comparisons between SMC's Year 1 and Year 2 balance sheets. Further information was determined by examining the company's Year 2 income statement.

1. The amount of cash dividends paid to the stockholders.
2. The amount of a decrease in the balance of an Unearned Revenue account.
3. The amount of an increase in the balance of an Inventory account.
4. The amount of an increase in the balance of a Land account.
5. The amount of a decrease in the balance of a Prepaid Rent account.
6. The amount of an increase in the balance of a Treasury Stock account.
7. The amount of an increase in the balance of the Accounts Receivable account.
8. The amount of a loss arising from the sale of land.
9. The amount of an increase in the balance of the Other Operating Expenses Payable account.

10. The amount of a decrease in the balance of the Bonds Payable account.

11. The amount of depreciation expense shown on the income statement.

Required

For each item described in the preceding list, indicate whether the amount should be added to or subtracted from the amount of net income when determining the amount of net cash flow from operating activities using the indirect method. Also identify any items that do not affect net cash flow from operating activities because they are reported as investing or financing activities.

Exercise 12-2A Use the indirect method to determine cash flows from operating activities

LO 12-1

Alfonza Incorporated presents its statement of cash flows using the indirect method. The following accounts and corresponding balances were drawn from the company's Year 2 and Year 1 year-end balance sheets:

Account Title	Year 2	Year 1
Accounts receivable	$16,200	$17,800
Accounts payable	7,600	9,100

The Year 2 income statement showed net income of $31,600.

Required

a. Prepare the operating activities section of the statement of cash flows.

b. Explain why the change in the balance in accounts receivable was added to or subtracted from the amount of net income when you completed requirement *a*.

c. Explain why the change in the balance in accounts payable was added to or subtracted from the amount of net income when you completed requirement *a*.

Exercise 12-3A Use the indirect method to determine cash flows from operating activities

LO 12-1

Shim Company presents its statement of cash flows using the indirect method. The following accounts and corresponding balances were drawn from Shim's Year 2 and Year 1 year-end balance sheets:

Account Title	Year 2	Year 1
Accounts receivable	$36,000	$37,200
Prepaid rent	2,400	1,800
Interest receivable	600	400
Accounts payable	9,300	10,400
Salaries payable	4,500	5,200
Unearned revenue	3,600	5,400

The income statement reported a $1,500 gain on the sale of equipment, an $800 loss on the sale of land, and $3,600 of depreciation expense. Net income for the period was $47,300.

Required

Prepare the operating activities section of the statement of cash flows.

Exercise 12-4A Use the direct method to determine cash flows from operating activities

LO 12-2

The following accounts and corresponding balances were drawn from Avia Company's Year 2 and Year 1 year-end balance sheets:

Account Title	Year 2	Year 1
Unearned revenue	$7,600	$6,200
Prepaid rent	2,400	3,600

During the year, $46,000 of unearned revenue was recognized as having been earned. Rent expense for Year 2 was $18,000.

Required

Based on this information alone, prepare the operating activities section of the statement of cash flows assuming the direct approach is used.

LO 12-2

Exercise 12-5A *Use the direct method to determine cash flows from operating activities*

The following accounts and corresponding balances were drawn from Marinelli Company's Year 2 and Year 1 year-end balance sheets:

Account Title	Year 2	Year 1
Accounts receivable	$35,200	$31,600
Interest receivable	4,200	4,800
Other operating expenses payable	21,000	18,500
Salaries payable	6,500	7,200

The Year 2 income statement is shown next:

Income Statement	
Sales	$ 530,000
Salary expense	(214,000)
Other operating expenses	(175,000)
Operating income	141,000
Nonoperating items: Interest revenue	16,500
Net income	$ 157,500

Required

a. Use the direct method to compute the amount of cash inflows from operating activities.

b. Use the direct method to compute the amount of cash outflows from operating activities.

LO 12-1, 12-2

Exercise 12-6A *Direct versus indirect method of determining cash flows from operating activities*

Expert Electronics, Inc. (EEI) recognized $3,800 of sales revenue on account and collected $2,100 of cash from accounts receivable. Further, EEI recognized $900 of operating expenses on account and paid $700 cash as partial settlement of accounts payable.

Required

Based on this information alone:

a. Prepare the operating activities section of the statement of cash flows under the direct method.

b. Prepare the operating activities section of the statement of cash flows under the indirect method.

LO 12-1, 12-2

Exercise 12-7A *The direct versus the indirect method of determining cash flows from operating activities*

The following accounts and corresponding balances were drawn from Jogger Company's Year 2 and Year 1 year-end balance sheets:

Account Title	Year 2	Year 1
Accounts receivable	$57,000	$62,000
Prepaid rent	1,100	1,300
Utilities payable	900	750
Other operating expenses payable	21,300	22,400

The Year 2 income statement is shown next:

Income Statement	
Sales	$268,000
Rent expense	(36,000)
Utilities expense	(18,300)
Other operating expenses	(79,100)
Net Income	$134,600

Required

a. Prepare the operating activities section of the statement of cash flows using the direct method.
b. Prepare the operating activities section of the statement of cash flows using the indirect method.

Exercise 12-8A *Determining cash flow from investing activities*   LO 12-3

On January 1, Year 1, Shelton Company had a balance of $325,000 in its Land account. During Year 1, Shelton sold land that had cost $106,500 for $132,000 cash. The balance in the Land account on December 31, Year 1, was $285,000.

Required

a. Determine the cash outflow for the purchase of land during Year 1.
b. Prepare the investing activities section of the Year 1 statement of cash flows.

Exercise 12-9A *Determining cash flows from investing activities*   LO 12-3

On January 1, Year 1, Bacco Company had a balance of $72,350 in its Delivery Equipment account. During Year 1, Bacco purchased delivery equipment that cost $22,100. The balance in the Delivery Equipment account on December 31, Year 1, was $69,400. The Year 1 income statement reported a gain from the sale of equipment for $5,000. On the date of sale, accumulated depreciation on the equipment sold amounted to $22,000.

Required

a. Determine the original cost of the equipment that was sold during Year 1.
b. Determine the amount of cash flow from the sale of delivery equipment that should be shown in the investing activities section of the Year 1 statement of cash flows.

Exercise 12-10A *Determining cash flows from investing activities*   LO 12-3

The following accounts and corresponding balances were drawn from Delsey Company's Year 2 and Year 1 year-end balance sheets:

Account Title	Year 2	Year 1
Investment securities	$110,000	$116,500
Machinery	486,000	437,000
Land	160,000	100,000

Other information drawn from the accounting records:

1. Delsey incurred a $6,000 loss on the sale of investment securities during Year 2.
2. Old machinery with a book value of $8,000 (cost of $36,000 minus accumulated depreciation of $28,000) was sold. The income statement showed a gain on the sale of machinery of $4,500.
3. Delsey did not sell land during the year.

Required

a. Compute the amount of cash flow associated with the sale of investment securities.
b. Compute the amount of cash flow associated with the purchase of machinery.
c. Compute the amount of cash flow associated with the sale of machinery.
d. Compute the amount of cash flow associated with the purchase of land.
e. Prepare the investing activities section of the statement of cash flows.

LO 12-4

Exercise 12-11A *Determining cash flows from financing activities*

On January 1, Year 1, DIBA Company had a balance of $450,000 in its Bonds Payable account. During Year 1, DIBA issued bonds with a $200,000 face value. There was no premium or discount associated with the bond issue. The balance in the Bonds Payable account on December 31, Year 1, was $400,000.

Required

a. Determine the cash outflow for the repayment of bond liabilities assuming that the bonds were retired at face value.
b. Prepare the financing activities section of the Year 1 statement of cash flows.

LO 12-4

Exercise 12-12A *Determining cash flows from financing activities*

On January 1, Year 1, Hardy Company had a balance of $150,000 in its Common Stock account. During Year 1, Hardy paid $20,000 to purchase treasury stock. Treasury stock is accounted for using the cost method. The balance in the Common Stock account on December 31, Year 1, was $175,000. Assume that the common stock is no par stock.

Required

a. Determine the cash inflow from the issue of common stock.
b. Prepare the financing activities section of the Year 1 statement of cash flows.

LO 12-4

Exercise 12-13A *Determining cash flows from financing activities*

The following accounts and corresponding balances were drawn from Dexter Company's Year 2 and Year 1 year-end balance sheets:

Account Title	Year 2	Year 1
Bonds payable	$350,000	$400,000
Common stock	450,000	420,000

Other information drawn from the accounting records:

1. Dividends paid during the period amounted to $50,000.
2. There were no bond liabilities issued during the period.

Required

a. Compute the amount of cash flow associated with the repayment of bond liabilities.
b. Compute the amount of cash flow associated with the issue of common stock.
c. Prepare the financing activities section of the statement of cash flows.

PROBLEMS—SERIES A

Problem 12-14A The direct versus the indirect method of determining cash flow from operating activities

LO 12-1, 12-2

Green Brands, Inc. (GBI) presents its statement of cash flows using the indirect method. The following accounts and corresponding balances were drawn from GBI's Year 2 and Year 1 year-end balance sheets:

Account Title	Year 2	Year 1
Accounts receivable	$48,000	$52,000
Merchandise inventory	78,000	72,000
Prepaid insurance	24,000	32,000
Accounts payable	31,000	28,000
Salaries payable	8,200	7,800
Unearned service revenue	2,400	3,600

CHECK FIGURE
Net Cash Flow from Operating Activities: $105,200

The Year 2 income statement is shown next:

Income Statement

Sales	$720,000
Cost of goods sold	(398,000)
Gross margin	322,000
Service revenue	6,000
Insurance expense	(36,000)
Salaries expense	(195,000)
Depreciation expense	(12,000)
Operating income	85,000
Gain on sale of equipment	4,500
Net income	$ 89,500

Required

a. Prepare the operating activities section of the statement of cash flows using the direct method.
b. Prepare the operating activities section of the statement of cash flows using the indirect method.

Problem 12-15A Determining cash flows from investing activities

LO 12-3

The following information was drawn from the year-end balance sheets of Mass Trading Company:

Account Title	Year 2	Year 1
Investment securities	$ 47,200	$ 42,400
Equipment	246,000	218,000
Buildings	646,000	720,000
Land	95,000	72,000

CHECK FIGURES
b. $4,700
c. $10,000

Additional information regarding transactions occurring during Year 2:

1. Investment securities that had cost $6,100 were sold. The Year 2 income statement contained a loss on the sale of investment securities of $1,400.
2. Equipment with a cost of $38,000 was purchased.

3. The income statement showed a gain on the sale of equipment of $8,000. On the date of sale, accumulated depreciation on the equipment sold amounted to $8,000.
4. A building that had originally cost $210,000 was demolished.
5. Land that had cost $30,000 was sold for $27,000.

Required

a. Determine the amount of cash flow for the purchase of investment securities during Year 2.
b. Determine the amount of cash flow from the sale of investment securities during Year 2.
c. Determine the cost of the equipment that was sold during Year 2.
d. Determine the amount of cash flow from the sale of equipment during Year 2.
e. Determine the amount of cash flow for the purchase of buildings during Year 2.
f. Determine the amount of cash flow for the purchase of land during Year 2.
g. Prepare the investing activities section of the Year 2 statement of cash flows.

LO 12-4

CHECK FIGURES
c. $15,000
e. Net Cash Flow from Financing Activities: ($206,000) outflow

Problem 12-16A *Determining cash flows from financing activities*

The following information was drawn from the year-end balance sheets of Fox River, Inc.:

Account Title	Year 2	Year 1
Bonds payable	$600,000	$800,000
Common stock	210,000	180,000
Treasury stock	20,000	5,000
Retained earnings	86,000	75,000

Additional information regarding transactions occurring during Year 2:

1. Fox River, Inc. issued $100,000 of bonds during Year 2. The bonds were issued at face value. All bonds retired were retired at face value.
2. Common stock did not have a par value.
3. Fox River, Inc. uses the cost method to account for treasury stock.
4. The amount of net income shown on the Year 2 income statement was $32,000.

Required

a. Determine the amount of cash flow for the retirement of bonds that should appear on the Year 2 statement of cash flows.
b. Determine the amount of cash flow from the issue of common stock that should appear on the Year 2 statement of cash flows.
c. Determine the amount of cash flow for the purchase of treasury stock that should appear on the Year 2 statement of cash flows.
d. Determine the amount of cash flow for the payment of dividends that should appear on the Year 2 statement of cash flows.
e. Prepare the financing activities section of the Year 2 statement of cash flows.

LO 12-1, 12-3, 12-4

Problem 12-17A *Preparing a statement of cash flows*

The following information can be obtained by examining a company's balance sheet and income statement information:

a. Increases in current asset account balances, other than cash.
b. Decreases in current asset account balances, other than cash.
c. Cash outflows to purchase long-term assets.
d. Decreases in current liability account balances.
e. Cash outflows to repay long-term debt.
f. Gains recognized on the sale of long-term assets.
g. Noncash expenses (e.g., depreciation).
h. Cash outflows to purchase treasury stock.

i. Increases in current liability account balances.
j. Cash inflows from the sale of long-term assets.
k. Cash inflows from the issue of common stock.
l. Cash outflows to pay dividends.
m. Losses incurred from the sale of long-term assets.
n. Cash inflows from the issue of long-term debt.

Required

Construct a table like the one shown next. For each item, indicate whether it would be used in the computation of net cash flows from operating, investing, or financing activities. Also, indicate whether the item would be added or subtracted when determining the net cash flow from operating, investing, or financing activities. Assume the indirect method is used to prepare the operating activities section of the statement of cash flows. The first item has been completed as an example.

Item	Type of Activity	Add or Subtract
a.	Operating	Subtract
b.		

Problem 12-18A Using financial statements to prepare a statement of cash flows—indirect method

LO 12-1, 12-3, 12-4

The comparative balance sheets and income statements for Gypsy Company follow:

CHECK FIGURES
Net Cash Flow from Operating Activities: $32,200
Net Increase in Cash: $16,200

Balance Sheets
As of December 31

	Year 2	Year 1
Assets		
Cash	$ 32,500	$16,300
Accounts receivable	4,750	2,800
Inventory	11,200	9,800
Equipment	45,000	52,000
Accumulated depreciation—equipment	(17,800)	(21,800)
Land	28,000	12,000
Total assets	$103,650	$71,100
Liabilities and equity		
Accounts payable (inventory)	$ 3,750	$ 4,900
Long-term debt	5,800	7,800
Common stock	47,000	25,000
Retained earnings	47,100	33,400
Total liabilities and equity	$103,650	$71,100

Income Statement
For the Year Ended December 31, Year 2

Sales revenue	$ 61,200
Cost of goods sold	(24,500)
Gross margin	36,700
Depreciation expense	(12,000)
Operating income	24,700
Gain on sale of equipment	1,500
Loss on disposal of land	(100)
Net income	$ 26,100

Additional Data

1. During Year 2, the company sold equipment for $21,500; it had originally cost $36,000. Accumulated depreciation on this equipment was $16,000 at the time of the sale. Also, the company purchased equipment for $29,000 cash.
2. The company sold land that had cost $6,000. This land was sold for $5,900, resulting in the recognition of a $100 loss. Also, common stock was issued in exchange for title to land that was valued at $22,000 at the time of exchange.
3. Paid dividends of $12,400.

Required

Prepare a statement of cash flows using the indirect method.

LO 12-1, 12-3, 12-4

Problem 12-19A *Using financial statements to prepare a statement of cash flows—indirect method*

The comparative balance sheets and an income statement for Raceway Corporation follow:

CHECK FIGURES
Net Cash Flow from Operating Activities: $45,900
Net Decrease in Cash: $42,100

Balance Sheets
As of December 31

	Year 2	Year 1
Assets		
Cash	$ 6,300	$ 48,400
Accounts receivable	10,200	7,260
Merchandise inventory	45,200	56,000
Prepaid rent	700	2,140
Equipment	140,000	144,000
Accumulated depreciation	(73,400)	(118,000)
Land	116,000	50,000
Total assets	$245,000	$189,800
Liabilities		
Accounts payable (inventory)	$ 37,200	$ 40,000
Salaries payable	12,200	10,600
Stockholders' equity		
Common stock, $50 par value	150,000	120,000
Retained earnings	45,600	19,200
Total liabilities and equity	$245,000	$189,800

Income Statement
For the Year Ended December 31, Year 2

Sales	$ 480,000
Cost of goods sold	(264,000)
Gross profit	216,000
Operating expenses	
Depreciation expense	(11,400)
Rent expense	(7,000)
Salaries expense	(95,200)
Other operating expenses	(76,000)
Net income	$ 26,400

Other Information

1. Purchased land for $66,000.
2. Purchased new equipment for $62,000.

3. Sold old equipment that cost $66,000 with accumulated depreciation of $56,000 for $10,000 cash.
4. Issued common stock for $30,000.

Required

Prepare the statement of cash flows for Year 2 using the indirect method.

Problem 12-20A *Using transaction data to prepare a statement of cash flows—direct method*

LO 12-2, 12-3, 12-4

York Company engaged in the following transactions for the year Year 1. The beginning cash balance was $86,000 and the ending cash balance was $59,100.

CHECK FIGURE
Net Cash Flow from Operating Activities: $(900)

1. Sales on account were $548,000. The beginning receivables balance was $128,000 and the ending balance was $90,000.
2. Salaries expense for the period was $232,000. The beginning salaries payable balance was $16,000 and the ending balance was $8,000.
3. Other operating expenses for the period were $236,000. The beginning other operating expenses payable balance was $16,000 and the ending balance was $10,000.
4. Recorded $30,000 of depreciation expense. The beginning and ending balances in the Accumulated Depreciation account were $12,000 and $42,000, respectively.
5. The Equipment account had beginning and ending balances of $44,000 and $56,000, respectively. There were no sales of equipment during the period.
6. The beginning and ending balances in the Notes Payable account were $36,000 and $44,000, respectively. There were no payoffs of notes during the period.
7. There was $4,600 of interest expense reported on the income statement. The beginning and ending balances in the Interest Payable account were $8,400 and $7,500, respectively.
8. The beginning and ending Merchandise Inventory account balances were $22,000 and $29,400, respectively. The company sold merchandise with a cost of $83,600 (cost of goods sold for the period was $83,600). The beginning and ending balances in the Accounts Payable account were $8,000 and $6,400, respectively.
9. The beginning and ending balances in the Notes Receivable account were $60,000 and $100,000, respectively. Notes receivable result from long-term loans made to employees. There were no collections from employees during the period.
10. The beginning and ending balances in the Common Stock account were $120,000 and $160,000, respectively. The increase was caused by the issue of common stock for cash.
11. Land had beginning and ending balances of $24,000 and $14,000, respectively. Land that cost $10,000 was sold for $6,000, resulting in a loss of $4,000.
12. The tax expense for the period was $6,600. The Taxes Payable account had a $2,400 beginning balance and an $2,200 ending balance.
13. The Investments account had beginning and ending balances of $20,000 and $60,000, respectively. The company purchased investments for $50,000 cash during the period, and investments that cost $10,000 were sold for $22,000, resulting in a $12,000 gain.

Required

a. Determine the amount of cash flow for each item and indicate whether the item should appear in the operating, investing, or financing activities section of a statement of cash flows. Also identify any items that do not affect the cash flow statement. Assume York Company uses the direct method for showing net cash flow from operating activities.
b. Prepare a statement of cash flows based on the information you developed in requirement *a*.

Problem 12-21A *Using financial statements to prepare a statement of cash flows—direct method*

LO 12-2, 12-3, 12-4

The following financial statements were drawn from the records of Matrix Shoes:

CHECK FIGURES
Net Cash Flow from Operating Activities: $56,200
Net Increase in Cash: $80,200

Balance Sheets
As of December 31

	Year 2	Year 1
Assets		
Cash	$ 94,300	$ 14,100
Accounts receivable	36,000	40,000
Merchandise inventory	72,000	64,000
Notes receivable	0	16,000
Equipment	98,000	170,000
Accumulated depreciation—equipment	(47,800)	(94,000)
Land	46,000	30,000
Total assets	$298,500	$240,100
Liabilities		
Accounts payable	$ 24,000	$ 26,400
Salaries payable	15,000	10,000
Utilities payable	800	1,400
Interest payable	0	1,000
Notes payable (long-term)	0	24,000
Common stock	150,000	110,000
Retained earnings	108,700	67,300
Total liabilities and equity	$298,500	$240,100

Income Statement
For the Year Ended December 31, Year 2

Sales revenue	$ 300,000
Cost of goods sold	(144,000)
Gross margin	156,000
Operating expenses	
Salary expense	(88,000)
Depreciation expense	(9,800)
Utilities expense	(6,400)
Operating income	51,800
Nonoperating items	
Interest expense	(2,400)
Loss on the sale of equipment	(800)
Net income	$ 48,600

Additional Information

1. Sold equipment costing $72,000 with accumulated depreciation of $56,000 for $15,200 cash.
2. Paid a $7,200 cash dividend to owners.

Required

Analyze the data and prepare a statement of cash flows using the direct method.

EXERCISES—SERIES B

LO 12-1

Exercise 12-1B *Use the indirect method to determine cash flows from operating activities*

An accountant for Farve Enterprise Companies (FEC) computed the following information by making comparisons between FEC's Year 2 and Year 1 balance sheets. Further information was determined by examining the company's Year 2 income statement.

1. The amount of an increase in the balance of a Prepaid Rent account.
2. The amount of an increase in the balance of a Treasury Stock account.

3. The amount of a decrease in the balance of the Accounts Receivable account.
4. The amount of a gain arising from the sale of land.
5. The amount of an increase in the balance of the Salaries Payable account.
6. The amount of an increase in the balance of the Bonds Payable account.
7. The amount of depreciation expense shown on the income statement.
8. The amount of cash dividends paid to the stockholders.
9. The amount of an increase in the balance of an Unearned Revenue account.
10. The amount of a decrease in the balance of an Inventory account.
11. The amount of a decrease in the balance of a Land account.

Required

For each item in the preceding list, indicate whether the amount should be added to or subtracted from the amount of net income when determining the amount of net cash flow from operating activities using the indirect method. Also identify any items that do not affect net cash flow from operating activities because they are reported as investing or financing activities.

Exercise 12-2B *Use the indirect method to determine cash flows from operating activities*

LO 12-1

Napoleon Incorporated presents its statement of cash flows using the indirect method. The following accounts and corresponding balances were drawn from the company's Year 2 and Year 1 year-end balance sheets:

Account Title	Year 2	Year 1
Accounts receivable	$31,400	$28,600
Accounts payable	10,300	9,800

The Year 2 income statement showed net income of $41,500.

Required

a. Prepare the operating activities section of the statement of cash flows.
b. Explain why the change in the balance in accounts receivable was added to or subtracted from the amount of net income when you completed requirement *a*.
c. Explain why the change in the balance in accounts payable was added to or subtracted from the amount of net income when you completed requirement *a*.

Exercise 12-3B *Use the indirect method to determine cash flows from operating activities*

LO 12-1

Pella Company presents its statement of cash flows using the indirect method. The following accounts and corresponding balances were drawn from Pella's Year 2 and Year 1 year-end balance sheets:

Account Title	Year 2	Year 1
Accounts receivable	$24,000	$21,000
Prepaid rent	1,650	1,900
Interest receivable	900	1,200
Accounts payable	10,200	8,500
Salaries payable	2,700	2,900
Unearned revenue	2,000	1,800

The income statement reported a $700 loss on the sale of equipment, a $900 gain on the sale of land, and $2,500 of depreciation expense. Net income for the period was $36,500.

Required

Prepare the operating activities section of the statement of cash flows.

LO 12-2

Exercise 12-4B *Use the direct method to determine cash flows from operating activities*

The following accounts and corresponding balances were drawn from Osprey Company's Year 2 and Year 1 year-end balance sheets:

Account Title	Year 2	Year 1
Unearned revenue	$4,500	$6,000
Prepaid rent	5,200	3,600

During the year, $84,000 of unearned revenue was recognized as having been earned. Rent expense for Year 2 was $24,000.

Required

Based on this information alone, prepare the operating activities section of the statement of cash flows assuming the direct approach is used.

LO 12-2

Exercise 12-5B *Use the direct method to determine cash flows from operating activities*

The following accounts and corresponding balances were drawn from Pixi Company's Year 2 and Year 1 year-end balance sheets:

Account Title	Year 2	Year 1
Accounts receivable	$62,000	$56,000
Interest receivable	8,000	6,000
Other operating expenses payable	26,000	29,000
Salaries payable	12,000	9,000

The Year 2 income statement is shown next:

Income Statement	
Sales	$ 650,000
Salary expense	(420,000)
Other operating expenses	(110,000)
Operating income	120,000
Nonoperating items: Interest revenue	15,000
Net income	$ 135,000

Required

a. Use the direct method to compute the amount of cash inflows from operating activities.
b. Use the direct method to compute the amount of cash outflows from operating activities.

LO 12-1, 12-2

Exercise 12-6B *Direct versus indirect method of determining cash flows from operating activities*

Ragg Shop, Inc. (RSI) recognized $3,800 of sales revenue on account and collected $2,950 of cash from accounts receivable. Further, RSI recognized $1,200 of operating expenses on account and paid $900 cash as partial settlement of accounts payable.

Required

Based on this information alone:

a. Prepare the operating activities section of the statement of cash flows under the direct method.
b. Prepare the operating activities section of the statement of cash flows under the indirect method.

Exercise 12-7B The direct versus the indirect method of determining cash flows from operating activities

LO 12-1, 12-2

The following accounts and corresponding balances were drawn from Geneses Company's Year 2 and Year 1 year-end balance sheets:

Account Title	Year 2	Year 1
Accounts receivable	$65,000	$72,000
Prepaid rent	1,400	1,950
Utilities payable	3,200	3,800
Other operating expenses payable	27,000	31,500

The Year 2 income statement is shown next:

Income Statement	
Sales	$ 420,000
Rent expense	(52,000)
Utilities expense	(45,300)
Other operating expenses	(195,000)
Net income	$ 127,700

Required

a. Prepare the operating activities section of the statement of cash flows using the direct method.
b. Prepare the operating activities section of the statement of cash flows using the indirect method.

Exercise 12-8B Determining cash flow from investing activities

LO 12-3

On January 1, Year 1, Poole Company had a balance of $178,000 in its Land account. During Year 1, Poole sold land that had cost $71,000 for $95,000 cash. The balance in the Land account on December 31, Year 1, was $210,000.

Required

a. Determine the cash outflow for the purchase of land during Year 1.
b. Prepare the investing activities section of the Year 1 statement of cash flows.

Exercise 12-9B Determining cash flow from investing activities

LO 12-3

On January 1, Year 1, Sanita Company had a balance of $76,300 in its Office Equipment account. During Year 1, Sanita purchased office equipment that cost $30,300. The balance in the Office Equipment account on December 31, Year 1, was $75,400. The Year 1 income statement contained a gain from the sale of equipment of $6,000. On the date of sale, accumulated depreciation on the equipment sold amounted to $14,400.

Required

a. Determine the cost of the equipment that was sold during Year 1.
b. Determine the amount of cash flow from the sale of office equipment that should be shown in the investing activities section of the Year 1 statement of cash flows.

LO 12-3

Exercise 12-10B *Determining cash flows from investing activities*

The following accounts and corresponding balances were drawn from Teva Company's Year 2 and Year 1 year-end balance sheets:

Account Title	Year 2	Year 1
Investment securities	$102,000	$110,000
Machinery	480,000	465,000
Land	75,000	95,000

Other information drawn from the accounting records:

1. Teva incurred a $3,000 loss on the sale of investment securities during Year 2.
2. Old machinery with a book value of $8,000 (cost of $34,000 minus accumulated depreciation of $26,000) was sold. The income statement showed a gain on the sale of machinery of $7,500.
3. Teva incurred a loss of $4,000 on the sale of land in Year 2.

Required

a. Compute the amount of cash flow associated with the sale of investment securities.
b. Compute the amount of cash flow associated with the purchase of machinery.
c. Compute the amount of cash flow associated with the sale of machinery.
d. Compute the amount of cash flow associated with the sale of land.
e. Prepare the investing activities section of the statement of cash flows.

LO 12-4

Exercise 12-11B *Determining cash flows from financing activities*

On January 1, Year 1, Van Company had a balance of $800,000 in its Bonds Payable account. During Year 1, Van issued bonds with a $300,000 face value. There was no premium or discount associated with the bond issue. The balance in the Bonds Payable account on December 31, Year 1, was $600,000.

Required

a. Determine the cash outflow for the repayment of bond liabilities assuming that the bonds were retired at face value.
b. Prepare the financing activities section of the Year 1 statement of cash flows.

LO 12-4

Exercise 12-12B *Determining cash flows from financing activities*

On January 1, Year 1, Milam Company had a balance of $300,000 in its Common Stock account. During Year 1, Milam paid $18,000 to purchase treasury stock. Treasury stock is accounted for using the cost method. The balance in the Common Stock account on December 31, Year 1, was $350,000. Assume that the common stock is no par stock.

Required

a. Determine the cash inflow from the issue of common stock.
b. Prepare the financing activities section of the Year 1 statement of cash flows.

LO 12-4

Exercise 12-13B *Determining cash flows from financing activities*

The following accounts and corresponding balances were drawn from Cushing Company's Year 2 and Year 1 year-end balance sheets:

Account Title	Year 2	Year 1
Bonds payable	$200,000	$150,000
Common stock	650,000	400,000

Other information drawn from the accounting records:

1. Dividends paid during the period amounted to $50,000.
2. There were no bond liabilities repaid during the period.

Required

a. Compute the amount of cash flow associated with the issue of bond liabilities.
b. Compute the amount of cash flow associated with the issue of common stock.
c. Prepare the financing activities section of the statement of cash flows.

PROBLEMS—SERIES B

Problem 12-14B The direct versus the indirect method of determining cash flows from operating activities

LO 12-1, 12-2

The following accounts and corresponding balances were drawn from Crimson Sports, Inc.'s Year 2 and Year 1 year-end balance sheets:

Account Title	Year 2	Year 1
Accounts receivable	$31,000	$36,000
Merchandise inventory	70,000	65,000
Prepaid insurance	25,000	24,000
Accounts payable	18,000	20,000
Salaries payable	5,100	4,500
Unearned service revenue	10,200	9,500

The Year 2 income statement is shown next:

Income Statement

Sales	$ 495,000
Cost of goods sold	(215,000)
Gross margin	280,000
Service revenue	20,000
Insurance expense	(42,000)
Salaries expense	(122,000)
Depreciation expense	(12,000)
Operating income	124,000
Gain on sale of equipment	1,500
Net income	$ 125,500

Required

a. Prepare the operating activities section of the statement of cash flows using the direct method.
b. Prepare the operating activities section of the statement of cash flows using the indirect method.

Problem 12-15B Determining cash flows from investing activities

LO 12-3

The following information was drawn from the year-end balance sheets of Vigotti Company:

Account Title	Year 2	Year 1
Investment securities	$ 51,000	$ 60,000
Equipment	310,000	275,000
Buildings	980,000	950,000
Land	135,000	110,000

Additional information regarding transactions occurring during Year 2:

1. Investment securities that had cost $11,300 were sold. The Year 2 income statement contained a loss on the sale of investment securities of $800.
2. Equipment with a cost of $80,000 was purchased.
3. The income statement showed a gain on the sale of equipment of $9,500. On the date of sale, accumulated depreciation on the equipment sold amounted to $38,000.
4. A building that had originally cost $90,000 was demolished.
5. Land that had cost $20,000 was sold for $15,000.

Required

a. Determine the amount of cash flow for the purchase of investment securities during Year 2.
b. Determine the amount of cash flow from the sale of investment securities during Year 2.
c. Determine the cost of the equipment that was sold during Year 2.
d. Determine the amount of cash flow from the sale of equipment during Year 2.
e. Determine the amount of cash flow for the purchase of buildings during Year 2.
f. Determine the amount of cash flow for the purchase of land during Year 2.
g. Prepare the investing activities section of the Year 2 statement of cash flows.

LO 12-4

Problem 12-16B *Determining cash flows from financing activities*

The following information was drawn from the year-end balance sheets of Long's Wholesale, Inc.:

Account Title	Year 2	Year 1
Bonds payable	$400,000	$600,000
Common stock	190,000	150,000
Treasury stock	20,000	15,000
Retained earnings	96,000	80,000

Additional information regarding transactions occurring during Year 2:

1. Long's Wholesale, Inc. issued $90,000 of bonds during Year 2. The bonds were issued at face value. All bonds retired were retired at face value.
2. Common stock did not have a par value.
3. Long's Wholesale, Inc. uses the cost method to account for treasury stock. Long's Wholesale, Inc. did not resell any treasury stock in Year 2.
4. The amount of net income shown on the Year 2 income statement was $49,000.

Required

a. Determine the amount of cash flow for the retirement of bonds that should appear on the Year 2 statement of cash flows.
b. Determine the amount of cash flow from the issue of common stock that should appear on the Year 2 statement of cash flows.
c. Determine the amount of cash flow for the purchase of treasury stock that should appear on the Year 2 statement of cash flows.
d. Determine the amount of cash flow for the payment of dividends that should appear on the Year 2 statement of cash flows.
e. Prepare the financing activities section of the Year 2 statement of cash flows.

LO 12-1, 12-3, 12-4

Problem 12-17B *Preparing a statement of cash flows*

The following information can be obtained by examining a company's balance sheet and income statement information:

a. Increases in current asset account balances, other than cash.
b. Cash outflows to purchase noncurrent assets.
c. Decreases in current liability account balances.
d. Noncash expenses (e.g., depreciation).
e. Cash outflows to purchase treasury stock.

f. Gains recognized on the sale of noncurrent assets.
g. Cash outflows to pay dividends.
h. Cash inflows from the issue of common stock.
i. Cash inflows from the sale of noncurrent assets.
j. Increases in current liability account balances.
k. Cash inflows from the issue of noncurrent debt.
l. Losses incurred from the sale of noncurrent assets.
m. Decreases in current asset account balances, other than cash.
n. Cash outflows to repay noncurrent debt.

Required

Construct a table like the one shown next. For each item, indicate whether it would be used in the computation of net cash flows from operating, investing, or financing activities. Also, indicate whether the item would be added or subtracted when determining the net cash flow from operating, investing, or financing activities. Assume the indirect method is used to prepare the operating activities section of the statement of cash flows. The first item has been completed as an example.

Item	Type of Activity	Add or Subtract
a.	Operating	Subtract
b.		

Problem 12-18B Using financial statements to prepare a statement of cash flows—indirect method

LO 12-1, 12-3, 12-4

The following financial statements were drawn from the records of Culinary Products Co.:

Balance Sheets
As of December 31

	Year 2	Year 1
Assets		
Cash	$24,200	$ 2,800
Accounts receivable	2,000	1,200
Inventory	6,400	6,000
Equipment	19,000	42,000
Accumulated depreciation—equipment	(9,000)	(17,400)
Land	18,400	10,400
Total assets	$61,000	$45,000
Liabilities and stockholders' equity		
Accounts payable (inventory)	$ 2,600	$ 4,200
Long-term debt	2,800	6,400
Common stock	22,000	10,000
Retained earnings	33,600	24,400
Total liabilities and stockholders' equity	$61,000	$45,000

Income Statement
For the Year Ended December 31, Year 2

Sales revenue	$ 35,700
Cost of goods sold	(14,150)
Gross margin	21,550
Depreciation expense	(3,600)
Operating income	17,950
Gain on sale of equipment	500
Loss on disposal of land	(50)
Net income	$ 18,400

Additional Data

1. During Year 2, the company sold equipment for $18,500; it had originally cost $30,000. Accumulated depreciation on this equipment was $12,000 at the time of the sale. Also, the company purchased equipment for $7,000 cash.
2. The company sold land that had cost $4,000. This land was sold for $3,950, resulting in the recognition of a $50 loss. Also, common stock was issued in exchange for title to land that was valued at $12,000 at the time of exchange.
3. Paid dividends of $9,200.

Required

Prepare a statement of cash flows using the indirect method.

LO 12-1, 12-3, 12-4

Problem 12-19B *Using financial statements to prepare a statement of cash flows— indirect method*

The comparative balance sheets and an income statement for Wang Beauty Products, Inc. are shown next.

Balance Sheets
As of December 31

	Year 2	Year 1
Assets		
Cash	$ 68,800	$ 40,600
Accounts receivable	30,000	22,000
Merchandise inventory	160,000	176,000
Prepaid rent	2,400	4,800
Equipment	256,000	288,000
Accumulated depreciation	(146,800)	(236,000)
Land	192,000	80,000
Total assets	$ 562,400	$ 375,400
Liabilities and equity		
Accounts payable (inventory)	$ 67,000	$ 76,000
Salaries payable	28,000	24,000
Stockholders' equity		
Common stock, $50 par value	250,000	200,000
Retained earnings	217,400	75,400
Total liabilities and equity	$ 562,400	$ 375,400

Income Statement
For the Year Ended December 31, Year 2

Sales	$1,500,000
Cost of goods sold	(797,200)
Gross profit	702,800
Operating expenses	
Depreciation expense	(22,800)
Rent expense	(24,000)
Salaries expense	(256,000)
Other operating expenses	(258,000)
Net income	$ 142,000

Other Information

1. Purchased land for $112,000.
2. Purchased new equipment for $100,000.
3. Sold old equipment that cost $132,000 with accumulated depreciation of $112,000 for $20,000 cash.
4. Issued common stock for $50,000.

Required

Prepare the statement of cash flows for Year 2 using the indirect method.

Problem 12-20B *Using transaction data to prepare a statement of cash flows—direct method*

LO 12-2, 12-3, 12-4

The Electric Company engaged in the following transactions during Year 2. The beginning cash balance was $43,000 and the ending cash balance was $48,600.

1. Sales on account were $274,000. The beginning receivables balance was $86,000 and the ending balance was $74,000.
2. Salaries expense was $115,000. The beginning salaries payable balance was $9,600 and the ending balance was $7,500.
3. Other operating expenses were $118,000. The beginning Other Operating Expenses Payable balance was $8,500 and the ending balance was $6,000.
4. Recorded $25,000 of depreciation expense. The beginning and ending balances in the Accumulated Depreciation account were $18,000 and $43,000, respectively.
5. The Equipment account had beginning and ending balances of $28,000 and $42,000, respectively. There were no sales of equipment during the period.
6. The beginning and ending balances in the Notes Payable account were $38,000 and $32,000, respectively. There were no notes payable issued during the period.
7. There was $4,600 of interest expense reported on the income statement. The beginning and ending balances in the Interest Payable account were $6,400 and $6,200, respectively.
8. The beginning and ending Merchandise Inventory account balances were $26,000 and $32,500, respectively. The company sold merchandise with a cost of $119,000. The beginning and ending balances in the Accounts Payable account were $10,000 and $12,500, respectively.
9. The beginning and ending balances in the Notes Receivable account were $80,000 and $20,000, respectively. Notes receivable result from long-term loans made to creditors. There were no loans made to creditors during the period.
10. The beginning and ending balances in the Common Stock account were $140,000 and $190,000, respectively. The increase was caused by the issue of common stock for cash.
11. Land had beginning and ending balances of $48,000 and $28,000, respectively. Land that cost $20,000 was sold for $16,000, resulting in a loss of $4,000.
12. The tax expense for the period was $6,600. The Tax Payable account had a $3,200 beginning balance and a $2,800 ending balance.
13. The Investments account had beginning and ending balances of $10,000 and $30,000, respectively. The company purchased investments for $40,000 cash during the period, and investments that cost $20,000 were sold for $26,000, resulting in a $6,000 gain.

Required

a. Determine the amount of cash flow for each item and indicate whether the item should appear in the operating, investing, or financing activities section of a statement of cash flows. Also identify any items that do not affect the cash flow statement. Assume The Electric Company uses the direct method for showing net cash flow from operating activities.

b. Prepare a statement of cash flows based on the information you developed in requirement *a*.

Problem 12-21B *Using financial statements to prepare a statement of cash flows—direct method*

LO 12-2, 12-3, 12-4

The following financial statements were drawn from the records of Boston Materials, Inc.:

Balance Sheets
As of December 31

	Year 2	Year 1
Assets		
Cash	$ 99,700	$ 25,400
Accounts receivable	72,000	60,000
Inventory	86,000	75,000
Notes receivable (long-term)	0	24,000
Equipment	104,000	152,000
Accumulated depreciation—equipment	(67,500)	(75,000)
Land	60,000	45,000
Total assets	$354,200	$306,400
Liabilities and equity		
Accounts payable	$ 35,300	$ 36,200
Salaries payable	18,200	15,500
Utilities payable	1,400	2,800
Interest payable	600	1,200
Notes payable (long-term)	0	36,000
Common stock	120,000	100,000
Retained earnings	178,700	114,700
Total liabilities and equity	$354,200	$306,400

Income Statement
For the Year Ended December 31, Year 2

Sales revenue	$ 450,000
Cost of goods sold	(212,000)
Gross margin	238,000
Operating expenses	
Salary expense	(96,000)
Depreciation expense	(18,500)
Utilities expense	(7,500)
Operating income	116,000
Nonoperating items	
Interest expense	(3,500)
Gain on sale of equipment	1,500
Net income	$ 114,000

Additional Information

1. Sold equipment costing $48,000 with accumulated depreciation of $26,000 for $23,500 cash.
2. Paid a $50,000 cash dividend to owners.

Required

Analyze the data and prepare a statement of cash flows using the direct method.

ANALYZE, THINK, COMMUNICATE

ATC 12-1 Business Applications Case *Understanding real-world annual reports*

Required

Obtain the Target Corporation's annual report at http://investors.target.com using the instructions in Appendix B, and use it to answer the following questions:

a. For the year ended January 28, 2017 (2016), which was larger, Target's *net income* or its *cash flow from operating activities?* By what amount did they differ?

b. What two items are most responsible for the difference between Target's *net income* and its *cash flow from operating activities* in 2016?

c. Target generated approximately $5.4 billion in cash from operating activities, and its cash balance decreased by $1.5 billion. How did the company use this $6.9 billion in cash?

ATC 12-2 Real-World Case *Following the cash*

Tesla, Inc. began operations in 2003 but did not begin selling its stock to the public until June 28, 2010. It has lost money every year it has been in existence, and by December 31, 2016, it had total lifetime losses of approximately $3 billion. In addition to making automobiles, Tesla makes energy storage systems. Tesla's statements of cash flows for 2014, 2015, and 2016 follow.

TESLA, INC.
Consolidated Statements of Cash Flows
(in thousands)

For the Years Ending December 31

	2016	2015	2014
Cash flows from operating activities:			
Net loss	$ (773,046)	$ (888,663)	$ (294,040)
Adjustments to reconcile net loss to net cash used in operating activities:			
Depreciation and amortization	947,099	422,590	231,931
Stock-based compensation	334,225	197,999	156,496
Amortization of discount on convertible debt	87,286	72,063	69,734
Inventory write-downs	65,520	44,940	15,609
Loss on disposal of property and equipment	34,633	37,723	14,178
Foreign currency transaction (gain) loss	(29,183)	55,765	(1,891)
Gain on the acquisition of SolarCity	(88,727)	—	—
Non-cash interest and other operating activities	(7,775)	26,373	7,471
Changes in operating assets and liabilities, net of effect of business combinations			
Accounts receivable	(216,565)	46,267	(183,658)
Inventories and operating lease vehicles	(2,465,703)	(1,573,860)	(1,050,264)
Prepaid expenses and other current assets	56,806	(29,595)	(60,637)
MyPower notes receivable	3,468	—	—
Other assets	(52,821)	(24,362)	(4,493)
Accounts payable and accrued liabilities	750,640	263,345	414,856
Deferred revenue	382,962	322,203	209,681
Customer deposits	388,361	36,721	106,230
Resale value guarantee	326,934	442,295	249,492
Other long-term liabilities	132,057	23,697	61,968
Net cash flows from operating activities	(123,829)	(524,499)	(57,337)
Cash flows from investing activities:			
Purchases of property and equipment excluding capital leases, net of sales	(1,280,802)	(1,634,850)	(969,885)
Purchase of solar energy system, to be leased	(159,669)	—	—
Purchase of short-term investments and marketable securities	—	—	(205,841)
Maturities of short-term marketable securities	16,667	—	189,131
Increase in restricted cash	(206,149)	(26,441)	(3,849)
Cash acquired through (used in) business combinations	213,523	(12,260)	—
Net cash flows from investing activities	(1,416,430)	(1,673,551)	(990,444)
Cash flows from financing activities:			
Proceeds from issuance of common stock in initial public offering	1,701,734	730,000	—
Proceeds from issuance of convertible and other debt	2,852,964	318,972	2,300,000
Repayments of convertible and other debt	(1,857,594)	—	—
Collateralized lease borrowing	769,709	568,745	3,271
Proceeds from exercise of stock options and other stock issuances	163,817	106,611	100,455
Principal payments on capital leases	(46,889)	(203,780)	(11,179)
Common stock and debt issuance costs	(20,042)	(17,025)	(35,149)
Proceeds from issuance of warrants	—	—	389,160
Proceeds from issuance of common stock in private placements	—	20,000	—
Purchase of convertible note hedges	—	—	(603,428)
Proceeds from investment by noncontrolling interests in subsidiaries	201,527	—	—
Distributions paid to noncontrolling interests in subsidiaries	(21,250)	—	—
Net cash flows from financing activities	3,743,976	1,523,523	2,143,130
Effect of exchange rate changes on cash and cash equivalents	(7,409)	(34,278)	(35,525)
Net increase (decrease) in cash and cash equivalents	2,196,308	(708,805)	1,059,824
Cash and cash equivalents at beginning of period	1,196,908	1,905,713	845,889
Cash and cash equivalents at end of period	$3,393,216	$1,196,908	$1,905,713

a. As this chapter explained, many companies that report net losses on their earnings statements report positive cash flows from operating activities. How do Tesla's net incomes compare to its cash flows from operating activities?

b. Based only on the information in the statements of cash flows, does Tesla appear to be growing the capacity of its business? Explain.

c. In 2016, Tesla paid off $1.9 billion of "convertible and other debt." Where did it get the funds to repay this debt?

d. All things considered, based on the information in its statements of cash flows, does Tesla's cash position appear to be improving or deteriorating?

ATC 12-3 Group Assignment *Preparing a statement of cash flows*

The following financial statements and information are available for Blythe Industries Inc.:

Balance Sheets
As of December 31

	2017	2016
Assets		
Cash	$ 160,200	$120,600
Accounts receivable	103,200	85,000
Inventory	186,400	171,800
Marketable securities (available for sale)	284,000	220,000
Equipment	650,000	490,000
Accumulated depreciation	(310,000)	(240,000)
Land	80,000	120,000
Total assets	$1,153,800	$967,400
Liabilities and equity		
Liabilities		
Accounts payable (inventory)	$ 36,400	$ 66,200
Notes payable—Long-term	230,000	250,000
Bonds payable	200,000	100,000
Total liabilities	466,400	416,200
Stockholders' equity		
Common stock, no par	240,000	200,000
Preferred stock, $50 par	110,000	100,000
Paid-in capital in excess of par—Preferred stock	34,400	26,800
Total paid-In capital	384,400	326,800
Retained earnings	333,000	264,400
Less: Treasury stock	(30,000)	(40,000)
Total stockholders' equity	687,400	551,200
Total liabilities and stockholders' equity	$1,153,800	$967,400

Income Statement
For the Year Ended December 31, 2017

Sales revenue		$1,050,000
Cost of goods sold		(766,500)
Gross profit		283,500
Operating expenses		
Supplies expense	$20,400	
Salaries expense	92,000	
Depreciation expense	90,000	
Total operating expenses		(202,400)
Operating income		81,100
Nonoperating items		
Interest expense		(16,000)
Gain from the sale of marketable securities		30,000
Gain from the sale of land and equipment		12,000
Net income		$ 107,100

Additional Information

1. Sold land that cost $40,000 for $44,000.
2. Sold equipment that cost $30,000 and had accumulated depreciation of $20,000 for $18,000.
3. Purchased new equipment for $190,000.
4. Sold marketable securities that were classified as available-for-sale and that cost $40,000 for $70,000.
5. Purchased new marketable securities, classified as available-for-sale, for $104,000.
6. Paid $20,000 on the principal of the long-term note.
7. Paid off a $100,000 bond issue and issued new bonds for $200,000.
8. Sold 100 shares of treasury stock at its cost.
9. Issued some new common stock.
10. Issued some new $50 par preferred stock.
11. Paid dividends. (*Note:* The only transactions to affect retained earnings were net income and dividends.)

Required

Organize the class into three sections and divide each section into groups of three to five students. Assign each section of groups an activity section of the statement of cash flows (operating activities, investing activities, or financing activities).

Group Task

Prepare your assigned portion of the statement of cash flows. Have a representative of your section put your activity section of the statement of cash flows on the board. As each section adds its information on the board, the full statement of cash flows will be presented.

Class Discussion

Have the class finish the statement of cash flows by computing the net change in cash. Also have the class answer the following questions:

a. What is the cost per share of the treasury stock?
b. What was the issue price per share of the preferred stock?
c. What was the book value of the equipment sold?

ATC 12-4 Business Applications Case *Identifying different presentation formats*

In *Statement of Financial Accounting Standards No. 95,* the Financial Accounting Standards Board (FASB) recommended but did not require that companies use the direct method. In Appendix B, Paragraphs 106–121, the FASB discussed its reasons for this recommendation.

Required

Obtain a copy of *Standard No. 95* and read Appendix B Paragraphs 106–121. Write a brief response summarizing the issues that the FASB considered and its specific reaction to those issues. Your response should draw heavily on paragraphs 119–121.

ATC 12-5 Writing Assignment *Explaining discrepancies between cash flow and operating income*

The following selected information was drawn from the records of Fleming Company:

Assets	2016	2017
Accounts receivable	$ 400,000	$ 840,200
Merchandise inventory	720,000	1,480,000
Equipment	1,484,000	1,861,200
Accumulated depreciation	(312,000)	(402,400)

Fleming is experiencing cash flow problems. Despite the fact that it reported significant increases in operating income, operating activities produced a net cash outflow. Recent financial forecasts predict that Fleming will have insufficient cash to pay its current liabilities within three months.

Required

Write an explanation of Fleming's cash shortage. Include a recommendation to remedy the problem.

ATC 12-6 Ethical Dilemma *Would I lie to you, baby?*

Andy and Jean Crocket are involved in divorce proceedings. When discussing a property settlement, Andy told Jean that he should take over their investment in an apartment complex because she would be unable to absorb the loss that the apartments are generating. Jean was somewhat distrustful and asked Andy to support his contention. He produced the following income statement, which was supported by a CPA's unqualified opinion that the statement was prepared in accordance with generally accepted accounting principles.

CROCKET APARTMENTS
Income Statement
For the Year Ended December 31, 2016

Rent revenue		$ 580,000
Less: Expenses		
Depreciation expense	$280,000	
Interest expense	184,000	
Operating expense	88,000	
Management fees	56,000	
Total expenses		(608,000)
Net loss		$ (28,000)

All revenue is earned on account. Interest and operating expenses are incurred on account. Management fees are paid in cash. The following accounts and balances were drawn from the 2015 and 2016 year-end balance sheets:

Account Title	2015	2016
Rent receivable	$40,000	$44,000
Interest payable	12,000	18,000
Accounts payable (oper. exp.)	6,000	4,000

Jean is reluctant to give up the apartments but feels that she must do so because her present salary is only $40,000 per year. She says that if she takes the apartments, the $28,000 loss would absorb a significant portion of her salary, leaving her only $12,000 with which to support herself. She tells you that, while the figures seem to support her husband's arguments, she believes that she is failing to see something. She knows that she and her husband collected a $20,000 distribution from the business on December 1, 2016. Also, $150,000 cash was paid in 2016 to reduce the principal balance on a mortgage that was taken out to finance the purchase of the apartments two years ago. Finally, $24,000 cash was paid during 2016 to purchase a computer system used in the business. She wonders, "If the apartments are losing money, where is my husband getting all the cash to make these payments?"

Required

a. Prepare a statement of cash flows for the 2016 accounting period.

b. Compare the cash flow statement prepared in requirement *a* with the income statement and provide Jean Crocket with recommendations.

c. Comment on the value of an unqualified audit opinion when using financial statements for decision-making purposes.

ATC 12-7   Research Assignment   *Analyzing cash flow information*

In 2016 and 2015, Sears Holding Corporation reported net losses and negative cash flows from operating activities. Using the company's Form 10-K for the fiscal year ended January 28, 2017 (2016), complete the requirements shown in the following. The Form 10-K can be found on the company's website. It can also be obtained using the EDGAR system following the instructions in Appendix A.

Required

a. Determine Sears' net incomes and cash flow from operating activities for 2016 and 2015.

b. How was Sears able to pay its bills given that it has such large, negative net cash flows from operating activities in 2016 and 2015? Provide a separate answer for each year.

Design Elements: Abstract texture: ©Ingram Publishing; Video Camera icon: ©McGraw-Hill Education; Check mark: ©McGraw-Hill Education; Look forward/backward icon: ©McGraw-Hill Education; Globe with view of North and South America: ©Design Pics/Don Hammond; Globe with magnifying glass icon: ©McGraw-Hill Education; Pen and paper icon: ©McGraw-Hill Education; Business Applications icon: ©McGraw-Hill Education; Group Assignment icon: ©McGraw-Hill Education; Globe icon 2: ©McGraw-Hill Education

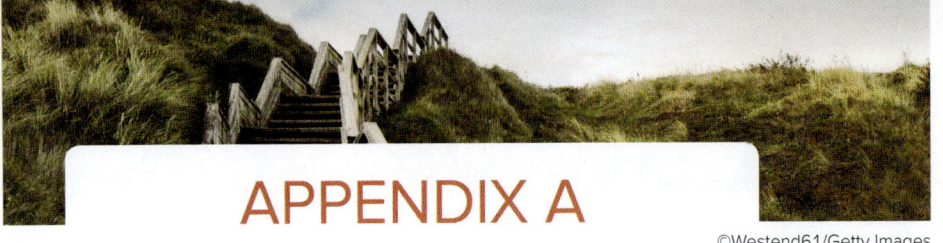

APPENDIX A

©Westend61/Getty Images

ACCESSING THE EDGAR DATABASE THROUGH THE INTERNET

Successful business managers need many different skills, including communication, interpersonal, computer, and analytical skills. Most business students become very aware of the data analysis skills used in accounting, but they may not be as aware of the importance of "data-finding" skills. There are many sources of accounting and financial data. The more sources you are able to use, the better.

One very important source of accounting information is the EDGAR database. Others are probably available at your school through the library or business school network. Your accounting instructor will be able to identify these for you and make suggestions regarding their use. By making the effort to learn to use electronic databases, you will enhance your abilities as a future manager and your marketability as a business graduate.

These instructions assume that you know how to access and use an Internet browser. Follow the instructions to retrieve data from the Securities and Exchange Commission's EDGAR database. Be aware that the SEC may have changed its interface since this appendix was written. Accordingly, be prepared for slight differences between the following instructions and what appears on your computer screen. Take comfort in the fact that changes are normally designed to simplify user access. If you encounter a conflict between the following instructions and the instructions provided in the SEC interface, remember that the SEC interface is more current and should take precedence over the following instructions.

Most companies provide links to their SEC filings from their corporate website. These links are often simpler to use and provide more choices regarding file formats than the SEC's EDGAR site. On company websites, links to SEC filings are usually found under one of the following links: "Investor Relations," "Company Info," or "About Us."

1. Connect to the EDGAR database through the following address: **http://www.sec.gov/.**
2. After the SEC homepage appears, click on **Company Filings.**
3. On the screen that appears, enter the name of the company whose file you wish to retrieve.
4. The next screen will present a list of companies that have the same name as the one you entered, along with companies that have similar names. Identify the company you want and click on the CIK number beside it.
5. Enter the SEC form number that you want to retrieve in the window titled **Filing Type** that appears in the upper left portion of the screen. For example, if you want Form 10-K, which will usually be the case, enter **10-K** and click on the **Search** button.
6. A list of the forms you requested will be presented, along with the date they were filed. Click on the **Document** button next to the file you wish to retrieve.
7. Once the 10-K has been retrieved, you can search it online or save it on your computer.
8. Often, the 10-K will have a table of contents that can help locate the part of the report you need. The financial statements are seldom located at the beginning of the Form 10-K. They are usually in either Section 8 or Section 15.

APPENDIX B

PORTION OF THE FORM 10-K FOR TARGET CORPORATION

This appendix contains a small portion of the Form 10-K for the Target Corporation that was filed with the Securities and Exchange Commission on March 8, 2017. This material relates to the company's fiscal year ended January 28, 2017. Throughout the text, this is referred to as the company's 2016 fiscal year. **This material in this appendix is included for illustrative purposes, and it is intended to be used for educational purposes only.**

For the ATC-1 problem in each chapter, you will need the complete version of Target's Form 10-K, which can be found online at http://investors.target.com. Once on the "sec filings" page, under "filter by form type" drop-down window, select "Annual filings," and then select the "10-K" that has a filing date of "03/08/17." Several versions of this 10-K are available, but the pdf format works best for the purposes of this text. The authors suggest you download and save this file so that you do not need to look it up each time you need it. The Form 10-K may be also obtained from the SEC's EDGAR website, using the procedures explained in Appendix A.

UNITED STATES
SECURITIES AND EXCHANGE COMMISSION
Washington, D.C. 20549

FORM 10-K

(Mark One)

☒ **ANNUAL REPORT PURSUANT TO SECTION 13 OR 15(d) OF THE SECURITIES EXCHANGE ACT OF 1934**

For the fiscal year ended February 1, 2014

OR

☐ **TRANSITION REPORT PURSUANT TO SECTION 13 OR 15(d) OF THE SECURITIES EXCHANGE ACT OF 1934**

For the transition period from _____ to _____
Commission file number **1-6049**

TARGET CORPORATION
(Exact name of registrant as specified in its charter)

Minnesota	41-0215170
(State or other jurisdiction of incorporation or organization)	(I.R.S. Employer Identification No.)
1000 Nicollet Mall, Minneapolis, Minnesota	**55403**
(Address of principal executive offices)	(Zip Code)

Registrant's telephone number, including area code: 612/304-6073

Securities Registered Pursuant To Section 12(B) Of The Act:

Title of Each Class	Name of Each Exchange on Which Registered
Common Stock, par value $0.0833 per share	New York Stock Exchange

Securities registered pursuant to Section 12(g) of the Act: **None**

Item 8. Financial Statements and Supplementary Data

Report of Management on the Consolidated Financial Statements

Management is responsible for the consistency, integrity, and presentation of the information in the Annual Report. The consolidated financial statements and other information presented in this Annual Report have been prepared in accordance with accounting principles generally accepted in the United States and include necessary judgments and estimates by management.

To fulfill our responsibility, we maintain comprehensive systems of internal control designed to provide reasonable assurance that assets are safeguarded and transactions are executed in accordance with established procedures. The concept of reasonable assurance is based upon recognition that the cost of the controls should not exceed the benefit derived. We believe our systems of internal control provide this reasonable assurance.

The Board of Directors exercised its oversight role with respect to the Corporation's systems of internal control primarily through its Audit Committee, which is comprised of independent directors. The Committee oversees the Corporation's systems of internal control, accounting practices, financial reporting and audits to assess whether their quality, integrity, and objectivity are sufficient to protect shareholders' investments.

In addition, our consolidated financial statements have been audited by Ernst & Young LLP, independent registered public accounting firm, whose report also appears on this page.

Brian C. Cornell
Chairman and Chief Executive Officer
March 8, 2017

Cathy R. Smith
Executive Vice President and
Chief Financial Officer

Report of Independent Registered Public Accounting Firm on Consolidated Financial Statements

The Board of Directors and Shareholders

Target Corporation

We have audited the accompanying consolidated statements of financial position of Target Corporation and subsidiaries (the Corporation) as of January 28, 2017 and January 30, 2016, and the related consolidated statements of operations, comprehensive income, cash flows, and shareholders' investment for each of the three years in the period ended January 28, 2017. These financial statements are the responsibility of the Corporation's management. Our responsibility is to express an opinion on these financial statements based on our audits.

We conducted our audits in accordance with the standards of the Public Company Accounting Oversight Board (United States). Those standards require that we plan and perform the audit to obtain reasonable assurance about whether the financial statements are free of material misstatement. An audit includes examining, on a test basis, evidence supporting the amounts and disclosures in the financial statements. An audit also includes assessing the accounting principles used and significant estimates made by management, as well as evaluating the overall financial statement presentation. We believe that our audits provide a reasonable basis for our opinion.

In our opinion, the financial statements referred to above present fairly, in all material respects, the consolidated financial position of Target Corporation and subsidiaries at January 28, 2017 and January 30, 2016, and the consolidated results of their operations and their cash flows for each of the three years in the period ended January 28, 2017, in conformity with U.S. generally accepted accounting principles.

We also have audited, in accordance with the standards of the Public Company Accounting Oversight Board (United States), the Corporation's internal control over financial reporting as of January 28, 2017, based on criteria established in *Internal Control—Integrated Framework* issued by the Committee of Sponsoring Organizations of the Treadway Commission (2013 Framework), and our report dated March 8, 2017, expressed an unqualified opinion thereon.

Ernst & Young LLP

Minneapolis, Minnesota
March 8, 2017

Report of Management on Internal Control over Financial Reporting

Our management is responsible for establishing and maintaining adequate internal control over financial reporting, as such term is defined in Exchange Act Rules 13a-15(f). Under the supervision and with the participation of our management, including our chief executive officer and chief financial officer, we assessed the effectiveness of our internal control over financial reporting as of January 28, 2017, based on the framework in *Internal Control—Integrated Framework (2013)*, issued by the Committee of Sponsoring Organizations of the Treadway Commission (2013 framework). Based on our assessment, we conclude that the Corporation's internal control over financial reporting is effective based on those criteria.

Our internal control over financial reporting as of January 28, 2017, has been audited by Ernst & Young LLP, the independent registered public accounting firm who has also audited our consolidated financial statements, as stated in their report which appears on this page.

Brian C. Cornell
Chairman and Chief Executive Officer
March 8, 2017

Cathy R. Smith
Executive Vice President and
Chief Financial Officer

Report of Independent Registered Public Accounting Firm on Internal Control over Financial Reporting

The Board of Directors and Shareholders

Target Corporation

We have audited Target Corporation and subsidiaries' (the Corporation) internal control over financial reporting as of January 28, 2017, based on criteria established in *Internal Control—Integrated Framework* issued by the Committee of Sponsoring Organizations of the Treadway Commission (2013 Framework) (the COSO criteria). The Corporation's management is responsible for maintaining effective internal control over financial reporting, and for its assessment of the effectiveness of internal control over financial reporting included in the accompanying Report of Management on Internal Control over Financial Reporting. Our responsibility is to express an opinion on the Corporation's internal control over financial reporting based on our audit.

We conducted our audit in accordance with the standards of the Public Company Accounting Oversight Board (United States). Those standards require that we plan and perform the audit to obtain reasonable assurance about whether effective internal control over financial reporting was maintained in all material respects. Our audit included obtaining an understanding of internal control over financial reporting, assessing the risk that a material weakness exists, testing and evaluating the design and operating effectiveness of internal control based on the assessed risk, and performing such other procedures as we considered necessary in the circumstances. We believe that our audit provides a reasonable basis for our opinion.

A company's internal control over financial reporting is a process designed to provide reasonable assurance regarding the reliability of financial reporting and the preparation of financial statements for external purposes in accordance with generally accepted accounting principles. A company's internal control over financial reporting includes those policies and procedures that (1) pertain to the maintenance of records that, in reasonable detail, accurately and fairly reflect the transactions and dispositions of the assets of the company; (2) provide reasonable assurance that transactions are recorded as necessary to permit preparation of financial statements in accordance with generally accepted accounting principles, and that receipts and expenditures of the company are being made only in accordance with authorizations of management and directors of the company; and (3) provide reasonable assurance regarding prevention or timely detection of unauthorized acquisition, use or disposition of the company's assets that could have a material effect on the financial statements.

Because of its inherent limitations, internal control over financial reporting may not prevent or detect misstatements. Also, projections of any evaluation of effectiveness to future periods are subject to the risk that controls may become inadequate because of changes in conditions, or that the degree of compliance with the policies or procedures may deteriorate.

In our opinion, the Corporation maintained, in all material respects, effective internal control over financial reporting as of January 28, 2017, based on the COSO criteria.

We also have audited, in accordance with the standards of the Public Company Accounting Oversight Board (United States), the consolidated statements of financial position of Target Corporation and subsidiaries as of January 28, 2017 and January 30, 2016, and the related consolidated statements of operations, comprehensive income, cash flows and shareholders' investment for each of the three years in the period ended January 28, 2017, and our report dated March 8, 2017, expressed an unqualified opinion thereon.

Ernst & Young LLP

Minneapolis, Minnesota
March 8, 2017

Consolidated Statements of Operations

(millions, except per share data)	2016	2015	2014
Sales	$69,495	$73,785	$72,618
Cost of sales	48,872	51,997	51,278
Gross margin	20,623	21,788	21,340
Selling, general and administrative expenses	13,356	14,665	14,676
Depreciation and amortization	2,298	2,213	2,129
Gain on sale	—	(620)	—
Earnings from continuing operations before interest expense and income taxes	4,969	5,530	4,535
Net interest expense	1,004	607	882
Earnings from continuing operations before income taxes	3,965	4,923	3,653
Provision for income taxes	1,296	1,602	1,204
Net earnings from continuing operations	2,669	3,321	2,449
Discontinued operations, net of tax	68	42	(4,085)
Net earnings / (loss)	$ 2,737	$ 3,363	$ (1,636)
Basic earnings / (loss) per share			
Continuing operations	$ 4.62	$ 5.29	$ 3.86
Discontinued operations	0.12	0.07	(6.44)
Net earnings / (loss) per share	$ 4.74	$ 5.35	$ (2.58)
Diluted earnings / (loss) per share			
Continuing operations	$ 4.58	$ 5.25	$ 3.83
Discontinued operations	0.12	0.07	(6.38)
Net earnings / (loss) per share	$ 4.70	$ 5.31	$ (2.56)
Weighted average common shares outstanding			
Basic	577.6	627.7	634.7
Dilutive effect of share-based awards	4.9	5.2	5.4
Diluted	582.5	632.9	640.1
Antidilutive shares	0.1	—	3.3
Dividends declared per share	$ 2.36	$ 2.20	$ 1.99

Note: Per share amounts may not foot due to rounding.
See accompanying Notes to Consolidated Financial Statements.

Consolidated Statements of Comprehensive Income

(millions)	2016	2015	2014
Net income / (loss)	$2,737	$3,363	$(1,636)
Other comprehensive (loss) / income, net of tax			
Pension and other benefit liabilities, net of tax benefit of $9, $18, and $90	(13)	(27)	(139)
Currency translation adjustment and cash flow hedges, net of provision for taxes of $2, $2, and $2	4	(3)	431
Other comprehensive (loss) / income	(9)	(30)	292
Comprehensive income / (loss)	$2,728	$3,333	$(1,344)

See accompanying Notes to Consolidated Financial Statements.

Consolidated Statements of Financial Position

(millions, except footnotes)	January 28, 2017	January 30, 2016
Assets		
Cash and cash equivalents, including short-term investments of $1,110 and $3,008	$ 2,512	$ 4,046
Inventory	8,309	8,601
Assets of discontinued operations	69	322
Other current assets	1,100	1,161
Total current assets	11,990	14,130
Property and equipment		
Land	6,106	6,125
Buildings and improvements	27,611	27,059
Fixtures and equipment	5,503	5,347
Computer hardware and software	2,651	2,617
Construction-in-progress	200	315
Accumulated depreciation	(17,413)	(16,246)
Property and equipment, net	24,658	25,217
Noncurrent assets of discontinued operations	12	75
Other noncurrent assets	771	840
Total assets	**$ 37,431**	**$40,262**
Liabilities and shareholders' investment		
Accounts payable	$ 7,252	$ 7,418
Accrued and other current liabilities	3,737	4,236
Current portion of long-term debt and other borrowings	1,718	815
Liabilities of discontinued operations	1	153
Total current liabilities	12,708	12,622
Long-term debt and other borrowings	11,031	11,945
Deferred income taxes	861	823
Noncurrent liabilities of discontinued operations	18	18
Other noncurrent liabilities	1,860	1,897
Total noncurrent liabilities	13,770	14,683
Shareholders' investment		
Common stock	46	50
Additional paid-in capital	5,661	5,348
Retained earnings	5,884	8,188
Accumulated other comprehensive loss		
Pension and other benefit liabilities	(601)	(588)
Currency translation adjustment and cash flow hedges	(37)	(41)
Total shareholders' investment	10,953	12,957
Total liabilities and shareholders' investment	**$ 37,431**	**$40,262**

Common Stock Authorized 6,000,000,000 shares, $0.0833 par value; 556,156,228 shares issued and outstanding at January 28, 2017; 602,226,517 shares issued and outstanding at January 30, 2016.
Preferred Stock Authorized 5,000,000 shares, $0.01 par value; no shares were issued or outstanding at January 28, 2017 or January 30, 2016.
See accompanying Notes to Consolidated Financial Statements.

Consolidated Statements of Cash Flows

(millions)	2016	2015	2014
Operating activities			
Net earnings / (loss)	$2,737	$3,363	$(1,636)
Earnings / (losses) from discontinued operations, net of tax	68	42	(4,085)
Net earnings from continuing operations	2,669	3,321	2,449
Adjustments to reconcile net earnings to cash provided by operations:			
Depreciation and amortization	2,298	2,213	2,129
Share-based compensation expense	113	115	71
Deferred income taxes	41	(322)	7
Gain on sale	—	(620)	—
Loss on debt extinguishment	422	—	285
Noncash (gains) / losses and other, net	—	57	40
Changes in operating accounts:			
Inventory	293	(316)	(512)
Other assets	36	227	(115)
Accounts payable and accrued liabilities	(543)	579	803
Cash provided by operating activities—continuing operations	5,329	5,254	5,157
Cash provided by / (required for) operating activities—discontinued operations	107	704	(692)
Cash provided by operations	5,436	5,958	4,465
Investing activities			
Expenditures for property and equipment	(1,547)	(1,438)	(1,786)
Proceeds from disposal of property and equipment	46	28	95
Proceeds from sale of businesses	—	1,875	—
Cash paid for acquisitions, net of cash assumed	—	—	(20)
Other investments	28	24	106
Cash (required for) / provided by investing activities—continuing operations	(1,473)	489	(1,605)
Cash provided by / (required for) investing activities—discontinued operations	—	19	(321)
Cash (required for) / provided by investing activities	(1,473)	508	(1,926)
Financing activities			
Change in commercial paper, net	—	—	(80)
Additions to long-term debt	1,977	—	1,993
Reductions of long-term debt	(2,641)	(85)	(2,079)
Dividends paid	(1,348)	(1,362)	(1,205)
Repurchase of stock	(3,706)	(3,483)	(26)
Stock option exercises	221	300	373
Cash required for financing activities	(5,497)	(4,630)	(1,024)
Net (decrease) / increase in cash and cash equivalents	(1,534)	1,836	1,515
Cash and cash equivalents at beginning of period[a]	4,046	2,210	695
Cash and cash equivalents at end of period	$2,512	$4,046	$2,210
Supplemental information			
Interest paid, net of capitalized interest	$ 999	$ 604	$ 871
Income taxes paid / (refunded)	1,514	(127)	1,251
Property and equipment acquired through capital lease obligations	238	126	88

[a] Includes cash of our discontinued operations of $25 million at February 1, 2014.
See accompanying Notes to Consolidated Financial Statements.

Consolidated Statements of Shareholders' Investment

(millions)	Common Stock Shares	Stock Par Value	Additional Paid-in Capital	Retained Earnings	Accumulated Other Comprehensive (Loss)/Income	Total
February 1, 2014	632.9	$53	$4,470	$12,599	$(891)	$16,231
Net loss	—	—	—	(1,636)	—	(1,636)
Other comprehensive income	—	—	—	—	292	292
Dividends declared	—	—	—	(1,273)	—	(1,273)
Repurchase of stock	(0.8)	—	—	(46)	—	(46)
Stock options and awards	8.1	—	429	—	—	429
January 31, 2015	640.2	$53	$4,899	$9,644	$(599)	$13,997
Net earnings	—	—	—	3,363	—	3,363
Other comprehensive loss	—	—	—	—	(30)	(30)
Dividends declared	—	—	—	(1,378)	—	(1,378)
Repurchase of stock	(44.7)	(4)	—	(3,441)	—	(3,445)
Stock options and awards	6.7	1	449	—	—	450
January 30, 2016	602.2	$50	$5,348	$8,188	$(629)	$12,957
Net earnings	—	—	—	2,737	—	2,737
Other comprehensive loss	—	—	—	—	(9)	(9)
Dividends declared	—	—	—	(1,359)	—	(1,359)
Repurchase of stock	(50.9)	(4)	—	(3,682)	—	(3,686)
Stock options and awards	4.9	—	313	—	—	313
January 28, 2017	556.2	$46	$5,661	$5,884	$(638)	$10,953

See accompanying Notes to Consolidated Financial Statements.

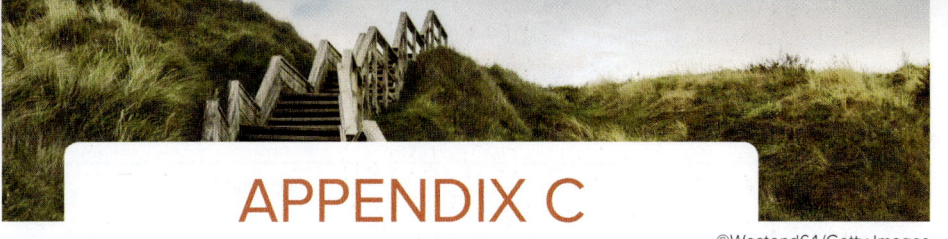
©Westend61/Getty Images

APPENDIX C

SUMMARY OF FINANCIAL RATIOS

CHAPTER 3

Debt-to-Assets Ratio

The debt-to-assets ratio reveals the percentage of a company's assets that is financed with borrowed money. The higher the debt-to-assets ratio is, the greater its financial risk, other things being equal. The debt-to-assets ratio is defined as

$$\frac{\text{Total debt}}{\text{Total assets}}$$

Return-on-Assets Ratio

The return-on-assets ratio (ROA) helps measure how well a company is using the assets available to it. The greater the amount of earnings that can be obtained for a given amount of assets, the better a company is doing at utilizing its assets. So, in general, the higher a company's ROA, the better. The ROA ratio is defined as

$$\frac{\text{Net income}}{\text{Total assets}}$$

Return-on-Equity Ratio

The return-on-equity ratio (ROE) helps to measure how much the owners of a company are earning on the money they have invested in the business. The higher a company's ROE, the better. The ROE is defined as

$$\frac{\text{Net income}}{\text{Stockholders' equity}}$$

CHAPTER 4

Gross Margin Percentage

The gross margin percentage helps explain a company's pricing strategy. It compares the amount a company pays for the goods it sells to the price the company is able to charge for those goods. The more a company marks up its goods, the higher the gross margin percentage will be. Specialty shops tend to have higher gross margin percentages, while discount stores tend to have lower percentages. This ratio is sometimes called the gross profit percentage. The gross margin percentage is defined as

$$\frac{\text{Gross margin}}{\text{Net sales}}$$

Return-on-Sales Ratio

The return-on-sales ratio, expressed as a percentage, indicates how much of each dollar of sales remains as profit after all expenses have been deducted. Discount stores do not necessarily have lower return-on-sales percentages than specialty shops. The higher the return-on-sales ratio percentage, the better. The return-on-sales ratio is defined as

$$\frac{\text{Net income}}{\text{Net sales}}$$

CHAPTER 5

Inventory Turnover Ratio and Average Days to Sell Inventory

The inventory turnover ratio and the average days to sell inventory ratio indicate how long a company takes to sell the goods it has in merchandise inventory. The first ratio, inventory turnover, explains how many times per year a company's inventory is sold, or "turned over"; generally, the *higher* this ratio is, the better. Because the inventory turnover ratio is not easily understood by everyone, the second ratio, average days to sell inventory, is often used. However, the average days to sell inventory ratio cannot be computed without first computing the inventory turnover ratio. Generally, the *lower* the average days to sell inventory ratio is, the better. The inventory turnover ratio is defined as

$$\frac{\text{Cost of goods sold}}{\text{Inventory}}$$

The average days to sell inventory ratio is defined as

$$\frac{365 \text{ days}}{\text{Inventory turnover}}$$

A company's operating cycle is the time it takes it to convert cash into inventory, sell the inventory, and collect the cash from accounts receivable that resulted from the sale of the inventory. The time it takes a business to do this can be computed by adding the *average days to sell inventory* and the *average days to collect accounts receivable*.

CHAPTER 7

Accounts Receivable Turnover Ratio and Average Days to Collect Receivables

The accounts receivable turnover ratio and the average days to collect receivables ratio indicate how long a company takes to collect its accounts receivable. The first ratio, accounts receivable turnover, explains how many times per year a company's receivables are collected, or "turned over"; generally, the *higher* this ratio is, the better. Because the accounts receivable turnover ratios are not easily understood by everyone, the second ratio, average days to collect receivables, is often used. However, the average days to collect receivables ratio cannot be computed without first computing the accounts receivable turnover ratio. Generally, the *lower* the average days to collect receivables ratio is, the better. The accounts receivable turnover ratio is defined as

$$\frac{\text{Sales}}{\text{Accounts receivable}}$$

The average days to collect receivables ratio is defined as

$$\frac{365 \text{ days}}{\text{Accounts receivable turnover ratio}}$$

CHAPTER 9

Current Ratio

Liquidity refers to how quickly noncash assets can be converted into cash. The more quickly assets can be converted into cash, the more liquid they are and the more useful they are for paying liabilities that must be paid in the near future. The current ratio provides a measure of how much liquidity a company has. Specifically, it compares a company's more liquid assets (current assets) to its current liabilities. Other things being equal, the higher a company's current ratio, the easier it can pay its currently maturing debts. The current ratio is defined as

$$\frac{\text{Current assets}}{\text{Current liabilities}}$$

CHAPTER 10

Times-Interest-Earned Ratio

The times-interest-earned ratio helps assess a company's ability to make interest payments on its debt. Failure to make interest (or principal) payments can cause a company to be forced into bankruptcy. Other things being equal, a company with a higher times-interest-earned ratio is considered to have lower financial risk than a company with a lower ratio.

EBIT is an acronym for "earnings before interest and taxes." In other words, it is what net earnings would have been if the company had had no interest expense or income tax expense. Because net earnings are calculated after interest has been subtracted, a company might have $0 of earnings and still have been able to make its interest payments. Thus, the times-interest-earned ratio is based on EBIT and is defined as

$$\frac{\text{EBIT}}{\text{Interest expense}}$$

Return-on-Assets Ratio (refined)

As discussed in detail in Chapter 3, the return-on-assets ratio (ROA) helps measure how well a company is using the assets available to it. The greater the amount of earnings that can be obtained for a given amount of assets, the better a company is doing at utilizing its assets, so the higher this ratio is, the better. Throughout most of this textbook, ROA has been based on net earnings. However, the use of net earnings creates an ROA that is biased against companies with relatively more debt versus equity financing. Because the ROA ratio is intended to help assess how efficiently a company is using its assets, not how it is financed, the ROA that is used in the business world is often defined as

$$\frac{\text{EBIT}}{\text{Total assets}}$$

CHAPTER 11

Price-Earnings Ratio

The price-earnings ratio (P/E ratio) gives an indication of how optimistic the financial markets are about a company's future earnings. The higher a company's P/E ratio is, the more investors are willing to pay for each dollar of earnings that the company generates. Typically, investors are willing to pay this higher price because they think the company will grow in the future. Lower P/E ratios indicate investors are less optimistic about the company's future growth. The price-earnings ratio is defined as

$$\frac{\text{Market price of one share of stock}}{\text{Earnings per share}}$$

Earnings per Share Ratio

The earnings per share ratio (EPS) provides an indication of the amount of a company's earnings that are attributable to each share of common stock outstanding. Obviously, the higher this ratio is, the better. In companies that have complex equity structures, such as convertible preferred stock and stock option plans, the computation of EPS can be very complex, but in its simplest form, EPS is defined as

$$\frac{\text{Net earnings}}{\text{Outstanding shares of common stock}}$$

APPENDIX D

ANNUAL REPORT AND FINANCIAL STATEMENT ANALYSIS PROJECTS

ANNUAL REPORT PROJECT FOR THE TARGET CORPORATION (SEE APPENDIX B FOR THE TARGET ANNUAL REPORT)

Target's 2014, 2015, and 2016 Statements of Operations and Statements of Financial Position have been loaded in Excel spreadsheets and are available in the *Connect* library. The statements in the spreadsheets have been revised to better reflect the format and wording used in the course textbook. The Excel spreadsheets provide a starting point for the vertical and horizontal analysis required in the project.

Please note: All references to the company's year-end data pertain to the fiscal year-end. For example, the company's 2016 financial statements are dated January 28, 2017, which is the company's fiscal closing date. Likewise, the 2015 financial statements apply to the fiscal year-ending January 30, 2016.

Company Overview and Management's Discussion and Analysis

The annual report for Target Corporation opens with a general description of business operations, risk factors, stock market registration, and selected financial data. This is followed by Management's Discussion and Analysis of Financial Condition, in which management talks about financial results, including segment results, liquidity, and other matters deemed necessary to provide adequate disclosure to users of the report. Refer to these items to answer Questions 1–6.

1. How many employees did Target have in 2016?
2. Identify at least five risk factors for Target.
3. On what stock market exchange is the company's stock traded? What is Target's symbol?
4. Who operates the pharmacies located in Target's stores?
5. According to the Consolidated Statements of Operations, sales decreased from $73,785 million in 2015 to $69,495 million in 2016. Identify the main factor for this decline.
6. Target provides information about its capital expenditures related to three major categories: existing stores, new stores, and technology and supply chain. What percentage of capital expenditures was spent on each category in 2016 and in 2014? What has been the trend in Target's capital expenditures over the past three years?

Report of Independent Registered Public Accounting Firm on Consolidated Financial Statements (Auditors)

7. What is the name of the company's independent auditors?
8. Who is responsible for the financial statements?
9. What is the outside auditors' responsibility?

10. What type of opinion did the independent auditors issue on the financial statements (unqualified, qualified, adverse, or disclaimer)? What does this opinion mean?
11. The auditors' report indicates the audit was concerned with material misstatements rather than absolute accuracy in the financial statements. What does "material" mean?

Income Statement—Vertical Analysis

12. Using Excel, compute common-size income statements for all three fiscal years. In common-size income statements, net sales is 100 percent and every other number is a percentage of sales. Attach the spreadsheet to the end of this project. (To help you get started, you can find Target's financial statements in Excel format in *Connect*. The financial statements have been slightly reformatted to conform to the multi-step income statement format utilized throughout the textbook.)
13. Using the common-size income statements, identify the significant trends.
14. What was the gross margin (gross profit) and the gross margin percentage for fiscal years 2016, 2015, and 2014?
15. If the gross margin percentage changed over the three-year period, what caused the change? (*Hint:* Changes in either the numerator or denominator reveal what caused the change in the gross margin percentage.)
16. What was the percentage return on sales for fiscal years 2016, 2015, and 2014? What do these ratios indicate about Target?

Income Statement—Horizontal Analysis

17. Using Excel, compute annual changes for each line item on the income statement. For each of the two most recent years, insert a column for changes in absolute dollars and insert another column for the percentage changes. Attach the spreadsheet to the end of this project. (You can find Target's financial statements in Excel format in *Connect*.)
18. What were the absolute dollar and the percentage changes in revenues between fiscal years 2016 and 2015 and between 2015 and 2014?
19. Describe the trend in revenues. Be specific (e.g., slight/steady/drastic increase or decrease each year, or fluctuating with an initial modest/significant increase or decrease followed by a modest/significant increase or decrease, etc.) to precisely describe the company's situation.
20. What were the absolute dollar and the percentage changes in cost of sales (cost of goods sold) between fiscal years 2016 and 2015 and between 2015 and 2014?
21. Describe the trend in cost of sales (cost of goods sold). Be specific (e.g., slight/steady/drastic increase or decrease each year, or fluctuating with an initial modest/significant increase or decrease followed by a modest/significant increase or decrease, etc.) to precisely describe the company's situation.
22. What were the absolute dollar and the percentage changes in selling, general, and administrative expenses (operating expenses) between fiscal years 2016 and 2015 and between 2015 and 2014?
23. Describe the trend in selling, general, and administrative expenses. Be specific (e.g., slight/steady/drastic increase or decrease each year, or fluctuating with an initial modest/significant increase or decrease followed by a modest/significant increase or decrease, etc.) to precisely describe the company's situation.
24. What were the absolute dollar and the percentage changes in net income between fiscal years 2015 to 2016 and 2014 to 2015?
25. How would you describe the trend for net income? Be specific (e.g., slight/steady/drastic increase or decrease each year, or fluctuating with an initial modest/significant

increase or decrease followed by a modest/significant increase or decrease, etc.) to precisely describe the company's situation. Do you expect the trend to continue?

26. Which items had the largest percentage change from 2014 through 2016, revenues or expenses (such as selling, general, and administrative expenses or cost of sales)?

27. Summarize what is causing the changes in net income from fiscal year 2014 to 2015 and 2015 to 2016 based on the percentages computed in Questions 18 through 26. Do you expect the trend to continue?

Balance Sheet—Vertical Analysis

28. Using Excel, compute common-size balance sheets for the years ended January 28, 2017, and January 30, 2016. In common-size balance sheets, total assets is 100 percent and every other number is a percentage of total assets. Attach the spreadsheet to the end of this project. (You can find Target's financial statements in Excel format in *Connect*.)

29. Current assets constituted what percentage of total assets at January 28, 2017, and January 30, 2016? Which current asset had the largest balance at each fiscal year-end?

30. Long-term assets constituted what percentage of total assets at January 28, 2017, and January 30, 2016? (*Note:* solutions for percentages calculated for items 29 and 30 should total 100 percent.) Which long-term asset had the largest balance at each fiscal year-end?

31. Which category of assets (single line item) on the balance sheet is the largest as of January 28, 2016? Explain why a simple comparison of the percentage amounts for each asset line may lead to misleading results for answering the question, "Which category is largest?"

32. Current liabilities constituted what percentage of total assets at January 28, 2017, and January 30, 2016? Which long-term liability had the largest balance at each fiscal year-end?

33. Long-term liabilities constituted what percentage of total assets at January 28, 2017, and January 30, 2016? Which long-term liability had the largest balance at each fiscal year-end?

34. Calculate the ratio of stockholders' equity to total assets on January 28, 2017, and January 30, 2016. Identify whether Target finances its assets mostly with debt or equity.

Balance Sheet—Horizontal Analysis

35. Using Excel, compute annual changes for each line item on the balance sheet. Insert a column for changes in absolute dollars and insert another column for the percentage changes. Attach the spreadsheet to the end of this project. (You can find Target's financial statements in Excel format in *Connect*.)

36. What was the absolute dollar and the percentage change between the January 30, 2016, and January 28, 2017, of "Assets of discontinued operations" in current assets, and "Noncurrent assets of discontinued operations," in long-term assets? Was the change an increase or decrease? What was the nature of the discontinued operations at Target? You will need to read the Notes to Consolidated Financial Statements to answer this.

37. What was the absolute dollar and the percentage change between the January 28, 2017, and January 30, 2016, balances for inventory? Was the change an increase or decrease? What line item (account) on the income statement is directly related to inventory? Did this account change in a similar direction as inventory?

38. Compared to the January 30, 2016, balances, did the amounts reported for the following long-term assets increase or decrease? By how much? Include dollar amounts for each item.

	Year Ended January 28, 2017	
	Dollar Amount	Increase or Decrease
Property, plant, and equipment, net		
Other noncurrent assets		
Total long-term assets		

What line item on the income statement is directly related to property, plant, and equipment? Did this account change in a similar direction as property, plant, and equipment?

39. What were the absolute dollar and the percentage changes of long-term liabilities from January 28, 2017, to January 30, 2016? Were the changes increases or decreases? What line item (account) on the income statement is closely related to the long-term liabilities? Did this account change in the same direction as long-term liabilities?

40. What was the amount of the change in the balance in retained earnings between January 28, 2017, and January 30, 2016? What caused this change?

Balance Sheet—Ratio Analysis

41. Compute the current ratio at January 28, 2017, and January 30, 2016. What does this ratio indicate about Target?

42. Calculate the debt-to-assets ratios for the years ended January 28, 2017, and January 30, 2016. In which year did Target appear to have the highest financial risk?

43. Calculate the inventory turnover ratios and the average number of days to sell inventory for the years ended January 28, 2017, and January 30, 2016. In which year was the turnover and days to sell inventory more favorable?

Balance Sheet—Stockholders' Equity Section

44. Does the company's common stock have a par value? If so, how much was the par value per share?

45. How many shares of common stock were issued as of January 28, 2017, and January 30, 2016?

46. How many shares of treasury stock did the company have as of January 28, 2017, and January 30, 2016? How were the treasury stock purchases reflected on the statement of cash flows? Include the type of cash flow activity.

47. What percentage of stockholders' equity do the following items represent at each year-end (January 28, 2017, and January 30, 2016)?

	2017	2016
Total paid-in capital	%	%
Retained earnings		
Other items	100%	100%

Statement of Cash Flows

48. Does Target report cash flows from operating activities using the direct or the indirect method? Describe how you can tell.

49. What was the dollar amount of the increase or decrease in cash and cash equivalents for the fiscal years 2016, 2015, and 2014?

50. Does the ending balance of cash and cash equivalents agree with the amount reported on the balance sheet for years ended January 28, 2017, and January 30, 2016?

	2017	2016
Balance sheet	$	$
Statement of cash flows		

51. Identify the four largest individual cash flow items (inflows or outflows) for the year ended January 28, 2017.

52. On what statement(s) would you expect to find information regarding the declaration and payment of dividends? What amount of dividends did Target pay in 2016? What amount of dividends did Target declare in 2016? Briefly explain why these amounts are not the same.

Notes to the Financial Statements

53. In your own words, briefly summarize two significant accounting policies.

54. When does Target recognize the revenue earned from the sale and use of "gift cards"?

55. While there are Target-brand credit cards, Target does not actually own or administer them. Who does, and how much did Target earn in 2016 and 2015 from Target-branded credit cards?

56. Using the following schedule, identify which accounts on the balance sheet and income statement are affected by a company's inventory cost flow assumption. Also, identify the effects that the three inventory cost flow assumptions, FIFO, weighted-average, and LIFO have on the amounts reported on the balance sheet and income statement. Specifically, identify which cost flow assumption results in the highest, lowest, and middle dollar amount that is reported in the relevant account on each statement. Assume that prices are rising.

	Effect of Cost Flow Assumptions		
Account Affected	FIFO	AVG	LIFO
1. Balance Sheet:			
2. Income Statement:			

57. What inventory cost flow method does Target use?

58. What are the estimated useful lives of the company's depreciable assets?

59. Using the following schedule, identify which accounts on the balance sheet and income statement are affected, given the two types of depreciation methods a company may use (accelerated versus straight-line). Also, assuming it is the first year a depreciable asset is used, identify the effects that the two depreciation methods have on the amounts reported on the balance sheet and income statement. Specifically, identify which method results in the highest dollar amount reported, and which results in the lowest.

	Effect of Depreciation Methods	
Account Affected	Accelerated	Straight-Line
1. Balance Sheet:		
2. Income Statement:		

60. What method of depreciation does Target use?
61. Did the balance in the goodwill account increase or decrease? Speculate as to what caused this change.
62. In addition to goodwill, what kinds of intangible assets does the company have? What are their estimated lives?
63. Identify three different accrued expenses.
64. Identify two kinds of commitments and contingencies.
65. What is the amount of available unsecured revolving credit? What was the balance outstanding at the end of each fiscal year?
66. What is the amount of total long-term borrowings at January 28, 2017? What was the weighted-average interest rate on Target's notes payable and debentures for 2016? Other than "long-term debt and other borrowings," what are the other long-term liability items reported on the balance sheet?

Performance Measures

67. Compute the return-on-assets ratio (use net income rather than EBIT in the numerator) for the years ended January 28, 2017, and January 30, 2016.
68. Compute the return-on-equity ratio for the years ended January 28, 2017, and January 30, 2016.
69. Were the return-on-equity ratios greater or lesser than the return-on-assets ratios? Explain why.
70. What were Target's basic earnings per share (EPS) for the years ended January 28, 2017, and January 30, 2016? Identify what caused the ratio to change.

FINANCIAL STATEMENTS PROJECT (SELECTION OF COMPANY TO BE DECIDED BY INSTRUCTOR)

Date Due: _____

Required

Based on the annual report of the company you are reviewing, answer the following questions. If you cannot answer a particular question, briefly explain why. If the question is not applicable to your company's financial statements, answer "N/A."

Show all necessary computations in good form. Label all numbers in your computations. If relevant, reference your answers to the page(s) in the annual report.

"Current year" means the most recent fiscal year in the company's annual report. "Prior year" means the fiscal year immediately preceding the current year.

1. What products or services does the company sell? Be specific.
2. What do you think the outlook is for these products or services? Why do you think so?
3. By what percentage have sales increased or decreased in each of the last two fiscal years?
4. If the company reported sales by segments, which segment had the largest percentage of total sales? Which segment had the smallest percentage of total sales? **Show computations of the relevant percentages.**

   Largest segment _____   Percentage of total sales _____

   Smallest segment _____   Percentage of total sales _____

5. What is net income for the current year? _____
6. Did the current year's net income increase or decrease since the prior year? By how much? What caused the change?

7. If the company reported earnings by segments, which segment had the largest percentage of total earnings? Which segment had the smallest percentage of total earnings? **Show computations of the relevant percentages.**

   Largest segment _____ Percentage of total earnings _____

   Smallest segment _____ Percentage of total earnings _____

8. Did the company report any special, unusual, or otherwise nonroutine items in either current or prior year net income? If so, explain the item(s).

9. For the current year, how does net income compare to net cash provided (used) by operating activities?

10. For the current year, what one or two items were most responsible for the difference between net income and net cash provided (used) by operating activities?

11. Did the company pay cash dividends during the current year? If so, how much were they?

12. If the company paid cash dividends, what percentage of net income were the cash dividends? If the company did not pay cash dividends, why do you think it did not?

13. Which of the following is the company's largest asset category: accounts receivable, inventory, or land? What is the amount of that asset category?

14. If the company reported assets by segments, which segment had the largest percentage of total assets? Which segment had the smallest percentage of total assets? **Show computations of the relevant percentages.**

    Largest segment _____ Percentage of total assets _____

    Smallest segment _____ Percentage of total assets _____

15. How much **cash** did the company invest in property, plant, and equipment during the current year?

16. Which inventory method(s) did the company use?

17. Which depreciation method(s) did the company use?

18. If the company has any intangible assets, what kind are they?

19. Did the company report any contingent liabilities ("contingencies")? If so, briefly explain.

20. Does the company have any preferred stock authorized? If so, how many shares were authorized?

21. Does the company's common stock have a par value? If so, what was it?

22. In what price range was the company's common stock trading during the last quarter of the current year?

23. What was the market price of the company's common stock on DD/MM/Year?

24. Where (on what stock exchange) is the company's stock traded?

25. Who was the company's independent auditor?

26. Develop one question about the company's financial report that you do not know how to answer.

27. Compute the following ratios for the current year and the prior year. Show the appropriate formulas in the first column. Show all supporting computations in the second and third columns.

Appendix D

Ratio	Current Year	Prior Year
Gross Profit Formula:		
Inventory Turnover Formula:		
Current Ratio Formula:		
Debt to Equity Formula:		
Return on Assets Formula:		
Return on Equity Formula:		

APPENDIX E

ACCOUNTING FOR INVESTMENT SECURITIES

TYPES OF INVESTMENT SECURITIES

A financial investment occurs when one entity provides assets or services to another entity in exchange for a certificate known as a *security*. The entity that provides the assets and receives the security certificate is called the **investor.** The entity that receives the assets or services and gives the security certificate is called the **investee.** This appendix discusses accounting practices that apply to securities held by investors.

There are two primary types of investment securities: debt securities and equity securities. An investor receives a **debt security** when assets *are loaned* to the investee. In general, a debt security describes the investee's obligation to return the assets and to pay interest for the use of the assets. Common types of debt securities include bonds, notes, certificates of deposit, and commercial paper.

An **equity security** is obtained when an investor acquires an *ownership interest* in the investee. An equity security usually describes the rights of ownership, including the right to influence the operations of the investee and to share in profits or losses that accrue from those operations. The most common types of equity securities are common stock and preferred stock. In summary, **investment securities** are certificates that describe the rights and privileges that investors receive when they loan or give assets or services to investees.

Transactions between the investor and the investee constitute the **primary securities market.** There is a **secondary securities market** in which investors exchange (buy and sell) investment securities with other investors. Securities that regularly trade in established secondary markets are called **marketable securities.** Investee companies are affected by secondary-market transactions only to the extent that their obligations are transferred to a different party. For example, assume that Tom Williams (investor) loans assets to American Can Company (investee). Williams receives a bond (investment security) from American Can that describes American Can's obligation to return assets and pay interest to Williams. This exchange represents a primary securities market transaction. Now assume that, in a secondary-market transaction, Williams sells his investment security (bond) to Tina Tucker. American Can Company is affected by this transaction only to the extent that the company's obligation transfers from Williams to Tucker. In other words, American Can's obligation to repay principal and interest does not change. The only thing that changes is the party to whom American Can makes payments. *An investee's financial statements are not affected when the securities it has issued to an investor are traded in the secondary market.*

The **fair value,** also called **market value,** is the amount that the investor would receive if the securities were sold in an orderly transaction. More specifically, the fair value is based on the amount that would be collected (an exit value) from the sale of an asset as opposed to the cost necessary to acquire a comparable asset. For a more detailed definition of fair value, see *FASB Accounting Standards Codification Topic 820,* "Fair Value Measurements and Disclosures." Whether securities are reported at fair value or historical cost depends on whether the investor intends to sell or hold the securities. Generally accepted accounting principles require companies to classify their investment securities into one of three categories: (1) held-to-maturity securities, (2) trading securities, and (3) available-for-sale securities.

Held-to-Maturity Securities

Because equity securities representing ownership interests have no maturity date, the held-to-maturity classification applies only to debt securities. Debt securities should be classified as held-to-maturity securities if the investor has a *positive intent* and the *ability* to hold the securities until the maturity date. **Held-to-maturity securities** are reported on the balance sheet at *amortized historical cost*.[1]

Trading Securities

Both debt and equity securities can be classified as *trading securities*. **Trading securities** are bought and sold for the purpose of generating profits on the short-term appreciation of stock or bond prices. They are usually traded frequently and within short time spans from the time when they are acquired. Trading securities are reported on the investor's balance sheet at their fair value on the investor's fiscal closing date.

Available-for-Sale Securities

All marketable securities that are not classified as held-to-maturity or trading securities must be classified as **available-for-sale securities.** These securities are also reported on the investor's balance sheet at fair value as of the investor's fiscal closing date.

Two of the three classifications, therefore, must be reported at fair value, which is a clear exception to the historical cost concept. Other exceptions to the use of historical cost measures for asset valuation are discussed in later sections of this appendix.

REPORTING EVENTS THAT AFFECT INVESTMENT SECURITIES

The effects on the investor's financial statements of four distinct accounting events involving marketable investment securities are illustrated in the following section. The illustration assumes that the investor, Arapaho Company, started the accounting period with cash of $10,000 and common stock of $10,000.

EVENT 1 Arapaho paid $9,000 cash to purchase marketable investment securities.

This event is an asset exchange. One asset (cash) decreases, and another asset (investment securities) increases. The income statement is not affected. The $9,000 cash outflow is reported as either an operating activity or an investing activity, depending on how the securities are classified. Because *trading securities* are short-term assets that are regularly traded for the purpose of producing income, cash flows from the purchase or sale of trading securities are reported in the operating activities section of the statement of cash flows. In contrast, cash flows involving the purchase or sale of securities classified as *held to maturity* or *available for sale* are reported in the investing activities section of the statement of cash flows. The only difference among the three alternatives lies

---

[1] Debt securities are frequently purchased for amounts that are more or less than their face value (the amount of principal due at the maturity date). If the purchase price is above the face value, the difference between the face value and the purchase price is called a *premium*. If the purchase price is below the face value, the difference is called a *discount*. Premiums and discounts increase or decrease the amount of interest revenue earned and affect the carrying value of the bond investment reported on the balance sheet. The presentation in this appendix makes the simplifying assumption that the bonds are purchased at a price equal to their face value. Accounting for discounts and premiums is discussed in Chapter 10.

in the classification of the cash outflow reported on the statement of cash flows, as shown in the following statements model:

Event No.	Type	Assets			=	Liab.	+	Equity	Rev.	−	Exp.	=	Net Inc.	Cash Flow
		Cash	+	Inv. Sec.										
1	Held	(9,000)	+	9,000	=	NA	+	NA	NA	−	NA	=	NA	(9,000) IA
1	Trading	(9,000)	+	9,000	=	NA	+	NA	NA	−	NA	=	NA	(9,000) OA
1	Available	(9,000)	+	9,000	=	NA	+	NA	NA	−	NA	=	NA	(9,000) IA

EVENT 2 Arapaho earned $1,600 of cash investment revenue.

Investment revenue is reported the same way regardless of whether the investment securities are classified as held to maturity, trading, or available for sale. Investment revenue comes in two forms. Earnings from equity investments are called **dividends.** Revenue from debt securities is called **interest.** Both forms have the same impact on the financial statements. Recognizing the investment revenue increases both assets and stockholders' equity. Revenue and net income increase. The cash inflow from investment revenue is reported in the operating activities section of the statement of cash flows regardless of how the investment securities are classified.

Event No.	Assets	=	Liab.	+	Equity	Rev.	−	Exp.	=	Net Inc.	Cash Flow
	Cash	=			Ret. Earn.						
2	1,600	=	NA	+	1,600	1,600	−	NA	=	1,600	1,600 OA

EVENT 3 Arapaho sold securities that cost $2,000 for $2,600 cash.

This event results in recognizing a $600 realized (actual) gain that increases both total assets and stockholders' equity. The asset cash increases by $2,600 and the asset investment securities decreases by $2,000, resulting in a $600 increase in total assets. The $600 realized gain is reported on the income statement, increasing net income and retained earnings. The $600 gain does not appear on the statement of cash flows. Instead, the entire $2,600 cash inflow is reported in one section of the statement of cash flows. Cash inflows from the sale of held-to-maturity and available-for-sale securities are reported as investing activities. Cash flows involving trading securities are reported as operating activities. These effects are shown next:

Event No.	Type	Assets			=	Liab.	+	Equity	Rev. or Gain	−	Exp. or Loss	=	Net Inc.	Cash Flow
		Cash	+	Inv. Sec.										
3	Held	2,600	+	(2,000)	=	NA	+	600	600	−	NA	=	600	2,600 IA
3	Trading	2,600	+	(2,000)	=	NA	+	600	600	−	NA	=	600	2,600 OA
3	Available	2,600	+	(2,000)	=	NA	+	600	600	−	NA	=	600	2,600 IA

EVENT 4 Arapaho recognized a $700 unrealized gain.

After Event 3, the historical cost of Arapaho's portfolio of remaining investment securities is $7,000 ($9,000 purchased less $2,000 sold). Assume that at Arapaho's fiscal closing date, these securities have a fair value of $7,700, giving Arapaho a $700 unrealized gain on its investment. This type of gain (sometimes called a *paper profit*) is classified as *unrealized* because the securities have not been sold. The treatment of **unrealized gains or losses** in the financial statements depends on whether the securities are classified as held to maturity, trading, or available for sale. Unrealized gains or losses on securities classified as *held to maturity* are not recognized in the financial statements; they have no effect on the balance sheet, income statement, and statement of cash flows. Even so, many companies choose to disclose the market value of the securities as part of the narrative description or in the notes that accompany the financial statements. Whether or not the market value is disclosed, held-to-maturity securities are reported on the balance sheet at amortized cost.

Investments classified as trading securities are reported in the financial statements at fair value. Unrealized gains or losses on *trading securities* are recognized in net income even though the securities have not been sold. In Arapaho's case, the $700 gain increases the carrying value of the investment securities. The gain increases net income, which in turn increases retained earnings. Unrealized gains and losses have no effect on cash flows.

Investments classified as available-for-sale securities are also reported in the financial statements at fair value. However, an important distinction exists with respect to how the unrealized gains and losses affect the financial statements. Even though unrealized gains or losses on available-for-sale securities are included in the assets on the balance sheet, they *are not* recognized in determining net income.[2] On Arapaho's balance sheet, the $700 gain increases the carrying value of the investment securities. A corresponding increase is reported in a separate equity account called Unrealized Gain or Loss on Available-for-Sale Securities. The statement of cash flows is not affected by recognizing unrealized gains and losses on available-for-sale securities.

The effects of these alternative treatments of unrealized gains and losses on Arapaho's financial statements are shown next:

Event No.	Type	Assets	=	Liab.	+	Equity			Rev. or Gain	−	Exp. or Loss	=	Net Inc.	Cash Flow
		Inv. Sec.	=			Ret. Earn.	+	Unreal. Gain						
4	Held	NA	=	NA	+	NA	+	NA	NA	−	NA	=	NA	NA
4	Trading	700	=	NA	+	700	+	NA	700	−	NA	=	700	NA
4	Available	700	=	NA	+	NA	+	700	NA	−	NA	=	NA	NA

FINANCIAL STATEMENTS

As the preceding discussion implies, the financial statements of Arapaho Company are affected by not only the business events relating to its security transactions but also the accounting treatment used to report those events. In other words, the same economic events are reflected differently in the financial statements depending on whether the securities are classified as held to maturity, trading, or available for sale. Exhibit E.1 displays the financial statements for Arapaho under each investment classification alternative.

---

[2]GAAP permits companies to report unrealized gains and losses on available-for-sale securities as additions to or subtractions from net income with the result being titled *comprehensive income*. Alternatively, the unrealized gains and losses can be reported on a separate statement of net income and other comprehensive income.

EXHIBIT E.1

ARAPAHO COMPANY
Comparative Financial Statements

Income Statements

Investment Securities Classified as	Held	Trading	Available
Investment revenue	$1,600	$1,600	$1,600
Realized gain	600	600	600
Unrealized gain		700	
Net income	$2,200	$2,900	$2,200

Balance Sheets

	Held	Trading	Available
Assets			
Cash	$ 5,200	$ 5,200	$ 5,200
Investment securities, at cost (market value $7,700)	7,000		
Investment securities, at market (cost $7,000)		7,700	7,700
Total assets	$12,200	$12,900	$12,900
Stockholders' equity			
Common stock	$10,000	$10,000	$10,000
Retained earnings	2,200	2,900	2,200
Unrealized gain on investment securities			700
Total stockholders' equity	$12,200	$12,900	$12,900

Statements of Cash Flows

	Held	Trading	Available
Operating Activities			
Cash inflow from investment revenue	$ 1,600	$ 1,600	$ 1,600
Outflow to purchase securities		(9,000)	
Inflow from sale of securities		2,600	
Investing Activities			
Outflow to purchase securities	(9,000)		(9,000)
Inflow from sale of securities	2,600		2,600
Financing Activities*	0	0	0
Net decrease in cash	(4,800)	(4,800)	(4,800)
Beginning cash balance	10,000	10,000	10,000
Ending cash balance	$ 5,200	$ 5,200	$ 5,200

*The $10,000 of common stock is assumed to have been issued prior to the start of the accounting period.

The net income reported under the trading securities alternative is $700 higher than that reported under the held-to-maturity and available-for-sale alternatives because unrealized gains and losses on trading securities are recognized on the income statement. Similarly, total assets and total stockholders' equity are $700 higher under the trading and available-for-sale alternatives than they are under the held-to-maturity category because the $700 unrealized gain is recognized on the balance sheet for those two classifications. The gain is not reported on the income statement for available-for-sale securities; it is reported on the balance sheet in a special equity account called Unrealized Gain on Investment Securities. The statements of cash flows report purchases and sales of trading securities as operating activities, while purchases and sales of available-for-sale and held-to-maturity securities are

EXHIBIT E.2

Investment Category	Types of Securities	Types of Revenue Recognized	Reported on Balance Sheet at	Recognition of Unrealized Gains and Losses on the Income Statement	Cash Flow from Purchase or Sale of Securities Classified as
Held to maturity	Debt	Interest	Amortized cost	No	Investing activity
Trading	Debt and equity	Interest and dividends	Market value	Yes	Operating activity
Available for sale	Debt and equity	Interest and dividends	Market value	No	Investing activity

investing activities. Exhibit E.2 summarizes the reporting differences among the three classifications of investment securities.

Alternative Reporting Practices for Equity Securities

If an investor owns 20 percent or more of an investee's equity securities, the investor is presumed able, unless there is evidence to the contrary, to exercise *significant influence* over the investee company. Investors owning more than 50 percent of the stock of an investee company are assumed to have control over the investee. The previous discussion of accounting rules for equity securities assumed the investor did not significantly influence or control the investee. Alternative accounting rules apply to securities owned by investors who exercise significant influence or control over an investee company. Accounting for equity investment securities differs depending on the level of the investor's ability to influence or control the operating, investing, and financing activities of the investee.

As previously demonstrated, investors who do not have significant influence (they own less than 20 percent of the stock of the investee) account for their investments in equity securities at fair value. Investors exercising significant influence (they own 20 to 50 percent of the investee's stock) must account for their investments using the **equity method.** A detailed discussion of the equity method is beyond the scope of this text. However, *be aware that investments reported using the equity method represent a measure of the book value of the investee rather than the cost or fair value of the equity securities owned.*

Investors that have a controlling interest (they own more than 50 percent of the investee's stock) in an investee company are required to issue **consolidated financial statements.** The company that holds the controlling interest is referred to as the **parent company,** and the company that is controlled is called the **subsidiary company.** Usually, the parent and subsidiary companies maintain separate accounting records. However, a parent company is also required to report to the public its accounting data along with that of its subsidiaries in a single set of combined financial statements. These consolidated statements represent a separate accounting entity consisting of the parent and its subsidiaries. A parent company that owns one subsidiary will produce three sets of financial statements: statements for the parent company, statements for the subsidiary company, and statements for the consolidated entity.

KEY TERMS

Available-for-sale securities 720
Consolidated financial statements 724
Debt security 719
Dividend 721
Equity method 724
Equity security 719
Fair value 719
Held-to-maturity securities 720
Interest 721
Investee 719
Investment securities 719
Investor 719
Market value 719
Marketable securities 719
Parent company 724
Primary securities market 719
Secondary securities market 719
Subsidiary company 724
Trading securities 720
Unrealized gains or losses 722

EXERCISES

Exercise E1 Identifying asset values for financial statements

Required

Indicate whether each of the following assets should be valued at fair market value (FMV), lower of cost or market (LCM), or historical cost (HC) on the balance sheet. For certain assets, historical cost may be called amortized cost (AC).

Asset	FMV	LCM	HC/AC
Buildings			
Available-for-sale securities			
Office equipment			
Inventory			
Supplies			
Land			
Trading securities			
Cash			
Held-to-maturity securities			

Exercise E2 Accounting for investment securities

Norris Co. purchased $36,000 of marketable securities on March 1, Year 1. On the company's fiscal year closing date, December 31, Year 1, the securities had a market value of $27,000. During Year 1, Norris Co. recognized $10,000 of revenue and $2,000 of expenses.

Required

a. Record a +, −, or NA in a horizontal statements model to show how the purchase of the securities affects the financial statements, assuming that the securities are classified as (1) held to maturity, (2) trading, or (3) available for sale. In the Cash Flow column, indicate whether the event is an operating activity (OA), investing activity (IA), or financing activity (FA). Record only the effects of the purchase event.

Event No.	Type	Cash	+	Inv. Sec.	=	Liab.	+	Equity	Rev.	−	Exp.	=	Net Inc.	Cash Flow
1	Held													
2	Trading													
3	Available													

b. Determine the amount of net income that would be reported on the Year 1 income statement, assuming that the marketable securities are classified as (1) held to maturity, (2) trading, or (3) available for sale.

Exercise E3 Effect of investment securities transactions on financial statements

The following information pertains to Botter Supply Co. for Year 1:

1. Purchased $100,000 of marketable investment securities.
2. Earned $10,000 of cash investment revenue.
3. Sold for $30,000 securities that cost $25,000.
4. The fair value of the remaining securities at December 31, Year 1, was $89,000.

Required

a. Record the four events in a statements model like the following one. Use a separate model for each classification: (1) held to maturity, (2) trading, and (3) available for sale. The first event for the first classification is shown as an example.

Held to Maturity

Event No.	Cash	+	Inv. Sec.	=	Liab.	+	Ret. Earn.	+	Unreal. Gain	Rev. or Gains	−	Exp. or Loss	=	Net Inc.	Cash Flow
1	(100,000)	+	100,000	=	NA	+	NA	+	NA	NA	−	NA	=	NA	(100,000) IA

b. What is the amount of net income under each of the three classifications?
c. What is the change in cash from operating activities under each of the three classifications?
d. Are the answers to requirements *b* and *c* different for each of the classifications? Why or why not?

Exercise E4 *Preparing financial statements for investment securities*

Molten, Inc. began Year 2 with $100,000 in both cash and common stock. The company engaged in the following investment transactions during Year 2:

1. Purchased $20,000 of marketable investment securities.
2. Earned $600 cash from investment revenue.
3. Sold investment securities for $14,000 that cost $10,000.
4. Purchased $7,000 of additional marketable investment securities.
5. Determined that the investment securities had a fair value of $22,000 at the end of Year 2.

Required

Use a vertical statements model to prepare income statements, balance sheets, and statements of cash flow for Molten, Inc. assuming the securities were (*a*) held to maturity, (*b*) trading, and (*c*) available for sale.

Exercise E5 *Differences among marketable investment securities classifications*

Complete the following table for the three categories of marketable investment securities:

Investment Category	Types of Securities	Types of Revenue Recognized	Value Reported on Balance Sheet	Recognition of Unrealized Gains and Losses on the Income Statement	Cash Flow from Purchase or Sale of Securities Is Classified as
Held to maturity	Debt	Interest	Amortized cost	No	Investing activity
Trading					
Available for sale					

Exercise E6 *Effect of marketable investment securities transactions on financial statements*

The following transactions pertain to Harrison Imports for Year 1:

1. Started business by acquiring $30,000 cash from the issue of common stock.
2. Provided $90,000 of services for cash.
3. Invested $35,000 in marketable investment securities.
4. Paid $18,000 of operating expense.
5. Received $500 of investment income from the securities.
6. Invested an additional $16,000 in marketable investment securities.

7. Paid a $2,000 cash dividend to the stockholders.
8. Sold investment securities that cost $8,000 for $14,000.
9. Received another $1,000 in investment income.
10. Determined the market value of the investment securities at the end of the year was $42,000.

Required

Use a vertical statements model to prepare a Year 1 income statement, balance sheet, and statement of cash flows, assuming that the marketable investment securities were classified as (a) held to maturity, (b) trading, and (c) available for sale. (*Hint:* Record the events in T-accounts prior to preparing the financial statements.)

Exercise E7 *Comprehensive horizontal statements model*

Woody's Catering experienced the following independent events:

1. Acquired cash from issuing common stock.
2. Purchased inventory on account.
3. Paid cash to purchase marketable securities classified as trading securities.
4. Recorded unrealized loss on marketable securities that were classified as available-for-sale securities.
5. Recorded unrealized loss on marketable securities that were classified as trading securities.
6. Recorded unrealized loss on marketable securities that were classified as held-to-maturity securities.
7. Wrote down inventory to comply with lower-of-cost-or-market rule. (Assume that the company uses the perpetual inventory system.)
8. Recognized cost of goods sold under the weighted-average method.
9. Recognized cost of goods sold under FIFO.

Required

a. Show the effect of each event on the elements of the financial statements using a horizontal statements model like the following one. Use + for increase, − for decrease, and NA for not affected. In the Cash Flow column, indicate whether the item is an operating activity (OA), investing activity (IA), or financing activity (FA). The first transaction is entered as an example.

Event No.	Assets	=	Liab.	+	Equity	Rev. or Gain	−	Exp. or Loss	=	Net Inc.	Cash Flow
1	+		NA		+	NA		NA		NA	+ FA

b. Explain why there is or is not a difference in the way Events 8 and 9 affect the financial statements model.

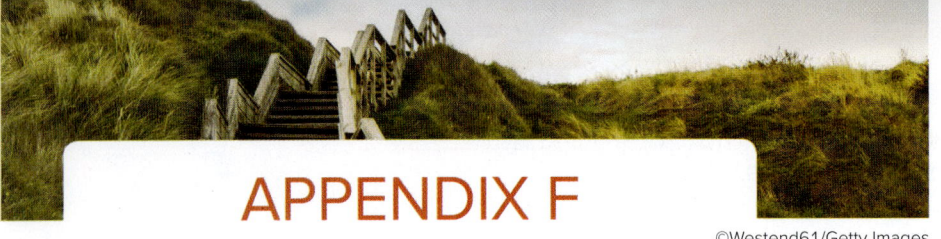

APPENDIX F

TIME VALUE OF MONEY

Future Value

Suppose you recently won $10,000 cash in a local lottery. You save the money to have funds available to obtain a masters of business administration (MBA) degree. You plan to enter the program three years from today. Assuming you invest the money in an account that earns 8 percent annual interest, how much money will you have available in three years? The answer depends on whether your investment will earn *simple* or *compound* interest.

To determine the amount of funds available assuming you earn 8 percent **simple interest,** multiply the principal balance by the interest rate to determine the amount of interest earned per year ($10,000 × 0.08 = $800). Next, multiply the amount of annual interest by the number of years the funds will be invested ($800 × 3 = $2,400). Finally, add the interest earned to the principal balance to determine the total amount of funds available at the end of the three-year term ($10,000 principal + $2,400 interest = $12,400 cash available at the end of three years).

Investors can increase their returns by reinvesting the income earned from their investments. For example, at the beginning of the second year, you will have available for investment not only the original $10,000 principal balance but also $800 of interest earned during the first year. In other words, you will be able to earn interest on the interest that you previously earned. Earning interest on interest is called **compounding.** Assuming you earn 8 percent compound interest, the amount of funds available to you at the end of three years can be computed as shown in Exhibit F.1.

EXHIBIT F.1

Year	Amount Invested	×	Interest Rate	=	Interest Earned	+	Amount Invested	=	New Balance
1	$10,000.00	×	0.08	=	$ 800.00	+	$10,000.00	=	$10,800.00
2	10,800.00	×	0.08	=	864.00	+	10,800.00	=	11,664.00
3	11,664.00	×	0.08	=	933.12	+	11,664.00	=	12,597.12
Total interest earned				=	$2,597.12				

Obviously, you earn more with compound interest ($2,597.12 compound versus $2,400 simple). The computations required for **compound interest** can become cumbersome when the investment term is long. Fortunately, there are mathematical formulas, interest tables, and computer programs that reduce the computational burden. For example, a compound interest factor can be developed from the formula

$$(1 + i)^n$$

where i = interest

n = **number of periods**

The value of the investment is determined by multiplying the compound interest factor by the principal balance. The compound interest factor for a three-year term and an 8 percent interest rate is 1.259712 (1.08 × 1.08 × 1.08 = 1.259712). Assuming a $10,000 original investment, the value of the investment at the end of three years is $12,597.12 ($10,000 × 1.259712).

This is, of course, the same amount that was computed in the previous illustration (see the final figure in the New Balance column of Exhibit F.1).

The mathematical formulas have been used to develop tables of interest factors that can be used to determine the **future value** of an investment for a variety of interest rates and time periods. For example, Table I (shown at the end of Appendix F) contains the interest factor for an investment with a three-year term earning 8 percent compound interest. To confirm this point, move down the column marked n to the third period. Next, move across to the column marked 8 percent, where you will find the value 1.259712. This is identical to the amount computed using the mathematical formula in the preceding paragraph. Here also, the value of the investment at the end of three years can be determined by multiplying the principal balance by the compound interest factor ($10,000 × 1.259712 = $12,597.12). These same factors and amounts can be determined using computer programs in calculators and spreadsheet software.

Clearly, a variety of ways can be used to determine the future value of an investment, given a principal balance, interest rate, and term to maturity. In our case, we showed that your original investment of $10,000 would be worth $12,597 in three years, assuming an 8 percent compound interest rate. Suppose you determine this amount is insufficient to get you through the MBA program you want to complete. Assume you believe you will need $18,000 three years from today to sustain yourself while you finish the degree. Suppose your parents agree to cover the shortfall. They ask how much money you need today in order to have $18,000 three years from now.

Present Value

The mathematical formula required to convert the future value of a dollar to its **present value** equivalent is

$$(1 + i)^n$$

where i = interest

   n = number of periods

For easy conversion, the formula has been used to develop Table II, Present Value of $1 (shown at the end of Appendix F). At an 8 percent annual compound interest rate, the present value equivalent of $18,000 to be received three years from today is computed as follows: Move down the far left column to where $n = 3$. Next, move right to the column marked 8 percent. At this point, you should see the interest factor 0.793832. Multiplying this factor by the desired future value of $18,000 yields the present value of $14,288.98 ($18,000 × 0.793832). This means if you invest $14,288.98 (present value) today at an annual compound interest rate of 8 percent, you will have the $18,000 (future value) you need to enter the MBA program three years from now.

If you currently have $10,000, you will need an additional $4,288.98 from your parents to make the required $14,288.98 investment that will yield the future value of $18,000 you need. Having $14,288.98 today is the same as having $18,000 three years from today, assuming you can earn 8 percent compound interest. To validate this conclusion, use Table I to determine the future value of $14,288.98, given a three-year term and 8 percent annual compound interest. As previously indicated, the future value conversion factor under these conditions is 1.259712. Multiplying this factor by the $14,288.98 present value produces the expected future value of $18,000 ($14,288.98 × 1.259712 = $18,000). The factors in Table I can be used to convert present values to future values, and the corresponding factors in Table II are used to convert future values to present values.

Future Value Annuities

The previous examples described present and future values of a single lump-sum payment. Many financial transactions involve a series of payments. To illustrate, we return to the example in which you want to have $18,000 available three years from today. We continue the assumption that you can earn 8 percent compound interest. However, now we assume that you do not have $14,288.98 to invest today. Instead, you decide to save part of the money during each of the next three years. How much money must you save each year to have $18,000 at the end of three years? *The series of equal payments made over a number of periods in order to acquire a future value is called an* **annuity.** The factors in Table III, Future Value of an Annuity of $1 (shown at the end of Appendix F) can be used to determine the amount of the annuity needed to produce the desired $18,000 future value. The table is constructed so that future values can be determined by multiplying the conversion factor by the amount of the annuity. These relationships can be expressed algebraically as follows:

Amount of annuity payment × Table conversion factor = Future value

To determine the amount of the required annuity payment in our example, first locate the future value conversion factor. In Table III, move down the first column on the left-hand side until you locate period 3. Next, move to the right until you locate the 8 percent column. At this location, you will see a conversion factor of 3.2464. This factor can be used to determine the amount of the annuity payment as indicated in the following:

Amount of annuity payment × Table conversion factor = Future value

Amount of annuity payment = Future value ÷ Table conversion factor

Amount of annuity payment = $18,000.00 ÷ 3.2464

Amount of annuity payment = $5,544.60

If you deposit $5,544.60 in an investment account at the end of each of the next three years,[1] the investment account balance will be $18,000, assuming your investment earns 8 percent interest compounded annually. This conclusion is confirmed by the following schedule:

End of Year	Beg. Acct. Bal.	+	Interest Computation	+	Payment	=	End. Acct. Bal.
1	NA	+	NA	+	$5,544.60	=	$ 5,544.60
2	$ 5,544.60	+	$ 5,544.60 × 0.08 = $443.57	+	5,544.60	=	11,532.77
3	11,532.77	+	11,532.77 × 0.08 = 922.62	+	5,544.60	=	18,000.00*

*Total does not add exactly due to rounding.

PRESENT VALUE ANNUITIES

We previously demonstrated that a future value of $18,000 is equivalent to a present value of $14,288.98, given annual compound interest of 8 percent for a three-year period. If the future value of a $5,544.60 annuity for three years is equivalent to $18,000, that same annuity should have a present value of $14,288.98. We can test this conclusion by using the conversion factors in Table IV, Present Value of an Annuity of $1 (shown at the end of Appendix F). The present value annuity table is constructed so that present values can be determined by multiplying the conversion factor by the amount of the annuity. These relationships can be expressed algebraically as follows:

Amount of annuity payment × Table conversion factor = Present value

To determine the present value of the annuity payment in our example, first locate the present value conversion factor. In Table IV, move down the first column on the left-hand side until you locate period 3. Next, move to the right until you locate the column for the

---

[1] A payment made at the end of a period is known as an *ordinary annuity*. A payment made at the beginning of a period is called an *annuity due*. Tables are generally set up to assume ordinary annuities. Minor adjustments must be made when dealing with an annuity due. For the purposes of this text, we consider all annuities to be ordinary.

8 percent interest rate. At this location, you will see a conversion factor of 2.577097. This factor can be used to determine the amount of the present value of the annuity payment, as indicated:

Amount of annuity payment × Table conversion factor = Present value

$5,544.60 × 2.577097 = $14,288.97*

*The 1 cent difference between this value and the expected value of $14,288.98 is due to rounding.

In summary, Tables III and IV can be used to convert annuities to future or present values for a variety of different assumptions regarding interest rates and time periods.

BUSINESS APPLICATIONS

Long-Term Notes Payable

In Chapter 10, we considered a case in which Blair Company borrowed $100,000 from National Bank. We indicated that Blair agreed to repay the bank through a series of annual payments (an *annuity*) of $25,709 each. How was this amount determined? Recall that Blair agreed to pay the bank 9 percent interest over a five-year term. Under these circumstances, we are trying to find the annuity equivalent to the $100,000 present value that the bank is loaning Blair. The first step in determining the annuity (annual payment) is to locate the appropriate present value conversion factor from Table IV. At the fifth row under the 9 percent column, you will find the value 3.889651. This factor can be used to determine the amount of the annuity payment as indicated in the following:

Amount of annuity payment × Table conversion factor = Present value

Amount of annuity payment = Present value ÷ Table conversion factor

Amount of annuity payment = $100,000 ÷ 3.889651

Amount of annuity payment = $25,709

There are many applications in which debt repayment occurs through annuities. Common examples with which you are probably familiar include auto loans and home mortgages. Payment schedules for such loans may be determined from the interest tables, as demonstrated here. However, most real-world businesses have further refined the computational process through the use of sophisticated computer programs. The software program prompts the user to provide the relevant information regarding the present value of the amount borrowed, number of payments, and interest rate. Given this information and a few keystrokes, the computer program produces the amount of the amortization payment along with an amortization schedule showing the amounts of principal and interest payments over the life of the loan. Similar results can be obtained with a spreadsheet software application such as Excel. Even many handheld calculators have present and future value functions that enable users to quickly compute annuity payments for an infinite number of interest rate and time period assumptions.

Bond Liabilities: Determine Price

In Chapter 10, we discussed the use of discounts and premiums as a means of producing an effective rate of interest that is higher or lower than the stated rate of interest. For example, if the stated rate of interest is lower than the market rate of interest at the time the bonds are issued, the issuer can increase the effective interest rate by selling the bonds for a price lower than their face value. At maturity, the issuer will settle the obligation by paying the face value of the bond. The difference between the discounted bond price and the face value of the bond is additional interest. To illustrate, assume that Tower Company issues $100,000 face value bonds with a 20-year term and a 9 percent stated rate of annual interest. At the time the bonds are issued, the market rate of interest for bonds of comparable risk is 10 percent annual interest. For what amount would Tower Company be required to sell the bonds in order to move its 9 percent stated rate of interest to an effective rate of 10 percent?

Information from present value Tables II and IV is required to determine the amount of the discount required to produce a 10 percent effective rate of interest. First, we identify the future cash flows that will be generated by the bonds. Based on the stated interest rate, the bonds will pay $9,000 ($100,000 face value × 0.09 interest) interest per year. This constitutes a 20-year annuity that should be discounted back to its present value equivalent. Also, at the end of 20 years, the bonds will require a single $100,000 lump-sum payment to settle the principal obligation. This amount must also be discounted back to its present value in order to determine the bond price. The computations required to determine the discounted bond price are shown next:

Present value of principal	$100,000 × 0.148644 (Table II, $n = 20$, $i = 10\%$)	= $14,864.40
Present value of interest	$9,000 × 8.513564 (Table IV, $n = 20$, $i = 10\%$)	= 76,622.08
Bond price (proceeds received)		$91,486.48

Tower Company bonds sell at an $8,513.52 discount ($100,000 − $91,486.48) to produce a 10 percent effective interest rate. Note that in these computations, the stated rate of interest was used to determine the amount of cash flow, and the effective rate of interest was used to determine the table conversion factors.

TABLE I — Future Value of $1

n	4%	5%	6%	7%	8%	9%	10%	12%	14%	16%	20%
1	1.040000	1.050000	1.060000	1.070000	1.080000	1.090000	1.100000	1.120000	1.140000	1.160000	1.200000
2	1.081600	1.102500	1.123600	1.144900	1.166400	1.188100	1.210000	1.254400	1.299600	1.345600	1.440000
3	1.124864	1.157625	1.191016	1.225043	1.259712	1.295029	1.331000	1.404928	1.481544	1.560896	1.728000
4	1.169859	1.215506	1.262477	1.310796	1.360489	1.411582	1.464100	1.573519	1.688960	1.810639	2.073600
5	1.216653	1.276282	1.338226	1.402552	1.469328	1.538624	1.610510	1.762342	1.925415	2.100342	2.488320
6	1.265319	1.340096	1.418519	1.500730	1.586874	1.677100	1.771561	1.973823	2.194973	2.436396	2.985984
7	1.315932	1.407100	1.503630	1.605781	1.713824	1.828039	1.948717	2.210681	2.502269	2.826220	3.583181
8	1.368569	1.477455	1.593848	1.718186	1.850930	1.992563	2.143589	2.475963	2.852586	3.278415	4.299817
9	1.423312	1.551328	1.689479	1.838459	1.999005	2.171893	2.357948	2.773079	3.251949	3.802961	5.159780
10	1.480244	1.628895	1.790848	1.967151	2.158925	2.367364	2.593742	3.105848	3.707221	4.411435	6.191736
11	1.539454	1.710339	1.898299	2.104852	2.331639	2.580426	2.853117	3.478550	4.226232	5.117265	7.430084
12	1.601032	1.795856	2.012196	2.252192	2.518170	2.812665	3.138428	3.895976	4.817905	5.936027	8.916100
13	1.665074	1.885649	2.132928	2.409845	2.719624	3.065805	3.452271	4.363493	5.492411	6.885791	10.699321
14	1.731676	1.979932	2.260904	2.578534	2.937194	3.341727	3.797498	4.887112	6.261349	7.987518	12.839185
15	1.800944	2.078928	2.396558	2.759032	3.172169	3.642482	4.177248	5.473566	7.137938	9.265521	15.407022
16	1.872981	2.182875	2.540352	2.952164	3.425943	3.970306	4.594973	6.130394	8.137249	10.748004	18.488426
17	1.947900	2.292018	2.692773	3.158815	3.700018	4.327633	5.054470	6.866041	9.276464	12.467685	22.186111
18	2.025817	2.406619	2.854339	3.379932	3.996019	4.717120	5.559917	7.689966	10.575169	14.462514	26.623333
19	2.106849	2.526950	3.025600	3.616528	4.315701	5.141661	6.115909	8.612762	12.055693	16.776517	31.948000
20	2.191123	2.653298	3.207135	3.869684	4.660957	5.604411	6.727500	9.646293	13.743490	19.460759	38.337600

TABLE II — Present Value of $1

n	4%	5%	6%	7%	8%	9%	10%	12%	14%	16%	20%
1	0.961538	0.952381	0.943396	0.934579	0.925926	0.917431	0.909091	0.892857	0.877193	0.862069	0.833333
2	0.924556	0.907029	0.889996	0.873439	0.857339	0.841680	0.826446	0.797194	0.769468	0.743163	0.694444
3	0.888996	0.863838	0.839619	0.816298	0.793832	0.772183	0.751315	0.711780	0.674972	0.640658	0.578704
4	0.854804	0.822702	0.792094	0.762895	0.735030	0.708425	0.683013	0.635518	0.592080	0.552291	0.482253
5	0.821927	0.783526	0.747258	0.712986	0.680583	0.649931	0.620921	0.567427	0.519369	0.476113	0.401878
6	0.790315	0.746215	0.704961	0.666342	0.630170	0.596267	0.564474	0.506631	0.455587	0.410442	0.334898
7	0.759918	0.710681	0.665057	0.622750	0.583490	0.547034	0.513158	0.452349	0.399637	0.353830	0.279082
8	0.730690	0.676839	0.627412	0.582009	0.540269	0.501866	0.466507	0.403883	0.350559	0.305025	0.232568
9	0.702587	0.644609	0.591898	0.543934	0.500249	0.460428	0.424098	0.360610	0.307508	0.262953	0.193807
10	0.675564	0.613913	0.558395	0.508349	0.463193	0.422411	0.385543	0.321973	0.269744	0.226684	0.161506
11	0.649581	0.584679	0.526788	0.475093	0.428883	0.387533	0.350494	0.287476	0.236617	0.195417	0.134588
12	0.624597	0.556837	0.496969	0.444012	0.397114	0.355535	0.318631	0.256675	0.207559	0.168463	0.112157
13	0.600574	0.530321	0.468839	0.414964	0.367698	0.326179	0.289664	0.229174	0.182069	0.145227	0.093464
14	0.577475	0.505068	0.442301	0.387817	0.340461	0.299246	0.263331	0.204620	0.159710	0.125195	0.077887
15	0.555265	0.481017	0.417265	0.362446	0.315242	0.274538	0.239392	0.182696	0.140096	0.107927	0.064905
16	0.533908	0.458112	0.393646	0.338735	0.291890	0.251870	0.217629	0.163122	0.122892	0.093041	0.054088
17	0.513373	0.436297	0.371364	0.316574	0.270269	0.231073	0.197845	0.145644	0.107800	0.080207	0.045073
18	0.493628	0.415521	0.350344	0.295864	0.250249	0.211994	0.179859	0.130040	0.094561	0.069144	0.037561
19	0.474642	0.395734	0.330513	0.276508	0.231712	0.194490	0.163508	0.116107	0.082948	0.059607	0.031301
20	0.456387	0.376889	0.311805	0.258419	0.214548	0.178431	0.148644	0.103667	0.072762	0.051385	0.026084

TABLE III — Future Value of an Annuity of $1

n	4%	5%	6%	7%	8%	9%	10%	12%	14%	16%	20%
1	1.000000	1.000000	1.000000	1.000000	1.000000	1.000000	1.000000	1.000000	1.000000	1.000000	1.000000
2	2.040000	2.050000	2.060000	2.070000	2.080000	2.090000	2.100000	2.120000	2.140000	2.160000	2.200000
3	3.121600	3.152500	3.183600	3.214900	3.246400	3.278100	3.310000	3.374400	3.439600	3.505600	3.640000
4	4.246464	4.310125	4.374616	4.439943	4.506112	4.573129	4.641000	4.779328	4.921144	5.066496	5.368000
5	5.416323	5.525631	5.637093	5.750739	5.866601	5.984711	6.105100	6.352847	6.610104	6.877135	7.441600
6	6.632975	6.801913	6.975319	7.153291	7.335929	7.523335	7.715610	8.115189	8.535519	8.977477	9.929920
7	7.898294	8.142008	8.393838	8.654021	8.922803	9.200435	9.487171	10.089012	10.730491	11.413873	12.915904
8	9.214226	9.549109	9.897468	10.259803	10.636628	11.028474	11.435888	12.299693	13.232760	14.240093	16.499085
9	10.582795	11.026564	11.491316	11.977989	12.487558	13.021036	13.579477	14.775656	16.085347	17.518508	20.798902
10	12.006107	12.577893	13.180795	13.816448	14.486562	15.192930	15.937425	17.548735	19.337295	21.321469	25.958682
11	13.486351	14.206787	14.971643	15.783599	16.645487	17.560293	18.531167	20.654583	23.044516	25.732904	32.150419
12	15.025805	15.917127	16.869941	17.888451	18.977126	20.140720	21.384284	24.133133	27.270749	30.850169	39.580502
13	16.626838	17.712983	18.882138	20.140643	21.495297	22.953385	24.522712	28.029109	32.088654	36.786196	48.496603
14	18.291911	19.598632	21.015066	22.550488	24.214920	26.019189	27.974983	32.392602	37.581065	43.671987	59.195923
15	20.023588	21.578564	23.275970	25.129022	27.152114	29.360916	31.772482	37.279715	43.842414	51.659505	72.035108
16	21.824531	23.657492	25.672528	27.888054	30.324283	33.003399	35.949730	42.753280	50.980352	60.925026	87.442129
17	23.697512	25.840366	28.212880	30.840217	33.750226	36.973705	40.544703	48.883674	59.117601	71.673030	105.930555
18	25.645413	28.132385	30.905653	33.999033	37.450244	41.301338	45.599173	55.749715	68.394066	84.140715	128.116666
19	27.671229	30.539004	33.759992	37.378965	41.446263	46.018458	51.159090	63.439681	78.969235	98.603230	154.740000
20	29.778079	33.065954	36.785591	40.995492	45.761964	51.160120	57.274999	72.052442	91.024928	115.379747	186.688000

TABLE IV — Present Value of an Annuity of $1

n	4%	5%	6%	7%	8%	9%	10%	12%	14%	16%	20%
1	0.961538	0.952381	0.943396	0.934579	0.925926	0.917431	0.909091	0.892857	0.877193	0.862069	0.833333
2	1.886095	1.859410	1.833393	1.808018	1.783265	1.759111	1.735537	1.690051	1.646661	1.605232	1.527778
3	2.775091	2.723248	2.673012	2.624316	2.577097	2.531295	2.486852	2.401831	2.321632	2.245890	2.106481
4	3.629895	3.545951	3.465106	3.387211	3.312127	3.239720	3.169865	3.037349	2.913712	2.798181	2.588735
5	4.451822	4.329477	4.212364	4.100197	3.992710	3.889651	3.790787	3.604776	3.433081	3.274294	2.990612
6	5.242137	5.075692	4.917324	4.766540	4.622880	4.485919	4.355261	4.111407	3.888668	3.684736	3.325510
7	6.002055	5.786373	5.582381	5.389289	5.206370	5.032953	4.868419	4.563757	4.288305	4.038565	3.604592
8	6.732745	6.463213	6.209794	5.971299	5.746639	5.534819	5.334926	4.967640	4.638864	4.343591	3.837160
9	7.435332	7.107822	6.801692	6.515232	6.246888	5.995247	5.759024	5.328250	4.946372	4.606544	4.030967
10	8.110896	7.721735	7.360087	7.023582	6.710081	6.417658	6.144567	5.650223	5.216116	4.833227	4.192472
11	8.760477	8.306414	7.886875	7.498674	7.138964	6.805191	6.495061	5.937699	5.452733	5.028644	4.327060
12	9.385074	8.863252	8.383844	7.942686	7.536078	7.160725	6.813692	6.194374	5.660292	5.197107	4.439217
13	9.985648	9.393573	8.852683	8.357651	7.903776	7.486904	7.103356	6.423548	5.842362	5.342334	4.532681
14	10.563123	9.898641	9.294984	8.745468	8.244237	7.786150	7.366687	6.628168	6.002072	5.467529	4.610567
15	11.118387	10.379658	9.712249	9.107914	8.559479	8.060688	7.606080	6.810864	6.142168	5.575456	4.675473
16	11.652296	10.837770	10.105895	9.446649	8.851369	8.312558	7.823709	6.973986	6.265060	5.668497	4.729561
17	12.165669	11.274066	10.477260	9.763223	9.121638	8.543631	8.021553	7.119630	6.372859	5.748704	4.774634
18	12.659297	11.689587	10.827603	10.059087	9.371887	8.755625	8.201412	7.249670	6.467420	5.817848	4.812195
19	13.133939	12.085321	11.158116	10.335595	9.603599	8.905115	8.364920	7.365777	6.550369	5.877455	4.843496
20	13.590326	12.462210	11.469921	10.594014	9.818147	9.128546	8.513564	7.469444	6.623131	5.928841	4.869580

KEY TERMS

Annuity 730
Compound interest 728
Compounding 728
Future value 729
Present value 729
Simple interest 728

EXERCISES

 All applicable Exercises are available in Connect.

Exercise F1 *Future value and present value*

Required

Using Tables I, II, III, or IV in this appendix, calculate the following:

a. The future value of $30,000 invested at 8 percent for 10 years.
b. The future value of eight annual payments of $2,000 at 9 percent interest.
c. The amount that must be deposited today (present value) at 8 percent to accumulate $60,000 in five years.
d. The annual payment on a 10-year, 6 percent, $50,000 note payable.

Exercise F2 *Computing the payment amount*

Barry Rich is a business major at State U. He will be graduating this year and is planning to start a consulting business. He will need to purchase computer equipment that costs $25,000. He can borrow the money from the local bank but will have to make annual payments of principal and interest.

Required

a. Compute the annual payment Barry will be required to make on a $25,000, four-year, 8 percent loan.
b. If Barry can afford to make annual payments of $8,000, how much can he borrow?

Exercise F3 *Saving for a future value*

Billy Dan and Betty Lou were recently married and want to start saving for their dream home. They expect the house they want will cost approximately $325,000. They hope to be able to purchase the house for cash in 10 years.

Required

a. How much will Billy Dan and Betty Lou have to invest each year to purchase their dream home at the end of 10 years? Assume an interest rate of 9 percent.
b. Billy Dan's parents want to give the couple a substantial wedding gift for the purchase of their future home. How much must Billy Dan's parents give them now if they are to reach the desired amount of $325,000 in 12 years? Assume an interest rate of 9 percent.

Exercise F4 *Sale of bonds at a discount using present value*

Carr Corporation issued $50,000 of 6 percent, 10-year bonds on January 1, Year 1, for a price that reflected a 7 percent market rate of interest. Interest is payable annually on December 31.

Required

a. What was the selling price of the bonds?
b. Prepare the journal entry to record issuing the bonds.
c. Prepare the journal entry for the first interest payment on December 31, Year 1, using the effective interest rate method.

GLOSSARY

©Westend61/Getty Images

absolute amounts Dollar totals reported in accounts on financial reports that can be misleading because they make no reference to the relative size of the company being analyzed.

accelerated depreciation method Depreciation method that recognizes more depreciation expense in the early stages of an asset's life than the straight-line method, and less later in the asset's life.

account Record of classified and summarized transaction data; component of financial statement elements.

account balance Difference between total debit and total credit amounts in an account.

accounting Service-based profession developed to provide reliable and relevant financial information useful in making decisions.

accounting controls Procedures companies implement to safeguard assets and to ensure accurate and reliable accounting records and reports.

accounting equation Algebraic relationship between a company's assets and the claims on those assets, represented as Assets = Liabilities + Equity.

accounting event Economic occurrence that changes a company's assets, liabilities, or equity.

accounting period Time span covered by the financial statements; normally one year, but may be a quarter, a month, or some other time interval.

accounts receivable Expected future cash receipts arising from permitting customers to *buy now and pay later;* typically relatively small balances due within a short time period.

accounts receivable turnover Financial ratio that measures how fast accounts receivable are collected in cash; computed by dividing sales by accounts receivable.

accrual Recognition of events before exchanging cash.

accrual accounting Accounting system that recognizes expenses or revenues when they occur regardless of when cash is exchanged.

accrued expenses Expenses that are recognized before cash is paid. An example is accrued salaries expense.

accrued interest Interest revenue or expense that is recognized before cash has been exchanged.

accumulated depreciation Contra asset account that shows the sum of all depreciation expense recognized for an asset since the date of acquisition.

acid-test ratio Measure of immediate debt-paying ability; calculated by dividing very liquid assets (cash, receivables, and marketable securities) by current liabilities.

adjusting entry Entry that updates account balances prior to preparing financial statements; a bookkeeping tool. Adjusting entries never affect the Cash account.

administrative controls Procedures companies implement to evaluate performance and monitor compliance with company policies and public laws.

adverse opinion Opinion issued by a certified public accountant that means one or more departures from GAAP in a company's financial statements are so very material the auditors believe the financial statements do not fairly represent the company's status; contrast with *unqualified opinion.*

aging of accounts receivable Classifying each account receivable by the number of days it has been outstanding. The aging schedule is used to develop an estimate of the amount of the allowance for doubtful accounts.

Allowance for Doubtful Accounts Contra asset account used to record the amount of accounts receivable estimated to be uncollectible.

allowance method of accounting for uncollectible accounts An accounting practice that recognizes an estimated rather than the actual amount of uncollectible accounts expense. Estimated expenses are used to improve matching of revenues and expenses and/or to more accurately reflect the net realizable value of accounts receivable.

American Institute of Certified Public Accountants (AICPA) National association that serves the educational and professional interests of members of the public accounting profession; membership is voluntary. See also *Code of Professional Conduct.*

amortization (1) Systematic and periodic allocation of the costs of intangible assets to expense over their useful lives; (2) periodically transferring the discount on a note or a bond to interest expense.

amortizing Systematically allocating the cost of intangible assets to expense over their useful lives; also a term for converting the discount on a note or a bond to interest expense over a designated period.

annual report A document companies publish to provide information, including financial statements, to stockholders.

annuity Series of equal cash flows received or paid over equal time intervals at a constant rate of return.

appropriated retained earnings Retained earnings restricted by the board of directors for a specific purpose (e.g., to repay debt or for future expansion); part of total retained earnings, but not available for distribution as dividends.

articles of incorporation Information about a proposed corporation, such as its name, purpose, location, expected life, proposed capital stock, and a list of the members of its board of directors, filed with a state agency when applying for the legal formation of the corporation.

articulation Characteristic of financial statements that means they are interrelated. For example, the amount of net income reported on the income statement is added to beginning retained earnings as a component in calculating the ending retained earnings balance reported on the statement of changes in stockholders' equity.

asset Economic resource used to produce revenue that is expected to provide a future benefit to the business.

asset exchange transaction A transaction, such as the purchase of land with cash, that decreases one asset and increases another asset; total assets remain unchanged.

asset source transaction A transaction that increases both an asset and a claim on assets; the three types of asset source transactions are acquisitions from owners (equity), borrowings from creditors (liabilities), or earnings from operations (revenues).

asset turnover ratio The amount of net sales divided by average total assets.

asset use transaction A transaction that decreases both an asset and a claim on assets; the three types of asset use transactions are distributions (transfers to owners), liability payments (to creditors), or expenses (costs incurred to operate the business).

audit Detailed examination of some aspect of a company's accounting records or operating procedures in order to report the results to interested parties. See also *financial statements audit.*

Glossary

authority manual Written documentation outlining levels of authority and responsibility. The authority manual provides specific guidelines, such as those for a personnel officer, as well as general guidelines, such as giving all vice presidents authorization to approve up to a designated spending limit.

authorized stock Number of shares of stock a corporation has state approval to issue.

available-for-sale securities Classification for marketable securities that are not considered held-to-maturity or trading securities.

average days to collect accounts receivable (average collection period) Measure of how quickly, on average, a business collects its accounts receivable; calculated as 365 divided by the accounts receivable turnover.

average days to sell inventory (average days in inventory) Financial ratio that measures the average number of days that inventory stays in stock before it is sold.

balance sheet Financial statement that reports a company's assets and the corresponding claims (liabilities and equity) on those assets as of a specific date (usually as of the end of the accounting period).

bank reconciliation Schedule that identifies and explains differences between the cash balance reported by the bank and the cash balance in the company's accounting records.

bank statement Record issued by a bank (usually monthly) of all activity in the bank account for that period.

bank statement credit memo Bank statement enclosure that describes an increase in the account balance.

bank statement debit memo Bank statement enclosure that describes a decrease in the account balance.

basket purchase Acquiring several assets at once for a single purchase price; no specific cost is attributed to the individual assets.

board of directors Group of individuals elected by the stockholders of a corporation to oversee its operations.

bond certificate Debt security used to obtain long-term financing in which a company borrows funds from a number of lenders, called *bondholders;* usually issued in denominations of $1,000.

bond discount Difference between the selling price and the face amount of a bond sold for less than the face amount.

bond premium Difference between the selling price and the face amount of a bond sold for more than the face amount.

bondholder The party buying a bond (the lender or creditor).

book of original entry A journal in which a transaction is first recorded.

book value Historical (original) cost of an asset minus accumulated depreciation to date.

book value per share An accounting measure of a share of common stock, computed by dividing total stockholders' equity less preferred rights by the number of common shares outstanding.

call premium Difference between the call price (the price that must be paid for a called bond) and the face amount of the bond.

call price Specified price an issuer must pay to call bonds; usually higher than the face amount of the bonds.

callable bonds Bonds that the issuer, at its option, may pay off prior to maturity.

capital expenditures (for an existing asset) Substantial amounts spent to improve an asset's quality or to extend its life.

carrying value Face amount of a bond liability less any unamortized bond discount or plus any unamortized bond premium.

cash Coins, currency, checks, balances in checking and certain savings accounts, money orders, bank drafts, certificates of deposit, and other items that are payable on demand.

cash discount Price reduction on merchandise sold offered by sellers to encourage prompt payment; when taken, represents a sales discount to the seller and a purchase discount to the buyer of the merchandise.

cash inflows Sources of cash.

cash outflows Uses of cash.

Cash Short and Over Account used to record the amount of cash shortages or overages; shortages represent expenses and overages represent revenues.

certified check Check guaranteed by a bank to be drawn on an account with sufficient funds to pay the check.

certified public accountant (CPA) Accountant who, by meeting certain educational and experiential requirements, is licensed by the state government to provide audit services to the public.

chart of accounts List of all ledger accounts and their corresponding account numbers.

checks Prenumbered forms, sometimes multicopy, preprinted on the face with the name of the business issuing them, authorizing the bank to disburse funds from the issuer's account. The issuer enters the transaction date, the desired payee, and the amount in the appropriate places on the check form.

claims Owners' and creditors' interests in a business's assets.

claims exchange transaction A transaction that decreases one claim and increases another claim; total claims remain unchanged. For example, accruing interest expense is a claims exchange transaction; liabilities increase, and the expense recognition decreases retained earnings.

classified balance sheet Balance sheet that distinguishes between current and noncurrent items.

closely held corporation Corporation whose stock is exchanged among a limited number of individuals.

closing entries Entries that transfer the balances in the temporary accounts (Revenue, Expense, and Dividends accounts) to the Retained Earnings account at the end of the accounting period.

closing the books; closing Bookkeeping technique of transferring balances from the temporary accounts (Revenue, Expense, and Dividends) to the permanent account (Retained Earnings).

Code of Professional Conduct Guidelines established by the American Institute of Certified Public Accountants (AICPA) to promote ethical conduct among certified public accountants; AICPA members agree to adhere to this code, which goes beyond legal requirements.

collateral Assets pledged as security for a loan.

common size financial statements Financial statements in which dollar amounts are converted to percentages to aid in comparing financial data among periods and among companies.

common stock Basic class of corporate stock that has no preferential claim on assets or dividends; certificates that evidence ownership in a company.

compound interest Interest earned on interest by reinvesting interest so that it is added to the initial principal. Contrast with *simple interest.*

compounding Earning interest on interest.

confidentiality Code of ethics requirement that prohibits CPAs from voluntarily disclosing information they acquire as a result of accountant–client relationships.

consistency The generally accepted accounting principle that a company should, in most circumstances, continually use the same accounting method(s) so that its financial statements are comparable across time.

consolidated financial statements Financial statements that represent the combined operations of a parent company and its subsidiaries.

contingent liability Obligations with amounts due that depend on events that will be resolved in the future.

continuity Presumption that a corporation's existence may extend well beyond the time at which any particular shareholder retires or sells his or her stock.

contra asset account Account used to reduce the reported value of the asset to which it relates (e.g., subtracting the contra asset Allowance for Bad Debts from Accounts Receivable reduces receivables to their net realizable value).

contra liability account Account used to reduce the reported value of the liability to which it relates (e.g., subtracting the contra liability Discount on Notes Payable from Notes Payable reduces the amount of liabilities on the balance sheet).

convertible bonds Bonds that bondholders can convert (exchange) to ownership interests (stock) in the corporation.

copyright Legal protection of writers' works, musical compositions, and other intellectual property for the exclusive use of the creator or persons assigned the right by the creator.

corporation Legal entity separate from its owners, created by the state pursuant to an application submitted according to state laws by a group of individuals with a common purpose.

cost An amount paid to acquire a resource (asset) or to pay for a resource that has been consumed. Incurring cost results in an asset exchange or expense recognition.

cost method of accounting for treasury stock Method of accounting for treasury stock in which treasury stock purchases are recorded in the Treasury Stock account at their cost to the company without regard to the original issue price or par value.

cost of goods available for sale Total costs paid to obtain goods and ready them for sale, including the cost of beginning inventory plus purchases and transportation-in costs, less purchase returns and allowances and purchase discounts.

cost of goods sold Total cost incurred for the goods sold during a specific accounting period.

credit Entry on the right side of an account; increases liability and equity accounts or decreases asset accounts.

creditor Individual or organization that has loaned goods or services to a business.

cumulative dividends Preferred dividends that accumulate from year to year until paid.

current (short-term) asset Asset that will be converted to cash or consumed within one year or an operating cycle, whichever is longer.

current (short-term) liability Obligation due within one year or an operating cycle, whichever is longer.

current ratio (working capital ratio) Measure of liquidity; calculated by dividing current assets by current liabilities.

date of record Date that establishes who will receive the dividend payment: shareholders who actually own the stock on the record date will receive the dividend even if they sell the stock before the dividend is paid.

debenture Unsecured bond backed by the general credit of the issuing company.

debit Entry on the left side of an account; increases asset accounts or decreases liability and equity accounts.

debt security Type of financial instrument that represents a liability to the investee company.

debt-to-assets ratio Financial measure of a company's level of risk, calculated as total debt divided by total assets.

debt-to-equity ratio Financial ratio that compares creditor financing to owner financing, expressed as the dollar amount of liabilities for each dollar of stockholder's equity.

declaration date Date on which the board of directors declares a dividend.

deferral Recognition of revenue or expense in a period after the cash is exchanged.

deferred tax liability Income tax payment postponed until future years because of the difference in accounting methods selected for financial reporting and methods required for tax purposes (e.g., a company may use straight-line depreciation in financial statements but use MACRS for tax reporting).

depletion The removal of natural resources from the land; the depletion costs of the natural resources are systematically transferred to expense as the resources are removed.

deposit ticket Bank form submitted along with funds that identifies the account number, account name, and a record of the checks and cash being put in the account.

deposits in transit Deposits added to a depositor's books but not received and recorded by the bank prior to the date of the bank statement.

depreciable cost Original cost minus salvage value (of a long-term depreciable asset).

depreciation Decline in value of long-term tangible assets such as buildings, furniture, or equipment. It is systematically recognized by accountants as depreciation expense over the useful lives of the affected assets.

depreciation expense Portion of the original cost of a long-term tangible asset allocated to an expense account in a given period.

direct method Method of reporting cash flows from operating activities on the statement of cash flows that shows individual categories of cash receipts from and cash payments for major activities (collections from customers, payments to suppliers, etc.).

direct write-off method Accounting practice of recognizing uncollectible accounts expense when accounts are determined to be uncollectible, regardless of the period in which the related sale occurred.

disclaimer of opinion Report on financial statements issued when the auditor is unable to obtain enough information to determine if the statements conform to GAAP; is neither positive nor negative.

discount Amount of interest included in the face of a discount note; the discount (interest) is subtracted from the face amount of the note to determine the amount of cash borrowed (principal).

discount note Note with interest included in its face value, which is also the maturity value.

Discount on Bonds Payable Contra liability account used to record the amount of discount on a bond issue.

Discount on Notes Payable Contra liability account subtracted from the Notes Payable account to determine the carrying value of the liability.

dividend Transfer of wealth from a business to its owners.

dividend yield Ratio for comparing stock dividends paid in relation to the market price; calculated as dividends per share divided by market price per share.

dividends in arrears Cumulative dividends on preferred stock that were not paid in prior periods; must be paid before paying any dividends to holders of common stock.

double taxation Recognition that corporate profits distributed to owners are taxed twice, once when the income is reported on the corporation's income tax return and again when the dividends are reported on the individual's return.

double-declining-balance depreciation Depreciation computations that produce larger amounts of depreciation in the early years of an asset's life and progressively smaller amounts as the asset ages.

double-entry accounting (double-entry bookkeeping) Recordkeeping system that provides checks and balances by recording two sides for every transaction.

earnings (net income) The difference between revenues and expenses. Sometimes called *profit*.

earnings per share (EPS) Measure of the value of a share of common stock in terms of company earnings; calculated as net income available to common stockholders divided by the average number of outstanding common shares.

effective interest rate Yield rate of bonds, equal to the market rate of interest on the day the bonds are sold.

effective interest rate method Method of amortizing bond discounts and premiums that bases interest computations on the carrying value of the liability. As the liability increases or decreases, the amount of interest expense also increases or decreases.

elements The primary financial statement categories: assets, liabilities, equity, contributed capital, revenue, expenses, gains, losses, distributions, and net income.

employee An individual whose labor is supervised, directed, and controlled by a business.

Employee's Withholding Allowance Certificate, Form W-4 A form used by an employee to report the number of withholding allowances claimed by the employee. Each withholding allowance reduces the amount of income tax withheld from the employee's pay.

Employer's Quarterly Federal Tax Return, Form 941 The form used to show the amounts due and paid to the government for federal tax withholdings.

equity method Method of accounting for investments in marketable equity securities required when the investor company owns 20 percent or more of the investee company. Under the equity method, the amount of the investment asset represents a measure of the book value of the investee rather than the cost or market value of the investment security.

equity security Type of financial instrument that evidences an ownership interest in a company, such as a common stock certificate.

estimated useful life Time period for which a business expects to use an asset.

ex-dividend Stock traded after the date of record but before the payment date; does not receive the benefit of the upcoming dividend.

expense An economic sacrifice (decrease in assets or increase in liabilities) that is incurred in the process of generating revenue.

face value (of bond) Amount to be paid to the bondholder at bond maturity; base for computing periodic cash interest payments.

fair value The price at which securities or other assets sell in free markets. Also called *market value*.

Federal Unemployment Tax Act (FUTA) The act that requires employers to pay unemployment tax for the establishment of a fund that is used to provide temporary relief to qualified unemployed persons.

fidelity bond Insurance policy that a company buys to insure itself against loss due to employee dishonesty.

financial accounting Branch of accounting focused on the business information needs of external users (creditors, investors, governmental agencies, financial analysts, etc.); its objective is to classify and record business events and transactions to produce external financial reports (income statement, balance sheet, statement of cash flows, and statement of changes in equity).

Financial Accounting Standards Board (FASB) Private, independent standard-setting body established by the accounting profession that has been delegated the authority by the SEC to establish most of the accounting rules and regulations for public financial reporting.

financial leverage Principle of increasing earnings through debt financing by investing money at a higher rate than the rate paid on the borrowed money.

financial resources Money or credit supplied to a business by investors (owners) and creditors.

financial statements Reports used to communicate a company's financial information to interested external parties. The four general-purpose financial statements are the income statement, statement of changes in equity, balance sheet, and statement of cash flows.

financial statements audit Detailed examination of a company's accounting records and the documents that support the information reported in the financial statements; includes testing the reliability of the underlying accounting system used to produce the financial reports.

financing activities Cash inflows and outflows from transactions with investors and creditors (except interest), including cash receipts from issuing stock, borrowing activities, and cash disbursements to pay dividends; one of the three categories of cash inflows and outflows reported on the statement of cash flows. This category shows the amount of cash supplied by these resource providers and the amount of cash that is returned to them.

first-in, first-out (FIFO) cost flow method Inventory cost flow method in which cost of goods sold is computed as if the earliest items purchased are the first items sold.

fiscal year The annual time period for which a company provides financial statements.

fixed interest rate Interest rate (charge for borrowing money) that remains constant over the life of the loan.

FOB (free on board) destination Shipping term that means the seller bears the freight (transportation-in) costs.

FOB (free on board) shipping point Shipping term that means the buyer bears the freight (transportation-in) costs.

franchise Exclusive right to sell products or perform services in certain geographic areas.

full disclosure The accounting principle that financial statements should include all information relevant to an entity's operations and financial condition. Full disclosure frequently requires adding footnotes to the financial statements.

future value Amount an investment will be worth at some point in the future, assuming a specified interest rate and the reinvestment of interest each period that it is earned.

gains Increases in assets or decreases in liabilities that result from peripheral or incidental transactions.

general authority Company guidelines that apply to various levels of a company's management, such as requiring everyone at that level to fly coach class.

general journal Book of original entry in which any accounting transaction could be recorded, though commonly limited to adjusting and closing entries and unusual transactions.

general ledger The set of all accounts used in a given accounting system, typically organized in financial statement order.

general uncertainties Uncertainties such as competition and damage from storms. These uncertainties are distinguished from contingent liabilities because they arise from future rather than past events.

generally accepted accounting principles (GAAP) Rules and practices that accountants agree to follow in financial reports prepared for public distribution.

going concern assumption Accounting presumption that a company will continue to operate indefinitely, benefiting from its assets and paying its obligations in full; justifies reporting assets and liabilities in the financial statements.

goodwill Intangible added value of a successful business attributable to such factors as reputation, location, and superior products that enables the business to earn above-average profits; measured by an entity acquiring the business as the excess paid over the appraised value of the net assets.

gross earnings The total amount of employee wages or salaries before any deductions or withholdings. Gross earnings include the total of regular pay plus any bonuses, overtime, or other additions.

gross margin (gross profit) Difference between sales revenue and cost of goods sold; the amount a company makes from selling goods before subtracting operating expenses.

gross margin method Technique for estimating the ending inventory amount without a physical count; useful when the percentage of gross margin to sales remains relatively stable from one accounting period to the next.

gross margin percentage Expressing gross margin as a percentage of sales by dividing gross margin by net sales; the amount of each dollar of sales that is profit before deducting any operating expenses.

gross profit See *gross margin*.

half-year convention Tax rule that requires recognizing six months of depreciation expense on an asset both in the year of purchase and in the year of disposal regardless of the actual purchase date.

held-to-maturity securities Classification for marketable debt securities the purchasing company intends to hold (rather than sell) until the securities mature.

historical cost concept Accounting practice of reporting assets at the actual price paid for them when purchased regardless of estimated changes in market value.

horizontal analysis Analysis technique that compares amounts of the same item over several time periods.

horizontal statements model Concurrent representation of several financial statements horizontally across a page.

imprest basis Maintaining an account at a specified fixed amount, such as periodically replenishing a petty cash fund to its imprest amount.

income Increase in value created by providing goods and services through resource transformation.

income statement Financial report of profitability; measures the difference between revenues and expenses for the accounting period (whether or not cash has been exchanged).

independent auditor Licensed certified public accountant engaged to audit a company's financial statements; not an employee of the audited company.

independent contractor An individual who is paid by a business but retains individual control and supervisory authority over the work performed.

indirect method Method of reporting cash flows from operating activities on the statement of cash flows that starts with the net income from the income statement, followed by adjustments necessary to convert accrual-based net income to a cash-basis equivalent.

information overload Situation in which the presentation of too much information confuses the user of the information.

installment notes Obligations that require regular payments of principal and interest over the life of the loan.

intangible assets Long-term assets having no physical substance that benefit their owners through providing rights and privileges, such as a trademark.

interest Fee paid for the use of funds; represents expense to the borrower and revenue to the lender.

interest-bearing notes Notes that require face value plus accrued interest to be paid at maturity.

internal controls Policies and procedures companies establish to provide reasonable assurance of reducing fraud, providing reliable accounting records, and accomplishing organization objectives.

International Accounting Standards Board (IASB) Private, independent body that establishes International Financial Reporting Standards (IFRS). The IASB's authority is established by various governmental institutions that require or permit companies in their jurisdiction to use IFRS. To date, over 100 countries require or permit companies to prepare their financial statements using IFRS. One notable exception is the United States of America.

International Financial Reporting Standards (IFRS) Pronouncements established by the International Accounting Standards Board that provide guidance for the preparation of financial statements.

inventory cost flow methods Alternative ways to allocate the cost of goods available for sale between cost of goods sold and ending inventory.

inventory turnover A measure of sales volume relative to inventory levels; calculated as the cost of goods sold divided by average inventory; indicates how many times a year, on average, the inventory is sold (turned over).

investee Company that receives assets or services in exchange for a debt or equity security.

investing activities Cash inflows and outflows associated with buying or selling long-term assets, and cash inflows and outflows associated with lending activities and investments in the debt and equity of other companies; one of the three categories of cash inflows and outflows reported on the statement of cash flows.

investment securities Certificates that describe the rights and privileges that investors receive when they loan or give assets or services to investees.

investor Company or individual who gives assets or services in exchange for security certificates representing ownership interests.

issued stock Stock a company has sold to the public.

issuer (of a bond) Party that issues the bond (the borrower).

journal Book (or electronic record) of original entry in which accounting data are entered chronologically before posting to the ledger accounts.

labor resources The intellectual and physical efforts of individuals used in the process of providing goods and services to customers.

last-in, first-out (LIFO) cost flow method Inventory cost flow method in which cost of goods sold is computed as if the most recently purchased items are the first items sold.

legal capital Amount of assets that should be maintained as protection for creditors; the number of shares multiplied by the par value.

liabilities Obligations of a business to relinquish assets, provide services, or accept other obligations.

limited liability Concept that investors in a corporation may not be held personally liable for the actions or debts of the corporation; stockholders' liability is limited to the amount they paid for their stock.

limited liability company (LLC) Organizational form that offers many of the favorable characteristics and legal benefits of a corporation (e.g., limited liability and centralized management) but is permitted by federal law to be taxed as a partnership, thereby avoiding double taxation of profits.

line of credit Preapproved financing arrangement with a lending institution in which a business can borrow money up to the approved limit by simply writing a check.

liquidation Process of dividing up an organization's assets and returning them to the resource providers. In business liquidations, creditors normally have first priority; after creditor claims have been satisfied, any remaining assets are distributed to the company's owners (investors).

liquidity Ability to convert assets to cash quickly and meet short-term obligations.

liquidity ratios Measures of short-term debt-paying ability.

long-term liabilities The dollar value of long-term assets per each dollar of long-term debt. A high ratio suggests that there is a sufficient amount of long-term assets available to pay off long-term debt.

long-term operational assets Assets used by a business, normally over multiple accounting periods, to generate revenue; contrast with assets that are sold (inventory) or held (investments) to generate revenue; also called *productive assets*.

losses Decreases in assets or increases in liabilities that result from peripheral or incidental transactions.

lower-of-cost-or-market rule Accounting principle of reporting inventory at its replacement cost (market) if replacement cost has declined below the inventory's original cost, regardless of the cause.

maker The party issuing a note (the borrower).

management's discussion and analysis (MD&A) Section of a company's annual report in which management explains many different aspects of the company's past performance and future plans.

managerial accounting Branch of accounting focused on the information needs of managers and others working within the business; its objective is to gather and report information that adds value to the business. Managerial accounting information is not regulated or reported to the public.

manufacturing businesses Companies that make the goods they sell customers.

market Group of people or entities organized to buy and sell resources.

market interest rate Interest rate currently available on a wide range of alternative investments with similar levels of risk.

market value The price at which securities sell in the secondary market; also called *fair value*.

marketable securities Securities that are readily traded in the secondary securities market.

matching concept Accounting principle of recognizing expenses in the same accounting period as the revenues they produce, using one of three methods: match expenses directly with revenues (e.g., cost of goods sold); match expenses to the period in which they are incurred (e.g., rent expense), and match expenses systematically with revenues (e.g., depreciation expense).

materiality The point at which knowledge of information would influence a user's decision; can be measured in absolute, percentage, quantitative, or qualitative terms. The concept allows nonmaterial matters to be handled in any convenient way, such as charging a pencil sharpener to expense rather than recording periodic depreciation over its useful life.

maturity date The date that a liability is due to be settled (the date the borrower is expected to repay a debt).

Medicare Health insurance provided by the government primarily for retired workers.

merchandise inventory Finished goods held for resale to customers.

merchandising businesses Companies that buy and resell merchandise inventory.

modified accelerated cost recovery system (MACRS) Prescribed method of depreciation for tax purposes that provides the maximum depreciation expense deduction permitted under tax law.

mortgage bond Type of secured debt that conditionally transfers title of designated property to the bondholder until the bond is paid.

multistep income statement Income statement format that matches various revenues with related expenses in order to present subtotals (steps) such as gross margin and operating income; distinguishes between routine operating items and nonoperating items such as gains, losses, and interest. Contrast with *single-step income statement*.

natural resources Wasting assets originally attached to land such as mineral deposits, oil and gas reserves, and reserves of timber, mines, and quarries; the land value declines as the resources are removed.

net income Increase in equity resulting from operating the business.

net income percentage See *return on sales*.

net loss Decrease in equity resulting from operating the business.

net margin Profitability measurement that indicates the percentage of each sales dollar resulting in profit; calculated as net income divided by net sales.

net pay Employee's gross pay less all deductions (withholdings).

net realizable value The amount of accounts receivable a company expects to actually collect in cash; the face amount of receivables less an allowance for estimated uncollectible accounts.

net sales Sales less returns from customers and allowances or cash discounts given to customers.

non-sufficient-funds (NSF) check Customer's check deposited but returned by the bank on which it was drawn because the customer did not have enough money in his or her account to pay the check.

noncash investing and financing activities Certain business transactions, usually long-term, that do not involve cash, such as exchanging stock for land or purchasing property by using debt; reported separately on the statement of cash flows.

not-for-profit entities Organizations (also called *nonprofit* or *nonbusiness entities*) established primarily for motives other than making a profit, such as providing goods and services for the social good. Examples include state-supported universities and colleges, hospitals, public libraries, and public charities.

note payable Liability represented by a legal document called a *note* that describes pertinent details such as principal amount, interest charges, maturity date, and collateral.

notes receivable Notes that evidence rights to receive cash in the future; usually specify the maturity date, rate of interest, and other credit terms.

notes to financial statements Written explanations accompanying the financial statements that provide information about such items as estimates used and accounting methods chosen when GAAP permits alternatives.

operating activities Cash inflows from and outflows for routine, everyday business operations, normally resulting from revenue and expense transactions including interest; one of the three categories of cash inflows and outflows reported on the statement of cash flows.

operating cycle Process of converting cash into inventory, inventory into receivables, and receivables back to cash; its length can be measured in days using financial statement data.

operating income (or loss) Income after subtracting operating expenses from operating revenues. Gains and losses and other peripheral activities are added to or subtracted from operating income to determine net income or loss.

opportunity An element of the fraud triangle that recognizes weaknesses in internal controls that enable the occurrence of fraudulent or unethical behavior.

outstanding checks Checks the depositor company has written and deducted from its cash account balance that have not yet been presented to its bank for payment.

outstanding stock Shares of stock a corporation has issued that are still owned by outside parties (i.e., all stock that has been issued less any treasury stock the corporation has repurchased).

Paid-In Capital in Excess of Par (or Stated) Value The account in which a company records any amount received above the par or stated value of stock when stock is issued.

par value Arbitrary value assigned to stock by the board of directors; like *stated value*, designates *legal capital*.

parent company Company that holds a controlling interest (more than 50 percent ownership) in another company.

partnership Business entity owned by at least two people who share talents, capital, and the risks of the business.

partnership agreement Legal document that defines the rights and responsibilities of each partner and describes how income and losses are to be divided.

patent Legal right granted by the U.S. Patent Office ensuring a company or an individual the exclusive right to a product or process.

payee The party collecting cash.

payment date Date on which a dividend is actually paid.

percent of receivables method A method of estimating the amount of uncollectible accounts by taking a percentage of the outstanding receivables balance. The percentage is frequently based on a combination of factors such as historical experience, conditions of the economy, and the company's credit policies.

percent of revenue method A method of estimating the amount of uncollectible accounts by taking a percentage of revenue that was earned on account during the accounting period. The percentage is frequently based on a combination of factors such as historical experience, condition of the economy, and the company's credit policies.

percentage analysis Analysis of relationships between two different items to draw conclusions or make decisions.

period costs Expenses recognized in the period in which they are incurred regardless of when cash payments for them are made; costs that cannot be directly traced to products.

periodic inventory system Method of accounting for inventory that requires a physical count of goods on hand at the end of the accounting period in order to determine the amount of cost of goods sold and to update the Inventory account.

permanent accounts Balance sheet accounts; contain information carried forward from one accounting period to the next (the ending account balance of one period becomes the beginning account balance of the next period).

perpetual inventory system   Method of accounting for inventory in which the amount of cost of goods sold is recorded for each sale of inventory; the Inventory account is increased and decreased with each purchase and sale of merchandise.

petty cash fund   Small amount of currency kept on company premises to pay for minor items when writing checks is not practical.

petty cash voucher   Document that verifies a petty cash disbursement, signed by the person who received the money. Supporting documents, such as an invoice, restaurant bill, or parking fee receipt, should be attached to the petty cash voucher.

physical flow of goods   Physical movement of goods through a business, normally on a FIFO basis so that the first goods purchased are the first goods delivered to customers, reducing the likelihood of inventory obsolescence.

physical resources   Natural resources businesses transform to create more valuable resources.

posting   Copying transaction data from journals to ledger accounts.

preferred stock   Class of stock, usually nonvoting, that has preferential claims (usually to dividends) over common stock.

Premium on Bonds Payable   A liability account that represents reductions in the stated rate of interest.

prepaid items   Deferred expenses. An example is prepaid insurance.

present value   A measure of the value today of an amount of money expected to be exchanged on a specified future date.

pressure   An element of the fraud triangle that recognizes conditions that motivate fraudulent or unethical behavior.

price-earnings (P/E) ratio   Measure that reflects the values of different stocks in terms of earnings; calculated as market price per share divided by earnings (net income) per share; a higher P/E ratio generally indicates that investors are optimistic about a company's future.

primary securities market   Market in which investee companies issue debt and equity securities to investors in exchange for assets; contrast with *secondary securities market*.

principal   Amount of cash actually borrowed, to be repaid in the future with interest.

procedures manual   Written documentation of a company's accounting policies and procedures.

proceeds   The amount of cash received. An example is the principal amount borrowed on a discount note payable.

product costs   All costs directly traceable to acquiring inventory and getting it ready for sale, including transportation-in. Contrast with *selling and administrative costs*.

profit   Value added by transforming resources into products or services desired by customers.

profitability ratios   Measurements of a firm's ability to generate earnings.

promissory note   A legal document representing a credit agreement between a lender and a borrower. The note specifies technical details such as the maker, payee, interest rate, maturity date, payment terms, and any collateral.

property, plant, and equipment   Assets such as machinery and equipment, buildings, and land used to produce products or to carry on the administrative and selling functions of a business; sometimes called *plant assets*.

purchase discount   Reduction in the gross price of merchandise offered to a buyer if the buyer pays cash for the merchandise within a stated time (usually within 10 days of the date of the sale).

purchase returns and allowances   A reduction in the cost of purchases resulting from dissatisfaction with merchandise purchased.

qualified opinion   Opinion issued by a certified public accountant that means the company's financial statements are, for the most part, in compliance with GAAP, but there is some circumstance (explained in the auditor's report) about which the auditor has reservations; contrast with *unqualified opinion*.

quick ratio   Measure of immediate debt-paying ability; calculated by dividing very liquid assets (cash, receivables, and marketable securities) by current liabilities.

ratio analysis   Analysis of relationships between two different items to draw conclusions or make decisions.

rationalization   An element of the fraud triangle that recognizes a human tendency to justify fraudulent or unethical behavior.

realization   Accounting term that usually refers to actual cash collection (e.g., collecting accounts receivable).

recognition   Reporting an accounting event in the financial statements.

reinstate   Recording an account receivable previously written off back into the accounting records, generally when cash is collected long after the original due date.

relative fair market value method   Method of allocating the purchase price among individual assets acquired in a basket purchase; each asset is assigned a percentage of the total price paid for all assets. The percentage assigned equals the market value of a particular asset divided by the total of the market values of all assets acquired in the basket purchase.

reporting entities   Businesses or other organizations for which financial statements are prepared.

restrictive covenants   Provisions specified in a loan agreement that are designed to reduce creditor risk, such as limiting additional borrowing or dividend payments.

retail companies   Businesses that sell merchandise directly to consumers.

retained earnings   Portion of stockholders' equity that includes all earnings retained in the business since inception (revenues minus expenses and distributions for all accounting periods).

return on investment   Measure of profitability based on the asset base of the firm; calculated as net income divided by average total assets. ROI is a product of net margin and asset turnover.

return on sales   Profitability measure that reflects the percentage of net income each sales dollar generates; computed by dividing net income by net sales. Also called *net income percentage*.

return-on-assets ratio   Profitability measure based on earnings a company generates relative to its asset base; calculated as net income divided by average total assets.

return-on-equity ratio   Profitability measure based on earnings a company generates relative to its stockholders' equity; calculated as net income divided by average stockholders' equity.

revenue   The economic benefit (increase in assets or decrease in liabilities) gained by providing goods or services to customers.

revenue expenditures   Costs incurred for repair or maintenance of long-term assets: recorded as expense and subtracted from revenue in the accounting period in which incurred.

salaries   A term used to describe the amount due employees who are paid a set amount per week, month, or other earnings period regardless of how many hours they work during the period.

salaries payable   Amounts owed but not yet paid to employees for services they have already performed.

sales discount   Cash discount offered by the seller of merchandise to encourage a customer to pay promptly. When the customer takes the discount and pays less than the original selling price, the difference between the selling price and the cash collected is the sales discount.

sales returns and allowances   A reduction in sales revenue resulting from dissatisfaction with merchandise sold.

salvage value   Expected selling price of an asset at the end of its useful life.

Sarbanes–Oxley Act of 2002 Federal legislation enacted to promote ethical corporate governance and fair financial reporting. The act requires a company's chief executive officer (CEO) and chief financial officer (CFO) to certify in writing that the financial reports being issued present fairly the company's financial status. An executive who falsely certifies the company's financial reports is subject to significant fines and imprisonment. The act also establishes the Public Company Accounting Oversight Board (PCAOB), which has the primary responsibility for developing and enforcing auditing standards for CPAs who audit SEC companies. The Sarbanes–Oxley Act also prohibits auditors from providing most types of nonaudit services to companies they audit.

schedule of cost of goods sold Internal report used with the periodic inventory system that reflects the computation of cost of goods sold.

secondary securities market Market in which investors exchange securities with each other; contrast with *primary securities market*.

secured bonds Bonds secured by specific identifiable assets.

Securities Act of 1933 Federal legislation passed after the stock market crash of 1929 to regulate the issuance and subsequent trading of public company stocks and bonds; created the Securities and Exchange Commission (SEC).

Securities and Exchange Commission (SEC) Federal agency authorized by Congress to establish financial reporting practices of public companies; requires companies that issue securities to the public to file audited financial statements with the government annually.

Securities Exchange Act of 1934 See *Securities Act of 1933*.

segregation of duties Internal control feature of assigning the functions of authorization, recording, and custody to different individuals.

selling and administrative costs Costs such as advertising expense and rent expense that cannot be directly traced to inventory; recognized as expenses in the period in which they are incurred. Contrast with *product costs*.

serial bonds Bonds that mature at specified intervals throughout the life of the total issue.

service businesses Organizations such as accounting and legal firms, dry cleaners, and insurance companies that provide services to consumers.

service charges Fees charged by a bank for such things as services performed or penalties for overdrawn accounts or failure to maintain a specified minimum cash balance.

shrinkage Decreases in inventory for reasons other than sales to customers.

signature card Bank form that documents the bank account number and signatures of persons authorized to write checks on an account.

simple interest Interest computed by multiplying the principal by the interest rate by the number of periods. Previously earned interest is not added to the principal, so no interest is earned on the interest of past periods. Contrast with *compound interest*.

single-step income statement Income statement format that presents net income in one step, the difference between total revenues and total expenses. Contrast with *multistep income statement*.

sinking fund Fund to which the bond issuer contributes cash annually to ensure sufficient funds will be available to pay the face amount on the maturity date.

Social Security Insurance provided by the federal government to qualified individuals. Also called old age, survivors, and disability insurance (OASDI).

sole proprietorship Business (usually small) owned by one person.

solvency Ability of a business to pay liabilities in the long run.

solvency ratios Measures of a firm's long-term debt-paying ability.

source document Record such as a cash register tape, invoice, time card, or check stub that provides accounting information to be recorded in the accounting journals and ledgers.

special journals Journals designed to improve recording efficiency for specific routine, high-volume transactions such as credit sales.

specific authorizations Policies and procedures that apply to designated levels of management, such as the policy that only the plant manager can authorize overtime pay.

specific identification Inventory costing method in which cost of goods sold and ending inventory are computed using the actual costs of the specific goods sold or those on hand at the end of the period.

spread Difference between the rate a bank pays to obtain money (e.g., interest paid on savings accounts) and the rate the bank earns on money it lends to borrowers.

stakeholders Parties interested in the operations of a business, including owners, lenders, employees, suppliers, customers, and government agencies.

stated interest rate Rate of interest specified in the bond contract that is the percentage of face value used to calculate the amount of interest paid in cash at specified intervals over the life of the bond.

stated value Arbitrary value assigned to stock by the board of directors; like *par value*, designates *legal capital*.

statement of cash flows The financial statement that reports a company's cash inflows and outflows for an accounting period, classifying them as operating, investing, or financing activities.

statement of changes in stockholders' equity Statement that summarizes the transactions that affected the owners' equity during the accounting period.

stewardship Refers to a business's duty to protect and use the assets of the company for the benefit of the owners (the firm's stockholders).

stock certificate Document showing ownership interest issued to an investor in exchange for contributing assets to a corporation; describes ownership rights and privileges.

stock dividend Proportionate distribution of additional shares of the declaring corporation's stock.

stock split Corporate action that proportionately reduces the par value and increases the number of outstanding shares; designed to reduce the market value of the split stock.

stockholders Owners of a corporation.

stockholders' equity The interest in a corporation's assets that is owned by the stockholders.

straight-line amortization Method of amortization in which equal amounts of the account being reduced (e.g., Bond Discount, Bond Premium, Patent) are transferred to the appropriate expense account over the relevant time period.

straight-line depreciation Depreciation computations that produce equal amounts of depreciation to allocate to expense each period over an asset's life; computed by subtracting the salvage value from the asset's cost and then dividing by the number of years of useful life.

subordinated debentures Unsecured bonds with a lower claim on assets than general creditors; in the case of liquidation, holders are paid off after the general creditors are paid.

subsidiary company Company controlled (more than 50 percent owned) by another company.

T-account Simple account representation, using two bars arranged in the form of the letter "T"; the account title is written across the top on the horizontal bar, debit entries are recorded on the left side of the vertical bar, and credit entries on the right side.

tangible assets Assets that have physical form, such as equipment, machinery, natural resources, and land.

temporary accounts Accounts used to collect retained earnings data applicable to only the current accounting period (revenues, expenses and distributions); sometimes called *nominal accounts*.

term bonds Bonds in an issue that mature on a specified date in the future.

times-interest-earned ratio Ratio that measures a company's ability to make its interest payments; calculated by dividing the amount of earnings available for interest payments (net income before interest and income taxes) by the amount of the interest payments.

trademark Name or symbol that identifies a company or an individual product.

trading securities Classification for marketable securities companies plan to buy and sell quickly to generate profits from short-term appreciation in stock and bond prices.

transaction Business event that involves transferring something of value between two entities.

transferability Characteristic of corporations referring to the ease of exchanging ownership interests because ownership is divided into small, readily traded ownership units (shares of stock).

transportation-in (freight-in) Cost of freight on goods purchased under FOB shipping point terms; a product cost usually added to the cost of inventory.

transportation-out (freight-out) Freight cost for goods delivered to customers under FOB destination terms; a period cost expensed when incurred.

treasury stock Stock previously issued to the public that the issuing corporation has bought back. Contrast with *outstanding stock*.

trend analysis Study of the performance of a business over a period of time.

trial balance Schedule listing the balances of all ledger accounts; verifies mathematical accuracy of the accounting records and provides a convenient reference of current account balances.

true cash balance Actual amount of cash owned by a company at the close of business on the date of the bank statement.

unadjusted bank balance Depositor's cash balance reported by the bank as of the date of the bank statement.

unadjusted book balance Cash account balance in the depositor's accounting records as of the date of the bank reconciliation before making any adjustments.

uncollectible accounts expense Expense associated with uncollectible accounts receivable; amount recognized may be estimated using the allowance method, or actual losses may be recorded using the direct write-off method.

unearned revenue Liability arising when customers pay cash in advance for services a business will perform in the future.

units-of-production depreciation Depreciation computations that produce varying amounts of depreciation based on the level of an asset's usage each period rather than a measure of time; for example, automobile depreciation may be based on total estimated miles to be driven rather than total estimated years to be used.

unqualified opinion Opinion issued by a certified public accountant that means the company's financial statements are, in all material respects, in compliance with GAAP; the auditor has no reservations. Contrast with *qualified opinion*.

unrealized gains or losses Paper gains or losses on investment securities the company still owns; not realized until the securities are sold or otherwise disposed of.

unsecured bonds (debentures) Bonds backed by the general credit of the organization.

unsubordinated debentures Unsecured bonds with claims on assets equal to those of general creditors.

useful life The period of time over which an asset is expected to be used in the normal operation of a business.

users Individuals or organizations that use financial information for decision making.

variable interest rate Interest rate that fluctuates (changes) from period to period over the life of the loan.

vertical analysis Analysis technique that compares items on financial statements to significant totals.

vertical statements model Concurrent representation of several financial statements shown vertically on a page.

Wage and Tax Statement, Form W-2 Form used by employers to notify each employee of the amount of his or her gross earnings for the year and the amounts withheld by the employer.

wages A term used to describe amounts due employees who are paid according to the number of hours they actually work.

warranties Promises to correct deficiencies or dissatisfactions in quality, quantity, or performance of products or services sold.

weighted-average cost flow method Inventory cost flow method in which the cost allocated between inventory and cost of goods sold is based on the weighted average cost per unit, which is determined by dividing the total cost of goods available for sale during the accounting period by the total units available for sale during the period. If the weighted average is recomputed with each successive purchase, the result is a moving average.

wholesale companies Companies that sell goods to other businesses.

withdrawals Distributions of assets to the owners of proprietorships and partnerships.

working capital Current assets minus current liabilities.

working capital ratio Another term for the current ratio: calculated by dividing current assets by current liabilities.

INDEX

A

Abercrombie & Fitch, Co., 142
Accelerated depreciation methods, 426
Account balance, 148
Accounting. *see also* Accrual accounting; Deferral accounting
  careers in, 6–8
  cash basis, 71
  defined, 3
  financial vs. managerial, 6, 7
  as information provider, 5–7
  measurement rules in, 8
  nonprofit, 6, 7
  terminology in, 10, 11
Accounting controls, 316
Accounting cycle, 79–82
Accounting equation
  adjusting entries and impact on, 75
  creation of, 11–12
  interpretation of information in, 17–19
  left vs. right side of, 17
  recording business events under, 13–16
Accounting events, 13
Accounting period, 23
Accounts, information gathering from, 10–11
Accounts payable, 154, 655–656
Accounts receivable, 362–385. *see also* Notes receivable
  accrual accounting for, 73
  adjustment to uncollectible accounts expense, 370
  aging, 373–374
  average number of days to collect, 383
  cash collected from, 152
  collection of, 365, 369, 370
  credit card sales and, 381–384
  defined, 362
  direct write-off method to estimate uncollectible expenses, 375–376
  financial statements and, 367–368, 372
  net realizable value of, 364
  percent of receivables method to estimate uncollectible expenses, 372–374
  percent of revenue method to estimate uncollectible expenses, 364–372
  real-world data on, 383–384
  recognition of uncollectible accounts expense, 365–366
  reconciliation of, 326, 328, 654–655
  recording and reporting, 367, 371
  recovery of uncollectible accounts, 369–370
  reinstatement of, 369–370
  revenue recognition and, 364, 369
  turnover ratio, 383, 385, 709
  write-off of uncollectible accounts, 368
Accounts receivable turnover ratio, 383, 385, 709
Accrual accounting, 71–81
  accounting cycle for, 79–81
  for accounts receivable, 73
  for advertising expenses, 74
  balance sheets and, 77
  closing process in, 79, 80
  for consulting services, 75
  defined, 71
  financial statements in, 76–79
  in general ledger, 76, 77
  income statements and, 76
  matching concept and, 80–81
  overview, 72
  for payables, 74–75
  for salary expenses, 74–75
  statement of cash flows and, 79
  statement of changes in stockholders' equity and, 76
  vertical statements model and, 76, 78
Accruals, defined, 71
Accrued expenses, 75
Accrued interest, 378
Accumulated depreciation, 99–100, 424
ACS (American Cancer Society), 2, 11
Adjusted ledger account balances, 76
Adjusting entries, 75, 378, 501, 502–503
Adjustments
  to bank balance, 325, 327
  to book balance, 325–328
  for lost, damaged, or stolen inventory, 226–227
  for salary expenses, 74–75, 155–156
  in T-accounts, 155–157
  to uncollectible accounts expense, 370
Administrative controls, 316
Administrative costs, 215, 218
Advance Auto Parts, Inc., 586
Advanced Micro Devices, Inc., 532

745

Index

Adverse opinions, 334
Advertising expenses, 74
Aetna, 166–167
Aflac, 166–167
Aging accounts receivable, 373–374
AICPA (American Institute of Certified Public Accountants), 94
Alaska Air Group, 443
Allowance for doubtful accounts, 364, 366, 368
Allowance method of accounting for uncollectible accounts, 364
Alphabet, Inc., 356–357, 587, 610
Amazon.com, 20, 640, 668
American Cancer Society (ACS), 2, 11
American Eagle Outfitters, Inc., 142, 498
American Electric Power, 498
American Greetings Corporation, 472
American Institute of Certified Public Accountants (AICPA), 94
Amgen, Inc., 206
Amortization
   of bond discounts, 548–553, 556–557
   of bond premiums, 553–554, 557–559
   of bond redemptions, 554–555
   defined, 420, 537
   of discounts, 501
   effective interest rate method of, 555–561
   straight-line, 548–555
Amtrak, 447
Anadarko Petroleum Corporation, 472
Annual reports, 30–32, 332–335
Annuities, 729–731, 734
Apache Corporation, 614
Apple, Inc., 64
Appropriated retained earnings, 611–612
Arley Water Works, 223
Articles of incorporation, 596
Articulation relationships, 25
Asset exchange transactions
   accounts receivable collection, 73, 328
   characteristics of, 93
   effects of, 14, 20
   inventory purchases, 217
   land purchases, 151, 218
   in T-accounts, 151–152
Assets. see also Depreciation; Intangible assets; Long-term operational assets; Useful life of assets
   assessment of effective use of, 165
   as collateral, 377
   current (short-term), 418, 495
   defined, 11
   disposal of, 430

   fixed, 420
   gains and losses from sale of, 658
   inventory costs allocated to, 216
   liquidations resulting from mismanagement of, 19
   measurement of, 374
   physical control of, 320
   preferred stock and, 602
   sources of, 11–12, 148
   tangible, 420
   in transactions, 13–16, 20, 72–74
   transfers in closing process, 14, 15, 25–28
   write-off of, 91
Asset source transactions
   characteristics of, 93
   effects of, 13–14, 20
   revenue recognition, 73, 150
   stock issues for cash, 72, 148–149, 216
   supply purchases, 82, 149
   in T-accounts, 148–151
Asset use transactions
   advertising expenses, 74
   characteristics of, 93
   effects of, 15–16, 20
   salary expenses, 74, 82, 153
   selling and administrative costs, 218
   supply expenses, 83
   in T-accounts, 152–154
AT&T, Inc., 267, 598
Audit opinions, 334
Audits, 333–335
Audit services, 7, 95
Authority manuals, 320
Authorized stock, 601
AutoNation, Inc., 213–214, 216, 236
AutoZone, Inc., 414, 533
Available-for-sale securities, 720, 722
Average number of days to collect receivables, 383, 709
Average number of days to sell inventory, 287, 288, 709
Avon, 561

B

Backward balance sheets, 497
Bahama Breeze, 472
Balance sheets. see also Financial statements
   accrual accounting and, 77
   alternative names for, 10
   backward, 497
   classified, 496
   deferral accounting and, 91, 92–93
   example of, 22
   inventory cost flow and, 275

Balance sheets—Cont.
   liabilities and, 495–496
   long-term assets on, 441
   for merchandising businesses, 231
   notes receivable and, 380–381
   preparation of, 23–24
   Target Corporation annual report, 713–714
Ball Co., 243
Bank balance, adjustments to, 325, 327
Bank of America Corp., 447, 531
Bank reconciliation, 325–330
Bank statements, 324
Basket purchases, 421–422
Berkshire Hathaway, 640
Bernard Madoff Investments, 334
Best Buy, 12, 169, 488
Biogen Idec, Inc., 206
Bloomin' Brands, Inc., 267
Board of directors, 598
Boeing, 413
Bojangels', Inc., 587
Bond certificates, 542, 543
Bond discounts, 548–553, 556–557
Bonded employees, 319
Bondholders, 542
Bond premiums, 553–554, 557–559
Bond redemptions, 554–555
Bonds, 542–555
   advantages of, 542–543
   amortization of, 548–555
   callable, 544
   convertible, 544
   face value of, 542, 545, 549–550
   financial statements and, 547–548, 552–553
   in journal entries, 545–547, 549–551
   mortgage, 543
   price determination of, 549, 731–732
   ratings, 545
   restrictive covenants and, 545
   security of, 543
   serial, 543
   special features of, 544
   term, 543
   timing of maturity, 543–544
   unsecured, 543
Bonds payable, 664–665
Bonefish Grill, 267
Book balance, adjustments to, 325–328
Books of original entry, 158
Book value, 99–100, 424, 601
BorgWarner, Inc., 414
Bosch, 322

Buffalo Wild Wings, Inc., 141–142
Burger King, 6, 384
Business liquidations, 18–19
Business organizations, 594–615. *see also* Corporations; Merchandising businesses
   financial statements of, 599–600
   forms of, 596–600
   limited liability companies, 597
   manufacturing, 29
   overview, 594
   partnerships, 596, 600
   service businesses, 29
   sole proprietorships, 596, 599
Business resource usage, 4–5

C

Callable bonds, 544
Call premiums, 544
Call price, 544
Capital expenditures, 434
Capitalized costs, 434–435, 438
Capital raising abilities of corporations, 598–599
Capital stock, 600–601
Careers in accounting, 6–8
Carmike Cinemas, Inc., 11
Carrabba's Italian Grill, 267
Carrying value, 100, 424, 549
Cash
   accounting for, 321–324
   accounts payable settled with, 154
   collection from accounts receivable, 152
   controlling, 321–323
   cost of protecting, 323
   defined, 321
   dividends as, 15, 17–18, 153, 609
   operating expenses, 500, 504
   petty cash, 330–332
   short and over, 329–330
   stock issues for, 72, 148–149, 216
Cash basis accounting, 71
Cash discounts, 222
Cash flow, 24, 79, 646. *see also* Statement of cash flows
Cash service revenue, 500–501, 503
Caterpillar, 447, 669
Certified checks, 326
Certified Internal Auditor (CIA) designation, 8
Certified Management Accounting (CMA) designation, 8
Certified public accountants (CPAs), 6–7, 333, 335
Chain of command, 320
Chart of accounts, 160
Checks and checking accounts, 323–324, 326, 329

Chesapeake Energy Corporation, 472
Chevron, 166, 610, 669, 670
Christensen, H. B., 432
CIA (Certified Internal Auditor) designation, 8
Claims exchange transactions, 75, 93, 154–155
Claims on assets, 12
Classified balance sheets, 496
Closely held corporations, 596
Closing entries, 161–164
Closing process
   in accrual accounting, 79, 80
   asset transfers in, 14, 15, 25–28
   in deferral accounting, 91–93
   in trial balance, 161–164
CMA (Certified Management Accounting)
    designation, 8
Coca-Cola Company, 269, 420, 438, 639
Code of Ethics (Institute of Internal Auditors), 94
Code of Professional Conduct (AICPA), 94
Colgate-Palmolive Company, 413
Collateral, 377, 545
Comcast Corp., 443
Commissions for extended warranty sales, 488
Committee of Sponsoring Organizations of the
    Treadway Commission (COSO), 318–319
Common size financial statements, 234–235
Common stock, 12, 91, 148–149, 216, 601–602, 665
Comparative income statements, 213–215
Competition, price, 237
Compound interest, 728
Comprehensive income, 30
Confidentiality rules for CPAs, 335
Consistency principle, 279–280
Consolidated financial statements, 724
Consulting services, 7, 75
Consumers, use of resources by, 4, 5
Contingent liabilities, 483–484
Continuity of corporations, 598
Contra asset accounts, 99–100, 366, 369–370, 424
Contra liability accounts, 500, 501
Control. *see* Internal control
Convergence, 81
Conversion agents, 4, 5–6
Convertible bonds, 544
Copyrights, 438
Corporate governance, 94–97
Corporations, 596–615. *see also* Stock
   capital raising abilities of, 598–599
   cash dividends and, 609
   closely held, 596
   continuity of, 598
   control through stock ownership, 615
   double taxation of, 597
   features of, 596
   financial statements for, 605–606, 612–613
   limited liability of, 598
   management structure of, 598
   ownership transferability in, 598
   presentation of stockholders' equity in, 600
   price-earnings ratio for, 614–615, 710
   regulation of, 596–597
   retained earnings appropriation and, 611–612
   S Corporations, 597
Correction of errors, in bank reconciliation, 326
COSO (Committee of Sponsoring Organizations of the
    Treadway Commission), 318–319
Costco Wholesale Corporation, 287, 297, 311
Cost flow methods for inventory. *see* Inventory cost
    flow methods
Cost method of accounting for treasury stock, 607–608
Cost of goods available for sale, 216, 276–278
Cost of goods sold, 216, 217, 235, 240, 272, 420
Costs. *see also* Expenses
   administrative, 215, 218
   capitalized, 434–435, 438
   of credit sales, 382
   defined, 84
   depreciable, 422
   inventory cost allocation, 216
   of inventory financing, 223
   long-term operational assets, 421–422
   period, 81, 215
   product, 215
   of protecting cash, 323
   research and development, 438
   selling and administrative, 215, 218
   transportation, 223–226
CPAs (certified public accountants), 6–7, 333, 335
Cracker Barrel Old Country Store, 141
Credit balances, 158
Credit cards, accounting for sales by, 381–384
Credit lines, 541–542
Credit memos, on bank statements, 324
Creditors, 4–5, 11, 18–19, 148
Credits, in T-accounts, 148, 157–158
Credit terms, 222
Criminal and ethical misconduct, 95–97
CSX Corporation, 472
Cumulative dividends, 602
Curious Accountant feature
   accounts receivable, 363, 365
   accruals and deferrals, 72, 92
   debt interest payments, 537, 539
   fiscal year, 147, 163

Curious Accountant feature—*Cont.*
　inventory cost flow methods, 273, 287
　long-term operational assets, 419, 437
　losses, 647, 653
　payroll, 479, 495
　profit margins, 213, 236
　Sarbanes–Oxley Act, 317, 322
　stakeholders, 2, 11
　stock investments, 595, 597
　transactions, 20
Current ratio, 497–498, 709–710
Current (short-term) assets, 418, 495
Current (short-term) liabilities, 495–496
CVS Caremark, 237

D

D. R. Horton, 288, 384
Darden Restaurants, Inc., 472
Date of record for dividends, 609
Debentures (unsecured bonds), 543
Debit balances, 158
Debit memos, on bank statements, 324
Debits, in T-accounts, 148, 157–158
Debt, 536–561. *see also* Bonds; Liabilities
　EBIT and ratio analysis, 560
　effective interest rate amortization, 555–561
　financial leverage and tax advantage of, 559–560
　installment notes payable, 538–540
　interest on, 537, 539
　lines of credit, 541–542
　overview, 536–537
　refinancing, 495–496
　risk assessment of, 165–166
　straight-line amortization of, 548–555
　times-interest-earned ratio and, 561
Debt securities, 719
Debt-to-assets ratio, 166–168, 708
Declaration date for dividends, 609
Deere & Company, 267, 472
Deferral accounting, 81–93
　balance sheets and, 91, 92–93
　closing process in, 91–93
　defined, 71
　financial statements in, 87–93
　in general ledger, 87–88
　overview, 81
　for prepaid items, 84–85
　for salary expenses, 82
　for supplies, 82–83
　for unearned revenue, 86–87
　vertical statements model and, 89–91

Deferrals, defined, 71
Deferred tax liability, 433
Deflation, 279
Delta Air Lines, 531
Depletion of natural resources, 420, 436–437
Deposits in transit, 325
Deposit tickets, 323
Depreciable cost, 422
Depreciation, 422–431
　accelerated methods of, 426
　accumulated, 99–100, 424
　comparison of methods of, 430–431
　defined, 422
　disposal of assets and, 430
　double-declining balance, 422, 426–427
　on financial statements, 425–427, 429
　illustration of, 423
　journal entries for, 169
　modified accelerated cost recovery system for, 431–433
　overview, 422
　for property, plant, and equipment, 420
　straight-line, 99, 422, 423–425
　units-of-production, 422, 428–429
Direct method for statement of cash flows, 648–649, 661, 666–667
Direct write-off method to estimate uncollectible accounts expense, 375–376
Disclaimer of opinion, 334
Disclosure, 279–280, 443, 669
Discount merchandisers, 287
Discount notes, 499–505
Discounts
　amortization of, 501
　bond, 548–553, 556–557
　cash, 222
　computation of, 499
　on notes payable, 500
　purchase, 222
　sales discounts, 231, 233–234
Dividends
　as asset distribution, 12, 15
　cash, 15, 17–18, 153, 609
　cumulative, 602
　on financial statements, 612–613
　investment securities and, 721
　limitations on retained earnings, 17–18
　on preferred stock, 602
　receiving, 613
　retained earnings appropriation and, 611–612
　stock, 610–611
Dividends in arrears, 602
Dollar General Corporation, 165

Dominion Resources, 498
Double-declining balance depreciation, 422, 426–427
Double-entry accounting system, 146–168
    adjustments in, 155–157
    asset exchange transactions in, 151–152
    asset source transactions in, 148–151
    asset use transactions in, 152–154
    claims exchange transactions in, 154–155
    closing entries in, 161–164
    debit/credit terminology in, 148
    debt risk assessment in, 165–166
    effective use of assets in, 165
    error detection tools in, 149
    general journal in, 158–160
    overview, 146–147
    post-closing trial balance in, 164
    T-accounts in, 148–158
    trial balance and financial statements in, 160–168
    uncollectible account events in, 367, 371
Double-entry bookkeeping system, 13
Double taxation, 597
Dow Jones Industrial Average, 164, 610

E

Earnings. see also Income; Salaries and wages
    as added value, 4
    gross, 488
    net increases in assets as, 12
    retained, 12, 17–18, 611–612, 665
Earnings before interest and taxes (EBIT), 560
Earnings per share ratio (EPS), 614, 710
Ebbers, Bernie, 318
EDGAR (Electronic Data Gathering, Analysis, and Retrieval) database, 335, 700
Effective interest rate, 549, 555–561
Electronic Data Gathering, Analysis, and Retrieval (EDGAR) database, 335, 700
Elements of financial statements, 10–12
Embezzlement, 319, 320
Emissions defeating software scandal, 317, 322
Employees. see also Payroll
    bonded, 319
    fringe benefits for, 479, 494
    identification of, 487–488
    quality of, 319
    required absences for, 319
Employee's Withholding Allowance Certificate, Form W-4, 489, 490
Employer payroll taxes, 493
Employer's Quarterly Federal Tax Return, Form 941, 490
Ending balance of inventory, 285–289

Enron, 94–95, 318
Enterprise Risk Management (ERM)–An Integrated Framework (COSO), 318–319
Environmental Protection Agency (EPA), 317
EPS (earnings per share ratio), 614, 710
Equity method of reporting, 724
Equity securities, 719, 724
Error correction, in bank reconciliation, 326
Esteé Lauder, 561
Estimated useful life, 422
Estimation of ending inventory balance, 285–289
Ethan Allen, 413
Ethical issues, 94–97
Ex-dividend trades of stock, 609
Expenses. see also Costs; Depreciation; Uncollectible accounts expense
    accrued, 75
    advertising, 74
    asset write-offs and, 91
    cash operating, 500, 504
    defined, 15, 75
    interest, 100–102, 169–170
    inventory costs allocated to, 216
    noncash, 658
    plant asset expenditures, 434
    recognition of, 217
    research and development, 438
    salary, 74–75, 82, 153, 155–156
    supplies, 82–83, 149, 156
Expenses payable, 656–657
Extended warranties, 488
External users of accounting information, 6
ExxonMobil, 166, 167, 234, 598, 614, 640

F

Facebook, Inc., 447, 587, 610, 669
Face value
    of bonds, 542, 545, 549–550
    of notes, 499, 502, 503
FAF (Financial Accounting Foundation), 8
Fair value, 719
FASB. see Financial Accounting Standards Board
FCX (Freeport-McMoRan Copper & Gold, Inc.), 419, 437
Federal income tax withholdings, 488–490
Federal Insurance Contributions Act (FICA), 490–491
Federal Reserve, 498
Federal Unemployment Tax Act (FUTA), 493
FICA taxes, 490–491
Fidelity bonds, 319

FIFO cost flow method. *see* First-in, first-out cost flow method
Financial Accounting Foundation (FAF), 8
Financial Accounting Standards Board (FASB)
   Accounting Standards Codification 606, 71, 81
   Accounting Standards Codification 820, 719
   comparison with IASB, 9
   on direct method for operating activities, 649
   on disclosure of cash flow per share, 669
   measurement rules established by, 8
   Securities and Exchange Commission deferral to, 597
Financial leverage, 166, 167–168, 559–560
Financial reports, 2
Financial resources, 4–5
Financial statements. *see also* Balance sheets; Income statements; Statement of cash flows
   in accrual accounting, 76–79
   bonds and, 547–548, 552–553
   capital structure in, 599–600
   closing process following preparation of, 25–28
   common size, 234–235
   consolidated, 724
   for corporations, 605–606, 612–613
   in deferral accounting, 87–93
   depreciation on, 425–427, 429
   discount notes and, 501–502, 504–505
   dividends on, 612–613
   in double-entry accounting system, 160–168
   elements of, 10–12
   examples of, 22
   function of, 20
   horizontal model for, 28–32
   inventory cost flow and, 275, 278–280
   inventory transactions in, 218–219
   investment securities and, 722–724
   liabilities and, 486
   long-term operational assets and, 425–427, 429
   notes receivable and, 380–381
   notes to, 333
   project parameters, 716–718
   real-world, 29–30
   statement of changes in stockholders' equity, 10, 22, 23, 76
   stock transactions on, 605–606
   Target Corporation annual report, 702–707
   uncollectible accounts expense and, 367–368, 372
Financial statements audit, 333–334
Financial vs. managerial accounting, 6, 7
Financing activities
   cash, 24, 25, 72, 649–650, 663–665
   noncash, 650, 668
First-in, first-out (FIFO) cost flow method, 274, 276–277, 279, 280–281, 283

Fiscal year, 147, 163
Fitch rating agency, 545
Fixed assets, 420
Fixed interest rate, 536
Fixtures, 662
Fleming's Prime Steakhouse and Wine Bar, 267
FOB destination, 223, 225
FOB shipping point, 223–224
Foot Locker, Inc., 586
Forbes magazine, 6
Ford Motor Company, 9, 64, 91, 213, 215–216, 236, 640–641
Form 941, Employer's Quarterly Federal Tax Return, 490
Form W-2, Wage and Tax Statement, 489–491
Form W-4, Employee's Withholding Allowance Certificate, 489, 490
Franchises, 439
Fraud
   accounting, 318
   embezzlement, 319, 320
   emissions defeating software scandal, 317, 322
   inventory, 284–285
Fraud triangle, 95–97
Freeport-McMoRan Copper & Gold, Inc. (FCX), 419, 437
Fringe benefits, 479, 494
Full disclosure, 279–280
FUTA taxes, 493
Future value annuities, 729–730, 734
Future value of money, 728–729, 733

G

GAAP. *see* Generally accepted accounting principles
Gains
   from asset sales, 658
   in merchandising businesses, 227–231
   unrealized, 722
Gap, Inc., 147, 163, 313, 498
GEICO Insurance, 13
General authority, 320
General Electric, 282, 333, 597
General journals, 158–160, 239
General ledgers
   accrual accounting and, 76, 77
   deferral accounting and, 87–88
   defined, 16, 160
   discount notes and, 501–502, 504–505
   example of, 160
   inventory transactions in, 218–219
   journals and, 158, 160
   liabilities accounting in, 486

Generally accepted accounting principles (GAAP)
   on accrual accounting, 71
   on disclosure of accounting policies, 443
   financial statement preparation in accordance with, 333
   full disclosure and consistency, 279–280
   global, 9
   historical cost concept and, 432
   on historical cost rule, 16
   IFRS vs., 81, 167
   on interest reporting, 230
   inventory cost flow methods and, 282, 287
   for public financial reports, 8
   on research and development costs, 438
   on stock split timing, 611
General Mills, 561, 639
General Motors, 4, 91, 316, 413
General uncertainties, 483
GlaxoSmithKline, 237
Going concern doctrine, 19, 478
Goldman Sachs, 610
Goodwill, 439–440
Google, Inc., 356–357, 587, 610
Governance, corporate, 94–97
Great Depression, 596
Green Bay Packers, 31
Gross earnings, 488
Gross margin, 216, 227, 229, 289
Gross margin method, 285–286
Gross margin percentage, 235–237, 708
Gross profit, 216

H

Half-year convention, 432
H&R Block, Inc., 142–143
Harley-Davidson Co., 385, 459
Healthy Choice, 439
Held-to-maturity securities, 720, 722
Hershey Foods Corporation, 413
Historical cost concept, 9, 15–16, 421, 432, 439
Home Depot, Inc., 498, 589
Horizontal statements model, 28–32

I

IASB (International Accounting Standards Board), 9, 81
IBM (International Business Machines, Inc.), 4, 64
Identifiable useful lives of intangible assets, 420, 440
IFRS. *see* International Financial Reporting Standards
Imprest basis, maintenance of petty cash funds on, 330
Income. *see also* Earnings; Revenue; Salaries and wages
   comprehensive, 30
   net, 21, 79, 229
   operating, 229
   from operations, 12
   from resource transformation process, 4
Income statements. *see also* Financial statements
   accrual accounting and, 76
   alternative names for, 10
   comparative, 213–215
   example of, 22
   inventory cost flow and, 275, 279
   matching concept and, 21
   for merchandising businesses, 213–215, 227, 229–230
   multistep, 230
   notes receivable and, 380
   preparation of, 21, 23
   single-step, 230
   Target Corporation annual report, 712–713
   tax returns vs., 279
Income taxes, 279, 431–433, 488–490
Indefinite useful lives of intangible assets, 420–421, 441
Independent auditors, 333–335
Independent contractors, 487–488
Indirect method for statement of cash flows, 648–649, 652–659, 666
Inflation, 279
Initial public offerings (IPOs), 31
Installment notes payable, 538–540
Institute of Internal Auditors, 8, 94
Institute of Management Accountants, 8, 94
Insurance policies, 84, 152, 156, 656
Intangible assets, 437–441
   balance sheets and, 441
   copyrights, 438
   defined, 420
   expense recognition for, 440–441
   franchises, 439
   goodwill, 439–440
   identifiable useful lives of, 420, 440
   indefinite useful lives of, 420–421, 441
   overview, 437
   patents, 438
   trademarks, 438
Intel, 474
Interest. *see also* Interest rates; Time value of money
   accounting for, 100–102
   on accounts receivable, 365
   accrued, 378
   in bank reconciliation, 326
   on borrowed resources, 4
   collection on maturity date, 379
   compound, 728
   on debt, 537, 539
   on discount notes, 499

Interest—*Cont.*
   fixed, 536
   investment securities and, 721
   journal entries for, 169–170
   on lines of credit, 541
   on notes, 377
   semiannual payments of, 553
   simple, 728
   on unpaid receivables, 385
   variable, 536
Interest-bearing notes, 499
Interest payable, 657
Interest rates
   effective, 549, 555–561
   fixed, 536
   market, 554, 556
   stated, 542
   variable, 536
Interest receivable, 655
Intermittent sales and purchases, 280–282
Internal control, 316–335
   annual reports and, 332–335
   audits and, 333–335
   authority and responsibility in, 320
   bank account reconciliation and, 325–330
   bonded employees and, 319
   cash accounting and, 321–324
   categories of, 316
   checking account documents and, 323–324
   for criminal and ethical misconduct prevention, 95–96
   defined, 316, 318
   key features of, 318–320
   limitations of, 320
   performance evaluations and, 320
   petty cash and, 330–332
   physical control of assets and, 320
   prenumbered documents in, 320
   procedures manuals for, 319
   quality of employees and, 319
   required absences and, 319
   segregation of duties and, 319
Internal Control–An Integrated Framework (COSO), 318
Internal Revenue Service (IRS), 2, 279, 560
Internal users of accounting information, 6
International Accounting Standards Board (IASB), 9, 81
International Business Machines, Inc. (IBM), 4, 64
International Financial Reporting Standards (IFRS)
   GAAP vs., 81, 167
   growth of, 9
   on last-in, first-out cost flow method, 282
   lower-of-cost-or-market rule and, 284
   on property, plant, and equipment accounting, 432
   on research and development costs, 438
   on stock split timing, 611
   on terminology differences, 385
International issues
   backward balance sheets, 497
   global generally accepted accounting principles, 9
   IFRS vs. GAAP, 167
   last-in, first-out cost flow method, 282
   lower-of-cost-or-market rule, 284
   property, plant, and equipment accounting, 432
   research and development costs, 438
   stock split timing, 611
   terminology differences, 385
Intuit, Inc., 142–143
Inventory, 272–289. *see also* Inventory cost flow methods
   allocation of cost between asset and expense accounts, 216
   average number of days to sell, 287, 288, 709
   cost of goods available for sale, 216, 276–278
   counting services, 230
   estimating ending balance of, 285–289
   expense recognition of, 217
   financial statements and, 275, 278–280
   financing, 223
   fraud prevention in, 284–285
   with intermittent sales and purchases, 280–282
   in ledger accounts and financial statements, 218–219
   lost, damaged, or stolen, 226–227
   lower-of-cost-or-market rule for, 282–284
   periodic system of, 238–240
   perpetual system of, 216, 240, 285
   purchase of, 217
   real-world data on, 288–289
   reconciliation of, 655–656
   revenue recognition from sale of, 217
   transactions involving, 215–220
   turnover ratio, 287, 709
Inventory cost flow methods, 274–282
   allocation of cost of goods available for sale, 276–278
   financial statements affected by, 275, 278–280
   first-in, first-out, 274, 276–277, 279, 280–281, 283
   full disclosure and consistency of, 279–280
   inflation vs. deflation in, 279
   with intermittent sales and purchases, 280–282
   last-in, first-out, 274, 277, 279, 281–283
   for multiple layers with multiple quantities, 276
   physical flow of goods, 274–275
   ratio analysis and, 289
   relative use of, 275
   specific identification, 274
   weighted average, 274, 278, 281–282

Inventory turnover ratio, 287, 709
Investees, 719
Investing activities
  cash, 24, 25, 649, 661–663
  noncash, 650
  stock, 595, 597
Investment securities, 719–724
  available-for-sale, 720, 722
  defined, 719
  financial statements and, 722–724
  held-to-maturity, 720, 722
  reconciliation of, 662
  reporting events affecting, 720–722
  trading, 720, 722
  types of, 719–720
Investors, 4–5, 12, 18–19, 719
IPOs (initial public offerings), 31
IRS (Internal Revenue Service), 2, 279, 560
Issued stock, 601
Issuers, 480, 542

J

J. M. Smucker Company, 358–359
JCPenney, 213
Johnson & Johnson, 237, 586
Journals and journal entries
  bonds in, 545–547, 549–551
  defined, 158
  general, 158–160, 239
  inventory transactions in, 218–219
  for long-term assets and depreciation, 169
  for notes payable and interest expense, 169–170

K

Kellogg's, 561
Kelly Services, 443
Kleenex, 438
The Kroger Company, 268, 273, 287, 384

L

Labor resources, 5
Land
  purchase of, 151, 218
  reconciliation of, 662–663
  as tangible asset, 420
Last-in, first-out (LIFO) cost flow method, 274, 277, 279, 281–283
Las Vegas Sands Corporation, 544
Late payment penalties, 223
Lawsuits, as contingent liabilities, 483

Legal capital, 601, 604
Levi Strauss, 147, 163
Liabilities, 478–498. *see also* Bonds; Debt; Payroll
  balance sheets and, 495–496
  contingent, 483–484
  current (short-term), 495–496
  defined, 11
  expenses vs., 75
  financial statements and, 486
  in general ledger T-accounts, 486
  liquidity vs. solvency of, 497–498
  long-term, 536
  notes payable, 169–170, 480–481, 731
  overview, 478–479
  real-world data on, 498
  sales tax, 482–483
  warranty obligations, 484–485, 488
LIFO cost flow method. *see* Last-in, first-out cost flow method
Limited liability, 598
Limited liability companies (LLCs), 597
Lines of credit, 541–542
Liquidations, 18–19
Liquidity, 24, 380, 497–498
LLCs (limited liability companies), 597
Loans, 377–378
Lockheed Martin Corporation, 363, 365
LongHorn Steakhouse, 472
Long-term liabilities, 536. *see also* Debt
Long-term notes payable, 731
Long-term operational assets, 418–443. *see also* Intangible assets
  basket purchase of, 421–422
  cash purchases of, 98–99
  continuing expenditures for, 434–435
  cost determination of, 421–422
  defined, 418
  depreciation of, 422–431
  disposal of, 430
  financial statements and, 425–427, 429
  income tax considerations, 431–433
  industry characteristics and, 443
  interest expenses for, 100
  journals for, 169
  judgment and estimation effect for, 442–443
  natural resources, 420, 436–437
  overview, 418–419
  property, plant, and equipment, 420, 432, 434–435
  recognition of expenses for, 99–100
  renting, 99
  revision of estimates for, 433–434
  tangible, 420

Losses
  from asset sales, 658
  business liquidations resulting from, 18–19
  in merchandising businesses, 227–231
  from operations, 12
  unrealized, 722
Lower-of-cost-or-market rule, 282–284
Lowe's, 169, 498

M

MACRS (modified accelerated cost recovery system), 431–433
Macy's, 237, 288–289, 384
Makers of notes, 377
Management's discussion and analysis (MD&A), 31, 333, 335, 711
Management structure of corporations, 598
Managerial vs. financial accounting, 6, 7
Manpower, Inc., 443
Manufacturing businesses, 29
Marathon Oil, 166
Marketable securities, 719
Market interest rate, 554, 556
Markets, defined, 4
Market value, 15–16, 601, 719
Marriott International, 561
Matching concept, 21, 80–81, 378
Matching revenues and expenses, 374
Materiality, in financial statements audits, 334
Maturity date, 377, 379
Maturity of bonds, 543–544
McDonald's Corporation, 64, 288–289, 383–384, 420, 607, 641
MD&A (management's discussion and analysis), 31, 333, 335, 711
Mead Johnson Nutrition Co., 439
Measurement rules, 8
Medicare taxes, 490–491
Merchandise inventory, 213
Merchandising businesses, 212–240. *see also* Inventory
  balance sheets for, 231
  common size financial statements for, 234–235
  defined, 29
  discount merchandisers, 287
  events affecting sales in, 231–237
  fraud prevention in, 284–285
  gains and losses in, 227–231
  income statements for, 213–215, 227, 229–230
  net sales in, 234
  overview, 212–213
  purchase discounts in, 222
  real-world data on, 236–237
  returns and allowances in, 221, 232–233
  revenue generation by, 212–213
  sales discounts in, 231, 233–234
  statement of cash flows for, 231
  transportation costs in, 223–226
Merck & Company, 30, 237
Meredith Corporation, 72, 92–93
Microsoft Corporation, 64, 269, 474
Model Business Corporations Act of 1950, 596
Modified accelerated cost recovery system (MACRS), 431–433
Molson Coors Brewing Company, 472
Money, time value of. *see* Time value of money
Moody's rating agency, 545
Mortgage bonds, 543
Mortgage payable, 664
Multistep income statements, 230

N

Natural resources, 5, 420, 436–437
Neiman Marcus, 238, 287
Netflix, Inc., 143–144, 206, 669, 670
Net income, 21, 79, 229
Net income percentage, 235
Net loss, 21
Net pay, 492
Net realizable value of accounts receivable, 364
Net sales, 234
Newell Brands, Inc., 531
Newmont Mining Corporation, 531
New York Stock Exchange, 16, 596
Nike Company, 208, 438
Nikolaev, V., 432
Nonbusiness resource usage, 6
Noncash activities, 650, 668
Noncash expenses, 658
Nonprofit accounting, 6, 7
Non-sufficient-funds (NSF) checks, 326, 329
No-par stock, 605
Notes payable
  accounting for, 480–481
  installment, 538–540
  journal entries for, 169–170
  long-term, 731
Notes receivable, 376–381
  defined, 363
  financial statements and, 380–381
  promissory notes, 376–377
  recording and reporting, 377–379
Notes to the financial statements, 333

Index

Not-for-profit entities, 6, 11
NSF (non-sufficient-funds) checks, 326, 329

O

Office Depot, 169, 237
OfficeMax, 344
Old age, survivor's, and disability insurance (OASDI), 490
Olive Garden, 472
Operating activities
　cash, 24–25, 73, 74, 79
　direct method for, 648–649, 661
　indirect method for, 648–649, 652–659
　reconciliation approach for, 654–658
　rule-based approach for, 658–659
　as source of assets, 12, 148
　on statement of cash flows, 648–649, 652–661
Operating cycle, 384, 495
Operating income, 229
Opportunity, in criminal and ethical misconduct, 95–97
Outback Steakhouse, 267
Outstanding checks, 325
Outstanding stock, 601
Ownership transferability in corporations, 598
Owners of resources, 4, 5

P

Papa John's International, Inc., 415
Paper profits, 722
Parent companies, 724
Partnership agreements, 596
Partnerships, 596, 600
Par value of stock, 600–601, 604
Patents, 438
Payees, 377
Payment date for dividends, 609
Payments
　cash, 322–323
　debt interest payments, 537, 539
　late payment penalties, 223
　semiannual interest, 553
Payroll, 487–494. see also Salaries and wages
　employer payroll taxes, 493
　federal income tax withholdings, 488–490
　fringe benefits and, 479, 494
　gross earnings, 488
　identification of employees for, 487–488
　net pay computations, 492
　overview, 487
　recording and reporting, 493
　Social Security and Medicare taxes, 490–491
　voluntary withholdings, 491–492
PCAOB (Public Company Accounting Oversight Board), 95, 335, 597
Penalties, for late payments, 223
Penske Automotive Group, Inc., 311
PepsiCo, 640
P/E ratio (price-earnings ratio), 614–615, 710
Percent of receivables method to estimate uncollectible accounts expense, 372–374
Percent of revenue method to estimate uncollectible accounts expense, 364–372
　adjustment to uncollectible accounts expense, 370
　collection of receivables and, 365, 369, 370
　financial statements and, 367–368, 372
　recognition of uncollectible accounts expense, 365–366
　recording and reporting, 367, 371
　recovery of uncollectible accounts, 369–370
　revenue recognition and, 364, 369
　write-off of uncollectible accounts, 368
Performance evaluations, 320
Period costs, 81, 215
Periodic inventory system, 238–240
Permanent accounts, 26
Perpetual inventory system, 216, 240, 285
Petco, 243
Petty cash, 330–332
Physical control of assets, 320
Physical flow of goods, 274–275
Physical resources, 5
Plant assets, 420, 434–435
Polo Ralph Lauren, 163, 438
Post-closing trial balance, 164
Posting process, 160
PPE (property, plant, and equipment), 420, 432, 434–435
Preferred stock, 602–603
Premiums, 544, 553–554, 557–559
Prenumbered documents, 320
Prepaid items, 84–85, 152, 156, 656
Present value annuities, 730–731, 734
Present value of money, 729, 733
Pressure, in criminal and ethical misconduct, 96–97
Price competition, 237
Price-earnings ratio (P/E ratio), 614–615, 710
Price increases of stock, 613–614
Primary securities market, 719
Princess Cruise Lines, 459
Principal, 377, 379, 499
Principles of Professional Conduct (AICPA), 94
Private accounting, 7–8

Procedures manuals, 319
Proceeds, 499
Product costs, 215
Profit, 4, 216, 289, 722
Profit margins, 213, 236
Progressive, 166
Promissory notes, 376–377
Property, plant, and equipment (PPE), 420, 432, 434–435
Public accounting, 6–7
Public Company Accounting Oversight Board (PCAOB), 95, 335, 597
Publix, 284
Purchase discounts, 222
Purchase returns and allowances, 221
Purchases, intermittent, 280–282

Q

Qualified opinions, 334
Quality improvements, 434–435
Quality of employees, 319
QuickBooks, 142–143, 158

R

R&D (research and development) costs, 438
Ratings for bonds, 545
Ratio analysis, 235, 289, 560
Ratio covenants, 544
Rationalization, in criminal and ethical misconduct, 96–97
Reality Bytes feature
    asset write-offs and stock prices, 91
    cost of protecting cash, 323
    debit and credit entry systems, 158
    dividends, 610
    goodwill, 439
    interest on unpaid receivables, 385
    inventory cost flow methods, 283
    inventory counting services, 230
    late payment penalties, 223
    noncash transactions, 668
    ratio covenants, 544
    Snapchat, 31
    treasury stock, 607
    warranties, 488
Receipts, cash, 321
Receivables. see Accounts receivable; Notes receivable
Reckitt Benckiser Group, PLC, 439
Recognition
    of cost of goods sold, 217
    of revenue, 71, 73, 81, 150, 217, 364, 369
    of uncollectible accounts expense, 365–366

Reconciliation
    of accounts payable, 655–656
    of accounts receivable, 326, 328, 654–655
    of bank accounts, 325–330
    of bonds payable, 664–665
    of common stock, 665
    of interest payable, 657
    of interest receivable, 655
    of inventory, 655–656
    of investment securities, 662
    of land, 662–663
    of mortgage payable, 664
    of prepaid insurance, 656
    of retained earnings, 665
    of salaries payable, 656
    of store fixtures, 662
    of treasury stock, 665
    of unearned rent revenue, 657–658
Reconciliation approach for operating activities, 654–658
Recovery of uncollectible accounts, 369–370
Reevaluation model for PPE accounting, 432
Refinancing short-term debt, 495–496
Reinstatement of receivables, 369–370
Relative market value method, 421
Rent-A-Center, 382–383, 537, 539, 668–669
Rent revenue, unearned, 657–658
Reporting. see also Financial statements
    equity method of, 724
    investment securities and, 720–722
    notes receivable, 377–379
    payroll taxes, 493
    statement of cash flows format, 650–651
    uncollectible accounts expense, 367, 371
Reporting entities, 8–10
Required absences for employees, 319
Research and development (R&D) costs, 438
Resource owners, 4, 5
Resource usage, 4–6
Restaurant Brands International, 288–289, 383–384
Restrictive covenants, 545
Retail companies, 213. see also Merchandising businesses
Retained earnings, 12, 17–18, 611–612, 665
Return-on-assets ratio (ROA), 165, 560, 708, 710
Return-on-equity ratio (ROE), 166–168, 708
Return-on-sales ratio, 235, 236–237, 708
Returns and allowances, 221, 232–233
Revenue. see also Income
    cash service, 500–501, 503
    defined, 14, 87
    recognition of, 71, 73, 81, 150, 217, 364, 369
    unearned, 86–87, 92, 149–150, 657–658

Revenue expenditures, 434
RIGIS, LLC, 230
Risk assessment of debt, 165–166
Rite Aid, 237
ROA (return-on-assets ratio), 165, 560, 708, 710
ROE (return-on-equity ratio), 166–168, 708
Roy's, 267
Ruby Tuesday's, Inc., 312
Rule-based approach for operating activities, 658–659

S

Safeway, 283
Salaries and wages. *see also* Earnings; Income; Payroll
    adjustments for, 74–75, 155–156
    defined, 488
    reconciliation of, 656
    in second accounting cycle, 82
    in T-accounts, 153, 155–156
Sales
    events affecting, 231–237
    intermittent, 280–282
    net, 234
    real-world data on, 236–237
Sales discounts, 231, 233–234
Sales returns and allowances, 232–234
Sales tax, 482–483
Salvage value, 98, 422, 426, 429, 434
Sam's Club, 213
Sanders, Jeffery, 6
Sarbanes–Oxley Act of 2002 (SOX), 94–95, 317, 318, 322, 335, 597
Schedule of cost of goods sold, 240
S Corporations, 597
Sears, 13, 213, 459, 699
SEC. *see* Securities and Exchange Commission
Secondary securities market, 719
Secured bonds, 543
Securities. *see* Investment securities
Securities Act of 1933, 596
Securities and Exchange Commission (SEC)
    audit standards from, 335
    corporate regulation by, 596–597
    creation of, 596
    reporting requirements from, 31, 167, 335
    as stakeholder, 2
Securities Exchange Act of 1934, 596
Segregation of duties, 319
Selling and administrative costs, 215, 218
Semiannual interest payments, 553
Serial bonds, 543
Service businesses, 29

Service charges, 326, 329
Shake Shack, Inc., 641
Short-term (current) assets, 418, 495
Short-term (current) liabilities, 495–496
Short-term debt, refinancing, 495–496
Shrinkage, of inventory, 226
Signature cards, 323
Signet Jewelers Limited, 312
Simple interest, 728
Single-step income statements, 230
Sinking funds, 544
Six Flags, Inc., 205
Snap, Inc., 31, 597, 647, 653–654
Snapchat, 31
Social Security taxes, 490–491, 495
Sole proprietorships, 596, 599
Solvency, 497–498
Sonic Drive-In, 67
Source documents, 158
Southwest Airlines, 443, 459
SOX. *see* Sarbanes–Oxley Act of 2002
Special journals, 158
Specific authorizations, 320
Specific identification inventory method, 274
Splits, stock, 611
Spread, 559
Stakeholders, 2, 5–6, 10, 11, 30
Standard & Poor's, 545, 586
Standards of Ethical Conduct (Institute of Management Accountants), 94
Staples, 237
Starbucks Corporation, 2, 11, 267, 288–289, 384, 642–643
Stated interest rate, 542
Stated value of stock, 601, 605
Statement of activities, 11
Statement of cash flows, 646–670. *see also* Financial statements
    accrual accounting and, 79
    classification scheme for, 25
    direct method for, 648–649, 661, 666–667
    example of, 22
    financing activities in, 649–650, 663–665
    indirect method for, 648–649, 652–659, 666
    investing activities in, 649, 661–663
    for merchandising businesses, 231
    noncash activities in, 650
    for not-for-profit entities, 11
    operating activities in, 648–649, 652–661
    overview, 646
    preparation of, 24–25, 651–652
    real-world data on, 668–670
    reconciliation approach in, 654–658

Statement of cash flows—*Cont.*
    reporting format for, 650–651
    rule-based approach for, 658–659
    Target Corporation annual report, 714–715
Statement of changes in stockholders' equity, 10, 22, 23, 76
Statement of financial position, 11
Stewardship function, 19
Stock. *see also* Corporations
    authorized, 601
    capital, 600–601
    classification of, 604–605
    common, 12, 91, 148–149, 216, 601–602, 665
    control through ownership of, 615
    dividends as, 610–611
    ex-dividend trades of, 609
    on financial statements, 605–606
    investment in, 595, 597
    issued, 601
    no-par, 605
    outstanding, 601
    par value of, 600–601, 604
    preferred, 602–603
    price increases, 613–614
    stated value of, 601, 605
    transactions, 604–606
    treasury, 601, 606–608, 665
Stock certificates, 596
Stockholders, 12, 148, 598
Stockholders' equity, 10, 12, 22, 23, 76
Stock splits, 611
Store fixtures, 662
Straight-line amortization, 548–555
    of bond redemptions, 554–555
    of bonds issued at a premium, 553–554
    of bonds issued at discount, 548–553
Straight-line depreciation, 99, 422, 423–425
Subordinated debentures, 543
Subsidiary companies, 724
Suppliers, 212
Supply expenses, 82–83, 149, 156

T

T-accounts, 148–158
    adjusting, 155–157
    asset exchange transactions in, 151–152
    asset source transactions in, 148–151
    asset use transactions in, 152–154
    claims exchange transactions in, 154–155
    credit and debits in, 148, 157–158
    defined, 148

    discount notes and, 501–502, 504–505
    error detection tools in, 149
    liabilities in, 486
Tangible assets, 420
Target Corporation
    auditors for, 711–712
    balance sheet, 713–714
    company overview, 711
    exercises with, 30, 63, 140, 204, 266, 310, 355–356, 412, 471, 529, 585, 639, 694
    financial statements and supplementary data, 702–707
    gross margin percentage, 235
    income statement, 712–713
    management's discussion and analysis, 711
    notes to financial statements, 715–716
    performance measures, 716
    statement of cash flows, 714–715
    as wholesale company, 213
Taxes
    deferred tax liability, 433
    double taxation, 597
    employer payroll, 493
    income, 279, 431–433, 488–490
    long-term debt advantage, 559–560
    sales tax, 482–483
    Social Security and Medicare, 490–491, 495
Tax returns, 279
Tax services, 7
Temporary accounts, 26
10-K reports, 31–32
Term bonds, 543
Tesla, Inc., 586, 695
Texas Instruments, Inc., 532
Tiffany & Company, 267
Times-interest-earned ratio, 561, 710
Time value of money, 728–734
    bond liabilities and, 731–732
    business applications, 731–732
    future value, 728–729, 733
    future value annuities, 729–730, 734
    long-term notes payable and, 731
    present value, 729, 733
    present value annuities, 730–731, 734
    tables for, 733–734
Tim Horton, 384
Toll Brothers, Inc., 205, 288, 384
Tommy Hilfiger, 163
Toyota Motor Corporation, 91
Toys R Us, Inc., 205
Trademarks, 438
Trading securities, 720, 722

760 Index

Transactions. *see also* Asset exchange transactions; Asset source transactions; Asset use transactions
   claims exchange, 75, 93
   classification of, 93
   defined, 13
   inventory, 215–220
   journals as chronological record of, 158
   stock, 604–606
Transferability of ownership, 598
Transportation costs, 223–226
Transportation-in, 223
Transportation-out, 224
Treasury stock, 601, 606–608, 665
Trial balance, 160–168
   closing entries in, 161–164
   debt risk assessment in, 165–166
   defined, 160
   effective use of assets in, 165
   overview, 160–161
   post-closing, 164
   with real-world data, 166–168
True cash balance, 325
Turbo Tax, 142–143
Turnover ratio, 287, 383, 385, 709
Twitter, 669

U

Unadjusted bank balance, 325, 327
Unadjusted book balance, 325–328
Uncollectible accounts expense
   adjustments to, 370
   collection of receivables and, 365, 369, 370
   direct write-off method for estimation of, 375–376
   financial statements and, 367–368, 372
   percent of receivables method for estimation of, 372–374
   percent of revenue method for estimation of, 364–372
   recognition of, 365–366
   recording and reporting, 367, 371
   recovery of, 369–370
   revenue recognition and, 364, 369
   write-off of, 368
Under Armour, Inc., 613–614
Unearned revenue, 86–87, 92, 149–150, 657–658
United Airlines, 20
Units-of-production depletion, 436–437
Units-of-production depreciation, 422, 428–429
Unqualified opinions, 334
Unrealized gains or losses, 722

Unsecured bonds, 543
Unsubordinated debentures, 543
U.S. Bureau of Labor Statistics, 495
U.S. Patent Office, 438
Useful life of assets
   defined, 98
   estimated, 422
   extension of, 435
   intangible assets, 420–421
   revision of, 433
Users of accounting information, 5–6

V

Vail Resorts, Inc., 205
Value Line Investment Survey, 669
Variable interest rate, 536
Vaseline, 438
Verizon Communications, Inc., 140–141, 443, 640
Vertical statements model, 76, 78, 89–91
Volkswagen AG, 317, 322
Voluntary withholdings, 491–492
Voucher, petty cash, 331
Vulcan Materials Co., 283

W

Wage and Tax Statement, Form W-2, 489–491
Wages. *see* Salaries and wages
Walgreens, 237
The Wall Street Journal, 322
Wal-Mart Stores, Inc.
   earnings for, 614
   exercises with, 306
   gross margin percentage, 235, 237, 238
   internal control for, 316
   inventory turnover, 288, 289
   marketing distribution system, 598
   materiality in financial statements audits, 334
   as merchandising business, 169
   operating cycle, 384
   return-on-assets ratio, 165
The Walt Disney Company, 65
Warranties, 484–485, 488
The Weather Company, 64
Weighted-average cost flow method, 274, 278, 281–282
Weight Watchers International, Inc., 472
The Wendy's Company, 6, 639, 669
Whirlpool Corporation, 415
Whole Food Market, Inc., 64, 268

Wholesale companies, 213. *see also* Merchandising businesses
Winterkorn, Martin, 322
Withdrawals, 599
Workers' compensation insurance, 495
WorldCom, 95, 318
Write-off of uncollectible accounts, 368

www.colgatepalmolive.co.in, 497
www.itvpic.com, 497
Wyndham Worldwide, 561

X

Xerox, 438